This book is accompanied by  **CD-ROM(s)**
Check on Issue and Return

ONE WEEK LOAN

Securitization

The Financial Instrument
of the Future

Securitization

The Financial Instrument of the Future

Vinod Kothari

WILEY

John Wiley & Sons (Asia) Pte Ltd

Other Wiley Editorial Offices

John Wiley & Sons, 111 River Street, Hoboken, NJ 07030, USA
John Wiley & Sons, The Atrium Southern Gate, Chichester P019 8SQ, England
John Wiley & Sons (Canada) Ltd, 5353 Dundas Street West, Suite 400, Toronto, Ontario M9B 6HB, Canada
John Wiley & Sons Australia Ltd, 42 McDougall Street, Milton, Queensland 4064, Australia
Wiley-VCH, Boschstrasse 12, D-69469 Weinheim, Germany

Library of Congress Cataloging-in-Publication Data

ISBN-13: 978-0-470-82195-7
ISBN-10: 0-470-82195-4

Typeset in 10.5/13 points, Palatino by C&M Digitals (P) Ltd.
Printed in Singapore by Markono Print Media Pte Ltd
10 9 8 7 6 5 4 3 2 1

Anju and Vishes
You bear a lot when I go into
writing mode; I owe it to you

Table of Contents

Register for free updates

In the fast changing world of securitization, the only continuity is change. The book in your hands deals with a wide array of issues and rules that are constantly evolving.

Should you wish to receive free updates of the book, register yourself at the link below:

http://vinodkothari.com/secbook.htm

Disclaimer: The update service is purely voluntary on the part of the author, and there is no commitment as to frequency or period during which the updates will be sent. Your purchase of the book does not constitute any payment towards the update service. There will be no updates once the author/publisher have decided upon bringing out a new edition of the book.

Preface to the second edition

Securitization is growing in its reach, geographically and in terms of industry segments. Its relevance in integrating mortgage lending markets with the capital markets is well established the world over, but it is interesting to see the application of securitization technology in traditional domains of corporate and project finance. In a much broader sense, securitization is a by-product of a larger tendency of the preponderance of the markets, because securitization builds that bridge whereby capital markets become connected to the market for the application of funds.

Geographically, securitization is actively practiced in most developed and emerging markets. It is being advocated by multilateral developmental agencies too. Unarguably, securitization will continue to grow – there is no doubt about the *future* of this instrument, dubbed in this book as the instrument of the future.

Securitization is a preferred form of funding – the preferential treatment owes itself to several of the oft-cited benefits, such as bankruptcy remoteness, off-balance sheet treatment and extended leverage. Most of these are derived from the technicality of the instrument. The history of the development of any financial product initially emphasizes those technical benefits, which, in the course of the product maturity, are either ruled out or subjected to extensive limitations by regulations or accounting standards. This is beginning to happen in the case of securitization. Bankruptcy remoteness has not been questioned on any significant scale, but accounting standards have put tougher conditions on off-balance sheet treatment. Over time, on-balance sheet treatment may put in doubt bankruptcy remoteness as well; it may be questioned as to how something that remains on the balance sheet be excluded from the purview of the bankruptcy court's jurisdiction. The process of maturity of any instrument is a tendency towards convergence, that is, from difference to indifference.

In presenting this new edition, I have received substantial support from many people, but I must mention one. Martin Rosenblatt, the world's number one expert on accounting for securitization, took time off to go through the whole chapter on accounting issues and made extensive suggestions for improvement. To Martin I remain obliged.

This edition is being published by John Wiley & Sons and as the world's leader in financial publishing, it is hoped that the book is more accessible and reader-friendly. The title has also been changes: from *Securitisation: The Financial Instrument of the New Millennium* to *Securitization: The Financial Instrument of the Future*.

I will look forward to constructive suggestions from readers.

Vinod Kothari
Kolkata
July 2006

Preface to
the first edition

The development of securitization as a financial instrument, coupled with other devices such as derivatives and alternative risk transfers, is part of the transformation of global financial markets. From the traditional form of financial intermediation, markets are growing into financial commoditization. Lending relationships are being converted into investment products at great pace and efficiency in many countries, with resultant benefits for the system as a whole.

Mortgage-backed securities are already the second-largest fixed income investment in the United States. Leaving aside other developed financial markets, mortgage securitization is attracting attention everywhere in the world including emerging markets. This activity demonstrates that securitization not only pleases maverick investment bankers and the world of high finance, but it also does good for society as it connects housing finance markets with capital markets. The key benefit of securitization is connectivity: it connects capital markets with housing finance markets, banking with insurance, private equity with bond markets and so on.

As the instrument becomes increasingly important, industry players have to attend to some of its sensitive spots. I would like to take opportunity to mention two of these here although the book has dealt with these as well as other issues at length.

Soon after the Enron debacle, securitization became associated with off-balance sheet financing and special purpose vehicles. Popular perception of off-balance sheet financing is that it is something dubious, something curious, like the "invisible man", and special purpose vehicles are devices to achieve off-balance sheet financing. There is no doubt that existing accounting standards in most parts of the world require that securitization leads to off-balance sheet funding. In reality, no funding is completely off the balance sheet, as what goes off the balance sheet of a bank is on the balance sheet of a special purpose entity. But again, public perception is often that special purpose vehicle is an obscure and opaque entity.

Personally, I do not see why securitization has to be off-balance sheet. Synthetic securitizations do not lead to off-balance sheet assets, and they still serve the purpose of risk transfer. What is more important is bankruptcy protection. Accounting treatment cannot be an objective by itself – it is merely the consequence of a series of steps designed for bankruptcy remoteness. As long as asset-based, entity-independent ratings are possible, on-balance sheet accounting should be just as applicable. We should seriously think in that direction.

The second area of public critique is sub-prime lending. The popular perception is that banks originate more sub-prime credits today than ever before, and the reason is that these loans are, soon after origination, parceled out into securitization vehicles. Unsurprisingly, home equity lending is a large component of the asset-backed market in the U.S. It is contended that the credit standards used by banks are not the same for the assets, including securitizable assets, that stay on the books.

The only way to check against this possibility is to maintain a strict fire wall between the lending desk and the securitization desk. This is easier said than done, but that does not reduce the need to say it or the seriousness required to implement it.

Over the last five to six years, my association with securitization industry has been quite intensive, partly due to my website and partly due to the interaction at my training courses and conferences. Many have said I live and breathe securitization to which I add: I also drink and eat it! I can only hope that this book will strengthen my nexus with the industry which I hold so dear.

There are many personalities in the small world of securitization from whom I draw tremendous inspiration and get unstinted support. To name them and to record my gratitude would be the least I could do in return. **Martin Rosenblatt** is a great source of information, and his expertise is not limited to accounting, in which he is unrivalled. **Professor Steven Schwarcz** is the encyclopedia of securitization law who has enriched my knowledge in that area. **Mark Adelson** has tremendous depth in securitization and I have benefited a lot from his writings. **Luke Mellor** is a remarkable personality who is always ready to help. **Manoj Mandal** has done commendable hard work on the script.

It would be a great pleasure if readers have something to share or say.

Vinod Kothari
Kolkata
September 4, 2003

Part I: Securitization: Concepts and Markets

Chapter 1

Securitization and Structured Finance

Just as the electronics industry was formed when the vacuum tubes were replaced by transistors, and transistors were then replaced by integrated circuits, the financial services industry is being transformed now that securitized credit is beginning to replace traditional lending. Like other technological transformations, this one will take place over the years, not overnight. We estimate it will take 10 to 15 years for structured securitised credit to replace to displace completely the classical lending system – not a long time, considering that the fundamentals of banking have remained essentially unchanged since the Middle Ages.

Lowell L. Bryan

Innovation, supported by technology, is constantly changing the face of the world of finance. Today it is more a world of transactions than a world of relations. Most relations have been transactionalized.

Transactions mean the *coming together* of two entities with a common purpose, whereas relations mean *keeping together* of these two entities. For example, when a bank provides a loan to a user, the transaction leads to a relationship – that of a lender and a borrower. However, the relationship is terminated when that very loan is replaced by a bond. The bond is not a relation; it is a commodity, capable of acquisition and disposal.

If we look around us, we also find innumerable instances in the personal world where relations have been replaced by mere transactions. Marriage is one of the oldest optional relationships, increasingly being replaced by "friendships." Employment is another relationship that takes a larger part of the working day, being replaced by outsourcing. Relationships require tolerance, so scarce in a world that is increasingly stressed and intolerant.

The transactionalization of financial relationships is also a reflection of this larger trend. Financial markets in the world today are replete with products that were relations at one time. Insurance risk has always been a relation – of providing and seeking protection. Today, this relation is tradable as a commodity. Aided by derivatives devices, more such risks and relations are placed in the capital markets today, signaling a broader trend: The trend of commoditization, of securitization.

Thus, securitization is not just a funding device or an alternative to secured funding; it is a new-found way of lending a tradable character to business relationships, not limited to financial relationships. This trend has grown tremendously over time and is only expected to expand as more and more relationships get converted into tradable paper.

Basic meaning of securitization

"Securitization" in its widest sense implies every process that converts a financial relation into a transaction.

The history of the evolution of finance and corporate law – the latter being supportive of the former – gives other instances where relations have been converted into transactions. In fact, this was the earliest, and by far unequalled, contribution of corporate law to the world of finance – the ordinary share, which implies piecemeal ownership of the company. The ownership of a company is a relation, packaged as a transaction by the creation of the ordinary share. This earliest instance of securitization was so instrumental in the growth of the corporate form of doing business – and hence industrialization that someone rated it as one of the two greatest inventions of the 19th Century – the other one being the steam engine.[1] That truly reflects the significance of the ordinary share, and if the same idea is extended, to the very concept of securitization; it as important to the world of finance as motive power is to industry. In many respects, the present day concept of securitization still draws upon the concept of equity share.[2]

Tradable loans in the form of debentures formed another very significant innovation in the world of finance, which are also a generic instance of securitization. Highlighting the significance of the bond as an innovation, Henry Dunning McLeod said: "The man who first discovered that a debt is a saleable commodity … made the discovery which has most deeply affected the fortunes of human race."

Other instances of securitization of relationships are commercial paper that securitizes a trade debt.

Asset securitization

The wide meaning of securitization explained above was in vogue before the 1980s.[3] John Reed, the-then chairman of Citicorp, defined securitization as "the substitution of more efficient public capital markets for less efficient, higher cost, financial intermediaries in the funding of debt instruments."[4]

He was obviously referring to the generic meaning of securitization as replacing intermediated funding by direct funding from capital markets by issuance of securities.

However, in the sense in which the term is used in present day capital market activity, **securitization** has acquired a typical meaning of its own, which is at times, for the sake of distinction, called **asset securitization**. It is taken to mean a device of structured financing in which an entity seeks to pool together its interest in identifiable cash flows over time, transfer the same to investors either with or without the support of further collaterals, and thereby achieve the purpose of financing. Though the end-result of securitization is financing, it is not "financing" as such because the entity securitizing its assets is not borrowing money but selling a stream of cash flows that was otherwise to accrue to it.

> The simplest way to understand the concept of securitization is to take an example. Let us say, I want to own a car to run it for hire. I could take a loan with which I could buy the car. The loan is my obligation and the car is my asset, and both are affected by my other assets and other obligations. This is a case of simple financing.
>
> On the other hand, I might analytically envisage the car – my asset in the instant case – as claim to value over a period of time, that is, the ability to generate a series of hire rentals. This claim to value represents at least four major elements:
>
> (a) originating the transaction that is, spotting a potential hiring opportunity, buying a suitable car for the said purpose, etc;
> (b) servicing the transaction that is, running the car for hire and doing all that is required in regard to client servicing;
> (c) funding the transaction that is, generating sufficient returns to pay off the investment inherent in buying the car;
> (d) residual value that is, the value left over after paying off the investment.
>
> If I were to sell off so much of the cash flow via hire rentals such that the funding part in (c) above is accounted for, I am still left with (a), (b) and (d), and properly speaking, in most businesses, the profit of the operator of the business lies in these elements rather than the funding. Hence, the investment becomes self-liquidated by way of the cash flow, and as an operator of the business, I still have my cream.

So, what is asset securitization? Literally, as the word implies, it is a process of converting something into a security, that is, when something which is not a security is converted into one, it is securitization. A "security" is a capital market instrument. In the example we have taken above, if the cash flow on account of hiring of the car would be converted into a security, and this security was then offered in the capital market, we have securitized the cash flow or securitized the asset. Thus, securitization is the process that transforms an asset into a security, and the security that results is typically called an "asset-backed security."

What is an asset-backed security?

The security at the end of the process of securitization is an asset-backed security. This security is significantly different from a usual capital market instrument, which is an exposure in the business of the issuer. An asset-backed security is simply an exposure in an asset, or, as the case may be, a bunch of assets. Going back to the example above, the investor who acquires the cash flow generated by the hiring of the car, reincarnated as a security, is not concerned with the generic risks of the business of the operator. The investor is exposed to the risks of the asset in question, but not the risks of the operator's business. Therefore, an asset-backed security is not a claim on an entity but an asset.

Two important points come up here. At the end of day, any claim on an asset is a claim on an entity as no asset is a value by itself. For instance, if the security in the example is not a claim on the car operator's business, it is a claim on the car hirer's business, and therefore, ends up into a claim on an entity. This point is answered by the "portfolio" nature of the asset, that is, if the hire rentals in the example above represent those from a portfolio of hirers, the investor in the security has a claim on a diversified portfolio of hirers, thus he is obviously better off than one with a claim on the operator.

The second issue is an offshoot of the answer to the first. If we say that the asset-backed investor is better off as he has a claim on a diversified portfolio of hirers, then we are not very far from a traditional investor, say, in a corporate bond. Only if the "diversified portfolio of hirers" is extended to cover the entire assets of the operator, there is no difference between the two investors. The one who invests in a traditional bond issued by the operator is also, in essence, backed by the entire assets of the operator. If and to the extent – these assets do not pay, both the investors would suffer losses, and almost likewise.

This discussion leads to an important feature of an asset-backed security: Whether asset-backed or entity-backed, there is no value-added merely by securitizing assets. The only source of value-addition is by a sort of *inter-creditor arrangement* whereby an asset-backed investor is put to two advantages – *legal preference* and *structural preference*.

Legal preference refers to the preference that an asset-backed investor enjoys over a traditional investor as a claimant on the assets of the operator. A traditional investor essentially has a claim against the operator. If the operator were to run into financial problems, the

---

Box 1.1 Concept of asset-backed security

- Analytically, every claim against an entity is a claim on assets – going by options theory, a loan is a claim on the assets of the entity.

- In ultimate analysis, every claim on assets is a claim on entities – someone has to pay for the asset.

- Distinction between corporate finance and asset-backed securitization is essentially the scope and definition of "asset."

- Securitization narrows it down to a specific pool, usually of assets already created, thus eliminating the risk inherent in creating assets.

- The fact that the pool is narrowed down itself reduces much of the risks, or at least perceived risks, as specific pools are less risky than entity-wide pools

investor's claim is subject to bankruptcy administration, which in most countries is a time-consuming process and might be legally preceded by other statutory claims. An asset-backed operator has a claim over the assets of the operator, as those assets have been hived off and made legal property of the investors. Therefore, these assets subserve the claims of the investors before they can be claimed by anyone else. Creating this legal preference is the key to securitization.

Structural preference refers to the qualitative attributes of the assets transferred to the investors in asset-backed securities. Though theoretically these assets are not "cherry-picked," the assets obviously answer to some qualitative standards, and therefore, the claims of the asset-backed investors are on assets that are either historically seen as good assets or prospectively believed to be good assets. In other words, securitization creates a structural preference for the investors in asset-backed securities by sort of de-constructing a corporation and making its specific assets exclusively available to asset-backed investors.

We used the words *inter-creditor arrangement* above as the genesis of the two preferences noted in the preceding paragraphs. That an asset-backed investor enjoys a legal and structural preference over the traditional investor is a matter of mutual arrangement among the various "creditors" (including, for this purpose, the asset-backed investor) of an entity. A preference is understandably an advantage that one has over the other, and looked at the other way around, it is only gained by the acceptance of deference by the other creditors. Therefore, the advantage that asset-backed investors gain is at the cost of the other creditors. Does this mean that the sum of the parts is no different from the whole? This issue will be discussed later in this chapter.[5]

Legal preference by isolation

As discussed earlier, the legal preference of the asset-backed investor over a traditional investor is key to the very economics of securitization. Much of the need for the present-day methods of securitization – isolation, etc. would disappear if it were possible to allow a certain group of investors a bankruptcy-proofing device whereby certain assets, or all assets, of a corporation would be used to pay them off first.[6] Thus, securitization strives at arbitraging the law by ensuring that at least some specific assets are free from any other claim and can be used to pay off only the asset-backed investors.

The device used for creating this legal preference is simple: Transfer of assets. The operator in the example above transfers a stream of hiring receivables to the investors. This transfer should be a legally recognized transfer, such that the receivables now become the legal property of the investors. Being the property of the investors, obviously, the receivables are not affected by any bankruptcy of the operator, or claims of the general creditors of the operator.

In securitization parlance, this legal transfer is often referred to as "isolation." Isolation is only a perfected, irreversible legal transfer. That the receivables are isolated from the operator means the receivables are beyond the legal powers of either the operator, or the operator's liquidator, or creditors, or for that matter, anyone with a claim against the operator.

Capital market window

Securitization has the law in its head and the capital market in its heart. The very idea of converting an asset into a capital market security is to raise money from the capital markets. A preliminary question is – why convert assets into securities? If the only intention is to sell an asset to an investor, it could well be done by discounting the receivables with a bank or similar investor.

Securitization, as the name implies, has a capital market window. The idea is to create a security and take the asset out into the market. In other words, the idea is to move funding from the banking world to the investment-banking world. This is simply explained by the growing preponderance of the capital markets – an obvious by-product of the institutionalization of finance, which is discussed in more detail later.

Use of special purpose vehicles

The twin objectives of transferring assets to investors and at the same time creating a capital market instrument can only be achieved by using a transformational device known as a special purpose vehicle. The special purpose vehicle is a legal outfit, specifically and solely created for the purpose of holding the assets sought to be transferred by the originator, and the issuance of securities by the special purpose vehicle, such that the securities are no different from a claim over those assets. Thus, investors do not have to acquire or hold the assets of the originator directly, but they do so indirectly through the vehicle. The vehicle, as an intermediary between the originator and the investors, sits with the assets as a sort of legalized facade for the multifarious and nebulous body, which is the investors.

Some definitions of securitization

- The composite name to a series of steps whereby the asset or assets of one or more originators are pooled and transferred into a separate legal vehicle; this is usually structured as independent, bankruptcy-remote and insulated against bankruptcy risk of the originator(s), and creation of different securities by such a vehicle, usually implying differential reallocation of risk and returns of such assets to such different securities, so that the securities are repaid from the pool of assets and not from the general funds of the originator(s) or the issuing vehicle.

- The process by which (relatively) homogeneous, but illiquid, assets are pooled and repackaged, with security interests representing claims to the incoming cash flow and other economic benefits generated by the loan pool sold as securities to third-party investors. Such asset-backed securities (ABS) may take the form of a single class offering, in which all investors receive a *pro rata* interest in the incoming revenues from the asset pool, or a multi-class offering, whereby two or more classes or *tranches* are granted different (and, in some cases, uncertain) claims, each with its own pay-out and risk characteristics.[7]
- **Standard & Poor's** explain the concept of asset-backed securities: "Typically, investors in corporate bonds are repaid from an issuer's general revenues. In contrast, investors in securitized bonds, also called structured financings, are repaid from the cash flow generated by a specific pool of assets. An originator sells its assets to a trust or corporation, which then issues securities backed by these assets. The securities are usually obligations that have been issued by these special-purpose entities. In a traditional securitization, investors do not usually have recourse to the seller of the assets, only to the assets contained within the trust."[8]
- UK accounting standard FRS 5 defines it from the viewpoint of investors as "a means whereby providers of finance fund a specific block of assets rather than the general business of a company."
- The word has found its way into a common man's dictionary as well. The **Concise Oxford Dictionary** has the following meaning of the word "securitize" "v. Convert (an asset, specially a loan) into marketable securities, typically for the purpose of raising cash."

Securitization of receivables

Much of the asset-backed securitization discussed earlier is, in fact, securitization of financial claims, that is, receivables. Obviously, this has been mainly used by entities where receivables form a large part of the total assets, such as banks and financial intermediaries. In addition, to be packaged as a security, the ideal receivable is one that is repayable over or after a certain period of time, and there is contractual certainty as to payment. Hence, the application of a securitization device was by tradition principally directed towards housing/mortgage finance companies, car rental companies, equipment leasing companies, credit cards companies, hotels, etc. Soon, electricity companies, telephone companies, real estate companies, aviation companies, etc. also joined as users of securitization. Insurance companies are the latest of the lot to make an innovative use of securitization of risk and receivables, although the pace at which securitization markets is growing, use of the word "latest" is not without risk of becoming stale soon.

The generic meaning of securitization is every such process whereby financial claims are transformed into marketable securities, but in the sense that the term is used here, securitization is a process by which cash flows, or claims against third parties of an entity, either existing or future, are identified, consolidated, separated from the originating entity, and then transformed into "securities" to be offered to investors.

The involvement of debtors in the receivable securitization process adds unique dimensions to the concept, of which at least two deserve immediate mention. One is the very legal possibility of transforming a claim on a third party as a marketable document; it is easy to understand that this dimension is unique to securitization of receivables, as there is no legal difficulty when an entity creates a claim on itself, but the scene is totally changed when rights on other parties are being turned into a tradable commodity. Two, it affords the issuer the ability to originate an instrument that hinges on the quality of the underlying asset. Simply, as the issuer is essentially marketing claims on others or a claim on the assets, the quality of his own commitment becomes subsidiary. Hence, it allows the issuer to make his own credit rating insignificant or less significant, and the intrinsic quality of the asset more critical. This is referred to as **asset-backed finance**, discussed later in this chapter.

Quick guide to jargon

Although there is a complete terminology appended to this chapter, this section will help the reader to quickly get familiarized with the essential securitization jargon.

The entity securitizing its assets is called the **originator;** the name signifies that the entity was responsible for originating the claims ultimately to be securitized. The originator is the one who transfers receivables to the issuing entity, discussed below. In many cases, the transferor may not be the *originator*, that is, original underwriter of the claim or the asset, but might simply be a *re-packager*, the one who buys assets from the market for the purpose of securitising them.

There is no distinct name for the investors who put money into the instrument; therefore, they may simply be called **investors**. The securities are backed by specific assets and are repayable from such assets only. Hence, they are called **asset-backed securities.**

The claims that the originator securitizes can either be existing claims or existing assets (in the form of claims), or expected claims over time. In other words, the securitized assets could be either existing receivables, or receivables to arise in the future. The latter, for the sake of distinction, is sometimes called **future flows securitization**, in which case the former is **existing asset securitization**.

In U.S. markets, another distinction is common between **mortgage-backed securities** (MBS) and **asset-backed securities** (ABS). This is only to indicate asset classes that are different; the former relates to securities based on mortgage receivables. Elsewhere, the acronym ABS typically includes all kinds of receivables including mortgage-backed receivables.

The assets or receivables that back up the securities are called **collateral**. Different types of asset-backed securities may also be analyzed based on the type of the collateral.[9]

It is important for the entire exercise to be a case of transfer of receivables by the originator, not a borrowing on the security of the receivables, so there is a legal **transfer of the receivables** to a separate entity. In legal parlance, it is the transfer of receivables achieved by a method called **assignment of receivables**. It is also necessary to ensure that the transfer of receivables is respected by the legal system as a genuine transfer and not as mere eyewash when the reality is only a mode of borrowing. In other words, the transfer of receivables has to be a **true sale** of the receivables, and not merely a financing against the security of the receivables.

Securitization involves a transfer of receivables from the originator, so it would be inconvenient, to the extent of being impossible, to transfer such receivables to the investors directly, as the receivables are as diverse as the investors themselves. In addition, the base of investors could keep changing as the resulting security is essentially a marketable security. Therefore, it is necessary to bring in an intermediary that would hold the receivables for the benefit of the end investors. This entity is created solely for the purpose of the transaction; therefore, it is called a **special purpose vehicle (SPV)** or a **special purpose entity (SPE),** which could be a trust or a company, thus the phrase **special purpose company (SPC)**. The function of the SPV in a securitization transaction could stretch from being a pure conduit or intermediary vehicle, to a more active role in reinvesting or reshaping the cash flow arising from the assets transferred to it, something that would depend on the end objectives of the securitization exercise.

The originator transfers the assets to the SPV, which holds the assets on behalf of the investors, and issues to the investors its own securities. Therefore, the SPV is also called the **issuer**.

There is no uniform name for the securities issued by the SPV as such securities take different forms. These securities could represent a direct claim of the investors on all that the SPV collects from the receivables transferred to it – in this case, the securities are called **pass through certificates** or **beneficial interest certificates** as they imply certificates of proportional beneficial interest in the assets held by the SPV. Alternatively, the SPV might be re-configuring the cash flow by reinvesting it, so as to pay the investors on fixed dates, not matching the dates when the transferred receivables are collected by the SPV. In this case, the securities held by the investors may be called **pay through certificates**. Alternatively, as these securities are essentially the obligations of the SPV that are discharged by the receivables from the assets transferred to it, the obligations could be referred to generically as **asset-backed obligations**, and specifically as **asset-backed bonds** or **asset-backed notes**. The securities issued by the SPV could also be named based on their risk or other features, such as **senior notes, junior notes, floating rate notes**, etc. Yet another way of referring to asset-backed securities is based on the term of the paper concerned; if the paper is short-term commercial paper, it is referred to as **asset-backed commercial paper,** otherwise referred to as **term paper.**

Another phrase commonly used in securitization exercises is **bankruptcy remoteness**. This means the transfer of the assets by the originator to the SPV is such that even if the originator goes bankrupt, or falls into other financial difficulties, the rights of the investors on the assets held by the SPV are not affected. In other words, the investors would continue to have a paramount interest in the assets irrespective of the difficulties, distress or bankruptcy of the originator. Bankruptcy remoteness could also be related to the issuer, that is, the special purpose vehicle is ideally so structured that it cannot go bankrupt. Technically, it is never possible to guarantee that the SPV will not go bankrupt, but the structural protection against bankruptcy relies on a basic tenet of life that we often forget: All worries are associated with wealth. If the SPV is so structured that it can have no wealth and no liabilities, it obviously can have no worries, including worries as to bankruptcy.

Securitization and asset-backed finance

Three features combine to make securitization:

- Asset-backed financing
- Capital market financing
- Structured financing.

The fact that the word "securitization" literally implies issuing securities, and so the funding in case of securitization comes from the capital markets, has been discussed already. The first feature is discussed under this heading, and the third feature in the next one.

Securitization is a device of asset-backed financing. The meaning of asset-backed finance, as opposed to entity-backed finance, is that the financier or investor is essentially exposed to the risks inherent in the asset. In all forms of funding, the financier takes exposure in the entity that raises the funding, and the assets that the entity builds out of such funding. The latter is significant because no entity can be persistently better than its assets. However, depending on what is the primary source of comfort of the financier, funding methods can be broadly looked as entity finance and asset finance.

As in asset-based methods of funding, the financier is primarily exposed to the assets, such funding methods are designed to ensure that:

- The assets are tangible, valuable and have marketable value;
- The financier has a close legal control on the value of the asset;
- This legal control also implies that the ability of the borrower to create parallel or senior interests of others over the asset can be controlled;
- The legal system of the jurisdiction allows the financier to convert the claim on the asset into cash.

One of the most traditional methods of asset-backed funding may be a secured loan. A secured loan is backed by the security of a tangible asset. The terms of the security interest allow the lender to access the asset and dispose it off to realize the outstanding amount due. The enforcement of security interests is typically governed by either common law or a specific law and its efficiency must be analyzed. Thus, a secured lender may look at the asset as the primary exposure and expose himself based on a certain loan-to-value (LTV) ratio.

Equipment leasing is another form of asset-backed finance. The lessor has legal control over the asset as its legal owner. Most leasing is based on the principles of asset-backed lending as the primary exposure of the lessor is on the asset.

Securitization takes the concept of asset-backed finance to a new level; while secured lending and equipment leasing are mostly restricted to fixed and tangible assets, securitization is applied for funding of working capital or receivables. Pools of such receivables are taken into a separate legal vehicle, thus creating sole and predominant legal control thereon by the investors. In addition, securitization takes the concept of asset-backed finance to its logical conclusion: The investors can look at the asset, and only the asset. In our example above on the secured loan, the lender may seek to realize the loan by disposal of the secured asset, and may still seek the deficit from the borrower. In securitization, the rights of investors are limited to merely the assets isolated into the SPV.

Thus, securitization results in a **mutually exclusive** asset-backed finance, the beneficiary entity does not have any claim on the assets transferred into the SPV, and the investors do not have any claim on any other assets of the beneficiary.

Securitization and structured finance

Securitization is a "structured financial instrument." "Structured finance" which has become a buzzword in today's financial market means a financial instrument structured or tailored to the needs of the issuer as opposed to a generic, on-tap product. From the investor's perspective, it also means an instrument structured to meet the risk-return and maturity needs of the investor, rather than a simple claim against an entity or asset. In present-day capital market jargon, the word "structured finance" is almost used as an alternative to securitization and other asset-backed products.

What is structured finance? When the rights of different investors in a transaction are differentiated, the result is structured finance. Re-allocation of risk and return to different investors obviously has to do with different risk appetite and yield expectations of investors; therefore, structured finance tries to "create" securities that are aligned closely to investor needs.

Let's take the example of the most basic form of structuring – **senior** and **junior** securities. Junior securities are subordinated; they will receive cash flow after the senior securities have been paid off. On the other hand, they will also be hit by losses before the senior securities.

Imagine a single-storey house at the seashore. If a tsunami hits and the water level goes up, it is likely that all living in the house will be affected. Now, think of a two-storey house and the tsunami. It is likely that the family living on the ground floor will be affected, but those on the second storey may not be. The position of the second floor is similar to the senior securities discussed above. The second floor is senior because the ground floor is junior. What makes the senior investor senior is that there is someone prepared to make himself subordinated. Once again, the family living on the second floor is unlikely to be affected unless those on the ground floor drown.

In other words, the ground floor takes more risk, so that the second floor may take less, but there may be corresponding benefits too. The same holds true for the senior and junior securities; the junior investor sacrifices himself to protect the senior investor, but obviously does so for higher returns.

Since everyone has their own preferences, prejudices and predicaments, we have so many differentiations of just about everything and all are adaptations to suit those preferences. Likewise, structured finance does not merely have securities come out of a transaction; it actively reconfigures securities to make them suit investors' need for risk and return.

In practice, the words "structured finance" and securitization are almost used interchangeably, as are the words "securitized instrument" and "structured product."

Some quick features of securitization

Before barging into a full-scale discussion on securitization, it makes sense to familiarize ourselves with some broad features.

What receivables are securitizable

A number of present-day securitizations seem to break all the rules as to what receivables are amenable to securitization; the traditional securitizable receivables possess the following features:

- **Substantial investment in receivables**: The entity must be having a substantial part of its assets in the form of receivables. Entities for which receivables are just a fraction of working capital may not find it economical to look at the securitization option primarily due to scalar economies. Such entities usually participate in the securitization market through *conduit* activity, where one conduit manager buys receivables of several originators, pools them, and then securitizes the same.
- **Receivables in future for value already provided**: The generic form of receivables securitized is receivables already created, that is, the existing right to receive over time, for something already done by the originator. This is to ensure that the receivables are independent of the performance or existence of the originator. This is different from a *future flow* that securitizes receivables yet to be generated. Future flows are also securitized, but the essentials in future flow securitization are very different from an existing receivable securitization.[10]

- **Reasonable predictability**: To be securitizable, the receivables must have a reasonable predictability. Normally, the receivables in question are backed by payment schedule, such as repayment of housing loans. There are cash flows that are not based on a payment schedule, but which can be modeled based on experience, such as rentals from real estate. Absolutely unpredictable receivables will be difficult to securitize, as it is difficult to envisage a security backed by such cash flow.
- **Diversification**: This is not a necessary feature, but usually it is preferred that the receivables are diversified, both geographically and in terms of the obligors. No single obligor, or few obligors having correlation, should be able to disrupt the payment stream substantially so as to adversely affect the investors. Receivables that are essentially backed by a single or a few are dependent upon the risk of the obligor(s) in question and will not have the benefit of diversification. Note that in absence of diversification, structured finance securities cannot be created, but one of the fundamental principles of structuring is diversity.

Creation of security

A significant distinction between securitization and asset sales is that the former results in creation of marketable securities, and hence the name "securitization." "Asset sales" is the broad term given to transfer of an asset, or portfolio of assets, usually by banks and financial intermediaries to raise liquidity or manage risks. These are mostly bilateral transactions.

On the other hand, the very purpose of securitization is to ensure marketability to financial claims. Hence, the instrument is structured so as to be marketable. The concept of marketability involves two postulates: (a) the legal and systemic possibility of marketing the instrument; (b) the existence of a market for the instrument. Securitized products are issued as transferable securities; in certificate form or in a bond or note form. However, the existence of a secondary market in securitized products is a case-specific phenomenon. Many securitized products are privately placed to institutional investors who intend to hold them to maturity.

Special purpose vehicle

A vehicle, whether special purpose or general purpose, is not required in case of asset sales in general, but is required for securitization transactions.

Creation of marketable securities is not possible without a conduit or vehicle that will house the assets

---

Box 1.3 Why special purpose vehicles?

- Special purpose vehicle is a transformation device; it is not an entity with substance, assets or income. It is a mere legal fiction that holds assets and issues securities.

- It does not add any credit, value or support to the assets.

- The result is that assets get *converted* into securities, the special purpose entity acting as a conversion device.

- The only backing of the securities issued by the entity is the assets, so these securities are asset-backed securities.

transferred by the originator and create securities based on such assets. Therefore, a vehicle is required to serve as an intermediary between the originator and the investors. But for such a vehicle, a transfer of assets between the originator and the investors will be a direct bilateral transfer and any further disposal thereof by the investors will be fraught with problems. We will discuss more of these problems later.

That is why we need a vehicle, but why a special purpose vehicle? The idea of a special purpose vehicle is to clothe an asset(s) with the garb of incorporation, so that one who owns the securities of the vehicle really owns the assets, no more and no less. A general purpose, or operating company, is not fit to hold securitized assets as such a company might have other assets and other liabilities, each of which might interfere with the exclusivity of rights over the assets that the transaction intends to give to the investors.

If an operating company holds assets, it might incur expenses, and/or incur liabilities, and might go bankrupt, thereby destroying the transaction. By its very nature, a special purpose vehicle is a legal shell with only the specific assets transferred by the originator, and those assets are either beneficially held by the investors or collateralize the securities of the vehicle; there is nothing left in the vehicle for anyone to have an interest in. A special purpose vehicle is a legal entity, but a substantive non-entity. This is what makes a special purpose vehicle bankruptcy-remote: Taking the special purpose vehicle to bankruptcy is almost the same as taking legal action against a pauper.

Re-distribution of risks

If there is a transfer of assets from the originator to the SPV (and from there, beneficially or indirectly to the investors), it should follow that there is a transfer of risk as well. For most financial assets, there is an element of credit risk, interest rate risk, or similar risks. How then are these risks re-distributed upon securitization?

In most securitization transactions, the risks are transferred in a structured fashion: Who takes the first hit, the next one, and thereafter until the last one is concerned or affected. Based on these priorities, risks are referred to as **first loss risk**, the second or subsequent loss risk, and so on. The one who takes the first loss risk is a **junior** holder, and the one who takes subsequent risk is a **senior** one. There might be one or more **mezzanine** security holders; if there are more than three classes, for want of better English terminology, the different classes can be referred to as **A Class, B Class, C Class** and so on, the first being the senior-most.

It is quite common for the originator to retain or re-acquire the first loss risk, that is, to the extent the total loss in the portfolio does not exceed the first loss limit, and the hit will be taken by the originator. This is done by one of the several methods of **credit enhancements** provided by the originator. The extent and nature of credit enhancement depend on the nature of the portfolio, underlying asset, and desired rating of the resultant securities and so on.

The essence of securitization is that unlike unstructured securities, investors do not take the same or similar exposure in the portfolio.

Rating

The need for rating of securitized products is clearly appreciated; investors expose themselves solely on the quality of the assets with a limited right of looking back at the originator. Therefore, it is natural that the investors must understand the quality of the portfolio. In some jurisdictions, regulations require asset-backed offerings to be rated.

There is, however, yet another aspect of rating in securitization transactions; if the securities being issued are structured, the rating of the senior security [see above] is a function of the loss protection it has from the junior one. That is, the higher the loss protection granted by the senior security, the greater the credit enhancement of the senior one. In essence, the rating of the senior security is a function of the amount of securities junior to it, which implies that in securitization transactions the rating of the senior securities is itself a derivative. In other words, you do not have to *arrive* at a rating, you can *target* a rating and structure the senior-junior hierarchy accordingly.

Securitization results in a rating arbitrage; ratings are raised because of and to the extent of subordination created. As the motivation for securitization is to see a rating upgrade, it is common to see securitization transactions rated.

The big picture of securitization of finance

In this section we see securitization in the setting of a larger transformation taking, place in global financial markets. Securitization is a part of this transformation.

Changing structure of financial markets

Institutionalization of savings

During the 1990s, a very significant change took place in U.S. financial markets – a replacement of traditional financial instruments with securitized instruments. Money markets, corporate bond markets, venture capital, and public equity substantially displaced the traditional financial instruments – bank deposits and loans – as both savings vehicles and sources of corporate finance. See Table 1.1.

Behind this change was a larger shift in the savings pattern – households putting an ever-increasing part of their savings into institutional vehicles, notably mutual funds. The share of mutual funds in total household savings has increased dramatically and as the data reveals, the money has moved away from traditional time and demand deposits in banks into institutional investments and capital markets.

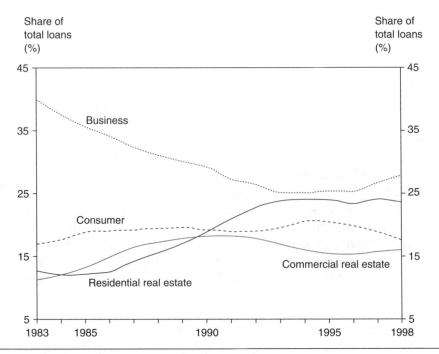

Figure 1.1   Types of Lending at U.S. Commercial Banks

Source: Reports of Condition and Income for banks

Box 1.4 Securitization and institutionalization of finance

- Securitization specifically, and capital market predominance in general, are the result of the growing institutionalization of finance.

- This is reflected in both the asset and liability sides of the banking system.

- Retail deposits fell significantly as money moved into institutional modes of savings.

- Thus, banks were forced to move their assets into capital markets.

- This led to commoditization of finance on both sides of the banking balance sheet.

The change in composition of household savings also led to an understandable change in composition of intermediaries. Banks received less money from depositors, and hence, their lending power fell substantially. Money passed on to the institutions, which gained more power. In 1999, traditional bank loans to U.S. companies fell to barely 12% of GDP, while the U.S. stock and bond markets each soared to values of more than 150% of GDP. Therefore, banks were both forced and motivated to access money from institutional intermediaries, that is, through capital markets rather than through deposits. These two changes took place slowly but surely and were self-reinforcing: one helped the other. See Figure 1.1.

Changes in corporate borrowing

This clearly meant that the corporate sector was depending less and less on banks as intermediaries, and seeking funding from a different, arguably more efficient, process of intermediation – capital markets.

The growing significance of capital market instruments as a means of funding the non-banking sector's balance sheet is visible in advanced markets and even

Table 1.1   Assets and liabilities of households, 1984–2004 (1) (US$ billions, end of year)

	Value			Percent of total		
	1984	*1994*	*2004*	*1984*	*1994*	*2004*
Total financial assets	**$6,699.5**	**$16,166.3**	**$32,876.7**	**100.0%**	**100.0%**	**100.0%**
Foreign deposits	6.9	18.8	101.4	0.1	0.1	0.3
Checkable deposits and currency	353.2	692.0	719.8	5.3	4.3	2.2
Time and savings deposits	1,875.3	2,220.9	4,463.7	28.0	13.7	13.6
Money market fund shares	191.0	367.6	943.6	2.9	2.3	2.9
Securities	1,565.2	5,904.5	12,245.7	23.4	36.5	37.2
Open market paper	42.0	46.7	126.8	0.6	0.3	0.4
U.S. savings bonds	74.5	179.9	204.4	1.1	1.1	0.6
Other Treasury securities	189.2	684.0	310.0	2.8	4.2	0.9
Agency- and GSE (2) -backed securities	12.7	49.5	349.3	0.2	0.3	1.1
Municipal securities	251.6	484.7	665.5	3.8	3.0	2.0
Corporate and foreign bonds	27.5	396.2	497.8	0.4	2.5	1.5
Corporate equities (3)	863.1	3,081.6	6,521.6	12.9	19.1	19.8
Mutual fund shares	104.6	981.9	3,570.4	1.6	6.1	10.9
Private life insurance reserves	236.1	491.5	1,067.3	3.5	3.0	3.2
Private insured pension reserves	328.3	796.6	2,002.8	4.9	4.9	6.1
Private non-insured pension reserves	897.4	2,470.9	4,490.6	13.4	15.3	13.7
Govt insurance and pension reserves	501.8	1,645.2	3,186.0	7.5	10.2	9.7
Investment in bank personal trusts	331.1	699.4	958.6	4.9	4.3	2.9
Miscellaneous and other assets	413.2	859.0	2,697.4	6.2	5.3	8.2
Total liabilities	**$3,092.5**	**$6,217.4**	**$14,542.7**	**100.0%**	**100.0%**	**100.0%**
Mortgage debt on nonfarm homes	1,317.9	3,289.3	8,049.0	42.6	52.9	55.3
Other mortgage debt (4)	607.8	857.8	1,652.8	19.7	13.8	11.4
Consumer credit	526.6	1,021.0	2,151.4	17.0	16.4	14.8
Policy loans	55.6	86.4	107.1	1.8	1.4	0.7
Security credit	31.8	75.1	263.4	1.0	1.2	1.8
Other liabilities (4)	552.7	887.9	2,319.0	17.9	14.3	15.9

(1) Combined statement for household sector, non farm and non corporate business and farm business. (2) GSE = Government Sponsored Enterprise. (3) Only those directly held and those in closed-end and exchange-traded funds. Other equities are included in mutual funds, life insurance and pension reserves, and bank personal trusts. (4) Includes corporate farms.

Source: Board of Governors of the Federal Reserve System. Available at http://www.financialservices facts.org/financial2/savings/ah/?table_sort_657060=9, last visited December 18, 2005.

Table 1.2   Rival sources of finance for the non-bank private sector[11]

	Borrowing from domestic banks[12] 1995–2000		Borrowing from international banks[13] 1995–2000		Borrowing from bond issuance[14] 1995–2000	
China	88	125	10	6	15	26
India	23	27	5	5	23	29
Russia	8	12	14	14	1	11
Hong Kong	144	154	368	118	12	23
Singapore	101	100	338	239	55	25
Indonesia	53	21	24	27	2	7
Korea	51	74	17	14	44	73
Malaysia	84	100	21	23	53	75
Philippines	39	45	11	22	3	18
Thailand	98	86	55	23	4	10
Argentina	20	23	13	17	10	25
Brazil	31	30	10	16	1	7
Chile	53	67	21	26	1	11
Colombia	18	19	11	15	1	8
Mexico	37	12	26	10	12	16
Peru	16	26	9	13	0	0
Venezuela	9	10	15	11	4	9
CzechRepublic	75	52	15	19	10	19
Hungary	24	36	18	30	57	49
Poland	18	30	6	10	11	18
Israel	70	87	5	8	1	4
Saudi Arabia	25	29	11	16	0	0
South Africa	58	68	10	15	2	4

Sources: IMF International Financial Statistics; national data; BIS statistics.

in emerging markets, as shown in the Table 1.2. The overall trend towards end-user corporates accessing resources from capital markets by offering various forms of securities is called *disintermediation*.

Securitization and disintermediation

Securitization has contributed to the pressures of disintermediation in more ways than one. Firstly, it allowed well-rated corporates to access resources cheaper than traditional capital market instruments such as bonds, and therefore, offered an added incentive to disintermediate. Secondly, it allowed even lower-rated corporates or corporates from emerging markets to sell their securities in the capital markets. Thirdly, the working capital needs that were mostly funded by the banking system have also moved into capital markets by devices such as asset-backed commercial paper. Fourthly, capital markets are still by and large closed for the start-up capital needed by small and medium enterprises that depends largely on the commercial banking system. Even this need is increasingly being met by capital markets through new instruments such as *primary market CDOs* as practiced in South Korea, for example.

Changes in bank liability structure

Like the corporates, even banks reduced their dependence on the traditional deposit. *ABA Banking Journal* ran a survey in May and June 1998 titled: "Has traditional funding become a "toast"?" [this probably referred to the toaster's apparent obsolescence due to the microwave]. The survey showed that six out of ten banks saw loan demand outstripping available deposits and nearly half of the banks surveyed were tapping non-deposit sources for funding. And this was mid-1998!

The institutionalization of savings had yet another visible impact – reducing the share of bank funding to larger corporates, who were trying to reduce their cost of borrowing by approaching the capital markets by issuing corporate bonds and commercial paper, and securitization. As seen in the chart above, the share of corporate loans in banks' total assets came down from over 40% in 1983 to just about 25% near 1998. Larger corporate clients of banks simply moved away from the banks to the capital markets.

With more money flowing through the capital markets, securitization was bound to happen on the scale at which we are seeing it today. Part of the demand for securitization comes from those financial intermediaries who are trying to keep up their lending, in spite of falling deposits, through securitization. In part, the demand comes from corporates looking at securitization as an efficient, cost effective, capital market-driven means of funding.

Securitization: changing the face of banking

Note the quotation that began this chapter, which says: Securitization is slowly but definitely changing the face of modern banking and by the new millennium would transform banking into a new-look function.

Banks are increasingly facing the threat of disintermediation. When asked why he robbed banks, the infamous American criminal Willie Sutton replied: "That's where the money is." No longer, banks would say! In a world of securitized assets, banks have diminished roles and the distinction between traditional bank lending and securitized lending clarifies this situation.

Traditional bank lending has **four functions:** originating, funding, servicing and monitoring. Originating means making the loan; funding implies that the loan is held on the balance sheet; servicing means collecting the payments of interest and principal, and monitoring refers to conducting periodic surveillance to ensure that the borrower has maintained the financial ability to service the loan. Securitized lending introduces the possibility of selling assets on a bigger scale and eliminating the need for funding and monitoring.

The securitized lending function has only **three steps** – originate, sell and service. This change from a four-step process to a three-step function has been described as the **fragmentation** or separation of traditional lending.

Capital markets fuels securitization

The fuel for the disintermediation market has been provided by the capital markets.

- Professional and publicly available ratings of borrowers have eliminated the informational advantage of financial intermediaries. Imagine a market without rating agencies: Anyone who has exposure in any product or entity has to appraise that entity. Obviously, only those who are able to employ advanced analytical skills will survive. However, the availability of professional and systematically conducted ratings has enabled lay investors to rely on the rating company's professional judgment and invest directly in the products or instruments of the user entities rather than to go through financial intermediaries.
- The development of capital markets has re-defined the role of bank regulators. A bank supervisory body is concerned about the risk concentrations taken by a bank. The more the risk undertaken, the more is the requirement of regulatory capital. On the other hand, if the same assets were distributed through the capital market to investors, the risk is divided and the only task of the regulator is that the risk inherent in the product is properly disclosed. The market sets its own price for risk – the higher the risk, the higher the return required.

Capital markets tend to align risk to risk takers. Free of the constraints imposed by regulators and risk-averse depositors and bank shareholders, capital markets efficiently align risk preferences and tolerances with issuers (borrowers) by giving providers of funds (capital market investors) only the necessary and preferred information. Any remaining informational advantage for banks is frequently offset by other features of the capital markets – the variety of offering methods, flexibility of timing and other structural options. For borrowers able to access capital markets directly, the cost of capital will be reduced according to the confidence that the investor has in the relevance and accuracy of the provided information.

As capital markets become more complete, financial intermediaries become less important as contact points between borrowers and savers. They become more important, however, as specialists that (1) complete markets by providing new products and services, (2) transfer and distribute various risks via structured deals, and (3) leverage their traditional skills of creation of credit assets by an underwriting process that selects the good borrowers and rejects the bad ones. These changes represent a shift away from the administrative structures of traditional lending to market-oriented structures for allocating money and capital.

In this sense, securitization is not really synonymous with disintermediation, but distribution of intermediary functions among specialist agencies.

Securitization and financial disintermediation

Securitization is often said to result in financial disintermediation, by allowing corporate customers to raise resources directly from the capital markets. This concept needs to be elaborated. The best way to understand this concept is to take the case of corporate bonds, a well-understood security.

As was discussed earlier, if one imagines a financial world without securities (and such a world is only imaginary), all financial transactions will be carried only as one-to-one relations. For example, if a company needs a loan, it will have to seek such a loan from lenders, and the lenders will have to establish a one-to-one relationship with the company. Each lender has to understand the borrowing company, and to look after his loan. This is often difficult, and hence, there appears a financial intermediary, such as a bank in this case, which pools funds from a group of such investors, and uses these pooled funds to lend to the company. Now, let us suppose the company securitizes the loan, and issues debentures to the investors. Will this eliminate the need for the intermediary bank? Investors can each lend to the company directly in small amounts, in the form of a security that is easy to appraise and is liquid.

Utilities added by financial intermediaries

A financial intermediary initially came into the picture to avoid the difficulties in a direct lender-borrower relationship between the company and investors. The difficulties could have been one or more of the following:

(a) **Transactional difficulty**: An average small investor would have a small amount to lend, whereas the company's needs are massive. The intermediary bank pools the funds from small investors to meet the typical needs of the company. The intermediary may issue its own security of smaller value.

(b) **Informational difficulty**: An average small investor would either be unaware of the borrower company or would not know how to appraise or manage the loan. The intermediary fills this gap.

(c) **Perceived risk**: The risk investors perceive in investing in a bank may be much less than that of investing directly in a company, although in reality the financial risk of the company is transposed on the bank. However, the bank is a pool of such individual risks, and so the investors' preference of a bank to the borrower company is reasonable.

Securitization of the loan into bonds or debentures fills all the three difficulties mentioned above, and so avoids the need for direct intermediation. It avoids the transactional difficulty by breaking the lumpy loan into marketable lots. It avoids informational difficulty because the securitized product is offered generally by way of a public offer, and its essential features are well disclosed. It avoids the perceived risk difficulty

> **Box 1.5 Securitization and disintermediation**
>
> - No doubt, securitization adds power to the process of disintermediation, as it moves more and more assets into the capital market directly.
>
> - However, securitization merely changes the role of financial intermediaries.
>
> - They partly become asset creators and processors, as in the mortgage markets.
>
> - And partly, they become facilitators of the process of securitization, as in the case of asset-backed commercial paper.

also, as the instrument is generally well secured and is rated for the investors' satisfaction.

Securitization changes the function of intermediation

It is true that securitization leads to a degree of disintermediation. Disintermediation is one of the important aims of a present-day corporate treasurer, as by leap-frogging the intermediary, the company intends to reduce the cost of its finances. Hence, securitization has been employed to disintermediate.

It is, however, important to understand that securitization does not eliminate the need for the intermediary; it merely redefines the intermediary's role. Let us revert to the above example. If the company mentioned above is issuing debentures to the public to replace a bank loan, is it eliminating the intermediary altogether? It may possibly avoid the bank as an intermediary in the financial flow, but would still need the services of an investment banker to successfully conclude the issue of debentures.

Hence, securitization changes the basic role of financial intermediaries. Traditionally, financial intermediaries have emerged to make a transaction possible by performing a pooling function and have contributed to reduce the investors' perceived risk by substituting their own security for that of the end user. Securitization puts these services of the intermediary in the background by making it possible for the end-user to offer these features in the form of the security; in which case, the focus shifts to the more essential function of a financial intermediary – distributing a financial product. As in the above case, where the bank acting as the earlier intermediary was eliminated and the services of an investment banker were sought to distribute a debenture issue, the focus shifted from the pooling utility provided by the banker to the distribution utility provided by the investment banker.

This has happened to physical products as well. With standardization, packaging and branding of physical products, the role of intermediary traders, particularly retailers, shifted from those who packaged smaller qualities or provided the customer assurance as to the quality, to ones who basically performed the distribution function.

Securitization seeks to eliminate fund-based financial intermediaries by fee-based distributors. In the above example, the bank was a fund-based intermediary – a reservoir of funds, whereas the investment banker was a fee-based intermediary, a catalyst or a pipeline of funds. Thus, with the increasing trend towards securitization, the role of fee-based financial services has been brought into focus.

In case of a direct loan, the lending bank was performing several intermediation functions noted above: It was distributor in the sense that it raised its own finances from a large number of small investors; it appraising and assessing the credit risk in extending the corporate loan, and having extended it, managed the same. Securitization splits each of these intermediary functions with each to be performed by separate specialized agencies; the distribution function will be peformed by the investment bank, the appraisal function by a credit-rating agency and management function possibly by a mutual fund that manages the portfolio of security investments by the investors. Hence, securitization replaces fund-based services by several fee-based services.

Securitization as a tool of risk management

Securitization is more than just a financial tool. It is an important element in risk management for banks, allowing them to not only remove substantial concentrations and values at risk, but also permits them to acquire securitized assets with potential diversification benefits. When assets are removed from a bank's balance sheet with a defined recourse or first loss risk, the bank limits its loss exposure to the amount of recourse or first loss protection provided by it[15]. Credit and interest rate risks are the key uncertainties that concern domestic lenders. By passing on these to investors, or to third parties when credit enhancements are involved, financial firms are better able to manage their risk exposure.

In today's banking, securitization is increasingly resorted to by the banks, along with other innovations such as **credit derivatives,** to manage credit risk.

Securitization and credit derivatives

Credit derivatives were developed along the lines of other OTC derivatives but have found an excellent companion in securitization. A credit derivative is a non-fund based contract in which one party agrees to undertake, for a fee, the risk inherent in a credit without acting or taking over the credit. This could be either the risk of specified *credit events* such as bankruptcy or failure to pay or could be the risk of any deviation in the total return from a credit asset.

The party that provides protection against such risk is called the *protection seller* and the party that buys such protection, normally but not necessarily the originator of the credit asset, is called the *protection buyer*.

The concept of credit derivatives is discussed at length in Vinod Kothari's book *Credit Derivatives and Synthetic Securitisation*.[16]

In a sense, credit derivatives seem to contradict securitization. Securitization results in the transfer of the assets of the originator, while the risk is largely retained by one or more credit enhancements of the originator. Credit derivatives, on the other hand, do not result in a transfer of the assets but transfer of the risk. Therefore, the two operate apparently in opposite directions.

Synthetic securitization

In reality, the marketplace has seen interesting and rapidly increasing application of securitization, combined with credit derivatives, in synthetic securitization.

Synthetic securitization can be explained in various ways – as a synthesis of securitization and credit derivatives, securitization of credit derivatives, or embedding credit derivatives in securities. All of these descriptions are correct, but what goes to the root of the term "synthetic security" is the idea of synthetically creating an asset by a credit derivative transaction. If the soul of an asset is really a bundle of risks and rewards (leave aside the body of an asset – the funding), a protection seller in a credit derivative transaction exposes himself to the credit risk of a credit asset, and logically enjoys the credit spread inherent in the asset. Therefore, though the protection seller does not buy the asset as such, he synthetically creates or buys the asset that is actually held by the protection buyer. As opposed to a traditional or *cash securitization* that is achieved by transfer of the assets of the originator, a synthetic securitization is accomplished by a synthetic transfer of such assets, and so the term synthetic securitization.

We discuss synthetic securitization at length in Chapter 22.

Economic impact of securitization

Securitization is as necessary to the economy as any organized markets are. While this sums up the economic significance of securitization, the following are the economic merits of securitization:

1. Facilitates creation of markets in financial claims

By creating tradable securities out of financial claims, securitization helps to create markets in claims that would, in its absence, have remained bilateral deals. In the process, securitization makes financial markets more efficient by **reducing agency costs**.

It makes financial assets tradable and also reduces the liquidity risk in the financial system. Liquidity-related problems have been responsible for a number of economic crises, such as those occurred in Southeast Asia in 1997. Securitization can help financial intermediaries to better manage asset liability mismatches and therefore avert liquidity problems. The result is that the need for risk capital, among other things, to support liquidity is also reduced.

2. Disperses holding of financial assets

The basic intent of securitization is to spread financial assets among as many savers as possible. With this end, the security is designed in marketable lots, which result in dispersion of financial assets.

One should not underestimate the significance of this factor because most of the recently developed securitizations have been lapped up by institutional investors. Lay investors need a certain cooling-off period before they understand a financial innovation. While other esoteric securitization classes may be too sophisticated for retail investors to understand, matured asset classes such as mortgages are attractive to retail investors.

3. Promotes savings

The availability of financial claims in a marketable form, with proper assurance on quality in the form of credit ratings and with the double safety net of trustees or others, makes it possible for the lay investors to invest in direct financial claims at attractive rates. This has a salubrious effect on savings.

4. Reduces costs

As discussed above, securitization tends to eliminate fund-based intermediaries and leads to specialization in intermediation functions. This saves the end-user company from intermediation costs, as the specialised-intermediary costs are service-related and generally lower. Securitization connects a lending activity directly to capital markets, thereby more efficiently connecting the provider of funds (the capital markets) with the user of funds (borrowers in the system). More will be explained later in this chapter on the impact of securitization on the cost of funding in a system.

Another reason why securitization is believed to reduce costs is the tranching of risk or structuring of securities. This is an important attribute of securitization and this is where the alchemy of securitization lies (see the next section).

5. Diversifies risk

Financial intermediation is a case of diffusion of risk because of accumulation by the intermediary of a portfolio of financial risks. Securitization further diffuses such diversified risk to a wide base of investors, and the result is that the risk inherent in financial transactions gets widely diffused. The former chairman of the Federal Reserve, Alan Greenspan, lauded the risk-modulating impact of securitization thus: "These instruments (securitization, CDOs) have been used to disperse risk to those willing, and presumably able, to bear it. Indeed, credit decisions as a result are often made contingent on the ability to lay off significant parts of the risk. Such dispersal of risk has contributed greatly to the ability of banks – indeed of the financial system – to weather recent stresses. More generally, the development of these instruments and techniques has led to greater credit availability, to a more efficient allocation of risk and resources, and to stronger financial markets."[17]

6. Focuses on use of resources, not their ownership

Once an entity securitizes its financial claims, it ceases to be the owner of such resources and becomes merely a trustee or custodian for the several investors who thereafter acquire such claims. Imagine securitization being carried not only financial claims but further to claims in physical assets being securitized, wherein the entity needing use of the physical assets acquires such without owning the property. The property is diffused over an investor group.

In this sense, securitization carries Gandhi's idea of a capitalist being a trustee of resources and not the owner.

7. Smooths the impact of recession

In 1991, when the U.S. economy was passing through recession, securitization was booming. A December 1991 article in *Institutional Investor* said: "The asset-backed securities market is roaring its way through the recession with record issuance and reliable performance that prove it has come of age." In 2001-2002, the global economy passed through multifarious problems such as large bankruptcies and terrorism, but securitization markets have continued to grow, and the growth has been widespread across different sectors. Evidently, more money is being raised by credit card securitization than in the past, which means consumer spending is being propped up by the capital markets. More auto loans have been securitized in 2002 than in the past, so auto sales have been supported by securitization. All this tends to ease the impact of economic recession.

The alchemy of securitization: Is the sum of parts more than the whole?

An essential economic question often raised is: Does securitization lead to any overall social benefit? After all, securitization breaks a company – a set of various assets into various subsets of classified assets, and offers them to investors. Imagine a world without securitization: Each investor taking a risk in the unclassified, composite company as a whole. So, how does it serve an economic purpose if the company is "de-composed" and sold to different investors?

We have discussed earlier that securitization essentially involves putting a section of investors in a position of priority over others. If there is any advantage for these investors, it is at the cost of the other investors, and therefore, the sum of the risk-return profile of these different investors should add back to that of the firm as a whole.

The alchemy of structured finance

Structured finance, generically, relies on the essential principle that there is an arbitrage in risk-reward tranching, and that the sum of the parts is different from the whole. Like the rest of our society, the investor fraternity is made of inequalities all around, such as unequal risk-return appetite, unequal preference to a payback period and pattern, etc. Therefore, structuring – carving out different statures or priorities, patterns and preferences for different investors, makes eminent sense.

The most evident example of the alchemy of securitization is arbitrage activity. An arbitrage vehicle buys assets, and finances the same issuing asset-backed securities, thereby making an arbitrage profit in the process. Obviously, there is no reason for the weighted average cost of the funding to be lower than the weighted average return from the assets, but the market proves

> Box 1.6 Is the sum of parts greater than the whole?
>
> - The firm itself is a pool and all that securitization does is decompose it into various asset pools.
>
> - The sum of these pools must be equal to the sum of the parts, because logically there cannot be any arbitrage in mere differentiation and integration.
>
> - However, markets are not arbitrage free. Experience proves that there is arbitrage in segmentation.
>
> - This is the same as there are classes for every walk of life.

that there is an arbitrage involved in stratification of the risks in the asset portfolio.

Structured finance

The principle of structured finance believes in structural arbitrage, which may be theoretically disputed but has been practically observed quite clearly.

Professor Steven Schwarcz in his book *Structured Finance*[18] has argued at length that securitization does reduce funding costs for an organization and therefore is not a zero sum game. His arguments essentially hinge on the economic rationale for secured lending, as any secured lending by definition puts the secured lender at priority to the unsecured one. Also, securitization creates a capital market avenue, and certainly capital market funding is more efficient than funding by intermediaries. The role of intermediaries is important for credit creation and capital allocation, but funding should come from where it eventually comes – households.

Lower costs due to higher leverage

After the bankruptcy of Enron in late 2001, securitization came into sharp focus and academicians on one hand and investment bankers on the other entered into the popular duel of whether securitization reduces lending costs at all. Rating agency Moody's released a compendium of its views on securitization called *Moody's Perspective 1987–2002: Securitization and its Effect on the Credit Strength of Companies.* In response to its own question, Moody's had the following comment to make:

> **Does securitization provide access to low-cost funding?**
> Not really. Many in the market believe that securitization offers "cheap funding" because the pricing on the debt issued in a securitization transaction is typically lower than pricing on the company's unsecured borrowings. However, the securitization debt is generally backed by high-quality assets, cash held in reserve funds, and may be over-collateralized. This means that the relatively lower pricing comes at the expense of providing credit enhancement to support the securitization debt.

It is true that credit enhancement by way of over-collateralization or otherwise is an inherent cost for the securitization transaction, but it is important to understand the nature of credit enhancement. In normal corporate funding, the equity of the firm is the credit enhancement for the lender, as equity is the first loss capital of the firm. The extent of such credit enhancement – appropriate leverage ratios for the firm – is in general extraneously fixed either by regulation or lending practices. For example, a straight-jacket debt/equity norms of a traditional lender, or the capital adequacy norms of financial regulators, put limits on the leverage. Thereby, firms are forced to require much higher credit enhancements in the form of equity than warranted. In the case of securitization, the required credit enhancement is related to the expected losses in the portfolio, and so it is directly connected with the risks of the portfolio.

Box 1.7 Securitization and leverage

- Behind the sophisticated argument of structured finance, there is a greater urge of raising higher leverage.

- Traditional corporate finance is concerned with entity-wide risks and therefore puts limits on the extent of leverage.

- Securitization structures take a more portfolio-specific view of the risks, and permit higher leverage by requiring lower credit enhancements.

- The result is that entities may build bigger asset bases with a meager amount of capital.

If we believe that equity is a costlier funding source than external funding, the higher leverage requirements imposed by traditional lending or regulatory capital requirements impose higher-weighted average funding costs on the firm. Securitization allows the firm to leverage itself more, and therefore attain a lower funding cost or attain correspondingly higher returns on equity. However, it is necessary to understand that such higher returns do not arise from more efficient operations but from higher leverage.

Securitization results in lower-weighted average costs for the following reasons:

- Rating arbitrage: Securitization allows entity ratings to remain unaffected and the transaction to ratings solely on the strength of its assets and the inherent credit enhancements. The best example of this was in May 2005, when the U.S. auto giants General Motors and Ford were downgraded, but that did not reduce their securitization volume; in fact, the volumes increased and the securities received a AAA rating. In fact, the existing securities from some existing transactions were upgraded to AAA level, essentially because of an increase in credit support levels.

- The rating arbitrage is understandable due to isolation of assets from the originator, bankruptcy risk and underlying credit support in the transaction.

- Because of the isolated pool and the insulation this provides against general entity-wide risks, the inherent leverage of a securitization transaction – the extent of funding built upon economic equity of the transaction is much higher.

- The higher the leverage, the lower the weighted-average cost.

Capturing scale and volume efficiencies

In a capital structure framework, higher returns on equity by taking higher leverage as well as higher risk, – is really no efficiency. Therefore, we seem to be back at where we started – a zero sum game. However, there is also potential for more efficient operations – the larger the scale of operations, which can be particularly significant in retail lending. Certainly, entities active in securitization have grown quickly and have attained a size by which they have economies of scale and scope.

Risks inherent in securitization

The **Bank for International Settlements** in a 1992 publication titled *Asset Transfers and Securitization* had the following to say:

The possible effects of securitization on financial systems may well differ between countries because of differences in the structure of financial systems or because of differences in the way in which monetary policy is executed. In addition, the effects will vary depending upon the stage of development of securitization in a particular country. The net effect may be potentially beneficial or harmful, but a number of concerns are highlighted below that may in certain circumstances more than offset the benefits. Several of these concerns are not principally supervisory in nature, but they are referred to here because they may influence monetary authorities' policy on the development of securitization markets.

While asset transfers and securitization can improve the efficiency of the financial system and increase credit availability by offering borrowers direct access to end-investors, the process may on the other hand lead to some diminution in the importance of banks in the financial intermediation process. In the sense that securitization could reduce the proportion of financial assets and liabilities held by banks, this could render more difficult the execution of monetary policy in countries where central banks operate through variable minimum reserve requirements. A decline in the importance of banks could also weaken the relationship between lenders and borrowers, particularly in countries where banks are predominant in the economy.

One of the benefits of securitization, namely the transformation of illiquid loans into liquid securities, may lead to an increase in the volatility of asset values, although credit enhancements could lessen this effect. Moreover, the volatility could be enhanced by events extraneous to variations in the credit standing of the borrower. A preponderance of assets with readily ascertainable market values could even, in certain circumstances, promote liquidation as opposed to going-concern concept for valuing banks.

Moreover, the securitization process might lead to some pressure on the profitability of banks if non-bank financial institutions exempt from capital requirements were to gain a competitive advantage in investment in securitized assets.

Although securitization can have the advantage of enabling lending to take place beyond the constraints of the capital base of the banking system, the process could lead to a decline in the total capital employed in the banking system, thereby increasing the financial fragility of the financial system as a whole, both nationally and internationally. With a substantial capital base, credit losses can be absorbed by the banking system. But the smaller that capital base is, the more the losses must be shared by others. This concern applies, not necessarily in all countries, but especially

> **Box 1.8 Securitization and sub-prime lending**
>
> - One common fear about securitization is that it may, or it does encourage sub-prime (junk) lending.
>
> - Banks generate credits that they would not tolerate on their balance sheets and parcel them off into securitization vehicles.
>
> - Several securitization conduits are administered by investment bankers rather than by the hardened, older bankers of yesteryear.
>
> - And the ultimate investors who put money into these conduits are unduly impressed by the sophistry of the transaction structure, with elaborate credit enhancements and rating rationale.

in those countries where banks have traditionally been the dominant financial intermediaries.

The above highlights the risks inherent in securitization. BIS has expressed concern about the relatively smaller capital base of the banking system supporting a much larger asset size. From a macro-economic perspective, this is not the only concern, as several other concerns are engaging the attention of banking regulators and academicians worldwide.

Abdication of credit – sub-prime lending created and sold

One of the oft-repeated concerns is that securitization has motivated banks and non-banks to create bad credits. The rationale is simple: Securitization motivates banks to create loans that they would hate to hold on their balance sheet. Given their ability to push junk assets into the capital market with a given amount of credit enhancement (a large part of which is nothing but the banks' profit in creating the credit, called *excess spread*), banks are generally seen to have abdicated their prime responsibility – credit.

That banks are eager to securitize their relatively riskier assets is easily established by the extent of sub-prime lending being securitized into manufactured home loans, sub-prime loans, sub-prime credit card receivables and auto loan receivables, home equity loans and others. "Sub-prime lending can be a pretty sleazy business. Lenders seek out customers with either spotty credit histories or no credit histories at all – typically low-income people – and often charge exorbitant interest rates and fees to compensate for the risk of default. It's not a new idea, as finance companies were built on sub-prime loans made during the Depression, although nobody used the term then. But once credit cards became a ubiquitous part of American life, and companies improved in use of demographics to target potential borrowers, the business really began to flourish."[19] And the fact is that most of the sub-prime lending portfolios finally found their way into the securitization markets.

Banking regulators have been aware of this risk for quite sometime; in a letter **SR 97-21 (SUP) July 11, 1997,** the U.S. Department of Banking Supervision and Regulation cautioned: "The heightened need for management attention to these risks is underscored by reports from examiners, senior lending officer surveys, and discussions with trade and advisory groups that have indicated that competitive conditions over the past few years have encouraged an easing of credit terms and conditions in both commercial and consumer lending."

Yet another fact serves this point: The case of Superior Bank, which failed and was closed in July 2001 (see below).

A **Business Week** article[20] titled *The Breakdown in Banking* says securitization is a US$7 trillion business today, a large part of which are the loans, credit card debt, sub-prime debt and mortgage loans written by banks that are converted into securities and sold off in the capital market. The spin-off of this process is that banks do not absorb the risks of the credits they create. The authors of the article say: "By selling off their loans, banks were able to lend to yet more borrowers because they could reuse their capital over and over. But it also meant that they made lending decisions based on what the market wanted rather than on their own credit judgements. The wholesale offloading of risk made the banking system less of a buffer and more of a highly streamlined transmitter of the whims of the market."

"Besides re-use of capital which creates excessive leverage on the whole, there is an inevitable question of moral hazard – the creation of credit without enough at stake. This leads to a temptation for banks to scrutinize borrowers less carefully than when their own money was at stake. The banks abdicated credit judgement and the people to whom they sold the paper had no credit judgement," says Martin Mayer, a guest scholar at the Brookings Institution and author of *The Bankers*.

The threat of unhealthy banking assets being pushed into securitization markets became more worrying in 2004 and 2005 as U.S. banks more aggressively and increasingly wrote poor quality mortgage loans with features such as optional adjustability, negative amortization and interest-only payment. Banks were pushing more of these loans into the securitization market.

Trading on thin capital

We have noted earlier that securitization creates for banks an ability to leverage their existing capital and resources to create more assets. This leads to excessive leverage. Excessive leverage can be compared to a multi-storey civic structure. If you intend to construct the 90-storey Petronas Tower, you obviously need a broad base to build on. The risk capital of a bank is its foundation, its base. In physics, a cone resting on its vertex is an unstable equilibrium; for an object to be stably placed on ground, its center of gravity must be closest to the base. The same rule applies to business entities: There is an imaginary center of gravity in an enterprise based on its size and this center must lie somewhere close to the base, which is the equity capital of the enterprise. There is no doubt that with the higher leverage attained due to off-balance sheet exposure, banks have become extremely vulnerable to economic cycles.

Off-balance sheet financing

Off-balance sheet assets of leading banks came into sharp focus after the Enron debacle, which was mainly related to off-balance sheet risks. During these discussions, Standard and Poor's published data about off-balance sheet assets of the 30 top securitizers in the U.S. (see Table 1.3). There were some banks whose off-balance sheet assets exceeded those on the balance sheet, bringing home the point that the retained risks in these transactions might put pressure on the capital of the banks:

Table 1.3 Off-balance sheet assets of certain U.S. banks

Company	Total securitized incl. CP (US$)	Assets (%)
Citigroup Inc.	129,452	12.1
ABN-Amro Bank N.V.	92,304	17.8
J.P. Morgan Chase & Co.	80,652	10.1
Bank One Corp.	78,998	29.2
MBNA Corp.	73,534	170.6
Bank of America Corp.	43,066	6.7
Wachovia Corp.	39,757	12.2
Countrywide Credit Industries Inc.	36,032	100.6
Deutsche Bank AG	33,041	6.4
Morgan Stanley Dean Witter & Co.	30,650	6.4
Abbey National PLC	29,255	9.6
Credit Suisse Group	29,097	4.8
Royal Bank of Scotland Group PLC	23,929	4.5
FleetBoston Financial Corp.	19,976	9.9
U.S. Bancorp	18,622	11.1
Westdeutsche Landesbank Girozentrale	17,984	4.6
Rabobank Nederland	17,679	5.6
Wells Fargo & Co.	17,050	5.7
Canadian Imperial Bank of Commerce	15,913	8.4
Bayerische Hypo- und Vereinsbank AG	14,771	2.3
Bank of Montreal	14,002	9.0
Toronto-Dominion Bank	13,007	6.4
Bank of Nova Scotia	11,789	6.2
AmSouth Bancorp	9,196	24.0
KeyCorp	8,052	9.6
GreenPoint Financial Corp.	7,223	36.1
Royal Bank of Canada	6,804	2.9
Zions Bancorp.	6,762	27.9
SunTrust Banks Inc.	6,467	6.3
Mellon Financial Corp.	6,216	13.0
HSBC Holdings PLC	5,071	1.8

Securitization, under its current accounting standards, not only permits but also requires off-balance sheet funding. Off-balance sheet funding became a dirty word in reaction to Enron's collapse;[21] there were several investigations into potential misapplication of the concept of SPVs. There is even an attempt to re-define qualifying SPEs for U.S. Accounting Standards whereby the QSPE status will be denied to several SPEs.[22]

Increases opaqueness of banks

Banks that securitize assets and still retain significant risks get into a serious situation where the assets disappear from the books and the risks stay. There is no better way of measuring risk than the accountant's rudimentary tool – the balance sheet. Securitization demolishes the accountant's balance sheet as a risk-measuring device and stretches out to off-balance sheet assets. The predicament is that a bank may carry inordinate risks not reflected on the face of its balance sheet.

These retained risks are reflected in the valuation of retained or residual interests in securitization. Simply, as banks retain risks post-securitization, they also retain rewards, that is, the residual cash flow after paying off external investors. As this is residual or subordinated, the risk referred to earlier should actually hive off from the residual value. There have been at least three cases of bank failures in the U.S. because of improper valuation of the residuals, or bluntly, improper appreciation of the risk on securitized assets: Superior Bank, First National Bank of Keystone, and Pacific Thrift and Loan.

Securitization makes a bank more opaque to a regulator. "Major banks have increased their opacity to regulators and the securities markets by (i) increasing their lending exposures to below-investment-grade companies and sub prime consumers, (ii) securitizing their assets, and (iii) expanding their dealing and trading activities in securities and OTC derivatives."[23]

The case of Superior Bank[24]

The case of Superior Bank easily highlights the risk inherent in securitization. The bank was virtually romancing with sub-prime lending behind the securitization facade. In 1993, it began to originate and securitize sub-prime home mortgages in large volumes and later, finding that there were investors who buy up what the bank itself hated to keep on its balance sheet, it expanded its activities to include sub-prime automobile loans as well. As usual, the bank was supporting its securitization business with residual interests and over-collateralization. Superior's residual interests represented approximately 100% of Tier-1 capital on June 30, 1995. By June 30, 2000, residual interest represented 348% of Tier 1 capital, which meant that the risk on the asset side was $3\frac{1}{2}$ times the risk on the liability side. After all, we have discussed earlier in this chapter, the first loss risk retained by the originator in a securitization transaction is comparable to equity in a corporation. If Tier 1 capital is the first loss support to the bank, the equity holders in Superior Bank agreed to absorb first loss risk of $1, and correspondingly, the bank went out in the market to bear first loss risk to the extent of $3.48. To a layman, it would mean having $1 in my pocket and going to the casino and putting down a bet of $3.48. However, the regulators did not see this for quite sometime.

Not only did the bank's financials hide the risk, on the contrary, they continued to book profits on the sale of sub-prime loans, which is allowed and required under U.S. Accounting Standards. "Superior's practice of targeting sub prime borrowers increased its risk. By targeting borrowers with low credit quality, Superior was able to originate loans with interest rates that were higher than market averages. The high interest rates reflected, at least in part, the relatively high credit risk associated with these loans. When these loans were then pooled and securitized, their high interest rates relative to the interest rates paid on the resulting securities, together with the high valuation of the retained interest, enabled Superior to record gains on the securitization transactions that drove its apparently high earnings and high capital. A significant amount of Superior's revenue was from the sale of loans in these transactions, yet more cash was going out rather than coming in from these activities."[25]

The bubble burst when regulators required the bank to revalue its residual interests when the bank became undercapitalized and was ordered to be closed.[26]

Cross-sector risk transfers

It is contended, though without compelling evidence, that the dispersal of risk resulting due to securitization its distribution into unrelated segments pose threats to the stability of the system, as a shock to the banking sector may quickly spread to completely unrelated sectors. It is a fact that due to securitization, particularly the synthetic CDOs, risks in banking assets have been transferred to insurance companies, investment companies, venture capital funds and the like who buy these securities.[27] On the one hand, Alan Greenspan thinks that the system has become more resilient with the spread of risk. On the other hand, there are some who are concerned about making the entire system more susceptible to shocks from cross-sector risk transfers.

Monetary policy sterilized

There is a contention that securitization reduces the efficacy of monetary policy as banks derive more of their funding from capital markets, and likewise, as disintermediation results in more direct funding by capital markets rather than through banks. If monetary policy is concerned with changing the market conditions for banks with a certain objective, securitization provides banks with an added flexibility of seeking a capital market access.

In sum, securitization is an interesting financial instrument and is today an indelible global phenomenon. However, there is no doubt this development has posed new challenges for all concerned – investors, regulators and banks. Years ago, in an article titled **On the Frontiers of Creative Finance: How Wall Street Can Securitise Anything**[28] Kim Clark noted: "Investors do need to beware, of course. Financial markets are notorious for pushing investment ideas into the absurd. Some of these exotic securities will undoubtedly collapse, which will undoubtedly cause a backlash."

Notes

1   The joint-stock form of ownership seems to have originated in the 12th Century in Italy; There is evidence that construction and operation of ships were funded by jointly contributed capital or stock. However, the idea of a tradable instrument such as a share of a fixed denomination seems to have become popular much later – around the 16th Century. The Joint East India Company in 1602 was funded by thousands of shareholders, contributing a total of 6.5 million florins.

2 Conceptually, an equity share is an obligation to distribute while debt is an obligation to pay. The simplest form of securitized instruments, *pass-through certificates,* also imply an obligation to distribute and hence are closer to equity than debt.

3 See, for example, the OECD publication titled Trends and Developments in Securitization, Financial *Market Trends,* No. 74, October 1999: "Initially, the term was applied to the process of disintermediation, or the substitution of security issues for bank lending. More recently, the term has been used to refer to so-called "structured finance"".

4 Quoted in Kendall, Leon T and Michael J Fishman (ed): *A Primer on Securitization* 1996.

5 See section title Alchemy of Securitization

6 Covered bonds are generally used in some European countries and have arguably served as an effective alternative to isolation-type securitization devices. This is discussed in a later chapter.

7 OECD publication titled Trends and Developments in Securitisation, *Financial Market Trends,* No. 74, October 1999

8 **What Is Securitization?** Commentary dated November 28, 2000

9 See details in Chapter 2.

10 See in Chapter 19 for details. See also Chapter 23 on Legal Issues in Future flows.

11 As percentage to GDP end-year data.

12 Domestic credit to the private sector.

13 Liabilities to BIS reporting banks

14 Domestic and international securities on issue

15 For more on the impact of securitization on economic capital, see Chapter 21 on Regulatory Capital

16 See for details at http://credit-deriv.com/crebook.htm

17 "The Continued Strength of the U.S. Banking System" by Alan Greenspan was delivered at the American Bankers Association conference in Phoenix, October 7, 2002. Greenspan has praised CDOs, mortgage-backed securities and other instruments for risk dispersion.

18 Third edition, 2002, Appendix A

19 Suzanne Koudsi, **Sleazy Credit**: *Fortune*; March 4, 2002.

20 Internet edition October 7, 2002

21 Here is an example of a public outcry against off-balance sheet funding from *Business* Week January 28, 2002: "When energy trader Enron Corp. admitted to hiding billions of dollars of liabilities in mysterious off-book entities, it trotted out the lame excuse of scoundrels: Everyone does it. And this time, it was the gospel truth . . . Hundreds of respected U.S. companies are ferreting away trillions of dollars in debt in off-balance-sheet subsidiaries, partnerships, and assorted obligations, including leases, pension plans, and take-or-pay contracts with suppliers. Potentially bankrupting contracts are mentioned vaguely in footnotes to company accounts, at best. The goal is to skirt the rules of consolidation, the bedrock of the American financial reporting system and the source of much its credibility."

22 See Chapter 27 on Accounting Issues

23 Controlling Systemic Risk in an Era of Financial Consolidation, July 2002 paper by Prof. Arthur E. Wilmarth, Jr.

24 There are more cases from the securitization "hall of shame" at http://vinod-kothari.com/sadepisodes.htm

25 Analysis of the Failure of Superior Bank: Statement of Thomas J.McCool, Managing Director, Financial Markets and Community Investment before the Committee on Banking, Housing, and Urban Affairs, U.S. Senate, Feb 7 2002

26 See also a detailed investigation report of the Inspector General, FDIC: *Issues Relating to the Failure of Superior Bank* February 6, 2002, at http://www.fdicig.gov/reports02/02-005.pdf, last visited Dec 18, 2005

27 Financial Services Authority, UK issued a discussion paper in May 2002 on cross sector risk transfers. Insurance regulators – Joint Forum of International Association of Insurance Supervisors – also published a paper titled *Risk Management Practices and Regulatory Capital: Cross-Sectoral Comparison* (Nov 2001). The Financial Stability Forum has also included cross-sectoral risk transfer as an area for further study. These issues are discussed at length in Vinod Kothari's *Credit Derivatives and Synthetic Securitisation.*

28 *Fortune*, April 28, 1997.

Securitization Terminology

A

A Notes – Class A of notes, that is, senior notes. Notes or securities which are senior to the other classes, such as Class B, and so on.

ABCP – See **Asset-backed Commercial Paper**

ABS – See **Asset-backed Securities**.

Acceleration – Generally refers to the underlying covenant in reinstating assets securitization and future flows securitization that the repayment of principal to the investors in a transaction will be accelerated upon the happening of certain events, normally events such as a fall in the degree of over-collateralization and under-performance events. **Acceleration** can also be used to indicate a stricter action where the entire amount invested by investors becomes immediately due.

Actionable Claims – A legal word for receivables, right to claim.

Adjustable Rate Mortgages – Is a mortgage loan which has a coupon or interest rate that is subject to change on predetermined reset dates, on the basis of variations in a reference rate. These loans use interest rate indices as the reference rate. **Adjustable rate loans** may have cap and floor features.

Administrator – Loosely refers to the entity doing **servicing** functions in a securitization; in case of a **conduit** program, might refer to the party doing administrative functions such as maintaining the bank accounts into which payments received from securitized assets are deposited, making payments to the investors using this cash flow, and monitoring the performance of the securitized assets.

Advance Rate – The extent to which an advance, that is, a loan was given against the value of an asset. Similar to **LTV Ratio**.

Adverse Selection – The possibility that due to information symmetry, an **originator** will transfer low quality assets to a securitization pool, or that better quality assets are likely to prepay over time, leaving pool quality assets in the pool.

Agency – Refers to the U.S. government agencies for promoting mortgage secondary markets. In market language, it may also refer to a security issued by these organisations. These organisations include: the **Federal Home Loan Mortgage Corporation (FHLMC or Freddie Mac),** the **Federal National Mortgage Association (FNMA or Fannie Mae),** the **Government National Mortgage Association (GNMA or Ginnie Mae)**.

Agency Securities – In the U.S. parlance, refers to the mortgage-backed securities issued by agencies. Compare with **Private Label Securities**.

All-in Cost – All-inclusive cost of a securitization, after taking into account the upfront cost.

Amortization – Repayment of principal on an investment inherent in regular periodic payments. **Amortization** is often classified as scheduled **amortization** and prepayment, with the former meaning the **amortization** if the payments were to be made as per schedule of payments fixed under each of the original loan transactions.

Amortization Period – In the context of reinstating transactions, the period after the reinstatement period, during which the cash flows arising out of **amortization** of assets will be used to amortize the securities.

Arbitrage Transactions – Transactions of securitization where assets are acquired from various **originators**, or from the market, and are securitized with the motive of making an arbitrage profit being the difference between the weighted average return of the assets and the weighted average coupon on the liabilities.

Arbitrage CDO – A CDO for the purpose of arbitraging. Compare with **Balance Sheet CDO**.

Asset-backed Commercial Paper – Where assets, usually short-term receivables such as trade receivables, are pooled into a vehicle that issues **commercial paper** typically of 90 days to 180 days maturity, such commercial paper, in tune with asset-backed securities is called asset-backed commercial paper. The vehicle may be a **conduit** for a single-seller, or various sellers of receivables, in which case it is called multi-seller ABCP conduit.

Asset-backed Securities (ABS) – Generically, any security backed by assets rather than a general obligation of someone to pay. Securitized instruments are asset-backed securities. In U.S. market parlance, MBS and ABS are distinctively used with ABS referring to securities backed by non-mortgage receivables.

Assignment – In relation to receivables, it means the legal action of transfer of receivables from one person to another. In relation to a mortgage, it would mean the transfer of a mortgage by the mortgagee (borrower and occupier) to another person.

Attachment Point – A term commonly used in case of **synthetic CDOs,** it means the level at which losses in a pool will attach to the particular class of securities. Contrast with **Detachment Point**.

Average Maturity – See **Weighted-Average Maturity**.

Average Life – The duration of a securitization investment, that is, weighted-average time outstanding for the principal invested.

B

B Notes – Compare with **A notes**.

Backstop Facility – A stand-by facility, that is, a liquidity arrangement whereby another party agrees to make a payment should the primary party not be able to do so, essentially for providing liquidity.

Back-up Servicer – In securitization transactions, it is customary for the **originator** to continue to service the original transaction with the **obligor**. However, the **SPV**/trustees are empowered, in certain predefined events, to remove the **originator** as **servicer** and bring in a back up servicer, that is, an entity other than the **originator**.

Balance Sheet CDO – A CDO that intends to transfer assets off the balance sheet of an **originator**, that is, from a single party, as opposed to an **arbitrage CDO**. The purpose of the CDO is to reduce the size of the balance sheet of the **originator**.

Balance Sheet Securitization – Similar to a **Balance Sheet CDO**, a securitization transaction aimed at transferring assets from the balance sheet of an **originator**.

Bankruptcy Remote Entity – An entity which is not engaged in any substantive business activity, does not have employees or recurring expenses, cannot issue liabilities. In other words, it cannot, in usual course, run into a situation where its liabilities exceed its assets. Besides, it is so owned or managed that it does not have any clear identifiable owner or holding company with which it can get into a substantive **consolidation**. If chances of bankruptcy or consolidation with a bankrupt, of an entity have been made remote, the entity is a bankruptcy remote entity. See also **Non-Petition**.

Basle II – Refers to the new capital standard of the Bank for International Settlements whereby the 1988 capital requirements for banks are to be replaced by new requirements more closely aligned with economic risk of an asset.

Balloon Loan – Leases or loans where a substantial payment is to be made on maturity. **Commercial mortgage loans** typically contain a balloon repayment.

Beneficial Interest – Contrasted with legal interest, means the right to stand to benefit, short of legal title. In a securitization deal, the receivables/cash flows or security interest thereon are legally held by the **SPV** or trust, for the benefit of the investors; hence, the investors are beneficiaries and their interest is beneficial interest.

BIS – Bank for International Settlements.

Billet de Tresorie – Literally meaning treasury bills, or commercial paper in the French market.

Black Box – A securitization issue where no or scanty details are known about the **obligor**s forming part of the collateral, except the selection criteria. Normally this is the case for many CDOs where disclosures are not made about the constitution of a portfolio for bank secrecy reasons.

Bullet – Is a type of credit security that repays the entire principal on the maturity date. Prior to the maturity or prepayment of the bond, interest payments are to be made in accordance with the payment schedule. See also **Hard Bullet**, **Soft Bullet**.

Burnout – Mortgage market phenomenon representing the tendency of mortgage pools to become less sensitive to interest rates as they tend to maturity. The older the pool, the more burnt out is the sensitivity to interest rate changes.

Buy-back Option – See **Call Option**.

C

Call Option – Generically, an option to buy or buy-back an asset. In context of securitization, can refer to (a) issuer's right to call back the securities and redeem them; or (b) **originator's** right to buy back assets transferred for securitization. An **originator's** call option may be fatal to the true sale character of the transaction.

Callable – A callable loan or a callable security is one which carries a call option, that is, one which can be prepaid wholly or partly before its scheduled maturity.

Callability Risk – In context of asset-backed securities, the risk of prepayment of the securities due to prepayment risk.

Capital Adequacy – In case of banks or financial institutions, the minimum amount of capital required as per bank regulations. The capital is generally computed based on risk-weighted value of assets.

Capital Relief – In context of banks of financial intermediaries, the amount by which the minimum capital required for capital adequacy is reduced, e.g., when assets are securitized.

Cash Collateral – In a securitization transaction, the amount of cash deposit put by the **originator** to serve as a cushion for the investors; a device of **credit enhancement**. Generally, the collateral is retained out of the amount payable by the **SPV** for purchase of the receivables of the **originator**.

Cash Flow Waterfall – See **Waterfall**.

Cat Bonds – See **Catastrophe Bonds**.

Catastrophe Bonds – A bond whereby the risk of losses faced by an insurer (or several insurers) on account of certain catastrophe insurance policies, or the risk as indicated by an industry index of such losses, is transferred to investors by a provision that entitles the issuer to set-off such loss against the interest, or principal, or both payable to the investors in such bonds.

CBO – See **Collateralized Bond Obligations**.

CDO – See **Collateralized Debt Obligations**.

CFO – See **Collateralized Fund Obligations**.

Cherry Picking – Picking up, as cherries are picked, selected quality assets for the purpose of securitization and leaving behind low grade assets. Cherry picking of assets for securitization is frowned upon by creditors of the **originator** as also the shareholders. In some countries, cherry picking for securitization is prohibited by regulation.

Choses in Action – A legal expression for actionable claims or receivables.

Clean up Buyback or Call – An option with the **originator** in securitization transactions where the **originator** can buy back the outstanding securitized instruments when the principal outstanding has been substantially amortized, leaving a small uneconomic amount to be serviced. Normally, a **clean up call** is exercised when the outstanding principal falls below 10% of the original.

CLN – see **Credit-linked Note**.

CLO – See **Collateralized Loan Obligations**.

CMBS – See **Commercial Mortgage-backed Securities**.

CMO – See **Collateralized Mortgage Obligation**.

Cohort – All the pools from a certain **agency,** with a specific coupon and issue year, form a cohort (e.g. FHLMC Gold 6.5s from 2001). Cohorts are often used for prepayment reporting purposes.

Collateral – Is the underlying security, mortgage, or asset for the purposes of securitization or borrowing and lending activities. In respect of securitization transactions, it means the underlying cash flows.

Collateral Manager – In certain transactions, particularly in arbitrage transactions, the vehicle makes regular purchase and sale of the collateral which is managed by the collateral manager.

Collateralized Bond Obligations – Obligations, usually structured obligations, of an issuer that are collateralized, that is, backed by a portfolio of bonds transferred by an **originator**, or bought from the market, with an intent of securitizing the same.

Collateralized Debt Obligations – A generic name for collateralized bond obligations and collateralized loan obligations.

Collateralized Fund Obligations – Obligations, usually structured obligations, of an issuer that are collateralized, that is, backed by a portfolio of hedge fund or equity fund investments, transferred by an **originator** or bought from the market with an intent of securitizing the same.

Collateralized Loan Obligations – Obligations, usually structured obligations, of an issuer that are collateralized, that is, backed by a portfolio of loans transferred by an **originator** or bought from the market, with an intent of securitizing the same.

Collateralized Mortgage Obligations – Is a securitization payment method where the cash inflows of the **SPV** are divided into several tranches, each tranche having different payback period and seniority profile. These tranches, which are often designated as A to Z pieces or securities, normally in the form of bonds. For example, the A bonds might be the senior most in terms of security, and is expected to pay off faster than other bonds. The different tranches can be structured as per the objectives of the investors as to pay back period and the risk inherent. The common CMO structures are: **Interest Only, Principal Only, Floater, Inverse Floater, Planned Amortization Class, Support, Scheduled, Sequential, Targeted Amortization Class, and Z or Accrual Bond.**

Co-mingling – Where the **originator** in a securitization is also the servicer, the cash collected by the **originator** may at times co-mingle, or may deliberately be mixed up with that of the **originator** himself, leading to no clear identification of the cash collected on behalf of the **SPV**. This is called co-mingling.

Co-mingling Risk – The risk that the cash flows collected by the **originator** gets co-mingled with that of the **originator**; hence, in bankruptcy, such cash would become the part of the bankruptcy estate of the **originator** and would not be available, for lack of traceability, to the **SPV**, although it belongs to the **SPV**.

Commercial Mortgage-backed Securities (CMBS) – A section of Mortgage-backed Securities, the word is used to distinguish these from Residential Mortgage-Backed Securities (RMBS). Commercial mortgages represent mortgage loans for commercial properties such as multi-family dwelling, shops, restaurants and showrooms.

Conduit – A securitization vehicle usually operated by third parties as a ready-to-use medium for securitization, usually for assets of multiple **originator**s. Commonly used in case of asset-backed commercial paper, CMBS.

Conforming Loans – In U.S. MBS parlance, means the mortgage loans that conform to the criteria set up by the agencies. Usually, non-conforming loans are taken into the market through **private label transactions**.

Consolidation – (1) (legal sense) The action of a judicial authority in treating the subsidiary (for example, **SPV**) and the holding company (example, the **originator**) as the same entity by applying a legal concept called lifting or piercing the corporate veil. If consolidation is ordered by a Court in a securitization transaction, the transfer of assets by the **originator** to the **SPV** would become unfructuous.

(2) (Accounting sense)The consolidation of the accounts of the subsidiary or quasi-subsidiary with those of the holding company. See also **Qualifying SPV, SIC 12, FIN 46**.

Constant Prepayment Rate (CPR) – A prepayment measure calculated by assuming that a constant portion of the outstanding mortgage loans will prepay each month. See also **PSA Prepayment Speed**.

Controlled Amortization – Transaction structures where the **amortization** of a security will be done not based on the **amortization** of the underlying collateral but based on a certain plan, by diverting cash flows to another class.

Covered Bonds – see **pfandbrief**.

Credit Default Swap – A credit derivative deal whereby on happening of certain credit events, mainly indicative of a credit default by a reference **obligor**, a specific obligation of the **obligor** will be swapped between the counterparties against cash, or a compensatory payment will be made by one party to the other.

Credit Enhancement – Refers to one or more initiatives taken by the **originator** in a securitization structure to enhance the security, credit or the rating of the securitized instrument, e.g., by providing a cash collateral, profit retention, and third-party guarantee. Credit enhancement could be structural credit enhancement, **originator** credit enhancement or third party credit enhancement.

Credit Derivative – A derivative contract whereby one party tries to transfer to another the credit risk, or variation in returns on a credit asset, to another. See also **Credit Default Swap, Credit Linked Note, Synthetic Assets**.

Credit Linked Note – A note or debt security which allows the issuer to set-off the claims under an embedded credit derivative contract from the interest, principal, or both, payable to the investor in such note.

Cash Flow Waterfall – see **waterfall**.

D

Deferred Purchase Price – A device of **credit enhancement** where a part of the purchase price for the receivable payable by the **SPV** to the **originator** is retained by the **SPV** to serve as a **cash collateral**.

De-recognition – In accounting sense, means putting an asset or liability off the balance sheet. In context of securitization, it relates to the de-recognition of assets securitized by the **originator** when they are sold for securitization. Accounting standards put up pre-conditions before a de-recognition is allowed. See also **Sale Treatment, FAS 140, IAS 39**.

Default – A contractual default, for example, the failure to pay on the contracted date. In context of securitization transactions, a default will be declared on a hard bullet payment date, or on legal final maturity. In market parlance, default also includes where a security is rated with a default rating by the rating agencies.

Defeasance – The prepayment of a liability by setting aside a fund which at a certain rate of return will repay the liability.

Delinquency – Failure to pay a debt when due.

Detachment Point – A term used in connection with synthetic CDOs, means the point at which losses in a pool will cease to apply to the class of securities in question. Contrast with **Attachment Point**.

Direct Credit Substitute – In the sense in which bank regulators use it, it means forms of extending support to a client which is effectively an alternative to direct lending. For example, an irrevocable guarantee or a letter of credit A direct credit substitute is converted into a credit equivalent for computation of risk-based capital.

Discrete Trust – A trust or **SPV** that holds only such assets as are related to a particular securitization transaction, and would usually be co-terminus with the tenure of a particular issuance. Compare with a **Master Trust**.

Diversity Score – In the context of CDOs, refers to a measure used by rating agency Moody's to indicate level of diversification of assets in a pool, by slotting the assets in the pool into different industry clusters, which are presumed to be mutually uncorrelated, and applying coefficients depending on the number of assets in each industry cluster.

Dollar Roll – The simultaneous sale and repurchase of a mortgage security, with sale on one settlement date and the repurchase on another, in order to refinance the holding, is called a dollar roll.

Duration – In fixed income investments, the weighted-average life of an investment. For instance, the duration of a 5-year bullet repaying bond is 5 years, but if the bond is amortized, say, equally every year, the duration will be the weighed average of the time for which the initial principal is outstanding. See also **Average Life**.

Dynamic Pool – A pool the constituents of which will be varied over time, based on pre-fixed selection criteria.

E

Early Amortization Event – In case of reinstating asset securitizations that allow reinvestment of the cash flows by the **SPV**, an early **amortization** trigger will put an immediate end to the **reinvestment period** and will start amortizing the securities. Compare with **Acceleration**.

Economic Capital – Capital computed under the internal risk assessment models of a bank or a financial intermediary, to cover the bank, in view of the probability distribution of losses out of an asset or pool of assets, against losses up to a particular level of confidence, that is, range of probabilities. Compare with **Regulatory Capital**.

Eligibility Criteria – The criteria for selection of receivables which are to be assigned by the **originator** to the **SPV**. These are normally contained in the **receivables sale agreement** with a provision that a breach of the criteria would amount to breach of warranties by the **originator**, obliging the **originator** to buy-back the receivables.

Embedded Option – Is an option whose characteristics are implied but not explicitly specified. For example, the option to prepay a mortgage loan.

Equipment Trust Certificate – Is a security which is collateralized by ownership of specific equipment, often capital in nature. Normally used in aviation revenues securitization, this would involve the ownership of the asset, e.g., aircraft, being transferred to the **SPV** which would issue certificates indicating beneficial ownership of the asset. The asset is leased out by the **SPV** to the aviation company normally under a full payout dry lease.

Equitable Assignment – An **assignment** of receivables that does not complete the legal requirements for an assignment, for example, a formal stamped instrument, or a notice to **obligors**. English common law recognizes equitable assignment as creating an equity between the assignor and the assignee, though it cannot have any standing in relation to either the **obligor** or any third parties.

Equitable Mortgage – A **mortgage** which has not been completed in accordance with legal requirements – say, stamping, filing or registration. English common law permits recognition of interest of a mortgagee even if the mortgage is not duly completed in law. However, perfect legal claim in priority over rights of all others can be obtained only by a **legal mortgage**.

Estate in Bankruptcy – Or bankruptcy estate, means the properties included in the properties of a bankrupt for the purposes of realisation and distribution by an administrator or liquidator appointed by the bankruptcy court.

Excess Spread – Refers to the excess of the income inherent in the portfolio of receivables, over and above the coupon payable to the investors and the expenses of the transaction.

Excess Servicing Fee – Refers to the excess of the coupon being earned on the collateral, over the **servicing fee** as well as the interest payable to investors.

Expected Maturity – The time period within which, based on the cash flows expected from assets transferred to the issuer, the securities are expected to be fully paid off. However, the expected maturity is not the **legal final maturity** as the rating of the transaction is not based on repayment by the expected maturity. See also **Hard Bullet, Soft Bullet**.

Extension Risk – The possibility that prepayments will be slower than an anticipated rate, causing later-than-expected return of principal. This usually occurs during times of rising interest rates. Opposite of **Prepayment Risk**.

External Credit Enhancement – **Credit enhancement** that is provided by enhancers other than the **originator** or investors by way of **subordination**. For example, a guarantee by a **monoline insurer** or a letter of credit from a bank.

F

Facility – In banking parlance, means the arrangement with a borrower to provide a particular kind of credit support to the borrower.

FAS 140 – Is the U.S. accounting standard on accounting for transfer of financial assets in a securitization transaction.

FASIT – Financial assets investment securitization trust. A U.S. tax vehicle that can treat certain interests as debt classes and hence aim at a tax neutral securitization vehicle. FASIT provisions have since been made dormant.

Fast-pay Structure – A structure that allows for allocation of the principal collections to certain classes, usually senior classes, such that that class amortizes faster than other classes. Compare with **Slow-pay Structure, Sequential Payment Structure**.

FICO Scores – A credit score given by one of the well known consumer credit scoring companies, Fair Isaacs and Company.

FIN 46 or FIN 46R – A U.S. accounting interpretation where the accounts of certain **SPVs**, called variable interest entities, are to be consolidated based on the holding of variable interest in the entity rather than voting right or equity.

Financing Treatment – A securitization transaction is said to have been given a financing treatment when it is treated as a financial transaction either for legal, tax or accounting purposes. Compare with **True Sale Treatment**.

First-loss Risk – If the risks in a portfolio of assets are structured into several classes, the first-loss risk to a certain extent is borne by a particular class before it can affect any other class. The first-loss class must be fully wiped off first, and then the loss affects other classes. The first-loss class is comparable to equity in a business and provides credit support to the other classes.

Fixed Allocation Percentage – In any revolving asset securitizations, refers to the fixed proportion in which principal collected every period will be allocated to amortize the outstanding investment of the investors, and the amount released to acquire new assets or reinvested otherwise.

Fonds Commun de Créance (FCC) – Securitization vehicles as known under French law.

Foreclosure – The exercise by an owner or secured creditor of the right to treat a **facility** as having been defaulted by the **obligor** and foreclosing the same, while exercising the rights available under the agreement to recover the outstanding sums. For example, in context of mortgages, the seizure of the mortgaged property; in case of leases, the repossession of leased property.

FRS 5 – The U.K. accounting standard on accounting for substance of transactions; has a specific section dealing with securitization.

Fund of Funds – See **Collateralized Fund Obligations**.

Future Flows Securitization – Refers to securitization of receivables that do not exist; that will arise over time.

G

Grantor Trust – A U.S. **tax-transparent** trust that is a passive non-business entity, normally used in **pass-through** securitization; a non-discretionary pass-through device that transfers fractional beneficial interest to the investors and does no more than simply allocate the receivables among the investors.

Green – Is a mortgage-backed securities term that indicates mortgages which are not seasoned yet. Typically, a mortgage that is less than 30 months old is considered green.

Gross WAC – See under **WAC**

Guarantee Fee – Generally, the fee any guarantor charges for guaranteeing obligations. In **pass-through** language, it refers to the fee the **agencies** charge for their guarantee and securitization function.

Guaranteed Investment Contract – A contract guaranteeing a particular rate of return on investments.

H

Hair Cut – In context of capital adequacy requirements, means the extent of marginal capital needed for a particular asset. For example, the haircut for a regular loan given by bank is 8%; in case of lower risk-weighted assets, the haircut is lesser.

Hard Bullet – In case of a bullet payment structure, if the repayment date is firm and the rating agency rates the ability of the issuer to redeem the security on such agreed date, the security is said to be hard bullet. Compare with **Soft Bullet**. The comparison is the similar to **expected maturity** and **final maturity** in case of non-bullet structures.

Home Equity Loans – A loan granted based on the "equity" a home owner has built into his owned house, i.e., the excess of the market value of the house over the loans already taken. Typically, the home equity lender takes a secondary charge over the house if already mortgaged to a primary lender.

I

Interest Coverage Test – A coverage ratio in a **CDO** whereby the interest receivable on the assets of the CDO must cover the interest payable on the rated liabilities (or a particular class of liabilities) by a certain ratio, or otherwise the CDO will be required to reduce its liabilities to be compliant with the said coverage ratio. See also **Over-collateralization Ratio**.

Interest Only – If the cash flow in a pool is stripped by principal and interest separation, securities based on or backed by the interest flows are called Interest Only or IOs. Compared with **Principal Only**.

IO – See **Interest Only**.

Internal Credit Enhancement – **Credit enhancements** by the structure of the transaction rather than by any **originator** or external support.

IRB Approach – Internal Ratings based approach to computing capital. A term used under **Basle II** to compute capital based on internal rating, as opposed to ratings assigned by external rating agencies, to a particular asset or a pool.

Issuer – In context of securitizations, refers to the **SPV** which issues the securities to the investors.

J

Junior Bonds – Bonds which are **subordinated** to **senior bonds**.

Jumbo Mortgage Loan – A big size residential mortgage loan that otherwise complies with the **conforming** conditions of the **agencies,** but disqualifies because of its size. Jumbo loans are securitized in the **private label market**.

K

L

Legal Final Maturity – The final maturity by which a security must be repaid to avoid a default of the contractual obligation. Typically, in securitization transactions, the legal maturity is set at some months after the **expected maturity** to allow for delinquent assets to pay off and to avoid contractual default which can lead to winding up of the transaction.

Lifting or Piercing the Corporate Veil – See under **Consolidation**.

Limited Recourse – The right of **recourse** limited to a particular amount or a particular extent. For example, in a securitization transaction, the right of recourse being limited to the **over-collateralization** or **cash collateral** placed by the **originator** is a case of a limited recourse.

Linked Presentation – A provision under U.K. Accounting standard **FRS 5** requiring the amount of securitized assets being netted off by the amount raised by selling them off, instead of removing the assets from the balance sheet. If the maximum loss the **originator** can suffer can be demonstrated to be capped, the securitization qualifies for a linked presentation.

Liquidity Facility – Refers to a short-term liquidity or overdraft facility granted by a bank (or, sometimes, the **originator**) to an **SPV** to meet the short-term funding gaps and pay off its securities. Liquidity facilities can sometimes be substantial and can be the sole basis of redemption of securities – for example, in case of **ABCP Conduits**.

Loan to Value Ratio – In case of asset-based lending, means the amount of loan as a percent of the value of the asset on which the loan is secured.

LTV – See **Loan to Value Ratio**.

M

Master Trust – A common pot into which a large amount of receivables is thrown by the **originator**, much larger than the value of the receivables being securitized, and the trust in turn creates an **investor interest** (value of receivables being securitized) and **seller interest** (the remaining, fluctuating part of the pot). This allows for the repayment pattern of the securities to be unconnected with the payback period of specific receivables. Compare with a **Discrete Trust**.

MBS – See **Mortgage-backed Securities**.

Medium-Term Note – A fixed income market term implying securities offered by an investor for various maturities ranging from a year to several years.

Mezzanine Bonds – Bonds that rank after **senior bonds** in priority, but before **junior bonds**.

Monoline Insurer – An insurer writing only a single line of insurance contracts, mostly credit insurance.

Mortgage-backed Securities (MBS) – Is a broad term that encompasses securities carved out of receivables backed by mortgage loans. MBS are further classified into **residential mortgage-backed securities** and **commercial mortgage-backed securities**.

Mortgage Bonds – See **pfandbrief**.

Multi-Seller Conduit – A conduit where assets are sold by multiple sellers, are consolidated at the conduit level and then securitized.

N

Negative Amortization – A term in mortgage funding (or any other asset-backed funding) where total collections from the **obligor** during a period are les than interest accrued, leading to a negative recovery of principal, that is, an inherent accretion to or reinvestment of principal.

Non–petition Undertaking – An undertaking obtained from the persons providing any services to an **SPV** that said person shall not file a petition for bankruptcy of the **SPV** until the investors in the **SPV** have been paid off. A feature required to ensure that the **SPV** is **bankruptcy remote**.

Novation – A term in English law meaning the substitution of one party to a contract by another, with the consent of the other contracting party. For example, A and B have a contract, and now A wants to transfer his rights and obligations under the contract with the sanction of C – this is a case of novation. Novation is required where A wants to transfer both the rights and obligations under the contract. Compare with **Assignment**. Also see **Sub-participation**.

O

OAS – See **Option Adjusted Spread**

Obligor – The debtor from whom the **originator** has right to receivables.

Obligor Notification – Giving of notice to **obligors** that the receivables have been **assigned** to the transferee. Usually **obligor** notification is reserved to be done only in emergencies. See also **Equitable Transfer**.

OC Test – See **Over-collateralization Test**.

Off Balance Sheet – A debt or asset which does not show up on the balance sheet of the entity that originated the asset or debt. In a securitization transaction, if the transaction qualifies for a **sale treatment**, the assets transferred by the **originator** are off the balance sheet of the **originator**, and so is the amount received on account of such transfer.

Option-adjusted Spread – As asset-backed investments have an inherent **callability** risk, there is an option embedded to prepay the instrument. Option adjusted spread looks at the spread of an investment after deducting the spread attributed to the optionality. The spread related to the option is computed by standard option pricing methods.

Originator – The entity assigning receivables in a securitization transaction.

Originator Advances – A **liquidity facility** provided by an **originator** to a securitization transaction where the **originator** pays a certain month(s)'s expected collections by way of an advance and later appropriates the actual collections to reimburse himself.

Originator Credit Enhancement – Refers to **credit enhancement** provided by the **originator**, such as **cash collateral**, **over-collateralization**,.

Orphan Company – A company which has no identifiable shareholder/ owners – e.g., an **SPV** owned by a charitable trust. A device normally used to avoid consolidation of the **SPV** with any entity.

Over-collateralization – A method of **credit enhancement** in a securitization transaction where the **originator** transfers an extra **collateral** to the **SPV** to serve as security in the event of delinquencies.

Over-collateralization Test – A coverage ratio required to be maintained in a **CDO** transaction, whereby the par value of assets of the CDO must at all times cover the rated liabilities (or a certain class of rated liability) by a certain ratio, or otherwise, the CDO will be obliged to reduce its liabilities to be compliant with the said coverage ratio. See also **Interest Coverage Test**.

P

P&I – Are principal and income payments or principal and interest. Compare with **Principal Only**, **Interest Only**.

PAC – See **Planned Amortization Class Security**.

PAC POs – Are **Principal Only** issues which are predicated on a predetermined **PAC** prepayment schedule, range, or collar.

Pass Through – Refers to the securitization structure where the **SPV** makes payments, or rather, passes payments to the investors, on the same periods, and subject to the same fluctuations, as are there in the actual receivables. That is to say, amount collected every month is passed through to investors, after deducting fees and expenses. Compare with **Pay Through**.

Pass-through Rate – The rate of coupon inherent in the pool, minus the expenses and the servicing fee, which is passed on to the investors.

Pay Through – A securitization structure where the payments used by the issuer to pay off the investors on a certain pre-fixed maturity and pattern, not reflective of the payback behavior of the receivables. Obviously, during the intervening periods, the **SPV** reinvests the receivables, mostly in passive and pre-programmed modes of investment.

Pfandbrief – A German traditional secondary market mortgage product where the investor is granted rights against the issuer as also against the underlying mortgage. Comparable instruments are generically known as **covered bonds** or **mortgage bonds**.

Planned Amortization Class – Is a class of securities which has a planned **amortization** schedule, so that the cash flows emanating from the assets are used to pay-off such class as per the schedule, and the remaining cash flows are diverted to a **support class**. The planned class is not affected by prepayments or delayed payments which are absorbed by the support class.

PO – See **Principal Only**.

Pool Policy – An insurance policy that covers losses sustained on a pool of mortgage loans.

Pool – Portfolio of assets, that is, the collateral, backing up a securitization transaction.

Pool Factor – The percentage of the original outstanding of a pool that remains outstanding on a particular date.

Pooling and Servicing Agreement – The agreement between the **originator** and the transferee setting out the conditions on which the pool of receivables will be originated and pooled, and how it would be serviced.

Prepayment – Making of payments by the **obligor** ahead of the schedule fixed by the origination agreement, for example, the loan agreement.

Prepayment Rate – The rate at which prepayment takes place in a pool, measured by certain standard models, such as BMA model or the **PSA model**.

Prepayment Risk – Is the risk of loss of interest due to **prepayments** by a borrower. The **SPV** may either pass through the prepaid amounts to investors thus resulting in faster payment of principal than expected, and reduced income over time, or if the **SPV** were to reinvest this money, the reinvestment does not produce the rate of return as in the underlying receivables. Hence, prepayment is viewed as a risk in securitization. See also **Extension Risk**.

Principal Only – Similar to **Interest Only**.

Private Label Securities – **RMBS** issued other than through the **agencies**.

Profit Extraction – The extraction of the **originator**'s spread in the securitization transaction, that is, the excess of the underlying rate of return in the receivables over the **weighted-average coupon** at which the **SPV** issues the liabilities. Usually, the **originator** does not receive the whole of this profit upfront but uses one or more devices to extract the profit, such as **servicing fees, retained interests, residual interests**.

PSA Prepayment – A measure of the rate of prepayment of mortgage loans developed by the Public Securities Association. This model represents an assumed rate of prepayment each month of the then-outstanding principal balance of a pool of new mortgage loans. A 100% PSA assumes prepayment rates of 0.2% per annum of the then unpaid principal balance of mortgage loans in the first month after origination and an increase of an additional 0.2% per annum in each month thereafter (for example, 0.4% per annum in the second month) until the 30th month. Beginning in the 30th month and in each month thereafter, 100% PSA assumes a constant annual prepayment rate (CPR) of 6 percent. Multiples are calculated from this prepayment rate; for example, 150% PSA assumes annual prepayment rates will be 0.3% in month one, 0.6% in month two, reaching 9 % in month 30, and remaining constant at 9% thereafter. A zero% PSA assumes no prepayments.

Q

Qualifying SPV – A term under **FAS 140** setting conditions for an **SPV** to qualify under the standard. If the transfer of assets is made to a qualifying SPV, the latter does not come for consolidation with the transferor. Besides, if the transferee is not a qualifying **SPV**, the transferee must be free to sell or pledge the assets.

R

Ramp-up Period – In case of **arbitrage transactions**, after the issuance of the securities, the **collateral manager** takes some time before the intended size of the portfolio is fully acquired or ramped up. The time taken to acquire the required size of the portfolio is called the ramp-up time.

RAP – Regulatory accounting practices. Refers to treatment of assets or off-balance sheet exposures for the purposes of computing required regulatory capital by banking regulators. Since regulatory motives are different, there are certain differences between accounting for assets under **GAAP** and RAP.

Real Estate Investment Trust – Is a special structure that holds real properties. These properties can be apartments, shopping malls, office buildings or other acceptable real assets. There are often tax rules applicable to such structures – for example, that the trust must distribute 95% of its income to the shareholders in order to qualify for special tax treatment.

Real Estate Mortgage Investment Conduit – Is a U.S. tax vehicle for securitization of mortgage-backed receivables.

Receivables Sale Agreement – The agreement under which the **originator** sells the receivables to the **SPV**.

Re-characterization – Generally refers to the action of a judiciary in ignoring the legal form of a transaction and treating it as what the Court regards is the true nature of the agreement. In the context of securitization, it refers to the treatment of a securitization not as **true sale** but as **financing** transaction.

Recourse – The ability of an investor/purchaser to seek payment against an investment to the **originator** of the investment. For example, in a securitization transaction, the right of the investor to seek payment from the **originator**.

Regulatory Arbitrage – Ability of banks to bring down their regulatory capital requirements without any substantial reduction in real risks inherent in the portfolio – for example, a securitization deal where the economic risks of the portfolio have been substantively retained.

Regulatory Capital – Is the amount of capital required by banking regulators as the minimum capital – under current norms, the capital requirements are based on credit risk and market risk. The computation in either case is based on the risk-weighted value of on-balance sheet and off-balance sheet assets of banks applying certain pre-defined risk weights. See also **Economic Capital**.

Regulatory Capital Relief – The extent to which the **regulatory capital** requirements of a bank/financial intermediary get reduced due to securitization of assets.

REIT – See **Real Estate Investment Trust**.

Reinstating Assets – Refers to securitization structures where there is a **reinvestment period** during which the assets which are collected or amortized will be reinstated by further sales by the **originator**.

Reinvestment Period – The period during which the cash flows accruing to the **SPV** are reinvested in buying assets as per the terms of the scheme. Usually, the assets may be bought from the **originator** or, in case of **arbitrage transactions**, may be bought from the market.

REMIC – See **Real Estate Mortgage Investment Conduit**.

Replenishment – In **revolving asset securitizations**, refers to the use of the cash receipts to acquire fresh receivables in lieu of those paid off, instead of for amortizing the principal outstanding.

Resecuritization – A securitization deal where investments in other securitization transactions or **structured products** is securitized again. That is to say, securitization of investments in securitization transactions.

Residual Interest – Usually the **originator** agrees to a **profit retention** in a securitization transaction, and the retained profit is captured using one or more devices close to the wind-down of the transaction. This is called residuary interest.

Retained Interest – Any risks/rewards retained by the **originator** in a securitization transaction – for example, service fees, any retailed interest strip.

Reverse Mortgage Loan – A mortgage loan given based on the value of a house to an elderly person; normally provides for payments to be made by the lender over a certain time, say, during the lifetime of the individual, and thereafter, the house to be taken over the by the mortgage lender. Called reverse mortgage since regular payments are released by the lender over a period.

Revolving Assets Securitization – Securitization of assets which have very short payback periods, such as credit cards, so that, when the receivables are paid off, the amount is utilised for **replenishment** by acquiring fresh receivables rather than for **amortization** of the investment. Also refers to securitization of revolving credits, where the credit is of a revolving nature – such as in case of credit cards, home equity credits. Most revolving asset securitizations will have a **reinstating** structure.

Rule 3a-7 – A rule of the SEC in U.S. granting exemption to **SPV** from being regulated under the Investment Company Act, 1940.

S

Sale Treatment – In accounting standards for securitization, recognition of a securitization transaction as a sale of receivables would lead to recognition of upfront income (or losses) on the assignment, **de-recognition** of the assets and the corresponding liability. Compare with **Financing Treatment**.

Scheduled Amortization – See under **Amortization,** also see **Scheduled Principal**, **Scheduled Interest**.

Scheduled Principal – Is the principal repayment inherent in periodic instalments as per the schedule of payments. This is usually modified by applying a **prepayment rate** to project the cash flows of the investor. See also **Amortization**.

"Schuldschein" or "Schuldscheindarlehen" – German credit linked notes.

SDA Model – See under **Standard Default Assumption**.

Seasoned – Assets which have been on the books of the **originator** for some time before they are considered for securitization, thus giving the benefit of retrospect. Contrast with **Green**.

Securitization – Is the process whereby assets, usually financial assets, are converted into marketable securities by transferring them to a vehicle **SPV** which in turn issues such securities either representing beneficial interest in such financial assets, or securities whose repayment is solely backed by such financial assets.

Senior/Junior – Senior securities are those which rank prior to the claims of the junior securities in terms of cash flows as well as on liquidation of the **SPV**.

Senior – Is a class of securities which have high or the highest claim against a borrower or assets of the borrower. Often they are secured or collateralized, or have a prior claim against the assets.

Sequential Payment Structure – A payment structure where the cash flows collected are paid sequentially to the various classes, i.e., first to the senior-most class, and after retiring it fully, to the second class and so on.

Servicer – In a securitization transaction, refers to the entity that would continue to collect the receivables, service the **obligors**. Normally, the **originator** is also the servicer. See also **Back-up Servicer**.

Servicer Advances – Similar to **Originator Advances**.

Servicing Fees – The fees payable to the **servicer** for servicing the transaction.

Set-off – Generally, the right to offset a payable against a receivable. In context of securitizations, most refers to the right of the **obligor** to deduct an amount that the **originator** owes to him, from the amount he owes to the **originator**. Normally, the **receivables sale agreement** would contain a warranty that there is not right of set-off with the **obligor**.

SIC 12 – An accounting interpretation by the **International Accounting Standards Board** whereby **SPV**s which are supported or credit-enhanced by the **originator** are to be treated as quasi-subsidiaries of the **originator** and hence consolidated with the **originator**.

Slow-pay Structure – Contrast with **Fast Pay Structure**.

Soft-bullet Structure – In case of a bullet payment structure, if the repayment date is an expected date but not firm and final date, the rating agency is not concerned with the ability of the issuer to redeem the security on such agreed date, the security is said to have a soft bullet maturity. Compare with **Hard Bullet**. The comparison is the similar to **expected maturity** and **final maturity** in case of non-bullet structures.

SPC – An **SPV** organised as a company.

SPE – See **Special Purpose Entity** – same as **Special Purpose Vehicle**.

Special Purpose Entity – Same as **Special Purpose Vehicle**.

Special Purpose Vehicle – Is a legal entity formed with the special purpose of acquiring and holding certain assets for the sole benefit of investors in such vehicle, such that the investors have acquired nothing but such specific assets. The vehicle has no other assets, and no other obligations, and is contractually and constitutionally debarred from acquiring any other assets, interests or obligations.

Sponsor – With reference to a **conduit**, the entity that sponsors and runs the conduit.

SPV – See **Special Purpose Vehicle**.

Standard Default Assumption – The standard default assumption by the Bond Market Association with takes defaults in mortgage pools to be linearly increasing up to a particular level and then decreasing to the maturity of the pool.

Stated Maturity – See **Legal Final Maturity**.

Static Pool – Where the components of a pool will not be changed over time; contrariwise, it is called a **dynamic pool**.

Stress Testing – A process of altering, unfavourably, the key assumptions underlying a portfolio to see if the portfolio would sustain situations of stress. The amount of stress applied differs based on the target rating.

Strips – Same as **Stripped Mortgage-backed Securities**.

Stripped Mortgage-backed Securities – Are securities which are constructed from MBS pass-throughs. Essentially, these securities strip the cash flow stream into a separate **interest only** (IO) and **principal only** (PO) securities.

Structural Credit Enhancement – A technique of **credit enhancement** by creation of **senior** and **junior** securities, thereby enhancing the credit rating of the senior securities.

Structured Investment Vehicle (SIV) – An **arbitrage vehicle** that issues both commercial paper and medium term notes to fund its assets.

Structured Products – In general, refers to the securities created by securitization process.

Structured Product CDO – A **CDO** that primarily will invest in structured products such as **RMBS**, **CMBS** or **ABS**.

Sub-participation – A technique used mostly by bankers to allow several other banks to share the risks and the returns of a financial transaction, including the funding of the transaction. The principal contract between the originating bank and the borrower remains unaffected, the sub-participation a contract between the participating banks and the originating bank.

Subordinated – Is a class of securities which have lower priority or claim against a borrower. Typically, these are unsecured obligations. They are also called **Junior** notes and bonds. This compares to **Senior** securities.

Substantive Consolidation – See under **Consolidation**.

Substitute Servicer – See **Back-up Servicer**.

Support Class – Is a bond engineered to counterbalance or uphold **Planned Amortization Class**, **Targeted Amortization Class** or other superior bonds in a deal. Also, referred to as a **Companion Bond**.

Synthetic Asset – Where the risks and rewards in an asset or portfolio of assets are acquired while not buying such asset or portfolio, but by a credit derivatives transaction, the asset is said to be synthetically acquired, and therefore, is said to be a synthetic asset.

Synthetic CDO – A **CDO** that "invests" primarily in synthetic assets -that is, builds up a position of risks/rewards on assets by credit derivatives transactions.

T

TAC – Is a **Targeted Amortization Class** security.

Targeted Amortization Class – Similar to a **planned amortization class** but usually is subordinated to **Planned Amortization Class** bonds but superior to other tranches.

Tax Transparent Entity – An entity which is not taxed either in representative capacity or in its own capacity as a tax paying entity, but the tax is levied on the participants in the entity based on their share of income in the entity. See also **Grantor Trusts**.

Third Party Credit Enhancement – A **credit enhancement** provided in a securitization transaction by third party guarantees, such as bank letter of credit, or **monoline** insurance contracts.

Tranche – Is the piece, portion or slice of a deal or structured financing. The risks shared by different tranches in terms of losses, sequential payment of the cash flows, etc are different. Obviously, therefore, the coupon on different tranches is also different.

Trigger Event – An event that will lead to an **acceleration** or **early amortization**.

Trophy Asset – Applied in context of commercial mortgage transaction, where one of the properties is a highly reputed property, hence, a "trophy".

True Sale – While every securitization involves a sale of financial assets by the **originator**, such sale may at times be treated as a financing transaction as the **originator** does not divest himself of continued association or credit support to such transferred assets. If the sale is so structured that for legal or tax purposes, it will be respected as a sale, it is a true sale. See also **Sale Treatment**, **Re-characterisation**.

U

Unwinding of Transfers – A **bankruptcy code** provision that allows a Court to annul the transfers of assets made a certain time, say six months, prior to bankruptcy.

V

Variable Interest Entity (VIE) – A term used under the U.S. accounting interpretation **FIN 46R** to refer to those entities that have a residual interest other than equity. **Consolidation**, for accounting purposes, of such entities is done on the basis of such variable or residual interest, rather than voting capital as in the case of other entities.

W

WAC – See **Weighted-Average Coupon**.

Waterfall – The manner of allocation and appropriation of the cash flows of the **SPV**, in a certain order of priorities.

Weighted-Average Coupon (WAC) – The weighted average of the coupon payable on the various liabilities of the issuer. In **pass-through** jargon, the term refers to the weighted average coupon of the underlying mortgages in the pool. The **gross WAC** refers to the gross coupon in the pool, while the **net WAC** is the gross WAC after netting off guarantee fees and servicing fees.

Weighted-Average Foreclosure Frequency (WAFF) – The default rate, that is, the foreclosure frequency on a weighted average basis for the pool.

Weighted-Average Maturity (WAM) – In case of securities which are amortized over time, the weighted average maturity is the duration of the securities, that is, the outstandings at different points of time, weighted based on the period for which they remain outstanding. In context of mortgages, also used to refer to the weighted average of the remaining maturities of a mortgage pool.

Weighted-Average Loss Severity (WALS) – Loss severity is the loss suffered if an asset defaults, that is, one *minus* the recovery rate; when this is computed on a weighted average basis for the pool, we have the WALS.

Whole Loan – As compared to **pass-through** refers to the whole of a loan, and a fractional interest as a pass through. When whole mortgage loans are traded in the market without securitization, it is a whole loan.

Chapter 2

Securitization: Methodology, Structures, Motivators and Demotivators

W hile the history of development of capital markets is itself the evolution of "securities," securitization of receivables is one of the latest applications of the generic device of security-creation, meaning a great deal to capital markets. This device has, for the first time, brought to the fore the unlimited potential of the applicability of securitization to a diverse group of assets, risks and relations.

Modus operandi of securitization briefly explained

Visualize an entity having receivables as one of its major assets, say a housing finance or a leasing company. Suppose the company has already created such receivables (that is, it has a contractual right to collect these receivables). This means the company's working capital is tied in with the receivables.

Securitization will unlock this working capital and make it free for further asset-creation. In this sense, securitization is a mode of financing, or rather refinancing.

The company will select the receivables to be securitized, following a certain criteria (see below the criteria to be adopted for such selection). While selecting, a set of discriminants can be used, but generally it is not advisable to the company to cherry-pick assets, that is, select assets of the best quality and leave behind the poor ones. Understandably, cherry-picking is frowned upon by equity shareholders and banks having traditional loan facilities with the company.

Such selected receivables will be transferred to a special purpose conduit, which could be a trust or a special purpose corporation. In this book, we call this entity a **special purpose vehicle (SPV)**. The SPV is either created by the company or is a specialized firm that offers SPV management services. The sole purpose of an SPV is holding receivables for the investors and safe-guarding their interests.

So, once the receivables are transferred by the originating company to the SPV, it is the SPV that now becomes the owner of the receivables.

While the SPV holds the receivables, investors acquire a beneficial right therein by paying for the present value of the receivables. The present value is computed at (a) the rate of return the company wants to offer the investors; and (b) the **excess spread** that the structure should have as a credit support. We will return later to the concept of excess spread and the way it serves as a credit support. Thus, the aggregate rate of return at which the SPV acquires the receivables may be the same or lower than the inherent rate of return of the receivable. If the SPV's discount rate is lower than the rate inherent in the pool, there is an immediate cash profit for the originator company.

The SPV issues certificates to investors indicating the money value of their beneficial interest in the pool of receivables. Alternatively, the SPV may issue debt instruments that pay off on stipulated dates with the payment for such debt securities to come from the sums received by the SPV. These may be called asset-backed notes or asset-backed securities. In this book, these will henceforth be referred to as **asset-backed securities (ABS)**. In ABS, we include both mortgage-backed and non-mortgage-backed securities, and unless we specifically refer to term paper, we include asset-backed commercial paper as well.

ABS are marketable instruments, just like any other capital market security. The SPV may create a modality for *inter-se* transfers of these certificates. The originator usually continues to act as the **servicer**; collecting receivables and remitting the proceeds to the investors.

The transfer of receivables to the SPV and creation of beneficial rights therein involve complicated legal issues in most countries. Hence, there may be lengthy legal documentation and stamping involved to complete the transfer. These issues are examined in subsequent chapters.

The transfer of receivables by the originator to the SPV is normally without recourse, but may sometimes be with limited recourse as well; again, this will be examined later under **credit enhancements**.

As the servicing is mostly done by the originating company, the debtors may often be unaware of securitization unless they are notified. The servicer continues to collect the receivables, mostly in a separate escrow account, from where the collections are drawn by the SPV. The SPV uses this collection either to pay off the investors proportionately (as in case of **pass-through** securitization) or to reinvest the money to pay the investors on stated intervals (as with **pay-through** or bond-structure securitization). For pass-through, as the SPV makes a proportionate payment to investors every period, the transaction automatically comes to an end when substantially all receivables are paid off. For pay-through securitizations, generally the originator would have provided some of his own cash, including his retained spread or an over-collateralization support, or simply an equity contribution to the SPV; therefore, the residual cash with the SPV at the end of the transaction is the originator's residual cash inflow.

If any enforcement is required against debtors, the SPV as the legal owner of the receivables will bring action against them, but here again, the actual physical and administrative action may be taken by the originator as the servicer of the SPV.

The basic process of securitization is illustrated below[1]:

Table 2.1   The basic process of receivables securitization

Step 1	The originator either has or creates the underlying assets – the transaction receivables that are to be securitized.
Step 2	The originator selects the receivables to be assigned.
Step 3	A special purpose entity is formed.
Step 4	The special purpose company acquires the receivables at their discounted value.
Step 5	The special purpose vehicle issues securities, either back to the originator who then takes it to the market or to the investors; these are either debt type securities or beneficial interest certificates, which are publicly offered or privately placed.
Step 6	Most significantly, the securities offered by the SPV are structured – usually Class A, B, C (senior, mezzanine, junior). This hierarchy of securities provides credit enhancement to each senior class; for example, Class A is protected by Class B and C. If the size of Class B and C is sufficient to absorb the expected losses of the pool at a certain degree of probability coverage (**confidence level**), Class A securities see the desired rating. Thus, the ratings are driven by the size of credit support, which is, in turn, driven by the expected losses from the pool, which are driven by the inherent risk of default in the pool.
Step 7	The servicer for the transaction is appointed, and is normally the originator.
Step 8	The debtors of the originator or **obligors** are not notified depending on the legal requirements of the country concerned. Most likely, the originator will try to avoid notification.
Step 9	The servicer collects the receivables, usually in an escrow mechanism, and pays off the collection to the SPV.
Step 10	The SPV passes the collections to the investors or reinvests the same to pay off the investors at stated intervals. The pay-down to investors will follow the formula fixed in the transaction, which may either **sequentially** pay Class A, B and C, or pay them **proportionally**, or in any other pattern. Alternatively, inside Class A, there may be several sequential tranches that have different pay back periods for different tranches.

Step 11	In case of default, the servicer takes action against the debtors as the SPV's agent. If losses are realized, they are distributed in the reverse order of seniority, that is, the subordinated class taking the loss first. Depending on the extent of the losses, the subordinated class is written off.
Step 12	When only a small amount of outstanding receivables are left to be collected, the originator usually cleans up the transaction by buying back the outstanding receivables.
Step 13	At the end of the transaction, the originator's profit, if retained and subject to any losses to the extent agreed by the originator, in the transaction is paid off.

Economic substance of securitization: Where does the alchemy lie?

The economic substratum of securitization lies in isolation of the assets of the entity into a separate pool. It is not difficult to understand that the rest of the features of securitization are not different from traditional corporate finance.

Commonly speaking, the following factors are cited as being responsible for the economic benefits of securitization:

- Better ratings
- Use of structured finance principles with required credit enhancements, made to measure as per investor needs
- Higher leverage
- Lower effective cost
- Bankruptcy remoteness

Each of these features, except the isolation of assets, is subject to successful counter argument. Let's first have a look at structured finance principles. In securitization transactions, we create a hierarchy of liabilities split into various classes such that each senior class sees credit support from each junior class. As a result, we are able to see the desired ratings for the senior-most class. This is not unique to securitization; in corporate finance also we have equity as the first to absorb losses and provide support to each class of liability. Then follow a series of liabilities, mutually prioritized, such as preferential capital, subordinated loans, senior unsecured loans, second secured loans (or floating charges), secured loans or fixed charges, preferred creditors and others. Thus, if credit enhancements and structured finance were all that was required to uplift the ratings of securities, the same is perfectly attainable in plain corporate finance as well.

Higher leverage and lower cost are both related and result from the same feature as well. The leverage for securitization is the reciprocal of the required extent of credit enhancement, which, in turn, is affected by the risk inherent in the assets. In corporate finance, the required credit enhancement – equity capital – is high because the corporate faces the risks of the entity-wide assets.

As we are on the issue of risk – does the fact that a part of the overall pool of a corporate has been cut and hived into a separate entity, reduce the risk of the asset? If so, who has taken on the residual risk? It is difficult to have a mathematical and fundamental justification for this, but the process of nuclearization – breaking up a large lump into smaller, more easily understandable nuclei – makes each nuclei more efficient. The risk of isolated pools is more easily quantifiable and thus the lower required credit enhancements. The principle *small is beautiful* seems to hold well here.

Features of securitization of receivables

1. Mode of asset-based financing[2]

As financing markets become more organized and investing more institutionalized and thus professionalized, there is a clear trend towards asset-based financing, rather than entity-based financing. Traditional financing is entity-based. For example, when X gives a loan of a certain amount to Y, he looks at the credibility and worth of the commitment made by Y on the basis of his credit. He confides in Y, the borrower or user of the money. He does so because (a) he has the mechanics to know and understand the worth of Y's commitment; and/or (b) he does not have the mechanics to know and understand the worth of the application to which Y will put the borrower's money.

However, as investing becomes more professional, investors have the ability and propensity to understand the application of the sum borrowed.

Thus, they will place more weight on the use of money rather than who the user is. This is not to deny the role of the user of money as a source of comfort to the lender. However, strictly user-based risk cannot be afforded by the institutional investor for several reasons:

(a)   The professional investor does so on the basis of a logical assessment of the credit risk and not merely on hunches.
(b)   User-based financing is necessarily subjective, as the user is an entity and not an asset, and the credit-assessment of an entity is as subjective as face-reading. The professional investor cannot go by subjective appraisal.
(c)   An asset is a store of intrinsic value. Therefore, one who looks at the asset and not at the user stands a better chance of recovering his finances.

It is difficult to say with certainty that asset-based financing is superior to user-based financing, but there remains a worldwide drift towards such financing. The latest financial innovations in the world confirm this. Leasing, factoring, leveraged buyouts and securitization are all modes of asset-based financing.

The most important feature of asset-based financing is that the credit-worthiness of the user is becoming less significant, while the worth of the application – the asset – is becoming more.

Securitization is a mode of asset-based financing. In a securitization transaction, the originator offers the investors an asset against their money; as an entity, he does not take any obligation to pay. The investors' receivable is the cash flow of the portfolio transferred.

If there is not an entity risk on the originator, then there is an entity risk on the debtors; so, how does it become a case of asset-based financing? In the ultimate analysis, all claims are claims against an entity, as understandably no asset can pay all by itself. However, the risk of an obligation of the originator failing, and that of a diversified pool of debtors, is substantially different.

2. Mode of structured financing

Once financing is asset-based, it becomes possible for the originator to structure the financing based on assets or the needs of the investor. As the investor is looking at the asset rather than the entity, the investor's claim is against specific assets, and so it becomes possible for the user entity to offer assets suiting the needs of the investor.

Investor needs can be expressed in various ways. Let's say investor needs are clarified based on their attitudes towards risk. There may be aggressive investors willing to take risks for better returns, or there may be risk-averse, conservative investors. Securitization structure can accordingly carve out securities rated at the best possible level, and those that are junior, or speculative, although carrying a very high rate of return.

Investor needs can also be classified as short term or long term. Here again, securitization tranches can be categorized into those paying quickly, those paying income regularly but reinvesting principal, and the zero coupon bonds.

Securitization expands the structuring flexibility many times, as it splits the same asset into many. Therefore, it can create different classes of securities linked to the same asset application, such as different maturity periods and different preferential rights. For more on structured financing, see Chapter 1.

3. Securitization of claims against third parties

From the viewpoint of the legal structure of securitization, the single most important difference between securitization of receivables and any other security issuance is that the former seeks to market claims against third parties and not against the originator. In fact, there may not be, in the case of securitization of receivables, any claim against the originator.

This poses a unique legal problem. The right of receiving a certain sum under a contract is a property (as it is a claim against third parties), so there may be a specific procedure prescribed for transfer. Securitization transactions in most countries tend to become complicated on account of these legal procedures.

In addition, property laws of most countries require a written document to transfer a receivable; as such transfer is incapable of a physical manifestation like delivery of the receivable. This may also involve exorbitant stamp duties.

Except for negotiable trade instruments, laws have not visualized parties dealing in receivables. Hence, most laws have not addressed the difficulties that arise when a private asset such as a receivable is converted into a public asset, such as a security. Also, securitization itself does not have a long history, so many of the questions likely to arise may not have surfaced yet.

4. Limited Recourse

As a case of asset-based financing, most securitization originators would ideally like the investor only to look at the asset, and so as not to have any recourse to the issuer. Thus, the investor has a legally tenable right over the receivable and must recover his money only from the debtor. In the event of failure on the part of a debtor to pay, the investor has to exercise his rights through the special purpose intermediary – the trust holding rights over the receivables.

Non-recourse securitization, as far as the issuer is concerned, should not be taken as a means of financing, but as a means of financial restructuring. The originator incurs no obligation to the investors; in a way, he prepays the obligation by transferring the asset. As there is no instant or continuing credit obligation on the issuer, the financing mobilized by securitization is not taken as the issuer's debt, and thus securitization brings about a change in the D/E profile of the originator.

However, in most securitizations the originator is required to add an element of his liability to the structure as a tool of credit enhancement. This is by way of limited participation in the credit risk of the transaction, for which various devices, such as recourse, subordination and excess spread may be used. These are discussed later under **credit enhancements**.

5. Asset features

Over the years, the concept of securitization has been extended to a number of applications. A new innovative use of securitization hits the market every other day. If one thinks of assets that are capable of securitization, the list is a long one. Any asset that produces a cash flow over time is a securitizable asset. Given this basic attribute, securitization applications have been taken to extremely exotic and unimaginable extent.

For example see Box 2.1.

Box 2.1: A few examples of exotic securitization deals:

- The securitization market was taken by surprise in early 1998 when receivables from David Bowie's first 25 music albums were securitized and sold in the U.S. These were known as **Bowie bonds**.
- A European company issued bonds secured on proceeds of revenues from James Bond movies; these became popularly known as **Bond bonds**.
- The securitization of insurance risk is now common, although the insurance risk securitization is a distinct technology by itself. As these bonds were mostly applied to catastrophe insurance, they were called **cat bonds**.
- All records were broken when the Italian government decided in April 1999 to securitize its delinquent social security receivables; this was perhaps the first application of securitization to reduce the government deficit. [Note: the reduction of fiscal deficit by such transactions was itself made subject to EU rules later – see Chapter 21 on Securitization of Government Revenues.]
- Another innovative deal in 2000 was the securitization of a stock of champagne bottles by a French company.
- The now well-known device called whole business securitization has been used to securitize the residual profits of several operating businesses.
- Commercial properties under construction that are financed via securitization are no longer surprising.

For traditional transactions, assets that can be securitized have some basic attributes:

1. Assets should represent cash flow

The asset in question should give rise to cash flow over a period of time. Normally, the cash flow should be steady and easy to identify, but there are many assets that do not give rise to identifiable cash flows. These would be unsuitable for securitization as the investors have to look at identifiable series of cash flows.

2. Quality of the receivables

Securitization is primarily meant to create a derivative asset (the security) out of a basic asset (the receivables). As asset-backed securities typically have good ratings, it might seem apparent that the securitized receivables should also be of good value because the quality of the securities is no different from the quality of the assets.

However, the reality is different. The securitization sphere has both kinds of assets – prime and sub-prime assets. If by sub-prime assets, we mean assets of a substandard quality or assets not meeting certain norms, there are innumerable sub-prime asset securitizations that also have the highest ratings. Once we understand the principles of structured finance, this may not sound surprising. The quality of assets is reflected by the extent of credit support required for the asset; prime assets require more credit enhancements, but for sub-prime assets AAA-rated securities may also be issued. There have been several notable securitizations of non-performing loans in Japan, Italy and the U.S. where there are AAA tranches.

Hence, it is not that the securitized receivables should be of high quality, but that the required sizing of the various classes of securities and thus the overall cost of the transaction would be a function of the quality of the receivables.

3. Diversification of the portfolio

Like the quality of the portfolio, diversity is also a factor that determines the credit enhancement structure of the transaction.

The principle of diversification is easy to understand. Think of a structure that stands on 20 columns; it can possibly go 200 meters high into the sky. Now think of a structure that stands on just one column; its stability is in doubt beyond about 10 meters. The sustenance of the structures is a function of the distribution of their load. An organization built on a broad base of 50,000 employees can achieve a turnover of billions of dollars, whereas a one-man organization has to be content with a self-employment model and the limits of individuality.

Likewise, if the pool of assets has a high degree of diversification, it can sustain high degrees of leverage. Diversification is the equivalent to distribution, the more it is "distributed" horizontally, the more it can go vertically. Diversification counterbalances leverage as most securitization transactions attain a high degree of leverage on the strength of a high degree of diversification. Diversification implies all sources from which risk can arise, such as geographies, countries, currencies and industries.

What happens if the pool is not diversified or is not diversified enough? Diversification is the reciprocal of **correlation**; the best example of a perfectly correlated pool is a single obligor. In this case, any risk that affects the obligor also affects the transaction. Applying structured finance principles to a single obligor asset pool is the same as thinking that the second level of a ship is safer than its hull; if the ship sinks, possibly all levels will be equally affected.

If one has the task of selecting a pool, the objective should be to construct a balanced, diversified pool so that leverage can be maximized and cost minimized.

4. Size of individual receivable

This factor is a direct offshoot of the diversification feature discussed above. To ensure diversification, we will need to ensure that the size of each individual obligor is not large enough to disrupt the pool.

5. Maturity composition of the receivables

In securitization transactions, we are concerned with the **remaining maturity** of the assets, as these already have a degree of **seasoning,** that is, the time elapsed since the origination of the asset. In constituting the pool of assets, it does not make good sense to include assets with either too long or too short a maturity. In general, it does not make sense to include assets too different from the average. For example, if the targeted repayment period of the transaction is five years, it does not make sense to include loans or assets that pay off in just fifteen months. Including these assets makes the pool cash flow front heavy, resulting in fast depletion of outstanding principal, all of which have unpleasant consequences.

On the contrary, in a revolving or reinvestment-type structure, discussed later in this chapter, the transaction intends to reinvest in the assets. That is, if the assets pay off, the SPV acquires further assets, thereby making the maturity irrelevant. However, even in case of a revolving asset, a pool with greatly disproportionate maturities does not yield easily to efficient structuring.

6. Periodicity of payments

Generally, the asset in question should result in periodic cash flow over time. It is not necessary that the assets should be amortizing such as in case of housing or auto loans. For example, the assets may have a certain rate of periodic payment, as with credit cards. But if the assets do not have any payment for a fairly long period, it becomes difficult to provide for investors' service.

7. Homogeneity of the assets

The underlying assets should be by-and-large homogenous. For example, if it is a pool of car loans, it should have housing loans or home durables loans in it; in other words, the pool should have a definite characteristic. The advantage in homogenous assets is pooling and the analysis of the pool will be easier because historical data can be applied to project the risks in the portfolio.

8. No executory clauses

The underlying contracts to be securitized must work, even if the originator goes bankrupt. If there are certain obligations to be performed by the origina-tor before he has the right to the receivable, the receivables cannot be trans-ferred independent of such obligations. For example, if the pool is a pool of lease receivables, and the lease requires the lessor to maintain the asset, the rentals become conditional upon such maintenance.

If the receivables are based on this kind of continuing obligation on the part of originator, the securitization transaction cannot achieve the originator inde-pendence and bankruptcy remoteness that are among the essential motives.

Such a transaction may be structured as a **future flow** (discussed later in this chapter). But future flows have their own structural uniqueness and generally the rating of future flows is linked to the rating of the originator.

9. Capacity to assign

Securitization involves the transfer of a right to receive – a right against a third party to the assignee. Therefore, the law of the land or the contract between the parties must not prohibit the right to assign. Normally, the right to assign a receivable is an inherent property right, but there may be legal formalities required to achieve such assignment. There may also be contractual restric-tions on the right to assign, or rights such as set-off that are inconsistent with the assignment of receivables.

10. Independence from the originator

The on-going performance of the assets and the making of claims against the debtors must be independent of the existence of the originator. This tends to be a wider restriction than the example above about executory contracts. As far as possible, the underlying contracts should not require something to be done by the originator or should depend upon the originator as a running concern.

11. Assets should be free of withholding taxes/pre-paid taxes

The receivables should generally be free of withholding taxes. If withholding taxes are applicable on the payments to be made by the debtors, complicated questions will arise. One elementary complication is that of who will take the credit for the withholding tax. The payment is collected by the originator, but on behalf of the SPV, which in turn collects it on behalf of the investors. It would be logistically impossible to allow the benefit of set off to the investors directly. Therefore, the SPV or the originator will be forced to take the credit for the pre-paid tax, which may be technically objectionable.

Another major difficulty is when to take the set off. Usually, withheld taxes only qualify for a refund after the tax assessment is complete, which may take time. This would create difficulties in the securitization structure by creating a residuary receivable that may be collected long after expiry of the scheme.

Value added tax may create similar problems – if any value added tax is passed on to the SPV, which it cannot offset, it creates a tax inefficiency.

6. Originator features

1. Receivables as major assets

Securitization of receivables obviously pre-supposes that the originator has a bulk of assets or future assets in form of receivables. Also, the receivables must satisfy the features discussed above, and at a point of time, should be of economic quantity to justify securitization. Hence, the following companies find securitization a viable option:

(a) **Real estate finance companies:** Securitization of receivables originated with mortgage finance companies. These companies are best suited for it as they largely satisfy the features above. They are predominantly a receivable-oriented company. The receivables are long term and generally secured by way of mortgage over the property finance. In the U.S. where it originated, these mortgages were also secured by government guarantees. The receivables also satisfy the diversification features.

Based on excellent security – unencumbered real estate, it is possible for these companies to part with receivables on a non-recourse basis.

Even now, the market for real estate securitization is much larger than other varieties.

(b) **Non-mortgage finance companies**: Though it was made popular by the real estate companies, securitization was caught up by other finance companies, particularly automobile financing companies. Auto-loan (including auto-installment credit/hire-purchase finance companies) broadly fulfilled the features necessary in securitization. The security in these cases was also considered good, because of the title over a utility asset with ready remarketing possibilities.

Later, leasing companies entered the fray. Consumer asset financiers also found securitization a possible route, coupled generally with credit enhancement techniques such as collaterals and recourse provisions.

(c) **Car rental companies**: These companies rent out cars on contractual hiring terms and therefore are essentially securitizing not a pre-contracted car rental but an estimated rental value based on past experience. Hence, a future asset and not a pre-contracted receivable is being securitized.

(d) **Credit card companies**: This is an innovative use of the device of securitization. The average period of credit for a credit card is generally very short, maybe a month, but this credit is generally revolving. Hence, based on the past experience of the credit period, a securitized receivable is created. The structure in this case is a special **revolving structure**, as it is impossible to match the payment made by the cardholder with the payment to the investor.

(e) **Hoteliers and real-estate rentiers**: Based on occupancy experience in case of hotels and estimated rentals for real estate, future receivables have been securitized, generally with either a recourse provision or a collateral.

(f) **Electricity and telephone companies**: These companies have an excellent opportunity of securitizing electricity meter rentals and telephone rentals. The receivables in these cases are widely spread and the delinquency record is also very favorable.

(g) **Banks**: To overcome capital adequacy problems, maintain liquidity, gain-on-sale and other issues, banks have resorted to securitization of their loan portfolios. **Collateralized loan obligations (CLOs)** essentially developed as a device for securitizing bank loans.

The list is not exhaustive as whenever a reasonable sum of money is receivable over a certain period of time, the possibility of securitization always exists. Some of the latest applications of securitization include insurance risk, intellectual property rights and sports earnings. The applications of securitization are examined at length later.

2. Financial and organizational strength

As such, the financial strength of the issuer is not important in securitization. However, no securitization transactions (except those guaranteed by external agencies) are completely independent of the originator. The transaction depends on the originator for (a) generating sufficient volumes of assets to have an economic size of the pool to be securitized; (b) ongoing originations, particularly for revolving structures; and (c) servicing risk. Hence, the originator should be a reasonably strong entity, with a strong origination and servicing network.

The financial strength of the originator may not be very significant, but his organizational strength certainly is. The originator either takes care of servicing by himself or in certain cases, has a master servicer charged with the overall responsibility of ensuring effective servicing.

7. Issuer/SPV features

The following features of the securitization SPV are normally necessary from a bankruptcy remoteness viewpoint[1]:

- Prevention of trading, external funding, etc. so that the SPV cannot endanger the transaction by introducing new and different risk factors; the SPV is known as a **single-purpose entity** as it cannot engage in any activity other than holding and maintaining interest in the securitized portfolios;
- Sub-contracting all services required to maintain the SPV and its assets, such as administering its receivables and company secretarial work;

- SPVs are not permitted to have any employees or (normally) to have general fiduciary responsibilities to third parties (such as acting as a trustee);
- Any person who contracts with the SPV must agree not to take the SPV to bankruptcy court in the event that the SPV fails to perform under the contract (**non petition agreements** – see Chapter 23);
- All of the SPV's liabilities (present and future) should be quantifiable, and shown to be capable of being met from the resources available to it, including corporate tax, advance corporate tax and any value added tax; the extent to which the SPV is reliant on third parties to meet its obligations should be minimized (and in some circumstances limited to a reliance on either AAA-rated or other bankruptcy remote companies only); funds due to the SPV have to be separated and ring-fenced as soon as they are received.

As the SPV cannot have any employees, the administration of the SPV's assets is typically subcontracted and handled by the servicer. This is typically done under the pooling and servicing agreement, which defines the different tasks to be carried out by the servicer. Broadly, the servicer will carry out all functions in relation to the receivables required for their being kept effective and effectively turned into cash. These range from:

- The collection of cash each day;
- Operating bank accounts;
- Enforcing agreements with the underlying debtors (such as collecting security and chasing borrowers in arrears);
- Ministerial functions, including enforcement of any claim, upkeep of physical asset;
- Accounting;
- Taxation (depending upon the jurisdiction concerned, the taxes may include income-tax, VAT or stamp duty);
- Reporting to investors, rating agencies and trustees;
- Pool management (such as dealing with requests for additional funds, changes to asset contracts);
- Management of related insurance (depending upon the underlying contracts).

If the SPV also has to invest or reinvest cash flows, it may be important to hire the services of an investment manager or adviser.

The SPV's own corporate functions, such as holding meetings, preparing minutes and legal compliances accounting and auditing, are also typically outsourced.

8. Investor features

(a) **Professional investor**: Generally, investors in securitized products, except for mortgage-backed securities, are institutional investors. Small investors have shown no interest in it, perhaps because the product is new or due to absence of liquid secondary markets.

(b) **Fixed and regular income investor**: Securitization is essentially a fixed income product. Within this broad category, it offers several options – starting from very low risk and very low-yield products to those implying a very high degree of risk and return. Yield-hungry investors may invest in BBB- or BB-rated, asset-backed securities where the relative value provided has historically been high.

(c) **Investor for a fixed period**: In view of limited common-investor interest, secondary markets in securitization may not be vibrant. Hence, securitized products may not be very liquid. Two-way quotes for asset-backed securities are not common, and originators generally do not make a market because of legal and accounting barriers. Thus, investors essentially invest in securitization transactions with mark-to-market motive.

The scenario is different for U.S. agency-backed RMBS that has developed into a vibrant fixed income or treasury alternative. Other securitized products have been favored by most institutional investors, including savings institutions, pension funds, banks, mutual funds and insurance companies. Institutional investors need fixed income securities, for which securitization is ideal. In Chapter 30, we take a close look at the investor rationale behind their investment.

Securitization and factoring

Factoring is an age-old British concept, where the factor acquires the debts of a client, pays for the same instantly, and generally manages the same.

Though the device used for securitization and factoring is the same – the transfer of receivables – the nature and inherent purpose of the two are entirely different. A factor intends to offer services relating to the management of a client's portfolio, whereas the intention of securitization is to render marketable the receivable, while the creditor company (issuer) continues to manage the receivables. For factoring, financing is incidental, whereas for securitization, financing is the main objective.

Although factoring involves financing, it is like financing by the debt-portfolio of the client taken over. For securitization, the issuer transfers the carefully selected receivables only.

Securitization and ring fencing

Ring fencing is a term commonly used in bankruptcy statutes. It means segregation of the assets of the debtor in a manner acceptable to a bankruptcy court, so that the ring-fenced assets are outside the estate of the bankrupt or bankruptcy court's jurisdiction. Ring fencing does not involve the transfer of assets, as for securitization, and the assets continue to stay on the books of the debtor. The legal process of ring fencing depends on the bankruptcy law of the country concerned.

As there is no transfer of assets, there is no SPV in ring fencing devices.

Ring fencing devices are essentially those of secured borrowing; they cannot achieve the same effect that securitization can. As an item of borrowing on balance sheet, they do not achieve the capital relief result; an important feature of securitization. Therefore, except in certain European jurisdictions where traditional mortgage funding instruments such as *pfandbriefe* have existed over years or where the cost of securitization is quite high or logistics make securitization difficult, ring fencing devices have not found a wide acceptance.[4]

The traditional mortgage funding devices in certain European countries – called *pfandbriefe* in Germany[5] – are essentially ones of ring fencing, as they are backed by local statutes that permit segregation of assets, funded by such bonds, to be applied for the benefit of the bondholders.

Asset classes

Please see Figure 2.1, which shows the composition of the securitization market. A detailed study of various securitization applications will be taken up in later chapters, but this is just an overview.

One of the key distinctions to be made is based on the existence of the asset; existing asset securitization and future flow securitization differ substantially. In an existing asset securitization, the cash flow from the asset exists and there is an existing claim to value. In a future flow securitization, there is no existing claim or contractual right to a cash flow; such contractual rights will be created in the future. For example, an airline company securitizing its future ticket sales is a case of a future flow securitization.

Future flow securitization is different from existing asset securitization in various ways, such as legal, accounting and tax implications and structuring features. In later modules, future flow securitization is discussed in detail.

The third main type is risk securitization where the issuer merely transfers risk by way of securitization, with no transfer of cash flow, and so, no funding. This is also referred to as **synthetic securitization**, discussed at length in Chapter 22. The synthetic securitization device can be used not merely to transfer credit risk, but for other uses, such as insurance risk and commodities risk.

Within existing-asset securitization, distinction is often made in U.S. market parlance between mortgaged-backed securities and asset-backed securities. The former refers to securitization of mortgage loans, including commercial as well as residential mortgages. The latter is mostly taken to mean securitization of non-mortgage assets. Outside the U.S., the term asset-backed securities covers generically all types of asset-backed notes.

The difference lies in the U.S. practices. The U.S. mortgage market is considered very safe as the mortgages are guaranteed by agencies such as GNMA, FNMA or FHLMC. Therefore, mortgage-backed securities are not collateralized usually and are mostly risk-free except for prepayment risk. However, for non-mortgage securities, over-collateralization is normally insisted upon.

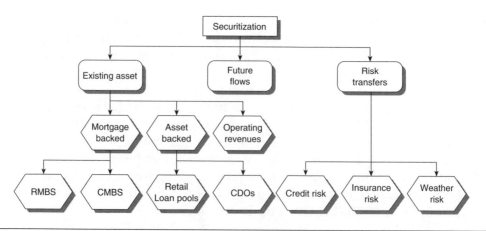

Figure 2.1 ABS types based on collateral

The existence of collateral requirements obviously leads to a difference in structure depending on the form of the collaterals. Apart from this, in agency structures, the agencies themselves act as managers of the SPV. In other words, the agencies set up trusts to issue notes to investors and with the money so raised, they buy the mortgages created by the mortgage financiers/ credit unions. Thus, once securitized, the mortgage creator is completely hived off from any responsibility in administration of the SPV.

A third type, practiced mostly in Europe right now, is securitization of all the revenues of an operating company, also known as operating revenues securitization or whole business securitization. Whole business securitization is by nature partly an existing asset securitization but largely a future flow.

Balance sheet and arbitrage transactions

It is possible to classify securitization structure into balance sheet and arbitrage structures. Balance sheet structures are transactions in which assets of a single originator are transferred for the purpose of refinancing the same. As these assets were on the balance sheet of the originator and the purpose of the transaction is to reduce balance sheet size, these are termed as balance sheet transactions.

On the other hand, if an SPV is structured to buy assets from various originators, pool such assets and refinance them with the objective of reaping the residual profit – arbitrage returns, the transaction is called an arbitrage transaction.

Analytically, every balance sheet transaction is intended for arbitrage, for example, the cost of funding. Again, every arbitrage transaction has an impact on someone's balance sheet, but the distinction in practice is made mainly to indicate the immediate purpose on hand.

Asset-backed securities and asset-backed commercial paper

Yet another term commonly prevailing in securitization parlance is **asset-backed commercial paper (ABCP)**[6]. Every asset-backed security that is structured as "commercial paper" is an ABCP. The distinction between **term**

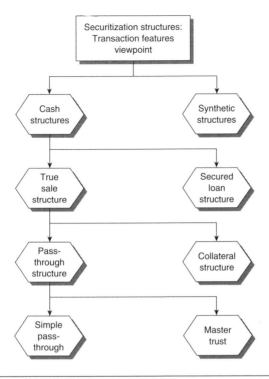

Figure 2.2 Securitization structures

paper, CP, or medium term notes (MTNs) is essentially one of tenure. So, if asset-backed securities are long term (typically, more than 12 months), they are called term paper; if they are expected to be paid off in 12 months or less, they are normally referred to as commercial paper.

Broad types of securitization structures

We discuss below the main types of securitization structures and then take up some of these structures in detail. Please see Figure 2.2 for a view of the branching of these various structural types.

Cash vs. synthetic structures

The concept of synthetic asset or synthetic securitization was briefly referred to in Chapter 1.[7] One can buy and sell assets for cash in the traditional, commonly understood way, or using derivatives, one can synthetically buy or sell assets. In a synthetic transaction, the seller does not sell assets for cash; in other words, the seller keeps his title and investment on the asset unaffected. He merely sells the asset synthetically – transfers risk/reward relating to the asset by entering into a derivative transaction. When securities that carry such an embedded derivative are issued, it becomes a synthetic securitization.

Most securitization globally follows the traditional cash structure under which the originator or repackager sells assets and receives cash instead. However, synthetic securitization is a fast growing structure, particularly in Europe and Asia.

True sale vs. secured loan structures

Usually, securitization transactions are structured as a sale of the subject asset by the originator. This is obviously intended to protect the assets from the bankruptcy of the originator because, as long as the assets are owned by the originator, they are a part of the bankruptcy estate. In certain jurisdictions, however, it is possible to create acceptable protection against bankruptcy by creating an all-pervasive security interest, one that covers the whole undertaking of the originator.[8] In such cases, secured loan structures are also used sometimes.

In a secured loan structure, the originator takes a loan similar to any other secured lending. Investor rights are protected by creating a fixed and floating charge over the undertaking of the originator in favor of a security trustee. Obviously, the assets intended to be securitized are not a specific asset pool as in the case of a true sale structure, but generic assets of the originator. As the assets are generically subject to the security interest of the security trustee, and the indenture of charge empowers the trustee to do so, the trustee may take possession of the assets on certain trigger events and prevent the assets from being encumbered any further by the originator or a bankruptcy court.

Obviously, the ability to use the secured loan structure will depend on the legal provisions of the country concerned. The U.K. is prominent among the countries using this structure, and some people feel that it can be used in several other countries having U.K.-type corporate and insolvency laws.

Pass-through vs. collateral structure

In a pass-through structure, the investors are made to participate proportionally in the cash flows emanating out of the specific assets of the originator. The special purpose vehicle is simply a distribution device. The investors are the beneficial, rateable owners of the pool.

In a collateral structure, the special purpose vehicle buys the assets of the originator in the same manner as a pass-through structure, but instead of rateably distributing the cash flow among the investors, it issues debt collateralized by the assets transferred by the originator. In other words, the special purpose vehicle does what any other corporate does – acquires assets funded by liabilities. The only difference between a regular corporate and the special purpose entity is that the special vehicle makes only such reinvestments as required to bridge the mismatch between the maturity of the assets and liabilities.

The pass-through structure is the most basic device of securitization. In the mortgage market, most transactions still take the pass-through route. However, in asset classes where cash flows are erratic, the pass-through cash flow structure is not very investor-friendly. Therefore, the collateral method is more frequently used outside of the mortgage market.

The collateral structure can also be called the pay-through structure. In the mortgage market, this structure is also called the CMO structure or the REMIC structure.

Discrete trust vs. master trust

A discrete trust implies one SPV for one pool, where investors clearly participate in the cash flow of an identified pool. In a master trust, the originator sets up a large fund, in which he transfers a big chunk of receivables, much larger than the size of funding raised from investors. From this larger fund, several security issuances can be created, either simultaneously or successively, so that all of them together equal the assets in the larger pool, but not singularly. At any point of time, the size of the investor funding raised is usually much smaller than the total size of assets in the pool; thus, a residual share is owned by the originator himself.

The master trust is a device to create mismatch between the repayment structure and the tenure of the securities and the assets in the pool. The master trust is a sort of a going concern to which the originator consistently keeps transferring assets, and holds a *seller share* that is the unfunded portion of the assets he transferred.[9] Master trusts are more flexible; therefore, they are finding more acceptability in several countries.

Direct portfolio transfers

Direct portfolio transfers, or asset sales, are not securitization as there is no creation of security or conversion of assets into securities. However, it is a common practice in the banking world. Smaller regional banks often sell their portfolio or individual transactions to larger ones.

No SPV is required for a discrete portfolio sale. We have noted before that an SPV is essentially a vehicle between the originator and the investors to render marketability to the assets. As with direct portfolio transfers there is no creation of security, so the target assets may be sold directly to the buyer.

Sometimes a direct portfolio transfer may be a precursor to securitization; a bank or repackager may collect enough transactions to securitize.

There is yet another common banking practice of syndicated loans or loan participation agreements different from a portfolio transfer. In a portfolio transfer, there is an assignment of assets from the transferor to the transferee. In syndicated loans, the common practice is to have one bank acquire an asset and let the members of the syndicate participate in the same by participation rights.

The legal process of assignment of receivables is necessary in a direct portfolio transfer, in the same way as securitization, except that the formalities of setting up an SPV are avoided. The accounting consequences of off-balance sheet accounting and gain-on-sale are applicable to direct portfolio transfers as well as to the accounting standards that do not make any substantial difference between transfers to an SPV for securitization and transfers to an operating company. For bank regulatory purposes as well, a direct portfolio transfer might have the same impact, with the difference to the advantage of the transferor that the often-stringent requirements relating to SPVs are avoided.

Quite often in market practice, a transfer may have a single, or few, investors for whom the entire collateral is housed and who will hold it to maturity. In such cases, there is no need to enter the rigmarole of securitization, as the intended purpose can be achieved by a direct portfolio transfer. On the other hand, if the objective of the investors is to buy a liquid, capital market instrument, they should not opt for a portfolio transfer.

Table 2.2 juxtaposes direct portfolio transfers and securitization:

Table 2.2   Direct portfolio transfers versus securitization

	Direct portfolio transfers	Securitization
Objective	To transfer one or more assets to another entity, normally in an over-the-counter, negotiated transaction	To convert a portfolio of assets into capital market securities so as to offer them to capital market investors – institutional or retail.
Likely investors	Usually entities in the same business as the originator	Usually institutional investors in the investment business.
Parties to the transaction	Does not need any SPV – bilateral transfer between the transferor and the transferee	SPVs are needed to hold the receivables while the resulting securities are made tradable to avoid trading in the assets themselves.
Legal process	Assignment of receivables to the transferee	Assignment of receivables to the SPV; issuance of beneficial interest certificates/debt securities by the SPV.
Accounting treatment	Achieves off-balance sheet accounting for the originator, subject to necessary preconditions	Achieves off-balance sheet accounting for the originator, subject to necessary preconditions.
Regulatory treatment	Grants capital relief subject to conditions. No SPV conditions.	Grants capital relief subject to conditions. Among conditions, there are usually stringent requirements relating to the independence of the SPV.

Direct portfolio transfers were very common among European banks. Recent advances in securitization structures have made direct portfolio transfers less common as the originator may achieve better pricing through securitization.

Pass-through structure

As discussed earlier, the pass-through method is the easiest and most basic form of securitization. Though it is commonly believed that the pass-through method was originated in U.S. mortgage markets, there has been use of participation certificates in bank loan sales for a longer time.

The name is derived from the nature of securitization; the issuer – the SPV – passes to investors the entire interest in and cash flow from the securitized portfolio. The investors are rateable beneficial owners of the assets transferred to the SPV, in proportion to the value of pass-through certificates held by them. The SPV does not reconfigure cash flow or create a mismatch in the maturities of the assets and the repayment on the certificates; during the servicing period of the transaction, the SPV continues to receive and redirect all principal collections to the investors. For example, if there are 1,000 pass-through certificates in a particular issue and for any particular month, the SPV collects US$15,406,000, each certificate will be entitled to $15,406. In the next month, collection will also be distributed accordingly. In other words, what investors receive and how they receive is the same for the SPV, period after period.

The investors' entitlement in a pass-through transaction is the right to participate in the cash flows; therefore, securities issued in a pass-through transaction are, from legal viewpoint, proportional, classified interest, in the pool of assets held by the SPV. It is a proportional interest because, the right of each investor is defined by the amount of certificates they hold. It is a classified interest because, the interests of each class of investors may not be uniform and subjected to order of priorities, such as senior or junior interest. These certificates are evidence of the beneficial interest held by the investors, so they are also known as *beneficial interest certificates*.

The pass-through SPV is also known as a *grantor trust* or *non-discretionary* trust, as the trustees in such a trust do not have any discretion as to the application of the cash flow. The term "grantor trust" is a tax term and will be taken up in Chapter 26 on Tax Issues.

Steps in a pass-through transaction

The steps in a pass-through transaction are enumerated below (see Figure 2.3 and Figure 2.5):

AT THE INCEPTION:

- The originator selects the receivables to be securitized.
- The originator sets up a special purpose vehicle (SPV). This is generally a pass-through trust, with the single purpose of holding the selected receivables on behalf of the investors. The trust is passive; it does not reinvest any of the cash flow.
- The originator transfers the receivables to the SPV, and in turn, the SPV issues the pass-through certificates to the owner. [Alternatively, the SPV might issue pass-through certificates to the investors directly, in which case, the offer for sale of the pass-through certificates by the originator is

not required]. The certificates represent undivided beneficial interest (denominated in terms of money) in the pool of receivables held on behalf of the investors by the SPV.

- The originator now has the pass-through certificates instead of the receivables. The originator makes an offer for sale of these pass-through certificates to the investors.

AT THE TIME OF PAYMENT FOR RECEIVABLES:

- The payment is collected on the due date by the originator/servicer.
- After deducting service charges, if any, the installment collected is passed through to the investors.
- The amount received by the investors has as much interest and principal elements as the gross total of the installments collected by the issuer. Before remittance to the investor, a certain time may be allowed for aggregation of all collections and for compilation of records.
- If there are any prepayments, that is, premature closures of the contracts, the amount received as a result will be passed-through to the investors.

AT THE TIME OF DELINQUENCY/ DEFAULT:

- If there is a delinquency on a receivable (temporary delay), and the transaction has one or more methods of liquidity enhancements,[10] the SPV will draw upon the liquidity enhancements to make up for the delinquent receivable.
- However, if as per the terms of the servicing agreement, the delinquency is such that it amounts to a default, the following steps follow.
- If there was a limited recourse or substitution provision, the SPV requires the originator to pay up, and in that case, the defaulted receivable will be reassigned to the originator.
- If there is no recourse to the issuer, the SPV will require the servicer to proceed against the defaulting debtor.
- On collection, the SPV will remit the funds to investors.

Nature of pass-through certificates

By structure and intent, a pass-through structure transfers interest in the receivable in favor of the investors through the SPV. The investors in a pass-through transaction acquire the receivables subject to all their fluctuations and prepayment. This is not to say there cannot be a layer of credit enhancement provided by the originator. But the timing risk in the asset portfolio, such as the pattern of repayment and risk of prepayment, are transferred to the investors. **In accounting jargon, pass-throughs are also called proportional redirection of cash flows.**[11]

It is notable that the nature of a securitization transaction, as far the originator is concerned, is the same irrespective of whether the structure of payments to investors is on a pass-through basis or bonds basis. Therefore, for the originator, in either case it is the same – he is paid for sale of the asset.

In the hands of investors, a pass-through is akin to proportional interest in the pool of receivables. Through the collective medium of the SPV, a pass-through investor is investing in the receivables directly. Therefore, the nature of the investment made by the investor is the acquisition of beneficial interest in the pool of receivables. The nature of income received by the investor is the same as the nature of income that would have been collected by the originator had the transfer of receivables not taken place.

The SPV in a pass-through transaction is merely a collective device, a compendious way for investors to pool funds to acquire the receivables. If the investors were to be presumptively taken as a single block, it is like a transaction directly between the block of investors and the originator, with the SPV being merely a pass-through and the trustee holding legal title over the receivables. This has an important implication on the asset/liability accounting of the SPV (see Chapter 27, Accounting by the SPV).

For tax purposes, the pass-through certificates are treated at par with equity or ownership interests, as the holder of a pass-through certificate is the beneficial owner of the assets of the SPV. Therefore, payments to pass-through certificate holders do not amount to payment in relation to a debt, so for tax purposes, the distribution of income on a pass-through certificate is not treated as a charge against income but as an allocation of income; the distinction is the same as with payment to a bondholder and that to an equity owner.

Advantages and difficulties in the pass-through structure

The pass-through method is the simplest, most transparent way of structuring a securitization transaction. As the SPV does not recycle cash flow, it remains a merely dormant redirection device and investors may be seen as collectively holding the pool of assets once held by the originator.

The strongest argument in favor of the pass-through structure is its economic efficiency – in the context of the efficiency of a pay-through or bond-type structure.

The pass-through method is used extensively in securitization transactions, mainly where the receivables have a defined monthly stream of payments. In RMBS, auto loans and other amortizing transactions, the principal collections are passed through to investors over time.

However, the biggest difficulty with the pass-through structure is the erratic and unpredictable cash flow structure, and the periodicity of the cash flow that coincides with payments on the underlying receivables. So, if the underlying receivables are payable every month, the investors are repaid every month. The other significant difficulty is that the amount of principal paid to investors every month is not consistent. This is for two reasons:

- In most retail portfolios, based on equal payment structure, the amount of principal increases every month.
- Also, as receivables are subject to prepayment, the prepayment of principal by investors, uncertain in itself, leads to investors receiving prepayment of principal.

The essence is that every month investors in pass-through transactions see an uncertain amount of principal. It is not difficult to understand that fixed income investors usually frown upon a monthly repayment of principal, as it means both reinvestment costs and loss of net present value.

Refinements in the pass-through structure

The essential problem with the pass-through structures is that the investment amortizes every month, at an unknown rate, as unscheduled payments (prepayments) affect the amount of principal paid.

The scheduled, amortization of the loan pool being repatriated to investors is an inherent feature of all securitizations, and the alternative – reinvestment-type or pay-through bonds (note the economic inefficiency argument explained later) – is too costly to be preferred. However, the prepayment risk remains a problem area for pass-through's for which some structures have evolved in the marketplace. The refinement of the most basic pass-through methods discussed below is either trying to differentially allocate prepayment risk or create securities with different risk and payback periods, while retaining the overall pass-through nature.

Senior and junior pass-through certificates: In the crudest sense, a pass-through certificate may mean that each investor is a proportional owner of the entire chunk of receivables, and there is no distinction between different investors.

However, that is not the case. In essence, securitization tries to create credit enhancements by subordination, so there are at least two classes of pass-throughs in every transaction – senior and junior. The junior certificate holders receive their payment after the senior ones have been paid. For interest payment, the due coupon (commonly called the **pass-through rate**) is paid first out of available income to the senior certificate holders, and then to the junior certificate holders from the remaining collections. If the collections for any month fall short of the scheduled collections, even after drawing from available liquidity enhancements, the accrued coupon is carried forth to the next month.

For principal payments, the principal may be paid **sequentially**, meaning all principal will go to the senior class until it is fully paid off, or **proportionally**, meaning the principal will be proportionally split between the senior and junior classes. Proportionality means, if there is no default or realized losses, there is a proportional distribution; if there is a loss, it is absorbed by writing off the junior class, thereby reducing its claim.

Despite classes of certificates, the overall nature of the transaction is still a pass-through.

Presence of various time tranches: Apart from creating different classes, it is also possible to create different time tranches – classes structured with different timing of cash flow. Assume two classes – senior and junior pass-throughs. If the paydown structure between the two is proportional and the assets pay off in 120 months, we expect both to pay off in 120 months. We may want to create a senior certificate that pays in just about five years. If we create two parts of the senior certificate, say Senior 1 and Senior 2, such that all cash flow, proportionally allocated to the senior class, is taken sequentially to Senior 1, and once fully paid, to Senior 2, we thereby ensure that Senior 1 will have a shorter payback period. Senior 2 will start receiving principal after Senior 1 has been paid off and hence, will have a longer payback. See Chapter 8 for numerical illustrations of sequential time tranches.

Stripped interest pass-throughs: Simple mortgage pass-throughs are affected by prepayments and delayed payments. While delayed payments may be offset by liquidity facilities, prepayments could affect the returns of the investors. If the underlying loans or mortgages prepay, such prepayment would have been passed over to the investors. These mortgages will not earn interest for the future, because it would mean a loss of opportunity for the investor, unless they are able to plough back the principal at effectively the same rate.

Prepayment risk is significant when rates of interest decline; existing borrowers find it worthwhile to prepay an existing fixed rate mortgage, and then take another mortgage at reduced rates. While investors in pass-throughs receive prepayment of principal, they are unable to reinvest the prepaid amount at the original rate because the interest rate has come down.

To eliminate the risk of interest rate loss due to prepayments, stripped pass-through certificates were devised. A stripped pass-through structure issues undivided interest certificates separately for the principal part (**principal only or POs**) and separately for the interest part (**interest only or IOs**). The holders of POs are proportional owners of the principal collected every month, and holders of IOs are holders of interest collected every month.

It is easy to understand that the risk of interest rate movement is taken entirely by the IOs, who face the loss of interest if a prepayment takes place. On the other hand, the holders of POs stand to a benefit on account of prepayment, as they get back the principal faster than projected without any corresponding impact on their interest earnings. PO strips will be presumably acquired by investors who anticipate a decline in interest rates; any decline in interest rates increases the market value of POs, as there will be an increase in the speed of prepayments. IO strips are bought by investors who eye higher interest rates; if this happens, the rate of prepayments will be less than projected at the time of pricing the transaction, so investors will stand to gain.

There is yet another class of stripped pass-throughs where each investor has a fixed share of the principal and a fixed share of the interest.

Prepayment protected classes: It is also possible to redistribute the mutual returns of various classes of investors by creating a prepayment-protected class, and a class taking all prepayments or all above a pre-specified prepayment. These are discussed later under **planned amortization class** and **target amortization class**.

Pay-through structure

The concept of pass-throughs and pay-throughs is more the model adopted by the transaction to relegate the cash flow to investors; as might be obvious, in practice one does not have to swear by any such clear distinction.

The name "pay-throughs" includes all securitization structures where the cash flow of the transaction is reconfigured at SPV level and paid to investors on a time pattern that is unmatched with the payback structure of the pool assets. In other words, it is a deliberate and managed mismatch in the maturities of assets and liabilities of the transaction.

The difficulty with pass-throughs is the direct association of the pay-in structure of the assets with the payback structure of the securities. The result is a chaotic structure of principal payments month after month, including unscheduled cash flow.

Monthly amortization of principal is not suitable for investor needs, all the more so when it is uncertain. Fixed income investors, accustomed to corporate bonds and fixed maturity paper are more comfortable with fixed and definite maturities.

In addition, in pass-through structures, the originator is passing the entire burden of asset liability mismatches to investors, while asset liability management is intrinsically the function of the originator as a financial intermediary.[12]

Thus, the market searched for methods that permitted dissociation between recoveries and repayments; the timing of the cash inflow for receivables needed to be segregated from repayment to investors. That repayment needed smoothing, but not necessarily following the same repayment period as the underlying receivables. In short, the cash flow from the receivables had to be re-configured.

This led to the super-imposition of a loan structure on a securitization device; the SPV instead of transferring undivided interest on the receivables issued debt securities, normally bonds, repayable on fixed dates. Such debt securities in turn were backed by the assets transferred by the originator to the SPV. In other words, as with the pass-through structure, the originator transferred the mortgages to the SPV. The SPV ran its own treasury – collected cash on regular basis, reinvested cash into temporary reinvestments (to the extent required for bridging the gap between the date of payments on out of assets and the date of servicing of the bonds), and using the cash flow from the assets along with the income out of reinvestment (and, to the extent required, by dipping into a liquidity facility) to retire the bonds. Such bonds were called **mortgage-backed bonds,** or **collateralized mortgage obligations;** this practice was used in the U.S. mortgage securitization market. The word "pay-through" contrast with pass-through as the payment for the mortgages is simply passed through the SPV to investors; in the present case, it is paid through the SPV to the investors. The SPV is not merely a passive conduit, but receives, reinvests and pays money, managing the implicit mismatch. See Table 2.3 for differences between the pass-through and pay-through structures.

The following features explain the pay-through process (see Figure 2.4):

AT THE INCEPTION:

- The originator selects the receivables to be securitized.
- The originator sets up a special purpose vehicle (SPV). This is generally an owner trust (a U.S. tax term) or a corporation, with the single purpose of holding the selected receivables on behalf of the investors. The trust is empowered to make reinvestment of the cash flows.
- The originator transfers the receivables to the SPV, and in turn, the SPV issues asset-backed notes or asset-backed bonds to the originator. [Alternatively, the SPV may issue notes or bonds to the investors directly, in which case the offer for sale of the securities by the originator is not required]. These bonds or notes (securities) represent SPV debt backed by the pool of receivables held on its own behalf by the SPV.
- The originator now has securities instead of receivables. The originator makes an offer for sale of these securities to the investors.

AT THE TIME OF PAYMENT:

- Payment is collected on the due date by the originator/servicer, who has also agreed to service the receivables.
- After deducting service charges, if any, the installment is passed over to the SPV.
- The SPV reinvests the amount so collected, usually in a **guaranteed investment account** or other specified modes of investment.
- On the date of scheduled payment to the investors, the payment is released from the bank account.
- The amount received by the investors has as much interest and principal as in a regular bond or loan structure.
- If there are any prepayments – premature closures of the contracts, the amount received as a result is deposited in the Reinvestment account and repaid as per scheduled payment dates.

Again, for the originator, it hardly matters whether the repayment structure at SPV level is distributive or deployment-oriented.

There is a significant difference on the role and structure of the SPV. A pass-through trust is a mere collective instrumentality, but the SPV in a pay-through structure is almost like an investment conduit, the only difference that it has a limited purpose and business. It collects and invests cash flows, trying to smooth the repayments to investors. By issuing debt securities repayable on fixed dates, it takes upon itself an obligation similar to a liability.

The nature of an investors' interest in a pay-through securitization is also clearly different; the investor has the right to receive interest and principal on fixed dates, although such interest and principal is backed by the payments on the assets transferred to it held by the SPV. Investors' interest and principal

Table 2.3   Main differences between pass through and pay-through structures:

	Pass-through	*Pay-through*
Role of the SPV	Merely a collective and distributive device; the SPV is passive and does not deal with the cash collection.	The SPV reinvests cash and pays off investors on stated dates.
Organizational structure of SPV	Usually as a tax transparent trust.	Usually as a body corporate or owner trust.
Manner of payment to investors	Investors are paid proportionately out of periodic collections. The investors' cash inflows are erratic with the same fluctuations as underlying receivables.	Investors are paid on stated dates from collections/accumulations out of reinvestment. Investor inflows are smoothed by a collection and reinvestment account acting as a sort of "spike buster."
Tax status of SPV	Generally, the SPV is tax transparent.	Generally, the SPV is taxed, either in representative capacity or as an entity.
Accounting for SPV	Generally, the SPV is not required to prepare accounts, as it does not have any asset/liability as such.	The fixed repayment date obligation taken by SPV is, or is similar, to a debt security, so there is an asset and liability treatment by the SPV.
Nature of investors' investment	Investors acquire a proportionate share of underlying receivables.	Investors acquire claims against the SPV.
Withholding tax on payments by the SPV	Generally not applicable.	Generally applicable.

receipts do not necessarily coincide with the interest and principal collections of the SPV.

Economic argument against pay-throughs

The essence of the pay-through method is that the SPV does reconfigure the cash flow; it creates and manages a mismatch between the inflows and outflows of the transaction. Where does the SPV reinvest the cash flows to bridge the mismatch? It is not difficult to see that the SPV's rights of reinvestment are greatly restricted.

- It can reinvest in buying further assets from the originator, which means the transaction becomes a revolving one where the limitations of revolving transactions will be applicable (see the later part of this chapter).
- It can reinvest in some liquid but passive modes of safe reinvestment such as bank deposits and money market accounts.
- It cannot lend this money or take exposure in the originator as that would amount to a risk on the originator.
- It cannot invest in other aggressive investments such as stocks, bonds or corporate loans, as doing so would mean the risk attributes of such investments overlay the risk on the pool.

So, in non-revolving structures, practically the only option the SPV has is to make passive investments in safe, nearly default-free financial assets.

As the coupon the SPV pays on the notes or weighted-average cost of the transaction is invariably higher than the return the SPV earns from such passive reinvestment, every dollar so reinvested results in a negative carry. Thus, the overall economics of the transaction is adversely affected by reinvestment. In fact, if substantial reinvestments are made, the negative carry might overtake the excess spread from the asset and result in a negative excess spread.

The investor-friendly feature of pay-through securities must be assessed carefully with this negative feature. This applies to the bond structure as well, which is discussed below.

Collateralized mortgage obligation bonds

As the pay-through structure had already mixed and matched an element of traditional debt with securitization, the next logical development was to add an element of financial engineering resulting in the creation of sequentially paying collateralized mortgage obligation (CMO) bonds. The CMO structure was first tried in the mortgage market in 1983. Replication has been done in several other asset classes over time, as the CDO device has used the CMO technique.

The pay-through mechanism solved one of the major difficulties of the pass-through – mismatching the recoveries and repayments. It still did not allow investors the facility of different tenure and repayment choices. Some investors may prefer a short-term investment, whereas some may invest for a longer period. Passing on equal payment to all is to ignore their different needs.

Collateralized Mortgage Obligation (CMO) bonds solved this difficulty. Notably, the term "mortgage obligation" is only to use the usual jargon for these bonds; there is no reason why the application of this device should be limited only to mortgage obligations. For example, when these bonds are backed by a portfolio of loans transferred by the originator, they are called **collateralized loan obligation** or **collateralized debt obligation** bonds, or CLO/CBOs for short.

The CMO structure breaks the investors into different tranches or different series of investors based on the duration for which they want to invest. The CMO structure proceeds on the principle of paying interest to all investors (excluding zero coupon bond holders), but principal is paid sequentially based on the priorities of different investors. For example, the A series of investors would be repaid first, so the entire principal collected, including pre-paid principal, is first used to pay off A-class investors. Once A-class is fully retired, repayments are made to B-class, with as many sequential classes as required. The last is Z-class, which receives a bullet payment at the end of the transaction. In the meantime, interest collected may be passed on to all the investors as per their outstanding investment.

Obviously, this structured investment option allows investors to invest as per their objectives. Short-term investors carrying less risk are paid back first and so expect a lesser rate of return. Medium-term investors have more risk to shoulder, as their investment is subject to all risks remaining after paying off A-class investors. It is Z-class investors (normally the originator himself) who takes all the risk and can target the highest rate of return.

In addition to the Z-class, there may also be an equity class in a CMO scheme. Although the Z bond is substantively no different from equity (a serious tax question, discussed at length in the chapter on tax issues), the equity class is brought to justify the debt classification of the other classes. Obviously, one cannot have debt unless one has equity in any vehicle.

The CMO structure is generically a variant of the pay-through method. The sizes of A, B, C through Z are all determined by modeling the cash flow which alone is a reiterative, involved exercise but is very significant. The overall economics of the transaction for the originator is directly governed by the segmentation of the investments. Class-A bonds are the best rated, and so the cheapest. The latter classes have a lower rating and higher cost. The Z-class, for example, is either not rated or rated below investment grade. There is an interesting trade off between the rating of the senior classes and the cost of the transaction. Each junior class is a protection for the senior class, while the junior-most class (the Z- class) is a credit enhancement for all others. Hence, more than the amount of the Z-class, the rating of the senior classes improves and thus the cost of the senior classes comes down. However, the cost of the junior classes goes up. The objective of the originator is to work through the least weighted-average cost of the transaction, so the structuring of the various classes assumes a great significance.

The other important aspect of structuring these various classes is the taxation of the SPV. The payments to the various debt classes is a tax-deductible charge, as payments coming into the SPV are taxable income. The objective of the SPV is to minimize or neutralize the impact of taxation on the transaction by nearly matching the incomes and expenses, so as to leave the least possible taxable income in the SPV.

The following features explain the CMO structure (see Figure 2.6):

AT THE TIME OF CREATION:

- Similar to the pay-through structure.

AT THE TIME OF PAYMENT:

- The payment is collected on the due date by the originator/servicer, who has also agreed to service the receivables.
- After deducting service charges, if any, the installment is passed over to the SPV.
- The SPV first uses the collections for servicing interest to all bondholders, except the zero coupon holders (if any).
- The remaining amount is first used to retire A-class bondholders proportionately.
- When A class bonds are fully amortized, the amortization of B class starts, and so on.
- The final remaining cash flow is used to pay off Z-class or zero coupon bondholders. If the Z-class is different from the equity class, the residual cash is taken over by the equity holders.

The bond structure represents a sizeable part of asset-backed transactions in international securitization.

Refinements in CMO structure

The CMO and its equivalent in other asset-backed securitizations have been quite widely used. The above tranched CMO structure, which pays back to investors in a sequential manner, is known as a **plain vanilla structure** or **sequential** structure. Over a period of time, various add-on features have been introduced in the CMO structure, essentially from the viewpoint of meeting the investors' need to seek repayment of their investments in a particular fashion. Some of these refinements are discussed below:

Planned amortization class

This variety was introduced around 1986 in U.S. mortgage markets. Essentially, planned amortization class (PAC) bonds are also bonds that are protected against prepayments, but protection comes not by sequencing payments but by transferring the fluctuations in prepayments to a class of bonds, called **support class** or **support bonds** (also called **companion bonds**). Thus, while a simple tranched CMO structure would make sequential payments to different classes of bond holders, the PAC structure essentially has two parts in the issuance – PAC bonds and support bonds. The PAC bonds have a planned amortization schedule. If the principal available for allocation for a month is more than the required amount as per the plan, the excess is diverted and paid to the support class. If the principal available is less than the required amortization, the shortfall is drawn out of the principal available for the support class. Thus, if the prepayment speed is more than the projected speed, the support class is repaid over a shorter maturity, and conversely, the support class has a longer maturity. In other words, the increase or decrease in prepayment speed is negotiated to the support class. Normally, the band of such increase or decrease is fixed for the support class, so that any increase or decrease in excess of the band is absorbed by the PAC bonds and not transferred to the support class.

The PAC structure has been the most widely used structure of CMOs; the PAC class has the advantage of cash flow certainty, while the support class is attractive to investors looking for higher yields.

Targeted amortization class

Another variant of the CMO structure is the targeted amortization class (TAC) bonds. These bonds are similar to the PAC class, with the only difference that TAC bonds do not provide protection against a drop in prepayment rates compared to the expected speed. Thus, if prepayment exceeds the projected rate, the excess principal is repaid to the support class. If the maturity extends due to a decline in prepayment, the support class is not affected. Thus, the purpose is only to protect against acceleration of a targeted amortization.

Accrual bonds or accretion bonds

An accrual bond or **Z-bond** is a zero coupon bond that has principal and interest locked out for a certain number of years. It is only towards the end of the structure that the bond starts paying coupon and repaying interest.

Normally the Z-bond is used as a shock absorber for sequential class CMOs. Z-bonds could also be used to support PAC or TAC bonds.

Floaters and inverse floaters

There is yet another innovation in CMO structures to break up the CMOs into floaters and inverse floaters. Floaters, or floating rate CMOs, are those whose rate of return will vary as per variations in the base rate. The base rate could be a representative rate, such as LIBOR (or EuriBOR) or treasury rates.

Fluctuations in interest rates are not absorbed by a swap counterparty, but by other section of CMOs – the inverse floaters. For every floater, there is an inverse floater. It is the inverse floaters that absorb the variations passed on to the floating class. For example, if interest rates go up, the floating class will have an increase in interest payments, which will be compensated by reducing the rate of interest payable on the inverse floating class. For declining interest rates, floating class payments will come down, and the inverse floating class will be benefited.

Investors, who believe interest rates will go up, prefer a floating rate investment. Those who are bearish on interest rates prefer an inverse floater to benefit from the decline in interest rates on the floating class. Inverse floating investors may also use the investment as a hedge against other floating class investments held by them.

This structure eliminates the costs that would otherwise have been payable on buying an interest rate swap.

Revolving structure

A revolving structure is used for short-lived assets such as credit card receivables, trade receivables and short-term lease rentals. It is understandable that the use of the usual pay-through or pass-through structure will be inappropriate as it is not economical to match the maturities of the assets and the securities. In such cases, the originator passes interest to the investors in a revolving pool of assets, where assets pay off, but are re-instated by a fresh stock of receivables.

The best example is that of credit cards. Credit card receivables typically pay off within 3–4 months or so. The entire principal along with the interest is paid off within this time. On the other hand, investors would like to lock in their money for a reasonably long period, say 3 years. The money is pooled with the SPV, which buys the requisite amount of credit card receivables from the originator. Once these are paid off, it retains the interest for servicing the investors, but releases the principal to buy fresh receivables for replenishment. The structure keeps revolving during the **revolving period** until the targeted **amortization period arrives**.

When it is time to amortize the receivables, the principal collected is used to pay off the principal to investors. The principal can be repaid either in several installments or in a single bullet payment. If it is a bullet repaying structure, there can be some accumulation and reinvestment of the principal, as it is unlikely that the entire principal will be collected at once.

> **Box 2.2: Reinstating-type securitization**
>
> - A reinstating-type securitization converts a short term asset into long-term security, thus providing a revolving funding to the originator.
> - Usually, the asset is also a revolving credit with a short term of each receivable, but the facility revolves on a continuing basis.
> - Thus, during the revolving period, the principal collected is churned back into business against a fresh lot of assets and the interest flows out to the investors.

Most revolving asset securitizations have a right to acceleration of principal repayment; in case of certain events, the SPV may use the principal repayments in any month, not for acquiring fresh receivables but to pay off investors before the scheduled repayment date. This is a basic protection needed, given the assets are of a revolving nature, and every month or so the investors' asset cover in the form of receivables is being depleted until it is replenished. This results in an originator's performance risk; if the originator exits business, or does not produce enough new receivables to replenish those paid off, investors may have no asset-backing for their investments. To take care of such a contingency, there may be a trigger event, such as a decline in receivables generated over a certain period that would lead to acceleration of repayment to the investors, that is, instead of releasing the collections to the originator, the SPV will pay off the principal to the investors.

An **early amortization trigger** is essential for any revolving structure. When these triggers have been hit, the transaction comes out of the revolving period and enters the amortization period. An early amortization period is a sort of pre-default acceleration clause – preventative rather than curative.

Box 2.3: Future flows securitization

- Future flows securitization differs greatly from asset-backed transactions, as the asset does not exist now but in the future.
- Therefore, the asset backing is only meaningful when assets actually come into being.
- Future flows, however, are based on a contingency plan that if the asset generation declines, the trustees will be able to take preventive action.
- A substantial amount of over-collateralization and cash flow trapping are the mainstays of future flow transactions, rather than asset backing.

For revolving transactions, there is an equalization element called a **seller's share** to take care of the fluctuations in the volume of assets originated month on month. The seller's share is the excess of total assets in the pool over and above the funding in the transaction. For example, if the total funding raised by a transaction is $100, the asset transferred is $110, and the extra $10 is the seller's share that takes care of fluctuations in monthly originations. In other words, month after month, the seller's share will be the actual value of assets in the pool ($100). Notably, the seller's share is not necessarily a subordination or over-collateralization[13] as it is at par with the investor interest; it is merely there to smooth the monthly fluctuations.

Credit card receivables apart, a revolving securitization device is also used for the securitization of consumer credits that also typically pay off over a short tenure. There are a number of lease securitizations that also use the revolving device for some time before turning into a bond structure; that is, all cash collected during a part of the transaction will be revolved back before the cash is released for principal repayment.

Impact and suitability of the revolving structure

The impact of the revolving structure is:

- To provide the originator with a revolving line of credit, such that the principal collected over the amortization period need not be returned to the SPV but may be retained by the originator, as if the originator has availed a fixed amount of facility; and
- To extend the term of the liabilities and make it longer than the term of the assets.

At the same time, an essential limitation of the revolving method should be noted. Assume we have a case of auto loans, with an average term of each loan being 48 months. If we use the revolving structure here, and have a revolving period of three years, it would mean the loans bought in the 36th month would continue for the next 48 months, thereby extending the total tenure of the transaction to seven years. Therefore, revolving structures are typically used only in cases where assets pay off in a few months, or where the assets can be sold off[14] if they do not pay up by the expected amortization date.

Future flows securitization

Over the past few years, another interesting application of the securitization device is future flows securitization. This is very different from traditional securitization applications, as compared with normal securitization of receivables in that a future flows securitization is one where the entity does not have any identifiable receivables as of date. From past conduct or by way of a reasonable expectation, it is likely the entity will have a certain amount of cash flow arising over time, but there is no debtor against whom there is any claim, either payable immediately or in the future. In other words, the basic subject matter of the securitization transaction – the receivables – is yet to come into existence (see Table 2.4).

This feature will obviously make a substantial difference to the motive, economics and structure of such transactions. The motive in a traditional securitization would be to source for funds against a portfolio of receivables on the strength of such a portfolio, but that of a future flows transaction cannot depend on the quality of the portfolio, as it is not in existence yet. Traditional securitizations can be motivated by off-balance sheet objectives; future flows securitization will never be off-balance sheet, as no transfer of assets has taken place as of date.

Motivations for future flows may be either a higher amount of funding as compared to traditional methods of funding, or cheaper funding.

Future flows are broadly of two types – domestic future flows and cross border future flows. Cross-border future flows relate to securitization of cash flow coming from other countries, typically hard-currency countries.

The economics of cross-border future flows securitization is totally different; most such future flows securitization deals have been originated from countries where domestic economic conditions have resulted in very low sovereign ratings, and therefore, an investor would either not be comfortable in lending to an entity in such a country, or if he does, the premium demanded would be abnormally high considering the rating of the country. In other words, the rating of the sovereign casts its shadow on the borrowing costs of the entities.

Say a Mexican company needs to borrow against future receivables – earnings on exports. The receivables have not been generated as the exports are yet to be sent. If the company resorts to traditional funding, it is likely to pay heavy costs because of the poor credit rating of the country. However, the earnings of the entity are to come from hard currency countries, such as exports to the U.S.

This creates opportunities for a future flows securitization. If the earnings of the company in dollars, from hard currency areas, could be trapped outside of Mexico, so that the company creates a lawful obligation for an at-source deduction in favor of the SPV, the investors would have a legally enforceable right over earnings of the company in dollars. The investors would not be affected by the exchange risk, as the earnings are in dollars. The investors would not be affected by political or other sovereign risks, as the earnings are being lawfully sourced from outside of Mexico. The only risk is that the company is not exporting: as a protection, the SPV could have a sizeable over-collateralization. That is, if the transaction is sufficiently over-collateralized, say, three times (meaning, the average dollar earnings received outside Mexico by the SPV is thrice the amount of servicing required for the investors), the investors can be reasonably certain of return of interest and principal. Besides, there could also be a provision for acceleration of principal repayment. As such, the transaction can achieve a rating that is far superior to the rating of the sovereign, and hence, be able to borrow at much better costs.

As is evident, the basic objective of a future flows securitization is to avail a rating improvement over the rating of the sovereign, and so source inter-national financing. Accordingly, opportunities for future flows securitization arise when:

- There is an entity in an emerging market;
- There is a steady receivable from hard currency areas in hard currency;
- There is an asset or framework that exists;
- The sovereign is rated below investment grade; and
- And it is legally permissible to create an at-source payment in the country of origin or another hard currency country.

Table 2.4   Main differences between asset-backed securitization and future flows securitization

	Asset-backed securitization	*Future flows securitization*
Legal nature	Sale of existing receivables	Agreement to sell receivables
Nature of receivables	Receivables for something done or service rendered	Any receivables from a hard currency country
Intent of the transaction	To sell a right in receivables and to pass on risk/reward in the receivables to investors	To provide investors with a mechanism of trapping receivables at the source, eliminating exchange rate and sovereign risk
Nature of amount received by originator	Consideration for sale of receivables	Advance against an agreement to sell receivables
Accounting treatment	Normally off-balance sheet	On-balance sheet
Typical usage	Developed/emerging markets	Emerging markets
Typical ratings	AA/AAA	BBB/A-
Extent of over-collateralization	Usually low	Usually very high

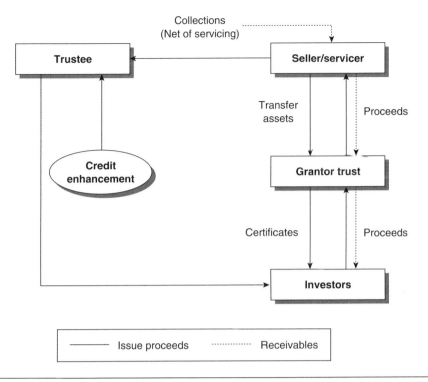

Figure 2.3   Pass-through Structure

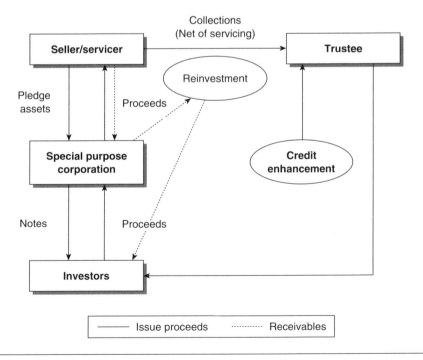

Figure 2.4   Pay-through Structure

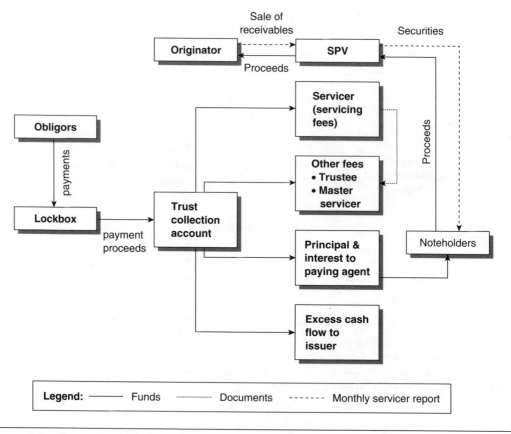

Figure 2.5   Cash and Data flow chart in a typical deal

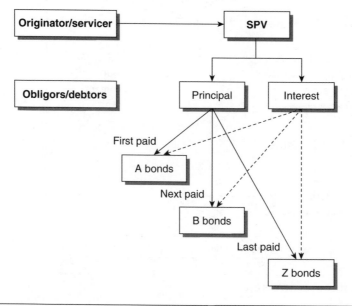

Figure 2.6   Illustration of Sequential Pay CMOs

For domestic future flows, the motivation generally is to find funding against assets that are typically not bankable, or a higher extent of funding because the regular approach of balance sheet lenders is to look at the value of assets on the balance sheet. A future flows investor looks at the cash flow not showing up on the balance sheet.

The legal, accounting and tax considerations that apply to future flows securitization are quite different from those applicable to normal securitization transactions (see Box 2.3).

Advantages of securitization for the issuer

Lower cost

Cost reduction is one of the most important motivations in securitization. Securitization seeks to break an originating company's portfolio into echelons of risk, trying to align them to different risk appetites. This alchemy supposedly works – the weighted overall cost of a company that has securitized its assets seems to be lower than a company that depends on generic funding. It is important to note here that one of the most tangible effects of securitization is to reduce the extent of risk capital or equity required (being off-balance sheet for regulatory purposes, requirements for which are dealt with separately in later chapters) for a given volume of asset creation. Assuming equity to be the costliest of all sources of capital, lower equity requirements result in lower costs.

Securitization enables the originator to achieve a rating arbitrage – obtain a rating that a generic funding could not have. Such a rating is possible due to the credit and structural enhancements in the transaction.

The direct impact of lower borrowing costs is on lower lending costs. Mortgage rates in many countries fell after securitization was introduced or became popular. Many banks also claim to be running on lower lending costs due to securitization.

A study published in the journal *Real Estate Economics in 2001* (Spring), relating to mortgage markets, states: "In the case of adjustable-rate mortgages, we find no evidence that securitization lowers coupon rates. Moreover, we find no association between securitization and the coupon rates on fixed-rate mortgages. Instead, securitization appears to lower mortgage loan origination fees, resulting in substantial savings for homebuyers. A 1% increase in the monthly level of pass-through creation is associated with a 0.5-basis-point reduction in loan origination fees. In 1993 alone, securitization

> **Box 2.4: Reasons why securitization may lower the cost**
>
> - Securitization is based on three essential arbitrages: Arbitrage by stratification, arbitrage by leverage, and arbitrage by higher ratings.
> - A possible impact on cost of capital.
> - Structured finance results in stratified, made-to-fit securities to address various investor groups.
> - Securitization allows the firm to attain higher effective leverage, thereby bringing down weighted-average cost.
> - Securitization allows the firm to attain higher ratings, and thus raise lower-cost funding.
> - Finally, securitization raises funding from capital markets, a presumably more efficient source, particularly for better-rated securities.

likely produced consumer savings of more than $2 billion in loan origination fees."[15]

There are many other articles and research on this issue, notably:

- Hendershott, P. H., and J. D. Shilling (1989), "The impact of agencies on conventional fixed-rate mortgage yields," Journal of Real Estate Finance and Economics 2:101–115.
- Sirmans, C. F. and J. D. Benjamin (1990), "Pricing fixed rate mortgages: Some empirical evidence," Journal of Financial Services Research 4:191–202.
- Jameson, M., S. Dewan, and C. F. Sirmans (1992), "Measuring welfare effects of "unbundling" financial innovations: The case of Collateralized Mortgage Obligations," Journal of Urban Economics 31:1–13.
- Credit Scoring and Mortgage Securitization: Implications for Mortgage Rates and Credit Availability, December 21, 2000, Andrea Heuson[16].
- GSEs, Mortgage Rates and the Long-Run Effects of Mortgage Securitization by Wayne Passmore and others[17], arguing that GSEs generally, though not necessarily, reduce the cost of mortgage lending.

There are also applications such as future flows securitization, in which the objective of the originator is to achieve ratings higher than that of the entity or the rating of the country to which the originator belongs. As securitization makes such higher ratings possible, it enables the originator to borrow at lower costs.

Alternative investor base

Without disturbing existing lenders, securitization extends the pool of available funding sources to an entity by bringing in a new class of investors. For many entities, typical securitization investors such as insurance companies, asset managers, pension funds and the like may not be available for access, other than for investment in a securitization program.

Perfect matching of assets and liabilities

Asset liability mismatch is a serious issue for financial intermediaries such as banks and finance companies. It refers to the maturity mismatch between assets and liabilities. Mismatch spells either higher risk or cost, and so intermediaries try to strike a near perfect match between maturities of assets and liabilities.

It is important to understand that the problem of asset liability mismatch is not eliminated by securitization; it is simply transferred to the investors. We return to this issue when discussing the limitations of securitization.

Makes the issuer- rating irrelevant

As an asset-based financing, securitization may make it possible even for a low-rated borrower to seek cheap finance, purely on the strength of the asset-quality. Hence, the issuer makes itself irrelevant in a properly structured securitization exercise. One of the common statements rating companies have to make is that in a normal debt issuance, a product is rated. In structured finance issues, the issuer dictates the rating and the structure is worked out accordingly. In other words, it is possible to obtain a AAA rating for securitized products, irrespective of the rating of the originator; all that is required to be insured is adequate legal protection against the bankruptcy of the originator and an adequate level of credit enhancement. The best instance of this was when U.S. automakers General Motors and Ford were downgraded to junk status in May 2005, several of their securitization transactions were actually upgraded.

Multiplies asset creation ability

As discussed earlier, securitization reduces the required economic equity of the transaction and thus the required equity support, making it possible to grow much larger asset holdings on a given amount of equity. In traditional borrowing or on-balance sheet sources of funding, both the required amount of equity support and the regulatory capital requirements serve as a cap on the maximum extent of assets one can have with given capital. In terms of traditional capital standards,[18] with $1,000 of capital, one can create assets of $12,500 (8% minimum capital requirements). However, for securitization, if the originator provides an enhancement of 5% out of his capital, $1,000 of capital can enable him to create $20,000 of assets. Thus, as the required credit enhancement is reduced, the asset generation ability is magnified.

Allows higher funding

A traditional financier looks at assets on the balance sheet and lends a fraction thereof. A typical bank funding working capital will look at the working capital gap and fund a certain percentage. Securitization investors look at the future cash flow, which is not necessarily on the balance sheet, so the issuer might end up receiving greater funding through securitization than by conventional funding methods.

Off-balance sheet financing

Financial intermediaries look at securitization essentially as an off-balance sheet funding method. Off-balance sheet features can be seen from an accounting standards viewpoint or from a regulatory viewpoint. The latter is relevant for computation of regulatory capital or capital adequacy requirements, coming next. This point covers off-balance-sheet funding from an accounting standards viewpoint.

The tendency of financial institutions and others to prefer off-balance sheet funding over on-balance sheet funding is because the former allows higher returns on assets and higher returns on equity, without affecting the debt-equity ratio. As tools of managerial performance, these have a definite relevance.

Securitization allows a firm to create assets, make income thereon, and yet put the assets off the balance sheet the moment they are transferred through a securitization device. Thus, the income from the asset is accelerated and the asset disappears from the balance sheet, leading to improvement in both income-related ratios and asset-related ratios.

Appropriately, the off-balance-sheet feature does not – by itself – have much merit. Its consequence is more important. Any method of off-balance sheet liability also means off-balance sheet assets; what one loves to achieve is not off-balance sheet assets, but off-balance sheet liabilities. By keeping liabilities off the balance sheet, an entity can manage and earn income on a higher value of assets, without making it apparent. Thus, the inner motive of off-balance sheet financing is increased leverage.

Helps in capital adequacy requirements

Capital adequacy requirements relate to the minimum regulatory capital for financial intermediaries. One of the very strong motivations for securitization is that it allows the financial entity to sell off some of its on-balance sheet assets, and thus remove them from the balance sheet and reduce the amount of capital required for regulatory purposes. For securitization, the required capital is the extent of first loss support or subordination provided by the originator. The extent to which capital requirements come down due to securitization of assets is called **capital relief.** Alternatively, if the amount raised by selling on-balance sheet assets is used for creating new assets, the entity is able to increase asset creation without needing increased capital, thus putting regulatory capital to more efficient use.

Motivated by this, large commercial banks have made extensive use of securitization for what is known as **regulatory arbitrage.** This practices led banking supervisors in many countries to lay down regulations on capital requirements for securitization, ultimately culminating in the issuance of new capital standards – Basle II.

Improves capital structure

Able to market an asset outright (while not losing the stream of profits therein), securitization avoids the need to raise a liability, and so improves the capital structure. Alternatively, if securitization proceeds are used to pay off existing liabilities, the firm achieves a lower debt-equity ratio.

The improvement of capital structure as a result of a lower debt-equity ratio may not be a mere accounting gimmick; if securitization results in transfer of risks inherent in assets or capping of such risks, there is a real re-distribution of risks taking place, leaving the firm with a healthier balance sheet and reduced risk.

Better opportunity of trading on equity with no increased risk

This point is a re-statement of the accounting and capital adequacy-related benefits of securitization, discussed above. The ability to create assets, as a result of off-balance sheet treatment and regulatory freedom, results in more profits and hence a stronger firm.

Extends credit pool

Securitization keeps the other traditional lines of credit undisturbed, thus increasing the total financial resources available to the firm. Securitization has been tried by many firms in addition to regular borrowings, not in place of.

Not treated as a loan for regulatory purposes

If there is any regulation relating to borrowing powers, or borrowing from the public, securitization is not taken by regulation to be debt. For example, a regulation relating to public borrowings will not apply to securitization, as a securitization is not a case of borrowing.

Reduces credit concentration

Securitization has also been used by many entities for reducing credit concentration. Concentration, either sectoral or geographical, implies risk. Securitization by transferring on a non-recourse basis exposure by an entity has the effect of transferring risk to capital markets.

Avoids interest rate risk

One of the primary motives in securitization of mortgage receivables is to transfer interest rate risk to investors. The lenders are subject to the risk, as mortgages carry a fixed rate of return, while the loans taken by lenders have a variable rate. When the mortgages are securitized, the originator completely avoids the price risk as the entire interest rate or prepayment risk inherent in the pool is transferred to capital markets.

Arbitraging by repackaging

Securitization has been used by a number of banks and finance professionals for arbitraging purposes: Buying up assets from the market at higher spreads, accumulating them, providing or organizing enhancements and securitizing them. These transactions are sometimes called *repackaging transactions,* giving a net arbitrage profit to the repackager.

Arbitraging on liquidity and term structure

A significant aspect of securitization structures, particularly related to long-term receivables, is that the originator or the conduit manager makes profits by arbitraging on the yield differences in the term structure of interest rates. In CMO tranches, for example, long-term mortgages were de-composed into shorter-term securities, each paying successively. In the process, the securitizer was able to lower his cost, and the arbitrageur was able to make profits. Looking at the arbitrage possibility, a commentator writes: "In the early 1980s, monetary policy eventually pushed short-term rates below long-term rates (partly because capital-short financial intermediaries became unwilling to make long-term loans). In that environment, securitization made it possible for stand-alone non-recourse structures to buy long-term mortgages and pay the purchase price by selling shorter term CMO securities. The earliest CMOs, for example, could be created by acquiring mortgages at about 98% of par, spending 0.5% on structuring and selling 100% of par worth of debt, with no retained risk. That's a 1.5% profit with 0% capital cost. Thus, the only limit to converting "lead" (mortgages) into "gold" (highly-rated and liquid securities) was the price of 'lead.'"[19]

Improves accounting profits

This point might well top the list: Securitization allows up-front recognition of profits. The profit is the difference between the average spread inherent in the financial asset and weighted-average return provided to the investors. Accounting standards permit the front-loading of this profit if the securitization transaction satisfies certain requisites. We take up this issue in a later chapter on accounting.

Advantages to the investors

Needless to say, advantages to the originating entity would not carry much relevance unless securitization makes an attractive option to investors as well. Global investors, particularly institutional investors, have shown active interest in investing in securitized products. Rating agencies have helped in promoting these interest levels as most securitized products have obtained good ratings, and in several cases, even with a downgrading of the entity, the structured finance offerings have not been downgraded.

Securitization offers three features that investors love: Good ratings, rating resilience and good spreads.

In this section, we will review some advantages investors look at:[20]

1. Better Security

Securitized instruments are devices of asset-based finance. Investors have a direct claim over a portfolio of assets, often diversified and reasonably credit-enhanced. Investors are not affected by any of the risks that beset the originator. Thus, securitization investments are far safer than investing directly in the debt or equity of the originator. This point is proven by history. Securitization withstood the Southeast Asian crisis of 1997, the Mexican crisis and so on. Companies in Thailand or Mexico that securitized their assets either restructured during the crises or went bust, but securitization investors were left largely unaffected.

2. Good ratings

As noted, many structured finance offerings have obtained good ratings. With the increasing institutionalization of investment functions, investments are managed by professionals preferring a formally rated instrument to an unrated one. Rated investments are now preferred because of a regulatory advantage conferred by a new capital adequacy framework proposed by the Bank for International Settlements. Thus, investment managers prefer rated structured finance products.

3. Rating resilience

This point is very significant. Rating resilience stands for the stability of a rating after issuance. In other words, if you buy an investment that is AAA today, what is the likelihood that it will not deteriorate over time or be downgraded? The likelihood of downgrades is mirrored by a past history of downgrades or upgrades (called **rating migration** or **rating transition**). For securitization issuance, both Moody's and Standard and Poor's published rating resilience studies that indicated securitization investment to be considerably safer than corporate debt.

4. Better matching with investment objectives

Securitized instruments have great flexibility to match with the investment objectives of the investors. Investors looking for a safe high-grade investment can pick up a senior-most, A-type product, while those looking for a mediocre risk but with a higher rate of return can opt for a B-type option. Similarly, investors can look at the short, medium or long term. It is even possible for investors to go for a fixed-rate investment, floating-rate investment or inverse floating-rate investment.

5. Good spreads

Securitized products have offered good yields with adequate security. Empirical data about securitization offerings reveal that an investor who maintained a good balance of emerging market and developed market offerings has been able to come out with good rates of return. Another high-yield product in the market has been several packages of CDOs. Securitized products have provided good relative value. Excess spread offered by most securitized products has come down over time, which is evidence of their growing popularity.

6. Few instances of default

History provides far fewer incidents of default and loss in securitization than in corporate debt. In Europe, for example, there is no instance of default at all in almost a decade of securitization issuance.

7. Moral responsibility

This is something that cannot be guaranteed in the long run, but in the past all concerned agencies – rating agencies, investment banks and the like – have tried greatly to prevent securitization transactions from running into trouble. The recent bankruptcy of LTV Corp. in the U.S. is another example of the originator trying to ruin the legal features of the transaction by litigation. Again, the entire industry rose up, and without letting the sensitive legal issue face the courts, had the matter resolved by replacing the securitization with a DIP funding.

Threats in securitization

It is important to appreciate the significant limitations of securitization:

1. Costly source 昂贵的来源

The aggregate cost of securitizing assets is theoretically expected to be lower than the cost of mainstream funding. But actually, securitization has proved to be a costly source, primarily in emerging markets. As a new product, investors demand a premium for the lack of understanding of the product. In addition, the costs of rating and legal fees also tend to be huge.

One of the reasons the cost of securitization is substantially higher, particularly in emerging markets, is an "ignorance premium" on investor returns. Securitization is still a new phenomenon in many countries and in view of lack of awareness and sophistication, investors demand higher returns from securitization transactions.

2. Uneconomical for lower requirements

Securitization is a capital market exercise, which requires setting up a separate legal vehicle, elaborate work on the information systems for separation of the assets securitized from the other assets of the originator and separation of banking accounts. In addition, there are huge upfront costs like rating fees and legal costs, including stamp duties where applicable, all of which add up to a heavy initial payment. Therefore, there is a certain minimum economic size below which securitization is not cost effective.

3. Passes on asset liability mismatch to investors

The creation and refinancing of all financial assets implies a mismatch; the cash flow that arises from the asset and the manner in which claims of the lenders are satisfied cannot be matched. If these claims were to be fully matched, there is little reason for a financial intermediary to exist. Therefore, mismatch management is a key function of financial intermediation.

Securitization transfers the problem of asset liability mismatch to investors. The profile of the repayment of principal to investors in a pass-through transaction replicates the payback pattern of the assets. The problem of mismatch is passed on from one who is more able to manage it to one less able.

4. Passes on database

One of the most important limitations of securitization is the loss of data. The data from the pool contains sensitive business information, and there is increasing insistence on huge chunks of information about the pool being transmitted in the course of securitization.[21] In addition to the disclosures required by regulators, there are disclosures to services, trustees, rating agencies, and in some circumstances, even to investors.

5. Leaves the entity with junk assets

One of the common concerns about securitization is if investors have preference for cherry-picked assets, securitization will leave the originator with junk assets. If one imagines an entity as a composite of good, medium and poor assets, if the good is chipped away, what remains is junk.

The Bank for International Settlements in a 1992 publication titled *Asset Transfers and Securitization* had the following to say:

> It is sometimes contended that banks in seeking a good market reception for their securitized assets may tend to sell their best quality assets and thereby increase the average risk in their remaining portfolio. Investor and rating agency demand for high quality assets could encourage the sale of an institution's better quality assets. Moreover, an ongoing securitization programme needs a growing loan portfolio and this could force a bank to lower its credit standards to generate the necessary volume of loans. In the end a capital requirement that assumes a well-diversified loan portfolio of a given quality might prove to be too low if the average asset quality has deteriorated.
>
> Such arguments are not easy to support with empirical evidence. Banks that have securitized large amounts of assets do not exhibit signs of lower asset quality. It should also be noted that banks, which constantly securitize assets, are necessarily interested in maintaining the quality of their loan portfolio. Any asset quality deterioration would affect their reputation and their rating and indeed the capital adequacy requirement imposed by their supervisors.

6. Poses liquidity threat

Originators relying on securitization, particularly revolving assets, may have assets abruptly coming back on their balance sheet in case early amortization triggers are hit. The way the early amortization triggers are set, they are activated when the business of the originator suffers. In other words, exactly when the originator needs more liquidity to surmount his business problems, he sees liquidity squeezed when a revolving facility becomes unavailable. The problem may be even more serious in the case of future flows where the trustees have the right to trap the excess cash flowing back to the originator. If the business scenario worsens, those trapping rights are activated and the claims of the investors are accelerated. This is fatal; imagine a case when, placed in financial difficulties, a business needs a debt moratorium, and instead has debt acceleration.

7. Bad in bad days

What is bad quickly turns worse in the case of securitization. We have discussed early amortization triggers and the trapping rights applicable in case of future flows. For banks and institutional lenders, they have realized the significance of long term partnership with their borrowers and are prepared to lend a helping hand in business emergencies. And they have the discretion to do so. In practice, there are innumerable instances of debt restructuring that help a business to survive. Securitization transactions, on the other hand, are looked after by professional trustees who do not have any discretion to allow time or skip payments. Restructuring provisions of bankruptcy laws also do not come to the rescue as most SPVs are structured as bankruptcy remote entities. It is important to understand that when a business starts bleeding, securitization transactions are like a scalpel rather than bandage.

8. Makes profit accounting volatile

Securitization accounting, as per current accounting standards, leads to upfront booking of profits. These profits represent not only the profits encashed while making the sale, but even estimated profits based on future profitability of the transaction. In other words, the originator accelerates future profits on the securitized portfolio and puts the same on books upfront. Unless a continued growth in volume of securitization is maintained, this impacts future profitability. That is why aggressive securitization is compared to tiger riding: To stay safe, you have to continue to ride!

Yet another drawback of securitization accounting is volatility, introduced by the need to regularly review and revise profit estimates made on past transactions. Thus, the quality and predictability of financial information is depleted by securitization transactions.

Notes

1   A good way to understand the process of securitization may be the series of steps listed below (p. 59), in conjunction with the numerical examples in Chapter 8.
2   See Chapter 1 for more on asset-based financing.
3   See Chapter 23 on Legal Issues

4 Rating agency Moody's issued a Special Report on March 22, 2001, titled Non-Bankruptcy-Remote Issuers In Asset Securitization suggesting that it was possible for an operating company, without involving a bankruptcy remote special purpose vehicle, to issue notes that could serve the same purpose as securitization – achieve higher ratings than that of the issuer. The Moody's report said that this was relevant for the insolvency laws of England & Wales, and countries with similar insolvency legal systems, such as the Cayman Islands, Hong Kong, Singapore, Australia, Malaysia and Bermuda. Legal experts were not in agreement and the market also did not take it very seriously.

5 *Pfandbriefe* and traditional mortgage funding instruments in Germany are discussed in detail in Chapter 3 under Germany, and also in Chapter 6 on RMBS.

6 ABCP is commonly issued by ABCP conduits – discussed in Chapter 18. Also, see Chapter 4 for more on expected and legal maturity of asset-backed securities.

7 Also discussed in Chapter 22.

8 See the section on secured loan structures in Chapter 23 on Legal Issues. Also *pfandbriefs* in Germany in Chapter 12 on Residential Mortgage-backed Transactions.

9 In the case studies taken up in Chapter 6 on Residential Mortgage-backed Securities, the Abbey National's Holmes transaction uses a master trust structure. Master trust structures have almost become the rule in credit card transactions.

10 See Chapter 4 on Liquidity Enhancements.

11 The term "pass-through" is covered in IAS 39 – see Chapter 27 under IAS 39.

12 We will return to asset liability mismatches later under Advantages of Securitization.

13 Over-collateralization is a form of credit enhancement discussed in Chapter 4.

14 For CDOs, the revolving structure is used, and the assets are corporate loans or bonds. If the bonds or loans do not amortize during the amortization period, they are sold, usually by way of an auction, called **auction call**.

15 Steven Todd: The Effects of Securitization on Consumer Mortgage Costs, http://papers.ssrn.com/sol3/papers.cfm?abstract_id=223585, last visited December 19, 2005.

16 http://www.federalreserve.gov/Pubs/FEDS/2000/200044/200044pap.pdf, last visited December 19, 2005.

17 http://www.federalreserve.gov/pubs/feds/2001/200126/200126pap.pdf, last visited December 19, 2005.

18 The new capital standard Basle II seeks to relate capital requirements not just to the value of assets, but the risk-weighted value, while the risks will be calculated based on external or internal rating of the asset. See Chapter 29.

19 Frederick Feldkamp in Securitization: The Alchemist's Dream; *International Financial Law Review*; London; 2000.

20 We shall take up investors' experience, including performance and returns, in Chapter 30.

21 For example, Regulation AB requires several disclosures – see Chapter 28.

Chapter 3

The World of Securitization[1]

T he market for securitization has grown dramatically since its onset about three decades ago, with the total outstanding issuance of securitized assets soon expected to reach US$9 trillion.[2] Notably, new issuers from new geographical territories are coming into the market, and at the same time, new applications of securitization beyond the traditional mainstream areas are keeping the markets vibrant. Synthetic securitization has given a totally new dimension to securitization methodology and has registered dramatic growth in recent years.

The purpose of this chapter is to take a quick look at the market developments, generally in regions and specific countries.

Arguably, mortgage financiers in the U.S. were the first securitizers, transforming themselves from portfolio lenders to mortgage originators. Constrained by regulatory growth restrictions, credit card (or non-bank entities) soon followed by securitizing excess production and adding upward of 30% a year to their portfolio. Specialty finance companies later emerged as increased market efficiency, advanced technology, structural improvements, and investor demand expanded the securitization market to include automobile, home equity, and other asset classes. These lenders used securitization aggressively as a low-cost funding source that effectively eliminated balance sheet constraints to growth.

Most recently, as investors became increasingly comfortable with newer asset classes and innovative structures, the securitization of commercial assets emerged. This market has also migrated from the U.S. to Europe and now Asia and other parts of the world. Motivated by regulatory capital relief and efficient capital allocation, commercial banks' issuance of collateralized loan obligations (CLOs) and collateralized bond obligations (CBOs) are adding new excitement in the market. Synthetic technology has taken securitization to arbitraging desks where extremely interesting combinations of synthetic assets are taken to market mimicking traditional credit assets.

History of securitization

The history of securitization depends on the meaning of securitization adopted. One could take a broad meaning as to include securitized loans or every securitized instrument, in which case, securitization goes as deep in history as the very concept of a corporate body.

However, in the sense it is understood presently – as a tool of structured finance-securitization developed in the U.S. real estate financing market—it spread not only all over the world but to diverse applications.

However, in Europe a form of mortgage funding has existed for many years that has remarkable similarities to the present form of securitization, although the two are not the same. This instrument has existed in Denmark for more than 200 years. Likewise, the German *pfandbrief* instrument has a long history. For more details, see the country profiles for Germany and Denmark later in this chapter.

Deeper in history

It remains interesting that securitization in Denmark has a history of 200 years, much longer than the U.S. mortgage-backed securities (see the country profile for Denmark). Similarly, Germany has a traditional mortgage financing instrument called *pfandbrief* that too has a very long history and is alive even today (see the country profile for Germany).

A form of transfer of interest in land seems to have an even deeper history than *pfandbrief*. In a paper titled The Capital Market Before 1600,[3] it says that sale of rentals out of land emanated in Northern France in the 12th Century, as an escape from increasing assaults on mortgage loans on account of usurious lending. "For example, rather than selling land for cash, it could be sold in exchange for a rent constituted on it – a *bail à rente* or rent-sale. Or, rents could be made the basis for a loan: a lord could assign rents due to him from his vessels to a third party in exchange for a capital sum, or he could constitute a rent on his land and sell this in exchange for a capital sum." The author says this was not viewed as a sale. "Because it was considered a sale rather than a loan, the creditor had less difficulty in seizing the property on which the annuity was drawn in case of default."

The U.S. mortgage market

The first efforts towards securitizing financial assets were made in the U.S., originating in the mortgage financing markets of the country. The instrument was developed with a need to create a secondary market in mortgage financing. In the process the catalysts were government agencies formed for buying and selling federally insured mortgages.

The history of U.S. government efforts to introduce a secondary market in mortgages goes back to the 1930s. Originally, mortgages in the U.S. were originated by savings and loans associations that financed their operations through retail deposits. During the Depression, deposit markets collapsed. To allow originators to fund mortgages, the Congress enacted the National Housing Act to create a secondary market in mortgages. Subsequently, it created the Federal Housing Administration (FHA). The FHA insured housing loans made by private lenders and thus absorbed the inherent risks in housing finance. In 1938, the Federal National Mortgage Association was created to buy and sell federally-insured mortgages. In 1968, the erstwhile Federal National Mortgage Association (FNMA) was split into two parts – a new FNMA and the Government National Mortgage Association (GNMA).

It was these agencies, FNMA (colloquially called Fannie Mae) and GNMA (colloquially called Ginnie Mae), which were responsible for the present-day development of securitization markets.

Ginnie Mae's first securitization initiative

In 1970, GNMA did its first securitization transaction on a "pass-through" structure. GNMA's pass-throughs were securities backed by mortgages insured by FHA. These pass-throughs had the full credit and the backing of the U.S. government, as GNMA guaranteed both the repayment of principal and timely payment of interest.

The 1970 program (GNMA-I) is still in operation. In 1983, GNMA launched another pass-through program called GNMA-II. GNMA II had a range of interest rates and sellers, while GNMA-I was designed for a single seller and a single rate of interest. These programs are further classified based on the type of mortgages pooled therein, such as single family (SF) loans and multi-family (MF) loans.

Fannie Mae's securitization deals

Though the FNMA was the oldest of all the U.S. government agencies, it was the last to enter the securitization market. In 1968, the original FNMA was split into a new FNMA and GNMA, with FNMA privately owned and its shares quoted on the New York Stock Exchange. However, due to implicit support from and historical affiliation with, the U.S. government, the credit standing of FNMA is seen as better than private corporations, although slightly inferior to government agencies like GNMA.

The first FNMA mortgage-backed security (MBS) was issued in 1981. The agency played a crucial role in promoting securitization of adjustable-rate mortgages (ARMs) and variable rate mortgages (VRMs).

The Freddie Mac

The FHLMC was created in 1970 to promote an active national secondary market in residential mortgages and has been issuing mortgage-backed securities since 1971.

Spreads over to non-mortgage assets

Securitization spread to non-mortgage assets in 1985. The first non-mortgage securitization deal was in March 1985, when Sperry Corporation issued $192.5 million in securities backed by computer lease receivables.

Securitization through recession

Since September 11, 2001, the U.S. economy was seen as passing through a recessionary phase. However, this did not affect securitization volumes. On the contrary, it is felt that securitization is helping maintain the growth in consumer spending by supplying capital to the credit card industry through securitization of credit cards. The percentage of securitization in the credit card segment has recorded a sharp increase.

Like the U.S., Japan and a number of Asian and European countries are equally concerned about recession.

That securitization is resilient through recession was noticed in 1991 and proven beyond a doubt in 2001. A December 1991 article in the *Institutional Investor* said: "The asset-backed securities market is roaring its way through the recession with record issuance and reliable performance that prove it has come of age."

Securitization volumes continued to grow, unimpeded by the economic slowdown in the early years of the decade. Rather than being identified as a cause of financial catastrophe, securitization has played a major role in improving the financial condition of distressed economies. Another striking feature is the growing number of securitization issues by sovereigns. Synthetic deals are also becoming increasingly popular. There can be no doubt that securitization has matured from being a complicated transaction veiled in complications and viewed with scepticism to an instrument used across the globe.

The life cycle of securitization

The life cycle of the development of securitization is shown in Figure 3.1:

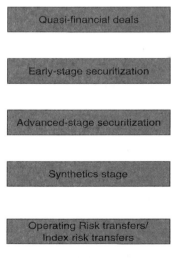

- Unrated, Bilateral transfers
- Full originator backing
- Purpose: off-balance sheet; exploiting excess spread, etc

- Transfers through SPV route
- High degree of credit enhancement/cash participation by originators
- Purpose: off balance sheet; better ratings

- Credit enhancements dwindle; lower classes take risk
- Synthetics; arbitrage activity enter the stage
- Purpose: economic capital; better capital/risk management

- Separation of funding and risk tranfers
- Synthetics answer regulatory concerns more easily
- In traditional cash structures, transaction models are built around securitisation mechanics: orignation/servicing split

- More stress on risk tranfers
- risks of operating businesses: retail credits, performance-oriented businesses are transferred
- Distinction bet. banking and insurance becomes less clear

Figure 3.1   Life cycle of asset-backed securitization

Present state of securitization

North America

U.S.

The United States of America is the largest securitization market in the world. In terms of depth, it is the only market in the world where securitization draws participation from both institutional as well as individual investors. In terms of width, the U.S. market has far more applications of securitization than any other market.

Approximately 75% or more of the global volume in securitization have originated from the U.S. This by itself indicates the tremendous significance of the U.S. in the global securitization market. Also, securitization issues originating from Japan, Europe and a few other emerging markets, draw investors from the U.S.

The historical beginning of the securitization pass-through market in U.S. mortgages has already been noted. Needless to say, mortgage markets might have existed in Europe for years, but the concept of securitization has matured in the U.S. and even developments such as securitization of insurance risk and public utility stranded costs, have taken place in the U.S.

We have noted the early beginning of securitization in 1970s, as well as the role of the government in promoting the concept through its agencies.

In the 1980s, securitization deals also received legislative support from the government. In 1983, the Securities and Exchange Commission made the benefits of shelf registration available for mortgage-related securities. In 1984, Congress adopted the Secondary Mortgage Market Enhancement Act (SMMEA), which provided for the exemption of highly rated mortgage-backed securities from the registration requirements of most state securities laws and made them eligible for investment by certain regulated entities. Then, as part of the Tax Reform Act of 1986, Congress enacted new tax legislation permitting the creation of real estate mortgage investment conduits — "REMICs" — facilitating the issuance of multi-class, pass-through securities. These early legislative actions benefited only mortgage-backed transactions. During the time when these laws were being debated and adopted, however, the first non mortgage-backed asset securitization transactions occurred, and the next round of legal changes was not limited to transactions involving mortgage loans.

In October 1992, the SEC amended its rules to permit specifically the shelf registration of investment grade "asset-backed securities."

In 1994, Congress amended SMMEA to provide an exemption from state securities laws for highly rated securities backed by certain lease receivables and small business loans, similar to the exemption already enjoyed by mortgage-backed securities.

Later, tax-efficient vehicles for non-mortgage securitization were permitted in 1996 (regulations were framed in 2000) called FASITs. However, FASITs came under a lot of criticism after the Enron debacle, and ultimately, the FASIT legislation was repealed in 2005.[4]

There is no doubt that the success of securitization in the U.S. has been helped by successive government support.

In recent years, particularly after the collapse of Enron, securitization earned a vicarious bad name due to special purpose entities run by Enron. Soon afterwards, there was an academic debate about whether to allow a bankruptcy safe-harbor to securitization transactions. This debate blew up into whether securitization is good for the country or not. Possibly for the first time, people had to write whether and why securitization is good. However, as stated above and evident from the data quoted elsewhere in this chapter, there has been no decline in securitization activity in the post-Enron years.

It is customary in the U.S. to classify securitization markets into mortgage-backed and asset-backed (other than mortgage) market. The issue of mortgage-backed securities in 2002 was a record high, which scaled a peak in 2003. Figure 3.2 shows the MBS (new issuance) until early 2003.

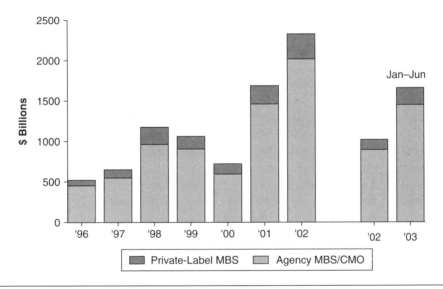

Figure 3.2 Issuance of mortgage-related securities, 1996–2003:Q2

Source: Bond Market Association

However, in 2004 the issuance of agency paper declined. The volume of agency paper in 2003 was US$2.13 trillion. However, the agency volume declined to US$1.01 trillion in 2004, and the volume until September 2005 was US$715 billion. U.S. mortgage financing activity moved from traditional mortgage funding products to innovative products such as ARMs and interest only mortgages, the private label sector. The growth of the private label MBS has also been dramatic. According to the Bond Association, issuance by private label issuers totalled US$415.4 billion by the first half of 2005, a hike of 52.7% from US$272.1 billion during the same period the previous year.

Likewise, the ABS segment activity has been scaling new heights as shown in Figure 3.3:

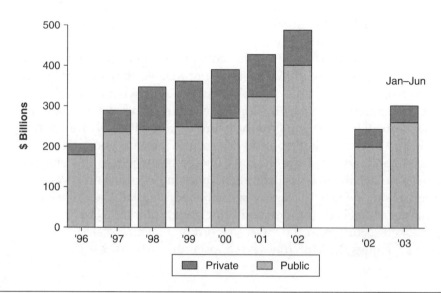

Figure 3.3   Issuance of asset-backed securities, 1996–2003:Q2

Source: Bond Market Association

The securitization market has continued to grow. According to the Bond Market Association, total volumes of securitization in the first three quarters of 2005 totaled US$831.9 billion and the total volume for 2005 was US$1,103.4 billion, substantially higher than US$902.6 billion registered in 2004. Amongst asset classes, the Home Equity Loan Sector accounted for US$329.3 billion and the Bond Association feels that this class contributed 40% of the total volume of asset-backed securities. The other major asset classes were Auto Loan (US$66.4 billion), Student Loan (US$45.7 billion) and Credit Cards (US$41.8 billion).

Canada

Canadian financial markets were quick to capture U.S. financial innovations. However, securitization had a slow start in Canada primarily due to the absence, for a long time, of agencies comparable to the GNMA that promoted the secondary market in mortgages.

Following the U.S. example, Canada formed a crown corporation called Canada Mortgage and Housing Corporation, essentially on the lines of Fannie Mae. This corporation is engaged in acquiring and securitizing housing mortgages.

In its report *Canadian Securitization — State of the Market* of March 2001, the credit agency Fitch said: "Fitch expects to see continued growth within asset classes already securitized, with particularly high growth rates expected in CMBS. Other asset classes with potential for growth include collateralized debt obligations (CDOs) and whole business transactions." In its April 2001 issue of *Global Securitization Quarterly*, Fitch further remarked that the term issuance in year 2000 outpaced ABCP in Canada. A study by the Dominion Bond Rating Service emphasized that Canadian asset-backed market has grown eight-fold in just five years and the value of securities outstanding at the end of 2000 stood at C$79.4 billion

The Canadian securitization market continued to grow. A leading authority on Canadian securitization reports that its ABS market would cross the C$100 billion market by March 2005.[5] In addition, the value of ABCP would be around C$101.7 billion.

Commercial mortgages, credit card receivables and banking assets are being securitized in larger volumes.

Accounting issues

The Canadian accounting standard on securitization transactions entitled "Accounting Guideline AcG-12, Transfers of Receivables", is based on FASB Statement 140. It aims to harmonize Canadian and U.S. practices. It is not applicable to securitizations of non-financial assets. A new accounting standard, called the AcG-15 has introduced the concept of Variable Interest Entity (VIE).[6] According to this rule, any entity that has a variable interest in any other entity would be obliged to disclose whether it is the sole beneficiary of such VIE. Further, if the entity is the sole beneficiary of the VIE, the latter would have to be consolidated with the former. The Canadian Accounting Standards body has stated that an entity would be considered as a VIE if:

- the equity is not enough to permit that entity to finance its activities without external support; or
- equity investors lack either voting control, an obligation to absorb expected losses, or the right to receive expected residual returns.

To preserve securitization assets off the balance sheet, it is imperative that SPVs be structured in a way that does not lead to consolidation under this rule.

Legal developments

The court of Appeal in Ontario upheld the judgment of the lower Court in the BC Tel's case (Metropolitan Toronto Police Widows and Orphans Fund vs. Talus Communications) and held the "true sale" characterization of the transaction valid.[7] The Judgment will encourage such "classical Canadian" transactions in the country, but is unlikely to be relied on by other common law courts.

Europe

Though securitization is today a buzzword in capital markets all over the world, it is interesting to note its acceptance by investors, investment bankers and issuers outside the U.S., the birthplace of securitization.

Origins of European securitization

Is the U.S. the birthplace of securitization? Any European may proudly claim that securitization originated in Denmark, where a mortgage credit system has existed for over 200 years now. There is also the *pfandbrief* market in Germany, a secondary mortgage market, but the Danish mortgage trading system is very close to the U.S. concept of pass-throughs.

Although a form of securitization has been in existence in the German and Danish mortgage markets for a long time, securitization in the modern sense only emerged in Europe in the mid-1980s with the issuance of the first LT. K. mortgage-backed securities.

Growth of securitization in Europe

The one-time snail's pace market in Europe is now evolving into a viable and rapidly advancing sector.

According to estimates by Moody's Investors Services, annual issuance of European MBS/ABS was less than US$10 billion until 1996, when it jumped to US$30 billion, then further increased to US$45.4 billion in 1997. Volume for 1998, however, was about the same as 1997 at US$46.6 billion, as the flight to quality towards the end of 1998 led to a dramatic widening in ABS spreads and reduced issuance to a trickle.

The European Market continued to register dramatic growth. According to the European Securitization Forum[8] (ESF), total volume of securitization was €243.5 billion in 2004. The volumes continued to increase through 2005; the ESF estimates that the volumes for 2005 would be around €255 billion. Mortgage-Based Securities had volumes of €138.5 billion, a 10.2% increase from €125.6 billion in 2004. New issuance of non-mortgage recorded a volume of €105.1 billion, a 15% increase from last year. RMBS accounted for about 50% of the total issues in the securitization market and continued to dominate the market. RMBS was followed by securitization of receivables due from lease, utility and aircraft, which accounted for 13% of the total volume of securitization issued. The CDO market also continued to increase and totaled €25.2 billion. In 2005, CDO issuance zoomed up to €46.8 billion.

Issuers continued to utilize the securitization market to lower their funding costs. Investors are attracted to securitized products because of their risk profile, characterized by higher investment ratings and less price volatility.

In Europe, the previous action in the ABS market had centered mainly on residential mortgages and, to a lesser extent, on the credit card-backed issues that are popular in international ABS circles. Also, it should be noted that in Europe, unlike the U.S., all deals use an ABS-structure, making no distinction between mortgage-backed and asset-backed securities.

The U.K. continues to top the market in Europe, with Italy having taken the second position. Germany ranks at a lower end, but it is apparent that European Securitization Forum data do not include the notional value of synthetic transactions, which is prominently the case in Germany.

United Kingdom

The U.K. is not only the largest market in Europe, but it is also making a number of innovative deals. The range of assets, which have been the subject of securitization in the U.K., is growing rapidly. New issues of securitized debt consists of collateral from the U.K., totaling the equivalent of €21.5 billion in the first quarter of 2003, a 75.4% increase from the €12.3 billion securitized in the first quarter of 2002. The data for the first half of 2003 shows U.K. issuance of €39.3 billion, about 47% of the total European market. Collateralized securitization issuance in the U.K. amounted to 50% of total European issuance in the first quarter.

In terms of asset classes, the U.K. can be said to be the securitization laboratory of the world, as some of the most interesting and innovative transactions have taken place there. From securitization of student rentals (Keele University) to death bonds (securitization of receivables of a funeral service operator), from the largest water utility securitization to the largest number of whole business transactions, the U.K. has never shied away from dreaming things as they never were, and asking, why not?[9]

Historically, securitization was slow to catch up in the U.K. Mortgage-backed securitization activity picked up there in the later part of 1980s. In 1986, Salomon Brothers set up a private company called The Mortgage Corporation, as a specialized conduit like Fannie Mae for acquiring and securitizing mortgages. Non-mortgage securitization was even slower to get cracking. As of mid-1993, it was estimated that there were only seven term securitizations involving non-mortgage assets, adding up to £1.38 billion. However, there were certain ABCP programs.

The U.K. has retained its position as the leader of the European securitization market. According to the ESF[10] the total volume of securitization in U.K. in 2004 was €105.3 billion, an increase of 38.5% from €76 billion issued in 2003. Mortgage-backed securities amounted to €77.4 billion, a 40% increase from €55.3 billion in 2003. Asset-backed securities in the U.K. were around €27.8 billion, a 37% increase over the previous year. In 2005, U.K. securitization volume was €145 billion.

Legal systems and initiatives

The English legal system is known the world over as common law. English common law distinguishes between tangible and intangible property – in possession and in action. The latter are transferable only by a written conveyance. Thus, the Law of Property Act 1925 requires a written agreement to transfer actionable claims. Notice to debtors is also required. Details of the common law provisions are discussed in the chapter on Legal Issues.

However, traditional English law has always recognized equitable transfers, those transfers not complying with the legal requirement of law but recognized as setting up a legal relationship between the transferor and transferee. Equitable transfers do not result in a right against the world at large, but a personal right – the right of the assignee under an equitable transfer is a right against the assignor, and not a independent right against any and all.

No specific legal amendments have been carried out to this age-old law.

Taxation

Another issue for securitization transactions in the U.K. has been the stamp duty issue. A stamp duty of 3.5 to 4% is payable on assignment of receivables. Parties normally contrive to avoid this by executing documents outside the jurisdiction, as the duty is payable at the place where the agreement is executed. However, there is a common stamp law provision that if an agreement executed outside the country but relating to property in the country comes to the country after execution, it will be stampable then. Thus, execution of the agreement outside the country defers the stamp duty implication until it is necessary to bring the document into the country for the purpose of enforcement.

In practice, however, stamp duty is not paid in U.K. as most securitization transactions are structured as equitable assignments and not as perfected legal transfers. Nevertheless, if and when the transactions are to be perfected into a full-fledged sale of receivables, the document will attract stamp duty; therefore, the originator is required to provide for full payment of duty. This is usually regarded as a theoretical tax – very rarely have circumstances arisen where the duty has actually become payable.

Several U.K. securitizations are structured initially as inter-company loans to a group company, to avoid problems of withholding tax. No withholding tax is charged for interest payments to SPVs located in countries with which the U.K. has a double tax avoidance treaty, such as the Netherlands.

VAT is not applicable on sale of receivables, but applies on servicing fees.

Originator taxation   The basic question to be decided for the originator is whether the disposition of the receivables will be taken as a sale or financing. The question would, in most cases, be decided by referring to the originator's accounting treatment. If the assets in question are business assets, and they are being transferred, business profits/loss may arise.

In certain cases, the asset being transferred may be held as capital assets, such as lease transactions. Ideally, in such cases, the physical asset and the receivables there should be split, and only the receivables should be transferred rather than the physical asset.

The other significant tax issue is the deductibility of the initial fees of the issue. Incidental costs of raising finance may, if properly structured, be deductible by the issuer under the FA 1996 rules. Accounting Standard FRS4 will generally require issue costs, and thus the tax deductions to be amortized over the period of the notes.

Investors' taxation   A U.K. investor's tax position will be reasonably straightforward. Notes will generally fall within the withholding tax exemption for quoted Eurobonds. In general, it is believed that the accounting method employed by the investor for books will be adopted for taxation too.

SPV taxation   A proper structuring of the SPV is crucial; the objective of all concerned parties is to ensure a tax-transparent SPV. This can be ensured only by matching incomes and expenses. Payments made by the SPV will be principal and interest on the bonds, of which interest will be tax deductible and principal will not.

Interest paid by the SPV on a participating loan, a loan with a right to participate in profits (normally given by the originator as his contribution), is not tax deductible. Such interest is also not taxable in the hands of the originator.

The tax characterization of the SPV – a trading company or investment company – is also relevant. The tax department has elaborate guidelines on the structuring of SPVs for entity classification.

In 2005 budget specific provisions were made to allow a moratorium on securitization SPVs from using IAS39; the changes will lead to a new method of accounting for hedges, which means income-expense mismatches for SPVs.

Accounting and regulatory treatment

Accounting treatment is governed by FRS 5, discussed separately in the chapter on accounting issues.

On the regulatory front, the Financial Services Authority has issued an elaborate statement on securitization. This is discussed later in the chapter on Regulatory Issues.

SPV structures

In most U.K. securitizations, the SPV is structured as "an orphan subsidiary" with the shareholding being transferred to a charitable trust. Therefore, although there is no direct control of the originator on the SPV, it is a matter of common knowledge that the SPV is a figment of the originator. The originator does maintain operational control over the SPV.

This ownership structure of the SPV is devised to avoid consolidation, both from bankruptcy as well as from an accounting viewpoint. However, as far as accounting consolidation is concerned, IASB's SIC 12 is inevitable if the originator provides credit enhancements in the form of subordinate securities as well. To avoid consolidation from a legal and accounting viewpoint, the originator must hold no equity interest and no residual interest in the SPV. Therefore, very convoluted methods are followed in the U.K. practice for extraction of the originator's profit from the transaction. These include deferred consideration, an intermediary trust holding legal interest on behalf of both the originator and the issuing SPV, interest swap, retained interest, management fees and brokerage.

Germany

Pfandbrief: The traditional German instrument

A traditional German mortgage-trading instrument called *Pfandbrief* has existed for over 200 years. It is said that the instrument was created by the order of Frederick the Great of Prussia in 1769. What is most remarkable is that since then, there has not been a single default in the *Pfandbrief* market.

Pfandbrief are asset-backed bonds. But unlike the U.S.-style securitizations, the underlying assets remain on the issuing bank's balance sheet. There is no special-purpose vehicle. The *Pfandbrief* institution is like one big SPV. Its designated mortgage or public-loan assets serve as an undifferentiated pool of collateral for all mortgage or public *Pfandbrief* at once. The bank has to manage that pool to make sure its value and cash flows cover all *Pfandbrief* liabilities.

A trustee appointed by the federal banking supervisor, BaKred, checks periodically that the collateral is adequate and registers all the assets in the pool. The bank needs the trustee's approval to sell any of those assets.

If the *Pfandbrief* issuer defaults, *Pfandbrief* holders have preferential access to the assets in the pool. If the registered collateral is inadequate to meet *Pfandbrief* liabilities, *Pfandbrief* holders get equal status with the highest creditors in the queue for the rest of the bank's balance sheet.

In fact, there hasn't been a *Pfandbrief* default since the instrument was created.

So popular are jumbo *Pfandbrief* among international investors now that the market is the seventh-biggest bond market in the world. About $1 trillion in *Pfandbrief* are outstanding. The ESF estimates that about €143.5 billion worth of *Pfandbrief* were issued in Germany in 2004, down 19.1% from 2003.[11] In 2005, the volume was €137.9 billion.

Modern securitization market

Germany is Europe's largest economy. With approximately DM1.9 trillion of mortgages, thousands of banks, some of the world's most powerful and sophisticated industrial and service corporations, and one of the leading financial centers in Europe, it is surprising that Germany ranks quite low in the European securitization market. Though the first securitization transaction by a bank in Germany seems to be the April 1995 securitization of mortgage receivables by a bank to a foreign SPV, the German securitization market in terms of volumes declined since 2001. However, this should not dishearten, as the last three years have witnessed quite a lot of synthetic securitization. German banks and mortgage lenders have taken to more of synthetic securitization (an unfunded nature where credit risk is traded as a marketable asset). Leading German bank KfW has presented good examples of synthetic securitization programs such as Promise and Provide.

While synthetic securitization is certainly the more popular way in Germany, there is an initiative for "true sale" securitizations (see later section in this chapter).

The *Bundesaufsichtsamt fhr das Kreditwesen*, the German Supervisory Authority for the Banking and Capital Markets Industry, has passed a rule that gives securitizations its official blessing and will contribute to acceptance of it as an effective commercial law financing instrument under German law.

German regulations on securitizations

On May 20, 1997, the BAK published "Circular Regarding the Sale of Customer receivables of Credit Institutions in Connection with ABS

Transactions," along with an explanatory letter. The stated purpose of the Circular is to provide credit institutions with planning and legal certainty in respect of central questions concerning ABS transactions and to enable their completion without the prior involvement of the BAK. The principal provisions of the BAK circular, applicable to credit institutions and banks, are discussed below:

ABS definition   The Circular defines ABS as "securities and certificates of indebtedness representing payment claims against a special purpose vehicle (SPV) serving exclusively the purposes of the ABS transaction." The payment claims are "backed" by a pool of "uncertified" receivables (assets) that are transferred to the SPV as security, principally for the benefit of the holders of the ABS. The word "uncertified" means the underlying securities are not certificates or securities themselves; this excludes them from the scope of the Circular transactions, whereby certificated securities are repackaged in ABS transactions.

   Under this regulation, there shall be no distinction between SPVs organized as trusts or as companies.

Capital requirements   German banks are supposed to maintain 8% capital against risk assets. This requirement shall be avoided completely in case of securitization transactions where the originator does not carry any direct or counterparty risk in the transferred receivables. That is to say, securitization shall be given an off-balance sheet treatment, subject to the satisfaction of certain conditions below:

- There must be a legally valid transfer of the receivables to the SPV (a "true sale").
- Recourse against the originator must be limited to liability for the legal existence of the receivables sold or their compliance with eligibility criteria set forth in the purchase agreement; in other words, the originator only gives certain warranties as to the existence and quality of the receivables at the time of their assignment, and no assurances regarding the subsequent quality of receivables.
- There must be no substitution by the originator of receivables sold to the SPV, other than substitutions for non-compliance with the contractually agreed eligibility criteria.
- Clean-up buyback is permitted, that is, repurchase of the receivables for the purpose of terminating the tail of receivables when their value falls to less than 10% of the receivables sold to the SPV at the initiation, is permitted. No other right of repurchase is allowed to the originator.
- Subject to certain exceptions (see below), neither the originator nor any of its affiliates must participate in the financing of the SPV during the transaction. Affiliates have been defined to mean credit institutions, financial institutions or enterprises engaged in ancillary banking services in which the originator directly or indirectly holds at least 40% of the capital shares

or which are controlled subsidiaries of the originator. "Financing of the SPV" this refers to any provision of financial means to the SPV during the transaction in the broadest sense, including the simple obligation to provide the SPV with financial means or giving a similar undertaking. The purpose of this regulation is to ensure that the credit risk transferred to the SPV does not fall back onto the originator in a different form.

The exceptions to the non-funding rule are as follows:

1. Subordinated loans can only be granted to the SPV before receivables are transferred to it and must only be repayable when the transaction is finalized. The granting of subordinated loans must be disclosed in the sales prospectus and the loan must be deducted in full from the (liable) own funds of the originator. That is to say, the capital of the bank will be reduced to the extent of subordinated loans granted.
2. Pure liquidity facilities can be provided by the originator to the SPV during the course of the transaction, such as to take the ABS out of the market and hold them for a short period of time.

   Further, the following credit enhancements taking the form of collateral structures, integral to the structure of the ABS transaction from its commencement, remain permissible:

   - **Over-collateralization**: the value of the receivables transferred to the SPV exceeds the nominal value of the securities issued by it;
   - **Purchase price discounts**: the purchase price paid by the SPV for the receivables is less than their book value;
   - **Subordination**: at least two different tranches of ABS – senior and junior – are issued; the junior tranche serves as a "buffer" for losses of the senior tranche; or
   - **Cash collateral account**: an account on which the difference between interest and principal repayments is collected from receivables debtors and the market rate to be paid by the issuer to the holders of the ABSs accrues. The credit balance can be used to cover any cash flow deficit of the SPV on a payment date.
   - The originator should not take the risk of underwriting the placement of the securities of the SPV. If the originator assumes the placement risk, in a firm commitment underwriting, capital relief will only be available to the extent that the ABS underwritten by the originator are completely placed on the market, or after the originator's underwriting obligation has expired.
   - Purchases of ABS by the originator in the secondary market must be at the current market price and must not involve the granting of credit to the SPV or the investors. Securities purchased by the originator must be backed by its own funds in accordance with Principle I.
   - Originators must take adequate measures to prevent any *de facto* obligation in order to assume economic responsibility for the receivables

sold in the ABS transaction, from arising, such as market pressure. In particular, the Circular requires that there be no corporate group, company law, capital or personal connection between the originator and the SPV or the trustee/collateral agent holding title to the receivables and other security in a fiduciary capacity. Nor must the name of the originator be similar to or identical with the name of the SPV. Finally, the ABS sales prospectus must indicate clearly that only the SPV is liable for claims of investors and that a guarantee obligation of the originator exists only to the extent expressly undertaken by it.

Retained market and liquidity risks must be backed by own funds, and capital requirements shall be applied to the extent of 100% of the retained risks.

No cherry-picking of receivables   One of the common apprehensions in securitization is that it leaves the bank with poor grade assets as all high quality assets would be sold away. As a safeguard, the BAK provides that the receivables be selected randomly from the originator's receivables portfolio. The random selection may, however, be made from those receivables satisfying certain contractual eligibility criteria or discriminants. The auditor's report on the audit of the annual accounts of the originator must comment on material deterioration, if any, in the portfolio caused by an ABS transaction; the BAK will assess whether "special circumstances" exist, requiring a revision of the own funds assessment.

Notification to the debtor   To facilitate ABS transactions by credit institutions, the Circular provides that no consent from the debtor of the receivable is required for the transmission of data.

On the common law requirement for notifying the debtor of any legal transfer of receivables, the Circular provides that no consent from the debtor of the receivable is required if the originator is also the servicer.

Not applicable to revolving assets   In a new circular no. 13/98, dated August 25, 1998, the German Banking Supervision Authority significantly limited the scope of ABS transactions of credit institutions. The new Circular clarifies that Circular no. 4/97 [see above] does not cover "revolving ABS transactions." A revolving transaction is one where a fixed volume with fixed maturity is backed by a pool of collateral comprising receivables of varying amounts and variable maturity periods. Credit card securitizations are an example of revolving securitization.

Impact of Basle II   The special rules of securitization by the German authorities regarding capital relief would be replaced by Basle-consistent rules. The EU has already passed the capital directive which is discussed in Chapter 29.

"True sale" initiative[12]   Thirteen leading banks formed a group called the "True Sale" Initiative (TSI) to advocate a friendlier legal framework for securitization transactions. The TSI has been able to achieve two significant developments in the German legislative framework, which would certainly encourage growth of securitization there.

German laws mandated that during securitization the name of the SPV must be entered into the land register to put it out of the insolvency estate of the securitizing bank. In other words, the interest of the SPV over real estate was perfected only when its name was entered as the owner of that estate in the land register. This made the process of securitization slow and expensive. Further, the law required that the obligor must be notified of the securitization deal, something any originator would be very uncomfortable to comply with. German legislators passed a law, called the Refinance Register Law, to amend this regulation. The new law has introduced the concept of refinance registers (*Refinanzierungsregister*). For an originating bank, the name of the SPV to which the assets are transferred shall be stated in the refinance register. In the event of insolvency of the originator bank, the assets entered into these registers will be kept out of the bankruptcy estate of the originator. The refinance registers will be supervised by the Banking Supervision Authority, the *BaFin*. Needless to say, this will go far in meeting the "true sale" criteria for securitization and thus encourage the growth of securitization. The second important amendment relates to the tax-related issues and is discussed below.

Tax aspects

Corporate income tax and trade tax are levied as for other businesses.

Foreign SPVs are subjected to German tax in the following cases only if their management is located in Germany (unlimited tax liability) or if they have German-sourced income to which assets and liabilities can be allocated (limited tax liability).

There are no stamp duties on transfer of receivables.

A recent important change in respect of tax issues is the amendment of the Trade Tax law. The German Tax regime considered half of the long-term debt as income for tax purposes. This imposed a tax, the rate of which varies according to the place of residence, on a purchaser of receivables backed by loans or securities. However, a 2003 amendment to this law was made inapplicable to purchasers of loans or credit risks originated by banks. After the amendment, the purchasers of securitized instruments originated by banks were exempt from trade tax. The TSI is lobbying to extend the immunity for securitization by non-bank originators.

Accounting aspects

The German Institute of Certified Public Accountants (IDW) issued a statement concerning the accounting treatment of asset-backed securities transactions in October 2002. It deals with the accounting treatment on the originator's balance sheet, and specifically how the originator can remove the assets from its balance sheet and as a result the treatment of purchase price discount. Key features are:

- The purchaser must have absolute ownership rights over the assets after the transfer;
- The sale and transfer must be final;
- The seller is not allowed to absorb the first-loss portion in respect of an asset by way of a guarantee or otherwise;
- The seller is not allowed to retain any default risk relating to the transferred assets.

Italy

State of the market and developments

Italy is second largest securitization market in Europe after the U.K., considering the volume of transactions that take place. One avid user of securitization in Italy is the government itself (see the chapter on Miscellaneous Asset Classes.[13])

The passage of the new securitization law (see below) has given a definitive boost to securitization activity in Italy. Banks have also made use of the new law and a lot of transactions continue to take place from banks and other financial institutions.

The first securitization transaction in Italy took place around 1990 and the first half of 1999; 19 transactions were outstanding with a volume of €3.4 billion.

Legal initiatives to promote securitization

Securitization Law No. 130 applies to securitization transactions.[14]

The law defines securitization as a process consisting of (i) any non-gratuitous transfer of credits or other non-negotiable financial assets that are likely to generate on-going periodic cash flow, and (ii) in the subsequent process of transforming such credits and/or assets into negotiable securities to be placed on the market.

The most apparent impact of the new law is to enact that the issuance of securitized instruments will be taken as a "financial instrument" and hence will not be subject to restrictions applicable to sourcing of public funds.

To be eligible for the favored treatment, the law requires securitization exercise to satisfy the following requirements:

- The special purpose vehicle to hold the transferred assets shall be a company satisfying the requisites provided by the Italian legislation governing financial intermediation, and in particular those provided by articles 106 and ff. of the Legislative Decree no. 385/1993 (the New Banking Law); therefore, the special purpose vehicle shall be an intermediary dealing exclusively with the management of one or more securitization processes;

- The credits and/or other financial assets concerned by each securitization transaction shall be considered as separate from both the special purpose vehicle's assets and those assets involved in other securitization transactions; therefore, the sums paid by the assigned debtors shall be exclusively employed for the satisfaction of the credit rights incorporated in the securities issued by the special purpose vehicle.

The law also makes provisions relating to the rights and obligations of the debtors, assignor and assignee:

1. The transfer of the concerned credits and/or assets is effective towards the assigned debtors from the date of publication of the notice of such transfer on the Official Journal; therefore, from that date, the transfer will be enforceable against the transferor's creditors and successors whose title is not prior in time than the transfer;
2. Payments made by the assigned debtors shall not be subject to the bankruptcy revocatory actions and therefore shall not fall within the scope of Art. 67 of the Italian Bankruptcy Law;
3. The transfers of the credits and/or assets will be subject to the bankruptcy revocatory actions, but with a significant reduction of the terms provided by Art. 67 of the Bankruptcy Law for carrying out the said actions (respectively the 2-year term will be reduced to 1 year and the 6-month term will be reduced to 3 months); obviously, all the provisions are aimed at guaranteeing more effective protection to investors involved in the securitization process.

The Bank of Italy issued the regulations on capital adequacy rules applicable to synthetic securitization structures by which an Italian bank acts as originator or subscriber of the notes issued by the SPV on December 31, 2001. Accordingly, it recognizes the "super-senior credit derivative, the 'SPV credit derivative.'" It also describes "risk-weighted portfolio" as the product with the highest risk-weighting percentage applicable to each asset of the reference portfolio and the total amount of the reference portfolio's assets.

A receiver has been empowered by the Bankruptcy Law to terminate a leasing contract that the originator has entered into, if the financial position of such an originator is not sound. If the originator becomes bankrupt, the Bankruptcy Law has the solution. (Articles 72 and 73).

Recent amendments to the corporate law[15]

Italian corporate law has been reformed recently and there has been a major change in the treatment of securitization. The Securitization Law permitted transactions in which the originator borrows from the SPV (this type of structure is very common in the case of whole business securitization). However, there was confusion as to whether the receivables backing such loans would be segregated from the bankrupt estate of the originator. The amended Italian Civil Code has clarified that it is permissible to securitize cash flow from a specific business activity. The Code has stated that a company can establish a specific pool of assets to back a specific business activity. However, the Code has also laid down that a company can segregate a maximum of 10% of a company's net assets for securitizing purposes.[16] The Code also permits use of a specific cash flow arising out of a business to fund the business of the company.

Covered bond transactions

Italian banks have recently been allowed to issue covered bonds by assigning certain classes of cash flows to an SPV incorporated under the Securitization Law. Article 3 of the Securitization Law insulates this portfolio of receivables from the bankruptcy of the originator. Article 4 lays down that the assignment of receivables shall be perfected against the originator bank, the assigned debtors and third party creditors, by way of publishing a notice of the assignment in the Official Gazette of the Republic of Italy. The Ministry of Economy and the Bank of Italy shall be issuing detailed regulations on covered bonds soon.[17]

Taxation of securitization

The new law also defines the taxability of securitization issues. The basic tax treatment of securitized instruments will be at par with corporate bonds. Withholding tax, as applicable on interest in case of corporate bonds – 12.5% on Italian resident individuals and institutions-will apply to payments on securitized notes. However, Italian commercial entities and non-resident entities from countries with which Italy has a double tax avoidance treaty will be exempt from the requirement. This removes one of the most important impediments to the growth of securitization.

In a recent circular letter 8/E issued on February 6, 2003, Italian tax authorities have cleared the issue of *de facto* tax neutrality of securitization vehicles under Securitization Law (Law 130, of April 30, 1999). The ruling is based on the so-called asset-segregation principle, as set out in the Securitization Law, pursuant to which any amount payable in connection with the receivables purchased by the securitization vehicle must exclusively be applied by the same securitization vehicle to satisfy the obligations towards note holders and other creditors, and to meet any related transaction costs.

Since the revenues of a particular transaction are dedicated solely to the benefit of the creditors of the transaction, there will be no income as far as the SPV is concerned unless the SPV brings any transaction for which there are no dedicated investors.

Denmark

The birthplace of securitization

It is said that the mortgage market in Denmark has existed for 200 years, so Denmark is the real birthplace of securitization. [also see **Europe**]. The structure of the Danish mortgage market is much similar to the present concept of the U.S. mortgage pass-throughs.

Historically, the development of the Danish mortgage market goes back to the 18th Century when the British set fire to Copenhagen. In the rebuilding of Copenhagen, borrowers needed funds, and they thought they would face better lending terms if they joined together in liability. The following table gives a brief history of the Danish mortgage market:

Table 3.1   History of the Danish mortgage system

Date	Event
1700	Great fire in Copenhagen – first mortgage institution funded as an association
1850	First Mortgage Credit Act – increasing numbers of regional mortgage institutions
1950	Mergers between mortgage institutions mean fewer national mortgage institutions
1990	Bank owned mortgage institutions are created
1995	First rating assigned to CMO's
1996	First rating assigned to MBS

Present state of the market

The amount of outstanding Danish fixed-rate MBSs was DKr 970 billion at the end of second quarter 1998, or about $150 billion, a remarkable amount for a nation of only five million people. Danish mortgage pools (or series) tend to be large in size, typically $1 billion or more initially (some issues are more than $10 billion). This size is achieved by keeping a series open for up to three years; new loans can be put into the pool anytime during a period of three years.

A report states that the Danish mortgage market has been booming, with a 20% net increase. A large proportion of issued bonds are callable as they allow borrowers greater flexibility.

Legal initiatives to promote securitization

The Danish Mortgage Credit Act has been amended several times and the latest amendment has allowed all mortgage banks to grant mortgage loans to agricultural property with a general maximum limit of 70% of the value of the property.

With regard to regulation, the Danish Ministry of Economic Affairs has set up a large committee with the task of examining the challenges that the financial sector will face after year 2000.

The Netherlands

The first securitization transaction in the Netherlands took place in 1996, when the Fortis group sold its receivables without notifying the respective debtors. This transaction was notable because the originator itself was not a rated company, while the issue obtained a high rating from the agencies. In 2001 there was a slight decline in volume compared to year 2000. The main constituent of the market remains RMBS, while synthetic securitization continues to spark interest.

General legal system

The country operates on a civil law system. The Civil Code introduced in 1992 a requirement for notifying debtors of any assignment.

> *The Dutch Ministry of Finance has issued a new exemption regulation under the Act on the Supervision of the Credit System. Effective as of July 18, 1997, it offers new potential for the establishment of securitization vehicles (SPVs) in the Netherlands. In addition, a recent Supreme Court judgment has clarified the legal position in the Netherlands on cross-border assignments of receivables and greatly facilitates these transactions. Both the new regulation and the recent Supreme Court judgment can be seen as strong incentives for securitization transactions in or through the Netherlands.*
>
> *The Supreme Court opinion ruled that in case of cross-border securitizations, parties may choose their jurisdiction and make assignment as per the law of the chosen jurisdiction.*

Exemption regulation for SPVs

Under the Dutch Act on the Supervision of the Credit System, a company that qualifies as a "credit institution" will either have to apply for a banking licence (for which, among other things, a minimum of own funds amounting to US$5.25 million is required) or be exempted under the Act. In principle, a company qualifies as a credit institution if – in the conduct of its business – it raises money (for instance through issuing debt instruments) to finance the granting of credit facilities and/or investment in assets.

This is a relatively broad definition compared to that applied in many other EU member states, where SPVs are generally exempted from banking supervisory legislation. An SPV established in the Netherlands for securitization purposes will be subject to banking supervision unless it is exempted under the Act.

One of the exemptions already available under the Act applies to companies receiving funds repayable at two years' notice or more from professional lenders only. Such companies are exempted from supervision because professional lenders are deemed to be capable of assessing the financial risks involved in a transaction. However, this exemption has the disadvantage that it only applies to long-term debt instruments. In securitization transactions, the receivables acquired by the SPV are very often short-term. The financing of short-term receivables by long-term funds creates a mismatch, which can now be overcome by applying the new regulation.

To provide opportunities for securitization in the Netherlands, the Dutch Central Bank asked the Ministry of Finance to issue an extra exemption regulation under Article 1(3) of the Act, which the Ministry has now promulgated.

Recently amendments were made to the securitization law. According to the recent notification (January 2, 2005), an entity would be exempt from the Regulations if it qualifies under any of the following conditions:[18]

- The funds of the entity are obtained from professional market parties (PMPs) or from a very small number of investors (called the "Closed Circle"); or
- The entity issues debt instruments to non-PMPs but: (1) over 95% of its balance sheet is lent to group companies to which the SPV belongs (2) and all borrowings are supported by eligible credit support.

As most SPVs are organized as orphan vehicles: they use the first condition.

"Silent assignment" law

An assignment is said to be silent when obligor notification is not given.[19] Article 3:94 of the Dutch Civil Code mandated that a transfer of receivables could be perfected only when the debtor is notified about such a transaction. Needless to say, this acted as a hindrance in securitization. The law was amended on October 1, 2004, and Article 3:94 was inserted into the law, removing the requirement of obligor notification in cases where (i) the receivables are either existing or arise out of a existing legal relationship; (ii) the deed of assignment is by way of a written contract or in a notarial form. The amendment has further noted that a debt assigned by the originator would be considered as a valid transfer even if the originator goes into bankruptcy before notification to the debtor.

Taxation

No stamp duty is charged on assignment of receivables.

No VAT is charged on transfer of receivables. The VAT will be chargeable on servicing fees.

There is no withholding tax on interest payments. Tax on profits of the securitization SPV will be liable to be taxed if the SPV has a permanent establishment in the country. Whether the SPV has a permanent establishment can be known by prior ruling of the tax authorities.

France

Under French practice, securitization is the same as in the U.S. – a sale of assets, generally a pool of receivables held by a bank, a financial institution, or a commercial company, to a dedicated vehicle that finances this purchase by issuing financial instruments on the market. Cash flow generated by the securitized assets is assigned to pay the principal and interest due under the financial instruments. On the basis of the U.S. securitization experience,

France enacted legislation in 1988 on the FCC (see below), making France and Great Britain the most advanced European countries in this field. Up to 1998 more than 120 FCC's have been set up by way of public offering (the only ones for which statistics are available), representing at that time approximately 150 billion French francs. The market should continue to grow significantly.

Legal initiatives

In general, France operates on a civil law system, which has typical difficulties for securitization transactions. French law not only requires notice to the debtor, but also prescribes the mode of service of notice through a court official. This method obviously had its own impracticalities, so until 1988 French securitizers used various alternatives such as subrogation (the entity acquiring receivables acquires them through the assignor, as a beneficiary of the assignor).

Legal developments have taken place aimed at removing the legal difficulties and advancing securitization markets in France. The original French legislation on securitization was implemented by the Act of December 23, 1988. Under this legislation, credit institutions, insurance companies and the *Caisse des dépôts et consignations* (a public entity) were permitted to sell their receivables to a tax-transparent vehicle, the *fonds commun de créances* or FCC (equivalent of the SPV in other markets), which would be financed by issuing units on the market.

Amendments in 1997 extended the scope of the legislation by taking into account most of the objections of market practitioners. It allowed an FCC to purchase and issue from time to time any type of receivables (including doubtful receivables or receivables of different types), whether denominated in French francs or in other currencies.

The 1998 amendments have further expanded the scope of securitization by making it possible for commercial companies to also use FCC to securitize their assets; earlier, the facility was limited to financial intermediaries such as credit institutions and insurance companies alone. Second, the originator is no longer required to notify the debtors of the assigned receivables of the transfer of their receivables, which was required earlier and found to be detrimental to the interests of the securitizer.

The French FCC

The French FCC is a legal process for conduct of securitizations. The creation and operation of an FCC requires the participation of (i) investors; (ii) a bank or financial institution where the funds of the FCC will be parked; (iii) a management company, the role of which is to conduct the investment policy of the FCC.

The FCC is a legal concept, not a legal entity – just like the British concept of trusts. In law, assets of the FCC are regarded as the joint ownership of the investors. Interest in an FCC – the interest held by the investors – is itself a transferable property. The activities of the FCC must consist exclusively of the co-ownership of receivables and not of other types of securities such as shares. The transfer mechanism provided for in the securitization law is inspired by the *Loi Dailly* mechanism. Title to the receivables is transferred by the execution and dating of a certain instrument, called *bordereau*.

The management company as mentioned above must obtain a license from the *Commission des Opérations de Bourse* to manage FCCs.

As an incentive, FCC is exempt from corporate income tax on its profit and from indirect taxation, such as the VAT on the fees paid to the management company, the custodian or the servicer of the receivables. There is no major obstacle to the transfer of a claim to an FCC. FCCs can acquire trade receivables, credit card receivables, mortgage-backed receivables, leasing receivables, receivables that are not transferable as a matter of law, doubtful or subject to litigation provided that the units issued by such FCC may only be subscribed to or held by the seller, non-French resident investors, or "qualified investors." A qualified investor means any legal entity with the necessary skills and means to assess the risks related to transactions of financial instruments, receivables denominated in a foreign currency (hedging is also permissible), export receivables and even future receivables. The receivables can be transferred to an FCC by way of a transfer deed. The originator must provide servicing to the transferred receivables in accordance with the terms of a servicing agreement entered into with the FCC. Units issued by FCCs are considered as securities and may be either in bearer or in the registered form.[20]

The French legislators have amended the law to make FCCs more attractive to foreign issuers. An article[21] on the subject states that the new amendments provide that:

- Receivables arising from any jurisdiction can be assigned to the FCC. Further, there shall be no requirement of any notification for the perfection of the assignment;
- The custodian can be located in any part of the world as long as the registered office of the custodian is in a member State of the European Economic Area;
- FCCs have been allowed to issue debt instruments governed by both French law and any other law.

Taxation issues

The French FCC is a collective conduit or a co-ownership. It does not have a legal personality. Therefore, no income tax is applicable on FCCs. FCCs are prohibited from borrowing.

Nominal stamp duty is applicable on assignment of receivables.

Withholding tax on interest is applicable but is avoidable in case of interest payments to offshore SPVs located in countries with whom France has a double tax avoidance treaty.

Synthetic securitization

The FCC may act as a synthetic securitization vehicle. It can now enter credit default swaps to cover its own exposure and the exposure of third parties.

Belgium

Development and state of the market

The Belgian securitization market is not very old, as the present form of securitization transactions originated in 1996. The first deal on record is BACOB's Atrium – 1, a securitization of housing loans guaranteed by the Flemish government. Soon thereafter, there was an auto loans securitization transaction originated by BBL.

The market got its momentum in 1997 with several issues – a mortgage-backed securitization deal structured on sequential CMO basis, and several asset-backed deals. The development process carried through to 1998, with transactions by *Kredietbank*, BACOB and SCA.

KBC is apparently a lead player in the Belgian market, responsible for some CLOs and synthetic transactions (Rosey Blue, discussed later in this book)

Legal initiatives

The general legal system in Belgium is civil law. As noted earlier in respect of several countries, civil law systems are not very conducive to securitization transactions. However, Belgian authorities have taken proactive steps not only to allow for the securitization of receivables but also to ensure that the hindrances found in the civil law rules relating to the formalities for transferring receivables be removed. On the other hand, a specific regulatory scheme has been created that has been made progressively more flexible and better adapted to international market practice.

Under Belgian law there is no general definition of securitization (titrization/effectisering). However, for several years now Belgian law has been adapted to allow for the securitization of receivables. On the one hand, the hindrances found in the civil law rules relating to the formalities for transferring receivables have been removed. Tax provisions have also been enacted to make securitization transactions practically tax neutral at the SPV level and more attractive to investors. The basic law of assignments is discussed below. The last important modifications to Belgian regulations were contained in the Law of December 12, 1996, implemented by the Royal Decree of 8th July 1997. Essentially, the law permits creation of two alternative securitization structures similar to a pass-through and corporate bond structures: SIC "Société d'Investissements en Créances" or an FPC "Fonds de Placement en Créances". The former is similar to a bond structure and the latter is a pass-through structure.

General law on assignment of receivables

The general scheme of Belgian law on assignment of receivables is as follows:

- **In case of all receivables**: Article 1690 of the Civil Code, on transfer of receivables in general covers the general rules regarding assignments.

Before the amendments made in 1994, this law required notification to debtors before any assignment could be effective. After amendments made in 1994, it is not necessary to notify debtors of an assignment. Under the new provisions, the transfer of receivables is effective with the mere consent of assignor and assignee, towards all third parties, including the creditors of both the assignor and assignee, with the sole exclusion of the debtor itself. The assignment is only effective as regards the debtor after it has either received notice of the assignment or has acknowledged it. In the absence of a notice or acknowledgment, the assignment is a 'silent' one, effective against all parties except the debtor. For most securitizations, it may not be necessary to notify the debtor at all as the servicing is mostly done by the originator himself.

- **In case of mortgage-backed receivables**: Article 51 of the Law of August 4, 1992, on transfer of receivables linked to (real estate) privileged or mortgage-backed loans. Here, the law requires registration of the transfer. This is a usual requirement in many countries. Registration would trigger a registration fee of 1%. This obstacle was also removed by the 1994 amendments that waived the registration requirement if the assignee is an SPV. A transfer of (real estate) privileged or mortgage-backed receivables by a regulated Belgian "mortgage enterprise" made in accordance with the above mentioned Article 51, however, requires the SPV to be licensed and subject to supervision as a 'mortgage enterprise' by the Office of the Control of Insurance. A Royal Decree facilitating the obtaining of a license of mortgage enterprise for securitization transactions is in preparation.
- **In case of consumer credit transactions:** Article 26 of the Law of June 12, 1991, on transfer of receivables from consumer credit agreements. This law was also amended in 1994. The transfer of receivables resulting from a consumer credit agreement to an SPV may be accomplished simply by applying the rules provided by Article 1690, as simplified by the Law of July 6, 1994. In such case, the more stringent transfer rules mentioned in Article 26 of the Law of June 12, 1991, do not apply.

Basic conditions concerning the receivables

The basic conditions concerning the receivables to be transferred are to be found in the agreements from which the receivables result and in the specific regulations on securitization.

These conditions for securitization can be outlined as follows:

- The receivables must be freely transferable and must not be of a personal (*intuitu personae*) character.
- The receivables should be "homogeneous." This implies that a single receivable cannot normally be securitized, although the BFC can permit otherwise. The requirement of homogeneity also implies that groups of receivables to be transferred should have similar characteristics, mainly from a financial point of view, although the regulations do not specify this. The conditions of repayment must be contractually determined as to their

due dates and amounts. It is therefore not sufficient that these conditions are determinable; they should be determined on the date of securitization.

- The securitization of future receivables is not possible under Belgian regulations.

Regulatory framework

Belgium adopted a regulatory framework modeled on French law for securitization transactions in receivables, which forms part of the regulations on collective investment undertakings found in Book III of the Law of December 4, 1990, relating to financial transactions and financial markets. The framework was introduced by the law of August 5, 1992, creating a new type of collective investment vehicle – the "collective investment undertaking in receivables" (OPCC/IBS). The Law of 1990 has been amended several times and most recently by the new law. Additional rules for undertakings for collective investments in receivables are set out in a Royal Decree of November 1993, as amended.

It should be noted that the application of the Belgian regulatory framework is not compulsory. A securitization transaction can thus be realized by Belgian entities through a foreign SPV structure, as indeed has been done in a few cases. However, there is a strong incentive to choose the Belgian regulatory framework because the tax advantages and certain simplified rules applicable to the transfer of receivables are conditional on application of the Belgian framework.

Under Belgian regulations, a securitization of receivables will require as a rule – at least in the event of a public transaction – the intervention of the originator (which does not have to be a credit institution), the SPV, a management company, a depository, a custodian, a supervisory company, an auditor, a rating agency and possibly a separate servicer and collecting agent and a representative of bondholders (see pg. 40 for a summary of conditions and functions that these different bodies must fulfill presently). The introduction of a management company is a unique feature of Belgian law.

Securitization of future receivables is not recognized in the Belgian system.

The Belgian legislature introduced some significant amendments to the law governing SPVs used for securitization purposes. The new law, (known as the UTIS Act) came into force in March 9, 2005, and is supposed to have significant impact on the securitization market of Belgium. Under the UTIS Act each securitization of SPVs will either have to (1) manage itself independently, or (2) appoint an external management licensed company to manage itself. An external management would be qualified to manage a company only if it satisfies the conditions laid down under the financial regulator. The new Act imposes restrictions on the nature of servicing contracts which the SPV can enter into with other parties and the originators. It further stipulates that in any share only the public must subscribe capital over and above the legally required minimum. In case the SPV has a share capital over and above the legally required minimum, the public must compulsorily hold such excess capital. These may act as bottlenecks in securitization transactions, but the Act also provides some positive stipulations. First, it allows "non-petition" agreements by the creditors of an SPV, which goes a long way in creating bankruptcy remote SPVs. Second, it allows the concept of "cell companies," which will encourage the use of a single SPV for multiple transactions. An author contends the new law will discourage use of public SPVs.[22]

Prudential regulation

The Belgian Banking and Financial Commission (BFC), the public body entrusted with the supervision of credit and other financial institutions and of public solicitation of savings, has extensive supervisory powers over securitization transactions. Not only will the intervention of different operators have to obtain its prior approval, but the SPV will also be submitted, like all other collective investment undertakings, to its prudential supervision.

The prudential norms require that the originator of a securitization transaction to qualify for off-balance sheet treatment should not be under any legal or moral obligation to support the transaction.

Taxation

Mortgage-backed receivables come under compulsory registration requirements – this entails a registration cost of 1%, while no registration requirements apply on non-mortgage securitizations.

Entity level tax on the SPV – SIC or FPC – can be avoided altogether. Further, the VAT is not chargeable on transfers of receivables, but servicing fees, as any other income, will be subject to the VAT.

Withholding taxes on interest are normally applicable, but FPCs being pass-through entities are not covered by the requirements. SICs have been granted exemption from withholding tax on interest received by them.

Originator taxation: The transfer of loans to SICs will be subject to the normal applicable fiscal provisions, which means a taxable gain or loss may arise upfront.

No indirect tax is payable on transfer of the receivables to the SPV.

SPV taxation: The SICs themselves are in principle subject to corporate income tax. However, the SICs are liable for income tax only on the total amount of the abnormal or gratuitous advantages received and disallowed expenses.

Investor taxation: Tax implications for investors depend on the nature of the instrument acquired by them. The return will be classified as interest or dividends, depending on whether the instrument was a share or a bond. A withholding tax of 15% may be applicable.

Portugal[23]

Portugal has been slow on securitization. The relevant legislation emerged only in 1999 (5 November 1999, Decree-Law 453/99). Earlier the Civil Code rules provided for the legislative requirement. The first mortgage-backed floating rate notes were issued through a Portuguese securitization vehicle only at the end of 2001 (Magellan). In 2002 (5 April Decree-Law n.82/02), important changes were made to the 1999 law.

Moody's in a February 22, 2001, special report entitled "2000 Year In Review 2001 Outlook Portuguese Structured Finance Market — Storm Ahead After the Break?" said there were only four issuances in 2000. Moody's says none of the issuances were under the new law as corresponding changes to the tax regime were still pending. In 2001, the market volume reached approximately US$3.6 billion, sparked by new CDOs. With the emergence of the amended law, it was observed that out of the 10 securitization transactions carried out in Portugal during 2002, only two followed the Civil Code structure, while eight of them followed the FTC structure. The law now allows for the securitization of credits, provided that such credits are of a monetary nature and have not been judicially seized, given as a guarantee, or pledged and are not subject to any legal or conventional restrictions concerning their assignment or to conditions. Non-performing credits are still governed by the Civil Code and not by the securitization law. Future receivables can be securitized, only if they arise out of presently existing legal relationships and if they can be estimated. Both the originators and non-originators are allowed to service the transaction subject to the necessary authorization from the Securities Market Commission (*Comissão do Mercado de Valores Mobiliários*). The securitization law has given two choices for the securitization structure, in what is referred to as the STCs (*Sociedades de Titularização de Créditos*) and the FTCs (*Fundos de Titularização de Créditos*). STCs are single purpose companies. They can purchase, service and transfer receivables solely. The FTCs are a little more complicated and regulated, and seem to be similar to mutual funds in nature, while STCs are SPV-structure vehicles. The STC structure seems to have been inspired by the Spanish law.

A Security Fund for Receivables Securitizations (under the Ministry of Finance) has been established by Decree-Law 188/02 of 21 August 2002, with the object of providing partial security to securitization transactions involving receivables originated by small and medium-sized companies. This will certainly reduce the receivables' credit risk and improve the ratings of such securitizations.

Corporate income tax for securitization vehicles is the same as that for commercial, industrial and agricultural companies. As per the Decree Law 219/01 of 4 August 2001, the originators – the sellers of the assigned credits – should consider the difference between the value of the receivables' assignment and the value of the assigned receivables as a profit or a cost in the tax year, in which the assignment occurred for tax purposes. Management fees earned by the originator are also to be treated as profits in the tax year in which the originator is entitled to receive such fees. Withholding tax on income derived from the assignment of credits is not required.

The assignment of credits for the purpose of securitization, interest charged/ credit granted by financial institutions to securitizations funds/financial institutions, commissions as per Article 5 of the Securitization Law, and the operations carried out by the custodians, as per Article 24 of the Securitization Law, are exempt from stamp duty.

The law allows the assignment of future receivables provided these are done out of the receivables from an existing relationship and are quantifiable or determinable. On a general reading, it seems that the criteria of "existing relationships" would be satisfied only if there is an existing contract between the originator and the obligor. However, it has been suggested that this requirement can be satisfied even in absence of a formal contract when there is "a *clientele relationship* that due to its solid and consistent nature will produce, over time and under reliable conditions, the future cash flows to be securitized"[24]

Unfortunately, Portugal does not match up to its European neighbors in terms of volume and diversity of assets.[25] The market is dominated by bank-originated securitizations. According to Portuguese law, any entity other than a bank or financial institution can assign receivables only after obligor notification. Obviously, this acts as an impediment in non-bank originated securitization.

Spain

State of the market

The traditional mortgage funding product in Spain was the *Pfandbrief*. Securitization of the U.S.-style was introduced only recently. Spain is one of those few markets where government initiatives have been behind growth in the securitization market. Securitization transactions originated around 1991, while the government passed an enabling law in 1992. Over a period of time, the government has reshaped and reformed the law, making it more permissive and market-friendly; the most recent legal initiative was taken in 1998 (see below).

The Spanish securitization market for many years has been a mortgage-dominated market. The first transaction in 1991 was one where *Citibank Hipotecas I* and *Sociedad Española* issued 19.8 billion pesetas (US$141 million) of "*Participaciones Hipotecarias* " (PHs) (participation certificates), secured by an issuer's specific portfolio of mortgage loans. There was an exceptional deal in 1996 to help the restoration of enterprises whose revenues were affected by the moratorium on the government's nuclear program.

Some innovative deals have been struck recently. For example, government subsidies to certain universities have been securitized, enabling the universities to raise immediate funds. There has also been a securitization of electricity bills receivables to partially finance the transition of the electric utilities; this is more or less on the lines of securitization of stranded costs by U.S. electric companies.

In 1998, the total volume of securitization in Spain was estimated at around US$ 4 billion. [Article in *Lawmoney*, April 1999].

In 2001, this volume reached approximately €10 billion, and the main market participants were banks and financial intermediaries, including the local version of savings and loans companies (*cajas*).

In 2002 securitization activities were strong, as the volume increased around 70% on year. Standards & Poor said it was by far the largest volume achieved in Spain, and over the last four years, issuance has quadrupled. Securitization of small business loans (PYMEs) and RMBS were the greatest contributors in 2002.

Spain has emerged as a major securitization market in Europe. According to the ESF, the total amount of Spanish issuance is approximately €32.5 billion in 2004. Spain is the third largest securitization market in Europe after the U.K. and Italy. In 2005, the volume was €42.45 billion.

Legal initiatives

Historically, Spain has been a country following the civil law tradition, but securitization law presents an attempted shoehorning of the U.K. common law into the Spanish legal framework. Not being a common law country, the concept of trusts is unknown in Spain. Similarly, mortgages of the U.K. common law type do not exist. Spain's own variant of land or property funding is called *hipoteca*, which has some similarities but many differences as compared with the U.K. mortgage system. The Spanish mortgage is limited only to immovable properties, cannot be negotiated, and needs compulsory registration. Under Spanish law, mortgages cannot be fractionalized or converted into securities as that would imply the creation of a trust. In other words, in Roman Dutch law or Spanish law, there is no distinction between legal and equitable interests in property.

Apparently, as in any Roman-Dutch legal system, securitization would have been impossible except for a specific law.

The government of Spain took early initiatives to promote securitization. A law permitting mortgage securitization was passed on July 7, 1992, enabling creation of *"Fondos de Titulización Hipotecaria,"* or mortgage securitization funds. This law not only permitted the transfer of mortgage receivables, but also provided for removal of the transferred receivables from the books of the originator, and also bankruptcy remote provisions.

In 1994, the scope of the law was extended to securitization of certain non-mortgage assets, particularly the nuclear moratorium compensation receivables.

However, most remarkable was the government's recent enactment of Royal Decree no. 926/1998 dated 14th May 1998. This enabled the creation of securitization *Fondos* (funds) that are comparable to trusts under English law. These funds are managed by *Sociedad Gestora de Fondos de Titulización* as trustees.

The major provisions are:

1) The permission to securitize all types of financial assets and future credit rights as trade receivables and toll road income. However, transactions based on future flows have to be notified to the Spanish Stock Exchange and to obtain the approval of the Spanish Ministry of Economy and Finance. The exception to this rule is the toll road income, already allowed in the Royal Decree.

2) The creation of open-ended structures. Previously, the *Fondo* expired once the bonds were redeemed. Now, the *Fondo* can add new assets (they must have similar features to the old ones) and issue a new series of bonds.

3) A rating company must asses the quality of the bonds issued by the *Fondo*. CNMV can require a minimum credit rating regarding the features of the assets and the bonds, although it is not yet clear what that minimum will be.[26] Because of typical limitations of Spanish law discussed above, the participation certificates from issuers in Spain do not exactly involve an SPV who acts as a trustee for the investors; in fact, each investor acquires a fractional interest in the mortgage, title in which continues to be held by the originator. Thus, the originator cannot transfer the whole of the mortgage, and at best can transfer only 99%. The investor, called the participant, can directly sue the obligor.

The 2002 Spanish Finance Act, passed in November 2002, gave recognition to mortgage transfer certificates ("*certificados de transmisión de hipoteca*"). The originators can now securitize both conforming and nonconforming loans through a *fondo de titulización de activos*.

The liquidator under the Spanish law had the power to annul contracts entered by the bankrupt company before the liquidation process began even if such contracts were legally valid. This power, often referred to as "clawback", is bestowed upon liquidators in several jurisdictions.[27] There is a risk that a securitization deal may be clawbacked by the liquidator even though the transaction satisfies "true sale" criteria. To remove this hitch, the Spanish legislature has enacted several changes to the existing laws regarding clawback. First, the amended law provides that only agreements that date up to two years prior to initiation of the insolvency proceeding can be crawled back. Second, only those transactions that are carried out in prejudice to the debtor and considered as harmful to the interests of the debtor can be clawed back by the liquidator. All agreements made without consideration are liable to be clawed back.[28]

Regulatory and accounting issues

The Bank of Spain, in a circular 4/91 of June 14, 1991, requires that to qualify for an off-balance sheet treatment transfers must be made with full risks and rewards attached to the assets. The originator is not allowed to support the assets nor agree to repurchase the assets.

There is no withholding tax in Spain for institutional investors, but it exists for retail investors.

Sweden

Legal and regulatory framework

Sweden, as a number of European markets, has a traditional mortgage funding instrument, called *Pandbrev* or *Pantbrev* (equivalent to the German *Pfandbrief*).

The mortgage market itself in Sweden is very well developed. The outstanding amount of mortgage loans forms more than 50% of the country's

GDP, based on a lecture by Lars Nyberg, Deputy Governor of the *Sveriges Riskbank*, on Economics Day at HSB Bank, Stockholm, on November 8, 2000. Sweden also has a very strong mortgage bond market (see *Pantbrev* above).

In March 1994, the government appointed a High Court judge to investigate the requisites of securitization for Sweden, and the judge produced a memo in May 1994 setting out his conclusions. However, nothing substantial has been done on the legislative front since then.

The new law was approved in January 2000 and was intended to alleviate difficulties under the existing law. Securitization is possible under existing legislation but costly, as the SPV is required to maintain a certain level of capital coverage. To avoid the capital costs, SPVs have so far been set up abroad where legislation permits this type of transaction without demand for capital coverage. Capital coverage – the regulatory capital required by banks against their assets – is the problem that pushed the jurisdiction of several transactions in the past.

Reportedly, there have been a number of deals in the Swedish market involving a variety of asset classes. However, Sweden has not emerged as a major securitization market in the European Union. Under Swedish regulations, any company that transacts "financing business" has to be registered with the Swedish Financial Supervisory Authority. This leads to a debate as to whether the SPV used in a securitization performs a "financing activity." It seems the FSA has not clarified this issue, but out of caution most SPVs clarify the issue with the FSA.[29]

Finland

In Finland, the Housing Fund of Finland raised through securitization in 1995 more than FIM 1.5 billion denominated in U.S. dollars and in 1996 did the first public securitization denominated in Finnish markka, when it securitized about FIM 1.5 billion of its loan receivables.

The 1995 transaction pooled together loans granted between 1973 and 1989, and so is considerably seasoned. By this time, the loan to value ratio had also considerably declined. Dublin was chosen as the location for the SPV for a number of reasons. Ireland, and especially the international finance center of Dublin, is well known to investors, an important factor when a new product is issued by a new issuer. The Irish legislation is 'securitization-friendly', and the country has a well-functioning securitization infrastructure, as a result of which the arrangements involved in the establishment of an SPV can be carried out quickly and smoothly. Another important reason was that the European Union had approved favourable tax treatment for companies in the International Finance Center of Dublin.

Legal system

The law requires notification to debtors.

There is no specific tax legislation concerning securitization. A Finnish SPV is liable to tax in Finland. The law does not allow for any exemption from this tax. It is not altogether clear, however, whether the income of the SPV should be taxed as business income, according to the Act on Taxation of Business Income, or as other income, according to the Act on Income Taxation. The differences between these two acts are notable, especially concerning accrual of income and expenses.

Because of these uncertainties and the fact that securitizations have been aimed at attracting foreign investors, most Finnish securitization transactions have been carried out through a SPV situated abroad. The relevant tax issues are then mainly determined by the tax regulations of the foreign jurisdiction in question, and by the tax treaty between Finland and that jurisdiction. A foreign SPV has limited tax liability in Finland and is only taxed in Finland on income deriving from Finland. Whether the income of the SPV is taxed in Finland depends, among other things, on whether the SPV is considered to be engaged in business activities in Finland. Under most tax treaties, however, business income is taxed only in the company's country of residence when the company has no permanent establishment in the other country. Thus, no Finnish tax will normally be due. As no tax treaties exist between Finland and most of the so-called tax havens, the taxation of a SPV located in such a jurisdiction would be determined according to domestic Finnish tax rules. The Mortgage Bank Act was passed in 1999, with an aim to regulate both mortgage banks and mortgage bonds. The German *Pfandbrief*-model has been the guiding force behind the structure of Finnish Mortgage bonds.

Switzerland

The Swiss legal system does not require notice to debtors. However, a debtor paying in absence of a notice to the originator sees a valid discharge.

There are no tax obstacles in Switzerland as offshore bodies are not taxed unless they have a permanent establishment in the country. There is no withholding tax on payments to foreign SPVs.

The Mortgage Bond Act provides for the arrangement of long-term mortgage loans at the most stable and lowest rate of interest possible for the property owner. In 1998 the mortgage bond institutes succeeded in convincing the Swiss Banking Commission, the EBK, the supervisory authority, that these requirements could best be met by a financing mix, whereby mortgage bonds with a duration of three to seven years at lower interest rates and those with a duration of eight to twelve years at slightly higher interest rates were issued. In a letter of November 1998, the EBK approved this system. Consequently, mortgage bonds with duration of three years or more can be issued.

There are two centralized mortgage bond issuing institutes working on the issuance of MBS.

Luxembourg[30]

Luxembourg is consciously being promoted by authorities as a jurisdiction of choice for securitization transactions. In 2004, the government enacted a law with a view to promote the jurisdiction as one of the most favored SPV jurisdictions.

The Securitization Law gives a very broad definition of the term "securitization." According to PwC, an SPV can be organized as a public limited company, a private limited company, a partnership limited by shares, or a "co-operative company organized as a public company." Conspicuously absent among the classes of SPV are trust companies, which are probably not recognized as in several other civil law countries. However, SPVs can be organized as a "securitization fund." The fund does not have a legal personality of its own, but can be managed by a management company. The law allows the concept of "cell companies," and funds from one source can be insulated from other sources.

An SPV, which issues securities to the public, would be governed by the rules of the Supervisory Commission of the Financial Sector (CSSF). The Articles of Association and other documents governing the SPV are to be filed with the CSSF. The details about the board of directors of the SPV should also be filed before the CSSF. Upon completion of all the formalities, the CSSF will register the entity in the official list of the CSSF.

The law does not put any limitation as to the types of assets that can be securitized. An important feature of the law is that it allows "non-petition provision" which goes a long way in achieving bankruptcy remoteness for the SPV. Further, the law allows non-recourse provisions that have significant impact on the rating enjoyed by a transaction. The law allows tax neutral treatment of the securitization.

Turkey[31]

Turkey has had several securitization transactions, particularly of future flows, over the last 10 years. The first securitization deal in Turkey was reported in 1993 for credit cards. There have been several credit card securitizations since, and most of these issues have been by commercial banks, generally involving foreign currency coming into the country. Securitization volumes out of Turkey continued to grow unabated by the lack of specific legislation on securitization. Major banks such as *Isbank* and *Akbank* have successfully securitized several million dollars of receivables. However, most transactions have been of future flows, especially financial future flows, where the objective is to raise international funding and eliminate sovereign risk.

Turkish banks have securitized items such as international credit card receivables, export receivables, cheques and travellers' cheques remittances and diversified payments in international financial markets.

An SPV does not require any licence to engage in securitization transactions.

As per Turkish law, a "true sale" takes place when there is assignment of existing and future receivables, such that the assignor makes such an assignment to the assignee without recourse to the assignor. However, in the event of the assignor's insolvency, bankruptcy, or non-performance, the assignee is allowed recourse against the assignor and this is no impediment for a "true sale".

As per Article 163 of the Turkish Code of Obligations (Law 818), to be a valid assignment, the assignor and assignee must enter into a written agreement.

The granting of security interest over present and future receivables is governed by The Turkish Civil Code (Law 4721). In case the originator grants an assignment of, or security interest in, the receivables to more than one purchaser or secured lender for any reasons whatsoever, the purchaser who notified the debtor at the earliest has priority over other purchasers. To be binding the assignment/pledge agreement with respect to the receivables must be notified properly.

The Execution and Bankruptcy Law (Article 280) provides that an assignment of receivables shall become null and void if the assignor makes it within the two years prior to its insolvency or bankruptcy with the intention of preventing the collection of claims by third-party creditors and the assignee is aware of this intention.

A stamp duty of 0.75% is levied. There is no tax on corresponding assignment of a security interest to secure the SPV note to the trustee.

Latvia

In Eastern European countries, securitization has developed more from the viewpoint of German *Pfandbrief* or mortgage-bonds tradition than the U.S. CMO or pass-through structure. This applies to Latvia also.

Total mortgage loans in Latvia as of April 1, 1999, were €52 million, including €6.5 million with the Mortgage Bank, with the average interest rate 14.4%. In 1998, total mortgage loans amounted to only about 1% of the GDP (in many countries it is as much as 60-90%; in the Czech Republic, housing loans alone make up 10%). The most important precondition for the development of mortgage lending in Latvia is appropriate financial resources. To ensure the security of the attracted resources and their purposeful usage (capitalization in real estate), the Cabinet of Ministers adopted a special concept of creating a mortgage lending system. In accordance with this concept, the Cabinet prepared and the Saeima passed in 1998, the Law on Mortgage Bonds, aimed at the protection of investors as the security of investments is the major factor that may promote a decline in interest rates on mortgage loans.

The most important feature of the system that distinguishes it from those of several other countries (like Germany and Denmark) using mortgage bonds as a financial instrument in the mortgage lending system, is that any bank complying with the provisions of the law, not only specialized mortgage banks, has the right to issue mortgage bonds. Banks have the right to issue mortgage bonds if they comply with the following rules:

- Capital of not less than €8 million;
- All financial transactions without restrictions are allowed;
- Approved rules of mortgage transactions are submitted;
- Rules of mortgage bond cover register are approved by the Bank of Latvia;
- Ensure management of cover in the register separate is from other assets.

Latvia has been using securitization to fund SMEs.

Poland[32]

Polish investment bank BRE in August 1999 lead managed what is believed to be the first structured finance transaction in the Polish capital markets. The Z10 million asset-backed commercial paper issue was the inaugural offering of the Z50 million trade receivables program for pharmaceutical concern Urtica. Polish power grid operator Polskie Sieci Elektronenergetyczne (PSE) has started to raise approximately US$1.5 billion in the international bond markets through the securitization of a new tax paid by electricity consumers in the year 2002 itself.

There is no direct law on securitization. Recently, a prospectus has been released by a task team of banks (affiliated with the Association of Polish Banks) to create a framework for securitization. Polish law does not recognize the concept of a trust. The legal framework for securitization in Poland needs to be worked out properly.

Fitch's December 2002 report states: "While securitization as a legal concept is not yet developed in Poland, there is marked interest by both the private sector financial community as well as the Polish regulatory authorities. Accordingly, Fitch Ratings understands the status of securitization to be at an early stage."

Looking at the prospects and problems in developing Polish securitization, the report stated: "Bank assets typically represent the bulk of securitizations and are thus most likely to be involved in Poland's expected securitization programmes. This would be for both funded programmes, with the aim of raising capital, as well as unfunded (synthetic) programmes, with the aim of relieving the capital adequacy ratio (CAR) through substantially reducing credit default risk from the bank's financials. In both cases, the future seems to provide even more motivation for such transactions, as the new Basle Accord's CAR is expected to rise.

However, synthetic and funded securitization of banking assets is hindered by a number of obstacles, including banking confidentiality laws. No information about obligors may be released by banks to a third party without the obligors' written approval to disclose such information. Accordingly, credit event information cannot be released. Practically, it is rather unlikely to obtain such an approval from current obligors and the incorporation of a consent clause into new lending contracts will be difficult as the receiver of such information (e.g. SPV, Servicer) has to be specified by name. In terms of consumer assets, apart from banking secrecy, there are strict regulations regarding the protection of individuals' data."

The Bond Act was revised in 2000, and accordingly one can now find revenue bonds, secured by future revenues of municipalities or municipal-related companies.

The transfer of assets to an SPV to achieve "true sale" for securitization purposes is possible. But it attracts a Civil Actions Tax of 1-2%.

According to the ESF the total volume of securitization in Poland would be approximately $0.6 billion as of 2003.

Austria

Article 22 (4) of the UCITS Directive has been fully implemented in Austria. At the request of the European Commission (DG Internal Market and Financial Services), the Federal Finance Ministry sent an up-to-date list of the issues falling under the scope of this provision to Brussels in a letter of 7 July 1999. Further legal developments in the first six months of 1998 included the following:

a. Amendment of the Mortgage Bank Act and the Mortgage Bond Act to allow cross-border mortgage lending activity.
b. Favorable weighting for mortgage bonds at 10%, including those issued after January 1, 1998.
c. Favorable weighting for commercial property loans at 50%.
d. Favorable weighting for MBS at 50%.

Nevertheless, the market in Austria continues to shrink. As a result of the repayment of loans, particularly in the public sector, issuing activity was adversely affected (down around 20% in 1998 compared with 1997). The volume of bonds issued by *Wohnbaubanken* (institutions specialized in housing finance, loans with tax advantages) in 1998 exceeded the volume of mortgage bonds for the first time. Under certain conditions, these bonds are exempt from withholding tax.

The rating of mortgage bonds has been considered, but to date the market has not implemented it.

According to the ESF, the volume of securitization would be $0.62 billion under the ABS category in 2004.

Czech Republic[33]

In the eastern part of Europe, the Czech Republic has not shown any substantial securitization activity. There is no specific securitization law in this country and even other laws do not indirectly refer to it. The February 2002 issue of a leading Czech business magazine *Ekonom* introduced the basic principles of securitization to the Czech Republic, identifying the major legal issues. It has been observed that Czech law doesn't favor complex methods of financing like securitization, and so it is not clear as to how the bankruptcy-remote requirement would be respected in bankruptcy proceedings. According to the ESF, the total volume of Securitization under the MBS would be around $0.03 billion.

Hungary[34]

The new Capital Markets Act (w.e.f. 01.01.2002) has liberalized the ABS market. Earlier the issues of securities in securitization transactions could not exceed private placements and hence public issues of ABS were not allowed. However, a financial institution was always allowed a public issue in an aggregate amount exceeding its capital.

In view of the new Capital Markets Act, certain important changes that affect securitization transactions were also introduced to the Hungarian Banking Act.

The "true sale" criteria is considered as satisfied, provided the transfer of assets is made at arms' length and the SPV is not a related party to the seller. Even the originator cannot have influence over the transferred assets. Notification of the debtors is essential upon the assignment of receivables.

The SPV is generally in the form of a company limited by shares with a minimum share capital of HUF 50 million. A factoring license is also required from the Hungarian Financial Supervisory Authority. The concept of a trustee is not popular here. A corporate income tax of 18% is levied on the SPV.

Hungary has not emerged as a major securitization market. A banker explains the reasons for the unpopularity of securitization as follows: "The market in Hungary is over-banked, and competition is very sharp. Cheap lending is available for whatever projects corporates want to undertake, and obtaining capital relief by moving assets off the balance sheet is not a hot topic for issuers here."[35]

Central and South America

Securitization has captured tremendous interest over all of Latin America. The Latin American market essentially consists of issuers trying to attract investors from developed markets. Most Latin American countries have speculative grade country ratings, so the issuers are essentially looking at ways of piercing their sovereign ratings through securitization.

Several Latin American transactions came to the market from 1997, but interest of investors was weakened due to several defaults and downgrades of Latin American transactions. Argentine sovereign action in early 2002 and a worsening situation for several economies such as Colombia have resulted in mixed securitization prospects for this part of the world.

Interest continues to be strong in Brazil and Mexico.

Origin of securitization in Latin America

Securitization in Latin America is not very old. Argentina witnessed the first securitization in late 1993 as Citicorp used an offshore vehicle to finance a pool of $50 million of auto loans generated within Argentina.

From 1995-97, there was a general lack of interest in the market since Latin American issuers depended largely on cross-border investors.

However, in 1997 and 1998, a number of transactions were reported, indicating both depth and width in the market. The range of applications includes auto loans, residential mortgages and commercial mortgages, credit cards, oil export income, oilfield royalties and air ticket securitization.

One of the distinctive features of the Latin American market is the popularity of future flows securitization. The genesis of this can be seen easily in originators having earnings from hard currency areas, then trying to shelter their earnings against foreign exchange and sovereign risks by trapping their cash flows in the country of origin. Most of these originators are those who have export receivables for either goods or services from hard currency areas. A Standard & Poor's report of July 1999, entitled "Lessons from the Past Apply to Future Securitizations in Emerging Markets," says: "In fact, approximately 90% of Latin American securitizations are backed by future flows."

Mexico

State of the market

Securitization is one of the hottest topics in Mexican finance today. Most of the securitizations in Mexico has been future flows or export receivables securitization. Mexico has the distinction of being the first country in the world to introduce the technology of future flows securitization. The first future flows securitization originated from Mexico in 1987, when there was hardly any substantial awareness about securitization. In 1994, Aeromexico, an airlines company, securitized its airline ticket receivables.

In 1997, there was an offer of $1.2 billion in future flow structured transactions. There was also a credit cards receivables deal by Banco Nacional de Mexico *S.A.* worth $215 million. Grupo Minero Mexico S.A. de C.V. came to market with $420 million in secured export notes. Industrias Peñoles S.A. de C.V., the Mexican silver mining company, issued a unique note where the payments to holders were to be made in kind – in silver.

In March 1998, a securitization was completed by Grupo Minero Mexico, the mining subsidiary of the Grupo Mexico conglomerate. The US$500 million guaranteed senior note issue was supported by warranties on the company's export receivables, principally copper, zinc, and silver.

As in other emerging markets (Turkey and Pakistan – see country pages), there have also been securitizations of foreign inward remittances; in October 1998 Banamex, a bank, issued US$300 million in remittance-backed securities.

The first publicly offered transaction in Mexico was towards end-1998 by consumer finance giant Grupo Elektra S.A. de C.V., which issued securities backed by trade receivables. With that success, within two years the same group also securitized its accounts receivables (Ps.350 million). In 2001, Mexican securitization volume grew 290%. The transaction was rated AAA (local) by Fitch IBCA.

Mexico has emerged as the largest securitization market in Latin America with a market size of US$4.1 billion.[36] S&P reports that investors purchased approximately US$9.9 billion in Mexican bonds.[37]

Legal initiatives

The Mexican government also has made a number of reforms aimed at creating a more efficient housing finance system. In the early 1990s, it authorized the creation of finance companies (SOFOLs) to encourage competition in the industry, and it is currently looking to reduce the cost and timing of foreclosure.

FOVI, the Mexican housing trust, has been trying to work out an MBS mechanism for financing SOFOLs.

The legal requirements for assignment of mortgages entailed notification to the obligor as also a compulsory registration, implying costs as well as inconvenience. Towards this, several of the states have begun modifying their civil codes to allow for the assignment of mortgages without the need for obligor notification and registration. Besides, mortgage foreclosure laws have also been amended by most of the states.

A majority of the states have passed laws that have removed difficulties surrounding the assignment of receivables, such as registration in local public registries. Another development has been creation of the debt security, the *Certificado Bursatil,* which emerged as the most important debt security in the Mexican market. In March 2005, the Ministry of Finance submitted a proposal which is supposed to further improve the legal framework for securitization.

Mortgage-backed securitization in Mexico

Rating agency Standard & Poor's in a report in *Structured Finance* July 2000 pointed to the following structural problems in securitization of mortgage receivables in Mexico:

- Difficulties in the securitization of standard mortgages that are adjusted according to two indices;
- Insufficient volume of mortgages originated through the government's new low-income housing program, due mainly to its recent creation;
- Need for increased liquidity in the banking system to allow for lending to resume;
- Present state of legal reforms, including frameworks for insolvency and foreclosures; and
- Further development of capital markets for long-term investments.

However, significant legal and capital market reforms have removed several of the difficulties mentioned above. Standard & Poor reports that investors purchased US$9.9 billion Mexican Structured Bonds. According to the rating agency, the country has emerged as the leader in the securitization market in Latin America. RMBS and ABS are backed by municipal securitizations and construction bridge loans. Mexican issuers are still frequent users of Future Flows securitizations and according to S&P these transactions would increase in the near future, while insurers are expected to wrap several of these.[38]

Tax issues

One of the significant issues in Mexican securitization will be the issue of withholding tax. The Income Tax Law provides that income in credit, obtained by a non-resident through the acquisition of a credit right of any kind, whether present, future or contingent, sold by a resident in Mexico, will be subject to a withholding tax rate of 10%. The income will be determined, generally, by subtracting the contractual price from the face value of the credit right. The law mentions that the withholding takes place when the accounts are considered sold. This issue is important in the case of selling future receivables.

Brazil

State of the market

Securitization in Brazil started sometime around 1993; Standard & Poor's in its report in *Structured Finance* July 2000 comments: "The prospects for the securitization of existing assets in Brazil are favorable, despite the fact that present volume of eligible assets is relatively low. Two, securitization laws enacted in Brazil in the late 1990s have served as catalysts for change, since they have helped spawn the right environment for credit-originating institutions. Mortgage foreclosures or auctions are now allowed in Brazil, and banks are authorized to transfer assets to non-financial institutions. Investors are now likely to be more interested in investing in MBS and ABS in Brazil than in the past." One of the first securitization transactions in the real estate segment, where receivables out of real estate transactions were sold to cross-border investors, was a February 1998 deal by *Cidadela*, which used the proceeds to promote installment sales of real estate developed by it.

Brazil has developed its own model of Fannie Mae: *Cibrasec* is a privately owned entity similar to the Fannie Mae. It completed its first purchase of mortgage loans in September 1998.

In its second quarter review for 2003, S&P commented: "It appears that Brazil's structured finance market is finally showing signs of rejuvenation, resuscitating after a period of political and economic uncertainty that put issuance on hold. New export future flow transactions are expected to take on new vigour."

According to S&P, Brazilian securitization volumes would be around $953 million, a whopping 247% increase over May 2004 volumes. S&P expects volumes to increase over the next few years. Major asset classes are trade receivables, consumer and personal loans, and S&P also mentions there may be new asset types of transactions such as future flow securitizations.[39]

Legal initiatives to promote securitization

In May 1998, the National Monetary Authority took the initiative to enact a law on securitization transactions. The purpose of the law was to enable transfer of receivables originated by banks, investment banks, leasing companies and mortgage companies.

Practitioners feel that the new law left a lot of loopholes – one provision is that the originator will not accept subordinated notes in exchange for the assets, which curtails one of the often accepted means of credit enhancement. The 1998 law was supplemental to the law already passed in November 1997, allowing banks to sell of their mortgage receivables to non-financial entities.

It may be noted that the Brazilian legal system is also not conducive to the trust concept; in absence of an enabling law, securitization deals in Brazil are prone to a number of legal impediments.

The new law permits the transfer of receivables to special purpose corporations, called *"Companhia Securitizadora de Créditos Financeiros* (Financial Credits Securitization Company)";again, the insistence on the corporate form is due to the absence of a pass-through trust in Brazilian law. The SPC, in turn, may either domestically issue shares or debentures, or internationally issue such securities permitted under the relevant law.

The Instruction nº 281 of June 4, 1998, issued by the Brazilian Securities Commission (CVM), provides for special procedures for registering issuance of debentures by securitization companies for public distribution. Accordingly, only debentures with a certain minimum nominal value may be registered (Art. 2 of the Instruction). The prospectus of the issue must make it clear that all payments under the debentures are conditioned (Art.6, III of the Instruction), and must also contain certain information regarding the underlying credits, such as their origin and the identity of the respective assignor (Art. 6, II, of the instruction).

Repurchase of receivables transferred to the SPC is not permitted.

Another notable legal initiative taken by the government is to make foreclosures of mortgages legal. This is expected to boost the real estate securitization market, which has so far been not very active.

Taxation of securitization

Around end-1998, the Brazilian government imposed a new tax on financial transactions, which was supposed to hit securitization transactions.

Future flows and Brazilian bankruptcy laws

Duff and Phelps in December 1999 issued a report entitled "Brazilian Bankruptcy Laws and Future Flow Securitization." The report discusses the impact of bankruptcy proceedings on future flows transactions, which is significant as future flow securitizations are not bankruptcy remote.

According to the report, there are three types of distress situations a Brazilian company may pass through – *insolvência, falencia or concordata. Concardata* is similar to a potential bankruptcy, like Chapter 11 of the US Bankruptcy Code.

Future flows are not immune from these proceedings, as the amount of existing receivables in a future flows transaction would never fully liquidate the investors' total receivables. Future flows, by their very nature, retire the investors' receivables by the originator's claims to arise in future. Thus, to the extent the receivables exist, the investors will have a senior or ownership claim thereon, but to the extent of the deficiency, that is, the difference between the total amount payable to the investors and the existing assets, it will only be an unsecured claim against the company. Any future flow transaction is always marked by a certain existing framework from which the flows arise in the future. For example, oil exports will arise from oil wells, which the originator might own. It is always advisable that the investors be given an ownership over the receivables that exist at the time of transfer, and a security interest in the framework from which the receivables arise. This would also greatly take care of performance risk, as if the originator goes out of business, the framework still exists and whoever operates it would be liable to pay investors.

Rating agencies would suggest the following further mitigants against bankruptcy risk in future flows:

- One important structural enhancement in all future-flow securitizations is the inclusion of early amortization triggers, which, upon breach thereof, cause the trustee to trap all offshore cash flows for the repayment of the future-flow debt. Early amortization triggers monitor, among others, the performance of the company's export levels to designated customers, the overall debt burden of the originating company and certain other financial covenants. These triggers are designed to detect potential negative performance by the underlying company and afford investors an "escape" before the company's situation deteriorated to the point of bankruptcy.
- Rating agencies normally insist that originators in future flows are strong companies with a good track record. For example, Duff and Phelps in their report above states: "These large companies are more likely to work through the concordata successfully. Furthermore, the company would be allowed to maintain its core operations, thereby generating the export receivables and offshore cash flows needed to repay the investors."

There are concerns as to whether "future flows" would be considered as "true sale" under the Brazilian law. However, both S&P and a reputed law firm have stated that "future flows" can be structured to avoid being hit by the non-true sale characterization.[40]

Asia

Asia is a huge block, economically and also culturally; it is a kaleidoscopic picture. As there are huge economic differences within the region, the same is true for stages of development of securitization. Japan is economically a different market altogether; the rest of Asia represents a mixed picture of some countries where market activity has reached a certain stage of development and others have yet to introduce the concepts.

On close study, it appears that the motivations that have driven banks and others into securitization markets elsewhere in the world may not be squarely applicable to Asia. For example, the U.S. mortgage market is a prime example of capital market-oriented mortgage lending activity. In Asia, the housing finance system still works on the basis of intermediated lending, either because of state-supported refinance institutions or because retail deposit-based banking is still predominant. Savings are yet to be institutionalized to the extent noticed in the U.S. market; therefore, disintermediation is less strong on either the asset side of banks or the liability side. Another reason for U.S. banks to aggressively enter securitization was capital adequacy. Asian banks are still not relieved of the mass of non-performing loans generated during the systemic crisis of 1997 or overall poor lending. Therefore, gaining capital relief through sale of good assets is much less a concern of banks in the region than cleaning up their balance sheet of bad assets.

For larger parts of Asia, securitization still means a mode of raising liquidity. It continues to be needed more for encashing future flows, funding infrastructural or developmental projects and industry, than for capital relief. Markets like Hong Kong, Singapore and South Korea are already showing interest in synthetic activity, but reasons for that are more for arbitrage than capital relief as such.

In terms of policy-makers, the most notable feature of Asian securitization over the last few years has been government legislative action. Most countries have either enacted laws or are in advanced stages of enacting legislation, presumably intended to remove roadblocks to securitization. Taiwan recently passed such law; Philippines is due to clear the securitization law soon; South Korea has enacted and successfully implemented its law; Malaysia works well with regulatory guidelines; India has enacted a combo piece of law that deals with several things, including securitization; Pakistan also has rules in place relating to SPVs; Thailand has an SPC law, although market practitioners feel there are still several bottlenecks; Singapore and Hong Kong have generally pro-market stances, more due to the absence of regulation than regulatory action.

Below, we take a quick look at market developments in some Asian countries:

Japan

General overview[41]

By U.S. securitization standards, Japan is still an emerging market because it has tremendous potential. By right, Japan should be the world's second largest securitization market as it is the world's second largest economy. Securitization in Japan dates as far back as 1931, when the Diet enacted the first legislation relating to mortgage securities. Prior to the implementation of the MITI Law in 1993, Japan had several types of structured financing techniques in practice. These included securitized commercial real estate mortgages, securitized residential real estate mortgages, residential mortgage trusts, and non-housing bank loan securitizations. Further, legal interests known as *kumiai* have sold divided interests in real property. Recently, however, most issues have had equipment leases as their underlying assets. Sakura Bank and Tokyo Mitsubishi Bank have used asset-backed debt to rebuild their balance sheets to meet the capital adequacy ratios instituted by the Bank of International Settlements (BIS). This method of raising cash is seen by the banks as necessary but expensive. The securitization market in Japan has assumed tremendous proportions in the last five years. The market has grown to encompass every major asset class that is securitized in developed markets around the world – trade receivables, equipment and vehicle leases, residential mortgages, commercial property, corporate loans and every kind of consumer finance. The recent takeover of Life Co., a collapsed consumer finance company, by finance company Aiful Corp was financed by securitization. The economy of Japan is geared up to experience growth with the help of structured finance.

Recent developments

The Japanese securitization market reached a volume of US$12.5 billion in 1998, and has been growing steadily since. Daiwa Securities predicts that the market could grow to US$770 billion in 5 to 10 years. The prime reasons why securitization should grow in Japan are (a) the new accommodative law; (b) and the problem of bad loans and capital adequacy that will force banks to use securitization to restructure their balance sheets.

The big news in the Japanese securitization market is that the Bank of Japan (BOJ) is willing to buy asset-backed paper representing the loan assets of Japanese banks, up to a total of ¥1 trillion.

According to a report by Fitch, the Japanese securitization market grew 50%, from ¥3.1 trillion in 2001 to over ¥4.6 trillion in 2002. CMBS issuance volume in 2002 was the same as in the previous year.

Japanese volumes have continued to grow. Moody reports that Japanese securitization volumes have reached ¥6.5 trillion.[42] Fitch says the volumes in the first 9 months of 2005 match that of issuance in 2004 at ¥5.5 trillion. RMBS is the largest asset class in Japan, accounting for 44.1% of transactions in 9M05.[43]

Like most other developed countries there has been considerable growth of arbitrage CDO volumes.

Legal aspects

To clearly understand the legal framework of securitization in Japan it is necessary to look to the past. Article 467 of the Japanese Civil Code requires that a transfer or assignment of claims will require a notice to, or consent from the obligor with a confirmed date certificate for the transfer or assignment to be effective against third parties, including a bankruptcy trustee or other insolvency officer of the originator. It did not provide a favourable environment for securitization. Hence, in 1993 the 'MITI Law' or the 'Specified Claims Law' (SCL) was enacted to allow transfer or assignment of certain specified claims, such as lease and credit card receivables, originated by non-bank finance companies, to be perfected against underlying debtors and against competing third party claims by publishing a notice in a daily newspaper circulated in Japan. It is known as the Specified Claims Law because it regulates the business concerning specified claims. The term MITI was actually the abbreviated form of the Ministry of International Trade and Industry. But the SCL or MITI law only applied to some specific assets and originators, not to all. It did not apply to loans originated by banks or consumer finance companies. Hence, the Perfection Law was passed in 1998 to facilitate the securitization of real estate and other assets outside the scope of the Specified Claims Law. The establishment of Japanese special purpose companies is permitted under the Special Purpose Company or TMK law, passed in 1998. The question of which party can service the assets has immense significance in case of securitization. According to the Practicing Attorney Law, only a qualified attorney can take up legal affairs; and a servicer's position could in part at least clash with an attorney. Thus, the Servicer Law was passed in February 1999. Accordingly, a corporation that met the requirements of having a minimum capital of ¥500 million and having a qualified lawyer on its board of directors, could be approved as a servicer. In May 1999, the "Non-Bank Bond Issuance Law" was enacted, which permitted non-bank consumer finance companies to raise funds for lending by issuing – among other things – ABS, making the erstwhile consumer loan securitizations legal as well as popular. However, Article 24(2) of the "Money Lending Law" makes it obligatory that an assignment of loans originated by a money lending company should be notified to the obligors.

The Diet amended the Trust law in late 2004. The amendment recognized the new type of trust company, the *kanri gata shintaku kaisha* (summery-type trust companies). As opposed to existing trust companies set up by banks and engaging in a wide spectrum of business, summary-type trust companies can engage in only a limited area of business. Some market participants feel that summary type trust companies may enter the securitization market to provide services where the services of the trustee are limited to being a "passive vehicle". The trust business law has also removed the restrictions on the types of asset classes that may be entrusted with trusts. This will surely encourage the growth of new asset classes. The amendment laid down specific duties and liabilities of trusts. The amendment has also laid down the same level of standard of care expected from parties that provide support services to trusts. Further, the trusts must be compulsorily registered with the FSA.

The Cabinet has clarified in the data protection law with respect to protection of data from individuals (the *Kojin Joho Hogo Hou)* and cases involving the transfer of receivables that no debtor notification is required for the transfer of receivables.[44]

Mortgage-backed loans

In recent years, there has been a number of securitizations of commercial mortgages, residential mortgages and non-performing and sub-performing property-related loans. But most of the CMBS transactions have been structured as secured loans and not as asset-backed transactions issued in the public markets. The residential mortgage-backed market has grown substantially, mainly due to the entrance of the state-owned Government Housing Loan Corp. The RMBS market in Japan grew by more than 40% in 2001, to around ¥500 billion. In July 2001, Shinsei Securities launched a MBS deal involving collateral of about 6,300 fixed and floating rate residential mortgages that it had acquired from Daihyaku Mutual Life, which had failed. For commercial property, the data revealed that in 2001, there were at least 20 performing and non-performing CMBS worth more than ¥600 billion. In 2000, the market was dominated by sale and leaseback deals from corporates, but the "5% rule" introduced in April 2001, changed the situation. It also must be noted that the first CMBS transaction in Japan that followed international standards was concluded in March 1999, just before the government activated its ¥60-trillion bank bailout package and the Bank of Japan introduced zero interest rates.

Taxation aspects

Since 1998, the Japanese Special Tax Measurement Law (JSTML) has been amended to facilitate special tax treatments for SPCs. According to the "90% Rule," dividends are considered as deductible expenses when they amount to more than 90% of net income. There have been constant reductions of real estate registration tax and acquisition tax for SPCs and REITs. They are also exempted from special land holding tax. In 2001 the real estate registration tax for investment companies (including J-REITs) was reduced and they were also exempted from a special land-holding tax.

Accounting aspects

In January 1999, the Business Accounting Deliberation Council (BADC) issued the Financial Instruments Standards. The Japanese Institute of Certified Public Accountants (JICPA) issued the implementation guidelines in January 2000. Now the originators could treat a securitization as sale subject to fulfilment of certain conditions. It resulted in achieving the off-balance sheet treatment, for non-consolidated statement purposes; the special purpose company (SPC) to which the assets are transferred could be excluded from consolidation. Guidelines for real estate securitization were issued by JICPA in July 2000. It says the "5%" will be applied to decide whether the originator can achieve sales treatment; the originator's risk exposure after the transfer should not exceed 5% of the fair value of the securitized real estate at the time of transfer. As per the existing Japanese GAAP, an SPC is not considered a subsidiary of the investor or the originator if the price for the asset transfer is fairly determined and the assignment is within the asset securitization purposes. This eliminates consolidation requirements. However, an assignor that securitizes real estate using a subsidiary SPC is not permitted to treat the transaction as a sale for non-consolidation purposes.

Others

In 2001, Shinsei Bank's CLO was initiated with a master trust structure, one of the world's largest securitization programs with ¥1.4 trillion ($11.5 billion) in loans. There have been several transactions using credit derivatives to securitize loan positions synthetically. The economy shows an increase in liquidity and diversification in the corporate bond market that allows the creation of a pool of secondary market bonds. Secondary CBOs will certainly continue, but with the increase in Asset-Backed Loans (ABLs), CDOs that incorporate a wide range of debt with both bonds and loans, will also become popular. The asset classes taking the Japanese securitization market by storm are auto loans, equipment leases and shopping credits. Asset-backed commercial paper (ABCP) is also a common phenomenon in Japanese securitization, as it is mostly purchased by the sponsoring banks or other banks, with little sold openly to investors in the capital market.

Singapore

General overview

Singapore has been seeing sporadic activity in the sphere of commercial mortgage-backed transactions, credit card deals and CDOs. Of these, the synthetic CDO deals recently (Merlion from JPMC/DBS Bank and another one from UOB) have received extensive international publicity as these are European-style arbitrage synthetic deals that herald the development of a strong credit derivatives market in the region. The commercial real estate deals from Singapore also, from viewpoint of structural features, are comparable to any international deals.

The Monetary Authority of Singapore (MAS) introduced guidelines for securitization on September 6, 2000 (MAS Notification No. 628, dated 06.09.2002 at www.mof.gov.sg for the text of the guidelines).

Legal aspects

Singapore, by and large, has the English common law system. Assignment of actionable claims requires legal notice to the debtor under section 4(6) of the Civil Law Act. Hence, to avoid debtor notification, assignments in Singapore are usually equitable assignment. [For meaning of equitable assignments, see Chapter 7 on Legal Issues.] Equitable assignment has its own risk, such as the existence of prior or superior claims and rights of set-off. Not being the legal owner of the receivables, the securitization SPV cannot bring claims against debtors in its own name and would have to depend on the originator. In case of mortgage loans, the transfer of receivables would also entail the transfer of the underlying mortgage, which would require compulsory registration with the Registrar of Titles and Deeds.

The securitization guidelines issued by MAS pursuant to section 54A(1) of the Banking Act must be adhered to with due care. The guideline starts with the definitions of various terms like ABS, MBS, seller, servicer and SPV. In the introductory part it explains the process of securitization in brief and talks about the role of banks in identifying, monitoring and managing the various types of risk arising from their involvement in securitization. The guideline applies to all banks acting as seller, servicer, provider of credit enhancement or liquidity facilities, manager or investor relating to any securitization transaction. For branches of foreign-incorporated banks, the treatment of securitization for capital adequacy purposes would be a matter for the home supervisor of the entity concerned. Nonetheless, branches of foreign-incorporated banks in Singapore must observe the requirements relating to disclosure, separation and, where applicable, any other conditions related to the provision of facilities and services as set out in this Notice. The most important part is that any bank proposing to act as seller or manager, either solely or jointly with other parties, in a securitization transaction must obtain prior approval from the MAS. To ensure that banks conduct securitization transactions in a prudent manner, the guidelines empower the MAS to impose supervisory limits on the volume or types of assets that may be securitized. MAS may also raise the capital adequacy requirements of a bank, when the totality of its activities suggests that its overall level or concentration of risk has become excessive relative to its capital. Various Disclosure Requirements, Separation Requirements (clear separation between the bank and the SPV) and other requirements have also been provided for.

Taxation aspects

The income tax implications involving the various transactions in an asset securitization arrangement are not adequately covered with clear-cut rules. There is no specific enactment that deals with the tax treatment of transactions involving asset securitization. One has to resort to the basic tax principles and available case laws to determine the tax treatment.

In general, it is considered advantageous for the SPV to be construed as a trading or business entity and not an investment holding company. In a normal business entity wholly engaged in the management of a continuous income stream derived from an asset that is acquired, its business expenses are allowable against its business income. Business losses not utilized during the current basis year can be used against future business income. This is not the case of a holding company where interest expenses incurred in the year are restricted to the amount incurred in the basis period for which the income is derived.

Management fees payable to a non-resident individual are subject to a 10% withholding tax.

There is a Goods and Services Tax (GST), which is not applicable on issue or transfer of "debt securities." It is felt that the definition of "debt securities" in Paragraph 3 of the Fourth Schedule to the GST Act is wide enough to exclude securitized notes from the applicability of GST. Stamp duties are applicable on the assignment of mortgages at a rate of S$500. Securitization of other receivables is exempt from stamp duty, pursuant to amendments made effective from February 28, 1998.

The Company Legislation and Regulatory Framework Committee (CLRFC) suggested in its report for granting of incentives for developing the asset securitization market by allowing a favorable tax treatment for special purpose vehicles (SPVs). It also suggested a lower effective tax rate of about 15% for the financial sector. On June 28, 2005, the MAS announced several concessions to SPVs, giving effect to the announcement of the Finance Minister in his 2004 Budget:

- The income of approved SPVs will be exempt until December 31, 2008.
- Provisions have been made to facilitate claim of GST by the SPVs.
- Stamp duty exemption has been granted on transfer of assets to SPVs.

To avail these benefits, there are several preconditions to be satisfied by the SPV.

Mortgage-backed securities

Singapore has witnessed a boom in the real estate market and mortgage loan market due to recent liberalization in the rulings relating to investment by employee benefit funds and other regulated financial intermediaries. This has led to the growth in the number of commercial mortgage-backed securitization (CMBS) deals. It has been accepted that there is a need as well as an opportunity to convert real estate assets with low liquidity into financial assets with high liquidity. The growth of CMBS in Singapore is intimately associated with the growth in REIT activity; REITs take the CMBS route to leveraging their property holdings.

Hong Kong

General overview

The journey of securitization in Hong Kong began in 1994 with the residential mortgage securitization for Bank of America. Gradually, the market observed residential mortgage deals of Citibank, Cheung Kong, Standard Chartered Bank and a credit card transaction for Chase. During the heydays of the Asian boom, Hong Kong led economic activity in the region. Obviously, Hong Kong remained at the center of securitization activity in Asia and a Fitch IBCA document estimated that in 1999, Hong Kong contributed approximately 60% of all securitization volume in Asia.

Securitization volumes of Hong Kong are not proportionate to its jurisdiction's position as a major economic center of Asia. Hong Kong banks are flush with funds and there is little motivation for them to tap the securitization market for capital relief purposes. However, some remarkable deals originate from Hong Kong. The most famous of these is the US$6 billion securitization of revenue from tolled tunnels and bridges by the Hong Kong government.[45]

Legal aspects

Currently, the permission of the HKMA is a precondition before securitization by banks, intending regulatory capital relief, is allowed. The legal system is based in general terms on English Law (with familiar concepts like equitable/legal assignment) making it quite straightforward to structure "true sale" transactions from a legal, regulatory and accounting perspective. The legal framework, in particular bankruptcy law, is well developed, with a mixture of legislation and case law. Most securitization transactions in Hong Kong follow the "equitable assignment" route, without giving a notice to the obligors. Registration of equitable assignments is not insisted upon. However, transfer of mortgages would require registration with the Land Registry offices. The regulatory environment is sophisticated, with a set of guidelines for regulatory off-balance sheet treatment for regulated institutions. These guidelines, issued by the Hong Kong Monetary Authority in 1995, revised in 1997, largely follow the Bank of England model. These guidelines put in certain conditions subject to which a securitization can give capital relief to the originator bank. Some of the prominent conditions are (a) transfer of the receivables to an unrelated party; (b) no right or obligation to buyback; (c) no recourse. The provision of credit enhancement by buying subordinated debt of the SPV would be directly deducted from the capital of the bank being a direct credit substitute. The Companies Ordinance and the Securities Ordinance also provide some requirements for securitization.

In 2003 the legislature amended the Companies Act, which has further encouraged the growth of securitization transactions.

Accounting aspects

Presently, Hong Kong has no set accounting guidelines for securitization. The Hong Kong Society of Accountants (HKSA) is ready to announce SSAP 39, based on IAS 39; SSAP 32 was renamed HKAS 27 in 2004. The Hong Kong Accounting standard laid down a very restricted definition of the word "subsidiary" for consolidation of accounts. According to the earlier definition, only corporate entities were considered as "subsidiaries". The accounting standard was amended with effect from December 1, 2005, under which a new category of entities called "subsidiary undertakings" was introduced under the definition of "subsidiaries." The word "undertaking" has been defined to include a body corporate, partnership or an un-incorporated carrying trade or business with or without a profit motive. Further, the Act provides that whether or not an entity is a subsidiary of another would depend on whether the parent entity has the "right to exercise dominant influence" over the other entity. "Right to exercise dominant influence" has been defined as the right to give directions regarding the operating and financial policy of an entity.[46] There are concerns as to whether an SPV's accounts would be consolidated with its sponsor after the implementation of these guidelines.[47] This requirement is similar to SIC 12 of the IASB, discussed in the chapter on Accounting Issues, and must be considered while planning an appropriate SPV structure.

Taxation aspects

Unlike virtually every other Asian country, Hong Kong has no withholding tax on interest payments to a non-resident, making the securitization off-shore of interest-bearing receivables much simpler. Further, there is also no VAT and no capital gains tax in Hong Kong. Stamp duties, generally a major irritant for securitization transactions, are levied on the transfer of land, but excluding mortgages. This trend is observed from the adjudications of Collector of Stamp Revenue. However, transfer of mortgages would be treated as transfer of interests in land, and would certainly attract stamp duty. Typical of Hong Kong's Income-Tax Law (Inland Revenue Ordinance), obligors whose payables have been securitized may not be able to claim a deduction for the interest paid by them unless the interest qualifies under section 16(2)(f) of the Inland Revenue Ordinance. One of the alternative conditions in the Ordinance is that the recipient of such interest should be liable to tax in Hong Kong. Thus, the SPV, even if it is incorporated in an off-shore location, would have to come forth for taxation in Hong Kong under Section 20A of Income-Tax Law (Inland Revenue Ordinance.) This leads to a necessary double taxation on the residuary income of the originator, as the SPV taxed in Hong Kong can only claim a deduction for the interest being paid by it. Apart from the provisions of the Inland Revenue Ordinance, other features of taxation are definitely securitization-friendly.

Mortgage-backed securities

One of the important developments in mortgage securitization in Hong Kong was the establishment of the Hong Kong Mortgage Corporation (HKMC) in March 1997. Earlier, the property market was suffering from falling prices and rents, which was not at all conducive. But gradually the situation has turned in favor of securitization. MBIA Assurance emerged as the first guarantor to wrap a Hong Kong MBS, when Société Générale brought a HK$800-million transaction repackaging mortgages granted by Hong Kong Telecom to its employees.

Most deals in Hong Kong are executed in U.S. dollars, which indicates that Hong Kong's home currency is yet to gain the required momentum. In December 2003, there was redemption through a call option for the deal launched by SPV Hong Kong Funding No.1 Ltd., which offered a $234 million, senior-tranche rated AAA by Moody's. The return to China of Hong Kong seems to have made little difference, as a large number of residential mortgage transactions were documented, some of which closed prior to the currency issues.

Thailand[48]

General overview

In Thailand, securitization really came alive in the autumn of 1996, partly with the closing in August of the Thai Cars auto receivables securitization for TISCO. Entities regulated by the Bank of Thailand were previously prevented from securitizing their assets (there was an absence of regulatory off-balance sheet guidelines) and initial transactions in 1996, including Thai Cars, were carried out by unregulated companies. Few securitization projects had begun in Thailand during 1996. Attempts were made on other transactions to try to develop "true sale" structures that did not have the VAT problem, but these met with little success. This may have limited the appeal of securitization in Thailand, as the Thai SPV was only a secured creditor of the originator and the structure did not provide the originator with off-balance sheet treatment. In addition, because it involved the originator in the creation of security, it was more likely to have negative covenant problems for the originator than a "true sale" deal. The Thai government has passed a new Securitization Law that certainly promotes the concept, but the VAT issue still remains and for certain assets and cross-border deals still so does a withholding tax problem. Unfortunately, the economic and currency crisis halted work on most transactions (consisting primarily of auto receivables and other consumer receivables) and to date the implications of the new law have not yet been fully explored. Legal aspects have since improved in favor of securitization, but the economic crisis in Thailand and the rest of Asia, did not allow securitization to prosper in full bloom.

The Thai securitization market is in revival mode and a number of important deals have taken place in recent years. Notable among these are the deals by the National Housing Authority and Aeon Thana Sinsap (Thailand) Public Company Limited. Further, Citibank recently carried its first credit card securitization. The Thai regulators permitted commercial banks to invest in CDOs and enter into credit default swaps, provided certain restrictions were observed. This will go a long way in developing the securitization market. However, tight foreign exchange regulations and a relatively small domestic credit volume are major impediments in the growth of the market and it is highly unlikely that Thailand would emerge as a major player in the Asian securitization market unless addressed.[49]

Legal aspects

Thailand has a civil law legal system, a codified system of law based on the reforms of King Chulalongkorn. The major Codes of Thailand are The Civil and Commercial Code, the Penal Code, the Civil Procedure Code, the Criminal Procedure Code, the Revenue Code and the Land Code. The Constitution is the supreme law of the land. The important feature to note is that there is separate Bankruptcy Court in Thailand. The Civil and Commercial Code and Securities and Exchange Commission Act (SECA) were the basic laws governing securitization transactions in Thailand until the emergence of The Emergency Decree on Special Purpose Juristic Person for Securitization (ED).

ED is more convenient and the reasons are evident. Section 306 of the Thai Civil and Commercial Code normally requires that either the assignor or assignee or both notify the obligor (debtor) when an assignment of his/her debt has been made, but under Section 15 of the Emergency Decree, this is not required. Even if the servicer changes in certain circumstances, for example due to merger/acquisition, there is no requirement for the SPV to notify each debtor of the transfer of claim. Section 17 of the ED provides exemptions to the originators and SPVs from paying the transfer fee.

In the securitization context, section 18 of the Emergency Decree on Special Purpose Vehicles for Securitization states: "In transferring assets pursuant to the authorized project in which the legal interest rate charged is over 15% per annum, the provisions under Section 654 of the Civil and Commercial Code shall not apply and the SPV is entitled to charge the interest on the assets at the rate of not more than the previous rate applicable and with the same interest calculation method." Thus, to the extent the originator has been legally entitled to charge interest beyond 15% per annum from the debtor (commercial banks and other financial institutions), when the securitization deal is in place, the SPV, although not a financial institution, is also entitled to charge the same rate of interest as that previously charged by the originator.

Section 9 of ED allows the establishment of an SPV in the form of either a limited company, a public limited company, a mutual fund or another juristic person as stipulated by the Security Exchange Commission (SEC). The SEC office currently has no policy to allow SPVs in the form of mutual funds, although it is expressly permitted by the legislation. Also, as an SPV is a legal entity set up temporarily to conduct the securitization process, it needs to be easy to set up and break down. For this reason, a public limited company is not viable as an SPV. Practically speaking, an SPV needs to take the form of a private limited company, established in accordance with the rules of the Thai Civil and Commercial Code. Sections 1096 to 1246 of the Civil and Commercial Code govern private limited companies in Thailand.

Another Emergency Decree on Corporation for the Secondary Market for Housing Loans, which intends to establish a governmental organisation (the "Corporation for the Secondary Market for Housing Loans") with the task of developing the secondary market for housing loans, also exists in Thailand, details are included under MBS in this part.

When a business is prepared to seek financing by way of securitization, Section 10 of the Emergency Decree says that only commercial banks, finance companies, credit financiers, securities companies, and any other juristic persons prescribed by the SEC can apply for securitization financing project approval. Nevertheless, the SEC has already announced that juristic persons set up under special laws, private limited companies or public limited companies are also able to apply for securitization under the Emergency Decree. The entity applying must fill out a securitization application form (No. 35-2-4) and attach various documents and submit the package to the SEC. The official name for Form 35-2-4 is "Application Form for the Securitization Project and the Application for the Permission to offer Newly Issued Debentures for Sale under the Securitization Project (for sale under the private placement basis or for sale to overseas investors)." Once the SEC has received the application form along with the relevant documents and evidence, it is required to notify the applicant within five working days as to whether or not the details given and documents filled out are correct and complete. If additional or corrected information is required, and this information is supplied, then the SEC must notify within three working days as to whether or not the new information is sufficient.

The SEC Office notifies the applicant within ten working days of receiving an adequate application whether or not the application is approved. If the project proposal is approved, the SEC office will issue an indication naming the juristic person stipulated to be authorized to issue new debentures for sale.

This juristic person will be registered as the SPV. If the application is in regard to offering the newly issued debentures on a private placement basis, the SEC office shall also issue evidence of registration of the restrictions on debenture transfer. Section 237-240 of the Civil and Commercial Code regulates "cancellation of fraudulent acts." A creditor is entitled to claim the cancellation by the court of any juristic act done by the debtor with knowledge that it would prejudice the creditor. This rule does not apply if (i) the person enriched by the act did not know at the time of the relevant facts that would make the act prejudicial to the creditor; and (ii) such act is not a gratuitous act. A third party acquiring a proprietary right in good faith is similarly exempt from cancellation under this section. Any cancellation ordered will work in favor of all creditors, and a claim must be brought within one year of the creditor's knowledge or within ten years of the occurrence of the event.

These provisions provide another means of protection for the investor (creditor) in the securitization scheme. If the asset behind the security is involved in an improper transaction, the investor may be able to claim cancellation and have the court so order. The Unfair Contract Terms Act applies in numerous circumstances, such as when a standard form contract has been used and there exists an ambiguous term; the contract is to be interpreted in favor of the party that did not draft the contract (interpretation *contra proferentum*). To determine what is fair in a contract, Section 10 of the Unfair Contract Terms Act says that consideration should be given to all the circumstances, including good faith, bargaining power, economic status, knowledge and understanding, foreseeability and past practice. In securitization context, this new legislation could have an impact. For example, if an obligor enters into a standard form agreement on the hire-purchase of an automobile with a bank, and a term of the agreement is later determined to be unfair, there could be repercussions for the investor who invested in this debt agreement as an asset. In practice, the Unfair Contract Terms Act simply means the contracts behind the securitization project in question will have to be scrutinized more closely.

Taxation aspects

The Thai Revenue Code outlines regulations for taxes to be imposed on income. Typically, incorporated firms ("juristic companies or registered partnerships") in Thailand pay income tax at a rate of 30% of net profits. A "juristic company or registered partnership" is a limited company, limited partnership, or registered ordinary partnership organized under Thai law or foreign law. This includes joint ventures and any profit seeking ventures undertaken by a foreign government. Foreign companies not registered or not residing in Thailand are subject to tax only on income from sources within Thailand. A juristic company or registered partnership organized under a foreign law whose employee, representative, correspondent or intermediary is carrying on business, and thereby deriving income or gains in Thailand, shall be deemed to be carrying on business in Thailand.

Parties in the securitization transaction need to factor in corporate income tax considerations to the securitization equation. Regular business expenses and depreciation allowances, at varying rates, can be deducted from the gross income. Taxes are due on a semi-annual basis within 150 days of the close of a six-month accounting period. Thai law prescribes a withholding tax of 15% for interest on a loan made to an offshore entity by a Thai entity.

The VAT is payable by suppliers and importers on the provision of goods and services of all kinds and services at all stages, as well as importation of goods. The standard rate is 7%. The definition of "goods" is sufficiently broad to include intangibles having value. Thus, the tax applies to the transfer of receivables in securitization transactions. The new securitization law allows for an exemption from payment of the VAT for transactions that fall under the definition of "securitization." If a particular transaction does not fall under the definition, it essentially renders the project impracticable because the VAT paid at the beginning of a transaction is not recoverable and eliminates profit margins.

To avoid the VAT problems in the past, securitization projects in Thailand were often structured in the form of loans.

Securitization transactions also attract Stamp Duty.

The Specific Business Tax (SBT) applies to various business revenues generated by those parties affected by the tax. For any business activity in the nature of banking, the tax rate is 3.3%. Securitization transactions also fall under SBT taxation. SBT is applied to the profit generated by the transfer of receivables – the difference between the discounting rate at which the assets are sold and the actual rate of return on the asset portfolio. Fees related to a securitization transaction have also to be taken into consideration. These include a registration fee of 2% for the transfer of an immovable property under the Land Code, and a fee associated with the machinery registration law. To promote securitization, the Thai government has passed Royal Decrees exempting securitization transactions such as The Royal Decree Under the Revenue Code on Exemption from the Value Added Tax (No. 333) B.E. 2541, The Royal Decree Under the Revenue Code on the Stipulation of Businesses to be Exempt from the Value Added Tax (No. 334) B.E. 2541, and The Royal Decree Under the Revenue Code on the Exemption of Revenue (No. 335) B.E. 2541. These decrees have to be implemented according to the rules, procedures and conditions of the director-general of the Revenue Department.

Mortgage-backed securities

In Thailand, there appears to be a primary mortgage market of sufficient size to make mortgage securitization feasible. The Government Housing Bank, Bangkok Bank and Thai Farmers Bank hold the majority of these mortgage assets. In the future, there exists potential to develop the secondary mortgage (securitization) aspect of this market. Issuing MBS could free up scarce capital resources for the originators (banks/financial institutions) to use in other projects. Unfortunately, at the present time, there are barriers to mortgage securitization in Thailand. The market is liquid, which means that many lenders would prefer not to sell their mortgage holdings. Mortgage loans currently attract a 50% risk weight, thus savings of capital are minimal. Conditions probably need to become more favorable before mortgage securitization can take off in Thailand. The *Bangkok Post* has reported cases of the Secondary Mortgage Corporation (SMC) picking up housing loans from commercial banks, securitizing them, and offering them, backed by a government guarantee, to the public. Thailand also has an Emergency Decree on Corporation for the Secondary Market for Housing Loans to establish a governmental organisation (the "Corporation for the Secondary Market for Housing Loans") with the task of developing that market. This is to be achieved through the transfer of assets in the form of "housing loans" (normally mortgaged loans) from financial institutions and real estate businesses to the "Corporation," and the securitization of these assets. The Emergency Decree on Corporation for the Secondary Market for Housing Loans represents another Thai government initiative aimed at making securitization transactions more feasible in Thailand.

Indonesia

General overview

The first securitization transaction in Indonesia was in August 1996 by PT Astra Sedaya Finance, which involved an unregulated finance company's auto loan receivables. The $200 million transaction via Automobile Securitized Finance, was wrapped up by the FSA and lead managed by BZW. Indonesia has both regulated and unregulated companies, although there are as yet no regulatory or accounting off-balance sheet guidelines. Like Thailand's SEC, Bapepam is keen to develop a domestic ABS market, both to facilitate off-balance sheet borrowing and to provide prime debt securities for insurance companies as well as money and pension funds to invest in. A supply of home grown ABS would lessen the pressure for institutions to commit themselves too heavily to the volatile property and equity markets.

There were two more transactions involving auto receivables in 1996 and 1997, as well as some credit card securitizations. As the market was poised for substantial growth, the Asian currency crisis of 1997 crashed all potential deals. There has been a lull in activity since, except for further attempts to promote securitization which is summarized below.

Recent developments

Indonesia is moving ahead with a plan to encourage securitization, particularly in the local market. *BAPEPAM*, the capital markets regulator, has already come out with a set of proposals for the regulation of on-shore securitization including a mechanism for establishing on-shore SPV's using some form of mutual fund. Currently, the volume of work is not substantial. The APEC Finance and Central Bank Deputies Meeting in September 2002 also resolved to promote securitization in Indonesia. Citibank privately placed $140 million of 10-year notes, backed by Bank International Indonesia's future Visa and MasterCard receivables in July 2002.

Legal aspects[50]

In general, the Indonesian legal environment, with a Roman-Dutch system, is friendly towards securitization. Receivables can be assigned in such a way that they would not be treated as part of the seller's estate if it becomes bankrupt. Indonesia's Bankruptcy Law (No. 4 of 1998) amends the 1906 Bankruptcy Law. Being a civil law jurisdiction, an assignment of a receivable under Indonesian law will be treated as a bilateral contract between the assignor and the assignee and will be binding upon the obligor only when a written notification has been done to the obligor or the obligor has given consent to the assignment. The formal method of notification permitted under law is reflective of the archaic Roman system; the notice will be delivered by the offices of the Court. This is impractical in most cases, so the assignee mostly keeps the assignment technically incomplete by not giving a notice of assignment up front, but reserving the right to give notice, in his own capacity or as holder of a power of attorney of the assignor at a later date, if the trigger events of default arise.

Indonesia also has some difficulty in defining the legal structure of the SPV. Trusts are not recognized in Indonesian law; some of the securitization SPVs have been incorporated as "multifinance companies," which means finance companies engaging in several financial services. One company considered a pioneer in securitization is ABS Finance Indonesia, mentioned later in this section.

Indonesia does not have the equitable/legal assignment distinction as such, but the consequences under Indonesian law of not giving notice of an assignment are essentially the same as under English law. Giving notice, however, is a more formal and complicated procedure in Indonesia than in some other jurisdictions. Indonesia also does not have the benefit of the common law concept of a trust.

There is no licensing requirement for an SPV to acquire receivables from an Indonesian company and most Indonesian lawyers are comfortable that the sale of receivables to an offshore SPV does not constitute a borrowing that requires government permission. This may still be an issue if any of the underlying obligors is an Indonesian company as opposed to an individual.

Taxation aspects

Two tax issues continue to prove problematic. There is no VAT on the sale price of the receivables. However, as in Thailand, a VAT of 10% is imposed on fees, including any servicing fee, and thus in most deals the excess spread in the transaction is paid to the originator as a deferred purchase price. A more difficult structuring challenge involves the issue of the withholding tax on interest payments off shore. One may avail exemption from this requirement by creating a taxable SPV in Indonesia and thereafter selling the interest as a separate strip to such exempt entity. But there is no official view of the tax authorities in this regard. There are currently no double tax treaties that could come to the rescue (the best was The Netherlands, which would bring the rate down to 10%) and because a "true sale" structure was being used, the introduction of yen as in the Thai Cars deal was not appropriate. The solution in most of the transactions was for the SPV, contemporaneously with the purchase of the receivables, to sell the future interest component to an Indonesian bank, which paid for the interest stream as and when it was collected.

Approximately 2.8% of Asian securitization volume originates from Indonesia.[51]

South Korea

General overview

South Korea flagged off securitization transactions with an SPC legislation towards September 1998. Thereafter, the Korean market developed briskly and is regarded by many as the largest securitization market in ex-Japan Asia. The setting up of KAMCO & KOMOCO, the enactment of ABS Act and the MBS Act have all made the atmosphere favorable. By the end of December 2002, KoMoCo had issued mortgage-backed securities amounting to W2.5 trillion. The various MBS issued by KoMoCo account for 80.5% of the market. The private-level MBS issued by SPCs, which were established by three non-bank mortgage lenders, accounted for 19.5%. In addition to mortgage-backed securities, Korean banks are also active in securitization of credit card receivables, which has been driven by growth in consumer lending. Auto loans securitization is a similar example.

The enactment of ABS Act and the MBS Act have made things easier.

For the mortgage market, Korea Mortgage Corporation (KoMoCo) was established in 1999. By the end of 2002, KoMoCo had issued mortgage-backed securities amounting to W2.5 trillion. The various MBS issued by KoMoCo account for 80.5% of the market share. KoMoCo has gained immense public confidence because the Korean government is its largest shareholder. The private-level MBS issued by SPCs, which were established by three non-bank mortgage lenders, accounted for 19.5%. This makes it clear that MBS issuance varies according to public confidence in an issuing company and also according to the quality of underlying assets. In contrast to commercial banks, non-banks have relatively strong incentive for securitization, because selling mortgage loans on origination can reduce or avoid funding burdens. The structure of the primary mortgage market has changed dramatically.

Prior to 1997, the primary mortgage market was clearly divided into the public and private sectors due to the difference in mortgage rates. However, the difference between these two sectors has continuously narrowed due to a different speed and range of rate adjustment. Further, Keun mortgage is also very popular in Korea. It serves a predetermined amount as collateral for several uncompleted obligations that will be created and extinguished in the course of continuous transactions, and whose remaining balance will be fixed at the settlement date of accounts. The MBS market is still very small in comparison to the ABS market due to low demand for mortgage securitization of banks and an insufficient legal and regulatory framework.

Korea accounts for almost 25% of all issuances from the continent. Of particular interest is the Korean NPL securitization market, which has been followed as a model in a number of countries.

Legal aspects

In September 1998, Korea passed the Asset-Backed Securitization Act (ABS Act) to promote the restructuring of firms and financial companies. According to this law, a Special Purpose Vehicle (SPV) could issue ABS based on assets transferred from the originator. It also provided a basic framework for securitization of mortgages. To provide a further boost to the ABS market, the Ministry of Finance and Economy (MoFE) revised the current ABS law in 1999. In April 1999, the Mortgage-Backed Securitization Act (also known as the MBS Company Act) was passed. to allow eligible companies to develop and sell mortgage-backed certificates, mortgage bonds and REIT (real estate investment trust) instruments; this facilitated the functioning of a domestic housing finance system in line with advanced countries. The MBS Act allowed the securitization of mortgage loans by a reliable permanent entity, rather than by an SPV with a limited life.

The notable features of the MBS Act are:[52]

1. Formation of an MBS Company requires authorization from the Financial Supervisory Commission (FSC). The FSC grants the consent, if the prescribed conditions are fulfilled and not otherwise. One such condition stipulates a minimum of W25 billion in equity capital and an 8% or higher level BIS capital adequacy ratio.
2. The plan of mortgage securitization has to be registered with the FSC to securitize mortgage loans.
3. An MBS Company is not allowed to run a mortgage portfolio investment business.
4. The MBS has to be issued by a trust and the MBS Company must be a trustee of such a trust.
5. The requirements of "True Sale" are clearly prescribed.
6. Special exceptions to the Civil Law regarding countermeasures against the transfer of credit and acquisition of mortgages have been provided.
7. An MBS Company is permitted to guarantee the payment of principal and interest of the MBS to a maximum of 30 times of its equity capital.
8. The MBS is also permitted to issue corporate bonds to a limit of 10 times of its equity capital and may borrow within the limit of its equity capital.

As mentioned, a mortgage-securitization body by the name of Korea Mortgage Corp. (KoMoCo) was set up as a joint venture with International Financial Corporation (IFC) and some domestic banks. The transfer of receivables by a Korean resident to a non-resident (such as the Cayman Islands) requires the consent of the Ministry of Finance and Economy (MOFE). However, during 1997 it became clear that MOFE was prepared to look more favorably on such transactions. During the second half of 1997, a number of transactions were worked on involving Korean merchant banks as sellers of equipment lease receivables (all U.S.dollar-denominated) owed by Korean corporations. The notice mechanics were relatively formal, requiring notarization with a fixed-date stamp. This may not be a problem when there are only a few obligors, but could give rise to difficulties if the pool contains a large number of obligors. In addition, in assigning the receivables it was necessary to also transfer title to some of the equipment, which in some cases such as, ships is logistically difficult and raises legal liability issues for the SPV. A positive feature of Korean law as observed in the MBS Act is that it recognizes trusts, which could be helpful in avoiding commingling risk, an issue grappled with in every jurisdiction.

The People's Republic of China

General overview

In the last edition of this book, we had stated: "No review of securitization in Asia would be complete without a discussion of the PRC." We are forced to change the sentence as in the past couple of years as China has emerged as one of the most important nations of the world. Hence, we say: "No review of securitization in the WORLD would be complete without a discussion of the PRC." The size of the country and its economy make it an obvious candidate for securitization.

In April 1997, China pioneered its first asset-backed securitization. China Ocean Shipping Company (COSCO), a shipping company owned by the Chinese government, completed an asset-backed securitization transaction that securitized COSCO's future shipping revenues derived from the U.S. and European operations[2]. By December 1997, COSCO announced plans for a second securitization for US$500 million in future shipping revenues. The progressive completion of the COSCO transaction sparked interest in raising more capital with domestic Chinese asset-backed securitization transactions, despite China's lack of a comprehensive legal system.

As a major emerging economy, China promises to be a good market for all types of asset classes. However, there is particular interest in the NPL securitization market of China, estimated to be around US$73.1 billion.[53] The four major banks of China are seriously considering securitization.[54] Moreover, the government has come up with a set of guidelines called the "administrative guidelines" which are very encouraging to securitization (see below for details). Hence, it seems that very soon China will emerge as a major securitization market. However, certain bottlenecks such as the near absence of a bond market continue to act as a roadblock.[55]

Recent developments

In recent times, there have been some remarkable deals from China and several "firsts" were registered. China Unicom's parent company inaugurated the latter market in September through the sale of 3.2 billion Yuan (HK$3.06 billion) of securities supported by mobile phone revenues. Newly-listed China Construction Bank, the nation's top property lender, has been earmarked to kick off the mortgage-backed market. Reports indicate that Construction Bank plans to sell more than US$371 million (HK$2.89 billion) of mortgage-backed securities. Further, there are also plans for an asset-backed issue by China Development Bank, a policy lender specializing in infrastructure financing, which has said it intends to issue securities worth 5.287 billion Yuan based on 62 loans it has made to 12 industries. Moreover, this, by all indications, is just the tip of the iceberg. From a press release of the People's Bank of China, dated December 22 2005, it seems two pilot projects had been approved during the year 2005. In 2006, the Chinese market appears well positioned to see several CDOs and some RMBS transactions, besides future flows deals, locally referred to as "enterprise receivables" deals.

Legal aspects

The 1995 Security Law, the 1997 Highway Law, the 1997 Project Finance Procedures, and the 1998 Foreign Security Implementing Rules provided a framework to structure a Chinese asset-backed securitization. Chinese laws and regulations have started addressing issues such as security interest creation, perfection by registration, priority rights by registration, designation of which entities may act as the Security Provider or issuer, and the adaptation of ad hoc trust laws by state banks to serve as special purpose vehicles. On January 1, 1998, SAFE issued the International Commercial Loans Procedures explaining and clarifying various issues relating to asset securitization.

Asset-backed securitization must have a legal structure capable of creating a security interest. Originally, China attempted to adapt its Civil Law to the needs of creating a security interest. The Civil Law serves as China's national gap-filling code and permits freedom of contract within its stipulated limitations. Article 89 of the Civil Law explicitly recognizes security interests and permits a debtor or a third party on the debtor's behalf to pledge certain types of assets as guarantees. In addition to recognizing security interests, section 2 of the Civil Law also offers rudimentary recognition of creditor's rights and the legal concept of priority in the case of insolvency. Although recognizing security interests and priority rights, the Civil Law remained silent regarding the application of security interest holder's priority rights in a dispute involving multiple security interest holders.

In 1995, the Standing Committee of the National People's Congress passed the National Security Law (NSL), which consolidated the treatment of security interests in China. The NSL law recognizes only five types of security interests – guarantee, mortgage, pledge, lien and deposit. As PRC bankruptcy laws are still underdeveloped, it acts as another legal hurdle in the process of securitization. The development of local market in China for asset-backed securities can be ensured by using an on-shore bankruptcy remote SPV. To achieve bankruptcy remoteness, SPV must be structured so that it is owned by a trust. It must also have independent directors and have restricted business activities. It seems difficult because the laws governing the establishment of limited-liability companies and partnerships are underdeveloped and furthermore because there is no concept of trusts.

One of the perceived major legal obstacles to achieving a "true sale" of receivables is the requirement that obligors give consent to the transfer of any receivables owed by them; however, it was recently clarified that all that was required was notification and not consent.

Securitization guidelines of the People's Bank of China

After several years of waiting, the Chinese central bank, the People's Bank of China, took the initiative to draft what is called the guidelines for Pilot Projects on securitization. These guidelines were promulgated in April 2005.[56]

The broad tenor of the guideline is very simple and permissive. It seeks to lay down the regulatory framework in a very easy manner with lots of flexibility. The directions are a complete code alone and lay down almost everything required such as investors rights, reporting by trustees and information documents. The simplicity and pragmatism of the guidelines are very appreciable.

Form of the special purpose entity

It is clear from the guidelines that special purpose vehicles will be formulated as trusts. China had recently adopted a trust law also; the broad concept of a special purpose trust will be similar to what is understood in other jurisdictions.

The law leaves the trust deed to provide for the basic rights of investors, originator and other parties.

The manner of transferring assets to the trust is by "undertaking a trust," the same as the English concept of declaration and acceptance of trust. By virtue of trust declaration, those assets will be demarcated from other assets of the trustor or the trustee. The law provides a clear bankruptcy remoteness – that the assets transferred into such a trust will not be affected by the bankruptcy of the trustee, originator, administrator or other service providers.

Most interestingly, there is also a ring fencing mechanism inherent in Article 7; it provides that claims and liabilities arising on account of one trust shall not be commingled with the claims or liabilities of other trusts. This means, effectively, there may be one trust entity taking care of several securitization transactions.

Article 16 provides that investment and trust companies registered with the CBRC can act as trustees.

Originators

The originators of credit assets for asset-backed securities will be financial institutions. From this, it seems other entities, such as corporates, will not fall under the current guidelines. Under the Chinese context, this may be treated either as a prohibition on securitization by other originators, or simply limitation to the scope of the present guidelines.

A very unclear statement appears in Article 12, saying that the originator will publish in national media the fact of securitization and thereby inform the relevant rights holders. It is not sure whether the Chinese regulators are trying to draw a leaf from Italian Law No 130. In Italy securitization transactions need to be registered with a public registry, which serves as a public notification device. Thereby, the need to notify the obligors is avoided. This purpose, obviously, cannot be met by a national media publication. It cannot be implied that the obligors would be named in the publication in question, and the intent of the clause remains strange.

China Banking Regulatory Commission

The overall supervision of securitization transactions is by the China Banking Regulatory Commission. The guidelines also provide that detailed rules on securitization shall be framed by the Commission

Trading in asset-backed securities

Asset-backed securities will be traded in the National Inter-bank Bond Market. Detailed rules for trading and information requirements have been laid out in Article 32 onwards. A credit rating is mandatory under Article 35.

Loan servicers

Detailed functions and duties of the servicers have also been laid down in the directions. These are mostly what the servicers have to do anyway in real securitization transactions.

However, one of the peculiar requirements comes from Article 24, which provides that the servicer will keep a specialized business department to separately manage securitized assets. That the securitized assets should not be commingled is understandable, but keeping a separate and specialized department is neither logistically required nor desirable, adding unwarranted cost to the transaction.

Taiwan

General overview

Taiwan has been far behind Japan, South Korea and Thailand, and its tax regime has significantly contributed to this backwardness. Apart from this, the lack of a proper legal structure and the availability of an alternative and cheap source of funding from local banks have been potentially discouraging factors. Taiwan is gradually converting itself from a labor-intensive economy to a capital – and technology-intensive economy. With the election of Chen Shui-bian as President in May 2000, there was an establishment of a democratic political system, the end of Kuomintang (KMT) rule, and preparation to join the World Trade Organization (WTO).

One of the notable developments is the passage of a securitization law, modeled on the Japanese pattern. In June 2003, a real estate securitization law was also passed.

Legal aspects

The Financial Asset Securitization Statute was proposed by the Ministry of Finance (MOF) to the Executive Yuan (Cabinet) on September 3, 2001, and it received legislative approval on June 21, 2002. It is based on the Japanese model and focuses on Trust Enterprises Laws. The basic features are as follows:

- Originators include banks, incorporated insurance firms, credit card service providers, securities firms and others approved by the MOF.
- Securitizable assets include housing and vehicle loans as well as credit cards and trade receivables.
- The MOF has been empowered to approve any other type of assets that can be securitized.
- Financial assets to be securitized must be transferred to an SPV which must be in the form of a trust.
- Thereafter, an SPV has to issue beneficiary certificates either to the public or any specific person or a group of persons not exceeding 50.
- Public offering needs the approval of the Securities and Futures Commission (SFC).
- The subscribers are also allowed to elect the supervisors, who are responsible for the management and supervision of financial assets.
- Before going for public offering the beneficiary certificates have to be subjected to Public Rating, as certified by the MOF.
- Beneficiary certificates are classified as securities, but some are also treated as short-term bills by the MOF. For short-term bills the profit on sales is subject to income tax at 25% for corporations and 40% for individuals. It is also not clear whether such beneficiary certificates may be treated overseas.
- As securities, all beneficiary certificates are subject to the Securities Exchange Law.
- Violation of the securitization laws and rules may lead to a punishment of a maximum seven years of imprisonment, apart from fines.

A separate Real Estate Securitization Law was passed in 2003.

Taxation aspects

The structure of the tax regime has greatly discouraged a securitization atmosphere in Taiwan. The crucial elements behind this negative tax regime have been the imposition of income tax, deed tax as well as a business tax on transfer of assets. This may have benefited the revenue but the cost of each deal was highly escalated and so securitization as a bundle of deals in itself could not be an exception. Further securities transaction tax is also applicable to all beneficiary certificates. Hence, the new law provides various concessions as follows:

- Exemption from business tax;
- Exemption from deed taxes, except in the context of transfers of real estate by the SPV;

- Exemption from stamp duty;
- Exemption from mortgage and other re-registration fees;
- Exemption (under current regulations) for securities transaction tax on the sale of securitized products; and
- Deferral of land value increment tax on REO.

The FASL also provides for additional tax benefits to the SPV and its beneficiaries, for instance, pass-through to beneficiaries of taxes on net income of the SPV.

Moody's Taiwan Corporation reports that securities worth over NT$50 billion (Taiwanese dollars) were issued in 2004, from around NT$30 billion in 2003. According to one article,[57] the Industrial Bank of Taiwan carried the first securitization offering in 2003. The Securitization law permits the use of use of REITS. It is reported that The Enforcement Rules of the Financial Assets Securitization Act (promulgated August 28, 2003) has extended the definition of an "asset" under the FASL to include "the future creditor rights that may be claimed against the obligor in monetary payments, set forth in the contract entered into between the originator and the obligor and when the conditions specified in the contract have been met."[58] This will encourage future flows securitizations.

India

Securitization in India is of recent origin but there have been deals that exhibit diversity as well market maturity. There have been two mainstays of the Indian market – RMBS deals and Auto-ABS deals. RMBS is now a standard and stable market with several players coming out with repeat issuance, either through the apex refinancing body, National Housing Bank, or directly. Auto-loans have been securitized since 1990; this is essentially a quasi-securitization market as the resulting paper is not marketable. However, there have been some interesting deals such as securitization of future flows, infrastructural projects and one CMBS deal. In June 2002, Credit Rating and Information Services of India rated the size of the Indian securitization market at over Rs. 172 billion. The new law – the Securitization, Asset Reconstruction & Enforcement of Security Interests Act – has just emerged, although it deals with enforcement of security interests as its focal point.[59] Securitization transactions as practiced in the marketplace are structured to fall outside the law, as the law is perceived more of a bottleneck than a facilitator.

From 2003 through 2005, the Indian market has registered dramatic growth in volumes. The growth has been stimulated by (a) the generally buoyant economy; (b) increasing acceptability of securitization investments among a wide range of investing institutions including banks.

The more important development directly affecting securitization is the special stamp duty regime that most states have formed for securitization. Six major Indian states have imposed a nominal 0.1% tax on assignment of debt for securitization purposes. This has definitely helped the securitization process become much cheaper. But for these changes in stamp duty, most securitization deals would have become economically unviable.

Amidst these encouraging developments, the spoilsport has been the RBI guidelines on securitization, finalized in February 2006. These guidelines do not address the real issues involved in securitization and will discourage securitization transactions by enhancing capital needs and prohibiting recognition of profits on sale.

The Indian securitization market is growing at a phenomenal rate. According to the rating agency ICRA,[60] the structured finance market grew 121% in the year 2005. The total volume of structured finance issues is reported to be around Rs 308 billion. Asset-backed securitization issuance is reported to be Rs 233 billion, accounting for 72% of the structured finance market. The MBS market reported growth of 13%. A noteworthy feature of the market is that the average ABS issue size has grown significantly. Increasing use of time tranching, prepayment protection, and introduction of re-securitizations are manifestations of the increasing maturity of the market.

There is a renewed interest in the Indian NPL market. Recently, the RBI allowed foreign ownership in Asset Reconstruction Companies to a maximum 49% of the equity of the ARC. However, investments by FIIs in ARCs require the prior permission of the Foreign Investment Promotion Board. FIIs "can invest up to 49% of each tranche of scheme of Security Receipts subject to condition that investment of a single FII in each tranche of scheme of SRs shall not exceed 10% of the issue." Encouraged by the positive legislative developments several major international finance companies such as Actis, Standard Chartered and PwC, are actively considering setting up ARCs.

Pakistan[61]

General overview

The October 1999 coup that again led to a military regime in Pakistan has ensured the way for regulatory and enabling legislation. However, the bottlenecks in the administrative machinery serve as an impediment to that development. ABS is not a totally new feature for the economy of Pakistan. On careful analysis, corporate debt issues by leasing companies, secured by way of assignment of specific lease rentals, closely resemble ABS. But they did not constitute a "true sale" by way of an SPV, and neither were they removed from the issuer's balance sheet. For these reasons the assignment of lease receivables cannot be considered an ABS in the real sense.

Securitization is slowly unfolding in Pakistan. Income tax laws and Islamic Laws are important hindrances, apart from the bottlenecks in the administrative machinery as mentioned above. The legal framework is certainly insufficient, still there remains hope that with the growth of stability in governance, as well as law and order, even securitization will grow to full bloom in Pakistan.

Recent developments

Until 1999 only two major ABS transactions were observed. Thereafter, the State Bank of Pakistan (SBP) amended the necessary guidelines for banks and DFIs. The revised guidelines permit total exposure of a bank/DFI to securities issued by an SPV to the least of the following:

(a) 5% of its own paid-up capital

(b) 15% of the total value of the ABS issued by the SPV.

The aggregate exposure to ABS cannot exceed 20% of the total paid-up capital of the bank/DFI. In June 2002, the specialized Companies Division of the SECP permitted the registration of the First Securitization Trust as the first special purpose vehicle under the Companies (Asset-backed Securitization) Rules, 1999 to raise funds for the Pakistan Industrial Leasing Corporation Ltd (PILCORP), up to 100 million rupees through issuance of debt instruments against the securitization of PILCORP's lease receivables.

In 2002-03, at least two future flow deals surfaced in Pakistan.

Legal aspects

The Companies (Asset-backed Securitization) Rules, 1999 was enforced by Statutory Regulatory Order 1338(I)/99. Though the Rules are short, containing only eleven sections, it is certainly a step in the right direction. The important provisions of the Rules are as follows:

1. Government-owned entities, Public Limited Company (SPC) or a Trust, (SPT) may register with the Securities & Exchange Commission of Pakistan (SECP) as an SPV.

2. Earlier SPCs had to function under Corporate Law Authority (CLA) formed as per the Companies Ordinance 1984. The SECP (created by the Securities and Exchange Commission of Pakistan Ordinance, 1997) has now replaced the CLA. It is the principal regulator of Equity and Investment in Pakistan.

3. The Ordinance governing SPCs contains provisions relating to Winding up and Insolvency, Schemes for Amalgamation and Disclosure. In certain situations the Ordinance also applies to SPTs .

4. Every SPC must have a minimum paid up capital.

5. An application for registration as an SPV is not entertained if its directors, officers or employees have been adjudged as insolvent, have suspended payment, compounded with creditors, have been convicted of fraud or breach of trust or of an offence involving moral turpitude.

6. SECP is empowered to bar an entity where the promoters, directors and trustees of such persons are, in its opinion, not persons of means and integrity and do not have special knowledge and experience of matters to be dealt with by an SPV.

7. Upon the receipt of the application a fact-finding inquiry is ordered.

8. Information relating to the Originator, Obligator, Trustee and other related parties in the transaction along with the details of the securitization transaction, are required upon application.

9. Various periodical reportings have to be made by the SPV to the SECP.

10. The SECP is also empowered to cancel the registration if the SPV fails to make a public offering of securities within the time and manner as prescribed in granting the certificate of registration.

11. If the SECP is satisfied that it would be in the public interest so to do, it may on its own motion, or on the application of the investors holding not

less than 10% of the securities issued by such SPV, by order in writing, cancel the registration. However, the SPV has the right of hearing before any such order is passed.

12. The originator and the SPV should not be "connected persons." Connected persons are defined as any person or company beneficially owning, directly or indirectly, 10% or more of the share capital of that SPV or able to exercise directly, or indirectly, 10% or more of the voting rights in that company.

13. The Pakistan Code of Good Corporate Governance, notified by the SECP is mandatory for SPCs.

14. Further, the Islamic principles of finance and investments should also be followed.

15. Advertisements, prospectuses and other invitations to the public to invest in a scheme, including public announcements, have to be submitted to the SECP for approval prior to their issue. The approval may be varied or withdrawn but not before a hearing. SPVs may at all times take legal recourse against the orders of the SECP.

16. Various prohibitions have also been prescribed for an SPV:

     i. Merging with, acquiring or taking over any other company or business, without prior approval of the Commission in writing to such scheme;

     ii. Pledging any of the assets held or beneficially owned by it except for the benefit of the investors;

     iii. Making a loan or advancing money to any person except in connection with its normal business;

     iv. Participating in a joint account with others in any transaction;

     v. Applying any part of its assets to real estate except property for its own use;

     vi. Making any investment with the purpose of having the effect of vesting the management, or control, in the Special Purpose Vehicle; and

     vii. Giving guarantees, indemnities or securities for any liability of a third party.

Taxation aspects

Since the passing of Finance Ordinance 2000, the income of an SPV is exempted from tax. They are also entitled to preferential withholding treatment. Stamp duties are applicable to the transfer of assets. Hence, a securitization transaction becomes a subject matter of stamp duty as well.

According to one thesis paper,[62] there have been a number of securitization deals by Pakistani companies. However, the political environment of the country has not improved, despite an "election" that led to the formation of a "civilian government." In the given circumstances, it is very unlikely that Pakistan would emerge as a major securitization market in the near future. However, the prospect of the use of Islamic financing techniques is bright.

The Pacific

Australia[63]

General overview

Australia has one of the most active securitization markets in the world. Over the years, investor interest in Australian issuances has increased dramatically and a significant portion of investors are from non-Australian jurisdictions. The Australian Securitization Forum points out that the level of interest in Australian issuances can be appreciated from the fact that most of the offers are oversubscribed. Australia is also the third largest RMBS market. Australian issuance in 2004 was around A\$64 million, a record. Although the level of issuance was slower in the first half of 2005, the Australian Securitization Forum expects volume to match the 2004 level.

The important contributing reasons for this growth are financial deregulation and the decline in the issue of Australian Government debt securities in the early part of the 1990s.

The first Australian securitization issue was completed by the Central Mortgage Registry in 1977. In 1984 the state governments of Victoria and New South Wales became interested in tapping into the capital market to fund their low cost housing schemes. The market reached new heights when National Mortgage Corporation (NMMC) was formed in 1984 and its first issue came out in 1985. At the same time in NSW, the First Australian National Mortgage Acceptance Corporation (FANMAC) was formed. FANMAC issued its first Mortgage-backed Security (MBS) in 1986. It is believed that the real secondary mortgage market commenced with the first NMMC issue, as issues prior to this had been backed by a single mortgage and were often sold to foreign investors. The recent trends, along with a great history, lead to the conclusion that Australia can work out new heights of securitization in the days to come.

Recent developments

Substantial legal/regulatory changes have taken place in recent times in Australia that have impacted securitization, while Australia does not have specific laws, like Italian Law.

In 2002, the Australian Securitization Forum (ASF) emerged as an incorporated association with an object to promote the development of securitization in Australia through the education of government, regulatory and other authorities, the public, investors, and others with an interest or potential interest, both in Australia and overseas.

Recent years have also seen Australia export its securitization expertise, with a number of prominent, domestically-based investment banks arranging and structuring securitization transactions in Asia and New Zealand. Australian securitization vehicles have been active in China, for example. According to one opinion, there are two new developing areas in Australian securitization: (1) Reverse mortgages and (2) SME loans.[64]

Legal aspects

There are no specific laws relating to securitization structures. Most securitization transactions are based on trust formations; therefore, they lean heavily on the trust law. Nominal stamp duty is payable on a declaration of trust for a securitization.

Mortgage-backed market

The Australian MBS market is one of the most efficient in the world, and given the fact that there are no state-sponsored vehicles as in the U.S., the level of sophistication attained by the mortgage securitization market is commendable. All major issuers have established Euro and Global MBS programs and Australia has the reputation of having the second largest MBS market in the world. New South Wales sponsored the growth of the mortgage-backed securities market by eliminating stamp duty on the issue and transfer of qualifying "mortgage-backed securities," and on the underlying transactions required to create such securities. The exemptions also appeared in a slightly different form in the *Duties Act* (see chapter on Legal Issues).

Taxation aspects

The Income Tax Assessment Act 1997 succeeds the Income Tax Assessment Act 1936. An SPC has to follow the tax rules normally applicable to corporations. To claim deductions for prior and/or current year losses and bad debts an SPC has to pass through the continuity of ownership test or continuity of business test. It means the tracing of controlling interests in the corporation through interposed entities and the application of the test is complex if shares are held (directly or indirectly) in a corporation by discretionary or charitable trusts (which generally happens in the case of securitizations). In case of trusts, tax is levied on the trustee if an Australian resident beneficiary is not presently entitled to the net income of the trust for tax purposes or where the trustee is taxed as a company for the purposes of Divisions 6B or 6C of the 1936 Tax Act. In such cases, the tax is levied on the trustee and not on the beneficiaries. In case an SPT incurs losses/bad debts and it desires to claim it as deduction, different tests have to be applied depending upon whether the trust is a fixed trust (where all income and capital of the trust are the subject of fixed entitlements) or a non-fixed trust (all trusts other than fixed trusts). The tests that must be passed by a non-fixed trust are generally more difficult to pass than those applicable to fixed trusts.

According to section 128B of the 1936 Tax Act, a non-resident of Australia who derives interest from a resident has to pay tax on that interest at 10%. This tax has to be withheld by the resident payer of the interest. This means that an Australian securitization vehicle must, unless it falls within an exemption under the Tax Act, deduct interest withholding tax from interest payments to non-resident holders of those securities. The exemptions are contained in section 128F of the Tax Act and Taxation Determinations: TD1999/8-26 (inclusive) and TD2001/3. The tax-sharing agreement would seek to determine tax liabilities of group members so that, say, a securitization trust was not burdened with the tax liabilities of other group members. Where a securitization vehicle is not wholly owned, then consolidation rules cannot be applied.

A Goods and Services Tax (GST) is also applicable for securitization. Stamp duty is also to be paid in respect of the transfer. It must be noted that as per section 282(3) no duty is chargeable under the Duties Act for the issue or making of a mortgage-backed security, the transfer or assignment, of or other dealing with a mortgage-backed security, or the discharge, cancellation or termination of a mortgage-backed security.

Accounting aspects

The Accounting Committee of the ASF has submitted an exposure draft to IASB on the lines of IAS 39. This was introduced as AAS 139 in September 2005.

New Zealand

General overview

The process of securitization in New Zealand is more or less similar to the U.S. and the U.K. New Zealand has been observing securitization activities, although in a very subtle manner. Personal Property Securities Act 1999 (PPSA) [see legal aspects below] and new accounting standards (see accounting aspects below) relating to consolidation of accounts have, however, done more harm than good to the existing securitization market in New Zealand. This is because the change has created some confusion, but with the passage of time, the situation should improve.

The New Zealand securitization market remains a young and feeble cousin of the Australian market. Even industry players themselves are not able to identify any specific reason for the low level of issuance.[65] Fitch reports that there have been only two issues during the third quarter of 2005.

Legal aspects

The PPSA is a law for enforcement of personal property security interests, modeled on Article 9 of the UCC.

The PPSA provides the rules for the creation, perfection and priority of security interests in personal property. An SPV, which is bankruptcy remote, is established for the only purpose of purchasing receivables. The SPV may be created in the form of a company or a trust. The trust remains an all time favorite. The purchase is funded by the issuance of debt securities in capital markets that may be either domestic or offshore. According to the provisions contained in the PPSA, a security interest exists where an interest is created or provided for by a transaction that in substance secures payment or performance of an obligation, without regard to the form of the transaction or the identity of the person who has title to the collateral. Certain interests are also deemed to be security interests; any transfer of accounts receivable creates a security interest. Accordingly, a transfer of assets that may have been previously (before the emergence of the PPSA) characterized as a "true sale" of the relevant assets is characterized under the PPSA as a secured loan, with the relevant SPV having a security interest in the receivables purchased.

Priority of security interests is determined by perfection of the relevant security interest on a "first in time" basis. Perfection would also render the transfer effective against the relevant originator and any liquidator of that originator. Consequently, an SPV will need to take steps to ensure that it has a perfected security interest for the purposes of the PPSA. So, it may register a financing statement on an electronic register, known as the Personal Property Securities Register or take possession of the collateral. Even then the concept of "true sale" is still important in terms of the position of the obligor, who remains entitled to a good discharge (in relation to an equitable assignment) by paying the originator until such time as it receives notice of the assignment (the assignment is perfected). In addition, if the relevant SPV does not perfect its security interest, and assuming that no perfected security interest in favor of another person exists, a "true sale" of the accounts receivable will be effective against the relevant originator and any liquidator of that originator.

The Reserve Bank of New Zealand (RBNZ) has also issued securitization guidelines for New Zealand registered banks. It basically covers two issues:

(i) Disclosure of information about securitization activities.

- The nature and amount of that bank's involvement in securitization structures;
- The arrangements in place to ensure that difficulties arising from its securitization activities do not impact adversely on it or other entities in the banking group;
- Whether financial services provided to SPVs are being provided at arms length terms and conditions and at fair value;
- Whether assets purchased from SPVs have been purchased on arms length terms and conditions and at fair value; and
- The funding (if any) provided to SPVs.

(ii) Ensuring that credit risk from securitization activities is included in the calculation of the banks' capital adequacy ratios.

The capital adequacy rules of the RBNZ set out guidelines as to what it considers as sufficient insulation from the credit risk arising from securitization activities.

The PPSA distinguishes between accounts receivable and chattel paper. Chattel paper refers to one or more writings that evidence both monetary obligation and security interest in, or lease of, specific goods. The sale of chattel paper by an originator to an SPV would involve the sale of the written security taken over the goods, which secures the payment for the goods (for example, a hire purchase agreement or a conditional sale and purchase agreement).

A security interest in accounts receivable may be defeated by a purchase money security interest. However, a security interest in chattel paper may gain priority over a purchase money security interest if the SPV takes possession of the chattel paper. Such possession must be for new value, without knowledge of the purchase money security interest and in the ordinary course of business. What constitutes possession for the purposes of the PPSA is still under review and the major issue will center on whether custodial arrangements are sufficient for this purpose.

Taxation aspects

For debt securities issued in off-shore markets, a non-resident withholding tax is levied on the interest paid. It can be avoided by an SPV by separating the acquiring vehicle and the offshore issuer. So the offshore issuer has to establish a branch in New Zealand. The acquiring SPV may also decide not to be funded from the offshore issuer and to fund itself, paying a 2% levy on interest in lieu of deducting non-resident withholding tax, with that 2% borne by the SPV or, more likely, passed on to the relevant originator.

Accounting aspects

The new accounting standard, FRS-37, came into effect December 31, 2002, and is modelled on SIC 12. It mainly deals with consolidation and provides that in some cases the accounts of an SPV has to be consolidated with those of the entity that controls the particular SPV. Hence, a subsidiary is an entity that is controlled by another entity. To determine whether an entity has control over an SPV or not the following two parameters have to be applied:

a. If the entity has the capacity to determine the financing and operating polices of an SPV, then the SPV is deemed to be controlled by such entity;
b. If the entity is entitled to a substantial level of ownership benefits from the activities of that SPV (current benefit or future benefit), then the SPV is deemed to be controlled by such entity.

Trends in global securitization

The world of securitization is moving very fast. Volumes, asset classes, investor classes – the acceptance of securitization as the financial instrument of the new millennium is growing at a very fast pace.

At this stage, some of the discernible trends are as follows:

1. Blurring distinction between structured finance and corporate finance

Convergence is the essential rule of development, and so as the markets are developing, there is an increasing convergence between securitization and corporate borrowing. Several applications of securitization resemble secured borrowing than to mainstream securitization. One noteworthy example is *whole business securitization*, where the entire cash flows of an operating company are securitized. A traditional lender also takes exposure on the entire cash flows of an operating company, leading to a very close similarity. There are certain single-obligor based mortgage securitizations that also amount to implicit lending to such an obligor. These instruments are hybrids between mainstream asset-backed products and corporate finance.

Investors are essentially looking at credit enhancements. For example, in whole business securitizations, investor comfort is the level of cash collateral, cash flow trapping and the inherent disincentives for the operator to default. As long as there are substantial credit enhancements, the instrument appeals to the investor – securitization or no securitization.

The key issue is: If credit enhanced borrowing is alright, why do we talk about securitization at all? The answer lies in originator's motivations. If the originator's approach is shaped by his own motivations of off-balance sheet funding, regulatory relief or gain on sale, he will rather go for a full-fledged securitization. On the other hand, if all he wants is a lower funding cost that is attainable with credit enhancements, collateralized borrowings or instruments with a hybrid character are acceptable.

2. Increasing use of derivatives in securitizations

An increasing number of securitizations are using the synthetic method – transferring risk using credit derivatives. Later, we will undertake a detailed discussion on synthetic securitization. Essentially, the purpose in a synthetic securitization may be either funding with a transfer of risk, or mere transfer of risk with no funding involved.

The central place of activity in synthetic securitization is Europe. At the beginning of 2001, synthetic CDOs were estimated to be occupying more than 50% of CDO volumes in Europe.[66] The reasons for increased acceptance of synthetic CDOs in Europe are not difficult to see; they do away with the tedious process of asset transfers and yet achieve the significant effects of capital relief, risk transfer and reduced concentration.

3. Increasing risk securitizations

Five years ago, securitization of risk appeared to be an innovation, but now it is a buzzword. The market is now seeing even more exciting forms of risk transfers, such as securitization of hedge funds or private equity funds.

A risk securitization device was first experimented with in the insurance market. To date, insurance risk securitization has been talked about more than practiced. But interestingly, outside the insurance world, the technique has found a number of interesting applications such as securitization of weather risk and credit risk.

4. Equity into debt, and debt into equity

Once again, it is the rule of convergence. A CDO essentially strips a portfolio of debts and converts it into several layers of debt, leaving an equity tranche. In other words, it carves an equity tranche into debt.

Recently, a path-breaking transaction was noted that carved out debt from equity. This was securitization of private equity investments, notable as the first such application of securitization. Prime Edge, a securitized portfolio of investments into private equity funds, made the headlines in innovative finance in June 2001.[67] By securitizing private equity investments, the transaction allows bond investors to participate in the area of private equity investments.

We are happy that most trends we had envisioned from our research have sustained over the years. The rule of convergence, we are proud to note, has lasted the test of time. In coming years there will be a number of issues affecting the securitization market. Even at the cost of going wrong, let's look at the crystal ball and see what might be in store for us. There are at least three emerging trends:

1. Emerging market volumes will increase

Emerging economies such as China, India, Brazil and Mexico will be employing securitization to address several issues that confront these countries. For example, there should be significant use of NPL securitization in China and India. Some of these emerging countries have already achieved investment grade, while most are rated a few notches below. The use of monoline insurers to wrap the transactions will help companies in these countries to achieve much better ratings for their securitized assets.

On the other hand, Basle-II guidelines will discourage the use of securitization by banks, as regulatory arbitrage possibilities will be eliminated. Further, some people believe that European volumes have already peaked and would either hit a plateau or start to fall.

After considering the two sides, we believe there will be a growth in numbers, while the debt of the market will also increase.

2. Increasing acceptability of on-balance sheet securitization

Basle–II will encourage the use of covered bonds by European banks. In general, with the increasing on-balance sheet treatment due to IAS 39, and Basle II rejecting gain-on-sale accounting, there will be increasing motivation on the part of securitizers to choose on-balance sheet structures. If countries implement laws similar to the German *pfandbrief* law, it would provide an efficient funding alternative with legal certainty. We expect governments to implement covered bonds law, as some European countries have already done.

3. Increasing use of arbitrage vehicles

Synthetic CDOs are increasingly used in developed markets. We are of the opinion that over time CDOs will be intensively used in the emerging markets as well. In addition, as the synthetic technology provides a convenient alternative to trading in credits, the use of synthetics as arbitrage vehicles will increase.

Notes

1   The information about various markets in this chapter is mostly based on secondary sources, primarily the Internet. Several of the author's colleagues have, over time, compiled this information. Part of this information may have become dated. Besides, we have relied upon the sources, quoted at relevant places. The author invites readers to help him know more about the markets that the readers may know better. Another good source of updates for various countries is the author's website: http://vinodkothari.com/secrep.htm

2   Author's estimate, taking into account U.S. and European data and ballpark figures of Asian and Latin American activity.

3   By Meir Kohn, Department of Economics, Dartmouth College

4   See <http://securitizationtax.com/supplement_5.pdf>

5   See Martin Fingerhut's "Canada's ABS Market Comes of Age" at the *International Financial Law Review* site http://www.iflr.com/?Page=17&ISS=17633&SID=524596 last visited July 12, 2005.

6   This is apparently comparable to the US FIN 46R – see chapter on Accounting.

7   See chapter on Legal Issues.

8   See European Securitization Forum *Data Report Winter 2005*

9   Exploring the reasons why the U.K. has experimented with so many different innovative applications, Hilda Mak and John Deacon in an article titled Developments in U.K. Securitization observe the reason lies in a stagnant mortgage market during the early 1990s, as a result of a general downturn in the mortgage business, by which securitization could not progress in its traditional mainstay – RMBS.

10 See ESF 2005 report supra.

11 For a further discussion on *pfandbriefs*, and the German *pfandbrief* law, see Chapter 12 on RMBS.

12 See the website of the true sale initiative at http://www.true-sale-international.de. Also, "Germany-yet to catch up in securitization," by Nina Siedler, Peter Jark, and Robert Hofbauer, Luter Rechtsanwaltsgesellschaft mbH, in *Global Securitization Review* 2005/2006 Euromoney Yearbooks pg. 103.

13 The website of the Department of Treasury contains a separate section on securitization, gives presentations, offers documents and investor reports for transactions. See http://www.dt.tesoro.it/ENGLISH-VE/Securitisa/index.htm, last visited December 28, 2005.

14 For materials on Italian securitization law, see Vinod Kothari's website at: http://vinodkothari.com/secitaly.htm.

15 See New Horizons for the Italian Securitization Market by Patrizio Messina, of Orrick, Herrington & Sutcliffe 2004. Published in the "Global Securitization and Structured Finance 2004" pg. 333.

16 Article 2447 BIS letter (a).

17 See, Changes in the Italian securitization legislation-new provisions on covered bonds. Umberto Mauro and Giuseppe Schiavello, Macchi di Cellere Gangemi.

Global Securitization Review pg. 143. Also Italian Securitization Law, by Freshfields Bruckhauseringer, October 2005.

18 See, Daphne Brinkhius" The Dutch Securitization Market and Developments of the Legal Framework"; Global Securitization Review 2005-2006, Euromoney Yearbooks pg. 120.

19 As to meaning of obligor notification and implications of not giving such notice, see the chapter on Legal Issues.

20 Based on the article by *Xavier de Kergommeaux and Gilles Saint Marc.*

21 See, Herve Touraine and Fabrico Grillo: Overview of the French Securitization Market: Recent Innovations and Market Trends, *Global Securitization and Structured Finance 2004.* Also, see Jean-Norbert Pontier: The Recent Changes in the French Securitization Regulatory Framework, at www.vinodkothari.com/french_securitization_law.htm.

22 Ivan Peeters "Changes in the Belgian Legal Framework for Securitization" Freshfields Briefing, May 2005.

23 Partly based on article by Miguel Castro Pereira and Inês Batalha Mendes.

24 See Paula Gomes Freire and André Figueiredo: Portugal ready to embrace new asset classes, *Securitization Guide* by IFLR.

25 See Supra.

26 Some useful information about Spanish securitization market in an article by Pablo Antolin, published in *World Securitization News and Comment*, June 1999.

27 See chapter on Legal Issues.

28 See Article by Íñigo Berrícano and Alejandro de Muns from Linklaters available on www. globalsecurtisation.com.

29 See Mattias Lampe, Olof Stenström and Christian Swartling: Securitization and Covered Bonds in Sweden, at www.globalsecuritization.com

30 Based on a paper entitled "Structuring Securitization Structures in Luxembourg by PwC available at www.vinodkothari.com.

31 Based on an article by *Ahmed Pekin, Senior Partner, Fethi Pekin, Partner and Melis Cosan Baban.*

32 Based on a Fitch Report, December 2002.

33 Based on an article by Michal Dlouhy, Petr Kuhn and Jan Vild.

34 Based on an article by *Bela Deri.*

35 Paul Sass, head of structured finance at OTP Bank, as quoted in The Banker. Available at www.thebanker.com/news/fullstory.php/aid/453/Securitization_gives_food_for_thought.html>.

36 Boris A. Otto of Thacher Proffitt: Asset Securitization in Mexico, *Global Securitization Review* 2005-2006 pg. 169 quoting Fitch report(supra).

37 See &P: Recent Securitization conference highlights rise of Mexico Plus Brazil's Expected Comeback, May 24, 2005.

38 S&P: Recent Securitization conference highlights rise of Mexico Plus Brazil's Expected Comeback, May 24, 2005.

39 S&P: Recent Securitization conference highlights rise of Mexico Plus Brazil's Expected Comeback, dated May 24, 2005 available at www.standardandpoor. com/ratingsdirect.

40 See S&P report supra and chapter on Brazil in the *International Comparative Legal Guide to Securitization 200*" available from www.securitization.net.

41   Based in part on International Structured Finance – Securitization in Japan: Special Report by Shinsei Bank, Japan.

42   See Moody's Reports: Japan's 2004 Securitization Market Grew To At Least ¥6.5 Trillion.

43   See, Fitch Report at www.fitchratings.com.

44   See, Toshifumi Ueda: A Legal Review of the Japanese Securitization Market: Overview of the Recent Legislation, *"Global Securitization Review*, published by Euromoney, 2005-2006 pg 193.

45   For details please see the website at <http://www.hklink2004.com.hk/eng/>

46   See KPMG Financial Reporting Update October 2005, issue 27 available from KPMG's Hong Kong website. For the text of the amendment please visit www. info.gov.hk.

47   See Reforms help Hong Kong Securitization, by Nicholas Chan and Susie Cheung: www.iflr.com/?Page=17&ISS=17633&SID=524604 →.

48   Partly based on an article by Chaipat Kamchadduskom.

49   See Generally, Stephen Jaggs and Matthew Waudby, Thai Structured Finance Renaissance?, "Published in 2005 Structured Finance Review available at www.iflr.com/?Page=17&ISS=17633&SID=524623–.

50   Based on Paul H. Brietzke – Securitization and Bankruptcy in Indonesia

51   Sarvar Ahmad, HSBC "Structured Capital Market in Asia".

52   Based on Joong-hee Lee (Housing Finance International – March 2003).

53   For an excellent paper on NPL Securitization in China , see Johnny P. Chen Non Performing Loan Securitization in the People's Republic of China, linked at www.vinodkothari.com/secchina.htm.

54   See China Takes Another Step Toward Financial Maturity," by William Pesek available at <http://www.iht.com/articles/2005/09/19/bloomberg/sxpesek.php>.

55   *ibid.*

56   See www.vinodkothari.com/seclaw.htm for the text of the Guideline.

57   See Securitization in Taiwan by Adrienne Showering, Berkeley Cox, Angela Kwan and Andrew O'Shea at www.globalsecuritization.com on the Asia Pacific Link.

58   See Supra.

59   For a complete discussion on the law of securitization in India, see Vinod Kothari's *Securitization Asst Reconstruction and Enforcement of Security Interests.*

60   See Update on Indian Structured Finance Market, July 2005 available on www. vinodkothari.com/secindia.htm, and www.icraratings.com.

61   Partly based on article written by Ahmed H. Ghazli, an attorney with the law firm of Afridi, Shah & Minallah, Lahore.

62   See Najmus Saquib: The Study of Prospects of Asset-backed Securitization in Corporate Sector of Pakistan" available on the international section of www.securitization.net.

63   Based in parts on Clayton Utz guide to Australian securitization market.

64   See Fabienne Michaux: Australian Securitization Update and Outlook, *Global Securitization Review* 2005 pg 180.

65   See "Securitization in New Zealand-the search for the Holy Grail" by the law firm Buddlefindlay.

66   *Synthetic CDOs: A Growing Market for Credit Derivatives*: a special report by Fitch, February 6, 2001.

67   See news item on http://vinodkothari.com/secnewsjune01.htm.

Part II: Financial Substance and Ratings

Chapter 4

Structuring and Credit-enhancing Securitization Transactions

This chapter describes the basic structuring elements of securitization, the agencies involved in a securitization transaction, and their role in a securitization transaction. We also take a quick look at the risks inherent in the stream of cash flows, and mitigation of such risks.

The structure of a securitization transaction is itself a function of the collateral type. We have taken up separately a study of the main collateral types in different chapters (Chapters 12–22); therefore, this chapter is only concerned with the basics of structuring.

Basics of securitization structuring

A securitization transaction is like a miniature corporation. Like for every corporate, the liabilities of the corporation will be paid from its assets, a securitization transaction will also raise liabilities that will be paid out of its assets. The analogy between securitization and a miniature corporation can be carried to quite an extent:

- A corporation is basically composed of assets and liabilities – the assets are refinanced by the liabilities.
- The assets of every corporate are dynamic – the assets are being created and realized on a regular basis.
- These assets fetch a certain rate of return, from which the costs of refinancing the liabilities is paid off.
- A corporation provides credit support – the ability to absorb losses on some of the assets:

- o In the first instance, we have the profits from other assets;
- o If the profits are not enough, we have the equity and the preference capital.

- Apart from credit support, we also have one or more sources of short-term liquidity that help to smooth temporary mismatches, such as cash not received from business assets to pay off monthly expenses.
- In addition, we have a management that regularly manages the whole show – both on the asset and liability side. The management negotiates assets and liabilities, monitors the same, and in case of difficulties, may negotiate a workout as well.
- The net profits of the corporation, which is like net result of its operation, are either drawn regularly or are partly retained and partly drawn, as per the decision of the management.
- The corporation thus goes on.

Securitization structures are similar, to a very large extent. The similarities and differences are:

- A securitization pool is composed of assets refinanced by liabilities.
- While the assets of every corporate are dynamic, the assets in a securitization pool may be either static or dynamic; however, even if they are dynamic, they have a static or well-defined character. Another significant difference is that for securitization, the assets are acquired by the securitization vehicle only after they have been originated; in other words, pre-origination risks do not affect investors.
- These assets fetch a certain rate of return, from which the costs of refinancing the liabilities are paid off. The difference between the rate of return from the assets and the cost of financing (plus other costs, which are not significant, except for servicing) is the **excess spread**.
- A securitization provides credit support, the ability to absorb losses on some of the assets:

  - o In the first instance, we have the excess spread from other assets (to the extent such excess spread is available for absorbing losses);
  - o If the excess spread is not enough, we have other sources of credit enhancement.

- Apart from credit support, we also have one or more sources of short-term liquidity that help to smooth temporary mismatches, such as cash not received from the pool assets to pay off the schedule monthly cash flow.
- Remarkably, in securitization transactions, there is no such thing called management. Securitization transactions are structured to be inanimate. There is a trustee overseeing the transaction, but the role of the trustee is no more than mere machine. There may be a degree of collateral management in some rare instances,[1] but generally there is no scope for management of the assets and negotiation of liabilities, as all liabilities are raised upfront and there is a rare possibility of negotiating a workout.
- The excess spreads left over after meeting all claims are either retained or swept by the seller as per the mechanism laid down by the transaction.

There is no scope for discretion of any "management", as this is also pre-programmed like every other feature of the transaction.

- The securitization transaction is not a going concern; once all assets are paid off, the transaction comes to closure.

As may be noted from the above analogy, the key difference between a corporation and a securitization transaction is the fact that the latter is completely non-discretionary. Discretion is the feature of entities and securitization transactions do not confide in entities but in assets. This significant feature leads to the following factors when structuring a securitization transaction:

- Identification of risk:

  o As in the case of corporate finance, so in case of securitizations – we need to identify the credit, liquidity and other risks that affect the securitization transaction.
  o We need to organize what will mitigate these risks:

    ◆ Credit support for credit risk
    ◆ Liquidity support for liquidity risk
    ◆ Measures to absorb any interest rate risk or exchange rate risk, if any

- As there is no scope for discretionary management of the risks by anyone, we need to:

  o Consider all such contingencies that might affect the transaction in the future
  o Formulate the responses to such contingencies

- In other words, the entire transaction is pre-formulated like a computer program.

Structuring variables

A brief identification and discussion of significant structuring variables for traditional securitization transactions follows. It is notable that in specific collateral classes, there might be unique elements. The following description is merely generic:

Asset pool

Identification of the assets that are to be securitized is the starting point of any securitization structure – the entire edifice is built *with* the assets. There are several factors related to the identification of the pool that merit careful consideration:

- The size of the pool is fixed keeping in view the funding needs, which, in turn is based on the intended application of the funding. In normal course, for an originator engaged in a regular business of origination, the proceeds of securitization are applied in funding further originations.

- There might be several questions to answer on what type of assets should be securitized, such as assets with high spread or low spread, prime assets or sub-prime assets. These questions are answered with reference to the objective of the originator. For example, if the objective is to capture the excess spread and maximize the gain on sale, obviously, securitization of sub-prime assets will be closer to the objective.
- A significant structuring issue is a static versus dynamic pool. If the transaction has a revolving period, the pool is essentially dynamic. However, the revolving structure has its limitations; it cannot be applied in case of assets with long durations. This point has been discussed in an earlier chapter.[2]
- Another significant feature is the **prefunding** or **ramp up** period. In case the originator does not have sufficient amount of pool assets to sell off immediately on the closing of the transaction, there might be a prefunding period, when one can originate and sell off assets. The prefunded amount is a sort of an advance against sale of the assets provided to the originator, normally kept in escrow and released as and when receivables are sold. Obviously, the prefunding feature adds a new dimension of risk – origination risk – and the rating agencies do stress this.

Selection criteria

In establishing the pool, it is important to apply selection criteria. We have already discussed the significance of diversification as an important attribute in selection of the receivables.[3] The pool should be so constructed as to provide a balanced spread of constituents with maximum possible diversity.

In addition, the following factors may be noted while selecting the pool:

- The selection criteria are typically set on a cut-off date. On the cut-off date, the rating agency is given the benefit of examining a **statistical pool**, normally larger than the actual value of funding to be raised, such that either the actual assets are selected from the statistical pool or the actual assets answer to the same description.
- The selection criteria should be fixed carefully, but not very aggressively or restrictively. The criteria should be definitive and capable of being quickly established. It is notable that the selection criteria will normally be put as **representations and warranties** in legal documents.
- The defining features of the pool quality are seasoning of the pool, current performance, and performance in the past. It is preferable to have a seasoned pool rather than an absolutely green pool, to have the benefit of retrospect. Seasoning also implies that the pool has been funded by the normal balance sheet of the originator before it was securitized, also a form of credit enhancement for the securitization transaction. The assets should usually be current –no overdue balances or more than a certain number of overdue days on the date of cut-off date. Besides, their past performance should not have more than a definite number of days overdue.
- The constituents of the pool should nearly answer the average characteristics of the pool. It is not ideal to have sharp departures from the average defining features of the pool quality.

Identification of risks[4]

Once the composition of the pool is fixed, the next significant task is (a) to analyze; and (b) to quantify all the risks that affect the pool. The risks relate to the nature of the collateral, but significant risk areas include the following:

- **Credit risk** – the risk of default, which is the risk of the obligor either declaring bankruptcy or not paying. If an obligor does not pay, it is a case of delinquency; when a delinquency is treated as a default and the recovery action follows is laid down by the servicing standards, based on the nature of the collateral. The recovery action may have several variables; the delinquent receivables are sold to a specialised servicer at a particular value (the specialized servicer may be the originator or his affiliate, or a third-party), or a foreclosure action legal suit or follow. Here, the objective is to quantify:

  - Default rate – the percentage of loans that go into default
  - Timing of the defaults or default rate over time – the default rate might have historically been a function of time, so is it possible to relate the default rate to the seasoning of the pool?
  - Recovery rate – should default happen, what is the likely recovery rate?
  - Recovery delay – the time between recognition of a default and actual recovery.

- The objective of all this analysis is to develop a cumulative loss percentage of the pool. The cumulative loss, based on validated assumptions, is called **expected loss**.
- **Prepayment risk:** Prepayment is a risk of a different kind; it is not a risk of losses, but losses of profits to investors. We have prepayment risk in a separate chapter (see Chapter 6). But with the risk of default, apart from studying the historical prepayment rate, we will also try to see the prepayment rate as a function of time.
- **Delayed payment risk:** This is essentially a risk of timing of the cash flow; the assets are not actually in default, but there is a temporary delay in payments. Delinquency risk may be divided into time buckets – 30 days, 60 days, 90 days and so on.
- **Interest rate risk:** A transaction is said to have interest rate risk in the following situations:

  - The assets or some of the assets have a fixed rate of interest, and the liabilities or some of the liabilities have a floating rate of interest;
  - The assets or some of the assets have a floating rate of interest, and the liabilities or some of the liabilities have a fixed rate of interest;
  - There is difference of basis or reset period; the base rate used for floating rate computation in case of assets and liabilities or reset periods, are different.

- **Exchange rate risk:** If the assets or some of the assets have a payment in one currency, and the liabilities or some of the liabilities have a denomination in a different currency, there is an exchange rate risk in the transaction.
- **Other risks:** Such risks as servicer migration and the disruption of servicing during that time, taxation risk and risk of stamp duties.

While understanding and quantifying each of these risks, it is important to understand the distinction between a static pool and dynamic pool. If the securitization pool is static, each of the risk attributes above will be studied with reference to a static pool – a fixed number of assets will be observed throughout their repayment cycle. If the pool is dynamic, then the risk attributes will be studied with reference to the relevant portfolio of the originator. The difference between a static and dynamic pool is that the static pool is seasoned over time but the dynamic pool largely remains unaffected by ageing as new assets are continuously added to the pool. For instance, if we had 1,000 assets in the pool, and the rate of prepayment is 2%, the rate is applied on a static portfolio over time. Therefore, default rates and prepayment rates become time vectors when they are applied to static pools.

Sources of credit support

The analysis of the default rate and expected loss, as discussed above, will give us input on the size of credit support required to absorb the losses, discussed in the next heading. However, before coming to the size of credit enhancements, it is important to understand the sources of enhancement. In this chapter, we would discuss several sources of enhancement, including enhancement by third parties. Significant sources of support may include excess spread, over-collateralization, subordination and recourse. Each of these might have different consequences on the economics of the transaction and need to be carefully compared.

Size of credit support

Unquestionably, the most significant structuring variable for any transaction is the size of the credit support. The size of the credit enhancement determines the economics of the transaction. The greater the credit enhancements, the more the weighted-average cost of the transaction is seen, because credit enhancement may mean either more coupon, or more infusion of originator equity, or more third-party cost if third-party enhancements are taken. At the same time, fewer enhancements mean a fragile transaction, with either low or fragile ratings. Therefore, the trade-off between the cost of the transaction and investor concerns is clear.

The credit enhancement decision is the same as capital structure decision for a firm. Like blood pressure, credit enhancement should be neither too low nor too high.

The size of credit enhancements relates directly to the rating of the securities, and is a function of the ratings. The size of the credit enhancement shall be discussed later in this chapter.

Financial structure – pass-through or reinvestment type

The meaning and implication of the financial structure of the transaction – pass-through versus bond-type – were discussed in the previous chapter.

Unless the nature of the payback from the securities is extremely irregular, it is not proper to use the pay-through or bond method, as the economics of the transaction is adversely affected by the problem of negative carry discussed in the previous chapter.

Classes of liabilities

By classes of liabilities, we mean the stacking order of different classes, such as senior, mezzanine and junior classes. The classification of liabilities is part of the credit enhancement structure, briefly discussed above and taken up in detail later in this chapter.

Determination of classes of liabilities, however, has another significant structuring issue: How many classes of liabilities will there be? The answer to this question is related to two things: What is the credit support level required at the senior most level and what is the least-rated class that can be sold in the capital market?

The structuring of classes of liabilities follows a step down approach. Let us suppose we are standing on the eighth rung of the ladder. How do we come down? Obviously, one step at a time. Likewise, let us suppose the required level of credit support to see the highest AAA rating is 8%. We also know that we will not be able to sell in the market securities with less than a BBB rating. Now, ideally, the stacking of liabilities should be:

Class	Rating	Required credit support	Size of the class
A	AAA	8%	92%
B	AA	6%	2%
C	A	5%	1%
D	BBB	4%	1%
E	Unrated	None	4%

In the table above, the size of Class A is given by the (1- credit support required), that is, 92%, since 8% of the total liabilities must be subordinated to class A. Now, we have the option of having just two classes – Class A and B, in which case, the size of class B will be 8%, and B will be an unrated class as there is no credit support available to B. Hence, B will not find a buyer and will have to be retained by the originator. But it is important to note that the objective of any originator in a securitization transaction is to minimize the retained class, as the retained class is effectively the equity of the transaction. We have discussed earlier why the minimization of the equity support is crucial to a lower weighted-average cost of any securitization transaction.

So, now we try and keep slicing the 8% support required for AAA rating. We climb one step down and ask, what is the support required for a AA rating? Say, the answer is 6%. In other words, class B must have a subordination of 6%. That gives us the size of class B (8%- 6% = 2%). Likewise, we ask for the level of credit support at each of the ratings, until we come to the BBB class. We know that we cannot go below BBB, as there are no buyers. Assuming the required support for the BBB class is 4%, it is the retained and unrated portion of the liabilities.

In practice, the higher the extent of subordination required at the AAA level, the more the number of classes – this seems very easy to understand.

Time tranching of liabilities

It may be noted that the thickest class in the above hierarchy is Class A. This is what we want to maximize, as this is the cheapest of all liabilities.

However, we may still like to do more structuring to reduce the weighted-average cost and align the securities to suit investor needs. Instead of expecting all Class A investors to be paid simultaneously, we might create further time tranches within Class A, such that there is a series payment to different classes one after the other. Say, if we have three such pieces as A-1, A-2 and A-3, all cash flow attributed to Class A are taken to retire A-1 first. There is redirection cash proportionally available for A-2 and A-3 into retiring A-1. Once A-1 is fully paid, we start retiring A-2 and so on. In the process, we create three securities, all with the same ranking and seniority and therefore, the same rating, but with three different payback periods.

Time tranching is done essentially to take advantage of the upwardly sloping **yield curve**, that is, investors expect higher rates of return for longer terms. Time tranching is mostly done on Class A, as it is the thickest. How many such tranches should be created is a question of the yield differences and investor preferences as to securities of different payback periods. It is quite common at least to have a tranche that pays off in just one year and so qualifies as a money market instrument.

Pay down of securities

How should the principal be paid down to the various classes of liabilities? This question is almost as significant as the decision of credit enhancement structure at the inception. The way the principal is paid down over time will determine the credit enhancement, and therefore the weighted-average cost of the transaction. The various pay-down options and their implications are discussed later in this chapter.

Liquidity support – need and sources

As credit support is needed for the risk of losses, so liquidity support is needed to finance the transaction to the extent of temporary shortfalls in collections. As in case of credit support, there are two significant considerations for liquidity support – size and sources. We will discuss liquidity support later in this chapter.

Apart from a shortfall in collections, the liquidity support is also required for temporary disruptions or apprehended liabilities. Disruptions may arise, for example, because of a possible changeover from a normal servicer to a backup servicer. It might be necessary to create liquidity for some apprehended liabilities such as stamp duty and taxes. It is notable that in case of apprehended external costs, the appropriate form of liquidity support will be cash reserve. Thus, liquidity problems may be either reversible – timing problems that are self-corrective such as delays in collections – or might be irreversible needs such as a provision for stamp duty liability.

Sometimes, liquidity is also created as cash is accumulated for a forthcoming repayment of liabilities. If liabilities call for bullet repayment, there might be an accumulation period to build cash to repay the same.

Every liquidity creation has an implicit or explicit cost. In case of internal liquidity sources such as cash reserve, the cost is the negative carry associated with the reinvestment of the cash. Therefore, the transaction must aim to establish just the required amount of liquidity.

Prepayment protection

The next significant structuring issue is whether it would be proper to have some prepayment-protected classes. The rule about prepayment protection is the same as for any other protection: we are safer when we are protected, but every protection has a cost. We need to ask if the real cost of protection is justified by the real risk that we are trying to protect against? As noted before, prepayment is not a risk of losses, but a loss of profits. If the investment is subject to a prepayment risk, investors increase their spread expectation by adding an implicit **cost of the prepayment option**.[5] On the other hand, if we create a prepayment-protected class, there has to be a prepayment-protecting class as well,[6] and obviously, the coupon expectation on this class will be higher than that on the protected class. So, one must analyze whether cost of the prepayment option implicitly borne on the entire portfolio is more than the cost of the entire prepayment burden transferred to just one class.

As prepayment leads to a significant impact on longer-term securities such as RMBS, the common use of prepayment protecting devices is restricted to long-term securities only.

Mitigation of other risks

As in the case of other risks of the asset pool, it is necessary to identify and mitigate other risks in the transaction. For example, if there is an interest rate risk, it is necessary to mitigate the same by entering into an interest rate swap. Issues of what should be the notional value of the swap, and who should be the swap counterparty would obviously arise. The notional value of the swap in case of asset-backed securities needs to be variable, as there is a prepayment risk that will reduce the size of the pool over time. The swap counterparty's choice is also significant, as the ratings of the counterparty will have an impact on the transaction.

Creation of cash reserve and investment

Cash reserve for a securitization transaction is the same as the liquidity needs for corporations. A cash reserve is both a liquidity and a credit-enhancer, which may be created either up front by retaining a part of the funding raised by the transaction, or may be created by pooling the excess profit. We have discussed the considerations relevant to cash reserve later in this chapter.

Wherever there is cash retained by the SPV, the associated significant issue is the reinvestment thereof. We have discussed before that reinvestment must be passive and highly rated, nearly risk-free.

Structural protection triggers

The structural protection triggers are like preventive steps to take care of imminent weaknesses in the transaction. As discussed, there is no "management" that might deal with problems that arise in the course of a securitization transaction. Therefore, responses to problems that might arise over time need to be pre-formulated. A structural protection trigger provides that if certain pre-specified weaknesses arise in the transaction, the structure of the transaction will be modified in a certain manner. For example:

- If the cumulative losses increase to a level of x% or above, the excess spread available to the originator will be trapped to either create or increase the cash reserve.
- If the cumulative losses increase to a level of x% or above, then the pay-down method will be changed from proportional to sequential – thereby providing increased credit enhancement to the senior classes.
- If the cumulative losses increase to a level of x% or above, there will be a lockout on the payments to a subordinated class.

Notably, these triggers are similar to the acceleration, a dividend freeze or similar covenants found in loan contracts.

Once again, too aggressive application of the triggers may exacerbate the performance of the transaction. To reiterate, as there is no scope for exercise of discretion, if the triggers are to apply, they will do so automatically[7] and indiscriminately.

Profit extraction methods

Profit extraction devices refer to the devices used by the originator to sweep the residual profit of the transaction, that is, the excess spread. Various options are available, and they might have different consequences on the legal structure, accounting treatment and the available credit enhancements. Commonly, a combination of methods may be used. These are discussed later in this chapter.

Clean up call

The clean up call is self-termination of the transaction when it has run down to an economic size. Generally, it is exercised when the outstanding value of pool assets has been reduced to a nominal value. If the clean up call is not exercised, the transaction drags on until the earlier of (a) every asset in the pool has been realized; or (b) legal final maturity.[8] It may not be efficient to carry the transaction to its legal maturity or realization of every asset, as servicing a transaction of an uneconomic size might be too costly.

Parties involved

A securitization transaction would involve the following parties:

Primary parties

- The originator – the party originating the transaction, who intends to securitize assets.
- The obligors – the debtors who must pay the originator. They are not active parties to the transaction, but their obligations to pay to the originator are transferred to the SPV.
- The special purpose vehicle – the vehicle or legal entity, either created or existing, for holding the receivables and issuing securities. Also called the issuer.
- The indenture trustee holding security interest – the trustee holding ownership or security interest on the assets of the issue for the benefit of the investors, and also maintaining a general surveillance on the transaction. In several countries, depending on the requirement of the jurisdiction, the trustee owning title over the asset and the one holding security interest over it may be different, respectively known as the **owner trustee** and **indenture trustee**.
- Investors acquiring the certificates – the investors who buy the notes issued by the issuer.
- Servicers and back-up servicers – the party that will take over the servicing, that is, the entire interface required with the obligors and investors on a regular basis including collections and remittances. Back up servicer is the one who will replace the main servicer should the contract with the main servicer be terminated for any reason.
- Swap counterparties – if there is an interest-rate or any other swap inherent in the transaction.

Supportive agencies

- Principal structuring advisor – no legal or necessary role, but generally the principal advisor on the structure.
- Underwriter/merchant banker – the dealmaker who undertakes to get the issuance subscribed.
- Rating company – the rating agency that rates the instrument. An almost necessary market feature of securitizations.
- Legal advisors – counsel who drafts the securitization documents and provides legal opinions.

- Credit-enhancer – one or more agencies that provide guarantee/insurance or other credit enhancement to the transaction.
- Banker – banker to operate the lock-box/escrow account where the collections will be deposited; where the guaranteed reinvestment contract will be maintained.
- Depository or custodian – the agency keeping the physical documents, such as mortgage deeds, relating to the transaction. It may also refer to the agency that will act depository to facilitate securities being held in a dematerialized form.

Steps in a securitization transaction

We have earlier noted the steps and the modus operandi in a securitization transaction (see Chapter 2). In this section, we go into the specifics of various steps and detailed analysis of the role of various parties in accomplishing them.

Figure 4.1 is a guide to show the steps in completing the securitization process. The steps are not necessarily sequential and a number of them can be initiated simultaneously. It must be noted that the time taken in accomplishing each step is a function of the extent to which a template for such transactions has been developed. The guide to time taken below is merely illustrative:

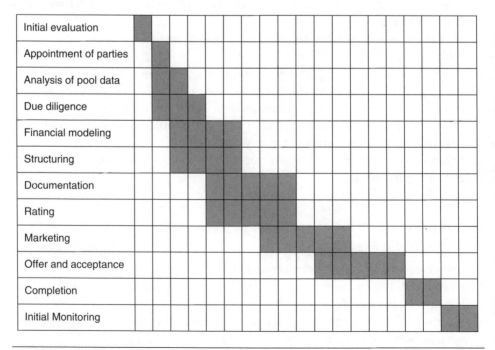

Figure 4.1 An activity chart for a proposed securitization transaction [Each small cell represents a week]

Initial feasibility study

Before launching upon the exercise at all, the originator must satisfy himself on the basic feasibility of the proposed securitization exercise. This requires a study of the following:

Objective of the originator

An originator may be looking at a securitization option with various objectives that may not be uniform. There may be various ways of serving such objectives. For example, the originator's objective may be an additional source of funding; an analysis needs to be done whether on-balance sheet sources of funding can lead to a lower weighted-average cost, a higher leverage and/or longer tenure. Obviously, securitization is not the right solution to all funding needs.

As a funding device, securitization is generally preferred for one or more of the following reasons:

- **It enables the firm to attain higher leverage**: The higher leverage comes due to securitization transactions looking at economic risk in a portfolio while traditional balance sheet lenders swear by standard debt-to-equity ratios. We live in a stressed, optimistic world, and higher leverage allows businesses to build more assets with less capital – just the thing that today's ambitious entrepreneur wants.
- **It enables funding for a longer term**: Several securitization transactions, for example whole business transactions, package cash flow over fairly long maturities resulting in a longer term of funding.
- **It reduces the weighted-average cost of funding**. This may be either the effect of arbitrage involved in structured finance or due to the higher rating obtained for structured finance transactions.

If the objective is funding, an originator must analyze whether the above reasons are true in his case. There are several securitizations that reduce aggregate leverage instead of increasing it, and increase weighted-average cost of capital instead of reducing it.

It is common that professional advisers – rating agencies, professional advisers or lawyers – are keen to suggest a securitization alternative in almost every case, in view of the larger role each has in a securitization option as compared to traditional alternatives. An originator must take a hard look at available options before launching upon the securitization option.

Legal feasibility

Legal feasibility is an important issue and should precede a financial evaluation. Common law systems are quite amenable to securitization. In civil law jurisdictions, various restraints may occur such as having to seek the approval of the debtor. These may be insurmountable problems. Assets may be a contingent or performance-based, which are not easily securitized except by facing the drag of the originator's rating. Sometimes, taxation issues might make a transaction unviable – for instance, transactions subject to withholding taxes.

Financial feasibility

This relates to a quick analysis of the costs involved in securitization including the upfront costs and the availability of investors to invest in the subject portfolio.

Systems feasibility

This is a very significant aspect of initial feasibility analysis and must be carefully analyzed. Securitization transactions, particularly retail, if done on a regular basis, are very demanding in terms of their systems needs. Being able to provide, collate and analyze pool data, have the ability to dissect originations into what is sold and what is not, as well as what is sold to Trust A and to Trust B for various series, might be a daunting task.

Key appointments

There are three key agencies whose advice is central to the transaction – investment bankers, rating agencies and legal advisors. Investment bankers normally take the issuer through the transaction. As these agencies will also help the originator in planning the structure, it will be important to do these appointments beforehand.

Asset analysis and selection

After having decided to securitize and appointed key advisors, the originator must begin a detailed examination of the asset pool.

The identification of assets depends on the class of targeted investors. In general, there are two basic concerns in selection of asset pool. First, the cash flow from the pool should generally be predictable. Second, the assets should by and large be homogenous and no asset should be large enough to substantially affect the total returns from the portfolio. In addition to the above, the selection of assets will be done based on certain discriminants or criteria, such as the age of the receivables, the remaining maturity, the last history of default and the amount per transaction.[9]

It is generally not advisable to allow the assets to be "cherry-picked," that is, selected other than by random sampling. In some cases, regulators (for example, bank regulators in permitting banks to securitize) specifically prohibit cherry-picking, understandably because if cherry-picked assets are removed, the credit quality of the assets that remain in the pool suffers.

It would be ideal to pick up assets that have a clean and standard documentation.

In revolving asset classes, it is necessary for the originator to transfer further assets into the pool over a period. Generally, these additional receivables are those that arise from designated accounts. For example, in case of credit cards receivables, the receivable is paid off in a short time, but further receivables are created on the same card. Thus, the originator may transfer all the receivables on designated accounts immediately, with an option with the SPV to acquire further receivables from such designated accounts over time.

The fixation of the discriminants based on which receivables are selected is premised on the loss history of the receivables. To choose the best discriminants, the originator must analyze the cash flow based on several criteria. For example, if the underlying pool represents cash flow from auto loans, the data should be classified based on the maturity of the case, LTV ratio, residence of the obligors, type of obligors – such as employees or self-employed individuals, model of the vehicle concerned or geographic location. To classify the data as many variables as possible should be used, as this will identify those that have the strongest predictive value for future cash flow.

The discriminants or selection criteria must not be too strict, as that will have the impact of selecting the best of the portfolio, the effect of which is the same as cherry-picking.

Due diligence audit

Normally, a due diligence audit of the transactions securitized would be insisted upon. The object of this is to ensure all transactions securitized are legally valid, comply with the pool selection criteria and that the underwriting standards are agreed upon; for securities collected, there must be no limitations against assignment or legal suits or counterclaims pending. The audit would also help to track the payment history of the selected receivables.

The due diligence process may undertake either a case-by-case examination or a sample test checking, depending upon the nature of the portfolio. Retail transactions are statistically tested, and are checked by sample checks as well portfolio level tests. However, wholesale and corporate exposures are checked on a case by case basis almost as a rule.

Besides due diligence on each transaction, the scope of due diligence reports may sometimes be wider, including a review of the general corporate health of the originator, the underwriting policies and business procedures.

An exemplary list of areas to be covered in due diligence study, apart from the general financial health of the originator, may relate to:

- Whether the originator's senior management or board is directly involved in decisions concerning the quality and types of assets to be securitized as well as those to be retained on the balance sheet.
- Ensure that written policies exist that:

    a. Outline objectives relating to securitization activities.

    b. Establish limits or guidelines for:

- Quality of loans originated
- Maturity of loans originated
- Geographic dispersion of loans
- Acceptable range of loan yields
- Credit quality
- Acceptable types of collateral
- Types of loans

- Determine whether the credit standards for loans to be securitized are the same as the ones for loans to be retained.

  a. If not, ascertain whether management consciously made this decision and that it is clearly stated in the securitization business plan.
  b. If higher quality loans are to be securitized to gain initial market acceptance, ensure that the originator limits lower quality loans it originates.

- Ensure that there is a complete separation of duties between the credit approval process and loan sales/securitization effort. Determine whether lending personnel are solely responsible for:

  a. The granting or denial of credit to customers.
  b. Credit approvals of resale counterparties.

- Ensure that loans to be sold or securitized are segregated or otherwise identified on the books of the originator.
- If loans are granted or denied based on a credit scoring system, ascertain whether the system was developed based on empirically derived data. Ensure that it is periodically revalidated.
- Ensure that the underwriting policies on originated transactions were well documented and there are internal controls to ensure that these are followed.
- Ensure that there are frequent and reliable credit reviews, inspections and physical verifications.
- Ensure that the MIS of the originator will generate reliable data on cash flow.

Determination of the structure

The next step, after the selection and tagging of receivables is to decide the basic securitization structure. The detailed consideration involved in structuring the transaction and the structuring variables have already been discussed above. At this stage, discussions with the investment bankers are also important as it decides the nature of the investors' instruments such as fixed rate instruments or floating rate notes and currency.

Credit enhancements

Credit enhancement is one of the most significant variables in a securitization structure. Detailed discussion on credit enhancement follows. The extent of credit enhancement is worked out with close association of the rating agencies. The extent and the form of credit enhancement have very significant implications on the overall cost of the transaction. Credit enhancement is comparable to equity in a business; therefore, the sizing of the enhancement is directly related to the weighted-average cost of the transaction, while its nature also has bearing on the originator's costs.

Intervening reinvestments

Depending on the nature of the transaction, the SPV will make reinvestments to cover the mismatches between the pay-in and pay-out, that is, collection and payment dates. The mismatches arise because of several reasons such as delays in collection, advance payments, mismatched scheduled dates and end-period continuing transactions when some transactions have already expired.

To take care of the mismatches in the cash flow, the SPV will make reinvestments into qualifying investments. This might include a guaranteed investment contract (GIC), normally with a bank, to reinvest the surplus cash available for more than a certain period, say 15 days, into a reinvestment account or fixed deposit. The various common types of reinvestment contracts are:

Guaranteed reinvestment contracts

Normally entered into with banks, this would be a typical short-term deposit with a bank at a spread over a base rate. The reinvestment rate is not fixed but variable with reference to a base rate. The base rate could typically be the central bank's discount rate.

Reinvestments in buying fresh receivables

In a number of securitizations, the repayment of a receivable is for a very short term, typically in case of credit card securitizations. Here, the redemption of the dues will be reinvested in buying fresh receivables.

Reinvestment in other permissible collateral

Alternatively, it could also be agreed that the cash surpluses will be reinvested in liquid securities at the relevant time available. The rating agencies also have a list of qualifying investments.

Fixing the legal structure

The next step is the determination of the legal details, such as the constitution of the SPV and process of assignment of receivables to it. In standard transactions, one might have a ready-to-use template, but it might be a tricky task in case of new transactions.

Determination of the important features of legal documentation may also be done at this time. This will include:

- Constitutional documents of the SPV;
- Assignment agreement for receivables/pooling and servicing agreement;
- Criteria for selection of receivables, and significant specific representations and warranties;
- Indenture of trust;
- Draft of the pass-through certificates or the bonds.

The actual legal methodology involved in transferring the receivables is mostly a complicated legal question. It has to depend on the laws of the relevant jurisdiction.

Anglo-Saxon jurisdictions, such as England, India, Australia, New Zealand and South Africa, distinguish between legal and equitable assignments. A legal assignment is a full-scale assignment following a legal conveyance. This may, however, require notices to the debtors. The process of serving notices on individual debtors is mostly considered undesirable, as any originator would like to maintain a continuing relation with the debtors and mostly would not even like the debtors to come to know of the fact of securitization. Besides, there might be heavy stamp costs involved in the case of legal assignments.

An equitable assignment, though recognized in law, creates only equitable interest in the receivables in favor of the SPV. Any suit by the SPV for recovery of debts would have to be filed either in the name of the originator, or after making the originator a defendant.[10] The other disadvantage with equitable assignments is the lack of clarity of tax laws in this case.

Unless, there are clear laws or precedents in the country regarding transfers of receivables, the choice is between a cumbersome and costly legal procedure, and a practical method that involves some legal risk but has prevailed long enough to be shrouded in apprehension.

Legal opinions

Typically, legal counsel will need to provide assurance, often through an opinion letter, that the transfer of assets to the SPV constitutes a true sale or a clean transfer strong enough to withstand any claw-back claims or allegations of voidable dispositions.[11]

The legal advisor has also to examine and report on the underlying transactions.

Rating

Rating is an indispensable part of securitization exercise. The various rating concerns and rating methodology are discussed in a later chapter. The rating rationale for most standard types of collateral is well known and is available on the websites of the rating agencies. In the case of CDOs, rating agencies have also come out with software that assists in working out portfolio risks – for instance, CDO Evaluator by Standard and Poor's, Vector by Fitch and CDO-ROM by Moody's.

Rating agencies provide a **presale rating report** that contains the detailed rating rationale of the transaction.

Offer

This is the consummation of a securitization transaction, and as for any capital market offering, requires detailed planning, roadshows and conferences, networking with investment bankers, dealers and brokers, and finally book-building.

Appointment of servicer/administrator

Every securitization requires the appointment of a servicer or administrator to:

- Collect and distribute obligor payments;
- The assets' performance; and
- Manage the collection of recoveries for defaulted monitor and report on receivables.

The appointment of the servicer is the implementation of something always integral to transaction features.[12]

Servicer capabilities

Typically, it is the originator who would be the servicer, and there are detailed servicer's requirements by most rating agencies. The servicer must be skilled in revenue collection, information processing and analysis. Rating agencies may insist on servicers that have the technology to monitor an ever-changing pool of assets and to spot early warning signs of the pool's slipping performance. It is a typical rating condition in public transactions to require a back-up servicer capable of stepping in and performing the replaced servicer's obligations on not more than 48 hours notice. If the servicer in question does not qualify under these norms, rating agencies may suggest appointment of a master servicer, responsible for the primary actual servicers.

Post completion routines

Once the transaction of securitization is complete, the prime burden is on the systems for earmarking the payments collected on behalf of the SPV; initially, the payments may not be deposited in the lock box account. The originator may also be concerned with the managing of the accounts and database of the SPV.

Ongoing reporting

Securitization transactions require reporting on an on-going basis by the servicer. The trustees will also be responsible for copious reporting work, done by the servicer and authenticated by the trustees (see Chapter 25 on Operational Issues).

Clean up call

Usually the structure would provide for an optional buy-back by the originator when the size of the transaction falls below a certain level.

Credit enhancements

Credit enhancements are not unique to securitization. They are there in any external lending or exposure. For example, in a loan transaction, the borrower's equity in the asset bought is the credit enhancement for the lender; the equity will absorb the risks before they hit the lender. In a loan to buy a car, the fact that the value of the car exceeds the amount of loan (1 – LTV ratio) is the credit enhancement of the lender. In plain corporate finance, the equity of the borrower is the credit enhancement for the lender. Credit enhancement for any business is the equity or economic capital present in the business.[13]

Likewise, credit enhancement is essential in securitization transactions. Securitization is a device of asset-based investment in which securitization investors are exposed to the isolated assets transferred by the originator. Isolation provides legal strength to the transaction, but conversely, also deprives the investors of any support from the originator to save a transaction from default. Therefore, in absence of credit enhancement, securitization investors would be in the nature of venture capitalists taking an absentee exposure in the business of the originator.

However, the key feature of structured finance is that the instrument offered to investors is structured, made-to-specification, and the specification is the credit quality or the rating that the investors want. Not every investor wants the best rating, as the best rating invariably also comes at the least coupon.

Credit enhancements bridge the gap between the stand-alone quality of the portfolio of assets transferred by the originator, and the target rating of the instrument based on needs of various investors. Thus, appreciably, there will be different credit enhancement levels for different classes of instruments.

The various types of credit enhancement are noted below. The nature and extent of credit enhancement required in cases would always be specific to the asset class and target investor class. Some credit

> **Box 4.1: Concept of credit enhancements**
>
> - Conceptually, credit enhancements are in every form of lending: the borrower's equity is the most basic form of credit enhancement in plain loans.
>
> - In securitization, primary form of credit enhancements play the same role as borrower's equity in the transaction; the credit enhancement determines the extent of leverage in transactions, the layer of protection against expected and unexpected losses.
>
> - As the required economic capital in balance sheet transactions is a function of required confidence level, so the size of credit enhancements depends on the desired rating.

enhancements, appropriate for a particular class, would be totally inappropriate for other classes. On the degree of protection required, every credit enhancement carries a cost – the resulting benefit is the higher rating and therefore the lower cost of funding. However, there may be a yielding point where the increase in cost may not be justified by the consequential reduction in cost of funding.

Hence, choosing the right type and extent of credit enhancement is a skilled task in itself. Most advisors would suggest a mixed enhancement strategy.

The sizing of the credit enhancements is based on several factors, notably:

- Various probabilities of losses, and the expected loss
- Standard deviation of the expected losses
- Loss severity – the extent of recovery if an asset turns bad
- Correlation factor between different assets in a pool

First, second and subsequent loss

Credit enhancement is comparable to the economic capital for a business, so the process of sizing credit enhancement is similar to that for fixation of economic capital. Different credit enhancements are required at different target ratings. For instance, to see a BBB rating, the probability of any losses in the portfolio hitting the BBB class must not be more than the standard historical probability of a BBB-rated investment defaulting. Thus, economic capital in the form of credit enhancement should be available to reduce the probability of default by absorbing standard deviation of the losses. The higher the desired rating, the probability of loss has to be lower, resulting in higher levels of enhancements. Sizing credit enhancements will be discussed later in this section.

Thus, credit enhancement is a stacking order; the first to bear the losses will be the one who provides credit enhancement at the lowest level. This risk is called the **first-loss risk**. Usually, first-loss risk is absorbed until the level at which the class seeing the benefit of enhancement becomes marketable. If the least marketable class in any market is BBB class, the first-loss risk absorbed must be such as to qualify the class for a BBB rating. This BBB class would itself be a credit enhancement for other senior classes; therefore, the BBB class bears the **second-loss risk** or **mezzanine risk.**

Internal and external credit enhancements

Credit enhancements could be:

- Originator-provided
- Structural
- Third party-provided

Originator-provided credit enhancements refer to those where a part of the credit risk is assumed by the originator.

Structural credit enhancements refer to the redistribution of risk among the investors, so that one section of investors provides credit enhancements to the other. Similarly, there might even be a bifurcation of risk among investors, such as IOs and POs, where the risk of prepayment speed or interest rate movements is split among investors.

Third-party credit enhancements refer to the assumption of specific risks, credit risks and interest rate risks by third parties.

The reliance of a securitization structure on each of the sources of credit enhancements also has its own implications. If a structure relies too heavily on the credit of the originator, the instrument may be controlled by the entity rating of the originator. Yet more importantly, the transaction may not qualify for an off-balance-sheet treatment in the hands of the originator. If a transaction relies heavily on a third-party support, the rating of the counterparty becomes very important; in the U.K. mortgage-backed market, a number of transactions were downgraded due to the downgrading of the insurance companies that insured these pools. Most securitization transactions make use of a combination of these three sources of enhancements, with third-party enhancements having a limited applicability – as noted later.

Originator credit enhancements

The essential meaning of all originator-enhancements is the same: the originator agrees to put in an equity contribution in the transaction. This "equity" may be put in the form of cash, assets or retained profits. In addition, it is most common for the originator to invest in the subordinated securities, discussed in the next heading. Eventually, in every form of credit enhancement, the originator puts either cash or its kind to support the transaction. There is no fundamental difference between transferring assets of $110, and being paid $100 (a case of over-collateralization), or transferring assets of $100 and getting paid $90 (a case of cash reserve), or transferring $100 and investing in subordinated securities worth $10. In fact, retained profits are also nothing but a sacrifice of the right to receive cash. However, in reality each of these different forms of enhancement has different consequences.

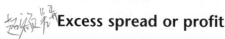### Excess spread or profit

The excess spread represents the excess of the inherent rate of return in the securitized portfolio over (a) the expenses of the transaction; (b) senior servicing fees; and (c) the rate of return offered to the investors.

> **Example 1**: Assume a pool of car loans has been contracted at inherent rates of return averaging 12%, and the originator expects a servicing fee of 2%, while the weighted-average funding cost of the SPV at 7%. Here, there is an element of excess spread, equaling to 3% (12% − 2% − 7%).

What will count as "excess spread"

It would be most usual for the originator to collect his service fee periodically, as that is the usual reward for continuing servicing function, normally matched by servicing costs. However, if the whole or a part of the servicing fee is subordinated,[14] that will also form part of the excess spread. In addition, if the coupon on junior subordinated notes is available for meeting the losses of the transaction, excess spread will be computed before such coupon.

The idea of excess spread is simple: Whatever is available from the income of the transaction, after meeting senior expenses, to meet losses on the assets, is credit-enhancing excess spread.

If the excess spread is not paid to the originator either up front or over a period, it is retained. It is retained by allowing the SPV to buy receivables at a discounting rate, in the above example at 12% (the same as the inherent rate of return of the pool); every interest collection leaves the SPV with a surplus of 3% after paying the servicing fees. The structure might provide for withdrawal of the retained spread either at the end of the transaction or on a periodic basis, or after the retained cash builds a reserve of a particular amount.

Does computation of excess spread necessarily imply the segregation of pool cash flow between principal and interest? By definition, excess spread is excess of income over expenses, excluding principal flows. Wherever the cash flow from the assets can be split into interest and principal, the computation of excess spread should be done based on the revenue cash flow only. In general, there is no question of there being an "excess principal" in a transaction; excess principal may only mean prepayment of principal, and so should be used to pay-down the securities rather than pay off as excess spread.

There are several ways for the originator to receive this excess profit – excess servicing fees, super profits on the subordinated debts acquired by the originator himself, interest on a subordinated loan, or the redemption price of a zero coupon bond; these are discussed later in the chapter.

Relevance of excess spread as a credit enhancement

Excess spread retention is by far the most common credit enhancement and is applicable for all those forms of collateral where revenue and principal collections can be segregated, such as RMBS, home equity, credit cards and auto loans.

Excess spread is the most natural form of enhancement. In every pool of assets, the income from the assets should take the losses on some assets, as in corporate finance, losses from some assets are taken care of by income from other assets. Unless the underwriting and pricing of the pool went fundamentally wrong, expected losses from every pool should sufficiently be covered by the expected excess profits, because the credit risk of every portfolio of assets are supposed to be priced out in the credit spreads.

Excess spread is also the least burdensome for the originator. Providing credit enhancement in other forms might have adverse consequences, for example, capital deduction for regulatory capital purposes. For instance, if the originator provides enhancement by over collateralization or by cash retention or subordinated investment, to the extent of such support provided, the capital of the originator suffers deduction. It is like the originator infusing equity into the asset. On the other hand, excess spread is only a loss of profits. There are no capital consequences if the excess spread serves as credit enhancement. If the excess spread is depleted in providing credit enhancement, it is only a loss of profit, while depletion of a subordinated investment will be a loss of capital.

Can excess spread suffice as a credit enhancement?

As discussed above, every pool should have sufficient excess spread at least to absorb the expected losses. However, the extent of excess spread is a function of (a) intensity of competition in the asset market; and (b) any senior expenses, senior IO or servicing fees that take a cut from out of the income before it is available for credit enhancement. It is notable that excess spread is usually only supposed to absorb the expected losses. Credit enhancement goes a step beyond – it has to provide for **unexpected losses** as well. That is to say, if things turn bad, and the loss levels rise, will the transaction go into a default? Credit enhancement, consistent with the rating of the transaction, indicates the tenacity of the transaction to withstand unexpected pressures. The concept is the same as that of economic capital[15] – while profits of an entity will usually absorb its losses, we need economic capital to absorb unexpected shocks.

Excess spread is usually considered **soft credit enhancement**. That is to say, while excess spread does provide credit enhancement, it cannot be trusted as a definitive source of support. All the more, it cannot be expressed as a percentage of the liabilities as it varies over time. As rating agency S&P puts it: "There is a distinction between "hard" and "soft" credit support. Hard credit support exists at closing (a reserve account initial deposit, overcollateralization, and subordination). Soft credit enhancement consists of excess spread that is available on a monthly basis to cover interest shortfalls and defaulted principal."[16]

Excess spread, even as a percentage of the outstanding asset balance, fluctuates over time. Excess spread may be compressed over time due to prepayments also – prepayment intensity is more for loans carrying higher rate of interest than those having lower interest; thus, the weighted-average rate of return on the pool may come down over time. Besides, all defaults and write offs also kill the excess spread, as there is no income from assets already defaulted.

Do rating agencies give credit to excess spread?

Rating agencies do give credit to excess spread, but not as much as in case of hard enhancements. As mentioned above, excess spread is itself liable to compression over time, and if the weighted-average rate of return in the pool has a high degree of standard deviation, the compression may be higher. While logically, it is impractical to think of a pool that does not have excess spread at least to cover expected losses, the structuring of a transaction may be more efficient, at least due to prevailing rating practices, if the excess spread was encashed and the hard enhancements were increased.

Can excess spread be controlled?

Is the excess spread of a pool completely origination-dependent or can it be controlled at the time of the transfer of the pool? The excess spread transferred to the SPV may easily be controlled at the time of transfer of the pool. Let us take the following examples to illustrate the point:

Example 2: Assume a pool of car loans has been contracted at inherent rates of return averaging 12%, but each of these loans are discounted at 10% and are sold to the SPV at a price equal to such discounted value The originator expects a servicing fee of 2%, while the weighted-average funding cost of the SPV is at 7%. Here, the excess spread is equal to 1% (10% − 2% − 7%). As the assets have been discounted at 10%, the SPV will get a return of only 10%. Excess spread equal to 2% was encashed upfront by the seller by selling the pool at a 10% discounting rate, which obviously means the pool was sold at higher than the par value.

Example 3: Assume a pool of car loans has been contracted at subvention rates, that is, to promote the sale of cars at low rates of return averaging 6%. However, each of these loans are discounted at 10% and are sold to the SPV at a price equal to such discounted value The originator expects a servicing fee of 2%, while the weighted-average funding cost of the SPV at 7%. Here, the excess spread is equal to 1% (10% − 2% − 7%). It is notable that while the original rate of return in the loans was much less because the loans were discounted at 10%, the seller took a loss at the time of sale but the SPV still sees a return of 10%.

Example 4: In example 2, the purpose may also be fulfilled by the originator creating a 2% IO strip, which is senior, such that the interest payable on the notional principal of the IO strip is paid before the excess spread is worked out. Obviously, this has the effect of reducing the excess interest by 2%.

It is clear from these examples that excess spread for any pool of assets can be controlled.

Cash collateral

Cash collateral, cash reserve or cash deposit refer to the SPV retaining a cash balance, which is subordinated to the interests of the investors. The cash reserve can be created either up front, by retention of a part of the funding of the transaction by the SPV, or by the originator making a subordinated loan to the SPV, or by building it up over the transaction by retention of the excess profits.

The initial cash collateral is a hard form of enhancement as it is available at the inception. If the cash collateral is to be built by retention of the excess profits, the size of the excess profits relative to the required cash collateral will determine the time expected to be taken to build it, but it can serve as reasonably certain form of enhancement.

Example 5: If a pool of car loans has an outstanding principal value of $100, and is transferred at par to the SPV. The SPV will raise a funding of $100, but retains a cash deposit of $100 and pays only $90 to the originator. In this case, there is a cash collateral to the extent of $10.

Cash collateral is economically burdensome

As noted, cash collateral is both a credit and liquidity enhancement. However, the relevance of the cash collateral is to be stressed more from a point of liquidity than a point of credit enhancement. As a source of credit enhancement, cash collateral is not a good choice as it implies a negative carry. It may be worthwhile comparing over-collateralization and cash collateral (see following capital on over-collateralization). As it implies negative carry, it has adverse impact on the excess spreads, and therefore, the overall economics of the transaction.

In a special report dated September 4, 2003, rating agency Fitch recounts two French transactions that went into early amortization due to excess spread compression. "Although not breaching any of the triggers applying to their assets, the cash accumulation hampered performance by reducing excess spread generated. As yields on cash are generally below those on receivables, the margins earned on both transactions narrowed markedly and the transactions became more vulnerable to deterioration in asset performance."

Credit-enhancing IO strip

A subordinated IO strip also serves the same purpose as excess spread. The IO strip is a security with no principal (however, notional principal to claim interest) that keeps claiming interest at the strip rate over time. If this interest claim is subordinated and may be deferred or waived to take care of losses, this is also a form of credit enhancement.

The nature of the subordinated IO strip is the same as excess spread, except that the IO strip is transferable and not necessarily held by the originator. However, the discussion above on the excess spread is applicable to the IO strip as well.

Over-collateralization

This refers to the originator transferring a higher value of receivables, but being paid for a lesser value and leaving the balance as a security interest with the SPV. As the most common form of margin, this is a common form of credit enhancement, particularly in emerging markets.

> **Example 6**: If a pool of car loans has an outstanding principal value of $110, and are transferred at par to the SPV. The SPV will raise a funding of $100 and pays $100 to the originator, retaining the balance of the assets as a collateral. Here, there is an over-collateralization to the extent of $10.

While the over-collateralization may seem like the cash collateral, there are significant, notable differences.

- Over-collateralization results in a collateral in kind, while cash collateralization results in a collateral in cash. The problem of negative carry inherent in cash collateral does not apply to over-collateralization.
- Assuming the cash collateral is invested for a fixed time, the percentage size of the cash collateral increases over time as the pool is paid down. This is the problem that the Fitch report cited has narrated. In case of

over-collateralization, as the size of the over-collateralised assets also simultaneously comes down, the percentage size of over-collateralization does not increase over time.

- In case of over-collateralization, what we have in the structure is both excess interest and excess principal, as principal is collected on assets worth $110 to pay principal on liabilities worth $100. If this excess principal collected, after being utilized to the extent required to absorb losses, is paid off, the transaction continues to have a 10% over-collateralization over time.

- Over-collateralization does not result in reduction of excess spread, as the in-kind assets broadly have the same rate of return as the rest of the pool. For cash reserves, the rate of return is markedly lesser than the coupon payable on the securities.

Treatment of over-collateralization by the originator

It is notable that in the legal sense, the extent of extra collateral transferred to the SPV is a transfer for the sake of security, not a legal transfer. Similarly, for accounting purposes, over-collateralization should be treated as deposit for security, rather than a transfer.

In addition, over-collateralization is a subordinated interest in the pool and not an investment. In accounting parlance, the over-collateralized pool will be treated as a part of the originated loans, although collateralized to secure a liability. Hence, mark-to-market rules applicable to investments in **available-for-sale** assets do not apply to over-collateralization stake.

Over-collateralization and early amortization triggers

Usually, a provision for over-collateralization may be accompanied by early amortization triggers. That is to say, if the performance of the pool worsens to an extent, then instead of the seller's subordinated interest in the principal being paid off, the same may be re-directed to pay off investors.

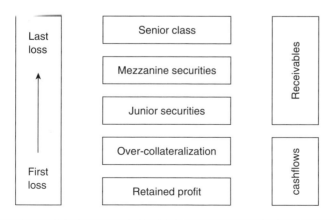

Figure 4.2 Illustration of a typiocal credit enhancement structure

Structural credit enhancements

When various classes of liabilities are issued with different priorities – such as Class A, Class B, Class C, the subordination of Class C provides a credit enhancement to Class B, and both of them provide enhancement to Class A. This credit enhancement comes from the structure of the liabilities, so it is called structured enhancement.

The most common form of credit enhancements for securitization transactions is the stratification of the securities into senior, mezzanine and junior or subordinated securities. As this is the very principle of structured finance – carving out securities with different risk/return attributes, structural enhancement is crucial to a securitization transaction.

The receivables will be used first to pay for the senior securities, which have a claim over the entire cash flow to be paid first. Obviously, senior securities are the safest of all, and would have to be contented with a very low rate of return. The subordinated securities are those paid after settling the claims of the senior and the mezzanine security holders. These are almost like equity holders in a company; they stand a chance of suffering a loss of principal and interest. The coupon rates are expected to increase as one goes down the ladder of the liabilities.

In terms of ratings, the stratification of liabilities is done so as to see a AAA rating for the senior most class. The rating for the junior-most rated class is what is sellable in the market.[17] The unrated class is typically retained by the originator.

The junior-senior structure is quite popular among securitizers. Where the junior-most securities are bought by the originator, such investment caps the risk of the originator. The rest of the credit risk is distributed among investors, and as the coupons offered on different classes of risks are different, there are investors for each class. The overall support required from the originator is much less in a stratified securitization than in case of a direct support provided by the originator. The originator can look at the weighted-average cost of funds. Besides, the structure meets the needs of different investors as per their own investment objectives. Most significantly, the senior notes may easily draw safety-minded investors such as charitable trusts, schools and churches.

Transaction-wide support vs. structural support

The different methods of originator enhancement, including excess spread, cash retention and over-collateralization, provide credit support to the entire

---

Box 4.2: Subordination structure

- Subordination is the most common feature in structured finance transactions.

- It creates a military-like set up of risk-takers: with each lower class providing protection for the senior classes.

- The only difference between a military set up and securitization structure is, securitizations are top-heavy: the most senior class is the thickest of all.

- Risks are absorbed bottom up – the junior-most take the risks first.

- And the rewards are distributed top-down – the senior-most class is the cheapest; the junior-most often also takes the residual returns.

transaction. On the other hand, structural support is different for each level of liabilities. Structural support is a case of re-allocation of risks – one is better at the cost of others.

Both have their own relevance – the pool-wide enhancements provide natural support to the transaction. If pool-wide enhancements are sufficient, even the junior-most class of liabilities may see an investment grade rating. However, a transaction backed solely by pool-wide enhancements fails to capture the real alchemy of structured finance.

Hence, most securitization transactions use a combination of excess spread retention and/or cash collateral, and a stratification of the investors.

Third-party credit enhancements

There are numerous types of third-party enhancements available. As securitization markets grow, the availability of third-party support to transactions is also growing.

Sources of external credit enhancements

The following is a quick description of the various sources of external support:

Pool insurance 保险

Insurance covers for the assets in the pool normally exist in case of mortgage assets. Insurance companies have been providing covers against mortgage assets in several forms. These policies typically cover the risk of foreclosure of a mortgage loan. The practices differ from country to country, but the broad types of insurance policies offered by insurance companies are:

- Primary insurance – the insurance company covering a particular loan. This may be a standard coverage or amortizing coverage, the latter meaning insured value is reduced over time.
- Portfolio insurance – provides insurance coverage on a pool of mortgages. Obviously, the cost of this is less than having each mortgage covered by insurance cover. This may be:
  - First-loss or stop-loss insurance – the insurance company takes losses up to a particular percentage of the initial loan size.
  - Excess of loss – exactly contrary to the above – as the insurance company takes losses exceeding a particular amount.

Mortgage insurance practices exist in several countries. In the U.S., mortgage insurance is provided by both public and private entities. The public insurers include federal, state, and governmental agencies, such as the Federal Housing Administration (FHA) and the Department of Veterans Affairs (VA). The private mortgage insurance industry predominantly consists of eight leading U.S. insurers.

The limitations of using insurance covers to shift the risk of the loans are:

- Under prevailing conditions, the benefit of insurance cover is mostly limited to mortgage markets.
- Whether the loans are insured or not, and under what terms, is the call of the originator taken based on his overall underwriting policies. Securitization is not necessarily in mind while making that decision.
- All insurance carries a cost: the originator needs to compare the cost of shifting the risk to an insurance company, or of redistributing the same to capital market investors.
- If insurance cover has been used as a credit enhancement, there is a dependence of the transaction on the rating of the insurance company.

Letters of credit

Here, the originator arranges for a letter of credit (LoC) from a third party, usually from an acceptable bank. Credit insurance is a little more advanced form of credit guarantees where the insurer may cover for such risks as interest rate variations. The considerations here are largely the same as those in case of insurance cover.

Related party guarantee

This refers to guarantees against defaults obtained by either the originator or a related party.

Monoline insurance

Monoline insurance companies originated in U.S. municipal markets and are so known because they are not engaged in traditional insurance functions but merely provide insurance against defaults in financial transactions. They are limited by charter [for example, by Article 69 of the State of New York] to provide only financial guarantees. Monolines have traditionally existed only in the U.S. but have recently expanded to European and certain Asian markets as well. A monoline insurance company would provide insurance cover to some of the securities in a securitization transaction which, based on the rating of the insurance company itself, would substantially upgrade the rating of the said securities.

The role of monolines and financial guarantee companies in the securitization market has grown over time. As per data on the website of the Association of Financial Guarantee Insurers (AFGI), "par value of outstanding asset-backed and mortgage-backed securities insured worldwide by AFGI members now totals more than $650 billion. This compares to $92 billion in par value in 1996."[18] The data of outstanding securities secured by AFGI insurers are:

Net par outstanding (Amounts in millions)	December 31, 2003
Structured finance	
Mortgage-backed securities - US	119,009
Other asset-backed - US	221,779
Mortgage-backed securities - international	31,244
Other asset-backed - international	104,061
Investor-owned utility obligations	40,530
Other - US	28,484
Other - International	58,175
Total structured finance	603,283
TOTAL	1,648,909

Credit derivatives

Another significant source of third-party credit enhancement is credit derivatives, the transfer of credit risk to a counter-party by way of a credit default swap transaction. The meaning of credit derivatives is discussed at length in Vinod Kothari's *Credit Derivatives and Synthetic Securitisation*.

Suitability of third-party enhancements

External credit enhancements are used commonly in mortgage markets. However, the use of insurance wraps for other securitization transactions can be viewed in light of the following:

- For emerging market transactions, insurance wraps or monoline guarantees are commonly used to make the securities acceptable to cross-border investors. For example, U.S. investors may be unwilling to accept a Korean transaction, even if it is credit-enhanced to a AAA level, except on the strength of an insurance company acceptable to them.
- Several future flow transactions are capped at the originator ratings. Insurance wraps allow such transactions to be rated at the AAA rating of the insurer.
- If due to its structural enhancements, a security at an A or AA level, the insurance wrap allows it to be uplifted. The insurance wrap is almost never the first-loss support to the transaction.

Sizing of credit enhancements

To reiterate, the size of the credit enhancement is one of the most critical factors in structuring of the transaction, and makes or mars its economics.

We have noted before that the size of credit enhancement is related to the expected rating of the security. In this section, we take up a closer look at how the exact size of credit enhancements related to rating levels are worked out. This section may be backed up by the numerical examples in Chapter 9, while Chapter 11 on rating may also be a useful companion.

The essence of quantification of credit enhancements is as follows: The enhancements imply the economic capital of the transaction, that is, the source that will absorb losses and keep the rated securities protected against losses. The losses are quantified based on the assumptions that are validated by the historical experience with a similar statistical static pool. However, we then stress the assumptions, and stress them so as to cover a particular range of probable scenarios. This range of probabilities is related to the rating of the securities.

Confidence level for different ratings

At the outset, we need to understand that there is nothing on which it is impossible to default. The best rating means highest safety, not absolute safety. With each level of rating, there remains a probability of default. The table below shows the historical probabilities of default on corporate bonds:

All Rated Corporate Bonds[a]

		Years after Issuance									
1977–2003		1	2	3	4	5	6	7	8	9	10
AAA	Marginal	0.00%	0.00%	0.00%	0.00%	0.03%	0.00%	0.00%	0.00%	0.00%	0.00%
	Cumulative	0.00%	0.00%	0.00%	0.00%	0.03%	0.03%	0.03%	0.03%	0.03%	0.03%
AA	Marginal	0.00%	0.00%	0.33%	0.17%	0.00%	0.00%	0.00%	0.00%	0.03%	0.02%
	Cumulative	0.00%	0.00%	0.33%	0.05%	0.05%	0.05%	0.05%	0.05%	0.53%	0.55%
A	Marginal	0.01%	0.11%	0.02%	0.09%	0.05%	0.10%	0.06%	0.21%	0.11%	0.06%
BBB	Marginal	0.04%	3.45%	1.58%	1.45%	0.98%	0.56%	0.28%	0.25%	0.16%	0.42%
BB	Marginal	1.22%	2.52%	4.44%	2.05%	2.55%	1.10%	1.65%	0.88%	1.72%	3.70%
	Cumulative	1.22%	3.77%	7.98%	9.87%	12.17	13.14%	14.57%	15.15%	16.61%	19.69%
B	Marginal	3.06%	6.92%	7.48%	8.58%	6.08$	4.18%	3.74%	2.31%	2.00%	0.88%
	Cumulative	3.06%	9.77%	16.52%	23.69%	28.32%	31.32%	33.89%	35.41%	36.70%	37.26%
CCC	Marginal	8.18%	15.57%	19.15%	12.18%	4.26%	10.25%	5.65%	3.15%	0.00%	4.28%
	Cumulative	8.18%	22.48%	37.32	44.96	47.30	52.70%	55.37%	56.78%	56.78%	58.63%

(a) Rated by S&P at Issuance
Based on 1.719 issues
Source: Standard & Poor's (New York) and E. Altman's Compilation

If we have a 5-year transaction, then historical levels of mortality, as shown by the above table, reflect the following table:

5-year PDs by S&P for bonds

	PD	Confidence level
AAA	0.03%	99.97%
AA	0.50%	99.50%
A	0.28%	99.72%
BBB	7.64%	92.36%
BB	12.17%	87.83%
B	28.32%	71.68%
CCC	47.30%	52.70%

That is to say, for AAA-rated bonds, the mortality rate is 0.03%, or recipro-cally, there is 99.97% confidence that the bond will survive (not necessarily with the same rating) at the end of five years. The confidence level for AA-rated bond is 99.5%, and that for BBB-rated bond is 92.36%.

In other words, if one has sufficient credit enhancement to cover 92.36% of the probable loss scenarios, the security at that level of credit enhancement may qualify for a BBB-rating.

Stress testing of retail portfolios

Retail loans, by definition, have a high granularity and the total pool amount is split into loans of insignificant sizes. Retail borrowers belong to different segments of the economy. Implicitly, it is assumed that there is a very low or no correlation between the different obligors. In addition, there is no compu-tation of the probability of default for each obligor individually, as all the obligors are presumed to have the same probability of default.

The rate of default for a retail pool is like a **hazard rate,** such as the rate of accidents in a city or the rate of deaths due to heart attack. The historical haz-ard rates may not hold good in the future, but the probability that the actual rate will be higher or lower than several multiples of the historical rate can be assessed.

Our idea is to stress the default rate so as to reach the confidence levels required for the desired rating. In case of retail pools, rating agencies do this stressing the application of multiples to the cumulative losses implied by the pool data. The process works as follows:

- We project the pool data, with normal assumptions of scheduled pay-ments, prepayments, and defaults.
- We compute the cumulative losses for the entire term of the pool. Note that the cumulative loss for the pool is not just the annual rate multiplied by the number of years – the loss rate is applied on an ever-reducing pool size, both due to amortization and prepayments.
- This cumulative loss is the expected loss, that is, loss without applying any stress.

- The stresses are now applied – the stress may be applied by multiplying the default rate, or by multiplying the expected loss, by multiples based on the required confidence levels. Rating agencies use multipliers to apply to the expected loss number.
- The typical multipliers used by Standard and Poor's in the case of auto loan transactions are given below; it is notable that the multipliers may be increased due to a lack of data and other relevant factors.

AAA	4–5x base case losses
AA	3–4x
A	2–3x
BBB	1.75–2x
BB	1.5–1.75x

Example 7: Let us assume, at a 0.5% rate of default (losses) per annum, the cumulative losses for a pool work out to 1.68%. Taking the above multipliers (higher of the range), the sizing of credit enhancements in shown below:

Base loss			1.68%
Rating (1)	*Multiplier* (2)	*Required support* (3)	*size of liabilities* (4)
AAA	5	8.40%	91.60%
AA	4	6.72%	1.68%
A	3	5.04%	1.68%
BBB	2	3.36%	1.68%
BB	1.75	2.94%	0.42%
Unrated			2.94%

The required support in Col. 3 of the above table has been worked out by multiplying the base case loss by the multipliers given in Col. 2. As Class A needs a credit support of 8.4%, the size of Class A is (1-8.4%). Likewise, the size of each class is computed by deducting, from the enhancement required at one level above, the enhancement required at the class level.

Sizing of enhancement for wholesale portfolios

The working of confidence levels required for each class of securities is the same as in the case of retail portfolios. However, the significant difference in case of wholesale portfolios is the computing of the probability distribution of the losses.

Wholesale portfolios are characterized by the following:

- Each obligor in the pool is different and has a different probability of default. It is possible to study the strength of each obligor, so it is possible to apply different probabilities of default to each obligor.
- If a default happens, the loss per obligor is given by (1-recovery rate), which is a function of several factors. The recovery rate for each obligor may also be different.
- If different obligors belong to the same or correlated industries, there is also a degree of correlation as between the obligors.
- Taking the probability of default of each obligor, and the correlations as input, the objective is to derive a distribution of probabilities of default for the pool.

The best example of a wholesale portfolio of credits is a CDO. Rating agencies use models to arrive at the distribution of probabilities based on the above input. These models essentially rely on simulation devices. The methodology used for arriving at the probabilities of default in case of CDOs, along with a description of the rating agency approaches, is discussed in Chapter 17 on CDOs.

Stepping up credit enhancements

In certain loan pools, particularly for unseasoned retain loan pools, the rate of default tends to go up over time. Hence, while a lower level of enhancement might be sufficient to kick-off the transaction, it may be necessary to increase the enhancement level to an increased level over the term of the transaction. This is usually ensured by sequential payment (see later in this chapter).

Liquidity enhancements

Almost as significant as the credit enhancements in a transaction is the liquidity enhancement, that is, the provision of liquidity for timely payment to the investors. Liquidity enhancements are only meant to provide a temporary cash facility and do not subordinate themselves to the external investors.

Typical sources of liquidity enhancements will include the following:

- **Servicer advances:** For retail portfolios, a common form of liquidity enhancement in a transaction is the servicer himself. Typically, servicers provide periodic advances to the structure from where the payments are made and the collections during the period go on to reimburse the servicer. Generally, the servicer has the first right to reimburse himself from the collections made during the period. Where the servicer provides liquidity, rating agencies take into consideration the rating of the servicer.
- **Bank facilities:** Servicing a securitization transaction, particularly those with pay-through features, is like running a treasury operation. To mitigate temporary liquidity problems, several structures need to arrange a liquidity facility with banks. This is quite common in case of conduits, or CDOs.

- **Cash reserve:** Building a real source of cash to meet periodic delinquencies is quite helpful, though, as we have noted, there is a cost of negative carry with cash reserves.

Pay-down structure

While the credit enhancement structure fixes the liabilities as at the start of the transaction, the pay down structure determines what will be the liability structure over time, because the pay-down structure is concerned with how the principal realized from the assets is distributed to various classes of liabilities. Therefore, the significance of the pay-down structure is the same as that of credit enhancements.

Notably, the pay-down question arises only where the liabilities will be amortized over time. If, for instance, the transaction provides for a bullet repayment of the liabilities, the pay-down sequence does not just matter.

The pay-down method relates to the principal collected over time. There are four broad pay-down choices (and there might be any combinations of these):

Box 4.3: Sequential vs. pro-rata pay-down	

Box 4.3: Sequential vs. *pro-rata* pay-down

- A sequential structure reduces the leverage inherent in the transaction as the pay-down starts; *pro-rata* structure maintains the leverage.

- Reduced leverage means higher weighted-average cost.

- If a certain level of leverage was found appropriate at the start-up, it should prevail, unless the transaction is perceived to be going wrong and needs extra layers of protection.

- Therefore, sequential pay-down is only a protective measure to be used as a corrective step to increase the relative thickness of senior classes.

Sequential pay-down

Sequential pay-down structure means the notes are paid down sequentially, top down. Nothing is paid to Class B notes until Class A is fully paid. It is sequential as amongst the various classes, and pro-rata within the class. The impact of a sequential pay-down is to reduce the leverage of the transaction, to increase the percentage credit enhancement of the senior classes, and to increase the weighted-average cost of the transaction.

A securitization transaction has a stacking order of investors, of which Class A is the senior most and the cheapest. Sequential pay-down means retirement of the highest-rated and therefore the cheapest debt class first. Obviously, this increases the protection available to the senior class as the relative size of debt to equity comes down. Simultaneously, as the cheapest class will be retired first, the weighted-average cost of the transaction goes up. The cost may go up to an extent as to completely dry down the excess spread.

Typically in a transaction the impact of a sequential pay-down on the weighted-average cost of the transaction may not be too substantial to be visible on the face of it, as the subordinated classes are not substantial in proportion alone. Yet the impact on weighted-average cost needs to be carefully studied.

Pro-rata pay-down

Pro-rata or proportional pay-down means the principal collections are distributed among the various classes in proportion to their respective outstanding capital. A *pro-rata* repayment structure maintains the relative share of various classes, the percentage credit enhancement available to the various classes, and the weighted-average cost of the transaction.

If the size of the subordinated classes is substantial, and the transaction has not hit any of the early amortization triggers, it might be sensible to do a proportional pay down.

Fast-pay/slow-pay structure

As a mid-point between sequential and proportional repayment, a fast-pay/slow-pay structure repays to both the senior and the junior classes, but more to the senior classes and less to the junior classes. Therefore, the senior class is the fast-pay class and the junior class is the slow-pay class. This method combines the advantages of the two methods discussed above.

Step-up structure

We have earlier talked about the need to step up credit enhancement over time. Here, we are trying to step-up the level of credit enhancement. For example, in Example 7, the credit support at the inception was 8.4%. Let us say, we have the objective of increasing the credit enhancement level to 12%. If so, we will do a sequential repayment of Class A until the size of Class A becomes 88% of the total liabilities, and thereafter, we do a proportional repayment. Thereby, we have increased the credit enhancement, and thereafter, remained at such an increased level.

Choice of the pay-down method

The choice of the pay-down method is critical. As noted from the discussion above, a completely sequential pay-down method, where the amortization period is long and the size of the subordinated securities is not purely nominal, may be fatal to the economics of the transaction. A fully proportional pay-down fails to meet the objective of increasing the enhancement to a higher level as the pool comes of age. Therefore, a combination of the two so that we achieve a step up but then a shift to the proportional method is an ideal choice.

Needless to say, the sequential method is the choice when the transaction has hit certain triggers.

Maturity of the securities

From the understanding of the concept of asset-backed securities, it is obvious that cash flow from the pool is used to pay off the securities over time. Depending on the transaction structure:

- The principal collected on the assets over time may be paid off to investors regularly.
- The principal collected over time may be reinvested, for example, in reinstating the pool.
- The principal collected over time may be accumulated to be paid off to investors by way of a bullet repayment.

In either event, as there is a dependence on the cash flow from the pool to pay off the securities, there is no fixed contractual maturity for repayment of the securities as in case of bonds or debentures. Hence, asset-backed securities have "expected maturity," that is, the date by which, based on the assumptions as to pay off of the assets, the securities are expected to be paid off. These assumptions include:

- The contractual scheduled cash flow, affected by delays, defaults and recoveries
- Prepayments
- Any clean up call option
- The manner of repayment of various classes of liabilities from the principal collections – will the principal be redirected to pay a particular class
- Early amortization triggers.

The expected maturity may be contracted because of more than expected prepayments, clean up call or early amortization. It may be extended because of factors like less-than-expected prepayment and non-exercise of the clean up call.

However, as expected maturities are completely definitive, it is necessary to come to that "judgement day" when the transaction will be ultimately wound up. This is the **final maturity**, or sometimes called **legal final maturity.** The legal final maturity is when the transaction is not expected to have any asset left over (in other words, provides time for delinquent receivables to have been paid off), and takes no prepayment or exercise of the call option to take place. In case of CMBS transactions, which have a refinancing feature,[19] as we expect no refinancing to take place, the legal final maturity is considerably longer.

Profit extraction devices

The excess spread inherent in the assets after meeting all costs and expenses is the residual profit of the transaction, which obviously should go to the originator. The originator may use various devices, or combinations thereof, to sweep this profit. Some possible devices are:

- Upfront encashment by transferring receivables at higher than their carrying value, or at a lower discounting rate than the weighted-average IRR
- Servicing fees

- Residual interest security – an investment in the SPV by way of a loan, zero coupon bond, or residual income bond that allows the originator to sweep the remaining profit in the SPV
- A clean up call, whereby all remaining receivables may be swept at a lower price
- Retention of an interest rate strip
- Interest on a subordinated loan
- Interest rate swap, whereby the actual interest income of the transaction is swapped by a lower interest rate
- Deferred sale consideration, the amount remaining with the SPV after repaying all investors is added to the consideration for sale of the asset as deferred sale consideration.

Each of these methods might have distinct legal, tax and accounting implications. While those technical implications are studied in respective chapters later, the substantive question from a structuring perspective is – should the entire excess spread be passed over to the SPV and then recaptured, or should a part of it be accelerated and encashed upfront? If the excess spread is quite high in view of the expected losses from the transaction, it is quite sensible to encash a part of the excess profit upfront. This is from several points of view. First, the sale consideration as between the seller and the SPV should be established as fair value; if the pool has high excess spread, it would mean the fair value is higher than the par value. Secondly, as in any event, the transaction will require a degree of hard enhancement, transferring more than required credit enhancement does not do any good. Third, if the excess spread is quite high, the recapture thereof in the form of service fees or returns on subordinated securities is likely to look artificially high, exposing the transaction to suspicion.

Cash flow waterfall

The cash flow waterfall is a reflection of the credit enhancement, principal priorities and structural protection. In other words, all the intended credit enhancement, priority or exceptional rights of investors of a particular class are all articulated in the waterfall clause. For instance, Class A is senior to Class B, because it is so provided in the sequential waterfall clause of the transaction. Examples of legal wording of the waterfall clause may be found in Chapter 24.

The cash flow waterfall has two sides, an interest waterfall and a principal waterfall. The interest inflows are used to meet the expenses of the SPV, to begin with those payable to external agencies, and thereafter, to pay interest to the various classes of investors. The servicer's service fees may be subordinated or may be senior, depending on whether it is a normal service fee or excess service fee.

The principal flows arise from out of the scheduled principal collection, prepayments, and any amount diverted from the revenue waterfall to meet losses of principal. The principal collected is used to pay off the principal on the securities.

As far as possible, a transaction should distinguish between the interest and principal waterfall. There is no difference between cash flow of an operating company and that of a securitization transaction from the viewpoint of waterfall; the significance of maintaining a distinction between revenue and capital flows in corporate finance reflects the same in case of securitization. We do not use principal flows to pay interest, but may use the excess of income over expenses – revenue flows – to pay off the principal.

Notes

1   As in the case of managed CDOs.
2   See Chapter 2 on Revolving Structures.
3   See Chapter 2 under Asset Features.
4   See Chapter 5 on Understanding the Nature and Risks of Asset-Backed Securities.
5   See more on computation of the option adjusted spread and cost of the prepayment option in Chapter 10.
6   See discussion in Chapter 2 on companion classes or support classes.
7   There might be procedures for noteholders voting to resolve such unapprehended problems.
8   See later in this chapter.
9   See also the preceding sections of this chapter.
10 See Chapter 23 on Legal Issues.
11 A model legal opinion for a securitization transaction is enclosed in the Appendix to Chapter 23 on legal issues.
12 The servicing and other operational aspects of securitization are taken up in Chapter 25.
13 For detailed analysis of the concept of economic capital, see Chapter 29 on Regulatory and Economic Capital.
14 Sometimes distinction is made between normal and excess service fees – the former senior and the latter junior.
15 See Economic Capital in Chapter 29.
16 Auto Loan Criteria, pg. 23
17 See earlier in this chapter on the classes of liabilities and the retained class.
18 At http://www.afgi.org/products-assetsec.htm, last visited December 20, 2005.
19 See details in Chapter 13.

Chapter 5

Understanding the Nature and Risks of Asset-backed Securities

This and the following two chapters develop analytical and numerical understanding of risks of asset-backed securities. This chapter is analytical, while the next two chapters are both analytical and numerical.

Asset-backed securities and the underlying collateral

Asset-backed securities are designed as structured, proportional claims on pools of assets; therefore, they carry the same risks as the asset pool in question. These risks are structured – they are not allocated uniformly to different classes of investors. But as investors tend to compare investment in asset-backed securities with other fixed income investors, it is important to understand the differential risks of investing in asset-backed paper.

Take the case of investment in mortgage-backed securities. If all the different classes of mortgage-backed paper are clubbed together, the sum of these securities is no different from the pool of mortgage loans originated and distanced by the originator. The originator himself, in turn, is also a pool of such pools. In a relatively straight-forward securitization transaction, asset-backed securities would represent cash flows that have passed through more than one filter of differentiation; the separation of the pool from the originator was itself one such filter, and then the structuring done at the transaction level was yet another. In more complex transactions, there might be several such layers of aggregation and segregation. For example, there may be assimilation of pools from different originators, credit enhancements at each such origination level, pooling them together into a conduit, creation of credit and liquidity enhancements at the pool-level and finally resulting in the securities.

The essence of asset-backed securities is a process of integration and differentiation. In fact, the essential process of creation of any financial instrument is the same integration and differentiation, but corporate finance itself is an integration of claims over the pool of corporate assets and differentiation thereof in two basic claims – ownership-type and debt-type, and within that, several other mutually-differentiated claims. On a more generic plain, this process of integration and differentiation is the very basis of nature – from vegetation to human body, all systems are designed to analyze substances, differentiate them, integrate them, and so on. This is because nothing is "created" – all creation is essentially differentiation and/or integration.

The essence of this discussion is to probe into a very basic question: Is the nature, and therefore, the underlying risk of an asset-backed security different from that of the business of the originator? The answer to the question cannot be singular. It is both yes and no.

Yes, the nature and risks of asset-backed securities are the same as those of the business of the originator. The mother source of cash flow is the pool of cash flow; that is, or was, an integral part of the business of the originator. It would be juvenile to expect the separated pool to be substantially different from the pools that have not been separated. Therefore, the business risk of the originator does have a clear reflection on asset-backed securities.

No, the nature and risks of asset-backed securities are not the same as those of the business of the originator. First of all, several things would have already been done before the pool was created, as in the mortgage lending business the securitization arises only after the pool has been created and seasoned for a while. Secondly and more significantly, the inherent risks and returns of the pool have been segregated into various classes and claims. That may mean either the risks have been mitigated or aggravated. Creation of several classes of claims obviously implies mutual allocation of such risk - with one class taking more risk than the other. Therefore, there might be leveraged risk for some classes and reduced risk for others.

The first point above gives us a significant message – that a clear understanding of the nature and risk of the collateral is important to understand the nature and risk of asset-backed paper. The second point provides another significant insight: These risks may actually have been structured, either reduced or increased. But as the source of the risks is the collateral, the need to understand the collateral cannot be over-emphasized.

Asset-backed securities emanate from different collateral classes, and the nature and risk of each collateral class are different. The broad generalization below suffers from over-simplification, but assuming it is of some value, here are some basic collateral classes from the viewpoint of nature and risk:

1. Asset-backed consumer credits – mortgage loans, auto loans, installment credit or hire purchase. At the pool-level, collateral quality is reflected by LTV ratio and debt-to-income ratio.
2. Non-asset-backed consumer revolving credits – such as credit cards and home equity line of credit. At the pool-level, collateral quality is reflected by consumer credit scores (such as FICO scores), and the extent of excess spread.
3. Non-asset-backed consumer term credits – such as student loans and home equity loans.

4. Asset-backed business loans – such as commercial mortgage loans, equipment leases, aircraft leases. Commercial mortgage-backed loans may be taken as a different class by itself, as the value of the mortgage property is independent of the nature of the business carried in it. But other asset-backed loans are substantially dependent on the businesses.
5. Non-asset-backed business exposures – such as CLOs, SME loans and leveraged loans.
6. CDOs and synthetic CDOs – a hand-picked sample of diversified business exposures, with a high degree of leverage, generally motivated by arbitrage.
7. Future flows and intellectual property – an obvious exposure in the direct business risks of the entity.
8. Whole business and similar transactions – a leveraged exposure in the business risks of the entity.

Risks in asset-backed securities

In most of these asset-backed securities, a common feature of the legal structure of the transaction is the isolation of the asset into a separate issuing vehicle. This is the "true sale" so-often talked about in context of any securitization. However, true sale only seeks to dedicate, to the exclusion of the other creditors of the originator, the cash flow of the pool to service the investors in the securitization transaction. But the more significant question is – will the cash flow come in? Sometimes, legal uniqueness of the transaction may cloud its inherent risks. Therefore, the brief discussion in this chapter, followed by more elaborate discussion in the following chapters, is extremely significant.

Will the cash flow come in or the credit risks?

As with any investment, the key question to understand is the volatility and unpredictability of the stream of cash flow. The uncertainty of cash flow at the pool-level is structured into claims of different classes of investors; therefore, it is necessary to understand what that uncertainty is.

Obviously, the credit risk of each collateral class is different. For most existing asset transaction, the credit risk is the risk of default by the obligors, but for several transactions, particularly future flows, the risk might actually be a performance risk on the part of the originator. Thus, in cases where the receivables are conditional upon performance of the part of the originator, the risk is two-fold – a primary risk on the originator's performance, and thereafter, a credit risk.

Who will get the cash flows in, or servicing risk?

The servicing function includes all that processes that are done post-origination until the receivables are actually collected. True sale or no true sale, the ability of the transaction to pay off investors depends on actual translation of the claims into cash. For different transactions, servicing might be a very different function; for example, for a typical consumer loan, the loan having been originated, the servicing function is largely limited to mere collection of the loan instalments over time and serving the information needs of the borrowers. But in case of several cash flows, servicing requires an intensive interface with the borrowers. To the extent the servicing task is not something that can easily be transferred, the isolation of the pool for legal purposes does not have much meaning. In other words, the transaction still remains anchored to the servicer, and so servicer-dependent.

Timing of the cash flow or prepayment risk

For several collateral classes, the prepayment risk might itself be a significant risk. If the underlying pool cash flow has a contractual or behavioral prepayment feature, the same is reflected on the cash flow of the pool. Prepayment risks can be very significant for longer-term cash flows, typically most significant in case of mortgage-backed securities.

Liquidity of the transaction

Liquidity implies whether the cash flow at any time will be sufficient to pay off scheduled interest and principal to the investors. Delinquency level is the basic reason for cash flow shortage.

Interest rate and other volatilities

If any of the assets and liabilities have an interest rate or basis mismatch, there is an interest rate risk in the transaction. Likewise, if any of the assets and liabilities of the transaction have a currency mismatch, there is an exchange rate risk.

Other risks

Depending on the nature of the transaction, there might be various other risks – such as collateral manager risk (in case of managed transactions), reinvestment risks (in case of transactionst that make substantial reinvestments) and others.

Modeling of asset risks

We take up the risk of prepayment in the next chapter. Chapter 7 takes care of the risk of default and delays. Servicing and other operational issues are taken up in Chapter 25. Interest rate mismatches and exchange rate mismatches are generic risks, not unique to securitization and thus are not discussed at length in this book.

Chapter 6

Understanding Prepayment Risk in Asset-backed Securities

Prepayment risk in case of asset-backed securities is one of most commonly talked-about risk. Historically, it has been one of the most misunderstood risks as well. Not appreciating the prepayment risk has led to colossal losses in mortgage-backed securities, as in case of Askin Funds. At the same time, adding presumptive, imaginary spreads for the implicit prepayment risk have made investors demand unjustified spreads in asset-backed securities. Hence, it is necessary to properly appreciate the prepayment risk.

Prepayment as a risk

To a common man, not receiving a promised cash flow on time or at all is a risk, but in the world of finance, receiving a cash flow before time is also, in a certain context, viewed as a risk. Prepayment means a loss of profit. For example, if L gave to B a loan of $100 for a period of 10 years at a rate of interest of 6%, and if the loan is prepaid at the end of six years, to L, the pre-paid loan means a loss of profit because evidently, L did this transaction because it meant a profit to him. In the business of lending, profits come from money that remains invested – therefore, every dollar that is prepaid reduces the money that remains invested, and so leads to a loss of profit. In fact, not only prepayment, even the scheduled repayment leads to a loss of profit, but what was scheduled was planned and thus expected. Prepayment is unscheduled cash inflow – the difference is the same as between retirement and retrenchment.

Prepayment leads to a loss of profit, not loss of profitability. In the example above, B would have surely paid interest for the six years – hence, L has still made the 6% return for the period for which the money remained invested.

One might ask, what stops L from reinvesting this money and still earn a 6% return? But unfortunately, one of the primary reasons for prepayment is that the rate of interest would have dropped down, so that L will not be able to earn 6% any more. So, if L had contracted a fixed-rate liability against this loan, L will be at a loss.

The following points may be notable as regards prepayment risk:

- Assuming that the borrower will exercise the prepayment option the moment the rate of interest falls, the cash flows of the lender become similar to that of a floating rate lender. The existing loans are repaid when rates of interest fall; the new loans carry reduced rates of interest.
- However, the significant difference between a floating rate loan and a prepayable fixed-rate loan is that in case of the former, the lender gets the benefit of the upside, that is, rates of interest increasing. For prepayable fixed-rate loans, if the rate of interest increases, the lender still gets the fixed rate; if the rate of interest falls, he has the lower rate. Therefore, the lender has the worse of the two scenarios.
- If the option is with the borrower, the borrower exercises the option only when it is profitable for him to do so. In other words, the option has a positive value for the borrower and a negative value for the lender. Therefore, a fixed-rate loan with a prepayment option has a greater risk than a floating rate loan.

Nature of the prepayment option

Contractual vs. behavioral prepayment option

The option to prepay may be either the contractual option of the borrower, granted as a part of the loan contract, or it may be viewed as a behavioral option.

The loan contract may, expressly or by default, grant the option to prepay. However what is relevant for analysis is the actual behavior of the borrower in prepayment. In many cases, even if the contract permits prepayment, a borrower may not reflect a behavior that matches perfectly with the "rational" behavior assumption. That is, the option may be exercised when rationally it should not be, and the option may not be exercised when it should be.

The behavior of the borrower might also indicate an inherent "leaper versus laggard" phenomenon. Indications of a lag in prepayment behavior are very common – that is, the option may not be exercised just when it should be, but after a time lag. Leapers, on the other hand, are those that just jump on the option the moment it becomes profitable to do so.

Some loans contractually rule out prepayment by putting a "prepayment lockout" clause, or might deter prepayments by putting a prepayment penalty (see below). In the latter case, prepayments might still happen – the borrower might find it worthwhile to pay the penalty. The penalty is a sort of a cost of prepayment; if the gains due to prepayment outweigh the costs, the borrower might still prepay. In addition, prepayment does happen for non-economic reasons.

Prepayment for economic and non-economic reasons

The other very important analysis of prepayment behavior is to distinguish between prepayment for economic reasons, and that for non-economic reasons. For instance, take the case of a mortgage loan taken at a fixed rate of interest. If interest rates go down, the prepayment happening as a result of the refinancing of the mortgage at cheaper rates is taking place for economic reasons. However, the same loan may be foreclosed even while the rates of interest remain fixed, or while rates of interest have gone up. For example, the borrower might be changing his location, so he has to pay off the loan and sell the house; he may like to move to a better or not as good location due to change in his social status; there might be a change in the marital status. When prepayment happens for factors other than the gain the borrower has due to prepayment, it is happening for non-economic reasons.

For mortgage financing, such non-economic prepayment is also called "turnover," implying the extent to which borrowers sell their houses and therefore, prepay the mortgage loans.

Significantly, prepayment happening for non-economic reasons does not cause any detriment to the lender, because such prepayment is unaffected by movement in interest rates. Therefore, such prepayment does not cause a financial loss to the lender, and might even result into a financial gain (as when interest rates have gone up).

Prepayment penalties

To deter a borrower from prepaying, a lender may put prepayment penalties. Prepayment penalties essentially take two forms – a fixed percentage of the outstanding loan, or a mark-to-market penalty.

The former is easily understandable, as it is just a fixed percentage on the outstanding loan amount. The latter is to compensate the lender for the loss of the spread due to prepayment. The penalty is computed as:

Penalty = (PV of remaining loan cash flow at the then prevailing interest rates) – outstanding principal.

As may be apparent, the above method completely protects the lender from the loss of mark-to-market gain. If the loan had marked-to-market rates of interest, the mark-to-market gain would have been equal to the present value of the loan at reduced rates of interest, minus outstanding contractual principal.

In some cases, instead of present-valuing the loan at the-then prevailing rates of interest, the loan is present-valued at an agreed, pre-specified rate of discounting (for example, if the loan was given at an interest rate of 6%, using a discounting rate of 5%), such that all the lender protects is his spread at the time of inception of the deal.

Prepayment and defeasance

Sometimes, to avoid the prepayment penalty or end a prepayment lockout, the borrower may defease a loan. Defeasance implies investing in some financial asset, the returns out of which repay the loan. Thus, the borrower has set aside money or an acceptable money-equivalent (for example, government treasury) with which the loan may be repaid.

Take, for instance, a $1,000 commercial mortgage interest-only (implying, no principal to be paid over the term; the entire principal to be paid at the end of the term) loan for 10 years, given at the rate of 7% per annum. After 2 years, the refinancing rates are down to 5%. The borrower still has to pay $70 per annum for the next 5 years, and $1,000 at the end of 5 years. Assuming the borrower may find treasury strips maturing at the end of each year, and the treasury has a yield of 4% per annum, he has to buy treasuries of the following amounts to fully defease the loan (see CD worksheet Chapter 6: Illustrating impact of defeasance):

Year	Interest	Principal	Reqd. investment in treasuries
3	70		67.31
4	70		64.72
5	70		62.23
6	70		59.84
7	70	1000	879.46

As may be obvious, defeasance itself involves a negative carry, as the return on treasuries is only 4% while the cost of refinancing is 5%. However, defeasance is usually not viewed as a refinancing alternative; it is mostly an alternative to paying the prepayment penalty in case the loan has to be liquidated to make a sale of the property or for any similar reason.

Prepayment risk in asset-backed securities

Asset-backed securities are derived from a pool of underlying loans, so if the loan pool prepays, the asset-backed securities prepay as well. Thus, contractual, behavioral or non-economic prepayment of a loan in the pool causes prepayments to be made to securitization investors too.

Additional factors that cause prepayment of asset-backed securities

However, apart from the prepayments in the pool, there are some additional reasons, for which investors in asset-backed securities might receive prepayment of principal:

1. Clean up call option: A clean up call option is usually exercisable when the outstanding balance of the pool falls below a particular percentage (mostly 10%, possibly lower) of the initial pool value. Such a call option if exercised also results in prepayment to the investor. Note, however, that the clean up call does not introduce any substantial prepayment risk as the clean up call happens only when the outstanding pool value becomes unsubstantial.

2. Early amortization triggers: Early amortization triggers may exist in case of revolving structures. Upon the triggers being hit, the cash flows otherwise being reinvested are released for amortization of investors – resulting in prepayment from the investors' viewpoint. In case of CDOs, the equivalent deleverage triggers may be asset cover/over-collateralization test and income/interest-cover test, which might curtail the reinvestment ability of the collateral manager and thus introduce prepayment risk.

3. Structural protection triggers: Most securitization transactions come with inbuilt structural protection triggers of some kind. To avoid a transaction from developing further weaknesses, the structure may provide for a sequential repayment mode or a payment lockout on the junior classes or diversion of the cash reserves. Thereby, the senior securities get an accelerated payment.

Note that both in early amortization triggers and structural redirection of cash flow to senior classes, the intent of the prepayment is additional protection to the transaction. Therefore, such a prepayment cannot be viewed as a risk from investors' viewpoint.

Analogy with callable securities

Investing in securitization paper may be compared with investing in callable corporate bonds. A callable bond carries a call option, and the issuer may call the bond when it is profitable to do so.

Analytically, the comparison between callable corporate bonds and asset-backed securities is understandable, the substantial difference between the two should be noted. When corporate bonds call, they typically pay up the whole of the outstanding principal. In case of asset-backed securities, prepayment risk implies an unpredictable amount of principal being returned. So, prepayment risk in asset-backed securities is more chaotic than callable bonds.

As in case of callable bonds, prepayment risk affects the **duration** of the asset-backed securities. If prepayment speeds are higher than expected,[1] the duration is reduced; if the prepayment speed is slower than expected, the duration is increased. Thus, prepayment introduces **contraction risk** or **extension risk** to the duration of the security.

Impact of prepayment risk on the pool

Apart from leading to a financial loss on account of loss of income, does prepayment have a bearing on the quality of the pool also? There are arguments that prepayment also adversely does affect the quality of the pool.

Prepayment implies some obligors exiting the pool by prepaying their loans. The pool consists of good obligors and bad obligors – good obligors will not default and bad obligors will not prepay. Hence, as prepayment happens, the percentage of defaults tends to increase. Notably, this would be true for a static pool, that is, a pool with specific loans. Securitization pools are generally static pools, so the impact of prepayment on the default rate seems logical.

This does not mean lower prepayment speeds mean better pools. In fact, between prepayment and default, prepayment is obviously preferable.

Prepayment has yet another impact that should matter to a static pool – it reduces the weighted-average rate of return for the pool. Once again, the reason is obvious – the pool consists of loans with high rates of interest and those with low rates. The prepayment intensity is higher with loans carrying higher rates of interest. Hence, the weighted-average rate of return for the loans would compress over time due to prepayment. The compression of the weighted-average rate of return would cause the reduction of the excess spread from the pool.

Prepayment risk in mortgage pools

The prepayment risk has been analyzed far more intensively in case of mortgage loans than for any other asset. This is obvious since mortgages represent a very long-term asset, and therefore, the impact of prepayment is the most obvious in case of mortgages.

Prepayments take place in mortgage pools for two basic reasons – turnover and refinancing. As we have discussed earlier, turnover is the simple tendency of long-term mortgage loans to be prepaid for reasons such as a borrower shifting location, moving to a new house, and change in social, personal or marital status. Refinancing is the tendency of the borrower to preclose a costly loan and see the property refinanced with a cheaper loan. The refinancing motive is interest-rate sensitive, whereas turnover is not.

If the mortgagor defaults on payments, the mortgagee takes a foreclosure action, which will generally result in sale of the house; foreclosure is also a case of prepayment.

Yet another form of prepayment is *curtailment*, that is, the mortgagor prepaying a part of the outstanding loan generally as a means of reinvesting the savings, or to park extraordinary inflows that the mortgagor might have.

Insurance payments also lead to a prepayment; if the house, for example, was to be damaged due to a hurricane or earthquake.

Thus, the aggregate prepayment can be viewed as the sum of:

- Turnover
- Refinancings
- Defaults and foreclosures
- Curtailments
- Insurance claims

Turnover

Turnover – the sale of homes – is affected by a complex interplay of several factors. The reasons for turnover are simple, such as mobility of population and social factors. However, the rate of turnover is affected by house prices (inflation in property prices gives more motivation to sell and encash the value of the property), mortgage affordability (ease in refinancing makes it easier for the buyer to buy a property).

Factors affecting turnover: refinancing rates

Data are copiously available on the U.S. housing market and turnover rates on an annual basis for several years have varied between 2% and 5%. However, the turnover rates do vary from year to year and those variations are often related to the prevailing economic scenario. There has been a particular spurt in the turnover rates in 2003 and 2004, explained partly by the so-called *housing bubble* – an inflation in house prices that arguably is unsustainable – and partly by mortgages becoming increasingly affordable due to historically low rates at that time. Alan Greenspan remarked: "We can have little doubt that the exceptionally low level of home mortgage interest rates has been a major driver of the recent surge of homebuilding and home turnover and the steep climb in home prices."[2]

The sequence is clearly appreciable; the policy of low interest rates and stiff competition among mortgage lenders to take market share in retail lending resulted in mortgages increasingly becoming more affordable, which, in turn, led to property price appreciation and high levels of home turnover.

Indicative of the levels of the turnover is the extent of refinanced homes as a percentage of the total originations. In a recent paper, Alan Greenspan and James Kennedy[3] did elaborate estimates of the extent of equity extraction in U.S. mortgage originations, which is provided in Figure 6.1 as to the share of refinance mortgage originations (in fractions, shown on Y-axis – .2 means 20%) to total mortgage originations in the U.S.):

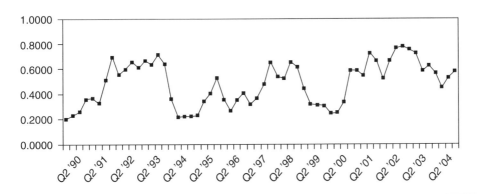

Figure 6.1 Share of refinance originations to total mortgage origination

Source: Greenspan and Kennedy: *ibid*

In projecting turnover rates, movement of mortgage rates and thus interest rates becomes significant. Thus, while prepayments resulting from the refinancing motive are interest rate-sensitive, the turnover factor is also, through a correlated web of macro-economic factors, impacted by interest rates.

Housing inflation

The relation between housing inflation and the rate of turnover is well established. One of the purposes of motivated turnover is the extraction of equity in the house, that is, the value of the house over the repayable mortgage loans. As housing inflation results in increasing equity, the homeowner is tempted to extract the equity out.

Inflation in property prices recently has been a near global phenomenon. An article in *The Economist*[4] recently gave data (Table 6.1) on property price rises in different countries and barring some exceptions most nations have seen a phenomenal increase in property prices over 2004 and 2005. This has apparently fuelled sale of existing homes by mortgagors to extract their equity.

Table 6.1 *The Economist's* house-price indices

% change:			
	on a year earlier		
	Q1 2005*	Q1 2004	1997–2005
South Africa	23.6	28.1	244
Hong Kong	19.0	17.4	−43
Spain	15.5	17.2	145
France	15.0	14.7	87
New Zealand	12.5	23.3	66
United States	12.5	8.4	73
Denmark	11.3	6.0	58
Sweden	10.0	7.7	84
China	9.8	7.7	na
Italy	9.7	10.8	69
Belgium	9.4	8.8	71
Ireland	6.5	13.2	192
Britain	5.5	16.9	154
Canada	5.2	5.7	47
Singapore	2.0	−1.5	na
Netherlands	1.9	5.5	76
Switzerland	1.0	3.4	12
Australia	0.4	17.9	114
Germany	−1.3[†]	−0.8[‡]	−0.2
Japan	−5.4	−6.4	−28

*Or latest [†]2004 average [‡]2003 average

Sources: ABSA: Bulwien; ESRI: Japan Real Estate Institute; Nationwide; Nomisma; NVM; OFHED; Quotable Value; Stadim; Swiss National Bank; government offices

Seasoning

The impact of seasoning – the number of months for which the mortgage has been in existence–on turnover is quite obvious. The reasons are partly logistics and inertia, and partly the costs and effort inherent in refinancing. As all turnover is explainable by one or more reasons, it would takes some time for the reasons to develop. Besides, there is a natural inertia for the mortgagor to close the mortgage, even if it might be profitable for him to do so. All refinancings involve both costs and effort.

The impact of seasoning is typically explained by the seasoning-based increase in mortgage rates. The most commonly used seasoning-based increase in turnover rates is the PSA ramp, discussed separately below. The PSA model, as discussed later, assumes a linear increase in the prepayment rate to reach a target level in the 30th month of origination; hence, one of the commonly used approaches to build the seasoning impact is to calculate the estimated turnover rate for the pool (**t**), and then adjust it for seasoning by multiplying the **t** as (the number .033 in equation below is 1/30):

$$t_n \ (n <= 30) = t *.033n$$

Seasonality impact

U.S. mortgages tend to have lower turnover in the months of August to February. The turnover rates start increasing in March and continue to increase until May or June.

Location

Besides other factors, prepayment speeds on account of turnover are also different for different locations. For example, in the U.S. market, certain states have a higher degree of turnover than the rest. Obviously, throughout the, world the tendency of borrowers to prepay mortgage loans differs.

Refinancing

As discussed, refinancing-triggered prepayment is the greatest concern for securitization pools. Refinancing is the prepayment that happens to take advantage of reduced mortgage rates. At pool-level, the refinancing advantage is defined as:

Refinancing advantage = Weighted-average coupon (WAC)
of the pool – current mortgage rates – refinancing cost

As the mortgage pool tends towards maturity, the outstanding value of the pool becomes very small; therefore, despite financial incentive in rate terms, there is not much absolute gain in having the house refinanced. This is called *burnout* – the pool becoming close to being fully burnt out.

A detailed analysis of the refinancing-related prepayment modeling is given below.

Prepayment modeling

In the projected cash flows of asset-backed securities, particularly those of a long-term nature, prepayments form a very significant portion. In addition, there might be several classes of securities that are particularly sensitive to prepayment. Therefore, prepayment modeling assumes a lot of significance in the analysis of asset-backed securities.

Prepayment modeling tries to project prepayments for a particular pool of receivables, based on relevant information. The relevant information may include characteristics of the pool such as projected mortgage rates, the weighted-average coupon of the pool, seasoning, extent of refinanced assets in the pool and location of the property, while projecting the prepayment rate for the pool.

We take up prepayment modeling below. As prepayment is an option of the borrower, investors in asset-backed securities might be interested to know what are their returns if the optionality is discounted; therefore, we discuss computation of the **option-adjusted spread** and other measures that build the optionality effect later.

Static prepayment models

The prepayment speed of a pool that is projected without taking into account the effect of refinancing rates or interest rate changes is the static prepayment speed; models that project such speed are static prepayment models. Depending upon the nature of the mortgage pool and the jurisdiction concerned, there are several static prepayment models in practice, enumerated below. Before we discuss these models, we will build a quick understanding of decompounding the annual prepayment rate into a monthly rate.

Annual and monthly prepayment rates

If we compute, using whatever model we are using, an annual prepayment rate of – say – 6%, what is the equivalent monthly rate?

The annualised prepayment speed is often referred to as the **conditional prepayment rate** or **CPR;** it should be noted that the CPR model is itself a prepayment model. This establishes the rate at which mortgages will prepay every year. The rate is conditional upon the maturity of the mortgage; mortgages exhibit a tendency to prepay more when they are seasoned and less when they are new. The rate is conditional upon the age of the mortgage, while the word "conditional" also refers to the survival rate; if x% of loans have already been prepaid in year 1, the rate in year 2 is applied on the balance of the loans and thus is conditional upon the loans surviving at the beginning of year 2.

The **CPR** is converted into a monthly rate called **single-monthly mortality rate** or **SMM**. While the CPR is projected, the SMM is derived from a given CPR. The SMM is computed as:

$$SMM = 1 - (1 - CPR) \wedge (1/12)$$

In other words, the monthly equivalent of the CPR is not just CPR/12. The above is a decompounding formula for decompounding anything that is a deductible. Notably, if one were to de-compound an additive, such as interest rate, we would:

$$Monthly\ rate = (1 + annual\ rate) \wedge (1/12) - 1.$$

In such cases, the monthly rate is a bit less than (annual rate/12). However, the decompounded monthly equivalent of a deductible is a bit more than (annual rate/12), as the monthly rate is applied on a ever-reducing balance.

From the above formula, the relation between the CPR and the SMM becomes clear:

$$CPR = 1 - (1 - SMM) \wedge 12$$

For example, if the CPR for mortgages of a particular age is 6%, the SMM would be:

$$1 - (1 - 6\%) \wedge (1/12) = 0.005143$$

The SMM is 0.5143%, which, if annually compounded, should result in pre-payments of 6%.

Note that the above decompounding method is applicable to all deductible rates.

How is the SMM information used to project yield:

Once we have a projected SMM or CPR of a portfolio, projecting the cash flows is not difficult; the outstanding mortgage balance is paid down to the extent of the SMM every month, along with the scheduled mortgage payments, including interest. Thus, we see the projected cash flows, from which the usual analysis of yield can be done. The various types of yields or spreads computed in case asset-backed securities are taken up later [see Chapter 10 on Investor Analysis].

Various static prepayment models:

There are several static prepayment models used in different markets and for different types of assets. The common ones are:

- **PSA model**: Propounded by the Public Securities Association, the model is commonly used in cases of RMBS transactions in the U.S. The model relates the prepayment speeds to the seasoning of the pool and takes a pool as fully seasoned at 30 months.

- **CPR model**: In this case, the prepayment rate is taken as a constant. Typically, this is used for home equity loans and student loans. In European transactions, CPR is very commonly used. The assumption here is that the seasoning-related ramp up has either already been reached or is not necessary in view of the nature of the collateral.
- **MPR or Monthly Prepayment Rate:** This is commonly used in case of non-amortizing pools such as credit cards.
- **ABS or Absolute Prepayment Rate:** As opposed to the CPR that applies on the reduced balance of the pool (and is therefore, conditional upon survival by the relevant year), the absolute prepayment speed relates to the initial balance of the pool. This is quite commonly used for non-mortgage pools such as auto loans.
- **HEP model:** Home Equity Model, which takes ramp up to 20% over 10 months. In other words, for a HEP of 100, the prepayment rate is taken as 2% in the first month, and then goes up to 20% in the 10th month of origination.
- **MHP model:** This is applicable for manufactured home loans. For MHP of 100, the rate in the first month is taken as 3.7% and then increases by 0.1% every month to reach 6% in the 24th month.

The PSA prepayment model

One of the most widely used benchmarks for projecting prepayment speed is PSA, or the Public Securities Association's model. Different prepayment assumptions are expressed in terms of PSA, thus the PSA is a sort of measuring tool. The PSA benchmark curve was introduced in 1985 to account for the seasoning (or ageing) pattern typically observed with residential loans.

The PSA benchmark is the rate of prepayment related to the maturity of the mortgage; the younger the mortgage, the slower the prepayment speed, since the speed will rise as the mortgage matures. The PSA benchmark assumes a linear relation between the prepayment rate and the age of the mortgage, building a simple benchmark as follows; if the CPR for a fully seasoned mortgage pool is 6%, it would take roughly 30 months from origination to reach the 6% level. The prepayment rate at origination is 0. If the ramp up over 30 months is taken to a linear spread, we see a simple step function of 0.2% every month. That is to say, the CPR is 0 to start with, 0.2% for a one-month-old mortgage, 0.4% for a 2-month-old mortgage and 0.6% for a 3-month-old mortgage. After 30 months, the rate reaches 6%, when we say the pool is fully seasoned.

The PSA does not project any prepayment speed for the pool, all it does is project the ramp up to the prepayment speed. In other words, the PSA model just projects the path to reach the speed for the pool.

As the model projects the relative path, the prepayment speed of the pool is referred to in terms of PSAs. If the pool has a prepayment rate of 100 PSA, the fully-seasoned pool is supposed to have a prepayment rate of 6%, which rises from 0.2% in the 1st month to 6% in the 30th month. Thereafter, it remains static at 6% (see Figure 6.2).

Projected speeds based on PSA

The PSA model is used as the market benchmark to project prepayment rates. The actual projected speed may differ from the PSA model due to several economic factors. A prepayment speed equal to PSA benchmarks is referred to as 100% of PSA, or **100 PSA**. If the projected speed is 150% of PSA, it will be referred to as **150 PSA**, and so on. Thus, a rate of 50 PSA means that the CPR is half that implied by 100 PSA; the monthly increments will also be half and the rate will eventually ramp up to 3%. A rate of 200 PSA means that the CPR is twice that implied by 100 PSA.

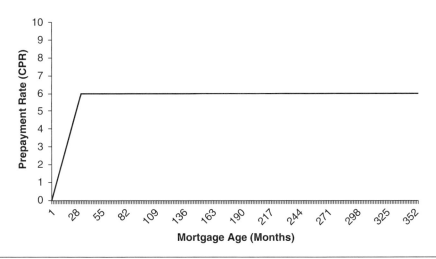

Figure 6.2   PSA Prepayment Model

Illustration 1

For a 5-month-old mortgage at 100 PSA, the SMM will be arrived at as follows:

CPR for a 5-month old mortgage = 0.2% * 5 = 1%
SMM for 1%   = 1 − (1−1%) ^ (1/12) = 0.000837

For a 20-month-old mortgage, the SMM will be arrived at as follows:

CPR for a 20-month-old mortgage = 0.2% * 20 = 4%
SMM for 1%   = 1 − (1−4%) ^ (1/12) = 0.0034

Illustration 2

Assume the PSA of the pool is 100; original maturity is 240 months and the pool is 10 months seasoned. The prepayment rates for the securitized pool are (see CD Chapter 6 worksheet showing prepayment ramp up):

month	Annual prepayment rate	monthly prepayment rate
1	2.200%	0.1852%
2	2.400%	0.2022%
3	2.600%	0.2193%
4	2.800%	0.2364%
5	3.000%	0.2535%
6	3.200%	0.2707%
7	3.400%	0.2878%
8	3.600%	0.3051%
9	3.800%	0.3223%
10	4.000%	0.3396%
11	4.200%	0.3569%
12	4.400%	0.3743%
13	4.600%	0.3917%
14	4.800%	0.4091%
15	5.000%	0.4265%
16	5.200%	0.4440%
17	5.400%	0.4615%
18	5.600%	0.4791%
19	5.800%	0.4967%
20	6.000%	0.5143%
21	6.000%	0.5143%
22	6.000%	0.5143%
23	6.000%	0.5143%
24	6.000%	0.5143%
25	6.000%	0.5143%
26	6.000%	0.5143%
27	6.000%	0.5143%
28	6.000%	0.5143%
29	6.000%	0.5143%
30	6.000%	0.5143%
31 onwards	6.000%	0.5143%

Note that the first month in the above table is not the first month of origination of the pool, but the first month of securitization.

The following points need to be noted about the PSA model:

- It may have been noted that the linear increase in the PSA model is that of the annual rates, while prepayments in any month are computed at the monthly rates, which are decompounded based on the linearly-increasing annual rates.

- The prepayment rates linearly increase through the term of the pool, until it reaches a seasoning of 30 months and thereafter, is the same as in the CPR model (see Figure 6.4).
- Note, however, that the prepayment rate is being applied on an ever decreasing pool balance. While prepayment rates are flat (having reached the 30-month ramp up), the actual amount of prepayment decreases at an increasing rate (because the outstanding principal value of an equated retail loan decreases at an increasing rate, with the interest coming down and the principal recovery going up). During the ramp up period, the combined impact of the linear increase in the prepayment rate and the decrease in the pool value makes the prepayment amount curvilinear. The graph looks like that below in Figure 6.3 (this is a 10-months seasoned pool, with a PSA of 100 and without considering any defaults):

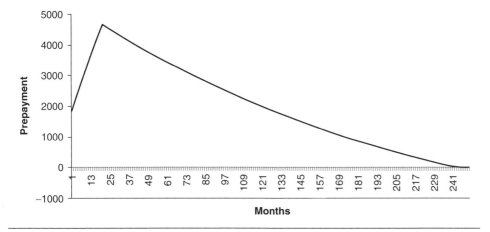

Figure 6.3 PSA prepayment rate

The CPR and other static models

The PSA ramp up is relevant only where the pool is reasonably green and most of the loans have a low seasoning. If the pool has significant seasoning, or if the pool consists of a large number of refinancing loans (where arguably the seasoning impact is not there as loans are seasoned as far as the mortgagee is concerned), the ramp up becomes irrelevant and so may apply to the CPR straight away.

Most non-U.S. pools, where it is an uncommon practice for banks to originate loans and securitize them soon after origination, have a CPR-type prepayment. For instance, for the U.K., the Council for Mortgage Lenders has been maintaining mortgage CPR data for 37 years and has recorded a CPR of 9.5% to 14% for about 85% of the time.

The CPR model is simple; the seasoning-based ramp up is not considered and the pool is taken to have a fixed prepayment rate all along. Once again, while the rates remain fixed, the prepayment amount comes down as applied on a reducing pool balance.

Illustration of CPR calculations

In the example above, if we take a CPR of 6%, the prepayment rate for all the months starting from the 1st month will remain static:

Annual prepayment rate: 6%
Equivalent monthly rate: 0.51430%

For workings, see CD worksheet showing impact of prepayment ramp up. The graphic of the CPR-based prepayments will appear as:

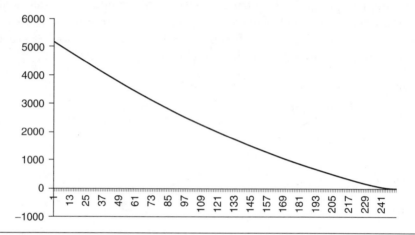

Figure 6.4   CPR-based prepayment

The other static models referred to above are trivial variations – either the ramp up period is different and/or the linear step is different.

For the ABS model, the prepayment rate is applied on the original balance of the pool. This would mean the prepayment amount will remain fixed, while in the case of the CPR model, the prepaid amount continues to decline.

Dynamic or econometric prepayment models

The PSA or the CPR models simply look at the ramp of the prepayment rate over the seasoning of the pool. These models are static; they do not project the behavior of the prepayment rate in response to factors that have a bearing on the prepayment rate. The models that project prepayments based on projected interest rate changes and other factors that have a bearing on prepayment are dynamic models. In fact, prepayment happens as a combination of turnover, which is interest-rate insensitive, and interest rate change; thus, prepayments are projected partly on a static PSA-type ramp up and partly in response to interest rate change.

Prepayment is an option with the mortgagor. In option-theory language, it is an option held by the mortgagor and written by the mortgagee. As with any option, the option is exercised when it is profitable for the option-holder to do so. If the current mortgage refinancing rate is lower than the coupon rate, the mortgagor has a financial motive in prepaying the mortgage and rational behavior predicates that the mortgagor should do so. However, there be various costs in prepaying the existing mortgage and in contracting the new mortgage (we will call them refinancing costs), such as prepayment penalty, fees, costs (for instance, inspection, valuation, documentation) or brokering that the mortgagor may have to pay for a new loan.

The net benefit in prepaying a mortgage is:

$$\text{Mortgagor's advantage} = \max[(\text{coupon rate - refinancing rate}) * \text{outstanding balance} - \text{refinancing costs}, 0]$$

As is quite evident from the above equation, the coupon rate of the mortgage being fixed, the mortgagor's advantage, is affected by the refinancing rate. Assuming the refinancing costs are fixed or at least partly fixed, the outstanding pool balance will also be a significant factor, as the net financial advantage in prepaying a mortgage with a small outstanding balance might be undone by the refinancing costs. Therefore, the seasoning of the loan is also a significant factor here; refinancing-related prepayment rates will be reduced when the size of the loan becomes substantially small.

There are two significant steps in a dynamic prepayment model:

- Projecting the relation between interest rates (or any other factor that has a bearing on prepayment rates) and prepayment rates;
- Projecting the interest rates.

Establishing relation between interest rates and prepayment rates

The relation between interest rates and prepayment rates is most commonly established using statistical regression analysis. Regression analysis looks at the dependence structure between two variables, so that changes in the dependent variable are explained by changes in the explaining variable. The dependent variable in our case is the prepayment or refinancing rate, and the explaining variable is the interest rate. The dependent variable is also called the regress and, while the causative or explaining variable is called the regressor. The objective of regression analysis is to predict prepayment rates given interest rate movements.

Meaning of linear regression

Regression analysis is supposed to be linear if the parameters that establish the relation between the regressor and regressand are linear. A regression model looks like:

$$Y_i = \beta_1 + \beta_2 x_i + \mu_I \tag{1}$$

Here, x is the explaining variable and y is the explained variable; β_1, β_2. are the parameters that establish the relation between the two. There is an error term μ_i that is the random deviation of the actual values of y around the expected values.

Prepayment as arctan function

Y as a function of x in the above equation is a linear function; functions may be of different types such as reciprocal function, logarithmic function and semi-logarithmic function. Prepayment as a function of interest rates is commonly seen to be an arc-tangent function. The arc-tangent function is an S-shaped trigonometric function that has a flattened shape on both ends of the curve, implying that as interest rates rise, prepayment falls but at a decreasing rate, finally to flatten to a minimal level; likewise, as interest rates fall, prepayments rise but at a decreasing rate, finally to reach a peak and flatten there as well. The shape of the arctan function can be seen in some of the models discussed below.

Some econometric prepayment models

Various prepayment models have tried to relate prepayment rates to the refinancing motive. The refinancing motive is the difference between the original coupon rate and the refinancing rate. As the refinancing motive increases, prepayment rates increase.

Inherent in all of these models is the *options theory*; prepayment is seen as an option that becomes beneficial to exercise when the net savings by refinancing the pool exceeds the net cost of refinancing. In other words, when the option is in-the-money, the option is exercised. However, if there was a perfectly rational behavior on the part of all mortgagors, then with the refinancing rates substantially coming down, all mortgages would be refinanced; that obviously does not happen. This is explained by the leaper-versus-laggard phenomenon discussed above.

Some prepayment models are discussed below (see also the implementation of the above models in Excel worksheets):

Asay, Guillaume and Mattu model (1987)

Relating the prepayment rate to the spread, that is, the difference between the original coupon rate and the refinancing rate, the authors relate the CPR as:

$$CPR = .3 - .16 \arctan (123.11 * (spread + .02)) \tag{2}$$

The working of prepayment under this model shows:

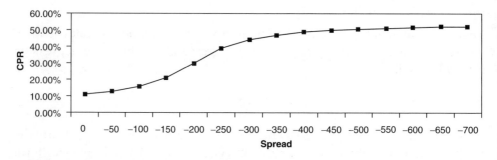

Figure 6.5   Assay, Guillaume and Mattu Model

Chinloy Model (1991)

This model looks at three factors that affect prepayments – the current refinancing rate (r), the rate at which the mortgage was initially contracted, and the seasoning of the mortgage.

$$\text{CPR} = .0813 + -1.7951(0.6735)r + .9063\ (.0688)\ \alpha + .0012\ (.0024)\ t \qquad (3)$$

Where r is the current rate for fixed rate mortgages, a is the rate at which the mortgage was originated, and t is the seasoning term [numbers in parentheses are standard error terms, as in equation (1) above].

Schwartz and Torous model

This model evaluates prepayment based on a proportional hazard model.

$$\text{CPR} = \{\lambda p\ (\lambda t)^{(p-1)}/(1+\lambda t)^p\} \quad \exp\left(\sum\nolimits_{h=1}^{4} \beta h V h\right) \qquad (4)$$

where

- $\lambda = 0.01496$
- $p = 2.31217$
- $\beta 1 = .38089$
- $\beta 2 = .00333$
- $\beta 3 = 3.57673$
- $\beta 4 = .26570$
- $V1 = c - 1(t\ \text{-}s)$, where c is the contracted mortgage rate, t is the current long term treasury rate with a lag of s (standard taken as 3)
- $V2 - V1^3$
- V3 Is the ln of the actual mortgage pool outstanding, divided by the outstanding that would have been there with no prepayments (that is, it tracks the history of prepayments in the pool).

Goldman Sachs model

This one is a commonly used model under which prepayment is a function of four factors – refinancing, seasoning, month factor (that is, monthly variations), and pool burnout. As we are concerned merely with the refinancing motive, we will look at the refinancing-related prepayments (RI). These are:

$$\text{RI} = .31234 - .20252 * \text{atan}\ (8.157 * \{- (c + s)/(p + f) + 1.20761\} \qquad (5)$$

- where c is average MBS coupon rate and s is the servicing fee taken out (which means c + s is the weighted-average rate for the loans in the pool
- p is the refinancing rate and f is the additional refinancing cost associated with refinancing

The prepayment rates as per this model is shown in Figure 6.6 (note the x-axis shows increasing refinancing rates, hence the curve has a downward slope to the right):

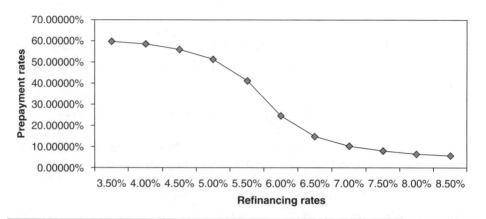

Figure 6.6   Refinancing rates and prepayment

OCC/OTS model

The formula used here is substantially the same as used in the Goldman Sachs model:

$$\mathrm{refi}_{n,t} = 0.2406 - 0.1389 \cdot \arctan\left[5.952 \cdot \left(1.089 - \frac{c}{m_{n,t-3}}\right)\right]$$

where c = coupon of the mortgage

$m_{n,t-3}$ = simulated mortgage refinancing rate[4]
            (lagged three months)

arctan = arctangent function   (6)

As may be noted, the mortgage refinancing rates over a period are simulated (as we discuss in the next section), and the impact of the current mortgage refinancing rates on the prepayment rates happens after a lag of three months.

Ignoring the lag (as we have taken annual numbers), the prepayment function as per the OCC formula is:

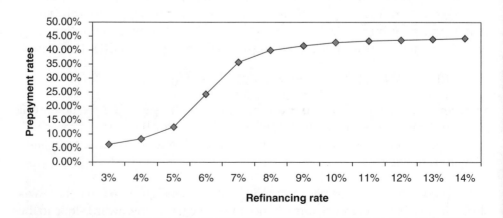

Figure 6.7   OCC model

We have used the above model in projecting prepayment and interest rates in the worksheet. Please see the worksheets (prepayment models on CD) for this chapter.

Projection of interest rates

As noted above, the critical issue in projection of prepayment is the interest rate path. Therefore, prepayment modeling is intrinsically connected with interest rate modeling. Interest rate modeling is a crucial issue in modern finance, as it is critical in pricing fixed rate securities as well as derivatives of interest rates. Copious research has gone into interest rate modeling, and by itself, this is an independent subject. Here, we go through a quick introduction of interest rate models to the extent it concerns prepayment modeling.

Which interest rate matters?

Specific to our context, what matters to us is the mortgage rate – the rate at which a fixed-rate mortgage is written. Logically, one might expect that the mortgage rate will a spread over the prevailing long-term rates of interest. As prepayment is affected by changes in mortgage rates over time, and assuming that the mortgage spread remains constant, prepayment rates are directly affected by movements in long-term interest rates over time. Hence, what is relevant for us is the long-term rate, but to reach that we must understand the behavior of short-term interest rates.

Interest rate models

The behavior of long-term interest rates or *term structure* is affected by movements in short-term interest rates. Short-term interest rates are *stochastic* – they randomly oscillate over time. The models that predict the behavior of interest rates are broadly classed as *general equilibrium* and *arbitrage-free* models. Equilibrium models hold that eventually interest rates in any economy are – though volatile – ultimately to settle into an equilibrium. Arbitrage-free models are in a way circular; they observe the current spreads on bonds or treasuries and then set a stochastic rate that explains the current rates.

Some of the common one-factor general equilibrium models are discussed below:

Generic form: Ito process

The generic form of stochastic interest rate changes over time is an Ito process as the following:

$$dr = \alpha\,(r)\,dt + \sigma(r)\,dz \tag{7}$$

The meaning of the above is simple. Here, r is an average or mean rate of interest, α is the drift away from the mean, and σ is the standard deviation – the volatility of interest rates. The last variable dz is a random number with a mean of 0 and standard deviation of 1, which has scaled the extent of volatility to the interest rates. The dz is the shock that causes interest rates to oscillate. Both α and σ are functions of r, but are independent of time.

One of the early interest rate models, the Rendelman and Bartter Model (1980), was of this type.

It is notable that in the pure Ito process models, interest rates take a random walk similar to stock prices. However, the analogy with stock movements does not hold good for interest rates, as interest rates, as a function of several economic factors, tend to converge to equilibrium. Therefore, the later family of models inserted a *mean reversion* feature. Mean reversion says that interest rates tend to revert to their long-term mean.

Mean reverting models

The mean reverting family include several models.

The general form of these models is:

$$r_{t+1} = r_t + \kappa \, (\theta - r_t)\Delta t + \sigma^* \Delta_t^{(.5)} {}^* r_t^\lambda {}^* z_t \qquad (8)$$

Here, θ is the level to which interest rates revert – the long term mean rate – κ is the speed with which they revert and σ is the standard deviation or volatility; λ will determine the reduction in volatility as rates drop.

If λ is set at 0.5, the equation becomes the CIR equation, also called the square-root model; if it is set at 1, it becomes the Vasicek equation. The working of the CIR model and the Vasicek model is illustrated in CD worksheet for Chapter 6: Illustrating the CIR and Vasicek Models.

Prepayments for adjustable rate mortgages

It might seem on the face of it that interest rate changes would not have an impact on adjustable rate mortgages (ARMs), but prepayment rates remain strong for ARMs also, as the role of interest rate changes cannot be denied.

First, non-economic factors such as turnover, and the related seasoning ramp effect, are equally applicable to ARMs. This is evident from Figure 6.8 showing prepayment rates on some of the 5/1 mortgage pools in the U.S. (from October 2005 to September 2005):

On the impact of interest rate change, it is important to understand that ARMs typically have an annually adjusting feature, preceded by a fixed interest rate period. That is to say, these mortgages are *hybrids*. Confirming the growing popularity of the hybrid ARM, a January 5, 2005, release by Freddie Mac says: "Over the last several years, annually adjusting ARMs with an initial "fixed-rate" period of more than one year, known as "hybrid" ARMs, have grown in popularity. According to the FHFB data, hybrid ARMs accounted for the majority of purchase-money ARMs by 2002. Within that product type, ARMs with an initial fixed-rate period of five years, known as "5/1" ARMs, have been the dominant choice of consumers."

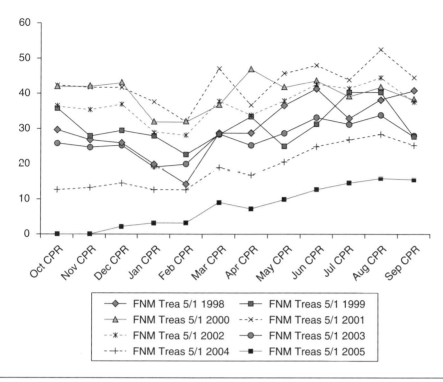

Figure 6.8   FNM ARM Prepayments

The five-of-one hybrid implies that the rate of interest will be fixed for the first 5 years, and then it will be adjustable on an annual basis. A typical hybrid ARM, under a situation of increasing long-term interest rates, will be priced at a rate cheaper than the fixed rate mortgage. With this in mind, there might be a refinancing motive for hybrids as well, explained by several factors:

- The yield curve at the time of origination versus refinancing: The borrower makes a selection of the ARM at the time of origination based on the yield curve. While he pays typically lower interest in an ARM, at least for the initial period, his projection is based on a certain yield curve slope. As the slope becomes steeper and the long-term interest rates start rising, an ARM becomes an eminently unprofitable proposition. The borrower might find a refinancing motive to shift to a fixed-rate loan, or another ARM with more favorable features such as a fixed period in a hybrid.
- The spread at the time of origination versus refinancing: The prevailing mortgage market spreads at the time of refinancing will also drive the borrower behavior. The refinancing advantage will increase, if the spreads have come down.

Thus, the familiar S-curve of regression between the refinancing motive and the CPR holds for ARMs also. A recent paper by JP Morgan Mortgage Research noted that for a given refinancing benefit, the prepayment rates were higher for ARMs than for 30-year fixed-rate loans, but as the incentive grew larger, the prepayment rate for ARMs became lesser.[5]

Prepayment model for commercial mortgages

The case of commercial mortgages is not substantively different from that of residential mortgages – prepayment is looked here as an option to be exercised when it is in-the-money. However, in case of commercial mortgages, the following distinguishing factors apply:

- The commercial mortgage borrower is more sophisticated. Unlike a residential house, there is no attachment or resistance to change.
- The factors for which turnover takes place in case of commercial properties are very different from those of residential properties.
- Commercial mortgage loans are typically characterized by a prepayment lock (a bar on prepayment for certain years), and prepayment penalty thereafter.
- The mortality rate of the business of the borrower might also be a reason for prepayment.
- Another strong reason in the case of commercial mortgages is to take out the equity inherent in the property. If the value of the property appreciates and the mortgagor finds it opportune to sell the property, he might prepay and release the property.

An alternative to prepayment for commercial loans is defeasance, where the borrower replaces the mortgaged property with a pool of treasuries or other acceptable securities that match the cash flow of the mortgages. Thus, the borrower prepays the loan in kind. While this is value for the mortgagor, it is not loss of value of the lender, as the lender may expect matching cash flows from the securities.

Unlike residential mortgages where prepayment data are copious, there are no generally-accepted prepayment models in the case of CMBS, understandable in view of the heterogeneity of the loans.

Prepayment models for non-U.S. pools

Prepayment practices in different countries differ based on several factors such as presence of prepayment penalties or yield maintenance provisions, documentation taxes and refinancing costs. Stamp duties, prevalent on mortgages and real estate in several countries such as the U.K., South Africa and India, serve as a demotivator for prepayments.

In the U.K. it is generally believed that prepayment rates hover around 18–20%; the difficulty of transparent prepayment data being available was recently highlighted by the Miles Review.[6] In other European markets, prepayments generally exist with a prepayment penalty – Denmark is notable as a EU country permitting prepayment without penalty.

Despite the barriers and demotivators, prepayment speeds have increased for European and Asian residential mortgages due to the historically low rates of interest around 2003 and 2004. Rating Agency S&P recently published data about the assumption made as to the CPR at the time of closing of certain transactions and the observed CPR rates, and the wide differences between the initial assumptions and the actuals are notable:[7]

Table 6.2 Sample Spread and Prepayment Data

| | | | | At closing date | | | As of August 2005 | | | |
| | | | | Assumed | Assumed WAL | Spread | Reported lifetime | Current WAL | Offered spread | |
Country	Issuer	Class	Closing date	CPR (%)	(years)	(bps)	CPR (%)	(years)	(bps)	Price
The Netherlands	Hermes VII B.V.	A1	October 2003	10.00	5.0	24.0	17.6	*3.0	11.0	100.38
	Hermes IX B.V.	A	February 2005	10.0	7.3	10.0	18.0	5.6	11.0	99.95
	Monastery 2004–1 B.V.	A1	September 2004	8.0	1.8	10.0	20.0	0.3	2.2	100.03
	Storm 2004-II B.V.	A	October 2004	7.0	5.4	15.0	2.5	5.6	12.0	100.16
Spain	UCI 7	A	October 2001	10.00	6.3	25.0	21.0	3.1	11.5	100.40
	UCI 10	A	May 2004	15.0	4.6	16.0	22.0	3.1	12.2	100.12
	UCI 12	A	Jult 2005	15.0	4.8	15.0	15.0	4.7	14.3	100.04
	Bancaja 6	A2	December 2003	10.0	6.0	25.0	15.0	2.9	11.5	100.42
Italy	BPM Securitisation S.r.l.	A	July 2001	16.0	3.5	26.0	8.0	0.9	4.5	100.19
	Seashell II S.r.l.	A	November 2001	2.0	4.8	30.0	4.0	2.4	8.0	100.52
U.K. Prime	Granite Mortgages 03-3 PLC	A	September 2003	20.0	4.2	19.0	50.0	*2.3	7.0	100.27
	Lothian Mortgages (No. 2) PLC	A3	September 2003	12.5	5.1	22.0	25.4	*3.2	8.0	100.43
U.K. Non-controlling	RMAC 2004-NSP4 PLC	A2	December 2004	**15.0-35.0	3.0	19.0	4.0	3.3	19.5	100.1
	Southern Pacific Securities H PLC	A2	November 2003	25.0	5.7	36.0	31.0	3.1	20.0	100.46

*To call date
**Assumed CPR at closing 15% for first 12 months, 35% thereafter.

Notes

1 As it is almost impossible to think of a retail loan pool with no prepayments at all, the prepayment risk is essentially the actual speed, higher or lower, than the projected one.
2 Remarks before American Bankers Association Annual Convention, Palm Desert, California (via satellite) September 26, 2005

3 Alan Greenspan and James Kennedy: Estimates of Home Mortgage Originations, Repayments, and Debt On One-to-Four-Family Residences, FEDS working paper No. 2005-41

4 June 16, 2005

5 Agency Hybrid ARM Prepayment Model, by John Sim and Rajan Dabholkar, March 12, 2004.

6 *The U.K. Mortgage Market: Taking a Longer-Term View*, a report by David Miles, March 2004

7 Prepayment Rates A Key Performance Driver In European RMBS Transactions, August 18, 2005

Chapter 7

Understanding Default Risk in Asset-backed Securities

W hile prepayment results in the mere loss of coupon, defaults may result in loss of principal as well. Losses on account of default are absorbed by the inherent credit enhancements, and to the extent not so absorbed, are allocated to investors. Therefore, investors are directly affected by the rate of losses in the pool.

Understanding the default risk is relatively less discussed than the risk of prepayments, because default risk is usually protected by credit enhancements, while prepayments risk is usually allowed to flow through. However, if credit enhancements are depleted due to default risk, even if the securities remain unaffected by default, their quality deteriorates and they may even suffer downgrades, resulting in mark-to-market losses. Thus, from an investors' viewpoint, it is not the mere risk of default being allocated to the securities, but the risk of downward changes in value of the securities which is equally significant.

Nature of default risk – default as an option

Arguably though, one of the significant contributions towards understanding the credit risk of assets is by Merton who looked at default as an option. Decomposing an entity into equity and debt, default is an option that the owners of the firm have to put the assets of the firm on the lenders. When a corporation declares bankruptcy or default, the equity holders have, in fact, exercised the option to default, because they find it profitable to do so; the assets of the corporation are worth less than its liabilities. Likewise, if we have taken a loan against a car, I would find it profitable to exercise the option to default if the value of the car has fallen below my outstanding loan amount. In other words, as the LTV ratio becomes more than 1, we would be in-the-money and would exercise the option to default.

The analogy between corporate bankruptcy and default on a car loan is not strictly comparable – corporates are limited liability entities. The shareholders cannot lose anything other than the equity that they put into the company. The company will be taken to winding up, which may not have any adverse implications for its shareholders. In case I default on the car loan, and the value of the car is not sufficient to cover my loan, I still have unlimited liability to repay the balance. If I fail to do so, there are several possibilities, such as legal proceedings for recovery, decline in my credit ratings and declaration of insolvency. Companies, being artificial bodies, can take the bankruptcy route out of business; individuals carry the stigma of insolvency as long as they live.

However, if one were to assume a limited recourse asset-backed credit where the right of the lender did not go beyond foreclosure action (like it should be in case of leases), the option to default in an asset-backed loan would be exactly comparable with corporate defaults.

Whether default is an economically efficient option or not, defaults happen in all types of obligations. Default rates are seen to be less in asset-backed obligations such as houses and cars, and more in unsecured obligations such as credit cards. Default rates are significantly low in case of residential mortgage loan pools with a reasonably good LTV ratio in most countries.

When the borrower loses income, employment or assets, does he first default on unsecured loans or on secured loans? The behavior of individuals and businesses may differ on this. When income depletes, borrowers choose among competing debt payments to remain financially solvent. This decision is made more difficult when the borrower is confronted by numerous debt-service obligations during an already stressful period. Many of these debts are not secured, but the vigorous collection initiatives used by credit card companies and the need to keep alive a great tool of convenience often cause the borrower to dedicate depleting funds to commitments other than the mortgage obligation.

The option to default on mortgages

In case of mortgages, if a default is viewed as a simple option to put the mortgaged asset on the lender, the pay-off of the option-holder (mortgagor) is:

His gain: Mortgage cash flows, valued at prevailing rates of interest
His loss: Value of the house + cost of default.

If the mortgage installments is represented as CF_i, refinancing rate at time i be r_i, the value of the house V, and the cost of default C, t is the time when we evaluate the default option and T is the maturity of the loan, then the motivation to default is given by:

$$\sum_{t}^{T} CFt * \exp(-rt) - V - C > 0 \qquad (1)$$

In the above equation, the factors bearing on the option to default are quite obvious:

LTV ratio

Of all factors, the LTV ratio is one of the most significant. As the excess value of the house over the mortgage balance is the borrower's equity in the asset, and the borrower loses the equity in case of default, the rule is – higher the extent of borrower equity, the lower the propensity to default. Thus, a conservative LTV fixation prevents a loan from defaulting.

The following table of rating agencies' assumption on default rates for BBB ratings in different countries shows the relation between the LTV ratio and default rates:[1]

Table 7.1   Rating Agency Default Probability Assumptions By LTV By Country For BBB Rating

LTV Ranges	Default Probabilities						Six country Averages Relative To 75.01–80%
	Australia	*Germany*	*Holland*	*Spain*	*UK*	*US*	
≤40	2.0%	2.0%	3.0%	3.0%	2.0%	1.2%	0.39
40.01–50	3.0%	3.0%	3.0%	3.0%	3.0%	1.8%	0.49
50.01–60	3.0%	3.0%	3.0%	4.0%	4.0%	2.5%	0.56
60.01–65	4.0%	3.0%	3.0%	4.0%	5.0%	3.0%	0.62
65.01–70	4.0%	4.0%	4.0%	4.0%	6.0%	3.7%	0.73
70.01–75	6.0%	4.0%	4.0%	5.0%	6.0%	4.6%	0.84
75.01–80	6.0%	5.0%	5.0%	6.0%	7.0%	6.0%	1.00
80.01–85	7.0%	6.0%	6.0%	7.0%	8.0%	8.1%	1.20
85.01–90	9.0%	7.0%	7.0%	8.0%	10.0%	11.0%	**1.48**
90.01–95	11.0%	9.0%	8.0%	10.0%	13.0%	15.1%	**1.88**
95.01–98	14.0%	10.0%	9.0%	12.0%	16.0%	20.6%	2.31
98.01–100	16.0%	12.0%	10.0%	16.0%	18.0%	23.2%	**2.69**

Movement of the loan-to-value ratio over time

The manner of amortization of the housing loan determines the way the principal of the loan is collected over time. Most housing loans are equal installment loans, but in a fiercely competitive world, loans with various kinds of options are offered in the market, such as interest-only loans, and negative amortization loans. As significant as the LTV ratio is at inception, also worth watching is the movement of the LTV ratio over time. By the cardinal principles of asset-backed lending, the amortization of the loan should be faster than the depletion in the value of the house. If it is the other way round, the LTV ratio increases over time, the impact of which is clearly seen in the default rates.

Prevailing mortgage rates

The reason why the prevailing mortgage rates are relevant for a default option is because the borrower has a fixed commitment for the remaining maturity of the loan to make mortgage payments. These payments include a certain rate of contracted interest. If the mortgage refinancing rates come down, the present value of the future obligations goes up. On the contrary, if the refinance rates have come down, the present value of the mortgage obligations comes down. So in evaluation of the default option, it is not the outstanding principal balance of the loan that is important, but the present value of the loan.

It is notable that interest rates have a bearing both on the prepayment option, as noted in the earlier chapter, and the default option. A decline in refinancing rates increases the prepayment benefit; we noted above it has the same impact on the motivation to default. In other words, the borrower either prepays or defaults – these two are mutually exclusive.

Housing prices

As a lower LTV ratio is a demotivator to default, an increase in the value of the house reduces the motivation to default. Thus property price inflation helps to keep default rates low. On the other hand, if the property bubble were to burst, there are fears that the default rates may substantially shoot up.

Cost of default

The cost of default includes several elements such as legal costs, and the non-quantitatives such as fear of legal action and loss of social status. In addition, loss of FICO scores, loss of collateral, implications to guarantors, might be deterrents to default.

Non-economic factors

The factors above are the economic factors that affect default as a rational choice. However, in many cases default is more a compulsion than a choice and may be caused by several factors, all essentially meaning the inability to pay, such as unemployment, loss of income or assets, prolonged sickness, bereavement or divorce.

Default rates as a function of seasoning

Do default rates also have a relation with seasoning? As in the case of a seasoning-based ramp up of prepayment rates, default rates also have a seasoning relationship as well.

For residential mortgages, one such model is the **standard default assumption (SDA)** of the Bond Market Association. The SDA model, like the static prepayment models discussed in the previous chapter, merely provides the path of the default curve over time.

A 100 SDA would mean the default rate for the pool will be 0.02% per annum at origination, and would be 0.6% in the 30th month. It will remain constant at that for the next 60 months, and then start linearly declining over the next 30 months to come to 0.03%. For the rest of the pool maturity, the rate will remain at that level.

For example, if the SDA for the pool were 150 SDA, then the pool will have a default rate of 0.03% in the 1st month, growing up to 0.9% in the 30th month, and the rate will decline from the 61st month to become 0.45% in the 120th month. See CD worksheet for Chapter 7. The default behavior under the SDA model is:

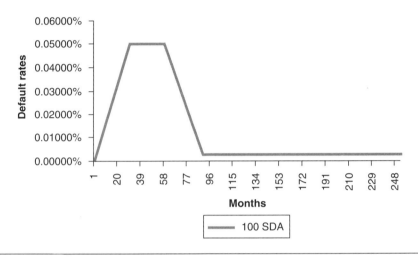

Figure 7.1   Prepayment under SDA model

If one were to compare the default behavior with different SDAs, it shows as:

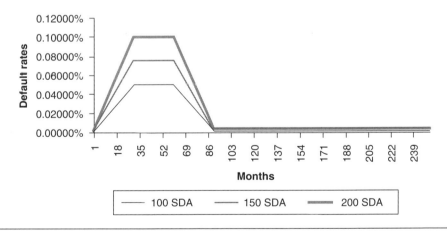

Figure 7.2   Prepayment under SDA model

Default risk for different securities

For asset-backed securities, the risk of default is split into securities of various classes. Thus, while the risk of default accumulates in the pool, each senior class sees protection from the junior classes. Thus, the size of the junior classes acts as the boundary and the losses will hit the particular class only if they exceed the boundary. This will require modeling of the losses at the pool-level, which was taken up in the case of retail loans, in Chapter 4, and for wholesale loans to be discussed in Chapter 17 on CDOs.

Note

1   Based on GE Capital Mortgage Corporation submission to Bank for International Settlements, dated March 31, 2001.

Cash flow Modeling for Asset-backed Securities

Securitization is the ability to discharge liabilities out of a closed-ended pool of cash flows, so the robustness of any securitization transaction depends on the expected cash flow from the pool. The cash flow has elements of volatility, which is normally related to some explaining variables. Hence, one of the prime objectives of cash flow modeling is to be able to project whether the cash flow from the pool will be sufficient to pay off the securities, and what extent of stress such cash flow can sustain.

Cash flow modeling is crucial to securitization from several viewpoints. It allows the originator to project his residual value from the transaction. It enables investors to project the extent to which investors can comfortably hope to be paid back. It is also important to project accounting values of several items – as we discuss later in our chapter on accounting issues.

The following is a step-by-step guide to cash flow modeling. We have taken several illustrative examples building various elements as we go, and then a real life case. The discussion below is backed by Excel worksheets. The use of Excel as a standard worksheet tool is well recognized, although we do not discourage use of other spreadsheet tools. In addition, use of VBA may enhance the power and flexibility of Excel to prepare cash flow models.

Constructing the cash flow model

The components of a securitization cash flow model will depend on the nature of the asset. From the viewpoint of its cash flow characteristics, assets may be of the following illustrative types:

- Amortizing loan pools, such as loans, leases.
- Non-amortizing, revolving pools, but with a payment rate such as credit cards and commercial paper.
- Protected income streams such as future flows, intellectual property.

- Correlation-sensitive pools with asset-specific probability of default such as CDOs.
- Residual income-based assets, such as whole business transactions, embedded value insurance securitizations.
- Synthetic transactions.

The components that the model will need to deal with include:

- Creation and Repayment of the asset over time
  - o Initial pool value plus any reinvestments over time, with ability to recognize if any pools that curb or curtail the reinvestment power are in place.
  - o Scheduled repayment of the asset over time.
  - o Unscheduled payments, such as delays, prepayments, and for income streams, volatility in income.
  - o For delay, realization over time.
  - o For default, the recovery rate and recovery are delayed.
- Cash inflows, wherever possible, distinguishing between:
  - o Interest and other revenue items.
  - o Principal items.
- Allocation of revenue:
  - o Ability to recognize if any triggers are in place.
  - o If no triggers are in place, the normal allocation priorities.
  - o If triggers are in place, the allocation as applicable for triggers.
  - o Diversion of excess spread to meet delinquency, if any, in principal account.
  - o Release of excess spread.
- Allocation of principal:
  - o Ability to recognize if any triggers are in place.
  - o If no triggers are in place, the normal allocation priorities:
    - Ability to understand if any step up sequential payment is required.
    - Allocation of principal as per the normal paydown, that is, sequential or proportional.
    - Sometimes, the allocation of principal may be more complicated; there might be several classes differentially coming for sequential repayment.
  - o If triggers are in place, the allocation as applicable for triggers:
- Generally if the triggers are in place, the structure may require allocation of principal on sequential basis.
  - o Diversion of excess spread to meet delinquency, if any, in principal account.
  - o Release of excess spread.

- Loss allocation:

  o Distribution of losses not absorbed by the excess spread to securities.

- Computation of the outstanding securities balances:

  o Allocation of principal payment and loss allocation to securities, and computation of their outstanding balances.

- Cash reserve:

  o Pooling of excess profit or creation of cash reserve otherwise by retention of money.
  o Any triggers for step up of the cash reserve.

Audit checks

As many cash flow models can be fairly complicated, it would be prudent to put in place several audit checks to see if there are any apparent errors of argument, structure or formulae.

One such quick check is the balance sheet of the SPV. As the assets and liabilities of the SPV must be equal all the time, the balance sheet throws any errors in the calculation.

The sum total of the scheduled amortization of the asset, prepayment and net losses and loss recoveries should equal the initial pool value for static pools, and the total value of assets acquired for revolving pools.

Likewise, one may think of similar audit checks that help to indicate errors before the model becomes very intricate.

Understanding the asset and its repayment over time

The foundation of any securitization transaction is the asset – therefore, the feedstock of the cash flow model is the asset details. The model must first draw up the scheduled cash flows from the asset.

For retail assets, such as housing loans and auto loans, the loans are mostly amortizing based on equal monthly payments. There might be various other payment options – equal repayment of principal over time starting from the n-th period of the loan or bullet payment of principal on the expiry of n-periods.

There might be several loans in the pool, and they might have different remaining maturities, different rates of interest, and therefore, different amortization periods. Ideally, it would be advisable to draw up the repayment details of each asset and then add up the monthly installments, interest and principal. However, sometimes for the sake of simplicity, the pool is taken as a single asset with the weighted-average remaining maturity as the term of the en-bloc loan.

Example 1: Loan cash flow for amortizing loan

Assume we have a pool of 100 mortgage loans, adding up to $1,000,000. Let us suppose the weighted-average remaining maturity of the pool is 300 months. The weighted-average coupon rate for the pool is 7%.

Chapter 8's Example 1 worksheet shows the calculation. The instalments are computed using Excel formula **PMT**. The rate of return for computing the PMT or the fixed monthly installment is the weighted-average coupon rate.

We do not de-compound the annual coupon rate into a monthly rate but just divide it by 12, because usually annualized percentage rates are expressed as multiples of the period rate for a year.

To allow the flexibility of recomputing instalments every month on a reducing pool balance, we have used the number of months as a variable instead of a fixed parameter. Likewise, the reference to the pool balance has also been kept a variable.

The interest and principal for each month may be calculated either by applying the interest rate on the pool balance, with the remaining amount of installment being principal recovery; the same may also be found by using Excel formulae **IPMT** and **PPMT**.

Note from the graph that the amount of interest decreases at an increasing rate, and the amount of principal increases at an increasing rate.

Example 2

If we were to re-do Example 1 as a real life pool actually appears, all the loans in the pool would have different coupon rates, different remaining maturities, and therefore, there would be separate installment, interest and principal calculations for all loans, which would add up to the pool values.

Let us suppose the loans in the pool range from size $8,000 to $12,000, but averaging about $10,000 per loan. The coupon rates range from 6% to 8%, averaging about 7% and the remaining maturities range from 200 months to 360 months, averaging about 300 months.

The results are given in the worksheet Example 2. Note that the outstanding amount, coupon rate and the remaining maturities for the loans, to look like a real life pool, were produced using random numbers [on Excel – Tools – Data Analysis – Randon Number Generation]. We used the normal distribution by putting the expected weighted-averages as the average, and a standard deviation. As may be seen, the actual weighted-averages for the pool are very close to what we expected. We have worked out the installments, principal repaid and interest paid for each loan in the pool, exactly the way they were worked out in Example 1, and then aggregated the information for the pool.

The factors that affect asset cash flows

Once we have plotted the scheduled cash flows from the asset, we need to incorporate all those factors for which the actual cash flows may be different from the scheduled cash flows. These factors would differ from case to case, but broadly for ascertainable cash flows like mortgage or auto loan payments, the volatility in cash flow may arise due to:

- Prepayments;
- Delays; and
- Defaults leading to foreclosures, and recoveries.

Incorporating prepayment in cash flow

The detailed models that have gone into projection of prepayment speeds and default rates have already been discussed in preceding chapters. Here, we take some examples to incorporate the prepayment factor in the projected cash flow.

Example 3: Incorporating seasoning-dependent prepayment

Let us work on Example 1. In addition, we assume that the weighted-average seasoning of the pool is 10 months, and that the prepayment rate applicable to the pool follows a PSA behavior. Take a prepayment rate of 100 PSA.

The workings are given in the Example 3 worksheet. The prepayment rate in PSAs and the seasoning are variable. From the PSA, as per the PSA-seasoning relationship, we compute the monthly prepayment rates. Note that the annual prepayment rates are based on seasoning (the month of the securitization transaction + weighted-average seasoning) and to get the monthly prepayment rates, we are de-compounding the annual rates using the de-compounding formula discussed in the preceding chapter on prepayment.

Why do we compute prepayment on the balance after the month's installment? Generally, one may expect prepayment and the monthly installment to coincide. The installments may be payable at different points of time during the month, but as we have taken all cash flow on an end-of-the-month basis, we take prepayment also at the end of the month. Obviously, the borrower has paid his installment for the month and prepays all future installments.

Example 4: Incorporating absolute prepayment

If it was not a pool of mortgages, but say a pool of asset-backed securities prepaying at an absolute rate (ABS rate), the working will be marginally different from what we have already done.

Let the original balances of the loans, at inception, be $1.2 million. The seasoning of the pool is not important if we assume that the prepayment rate triggers without being affected by the seasoning. The results are shown in Worksheet 4. Note that the question of de-compounding the annual rate does not arise, as the rate is not applicable to the reduced pool balance but on the initial loan balance. We have simply computed the monthly prepayment rate by dividing the annual rate by 12. The prepayment amount for the month has been set at the lower of the outstanding balance of the pool or the prepayment amount by applying the prepayment rate, for obvious reasons.

Incorporating delinquency

It is common for most asset cash flows to face delays. For modeling purposes, the impact of a delay to offset the cash flow and put them into "n" months after the scheduled date of payment. Accordingly, we may take several delay buckets – 1 month, 2 months and so on.

Example 5: Incorporating delay

Let us work on the cash flows as in Example 3. Let us assume the scheduled installment, consisting of interest and principal payment, is delayed at the rate of 5% for 1 month, 3% for 2 months, and 1.8% for 3 months. The first rate is inclusive of the second; that is, the total amount of cash flow delayed for 30 days is 5%, of which 3% spills over to 2 months, and of that, 1.8% remains unrecovered for 3 months. Very obviously, there will be no delays on the cash flow on account of prepayment. We are also making an assumption that there was no overdue amount as on the date of the securitization transaction.

The amounts that remain unrecovered for 3 months will obviously lead to a foreclosure action, which we are not considering in the present example (and which will be considered in a later chapter).

The results are in the Example 5 worksheet. As may be seen, the accumulated amount of debtors apparently continues to pile up, but that would be taken care of by the foreclosure action. As an audit check, we may see that the total accumulated amount of debtors is 1.8% of the total amount of installments.

Incorporating foreclosures and recoveries

The term foreclosure is essentially related to enforcement of security interest for loans backed by some security – such as mortgages. From delinquency to foreclosure, the process is normally dependent on the nature of the asset and the servicing practices prevailing in the asset segment. For instance, servicing standards may provide that if there is an overdue period of more than 3 months' receivables in any account, a foreclosure action will follow.

Foreclosure is the equivalent of a prepayment, in that all future installments are accelerated, and the action may lead to either recovery of the full outstanding or a loss. Any outstanding debtors on a foreclosed account are either recovered from the foreclosure proceeds or are written off.

Example 6: Incorporating foreclosures and recoveries

Let us work on Example 5 and suppose after the 3 month overdue period we initiate a foreclosure process; we end up with losing 0.5% pa of the asset. In other words, inclusive of the outstanding receivables and the future principal, there is a loss of 0.5% of the asset value. As there were no outstanding receivables on the day of securitization, this loss recognition starts from the fourth month. We may also incorporate the time taken in the foreclosure process and the delay in collecting the foreclosure value.

The results are shown in the Example 6 worksheet. Note that the amount in foreclosure is 1.8% of the asset balance, and the installments and interest are thereafter worked out only on the performing pool balance. There is no installment to compute on a case sent for foreclosure. Note that the 3 months' overdue receivables have been added to the total amount in foreclosure. The loss recognized is at the rate of 0.5% as given; both the foreclosure rate and loss rate have been decompounded.

We have also reduced the amount of overdue receivables carried over to the extent of the 3 months' overdues as that has been added to foreclosure losses.

Finally, to incorporate the delay in the recoveries on account of foreclosure, we have used the Excel function **Offset**.

Incorporating the impact of seasoning on foreclosure

In Chapter 7, we have seen the impact of seasoning on the foreclosure rate. As in the case of prepayment, the impact of seasoning on the foreclosure rate may be incorporated by relating the foreclosure rate to the month of the transaction.

Example 7: Incorporating seasoning ramp on foreclosures

We will redo Example 6 with the impact of seasoning in-built. Let us assume the weighted-average seasoning of the pool is 10 months, and that the pool follows SDA-type seasoning ramp, and that the pool has a foreclosure rate of 300 SDA. However, we have assumed there was no amount overdue as on the date of securitization, so we take the foreclosure from the fourth month, based on the then seasoning.

The results are shown in the Example 7 worksheet. We have put the default rate in a 4-step **IF** argument, with the function being different over the first 30 months, 31-60 months, 61-90 months, and beyond 90 months. This is as per the SDA model. The rest is self-explanatory.

The factors that affect the factors that affect cash flow

We have incorporated the impact of seasoning of the pool on the prepayment rates and default rates in the examples above. However, as noted in the previous chapters, there might be factors that affect the prepayment, delinquency and default rates, and it might be useful to model the behavior of these rates based on the independent variables that impact these rates.

Interest rates, for example, are one factor on which prepayment rates depend. There might be several other factors on which one might do a regression analysis to be able to predict prepayment, default and delinquency rates. As an example, we will construct a relation between interest rates and prepayment rates.

Interest rate volatility and prepayment

For the model to capture the impact of interest rate volatility on the prepayments, there are two things required – predicting interest rate behavior over time and building a relation between interest rates and prepayment rates.

There are several models on the interest rate or term structure modeling, which is an independent subject by itself and beyond the scope of this book. In the example below, we predict some possible interest rate scenarios and prepayments based on the same. The scenarios below have ignored the *shocks* in the interest rate path and simply modelled *drifts,* that is, long term movements in interest rates in a particular direction.

Example 8: Modeling interest and prepayment rates

Let us work on Example 7. We are doing two things in this working – modeling interest rate scenarios and relating prepayment rates to interest rates.

We take five arbitrary interest rate movements, defined as Steeply Rising, Moderately Rising, Flat, Moderately Falling and Steeply Falling. We take a CIR-type interest rate path; as we are not interested in taking the fluctuations in the short interest rate, we set the standard deviation to zero. The interest rate over time evolves as:

$$r_{t+1} = r_t + \kappa\,(\theta - r_t)\Delta t + \sigma * \Delta t^5 * r_t^{\lambda} * z_t$$

where θ is the long term mean that we set differently depending on the scenarios; κ is the tendency of the rates to move towards the mean, which we have set in the working at 0.3, and as we take the rates of interest every month, we have set Δt as ($^1/_{12}$). As we have assumed the standard deviation to be zero, the last item in the RHS does not concern us at all.

In addition, in each scenario, we have set peaks and the floor such that in a rising interest rate scenario, the interest will not go above the peak, and in a falling scenario the rate will not fall below the floor. Thus, the interest rates linearly rise or fall, and once they reach the peak or the floor as defined, they become flat.

The mortgage refinancing rates have been taken with a flat spread over the prevailing long term interest rate – 200 bps.

As for prepayment rates, we have taken them to be caused by two reasons – turnover and refinancing. The turnover phenomenon is unconnected with interest rates, but this has the seasoning ramp as already discussed. We set this to be 75 PSA. We then take the refinancing-related prepayment, taking a regression given by the following formula:

Prepayment rate = .2406–.1389*atan(5.952*(1.089–original coupon/ refinancing rate 6 months ago))

In other words, we have taken a 6-months time lag for interest rates to affect the prepayment rates. In addition, we have assumed that for the first six months of origination, the refinancing rates remain constant.

The results are in the Example 8 worksheet. The total prepayment rate is the sum of the turnover and the refinancing rate.

Understanding liabilities

As for any entity, the assets and the liabilities need to be matched. Securitization transactions are self-amortizing – the cash flows from the asset are to take care of the liabilities and there is no other way, except by adhoc liquidity support, by which liabilities can be paid off. Hence, understanding the liability structure is as significant as the modeling of the assets.

Generally speaking, the par value of the liabilities is the same as the par value or outstanding principal on the assets. In case the assets carry an over-collateralization, the excess collateral, if not used up to meet defaults, is returnable to the seller and represents a liability to the seller; therefore, in this case, the parity between assets and liabilities is established. As a matter of fact, due to the simple business rule that treats a business as a distinct entity from its stakeholders, and even the obligation to return any residual surplus to the equity stakeholder is treated as a liability, the assets and liabilities for every transaction must be equal.

Claims on revenue and claims on principal

As we have stated before, it would be advisable to maintain a distinction between the cash flow on account of revenue and that on account of principal; the cardinal rule that applies to all business entities is applicable here as well.

The liabilities of the transaction may also, accordingly, be analyzed into revenue liabilities and capital liabilities. Capital liabilities are related to reduction of the outstanding principal of the securities.

Revenue liabilities may include external fees and expenses, such as trustee fees, manager fees, servicer fees, and the coupon payable on the securities. Interest payable on the notional value of an IO security and payments to a swap counterparty are also revenue expenses. The revenue incomes will include the interest received from the assets, any late payment fees, any prepayment penalties, any other fees received and any swap counterparty inflows.

Likewise, on the principal account, the common liabilities may be:

- Liabilities to investors in form of repayment of principal on the asset backed securities; and
- Liability to return any residual surplus to the residual interest holder.

The sources of repayment of the liabilities are:

- Principal collected from the assets, whether scheduled or prepaid, including any recovery on account of foreclosures (except profits);
- Any liquidity support, for example, cash reserve, a line of credit or servicer advances;
- Any excess spread available as a credit enhancement; and
- Any other internal or external credit enhancements.

The total of these sources of repayment of liabilities is commonly termed as "distributable principal."

Manner of repayment of liabilities

The implications of various modes of repaying the liabilities – sequential, proportional or sequential up to a level – have been discussed in earlier chapters. The model must be able to allocate distributable principal based on the allocation model fixed by the transaction. Besides, the model must also be able to recognize if any triggers are in place when the payment allocation will be modified.

Loss allocation

The transaction provides when and how losses are recognized on the assets. Once a loss has been recognized, it either needs to be absorbed by the available credit enhancements or needs to be allocated to the securities. If there is a loss to be allocated, the same shall be allocated in the reverse order of seniority, that is to say, the junior most securities take the losses first.

To understand the manner of repayment of liabilities, the credit enhancement structure is more suitable, so we will take up the liability modeling along with the discussion on credit enhancement and any structural triggers.

Understanding transaction structure

There are certain other parts of the transaction structure that are crucial for modeling purposes. These are – the credit enhancement structure, any cash reserves and size and manner of creation thereof, any structural triggers that either lead to change in the payment waterfall, or curtail the ability of the originator to add any further assets.

Excess spread as a credit enhancement

As we have discussed in our chapter on credit enhancement, the excess spread provides the most natural and – commonly – the first layer of support for a transaction.

Whether the excess spread for absorbing the losses will be computed before the coupon on junior securities or the servicer's fees depends on the structure of the transaction.

Example 9: A simple pass through transaction

We will work on the numbers developed in Example 8. In addition, we have the following further information:

- We eliminate the delinquencies for the time being as we are not building any liquidity support in this example. We have also set the recovery rate on foreclosures at 30% of the amount in foreclosure; this allows the loss rate to also have the SDA-type pattern.

- We assume the liabilities are split into two classes – Class A and Class B – with respective sizes of $940,000 and $60,000. Coupon rates, respectively, are 5% and 8%.
- We have assumed a sequential paying structure; all distributable principal goes to Class A first, until Class A is fully paid, and then to Class B.
- In addition to the subordination structure above, the excess spread in the transaction will also be available for absorbing the defaults. On a regular basis, if there is a recognized loss during the month, the excess spread will be retained and redirected to meet the deficiency in the recovery; the remaining excess spread will be released to the residual interest holder on a monthly basis.
- The defaults that remain unabsorbed by the excess spread will be allocated to Class B first and then to Class A.

The results are in the Example 9 worksheet. The first sheet, containing assumptions and cash flows, is the same as in earlier examples except for the additional data on the securities and the coupon rates. In the second sheet, we have put the Revenue Waterfall, Principal Waterfall and the Loss Allocation. The revenue waterfall includes interest received as inflow, and the coupons as the outflow.

Note that the coupons are accrued and paid as per available income, in order of priorities. That is to say, a Class B coupon, for instance, is actually paid only to the extent of available income after paying the Class A coupon. Therefore, it may be noted that there remains an unpaid coupon towards the later part of the transaction due to a shortfall of income.

The excess spread that remains after paying the coupons (both senior and junior) is used to absorb losses. To the extent the excess spread is retained for meeting up defaults, it becomes a part of the principal recovered and is, therefore, added to the principal waterfall.

Thus, the principal waterfall has four items of inflow – scheduled principal recovery, prepayment, recoveries on account of foreclosure, and the losses recovered from excess spread. The allocation of the distributable principal takes the sequential form; we have implemented this by putting MIN formula in Excel, taking the lower of the available distributable principal and the outstanding balance of Class A, to repay Class A, and the balance to Class B. Note that before repaying principal to any class, we are allocating the losses as applicable to the class.

The loss allocation applies to such defaults as are not absorbed by the excess spread.

The securities balances reflect the monthly repayment and the loss allocation to the two classes. Finally, the balance sheet of the transaction reflects the assets and the liabilities, and is a very useful audit tool to test the model. For instance, as we make the monthly assets and liabilities, we are reminded to include the amount that has been debited on account of foreclosure, but the recovery whereof is pending. This amount is like asset balances in the foreclosure account. We have assumed that the loss is recognized immediately upon foreclosure; if not, the balances in the foreclosure account will reflect the losses pending recognition as well.

We note that there is an accrued and unpaid coupon on Class B towards the later part of the transaction. We also note that the excess spread becomes zero; in fact, considering the unpaid coupon on Class B, the excess spread turns negative. This results from the sequential payment structure. The coupon on Class B is higher than the income from the assets, so once Class A is paid off or nearly paid off, the excess spread turns negative as the weighted-average coupon exceeds the return from the asset.

Pooling excess spread into a reserve

In the example above, we released excess spread to the residual interest holder on a regular basis. Many transactions may accumulate the excess spread and build a cushion for any future shortfalls in cash flows. In other words, the excess spread is trapped up to a particular amount into a reserve and we highlight this below. Note that once we incorporate the cash reserve as well, we have three sources of credit enhancement in the transaction – subordination, excess spread and the cash reserve.

Example 10: Incorporating cash reserve

Let us work on the model developed in Example 9 and add to that the following:

- Let us suppose we pool the excess spread to create a cash reserve of 0.5% of the initial value of the transaction – 5,000.
- There will be obviously some reinvestment income from the cash reserve – say we earn an income of 3% on the cash reserve, which is understandably not "cash".
- We also incorporate a legal final maturity for the transaction. Upon the legal final maturity, we transfer the cash reserve back to the revenue waterfall.

The results are in the Example 10 worksheet. Let us first understand the pooling and withdrawal from the cash reserve. The target amount of the reserve is set at 0.5% of the asset balance, but once we reach the legal final maturity, it is set at zero. The new features of the revenue waterfall include income from the reinvestment of the reserve, which is based on the reinvestment rate times the opening balance. In addition, we have an amount drawn from the reserve. As the reserve was created to credit enhance the securities, we will dip into the reserve and draw an amount from there, if the income from the assets falls short of the accrued coupon. In addition, we will transfer the excess spread remaining after absorbing the defaults to the cash reserve until we reach the target amount of the reserve. Hence, the amount transferred to the reserve is the lesser of the available excess spread, and the difference between the target amount and actual cash reserve balance.

One may notice that with the creation of the cash reserve, the outstanding coupon on Class B that remained unpaid in Example 9 has disappeared. In fact, it would be interesting to note that the excess spread, which disappears for a while due to the Class B coupon, reappears towards the end due to the reinvestment income on the cash reserve. The cash reserve provides the benefit of over-collateralization for the transaction, and the income from there supports the excess spread.

The balance sheet of the transaction is also notable; a cash reserve adds to the assets of the transaction. At the same time, the cash reserve also represents the retained interest of the seller, so it is also a liability. The liability is contingent to the extent it may be utilized for meeting deficiencies. Hence, it is the actual balance of the reserve left after meeting up deficits, shown as the liability. Note that we have also incorporated a quick test to ensure that the balance sheet tallies.

Incorporating a clean up call

One may note from the Example 10 worksheet that the transaction drags on for several months, although the outstanding balance in the asset account becomes extremely small. A clean up call is to prevent uneconomic balances in the transaction from dragging on.

Example 11: Incorporating a clean up call

We have redone Example 10 with a clean up call at 1%; that is, when the outstanding asset value falls to 1% or less, the assets may be called up at their par value. We have treated this as akin to prepayment and added the flows on account of a clean up call along with the prepayment.

We have introduced one more refinement in the model; the cash reserve target is reduced to zero on the earlier of (a) securities being fully repaid; or (b) legal final maturity. This is because, with the clean up call, we expect the securities to be fully repaid substantially before legal final maturity.

The results are in the Example 11 worksheet, which is largely self-explanatory.

Modeling a real life case

The examples we have taken above provide us with the basis to prepare models for real life transactions. Each real life transaction will, understandably, have its own unique characteristics. We have oversimplified the models above by taking only two classes; real life transactions will have several classes with unique payment criteria.

Example of an auto loan securitization

The example below is based on a real life auto loan transaction.

Capital One Prime Auto Receivables Trust 2003–1

This is one of the standard auto loan securitization transactions. The facts below are based on the pre-sale rating report of Standard & Poor's dated March 26, 2003. Some facts have been assumed to complete the model.

		Liability Classes		
Class	Preliminary rating	Preliminary amount (mil. $)	Coupon	Credit support (%)
A-1	A-1+	220.0	3.5%	2.75 + excess spread
A-2	AAA	215.0	4.25%	2.75 + excess spread
A-3	AAA	350.0	4.55%	2.75 + excess spread
A-4	AAA	192.5	4.85%	2.75 + excess spread
B	A	22.5	6%	0.5 + excess spread

Extracts from the rating pre-scale report

Rationale The preliminary ratings assigned to the Capital One Prime Auto Receivables Trust 2003-1's asset-backed notes reflect credit support composed of the $22.5 million subordinated Class B notes, representing 2.25% of the cut-off date receivables balance; and a reserve account of $5.00 million, which is equal to 0.50% of the initial principal balance of the receivables. The ratings also take into account the adequacy of soft credit enhancement to cover net losses and the high credit quality of the 2003-1 securitized pool. In addition, the rating on the Class A-1 notes is based on internal credit support and conservative cash flow projections.

Transaction Structure Interest is paid on the notes on the 15th of each month; the first payment date is May 15, 2003. All classes are fixed-rate notes. Class A-1 will be money-market eligible notes maturing March 15, 2004. The remaining classes have the following final maturities:

- We Class A-2: July 15, 2004;
- We Class A-3: April 15, 2007;
- Class A-4: Sept. 15, 2009; and
- Class B: Sept. 15, 2009.

Principal within the Class A notes will be paid sequentially until the balance of each class is reduced to zero. Once the Class A-1 notes are paid off, principal will be paid pro rata between the senior Class A and Class B noteholders. The distribution to the senior Class A noteholders will be an amount equal to 97.75% of the pool balance as of the last day of the preceding calendar month. The allocation to the Class B noteholders will be an amount equal to 2.25% of the pool balance as of the last day of the preceding calendar month.

   If an event of default occurs resulting in an acceleration of the notes, interest on the Class A notes will be paid pro rata and principal payments will be made first to the Class A-1 notes until they are paid in full. Once Class A-1 is paid to zero, principal payments to Class A notes will be made pro rata based on their outstanding balances. After interest and principal on all of the Class A notes are paid in full, interest and principal payments will be made to the Class B noteholders.

Transaction Features   The 2003-1 transaction is initially a sequential payment structure. Once the Class A-1 notes are paid in full the principal distribution will be shared pro rata between the Class A and Class B noteholders as long as the reserve account is at its specified reserve account balance. This transaction also incorporates a reprioritization feature that will redirect cash flow away from paying Class B noteholders' interest to pay Class A noteholders' principal in the event of high losses.

Payment Structure   Distributions will be made from available funds in the collection account in the following order of priority:

1. Fees and reasonable expenses (not to exceed $150,000 per year) to the indenture trustee and owner trustee;
2. A servicing fee of 0.50% to the servicer;
3. Interest to the Class A noteholders;
4. Principal to the principal distribution account, which is an amount equal to the excess of the aggregate principal balance of the Class A notes over the pool balance of the receivables as of the last day of the preceding month;
5. Interest to the Class B noteholders;
6. Principal, first to the Class A-1 noteholders until the principal amount is reduced to zero; then, to the remaining Class A noteholders, sequentially, an amount equal to 97.75% of the pool balance as of the last day of the preceding calendar month;
7. The specified reserve account balance to the reserve account;
8. Principal to the Class B noteholders, in an amount equal to 2.25% of the pool balance as of the last day of the preceding calendar month; provided the Class A-1 notes have been reduced to zero and delinquency and charge-off rates are below 2.25%;
9. Expenses to the owner trustee and the indenture trustee that have not been previously paid; and
10. Any remaining amount to the equity certificate holder.

The specified reserve account balance is the greater of 0.50% of the initial pool balance and 0.85% of the outstanding pool balance. If the three-month average charge-off rate or the three-month average delinquency rate (greater than 60 days delinquent) exceeds 2.25%, then the specified reserve account balance increases to 3.50% of the outstanding pool balance. On each payment date, amounts on deposit in the reserve account are available to cover any shortfall in the amounts required to be paid on that payment date except for Class B principal. The reserve account can only be used to cover a shortfall to Class B principal at the final scheduled payment date for the Class B notes.

Performance   All of the receivables included in this pool were originated by PeopleFirst. As of December 31, 2002, Capital One's prime retail auto loan portfolio delinquencies greater than 30 days were 0.14% of principal amount outstanding versus 0.11% at December 31, 2001. Annual net losses (on a nongrowth-adjusted basis) were 0.12% of the average principal amount outstanding at December 31, 2002, versus 0.07% as of December 31, 2001. The performance reflects the high credit quality of the obligors. The prime loan portfolio grew to $2.1 billion at December 31, 2002, from $1.2 billion a year earlier.

Pool   As of the statistical cut-off date, the pool comprises $1.33 billion of fixed-rate retail auto loans with a weighted-average APR of 5.855%. The pool's weighted-average principal balance is $16,784, and the weighted-average remaining term is 53 months, with an average seasoning of approximately three months. The new car percentage is 24%. This pool is geographically well diversified except for a 17% concentration in California. All of the receivables were originated on the basis of loan applications received over the Internet. The actual receivables pool will be selected from the statistical pool and from receivables originated after the statistical cut-off date. The statistical distribution of the final pool will vary somewhat from the distribution of the pool as of the statistical cut-off date.

Further assumptions

We assume a prepayment rate of 2% ABS. We assume a charge-off rate of 0.12% of outstanding principal. We take up to 1 month delinquency as 0.2% and 1–2 months delinquency rate as 0.14%.

We also assume the cash reserve carries a reinvestment rate of 2.5%.

We assume the legal final maturity of the transaction to be 56 months.

Analysis of the transaction

We note the following features of the transaction:

- The initial value of the pool for this transaction would be $1 billion. One should not mistake the following sentence in the pre-sale report: "As of the statistical cutoff date, the pool comprises $1.33 billion of fixed-rate retail auto loans" to mean that the pool is over-collateralized, because the report clearly says that the loans to be transferred to the transaction will be selected from the statistical pool. In addition, over-collateralization is not a credit enhancement for this transaction.
- Correspondingly, the liabilities also add up to $1 billion. There is a mention of a residual income class, but obviously, that does not have a tangible issued amount.
- We take the pool at a weighted-average remaining maturity of 53 months and an annualized percentage rate (APR) of 5.855%
- The liabilities are essentially broken into two classes – Class A and Class B. Class A has been split into 4 time tranches with Class A being a money market instrument.
- The paydown structure is a combination of sequential and proportional structure. Initially, all cash flows go to pay off Class A-1. Once A-1 is fully

paid, the principal is allocated proportionally (the rating report perhaps loosely refers to 97.75% and 2.25% split, which the ratio between Class A and B at inception, but once Class A is fully paid, the ratio is no more that. Hence, we take the split to be in proportion to the actual outstanding amount of the two classes.

- The cash allocated to Class A will be split sequentially to pay off Class A-2 first, then A-3 and finally A-4.
- There is, however, a trigger that stops the payment of interest on Class B and directs the excess spread to pay off Class A principal if the delinquency and charge off rates are in excess of 2.25%.
- The cash reserve is set at 0.5% of the initial pool balance, or 0.85% of the outstanding pool balance, whichever is higher. We assume that the reserve is built by retaining the excess spread. There is a trigger that increases the amount of reserve in the event of the charge off or the delinquency rate being higher than 2.25%.
- As we have discussed earlier, it is structurally better for the transaction to have separate waterfalls for principal and interest. We will take items 1, 2, 3, 5, 7, 9 and 10 to the revenue waterfall. The meaning of item 4 is that to the extent the defaults have exceeded 2.25%, the interest to Class B and all subsequent items in the waterfall will be suspended and the amount will be diverted to pay principal to Class A. We will incorporate this feature into the waterfall.

Cash flow model

The cash flow model for the transaction is given in the Example 12 worksheet.

This model combines both delinquencies and defaults. As there are delinquencies, it was important for us to distinguish between the principal in arrears and the interest in arrears. The balance sheet of the transaction carries only the outstanding principal, as outstanding interest will require accrual of income not actually received, while the entire statements we have made are based on actual receipt basis.

Stress testing the model

Preparing the cash flow is simply putting the facts of the transaction into a template. However, one of the most significant objectives of the model is to be able to apply stress to the various assumptions that go behind the model.

The significant stress variables are:

- Compression of the rate of return inherent in the assets: Compression in rate of return on the pool may arise due to several reasons. First, as prepayment causes costlier loans in the pool to prepay faster, the weighted-average returns from the pool may decline. For similar reasons, defaults may also reduce the returns from the pool. Two, if the transaction has a revolving feature, compression in the pool may arise due to new loans carrying lower rates of return.

- Compression of the reinvestment income: If the transaction envisages any reinvestment of funds by the SPV, the reinvestment returns may decline over time.
- Prepayment rate: The prepayment rate may rise both due to the natural ramp up of prepayments and also because of changes in interest rates over time. The model may incorporate interest rate as a variable and vary prepayment rates as a function of interest rates – as discussed in our chapter on prepayments.
- Default rate: Like for prepayments, default rates are a function of seasoning as also variables that have a bearing on defaults, such as prices of the asset and movement in the LTV ratio.
- Delinquency rate: Rise in delinquencies is normally linked to economic phenomenon, as well as seasonality.
- Interest rates for any asset liability mismatches: In case there are any inherent interest rate mismatches, for example, partially floating rate assets, then using the interest rates as a stressing variable is quite important.
- Exchange rate for any exchange rate mismatches: The discussion above on interest rates applies to exchange rates also, in appropriate cases.

The Example 13 worksheet demonstrates the use of stress tests on the assumptions inherent in the Capital One case. Here, we have stressed the prepayments, defaults and have also compressed the rate of return on the pool.

Level of stress to apply

The extent of stress to apply will depend on the desired rating of the class. As we have noted in our chapter on ratings, ratings are assigned based on a confidence level that the security in question will not default on principal and/or interest. Therefore, the stresses applied will also have to absorb probabilities consistent with the desired ratings.

Rating agencies use proprietary methodologies for stress-testing the assumptions, which are normally published in the criteria for particular asset classes.

Chapter 9

Securitization: Financial Evaluation for the Originator

I n this chapter, we take up the financial evaluation of a securitization program from the point of view of the originator. This chapter is concerned with developing a framework on which the originator may compute the economics of a securitization program and have something to compare such economics with.

Securitization: The quantifiables and the non-quantifiables

In evaluating just about any funding option, it is important to understand that no funding option is directly comparable to any other option. For example, securitization may be compared with a borrowing option, but there are so many significant differences between borrowing and securitization that the two are not comparable. There is a degree of risk transfer in securitization, not in the case of loans. Securitization may be off-balance sheet, and that may be a value by itself.

As we go about comparing securitization with other comparable options, these differences have relevance. Many of these may not be quantifiable; for example, one cannot quantify the benefits of an off-balance sheet funding, but the non-quantifiable factors still provide us a framework for analysis.

The discussion below focuses on the quantifiable factors. However, any comparison between securitization and alternatives must bear in mind the fact that there are several non-quantifiable factors that are very significant, but their impact cannot be quantified explicitly to be placed in quantitative analysis. Each of the motivations listed in Chapters 1 and 2 are relevant here, but significant factors are:

- Securitization often caps the risk of the originator. Traditional borrowing sources are full recourse.
- Securitization may transfer asset liability mismatch, including the risk on account of prepayment, to investors.
- Securitization being off-balance sheet, results in all the benefits of off-balance sheet funding.
- Securitization may also result in capital relief.
- Securitization may also remove any interest rate risk inherent in the inevitable mismatches between assets and corresponding liabilities.

Securitization versus the unknown

In evaluating a securitization proposal, one of the most crucial questions is – what do we compare it with?

Broadly speaking, financial decisions are classed in two – investment decisions and financing decisions. Financing decisions relate to the mode of financing of a project or proposal. Investment decisions relate to whether or not to choose a project or proposal. In analysis of financial decisions, the proposal is compared with other financing options. Investment decisions are analyzed based on their net worth, alternative investment options and cost of capital.

There are several reasons why securitization cannot strictly be treated as a financing decision. The most significant is that it does not affect the ability of the entity to borrow by alternative means. The question of the securitization option being an alternative to a borrowing option would arise only when the entity could choose *either* securitization or traditional borrowing. When the entity could choose *both*, it is not a case of options at all. Securitization and borrowing are not mutually exclusive; hence, comparing them as options does not make sense.

The other reasons are the risk transfers and capital relief associated with securitization.

Securitization cannot be viewed as an investment decision. Investment decisions relate to investment of money for the sake of returns.

Securitization may be viewed, in a certain sense, as a disinvestment decision. Technically, a securitization is a sale of an asset, which is a case of disinvestment. In terms of cash flow, it amounts to unlocking investment put into an asset by acceleration of the value embedded in the asset. Hence, it is akin to a sale or disinvestment.

If securitization is treated as an investment decision, its analysis would, arguably, proceed on the basis of reinvestment returns. If we have a cash flow that can be sold at a discount of, say, 6%, it is worthwhile as long as we can invest the money, net of reinvestment costs, at more than 6%. In other words, instead of comparing the cost of the securitization with the cost of alternative funding options, one can compare it with reinvestment opportunities.

While the case for treating securitization as a disinvestment option appears to be tempting, there are several reasons why a disinvestment approach would lead to errant decisions. First of all, while a straightforward disinvestment decision does not retain any risks or returns in the sold asset, securitization transactions are technically structured as sales but do have retained interests as well as risks. Second and more significantly, the analogy of disinvestment of the securitized asset and reinvestment opportunities presuppose that the available investment opportunities are infinite. In real life situations, this is not the case. In a competitive business scenario, reinvestment opportunities are limited. Every player in a competitive business tries to grab his own share of the cake and essentially has to compare the means of refinancing such investment.

The analysis framework for a securitization proposal has to be based on a careful analysis of available options for the originator. Securitization versus other forms of on-balance funding may not be a sensible analysis if, due to capital limitations or balance sheet constraints, traditional balance sheet funding is not even available. Likewise, if investment opportunities are limited, the entity has limited options as to reinvestment and so it is the funding options that are competing to refinance the available investment.

In essence, it is important to understand where the competition lies. All analysis is to compare the relative advantages of two (or more) competing options. If a securitization option competes with other available funding options, and if investment options are limited, one would make a securitization versus other-financing-option analysis. On the other hand, if investment options are unlimited and securitization and other means of financing are not mutually exclusive, one would compare the cost of securitization with the returns on reinvestment.

In reality, securitization is perceived as an alternative to on-balance-sheet funding, or other means of off-balance sheet funding. For instance, alternative borrowing options may be closed, but it might be possible to think of a whole loans transfer.

Securitization versus cost of borrowing

References were made to the financial cost of securitization in Chapter 1 and Chapter 2. In practice, in many cases securitization is an alternative to other funding options. The aggregate cost of any funding option is a result of the following:

- Cost of the external funding option;
- Term of the funding option;
- Cost of equity required to support the funding;
- Movement of debt to equity ratio over time; and
- Impact of tax implications on the funding option.

We quickly attend to the last of the above bullets here. Tax is an important factor affecting the post-tax cost of a funding option. If taxation laws applying to two financial instruments are not the same (for example, loans and leases), their post-tax cost might differ, even if their pre-tax cost is the same. Thus, while taxation is quite a relevant factor in determining the post-tax cost of an option, in our discussion below on securitization costs, we have excluded the tax impact. There are two reasons – one, that the tax treatment to securitization is far from standard and there might be differences of jurisdiction impacting such treatment; and two, a properly structured securitization deal will be tax neutral – it would try to strike parity with a financing transaction. Hence, we do not envisage any incremental differences between taxation of securitization and that of a financing transaction.

To understand the cost of securitization, we will go through the following sequential process:

Equity is costlier than other sources of funding

One of the significant elements of funding costs is the cost of equity. Take a simple case of the following two options (See CD worksheet 1):

Option 1

Source of funding	Extent	Cost
Equity	20%	20%
Debt	80%	8%
Weighted-average cost		10.40%

Option 2

Source of funding	Extent	Cost
Equity	10%	20%
Debt	90%	8.50%
Weighted-average cost		9.65%

First of all, it is not difficult to understand that equity is costlier than other sources of funding. This is one of the most commonly understood notions in financial theory; equity bears the residual returns of the enterprise and therefore the returns are higher to compensate for the higher risks. From a post-tax perspective also, the cost of equity is higher as the servicing of equity does not qualify for tax deductions. The costs in our discussion have been converted into their pre-tax equivalent.

Therefore, debt to equity matters

As equity is costlier than any other source of funding, the debt-to-equity ratio or the extent of equity required to support a given level of debt, does matter substantially. If it is clear that the debt-to-equity ratio matters, it would also be evident that the way in which it varies over time in a funding proposition affects the cost of the proposal as well. It is rare for a debt-to-equity ratio to remain constant over time, because the manner of repayment of debt, and that of equity, is not the same.

There is a well known financial theory that the capital structure of the firm does not affect its cost of capital. If the extent of debt-to-equity is increased, equity carries more risk, and therefore, the returns on equity will be increased to hold the cost of capital constant. In other words, the cost of capital is affected by the risk underlying the assets and not by capital structure.

Whatever the merits of this theory, as far as securitization is concerned the impact of the equity contribution on the aggregate cost of funding is quite evident. The risk of the asset pool is the same, irrespective of whether the assets are funded by traditional funding methods or by securitization. Traditional funding methods may require higher capital support, due to the regulatory reasons (say, regulatory capital requirements) or due to the fact that traditional funding methods are subjected to originator's entity risks. Securitization, on the other hand, isolates the assets from the originator, but the originator still supports the minimal losses from the assets by way of an economic equity. It is a known fact that this economic equity is lower in case of securitization than in case of traditional funding, and it cannot be argued that the originator takes more risk in a securitization transaction than he does for traditional borrowing.

In other words, we hold the cost of equity constant – whether it is a securitization situation or traditional balance sheet financing.

What is equity in case of securitization?

The originator's retained interest or investment in a first-loss piece of a transaction is comparable to economic equity of the securitization transaction. Economically, equity is support for unexpected losses, so as to reduce the probability of losses exceeding such equity to a certain level.

Quite obviously, if the originator invests in mezzanine or senior securities of the transaction, which are already credit-enhanced, it is not equity, even if such securities are held by the originator.

Should the residual profits retained by way of a credit enhancement in the transaction also be treated as originator's equity? The answer to this decision depends on whether, in a competing proposition, residual profits can be extracted and encashed upfront. For instance, in a balance sheet borrowing transaction, the residual profits are encashed over time. If we compare a securitization option with an alternative borrowing option, we need to consider the par value of the asset minus the external funding as the equity component. For example, if a $1,000 asset is externally funded to the extent of 80%, the equity is 20%. If it was to be securitized, and the external investment in the securitization option is 95% with a 5% subordinated investment held by the originator, the equity component is 5%.

If the same example is compared with a whole loan transfer, and suppose the buyer of the whole loan is prepared to pay $1,050 for buying out the loan, the extent of residual profit inherent in the securitization transaction also becomes an equity component.

What is the cost of the originator's equity contribution?

An extremely significant point in analysis of the costs of securitization is the ascribing cost to the equity component. For example, if Class C, an unrated class, in a securitization transaction is held with the originator with a coupon of 8%, is it proper to take 8% to be the cost of Class C? If an unrated first-loss piece is held by the originator, its coupon is insignificant. The coupon on a retained piece is merely a way of sweeping the residual profits of the transaction. Hence, it is not the coupon rate that matters; the retained liability is equity support put in by the originator, so it must appropriately be priced at the cost of equity. Pricing the equity component at the cost of equity, and not at either the coupon rate or the weighted-average cost of capital of the originator, is an appropriate basis for pricing such equity component for several reasons.

First of all, it cannot be argued that the equity support to a securitization transaction has been funded by the overall balance sheet of the originator. External funding goes to fund on-balance sheet assets, but it would be hard to think of external funding available to finance residual interests in off-balance sheet assets. Second, for regulatory purposes, the residual first-loss interest requires deduction from capital, which means such investment is required to be funded 100% from out the originator's capital, though, for regulatory purposes, it is possible to use Tier 1 and Tier 2 capital in equal proportions for funding the same. However, as Tier 2 capital is quasi-equity, it would not be inappropriate, for costing purposes, to expect returns equal to those on regulatory capital on the equity support. Third, the volatility of returns on an equity piece is similar to that of equity in a business. The fourth reason is that the originator's equity support to a securitization transaction is like economic capital for the pool, and therefore, the pricing should be similar to returns on economic capital.

Thus, pricing the originator's equity contribution at returns on equity will provide a valid pricing measure.

A related question here is whether it is valid to take the returns on equity to be constant across different business segments or should it depend on the returns on economic capital from the portfolio? As different business segments require different doses of economic capital and have different portfolio returns, taking the return on equity capital for the business segment in question is more appropriate.

Relevance of debt-to-equity ratio

As we have elaborately discussed above, the debt-to-equity ratio matters in the aggregate cost of funding. Therefore, the movement of the debt-to-equity ratio over time would also matter. This movement is important because, unlike the revolving method of balance sheet funding where debt to equity remains nearly constant, for asset-backed funding the external debt may be repaid on an accelerated basis. For example, in a sequential paydown of securities, the equity remains constant until the debt is fully paid out, making the ratio/value of debt to equity zero over time.

One of the convenient ways of evaluating a method of financing with a varying debt-to-equity ratio over time is to use the NPV. Below, we compare securitization versus borrowing proposals using the NPV method.

The NPV of originator's residual interest

We will take a simple, almost oversimplified case, to understand the relative implications of the securitization option and the plain financing option. This example can give us a number of important implications:

A sequential paydown example

Example

Pool value	$1,000,000
Remaining term	5 Years
Weighted-average rate of return	10%
Cost of equity of the originator	20%
Securitization option	
External funding	90%
Cost of funding	7%
Originator funding	10%
Payment mode	sequential
Borrowing option	
Borrowed money	85%
cost of borrowed money	6.75%
Originator funding	15%
Repayment mode	constant D/E

The facts of the case are obvious. We are assuming a constant D/E ratio in case of the borrowing option, which is logical because on-balance sheet sources are diverse and usually any entity will leverage itself to the hilt. We are assuming, as for our first working, an 85:15 debt to equity ratio. As the recovery from the asset repays principal, we would be paying both the debt and equity in equal proportions. "Repaying equity" would mean the equity required to support the particular loan will be released and would be free to support other loans.

In case of the securitization option, we have taken a 10% equity as for the first working, and to illustrate the impact of the changing levels of credit enhancement (which is equivalent to the debt-equity ratio in case of the loan option), we choose a sequential mode of repayment.

The funding cost of the borrowing option is taken as 6.75%, whereas that of the securitization option is 7%; in other words, securitization has been taken as costlier by 25 basis points. On the face of it, it would appear that despite the cost of securitization being higher by 25 bps, securitization is still a better option as it allows for a higher leveraging on equity.

The results are shown in CD Worksheet 2. We have worked out both the equity IRR and the equity NPV in the two cases. In case of the loan option, these are:

Equity IRR	28.42%
NPV of equity flows	$26,649.36
NPV per dollar of investment	$0.1777

In case of the securitization option, these are:

Equity IRR	28.93%
NPV of equity flows	$24,447.26
NPV per dollar of investment	$0.2445

Quite obviously, the NPV itself is an absolute measure and does not have a value for the sake of comparing between two alternatives requiring either different levels of capital or different periods. Hence, we also compute the NPV per dollar of equity invested, and as apparent, despite the cost of securitization being higher, this results in a higher NPV per dollar. This is due to the higher leverage on equity permitted by securitization. It may be noted that the difference between the equity IRRs in the two options is not that sizeable, which is explained by the fact that the NPV is computed at the cost of equity of 20%. As the equity cash flow in the case of the securitization option is back-heavy, the discounting rate is lower than the rate implicit in the proposal, resulting in higher NPVs.

Now, let's change the assumptions a bit and increase the amount of on-balance sheet debt/equity to 87.5:12.5. On the face of it, it appears that the securitization option is still cheaper, based on the initial weighted-average cost. The initial weighted-average cost of the two options is:

Borrowing option	8.41%
Securitization option	8.300%

However, the NPVs and IRRs show that the borrowing option is better than the securitization option.

Borrowing option:

Equity IRR	32.75%
NPV of equity flows	$33,641.52
NPV per dollar of investment	$0.2691

Securitization option:

Equity IRR	28.93%
NPV of equity flows	$24,447.26
NPV per dollar of investment	$0.2445

The reason for the above is quite apparent; the initially cheaper cost of securitization quickly turns costlier as with sequential paydown, while the cost of the securitization option continues to increase over time.

Proportional paydown example

We will now take a proportional paydown example. All facts of the two alternatives above remain unchanged, except that for securitization, we have a proportional paydown. As is quite obvious, the proportional paydown maintains a constant credit enhancement and so a constant debt-to-equity in case of securitization. So, the initial weighted-average cost of securitization will continue to be the weighted-average cost throughout the transaction.

Taking the extent of borrowing in the borrowing option to be 85%, the results can be seen in CD Worksheet 3. The summary results are as follows:

Borrowing option:

Equity IRR	28.42%
NPV of equity flows	$26,649.36
NPV per dollar of investment	$0.1777

Securitization option:

Equity IRR	37.00%
NPV of equity flows	$35,884.29
NPV per dollar of investment	$0.3588

As can be seen, the borrowing option results have remained the same, but in case of securitization option, the proportional paydown provides a substantial improvement in the NPV per dollar of originator's equity.

Impact of prepayment

Strange though it may seem, prepayment, which is a factor affecting asset level cash flows, has an impact on the originator's economics.

It is easy to understand that prepayment has an impact on the profits from the asset itself. As the asset gives a positive return on equity, if the asset is prepaid rather than continued until conclusion, the net present value of the profit flowing from the asset stands reduced. In other words, an asset that continues to maturity gives more net present value (ignoring the returns from reinvestments) than an asset prepaid before maturity.

While the impact on prepayment on the net present value of the asset itself is understandable, that prepayment should tilt the comparative economics of a borrowing versus securitization option sounds strange on first instance. This impact is pronounced in case of a sequential paydown. A sequential paydown distorts the debt to equity of the securitization plan, and as prepayment accelerates the paydown of the asset, it results in a more accelerated decline of the level of external debt in securitization. As the debt to equity tumbles down faster, the cost of the securitization option rises.

We will take three situations to underscore this point. We have just recast the assumptions earlier to include a varying rate of prepayment and the results are in CD Worksheet 4. Choosing the sequential payment option, we have the following results with prepayment at 0%, 10% and 20%:

Prepayment at 0%

Borrowing option
Equity IRR	28.42%
NPV of equity flows	$26,649.36
NPV per dollar of investment	$0.1777

Securitization option
Equity IRR	28.93%
NPV of equity flows	$24,447.26
NPV per dollar of investment	$0.2445

Prepayment at 10%

Borrowing option
Equity IRR	28.42%
NPV of equity flows	$23,831.71
NPV per dollar of investment	$0.1589

Securitization option
Equity IRR	26.58%
NPV of equity flows	$17,751.86
NPV per dollar of investment	$0.1775

Prepayment at 20%

Borrowing option
Equity IRR	28.42%
NPV of equity flows	$21,378.96
NPV per dollar of investment	$0.1425

Securitization option
Equity IRR	24.52%
NPV of equity flows	$12,016.08
NPV per dollar of investment	$0.1202

The first option with prepayment at 0% is essentially the same that we have taken before. With the prepayment factor, as the profits from the asset decline, the NPV of equity falls both in case of the loan option and the securitization option, but it reduces far faster for the securitization option, such that with a 20% prepayment rate, the NPV per dollar for the securitization option is less than that of the loan option.

The accelerated decline of debt-to-equity, or increase of the credit enhancement, has that impact.

This problem, however, is not there for proportional payments, as there is no decline in debt/equity levels in that case As we see, the three instances of 0%, 10% and 20% prepayment do reduce NPVs, but the securitization option always remains better than the borrowing option.

0% prepayment

Borrowing option
Equity IRR   28.42%
NPV of equity flows $26,649.36
NPV per dollar of investment $0.1777

Securitization option
Equity IRR   31.93%
NPV of equity flows $29,040.90
NPV per dollar of investment $0.2904

10% prepayment

Borrowing option
Equity IRR   28.42%
NPV of equity flows $23,831.71
NPV per dollar of investment $0.1589

Securitization option
Equity IRR   31.04%
NPV of equity flows $24,690.59
NPV per dollar of investment $0.2469

20% prepayment

Borrowing option
Equity IRR   28.42%
NPV of equity flows $21,378.96
NPV per dollar of investment $0.1425

Securitization option
Equity IRR   30.36%
NPV of equity flows $21,207.37
NPV per dollar of investment $0.2121

Factors affecting originator's residual interest

As it is critical for the originator to minimize his aggregate cost of securitization, which is the same as the maximization of his residual value, we need to examine factors having a bearing on such residual interest. Incidentally, these factors are no different from those applicable to any investment and financing plan. It is only that the volatilities specific to securitization such as prepayment increase the intensity of some.

From the discussion above, some evident factors are:

1. The extent of leverage: As securitization is expected to permit a higher degree of leverage on equity, it may be expected to carry a lower cost, at least for the initial years of the transaction. This is despite the fact that the coupons payable on asset-backed securities are typically higher than those on traditional fixed income borrowing options.

2. The manner of repayment of the external funding relative to repayment or release of equity: As we have noted, the manner of repayment of external funding for on-balance sheet and off-balance sheet transactions is quite different. The higher initial leverage permitted by securitization transactions may abruptly come down, either because of a sequential paydown or because of any inherent transaction triggers. If the size of equity is significant, then sequential repayment does substantial damage.

3. Prepayment rates: As discussed above, prepayment rates accelerate the distributable cash flow, and therefore, also accelerate the paydown of principal in case of the sequential payment structure.

4. Any structural triggers that alter the manner of repayment of external funding or retain amounts payable to equity: Quite obviously, any of these triggers will have the impact of worsening the debt-to-equity ratio against the originator.

5. The originator's cost of equity: If the cost of the originator's equity is high, any structure that delays repayment of equity would be less preferred than one that accelerates the same.

Expected value of originator's residual interest

In the present valuation of the originator's residual interest, we have, at least on the face of it, not taken care of the contingency that the originator's residual interest may absorb the losses inherent in the assets. Almost as a universal feature of securitization transactions, the originator's excess spread bears the first layer of losses in the transaction. Even after the excess spread is exhausted, the originator provides the equity to the transaction, and is therefore liable to shoulder losses. In valuing the residual interest, should we not take into account the likelihood of losses eroding a part of this value?

In a certain way, we have already taken care of the contingencies affecting the residual. As the discounting rate we used for present valuation was the cost of equity, the volatility of equity flows incorporated in the discounting rate. In other words, the discounting rate was already risk-adjusted.

However, a more direct method of incorporating the risk on cash flow for the equity holder is to compute an expected value. In the expected value computation, we would:

- Identify the variables (for example, prepayment rate, default rate) that might have a bearing on the originator's residual value;
- Project different values for each of those variables;
- Assign a probability to each of those different values (each such probability and the related value of the variable being referred to as a scenario);
- Arrive at the value of the originator's residual in each scenario; and
- Multiply each of these scenario values by the probabilities and add up the results. This is the expected value of the originator's residual interest.

It is important to understand that as the risk of losses or contingencies is taken care of in the scenarios and the probabilities, the discounting rate to be used for valuation here should not be a risk-adjusted discounting rate.

Chapter 10

Investor Evaluation of Asset-backed Securities

Asset-backed securities are fixed income securities, in that they give rise to a fixed coupon or a fixed spread. A fixed coupon is applicable for fixed interest securities, and fixed spread is applicable for floating interest securities. While most asset-backed securities are fixed income securities, there cannot be a situation where there are fixed income securities alone. As in corporate finance, the very basis of distinction between debt and equity is based on some securities carrying a fixed obligation, and some are entitled to a residual distribution. One cannot envisage fixed income securities, unless there were some taking a residual variable income. It is equity-type securities that enable fixed income securities. The same is also true for securitization; to support the fixed income senior securities, there must be credit-enhancing, residual income securities. However, as most external securities are of fixed income nature, it is common-place to think of asset-backed securities as fixed income securities.

In corporate finance, the corporation provides treasury management to prevent the asset liability mismatches from affecting external investors. For securitization, there is minimal asset-liability management, so the prepayment and other volatilities inherent in the asset cash flow directly affect investors. From this viewpoint, asset-backed securities carry a different feature. They are fixed income, but not necessarily fixed-term securities.

Investors need to understand the impact of these volatilities on return and net present value. In addition, investors also need to take into account the fact that once the losses in the asset pool breach the equity levels, they are likely to hit investors. It is important to understand:

- The extent of credit enhancement;
- The nature of credit enhancement, that is, whether the enhancement is soft or hard;

- The source of credit enhancement – sometimes, the enhancement may be purely illusory, for example, any enhancement provided by the obligors; and
- The presence of correlation in the pool.

Essentially, investor analysis should at least cover:

- Understanding the spreads provided by the investment;
- Understanding the duration of the investment;
- Understanding the inherent prepayment risk, the consequential prepayment option-adjusted spread and the resulting negative convexity; and
- Understanding the correlation risk.

We take up each of these issues below.

Spreads inherent in asset-backed securities

Fixed income securities are typically evaluated on the basis of *spread*. Spread is a relative measure – it compares the returns of a particular fixed income security with the returns on a comparable risk-free security. To understand spreads, we must quickly refresh our understanding of *yields*.

In general, the yield of any fixed income security is its coupon rate, as long as the security is purchased at par. Yield is the implicit rate of return (IRR) of the investment in the security. A difference between IRR and the coupon rate may arise, illustratively, for the following reasons:

- If the security has been purchased at a price other than par value;
- If the bond is redeemed at a value other than the par value; and
- If the coupon payment dates on the security are different from the period over which the discounting rates are applied for IRR computation.

Example on computation of yield

Let us suppose we have three bond investment options for a bondholder who wants his cash flow on a quarterly basis (meaning, he wants to analyze a quarterly rate of return):

Option A: Purchase price and nominal value of the bond: $10,000. Coupon rate: 6%. Maturity: 5 years. Frequency of payment: quarterly. Redemption at par.

Option B: Nominal value of the bond: $10,000; Purchase price: $9,500. Coupon rate: 5.5%. Maturity: 5 years. Frequency of payment: quarterly. Redemption at par.

Option C: Nominal value and purchase price of the bond: $10,000. Coupon rate: 6.5 %. Maturity: 5 years. Frequency of payment: yearly. Redemption at par.

The workings are in CD Worksheet 1. Note that we have put all cash flows on a quarterly basis, as the bondholder wants to compute a quarterly rate of return. For Option C, this means writing zeros for the quarters where there was no coupon payment. The IRR computed for the quarter has been multiplied by four to annualize the same. The results are:

	Option A	*Option B*	*Option C*
Yield	6.00%	6.68%	6.35%

The yield for option A is the same as the coupon rate, for reasons we discussed earlier. However, Option A, while carrying a higher coupon rate than Option B, still gives a lower IRR than Option B due to the purchase discount for Option B. For Option C, there is a drop in the yield as compared to the coupon rate due to the annual payment of interest.

The securities above are 5-year securities. Let's say 5-year, risk-free securities. If the yield, as computed above, is compared with, say, 5-year treasury securities, the excess of the yield over the yield on a comparable risk-free security is referred to as the spread. For example, if 5-year treasury securities give a return of 5%, then the spreads for Option A, B and C, respectively, are 100 bps, 168 bps and 135 bps.

Treasuries are quite commonly used as the benchmark for expressing spreads, particularly for long-term fixed income securities. For securities whose maturity does not match with those of treasuries, interpolated treasury yields are used.

Another commonly used spread measure in the market is the *spread over swap rates*. This spread is conceptually similar to the spread over treasuries discussed above, except that it also reduces the swap spread for the relevant maturity. Once again, if swap spreads are not available for the given maturity, the same are interpolated.

Spreads for asset-backed securities

Adding another option to our analysis of the three bond options, let us say we have an Option D that is an amortizing bond. That is to say, it not only pays a coupon over its term, but also repays a part of the principal. Let us suppose this bond repays $582.46 per quarter, inclusive of interest and principal. That is to say, by paying 20 such quarterly instalments, the bond would have been fully redeemed.

We do a computation of yield for this option, and the computation is shown in CD Worksheet 2. We see a yield of 6%.

The computation of yields for asset-backed securities is similar to the amortizing bond example above. For asset-backed securities too, over time, the investor gets both coupon and principal. The additional differential is that the amount of principal repaid varies over time, and typically there is more of principal payout over time.

Let us use the worksheet that we developed for Chapter 9 – Worksheet 4. (While we keep prepayment neutral as of now, setting it to be zero), we will later see the impact of prepayment. We have renamed this worksheet as CD Worksheet 3 for this chapter; we have removed the loan cash flow as we are no longer interested in comparing securitization with borrowing. We are focusing on the cash flow for the external investor. Also, we have reduced the cost of external funding to 6% to make the case comparable to the bond options above. The cash flow of the external investors is shown in Worksheet 3, and briefly below:

Year 0	Year 1	Year 2	Year 3	Year 4	Year 5
–$900,000	$217,797.48	$224,349.38	$231,556.47	$239,484.27	$148,204.85

Without doing any adjustment for the fact that these cash flows are yearly, we see a yield of 6% on these cash flows.

Do we say the spread on Option A bonds, Option D bonds, and the ABS investment above is the same, as all of these have a 6% yield and all pay down fully in five years? In other words, what is the benchmark treasury rate with which we compare the yield given by Option D and ABS investment? It is quite obvious that the cash flows of Option A bonds and Option D bonds are very different. The cash flows of the Option D bonds, which provide a flat quarterly payment, are also different from the asset-backed securities, usually characterized by an increasingly periodic paydown, particularly for a sequential payment structure. The ABS investment, for example, returns a substantial amount of principal in the first year, so it is illogical to compare the return on this investment with a 5-year treasury. A crude answer to this problem might have been to look at the duration (as discussed below) of each of these options and to compare the spreads with treasuries of a like maturity, but that would ignore the upwardly sloping nature of the yield curve. That brings us to Z spread.

Understanding of Z spread

Due to the basic principles of macro-economics (e.g., liquidity preference), treasury yields for shorter maturities are lower than those for longer maturities. The upwardly sloping nature of yields for increasing terms is referred to as the *yield curve*.

In the computation of yields above, we were computing the implicit rate of return and inherently discounting all cash flows at such IRRs. On the other hand, as the treasury rates for different terms are different, it is illogical to use the same discounting rates for each period. This becomes particularly relevant when the investment option returns a sizeable principal over its term.

The Z spread, Zero-volatility spread (to distinguish this measure from option-adjusted spread discussed later in this chapter), looks at treasury rates for each period and adds a fixed spread to each of these rates to see the discounting rate for each period, such that the discounted values equal the initial investment. In other words, the Z spread is:

$$Z : C = \sum_{i=1}^{n} \frac{CF_i}{(1 + T_i + Z)^i}$$

where   C is the initial cash outflow for the investment
CF is the cash flow at time i
T is the treasury rate for time i
Z is the Z spread.

Example

Let us suppose the treasury rates for Year 1 to 5 are given below, and we have three alternative investment options, as given below:

Year	Yield		1	2	3	4	5
Treasury rates			4%	4.25%	4.50%	4.75%	5.00%
Bond A	6%	−10000	600.00	600.00	600.00	600.00	10600.00
Bond B	6%	−10000	$2,373.96	$2,373.96	$2,373.96	$2,373.96	$2,373.96
ABS cash flows	6%	−10000	$2,419.97	$2,492.77	$2,572.85	$2,660.94	$1,646.72

Clearly, the yield curve is a linear upwardly-sloping curve. Bond A is a coupon-paying, non-amortizing bond. Bond B is an equal annual payment bond. The third option is a securitization transaction with typically upward-bound cash flows. The yields as traditionally computed on these are 6%. However, as we compute the Z spreads for each of these, they seem substantially different.

The computation of Z spreads for these options is shown in Worksheet 4. Computation of the Z spread manually or on Excel involves a reiterative process. The process involves assuming a value for the Z spread, and then refining it upwards or downwards while narrowing the net present value to zero. An interpolation device has been used in Worksheet 4. The interpolation trick uses two guess rates of Z, and assumes that the difference in the two NPVs is evenly distributed over the difference in the two Zs. As the objective is to reach a zero NPV, the Z is incremented by the required basis points. In about 5-6 iterations, we should be able to get a zero NPV correct to some 5-6 decimal points.

The Z spreads for the three options are:

Bond A: 105.87019 bps
Bond B: 135.83451 bps
ABS: 139.61711 bps

These results are not surprising. As short-term interest rates are less than those for long term, and the yield of the investment option is constant at 6%, there is more of an NPV for the principal paid back sooner than later. Hence, an option that accelerates the principal payout will give a better spread than one, like Bond A, that pays out principal by way of a bullet repayment.

Comparing Z spread, NPV and yield

We have seen above that the **static yield**[1] of each of the investment options is 6% and, therefore, the static spread is also the same at 100 bps.

We may use yet another method of investment analysis, the static NPV. NPV is one of the most commonly used investment analysis tools, using a static rate of discounting, usually the weighted-average cost of capital of the investor.

In CD Worksheet 5, we have added NPV computation as well, computing NPVs of each of the options at a static rate of 5%. The results are:

	NPV at 5%
Bond A	$432.95
Bond B	$278.02
ABS cash flows	$267.68

As is apparent, from the viewpoint of NPV the first option is the best. This is obvious as the spread between the yield and the discounting rate of 5% is maximized for Bond A, which retains the investment right up to maturity. On the other hand, the ABS option accelerates the repayment of principal, so has the least NPV.

Given the conflicting results produced by the NPV analysis and the Z spread analysis, it is very important to understand what goes behind these two computations. The static yield as well as the static NPV have both ignored the fact that the intermediate rates of interest are not the same. The Z spread, on the other hand, has used dynamic discounting rates for each of the cash flows. Hence, in a situation of positively or negatively sloping yield curves, the Z spread analysis gives a more robust result.

Understanding of duration

As we have noted above, the present value, Z spread, and even the expected rate of return in fixed income securities are based on the weighted-average period for which the money invested in the investment option will remain invested. Hence, the concept of *duration* is very important in fixed income analysis.

Duration also explains the relation between yield and price of a fixed income security.

Mathematically, duration is the weighted average of the present values (PVs) of the cash flow, divided by the initial investment in the security. Duration (**D**) is defined as:

$$D = \sum_{i=1}^{n} i \times \frac{CF_i}{(1+r)^i} \times \frac{1}{B}$$

where B is the investment made in the bond or the security.

With a little reflection, one may understand that if in the above equation, r being the discounting is the same as the IRR implicit in the investment, by discounting each cash flow at the IRR, we see the principal component, such that the total of the principal components is equal to B or the investment made in the security. Hence, what we are computing is the weighted-average maturity for which the aggregate principal invested in the security was outstanding. However, the generic equation above allows for the discounting rate for duration computation to be different from the IRR of the investment.

Illustration

Assume the cash inflow for a mortgage with a principal of $1,000 over five years (principal + interest) is $280 per annum. The yield or IRR from the mortgage is 12.38% computed by a simple spreadsheet. The computation below shows the IRR as well as the duration:

Yield (IRR) Investment	(1)	12.38% −1000 (2)	PV of cash flows at IRR (3)	PV weighted by years (4)
Cash flows	1	280	249.163	249.163
	2	280	221.7221	443.4442
	3	280	197.3034	591.9101
	4	280	175.5739	702.2957
	5	280	156.2376	781.1879
		Duration		2.768001

Column 3 above is the present value of each cash flow discounted at the IRR. The products in column 4 is the said present value multiplied by the number of years for which they are outstanding; for example, the PV of the third inflow is $197.30 and is outstanding for three years before it is recovered. The sum of these products, divided by the total PV recovered, that is $1,000, is the duration that in the above working comes to 2.768 years.

Now, if the yield or the IRR is increased, obviously the present value of each of the cash flows will fall, resulting in a lower priced mortgage. The table below discounts the above cash inflows of $280 per annum at different discounting rates, starting from 10% to 13%. This can be accomplished on a simple spreadsheet formula using the **PV** function, specifying the discounting rate, number of years and the cash inflow.

Discounted values at different IRRs	
Discounting rate	Present value
10.00%	£1,061.42
10.50%	£1,048.00
11.00%	£1,034.85
11.50%	£1,021.97
12.00%	£1,009.34
12.50%	£996.96
13.00%	£984.82

If we plot them on a chart, we see a linear relation for any infinitesimal change in the yield. This linear relation is determined by the duration. This relation should be obvious, because by definition duration is obtained by dividing the price of the investment by the weighted average of the present values:

Duration = Sum of PVs or price of the investment / Sum of (Pvi + Time$i$), or
Duration * Sum of (Pvi + Time$i$) = price of the investment

Therefore, if the discounting rate, that is (1+r) is increased by ×%, the price of the investment should decrease by duration *times* ×%. That is to say, a 1% increase in (1+rate) should result in -, in the above example – a 2.768% decrease in the present value or price of the investment. This relation will hold good for a small, .001% increase in the price.

Understanding of convexity

When duration is used as a measure of the price-yield relationship, one of the important reasons for differences between the changed price of the security as a result of change in yield (or discounting rate) and the changed price as predicted by duration is the convexity of the investment. If duration were to hold as the relation between the price and yield, the relation would have been linear. However, the price/yield relation is curvi-linear and convex.

Hence, convexity measures the second momentum of the price/yield relationship.

Computation of convexity is shown in CD Worksheet 6.

Impact of prepayment on ABS investments

The reasons why prepayments happen and a detailed modeling of prepayment have been discussed in earlier chapters.

In our investment analysis of asset-backed securities, we noted the relevance of duration. Prepayment has a significant impact on the returns and value of ABS investments.

Impact of prepayment on duration

The relation between prepayment and duration is quite obvious; if prepayment speed increases, the payback is accelerated and duration comes down. If the prepayment speed is less than expected, the duration increases. Hence, prepayment introduces a **contraction risk** and reciprocally an **extension risk**.

The impact of prepayment on the duration is demonstrated in CD Worksheet 7. Worksheet 7 is based on Worksheet 3. The results are:

Prepayment rate	Duration
0 %	2.7784
5%	2.5713
10%	2.3792
20%	2.0381

Prepayment and yield

On the face of it, prepayment does not seem to be making an impact on yield. Investors' income is essentially the coupon, and investors see a coupon on what remains outstanding. If prepayment reduces the size of the investment, it also reduces the future coupon; hence, there does not seem to be a reason for the impact of prepayment on yield.

However, this presupposes that the coupon rate is the same as yield. This assumption does not hold in all cases where the acquisition cost of the investment is different from its par value. This may be so because of either an original issue premium or discount or may be due to secondary market transactions other than at par. For mortgage-backed pass throughs, it is common to have a single pass-through rate for various classes of securities, such that the coupon rate and the yield may be different.

In all such cases where the coupon rate and yield are different, changes in the prepayment rate also have an impact on yield.

Let's look at two situations to understand the impact: Where the yield is lower than the coupon rate (that is, the securities have been acquired at higher than par), and where the yield is higher than the coupon rate (where the securities have been acquired at lower than par). In the first case, we assume the securities were acquired at 105% of their face value, and in the second case, we assume the securities were bought at 95% of face value. Now, we may notice the impact of prepayment on the yields:

Prepayment rate	Securities bought at 105% of par	Securities bought at 95% of par
0%	4.17%	7.99%
5%	4.02%	8.15%
10%	3.86%	8.33%
20%	3.51%	8.72%

We may notice that with no prepayment rate, the yield in the first case is lower than the coupon rate (6%), and is higher than the coupon rate in the second case. We notice that in the first case, increasing prepayment speed reduces the yield, and in the second case, increasing prepayment speed increases the yield. The underlying reason for this is not difficult to understand. The yield reflects the value of money to the investors. If the yield is 4.17%, we may assume that is the rate at which investors are valuing money over time. When any cash flow is accelerated due to prepayment, what investors lose is the coupon, and what they gain is the time value of money. The gain in time value of money was priced at 4.17%, while the loss is 6%. As the loss is more than the gain, the yields are depressed.

For the second option, as the yield is higher than the coupon rate, increasing prepayment means more gain than loss, and hence, the yields have gone on increasing. Thus:

- Prepayment affects yields where pass-through rate/coupon rates are different from investors' yields.
- Higher prepayment leads to higher yield, if the yield was higher than the coupon rate.
- Higher prepayment leads to lower yield, if the yield was lower than the coupon rate.

Prepayment and negative convexity

From the discussion above on the relation between price and yields of fixed income securities, it should be evident that as yields decline, the price of a fixed income security increases, and as yields rise, the price declines. We noted that the linear relation between the yield and the price is given by the duration, but as the relation is curvilinear, we may also compute the convexity. Convexity implies that when the yields decline, the price of the security increases above what is indicated by the linear function, and vice versa.

For asset-backed securities, while a decline in yields should bring about an increase in the price of the asset-backed investment, it also has an impact on prepayment. We have noted in the earlier chapter on prepayment that this is substantially interest-rate sensitive. As interest rates decline, prepayment speeds up. As a result, an asset-backed investor is not able to capture the full impact of price appreciation that should have accompanied a reduction in yields. Hence, instead of benefiting from convexity, an asset-backed investor is hit by negative convexity, that is, the appreciation in the value of asset-backed investment is less than indicated by the linear price/yield function.

Prepayment and *Z* spread

As prepayment accelerates the payback of principal, it reduces net present value. We have noted before that the static net present value using a static discounting rate does not give very reliable returns. Hence, we may like to see the impact on prepayment on the Z spread.

We have shown the impact of prepayment on the Z spread in CD Worksheet 9. Worksheet 9 is built upon Worksheet 3 where we had computed the cash flow on asset-backed securities. To be able to compute the Z spread, we take the treasury rates for different maturities, taken the same as for Worksheet 4. The Z spreads at different prepayment speeds are:

Prepayment rate	Z spread
0%	139.6171
5%	144.64977
10%	149.86861
20%	160.73720

The above analysis is consistent with the fact that, in an increasing interest rate scenario, if prepayment rates are increased, the Z spread will increase. In fact, in an increasing interest rate scenario (implicit in the treasury rates going up over the longer term), prepayment rates should drop, causing the Z spread to come down.

Computation of option-adjusted spread

As we have noted earlier in the chapter on prepayment, this is an option with the borrower and will be exercised as per the option of the borrower, at his advantage; this means prepayment will increase when rates of interest decline, and prepayments will decrease when rates of interest increase.

In either case, the exercise of the option by the borrowers will reduce the Z spread of investors. Therefore, investors may want to project different scenarios of prepayment and Z spreads under each scenario. An option-adjusted spread is the value of the Z spread weighted by the probabilities of each of the prepayment scenarios. In other words, the option-adjusted spread (OAS) does not presume static prepayment rate, and so is no more zero-volatility (by definition, Z-spread means zero-volatility spread).

We have illustrated the computation of OAS in Worksheet 10. Let us suppose, given the rising interest rates, that we expect prepayment rates to stay limited to 10%. Now, we envisage five discrete scenarios. The scenario and the probability of each are given in the table below, which also computes the Z spreads under each of the scenarios in CD Worksheet 10:

Prepayment rate	Probability	Z spread	Product
3%	5%	142.6143234	7.13071617
6%	20%	145.6786771	29.13573542
10%	50%	149.868612	74.93430602
15%	20%	155.2721176	31.05442353
18%	5%	158.601765	7.93008825
Option-adjusted spread			150.1852694

As may be noted, in the table above, we have projected different prepayment scenarios and assigned probabilities to each of these scenarios. We have then computed the Z spreads under each scenario and multiplied the same by the probabilities to see the option-adjusted spread.

The reason why this spread is called the option-adjusted spread is because, by taking different scenarios of prepayment, we are trying to quantify the impact of the prepayment risk on the investors' spreads. As the prepayment option has thus been discounted, the spread that we are left is net of prepayment risk and hence is the term option-adjusted spread.

Understanding default risk

Like any other fixed income security, asset-backed securities are prone to risk of default. For asset-backed securities, allocation of losses to the securities is inherent in their very nature and is a part of the hierarchy of credit enhancements in the transaction.

An investor in an asset-backed security may like to analyze at what likely rate of default the available credit enhancements may be breached, so as to lead to losses of interest and/or principal to the investor. As excess spread also typically provides credit enhancements, and excess spread is impacted by the levels of prepayment, the investor may also like to manipulate (a) prepayment rates and their impact on the excess spread; (b) consequential depletion in the levels of credit enhancement; and (c) the available credit enhancements at the investors' level being completed eroded leading to an allocation of losses to the investor.

The analysis involves assigning probabilities to different values of prepayment rates and default rates, much the same as for OAS calculation. The only difference is that for analysis of default risk, it arises only where the prepayment and default rates go above a particular level. Thus, one may compute a *default adjusted spread*, applying probability to the loss allocation and the consequential loss of return. This would help the investor place a proper price to an asset-backed security.

Note

1   Signifying that the discounting rate is static.

Chapter 11

Rating of Securitization Transactions

Rating is almost indispensable in the process of securitization. All major international rating agencies are engaged in rating securitization transactions.

One of the significant features of securitization as a structured finance device is that the rating is a target, not a *fait accompli*. Every securitization transaction has a potential to result in a given rating. For example, if a AAA rating is targeted in an auto finance pool, originated by a A-rated issuer, it is quite possible to do so; all that is required is to work out the level of credit enhancements or subordinated interest.

For most securitization transactions, rating is the very objective of the transaction.

Structured finance ratings vs. other fixed income ratings

An issue often discussed is the difference between structured finance ratings and other fixed income ratings. If a structured security is rated AAA, is that different from a AAA-rating fixed income bond?

In fact, the very purpose of rating is objectivity and comparability. In some countries, rating agencies seek to distinguish structured finance ratings from other ratings on the ground that the ratings are derived from the structure of credit enhancements.[1] This distinction is at best illusory, and at worst deceptive. All ratings for fixed income securities are based on the probability, at a given confidence level, of payment of interest and principal. In all cases, these probabilities are assigned based on the existence of economic capital, and structured finance is no different.

As we have noted in the context of the sizing of credit enhancements (Chapter 4 for retail assets and Chapter 17 for CDOs), the essential rating consideration is to align the probability of default on the securities to those for bonds; thus, the question of any difference in meaning of ratings does not arise.

The table below shows the rating symbols used by the rating agencies. Note that the symbols do not distinguish between asset-backed securities and corporate paper:

Table 11.1 Rating Scales of the U.S. Rating Agencies

Agency	Investment Grade										Speculative Grade													
S & P	AAA	AA+	AA	AA–	A+	A	A–	BBB+	BBB	BBB–	BB+	BB	BB–	B+	B	B–	CCC+	CCC	CCC–	CC	C	D		
Moody's	Aaa	Aa1	Aa2	Aa3	A1	A2	A3	Baa1	Baa2	Baa3	Ba1	Ba2	Ba3	B1	B2	B3	Caa1	Caa2	Caa3	Ca		C		
Fitch	AAA	AA+	AA	AA–	A+	A	A–	BBB+	BBB	BBB–	BB+	BB	BB–	B+	B	B–	CCC+	CCC	CCC–	CC	C	DDD	DD	D

Rating agency concerns

Securitization is a structured finance device: Investors are not concerned with the entity except for the quality of the originated portfolio. Essentially, the rating agencies are concerned with the quality of the underlying pool.

It is often said that the rating of the originator is completely irrelevant for securitization transactions, but the originator quality, particularly the systems, strengths and procedures are relevant for evaluating the quality of the originated pool, as well as the abilities of the originator as servicer.

Rating considerations differ from asset to asset and generalizations, such as below, are only of a very preliminary significance.

Asset quality

The quality of the asset portfolio is the most important concern of the rating agency. The quality of the asset depends on the nature of the asset.

Rating agencies have long experience in rating securitization issues. They have developed a benchmark for different asset classes, available on their websites as rating criteria. For example, for mortgage assets, typical yardsticks for a pool selection will be shown in Table 11.2.

Solvency of the issuer

The solvency of the issuer, at the time of the transfer of receivables as well as within a certain time after the transfer of receivables, is a critical legal issue.

The corporate/bankruptcy laws of most countries stipulate against transfers made by an insolvent entity, or by a potentially insolvent company in apprehension of insolvency. These legal provisions make any transfers of assets made by an insolvent company or a company that becomes insolvent with a certain time after such transfer as legally invalid. If bankruptcy of the originator takes

Table 11.2 Typical criteria for mortgage pool selection

Mortgage type:	Fixed rate or adjustable rate, fully amortizing loans
Security	First mortgage over freehold property
Property	Residential, owner occupied; flats, semi-attached or detached housing
Loan purpose	Permanent financing for primary residence
Mortgagor characteristics	Person resident in the country
LTV ratio	Generally up to 80%
Loan size	In dollars
Income limit	Gross debt/income ratio – 30% if monthly income is < $40% if monthly income is > $
Property valuation	By recognized valuers
Geographic dispersion	Dispersion throughout the country commensurate with population distribution
Pool size	Minimum 300 loans
Mortgage performance	No loan > 30 days delinquency
Insurance	Fire insurance

place within this period, the transfer of receivables may be struck down leaving in the investors robbed of their basic property rights.

Thus, even for non-recourse assignments, the rating agency would like to ensure that there is no chance of the impending bankruptcy of the issuer.

In case of securitizations with recourse, the rating of the issuer is equally as important, if not more, as the rating of the portfolio.

Perfection of legal structure

Much time and money goes into legal opinions relating to securitizations. There are a number of legal issues involved, sometimes quite contentious, in a securitization process. These may include: (a) Whether there is a clear legal transfer of the receivables; (b) Whether the underlying contracts contain clear incontestable rights to receivables as well as inherent securities; (c) whether the securities are enforceable; (d) Whether the structure of the SPV is free from risk and legal liabilities.

Rating agencies would normally insist that the securitization exercise be vetted by some legal expert who is well versed with securitization structures. A detailed opinion relating to different aspects of the securitization deal is sought from legal experts. In **Annexure** to the chapter on Legal Issues, we give the model of a legal opinion relating to a securitization transaction in mortgage-backed securities. There will be specific variations for securitization of other assets.

Tax risks

The rating agency will also be concerned with the tax risks in the securitization exercise. Taxation provisions of many countries may not be clear in regard to the taxability of securitization transactions. More of this is taken up in the specific chapter devoted to taxation issues, but of immediate concern to the rating agency is whether the rights of investors to collect the flows guaranteed to them are likely to be jeopardised by any taxes, such as withholding tax, income tax or indirect taxes or duties.

If possible, the rating agency should insist on advance rulings. The system of advanced rulings exists in many countries. Alternatively, opinions from reliable tax experts with good understanding of securitization transactions should be sought.

Clean and prior title to the securitized portfolio

Associated with the legal risks, the rating agency would try to ensure that the investors, acting through the SPV would be able to enforce the claims and securities against the debtors when required. From this viewpoint, the constitution of the SPV becomes important. In several jurisdictions, it is not possible to organize the SPV as a company because of taxation difficulties. Also, legal enforcement of claims by an unincorporated body may not be very convenient, and so this issue should be examined in consultation with local advisers.

Another significant issue is the existence of prior charges or rights in the assigned debts. There might be claims of the liquidator of the assignor, statutory dues, and the employees of the originator or employee benefit funds. The rating agency would look at all possibilities where there could be prior claims that may rank superior to the rights of the SPV.

Risk of set-off

Set-off refers to the right of the debtor to set-off the obligation to pay, against any right of the debtor to receive any payment or service from the assignor. It is quite common for loan, lease and mortgage documents to provide that the installments are payable without any right of set off. However, sometimes common law or a statute may provide for a right of set off. The investors' right in the securitized portfolio would be jeopardised if the debtor could avail of the benefit of any set off against the installments payable by the debtor.

Risk of prepayment

Prepayment is seen as a distinct risk in securitizations. Prepayment refers to the option of the debtor to prepay the loan/lease/mortgage and thereby foreclose the transaction. Prepayment may either be an option under the contract, or even if not an express option, it may be an embedded or implicit option. Sometimes, even the statute requires a prepayment option to be given to the borrower.

In the event of prepayment, the prepaid principal has either to be reinvested by the SPV or passed through to the investors. In the former case, the prepayment risk refers to the inability of the SPV to reinvest the prepaid principal either immediately or at the same rate of return as the prepaid transaction. Both will have an impact on the rights of the investors.

Rating agencies measure the prepayment risk on the basis of historical data about prepayments and projection of factors that might cause prepayments. For example, interest rate variation is a very strong factor. If rates of interest come down, borrowers would be tempted to prepay past loans and take new loans at lower rates of interest. There might be other factors such as a housing loan prepaid due to a change of residence or marriage breaking up, a car loan prepaid on account of the model being unpopular or a substantial reduction in the prices of the car.

Executory contractual clauses

This issue, discussed in detail in the chapter on Legal Issues, refers to the existence of obligations on the part of the originator under the contract. The rating agency should cause the underlying agreement to be examined by competent legal experts from the point of view of action by the originator. The originator's unfulfilled obligations cannot be assigned to the assignee; at the same time, a consolidated assignment of rights along with obligations may not be legally valid.

Ratings of connected parties

Rating agencies are concerned with the ratings of the parties whose support is critical in the securitization program. If credit or liquidity support is provided by a party, the rating of such a party becomes important. If there are swap counterparties or insurance companies supporting the transaction, the rating of the swap provider or the insurance company in question becomes important.

Servicer or administrator rating

Servicing plays a very important role in ensuring that the underlying collateral continues to perform, so rating agencies place stress on the strengths of the servicer. If the originator is the servicer, the rating of the back-up servicer is also significant. We take up servicer ratings as a separate caption in this chapter.

Sovereign risks

Sovereign ratings are an important hurdle in the foreign currency rating of a transaction. The domestic rating of a transaction is relevant for domestic investors and is given based on the ratings of comparable domestic companies. International ratings are given based on ratings of comparable companies in international markets. International ratings are meant to be relied upon by international investors, so such ratings are conceptually not higher than the rating of the sovereign, as it can significantly affect the payment ability and operations of the company. To pierce sovereign ceilings, several securitization transactions either rely upon a trapping of cash flow outside the country or opt for political risk insurance by agencies such as OPIC.

The rating process

Review/presentation

The rating agencies will wish to visit the originator/administrator to assess the quality of the management, the way that the company is set up and to review the administrative procedures.

Prior to the visit, it is normal practice to prepare a file on the company including financial information, procedures, company history, senior staff biographies and example contracts. Collating and preparing this information normally takes several weeks.

Asset analysis or credit risk modeling

This is the one risk that rating agencies are prepared to take a commercial view on. This view is based upon an analysis of the asset pool proposed to be securitized, and a review of the historical performance of the originator's assets based upon certain assumptions. Generally the golden rules are:

- Present your data appropriately (detailed advice is required on this point, as the exact approach should be closely linked to the way that the transaction is to be structured); and
- Generate as much data as possible; irrelevant data can be discarded, but missing data are impossible to replace; rating agencies, in the absence of data, make conservative guesses (e.g.: 100% loss rates, no recoveries).

Once they have reviewed this information, the rating agencies will make an assessment of their worst-case expectations as to the performance of the portfolio, that is, how much stress needs to be applied to the normal assumptions to anticipate the worst-case scenarios depends on the volatilities underlying the assumptions. The structure then has to be designed to ensure that, should these losses appear, the rated debt is paid in full by the maturity date.

Here, the rating agency will come up with its computations of the expected loss, which will then be manipulated to compute the unexpected losses. The approach here is the same as the credit risk modeling of a pool of assets.

Transaction analysis or structural analysis

The structural analysis deal with how the credit losses of the pool will be allocated to various classes of securities.

The combination of the credit risk model with structural analysis involves the production of detailed computer models of the transaction, which are then used to determine the way in which the structure will behave in different stress environments. Typical variables are credit loss levels, delinquency levels, interest rates and corporation tax rates. Each rating level normally has associated with it a certain combination of stress assumptions, becoming more stressful for higher ratings.

Differences in the approaches/models used by the rating agencies, particularly on the computation of expected losses and the stress scenarios, do exist, but the essential focus of each rating agency is to ensure with a degree of confidence level that the rated securities are paid off. The confidence level, in turn, is dependent on the desired rating.

Legal and tax

It is now normal for the rating agencies to require detailed opinions on the transaction addressing both legal and tax risks. These opinions are extremely difficult documents for lawyers to write, as the levels of comfort required are higher than those that would be necessary from a commercial perspective. This is one of the expensive elements of a transaction.

The legal analysis of transactions could even involve cross-border laws. For example, in an aircraft lease securitization exercise, the rating agency insisted on obtaining legal opinions on the laws of all the countries where the aircraft could possibly land, and the result was 118 legal opinions!

Committee decision

As with all ratings, the final decisions are made by a credit committee or ratings committee on the basis of an assessment of instrument-specific documentation and other information provided by analysts. The committee's opinions may then be fed back into the rating process, for example through revision of standard assumptions. In addition, all ratings are ultimately mapped into an alphanumeric scale benchmarked to the historical performance of corporate bonds.

Rating models

The rating models built by the rating agencies are designed to compute the anticipated credit losses for different levels of credit rating.

A AAA-rating is supposed to withstand the worst-case scenario. The required credit support here or at different rating levels will be based on the anticipated **default frequency** and **loss severity**. Default frequency refers to the percentage of outstanding cases – in value terms – that will default. The estimated frequency will be higher at higher levels of rating, as the assumptions are most pessimistic for the highest level of rating.

At the assumed default frequency, the credit loss is given by the loss severity times the default frequency. The loss severity is the loss as a percentage of outstanding loan value. The loss is computed after taking into account the market value of the collateral, legal expenses in recovering, and loss of interest due to the time taken in foreclosure.

Evidently, the loss severity will be more at higher levels of rating as the assumptions are based on worst-case scenarios; the decline in the market value of the property will be taken as maximum, while legal costs and the time taken in enforcing the loan will be taken at the most as well.

Table 11.3   A sample of credit loss calculations for different ratings

Rating(1)	Default frequency(2)	Loss severity(3)	Credit loss(2) × (3)
AAA	15%	82.3%	12.3%
AA	10%	76%	7.6%
A	8%	71%	5.7%
B	6%	66%	4.0%

The levels of credit enhancement will be set up according to the expected credit losses.

Rating agencies have framed mortgage market models for most of the significant securitization markets; one can find the mortgage credit loss model for Netherlands, Spain, or for Mexico, and these models are available on the websites of the rating agencies.

Rating approaches for retail assets and wholesale assets

We have separately discussed the sizing of the credit enhancements for retail pools and for CDOs. This is a quick note on the major differences from viewpoint of rating model for the two types of assets.

For retail assets, the pool is diversified and granular. Hence, the idiosyncratic or diversifiable risk is not important. In any case, it is not possible to individually compute the risk of default of each asset. Hence, the approach here is based on actuarial principles. The loss and standard deviation thereof as reflected by the sample is taken to be representative of the population.

The CDOs and wholesale assets, on the other hand, require assessment of probabilities of default for each asset. There is a correlation risk as well and the approach used in most such cases is simulation.

Differences between structured finance and corporate finance ratings

In view of the nature of structured finance, there are some notable differences between structured finance ratings and corporate finance ratings.

First of all, structured finance securities are issued by bankruptcy remote entities, so the bankruptcy risk of the issuing entity is not in issue. The rating analyst looks at the ability of the structure to pay interest and principal by maturity. As for principal payment, there may not be a committed schedule of repayments – pass-through nature of securities might imply only an indicating or expected schedule. Therefore, rating agencies are concerned with evaluating the risk of payment by the final maturity of the transaction.[2]

In the case of structured finance ratings, rating agencies are concerned with a finite, static pool, as opposed to the dynamic pool and business of the operating company in case of usual fixed income securities. By its nature, structured finance is comparable to project finance more than corporate finance.

The BIS group on structured finance ratings assimilated the following differences between structured finance and corporate finance ratings:

Table 11.4 Structured finance versus traditional credit ratings: Commonalities and differences

Issue	Structured finance	Traditional
Rating process	Basically identical: Analyst review, credit committee	
Rating concept	Identical rating basis: Expected loss (EL) or default probability (PD)	
	Tranching can create securities with same expected loss, but much different unexpected loss properties	Expected loss may be a reasonable proxy for credit risk
Structural features	More "complex" - extensive analysis of "moving parts" required	Structural features, such as bond covenants, exist – but analysis less extensive
Credit risk analysis	Controlled environment enables more model-based, quantitative analysis of asset pool: emphasis on the relatively easily definable cash flow generated by the underlying asset pool; known maturity	More limited scope for quantitative analysis of overall balance sheet/franchise; emphasis on the cash flow generated by the obligor's ongoing business activities (issuing entity is going concern)
Conflicts of interest	Exist in both cases	
	Between originators, investors, third parties – more transparent, easier to control, requires structural mitigants	Between shareholders, different debt holders, management – more difficult to control (covenants)
Nature of rating	Pronounced ex ante nature (targeted ratings, iterative process, rating issued at inception); more model-based; greater flexibility to adjust structural factors	Ex post, though with ex ante elements (pre-rating feedback, issuer first rated in mid-life); more judgmental; limited issuer ability to adjust credit characteristics
Performance	More stable on average, but larger changes – significant instability of particular asset classes	Benchmark for structural finance ratings via EL/PD mapping

What credit ratings do not rate

Structured finance ratings, like all other credit ratings, are concerned with only the risk of default of the securities. They are not concerned with market risk – the loss in the market value or mark-to-market value of the securities.

Ratings are also not concerned with liquidity of the investment.

If the securities in question are subject to a prepayment risk, there might be a loss of value to the investor due to prepayments. Rating agencies are not concerned with prepayment risk, except the extent such risk might affect the excess spreads and thereby the levels of credit enhancement.

What rating upgrades of structured finance securities mean

In periodic review of ratings, rating agencies often upgrade or downgrade ratings. These are called rating transitions and these were referred to in Chapter 1 as one of the motivators for securitization transactions.

Notably, while a downgrade might mean deterioration in the quality of the asset pool, and in particular, depletion of the credit enhancement level, upgrades of ratings do not always mean improvement in the quality of the pool. For example, an upgrade may happen due to amortization of the pool and presence of a static cash reserve or sequential paydown structure of the transaction. Sometimes, as is commonly noted for CMBS transactions, an upgrade may also happen due to defeasance of the assets.

Servicer evaluation

In view of the significance of servicing quality, rating agencies have started placing increasing emphasis on effective servicing of the pools, and therefore, have developed criteria for servicer evaluation. The stress on servicer evaluation seems to be eroding the very line of distinction between asset-backed ratings and entity ratings.

All the rating agencies evaluate servicers. Standard & Poor's Servicer Evaluations are intended to assess a servicer's strengths, weaknesses, opportunities and limitations, through an examination of three key areas: "Management and Organization," "Loan/Asset Administration," and "Financial Position."[3] These three areas apply to all collateral classes.

Likewise, Fitch Ratings has listed the following to do a servicer evaluation:[4]

ABS Seller/Servicer Rating Criteria
Corporate Performance

- Company and management experience.
- Financial condition.
- Operational risk management.

Origination

- Origination and underwriting process.
- Risk management.
- Staffing and training.
- Technology.

Servicing

- Account maintenance.
- Customer service.
- Payment processing and cash management.
- Investor reporting and remitting.
- Collections and loss mitigation.
- Default loan management.
- Risk management.
- Staffing and training.
- Technology.

Role of ratings in structured finance

The role of ratings in structured finance has been hotly discussed over the past few years. While ratings have increasingly become relevant to capital markets and the new capital standards place increased stress on ratings, for structured finance rating arbitrage is by itself an essential motive. Hence, structured finance relies on ratings more than most other capital market participants. Obviously, structured finance ratings have become an important part of the income of rating agencies. "Structured finance ratings are now among the largest and fastest growing business segments for the three leading credit rating agencies and have developed into an important revenue source. Moody's annual report for 2003 documents that structured finance, at $460 million, accounted for more than 40% of ratings revenues. Between 1996 and 2003, structured finance revenue grew at an annual compound rate of nearly 30%. Although separate public accounts for the other two major rating agencies are not available, the 2003 annual report of Fimalac SA, the parent company of Fitch Ratings, indicates that Fitch earned more than 50% of its revenues from rating structured finance transactions. Similarly, McGraw-Hill's public reports suggest that structured finance is of comparable importance for its Standard & Poor's division."[5]

Despite the fact that the structured finance market to a very large extent is driven by ratings, there are some commonly noted differences in the approach of different rating agencies to structured finance ratings, particularly in case of CDOs. Why rating agency practices should have come under more scrutiny for CDOs than retail products is because CDOs are more arbitrage-driven and differences in ratings assigned by different rating agencies may lead to substantial differences in the arbitrage consequences to the investors.

Some areas of critique

As the role of rating agencies in the structured finance business was intensively discussed over in the past, some areas of critique are notable:

- It is contended that rating agencies not only provide ratings but also structuring advice, which leads to a conflict of interest. In addition, the nature of ratings in structured finance is *ex ante*, that is, the structure follows the ratings. Thus, the structuring of the transaction is driven by the ratings; the required enhancement levels are indicated by the rating agencies. While this may sound problematic, on an objective analysis, there is no difference between giving a rating based on a particular structure. For bond ratings, if the bond issuer infuses more capital, the rating may be revised. It is only that changes in capital structure can be more easily implemented in structured finance than in corporate balance sheets.
- **Notching practices**: In 2001 and 2002, there were intensive debates in the marketplace about notching practices, essentially notable in the CDO segment. A CDO may consist of bonds that are not rated by the rating agency in question. Instead of rating the bonds, the agency on the basis of more – or less – conservative standards used by it assigns shadow ratings several notches above or below such ratings. This practice of lowering or uplifting the notches came to be known as notching practice. A study by NERA Consulting Group on such practices was commissioned, which noted significant differences in the ratings of the leading three rating agencies.[6]

Notes

1 In India, for example, structured finance ratings are distinguished by a suffix AAA (SO), where SO stands for structured obligations.
2 Note the meaning of final maturity, and difference between expected maturity and final maturity, discussed in Chapter 4.
3 See S&P: Servicer Evaluations Ranking Criteria, September 21, 2004.
4 Fitch Ratings: Rating ABS Seller/Servicers, September 14, 2004.
5 Committee on the Global Financial System of the Bank for International Settlements: Role Ratings in Structured Finance, January 25.
6 Report dated November 6, 2003 by NERA: Credit Ratings for Structured Products.

Part III: Asset Classes

This part discusses some significant applications of securitization. It is notable that the applications of securitization are growing very fast, and therefore, the following applications may only be exemplary of a concept being applied extremely vigorously to very imaginative applications.

Chapter 12

Residential Mortgage-backed Securitization

Securitization of residential mortgages is the mother of all securitizations. They were the first application of the concept of securitization, and even today, the volumes of residential mortgage-backed securities far exceed the total value of any other securitization application, both in the U.S. market and in the most parts of the world.

Residential mortgage-backed securities (RMBS) are generally pass-through securities or bonds based on cash flow from residential home loans, as opposed to commercial real estate loans. The latter are known as commercial mortgage-backed securities (CMBS) and are taken up in the next chapter.

RMBS today is a major funding source for the residential mortgage market. The significance of RMBS for any economy is easily understood; housing is a basic need for civilized living, and mortgage lending – housing finance – enables

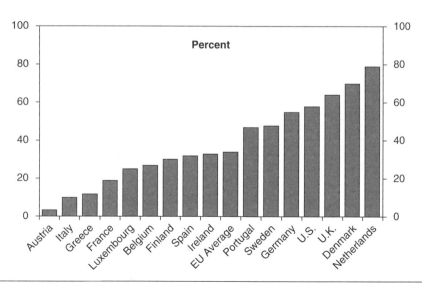

Figure 12.1 Ratio of outstanding residential mortgage debt to GDP, 2001
Source: Miles Review

people to affordably own houses. Securitization provides liquidity to the mortgage market, and therefore, it clearly relates to one of the basic needs of society. In short, as bank lending is the very life blood of industrialization, RMBS enjoys the same place in relation to housing needs.

RMBS is based on the idea of transfer of mortgages after their origination into the capital markets, so the RMBS system is sometimes also referred to as **secondary mortgage market**, implying a system whereby mortgages are originated and transferred.

Mortgage funding systems

Each country has a system of funding housing, and by commercial necessity, also a system of refinancing or provision of funding to these housing finance providers. The housing finance providers are often also referred to as the mortgage financiers. The chart below shows the ratio of residential mortgage debt to GDP in certain countries; the comparison, apart from the state of economic development, has a lot to do with the extent of urbanization, as economies with rural bases do not rely on formal methods of housing finance (see Figures 12.1 and 12.2):

Figure 12.2 shows the ratio of mortgage debt to GDP in some Asian countries:

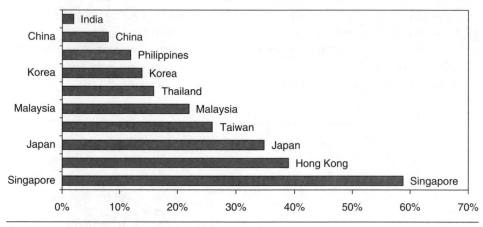

Figure 12.2 Ratio of Morgage debt to GDP

Source: Dr Bertrand Renaud

In different countries, there are different forms of housing finance entities – commercial banks, specialized housing finance entities, building societies, thrifts or cooperative credit societies.

Irrespective of the entity or institutional system that caters to housing finance needs, a common feature in all countries is housing finance is long-term, and is required generally in large amounts.

The traditional sources of funding for these mortgage financiers include:

- Deposits – term deposits from households
- Various forms of contractual savings plans – a sort of a deposit, but instead of being voluntary, it is contractual and generally monthly recurring, such as by way of a deduction from salaries. Normally contractual savings are supported by the government by tax relief.
- Issuance of traditional bonds/debentures by the financiers
- Lines of credit by way of refinance, refinancing loans.

The relative significance of these different sources of re-financing depends on the nature of the institution and way they have developed over time. Traditional building societies in several countries have depended, and still largely depend, on depository savings: "Specialist deposit funded institutions have traditionally dominated the provision of housing finance in English speaking countries (e.g., Australia, Canada, South Africa, the United States). The model for housing finance in these countries originated with the terminating building societies founded in England in 1775."[1]

In continental Europe, a unique mortgage-funding system by issuing mortgage bonds has prevailed for more than 200 years. These bonds are different from the traditional bonds issued in the capital market, as representing both a claim against the borrower and against the mortgage. Supported by specific law, these bonds ensure bankruptcy remoteness, and therefore, except for the off-balance sheet feature, provide the same incentives to the investor as securitization. These bonds are called by different names, commonly referred to as covered bonds, mortgage bonds, as also by their local-language names such as *pfandbriefes* in Germany, the oldest and the largest market for such bonds.

While capital markets, via mortgage-backed securities, are the largest supplier of resources to the US mortgage markets, in Europe and Asia, the mortgage system is still largely dependent on traditional methods of financing. In the U.S., the ratio of mortgage-backed securities to total mortgage debt outstanding has been more than 40% over the last 10 years or so (see the ratio of federally-related mortgage pools, GSEs and ABS issuers to the total mortgage assets):

Table 12.1 Home Mortgages by holder, 2000–2004 (1) ($ billions, end of year)

	2000	2001	2002	2003	2004
Total assets	**$5,126.3**	**$5,635.8**	**$6,309.6**	**$7,105.1**	**$8,071.1**
Household sector	87.4	94.9	103.6	113.1	123.5
Nonfinancial corporate business	21.4	23.0	24.0	25.0	26.0
Nonfarm noncorporate business	8.7	9.9	9.6	11.4	13.4
State and local governments	67.5	66.5	63.2	67.6	72.1
Federal government	17.7	17.1	16.2	15.3	14.8
Commercial banking	965.6	1,023.9	1,222.2	1,347.0	1,567.5
Savings institutions	594.2	620.6	631.4	703.4	875.8
Credit unions	124.9	141.3	159.4	182.6	211.2

	2000	2001	2002	2003	2004
Bank personal trusts and estates	2.3	2.5	2.3	1.9	1.9
Life insurance companies	4.9	4.9	4.7	4.4	4.7
Private pension funds	7.7	4.6	2.8	1.7	1.4
State and local govt retirement funds	7.1	6.9	6.8	6.3	6.8
Government-sponsored enterprises	205.1	225.6	271.1	363.3	367.8
Federally related mortgage pools	2,425.6	2,748.5	3,063.7	3,367.0	3,416.9
ABS issuers	426.3	496.1	551.8	683.2	1,071.9
Finance companies	130.6	120.1	135.0	152.2	190.2
Mortgage companies (2)	21.8	21.8	21.8	21.8	21.8
REITs	7.4	7.7	20.0	37.8	83.1
Home equity loans included above (3)	492.0	518.0	583.3	684.9	881.3
Commercial banking	235.0	258.6	303.3	366.0	483.6
Savings institutions	72.8	77.9	78.5	95.6	121.5
Credit unions	40.7	44.9	48.1	51.8	64.0
ABS issuers	12.9	16.5	18.5	19.2	21.9
Finance companies	130.6	120.1	135.0	152.2	190.2

(1) Mortgages on 1–4 family properties. (2) Not updated by the Federal Reserve System since 1997. (3) Loans made under home equity lines of credit and home equity loans secured by junior liens. Excludes home equity loans held by mortgage companies and individuals.
Source: Board of Governors of the Federal Reserve System.

On the other hand, in Europe mortgage finance is still largely dependent on bankers' traditional modes of savings and mortgage bonds. See Figure 12.3 below:

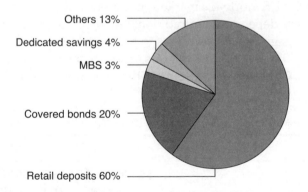

Others 13%
Dedicated savings 4%
MBS 3%
Covered bonds 20%
Retail deposits 60%

Figure 12.3 Mortgage funding sources in Europe
Source: Public Hearing on Mortgage Credit, Brussels, 7th Dec 2005

Government support to housing finance

In most countries, governments have tried to promote housing finance, by setting up specialized housing refinance bodies or secondary mortgage market bodies. The largest housing finance institution in the world, the Government Housing Loan Corporation of Japan, is a government-owned entity. The largest housing finance body in the U.S., Fannie Mae, is a government-sponsored entity. There are housing finance bodies of different descriptions throughout the world that are promoted, owned or supported by governments such as Hong Kong, Malaysia, India, France, South Korea and Spain.

Government support to housing finance is understandable as housing is a prime need and the governments owe it to their citizens to promote affordable housing.

Why secondary mortgage markets?

The traditional balance sheet funding system, whereby housing financiers rely either on deposits or on bonds, is seen as inefficient and costlier. Countries which have experimented with mortgage securitization systems have found that mortgage lending/servicing costs have come down and on the whole the mortgage system has become deeper and more efficient.

The impact of securitization in lowering mortgage costs has been academically argued by several researchers. Black, Garbade and Silber (1981)[2] and Passmore and Sparks (1996)[3] argue that the implicit government guarantee enhances liquidity. Within general asset markets, Greenbaum and Thakor (1987)[4] show that banks, by selling loans rather than funding them through deposits, can provide a useful signal of loan quality. Hess and Smith (1988)[5] show that asset securitization is a means of reducing risk through diversification. For a general literature review and some conclusions, see Andrea Heuson, Wayne Passmore, and Roger Sparks: *Credit Scoring and Mortgage Securitization: Implications for Mortgage Rates and Credit Availability* October 6, 2000. Yet another researcher studied the impact of CMOs on the mortgage costs and came to conclude that: "We find no association between securitization and the coupon rates on fixed-rate mortgages, instead, securitization appears to lower mortgage loan origination fees, resulting in substantial savings for homebuyers. A 1% increase in the monthly level of pass-through creation is associated with a 0.5-basis-point reduction in loan origination fees. In 1993 alone, securitization likely produced consumer savings of more than $2 billion in loan origination fees."[6]

The Hong Kong Monetary Authority in a April 1996 report[7] noted the advantages of a corporation for secondary mortgages: "The advantages of the mortgage corporation to the home buyers are apparent. It will help to ensure the availability of mortgage funds, which will in turn alleviate potential upward pressure on the mortgage interest rate. Over the long term, a lowering of mortgage rate may be possible because the improved liquidity of residential mortgage loans will allow a reduction in the risk premium on such loans."[8]

Countries that have lived with the secondary mortgage market system for several years have built the entire system of mortgage lending around their eventual aim at securitizing the mortgages. Apart from the U.S. mortgage market, the Australian market is a strong example of a system where a large part of the mortgage system is funded by securitization. This has led to a basic restructuring of the market. The mortgage origination, servicing and funding are split into various specialized agencies. Mortgages are typically originated by mortgage brokers who are neither banks nor non-banking financiers. They do not put in any funding of their own. Most of them are affiliates of some large mortgage retail network and simply originate a mortgage based on a set of well-defined underwriting standards. Having originated the mortgage, the retailer sells the mortgage to a "wholesaler." The wholesaler has either its own funding sources, or access to *warehousing* sources for funding the mortgages between their origination and ultimate securitization. The final source of funding, however, comes from the capital markets if a critical mass of mortgages is gathered.

This mortgage system, it is believed, minimizes agency costs. There is minimal equity put into the entire system, which is partly in the form of a subordinated capital typically put in by the wholesaler, and a contingent capital put in by the mortgage insurance company insuring the mortgage pool. The funding predominantly comes directly from the capital market.[9]

Origin of the secondary mortgage markets

There are two global examples of secondary mortgage markets – the government-sponsored agencies in the U.S. and the system of mortgage bonds or *pfandbriefes* in continental Europe. As the mortgage bond system is not exactly secondary trading in mortgages, it will be discussed later.

The secondary mortgage market in the U.S.

Agency market

The three government-sponsored agencies (GSEs), Government National Mortgage Association (GNMA) (nicknamed Ginnie Mae), Federal National Mortgage Association (FNMA) (nicknamed Fannie Mae), and Federal Home Loan Mortgage Corporation (FHLMC) (nicknamed Freddie Mac) are responsible for a huge secondary mortgage market in the U.S. The agencies are sponsored by the government and are referred to as Government Sponsored Entities, or GSEs.

In some primitive form, trading in mortgages seems to have existed in the U.S. even before the 1900s. "Mortgage-backed bonds were sold to the public even before 1900. After that time, mortgage participation certificates – which were very similar to the modern mortgage-backed securities – had been issued by mortgage-bankers. These securities were traded until 1930s, when the market collapsed with the Depression."[10]

The U.S. government set up Fannie Mae in 1938, soon after creation of the Federal Housing Administration (FHA) in 1934. The FHA started providing insurance coverage to 30-year fixed-rate mortgages, and Fannie Mae started purchasing these mortgages. However, Fannie Mae continued to work on the model of buying the mortgages, holding them and funding its own balance sheet with conventional debt.

In 1968, Fannie Mae was split into two; the first part continued as Fannie Mae but with a Federal charter and private shareholdings, while the second part as a government-owned agency called Ginnie Mae.

In 1970, Freddie Mac was created, with a primary focus towards the thrifts. The GNMA brought the first pass-through certificates into the market in 1970.

The secondary mortgage market presently runs with a combination of the agency-backed securities and non-agency securities, also known as *private label* securities.

The combination of agencies – FHA, Ginnie Mae, Fannie Mae and Freddie Mac – account for the vast and efficient mortgage funding system in the U.S. The FHA continues to insure both single-family and multi-family mortgages, which reduces the downpayment requirements and allows mortgages to be funded with higher LTV ratios. Ginnie Mae, still a government-body, continues to buy FHA/VA loans and issue MBS. Fannie Mae is the largest securitizer in the U.S. Both Fannie Mae and Freddie Mac are private corporations, although they have implicit government support.[11]

The non-agency market

Conforming loans are loans that meet up with the prescribed criteria, essentially with respect to loan size and the underwriting standards; they are usually bought by the agencies, which in general do not buy non-conforming loans. Ginnie Mae generally does not buy loans other than those insured by FHA/VA.

The non-agency market caters to these non-conforming mortgages, and these loans may be "jumbo" loans – loans of a higher amount that qualifies under the conformity standards – or B or C category loans, also called *sub-prime* loans, in the sense that they do not comply with the underwriting standards of the agencies as to a debt-to-income ratio, borrower history or LTV ratio. The non-agency originations may also include *no doc* or *low doc* originations, where the borrower either did not submit any basic document required for credit screening or the documentation was not complete.

Non-agency originations are obviously characterized by much higher spreads and much lower LTV ratios. These loans are taken to the capital market by larger originators directly, or by larger securitization specialists who buy out portfolios of smaller originators or retailers.

These are taken to the capital market with credit-enhancements. Notably, in the agency-backed market, credit-enhancements are not required as the agencies themselves guarantee repayment. However, in the private label market, various forms of enhancements include excess spread, higher subordination, and sometimes even third-party support: "Throughout the 1980s, third-party supports such as pool insurance, bond insurance, letters of credit (LOCs), and corporate guarantees were most frequently used. However, investors' heightened awareness of event risk (mostly due to bank and insurance company downgrades), combined with the withdrawal of many third-party credit-enhancement providers from the mortgage business in the aftermath of the Texas, New England, and California real estate debacles, resulted in a decisive turn towards subordination and other "standalone" (as opposed to external or third-party) credit-enhancement techniques that are internal to the structure itself."

The non-agency market originated in 1977 with the first securitization by Bank of America. From this period up to the mid-1980s, volumes of private-label securitization have been both thin and inconsistent, as most of the loans were originated and held with high spreads by thrifts. However, over time spreads in mortgages reduced and eventually turned negative, forcing the originators to look to the capital markets.

One of the difficulties in private label securitization was resolved by the Secondary Mortgage Market Enhancement Act of 1984 (SMMEA), which permitted shelf registration for bonds issued by the private securitizers. Before this, in case of private label securities, registration with the securities regulator was required for each issue separately, while for agency securities, as noted earlier, registration was completely exempted.

Private label securitization was highly credit-enhanced by subordination, so there were tax issues on the taxability of the pools as to whether a senior-junior classification could still be taken as tax-neutral, or a pass-through arrangement. However, when securitizers used the CMO device that broke up the mortgage cash flow into distinct bond-like classes, the possibility of the residual class being taxed as equity was much greater. This dis-incentive was also cleared by the government by enacting the Real Estate Mortgage Investment Conduit (REMIC) in 1987. Almost around the same time, rating agencies had come out with detailed guidelines on ratings based on subordination; they set up the multiples of expected losses that would need to be absorbed by the originators' enhancement. It thus became clear that even less credit-worthy or sub-prime portfolios could lead to AAA-rated securities, and thereafter, the private label market really boomed.

The next stage of development of the private label market was a structural change from the traditional concept of senior and junior pieces with the junior piece retained with the originator. Moody's in 1988 rated a transaction where the junior piece itself was tranched into two, leading to the mezzanine or B-class to be rated investment grade. The mezzanine class was a fast-pay class with maturity of less than 10 years, and the junior class was a slow-pay class extending right up to the longest maturity of the pool. Gradually, the market adopted the CMO method by converting the mortgage flows into fixed income securities, easily understood by Wall Street investors. "This shift to CMO issuance was itself the outward manifestation of several underlying trends that were changing the structure of the entire no agency MBS market:

1. A shift from adjustable-rate to fixed-rate originations in the nonconforming loan sector;
2. The related shift in loan origination market share from thrifts and other portfolio originators to secondary-market driven mortgage-banks and conduits;
3. Increased attention to no agency loan prepayment trends (although with varying degrees of success), which facilitated investor acceptance of increasingly prepayment-sensitive principal allocation structures."[13]

Proposal to regulate the GSEs

Over the last few years, controversy over the potential regulation of the GSEs raged in the U.S. While Ginnie Mae is effectively a government-owned company, Fannie Mae and Freddie Mac are regulated by the Housing and Urban Development (HUD) department of the government. The legal privileges of the GSEs are limited; they have a conditional access to funds up to $2.25 billion from the U.S. Treasury by way of line of credit and tax exemption. However, due to the public perception about their status as GSEs, they have been able to grow their funding at rates close to Treasury rates: "While the securities that the GSEs guarantee, and the debt instruments they issue, are explicitly not backed by the full faith and credit of the United States, such securities and instruments trade at yields only a few basis points over those of U.S. Treasury securities with comparable terms, based on the belief of many investors that the Federal government would intervene if a GSE were to become insolvent. Consequently, the GSEs are able to fund their operations at lower costs than other private firms with similar financial characteristics".[14]

Among others, former Fed Chairman Alan Greenspan has discussed at length the need to regulate the GSEs. In testimony before the Committee on Banking, Housing and Urban Affairs, the U.S. Senate, April 6, 2005, he stated: "Because Fannie and Freddie can borrow at a subsidized rate, they have been able to pay banks, thrifts, mortgage companies, and other home mortgage originators slightly higher prices for mortgages than their potential competitors have paid. This edge has enabled Fannie and Freddie to gain gradually but inexorably an ever-larger share of the home mortgage market. Investors have provided Fannie and Freddie with a powerful vehicle for pursuing profits through the rapid growth of their balance sheets, and the resultant scale has given them an advantage that their potential private-sector competitors cannot meet."

Chairman Greenspan saw a systemic risk in the size of the GSEs and the fact that they enjoyed subsidies in the marketplace; the ability of the GSEs to borrow essentially without limit has been exploited only in recent years. At the end of 1990, for example, Fannie's and Freddie's combined portfolios amounted to $132 billion, or 5.6% of the single-family home-mortgage market. By 2003, the GSEs' portfolios had grown ten-fold to $1.38 trillion, or 23% of the home-mortgage market.

Typically in a market system, lenders and investors monitor and discipline the activities, including leverage, of their counterparties to assure themselves of the financial strength of those to whom they lend. However, market discipline with respect to the GSEs has been weak to non-existent. Because the many counterparties in GSE transactions assess risk based almost wholly on the GSE's perceived special relationship to the government, rather than on the underlying soundness of the institutions, regulators cannot rely on market discipline to contain systemic risk.

That the growth of the GSEs has not resulted in benefits in terms of mortgage lending rates has been a cothetic argument favouring the withdrawal of their inherent subsidy. Greenspan says: "We have been unable to find any purpose for the huge balance sheets of the GSEs, other than profit creation through the exploitation of the market-granted subsidy. Some maintain that these large portfolios create a buffer against crises in the mortgage market. But that notion suggests that the spreads of home-mortgage interest rates against U.S. Treasuries, a measure of risk, would narrow as GSE portfolios increased. Despite the huge increase in the GSE portfolios, however, mortgage spreads have actually doubled since 1997, when comparable data for interest rate spreads on mortgage-backed securities first became available."

The above argument holds despite the fact the MBS market has done tremendous good to providing liquidity to the U.S. mortgage markets. He says: "The creation of mortgage-backed securities for public markets is the appropriate and effective domain of the GSEs. Deep and liquid markets for mortgages are made using mortgage-backed securities that are held solely by investors rather than the GSEs. Fannie's and Freddie's purchases of their own or each other's mortgage-backed securities with their market-subsidized debt do not contribute usefully to mortgage-market liquidity, to the enhancement of capital markets in the United States, or to the lowering of mortgages rates for homeowners. The bulk of the GSEs' portfolio growth over the past decade has occurred mainly through the acquisition of their own mortgage-backed securities, which reflects the AAA-rating of pools of home mortgages. As I indicated earlier, holding their own securities in portfolio often yielded Fannie and Freddie subsidized annual returns on equity of more than 25 percent, far in excess of the returns to purely private financial institutions from holding such securities."

H.R. 1461: Federal Housing Finance Reform Act of 2005 was introduced on April 5, 2005, and passed on October 26, 2005.[15] In the meantime, a 2,462-page report into the affairs of Fannie Mae, specially focused on accounting issues, was released in late February 2006.

Overview of the U.S. RMBS market

The RMBS market in the U.S. is broadly split into an agency market and non-agency market (see Figure 12.5 for segments). The agency market refers to the securities created by the GSEs, and the table below gives data about total outstanding agency-backed securities:

Table 12.2   Outstanding Volume of Agency Mortgage-Backed Securities 1980–2005* *($ Billions)*

	GNMA	FNMA	FHLMC	Total
1980	93.9	—	17	110.9
1981	105.8	0.7	19.9	126.4
1982	118.9	14.4	43	176.3
1983	159.8	25.1	59.4	244.3
1984	180	36.2	73.2	289.4
1985	212.1	55	105	372.1
1986	262.7	97.2	174.5	534.4

	GNMA	FNMA	FHLMC	Total
1987	315.8	140	216.3	672.1
1988	340.5	178.3	231.1	749.9
1989	369.9	228.2	278.2	876.3
1990	403.6	299.8	321	1,024.40
1991	425.3	372	363.2	1,160.50
1992	419.5	445	409.2	1,273.70
1993	414.1	495.5	440.1	1,349.70
1994	450.9	530.3	460.7	1,441.90
1995	472.3	583	515.1	1,570.40
1996	506.2	650.7	554.3	1,711.20
1997	536.8	709.6	579.4	1,825.80
1998	537.4	834.5	646.5	2,018.40
1999	582	960.9	749.1	2,292.00
2000	611.6	1,057.80	822.3	2,491.70
2001	591.4	1,290.40	948.4	2,830.20
2002	537.9	1,538.30	1,082.10	3,158.30
2003	473.7	1,857.20	1,162.10	3,493.00
2004	441.4	1,895.80	1,209.00	3,546.20
2005*	410.7	1,924.80	1,284.40	3,619.90

*As of September 30, 2005
Source: Bond Market Association

The following are data about the annual issuance of MBS by the agencies:

Table 12.3   Issuance of Agency Mortgage-Backed Securities 1980–2005* *($ Billions)*

	GNMA(1)	FNMA	FHLMC	Total
1980	20.6	—	2.5	23.1
1981	14.3	0.7	3.5	18.5
1982	16	14	24.2	54.2
1983	50.7	13.3	21.4	85.4
1984	28.1	13.5	20.5	62.1
1985	46	23.6	41.5	111.1
1986	101.4	60.6	102.4	264.4
1987	94.9	63.2	75	233.1
1988	55.2	54.9	39.8	149.9
1989	57.1	69.8	73.5	200.4
1990	64.4	96.7	73.8	234.9
1991	62.6	112.9	92.5	268

(Continued)

	GNMA(1)	FNMA	FHLMC	Total
1992	81.9	194	179.2	455.2
1993	138	221.4	208.7	568.1
1994	111.2	130.5	117.1	358.8
1995	72.9	110.4	85.9	269.2
1996	100.9	149.9	119.7	370.5
1997	104.3	149.4	114.3	368
1998	150.2	326.1	250.6	726.9
1999	151.5	300.7	233	685.2
2000	103.3	211.7	166.9	481.9
2001	174.6	528.4	389.6	1,092.60
2002	174	723.3	547.1	1,444.40
2003	218.6	1,198.60	713.3	2,130.50
2004	126.6	527.2	365.2	1,019.00
2005*	67.8	362.3	285.2	715.3

*As of September 30, 2005

One of the most notable features of the developments in the U.S. RMBS market over the last couple of years or so has been the surge in the non-agency RMBS issuance, as shown by the data below:

Non-agency RMBS issuance	
1999 (9 m)	64.9
2000	65.8
2001	143.1
2002	214.0
2003	297.1
2004	328.5
2005*	441.5

2005 data is provisional
Source: Asset-backed Alert at www.abalert.com

As may be noted, more than 40% of new issuance in the market currently comes from private label RMBS. This percentage was 20% or less a couple of years ago. The redirection of RMBS volumes to the non-agency market is explained by some fundamental changes that have taken place in the mortgage origination business: "The growth can be attributed to increases in jumbo mortgages above the conforming loan limit and adjustable rate, subprime and Alt-A mortgage volumes. Private-label issuers have the flexibility to focus on the larger and more credit-sensitive market niches. The MBA[16] reported that ARMs accounted for over one-third of total mortgage originations during the first three quarters of 2005."[17] The distinction between the conforming and non-conforming market, and jumbos and Alt-A are discussed below.

For agency securities, they are issued broadly in two forms – pass-throughs and collateralized mortgage obligations (CMOs – see later in this chapter). CMOs have increasingly grown in acceptance and with the tax rules on REMICs recently made more practical,[18] the growth in CMO volumes is expected to accelerate.

Agency and non-agency market

Broadly, RMBS are issued through agencies or the GSEs, or by private issues. Issuance by private issuers is called **non-agency**, or **private label** RMBS.

Agencies basically buy such residential mortgage loans that conform to their conditions. The agencies come out with both pass-throughs and CMOs.

Conforming and non-conforming markets

Mortgages that conform to the conditions laid down by the agencies – called conforming mortgages – are mostly sold to the agencies, but the private label or non-agency market consists of mortgages that for some reason do not qualify for purchase by the agencies. These are sold to private securitization majors from where they are securitized and brought into the market.

Illustrative features of mortgages purchased by the agencies are:

- The mortgages are on residential properties, most commonly one to four family homes (referred to as *single-family loans*). Multi-family mortgages, referred to as MFs, do not qualify for purchase by the agencies and generally come to the market as private label securities.
- The mortgages are generally 15-year and 30-year maturities that are fully amortizing;
- Mostly, the mortgages are fixed-rate mortgages, although adjustable-rate mortgages (ARMs) also qualify for purchase.
- Most mortgages have monthly payments;
- There are typically no prepayment penalties;
- The loans are due on the sale of the underlying property and cannot be assumed by the buyer of the property;
- Mortgage loans must be within the "conforming loan limit," which for one-unit homes in 2006 is $417,000. The loan limits for various conforming loans are as below:

Loan Limits for:	2006	2005*	2004
One-family	$417,000	$359,650	$333,700
Two-family	$533,850	$460,400	$427,150
Three-family	$645,300	$556,500	$516,300
Four-family	$801,950	$691,600	$641,650

- Mortgages of higher size are called *jumbo mortgages* and are generally brought into the market as private labels.
- Loans within the conforming loan limit generally satisfy other GSE specifications for loan documentation, credit information and property type, among other requirements. Loans not complying with the documentation requirement, called *low docs* or *no docs*, are generally privately securitized. The market term *Alternative A* or *Alt A* mortgage covers mortgages otherwise conforming and have a good credit score, but that do not qualify due to documentation deficiencies or a higher-than-permissible LTV ratio.

Prime, Alt-A and other components

In the non-agency market, the broad classes are: prime, Alt-A and subprime.

The prime class includes those loans that meet requirements for scores, and documentation, but do not conform to the requirements of the agencies. They are non-conforming primarily due to the jumbo nature, or because the loan has features such as an option ARM or negative amortization.

The Alt-A is a catch-all term that includes loans that satisfy the FICO scores requirement but are not treated as conforming for either prime or jumbo treatment. "The dominant approach for defining the alt-A mortgage loans makes reference to the characteristics (or combinations of characteristics) that would have disqualified a loan from traditional conforming or jumbo loan programs. Perhaps the most important of such characteristics is "documentation." A substantial proportion of traditional Alt-A loans were those where a borrower would not provide complete documentation of his assets or the amount or source of his income."[19] Other features of Alt-A loans include:

- Loan-to-value ratio (LTV) in excess of 80% but lacking primary mortgage insurance;
- Borrower who is a temporary resident alien;
- Secured by non-owner occupied property;
- Debt-to-income ratio above normal limits;
- Secured by a non-warrantable condominium unit or a condominium hotel; or
- LTV above permitted thresholds in combination with other factors.

The third category is subprime loans. These are also sometimes called B/C loans. These are in cases where the borrower does not have a history or does not have acceptable FICO scores. As in Figure 12.4, the volumes of sub-prime MBS have been increasing rapidly:

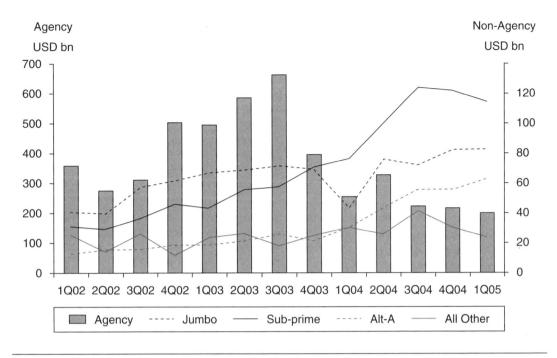

Figure 12.4   Growth of Agency and Non-Agency RMBS

Home equity loans are yet another category; we take this up later in this chapter:

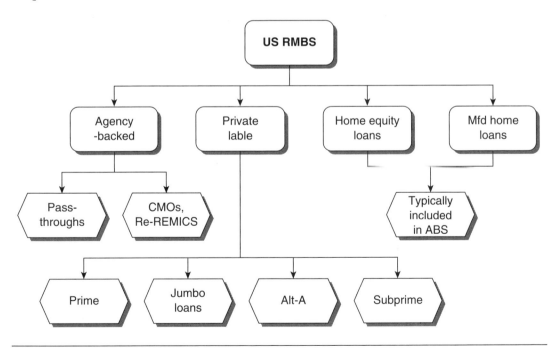

Figure 12.5   Quick snapshot of U.S. RMBS market

Secondary mortgage market in other countries

The U.S. model in promoting RMBS through agencies has been extremely successful in promoting housing finance, and consequently, housing. Housing is one of the most important developmental functions of the state, and many countries have shown an inclination to promote residential mortgage securitization. Many countries have emulated the U.S. model, while some have relied solely on privately-owned agencies.

Canada set up a crown corporation called **Canada Mortgage and Housing Corporation,** which essentially functions on the same basis as Fannie Mae. Some of the Latin American countries have set up Fannie Mae-type institutions. Hong Kong has set up a similar body, as well as Malaysia. India's National Housing Bank, though a housing finance body, also intends to promote securitization with a Fannie-Mae-type structure.

Besides agency-supported RMBS transactions, several large mortgage financiers run their own mortgage securitization programs. Most large mortgage banks and leading housing financiers in the U.S. securitizes their own housing finance receivables without resorting to the agency structure.

In several European countries, another form of mortgage funding device, in the form of *Pfandbriefe* in Germany, has existed for years. These are somewhat different from US pass-throughs as they are not off-balance-sheet instruments. In a *Pfandbriefe*, the mortgage financier issues debt securities secured by first right over the mortgages. The rights of the *Pfandbriefe* holders prevail over rights of any of the creditors of the originator; hence, the essential purpose of securitization is served, except for off-balance-sheet accounting. France has developed a similar device called *Obligations Fonciers*. Similar mortgage funding instruments exist in several other European countries such as Denmark, Spain and Belgium. Covered bonds are discussed in a later heading in this chapter.

But Dr. Michael Lea, who has done substantial work on secondary mortgage markets, says governments need to concentrate both on a healthy primary market and a healthy secondary market, the former before the latter. "(I)t is not possible to have a sustainable secondary mortgage market until there is a healthy and well-developed primary market. This does not mean that securitization is impossible as it may be possible to do a few transactions with a narrow range of collateral in the form of private placements. But a sustainable secondary market involves generating an on-going flow of transactions that will develop liquidity in the market, enhance investor and regulatory understanding and comfort and achieve the desired increase in availability of funds and decreased relative cost of mortgage credit. This can only be done if there is a sufficient volume of attractively priced, well-documented and underwritten mortgage loans that are serviced by competent and reputable organizations."[20]

Current size of the RMBS market in Europe

Compared to the U.S. RMBS market, the market in Europe or elsewhere in the world is considerably smaller. House ownership itself is not as highly leveraged in most other markets as the U.S. For instance, on a rough basis, mortgage loans are 53% of the GDP of the U.S., while it is only 36% in the EU. This is not due to any appreciable difference in the rate of house ownership – clearly reflecting much lower levels of leverage on house ownership in Europe.

There are two other prominent reasons why RMBS markets have not grown in Europe to the extent they have in the U.S. One is the presence of traditional mortgage bonds or *pfandbriefes,* and the other is the absence of any Fannie Mae-type agency in Europe.

The RMBS market formed in 2002 approximately 40% of the total securitization market in Europe. In the first half of 2003, this went up to almost 55%. Like the U.S. market, there was a spurt in new origination in Europe also. In 2004, RMBS issuance in Europe amounted to €120.1 billion. Up to the 3rd quarter of 2005, this was €94 billion.[21] *Pfandbrief* issuance, for the same period in 2005, was €180.6 billion; in other words, *pfandbriefs* are nearly twice as big as RMBS. The biggest originators of RMBS in Europe are in the U.K. (approximately half of total volume), followed by the Netherlands, Spain, Italy, France, Sweden and Germany. The data, of course, exclude the synthetic transactions done in Germany where synthetic RMBS activity dominates. It is notable that there are mega RMBS deals done by way of synthetic transactions all over Europe now. In addition, covered bonds have also become increasingly stronger.

RMBS in U.K.

The United Kingdom pioneered the use of mortgage securitization in Europe with the first transaction of MBS issued in January 1985. the market grew rapidly in the 1980s as several U.S.-headquartered banks entered the U.K. market and the housing market expanded substantially. Development of mortgage securitization in the U.K. was significant in 2000 and 2001, although currently MBS still account for less than 5% of total mortgage-balances. Substantial amounts of total European volume, reported above, come from the U.K.

Structuring of RMBS transactions

Residential mortgages are considered to be one of the safest financial claims in the world. The value of the mortgaged property could be subject to mortgage foreclosure procedures for which different countries may have different legal systems, but the important fact is that the funding is backed by a claim over a house where the borrower resides; his family peace is dependant upon his ability to perform under the loan. Properly underwritten residential mortgage loans are, therefore, quite safe. Investors in RMBS are investing in a widely diversified pool of loans backed by real estate; hence, they are making a very safe investment.

The structure of RMBS transactions would differ entirely based on whether it is an agency-backed transaction, and also based on the specifics of the system in the country concerned.

Structure of agency-backed securitization

Illustration of Fannie Mae MBS structure

The agency MBS market is a huge market in the U.S., and the largest segment of the fixed-rate investment grade bond market. Each agency has its own set of procedures and guidelines, but there is a broad harmony in the process. The following is a brief description of the MBS process of Fannie Mae, which largely represents the agency MBS system for all three agencies:[22]

> Mortgage-backed securities are sometimes called "mortgage pass-through certificates." This is because the security passes through to investors, at a specific coupon, the principal and interest scheduled for payment each month from mortgagors on the outstanding balance of the loans backing the security, and any unscheduled prepayments.
>
> An investor in an MBS owns an undivided interest in a pool of mortgages that serves as the underlying asset for the security. As an MBS holder, this investor receives a pro-rata share of the cash flows from the pool of mortgages.
>
> A nationwide network of lenders such as mortgage-bankers, savings and loan associations, and commercial banks originates the loans backing the MBS. Lenders submit groups of similar mortgage loans to Fannie Mae for securitization. Fannie Mae first ensures that the loans meet its credit quality guidelines and then securitizes the pool of mortgages. The loans are converted – or securitized – into liquid, very flexible instruments. The resulting MBS carries a guarantee of timely payment of principal and interest to the investor, whether or not there is sufficient cash flow from the underlying group of mortgages. Fannie Mae's obligation under this guarantee is solely Fannie Mae's and is not backed by the full faith and credit of the United States government.
>
> The securities thus created by Fannie Mae are taken into the capital market by securities dealers.
>
> Each pool of fixed-rate, single-family mortgages has a pass-through rate, or coupon, which is the interest rate passed on to the investor, usually on the 25th day after the end of the accrual period. The pass-through rate is lower than the interest rate on the underlying mortgages in the pool. This interest differential covers the guaranty fee paid to Fannie Mae, and the fee paid to the servicing institution for collecting payments from homeowners and performing other servicing functions. The lender that delivers the mortgages for securitization or sold to another institution can retain servicing of the loans.
>
> When fixed-rate mortgages are pooled together, Fannie Mae allows the interest rates on the underlying mortgages to fall within a 250-basis point range. The weighted-average coupon (WAC) of each security is the weighted-average of the mortgage note rates and is provided to the investor to help evaluate the cash flows of the pool. Further, the weighted-average maturity (WAM) is available as an indicator of the remaining terms (in months) of the mortgages underlying the MBS as of the issue date. The weighted-average loan age (WALA) and the weighted-average

loan term at origination (WALT) are also available to help analyze the potential cash flows of the pool.

Securities dealers sell Fannie Mae MBS to investors. Certificates issued in book-entry form initially will represent at least $1,000 of the unpaid principal amount of the mortgage loans in the pool.

Fannie Mae MBS issued in book-entry form are paid by wire transfer, which is both convenient and safe. Fannie Mae's central paying agent, the Federal Reserve Bank of New York, wires monthly payments to depository institutions on behalf of registered security holders on the 25th of each month, or the first business day after that if the 25th of a month is not a business day. This central paying agent concept simplifies accounting procedures because investors can receive just one payment monthly for all their book-entry MBS.

Typically, a mortgage originator accepts a mortgage application directly or through retailers. The mortgagors then take the mortgages to the agencies, and either sell the mortgages for cash or swap the mortgages against MBS. Here is what Fannie Mae's guide has to say on this:

When a lender enters into a transaction to sell mortgages (or participation interests in mortgages) to us to hold in our portfolio (or to later include in MBS pools we form), we will remit cash proceeds to the lender as the purchase price for the mortgages in accordance with the provisions of this Guide that are applicable to "portfolio" mortgages. When the lender enters into a transaction to sell mortgages (or participation interests in mortgages) to us that we will convey to an MBS trust under the terms of our MBS program, we will deliver to the lender (or its designee) mortgage pass-through certificates representing interests in the mortgages as the purchase price for the mortgages.

After the MBS has been put into the market, the next thing is servicing. Under agency-backed structures, servicing may be retained by the originator or handed over to specialized servicing agencies. The servicer mails mortgage bills to the homeowner, collects mortgage payments and possible late fees, then forwards the cash to the agency. In return, the servicer receives a small portion of the interest paid on each loan, typically a minimum of 25 bp of coupon[23] annually on each loan, paid in monthly instalments. This fee continues until the mortgage is prepaid; thus, the servicing fee component is akin to an IO in a mortgage that disappears when the mortgage is prepaid. It is typical for the servicer to place advances for delinquent payments by way of a liquidity enhancement to the transaction.

Secondary market in agency MBS

The agency-backed MBS market is very liquid and the volume of secondary market transactions is huge. An estimated US$254 billion in securities change hands every trading day.[24] This is the second largest in fixed income trades after Treasury securities.

Structure of non-agency pass-throughs

As noted, the non-agency market consists primarily of the jumbos, or home equity loans, or other non-conforming loans. There is a significant difference in the non-agency market; the credit of the agencies is not available and therefore, the transaction is to be based on credit enhancements. Obviously, the need for credit enhancement is also higher because of the apparent perception that the portfolio has higher embedded risk.

The non-agency market has a strong conduit activity, and also direct securitization by the larger originators. Conduit activity refers to cases where loans are originated by retailers who sell them over to wholesalers, who in turn take the mortgages to the capital markets. This results in a difference from a servicing viewpoint; the conduit manager is usually the master servicer in such cases.

Structure of CMOs

CMOs are issued in the agency and non-agency market. Structurally, the two are the same, so the discussion below applies generically to both.

Whether a CMO or a pass-through, every case of securitization is a pass-through as far as the servicer is concerned. Pay-through and pass-through are essentially the manners in which the SPV pays down the obligors. Hence, the role of the originator/servicer remains the same for CMO structures as well. In U.S. tax parlance, CMOs are covered by special tax provisions applicable to REMICs; therefore, CMOs are also referred to as REMICs, which is a tax term.[25] CMOs are also referred to as mortgage-pass-through derivatives, as the pay-out structure of a CMO is derived from the pay-in structure – the structure of the underlying pool.

A CMO is essentially a multi-class or multi-tranche repayment, each class represented by a debt security usually in the form of a bond. Each CMO is a set of two or more tranches, each having average lives and cash-flow patterns designed to meet specific investment objectives. Some CMOs issued have had more than 50 tranches.

The simplest of the CMO structures is **sequential payout**. As the name implies, repayments are directed to amortize the different classes sequentially, while the coupon is paid periodically to all classes, excluding the **zero coupon** class. So, the waterfall structure would provide for first paying the coupon rate of interest to the bondholders in each tranche. Thereafter, all scheduled and unscheduled principal payments (including the prepayments) go first to investors in the class (say Class A). Investors in Class B or later classes do not start receiving principal payments until Class A has been fully paid.

The time during which Class B investors do not receive any principal is called *principal lockout*.

The final tranche of a CMO often takes the form of a *Z-bond*, also known as an *accrual bond* or *accretion bond*. Holders of these securities receive no cash until the earlier tranches are paid in full. During the period that the other tranches are outstanding, the periodic interest accruals are added to the initial face amount of the bond but are not paid to investors. When the prior tranches are retired, the Z-bond receives coupon payments on its higher principal balance, plus any principal prepayments from the underlying mortgage loans.

The remaining cash flows that is the residual beneficial interest in the pool – is also sometimes issued as securities, called *residuals*.

U.K. RMBS

RMBS structures in different countries have evolved differently over time based on how the market adjusts to the environment. The U.K. does not have the agencies found in the U.S. market or the REMIC-type taxation convenience. Therefore, U.K. transactions have tried to cope with the regulatory and tax regime of the country by setting up CMO-type transactions. The issuance normally involves the issuance of bonds with a specific expected maturity and legal maturity extended by couple of years or so. For subordinate classes, there will be no expected maturity and the legal maturity would normally coincide with the maturity of the pool.

The U.K. housing market is primarily owner-occupied housing. At the end of 1998, 68% of dwellings were owner-occupied and 11% were privately rented. The remainder were some form of public/social ownership. Owner-occupation has been over 60% since 1984. The mortgage market, whereby loans are provided for the purchase of a property and secured on that property, is the major source of household borrowings in the U.K. At the end of 2000, mortgage loans outstanding amounted to £535 billion. Outstanding mortgage debt grew at an annual average rate of 6.20% between 1990 and 2001. At the end of 2001, 72% of outstanding mortgage debt was held with banks and 20% with building societies.

One of the distinctive features of U.K. RMBS is the use of the **master trust** device for issuing soft bullet securities out of a portfolio of mortgages. The market consists of both conforming and non-conforming or sub-prime mortgages. In addition, the pure pass-through method, whereby prepayments are passed on to investors straightaway, is uncommon in most European transactions. The U.K. market is itself dominated by variable rate mortgages; therefore, the effect of interest rates on prepayments is negligible.

Case studies of RMBS

Case study of a U.S. RMBS: Bank of America Funding 2005-1 Trust

This transaction was marketed via a prospectus dated January 26, 2005. The transaction is backed by a pool of conventional, fully amortizing, mortgage loans of one to four family units. Bank of America Funding Corp. is the seller of the loans into the pool.

The several classes of certificates and the issued amount of each are given in Table on next page:

Class		Initial bal. Class	Pass-Through Rate	Principal Types(2)	Interest Types(2)	Fitch	S&P
Offered Certificates							
Class 1-A-1	$	20,021,000	5.50%	Senior, Lockout Pay	Fixed Rate	AAA	AAA
Class 1-A-2	$	1,505,000	5.50%	Senior, Sequential Pay	Fixed Rate	AAA	AAA
Class 1-A-3	$	5,076,000	5.50%	Senior, Sequential Pay	Fixed Rate	AAA	AAA
Class 1-A-4	$	3,619,000	5.50%	Senior, Sequential Pay	Fixed Rate	AAA	AAA
Class 1-A-5	$	2,059,000	5.50%	Senior, Sequential Pay	Fixed Rate	AAA	AAA
Class 1-A-6	$	3,741,000	5.50%	Senior, Sequential Pay	Fixed Rate	AAA	AAA
Class 1-A-7		$145,293,000	5.50%	Senior, Sequential Pay	Fixed Rate	AAA	AAA
Class 1-A-8	$	5,370,000	5.50%	Senior, Sequential Pay	Fixed Rate	AAA	AAA
Class 1-A-9	$	5,067,000	5.50%	Senior, Sequential Pay	Fixed Rate	AAA	AAA
Class 1-A-10	$	1,000,000	5.50%	Senior, Sequential Pay	Fixed Rate	AAA	AAA
Class 30-IO		0	5.50%	Senior, Notional Amount	Fixed Rate, Interest Only	AAA	AAA
Class 30-PO	$	445,987	5.50%	Senior, Ratio Strip	Principal Only	AAA	AAA
Class 1-A-R	$	100	5.50%	Senior, Sequential Pay	Fixed Rate	AAA	AAA
Class B-1	$	3,304,000	5.50%	Subordinated	Fixed Rate	AA	AA
Class B-2	$	1,501,000	5.50%	Subordinated	Fixed Rate	A	A
Class B-3	$	701,000	5.50%	Subordinated	Fixed Rate	BBB	BBB
Total offered		198,703,087					

Non-Offered Certificates							
Class B-4	$	701,000	5.50%	Subordinated	Fixed Rate	BB	BB
Class B-5	$	500,000	5.50%	Subordinated	Fixed Rate	N/A	B
Class B-6	$	301,031	5.50%	Subordinated	Fixed Rate	None	None
Total		200,205,118					

The transaction is a pass-through, and such transactions have a common pass-through rate of 5.5% for all the classes as may be noted. This obviously means yield differences for various classes would have been created by issue price differentials.

Credit-enhancement structure and principal paydown

In terms of credit support structure, the classes may be seen as under:

		Ratings	*Credit support*
Class 1-A (10 tranches)	192,751,000	AAA	3.500%
IO	0	AAA	3.500%
PO	445,987	AAA	3.500%
Residual	100	AAA	3.500%
Class B-1	3,304,000	AA	1.850%
Class B-2	1,501,000	A	1.100%
Class B-3	701,000	BBB	0.750%
Class B-4	701,000	BB	0.400%
Class B-5	500,000	B	0.150%
Class B-6	301,031	Unrated	0
Total	200,205,118		

Class A has 10 sequentially paying pieces, the idea of which is to have securities with different expected maturities. The IO class simply strips interest on a notional principal value, which is at inception approximately 5% of the total pool size. The residual class is a mere nominality for REMIC qualification and for sweeping residual surplus, if any, in the transaction. The IO and PO both being senior, see the same rating as Class 1-A.

At the lowest level, class B-5, the credit support is only 0.15%, which allows a B rating. From there upwards, the credit-enhancement increases step-wise, to increase to 3.5% for the senior-most classes. Over time, the credit-enhancement will increase, following the pay down structure.

The paydown structure is that the prepayments received over the first 5 years, apportioned to the classes other than the PO class, will be allocated entirely to the AAA certificates (obviously, the IO class gets no principal). For the next 4 years, the prepayment allocation is more (percentage trickles down from the 6th year to the 9th year) to the AAA certificates than to the subordinated certificates. This would mean, to the extent of prepayments over the first 9 years, the senior certificates see more than proportional principal paydown, and therefore, there will be a step up in credit enhancement. This would, of course, depend on the prepayment speed.

The sequential allocation of principal to different tranches in class 1-A is designed to have different expected maturities. The sequential order is:

- Class 1-A-1 first gets paid to the extent of the shifting of prepayments for the first 9 years (see above).
- Class 1-A-7 thereafter, until reduced to zero.
- Thereafter, the allocated principal is split in ratio of 22.1124758538%: 77.8875241462%:

  o The former goes sequentially to class A-9 and A-10 in that order;
  o The latter goes sequentially to Class 1-A-8, Class 1-A-2, Class 1-A-3, Class 1-A-4, Class 1-A-5 and Class 1-A-6 Certificates, in that order.

- The balance goes to Class 1-A-1.
- In other words, Class A-1 sees all the principal payouts in the first 5 years and thereafter, a part for the next 4 years, and then is retired late in the sequence.

The result of this mix of sequences is that each of the different securities have differential prepayment sensitivity. Based on different PSA, the weighted-average life of the securities is indicated as:

Table 12.4 *Weighted-average Life (in years) under different PSA assumptions*

Class	0%	100%	300%	500%	800%
-A-1	20.91	15.65	11.05	8.9	5.09
-A-2	28.12	21.96	8.91	5.05	3.38
-A-3	28.49	23.36	10.01	5.38	3.52
-A-4	28.97	25.41	12.01	5.88	3.73
-A-5	29.28	26.9	14	6.31	3.88
-A-6	29.6	28.6	18.7	6.92	4.07
-A-7	17.13	8	3.43	2.38	1.75
-A-8	27.71	20.63	8.15	4.81	3.24
-A-9	28.43	23.3	10.29	5.4	3.51
-A-10	29.61	28.67	18.93	6.95	4.08
-A-R	0.08	0.08	0.08	0.08	0.08
30-IO	19.27	11.23	5.54	3.66	2.48
30-PO	18.81	10.99	5.41	3.54	2.38
B-1	19.16	14.44	10.32	8.65	7.2
B-2	19.16	14.44	10.32	8.65	7.2
B-3	19.16	14.44	10.32	8.65	7.2

Servicers

As is the common practice with RMBS pools, primary servicing is done by the originators. In this case, the primary servicers are Bank of America, National Association, National City Mortgage Co., Wells Fargo Bank, N.A., Chase Home Finance LLC and Countrywide Home Loans Servicing LP. The master servicer is Wells Fargo and Washington Mutual.

Mortgage pool

The pool has been originated or acquired by the different originators. The pool consists of 368 mortgage loans. The aggregate principal balance of the loans is exactly the same as the value of the securities – $200 million. The interest rates on the loans range from 5.25% to 6.875%, with a weighted-average of 6.039%. The loans had an original maturity of 20 to 30 years, and they have been seasoned for 0 to 20 months. The weighted-average remaining maturity is 357 months, which clearly means the proportion of 20-year loans is very small.

The servicing fee is 0.25% per annum. For some of the loans in the pool, master servicing fee is also applicable. In addition, there is a "securities administrator" fee of 1.75 bps.

Servicer advances are applicable to the transaction. The advances continue until foreclosure of the mortgage.

Clean up call option

Clean up call option is available when the principal balance of the mortgage loans falls below 1% of the initial principal balance. Clean up call at 1% is quite common for RMBS transactions.

Case study: Abbey National's Holmes Financing

Abbey National, one of the U.K.'s leading mortgage originators has come out with several RMBS transactions via its Holmes Funding and Holmes Financing series. As a case illustrative of the standard U.K. RMBS procedure, we take the Holmes Financing (No. 5) (here referred to as "Holmes 5") transaction, whereby Abbey raised funding in excess of GBP 2 billion by mortgage-backed notes, composed of 11 tranches. The transaction is the fifth issued from the Holmes residential mortgage master trust, which at the closing of the above transaction was to contain approximately GBP 18 billion of mortgage loans. A master trust is like a large common pot, almost representative of the asset side of the originating company,[26] from which the originator continues to issue securities, with the residual being the "seller share" retained by the originator. Thus, the originator has net-of-the-liabilities as his asset.

The transaction structure of Holmes 5 is shown below:

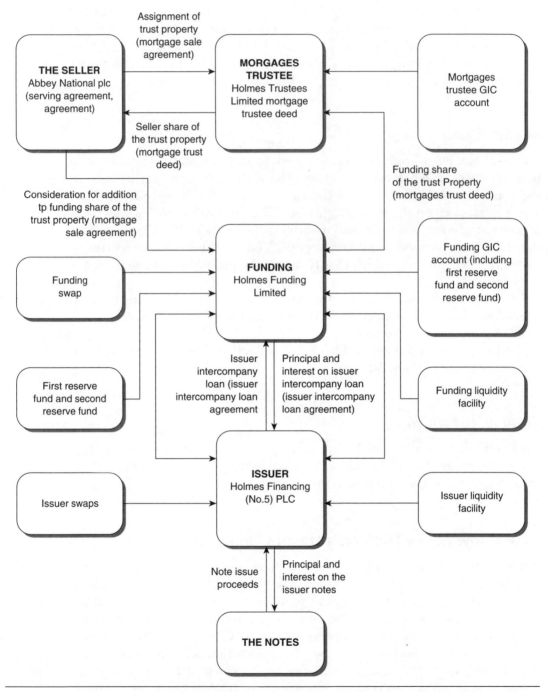

Figure 12.6   Transaction structure of Holmes 5

As seen in the figure, there are three intermediaries between the mortgage originator (Abbey) and the investors – a master trust, an intermediary borrowing company and the issuing company. In a number of U.K. transactions, especially those using the master trust structure, an intermediary lending vehicle is commonly used, which raises funding from the capital market and gives an inter-company loan; the borrowing company acquires the assets of the originator. The investors acquire security interest on the assets of the lending vehicle, the lending vehicle has security interest on the assets of the intermediary vehicle, and the intermediary vehicle is a beneficiary of the master trust which acquires the assets of the originator. The lending vehicle gives several different loans, which correspond by amount and maturity with the notes issued by the vehicle, each having the desired priority.

In Holmes 5, the notes were issued in various denominations – US$, GBP, CHF and Euros. The notes were altogether clustered into three classes as:

- $1,000,000,000 floating rate series 1 class A issuer notes due October 2002;
- $35,000,000 floating rate series 1 class B issuer notes due July 2040;
- $52,000,000 floating rate series 1 class C issuer notes due July 2040;
- $750,000,000 floating rate series 2 class A1 issuer notes due October 2006;
- $35,000,000 floating rate series 2 class B issuer notes due July 2040;
- $52,000,000 floating rate series 2 class C issuer notes due July 2040;
- €600,000,000 Fixed-floating rate series 3 class A1 issuer notes due October 2008;
- £500,000,000 floating rate series 3 class A2 issuer noted due July 2040;
- €53,000,000 floating rate series 3 class B issuer notes due July 2040; and
- €76,000,000 floating rate series 3 class C issuer notes due July 2040.

Special purpose vehicles

As explained above, this transaction and, generally, transactions using the master trust structure, have an additional borrowing vehicle between the issuing vehicle and the master trust. In this transaction, there are three special purpose vehicles – the master trust, the intermediary borrowing company, which also acquires the investor-share in the property held, and the issuing vehicle. All the special purpose vehicles have nominal capital of £2 paid up, held by a holding company that has a declared public charitable trust on the shares in favor of SPV Management. The directors of the SPVs are also provided by SPV Management. Thus, the SPVs satisfy independence criteria.

The loan portfolio

In view of the master trust structure, Abbey has transferred a substantial portfolio to the master trust (discussed below). The portfolio held before the issue date comprised 343,413 mortgage accounts having an aggregate outstanding principal balance of £22 billion as of that date. Approximately 70% of the loans have an outstanding principal balance of £25,000-75,000. Approximately 70% of the loans had an LTV ratio of more than 75% at origination, with 36% having an LTV of 90-95%. The loans in the portfolio were originated by Abbey between August 1, 1995 and June 24, 2001; in other words, some of the loans were not seasoned. This is also evident from the fact that about 57% of the loans have a remaining maturity of 20-25 years. No loan in the portfolio was delinquent or non-performing at the time it was assigned to the mortgages trustee. Again, in line with the master trust structure, even after the closing date, Abbey may assign new loans and their related security to the mortgages trustee.

A distinction between the U.K. and U.S. mortgage practice is the charging of prepayment fees. In the U.S. market, mortgages can be prepaid without any penalty, while in the U.K., it is common for mortgagees to insist on prepayment fees. Under the master trust structure, unscheduled principal repayments reduce the seller share and not the investor share; therefore, prepayment risk is completely absorbed by the seller. Hence, the prepayment fees are also retained by the seller in this instant case.

The structure also allows Abbey the liberty to make further advances to the existing borrower, with the limitation that no further advances shall be made if the LTV ratio, based on value re-assessed, is to exceed 95%.

In case of a product switch – the borrower switching from one loan option to another with Abbey, Abbey may repurchase the loan from the trust. This is one of the permitted cases of repurchase.

The loans in the portfolio are covered by a mortgage indemnity guarantee policy in all cases where the LTV ratio exceeds 75%.

Master trust and the transfer of assets

As noted before, the trust to which Abbey has transferred the mortgages is a master trust. The total amount of property in the trust is much larger than is required for redemption of the notes, because the originator intends to use the master trust as a warehouse of receivables from which further release via more issuance can be done as required; the remaining interest belongs to Abbey. Thus, at the closing of the issue, the share of the investor representative, representing all previous issues from the master trust, was 62.5% and the balance was the share of the seller.

As noted earlier, the notes in the instant case are bullet repayment notes. Under the master trust structure, allocation of all scheduled and unscheduled principal collections is made against the seller share, unless the accumulation period starts. The accumulation period is that which, at the determination of the trustees, the principal collections should be accumulated to prepare for the bullet repayment of the notes. Hence, on each distribution date, the seller share and investor share in the trust property are re-determined. Each principal collection, whether on account of prepayment or regular payment, reduces the seller share and accordingly, the entire principal collection is appropriated by the seller. If the seller transfers new loans into the master trust, the seller share goes up. If the seller issues any new notes from the master trust, the seller share comes down and the investor share goes up. In other words, at any time the investor share is only so much of the mortgage principal as is required to amortize the notes, and the balance is the seller share.

While the seller share seems to be the residual interest in the pool, in fact, it is not residual and subordinated – it ranks at par with the investor share. If there are any losses in the mortgage pool from the last distribution date to the current one, the same are divided pro-rata between the seller and the investors.

In the present case, the investor share is computed based on the following formula:

$$\text{Investor share} = A–B–C+D+E$$
$$\text{Seller share} = \text{Total trust property} – \text{Investor share}$$

A = the amount of investor share on the immediately preceding distribu-
    tion date;
B = the amount of any principal receipts on the loans distributed to fund-
    ing on the relevant distribution date;
C = the amount of losses sustained on the loans in the period from the last
    distribution date to the relevant distribution date and allocated to
    investor share;
D = any new loans assigned to the mortgages trustee on the relevant distri-
    bution date – any new issue of notes from the pool;
E = Acquisition by investor representative from the seller on the relevant
    distribution date of a portion of the seller's share of the trust property.

Usually, the seller's share in a master trust is only for structural convenience and does not provide any credit-enhancement. However, in the present case, a certain amount of "minimum seller share" is required to mitigate any risk on account of the borrower's deposits in Abbey (set-off risk).

There are two notable facts about the transfer; one, the transfer is an equitable transfer, and two, there is a deferred consideration for sale.

Equitable transfers are fairly common in the U.K. and courts have generally accepted an equitable transfer as conferring equitable interest in the transferee relating to the property. The legal title remains vested with the transferor, as there is no obligor notification, which is required to complete the legal transfer. In the meantime, the transferor gives an irrevocable power of attorney to the transferee, security trustee, and the intermediary. There are certain deficiencies of equitable transfer, noted in the chapter relating to legal issues. There is a provision for perfecting the transfer into a legal transfer (which, in U.K. parlance would mean notifying all obligors) in certain circumstances, listed below:

(A)   The service of an intercompany loan enforcement notice in relation to any intercompany loan or the notes under the present or previous issues out of the master trust;
(B)   The seller being mandatorily required by authorities to perfect legal title to the mortgages;
(C)   It being rendered necessary by law to take any of those actions;
(D)   The security under deed of charge or any material part of that security being in jeopardy and the security trustee deciding to take that action to reduce materially that jeopardy;
(E)   Unless otherwise agreed by the rating agencies and the security trustee, the termination of the seller's role as servicer under the servicing agreement;

(F)   The seller requesting legal transfer by notice to the concerned agencies;

(G)   The downgrade of Abbey below BBB-; and

(H)   The latest of the last repayment dates of the issuer intercompany loan, the previous intercompany loans and any new intercompany loans.

Deferred consideration is a commonly-used method of originator's profit extraction in the U.K. The loans in the instant case have been transferred at their carrying value, with a small amount of servicing fee charged. Thus, almost the entire profit of the originator is retained with the master trust and is embedded in the seller's share. This will be captured as deferred consideration at the time of termination of the transaction. Obviously, the deferred consideration provides both liquidity and credit enhancement to the transaction.

Home equity loans securitization

Securitization of home equity loans – a loan based on the value of a house over an existing outstanding funding – is a very common securitization application in many countries, predominantly the U.S. Home equity loans, along with several other forms of sub-prime lending are the assets that bankers originate and arbitrage upon by taking them to securitization markets.

In U.S. industry jargon, securitization of home equity loans is taken as a part of asset-backed securities rather than mortgage-backed securities. This is probably because the mortgage backing in this case is secondary and the loan is essentially a revolving-type credit to the obligor. It is, therefore, included in ABS volumes.

In the U.S. market, home equity is the largest component of the ABS (so defined) market, and the share of home equity financing has been growing, as is evident from the following table:

Table 12.5   Home Equity Securities Outstanding 1995–Q3, 2005

	Home Equity	% of Total ABS
1995	33.1	10.5%
1996	51.6	12.8%
1997	90.2	16.8%
1998	124.2	17.0%
1999	141.9	15.8%
2000	151.5	14.1%
2001	185.1	14.5%
2002	286.5	18.6%
2003	346.0	20.4%
2004	454.0	24.8%
2005:Q3	513.6	26.7%

All amounts in billions
Source: Bond Markets Association

Most of the U.S. home equity securitizers make use of the REMIC structure, which allows them to package classes with varying paybacks.

Home equity loans are of two types – closed-end loans against the non-mortgage value of the property (loans that have a fixed repayment period), and open-end mortgage loans, also called *home equity line of credit* (HELOC). In the closed-end type, first-lien loans and second-lien loans are both included. First-lien loans included in the home equity category are the B or C type loans with impaired credit that were discussed earlier.

Manufactured home loans

Manufactured housing loans are yet another residential house application in the U.S., but customarily included in the ABS category. The reason why they are not included in the mortgage segment is because by its nature a manufactured house is a chattel, not a mortgage property.

A manufactured house is essentially a house on wheels, a pre-fabricated, factory-made structure on chassis. It is wheeled to the housing site and installed on cement pads. Though meant to be mobile, it never actually moves. Manufactured houses are meant for low income groups as they cost substantially less than traditional site-built houses. There are elaborate safety guidelines in form of National Manufactured Home Construction and Safety Standards established by the U.S. Congress and administered by the Department of Housing and Urban Development.

As a collateral for securitization transactions, manufactured house loans are considered to be a sub-prime segment, in view of the high rates of interest and high credit risks. There is no structural difference between a traditional mortgage securitization and the manufactured home loan. The credit-enhancements typically employed are subordination and excess spread. This segment has also been responsible for a high rate of default (see Chapter 30).

Manufactured home loan transactions are also typically structured as REMICs.

Investing in the MBS market

Who invests in MBS?

While banks are the largest investors in mortgages (including MBS and unsecuritized whole loans), in the agency securitization market the GSEs themselves are the largest investors. The agencies have a stated objective of growing their mortgage portfolio size consistently. As long-term, hold-to-maturity investors in MBS, the GSEs purchase MBS and regularly issue bullet and callable debt against them, picking up the difference in yield. The agencies are allowed to leverage up to 40 times their Tier I capital.

In addition, banks and money managers are large investors in MBS. The banks are typical investors in 30-year MBS and are motivated by the spread and liquidity of the investment, in spite of the prepayment and negative convexity risk.

Other investors include life insurers, property and casualty insurers, thrifts and pension funds. The investor base remains overwhelmingly institutional. Investments in MBS are made for a variety of reasons. Some investors purchase MBS to hold long term in portfolios, while others purchase for short term trading purposes. MBS are also widely used for hedging purposes.[27]

In spite of the largely institutionalized market, the market is extremely liquid. There are almost US$100 billion in trades every day.[28]

Risks in investing in MBS

Investing in MBS could be a lot different from investing in other fixed income securities or substantively the same, depending on the structure of the MBS. There are four key questions to ask before investing in an MBS:

- Is there a prepayment/delayed payment risk inherent in the investment?
- What are the credit risks in the portfolio? Are the credit enhancements enough given the nature of the portfolio?
- Is the risk interest-rate sensitive?
- What is the interest-rate sensitivity of the investment?

In general, the U.K.-type MBS provides for a bullet repayment, while U.S. CMOs do not have an associated prepayment risk that is interest-rate sensitive. However, subordinated tranches of CMOs or inverse floaters can be highly interest-rate sensitive instruments. Similarly, on the credit or default risk, sub-prime investments such as home equity and manufactured housing can have substantial default risk involved.

There are several instances in the history of MBS investing where investors have burnt their fingers badly by not properly appreciating the inherent interest rate risk.

Orange County's bankruptcy

Orange County, California in December 1994 went into bankruptcy with a loss of US$1.6 billion. This was the largest loss ever recorded by a local government investment pool, and led to the bankruptcy of the county shortly thereafter.

Bob Citron, the County Treasurer, was entrusted with a US$7.5 billion portfolio belonging to county schools, cities, special districts and the county itself. Among others, Citron made heavy investments in inverse floaters. His strategy was based on a speculation that interest rates would either stay flat or come down. He was working on a leveraged portfolio with a high amount of repo borrowings. With investors' equity of US$7.5 billion, the asset size amounted to US$20.5 billion. During 1994, the Fed started a series of interest rate hikes – six interest rate hikes from February. When interest rates go up, the yield on inverse floaters falls, and falls more than proportionately. Due to the leveraged nature of the portfolio, the adversity was multiplied several times, which led to heavy losses for the county.

Askin Capital Management

Askin Capital Management is a case of wrong investment priorities in mortgage-backed securities and speculating on interest rates. David Askin was a mortgage trader who had floated investment funds, investing in high-quality mortgage securities. On the promise of high liquidity and low leverage, "risk neutral" investment strategies, investors handed over some US$630 million to Askin's hedge funds – Granite Partners, Granite Corporation and Quartz Hedge Fund.

Askin invested in PO strips of CMOs. PO strip market values are inversely proportionate to interest rates. As interest rates go up, prepayments decline, and so PO holds saw staggered principal repayments. On the other hand, if interest rates decline, prepayment speed increases, with PO holders getting faster unscheduled principal.

However, in 1994, interest rates, especially short-term rates, rose dramatically and PO values crashed. Four Askin funds with $600 million in assets filed for bankruptcy when the rising rates drove down the market values of POs. Investors lost virtually everything, and the collapse stopped the MBS market in its tracks, generating a string of lawsuits, some of which are still pending. Askin was barred by the SEC from the securities industry for two years, and agreed to pay a US$50,000 fine without admitting or denying guilt.

Beacon Hill Hedge fund

In October 2002, MBS market hedge fund Beacon Hill Asset Management LLC decided to wind up its heavy losses in MBS bonds. Though hedge fund affairs are not easily disclosed, it is estimated that the fund would have suffered losses of some US$400 million due to interest rate swings.

MBS vs. fixed income investments

So, MBS investment is not the same as investing in regular fixed income securities, as the investment is a prepayment-sensitive, pass-through. It should be noted that the prepayment-sensitivity of pass-throughs is itself dependant on the extent of prepayment penalties imposed by the mortgagees; in some markets, the prepayment penalties can be substantial and can de-motivate prepayments.

The Bond Market Association's guide to investing in MBS[29] makes a very interesting reading of investing in MBS:

> With fixed-income securities such as corporate bonds, an investor effectively lends money to the bond issuer in return for a stated rate of interest (the coupon rate) over the life of the bond. The investor receives a repayment of principal – namely, the "face value" of the bond – in a single lump sum when the bond matures.

Investors in mortgage securities also earn a coupon rate of interest, but they receive repayments of their principal in increments over the life of the security, as the underlying mortgage loans are paid off, rather than in a single lump sum at maturity.

Because the timing and speed of principal repayments may vary, the cash flow on mortgage securities is irregular. If homeowners whose mortgages are in a pool sell their homes, refinance their loans to take advantage of lower interest rates, prepay their mortgages for some other reason or default on their loans, the principal is distributed on a pro rata basis to investors in pass-through securities. Investors in CMOs and REMICs receive these principal repayments according to the payment priorities of each CMO or REMIC and the class of securities they own. When this happens, the investors' remaining interest in the pool is reduced by the amount of prepayments. Because the principal is reduced over the life of the security, the interest income also decreases in terms of absolute dollars paid to investors.

Mortgage securities are sold and traded in terms of their assumed "average life" rather than their maturity dates. The average life is the average amount of time that will elapse from the date of MBS purchase until principal is repaid based on an assumed prepayment forecast. In other words, average life is the average amount of time a dollar of principal is invested in an MBS pool. However, some mortgage loans could remain outstanding for the entire life of the original loans – typically, 30 years.

As with any fixed-income security, the yield on a mortgage security investment depends on the purchase price in relation to the coupon rate and the length of time the principal is outstanding.

To compare the value of a mortgage security with other fixed-income investments, some prepayment assumptions, based on historic prepayment rates, are factored into the price and yield. The more accurate the prepayment projections, the more realistic the yield estimates.

MBS and interest rates

Interest rate movements have been observed as affecting prepayment speed, which affects the cash flow of the mortgage investor. Therefore, mortgage investments are interest-rate sensitive.

The impact of interest rates on the MBS investors' yield will depend on whether the security was purchased at a premium or a discount, and whether the security is a plain pass-through or a structured security such as subordinated CMO tranches, strips, IOs and POs, inverse floaters and supported classes.

The fact that the mortgage investor may get his principal repaid before the scheduled maturity is akin to a call risk on a regular bond. In case of callable bonds, the option with the bond issuer to call the bond and pay it before maturity poses a reinvestment risk for the investor. Similarly, it is not an option with the mortgage-originator, but the pass-through of the option granted by the mortgage-originator to the mortgagor poses a similar call risk on the investors. Therefore, the prepayment risk is also referred to as *call risk*. The reciprocal of the call risk is the *extension risk* – that the prepayment speed will be less than what was projected, and thus, the repayment period will be extended.

We have discussed investors' evaluation of MBS in Chapter 10.

Mortgage bonds

A traditional but very significant source of mortgage funding in Europe, covered bonds deserve a very special mention, not only because they are responsible for refinancing a substantial part of the European market, but due to their growing significance. Interestingly, off-balance sheet financing becomes difficult under international accounting norms and the scope for regulatory capital arbitrage inherent in off-balance sheet funding comes down, mortgage bonds are expected to become even more popular in time to come.

The reason why covered bonds have so far been largely popular in continental Europe is obviously history; Germany and Denmark are the two countries with mortgage bonds for over 100 years. Until the mid-1990s, covered bonds remained largely limited to Germany and to a limited extent other continental European countries. Germany still remains the largest issuer of mortgage bonds, known as *pfandbriefs* in local parlance. *Pfandbriefs*, or *pfandbriefes*, as they are known in Germany, are known by various local European names as *pantbrevs*, *cedulas*, *obligations foncieres*, *lettres de gage*, mortgage bonds, covered bonds, asset-covered bonds and asset covered securities.

Literally, the word *pfandbrief* means a letter of pledge. The word "pledge" in English common law is given the meaning of a possessory security interest, so the *pfandbrief* should essentially mean mortgage; therefore, the legal basis of a *pfandbrief* is not very different from mortgages. In Germany and several European jurisdictions, the genesis of covered bonds is a specific legislation that grants a bankruptcy remoteness to the bond holders, but the essential idea is not unique; in the typical English law concept of secured lending, a secured lender has a bankruptcy-remote claim on the secured assets.

For covered bonds, a specific law regulates the entities that issue such bonds. Unlike securitization, there is no off-balance sheet treatment, as there is no true sale. The assets – the pool of mortgages – remain with the mortgage issuer, but there is a bankruptcy-remote claim that the bondholders have against the pool of mortgages.

Covered bonds and securitization – distinction

Table 12.7 summarizes the key differences between covered bonds and residential mortgage securitization:

Table 12.7 Differences between covered bonds and residential mortgage securitization

	Securitization	Covered bonds
Legal nature	Isolation achieved by transfer of a pool of assets to a bankruptcy-remote entity	There is no isolation of any specific pool – the claim of the bondholders extends to the entire floating pool of mortgage loans
Legal backing	Backed by common law or specific law that permits/recognizes sale of assets by the originator	Backed by either specific law or common law relating to issue of mortgage bonds
Common issuers	Securitization extends to various classes of assets and issuers	Covered bonds are presently mostly limited to mortgages and other assets as may be permitted by the relevant law, for example, three classes of *pfandbriefs* permitted by German law
Balance sheet treatment	Usually not recorded as a liability of the originator	Usually recorded as a liability of the originator
Recourse against the originator	Except for the credit enhancements, there is no recourse against the originator	In addition to rights against the pool of assets, the bond holders also have a claim against the originator
Common methods of credit enhancements	Excess spreads and subordination used as common credit enhancements	Excess spreads continue to benefit the originator's common revenue; the common equity capital of the originator serves as the credit-enhancement
Booking of gains on sale	Subject to accounting standards, gains on sale usually booked at the time of sale of the asset	As there is no sale, the question of booking any gain on sale does not arise
Separation of origination and servicing	Technically, the originator ceases to have any connection with the portfolio after sale – servicing is typically continued under a presumably independent relationship	As there is no legal isolation of the pool from the originator, the originator retains his originator-owner-servicer position on the portfolio

The covered bonds market

The *Pfandbrief* bond market is the biggest segment of the euro-denominated private bond market in Europe and rivals in size the individual European government bond markets. "Since the turn of the millennium the market for *Pfandbriefe* and *Pfandbrief*-like products in Europe has progressed to become one of the most dynamic asset classes in the European capital market. At end-2004, the volume of securities outstanding rose to over € 1,600 billion from more than 20 countries with active covered bond issuers."[30]

Covered bonds have quickly expanded and are gaining popularity in several European jurisdictions, but Germany is still the most predominant contributor to the market. The data published by the Association of German *Pfandbrief* Banks[31] make this obvious:

Market shares in the European *Pfandbrief* market
As at Dec 2004

	Outstanding in billion euros	*Percent share*
Germany	1,010	61.89%
Denmark	233	14.28%
France	101	6.19%
Spain	101	6.19%
Sweden	83	5.09%
Ireland	31	1.90%
Switzerland	29	1.78%
Luxembourg	20	1.23%
Great Britain	15	0.92%
Other countries	9	0.55%
Total	1,632	

Historically, in Germany and some other countries covered bonds have existed for over a century now. The widely circulated story is that the oldest *pfandbrief* decree was passed by Frederick II of Prussia in the 18th century who used the funding to finance the war. However, it was only in 1899 that Pfandbrief took its present form, when the Mortgage-bank Law was passed. The oldest law on *Pfandbrief*-style products is said to be have been issued in France in 1852 with the *Loi sur l'obligation foncière et communale*. The oldest mortgage credit market can be traced to Denmark, where there was massive housing finance needed for reconstruction after the Great Fire of 1789.

Most European markets provide a legal basis for covered bonds transactions. Germany has had a mortgage-banking law providing for *pfandbriefs* for some time. In July 2005, the provisions scattered in different laws were consolidated in a new *Pfandbrief* Act 2005. Spain and Denmark have also had covered bond laws for decades. In France the law governing *obligations foncières* was revised in 1999. In Luxembourg, a new-look law on *lettres de gage* of 1993 was passed in 1997. In Finland legislation on *Pfandbriefe* was introduced in 2000. In recent years, realizing the growing popularity of covered bonds, several other European countries have taken legislative measures. In Italy, the first covered bond was issued at the beginning of 2005, and the first step towards a general legal framework was taken midway through 2005. In Portugal, experts are expecting a completely overhauled legal basis to be passed before the end of 2005. The laws on the issuance of covered bonds were recently modernized in Sweden and Austria. In UK, it is felt that with rich common law tradition, a specific mortgage bond law is not required. Preparations for corresponding laws are well underway in Slovenia and Romania. In the Netherlands and Belgium, the introduction of covered bond laws is the subject of intense debate, while Turkey also is currently looking into the introduction of a product.

The most notable development in the *pfandbrief* market was the introduction of the *jumbo pfandbrief* in 1995, prior to which the market was limited to domestic boundaries. The *jumbo pfandbrief* essentially implies a *pfandbrief* issuance where the issuer continuously provides two way quotes, thus providing continuous liquidity to a market that was previously illiquid. In 1996, the association of *pfandbrief* issuers standardized the terms of jumbos to include only those issuances where the minimum issue size was DM 1 billion, and at least three banks agreed to act as market makers. Soon, the concept of jumbo issuance spread to other covered bond issuing countries as well. In the first quarter of 2005, the volume of jumbo covered bonds was estimated at €607 billion.

Structure of a *pfandbrief*

The legal and structural features of *pfandbriefs* essentially flow from the German law, so we discuss below the salient features of German *pfandbrief* legislation.

Under German law, *pfandbriefs* can be issued only by banks, also on the strength of a specific license issued on satisfaction of several conditions. These *pfandbrief* issues are expected on a regular and consistent basis, rather than on an opportunistic or sporadic one.

There are three different types of *pfandbriefs* permitted by the German *Pfandbrief* Act – mortgage *pfandbriefs*, public *pfandbriefs* and ship *pfandbriefs*. Mortgage and ship *pfandbriefs*, as the name implies, are backed by real estate and ships, respectively. Public *pfandbriefs* are those backed by claims against public sector authorities. Notably, the loan-to-value ratio in case of mortgage loans is limited to 60%.

The key feature of *pfandbriefs* is "covered assets," the collateral backing up the *pfandbriefs*. Depending on the type of *pfandbriefs*, the covered assets should be qualifying mortgages, public sector financial claims or mortgages on ships. In addition, within specific limits, claims against central banks, credit institutions and derivatives transactions are also recognized as covered assets.

The key to the bankruptcy remoteness of *pfandbriefs* lies in Sec. 30 of the *Pfandbrief* Act. This section provides that if insolvency proceedings are opened in respect of the *Pfandbrief* bank's assets, the assets recorded in the cover registers shall not be included in the insolvent estate. The claims of the *Pfandbrief* creditors must be fully satisfied from the assets recorded in the relevant cover register; they shall not be affected by the opening of insolvency proceedings in respect of the *Pfandbrief* bank's assets. *Pfandbrief* creditors shall only participate in the insolvency proceedings to the extent their claims remain unsatiated from the covered assets. Notably, this principle is very similar to the position of secured lenders under U.K. corporate insolvency laws.

There are independent administration provisions for the covered assets. Sec. 30.2 provides that the court of jurisdiction shall appoint one or two natural persons to act as administrators, whereupon the right to manage and dispose of the covered assets shall be transferred to the administrator.

Acquisition and disposal of covered assets is not illegal; the security interest of the *pfandbrief* holders on the covered assets is comparable to a floating charge under English law. However, once the appointment of the administrator has been done, the security interest crystallizes and any disposal of the assets subsequent to appointment of the administrator shall be invalid.

Rating of *pfandbriefs* by the rating agencies

A *pfandbrief* is an obligation of the issuer, but should it qualify for an asset-backed, structured finance rating? In view of the specific claim of the *pfandbrief* holders on the covered assets, the assets are ring-fenced. To the extent of the unsatiated claims of the bondholders, the law grants rights against the other assets of the issuer, so the net worth of the issuer should be viewed as credit enhancement.

Rating agencies are still grappling with the special features of *pfandbriefs*, which are close to structured finance instruments, on-balance sheet obligations of the issuer. Are corporate finance rating principles appropriate or structure finance? The answer is not yet completely clear. Unlike securitization transactions, there is no isolation of assets from the issuer; thus, the rating agencies feel that the management of the bank has the ability to influence the quality of the pool. Therefore, the risk profile of the bank as a whole must be considered while rating *pfandbriefs*.

None of the rating agencies have been comfortable in giving structured finance type ratings to *pfandbriefs*

Notes

1 Lea, Dr Michael: *Overview of Housing Finance Systems, at* www.countrywideinternational.com/article4_Overview.PDF (last visited October 23, 2002).
2 **The Impact of the GNMA Pass-through Program on FHA Mortgage Costs**: *Journal of Finance*, xxxvI, 2: 457–469.
3 Passmore, W. and R. Sparks. 1996. **Putting the Squeeze on a Market for Lemons: Government-Sponsored Mortgage Securitization**: *Journal of Real Estate Finance and Economics* 13: 27–43.

4   **Bank Funding Modes: Securitization versus Deposits** *Journal of Banking Finance*. 11: 379–402.

5   **Elements of Mortgage Securitization**: *Journal of Real Estate Finance and Economics.* 1: 331–346.

6   Todd, Steven **The effects of securitization on consumer mortgage costs:** *Real Estate Economics*; Spring 2001.

7   This seems to be a precursor to the setting up of Hong Kong Mortgage Corporation.

8   Para 3.10 of the Report titled Mortgage Corporation Proposal.

9   See also Chapter 1 on the the impact of securitization on lending costs.

10 Skarabot. Jure: *Securitization and Special Purpose Vehicle Structures*, paper April 29, 2002, quoting Shenker J., and A. Colletta: "Asset Securitization: Evolution, Current Issues and New Frontiers", *Texas Law Review*, 69, (1991), p. 1369–1429.

11 The support, given by law, includes the following: (a) The securities issued by the agencies do not require registration with the SEC; (b) The securities are exempt from both state and local taxes; (c) The Secretary of the State is authorized, but not required, to provide liquidity support to the GSEs by buying their securities up to US$2.25 billion each.

12 Bruskin, Eric, Anthony B. Sanders and David Sykes: *The Nonagency Mortgage Market: Background and Overview*, April 1999 (paper).

13 Bruskin, etc: *ibid.*

14 HUD Regulation of Fannie Mae and Freddie Mac, HUD website at http://www.hud.gov/offices/hsg/gse/gse.cfm, last visited December 22, 2005.

15 For status report, see http://www.govtrack.us/congress/bill.xpd?bill=h109-1461, last visited March 2, 2006.

16 Mortgage-bankers Association.

17 The Bond Market Association, Research Quarterly, November 2005.

18 See in Chapter 26 on Taxation Issues.

19 Nomura Fixed Income Research: A Journey to the Alt-A Zone, June 3, 2003.

20 Lea, Dr. Michael: *Prerequisites for a Successful SecondaryMortgage Market: The Role of the Primary Mortgage Market* (paper presented at Inter-American Development Bank conference) November 1999.

21 Culled from various periodic reports of European Securitization Forum: *at www.europeansecuritization.com.*

22 Based on Fannie Mae website.

23 Ginne Mae has a practice of servicing fee of 43 bps.

24 Data on Bond Market Association website at http://www.bondmarkets.com/story.asp?id=98 last visited December 22, 2005.

25 See chapter on tax issues.

26 In this particular case, the asset-base of Abbey is much larger than what is held by the master trust. Around the time of the issue discussed here, Abbey's mortgage portfolio was £68 billion.

27 Department of Treasury, SEC and Office of Federal Housing Enterprise Oversight Staff report on Enhancing Disclosure In The Mortgage-Backed Securities Markets, January 2003.

28 Deutsche Bank: *Guide to US Mortgage-backed Securities* January 2002.

29 http://www.investinginbonds.com/info/igmbs/versus.htm, last visited October 29, 2002.

30 *The Pfandbrief – Europe's Covered Bond Benchmark Facts and Figures, 2005;* Association of German *Pfandbrief* Banks, p. 37.

31 *Ibid, P. 37.*

Chapter 13

Commercial Mortgage-backed Securitization

W e use the acronym CMBS to mean commercial mortgage-backed securities and CRE to mean commercial real estate.

Of late, CMBS has drawn investor interest because of the exhibit strength of CMBS paper. Studies by rating agencies have shown that CMBS defaults and downgrade performance have been quite impressive, and for defaulted investments, the recovery performance has been sterling.[1] For several quarters in the past, the upgrades have been exceeding downgrades. A Nomura Securities report says: "In addition to the time honored safe havens of U.S. treasuries and grandma's mattress, there now seems to be another acceptable place to invest in time of trouble, CMBS."[2] We will revert to the recent performance of CMBS later in this chapter.

What is CMBS?

Commercial mortgage-backed securities (CMBS) are bonds or other debt instruments collateralized by commercial real estate, as opposed to residential real estate. Commercial property means property let out or managed for economic benefit as opposed to that for self-occupation, and includes multi-family dwelling units (apartments or condominiums), retail centers, hotels, restaurants, hospitals, warehouses and office buildings.

The distinction between RMBS and CMBS is made because of the significant differences between the two in terms of risks, structural features and type of obligors.

In a generic sense, CMBS includes various types of funding backed by commercial real estate, including loans against real estate, real estate lease receivables and rentals.

Differences between RMBS and CMBS

CMBS is structurally unique and differs substantively from RMBS or CDOs, or, for that matter, any of the other variants of ABS. While RMBS, credit cards and auto loans depend on consumer behavior, CMBS is essentially a business loan, extended against commercial properties. For office complexes, shopping plazas and the like, it is like funding an income-generating asset.

CMBS is a wholesale transaction, while RMBS and many other ABS represent diversified retail loans. While assessing the credit of these transactions, rating agencies and investors are more concerned with the strength of the underwriting standards and statistical history of losses. For CMBS, the income-earning capacity of the property is most important.

The essential features of CMBS transactions are based on the nature of the underlying loan, which may be a loan to construct a commercial property, or a loan against the value of a property. The underlying collateral may be one or just a few CRE loans, or a pool of loans backed by a CRE extended by a lender in the normal course of banking business.

Table 13.1   Differences between RMBS and CMBS

	RMBS	*CMBS*
Nature of the market	Largely standardized market with origination mainly by mainstream housing finance institutions	Scattered market with origination from banks and lenders
Conduit activity	Very little conduit activity; originators are securitizers	Large extent of conduit activity: in 1998, the peak year of CMBS issuance in the U.S., 91% of all CRE origination was by conduits.
Prepayment risk	High extent of prepayment risk, for several reasons including interest rate movements.	Comparatively lower prepayment risk; ticket size is large. Most CRE loans contain a prepayment lock in period and also a prepayment penalty.
Default risk	Very low default risk for prime mortgages; higher default risk in sub-prime mortgages. Due to a large number of small-ticket loans, the default rate at a pool-level is comparatively low.	While historical performance data are diverse, there is a small number of highly leveraged loans. So, a meltdown in the property market, or higher vacancy rates may mean substantial default risk.
Subordination levels	Much lower degree of subordination.	Much higher degree of subordination.
Classes of securities	Just a few classes of securities.	A large number of classes of securities.

Typical features

One of the significant attributes of CMBS as against RMBS is the lower degree of prepayment risk as most commercial mortgages are for a fixed term and have a prepayment lock-in and prepayment penalties. The credit attributes are also different as the collateral consists of a small number of CRE loans.

Unlike RMBS, CMBS issuance is not supported by government agencies in most countries; therefore, a hard look into the credit attributes of the mortgage pool is very important. Most CMBS issues are backed appropriately by ratings. Some of the significant distinguishing features of CMBS are noted below:

- **Lending against borrower versus lending against property**: Residential mortgage loans are loans against a borrower's credit and are usually underwritten after evaluating the borrower's debt/equity ratio. CRE loans are given against the income-earning potential of the property. In CRE jargon, a lender looks at the stabilized net cash flow of the property (see Box 13.1).
- **No agency support**: Most CMBS transactions do not have credit enhancements provided by government agencies. Hence, rating and internal credit enhancements become important.
- Fewer **Less number of transactions in the pool**: Quite expectedly, each commercial mortgage typically has a much higher value than for RMBS transactions. Therefore, the number of transactions in the pool is lesser and the value of the pool is higher, indicating larger concentration risk and the ability of performance of a single transaction to disrupt the performance of the entire pool is quite strong. Some CMBS have a single mortgage underlying the issue.
- **Heterogeneity**: While RMBS transactions pool mortgages that are more or less homogenous, commercial mortgages are mainly cases in themselves. They will have differential documentation, property features, LTV ratios and payback periods. The terms of commercial mortgages are mostly individually negotiated, while residential mortgages are more or less a standardized commodity.
- **High LTV ratios**: Most commercial mortgages are far higher leveraged than residential mortgages. The loan to-value (LTV) ratios are consequently far higher as compared to residential mortgages.

Box 13.1: How is a CRE loan originated?

1. PGI: Calculate the Potential Gross Income that a property is capable of generating (contract rent + vacant space at market rent).
2. Vacancy Reserve: Subtract from PGI the greater of the Actual, Market or Underwriting Guideline for Vacancy.
3. Normalizing: Remove any unusual, non-recurring income and expenses like Tax Refunds, Lease Buyouts, TI/LC costs, Replacement Reserves and Extraordinary Capital Expenditures.

4. Adjust for Inflation: Multiply the remaining expenses by three percent or the expected inflation rate.
5. Calculate NOI: Subtract from the PGI the Vacancy Reserve, and then subtract the inflation-adjusted expenses.
6. Apply Property-specific Underwriting Parameters: Management Fee (3-5%), Replacement Reserves (by square foot or by unit), and TI/LC Reserves (for Office, Industrial or Retail properties).
7. Calculate NCF: Subtract NOI from the Underwritten Fees and Reserves.

The value of the property is computed by capitalizing the NCF at a certain capitalization rate. Thereafter, the lender works at his standard LTV ratio to work out the amount of the loan.

CMBS and REITs

Real estate investment trusts (REITs) are originally a U.S. tax-term created way back in 1960s to encourage owning and funding of commercial property on a mutual fund basis. Being essentially a tax concept, REITs are required to invest only in qualifying property and comply with tax rules. REITs are companies that own, manage, and develop pools of properties, from apartments and office buildings. In exchange for following rigid tax guidelines, which include distributing a very high degree of their taxable income in dividends (for example, 95%) and earning that income primarily from leasing buildings, REITs are exempt from corporate taxation.

REITs are essentially tax-transparent property-owning vehicles, so there are clearly defined tax rules that lay down what they can or cannot do. While these regulations are jurisdiction-specific, countries largely have modelled their regulations on the U.S. system.

REITs are essentially property ownership vehicles, while CMBS is essentially property funding vehicle. REITs are generally allowed to borrow up to a certain percentage of their assets, so several REITs have resorted to CMBS for part-financing their properties. REITs are also a device of securitization, but securitization of the ownership of commercial real estate.

In many cases, REITs also raise funding by securitizing the properties under their management. REITs are allowed to leverage their assets up to a certain percentage. Securitization allows REITs to enhance the returns on equity.

REITs are quite significant in the commercial property market: we will discuss REITs in a following section in this chapter.

CMBS market

The CMBS market has globally enabled interaction between capital markets and commercial real estate. The coming together of CRE market and the capital market is very significant, as CRE represents real wealth.

So far, it is the U.S. market that has seen a very large contribution from CMBS, but there are portents of a very fast growing CMBS market in London, Tokyo and Singapore.

The U.S. CMBS market had steep growth until 1996; thereafter, volumes declined until 2000. The market then performed fairly well when on September 11, 2001, terrorists flew hijacked planes into the World Trade Center and thousands were killed. The WTC itself was partly funded by securitization money and more than US$1 billion worth of securitization-funded real estate was reduced to rubble. Despite the scenario of uncertainty that prevailed in the later part of 2001, U.S. CMBS volumes ended close to the 1998 level in 2001. From 2002 onwards, the market has grown at a brisk pace. The growth rate has continued from 2002 to 2005 with the volume in 2005 hovering around $130 billion.

The last few years have also been marked by rapid development of the CMBS market in other countries. Along with the traditional centers such as the U.K., France and Japan, there has been significant interest in CMBS in places like Singapore, Malaysia, and even China. Massive real estate investment is taking place in the Gulf region, part of which may find its way to the CMBS market in the near future.

Development of the CMBS market

U.S.

The history of the CMBS market in the U.S. is synonymous with the Resolution Trust Corporation (RTC) picking up commercial loans and securitizing them.

Ironically, the genesis of CMBS market lies in the failure of the savings and loans associations (or thrifts) in the U.S., when the assets of the latter were taken over by RTC, which used securitization as a method to sell the loans backed by real estate. RTC made the first securitization issue of multi-family mortgages in August 1991. By July 1993, the RTC had issued close to US$14 billion worth performing mortgage assets.

The RTC did its last securitization transaction in 1995 and then, having accomplished its limited purpose, went out of business. Despite RTC issues dissipating, the CMBS market has retained its vigor, using much of the RTC template. In 1993, about 80% of the total of the CMBS market was shared by private issuers. The role of the RTC in promoting commercial mortgage securitization is laudable and comparable to specialized federal agencies such as FNMA and GNMA.

Late development of the CMBS market

It may sound a little surprising that even while the RMBS market was already developed and doing quite very well, it took a while for the CMBS market to come up. In the U.S. at the end of 1992, there was $3.1 trillion outstanding in the residential mortgage market, of which around $1.5 trillion, or about 50%, was already securitized.

Against this, for CMBS there was a total $1 trillion outstanding, of which less than 3% was securitized.

The reasons for the late development of the CMBS market are:

1. Abundance of alternative sources of capital
2. Absence of consistence underwriting standards – commercial real estate financing mostly being big ticket transactions followed by a more personalized/informal lending approach.
3. Lack of standard loan documentation.
4. Poor historical performance data.
5. Excessive leveraging of real estate transactions.

Reasons for decline post-1998 in the U.S. market

In the U.S., the volume of issuance of CMBS was measured at $2 billion 1992, rising to $80 billion in 1998.

The reasons for the decline in CMBS issuance in 1998 and for the next 3 years were overcapacity and constant erosion of conduit profits.

A large part of the profits in the CMBS market came from conduit activity; conduits buy CRE loans and securitize them for the sake of arbitrage. Arbitrage opportunities existed pre-1998 due to the inefficient pricing of the CRE market, which in turn was due to the highly illiquid nature of CRE loans. In contrast with RRE loans, CRE lending was over-leveraged, highly illiquid and a heterogeneous market. The CMBS market introduced liquidity to CRE market, and therefore, got the opportunity of earning arbitrage profits.

The arbitrage profit dried over time, making conduit activity less profitable. This led to a shakeout and exit of those who had already built huge overheads on the promise of arbitrage profits. Accounting firm Ernst and Young says in *Commercial Mortgage-backed Securitization Update 2000–1*: "Looking back eight to 10 years, CMBS had two key goals. The first was for real estate owners to have access to the capital markets when the more traditional sources of funding, for whatever reason, dried up. The second was for lenders to be able to provide loans and generate fee income without incremental balance sheet exposure. The investment banks got residuary benefit from underwriting and trading revenues. And, as an added bonus, the fixed-income investment community got a new, highly diversified and highly rated instrument to add to their portfolios, typically at higher yields that similarly rated corporate debt. Eroding profit is a sign that the CMBS market has, in large part, achieved these goals. That the market has finally matured."

While global volumes were growing, U.S. volumes were $77.7 billion in 1998, down to $58.5 billion in 1999 and $48.9 billion in 2000. The trend was reversed in 2001, and after a decline in 2002, volumes started picking up again in 2003, which has continued.

Ernst and Young [in *Commercial Mortgage-backed Securitization Update 2000–1*] said: "Wall Street's withdrawal from CMBS will continue into 2001 and last as long as capital is readily available from alternative sources, typically financial institutions willing to commit their balance sheets. Given their

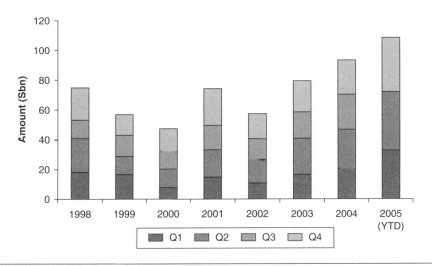

Figure 13.1   Domestic CMBS Issuance 1998–2005

Source: Nomura Fixed Income Research, September 2005 CMBS Monthly

investment in infrastructure, the investment banks will probably want to keep a CMBS placeholder. If the economy tanks, and real estate capital becomes scarce, they will jump back in to exploit that window of opportunity. In the meantime, most commercial mortgage lending, both portfolio and securitized, will continue to be provided by banks." This prediction, however, erred as CMBS volumes scaled up in 2001, and thereafter, have grown substantially.

Europe

In Europe as in the U.S., CMBS is a recent development. The volumes were negligible to non-existent before 1995. The tangible growth picked up during and after 1998. In 2000, it totaled about €10 billion (including approximately €3.6 billion of debt issuance from property-related operating company transactions or whole business transactions). This compares with issuance of only €5.7 billion in 1999 and represents a healthy growth of 75% compared to 1999.

There was significant growth in European CMBS volumes in 2005. In the first half of 2005, the U.K. itself accounted for €12.2 billion in issuance. The total European issuance in the first half of 2005 was €21.2 billion, 149% higher than the corresponding period the previous year.

The CMBS market in Europe is fragmented with each country having its different real estate leasing systems. The U.K. takes the lead where prime commercial real estate has been securitized in several recent transactions. The other jurisdictions are France, Germany and Italy.

Asia

There has been a substantial growth in CMBS activity in Asia over the past few years. The major markets are Singapore, Malaysia and Hong Kong.

In Singapore, the growth in CMBS has taken place simultaneously with REITs. Major REITs have resorted to CMBS to leverage their returns. Major commercial properties in Singapore have been funded by CMBS. The Malaysian market has also seen several CMBS transactions including refinancing-type transactions as well as liquidation-type transactions.

Types of CMBS

CMBS has taken various forms over time – loans backed by commercial property, rentals from commercial real estate, sale and leaseback of properties, whole-business cash flows based primarily on property income, loans granted for construction and sale of real estate, loans granted for construction and renting of real estate and securitization of properties pending liquidation. In short, in all cases where there is a commercial possibility of financing commercial real estate, there is a possibility of such financing bundled as a CMBS transaction.

The traditional picture of a CMBS transaction is a pool of loans backed by commercial properties. As in an RMBS transaction, in a traditional CMBS transaction too, there is a bank that originates the transaction by giving a loan to the owner/lessee of the CRE. For an RMBS deal, the borrower is a household who pays for the loan based on his other disposable income; for CMBS, the borrower is a CRE owner who has to earn from the property to pay off the loan. Therefore, the end-obligors for CMBS are the tenants or the persons using the CRE. The loan receivables are pooled and assigned to an SPV, which then issues securities in the market.

Several CMBS transactions are originated by the property-owners looking at refinancing an existing CRE. Alternatively, it might also be financing of the development of a CRE.

The typical classification, based on origination type, for the U.S. market is conduit and non-conduit or seasoned collateral. The classification for non-U.S. transactions is based on multi-borrower deals versus single-borrower deals. See Figure 13.2 for an overview of CMBS.

CMBS and construction financing

The use of CMBS in construction financing was first made by the U.K. CMBS transactions such as Canary Wharf. Here, the underlying facts were:

- There is a reputed property developer, with a property in an area that is a hot office location in the city.
- The construction is carried out by an internationally renowned construction firm. There are performance risk mitigants such as insurance coverage.
- A large part of the property has been pre-rented, as is common for major developments.
- The tenants are well-known global financial services players.
- Based on the above, the income from the property was securitized even before the property was completed.

This was an innovative application of securitization, essentially similar to financing a property development project.

In several Singapore transactions too, properties under development have been funded by way of securitization.

Balance sheet and conduit activity

Balance sheet transactions are usually originated by banks or financial intermediaries and consist of securitization of commercial property loans. Arbitrage or conduit activity refers to a conduit manager or arbitrageur picking up loans from various originators and securitizing them to make arbitrage profit.

The conduit activity has become very strong in the U.S. commercial real estate loans market. The conduits are typically the originators who originate mortgage loans expressly for the purpose of their sale to a securitization trust.

"Fusion conduit" type originations started in the late 1990s, notably towards 1998. The essential purpose of a fusion conduit deal is to attain a higher volume of issuance to achieve economies of scale. A fusion blends together conduit loans with other balance sheet loans and is a melting pot of loans, typically a much larger number of loans and broader geographic diversification. The fusion conduit activity has become so significant that in the first half of 2005, all 21 conduit deals were fusion conduit deals.[3]

Trophy assets vs. portfolio of assets

Securitization of a mortgage portfolio backed by a single property or a few properties with one primary attraction is commonly referred to as trophy property CMBS. The most prominent that comes to mind is the one backed by the ill-fated World Trade Center. In the U.K. as well, there have been several trophy deals such as the ones backed by Trafford Center shopping mall in Manchester, the Broadgate and Canary Wharf office complexes in London. This is also a common feature of CMBS transactions in Japan and Singapore.

By property sectors

Yet another way to typically classify CMBS transactions is by property sectors. Primarily, there are five property sectors – office, retail, industrial, hotel, and multi-family. The factors that affect the strength of the CMBS are different in these sectors with respect to:

- Rent levels, type of occupiers, stability of the cash flow and occupancy.
- Sensitivity of property performance to the business cycle.
- Likely future growth of demand for space and rents vs. future supply.
- Relationship between the property value and replacement costs in the local market.

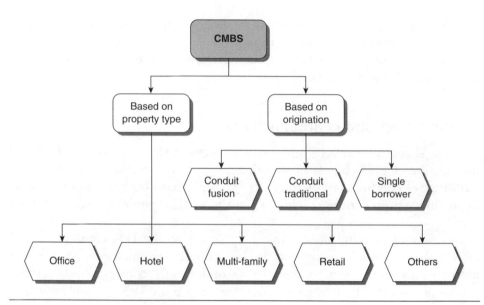

Figure 13.2   Overview of CMBS

Structure of a CMBS transaction

The basic source of cash flow forming the waterfall of the CMBS transaction is the estimated income from the property or properties. If the transaction consists of loans against properties, the repayment of the loans is based on the income from the properties; therefore, the potential cash flow from the property is the cash cow of the CMBS deal.

The cash flow from the property, called net operating cash flows (NOCF) or simply net cash flows (NCF, sometimes Net Operating Income or NOI) is the most significant element in the CMBS structure. While the NCF is estimated based on all surrounding factors, the rating agencies apply their own stress tests for the NCF.

Balloon loans

The best way to illustrate a CMBS transaction is to think of the valuation of a commercial property. Typically, a standard, good quality commercial property has a life of 25 to 30 years, and in valuation of the property, the lender looks at NCF for 25 to 30 years. Therefore, if a loan against commercial property were to be paid out of the cash flows of the property, it would take a good 25 years or longer to repay the same.

Therefore, if CMBS transactions had an amortizing structure, similar to RMBS pools, the transaction would have a very long duration. However, investors are generally looking at maturities of 5–7 years, so the normal structure of a CMBS is to have a partial amortization of the loan over the term of the transaction, with a balloon payment at the end of the term.

Thus, most CRE loans carry a balloon repayment structure with only the payment of coupon during the initial years and amortization of principal beginning later. Substantial repayment takes place at the end of the term with the refinancing of the property.

Typical credit enhancements

The structuring of a CMBS transaction is based essentially on corporate finance principles. The transaction is funding a property or a pool of properties. True sales might be significant in the legal structure, but other than an effective right to foreclose the mortgage, true sale does not mean much here. As corporate funding, the two major sources of credit support here are – LTV ratio and the debt-service coverage ratio. These are comparable to asset coverage and income coverage for project loans.

The typical credit enhancements in CMBS transaction are:

1. **Loan-to-value ratio**: This is a loan-level credit enhancement. If the value of the property is $100, and the lender gives a loan of $70, the LTV ratio is 70%. Reciprocally, it means there is an over-collateralization of 30% in the form of the borrower's equity in the property. Given the fact that CMBS is essentially securitization of the value of the property, the LTV ratio can surely be looked at as a credit enhancement for the transaction. If the LTV ratio at the transaction level is 70%, then, for each of the classes, the LTV ratio keeps declining in view of the subordination structure. In other words, senior classes benefited from reducing LTV ratio that implies higher extent of over-collateralization.
2. **Debt-service coverage ratio**: This implies the extent to which net operating cash flow of the property covers the debt service, that is, the repayment of securities. Once again, with the subordination structure, the DSCR is reduced for senior classes.

Table 13.2　Example of CMBS structuring:
An example of the structuring of a CMBS transaction is (results in Table 13.3 are in CD worksheet 1):

Net operating income	100,000 pm
Economic life	300 months
Capitalization rate	8%
Valuation	$12,956,452.26
Rounded off	$13,000,000.00
LTV ratio	70%
Capital market funding	$9,069,516.58
Rounded off	$9,000,000.00
% of NOI to be used in debt service	80%
Maximum possible debt service	$80,000.00
Term of the securities	60.00 months
Weighted-average coupon	4.450%
Total debt service over the term	$4,296,388.00
% of loan to be repaid at the end of term	52.26%

Table 13.3   Example of CMBS structuring

Securities		Rating	size	Coupon	subordination	LTV ratio	debt service required	DSCR
Class A	80%	AAA	$7,200,000.00	4%	20.0%	55.38%	$63,299.62	$1.580
Class B	4%	AA	$360,000.00	4.25%	16.0%	58.15%	$3,184.41	$1.504
Class C	4%	A	$360,000.00	4.50%	12.0%	60.92%	$3,203.91	$1.435
Class D	4%	BBB	$360,000.00	5.50%	8.0%	63.69%	$3,282.64	$1.370
Class E	4%	BB	$360,000.00	7%	4.0%	66.46%	$3,402.95	$1.309
Class F	4%	unrated	$360,000.00	10%	0.0%	69.23%	$3,651.42	$1.250

3. **Subordination**: Most CMBS transactions have several A and B pieces. The extent of credit enhancement required for a AAA-rated CMBS is typically quite high (as compared to an RMBS pool), so there are typically several classes of securities to minimize the extent of the below-investment-grade or retained tranche.

4. **Cash reserves**: Most CMBS transactions trap a part of the cash flow into a cash reserve to build a liquidity and credit enhancement into the deal.

Refinancing risk: how is it factored in the transaction structure?

As discussed earlier, most CMBS structures have an inherent balloon payment that is based on refinancing the property. In other words, repayment of the CMBS investors will depend on ability of the CRE owner to raise funding by refinancing the property. The refinancing may be in any form, including a re-run of the securitization transaction. This ability depends on several factors, including the prevailing value of the property the prevailing interest rates. All these factors contribute to the **refinancing risk** of the CMBS transaction.

Given the nature of an equated payment loan, the extent of principal composed in equated installments is low at the inception, and increases over time. Therefore, there is a substantial degree of outstanding principal or balloon repayment left. See the example below as illustration.

> **Example**: Take a loan of $1,000,000, repayable in equal instalments at interest rate of 6% over 360 months. The monthly instalment works out to $5,995.51. At the end of 120 months, there is still 83.61% outstanding principal as shown in the working below.
>
> See CD worksheet 2 for this chapter.

The working above is a categorical illustration of the nature of an equated payment loan. The period of 120 months is 1/3rd of the loan term, but the amortization is only 16% or almost 1/6th. Given the fact that the amortization rate of the property is very slow in first 1/3rd of the loan term, if the rate of depreciation in the value of the property is faster than the rate of amortization, the LTV ratio changes adversely (in other words, the LTV ratio increases).

The refinancing risk essentially comes from two sources, both a reflection of the same risk. If the rates of mortgage financing rise by the time the existing loan matures, the amount of loan that may be serviced by the NCF of the property may not be enough to repay the existing loan. The other reflection is the increase in **capitalization rate** (sometimes called the **cap rate**), the rate at which the NCF is capitalized to get the value of the property.

To factor the refinancing risk, rating agencies often discount the cash flows beyond the maturity of the current CMBS transaction at higher discounting rates, implying the increased refinancing cost. Thus, the balloon payment required to be repaid is computed as (the NCF * LTV ratio) discounted at such increased refinancing rate.

Diversification

Spatial diversification

In structuring CMBS transactions diversification of the geographical reasons where the properties are located is often an advantage. There could not have been a better way to learn this lesson than the September 11 disaster; transactions that had a high concentration in Manhattan were subject to greater surveillance than those having a diversified pool.

There are a number of single property or trophy property securitizations that relate to a single commercial property, such as the WTC. These obviously carry more risk.

Property-type diversification

The transaction could also be collateralized by different types of properties.

Servicers

Like all securitization transactions, servicing remains an important task in CMBS as well – with the significance increased due to need to monitor several covenants relating to the properties in question. As many CMBS transactions would have been originated by a broker networks, there might a sub-servicer, that is, the servicer who actually originated the loan (sometimes also called the Primary servicer), and a master servicer, a servicer at the conduit level. In addition, there might be a special or back up servicer as usual who will take up the servicing of the loans in exceptional cases, for example, for default.

Case study: GMAC's 2001-WTC transaction

We take up a case to understand the structure of a typical CMBS transaction. The transaction in this case funded the lease of the ill-fated World Trade Center that was destroyed less than one month after the conclusion of the securitization deal. Our intent here is merely to look at the structure of a typical

CMBS transaction and there is nothing in this case study that relates to the tragedy that was to follow.

The transaction structure is a pass-through, although treated as a REMIC for tax purposes. The certificates were called Mortgage Pass-Through Certificates, Series 2001-WTC, issued pursuant to the Trust and Servicing Agreement.

We understand from this case study that CMBS essentially hinges on the value of the property; it is a securitization of the property, so the transaction is as good as the value, both in stock and flow terms, of the property. We also learn from this case that despite being the sole property hit by a terrorist attack, the transaction has still survived due to the insurance coverage. Insurance is a necessary loan-level credit enhancement in CMBS transactions.

Collateral

This CMBS transaction is what is typically called a "trophy property." The sole property in this case is, or rather was, the World Trade Center (WTC). The WTC primarily consisted of seven buildings, and the collateral for this transaction was a mortgage loan in respect of four 99-year leasehold interests 1, 2, 4 and 5 WTC. The title to the Property and to the land where the Property is located was with The Port Authority of New York and New Jersey. The Port Authority gave a 99-year lease of the WTC to Silverstein Properties.

The initial value of the property was assessed at US$1.2 billion. Silverstein had taken the lease at an initial cost of US$491 million, but including the transfer taxes and the mandatory capital expenditure, the initial outlay of Silverstein was mentioned in the offer documents as US$896 million. Thus, Silverstein put in equity of US$125 million and the balance was lent by GMAC.

The mortgage loan is the only collateral backing up the certificates, and the leasehold interest in the WTC is the collateral backing up the mortgage.

The following Table 13.4 summarizes information about the collateral:

Table 13.4   Summary information for case study

Summary Information			
Loan Amount	$563,000,000	Appraised Value PSF	$117.90
Appraised Value	$1,200,000,000	Initial Loan PSF	$55.32
Date as of which Appraised	July 10, 2001	Maturity Date Loan PSF	$51.63
Property Size	10,178,056 square feet	Extended Maturity Date Loan PSF	$49.82
U/W NCF DSCR	2.53x	Initial LTV	46.92%
		Maturity Date LTV	43.79%
		Extended Maturity Date LTV	42.25%
		Initial LTV Ratio:	62.81%

The following is the NCF computation for the property as disclosed in the offer documents:

Table 13.5 Computation of net cash flow for case study

	1997 (1)	1998 (1)	1999 (1)	2000 (1)	U/W
Revenues					
Base Rental Income	$187,212,000	$216,258,000	$232,832,000	$252,542,000	$294,573,193
Recoveries	57,277,000	48,428,000	48,105,000	52,626,000	51,954,956
Other Income	11,185,000	12,646,000	15,144,000	12,975,000	13,806,311
Total Income	**$255,674,000**	**$277,332,000**	**$296,081,000**	**$318,143,000**	**$360,334,460**
Expenses					
Property Management Fees and Administration	15,342,000	18,136,000	17,762,000	18,511,000	6,626,745
Rent Under Net Lease	–	–	–	–	93,500,000
PA Percentage Rent	–	–	–	–	1,556,635
PILOT Payments	17,980,000	19,223,000	19,881,000	20,338,000	20,948,140
Insurance	4,600,000	3,994,000	2,679,000	3,168,000	10,116,582
Operating Expenses	122,810,000	124,508,000	121,686,000	133,489,000	110,340,000
Total Operating Expenses	**$160,732,000**	**$165,861,000**	**$162,008,000**	**$175,506,000**	**$243,088,102**
Net Operating Income	94,942,000	111,471,000	134,073,000	142,637,000	117,246,359
Capital Reserve	–	–	–	–	2,544,514
Retenanting Costs	–	–	–	–	15,081,000
Net Cash Flow	**$94,942,000**	**$111,471,000**	**$134,073,000**	**$142,637,000**	**$99,620,845**

The loan

GMAC Commercial Mortgage Corporation (Originator) gave a loan of US$563 billion to several shell companies incorporated as Delaware LLCs, belonging, under a complex tiering of ownership to Larry Silverstein on July 24, 2001. Each borrower is a single purpose company.[4] The loan has several components "Component A-1," "Component A-2A," "Component A-2B," "Component B,"

"Component C," "Component D," "Component E," "Component F," "Component G" and "Component H". The initial loan amount for each of these components corresponds to the initial funding raised by the respective certificates of the same class. The components carry interest based on LIBOR, which corresponds to the interest rates on the certificates, and interest strip retained by the originator and certain administration costs. However, the amortization of the loans is based on an assumed interest rate of 5.75% and an amortization period of 30 years. This means, the interest element for each month will be based on the LIBOR-based floating rate, while the remaining of the pre-fixed amortization amount will go towards principal.

The rates of interest for various components are LIBOR + the following:

Table 13.6   Coupon rates for various securities in case study

Component	Component Margin	Administrative Cost Rate	Class X-1 Strip Rate	Class X-2 Strip Rate	Gross Component Margin for Due Dates up to Prepayment Release Date	Gross Component Margin for Due Dates after Prepayment Release Date
A-1	0.22%	0.0536%	0.80%	0	1.073600%	0.273600%
A-2A	0.37%	0.0536%	0.80%	0	1.223600%	0.423600%
A-2B	0.37%	0.0536%	0.80%	0	1.660615%	0.860615%
B	0.60%	0.0536%	0.80%	0.437015%	1.890615%	1.090615%
C	1.10%	0.0536%	0.80%	0.437015%	2.390615%	1.590615%
D	1.35%	0.0536%	0.80%	0.437015%	2.640615%	1.840615%
E	1.90%	0.0536%	0.80%	0.437015%	3.190615%	2.390615%
F	2.25%	0.0536%	0.80%	0.437015%	3.540615%	2.740615%
G	2.60%	0.0536%	0.80%	0.437015%	3.890615%	3.090615%
H	3.00%	0.0536%	0.80%	0.437015%	4.290615%	3.490615%

Based on a weighted average of the above, the loan comes to Silverstein at the rate of LIBOR + 2.1276%

As with most CMBS loans, the loan is not fully amortizing over its maturity and will leave a large principal balance. In the present case, the loan will leave a balance of US$525,537,687 one month prior to its Maturity Date. The maturity is September 2006. This obviously explains the large mortgage-balance. In other words, the borrower will be required to make a large balloon payment on the maturity date, unless the borrower is able to seek refinancing on that date.

In addition, the loan is non-recourse; the lender has recourse against the property but not against the borrower. This, in any case, is given by the nature of the borrower as a limited purpose company.

The mortgage loan is unseasoned and was originated almost contemporaneously with the issuance of the certificates.

There is an additional capital expenditure loan of $200 million by GMAC to the same project that is not covered by the present issuance.

Prepayment protection

The mortgage loan in this instance is for a period of 60 months and is protected against prepayment up for to 54 months. There is a prepayment penalty for any prepayment over this lock-in period and thereafter the prepayment can be made without penalty.

The certificates

As noted the transaction is a pass-through, thus beneficial interest certificates have been issued by the trustee. The issuance was under rule 144A, which means it was offered to qualified institutional buyers on a private placement basis.

The terms of the certificates provided for a pass-through by the 9th of each calendar month, starting October 2001.

Particulars of the certificates are shown in Table 13.7:

Table 13.7 Particulars of various securities in case study

Class	Exp. Rating S&P/Fitch	Initial certificate balance	Pass-Through Rate	Expected WAL with No Extension (Yrs)	Cumul. LTV Ratio (%)	Cumul. DSCR
A-1	AAA/AAA	$38,140,000	L + 0.22%	2.71	27.30%	4.35x
A-2	AAA/AAA	$289,260,000	L + 0.37%	5.06	27.30%	4.35x
X-1	AAA/AAA	$563,000,000	0.80%	N/A	N/A	N/A
X-2	AAA/AAA	$505,600,000	0.44%	N/A	N/A	N/A
B	AA/AA	$50,975,000	L + 0.60%	5.06	31.50%	3.76x
C	A/A	$68,825,000	LIBOR + 1.10%	5.06	37.30%	3.18x
D	A−/A−	$23,000,000	L + 1.35%	5.06	39.20%	3.03x
E	BBB+/BBB+	$12,800,000	L + 1.90%	5.06	40.30%	2.95x
F	BBB+/BBB+	$12,600,000	L+ 2.25%	5.06	41.30%	2.87x
G	BBB+/BBB	$28,300,000	L + 2.60%	5.06	43.70%	2.72x
H	BBB/BBB−	$39,100,000	L + 3.00%	5.06	46.90%	2.53x

Retention of interests by the originator

There are several retained interests of the originator in the present case. There are two retained interest rate strips – X-1 and X-2. The servicing fees are not very high – 0.05%. The originator holds Class Q and R.

In addition, the originator is also the initial holder of classes F, G and H.[5]

Liquidity and credit enhancements

We have earlier mentioned that the insurance coverage itself is an essential loan-level credit enhancement. Liquidity reserves are also important for this type of transaction. It is a fact that after the 9-11 tragedy, the transaction could pay on the October and perhaps also the November 2001 dates solely out of liquidity reserves.

There are several liquidity and credit enhancements in this transaction:

- The $95 million liquidity reserve is a sort of undisbursed loan amount by the lender.
- A credit support reserve, in which all surplus cash left after mortgage payments are deposited. Any equity distribution – amounts calculated to give a 10% return on the borrower's equity that are to be made out of this account – can be withheld until there is any other item of priority requiring payment.
- In addition, there are several reserves required either to maintain the property or to meet statutory obligations.

Servicer advances also ensure liquidity. The servicer is required to make advances equal to scheduled monthly payments of both the interest and the principal. If the servicer fails to make the required advances, the trustee is required to make the advances.

The aftermath

What happened to the WTC shortly after the deal is well known, but this deal has so far remained unaffected by the tragedy. Initially there were concerns as to whether the insurance companies would find an excuse under the exclusion clauses, but it was generally thought that there was no specific exclusion for acts of terrorism under the insurance coverage.

By December 2001, all the insurers had paid their initial $75 million and the borrowers continued to pay under the mortgage loans uninterrupted. By January 31, 2002, the insurers had paid advances of $150 million.

In April 2002 GMAC arrived at a settlement with Silverstein on use of the insurance proceeds: "GMAC Commercial Mortgage Corporation, in its capacity as servicer for Wells Fargo Bank, Minnesota, Trustee, for the above referenced transaction, has agreed to settle the matter of GMAC Commercial Mortgage Corporation vs. 1 World Trade Center LLC et al. The lawsuit related to the $563 million mortgage loan GMACCM made to the Silverstein borrowers secured by the World Trade Center buildings 1, 2, 4 and 5 which forms the basis of the above-referenced securitization transaction. The dispute centered on to what extent the Silverstein borrowers had the right to use insurance proceeds for the payment of their ongoing expenses. Under the terms of the settlement, these insurance proceeds will be used to continue to pay rent due to the Port Authority of New York and New Jersey, PILOT payments, insurance payments, and debt service for the Mortgage Loan. The agreement calls for a portion of the remaining insurance proceeds to be used for ongoing expenses of the Silverstein Borrowers, such as legal and consulting fees and management expenses, and for a portion to be retained by GMACCM as additional security to be held in a newly established reserve security account as well as for the payment of expenses of the lender. The agreement relates only to insurance proceeds designated by the insureds to business interruption losses and does not pertain to property damage losses."

By July 2002, $644 million had been received from the insurers. It seems the transaction was terminated in January 2004.

Case Study: Canary Wharf – A typical U.K. CMBS

As with RMBS, U.K. CMBS transactions differ from U.S. deals in their structure. U.K. transactions use mostly loan-type structures with an intermediary lending company giving a loan to the borrower company, and the latter creating security interest in favor of the former.

Introduction to the transaction

This transaction is the securitization of several office buildings under construction[6] and the source of liquidation of the securities are rentals out of pre-let office space. A prime office area close to the City of London, the office space in this property had been pre-let to several leading investment banks and law firms, who signed rental contracts and agreed to start paying pre-fixed rentals irrespective of whether the construction was completed by that date or not. Therefore, the risk of completion of construction has been shifted to the tenants.

Like the WTC securitization, this is also a case of trophy property.[7]

The present case covers the following issuance of mortgage debentures by Canary Wharf Finance II PLC made in February 2002:

Table 13.8 Securities in UK CMBS case study

Class	Face value	Rating	Type	Maturity
A1	£527m	AAA	Fixed	2033
A3	£200m	AAA	Fixed	2037
A5	US$579m	AAA	FS*	2033
B	£150m	AA	Fixed	2033

Canary Wharf Finance II plc had earlier issued £475 million of fixed rate, stepped rate and floating rate notes in May 2000 and a further £875 million in June 2001. This case covers the issuance of debentures in Feb 2002, which is the second "tap" issue, including the US$ issue that amounted to £1.257 billion. That is to say, total funding raised in this issue under this vehicle was US$2.607 billion.

The structure of the transaction is the same as that for the original transaction.

Transaction structure

At first look, the transaction structure of Canary Wharf II PLC looks quite complicated with a plethora of loans and parties. Part of the complexity is that this is an existing transaction on which further collateral and financing has been mounted.

The simple vertical structure of the transaction is: Canary Wharf Finance II Plc (Issuer) has issued the debentures and raised funding from the capital markets. The issuer gives a loan to CW Lending II (Borrower), which in turn gives a loan to CWCB Finance (Intermediate Borrower). The Intermediate Borrower lends to the subsidiaries that are to own and let the properties under construction, called Charging Subsidiaries. As there are some existing charging subsidiaries, the structural diagram talks of Original Charging Subsidiaries, New Charging Subsidiaries and Second New Charging Subsidiaries.

The offer documents say the funding so raised by the charging subsidiaries will be used to repay the existing loans, or for other purposes, by the Canary Wharf group.

The would-be tenants of the would-be properties are, therefore, the tenants of the Second New Charging subsidiaries, which will direct the tenants to deposit the rentals into a Rental Receipt Account.

The properties

As said before, the properties are under various stages of construction. There are three basic contingencies for a building under construction: (a) What if the building is not completed on schedule? (b) What if the work is withheld because the contractee does not have required funding to carry on with the construction? (c) What if, post construction, the buildings are not let out. The transaction structure takes care of the first two risks. The third risk, in view of the prime nature of the property and the previous 100% underwriting experience, is negligible.

The failure to complete construction on schedule is answered by rental undertakings. The undertaking for rentals, in case the construction is not completed on schedule, has been given by Rental Undertaking facilitators: Lehman Brothers Holdings Inc., Morgan Stanley Dean Witter & Co., Citibank, N.A. and The Royal Bank of Scotland plc. The facilitators, in turn, have an indemnity agreement with Heron Quay. Therefore, the risk is ultimately with the Canary Wharf group, but is credit-enhanced by independent undertakings from reputed investment banks. In addition, advance payments to contractors are to be made only against a bond whereby the contractor is obliged to refund to the contractee the amount of advance, less value of work done, for contract not completed on schedule.

For DS5 and HQ2, the rental undertakings are further supported, for DS5, by a credit-linked note, and for HQ2, by a guarantee of a monoline guarantor.

As for any lack of funding by Canary Wharf group leading to a disruption of the work, it is provided in the structure that Canary Wharf group will put in 110% of the projected cost of construction on or before the issue closing date.

Cash flows

The primary source of cash flow with the charging subsidiaries is the rentals and the payments by the rental-undertaking providers, as well as the guarantors/ credit-risk mitigators as discussed above.

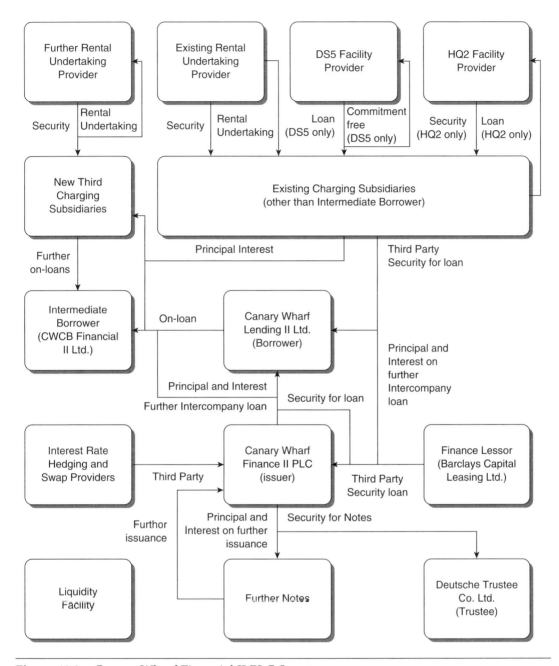

Figure 13.3   Canary Wharf Financial II PLC Structure

By way of liquidity enhancement, the transaction is also supported by a liquidity facility granted by Barclays Bank.

Investing in CMBS: Performance of CMBS

The risks in investing in CMBS are different from those in RMBS. As noted earlier, prime RMBS transactions have (a) negligible to non-existent default risk; and (b) a substantial amount of prepayment risk. For CMBS, the situation is virtually opposite – (a) there is a degree of default risk as the repayment of the loan is contingent upon the performance of the CRE; and (b) there is a negligible prepayment risk as the CRE loans typically have a protection against prepayment.

Prepayment protection in CRE loans

The protection against prepayments in CRE loans could come in several ways:

(a) Prepayment lockout: A certain lock-in/lock-out period during which the borrower cannot simply prepay the loan;
(b) Yield-maintenance clauses, that is, even if the loan is prepaid, the borrower is required to pay so much penalty as to maintain the original yield, after taking into account the prevailing yields. Thus, the mark-to-market losses on the loan are reimbursed by the borrower for a prepayment.
(c) Defeasance: Defeasance is a sort of prepayment of a liability by creating a sinking fund, or investing the required amount of money in acceptable collateral, such that the returns from the collateral repay the loan instalments. The effect is the same as discounting the loan instalments are prevailing yields from the specified investment.
(d) Another alternative is for the lender to charge a fixed penalty as a percent of the outstanding principal.

Delinquency in CMBS

As a study of prepayments is important for RMBS, so a study of delinquency rates is important for CMBS deals. CMBS investments are based on projected delinquency rates. It is generally believed that the delinquency rates start from 0% in the first year (no loan is delinquent when it is given or securitized) and the rate peaks around the 5th or 6th year, tapering off gradually as the mortgage matures.

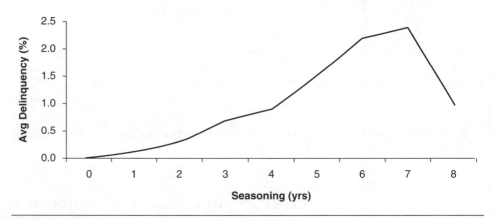

Figure 13.4   Avg Delinquency %–All Property Types

Nomura Fixed Income Research has done a study of mortgage loans from 1994 to 2002 to test the above hypothesis.[8] It concluded that the delinquency rates for different property types are different, and the research largely affirms the above understanding.

Performance of CMBS vs. other collateral classes

Over the last few years, performance of CMBS has been excellent, measured by most of the possible analytical measures. One, spreads on CMBS have been coming down. Two, the rating transition studies of most rating agencies show there have been a substantial number of upgrades relative to downgrades. Three, there have been a few cases of default, but wherever defaults have been there, recovery rates have been excellent.

Upgrades for CMBS transactions do not necessarily mean happiness. In several cases, upgrades happen as a result of defeasance of the underlying mortgage loan by the borrower. If the borrower finds attractive opportunities of refinancing the loan, and he is restrained by prepayment lock-out or penalties, he may defease the loan by buying and pledging some such securities that upon maturity will fully repay the loan. Thus, he sees a release of the mortgaged property by replacing the collateral with securities. As these securities are typically either Treasuries or AAA-rated securities, the rating agencies are forced to upgrade the rating of all the tranches in view of the rating of the collateral.

Nomura Fixed Income Research in a paper[9] compared the performance of CMBS with other collateral classes. It compared the spreads on AAA CMBS,

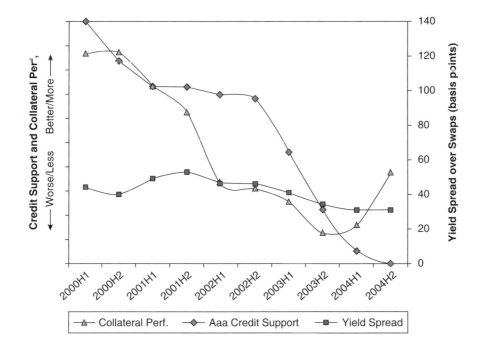

Figure 13.5   CMBS Trends

the credit support levels for AAA CMBS paper, and the performance of commercial property loans based on 60 to 90 days delinquency, foreclosure and REO[10] holdings. It says: "Of all the product categories, CMBS arguably appears to present the worst story during sample period.[11] Credit support levels declined significantly and collateral credit performance worsened as well. Meanwhile, yield spreads on CMBS actually *tightened* to a slight degree. In addition, gradual changes in underwriting practices and deal structures made newer deals somewhat weaker than older deals from an investor's perspective. Thus, from a value perspective, seemingly got worse along all dimensions during the sample period." Figure 13.5 shows the performance of CMBS as analyzed by the Nomura Fixed Income report.

Notes

1 See regular rating transition studies of Standard & Poor's. Also see Vinod Kothari's securitization site at: http://vinodkothari.com and later chapter on Investing in Securitization Transactions.

2 Nomura Fixed Income Research: *Tale of Two Cities: US Fixed Income Research Mid-year Review*, July 2002

3 Based on http://www.cmalert.com/Public/MarketPlace/Ranking/index.cfm?files=disp&article_id=79396, last visited October 15, 2005

4 This means the borrower is not a "special purpose company" as it owns the leasehold interest in the property and operates the same, but is limited to that purpose. Hence, it is called single purpose or a *limited purpose* company.

5 Offer Circular, page 52.

6 "The transaction represents the first securitization ever of uncompleted buildings." – A Clifford Chance Press release of June 12, 2001.

7 "After the terrorist attacks on the World Trade Center on September 11 there was some concern that securitizations of trophy real estate developments could suffer, either from fear of attacks or a downturn in investment banking. However, rating agencies have said subsequently that Canary Wharf's debt has not been affected." Finance Times (UK) report dated February 12, 2002.

8 Nomura Fixed Income Research: *Tale of Two Cities: US Fixed Income Research Mid-year Review*, July 2002.

9 Structured Finance Trends – Yield Spreads, Credit Support, and Collateral Performance – The Big Picture, June 27, 2005.

10 REO – Real estate owned, a term implying a real estate property taken over by a mortgagee.

11 The study relates to year 2000 to 2004.

Chapter 14

Credit Card Securitization

At first look, credit card receivables seem to be too short term an asset to be amenable to securitization, but not surprisingly credit card issuers have made good use of securitization markets almost everywhere. Credit card receivables are short term, but they are revolved into creation of fresh receivables on a fairly steady basis. If a card user swipes the card, the amount that he utilizes is payable within a certain time. However, a credit card is a revolving line of credit. Therefore, they represent a steady stream of cash flows, and are a good candidate for securitization.

Though unsecured, credit card companies make high interest income on account of the finance charges, fees, late fees and periodic membership fees. They have put in place systems whereby the card company has a constant watch on the account, and can immediately block a card or reduce its credit for delinquencies. The maximum amount that can be lost on a card is thus controlled. Thus, over time, card companies have positioned themselves very well to make money out of a very diversified base of plastic money users.

For credit card issuers, securitization is one of the very important avenues of sourcing funds, as most traditional financiers have shunned taking funding exposure on credit card receivables: "Credit card companies rely on securitization for funding and, if the window to the asset-backed market were to close over an extended period, their growth models would fail. However, the securitization market has proved resilient even in the face of the disruptions caused by Russia's default and the demise of Long-Term Capital Management in 1998 and the events of September 11 2001."[1] The receivables are unsecured, though they are very widely diversified.

As a component of the ABS market, credit cards, along with auto loans, are supposed to form the two pillars of the ABS market. From the viewpoint of resilience, the credit card market has been tested for quite some time; practices have largely been standardized and the default and downgrade history so far, barring some cases of fraud, has been quite satisfactory.

Credit card securitizations use a revolving structure where the amount of principal collected during a certain period is rotated back to the originator to acquire fresh receivables. The amortization starts after a fixed period. The revolving method used to securitize credit card receivables is also used for several other short-term receivables such as consumer finance and home equity lines of credit.

Nature of credit card debt

Credit card debt is essentially consumer revolving credit. The consumers view credit card and home equity loans as alternatives and many of them prefer home equity loans to credit cards in view of the longer term permitted by the latter.

From this viewpoint, credit card securitization has largely the same features as home equity loans.

A Deutsche Bank research paper lucidly points out some interesting features of credit card debt and credit card securitizations thus: "In the world of investing, credit card ABS are unique because credit card lending itself is unique. Unlike virtually any other consumer lender, a credit card company may, unilaterally, change the risk/reward relationship of its business at any time. For the most part a credit card lender can increase yield on its existing portfolio by changing the financing rate charged, as well as by changing late fees, overlimit fees and annual fees, all of which can be quite significant. The lender can reduce risk by closing accounts or preemptively lowering a cardholder's credit line. Moreover, credit card companies conduct constant and automated surveillance of daily purchase activity (how much, how often and where individual cardholders are spending money); a borrower's activity with other lenders can also be monitored through regular updates from the various credit bureaus. Relative to any other type of consumer lender, the credit card lender in many ways has a better and more current understanding of a borrower's creditworthiness, and greater flexibility to respond to changes as they occur."[2]

The credit card industry is internally a highly concentrated industry – larger players have the economies of scale, and as part of larger banking networks also the advantage of scope. Obviously, the credit card securitization market is also a highly concentrated market.

An overview of the market

The first case of credit card securitization dates back to 1986 when Salomon Brothers applied the fast emerging securitization device to buy credit card receivables from Banc One and sell them in the form of Certificates for Amortising Revolving Debts (CARDs) in a structured, credit-enhanced transaction. Since then, the market has never looked back. Credit card ABS has been the largest component of the U.S. ABS market for several years, but has

Table 14.1 U.S. credit card ABS Outstanding

	Credit Card	% of Total ABS
1995	153.1	48.4%
1996	180.7	44.7%
1997	214.5	40.0%
1998	236.7	32.4%
1999	257.9	28.6%
2000	306.3	28.6%
2001	361.9	28.2%
2002	397.9	25.8%
2003	401.9	23.7%
2004	390.7	21.4%
2005 (Q2)	365.2	19.6%

Source: Bond Market Association

lately given the first position to home equity loans, primarily due to the massive growth of the latter collateral class.

Credit card securitizations have been a significant asset class in Europe as well, although in terms of percentage of the total ABS market, it is much smaller. In the first half of 2003, for example, credit card ABS issuance was 9% of the total ABS market, excluding MBS transactions.[3] In 2004, credit cards formed 6% of the European non-MBS issuance.[4] The following table by Standard & Poor's shows the European credit card ABS data:

Table 14.2 Development of Credit Card Receivables Transactions

Year	Originators	Trusts	Transactions
1995	1	1	1
1996	1	1	3
1997	2	2	5
1998	2	2	8
1999	3	3	12
2000	4	4	17
2001	5	6	20
2002	7	9	27
2003	8	10	34

Transaction structure

A credit card debt is a retail asset. The credit card account is an ongoing service between the credit card company and the customer. When a card is used, the card company generates receivables from the customer; it is this receivable that is securitized. Therefore, the legal relation between the card company and the cardholder remains intact, and the card receivables are transferred to the trust.

The accounts that will be transferred to the trust are selected based on selection criteria. The criteria are mostly standard and would rule out only such accounts as have been treated as delinquent. For example, the following criteria may be taken as a sample:

An account is eligible, if on the date of transfer, the account:

- was in existence and maintained with the seller;
- is payable in U.S. dollars (or the currency of interest);
- is an account for which the customer has provided, as his most recent billing address, an address located in the U.S. (or a jurisdiction of interest);
- has not been classified by the seller as cancelled, counterfeit, deleted, fraudulent, stolen or lost;
- has either been originated by the seller or acquired by the seller from another institution; and
- has not been charged-off by the seller in its customary and usual manner for charging-off such account as of the cut-off date and, with respect to additional accounts, as of their date of designation for inclusion in the trust.

Revolving asset structure

The use of the revolving device, where over a certain reinvestment period, principal collections are not used to pay down the securities but are used to buy new receivables and *replenish* the principal balance of the asset pool, is not limited to credit cards. Apart from several other short-term assets, the revolving feature is increasingly used in several other cases, including CDOs.

A revolving asset structure is not really a future flow securitization. In a future flow transaction, the receivables transferred to the SPV at the inception is much less than the funding raised from the investors, as the transaction relies on receivables to be generated and sold in the future. For revolving transactions, however, at the inception the value of the asset transferred to the SPV equals (or, taking care of over-collateralization, exceeds) the funding raised from the investors. However, there are assets acquired by the SPV on an on-going basis until the amortization period starts.

A revolving asset securitization is, therefore, akin to a revolving credit arranged by the originator. On an ongoing basis, the originator will be able to avail of funding until the amortization period starts.

The portfolio of assets represents a revolving credit to consumers in which the outstanding principal may fall, so the trust deed contains provisions that the cash collected from the consumers will be trapped in the SPV unless the total amount of receivables in the trust is at least equal or greater than the total outstanding funding.

Seller's interest

In addition, to cover the contingency of the assets suffering a decline, a buffer is kept in the form of seller interest. The seller interest is the excess of receivables sold by the seller into the trust, over the total amount of funding outstanding. This excess is not by way of over-collateralization (which if required, may be additional), as the seller's interest is not subordinated to the investors. The seller's interest also levels off temporary fluctuations in the card balances, such as more card purchases during a holiday or festive season. The seller's interest also absorbs dilutions in the transferred accounts due to non-cash reasons, such as a reversal of debit to the card due to return of goods and processing errors.

Discrete and master trust structure

Credit card securitizations could either use a discrete trust or a master trust structure. Recently, the master trust structure has been the most widely used structure.

Where it is a discrete trust, the receivables transferred are to the extent required for the resulting securities, beneficially owned by the investors. A master trust uses a generic trust out of which securities can be created as and when demanded.[5]

In master trust mechanics, the master trust is an umbrella body covering various issuances under the trust. It may be likened to the extension of the originator's balance sheet. There is no demarcation of the assets attributable to particular issuer trusts or series trusts – the assets are held under a common melting pot of the master trust from where pro-rated allocation is done. The allocation of cash flow by the master trust to the various issuances or series is very similar to a corporation equitably allocating its cash flow to its various liabilities.

Allocation of interest

The allocation of the collections by the master trust to the various issuer trusts is done based on the outstanding amount of the relevant trusts, and the outstanding seller's interest. The finance charges and the fee income, net of the servicing fee and the charge offs, is distributed to each series. From this allocated amount, each series takes care of its own coupon, and the excess spread in the series is dealt with (retained or returned as the seller's interest), as per the terms of the scheme. Most master trusts also provide for utilization of the surplus excess spread, that is, over what is required as a condition to the rating, as a support to the other series under the master trust. This is a sort of a "loan" from one series to another, as the amount so lent by the lending series is recoverable whenever the recipient series has enough excess spread of its own. Thus, there is a cross-collateralization of the excess spread from one series to the other, implying an additional support granted by the seller to the series in need of support, as the excess spread was returnable to the seller. In addition, as a levelling provision, the master trust documents may also provide for the pro-rated allocation of the excess spread of each of the schemes, should the allocated interest in a particular month fall short of the coupon required to service investors.

Thus, the master trust method provides an inter-series enhancement to the investors.

Allocation of principal and prepayments

The various series under the master trust might have differing requirements of principal for amortization. Those that are still under a reinvestment period will not need any principal at all; thus, the principal is first allocated proportional to the outstanding investment of the series that are under an amortization period, either scheduled or early amortization. Notably, the proportions of "outstanding investment" here would mean proportions obtained as at the time when amortization started; otherwise, the schemes which have already partly amortized their outstanding investment will see a reduced allocation. Once again, the surplus principal so allocated to the various schemes may be distributed to the schemes in deficit – the schemes that have hit early amortization triggers. The remaining surplus principal is the principal available for replenishment, and is therefore released for purchasing assets from the originator.

Development of the master trust structure

The master trust structure was first developed by Citibank in 1991. In a discrete securitization of credit card receivables, to have a bullet repayment of the securities, there would have to be a substantial accumulation period. The creation of the master trust structure was a creative but natural solution to create asset-liability mismatches and to manage the same at the master trust level.

The master trust may be viewed as the larger balance sheet of the card issuer. The master trust has a substantial chunk of assets in it, funded by various transactions at different points of time.

In U.K. transactions as well, the master trust structure is almost universally used.

Delinked structure

A fully-ramped structure, the traditional picture of a securitization transaction, envisages simultaneous issuance of senior and subordinated securities. For master trusts, the single trust allows creation of various securities at different times, so the next stage of development is perfectly logical – the issue of senior and subordinated securities is delinked. In other words, subject to satisfaction of certain conditions, the senior securities may be issued without issue of subordinated securities that may be issued at an opportune time.

In a usual "linked" structure, the master trust issues matching amount of notes to the issuing vehicle. Assume a master trust has assets of $1 billion, and we desire to raise a funding of $200 million. Let us suppose, the Class A, B and C sizes to get the desired ratings are respectively 85%, 10% and 5%. To allow for issue of these securities, the master trust issues to the issuing vehicle, say SPV A, three classes of notes of $170 million, $20 million, and $10 million, respectively. The balance of the assets in the master trust represents the seller's share. Having thus acquired a $200 million share in the master trust, the SPV issues a like amount of notes to investors. In other words, for each Class A of funding vehicle, there is an identifiable Class B and Class C.

The "delinked structure" creates a common funding melting pot, which may continue issuing various series of Class A notes at different points of time, as long as there is a required extent of "collateralized interest," the value of assets exceeding the total amount of Class A funding.

One of the important differences between the traditional master trust structure and the de-linked structure is that, in the latter case, as the various class A series are issued from the same vehicle, the amount of excess spread for each series is the same. Also, there is an automatic sharing of the excess spread of the entire asset pool by each of the issued classes.

There are several features of the de-linked structure that merit a mention:

- Let us suppose the required subordination level for a AAA rating in a transaction is 10%, and for an A rating is 4%. In other words, we may have Class A of $90, Class B of $6, and Class C of $4:

Table 14.3   Required amount of subordination

	Rating	Required subordination	Size
Class A	AAA	10%	90
Class B	A	4%	6
Class C	None	0%	4
Total funding			100

- However, the issuer finds an opportunity of issuing Class C notes of $10. the delinked structure allows the issuer to issue Class C notes of $10. Hence, the total funding of the issuer vehicle now is:

Table 14.4   Actual amount of securities issued

	Actual size	Encumbered	Unencumbered
Class A	90		
Class B	6	6	0
Class C	10	4	6
Total funding	106		

The subordination required by way of Class C was only $4, the actual amount of Class C being $10, so the difference is "unencumbered," meaning it is available for further subordination to other issuances of Class A or Class B.

- Based on this available amount of subordination, the issuer may anytime create further Class A securities. The further amount of Class A securities that may be issued is:

Table 14.5   Further securities that may be issued

Only Class A	54
Class A & B	
Class A	135
Class B	9

- The delinked structure makes use of *scaling/sliding* credit enhancement. The meaning of sliding enhancement is that as long as there is sufficient subordination available to Class A, it does not matter what combination of Class B and C is issued by the issuer. For example, in the table above, if a $6 Class C is unencumbered, it may be used either for issuing Class A only in which case new class A-2 is $54 (10% subordination of Class C – the total subordination required for AAA rating), or the issuer may create Classes A and B, both in which the respective sizes are $135 and $9 – one may see that here also, both the securities have the required subordination for their respective rating.
- The concept of scaling enhancement is that if Class B notes, for instance, were unencumbered, their requirement of subordination from Class C is limited only to the extent Class B provides subordination to Class A. For instance, in the above example, if the actual size of Class B were $10 instead of $6, the size of credit enhancement required from Class C would be scaled down to 4% of the total asset pool, and not (10*4/6).

Components of a credit card structure

Below we discuss the various components of cash inflows and outflows/losses that impact the credit of a credit card portfolio. Notably, apart from the uniqueness of these components, the credit card debt itself is different in a way from regular loans, as it is a revolving credit.

Portfolio yield

The portfolio yield is the rate of return on the credit card portfolio, and in the context of securitization, those parts of income transferred to the trust. Typically, in almost every transaction, the credit card issuer transfers the finance charges, fees collected from the cardholders including late fees, over-limit fees, charges for bounced cheques, interchange or merchant discount (the discount deducted on payments to the merchants), and recoveries on previous charge-offs. Understandably, this yield differs from period to period and there is no fixed rate of return for credit card debt.

Here are the statistics for MBNA's master trust II:

Table 14.6 MBNA Master Credit Card Trust II Portfolio Statistics*

	2002	*2001*	*2000*	*1999*
Portfolio yield (%)	17.94	19.38	19.15	18.44
Avg. monthly payment rate (%)	13.63	13.03	13.01	13.17
Delinquencies of 30 days or more (%)	5.55	5.16	4.72	4.63
Net losses (%)	5.55	5.24	5.10	4.93

*Twelve months ended Dec. 31.

Source: S&P's presale report for MBNA Credit Card Master Note Trust $1 billion floating-rate Class A (2003–2) notes

The portfolio yield for U.S. credit card banks has stabilized in the 18–20% range. Moody's Investor Service published an industry average of the credit card yields of rated credit card securitization transactions – a total of $325 billion in credit card debt over 255 rated transactions.

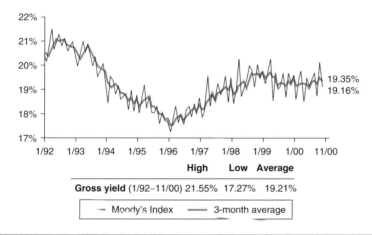

Figure 14.1 Portfolio yields of U.S. credit card banks

Source: Moody's Credit Card index

Rating agency Fitch also captures key portfolio performance index regularly in its newsletter *Credit Card Movers and Shakers*. The indices until mid-2003 are reflected in the figure below:

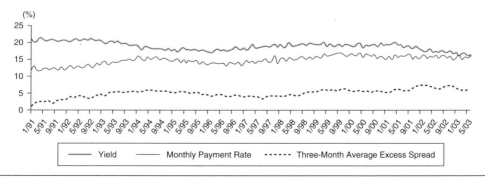

Figure 14.2 Fitch ratings credit card performance indexes

As may be noted, the yield has increased with increasing delinquency and charge offs and due to late fees. Similar data are available about European securitization, for example the following is from a report[6] by rating agency Standard & Poor's:

Table 14.7   Standard & Poor's European Credit Card Quality Indexes

	June 2001	December 2001	June 2002	December 2002	June 2003
Outstandings (£) million	13,916.83	14,416.68	16,817.68	18,800.27	21,908.60
Yield (%)	17.0	17.7	15.8	18.3	17.1
Charge-offs (%)	3.4	4.2	4.3	3.7	3.8
Weighted base rate (%)	5.3	4.0	4.0	4.0	3.8
Excess spread (%)	8.3	9.5	7.6	10.6	9.6
Delinquencies (%)	4.3	4.4	4.3	4.0	4.0
Payment rate (%)	19.1	18.0	16.3	15.3	18.0

Charge-offs

By the very nature of the credit card debt, there is a high amount of charge-offs, that is, debt written off as bad by the industry. There are periodical fluctuations in the loss rate reflecting the prevailing economic situations – unemployment and economic insecurity in general.

The Moody's index of 255 rated credit card securitization transactions also maps the weighted average charge-offs, given in the figure below:

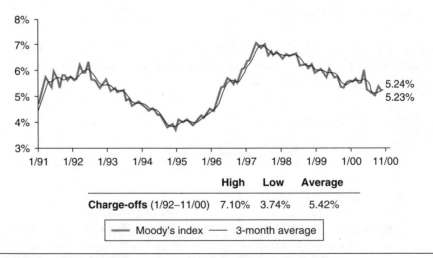

Figure 14.3   Charge-offs in select credit card deals

Source: Moody's Credit Card Index

The charge-off rate on credit cards is a sort of a barometer of consumer behavior. In June 2003, the U.S. charge-off rate reached 6.79%, which was the highest over a 5-year period. Fitch Ratings captures[7] credit card charge-off index as well as 60-day delinquency in an index below:

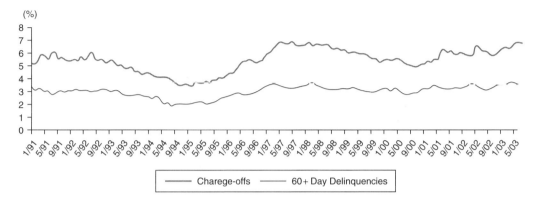

Figure 14.4   Fitch ratings credit card charge-off index

The charge-off rate also greatly differs between prime and sub-prime issuances. For sub-prime cards, for example, the charge-off rate in the month of June 2003 was 17.53%.

In addition, industry analysts also say the charge-off rate is related to the vintage of the card – how long the cardholder has been enrolled. It is believed that the charge-off rate starts from nil at the origination and peaks to something like 9% in the 18–24th month, and thereafter, settles at about 6% or the industry average.

Credit scores and the charge-off rate

Credit card origination is done partly by the data in possession of the card originators, and partly relying on a personal credit rating bureau. A personal credit rating bureau supplies credit score information on individuals, which, in most cases, is based on credit scoring models provided by Fair Isaac and Company. Hence, the scores provided by the said scoring agency are referred to as *FICO scores* – an individual with 500–800 points of score is considered to be quite good.

The correlation between FICO scores and the charge-off rate has been established by rating agencies. For example, a Standard & Poor's study shows the charge-off rate for bank cards to be close to 60% for a FICO score of less than 500, coming down to 0% for a score of over 800.

Payment rate

The payment rate is defined as the monthly payment of interest and principal, divided the total outstanding on the card. Card issuers typically require a certain minimum payment to be paid; in addition, cardholders are entitled to either clear off the full balance or any part thereof. The payment rate is relevant to a securitization transaction as it determines the period it will take for a transaction to amortize once the amortization period starts. The Fitch graphic above reflects the average payment rate – at approximately 15%. A higher payment rate is a strong attribute for a portfolio.

Servicing fee and base rate

It is typical of credit card securitizers to fix a servicing fee of 2%. A base rate implies the total of the servicing fee and the coupon payable to the investors, such that the portfolio yield, minus the charge-off rate, minus the base rate is the excess spread.

The coupon itself may be a fixed or floating rate. Credit enhancement levels required for floating rate issuances are slightly higher than those for a fixed rate, as rating agencies also stress the index rate.

The analysis of all the factors affecting the excess spread – yield, charge-off and coupon – is important in a transaction, as the early amortization events are generally linked with the excess spread.

Early amortization triggers

Hitting an early amortization trigger obviously spells a liquidity crisis for the originator, as the line of funding dries up as the trigger is hit. Hence, it is very important for the originator to avoid hitting the trigger. Early amortization is also obviously a prepayment risk for the investors. It is therefore understandable that early amortization has been a remote event; there are only 0.02% (two to three) cases of early amortization so far.

One common trigger is based on the excess spread, computed based on a 3-month rolling average. If this average spread falls to zero, the transaction enters an early payout.

The other common stress variable is the *purchase rate*, that is, the rate at which new receivables are originated by the originator for purchase by the trust.

Decline in seller's interest is also commonly a trigger. A complete inventory of common early amortization triggers is:

Seller/Servicer Events

1. Failure or inability to make required deposits or payments;
2. Failure or inability to transfer receivables to the trust when necessary;
3. False representations or warranties that remain unremedied;
4. Certain events of default, bankruptcy, insolvency, or receivership of the seller or servicer;

Legal Events

5. Trust becomes classified as an "investment company" under the Investment Company Act of 1940 (relevant for U.S. transactions – in other cases, refer to other regulatory statements);

Performance Events

6. Three-month average of excess spread falls below zero;
7. Seller's participation falls below the required level;
8. Portfolio principal balance falls below the invested amount.

Subordination structure and C Class

Traditionally, the credit card ABS market, like most other ABS segments, has known only two classes of security the senior and the subordinated securities. The junior class is a credit enhancement to the senior class, and is normally not sold. If the issuer intended to sell the junior class as well, the common source of credit enhancement was external – letters of credit or guarantees from monoliners. Alternatively or simultaneously, a significant amount of cash collateral was provided as an enhancement.

"In 1993, Household Bank became the first credit card securitizer to replace a portion of its cash enhancement with receivables. The Class C structure was born."[8] The significant advantage of Class C was that it was not retained cash but an interest in the receivables. This avoided negative carry, as also allowed the originator to remove a larger part of the assets from the balance sheet. Initially, the C class was not typically sold off in the capital market but was placed with the traditional credit enhancers. However, in the mid-1990s, a section of investors started buying the Class C with the objective of yield enhancement.

Investor experience in credit cards

In 2001, for the first time the credit card ABS in the U.S. had a case of a default. "For the first time in ABS history, credit cards experienced ten downgrades in a year, more than all downgrades recorded over the past 15 years. However, these downgrades were limited to just one issuer: a furniture retailer with two transactions and four credit classes (with two of their subordinate credit classes eventually being further downgraded to default). The reasons for all downgrades were the poor performance of collateral and the low quality of the servicer. They were isolated events and not related to overall conditions in bank credit cards."[9]

Commercial Financial Services

A charged-off credit card transaction sponsored by Commercial Financial Services ("CFS") was downgraded in 1999. After its bankruptcy filing in December 1998, CFS was liquidated in June 1999. CFS had been the largest securitizer of charged-off credit card receivables.

NextCard

Following breach of certain regulatory conditions, NextCard was in 2001 denied the low-level recourse treatment for its capital,[10] consequently making it an undercapitalized institution. Soon after, on February 7, 2002, the Office of the Comptroller of the Currency (OCC) closed the bank and appointed the FDIC as receiver. The trustees for its securitizations took this as an early amortization event; however, the FDIC notified the trustee for NextCard's securitizations that an "early amortization based solely on the insolvency or the appointment of the FDIC as receiver is not enforceable against the FDIC."

After some time, rating agencies downgraded all the classes, including AAA class, of NextCard.

Notes

1 Mason, Howard K. and Rick L. Biggs: *Credit Card Securitization: A Quick Primer* May 2002. p. 1.
2 Deutsche Bank Global Securitization Research: *The Essential Guide to Credit Card As Bs and Cs* January 2001.
3 European Securitization Forum data.
4 *ibid.*
5 Refer to the subject index for discussion at other places in this book on master trust structure.
6 Standard and Poor's *European Structured Finance Report* July 2003.
7 Fitch Ratings: *Credit Card Movers and Shakers* July 2003.
8 Deutsche Bank Global Securitization Research, *ibid* p. 11.
9 Rating Transitions 2001: U.S. ABS Credit Ratings Endure the Test of Recession, S&P commentary dated January 14, 2002.
10 See for details, Chapter 21 on Regulatory Issues.

Chapter 15

Auto Loan Securitization

Auto loan securitization is essentially a retail collateral, as auto finance is essentially a variant of consumer finance. Other consumer finance receivables include the receivables arising out of typical consumer finance and installment credit transactions.

Forms of installment credit have been prime movers of auto sales in recent years. At certain phases in the economic cycle, auto finance becomes the most important way of selling vehicles. In most markets, a larger part of vehicles sales are installment-funded rather than bought with consumer equity. In the U.K., this percentage was measured at some 57%.

If auto financing is the key to auto sales, auto loan securitization is the key to refinancing of auto loan transactions. Speaking of the significance of auto loan securitization, a report by rating agency Fitch says: "Since the inception of the asset-backed securities (ABS) market, auto-backed securitization has been a vital part of the total ABS volume. After experiencing a decreasing market share during the last half of the 1990s, auto ABS's market presence increased, leading public ABS volume in 2000 and finishing second behind home equities in 2001, with US$75.3 billion in new issuance and 24.3% of total ABS volume. The vibrant economy over most of this period led to record vehicle sales, while growing corporate challenges aided securitization. Investors flocked to auto deals for their consistent performance, shorter average lives, and innovative structures, which satisfied investors' needs, in many ways replacing corporate bonds. In spite of the slowing economy and ongoing manufacturer difficulties, these traits are expected to continue the growth of auto loan securitization in the future."[1]

As the above quote says, auto loan securitization is today the second most important component of non-MBS securitization in the U.S.[2], and the scenario is the same elsewhere.

Forms of car funding

In various countries, there prevail different modes of funding of vehicles such as:

- Secured loans
- Conditional sales
- Hire purchase
- Financial leases
- Operating leases

In a broad sense, auto loan securitization covers each of these methods of funding, except for the last one. Operating leases and rentals are a different product in view of the nature of the cash flow and the inherent risks.

Auto loans securitization market

Outside the mortgage-backed market, auto loan securitization was the second application of securitization, the first being computer lease securitization. Ever since, auto loans have formed an important segment in ABS market not only in the U.S. but all markets. The interesting features of auto loan markets are high asset quality and ease in liquidation of delinquent receivables. The emergence of an alternative in the form of asset-backed commercial paper has reduced the significance of auto loan securitizations, but the activity in this segment is still important.

The U.S. market

As said before, auto ABS has traditionally been the number one component in the U.S. ABS market, but was relegated to second in 2001.

In terms of the quality of the collateral, the market mostly consists of prime auto ABS – about 70% of the total issuance falls in this category. Relatively, the share of sub-prime auto ABS has been increasing over time.

Captive finance companies of the Big 3 — Ford Motor Credit Co., General Motors Corp., and DaimlerChrysler – are the leading issuers. In 2001, they shared among themselves 31% of all public ABS offerings. In 2002, the ratings of the leading automakers were downgraded, which made it costlier for them to raise straight debt in the capital markets. Therefore, the Big 3 increased their ABS presence. Downgrades of automakers have continued in 2005 – with bankruptcies of some major auto component suppliers and growing bankruptcy fears for some of the largest automakers.

Apart from creating asset-backed securities, another practice that gained prevalence recently is whole loan transfers by forming multi-investor syndicates.

Other countries

In Europe, out of asset-backed securities excluding MBS and CDOs, auto ABS constitutes an important asset class. In the U.K., the first Auto ABS transaction took place in 1997 by Ford Credit. In Asian markets, finance companies have been particularly active in securitization of auto loan receivables.

Table 15.1   U.S. Auto loan backed ABS (outstanding)

	Automobile	% of Total ABS
1995	59.5	18.8%
1996	71.4	17.7%
1997	77.0	14.4%
1998	86.9	11.9%
1999	114.1	12.7%
2000	133.1	12.4%
2001	187.9	14.7%
2002	221.7	14.4%
2003	234.5	13.8%
2004	232.1	12.7%
2005 Q3	226.0	11.8%

Source: Bond Market Association

Collateral quality

The quality of auto loans depends upon the quality of the underlying collateral, lending terms (loan-to-value ratio), and tenure. Recent years have seen tremendous competition in the auto loan financing segment with concomitant deterioration in the quality of the loans; there is an increasing proportion of used car loans versus new car loans, while the loan-to-value ratio has worsened and financings are for a longer period now. There is a big push to car sales given by zero APR schemes.

The most important factor that affects the quality of the auto loan pool is the quality of the underwriting systems followed by the financier. Vehicle financings proposals are generally originated at the dealer's floor. The finance company generally outsources the field investigation and then underwrites the loan based on documents and inspection reports. For prime loan pools, there are strict norms that the proposal must comply with in terms of LTV and debt-to-income ratios. Another way of distinguishing between prime and non-prime portfolios is based on the age of the vehicle; new vehicle financings are considered prime and used vehicles are taken as sub-prime.

One of the most critical factors in all asset-based financings is the movement of the LTV ratio over time. The initial LTV ratio is a reciprocal of the down payment. If the value of the vehicle and the down payment are both expressed as percentage of the same number, the initial LTV is (1-down payment). However, over a period of time, the rate of depreciation of the vehicle and the amortization of the loan would continue to affect the LTV ratio. The loan amortization of an equal-EMI structure will see an increasing principal recovery over time, and therefore, a slightly negatively convex outstanding balance.[3]

The significance of the LTV ratio impacting delinquency has also been discussed, elsewhere in this book, although in the context of MBS transactions.[4]

Typical structures

The payment structure of auto loans normally ranges three to six years, ideal for direct pass-throughs as well as collateralized bonds. In the U.S. market, most auto loan transactions have traditionally been structured as principal pass-throughs, but of late, there is an increasing use of the revolving feature to extend the maturity of the investment and soft bullet structures.

Credit enhancements

The most common forms of credit enhancements in auto loan securitizations are excess spread, cash reserve and subordination.

Auto loans are usually extended at APRs, which are significantly higher than the weighted-average cost of funding the securitization transaction. Therefore, trapping the excess spread is an easy yet powerful credit enhancement. The extent of excess spread to support a pool will be affected by prepayment rate. Prepayments lead to unscheduled termination of the contract, whereby the excess spread ceases. Excess spread also comes down due to involuntary pre-closure, that is, repossession that is affected by the delinquency rate.

There have been number of recent cases of subvention funding, where the captive finance company, or for that matter even an independent finance company, gives a low APR or zero APR financing to promote vehicle sales. This would lead to cases of negative excess spread – that is, the weighted average cost of the bonds being higher than the weighted average APR of the pool. This would necessitate the creation of a yield supplement in the pool, either by cash reserve or over-collateralization.

Specific issues in auto loan securitization

An important legal issue for auto loan securitization is whether the assignment of receivables achieves a "true sale" recognized by law. This would be particularly important in case of auto lease transactions where the ownership of the physical property may be registered in the name of the originator. In many countries, transfer of physical ownership of assets in lease and hire purchase transactions poses logistical problems. Therefore, a sale of receivables is done, but not backed by a sale of the underlying physical assets.

This is where legal examination is required as to whether the ownership of the asset retained by the originator will create either any disabilities on the part of the transferee or any concerns on the part of the originator.

Another significant legal issue is whether there are any obligations arising out of the physical asset, such as any qualitative obligations, or those arising out of insurance contracts, environmental or third party liabilities. As a general rule, for financial leases, such liabilities do not affect the financier, but the law is evolving in this regard and legal precedents differ in various countries.

Case study: Daimler-Chrysler Auto Trust

Daimler-Chrysler Services is one of the Big 3 captives active in auto loan securitization in the U.S. The present case is a prototypical prime auto loan securitization.

We pick up Daimler-Chrysler Auto Trust 2002-B for our case study, though by and large, most of these cases are essentially similar. The present case involved issuance of US$1.9199 billion securities (including certificates) of which public issuance was roughly $1.5 billion as shown below:

Table 15.2 Securities issued

	Face value	Coupon	Issue price to public	Public issue amount	Legal final maturity
	US$ mill.				
Class A-1	356.694	1.83%	na	na	Jun-03
Class A-2	675.000	2.20%	99.9962%	674.9744	Apr-05
Class A-3	430.000	2.93%	99.9865%	429.942	Jun-06
Class A-4	395.000	3.53%	99.9718%	394.8886	Dec-07
Subordinated certificates	62.369	0%	na	na	na
Total	1919.063			1499.805	

Of these, the A-1 notes and the Certificates were not publicly offered.

The collateral

Some basic facts about the collateral are:

Aggregate principal balance	$2000.014 million
Weighted-average APR	7.09%
Weighted-average original term	59.2 months
Weighted-average remaining term	54.17 months

The collateral consisted of both new and old vehicles. Roughly 21.5% of the receivables relate to used cars.

It is apparent that there is also a significant portion of subvention cases in the portfolio as the percentage of cars with 0% to 5% APR is 28%. However, the weighted-average APR leaves a significant excess spread.

The selection criteria used for selecting the receivables to be sold are:

- Each receivable was originally purchased by the seller from dealers in the ordinary course of its business.
- Interest on each receivable is computed using the simple interest method.
- As of the cut off date:
  - No receivable was more than 30 days past due (an account is not considered past due if the amount past due is less than 10% of the scheduled monthly payment);
  - No receivable was the subject of a bankruptcy proceeding;
  - Each receivable had a principal balance of at least $1,000; and
  - Each receivable had a scheduled maturity on or before June 30, 2008.

The net credit losses as a percentage of the annual liquidations, that is, principal repayments, have been lower than 2% for the last three years.

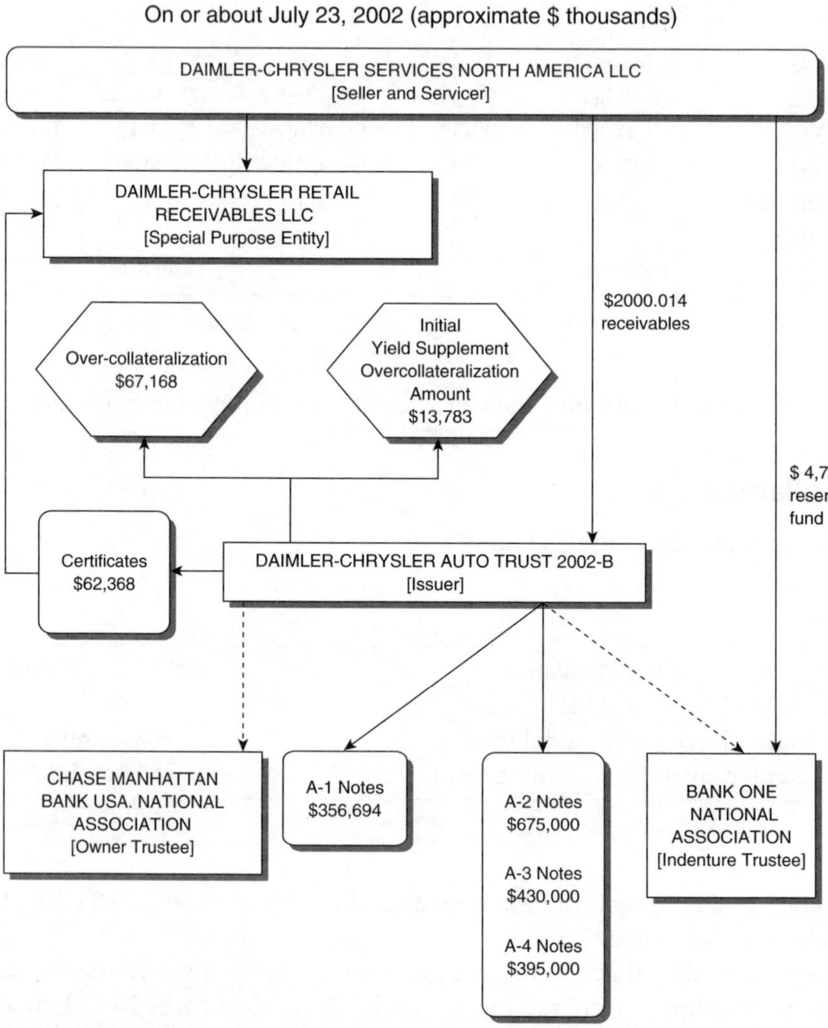

On or about July 23, 2002 (approximate $ thousands)

Figure 15.1 Transaction graphic of Auto Loan Securitization Case

Transaction structure

The transaction structure is as shown in Figure 15.1:

Issuer

Like many auto-loan securitizations, the structure of the transaction is a pay-through and not a pass-through. The issuing trust is a Delaware business trust.

Pay-down structure

The transaction follows a pay-through structure and will sequentially repay the various classes. The principal collections on the loans, plus excess spread, minus distribution on account of over-collateralization, are used to sequentially pay the various classes. The certificates will not receive any principal until their maturity. The legal final maturities mentioned above are the hard maturity dates for the notes.

Clean up call

There is a clean up call option with the servicer exercisable when the outstanding balance under the certificates falls to equal to or less than 10% of the initial balance of US$2 billion approximately. The servicer will exercise the clean up call by buying back Class A-2 and the certificates (as by then other notes would have already been redeemed fully).

Credit enhancements

The transaction has an all-inclusive credit enhancement of 7%, including over-collateralization, reserve fund and the subordinated certificates.

Over-collateralization

The extent of over-collateralization is given by the following:

Initial portfolio balance	$2000.014
Yield supplement	13.783%
Total funding balance	$1919.063
Over-collateralization	67.1677%

The trust is required to maintain a 4% over-collateralization. The excess of any cash collections over the required minimum over-collateralization will be released by the trust to the seller as over-collateralization distribution. In terms of the pay-down sequence, the over-collateralization comes at number 2, immediately after the A-1 notes.

Reserve fund

The transaction also maintains a reserve fund of US$4.797 million, which is 0.25% of the total funding balance. The initial reserve fund will be created from out of the funding raised by the transaction, and thereafter, it must be maintained from the collections before any excess interest is distributed.

Yield supplement

An over-collateralization by way of yield supplement has been provided here to the extent of $13.783 million. This is to support the transactions where their APR for the transaction is lower than the weighted-average coupon payable on the funding. The difference between a regular over-collateralization and the yield-supplement over-collateralization is that in this case, the principal repayment on such an account is also appropriated and distributed as if it were interest on the reference loans that these accounts seek to supplement. That is, the receivables from the supplemental accounts are simply added to those from the original loans such that all principal and interest on the supplemental loans become a part of the interest of the original loans. In the present case, the yield supplement amounts put the APR of the deals at 4%, which is well above the weighted-average funding cost of the transaction.

Excess interest

Excess interest will be used to pay off the note in sequence, which increases the credit enhancement available to the senior notes. Excess interest here is the excess of:

> Interest on all loans
> *Plus* principal on loans provided as yield supplement loans (as discussed above)
> *Plus* investment income out of reserve fund; and
> *Over* servicing fees

Such excess interest is used to pay off Class A-1 first, then the over-collateralization in excess of the required 4%, and then Class A-2 and so on.

Certificates

In addition, the certificates are subordinated to the notes. The certificates carry zero coupons and will not come for principal repayment until the complete amortization of all the notes. Hence, the certificates also provide a source of both liquidity and credit enhancement. The certificates are 3.25% of the total funding.

Cash flow waterfall

The cash flow waterfall for the transaction is:

- pay servicing fee
- pay accrued and unpaid interest on the notes
- replenish reserve fund, if necessary, up to the initial amount
- pay up to the outstanding principal amount of the A-1 notes
- pay the over-collateralization distribution amount, if any, to the seller
- pay up to the outstanding principal amount of the A-2 notes
- pay up to the outstanding principal amount of the A-3 notes
- pay up to the outstanding principal amount of the A-4 notes
- pay up to the outstanding principal amount of the certificates
- distribute remaining balance, if any, to the seller

Notes

1 Fitch Ratings: *A Road Map to Rating Auto Loan-Backed Securitizations*, March 13, 2002.
2 Auto loan ABS was No. 1 until 2000, and then moved to third position in 2001 onwards due to substantial growth in home equity loan securitization – see statistics later in this chapter.
3 For more details on the nature of capital recovery, see Vinod Kothari's *Lease Financing and Hire-purchase* 4th edition 1996.
4 See Chapter 30 on Investing in Securitization Transactions.

Chapter 16

Equipment Lease Securitization

Equipment lease securitization can be said to be the mother of all non-MBS securitizations, as in 1985 asset-backed securitization originated with a deal done by Sperry's Corporation. As securitization is a very significant mode of funding for the leasing companies, the volumes of lease securitization have a significant correlation with the growth of the leasing market itself.

Equipment leasing market

The global equipment leasing market is a huge market, matured over years and multi-faceted regulations and accounting standards. The global size of the equipment leasing market is estimated at approximately US$500-600 billion in new originations every year. See Figure 16.1.[1]

Equipment lease securitization market

The first case of securitization outside the mortgage market was a lease, as noted earlier. Securitization of equipment leases forms an increasing proportion

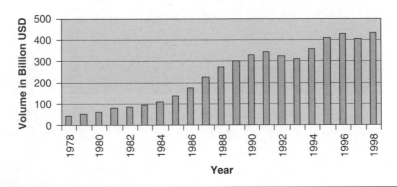

Figure 16.1   Global leasing volumes

of the total ABS market. In the U.S. alone in 1997, more than $7 billion of equipment lease-backed deals were completed. Currently, equipment lease securitization forms about 4-5% of total ABS. In Europe, data about lease securitizations are not separately captured, but equipment lease securitization is strong in several countries, notably the U.K. and Italy. The increasing investor interest in lease securitizations is witnessed in finer pricing, lesser credit enhancements and several issues actively traded in secondary markets.

Product structure

The features of equipment leases depend upon the type of leased product and transaction size. Generally, equipment leases are classified into small-ticket, medium-ticket and big-ticket leases.

Small-ticket leases include small transactions, normally of a retail variety, and would mostly have consumer leases. Here, both the product and the obligors are diversified, and the quality of the issuer is given the prime significance.

The medium-ticket segment covers leases of office equipment, printing machinery and small machinery items.

Big-ticket items are heavy industry machinery and high-cost medical equipment such as MRI equipments. There is a higher degree of concentration here and therefore increased risk.

Most lease securitization transactions are based on a specific industry focus, such as medical equipment and farming equipment.

Rating of equipment lease securitizations

Duff and Phelps Credit Rating (before merging into Fitch) had the following to say on rating lease securitization:

> The rating approach for analyzing equipment lease-backed securities is similar to that of other asset-backed transactions. Credit enhancement is generally sized based on analysis of historical losses and industry averages and an analysis of portfolio concentrations. DCR's analysis will also incorporate other quantitative and qualitative factors, including, but not limited to: historical portfolio performance; portfolio characteristics, concentrations and seasoning; origination sources, such as vendor programs and broker relationships; credit under-writing standards and related changes over time; servicing and collection procedures and related changes over time; management experience and the transaction's payment and legal structure.

To the extent available, historical portfolio performance is evaluated on a static pool basis to determine likely performance over the life of the transaction, including the expected timing of losses. Charge-off policies are also evaluated, as the timing of recognizing defaults and recoveries, if any, affect cash flows to the pool. Factors that determine the amount of credit given to recoveries include the nature of the equipment being financed, the originator's UCC filing thresholds, historical recovery rates and the strength of vendor programs and remarketing agreements.

Residual value risk in equipment lease securitizations

One of the special features of equipment lease securitization is the risk of residual values. This will be true for operating leases, and clearly, because of accounting standards, a growing proportion of international leasing volumes is operating leases. In an operating lease, the lessor retains a risk position on the value of the asset, for an amount that should be at least 10% in present value of the initial fair value of the asset.

The residual value management is an important aspect of leasing business. The relevance of this to securitization is clear; the residual value cash flow is kept out of securitization or the lessor obtains a guarantee or insurance for the residual value. Keeping the residual value of the equipment of the securitization pool may resolve problems of uncertainty, but creates legal issues as to the sharing of the beneficial interest in the asset.

If the residual value risk is not effectively sheltered, rating agencies tend to insist on higher levels of enhancement.[2]

Investing in equipment lease securitizations

Investors have pointed out that a prime reason for investing in equipment lease securitization has been the higher yield this class has over traditional credit card or auto loan transactions.[3] Investors have also cited two common concerns–illiquidity, and asset valuation problems. Most of the equipment lease issuances have been 144A issues.[4] Valuation difficulties pointed out by investors relate to the heterogeneity of the equipment backing up the collateral. While in case of cards, or cars, it is a standard loan, the features of equipment leases and the inherent risks vary across equipment types, making valuation a daunting task.

Valuation difficulties were exacerbated by the asset depreciation strategies for the variety of equipment.

Notes

1 For more on the leasing industry, see Vinod Kothari's *Lease Financing and Hire Purchase*. For latest edition and pricing, please see http://india-financing.com
2 The U.S. SEC regulation AB has made certain quantitative limits to residual risk in case of lease transactions. See Chapter 28.
3 This section is based on the research done by the Equipment Leasing Association, U.S.: see results in *The Securitization Marketplace 2002* by Equipment Leasing and Finance Foundation.
4 A U.S. securities market term for private placements.

Chapter 17

Collateralized Debt Obligations

More recently these transfers have taken more exotic forms, such as collateralized debt obligations (CDOs) or indeed synthetic CDOs. One investment banker recently described synthetic CDOs to me as "the most toxic element of the financial markets today" ... When an investment banker talks of toxicity, a regulator is bound to take a heightened interest.

Howard Davies, in speech dated January 29, 2002

Collateralized debt obligations (CDOs) are clearly one of the hottest collateral classes in asset-backed securities. CDOs make use of the securitization methodology to convert loans and bonds into capital market instruments. Apart from using securitization to parcel out loans held on the balance sheet of banks, the CDO methodology provided an excellent arbitraging opportunity thus giving a new dimension to securitization and creating new opportunities. Combined with credit derivatives technology, CDOs acquiring synthetic assets have given a new tool of convenience to ramp up CDOs. We take up synthetic securitization, along with synthetic CDOs, in a later chapter.

Over time the CDO methodology, originated for loan and bond portfolios, has found its logical extension into investment in private equity funds and hedge funds, which may well be an explosive growth area to come.

Needless to say, arbitrage CDOs and other investment vehicles using the securitization methodology provide a new growth engine to the global securitization business.

What is a CDO?

During the 1980s, creation of bonds backed by a portfolio of mortgages became popular. We have noted the concept and development of CMOs, or the REMICs where repayment of fixed income securities is derived out of a collateral of mortgages. The underlying idea and methodology in CDOs are the same – transfer of a portfolio of loans and bonds into a pool and issuance of debt based on the same. CDOs are capitalized by equity that provides the credit enhancement for the liabilities.

A CDO is a generic name for collateralized loan obligations (CLOs) and collateralized bond obligations (CBOs).

Differences between CLOs and CBOs

Structurally, a CDO based on loans and a CDO based on bonds are almost similar, but bonds are marketable negotiable securities while loans are not. Therefore, there are certain obvious differences in the process of transfer of loans as compared to bonds. Loans may not be whole loans but mere participation in a syndicated loan. These facts will present difficulties in assignment of the loan and therefore a complete de-linking of loans from the lender will be difficult to achieve.

The legal concerns for assignment of loans are also significant – banking laws mostly permit a set off right with the borrower in case the borrower has any deposits with the lender. Assignment of loans may not be backed by assignment of deposits, which may be another problem area.

In terms of the cash flow structure as well, repayment of loans is very different from that of bonds. The latter are typically bullet repayment securities, while loans have varying payment terms mostly structured to the needs of the borrower.

Loans are created based on heterogeneous and structured loan documents. Rating of the CLO would involve a case-by-case analysis of each constituent of the CLO, so the due diligence process will be both costly and time consuming and loans with very specific terms may be omitted from the CLO.

The other difficulty is that while bonds are mostly rated, loans may not be. Rating agencies often rely on the internal rating systems of the bank (which are refined over time to the satisfaction of the rating agency).

The market for loans is less liquid. This may pose difficulties in terms of reinvestment or the ramp up period. By the same logic the recovery rate on defaulted loans may be less than for bonds.

In reality, it is difficult to think of a CDO that consists only of loans, or one that consists only of bonds. Therefore, the generic term CDOs, which includes collateral in the form of loans, bonds and other loan-type exposures (for example, derivatives exposures, guarantees, etc.) has become more common.

Typical structure of a CDO

A CDO typically uses 20 to 500 loans or bonds to make the pool, as against traditional ABS, which has anything between 500 to 100,000 loans comprising the pool. The structure of the CDO has the following distinguishing characteristics:

- The composition of the pool will be determined by whether the CDO is meant for balance sheet or arbitrage purposes and the type of assets it pertains to.
- The selection of the assets is done so as to lead to a level of diversification.
- The levels of credit enhancements are computed by:

  o Assessing the probability of default of each loan
  o Assessing the intra-industry and inter-industry correlations
  o Drawing up a probability distribution
  o Sizing the enhancement so as to satisfy the required credit enhancement target.

- The maturity of the notes is generally by way of a bullet repayment, say, at the end of eight years.
- Over this time, the CDO manager will have the right to reinvest the principal proceeds.
- The CDO manager's right of reinvestment will normally be controlled by specifying the over-collateralization (OC) and interest coverage (IC) triggers.
- If the CDO is meant for arbitrage purposes, the residual income of the CDO, after the manager's fees, is the arbitrage revenue.

Types of CDOs

CDOs may be classified into various types from different perspectives:

- Based on mode of assets acquisition

  - Cash CDO
  - Synthetic CDO:
    - Fully tranched
    - Single tranche
  - Hybrid CDO

- Based on what it holds:

  - High-yield CDO
  - Investment grade CDO
  - Emerging market CDO
  - Structured finance CDO or CDO^2
  - Primary market CDO

- Based on purpose:

  - Balance sheet CDO
  - Arbitrage CDO

- Based on leverage structure

  - Cash flow structure
  - Market value structure

- Based on asset ramping
  - Fully ramped up
  - Partly ramped up
  - To be ramped up

Cash and synthetic CDOs

CDOs may acquire assets in cash or synthetically. The cash asset CDO acquires assets in a traditional manner – raising the funding required equal to the size of the CDO and investing the same in acquiring the assets. The assets are acquired either from one originator (as for balance sheet CDOs) or from the market (as for arbitrage CDOs).

For synthetic CDOs, the assets are acquired synthetically, that is, by signing up credit derivative deals selling protection against the assets. A synthetic mode of acquisition of assets is now well accepted as a mode of reaping credit spreads on assets without having to acquire them as such.

The basic difference between cash and synthetic CDOs is the amount of funding raised and the manner of its investment. A synthetic CDO does not have to pay for the assets it acquires unless the protection payments are triggered, so the amount of funding required for synthetic CDOs is much lower. Typically, the CDOs go for a cash funding from investors only to the extent required to have a AAA rating on the senior-most of its securities, as this funding is essentially a credit enhancement to absorb the risks of the portfolio of synthetic liabilities of the CDO. The difference between the total of synthetic assets and the cash funding of the CDO is covered by an unfunded protection bought on a swap, a sort of a synthetic liability or synthetic funding of the CDO. Thus, the cash funding or cash liabilities of the CDO are invested in cash assets (typically highly-rated collateral), and the total of synthetic assets is equal to the sum of funded liability as well as unfunded liability.

Synthetic CDOs are taken up in detail in Chapter 22.

Of late, another type of CDO gaining popularity is a hybrid CDO; it invests in the cash market and in the synthetic market. Hybrid securitization is also discussed in Chapter 22.

CDO types based on collateral

The collateral-based classification is, understandably, mostly related to arbitrage CDOs. Based on its investment objectives, CDOs may acquire investment grade assets or high-yield bonds (a more presentable name for junk bonds). CDOs may be specifically aimed at emerging market debt. At one time, CDOs structured on high-yield bonds were quite popular, but recent default rate for high-yield securities has limited new activity in that market.

Structured finance CDOs – CDOs buying securitized instruments – have been much in popularity of late. These CDOs re-securitize exposure in assets that have been securitized already, so these are also called *re-securitizations* or *CDO.*[2] Several CDOs also make investments in REITs or particular tranches of residential mortgage-backed securities. Structured finance CDOs are discussed at length later in this chapter.

Sometimes CDOs make investment in trust-preferred securities, a hybrid between preferred stock and subordinated debt. These may, accordingly, be called *trust preferred CDOs*.

Primary market CDOs create loans – that is, they do not buy loans that have already been given but originate a specific pool of loans.

Balance sheet and arbitrage CDOs

CDOs may be aimed at transferring the assets of a particular originator and thereby reducing the balance sheet size of the originator, or at earning arbitrage profits for the equity holders. Arbitrage CDOs ramp up their assets from the market; there is no bar on their picking up the assets of the sponsor. Quite often, before the CDO is brought to the market, the sponsor may have already ramped up at least a portion of the assets.

Balance sheet CDOs are aimed at, among other things, regulatory and/or economic capital relief, which cannot be a motive in arbitrage transactions. There is, of course, an implicit arbitrage for balance sheet CDOs as well, although this arbitrage is only the balance sheet; it replaces the existing balance sheet funding cost by presumably a lower weighted-average cost of the CDO.

Detailed discussion on balance sheet and arbitrage CDOs follows.

Par value and market value-based structures

The crux of CDOs lies in counter-balancing diversification and leverage. The diversification is on the asset side and the leverage is on the liability side. The leverage implies risk, which may go up during the life of the CDO if the quality of the assets on the asset side suffers. CDOs try to take corrective action to keep the leverage under check, and if required, to reduce it, by putting limits on leverage such as on over-collateralization test and interest coverage test. These are discussed later in this chapter. These tests may be based on the par value of the assets or on the market value of the assets; accordingly, CDOs may be referred to as market value CDOs or par value CDOs.

Growth of the CDO market

The CDO market originated in the late 1980s. However, during the early years, the total issuance hardly ever exceeded a few billion dollars. The real impetus came around 1996 when the risk return profile of the high-yield debt market and the pricing of a AAA floater created excellent arbitrage conditions. In 1998, the collapse of LTCM created premium for liquidity in the market. Around the same time, rating agencies became more comfortable with rating of CDOs including those for arbitrage purposes.

The following Figure 17.1 gives a pre-1997 view of the CDO market; as is evident, the real explosion came only in 1996:

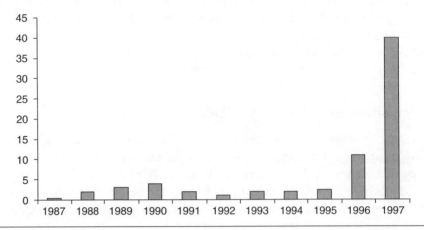

Figure 17.1   CDO issuance up to 1997

Since 1998, the growth has been phenomenal, although there have been ups and downs periodically:

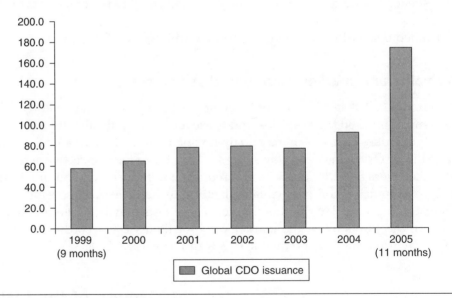

Figure 17.2   Global CDO issuance

Source: Market data at www.abalert.com

The boom in CDO issuance in 2005 is evident, as the market went to great extent in search of yields and diversification.

European CDO market

Europe has made a very significant contribution to the growth of the global CDO market. In the first half of 2001, Europe accounted for nearly 43% of the global CDO issuance. This position continues; in the first half of 2003, total European CDO issuance was measured at €11.7 billion.[1]

The key difference between the European market and the US market is the predominance of balance sheet activity in Europe. Europe does not have as big a market in high-yield debt; obviously, there is limited potential then in arbitrage CDO transactions. However, synthetic CDOs form a very large chunk of CDO activity, particularly in Germany.

The CDO market is largely global, and most CDOs relate to collateral from all over the world. In essence, the CDO market, unlike the retail ABS market, is completely globalized and has generally a homogenous character.

CDO market trends

Rating agency Fitch notes the following trends in the CDO market to watch in 2006 and beyond:

- Synthetic and Cash CDO markets are converging. Hybrid CDOs referencing a wider array of assets are expected to enter the market (hybrid synthetic securitization is discussed in Chapter 22).
- Leveraged Super Senior tranches of CDOs referenced to asset-backed securities are generating increasing interest; in synthetic securitizations, super senior tranches are mostly funded. However, in some recent transactions, the super senior tranche has been partly funded with the option of calling for further capital from the super senior investor should the underlying assets suffer losses beyond a particular level, or to wind up the transaction with mark-to-market losses.
- Heightened focus on the managers' role as CDO structures become more complex; more emphasis on quantitative methodologies for comparing and tracking manager performance.
- Increasing influence of hedge funds in the CDO market. Hedge fund managers who are venturing into the CDO space and vice-versa.
- The emergence of unrated collateral and investors' demand for more transparency.
- Regulatory and accounting changes.

CDO market and the health of banking

CDOs and their impact on the global financial system have been an intensively debated topic of late. We started this chapter with a quote from Howard Davies, who referred to CDOs as the toxic waste of investment banking. Alan Greenspan, on the other hand, has generally regarded risk transfers by CDOs and credit derivatives as responsible for maintaining the health of the global banking system. In a speech to the Federal Reserve Bank of Chicago's 41st Annual Conference on Bank Structure, Chicago, Illinois on May 5, 2005, he stated:

"As is generally acknowledged, the development of credit derivatives has contributed to the stability of the banking system by allowing banks, especially the largest, systemically important banks, to measure and manage their credit risks more effectively. In particular, the largest banks have found single-name credit default swaps a highly attractive mechanism for reducing exposure concentrations in their loan books while allowing them to meet the needs of their largest corporate customers. But some observers argue that what is good for the banking system may not be good for the financial system as a whole. They are concerned that banks' efforts to lay off risk using credit derivatives may be creating concentrations of risk outside the banking system that could prove a threat to financial stability. A particular concern has been that, as credit spreads widen appreciably at some point from the extraordinarily low levels that have prevailed in recent years, losses to nonbank risk-takers could force them to liquidate their positions in credit markets and thereby magnify and accelerate the widening of credit spreads."

Balance sheet CDOs

Balance sheet CDOs are not a new type of securitization but rather an application of the securitization methodology. Balance sheet CDOs parcel out a portfolio of loans, usually low-rated loans or emerging market credits, and below-investment grade bonds held by large banks. Balance sheet CDOs may be either cash CDOs or synthetic CDOs.

Traditional, cash CDOs

This structure was used for the first time by Nations Bank in 1997, then by LTCB (PLATINUM), IBJ (PRIME), Sumitomo (WINGS) Bankboston (BANK-BOSTON), Bank of Montreal (LAKESHORE), Sanwa (EXCELSIOR), and SG (POLARIS). The methodology in all of these was fairly simple – transfer of a near-homogenous portfolio of loans into an SPV and issuance of liabilities easily sellable to investors.

Type of SPV

Most traditional CDOs have made use of the master trust methodology with seller share and investor share and to be able to use the same SPV for a series of issuance over time and with no need to match the amount of liabilities issued with the amount of loans transferred.

Underlying assets

Usually portfolios of syndicated loans with ratings of BB to BBB are accumulated. Something like 500 loans may be pooled together to attain the required size.

Diversity score

The diversity score is a measure used by rating agencies to signify the lack of correlation, and therefore, as a measure of diversification of the portfolio. By their very nature, the economics of a CDO lie in the diversification of the portfolio. To measure diversification, rating agencies use not merely diversification of borrowers but diversification of industries. If there are 500 loans in the portfolio with a diversity score of 50, it might, in plain English, mean there are 50 mutually uncorrelated industries comprised in the portfolio.

The diversity score is based not merely on the number of industries in the portfolio but also the number of borrowers per industry. With a larger number of borrowers per industry, the average concentration per borrower comes down, and hence the diversity score goes up. That is, a diversity score is based both on the number of industries in a portfolio and the number of borrowers per industry. See Table 17.1 below for industry and borrower diversification published by Moody's:[2]

Table 17.1   Analysis of Trade-Off between Issuer and Industry Concentration

# of Issuers Per Industry	# of Industries	# of Issuers	Avg. Issuer Concentration	Diversity Score
5	25	125	0.80%	67
3	33	99	1.01%	66
4	20	80	1.25%	46
2	25	50	2.00%	38
1	33	33	3.03%	33

As could be seen above, with 25 industries represented by 125 borrowers, one sees a diversity score of 67 while the same number of industries, but with 50 borrowers produces a diversity score of only 38.

Besides concentration limits of the type mentioned before, a 2% per borrower and 8% per industry are also imposed.

Reinvestment period

Like traditional ABS such as credit cards, CDOs allow a certain reinvestment period because many of the loans may have sizeable principal repayments from the very first month of the CDO. During the reinvestment period, the originator may put in more loans into the CDO, but these loans are approved based on the preset conditions such as minimum rating and diversity score. In addition, the OC/IC triggers must also be in compliance.

The reinvestment period is typically one year before the repayment starts. That is, one year before the scheduled repayment, the trustees start building up cash in the CDO for forthcoming repayment. One year before repayment as well, there may be accumulation of cash to the extent of 50%, while the other 50% may be allowed to be reinvested. Therefore, the reinvestment may be 100% during the first 2 years, and 50% during the 3rd year. In the 3rd year, repayment of the 3-year paper may be made.

Typical stratification

The typical credit enhancement structure of CDOs has by and large standard-ized over time as follows:

Senior AAA securities	92%
Mezzanine A securities	3%
Junior BBB tranche	1.5%
Junior BB tranche	1.5%
Subordinated, unrated tranche	1%
Cash collateral account	1%
Originator's excess spread	NA

Thus the credit enhancement provided by the originator is 1% CCA, 1% junior unrated class, and the excess spread account. The excess spread is usually paid off by the trustees to the originator, but for a deterioration in the quality of the portfolio, this amount may be used to pay off the investors.

Usually all the rated tranches are repaid over two periods – three years and five years.

Early amortization triggers

The typical early amortization triggers in CDOs are (i) the selling bank is no longer able to generate new loans; (ii) the rating of the selling bank, manag-ing the cash, falls below A1/P1; (iii) the average quality of the portfolio falls below the predetermined quality level (Average Rating and Diversity Score). If the triggers are hit, the reinvestment period ends at the end of 3 years and the cash collections are distributed to the investors in order of priorities.

Structural tests

If the tests relating to the over-collateralization (OC) and interest cover (IC) are not satisfied, the CDO will use the cash flow waterfall to make a principal dis-tribution to the senior classes until the breach of the structural tests is corrected. The working of these structural triggers is discussed later in this chapter.

Cash flow waterfall

The cash flow waterfall for CDOs is similar to that for generic securitization. The differentiating element is the presence of the structural triggers. The illus-trations of a typical waterfall for arbitrage transactions (in the later part of this chapter) will be relevant to balance sheet CDOs as well.

Synthetic CDOs

Synthetic CDOs are discussed in a later chapter in this book.

Arbitrage CDOs

Making use of the technology provided by traditional asset-backed securiti-zations, but with the motive of making arbitrage opportunities provided by inefficient pricing of securities, particularly high-yield securities, there emerged in the market a new class of securitization product – arbitrage CDOs.

Arbitrage opportunities arise in every market, but the typical feedstock of arbitrage CDOs is high-yield debt; significant arbitrage opportunities are given by the implied default rates and expected default rates on high yield debt. The implied default rate is inherent in the pricing of the debt, whereas the expected default rate is based on the probability distribution of the downgrade of a particular rating.

Meaning of an arbitrage CDO

A CDO is a securitization product that creates obligations backed by a pool of bonds, loans or similar fixed income instruments. The collateral that backs CDOs is typically leveraged loans, high yield bonds, junior tranches of asset-backed paper or mortgage-backed securities, or junior tranches of other CDOs.

The purpose of a CDO is not to liquidate the assets held on the balance sheet of the originator, but to accumulate assets from proceeds of the CDO to make an arbitraging profit; that CDO is called an arbitrage CDO. Arbitrage CDOs can be issued by anyone, but most typically are issued by investment management boutiques, asset managers, investment banks, insurance companies and the like.

In a typical asset-backed transaction, the assets are originated by the originator and then securitized. The asset in question is a loan, mainly an originated loan or a bond, usually bought in the primary market. The word "originator" is inap-propriate for the arbitrage variety, as the portfolio of loans or bonds is mostly not originated by the entity bringing the CDO to market; instead it is picked up from the market. Hence, packager or repackager is the common term applied to the one who brings an arbitrage CDO to the market. In many cases, the portfolio of bonds or loans held by an arbitrage CDO is not static but is managed over time, so the packager is also called the "CDO manager" a standard market term as an equivalent of the originator in traditional asset-backed transactions.

Illustration of arbitraging

Typical funding structure

The key element in an arbitrage CDO is the equity tranche, equivalent to the first-loss piece in a traditional securitization transaction. In a traditional trans-action, the first-loss piece depends on the size of the transaction; in an arbi-trage CDO, the size of the transaction depends on the size of the equity piece, and the entire edifice of the transaction is built on the equity piece.

Depending on the nature of the portfolio, the equity piece may range between 3-8%. It is notable that the equity piece need not be structured as legal equity, but it must have the ability to sweep the residual returns of the transaction.

How and why arbitrage exists

The basic meaning of arbitraging in the context of CDOs is arbitraging between the rate of return on the collateral and the weighted-average cost of the CDO including the equity portion. The following Table 17.2 shows the returns on equity of a putative CDO, as in the example below, going as high as 20.88%.

Table 17.2   Arbitrage conditions for CDO equity investment

	Size	*Rate*	*Product*
Assets			
Portfolio of high-yield debt	500	10.50%	52.5
Liabilities			
AAA notes (assuming LIBOR = 5%)	350	5.45%	19.075
A notes	50	6.15%	3.075
BBB notes	25	7.15%	1.7875
BB notes	25	11%	2.75
Equity	50	0	0
Weighted-average funding spread on liabilities			5.93%
Weighted-average funding rate including equity			5.34%
Collateral yield			52.5
Less funding cost			26.6875
Less: base case losses and expenses		3.25%	16.25
Returns on equity			10.4375
Percentage return on equity		50	20.88%

The arbitrage income here is a result of the high leverage of the CDO; thus CDOs are appropriately described as leverage products. The leverage built on the CDO's equity of $50 is an asset-base of $500, that is, a gearing of 9:1. In many CDOs, this gearing would go up as high as 25:1. The return on equity is the compensation for the excessive volatility of the returns on equity with reference to the variability of the income side. By economic logic of arbitrage-free markets, the long-term, risk-adjusted return on equity should leave the equity holder without an arbitrage profit. But it is a known fact that the pricing of subordinated loans or investments in the market is not efficient, leaving a scope for arbitrage profits.

Emergence of arbitrage CDOs

Arbitrage CDOs have existed since the late 1980s. A Bank of America publication says: "For an asset class that has experienced explosive growth and has existed since the late 1980s, CDOs surprisingly are still referred to as an "emerging asset class."[3] However, the real explosive growth in arbitrage CDO issuance came after 1995.

In terms of market share, arbitrage activity has been growing in relation to the total CDO market size. The value of each deal for balance sheet CDOs is more; therefore, the share of balance sheet CDOs is more in terms of size than in number of deals.

Difference between arbitrage CDOs and balance sheet CDOs

- **Purpose**: As discussed above, the purpose of a balance sheet CDO is to liquidate the assets on the balance sheet of the originator. This itself is mostly motivated by capital adequacy concerns, like reducing cost of capital, liquidity. On the other hand, arbitrage CDOs are issued mostly by non-banks and therefore, do not have the typical asset-backed securitization motives; there is no capital relief objective, nor does the cost of capital, off-balance sheet treatment play any role. Thus, there is a very basic distinction between a balance sheet CDO and an arbitrage transaction.
- **Size**: Balance sheet CDOs are usually much larger in size so as to have a significant impact on the balance sheet and ROE of the bank, and the usual market practice is US$1 billion upwards. Arbitrage CDOs, on the other hand, try and package a small bunch of investments and may usually be anywhere between US$200-500 million.
- **Typical issues**: The typical issuers of balance sheet CDOs are banks and financial intermediaries. The typical sponsors of arbitrage CDO deals are insurance companies, mutual funds, asset managers and the like.
- **Significance of true sale**: From the viewpoint of structure, although arbitrage CDOs use a bankruptcy-remote SPV, there is obviously no true sale concern typical of asset-backed transactions. In asset-backed deals, true sale concerns arise because there are assets being held on the balance sheet of an originator being transferred. Therefore, there is a question as to whether such a transfer is a sale in law or not. For arbitrage CDOs that question is irrelevant as the portfolio of loans or bonds is acquired by the SPV itself from the market and usually is a stock of readily-transferable financial assets.
- **Consolidation concerns**: Similarly, the legal concerns that dominate a traditional ABS deal – the fear of equitable consolidation or clawback – are absent in an arbitrage CDO as the relation of the SPV to the originator is very different and the purpose and manner of transfer of assets to the SPV does not warrant any consolidation concern.
- **Nature of credit enhancements and warranties**: In a traditional asset-backed transaction, the assets are usually created by the originator as a part of the originator's business. For example, the auto loans securitized have been originated by the auto finance company. The deals are created by the financier, so there is an implicit/explicit warranty that receivables are created following a certain underwriting standard and that they are of an acceptable quality standard. The originator is required to give a number of warranties at the time of assignment of receivables to the SPV. Quite often, there is also an extent of credit enhancement in the form of either direct recourse, or

substitution/buyback by the originator as a mark of his first loss position and also continued involvement in the transaction. For understandable reasons, arbitrage transactions are without warranties from the CDO manager. Credit enhancements are mostly limited to the equity participation of the CDO manager, but there is no recourse atypical of an arbitrage CDO.

- **Servicing**: The usual servicing of assets is not there in the nature of an arbitrage CDO. The role of traditional servicer in an asset-backed transaction is replaced as manager in CDOs – one in the position of a portfolio manager. The significance of the manager in CDOs is the same as that of the servicer in traditional ABS.
- **Manner of placing**: As for traditional ABS, there have been public offers, 144A offers and private placements. However, for CDOs, they have mostly been privately placed to qualified institutional buyers.

Revolving period

In terms of methodology, CDOs are similar to credit card securitizations: they are mostly issued using the master trust structure and often involve a revolving period and redemption period. If the assets of the CDO are not fully amortized before maturity, there is an **auction call;** that is, the assets are auctioned.

Market value CDOs

We have briefly dealt with the distinction between a cash flow CDO and a market value CDO from the viewpoint of the paydown triggers. There are some structural differences between the two as well.

Structure of a market value CDO

A cash flow CDO has securities pooled at the beginning of the deal that remain static throughout the term. On the other hand, a market value arbitrage CDO is one where the CDO manager has a portfolio throughout the term of the CDO based on a specific investment policy and certain leverage ratios.

In cash flow CDOs there is a reinvestment period during which the cash inflows are reinvested, but this is like reinvestment in traditional CDOs.

On the other hand, in market value CDOs the entire portfolio is dynamically managed through the term of the CDO with the objective of maximizing the return on equity, for which the investment in equity is similar to a highly leveraged investment in capital market securities.

Market value CDOs have emerged only over the last four to five years, but their share in the arbitrage CDO market has grown phenomenally.

Market value CDOs are similar to hedge funds: in fact the concept looks deceptively similar to hedge funds. The focus of a CDO manager is on return on equity, without compromising the safety of the senior investors' interest. The focus of both senior investors and equity investors is the portfolio managers' quality. The portfolio manager in a cash flow deal focuses on securities that have a minimum likelihood of default. On the other hand, the manager in a market value deal is focused on market value appreciation. The manager may quite often select distressed debts or junk bonds, as liquidity is not an important portfolio management objective. "Given the severely illiquid nature of some of the market value portfolio managers' investment picks, they represent the extreme end of the spectrum among total-rate-of-return investors."[4]

The differing objectives of cash flow and market value CDOs also reflect the composition of the asset portfolio. Cash flow CDOs usually invest in rated and current, that is, currently non-defaulting investments. On the other hand, market value CDOs devote something like 25% of their investments into assets with higher chances of appreciation such as distressed debts and hybrid capital instruments.

Liabilities of cash flow and market value CDOs

Consistent with the nature of their investments, the liabilities of cash flow and arbitrage CDOs also differ. The extent of equity often required for cash flow CDOs is close to 8-12% while those for market value CDOs is 15–25%. Thus the leverage rate for cash flow CDOs is much more than for market value CDOs.

The typical liability structure of a market value deal is:

50% senior debt
x% term notes
y% equity

Ramp up period

The ramp up period implies the period over which the CDO manager will be allowed to invest the proceeds of the issuance into assets as per objectives of the CDO. Appreciably, there is no need for a ramp up period for balance sheet transactions, but in arbitrage transactions, the manager would need some time to line up the assets. This is the ramp up period.

Ramp up periods are typically more in market value deals and there is an active portfolio management that continues all through the period. In market value deals, the ramp up period can be typically between six months to one year; in some emerging market CDOs the ramp up period of even two years is allowed. A longer ramp up period means more risk: so rating agencies pull down the rating of the transaction if the ramp up period is long.

During the ramp up period, the cash raised will be invested in liquid, permissible investments.

In addition to the ramp up period, the CDO has a typical warehousing period, meaning a period before the issue of the securities when the sponsor starts collecting the collateral. Reinvestment and amortization periods are the same as for traditional securitizations.

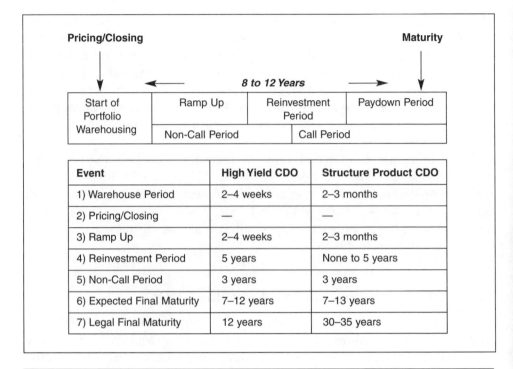

Figure 17.3 Illustrating CDO schematics

The CDO manager

The crucial agency in an arbitrage CDO is the CDO manager, who manages the portfolio of the CDO. The CDO manager is the investment adviser for the deal, and may be different from the issuer but is often an affiliate of the issuer.

The CDO manager may or may not be the equity investor of the CDO. The most common CDO managers are investment advisers and insurance companies seeking to expand the value of assets under their management. Their motivation is to increase their fee income, while having a negligible impact on the costs of the set up. "An insurance company with a high-yield bond portfolio already has the expertise in place for the purchase and monitoring of those credits. To create the model portfolio for a potential CDO, the insurance company can simply increase the size of every position, which is virtually cost-free. In doing so, the company creates an annuity stream of asset management fees lasting the life of the transaction. Executing a CDO is simply a way for the investment advisor to leverage off a fixed-cost base."[5]

Qualities of the CDO manager

Rating agencies look at experience, staffing and financial and managerial resources of CDO managers while rating a CDO issue. The size of an organization has obviously been an important factor.

The following are important manager attributes that play a significant role:

Experience

CDO management requires skills that are unique. Though skills of acquiring and managing a high-yield portfolio are important, it is often emphasized that CDO management skills are different from regular high-yield investments. Rating agency Moody's said: "We recognize further that high-yield experience outside the CDO environment may not translate into skill with CDOs. We have found several cases of seasoned managers who were successful within a mutual fund or separate account context but who failed as CDO managers."[6] In simple English, what this means is that those who have already proved their mantle as CDO managers are likely to be rated better than rookies. "The ability to analyze performance history in specific asset classes and performance within a structured credit vehicle (as opposed to a total return vehicle) is an important factor in the investment decision. As a result, repeat managers with solid performance records are gaining a strong advantage in the competition for fund management."[7]

Staffing

The rating agencies insist that CDO management teams are adequately staffed. Too many credits alloted to per person are frowned upon. If the team is too thin, the rating agencies often insist on a "keyman" provision where if a key person leaves the organization, it is treated as an event empowering noteholders to replace the key person.

Strong internal controls

Strong internal control systems are an essential part of the organization of CDO managers. Too much autonomy with any particular individual is avoidable. Periodic reviews by a credit committee, independent of the CDO yet understanding its business, is often considered desirable.

Technological investments

CDO managers would find it advisable to invest in technology products that facilitate identification of investment proposals, compliance with asset and collateral tests, and other requirements and triggers.

Financial resources

CDO managers need capital to be able to build a sound team and invest in technology.

Rating agency Standard & Poor's has listed [Standard & Poor's: *Global CBO/ CLO Criteria*, p. 15-6] a number of factors they would review in evaluating the manager:

The following information, modified for each transaction, should be assessed in an asset manager and originator/servicer review:

Overview of the Company

- Background of the company;
- Organizational structure and staffing;
- Financial strength;
- Rated CBO/CLO history and management of multiple-rated CBO/CLO transactions;
- Competitive position in managing high-yield bonds, bank loans, emerging markets assets and asset-backed securities;
- Prior experience as servicer, manager and/or investor, including volume and history of high-yield bond, bank loan, emerging market assets and asset-backed securities under management;
- Number of high-yield, bank loans and emerging markets funds under management;
- Industries covered and not covered;
- Number of credits/industries covered by each analyst (credit generalist versus industry specialists);
- Ability to expand expertise to cover industries required in a diversified CBO/CLO;
- Regions covered in emerging markets;
- Types of asset-backed securities;
- Performance results relative to peer group and indices;
- Experience of the company in corporate lending or managing portfolios of high-yield bonds, bank loans, emerging markets debt and asset-backed securities;
- Experience of staff in corporate lending or investing in and managing portfolio of high-yield bonds, bank loans, emerging markets assets and asset-backed securities including experience and performance results prior to joining the company;
- Similarities and differences in managing CBOs and existing funds;
- Strategic objectives of the company in extending credit or managing CBO portfolios; and
- Compensation arrangements for portfolio managers/servicers.

Underwriting/Investment Strategy and Objectives:

- Credit and approval policy;
- Underwriting guidelines;
- Investment strategy (credit versus yield);
- Investment style (buy and hold versus high turnover);
- Decision-making, selection and approval process for buy/sell/trade/lend decisions;

- Breakdown of loan book (bilateral vs. syndicated loans; agent bank role) and transaction book;
- Research methodology and capabilities;
- Sample credit and research reports;
- Credit processes;
- Presence of any subservicers on any of the lender's portfolio or sub-advisors on any of the company's managed funds;
- Depth and breadth of research;
- Audit status of the company's financial statements, and if audited, whether auditors issue any report on internal control;
- Hedging Strategy for interest rate and currency risks (Asset-specific vs. aggregate portfolio);
- Pricing sources; and
- Policies and procedures regarding securities valuation, segregation of duties.

Servicing and Credit monitoring capabilities:

- Procedures in place to service, administer and monitor the CBO/CLO securitization, and to ensure compliance with the CBO/CLO transaction documents;
- Identification of who performs the above servicing, administration, monitoring and compliance functions, along with whether they are contracted solely to the trustee or third party servicer, or are they jointly performed by the CBO/CLO sponsor (issuer asset manager or originator/servicer);
- Portfolio administration and report generation (credit/underwriting package and surveillance);
- Frequency and scope of credit review;
- Frequency of credit reviews for determining credit deterioration, improvement, change in risk standing or increase of credit line;
- Handling collection and disbursements;
- Managing Revolving Credit Facilities And Liquidity;
- Handling delinquencies (forbearance vs. write-off, loan modification and restructuring);
- Handling problem credits (Disposition: workouts vs. secondary market sale history);
- Handling "credit risk securities" and defaulted assets (liquidation strategy: transfer of assets to a workout specialist or "cradle to grave" philosophy);
- Historical portfolio performance (delinquencies/defaults/recoveries/timing);
- Systems and back-up capabilities;
- Conversion problems: actions and contingency plans; and
- Conversion problems for service providers such as the trustee.

Deutsche Bank Alex-Brown in their report [*Structured Product CDOs—Guide for Debt & Equity Investors* March 20, 2001] suggested an exhaustive list of questions to evaluate a CDO manager:

Table 17.3   Evaluation of CDO Manager

Collateral Management	Who will be managing the CDO?
	How are responsibilities divided between junior and senior staff?
	How much staff turnover has taken place?
	What experience does the manager have in underlying asset classes and how extensive has the experience been in subordinates?
	What has been the manager's historical performance in these assets?
	How much diversification will come from assets where the manager has less experience?
	What experience does the manager have in managing a CDO and how has performance deviated inside the CDO versus outside the CDO?
	How have credit deteriorations in the past been resolved?
	What other resources can the manager draw on within the organization with regard to structured products?
	What systems are in place to model and project prepayments?
	What experience does the manager have in distressed sales? Work outs?
Source of Assets	How was the portfolio sourced?
	Existing balance sheet? New purchases?
	Primary market versus secondary market?
	Has a disproportionate amount of the collateral been sourced from a single lead manager?
	What constitutes recent purchases of "dealer-aged" positions?
Moral Hazard	What is the motivation for issuing the CDO?
	How important is the CDO platform to the manager's overall funding strategy?
	What are the plans for future issuance?
	How have problems in existing deals been resolved and to the benefit of debt or equity holders?
	How much equity will the manager retain in the transaction?
	Will the manager be placing equity with existing clients or affiliates?
CDO Structure	How familiar is the manager with CDO technology?
	In what ways has the structure been tailored to accommodate the strengths of the manager?
	How will the manager balance the interests of debt and equity investors?
Infrastructure	How will the portfolio be monitored on a day-to-day basis?
	What systems/feeds are in place between the manager and the trustee?
	How frequently will the manager tie out with the trustee?
	What systems are in place to track rating changes and delinquencies on underlying pools?

Balancing between equity investors and debt investors

The CDO manager has to walk the tightrope of balancing between the needs of the noteholders and the equity holders. The equity holders are interested in value maximization while the noteholders are concerned about the regularity of payments. Their needs are conflicting. From the point of view of rating agencies, noteholder-friendly CDO managers are preferred; but the rating agencies' preference is understandable as they rate only the notes not the equity. It is difficult to decipher and distinguish between CDO managers who are noteholder friendly or otherwise, but some have acquired a particular reputation over time. Rating agency Moody's says: "Moody's looks for the collateral manager to possess the core competencies that will enable him/her to make sound investment decisions that are consistent with the spirit and letter of the governing documents. In turn, we then analyze the transaction assuming nothing more (or less) than such capable and effective management." [*Responses to Frequently Asked CDO Questions (Second of Series)* July 13, 2001]

In cases where the CDO manager owns equity in the CDO, the question of conflict becomes all the more glaring. Rating agencies have reviewed both the pros and cons of the manager holding equity in the CDO. Among the advantages are the facts that manager does not have the pressure of having to account for external equity holders, while having the understanding and support of equity investors if the manager has to strive to maintain the rating of the external notes.

At the same time, the cons are that the equity might have been sold with high-sounding promises and the temptation to give quick rewards to equity owners might conflict with the larger interest of the CDO, and therefore the ability to raise debt in the future. As rating agency Moody's puts it: "Collateral managers who fight the CDO structure to make immediate equity payments ("equity friendly"), while not trying to fix the deteriorating nature of their portfolios, ultimately harm the equity investor, the transaction and themselves. These managers may eventually turn off all payments to the equity investors with no reasonable chance of making any payments in the future. The short-sighted strategy of making immediate equity payments at the expense of a sound portfolio and structural integrity is very visible in the marketplace. Among the many ramifications to this approach is the difficulty, or impossibility, of raising debt at a reasonable cost for future deals. Basically, the CDO market may close for that manager."

The CDO manager's fees

The CDO manager's fees are among the first priorities in the waterfall. However, quite often the fees are broken into a primary fee and a secondary fee, with only the primary being senior to the noteholders and the secondary fee only payable out of the residual left after paying over the noteholders.

The adequacy of fees from a marketplace perspective is necessary both as a motivation to the manager to do his job well, as well as looking at the possibility of inviting a backup servicer to take the task for defaults by the primary servicer.

The CDO investors

The CDO equity investor obviously is driven by motivation of earning highly leveraged equity returns without committing substantial investments. Portfolio managers look at CDO equity for yield enhancement; American Express is known to have invested substantial amounts in junior classes of CDOs to enhance the returns of the bank as a whole.

CDOs offer a wide spectrum of ratings and maturities – from AAA to B and from 15 years to 4 years. Thus, they serve each investor's investment preferences.

Market practitioners confirm that there is very little secondary market activity in CDO tranches.

The CDO trustee

The trustee is one of the very significant agencies in CDOs, as for other asset-backed transactions. The trustee performs the functions of independent oversight over the manager, while also observing compliance with the indenture deed.

Rating agency Fitch has listed the following aspects that go into evaluating CDO trustees:

- Corporate affiliations;
- Primary assets types and total assets under management;
- Quality of systems used for bookkeeping;
- Performance history on past securitizations;
- Organizational chart and biographical information on key personnel;
- Management structure and philosophy;
- Experience of management and staff with respect to CDOs; and
- Crisis management and quality control. [DCR 's *Criteria for Rating Cash Flow CDOs* February 2000 DCR was later taken over by Fitch]

Authorization of trades

Trustees keep a constant vigil on new trades conducted, particularly the acquisition of new investments. The trustees have access to databases such as Bloomberg to independently verify credit ratings, maturity dates, type of security, default status, interest rates, currency and issuer domicile to ensure compliance with the indenture provisions.

Credit enhancer and swap counterparty

To take care of interest rate risk and provide additional credit enhancements, sometimes various forms of credit enhancements from external parties such as interest rate swaps and sureties may be brought in. Most of these enhancements in CDOs are investor-driven and as CDOs are privately placed, these enhancements are used only based on specific concerns of larger investors.

The role of credit enhancers in CDOs is similar to other CDO transactions. However, rating agencies often use the weakest-link approach to ratings, so there are certain preconditions for credit enhancers as follows:

- Ratings of parties should be at least as high as the desired rating of the senior notes;
- Replacement parties should be required to maintain a corresponding rating level; and
- Termination events associated with these contracts should not introduce additional risks to the CDO transaction. [DCR 's *Criteria for Rating Cash Flow CDOs* February 2000 DCR was later taken over by Fitch]

Typical credit enhancements in CDOs

The enhancement structure for balance sheet CDOs is similar to traditional securitizations. The common forms of credit enhancements for arbitrage CDOs include:

- Stratification or subordination, including the equity piece
- Excess spread account
- Cash collateral
- Financial guarantee contract or insurance wrap
- Other forms of enhancements

Subordination

The most common form of credit enhancement used in CDOs is stratification. Almost all CDOs use one senior tranche, and have one junior-rated tranche in addition to an unrated equity or economic equity tranche. There may also be more rungs between the senior and the junior tranches.

The subordination must be supported by appropriate paydown structure. There are basically three payment strategies followed – sequential pay, fast/slow pay and pro-rata paydown. Pro-rata paydown suggests that payments are made to the junior tranches as they are made to the senior tranches. Proportional paydown reduces the amount of cash available to the senior tranches as default rates often increase as the collateral achieves a particular vintage. Therefore, the pro-rata payment structure is not greatly favored.

Cash collateral

Cash collateral implies a proportion of the cash payable to the originator for transfer of the collateral is retained by the trustees to be used as an enhancement. Needless to say, there is no better security than cash for the investors: however, cash collateral is inefficient from the viewpoint of equity owners.

Cash collateral implies a "negative carry," which means the rate of return on the collateral is significantly less than the coupon payable to the debt tranches. The higher the cash collateral, the less the returns will be on equity class.

Excess spread

In CDOs, excess spread is the difference between the coupon earned on the collateral and the coupon payable to liabilities. Excess spread is seen in both balance sheet and arbitrage structures; it is obviously higher in arbitrage transactions. There are two ways of using excess spread – by creating a cash collateral and by subordination of excess spread to the noteholders to comply with the OC/IC metrics. The second use of excess spread is almost universal. The first use is tantamount to building up a cash collateral with the difference that the collateral amount increases as the transaction achieves a vintage that is in line with the observed tendency of CDOs.

Bond insurance or financial guarantee

Bond insurance, particularly for the senior-most tranche, is becoming increasingly common where the indication is that in absence of such cover, the senior tranche is likely to see a AA rating. From the viewpoint of the issuer, the trade off is between the lower cost arising due to higher rating, versus the cost of insurance coverage. Rating agencies have mostly assigned a wrapped transaction the rating of the insurer. There is also a degree of volatility in such wrapped ratings in that if the rating of the insurer were to suffer a downgrade, the notes will also be downgraded.

Managing the assets of CDOs

Selecting and monitoring of the assets of a CDO, either market value or cash flow, is one of the most essential secrets to the success of a CDO. A CDO is essentially a correlation (or rather, diversification) product – there is good arbitraging opportunity in high-yield debt but unless one builds a diversified portfolio, it carries high risk. It is difficult for any single investor to build a diversified portfolio requiring a huge investment. Hence, the essential idea of a CDO is to use external funding sources to fund the acquisition and hope to make arbitrage revenues for the equity.

"A Collateralized Debt Obligation is a correlation product. Investors in this product are buying correlation risk. To determine that they are getting a fair return for this risk, they must be able to measure the correlation risk."[8]

Asset quality tests

Minimum average rating test

This test stipulates the weighted-average rating of the portfolio. This rating is usually B to B+ in cash flow transactions.

Minimum recovery rate test

The recovery rate is the rate of recovery if there is a default in a security. The recovery rates are given by tabulations of rating agencies, and the minimum recovery rate test stipulates the minimum weighted-average recovery rate for the portfolio.

Industry and obligor concentration tests

These tests specify the maximum investment in a particular industry or an individual obligor. The typical industry concentration norm is 8% and the typical borrower concentration is 2.5%.

Minimum weighted average coupon

This stipulates the weighted-average coupon of the assets in the portfolio. A typical weighted average coupon for a bond portfolio is 9–9.5%, but these rates change with varying economic conditions.

Cash flow coverage tests

These are the tests that require regular adherence over the term of the CDO. There are two significant coverage tests, both in respect of the rated securities, discussed below:

Over-collateralization and interest coverage ratios

An over-collateralization test (OC test) is an important structural protection granted to the investors in the CDO. Every CDO is a leverage vehicle – the value of the various classes of liabilities are leveraged several times. However, the OC test puts a limit to the extent of leverage relative to the assets of the CDO. There are OC tests for various classes of rated liabilities. There is no OC test for the junior-most or unrated class. For any particular class, the OC test is defined as:

The OC Cover should be more than or equal to:

- The principal amount of performing assets plus the lower of the fair market value or assumed recovery rate of defaulted assets plus cash and short-term investments not comprising interest income
- Divided by the principal amount (including capitalized interest) of the respective class of notes plus principal amount of the classes senior to the respective class.

Note that for computing the value of the assets (numerator), we have taken the par value or book value of the assets, not their market value. Market value is the basis for the OC test for market value CDOs.

The value of the denominator takes into account the par value of all senior classes. So, the OC test for the senior most class will take the value of assets and the par value of the senior class. The same for the mezzanine class will take the value of the assets and the par value of the senior and the mezzanine class, and so on.

Illustration of the working of the OC test

Tranche A Over-collateralization Test	CDO Asset Par/Tranche A Par
Tranche B Over-collateralization Test	CDO Asset Par/Tranche A and B Par
Tranche C Over-collateralization Test	CDO Asset Par/Tranche A, B, and C Par

---

Let us assume there are four classes of liabilities in a CDO of which the last one is unrated, adding up as:

	Par value	*Minimum O/C*	*Present O/C*
Class A	50	1.5	2.2
Class B	30	1.2	2.2
Class C	15	1.1	1.157895
Class D	15	NA	
Total of liabilities	110		
Principal value of the assets	110		

Column 2 above is the minimum OC cover required; column 3 gives the OC as at beginning.

	Par value	*Minimum O/C*	*Present O/C*	
Class A	50	1.5	2	
Class B	30	1.2	1.25	
Class C	15	1.1	1.052632	BREACH
Class D	15	NA		
Total of liabilities	110			
Value of assets after default	100			

Let us now suppose some of the assets in the portfolio default and the (par value of the performing assets + recoverable value of non-performing assets) comes down to 100.

We can see above that the OC test for Class C is breached above.

When the OC test is breached, the transaction is to be de-leveraged. This means, instead of reinvesting the cash flow, the manager must now pay off cash to the various classes sequentially (or pro-rata, if the transaction documents provide for pro-rata paydown – see later under heading paydown structures) as per their priority order till the OC test is restored. Assuming the waterfall structure does not allow any principal to be paid on a junior class before the senior class is fully redeemed (sequential paydown structure), the position after de-leverage will emerge as shown in revised worksheet.

	Par value	Minimum O/C	Present O/C	
Class A	5	1.5	11	
Class B	30	1.2	1.571429	
Class C	15	1.1	1.1	pass
Class D	15	NA		
Total of liabilities	20			
Reduce asset worth	45			
Value of the assets after default	55			

The other similar structural protection is the interest cover test. The working of the interest coverage test is substantially similar, but is based on an inter-coverage ratio. That is, the interest receivable on the assets must cover the interest payable on a particular class in a certain proportion.

Illustration of the working of the IC test	
Tranche A Interest Coverage Test	CDO Asset Coupon/Tranche A Coupon
Tranche B Interest Coverage Test	CDO Asset Coupon/Tranche A and B Coupon
Tranche C Interest Coverage Test	CDO Asset Coupon/Tranche A, B, and C Coupon

A breach of this test will also lead to diversion of all interest to the senior classes to pay them off until the interest coverage ratio is restored.

For market value CDOs, the working of the OC test will be based on the market value of the collateral, instead of the par value. For assets where ready estimates of market value are not available, the CDO manager applies certain discounting factors to assess the market value.

What happens when tests are not met?

A continued compliance with the OC and IC test is the protection system of CDOs. The methodology has been borrowed from hedge funds that use deleveraging to tackle the breach of the triggers.

The OC test, for example, stipulates the ratio between the par value (or, for market value CDOs, the market value) of the non-defaulting collateral to the par value of the outstanding debt. The contingencies in which the OC test will be breached are:

- There is a default; if there is a default, the CDO will sell the defaulted collateral at a discounted price. If the default results into the OC test being breached, the cash collected on default as also the excess spread will not be reinvested or paid to the equity holders, but will be used to pay off so much principal to Class A so that the outstanding class A satisfies the OC test.
- There is call; if some of the collateral is called and prepaid, the CDO will be free to reinvest the excess cash as prepayment of the collateral – it does not violate the OC test.

Cash flow waterfall

Based on the structural features and the tests discussed above, the principal and interest waterfall of a CDO will be as shown in Figures 17.4 and 17.5.

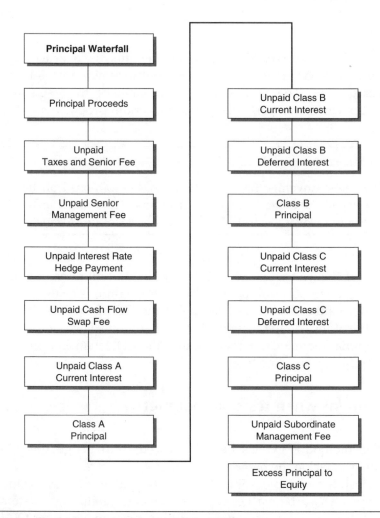

Figure 17.4 Typical principal waterfall in CDO

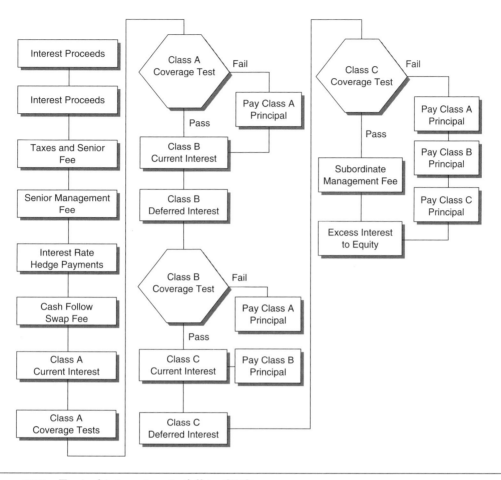

Figure 17.5 Typical interest waterfall in CDO

Resecuritization or structured finance CDOs

An interesting application of arbitrage CDOs is resecuritization, securitization of securitization investments. These are called structured product CDOs or resecuritizations. The collateral for resecuritizations is, mostly, subordinate tranches of RMBS, CMBS, CDOs and other ABS transactions.

Growth of structured product CDOs

The market for structured product CDOs has undergone unprecedented growth over the last five years or so. From virtually zero in 1998, the structured product CDO market recorded a volume of about US$10 billion in 2000, nearly 10% of the entire CDO market.

The resecuritization volumes have registered a sharp increase over 2001. The repackaging of ABS transactions during the first half of 2001 was a highlight of all CDO activity in this year. "The repackaging of structured finance

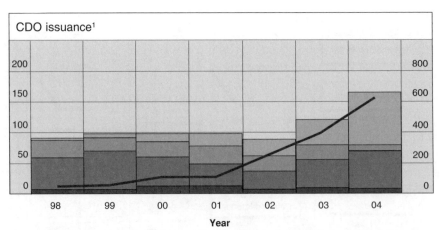

¹Categories refer to primary collateral composition of cash CDOs (except for synthetic CDOs); in billions of US dollars.   ²Investment grade.   ³High-yeild loans and bonds.   ⁴Total notional volume of synthetics (ie CDS protection sold to support issuance).

Figure 17.6   CDO Issurance data

and real estate securities in 2001 has become one of the fastest growing sectors of the CDO universe" [Standard & Poor's Commentary *Cash Flow CDOs: Continued Growth Despite Economic Risks* Dated August 7, 2001]. In 2001, three classes of repackaging transactions had for the most part emerged:

- CDO of CMBS/REIT/RMBS,
- CDO of CDOs, and
- CDO of ABS and real estate securities.

The arbitrage opportunities in resecuritizations arise because of the inefficient pricing of subordinate tranches. Deutsche Bank came out with a report entitled *Structured Product CDOs*, March 20, 2001, in which they analyze the increasing popularity of structured product CDOs. They see three reasons behind the growing popularity of structured product CDOs:

- Despite awareness about the strength and quality of mezzanine and junior tranches of ABS, their pricing in the market suffers primarily due to liquidity problems, lack of understanding of default, servicer and prepayment risks. By pooling them together and repackaging them as senior securities, the CDO manager allows investors to participate in this asset class.
- As compared to traditional corporate debt, the default rates and recovery rates in structured products have been far more comfortable.
- Investors have gravitated towards structured product CDOs to achieve greater diversification and returns. "Traditional CDOs backed by non-investment grade bonds and loans are a levered exposure to the high-yield market; defaults are typically triggered by a single discrete event such as a

bankruptcy filing. CDOs backed by ABS, CMBS and RMBS expose investors to risks which are generally a function of collateral deterioration much of which is actuarial in nature, occurs over time, and is factored into the structures of the underlying securities." [Deutsche Bank report entitled *Structured Product CDOs* March 20, 2001.]

From the viewpoint of an OC test, there is a typical issue for structured product CDOs; technically, a default arises in structured products only when the investment is not paid by the legal maturity, which may be postponing a realized weakness for a substantial time. There may be a prolonged deterioration in credit quality before the instrument counts as a default. Rating agency Moody's says it will treat an investment as having defaulted once it starts PIK-ing (paying in kind, typically allowed for structured finance investments.)

Structured finance CDOs have continued to grow – both in the cash flow form as also in the synthetic form. In the synthetic structured finance segment, structuring would hopefully become more standardized with ISDA's new protocol for credit default swaps on asset-backed securities.

Distressed debt CDOs

Of late, there has been a tremendous interest in the market for distressed product CDOs, that that is, CDOs whose collateral solely consists of distressed securities. Enticing expressions such as "spinning gold out of straw" have been given for such CDOs.[9] Fitch, Standard & Poor's, and Moody's have all come out with special reports on this very exciting subject.

The landmark distressed product CDO was the Ark CLO 2000-1 Ltd. This transaction was given confidential ratings in December 2000. Fleet Boston Corp was the originator that transferred a portfolio of distressed and defaulted bank loans in excess of US$1.5 billion to the SPV. Rating agency Standard & Poor's writes that Ark CLO was the first rated cash flow transaction based on a non-performing portfolio after nearly a decade – the last transaction was in the late 1990s originated by Grant Street Bank.

Over the last 2-3 years, the U.S. market has seen a deluge of defaulted high-yield bonds issued around 1997 and 1998. During the first 6 months of 2001, approximately US$46 billion worth of high-yield bonds defaulted. "Vulture funding" has been known in U.S. loan markets for quite some time and in various facets; takeovers of failed corporations, viatical insurance policy transfers – distressed debt CDOs are instances of a market looking for a business opportunity in all calamities.

Thus, distressed product CDOs represent the opportunities in the defaulted or near-to-default securities market.

What is distressed debt?

Distressed debt is not necessarily a debt that has been defaulted. Rating agency Fitch defines distressed securities as "those loans priced at less than $0.90 and bonds trading 1,000 basis points or more above treasuries." [Fitch

Special Report on *Framework for Rating Distressed Debt CDOs* July 27, 2001] Standard & Poor's, on the other hand, gives a more subjective definition: "A credit is considered distressed if the borrower's financial ability to honour its obligations/payments comes into question. Common indicators that a borrower may have financial difficulty in repaying its debt include a breach of financial covenants, a payment or technical default of other debt obligations, or a trading value for their debt significantly below other debt with similar coupon and maturity features". [Standard & Poor's Commentary titled *Distressed Debt CDOs: Spinning Straw Into Gold* May 7, 2001] Practically, these are securities or loans that carry a rating of CCC or below.

Distressed debt CDOs and securitization of non-performing loans

There have been several instances of securitization of non-performing loans in the U.S., Italy, Japan and some Asian countries. Here banks as originators, or asset reconstruction companies as acquirers of non-performing loans, have securitized non-performing loans usually with a very high degree of over-collateralization and/or a recourse or guarantees.

Distressed debt CDOs are usually arbitrage transactions and are therefore different from the securitization of NPLs. However, if a bank does a balance sheet transaction of distressed loans, it may be the same as a distressed debt CDO.

Motivations

Rating agency Standard & Poor's says: "Securitizing distressed assets provides a method by which a financial institution can limit its exposure to further losses. Through the capital markets, the risks and rewards of these problem debt instruments can be transferred to CDO investors. By structuring a transaction with different levels of subordination, reserves, and tiered repayment priorities, different ratings can be achieved for different classes of notes, attracting investors with different risk appetites. Of course, in these transactions as in all securitizations, investors expect that the asset pool, coupled with the ability of the collateral manager to recover sufficient value from the defaulted loans, will provide an attractive reward for the risk they undertake." [Standard & Poor's Commentary titled *Distressed Debt CDOs: Spinning Straw Into Gold* May 7, 2001]

Credit enhancement levels

The key issue in distressed debt CDOs is the computation of credit enhancement levels. Rating agencies have declared that the adequate level of credit enhancements are to be worked out based on a case by case analysis of the collateral. Basically, the collateral for a distressed debt CDO would consist of (a) defaulted debt; (b) distressed but not yet defaulted debt; and (c) non-distressed debt. For defaulted assets, the credit enhancement is based on the recovery rate and possible time taken in recovery, whereas in non-distressed debt, it is default probability followed by recovery rate and time in recovery.

The fair value of defaulted securities is computed based on bid prices, which in turn is discounted for the debt's stage in the distress cycle. Debt in a late stage of the cycle, that is, if sufficient time has elapsed since declaration of bankruptcy, usually see the market bid rates give a good indication of the terminal value of the securities. However, if the debts are in early stage of the cycle, the bid rates are not a very good indicator.

"As a general rule, for all securitizations, the total debt issued by the CDO must be less than the total purchase price or fair market value of the underlying collateral assets." [Fitch: *Special Report: Framework for Rating Distressed Debt CDOs*, July 27, 2001]

Typical issues in distressed debt CDOs

Rating agencies have indicated preference for the sequential payment method rather than proportional pay for distressed debt CDOs. [Standard & Poor's Commentary titled *Distressed Debt CDOs: Spinning Straw Into Gold* May 7, 2001] The payout structure of most distressed debt CDOs allows for payments in kind.

Reinvestment periods are not suitable for distressed debt CDOs in view of the illiquid nature of their investments.

Besides, the legal maturity of the CDO tranches is sufficiently long to allow the manager time to work out and resolve the distressed debt.

Among other specialities, taxation of distressed debt CDOs is a unique issue. Concerns have been expressed that a distressed debt CDO may be construed to be in the business of workouts, and therefore, may be treated as a taxable entity rather than as a conduit.

Evaluation of distressed debt CDO manager

Needless to stress, as in any other CDO, the evaluation of the CDO manager is extremely significant in a distressed debt transaction. Rating agency Standard & Poor's has listed [Standard & Poor's Commentary titled *Distressed Debt CDOs: Spinning Straw Into Gold* May 7, 2001] the following factors that would be used in evaluation of the CDO manager:

- How much experience does the manager have in working out distressed or defaulted debt and how good is its track record?
- What are the key loan selection criteria for selecting the loans that are included in the securitized pool?
- Has the collateral manager done its own due diligence review of each borrower/loan?
- Based on its review, does the collateral manager have a well-defined exit strategy for each potential problem loan?
- Does the exit strategy aim to maximize recovery values?
- Is the collateral manager relying on restructuring, liquidating, or refinancing of the troubled debt in its recovery maximization strategy?

- Is the manager anticipating selling the distressed loan under some circumstances?
- Does the manager have a controlling interest in the loan or will it be relying on following the majority of the credit group's decisions?
- Does the manager understand the cash flow requirements of a securitized transaction and is its strategy compatible with those requirements?
- What are the expected third-party professional fees and expenses?
- How will third-party fees be managed?
- Are the collateral manager's financial incentives aligned with the interests of the securitization investors?

Hedge fund CDOS or fund of funds

The CDO device has also been used outside of traditional debt securities, for example, to pick up other financial instruments such as hedge fund investments and private equity investments. To give a more generic scope to the term CDO, a new term prevails to include these devices – collateralized financial or fund obligations (CFOs), or hedge fund CDOs, or fund of funds.

Hedge funds are unregulated investment vehicles[10] that allow the fund manager a high degree of freedom to trade without restrictions, and generate high returns on equity to the investors. The hedge fund essentially captures arbitrage opportunities on a risk-neutral basis. Strategies adopted by hedge funds are broadly classed into directional strategies and non-directional strategies. The former takes an exposure on a certain security or segment based on perception of the manager, while the latter is purely arbitraging by exploiting discrepancies between different market segments (say, cash and synthetic market, spot and futures market).[11] The investors are typically high net worth individuals or aggressive investors looking at picking yields from this investment.

CFOs would make investments in several hedge funds, attain the benefit of diversification, and therefore, pick up arbitrage profits for the equity investors while still being able to pay a coupon to the senior classes. The hedge fund or private equity investment is in the nature of an equity investment, and the device of securitization repackages the equity investment, at least largely, into debt.

One of the first such transactions was Prime Edge.

Investing in CDOs

Investor motivations

CDO investments have been growing fast, and in spite of the fact that a number of high-yield debts are defaulting, the demand for CDOs has still been quite robust. There were lots of downgrades during 2000 and 2001, yet investors have shown a preference for CDO investments.

The following factors explain the investor preference for CDOs:

1. Strength and Stability

So far all concerned agencies have tried to maintain the sanctity of the CDO market by ensuring solid and strong portfolios in CDOs. Various over-collateralization and other metrics have been carefully applied to result in robust portfolios.

2. Diversification

CDOs enable an investor already active in traditional ABSs to diversify his portfolio as they are a class of asset not correlated with traditional ABSs. For example, credit rating agencies consider traditional ABSs and CDOs as two separate sectors, when they calculate a portfolio Diversity Score. Investing in structured product CDOs indirectly allows investors to invest in a much more diversified pool.

3. Standardization

Though they are still a very young product, CDO methodology, rating devices and structures have by and large been standardized. The credit enhancement levels, portfolio composition and diversity scores have been fairly uniformly been observed.

4. Deep market

Investors have access to a very deep market in CDOs in volumes that are very large and are growing steadily.

5. Yield

At the same rating, CDOs offer higher yields than traditional ABSs and so more than plain-vanilla securities. For instance, the indicative spreads as of December 2005 for a AAA, 5-year CDO varies from LibOR + 20bp to LibOR + 55bps, depending on the nature of the underlying and the management type. The spreads have been tightening over time, but the spread advantage is expected to continue for some time.

6. Transparency

The risk of each transaction is represented by a limited number of commercial debtors that can be analyzed on an issue-by-issue basis. In general, for investors in senior tranches, aggregate data suffice, but detailed information is given to investors in the more subordinated tranches who can fine-tune the monitoring of their investment carefully, or even model their risk profile themselves.

Risks in CDO investment – structure and collateral risks

Correlation risk

The quintessential risk in any CDO structure is the risk of correlation. CDOs are essentially correlation products; they create seemingly diversified asset pools and try to take advantage of the lack of correlation by stretching the leverage. Needless to say, high degrees of leverage can never be sustained with presence of correlation. So, if correlation is present in the CDO, the structure becomes extremely fragile.

Armed with CDO evaluation models of the rating agencies, CDO structurers have the advantage of doing a mix and match of assets to try and contrive a structure that under rating agencies' presumptions, has minimal asset correlation. For example, if obligors from different industry clusters are selected as per the rating agencies' definitions, the correlation is presumed to be either zero or minimal.[12]

In situations of economic downturn, most often, there are widespread inter-sector disturbances that cause generic losses to several segments. In adverse business cycles, the absence of correlations among industries will not hold, leading to a basic assumption being questioned.

Interest rate and basis mismatch

One of the primary interest rate risks in CDO collateral arises out of mismatch; interest rates on liabilities are often a floating rate, while that on the loans may either be fixed or may be floating with reference to a different base rate. While hedge agreements are often used to alleviate interest rate risk, the CDO manager must ensure that the hedge counterparty complies with the conditions set by rating agencies to give AAA rating to the senior tranches. See for example the conditions put up by Standard & Poor's in *Global CBO/ CLO Criteria*, pages 50-1.

Connected mismatches are mismatches in payment dates and payment periodicity. Running the CLO, to an extent, is like running an operating financial intermediation business and these mismatches are unavoidable. The mismatch spells a risk either way; if the assets repay more frequently than the liabilities, the transaction suffers from negative carry; if the assets repay less frequently than the liabilities, the transaction runs into liquidity problems. One possible solution is to enter into a TROR swap receiving payments matching with those on liabilities; however, the costs of the swap as well as the rating of the swap counterparty may both be issues of concern. If the swap counterparty is the issuer or an affiliate of the issuer, the swap will surely create problems of consolidation on bankruptcy.

High-yield transactions also suffer from "spread compression" risk, the risk of higher yielding investments either being called back or defaulting, while the reinvestment is in lower-yielding debt, and thus reducing the arbitrage spread. This is partly mitigated by the fact the coupon on the liabilities is also a floating rate.

Cross currency risk

Many CLO/CBO transactions are comprised of debt or loans from various countries particularly emerging markets. These are mostly hedged on a customized basis. Here again, the rating agencies' stipulation as to the rating of the hedge counterparty is important.

Liquidity risk

Liquidity risk arises in part from mismatches in coupon receipts and payments but more significantly may arise due to delays and defaults. The cash flow models that are made to analyze the default risk of a CDO do not capture the liquidity risk because it is essentially an intra-period risk – for example, the availability of cash during the half-year. The O/C and I/C tests also do not capture liquidity risks.

One of the ways usually adopted to minimize the liquidity problem is to ensure that when collateral is sold, the accrued interest portion inherent in the sale proceeds is not available for reinvestment but is retained for coupon payments. A certain minimum liquidity reserve may also be necessary.

Ramp up risks

The ramp up period may be anywhere between three to six months. In structured product CDOs the ramp up period is even longer. There is a much smaller ramp up period in balance sheet CDOs.

The risks during the ramp up period include the following: a negative carry during the ramp up period as the short-term investments carry much lower coupon; origination risk – the risk of bonds or assets not being available; concentration risk during the ramp up period; and adverse interest rate changes during the ramp up period.

Arbitrage transactions where ramp up risks are significant use various methods to reduce them. Among these are a staggered ramp up period, in which the aggregate ramp up is divided into smaller segments, each with a target ramp up period, so that if the ramp up is not achieved during that period, the excess must be returned.

Reinvestment risks during the revolving period

CDOs almost universally allow reinvestment by the CDO manager during a long enough period, usually during the first four to six years. The 100% reinvestment period is the period ending one year before the repayment begins, and thereafter, a proportion of the cash collected is reinvested. The reinvestment option with the CDO manager is supposedly quite useful. "Reinvestment of collateral cash receipts during this time has several advantages. Reinvestment can be used to maintain collateral quality and portfolio diversification, as rating changes, or as maturities, amortization, prepayments, or defaults reconfigure the pool. In addition, if prepayments during the revolving period are reinvested in eligible collateral, they may preserve yield for investors. The revolving period also enables a transaction to profit purely from limited trading activities, that is, buying and selling bonds and/or loans." [Standard & Poor's *Global CBO/CLO Rating Criteria*]

On the other hand, reinvestment option introduces several risks. These risks are redressed by introducing the collateral tests – OC, IC, weighted average coupon, weighted average maturity, tests. Besides, stringent criteria for selection of eligible collateral is followed which is also subject to authorization and surveillance of the trustees.

Lack of granularity

Most CDOs invest in a limited number of assets, which is by definition matched with the arbitrage objective. One cannot think of making arbitrage profits investing in a very broad cross-section of assets. The asset pool of a typical CDO will consist of 80 – 120 names. If there are 80 assets in the pool, default of any one asset will mean 1.25% of the assets defaulting. The asset pool is non-granular, so it exposes the structure risk.

Asset risks

The risks inherent in the collateral portfolio differ based on the composition of the portfolio. Essentially a portfolio of bonds or loans, apart from carrying the most basic and common risk – credit risk, carries the risk of interest rate variability, callability, convertibility and exchangeability.

Increasingly in CDOs, managers are including assets which, in rating jargon, have a bivariate risk probability. Bivariate risk probability is said to arise when an asset is subject to risk of two unconnected parties. For example, a loan participation is subject to the risk of the borrower as well as the risk of the other loan participant. Rating agencies would prefer to put a limit on such assets.

There are unrated assets and other opaque risks being introduced in CDOs.

Taxation of CDOs

This section may be best read after our chapter on Taxation of Securitization Transactions.

Taxation of CDOs is not very different from other asset-backed securities, with the difference that it is unlikely that the SPV will qualify for tax exemption as a conduit. It may be structured as a tax exempt FASIT but much of the structural flexibility required in CDOs will be lost in that case.

Therefore, in most cases the CDO is domiciled in a tax exempt jurisdiction to avoid entity level taxation. The jurisdiction preferred by U.S. securitizers is the Cayman Islands.

At the same time, to avoid treatment as foreign debt, a U.S.-based co-issuer is brought in for the securities. The issuance of securities is mostly done u/s 144A, as it is mostly a private placement and is offered to qualified institutional investors.

Legal issues specific to CDOs

We suggest that this section may also be taken up in conjunction with, and preferably after, the chapter on Legal Issues.

Bankruptcy remoteness

The bankruptcy remoteness condition is the same for CDO SPVs as for any other asset-backed transaction. While bankruptcy remoteness concerns are similar, the question of substantive consolidation is less relevant in arbitrage CDOs than in other securitizations as the assets are not transferred by any particular originator. Rating agencies insist on the same limited business/ limited purpose conditions and require separateness covenants as for other securitizations.

True sale opinion

True sale opinion is a key legal issue in regular asset-backed transactions; for CBOs where bonds have been purchased in open market transactions, this issue does not arise at all. Therefore, in CBOs a mere certificate from the sponsor that the bonds have been bought from open market is sufficient.

Transfer of loans and perfection

There is complete diversity between a CDO and CLO when it comes to transfer related issues. Bonds are transferable assets, loans are not. In U.S. practice, it is common to use two tier SPVs for CLOs originated by banks. The transfer of assets and the structuring of the SPVs for loans originated by the bank may be a significant question not only from a legal viewpoint but from an accounting viewpoint.

In our discussion on the legal issues in securitization, we have talked of several methods of transferring assets – assignment, novation and participation. In several loan securitizations, instead of transfer, participation interests are used. The reasons could be either restrictions on assignment in originating contracts, or difficulties by way of stamp duties. Issuance of participation rights does not stand at the same footing as a true sale, but in several jurisdictions participation rights are well regarded.

In U.S. as well as U.K. CLOs, participation rights have been used. In case of FDIC-insured banks, rating agencies sometimes seek affirmations from FDIC, so that the security interest created by the bank will not be avoidable in bankruptcy. Several lawyers have indicated that even participations may be structured as true sales. However, the widely prevailing view is that a participation may only be viewed as creation of equitable interest. Equitable transfer is based on the legal doctrine that if the transferor and transferee have intended a transfer, and all that is lacking is a legal compliance, courts would likely give effect to the intent of parties. Rating agency Standard & Poor's has listed the following requirements to treat participation as a sale:

- Segregation of funds: The funds received are earmarked separately and are not commingled with the funds of the transferor to give evidence of the intent to affect a transfer.
- Document segregation: The loan agreements as part of the securitized pool should be physically segregated from other transferor loans or participation agreements. These loan agreements should be held in custody by the transferor and clearly segregated in files conspicuously labelled to show that the loans or participations are held by the transferor as custodian for the issuing SPE and for the transferor as lender. The portion of each loan participation participated to the issuing SPE at any point in time should be specified in the loan or participation files.
- Promissory notes: To the extent there are promissory notes that are instruments under the applicable state's UCC for the loans being participated, the notes should be transferred to the issuing SPE or held pursuant to a formal custody agreement, with a third party acting as custodian for the benefit of both the transferor and the issuing SPE.
- Record keeping and reporting requirements: The transferor should keep complete, accurate and separate records for each loan, including records sufficient to monitor the amount of each loan participated to the issuing SPE, including the transfers of loan receivables from the transferor's general and custody/trust accounts to the issuing SPE, and use of such receivables for reinvestment during the revolving period.

Besides, as the originator remains the lender in relation to the borrower, there are several safeguards in such cases, for example:

- The lender will not agree to any variation, rescheduling or waiver that may in any way affect the interests of the transferee;
- The lender will not release any security;
- Waive any claim against the borrower or the guarantor;
- State clearly by way of a written document that the lender is a lender for record but is a servicer for the transferee.

Yet another method of transfer used sometimes in the U.K. is a declaration of trust by the lender. Sumitomo Bank used this in a European CLO called Aurora. Here the bank does not transfer the loans but merely declares trust on the loans and/or proceeds of the loans. There are issues as to whether this method will qualify for off-balance sheet accounting or regulatory relief.

Right of set off

Prima facie in loan transactions, the right of set off is an inherent right of the borrower. The right of set off exists unless a sale of the loan has been notified to the borrower. In some jurisdictions, there are rights of set off granted by law. These risks are redressed by providing for adequate credit enhancement.

Lender liability

A unique concern also exists in securitizations relating to liabilities of the lender, particularly for undrawn loan amounts. If a lender fails to allow draw-down of a partly drawn loan, it might expose the lender to liability, including damages. The concern in securitization is: whether such a liability can be reflected on the SPV, or can be converted into a right of set off with the borrower. This issue is jurisdiction specific and depends on the laws of the jurisdiction concerned.

CDOs and index trading

Index trading has become immensely popular over the last few years. Indices are the standard set of counterparty names for different markets, such as iTraxx, or DJ CDX.NA.IG These indices are comparable to standardized synthetic CDOs. It is possible to trade in the whole index or in specific tranches.

Index trading has a relative advantage, in that it is completely standardized. Synthetic CDOs and Index trades are discussed at length in Vinod Kothari: *Credit Derivatives and Synthetic Securitisation*.

Current problems facing the CDO sector

Increasing downgrades and defaults

The downgrades in the CDO sector have obviously kept pace with down-grades in the high-yield segment. High-yield defaults are increasing at a pace stronger than in the past, which might reflect on CDO tranches.

The table below shows downgrades by Standard & Poor's up to the second quarter of 2003.[13]

Table 17.4   U.S. CDO Downgrades and percentage of total ABS downgrades

Asset class	1Q02	2Q02	3Q02	4Q02	1Q03	2Q03	2002 (%)	2002 (#)	YTD 2003 (%)	YTD 2003 (#)
Cash flow CDO	29	29	46	39	56	72	20%	143	27%	128
Synthetics	19	45	81	40	27	29	26%	185	12%	56
Synthetic CDO	2	3	11	23	9	8	5%	39	4%	17
Total	102	132	290	199	142	342	100%	723	100%	484

As is apparent, downgrades, particularly of high-yield CDOs issued in 1997 and 1998, have marred the scene. The number of downgrades has grown, particularly in the second quarter of 2003.

In 2004 and 2005 as well, rating instability in the CDO segment has generally been higher than other classes of asset backed securities. The following data for 2005 from Standard & Poor's reveal this:

Table 17.5 Standard & Poor's 2005 Global CDO Rating Actions By Region, CDO Segment, and Reason (No.)

CDO segment	—U.S.— Down	Up	—Europe— Down	Up	—Japan— Down	Up	—Asia/ Australia/ New Zealand— Down	Up	—Global— Down	Up
Cash flow arbitrage corporate high-yield CBO	15	50	0	2	0	0	0	0	15	52
Cash flow arbitrage corporate high-yield CLO	2	16	0	1	0	0	0	0	2	17
Cash flow arbitrage corporate investment-grade CBO	0	1	0	0	0	0	0	0	0	1
Cash flow balance sheet corporate CDO	0	6	0	0	0	3	0	0	0	9
Cash flow CDO of ABS	70	31	0	0	0	0	0	0	70	31
Cash flow CDO of CDO	0	0	0	0	0	0	0	0	0	0
Cash flow CDO retranching	4	4	0	0	0	0	0	0	4	4
Cash flow other	4	0	0	0	0	0	0	0	4	0
Market value/ leveraged funds	0	0	0	0	0	0	0	0	0	0
Other CDOs	0	0	0	4	0	0	0	0	0	4
Synthetic balance sheet corporate CDO	0	0	4	9	0	0	4	3	8	12
Synthetic CDO of ABS	6	0	1	1		6	1		8	7
Synthetic CDO of CDO	6	0	40	9	5		2	1	53	10
Synthetic corporate investment-grade CDO	17	2	117	74	50	3	17	30	201	109
Synthetic emerging market CDO	21	0	0	4	0	0	0	0	21	4
Synthetic other CDOs	0	9	0	0	0	0	0	0	0	9
Total	145	119	162	104	55	12	24	34	386	269

Accounting worries

The CDO segment has been hit with several accounting worries over the last couple of years or so. To start with, one of the most significant problems facing CDO investors was the accounting rule called EITF 99-20,[14] which requires write-down through revenue account of all credit- and prepayment-sensitive ABS investments. Mark-to-market valuation is done based on projected cash flow that is reviewed on each reporting date. Subordinate tranches of CDOs are obviously credit-sensitive.

The second quarter of 2001 saw massive write downs owing to EITF 99-20. American Express was a leading name that wrote a massive amount to its revenue and the CEO admitted that it had not properly understood the risks of investing in CDO junior tranches.

Then, the FASB brought a new consolidation standard called FIN 46, later revised to FIN 46R, and then there was a proposed amendment of conditions for QSPEs – several CDO conduits may come up for consolidation under these accounting rules. See Chapter 27.

De-leveraging

An increasing number of transactions witnessed failures in coverage tests (such as the overcollateralization test) with several tranches de-levering as a result. The continuation of this trend will likely have a negative impact on the internal rate-of-return projections used to sell these deals and thus translate into potential ratings volatility.

Rating agencies approaches to CDOs

Rating agencies use different models to size the required credit enhancement for CDOs, but the inherent methodology in each case has the following underlying approach:

- Assessment of probability of default (PD): The probability of default for each obligor in the pool is established. This may be done based on data, or the ratings of each obligor, or the prevailing CDS or credit spreads for the obligor.
- Assumptions of correlations are punched in: The correlation assumption is a major input in the engine and so it is necessary to understand the rating agencies' approach to correlation.
- Currently, all three rating agencies use variations of simulation approaches to arrive at a probability distribution of the different number of defaults in the pool.
- Based on this distribution of default probabilities, the required size of enhancement, relative to the rating of the tranche, is worked out.

Historically, models have constantly been developed and refined, partly to accommodate new types of CDOs coming in the market, and partly to refine the correlation assumptions with changing market realities.

Moody's *binomial expansion technique* (BET) was one of the earliest and most transparent methods to size up the credit enhancement for CDOs. The inherent assumptions of this method were that it was possible to construct a theoretical model of obligors who did not have a correlation and who had a consistent probability of default, the binomial theory is applicable here. The binomial theory applies to several uncorrelated trials that have a fixed probability of success each time, such as tossing a coin or throwing dice. Likewise, for an obligor, the number of obligors in an uncorrelated pool is the number of trials, and the probability of default is the rate of success. Our objective is to assess the probability distribution of probabilities of a number of obligors in the pool defaulting, given by the *binomial distribution*.

The theoretical model, which supposedly eliminated the correlation in the pool, was called the *diversity score*.

S&P was using a simulation device all the time. While the binomial expansion device was very simple and easy to use, it had several inherent limitations; it did not allow for correlation as an input; it presumed the probability of default of obligors in the pool to be the same.

Moody's came out with several revisions of BET – first a multiple BET method and then a correlated BET. Finally, Moody's also adopted the simulation approach in November 2004 when it adopted the CDO ROM model.

Note the models discussed below are suitable for synthetic transactions. Cash transactions have cash flow features – cash flow waterfall, income, excess spread, reinvestment and OC/IC triggers – not relevant for synthetic transactions. The rating of cash transactions is based on stressing the cash flow and the defaults on the relevant bonds. Of course, simulation of default times may be done using the same methodology as explained below.

The models used by the different rating agencies are discussed below.

S&P's CDO Evaluator

The Evaluator uses the MC simulation device to arrive at a distribution of probabilities. The probabilities of default for each obligor are established based on the "default tables" inherent in the program.

Correlation inputs are 5% inter-industry and 30% intra-industry. The inputs of correlations are also different based on whether the industry is local, regional or global, based on industry classifications.

If the number of obligors in the pool is N, the simulation method takes a $N \times N$ matrix of correlation. It produces random numbers, which are then multiplied by a Cholesky decomposition of the correlation matrix, thus producing correlated random numbers. Such correlated random numbers are compared with the probability of default of each obligor to find if the obligor, based on the random number, defaults or survives.

The efficiency of simulations is based on the number of runs, so in each run the total number of defaults is counted. For instance, if the program had a total of 10,000 runs, we count cases of 0 defaults, 1 default, 2 defaults, 3 defaults and so on. The total number of observations for each number of defaults is divided by the total number of observations, to give the probability of default.

Thus, the probability distribution is the combined result of (a) PDs for each obligor; (b) correlation; (c) and randomness of the default scenarios.

The default of each obligor leads to a loss, and the loss is equal to (1-recovery rate). Recovery rate assumptions are different for each asset, based on several factors primarily location of the asset. In the new model, S&P simulates the recovery rates based on a beta distributed recovery rate, input being the mean and the standard deviation of the recoveries.

The result of the model will be a scenario default rate distribution for each class of ratings illustrated below:

Table 17.6   Scenario default rates for different ratings

Desired Rating	Rating Default Probability	Scenario Default Rate
AAA	0.271%	10.29%
AA+	0.341%	9.77%
AA	0.731%	7.93%
AA−	0.846%	7.71%
A+	0.949%	7.50%
A	1.070%	7.29%
A−	1.279%	7.07%
BBB+	1.775%	5.49%
BBB	2.406%	5.31%
BBB−	4.245%	5.14%
BB+	7.671%	3.60%
BB	11.014%	3.47%
BB−	12.681%	3.34%
B+	16.310%	2.14%
B	23.210%	2.06%
B−	26.996%	1.97%
CCC+	33.903%	1.89%
CCC	40.811%	0.90%
CCC−	60.541%	0.86%

The above table implies that for a given pool (for which the run on the model was done) to see a AAA rating, we will have to assume a 10.29% probability of default. That is, the credit enhancement should provide for (1-recovery rate) times the defaults.

Moody's CDO ROM model

The Moody's CDO ROM model is apparently suited for synthetic CDOs, both first level and CDO^2. The features of the model are:

- Analyzes both 1st and 2nd level synthetic CDO structures
- Monte Carlo simulation approach using asset correlation and look-through technology
- Default and loss probability based on Moody's ratings
- Correlated corporate recovery distribution based on domicile and seniority
- Integrated soft credit event[15] stresses and cheapest-to-deliver haircuts[16]
- Ability to run multiple tranche scenarios simultaneously

For asset correlation, which understandably is the most significant differentiating factor in the different rating agencies' approaches, Moody's divides industry clusters into low, medium and high intra-industry correlations. It also classifies into local, semi-local and global industries, as S&P does. "Asset correlations were derived through the integration of various mathematical approaches based on Moody's rating co-movements in conjunction with the expertise of Moody's analysts," says a Moody's presentation.

Are the ratings actually assigned to the deal differently from what transpires by a run on the model? The Moody's presentation says: "While CDOROM is the same tool used by Moody's analysts, the ratings are based on an integrated approach examining both qualitative as well as quantitative factors:

- The model allows analysts (as well as the market) to run various sensitivity analyses on the portfolios and attachment points
- Documentation and any ancillary legal, structural, collateral and counterparty risks are thoroughly reviewed and incorporated into the final ratings
- Adverse selection, mis-aligned incentives and other moral hazard risks are incorporated into the analysis."

Fitch VECTOR model

The Fitch Default VECTOR model ("VECTOR") is Fitch Ratings' main quantitative tool for evaluating default risk in credit portfolios backing CDOs. The model can be used for CDOs of corporate as well as asset-backed securities.

VECTOR, a multi-period Monte Carlo simulation model, simulates the default behavior of individual assets in a portfolio for each year of a transaction. It draws on a structural form methodology, which holds that a firm defaults if the value of its assets falls below the value of its liabilities (also referred to as the default threshold). Monte Carlo simulation is a widely used tool in finance and allows the modeling of the distribution of portfolio defaults and losses, taking into account default probability and recovery rates as well as the correlation between assets in a portfolio. The main output of VECTOR is the rating default rate ("RDR"), rating loss rate ("RLR") and the rating recovery rate ("RRR"), corresponding to each rating stress. The model output includes various portfolio statistics as well as a portfolio's default and loss distribution, and the aggregate distribution of defaults over time. VECTOR is not a cash flow model and does not take into account structural features such as payment waterfalls or excess spread. The RDR, RRR and timing of defaults are input to be used in the cash flow model. For synthetic deals that do not benefit from structural support, the RLR shows the calculation of the minimum credit enhancement for each rating.

VECTOR also allows a "look-through" analysis for synthetic CDOs of CDOs ("CDO squared") portfolios. The model simulates the universe of underlying assets that make up the "inner" CDOs and computes the loss on the "master" CDO, taking into account the attachment and detachment points of the individual "inner" CDO tranches. The correlation and recovery rate simulations on the "inner" CDOs are based on the individual underlying portfolios and no additional assumptions are required.

Notes

1 Data based on European Securitization Forum, Summer 2003 report, apparently excluding synthetic CDOs.
2 *Commonly Asked CDO Questions: Moody's Responds* February 23, 2001.
3 Banc of America Securities: **Collateralized Debt Obligations: An Introduction to Arbitrage CBOs and CLOs,** June 1999.
4 Banc of America Securities: *An Introduction to Arbitrage CBOs and CLOs* p. 6.
5 Banc America Securities: *Ibid.*
6 Moody's: *Responses to Frequently Asked CDO Questions (Second of Series)* July 13, 2001.
7 Standard & Poor's commentary titled *Cash Flow CDOs: Continued Growth Despite Economic Risks* August 7, 2001.
8 Richard K Skora: *Correlation – the hidden risk in Collateralized Debt Obligations.*
9 See, for example, Standard & Poor's Commentary titled *Distressed Debt CDOs: Spinning Straw Into Gold* dated May 7, 2001.
10 The U.S. SEC recently formulated rules about registration of funds that fall under certain criteria.
11 This might only serve as a broad classification, amplified through the use of leverage. The CSFB Tremont Hedge Fund Index identifies 10 major hedge fund strategies – convertible arbitrage, dedicated short bias, emerging markets, equity market-neutral, event-driven, fixed-income arbitrage, global macro, long-short equity, managed futures and multi-strategy.
12 S&P's new CDO Evaluator, version 3 supposes a 5% inter-industry correlation. The assumption was zero in earlier models.

13 Based on *Structured Finance Global Ratings Roundup Quarterly: Second-Quarter Performance Trends.*

14 See details in Chapter 27 on Accounting for Securitization.

15 Restructuring, for example, is not a hard credit event as it is not a default.

16 In physical delivery credit default swap transactions, usually the protection buyer has the option to deliver an asset that qualifies for the "deliverable obligation" characteristics. Obviously the protection buyer buys the cheapest asset prevailing in the market and delivers the same.

Chapter 18

Asset-backed Commercial Paper

Technically speaking, the distinction between asset-backed securities and asset-backed commercial paper (ABCP) is primarily one of the tenure of the paper – commercial paper by definition is short-term funding,[1] and is therefore mostly used for short-term assets such as trade receivables. However, in many cases ABCP tries to be exactly the opposite of credit card securitization. The former finances a short-term asset with longer-term securities, while ABCP conduits raise short-term funding and make at least partial investments in longer-term paper, thereby trying to capture the arbitrage possibilities. ABCP is most commonly run in the form of on-going conduit programs, mostly by leading commercial banks, where the conduit provides a window of short term trade receivables funding to the clients of the banks.

ABCP is a device of securitization of working capital and demonstrates how capital markets as an invading force have successfully made inroads into one of the historical domains of banks – working capital finance.

Genesis of asset-backed commercial paper

Asset-backed commercial paper (ABCP) is a device used by banks to see operating assets such as trade receivables funded by issuance of securities. Traditionally, banks devised ABCP conduits as a device to put their current asset credits off their balance sheets and yet provide liquidity support to their clients.

For example, assume Bank A has a client X, whose working capital needs are funded by the bank. If the bank wants to release the regulatory capital that is locked in this credit asset, the bank can set up a conduit, essentially an SPV that issues commercial paper. The conduit will buy the receivables of the client and see the same funded by issuance of commercial paper. The bank will be required to provide some liquidity support to the conduit, as it is practically impossible to match the maturities of the commercial paper to the realization of trade receivables. Thus, the credit asset is moved off the balance sheet, giving the bank regulatory relief.

Asset-backed commercial paper was originated in 1983 by Citibank [Citrioco LP, now Ciesco] to wean back corporates who migrated to capital markets for cheaper funding. In Europe, the first conduit was set up by Barclays [Sceptre] in late 1992. Today, asset-backed commercial paper conduits exist in all global financial centers, in some cases with local names such as BdT in France.

A Moody's special report *Asset-backed Commercial Paper: Understanding the Risks*[2] traces reasons as to why ABCP developed:

- Competition: Intensive interbank competition forced banks to find ways to reduce the cost of working capital funding to their prime clients. By using ABCP programs, the bank could allow its corporate customers to obtain working capital funded at prime rates, plus the fees for putting the program together.
- ABCP conduits could make the banks' balance sheets substantially leaner by pushing the funding off-balance sheet. The banks' capital requirements would be limited only to the extent of liquidity facilities, or to the extent the support granted to the conduit could be regarded as a direct credit substitute.[3]
- Fee income: The program would allow the bank to increase its fee income by way of managing the conduit. Fee-based income has a sizeable favorable impact on banks' financial statements.

The ABCP market

The ABCP market has gone through interesting stages in development. It grew very fast, to climb a steep growth curve over a very short time. According to U.S. market data, there was steep growth up to 2001, thereafter the growth curve started levelling off. The growth was affected by several reasons, including accounting concerns. The growth pattern is easily visible in Figure 18.1 below:

The current volume of outstanding ABCP in the U.S. ranges between US$750 billion to US$850 billion, as shown by Figure 18.1 (numbers in millions, source Bond Market Association):[4]

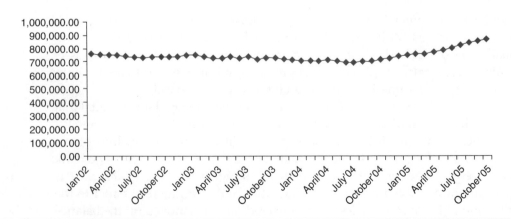

Figure 18.1   Outstanding US ABCP

A very large part of the commercial paper market today is asset-backed commercial paper. Figure 18.2 illustrates that this share has grown over time:

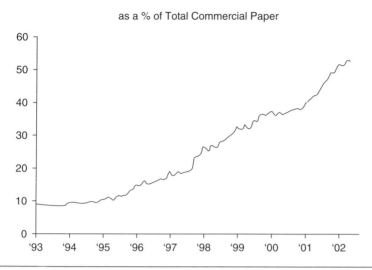

as a % of Total Commercial Paper

Figure 18.2 Asset-Backed Commercial Paper

At end of November 2005, the FRB reported a total CP outstanding of US$1.645 trillion wherein the share of ABCP outstanding was US$907 billion, over 55%.[5]

Besides the U.S., ABCP activity is popular in Europe, Japan and segments of Australia and Asia. A report by Standard and Poor's gives the following global data on ABCP volumes:

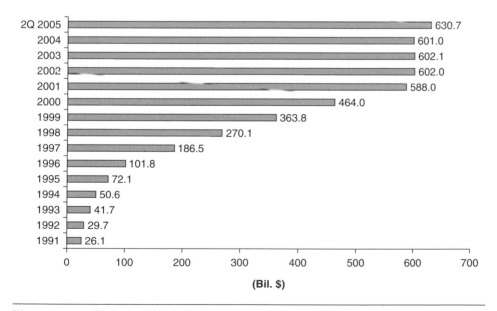

Figure 18.3 Global US$ ABCP outstanding

Source: S&P Report US$ ABCP Market Statistics: Outstandings Hit Record Highs in Second-Quarter 2005 October 17, 2005

Types of ABCP conduits

What is a conduit?

The issuance of ABCP is a standard and on-going feature, so banks mostly run on-going programs for ABCP issuance. These are run on the balance sheet as a specific entity, called the conduit. The conduit is a thinly-capitalized SPV, satisfying the general bankruptcy-remoteness criteria for bankruptcy remoteness. On a continuing basis, the conduit continues to acquire assets and funds the same by issuing CPs. However, there is almost necessarily an asset-liability mismatch, requiring the bank to provide liquidity support to the conduit.

Types of conduits

Depending upon whether the bank provides full or partial liquidity support to the conduit, ABCP can be either *fully supported* or *partly supported*.

ABCP conduits are virtual subsets of the parent bank. If the bank provides full liquidity support to the conduit, for regulatory purposes, the liquidity support given by the bank may be treated as a *direct credit substitute* in which case the assets held by the conduit are aggregated with those of the bank. Though the early ABCP conduits were directly and fully supported by the banks, subsequent regulation, essentially capital rules, have made fully supported conduits unpopular.

There also emerged a variant of fully supported conduits, which were supported, but not visibly or directly. For example, a support provider would either agree to purchase the outstanding paper, or would agree to provide a loan to redeem the paper. Such a support has a structural similarity to the fully supported type discussed above and therefore has the potential of being treated, for regulatory purposes, the same as fully supported conduits.

Not only are ABCP conduits set up by banks, there are also large issuers who set up their own conduits.

From the viewpoint of the number of originators throwing their receivables into the program, ABCP conduits are known as *single seller* and *multiple seller* conduits. In the latter case, the credit enhancements (and/or liquidity enhancements) are found both at the level of transfer by each originator (originator-level enhancement) and at the programme level. Figure 18.4 shows the structure of a multi-seller conduit:

The growth of multi-seller conduits has far outpaced that of single seller conduits.

The other type of conduit is called *arbitrage conduit*, which holds either high quality credit assets (hence *credit arbitrage*) or securities (hence, *securities arbitrage*), where the idea is to essentially gain regulatory or economic capital arbitrage by holding these assets in conduit balance sheets. S&P defines an arbitrage conduit as one where 95% or more of the assets are securities. Figure 18.5 shows the relative volumes of different types of conduits in the U.S. market:

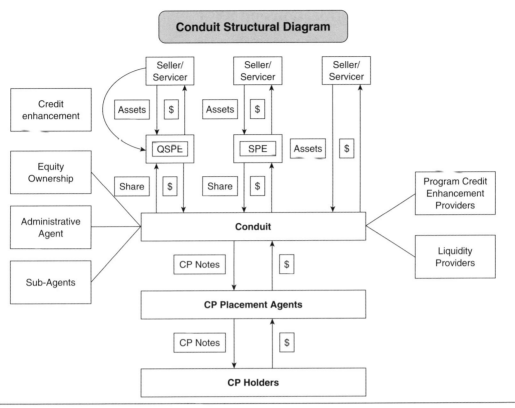

Figure 18.4   Conduit structural diagram

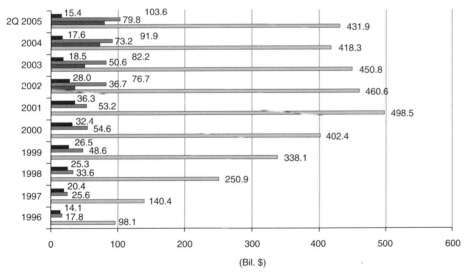

During second-quarter 2005, arbitrage programs were segmented from multiseller programs going back to December 2002. Aribitrage programs are identified as conduits in which 95% or more of the sellers are securities.

Figure 18.5   Global US$ ABCP Outstandings by program type at period end*

Traditional securitization and ABCP

ABCP has emerged over time as an independent class by itself. Though the basic legal structure and principles of structured finance used are similar, there are some very basic differences between ABS (also called *term securitization*, to distinguish from CP) and ABCP:

- Conduit investments are revolving and fluctuating, where ABS mostly has a fixed pool size.
- ABS collateral type is mostly homogenous. ABCP conduits buy a variety of assets.
- In ABS, it is common to see maturity matching, or to see short term assets such as card receivables funded by issuing long-term paper. Conduits do the contrary – they might fund long-term assets by issuing short-term paper, which they do on a continuous basis. The liquidity support of the sponsoring bank allows them to play with the mismatches.
- There is no scheduled amortization of the conduits' assets.
- Unlike term securitizations, ABCP conduits are going concerns with no fixed winding up date.

ABCP collateral

Asset-backed commercial paper was primarily designed to acquire and fund trade receivables of larger corporations. However, over time, the collateral composition has shifted heavily into investing in financial instruments. Today, ABCP conduits invest into all possible financial instruments such as CDO securities, lease receivables and corporate loans. Figure 18.6 on the collateral composition shows this. It is notable that conduits are increasingly being used to provide warehousing financing for mortgages, and for holding CDOs and equipment lease receivables.

It may be interesting to compare the 2005 collateral composition with 1993. A Moody's special report shows that the 1993 composition was as follows:

Trade and term receivables – 60%; credit card receivables – 12%; corporate loans – 12%; and others – 15%.

Credit enhancement structure

The issuer of commercial paper is called a *conduit*, because the program provides an issuance window to several seller-level trusts, each of which are special purpose vehicles. Typically, for multi-seller conduits the assets are pooled at the level of the seller and are transferred into individual SPVs. The sellers are, for a trade receivables conduit, the customers of the sponsor bank who want to see trade receivables funding. At this level, enhancement is done to an extent sufficient to ensure that the interest being sold from this SPV to the conduit will allow the conduit to see the desired rating. This means, unless the conduit itself is credit-enhanced, the rating of the interest sold by the SPVs to the conduit should match up with the desired rating of the CP to be issued by the conduit, say AAA. See Figure 18.6 for a typical multi-seller conduit credit support.

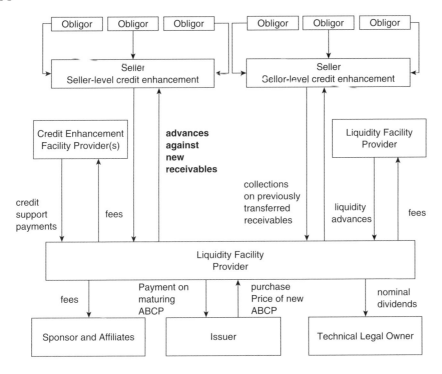

Figure 18.6 Partially supported, multiseller ABCP program structure

The enhancement granted at the seller level is called *seller level enhancement* or *pool-level enhancement*. When all these pool interests, duly credit enhanced, are sold to the conduit, there might be a credit or liquidity enhancement at that level too, which is called *programme level enhancement*.

The programme level enhancements may include both a credit enhancement and a liquidity enhancement. At the program level, the basic objective is to obtain a liquidity enhancement (as the interest sold to the conduit has already been credit enhanced), and the credit enhancement at this level is primarily required to be able to tie up liquidity facilities with independent banks. Liquidity support is discussed in the following heading.

It is important to understand that the credit-enhancement hierarchy is mostly relevant for partially supported conduits; as for fully supported conduits, what matters is the quality of the supporting bank.

Pool-level and program level enhancement

The pool-level enhancements provide support to the value of assets in the particular pool. The program-wide enhancement supports all outstanding paper at the given time, and therefore provides a fungible enhancement.

The pool-level enhancement should primarily cover the credit risk of the assets. In addition, where appropriate it should cover the exchange rate risk, interest risk, and for non-interest-bearing assets, the carrying costs. The normal methods of enhancement here are similar to those used for typical securitizations – over-collateralization, excess spread, recourse, subordination, or swaps with the originator. The pool-level enhancement may typically be done with a pool-level SPV that buys the receivables.

Program-wide enhancement covers all the outstanding paper in the pool and is designed to provide support when the losses out of a pool exceed the pool-level enhancement. The typical methods of enhancement here will include letters of credit, guarantee or insurance cover and cash collateral. The program-wide support also indicates the level of commitment of the sponsor to ensure the quality of the assets: "Presence of at least 5% program-wide credit enhancement of unrated pools of assets provides comfort that the program-wide, credit-enhancement provider is incentivized to keep the underwriting standards high."[6]

De-leverage triggers

As for CDOs, ABCP programs also have de-leverage triggers. These are in form of *stop-issuance* or *wind down* triggers, which stop the conduit from issuing any further CP or acquiring further assets, if and as long as the triggers are in place. Once again, in view of the two-tier nature of the conduit, the triggers may be set at the pool-level and the program level.

Pool-level triggers may include the following:

- Insolvency or bankruptcy of a seller/servicer.
- Downgrade of a seller's long- or short-term credit rating below a specified level.
- Cross-default of a seller under other debt obligations.
- Material adverse change in a seller/servicer's ability to perform its duties as servicer.
- Deterioration of portfolio assets below specified levels of write offs, delinquencies or dilution.
- Depletion of credit enhancement below a required minimum amount.
- Default or breach of any covenant, representation, or warranty by a seller or servicer.

Typical program-wide triggers are:

- Failure of the conduit to repay a maturing CP or an outstanding liquidity advance when due.
- Any program documents cease to be in full force and effect.
- Default or breach of any covenant, representation, or warranty by the conduit.
- The net worth of the conduit falls below a certain level.
- Draws on program-wide credit enhancement exceed a certain amount.

When the triggers are in place, the money collected from the assets will not be used for further asset creation but will be used to pay down the paper as it falls due.

Liquidity support

The liquidity support basically comes in form facilities to draw from a line of credit. The line of a credit provider, quite often, is the administrative agent himself.

For single-seller conduits, liquidity support is usually 100%.

The liquidity provider also needs to have a certain rating, and in the event of rating downgrade, the liquidity provider is required to collateralize the liquidity commitment with cash.

Depending on the way the liquidity facility is drawn up, it may go beyond mere liquidity support and provide credit support to the transaction as well. For example, sometimes the liquidity provider enters into an asset purchase agreement, which provides additional protection to the investors. "The liquidity provider also may be willing to provide an asset purchase agreement that provides added protection to investors. The liquidity facility provider's willingness to agree to such an arrangement will be based on the provider's independent document review and evaluation of the underlying pool of receivables. Though liquidity banks typically fund for non-defaulted receivables, the banks may be more willing to provide more than just protection against timing mismatches when the originator of the receivables has other banking arrangements with the provider and is an investment-grade client."[7]

Parties to an ABCP program

Program sponsor

The program sponsor is the one who originates the whole idea and refers assets to the conduit. The program sponsors are usually banks and financial intermediaries, who use the conduits as extensions of the bank's credit book to house specific assets with capital market funding.

It is not necessary for the conduit sponsor to own equity in the conduit. As SPVs are typically structured, the legal equity of the conduit is usually small and is owned by unaffiliated parties, such as charitable trusts. However, the sponsor does have material interest in the conduit, mostly by way of credit enhancements. These credit enhancements allow the bank to reap much of the excess spreads earned by the conduit, so the prime beneficiary of the conduit is mostly the sponsor. This practice led the accounting standard setters to put in place a different method for recognizing the economic equity of the conduit; rule FIN 46R is discussed in Chapter 27 on accounting issues.

Administrative agent

Like most securitization transactions have servicers, there is an administrative agent to handle the regular administration of the conduit. The administrative agent may be the program sponsor himself, or one of his affiliated entities, because the control on day-to-day affairs of the conduits vests in the agent. The functions of the administrative agent extend to issuing, managing and repaying the CP, advising on purchase of assets, as also handling the interface with the sellers.

The administrative agent's duties in connection with the day-to-day operations of the program include:

- Arranging for the execution and safekeeping of the program documents.
- Maintaining operating accounts.
- Investing excess funds in permitted investments.
- Maintaining general accounting records.
- Preparing financial statements and arranging audits.
- Preserving books and records.
- Giving notices to other key parties.
- Preparing monthly portfolio reports.

The administrative agent's duties in connection with the issuance and repayment of CP include:

- Instructing the issuing and paying agent and the depositary.
- Purchasing and selling assets.
- Extending loans to borrowers.
- Determining when draws on liquidity and credit enhancement facilities are necessary.

The administrative agent's role may also include credit advisory services such as:

- Identifying and referring new sellers to the conduit.
- Conducting due diligence reviews of prospective sellers.
- Structuring the acquisition of asset interests and any necessary hedging arrangements.
- Monitoring the ongoing performance of each transaction.

In short, the administrative agent does everything for the conduit that the bank would have done if the assets were housed on the bank's balance sheet.

Manager

The role of the manager, usually an independent, is from viewpoint of corporate governance. The manager is responsible for items like calling meetings of the executive committee.

Placement agent

This relates to the placing of commercial paper in the market. The placements are typically done through investment banks and money market brokers.

Issuing and paying agent

This is basically a settlement and record keeping function common to all fixed income issuance.

Rating of ABCP Conduits

As opposed to asset-backed securities where the rating is done based on a particular pool, for ABCP, the rating is given for the program. For obvious reasons, the quality of the management of the conduit, the fungible program-wide enhancement are relevant factors in the program rating. The distinction between traditional ABS rating and that of the program is quite obvious – the conduit rating is similar to the rating of corporates.

The significant aspects of rating of the conduit are:

Rating of the management

Unlike ABS where the inanimate pool of assets is responsible for ratings, ABCP conduits stress more the entity, that is, the quality of the management of the conduit. The administrator is the management of the program. Adding assets to the book of a conduit is similar to underwriting a credit asset in a bank, so the credit asset policy of the conduit becomes extremely significant here. It is necessary to ensure that the conduit is not being saddled with assets rejected by the regular credit assessment of the bank. S&P says: "In reviewing a conduit's underwriting criteria, assurances will be sought that the conduit's credit and investment policy is at least as conservative as that of the program administrator where the administrator is a financial institution."[8] Sound transaction underwriting would involve a thorough analysis of seller risks, including evaluation of overall creditworthiness, risk of fraud, product and performance risk, and the capacity of the seller to meet its representation and warranties.

Credit quality of assets

For multi-seller conduits, the asset quality will be driven by the underwriting standards used by each originator who sells receivables into pools. For each pool, an assessment of the experience of the originator and the underwriting standards for the assets become important. The sizing of the enhancement for each pool is done based on traditional ABS rating principles, that is, historical delinquency rates and loss severity. In assessing the quality of the pool, obligor concentration is one of the factors to specifically examine. Obligor concentration to a pool does what correlation does to CDOs. Transactions typically establish obligor concentration limits and industry concentration limits.

Receivables eligibility criteria

There is expected to be an ongoing acquisition of receivables in the pool, so it is significant to define the eligibility and – in particular – the ineligibility criteria. In view of the heterogeneous nature of receivables, it is not possible to standardize the criteria, but some of the common criteria will include:[9]

- Delinquent and defaulted accounts: Borrowing base calculations exclude defaulted receivables and receivables that are past due beyond a specified delinquency category;
- Excess concentration: To limit investor exposure to a default by a large obligor, most structures set size limitations for individual obligors. Such concentration limitations are generally set on the basis of the credit rating of the obligor and the credit enhancement floor;
- Unperformed contracts: Receivables billed before completion of service or delivery of a product are generally limited for two reasons; obligors are less likely to pay for a service or product that has not been received, and the receivables may be considered an executory contract[10] that could be rejected by the originator during its insolvency;
- Bill and hold receivables: In these instances, the supplier sells the goods to the customer but holds the inventory until the customer needs it. In the event of an insolvency of the supplier, the customer may attempt to stop payment on products that have not been shipped. In addition, collecting payment on other shipments to the customer may be difficult if there is a bill and hold inventory paid for but not in the possession of the customer;
- Tenor: The tenor of the receivables is limited to lower credit risk. For example, for an auto lease transaction, eligible leases might be limited to leases with an original tenor of 24 months. Generally, 60-month leases have more credit risk than 24-month leases because the originator is exposed to the default risk of the obligor for a longer period of time; and
- Obligor characteristics: Eligibility criteria also define obligor characteristics. For example, a pool may exclude receivables from affiliates of the originator or receivables from obligors who are past due on other receivables. A pool may also exclude receivables from obligors in a jurisdiction where it may be difficult to perfect the conduit's lien interest in such receivables.

Case study: Spinnaker Capital ABCP Program

Spinnaker Capital Pty. Ltd., Australia, runs an ABCP program. This study examines some salient features from its documents as of December 2005. The program intends to issue securities up to A$5 billion for maturities up to 95 days. Paper is issued by the program both in Australia and the U.S. The U.S. paper is issued by its U.S. subsidiary.

The collateral for the transaction is financial securities or receivables with a rating of AA–/A–1+.

The pool-level enhancement is over-collateralization or other forms enhancement, for example, insurance. For financial securities, the rating of the securities must at least be AA- /A–1+.

Program-wide support is in form of revolving cash advance facility provided by State Street Bank. The amount of this will be worked out in consultation with S&P.

In addition, State Street Bank also provides a liquidity facility to cover 102% of the par value of the paper. The liquidity facility is available for each trust – each pool. The liquidity facility is meant for the following:

- In respect of maturing Spinnaker Commercial Paper, if there is a mismatch in the timing of those obligations and the receipt of collections or other amounts received in respect of the relevant Receivables pool;
- To provide increased funding to the relevant Receivables Trust, or to make payments in respect of maturing Spinnaker Commercial Paper, if there is a disruption in the availability of funding in the commercial paper market;
- To pay amounts payable in respect of utilizations previously made under the relevant liquidity facility (the facility will be revolving in nature); and
- In respect of Intercompany Loan drawdowns, if there is a mismatch in the timing of those obligations and the issue of Spinnaker Commercial Paper, drawings under the Program Credit Enhancement Facility or income available from a Receivables Trust available for this purpose.

The administrator, State Street Capital Pty. Ltd, is also the receivables trustee and the manager of the trust.

Notes

1   The word "commercial paper" might have different meanings in different countries. It is typically taken to mean funding for a term up to 270 days, in some cases, going up to 365 days. The definition of the term "security" is in the U.S. Securities Act excludes securities with maturities up to 9 months – hence, CP of 270 days' maturity is exempt from securities regulation. Commercial paper is issued mostly in the form of promissory notes.
2   April 1993 by Mark Adelson.
3   For more on direct credit substitute and aspects of regulatory capital, see Chapter 21 on Regulatory Issues.
4   Recent commercial paper outstandings may be found on http://www. federalreserve.gov/releases/cp/default.htm#outstandings.

5   Analysis of data http://www.federalreserve.gov/releases/cp/table1.htm, last visited December 24, 2005.

6   S&P Global ABCP Criteria.

7   S&P Global ABCP Criteria.

8   Global ABCP Criteria, September 29, 2005.

9   Based on S&P: *ibid*.

10 See, for impact of executory clauses on the transfer, Chapter 23 on Legal Issues.

Chapter 19

Future Flows Securitization[1]

Over recent years, one of the most talked about applications of securitization, particularly from the emerging markets, has been future flows securitization. In a future flow transaction, the originator transfers a stream of cash flow, not necessarily an income, which will be dedicated to making payments to investors before the cash flow reaches the originator.

Take an electricity company securitizing electricity revenues, or an airlines company securitizing air ticket sales. The right to income does not exist today; it will exist over a period of time presuming the electricity company continues to sell power or the airlines continues to fly. If they do, the cash flows secured by sale of power in the first case and air tickets in the second will be trapped at the source, beyond the reach of the originator or its creditors, and used to pay off investors first, and then will be released to the originator for the rest of his requirements.

While traditional asset-backed transactions relate to assets that exist, future flows transactions relate to assets expected to exist. There is a source, a business, an infrastructure, from which the asset will arise. The source, business or infrastructure in question will have to be worked upon to generate the income; in other words, the income has not been originated and set apart such that repayment of the securities is a self-liquidating exercise. On the other hand, future flows is close to corporate funding in that there needs to be a performance on the assets or infrastructure to see the cash flow with which the securities will be paid.

What future flows are securitizable?

The essential premise in a future flow securitization is if a framework exists that will give rise to cash flows in future, the cash flow from such framework is a candidate for securitization. If the framework itself does not exist, the investors would be taking exposure in a dream; their rights would probably be worse than for secured lending. For example, if the cow exists, but not the milk, the milk can be securitized, as whoever owns the cow would be able to milk it. If both the milk and cow do not exist, it is not a proper candidate for securitization.

Thus, revenues from air ticket sales, electricity sales, telephone rentals, export receivables from natural resources, have been the subject of future flows securitization. However, in an apparent overdrive, sometimes, even something as integrally performance-based as the sales of goods or services are considered, out of businesses that require continued performance.

Some key features of future flows deals

Uncertain receivables

By its very nature, future flow receivables are uncertain, and largely unpredictable. Therefore, the originator transfers a certain portion of the receivables, and retains the excess over the transferred portion as the seller's interest. The transferred portion is the core receivable, which based on a past track record and after applying stress levels can be predictably certain. Thus, over a period the extent of the seller's interest varies based on the origination.

Box 19.1 Future flows: Selling a stream or selling a dream?

- By definition, future flows relate to cash flows yet to be originated.

- The distinction between asset-backed deals and future flows is almost the same as the traditional legal distinction between fixed and floating charges.

- As floating charges are generic, future flows are also generic in nature.

- Both are based on the ability to the lender to take timely action.

Cash flow trapping

A future flows deal, in its essence, is a cash flow trapping device. There is purportedly a mechanism of the sale of receivables – often backed by true sale opinions – but evidently, as what is being sold is yet to be generated, the whole concept will have no meaning unless the trustees could have physical trapping of the cash flows generated by the subject receivables, before they are routed to the originators.

Prioritization of the transferee

In a traditional asset-backed transaction, the transferee is concerned with only the cash flows that have been transferred. In a future flows transaction, the transferee is entitled, at least in the first stage, to the entire cash flow from the subject receivables, though the transferred interest is substantially lesser. After retaining the portion relating to the transferred interest, the trustees relay the balance of the cash to the transferor on account of the transferor's interest. It is from this amount that the transferor meets his regular operating expenses. In other words, by virtue of the cash flow trapping, the transferee gets a priority over even the operating expenses of the transferor.

High extent of over-collateralization

In most future flow transactions, the extent of overcollateralization is substantially higher than for asset-backed transactions. This is to safeguard against the fact that the investors are likely to be affected by the performance risk of the originator. Investors may have a cushion against the credit risks, but the fact that the airline does not fly at all or the electricity company does not generate power at all, is not guarded against, except by substantial over-collateralization or cash reserves.

Restrictions on the borrower's business

Being a quasi-lending type exposure, a future flow deal typically places restrictions on the borrower's ability to borrow and create encumbrances or liens, and similar covenants.

No originator independence

While asset-backed transactions are structured so as to be independent of the originator (except to the extent of servicing), future flows deals are substantially, if not completely, dependent on the originator. Therefore, seldom have future flow deals been able to traverse the rating of the originator; their motive is not to arbitrage the originator rating but the sovereign rating, as discussed in the next section. Or, alternatively, the motive is to achieve a higher extent of funding than permitted by traditional methods.

Not off-balance sheet

As future flow securitizations are not off-balance sheet, many of the typical merits of off-balance sheet financing – gain on sale and capital relief – do not apply.

Why future flow securitization?

The essential questions to ask in a future flow securitization are: What is the temptation of the originator in assigning future incomes? Would the originator not be better off in securing a traditional secured funding?

It is important to understand the answer to this question well, as it also highlights the proper application of future flows transactions. Conceptually, a future flow transaction would make sense for the originator if it helps the originator to reduce his overall cost of funding. This would be possible only if (a) the transaction helps the originator to borrow more; and/or (b) the transaction helps the originator to borrow at less cost.

The extent of borrowing possible in future flows deals is determined by the cash flows and the level of over-collateralization required. A traditional lender, on the other hand, is mostly concerned with values of assets on the balance sheet. For example, a typical working capital financing bank looks at the current assets on the balance sheet. If the balance sheet assets are four-months cash flow, a bank might provide 75% thereof, or three-months working capital. A securitization investor looks at cash flows for his regular servicing; with a collateralization of two times, a securitization transaction might result in funding of even 20-months cash flow. Therefore, it is quite possible for a future flow deal to result in an increased extent of borrowing.

On the cost of borrowing, the essential question is: Does future flow securitization remove any of the risks of traditional lending? All traditional lending is subject to the performance risk of the originator. If the originator does not perform or function at all, a lender would face default. The same is true for securitization also. However, future flows transactions remove two significant risks – credit risk and sovereign risk.

Credit risk, divested from the performance risk of the originator, implies a situation where the originator has cash flow, but does not pay up investors. This problem would be resolved in securitization if the transaction gives the SPV a legal right over the cash flow that is trapped at source.

Another important objective of future flow transactions has been to remove sovereign risk. This applies for cross-border lending, as most of the future flows transactions so far have been limited to cross-border investments. If an external lender gives a loan to a borrower, say, from an emerging market country, the risk the investor faces is that in the event of an exchange crisis the sovereign may either impose a moratorium on payments to external lenders or may redirect foreign exchange earnings. A future flow deal tries to eliminate this risk by giving investors a legal right over cash flow arising from countries other than the originator's, thereby trapping cash flow before it comes under the control of the sovereign.

As such, one of the motives in future flow securitization is to allow the originator, individually a strong company but based in a country with a poor sovereign rating, to pierce the sovereign rating. "In many cases, a future-flow securitization that encompasses strong legal and structural elements can achieve a rating that is above the sovereign ceiling otherwise applicable to foreign currency debt obligations issued directly by such company", says a report titled **Future-Flow Securitization Rating Methodology** (March 1999) by Duff and Phelps Credit Rating (before merger with Fitch).

Types of future flow deals

Domestic and cross-border future flows

One of the most common examples of a future flows securitization is securitization of cross border cash flow.

Take the instance of a typical transaction by say, a Mexican originator. The Mexican company has an option of borrowing from international markets, but the lenders would be concerned with currency risk (seen since 1997) and sovereign risks. This originator, say, exports crude oil to U.S. The cash flow emanating out of U.S. will be securitized and transferred to the SPV, set up in the U.S. The importers buying the crude oil from this originator would sign a notice and acknowledgement of assignment so as to subject them to U.S. law and force them to make payments to the SPV.

Now, the investors are secured against exchange risk, as the export receivables are in U.S. dollars. The investors are secured against sovereign risk as the cash flows are payable by U.S. companies subject to the sovereign's controls. The only risk the investors face is if the company is not producing and exporting at all, or the company redirects its exports to some other countries not covered by the legal rights of the investors.

While the above is a typical future flow deal based on sales of goods or services, the future flow transactions may be classified into the following broad heads:

Based on exports of goods or services

This is the most common type of future flow deals. Examples include the sale of pulp, oil or metals from Latin American countries.

Based on sales of goods or services

Several transactions taken place all over the world such as airline and train ticket receivables fall under this category.

Financial future flows

Financial future flows refer to flows to a financial intermediary, such as inward remittances to a bank. This is taken up in Chapter 21.

Other future flows

In addition, there are numerous examples such as the net settlement of telephone revenues and toll road receivables. Each of these receivables is a class by itself – the extent of dependence on the servicer may range from vital and essential to merely peripheral.

By country of origin, as per a report by Wachovia Securities,[2] the following countries have been the main suppliers of future flow securitizations, in order: Mexico, Brazil, Turkey, Venezuela, Argentina, Colombia, China, Peru, Chile and El Salvador.

Structural features

As future flow transactions are confronted with several risks relating to the originator as well as the obligors, most future flow transactions rely on structural features in addition to credit enhancements. These features include the following:

Subordination structures generally do not work

Based on the level of dependence the transaction has on the servicer, future flow transactions may either be completely originator-dependent or may have a peripheral dependence, although not essential. For example, a toll revenue securitization is a good case; here, the infrastructure giving rise to the income in the future already exists and all one has to do is to collect it to pay off investors. On the other hand, take the case of airline ticket receivables – there is a substantial performance risk on the entity. In the latter type cases, the rating of the transaction is generally capped at the entity rating of the originator.

If the originator's rating were to serve as a cap, subordination, which is basically intended to provide a rating upliftment, does not work for future flows.

Over-collateralization and cash reserve

One of the most significant forms of credit support to a future flow is the creation and maintenance of over-collateralization and a reserve. Over-collateralization implies the degree of DSCR of the transaction. In view of the fluctuating nature of income, after taking a base level of income (an easy approach may be to know some standard deviations from the average of the inflows), a degree of over-collateralization is reiteratively worked out to find the amount of funding. The debt service required should sufficiently be covered by expected income.

In addition, the excess of the inflows over the required debt service is typically pooled into a few months' cash reserve. The cash reserve helps smooth the temporary periods of volatility in the cash flow.

Early amortization triggers

The range and the scope of early amortization triggers (EATs) for future flow is often very wide. As for credit cards, early amortization is done by using the cash flow representing over-collateralization and trapping the cash representing the seller's interest. The triggers may include:

Cash flow-related early amortization triggers:

- If debt service coverage drops below the periodic required amount (e.g. 5.0x) for a payment period or below a monthly required amount (e.g. 3.0x).
- If any portion of interest and principal payments is not made in a timely manner.

Third party-related early amortization triggers:

- If a correspondent bank does not meet minimum credit rating requirements and that bank is not replaced in accordance with the terms of the transaction.

Company-related early amortization triggers:

- If litigation is instituted against the company that is likely to have a material adverse effect on the transaction.
- If the company becomes insolvent.
- Failure of the servicer to comply with terms of the transaction.

Sovereign-related early amortization triggers:

- If the sovereign interferes in any material way with the company's ability to direct cash flow to the transaction.
- If the sovereign takes over a substantial part of the business of the company.

What early amortization means to the originator

While the relevance of putting early amortization features in a transaction is understandable, it is necessary to realize that early amortization amounts to drying up the resources of the originator (by inherently calling back a loan or accelerating the repayment of the loan) when things start turning bad for him. The EATs are comparable to acceleration clauses in bank loans.

Reps and warranties of the seller

Compared with a traditional asset-backed deal, the representations and warranties of the seller in a future flow deal are far more comprehensive. This enables the transferee to relate a delinquency to a breach of the same and remit the delinquent receivables back to the seller.

Third-party guarantees a common feature

In several emerging market future flows, after a credit enhancement of the receivables to a volume for a AAA rating and making the transaction acceptable to international investors, obtaining an insurance wrap or a bond guarantee is quite a common feature. The use of guarantees is increasingly made in future flows; the Wachovia Securities document provides that 43% of the issuance in 2003 was wrapped.

Existing asset, future income: A case of toll revenues securitization

The spectrum of future flow securitization itself is very broad – every future flow transaction is a case by itself. One end of the spectrum includes toll revenues, where there is a mature infrastructure continuing to give rise to income in the future with a minimal performance risk on the part of the servicer. At the other extreme are export revenues from, say, textile exports that are completely dependent on the performance of the originator. In the former case, the transaction is technically structured as a future flow, but it is very comparable to a CMBS transaction wherein the value of the asset backs the investors. The asset in a CMBS is private property; the asset in toll revenues or infrastructure assets is a public utility and will rarely have a resale market.

"The toll road is operationally mature, and forms an integral part of the road transport network of a major city or interurban region. . . . The toll road has well defined and relatively low levels of future capital investment needs, at least during the expected period of the contemplated securitization. All toll roads require some reinvestment in order to maintain their peak operating capacity, and these capital improvements should be transparently incorporated into the financial forecast of the contemplated toll road debt securitization."[3] Thus, one of the primary risks in toll revenues securitization is the continuing need for regular capital investment, which must be provided for. However, this is also not significantly different from CMBS transactions, for which on-going repairs and maintenance costs are provided.

The Fitch report cited above has listed several instances of defaults in bonds by toll authorities – mainly because of factors such as a lack of economic development in the region. "In large part, these projects were built not to relieve existing traffic congestion, but to spur economic growth in underdeveloped areas.

Consequently, their less than satisfactory financial performance in their early-to-mid years is not surprising."[4]

We discuss in Chapter 21 an example of toll revenues securitization in Hong Kong.

Servicing risks in future flows

In future flows, the role of the servicer is much more comprehensive than the typical servicer in asset-backed transactions. The duties of the servicer are not limited to collections and posting; the servicer is also the operator of the asset. Depending on the nature of the transaction, a future flows might be no different from collateralized borrowing to the extent of risk it has on the servicer.

In Chapter 25, we discuss the operational issues concerning securitization.

The future flows market

A substantial part of securitization activity in emerging markets consists of future flow deals, as is clear in Figure 19.1.

A November 2003 report by Wachovia noted 249 transactions of future flows from emerging market countries after 1991 when this market first began.[5]

Legal taxation and accounting issues

From a legal viewpoint, a future flow securitization is a very tricky transaction. Experience with future flow transactions is still not very extensive and it is unlikely that a future flow deal has been tested for legal sanctity in a law court yet.

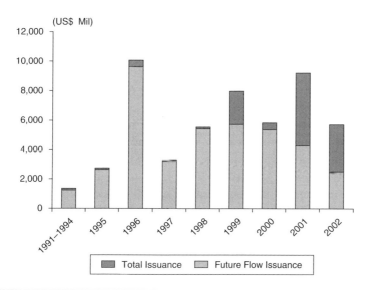

Figure 19.1   Annual Emerging-market issuance

Source: Fitch Ratings: Under Pressure: Structured

Transactions in Emerging-Market Stress-Update August 5, 2003

The basic legal issue to be examined is whether a future flow is assignable by itself. The general legal principle is: What exists can be transferred; what does not exist cannot be transferred, but there can be an agreement to transfer it. The future flow transaction remains an executory or promissory transaction; the income to be transferred does not exist. As and when it would exist, it would be transferred. But the key questions are: If the income to be transferred does not exist at all, will the investors have any recourse against the originator or the originator's assets? With such recourse, will terms be better than the rights of a secured or unsecured lender?

As stated, a future flow deal should be limited to cases where a framework that will give rise to cash flow in the future exists. If it does, all future income from it, whether earned by the present originator or by any other originator, may be assigned. By way of a fall back option, investors may also be given security interest on the framework. However, if investors do not have a right to claim back their money in the event the transferred cash flow does not arise at all, the investors will be worse than unsecured lenders.

From a taxation and accounting viewpoint, future flow securitization ranges somewhere in between collateralized lending and a transfer of cash flow, and to be more specific, it is closer to collateralized lending than to securitization. A future flow deal will be treated for tax purposes as akin to a borrowing transaction, and so for accounting as well.

Experience with future flows

Global experience with future flows has been mixed. Several transactions entered into unexpected contingencies at the time of the deals. There have been several ratings downgrades also. There were at least seven cases of default on future flows emanating from Argentina, and one case of default from Colombia.[6] Overall, the experience so far has been quite satisfactory. "Specifically, structures securitizing future receivables from an originating entity have proven to be the most reliable throughout various types of emerging-market distress."[7]

In the above publication, Fitch quoted examples of several securitization transactions that performed well despite extraordinary situations.

Petróleos de Venezuela S.A. was a Venezuelan company that had securitized oil receivables. In November 2002 to January 2003, the country passed through a period of civil discontent and the oil industry saw a major strike. In spite of the level of production and sale dipping substantially, this transaction survived due to very high levels of DSCR (in the worst period, it fell to 10x), high cash reserves built overseas, and a high amount of surplus cash pending return to the originator.

Pakistan Telecom's net settlement revenue securitization is also cited as an example, which concluded in 1997. In 1998, after its nuclear test, Pakistan faced economic sanctions and blocked multilateral funding. The transaction was rated BBB-, and was notably above the local currency rating of Pakistan Telecom, owing to the higher extent of net settlement inflows and the monopoly status of the company. From 1998-2001, the credit quality of Pakistan Telecom deteriorated, and so the transaction suffered downgrades. However, reports are that the transaction would have fully paid out by August 2003.

Yet another example is The Bank Internasional Indonesia (BII)'s credit card vouchers (a financial flow). The transaction has suffered several stresses including the massive deterioration of the rupiah, as well as travel restrictions from terrorist attacks in Bali and the SARS outbreak. This transaction has not defaulted to date, although the DSCR fell several times.

On the other hand, with the tough economic scenario such as for Argentina, export receivables securitization has paid off – the Aluar Aluminio Argentino S.A.I.C transaction was paid off in June 2004.

Notes

1 This chapter deals with the generic technology of future flows. See Chapter 21 for some specific forms of future flows such as intellectual property.
2 *ibid.*
3 Fitch Ratings: Toll Road Securitizations: Where the Future Flows, January 2004
4 Fitch Ratings, *Ibid.*
5 Wachovia Securities Structured Products Research: Emerging Market Future Flows Securitizations, November 20, 2003.
6 Avianca airlines filed for bankruptcy. Apart from a case of default, the transaction has also put to question the legal methodology of securitization transactions under a US jurisdiction. Notably, here, the transferee trust is domiciled in the U.S.
7 Fitch Ratings: Under Pressure: Structured Transactions in Emerging-Market Stress—Update 2003, dated August 5, 2003.

Chapter 20

Whole Business and Operating Revenues Securitization

Known by several names such as whole business securitization, corporate securitization, corporate entity securitization, operating revenues securitization, or hybrid finance, whole business securitization as a concept emerged essentially in the U.K. It has found limited application outside U.K., but of late, it has been of growing interest to the global securitization industry. Apart from continental Europe, whole business securitization has been successfully tried in Malaysia, and there are reports of deals even in the U.S. market.[1]

The device of whole business securitization sprang basically from the leveraged buyout (LBO) market and the crux of a whole business securitization is the securitization of an LBO. Whole business securitization captures the residual value of a business, that is, the valuation of the business, and creates securities that represent this residual value.

Given the ability to apply this device to the cash flow of almost any business, the concept virtually breaks down all limitations of securitization and extends it to almost any business that satisfies certain features.

Objectively, there is not much of difference between a plain secured borrowing and whole business securitization. In a plain borrowing, the borrower obliges himself to pay to the lender, and the obvious source of payment is the cash flow of the borrower. The lender might have security interest in all or some of the assets of the borrower to secure the loan so granted. In a securitization, on the other hand, the investor is given legal right over some of the assets of the originator which are legally isolated from the originator. In whole business securitization, as the idea is to make the whole of the cash flow of the business available for liquidating the securities, there is no question of isolating the assets of the originator. In other words, the investors are given a claim over all the cash flow of the originator, which remain within the legal and contractual control of the originator, and so the assets from which the cash flow arises. The only difference between secured lending and a whole business securitization is that in the latter case, investors acting through the SPV will have greater legal control over the originator, so that they can effectively assume the control of the originator's business in the event of default.

Market development

The idea of whole business securitization developed in the U.K. during the mid-1990s when the cash flow of a nursing home were securitized. This led to a spate of transactions in various spheres such as pubs, hospitals, entertainment and amusement sites, airports, theaters and ferry services. The idea essentially developed during the privatization exercise in U.K. when LBO funding, instead of being raised from traditional lenders, was raised from the capital markets.

The market for whole business securitization is still largely limited to Europe, and there too, with a concentration in the U.K.

In 2002, there were nine whole business transactions totaling €10.37 billion, 28% of the European ABS (excluding MBS) market. This was only 16% in 2001. The data for 2002 is biased by a huge whole business transaction – a €5.6 billion funding raised by water utility Anglian Water. According to a Moody's report, the total amount of funding in the U.K. by whole business transactions from 1998 to 2002 hit €26 billion.[2]

In a report dated January 17, 2005,[3] rating agency S&P reported a total of 132 ratings outstanding, on which the downgrade/upgrade history is as in Table 20.1:

Table 20.1 Rating Agency S&P: Lifetime Transition Matrix For Corporate Securitizations (end 2004)

From	Starting ratings (no.)	To AAA	AA	A	BBB	BB	CCC	CC	Upgrades	Stable	Downgrades
AAA	29	96.6	3.4						0.0	96.6	3.4
AA	10		100.0						0.0	100.0	0.0
A	50		4.0	82.0	4.0	2.0	8.0		4.0	82.0	14.0
BBB	37				91.9	2.7	2.7		0.0	91.9	8.1
BB	6					100.0			0.0	100.0	0.0
Ending ratings (no.)	132	28	13	41	36	8	5	0	2	119	11

Methodology

Secured loan structure

The common methodology in most whole business securitizations is for the issuer SPV to issue bonds in the market and with the funds so collected, provide a loan to the operator (originator). Whole business transactions are based on a loan structure rather than a true sale structure. While in a traditional securitization, the SPV purchases the assets of the originator, in a whole business transaction, the SPV gives a loan to the operating company against which it obtains a charge or security interest over substantially the whole of the assets of the operating company.

The originator agrees to repay the loan in fixed installments of interest and principal; these installments are used by the SPV to pay off the bonds. The central legal document in the transaction is the loan agreement whereby the SPV gives a loan to the operator. This loan agreement is backed by a fixed and floating charge over the entire estate of the operating company, which creates a special protection in bankruptcy.

An interesting question is why is the whole business securitization founded on secured loan and not a true sale? One needs to go to the root of the true sale issue before coming to an answer. As an essential feature of securitization, true sales have been used to isolate identified assets of an originator and put them into a separate vehicle that solely subserves for the benefit of investors. In a whole business securitization, first of all, the isolation of assets in impracticable as the assets in question are the operating assets of the originator from which the cash flow will emanate over time. These assets are virtually the entire estate of the originator. So if you are thinking of isolating the whole from the whole, you are either isolating nothing or leaving behind nothing.

Bankruptcy protection

More significantly, the key purpose of isolation by true sale is bankruptcy protection; the specific assets should be available for payment to the investors without being subject to any other claims. In the U.K. and such other jurisdictions, there is not exactly the same comfort as you would see in a true sale, but largely similar comfort can be obtained by a receivership device whereby, before the declaration of bankruptcy by the originator, a receiver would take possession of the whole or substantially the whole of the assets of the company and leave behind nominal assets, thereby leaving no motive on the part of the other creditors to take the operating company to bankruptcy.

Whole business securitizations are not designed to be bankruptcy remote as far as the originator is concerned; they cannot be, as there is no sale, and hence, no true sale, of the assets to the lending SPV. However, the security interest that the SPV holds gives it a specific power – to appoint an administrative receiver. This power is a typicality of the U.K. insolvency laws and is found in insolvency laws of certain other countries as well. See later in this chapter.

Table 20.2   Major differences between traditional securitization and whole business securitization

Basic nature	Isolation of specific and identifiable assets and dedicating these assets for payment to investors	Raising of funding for an operating company as an alternative to a traditional loan, with greater control over the assets of the operating company and hence higher rating
Legal feature	Based on a true sale of the identifiable assets	Based on a secured loan secured by a fixed and floating charge over substantially all the assets of the operating company
Cash flow securitized	Predictable cash flow from the identifiable assets	All the identifiable cash flow of the operating business
Motivations	Off-balance sheet; lower cost; additional source of funding	Alternative source of funding with probably higher leverage and cheaper cost
Countries where used	All over the world	U.K. and countries with similar corporate law and bankruptcy laws.
Investor comfort	Investors look at the identifiable assets; and investors do not have a general recourse against the originator	Investors have a general recourse against the operating company; however, investors are subject to preferential claims and other fixed charge holders
Accounting	Off-balance sheet	On-balance sheet
Typical maturities	Usually not very long; coterminous with that of the receivables	Usually long, going up to 25-30 years
Servicer responsibilities	Usually passive servicing; collection and repayment	Usually active handling of the receivables and the assets
Impact of operator bankruptcy	Designed so that the transaction is bankruptcy remote	Designed so that the receiver can pre-empt the bankruptcy of the operator and take control of the assets prior to actual bankruptcy; reduces risk of bankruptcy but does not avoid such risk altogether

Structural and Credit enhancements

Whole business securitizations are characterized more by structural protection, that is, a strong collateralized lending transaction, than by usual hierarchy of credit enhancements in traditional securitizations.

The relevance of subordination as a credit enhancement is highly limited, as the risk is not a pool of assets but in a single business; the probability "distribution" of risk of a single business has two extremes only – the business succeeds or fails. Several U.K. whole business transactions have been structured with subordinated notes, but for difficult business scenarios, the subordinated as well as the senior notes might have suffered downgrades,[4] a vindication of the principle stated above.

The stress is more on operational constraints, cash flow control and waterfall stipulations. Once again, these controls are common in project finance – securitization of whole business transactions uses a combination of structured finance and secured lending methodology to result in a more effective investor service.

The common structural enhancements used are as follows:

- **Breach of covenants: Administrative receivership:** As noted in the next heading, the ability of the trustees to appoint an administrative receiver is key to the presumable "bankruptcy remoteness" of whole business structures. The right to appoint an administrative receiver is given to a floating chargeholder, and therefore, the legal structure should clearly empower the chargeholder (trustee) to step in and appoint an administrative receiver. Detailed trigger events when this right will be available need to be specified.

  The security interest of the trustees is wide and comprehensive – apart from all hard and operating assets of the entity, it generally also includes, by an agreement with the holding company, a controlling block of equity of the operating company and dividends.

- **Financial covenants:** The transaction should constantly ensure maintenance of a debt service coverage. The whole business investors are paid out of residual profits, so the amount of cash flow, say free cash flow, available for investor service are the operational profits, after interest, depreciation (for capital assets replacement) and taxes. This cash flow should generally cover the debt service to investors at least 1.1 times or so. Failure of the covenant, remaining unrectified for a certain period, would amount to a default event, allowing the trustee to crystallize the security interest and appoint an administrative receiver. Of course, the issuer is always allowed ways of curing such breach, such as the posting of cash collateral.

- **Liquidity facilities**: Almost all whole business transactions are backed by liquidity support to save the transaction from failing on payments during periods of temporary stress, such as strikes and lock outs. Generally speaking, a liquidity facility of at least 12–18 months' service is insisted upon. Usual requirements for a rating of the liquidity provider will also be applicable.

- **Working capital facilities:** The operating business, based on its needs, should have adequate provision for working capital. It is notable that as the investors in whole business transactions are entitled to residual cash flow, in terms of waterfall, investors are relegated behind working capital lenders. However, in terms of powers, the investors in whole business transactions have substantial powers conferred by the all pervasive security interest.
- **Restrictive covenants:** To ensure that the business character of the operating company does not significantly change, covenants are placed restricting acquisition of unrelated businesses or assets, disposal of assets, payment of dividends unless certain DSCR norms are complied with.

Cash flow waterfall

The cash flow waterfall is, by itself, an effective structural protection in a whole business transaction and should be put very carefully. The rule on the "tightness" of the cash flow waterfall is the same as on young women's dress; it should not be too tight to strangulate the body and not allow breathing space or too loose to have no "effect." Generally speaking, the cash flow waterfall has three alternative scenarios: Pre-enforcement – meaning until the trustees' security interest has been enforced; Post-enforcement – meaning after the trustees have decided to invoke the security interest; and Post-acceleration – meaning if decided to take the business down the winding up route.

The pre-enforcement waterfall typically provides for the following priorities ("issuer" below refers to the SPV issuing notes to investors, and the cash flow to which the waterfall applies are those after regular operating expenses):

1. Security trustee fees, note trustee fees, fees and expenses of the paying agents and agent bank.
2. Other third-party obligations of the issuer and obligors.
3. Amounts due to working capital facility provider.
4. Interest and principal due under the issuer's liquidity facility.
5. Amounts due towards satisfaction of minimum capital expenditure spend.
6. Amounts due to swap counterparties.
7. Third party liabilities of the issuer.
8. Scheduled interest on senior-term advance.
9. Scheduled principal due on senior-term advance.
10. Scheduled interest due on junior-term advance.
11. Scheduled principal due on junior-term advance.
12. Issuer tax liabilities.
13. Payments to maintenance capital expenditure other than minimum capital expenditure spend.
14. Amounts due to swap counterparties in respect of termination payments as a result of a downgrade of a counterparty.
15. Any surplus to the borrower for general corporate purposes if the restricted payment condition is satisfied, including the payment of a dividend.

If the enforcement event has occurred, the trustees may remove any capital expenditure and the residual cash flow flowing back to the operating company from the waterfall. Instead, a cash collateral account may be created to trap the cash flow and retain it in the operating company.

If an acceleration event has occurred, the trustees may decide to direct all cash flow to the repayment of secured loans in priority to all unsecured claims.

The legal basis

The legal basis for whole business securitization is the ability of the SPV to cause the originator to give up his business in favor of an administrator to be appointed by the SPV, should a trigger event take place. This is similar to the concept of a backup servicer in usual securitizations; the originator continues to service the cash flow that he has transferred, but if something wrong happens, the SPV or the security trustee has the power to replace the originator by a back-up servicer. In whole business securitization, the operator or the originator continues to run his business, but if any of the trigger events happen, the trustee may cause the originator to give up the management of his business and hand over the same to an administrator, comparable to a backup servicer.

Administrative receivership

One of the key issues in traditional securitization is bankruptcy remoteness. Is whole business securitization bankruptcy remote? As there is no transfer of assets from the originator to the SPV, the assets of the originator are a part of the bankruptcy estate of the originator. However, whole business securitizations rely on a legal provision in U.K. bankruptcy law that allows a person holding a floating charge on the entire business of the bankrupt to ward off the jurisdiction of a bankruptcy receiver, and handover the management of the business to the person holding the floating charge. Thus, the whole business securitization device is premised on the ability of the SPV, as a holder of floating charge over all the assets of the originator, to assume administration of the business of the originator, should the originator file for bankruptcy.

The administrative receiver, under special provisions of U.K. law takes over the properties covered by the charge.

Law of receivership

The right to appoint an administrative receiver is conferred by debentures (bonds are also debentures, under U.K. corporate law) issued by a company. Section 29 (2) of the U.K. Insolvency Act 1986 defines an administrative receiver as "a receiver or manager of the whole (or substantially the whole) of a company's property appointed by or on behalf of the holders of any debentures of the company secured by a charge which, as created, was a floating charge, or by such a charge and one or more other securities." Thus, for the appointment of the administrative receiver to be effective, the bond or debenture-holders must have empowered their trustee, who holds a floating charge over the whole or substantially the whole of the properties of the company. The powers of the administrative receiver are given in Schedule 1 to the Act which among others includes a significant power – to take possession of the company's property and the power to sell or dispose of it.

A receiver is appointed under the terms of the debentures issued by the company. The receiver is the agent of the debenture-holders and steps in to take control of the property of the company for protecting the interests of the debenture-holders. The legal provisions about receivers are not unique to U.K. law, but are found in laws of several countries that have inherited or adopted U.K.-type corporate and insolvency laws.

Take India. Sec. 423 of the Companies Act makes reference to the powers of a receiver appointed by the debenture holders[5] to take over property conferred by the instrument securing the debentures.

How exactly does the appointment of a receiver take place? The bond trustee or the security trustee would usually be named or is empowered to appoint a receiver. In a whole business securitization case, the receiver will be more than just the administrator of the secured property; he must be even able to run the business of the failing company or at least ensure the assets are safe for the benefit of the investors.

Will the lending SPV be the receiver? No. Bankruptcy laws place a restriction on corporates being appointed as receivers; this is a legacy of the old regime where corporates were not allowed to become receivers and liquidators. Many countries these days allow corporates to become liquidators, but the bar for receiverships continues.

Fixed and floating charges

In whole business securitizations, it is a common practice for the security trustee to have a fixed and floating charge over the whole or substantially the whole of the assets of the operating company. A floating charge is like an umbrella charge: it floats over the assets of the company and fastens and becomes a fixed charge over the assets if the company goes into bankruptcy. A fixed charge is one that is fixed to specific assets.

The security trustee holds a floating charge to be able to appoint an administrative receiver: note sec. 29 (2), which says an administrative receiver is appointed by debenture-holders holding a floating charge over all or substantially all the assets of the company. The reason for the security trustee also holding a fixed charge is a fixed charge takes a priority over a floating charge. If all that the bondholders in a whole business securitization had was a floating charge, they would be subordinated to other creditors of the operating company holding a fixed charge. Thus, equipped with a fixed and floating charge over all or substantially all the assets of the originator, the investors see a first claim to both the possession and sale of the assets as also first priority.

Receivers are allowed by law to run the business of the company. More specifically, the loan agreement between the lending SPV and the operating company will allow the receiver to run the business should the trigger events take place. The loan agreement also places several restrictions on the business, borrowing ability and disposal of assets by the originator.

In addition, another central feature of whole business securitizations is the creation of an external liquidity facility to meet the bond repayments in the event of a delay in the takeover of business. Rating agencies require several months' servicing to be pooled in the liquidity facility.

Challenge to floating charges: the ruling in Brumark's case

The concept of floating charges securing transactions in general came under a serious legal challenge with the ruling in Brumark's case,[6] following by a subsequent ruling in Cosslett's case[7] and a more recent ruling in National Westminster Bank.

In the first case in Brumark (*Agnew* vs *Inland Revenue Commissioner*) the case arose in appeal against a New Zealand ruling wherein the HL discussed the nature of floating charges arising out of the age-old rulings of Lord Macnaughten. A floating charge necessarily implies a floating stock of property – mostly expressed as present and future property. When a charge allows the chargor the liberty to dispose of assets without the consent of the chargeholder, the charge must be construed as a floating charge.

This was a ruling in context of receivables. The HL extended the same ruling for machinery and equipment as well, in *Cosslett's* case. If the intent of the parties is that the chargor can dispose of assets, the charge in case of fixed assets should also be recharacterized as a floating charge.

Judicial recharacterization of a fixed charge into a floating charge may cast serious issues for whole business transactions, which are premised on a fixed and floating charge on the entire assets of an operating business. The fixed part may get recharacterized as a floating charge, if the intent was to allow the chargor to deal with the assets in the normal course of business. If that is done, that allows the chargor the liberty to create other fixed charges that rank in priority to the claims of the securitization investors. Of course this may be structured as an event of default, but quite often, this default is only like bolting the stable door after the horse has run away.

The idea of a charge creation is an inter-creditor arrangement. If the arrangement is such that a section of creditors has a claim over all the assets of the corporation, it is, by definition, a general claim. A specific charge is a specific claim, and should run faster than a general claim. The HL rulings have only refreshed this age-old concept of floating charges.

U.K. Insolvency law amendment and whole business transactions

As noted, the legal basis of a whole business transaction is the ability of a charge-holder holding floating charges on assets to have a receiver appointed and take the custody of the assets. This has been a feature of U.K. insolvency laws since the recommendations of the Kenneth Cork committee were implemented.

The amendments introduced after the Enterprise Bill 2002 have removed administrative receivership. Exceptions have, however, been made in respect of existing loans and capital market transactions. Whole business transactions would apparently be saved under the capital market exception.

Is a secured loan structure as safe as true sales?

While true sale structures have been tested in many cases and have survived many bankruptcies, none of the whole business securitizations so far have passed the bankruptcy test. There is a significant difference between a secured loan structure and true sale structure. In a true sale, once the assets are transferred by the originator, they are outside the control of the originator from every viewpoint. However, in a secured loan structure, the assets continue to be the assets of the originator. The originator's preferential creditors have a prior claim over the assets. Preferential creditors, defined by bankruptcy statutes, are usually government claims, and sometimes, even workmen's claims. In a situation of bankruptcy, it is quite likely that the assets of the bankrupt fall short of such claims; therefore, investors may have problems.

It is notable that in terms of legal interest, a whole business securitization is no better than a secured loan with a receivership right. Structured finance principles such as overcollateralization, liquidity and tranching are brought in to achieve good ratings.

Besides, there are onerous responsibilities cast by law on an administrative receiver. For a true sale, the bankruptcy of the originator does not concern the investors at all; even if the assets transferred to the SPV must be liquidated, the same can be done without any reference to the originator or other creditors of the originator. For administrative receivership, the receiver is primarily the agent of the bondholders, but he owes fiduciary duties to other creditors as well. First, he has to notify his appointment to all known creditors and also publish his appointment in newspapers. Then, within three months of appointment, he must call a meeting of creditors and submit the statement of affairs. In short, the role of a receiver is comparable to the role of a liquidator who runs the entire time-taking process of winding up of the company's affairs.

True sale securitizations are designed to survive the worst; whole business securitizations are designed to survive everything except the worst.

Businesses where whole business securitization is possible

In the U.K. market, so far, there have been a total of 36 whole business transactions rated by rating agencies, and the businesses involved spanned a wide range: Pubs, Service Stations, Hotels, Theme Parks, Ferry Service, London City Airport, Care Homes, Theaters, Food, Water, Ports and Shipping, Healthcare, Telecom Equipment, Real Estate and Timber.

It is difficult to define any central theme that connects these various businesses. However, Moody's[8] listed some significant features that makes a business a more likely candidate for whole business securitization:

- Predictable asset base and ease of replacing the borrower;
- Ability to place financial covenants, such as DSCR, in the loan document and restrict the rights of the borrower to be able to take pre-emptive action;
- Ability to place restrictions on operation of the business, such as Permitted disposals, Permitted indebtedness, Permitted business activities, Permitted merger and acquisitions, Minimum maintenance capex, Negative pledge, Change of control, and Amendments to main contracts;
- Sufficient amount of equity component in business; and
- Alternative use value of the properties – for instance, the fungibility of a nursing home into a house or office.

The concept of whole business securitization draws upon the long-term residual value of a business, so the business attributes of the entity to be a suitable for whole business candidate should be such that the entity itself is a good value. It is a good business even in different hands. On the contrary, if the business solely rests on managerial efficiency or personal talent, it is no different from issuance of secured bonds. The underlying concepts of a whole business securitization are essentially the same as valuation of a business for takeover or LBO. Some significant attributes for whole business securitization are:

- **Entry barriers**: To be value in itself, the business should be a sort of an oligopoly. The best examples are public utilities, established amusement properties and infrastructural assets. In any event, the business should be one that does not have appreciable risk of obsolescence or substitution.
- **Demonstration of successful presence:** The entity should have been in business successfully for several years to establish a track record of residual profits. "The business must be able to demonstrate a minimum of three years' stable trading, but 10 to 15 years is ideal. Preferably, this trading record will include periods of macroeconomic growth and decline to demonstrate business trends during different stages of an economic cycle."[9]
- **Maintainability of future profits**: Whole business transactions are essentially concerned with future sustainable profits, so it should be possible to project future profits with reasonable certainty. Transactions typically look at long maturities; therefore, the business should have a long-term future and should not be a long-term risk. Ideally, for a whole business securitization candidate it "is necessary for a low-risk strategy to be in place; to run a business as is, and not pursue risky options such as operational diversification, major acquisition trails or extensive development activity within the security group."[10]
- **Realizable asset value**: Clearly, a whole business transaction cannot substantially depend on the soft assets of the business, such as manpower and skill sets. It has to be backed by substantive hard assets. Two types of assets generally back whole business transactions – properties and operational assets. In the Madame Tussaud's transaction, apart from the properties at prime locations, the museum also has its operating assets – the wax models.

- **Brand value**: The entity must have a strong brand presence to sustain the profitability of the enterprise over the long run.
- **Management**: Lastly, stable management and efficient internal controls account for the long-term success of any business.

Why SPV in a whole business structure

Several people have opined that in a whole business securitization, it is not necessary to bring in a special purpose vehicle as there is no isolation of assets. The operating company may issue the bonds itself, and have a receiver designated as the security interest holder, and the structuring of the securities can be done as on the balance sheet of the originating company itself. Rating agency Moody's issued a paper in March 2001 entitled *Non-Bankruptcy Remote Issuers in Asset Securitisation* wherein they argued that it is not necessary except to meet the needs of a local legislation to involve an SPV at the issuing level in secured loan structures. This, according to Moody's, would simplify securitizations and reduce costs.

Truly, the need for a vehicle arose from the need to transfer and isolate assets, which is not being done in a whole business securitization.

Though an SPV is not required strictly speaking, but the legal fraternity in the country is still in favor of having SPVs, primarily for the apparent separation of issuance and origination and for organizing the credit enhancements at the SPV level rather than at the originator level.

Case study: South East Water (Finance) Ltd

Transaction structure

This transaction, given a preliminary rating by S&P in July 2004, is a whole business securitization of a U.K. water utility, South East Water (SEW). The bonds of £366 million have an underlying rating of BBB, but based on guarantee of Ambac, the bonds have been assigned a AAA rating. The bonds will be expected to be in two time tranches – £200 million for 15 years and £166 million for 25 years. The transaction goes to refinance the acquisition funding put in by Macquarie Bank, which acquired SEW in 2003.

Purpose of funding

SEW is a U.K.-based, regulated water-only company that serves about 594,000 properties in two geographically separate service regions in the southeast of England. It is the second largest water-only company in England and Wales. SEW Finance Ltd. is the SPV of a ring-fenced group of companies ultimately owned by the Macquarie Water (U.K.) Ltd (MWUK). The Macquarie European Infrastructure Fund, other Macquarie managed investors and Macquarie are the shareholders in MWUK. The funds raised will be upstreamed through a series of intercompany loans and loan repayments. The operating company has a long-term license to provide water in a defined area. The customer base is generally affluent.

There are debentures and finance leases outstanding with the operating company. It is expected that the finance lessors will sign up to an inter-creditor agreement proposed for the transaction, according to which they will rank pari passu with the new debt, or otherwise will be terminated and carved out of the securitization. The debenture holders will not be party to the inter-creditor agreement and payments of interest and principal to the debenture-holders will rank above senior bonds in the cash waterfall. The majority of the debenture instruments (£14.9 million or 96%) are redeemable over the course of the next nine years and SEW intends to repay each of the debentures at the earliest possible date for prepayment at par.

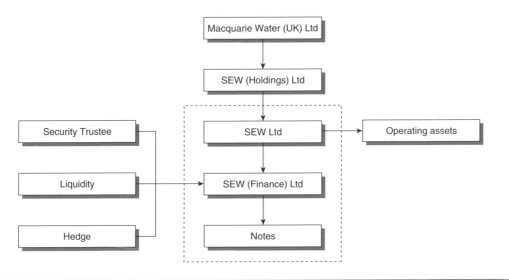

Figure 20.1 Transaction graphic of whole business securitization case

Liquidity support

There are two forms of liquidity support for the transaction. There is a debt service reserve, initially £15.9 million. This reserve provides support to interest payments and must be available to an amount at least equal to the aggregate of projected interest payments on the senior debt for the next 12 months less amounts available as cash on deposit under the first loss account (approximately £3.6 million at financial close). The other reserve facility is an O&M reserve facility that supports O&M payments and must also be available to an amount equal to 10% of projected operating and capital maintenance expenditure for the next 12 months.

The SPV will also initially have a £25-million funded capital expenditure reserve established to fund the first year's debt-funded capital expenditure. Thereafter, debt-finance capital expenditure will be funded through a £50-million term bank facility, which will periodically be refinanced through new bond issuance. A £10-million working capital bank facility will be available to fund ongoing working capital requirements.

Inter-creditor agreement

The key to the security interest creation lies in the inter-creditor agreement. The inter-creditor agreement dictates the rights and obligations of lenders to South East Water. By covering almost all creditors of the company it should, in times of financial stress, allow for orderly and considered decisions being made by the lending group without smaller creditors breaking rank and forcing the company into special administration. Importantly, the agreement outlines what is to happen during a standstill period. A standstill is specifically designed to reduce the likelihood of South East Water being forced into special administration. It prevents the secured creditors from taking any enforcement action or making claims against South East Water after an event of default has occurred. A standstill lasts for 18 months, unless 66.67% of lenders vote to terminate it early, or if the cause of the event of default is remedied. After 18 months the standstill will be automatically extended for a further 120 days unless a majority of lenders vote to terminate it. Further automatic extensions apply unless voted against by a decreasing margin of votes. The idea is that the standstill period gives the Security Trustee enough time to arrange an orderly disposal of the company while it is still operating satisfactorily, to maximize value for lenders.

The Security Trustee acts in accordance with instructions from the senior debt instructing group, which consists of senior lenders on a pound-for-pound basis. At the outset, for SEW it will be Ambac (the bond guarantee company that guarantees the bonds) who will dictate decisions of the senior debt instructing group.

Covenants

In all whole business transactions, the controls that the funding puts on the operating company are more significant than the security interest. The covenant package effectively provides three levels of protection for lenders, with progressively increasing levels of seriousness and consequences. The three levels are distribution *lock-up*, *trigger events*, and *events of default*.

The first covenant level is the distribution lock-up test, which bars the operating company from making an equity distribution in certain circumstances, namely:

- The level of debt as a proportion of the regulatory asset value (RAV) is greater than 85%;
- Where any drawings of liquidity are outstanding;
- Where the underlying credit rating is below investment grade (note that what is relevant here is the underlying rating, not the actual rating that piggy-backs on the guarantee); and
- Where an appeal of water regulatory authority's determination is being pursued.

The second covenant level is for the trigger events, the breach of which has more serious implications. Until remedied, the main consequence of a trigger event breach is (in conjunction with a distribution lock-up) the closer direct involvement in the business of the Security Trustee, who can request information and a remedial plan from the operating company, commission an independent review by technical advisers, discuss the remedial plan with water regulatory body, and can appoint additional non-executive directors if the trigger event is not remedied within six months. In short, the lenders (through the Security Trustee) effectively run the business until the trigger event has been remedied. The trigger events are numerous, the most important of which are:

- Breach of any of these financial tests – regulatory assets to net funded debt is greater than 90%; interest coverage ratio after required capital expenditure for maintenance purposes is less than 1.1x; average adjusted interest coverage ratio, as defined above, is less than 1.2x;
- Estimated capital expenditure exceeds regulator's allowance for any regulatory period by 10% or more;
- Available liquidity is insufficient to finance the following 12 months' capital expenditure, working capital or financing requirements;
- A drawdown on either the debt service reserve liquidity facility or the O&M reserve facility;
- The permitted non-regulated business limits are exceeded; and
- A material adverse effect on the business is likely to be felt from regulatory action, either through a pricing determination or through a change in the operating company's business permissions.

The third level of covenants is the event of a default, which represents the most serious level of breach. The main events of default include:

- Non-payment of amounts due;
- More severe breach of financial triggers;
- Cross-default to other indebtedness;
- Termination of business permission; forecast inability to meet the next six months' capital expenditure or working capital amounts;
- A change of control of the operating company; and
- A breach of the information provision or other general covenants, including the provision of compliance certificates, permitted business, permitted financial indebtedness, permitted disposals, restricted payments, and compliance with hedging policy.

The immediate consequence in the event of default is the commencement of a standstill period, as described above. Under a standstill, the rated bonds would continue to be serviced to the extent cash flow is available and in accordance with the cash waterfall outlined in the inter creditor agreement.

Cash flow waterfall

The cash flow waterfall is typical for these types of transactions. The first priority is O&M costs, recognizing the importance of keeping the business functioning and retaining its ongoing viability. The next priorities are the expenses of the various trustees, agent banks, and facility providers, recognizing the imperative to keep the structure and parties functioning as intended. Then follows the servicing of the first priority debt, the debenture stock of SEW. It is not practicable for the holders of the debentures to sign up to the inter-creditor agreement so they have to remain a priority. They are a minor part of the capital structure (there is about £15 million of debentures outstanding) and they will mature progressively over the next nine years and will not be replaced. The next priority is debt service of liquidity facility providers to the extent those facilities are used, and then payments to interest rate hedging counterparties follows. The next priority is debt service of the senior debt. Behind the senior debt service falls all other obligations including any subordinated debt service that may arise (none is envisaged at this stage) and replenishment of the debt service and O&M reserve.

Notes

1 See, of example, news reports at http://vinodkothari.com/secnewsfeb02.htm.
2 Moody's Special report: 2002 Review and 2003 outlook: European Whole Business Securitization, January 21, 2003.
3 Rating Transitions 2004: Upgrades Outnumber Downgrades For First Time In European Structured Finance.
4 See Fitch Ratings: Note Acceleration in Whole Business Securitization, April 2, 2004, graphic giving scenarios where different senior securities will suffer downgrade.
5 In law, debentures do not have to be marketable securities. A single loan instrument is also a debenture. The instrument acknowledging a floating charge is, by definition, a debenture.
6 Agnew v. Inland Revenue Commissioner, 2000 (7) SCC 291.
7 *Cosslett Contractors Ltd. (in administration)*, in re (2001) BCC 740.
8 *Whole Business Securitizations: A Unique Opportunity for U.K. Assets*, October 19, 2000.
9 Fitch Ratings: Criteria for Whole Business Securitization, January 28, 2004.
10 Fitch Ratings: *ibid*.

Chapter 21

Other Miscellaneous Asset Classes

In this last chapter on structured finance classes, we will look at some more significant classes. Needless to say, in the preceding classes discussed, we have not covered the exhaustive list of all asset types, which cannot be covered. The objective is to highlight that in structuring each such class, the crux is to understand the source of the cash flows, because the ultimate strength of the structure lies in ensuring return of the investors' money.

Securitization of intellectual property

The securitization of intangible property is the latest vista in the development of securitization. From mortgages and car loans to valuing and funding intangible property, the transition required is tremendous, but the market is increasingly finding comfort in properties backed by intangible assets. The reasons are not difficult to understand; the business world has increasingly become aware of the existence and significance of intangible assets. "A January 2003 Accenture survey of executives found that managing intangibles is one of their top three priorities. While nearly half the respondents said that intangible assets are what the company primarily relies on for shareholder wealth creation, only 5 percent reported their company had in place a robust system to measure and track all aspects of the performance of intangibles/intellectual capital."[1]

The share of intangible property securitization is still small, but the number of transactions is continuously increasing, and these transactions are remarkable. We discuss a few examples of the intangible asset market below.

Intellectual property revenues securitization market

In terms of glitz-appeal, securitization of royalties and other intellectual properties of music stars, performers, authors and cinema personalities has been quite impressive. David Pullman,[2] a New York-based financier claims to be the pioneer of music royalty-backed securitization, although in a court ruling, Pullman's claim that he had invented the method was rejected.[3] However, Pullman's Bowie Bonds have been a highly fascinating innovation in finance.[4]

Music royalties

Bowie Bonds

In 1997 David Pullman brought to the market bonds backed by the royalty income of the rock star David Bowie. The bonds involved the sale of existing publishing and recording rights to as many as 300 songs Bowie produced in his career. The financing was said to raise $55 million through issuance of 15-year notes, having an average life of approximately 10 years at a fixed-interest rate of 7.9%. The bonds were rated A3 by Moody's. The transaction not only created ripples in the world of finance, but gave a completely new dimension to the application of securitization in unimagined areas. In an article titled **Wall Street Can Securitize Anything**,[5] Kim Clark appropriately commented: "Financiers have shown remarkable ingenuity over the past decade in finding new and unusual things to turn into tradable securities. Home mortgages, car loans, and lottery winnings are just a few of the streams of income that have been "securitized" and peddled on Wall Street. The latest innovation in this usually arcane field even made it onto the nightly news: the $55 million of what will forever be known as "Bowie bonds" - securities backed by revenues from future sales of David Bowie's early albums. The rock star's highly publicized bonds are only a tiny part of a $150-billion-a-year-and-growing market of investments with the deceptively boring name of asset-backed securities, but they reveal how prevalent the practice of securitizing cash flow has become. The fact that Wall Street is getting into deals that, say, securitize the weird oeuvre of a weird rock star shows that 'securitization is going to change the world'."

The performance of such bonds is dependent on sales and royalties; Bowie bonds were downgraded by Moody's in 2004, citing lower than expected sales as the reason.

More instances of music securitization

David Bowie's transaction apart, there have been several music royalty securitizations, and some structured by Pullman's company. These include Scorpion, Iron Lady, Ron Isley and others.[6]

On the other side of the Atlantic, in March 2001 Royal Bank of Scotland structured a deal for Chrysalis PLC UK, labelled as the first deal from an international music publisher. This £60-million deal was funded by MUSIC Finance Corp and the collateral was the Chrysalis Group's International music catalogue and the revenues derived from the Catalogue – the Net Publishers Share (NPS) via the U.S. Commercial Paper market. The total facility of £60 million represents some 40% of the estimated current value of the catalogue and is non-recourse to the rest of the Chrysalis Group. In addition to unlocking the inherent value in the catalogue, the transaction allows

Chrysalis to maintain control over the administration and management of its various music-publishing subsidiaries. Like most other U.K. transactions, it uses a loan structure and not a true sale structure.

The 15-year transaction includes a three-year revolving period followed by a 12-year amortization period to a substantial residual amount. The effective interest rate after amortizing all fees and costs compared favorably to the Group's then-prevailing cost of borrowing.

Transaction structure

The basic structure of a royalty securitization transaction is not very different from a future flows-type structure. Here, the ownership of the special purpose vehicle is a lesser legal issue, as the transferor is an individual and does not come for consolidation rules either under bankruptcy[7] or accounting standards.[8] At the same time, the individual would see that valuable property is not permanently distanced from him. So, in a typical structure, the SPV might be owned by the individual concerned or by one of his family members.

The individual would then transfer his rights over his copyrighted, and preferably patented, intellectual property, for a purchase price to the SPV. Usual securitization devices are used here as well; there is a substantial over-collateralization, that is, the difference between the cash price paid by the SPV and the true market value of the intellectual property. The SPV, in turn, would grant licenses to use the property to relevant users – say a music publishing company. Preferably, these licenses are given on a long-term basis with some guaranteed payments, so that investors' share is taken care of. Essentially, the idea is that all the royalty income of the individual should be routed through the SPV, so that the investors' share therein is captured before the cash flows are routed to the individual in question.

As for regular securitization transactions, there is a servicer or administrator for this transaction – essentially the agency responsible for administering the collections and investor service. In addition, there will be a trustee holding security interest on the intellectual property under an indenture. Typically, the indenture documents will put the investor interest on the top of the author's interest in the property, thereby creating the benefit of subordination.

The crux of the whole process is to look at an income-producing individual as a corporation, the external investors as the lenders, and the individual himself holding equity to the extent of the excess of the value of his "business" over the liabilities.

Film financing

Bond bonds

An Italian company made an innovative use of securitization in March 1999 when it issued (for the first time in the world perhaps) bonds secured by revenues from several movies owned by it, including several James Bond movies. These bonds were called Bond Bonds. The following news report is based on *Lawmoney*:

The issue was made by Italian film producer the Cecchi Gori, the largest film producer in Italy. The size was £500 billion (US$280 million). The bonds were backed by revenues from cinema and video sales, as well as licensing films to television companies. Cecchi Gori owns the rights to more than 1,000 Italian and international films, including most of the James Bond movies.

DreamWorks

Big news was made also made in August 2002 by Steven Spielberg's DreamWorks, the Los Angeles entertainment group, which secured a US$1 billion funding by securitizing its future film revenues. According to a report in *Financial Times*, DreamWorks will securitize its new live action output and films already in its library, which typically generate revenue for years from releases in home video formats and repeat showings on television. Of the 30 films that have been placed in the transaction include *Gladiator*, *Shrek*, *American Beauty* and *Saving Private Ryan*.

The securitization depends on a well-established formula that allows several years' worth of revenues to be accurately predicted in the first few weeks following a film's theatrical release. Funds will be advanced in accordance with these calculations. The transaction has a three years' revolving period.

The funding was arranged by JP Morgan and FleetBoston. The senior tranche bears an insurance wrap from Ambac Insurance, which gives a AAA rating to the senior tranche.

Drug royalties securitization

Yet another variant of intellectual property securitization is drug royalties.

One of the notable transactions in this field is Royalty Securitization Trust I, issued by private equity firm Paul Capital Partners, which was successfully placed with investors late in 2004. The transaction was backed by Ambac guarantee. The US$229 million notes were backed by a portfolio of healthcare royalty interests and revenue interests in 23 biopharmaceutical products, medical devices and diagnostics selected from 13 of the 19 investments made by Paul Royalty Fund I, L.P.[9] This was the first securitization within this category.

Case study: Drug Royalty LLC

The pre-sale rating for this transaction, done by S&P, is dated February 24, 2005. The transaction envisages issuance of three classes of notes as below:

Table 21.1   S&P Preliminary Ratings as of February 24, 2005

Class	Preliminary rating	Preliminary amount (mil. $)	Stated final maturity date
A	A	42.600	July 15, 2014
B	BBB	16.00	July 15, 2014
C	BB	9.90	July 15, 2014

The notes of all the three classes have an expected maturity in October 2011.

The pool of assets is royalty from eight FDA-approved drugs. The income stream is by way of royalty is contingent. The eight royalty assets in the portfolio have been in the marketplace for an average of approximately 6.8 years. For the 12 months ended December 31, 2003, they generated approximately US$5.9 billion in sales and approximately US$18.3 million in royalty and contingent payment right revenues for the originator.

The revenue streams have been originated by Drug Royalty Corp, a Canadian company specialized in drug royalty financing. Drug Royalty, has operated since 1992. The principal business focus of the company is evaluating and acquiring royalty interests in both prescription and generic (non-prescription) pharmaceutical products. Drug Royalty targets inventors, universities, hospitals, biotech, pharmaceutical companies, and other owners that hold royalty interests in pharmaceutical products for acquisition, usually for cash. Typically, Drug Royalty or one of its affiliates purchases all or a portion of a seller's royalty assets, which entitle the owner to a specific percentage of, or payment based on, sales of the related pharmaceutical product. These royalty payments and contractual contingent payments are made either by the drug marketer or by the institution that receives royalty payments from the marketer.

There are three forms of credit enhancement for the transaction – over-collateralization to the extent of 26.6%, a liquidity reserve equal to six months' coupon service, and subordination as evident from the three classes of notes.

Others

In 1993, US fashion company Calvin Klein raised US$58 million with the securitization of royalties on perfume brands, arising from the exclusive right to use the Calvin Klein trademark on existing and future products.

Trademark and patent securitizations also have several instances. In early 2003, Guess? Inc., the Los Angeles apparel company, securitized royalty streams from 14 trademark license agreements - 12 domestic and two international agreements—for US$75 million dollars. Standard & Poor's rated the deal a BBB, and Guess? used the cash flow to retire some of its burdensome debt. The issuer of the securities is Guess? Royalty Finance LLC, the bankruptcy-remote SPV created for the purpose of this securitization.

Securitization of non-performing loans

There are three growth industries in Japan: funerals, insolvency and securitization.

> Dominic Jones, in an article in Asset
> Finance International *November 1998*

Recent securitization activity in several countries, including Japan, Korea, Italy, and lately China, is seeing a boost from a strange application:

Securitization of non-performing loans. Malaysia and India are also joining the fray. Mountains of bad loans are sitting on the balance sheets of banks all over the world, so obviously it makes great sense for the banks themselves.

The massive problem of bad loans

Non-performing or sub-performing loans have become a major problem for banking systems in many countries. In some countries, banks blame the lax recovery systems and legal infrastructure to a consistent accumulation of non-performing loans. In some cases, bad loans are said to be created during banking crises, and thereafter, these loans stay on the balance sheets of banks even as the crisis eases.

During the 1990s, the problem of non-performing loans with banks became particularly acute [in 1997, Japanese banks had an estimated US$1 trillion in nonperforming assets], and with securitization technology with structuring options finding increased acceptability, bankers world-over have been looking at financial restructuring options through securitization.

Recent estimates of NPLs by Ernst and Young[10] are given by the following Table 21.2:

Table 21.2   NPL amounts and reductions

Billions U.S.$	NPLs in all Financial Institutions	NPL in AMCS[1]	Gross reductions of NPLs in financial system since Asian financial crisis[2]
Japan	330 (b)	112 (c)	600
China	307 (a)	107	200
Taiwan	19.1	NAP	50
Thailand	18.8	5	95
Philippines	9	NAP	NAP
Indonesia	16.9	5	37
India	29.9	NAP	NAP
Korea	15	45	125
TOTAL	**746**	**274**	**1.107**

1. Estimated unresolved NPLs still in government AMCs
2. Estimated gross reduction in financial system nonperforming loans due to restructuring, reclassification, repayment, transfer to AMCs/Bad Banks, or write offs.
(a): No official government statistic available. Calculated estimate includes the 5-tier classification for. 4 SOCBs. 11 stock banks, and 3 policy banks as well as the 4-tier classification for the 112 city banks. Excludes financial institutions in rural areas.
(b): Based on ¥35.3 trillion as of March, 2003 at FOREX of ¥107=$1.
(c): Includes ¥4.6 trillion and ¥4.7 trillion in unpaid balance acquired by The Housing Loan & Credit Management Corporation (HLCMC) and the Resolution and Collection Bank (RCB), respectively, in addition to ¥2.5 trillion in unpaid balance acquired by the Resolution and Collection Corporation (RCC) at FOREX of ¥107=$1. HLCMC, which acquired loans from Housing Loan Finance Coorperatives; and the RCB, which acquired loans from the failed financial institutions were merged and created the RCC in April, 1999.
Source: Ernst and Young 2004 Asia Pacific Financial Solutions.

Resolution Trust Corp

Historically, the world's first securitization of non-performing loans could be said to be Resolution Trust Corporation's "N" series program of the 1980s. The RTC was essentially formed to market dud commercial mortgages of savings and loans associations in the U.S., bought at a deep discount and securitized in the market.

The RTC acquired almost 750 S&Ls and US$460 billion in assets and through bulk sales and securitization recovered almost 90%. The RTC was initially funded by issuance of government-guaranteed bonds [US$30 billion] and partly by the treasury [US$20 billion]. The total amount of assets of failed S&Ls acquired by it added to some US$460 billion.

Models in other countries

Japan

There have been several theoretical explanations as to how a securitization exercise could succeed in resolving the massive non-performing loan problem of Japanese banks. Kay Ellen Herr and Goe Miyazaki with Professor Edward Altman wrote an article [April 1999 – see on vinodkothari.com] titled *The Japanese Non-Performing Loans Problem: Securitization as a Solution*. The article suggested that several banks could pool their non-performing loan portfolios together and sell them into an SPV at fair market values. The loan to the obligors will thus be replaced by a loan to the SPV, and the SPV in turn may raise money by issuing asset-backed paper and thereby repay the loan from the parent bank. As the loans will be sold at their market values, the selling bank may get a tax shelter for the loss on sale, presuming the provisions are not allowed as an expense already. The selling banks also get a capital relief. The SPV tries to sell the real estate over time in a tie up with a real estate management company.

MSDW's securitization in Japan

What academicians such as Prof Altman were suggesting, MSDW put into practice. On November 25, 1999, Morgan Stanley Dean Witter (MSDW) launched and priced a ¥21.0 billion issue of floating rate structured notes for an SPV called International Credit Recovery - Japan One Ltd., a Cayman Islands-domiciled company. This was the first time a capital markets solution had been applied to the problem of non- and sub-performing loans. The MSDW deal was backed by non-performing loans backed on Japanese real estate, a total of 700 real estate assets of various types throughout Japan. MSDW had been buying these loans over time.

Resolution and Collection Corp. Japan

Largely modeled on the RTC experience, the government of Japan also sought to resolve its burgeoning non-performing loans through securitization. A body called Resolution and Collection Corp (RCC) was set up to partly resolve the ¥17.4 trillion worth of bad loans sitting with Japanese banks.

Under the plan, RCC would acquire non-performing loans from Japanese banks in exchange for beneficial interest certificates therein. The banks may either retain the same or sell them off in the market. The loan would be administered by RCC. RCC is expected not merely to collect, but possibly to resolve the bad loans, which may include debt-equity swap as well. Should that be agreed upon, RCC will transfer such shares acquired in exchange for the loans into a fund held jointly with private investors.

RCC's first securitization of bad loans kicked off in January 2002.

Kamco's Korean NPL securitization

The NPL problem in Korea and initiatives to clean up

The bank restructuring problem surfaced in Korea soon after the currency crisis of 1997. During the pre-1997 period, Korean banks weakened almost unnoticeably under decades of interventionist policy by the government under which banks were supposed to support development without looking at healthy banking principles. During the crisis, the economy went into recession and non-performing loans peaked near 20-30%.

During this time, the government forced banks to either reserve their non-performing loans, or to sell them off to Korean financial sector restructuring agency Korea Asset Management Company (KAMCO) at their perceived market value. Kamco was constituted as early as in 1962 as the intermediary

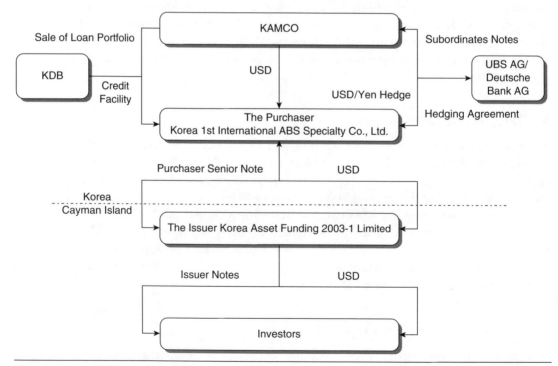

Figure 21.1   Korean NPL securitization transaction

agency of the Korea Development Bank (KDB) to dispose of distressed assets, but it was only in November 1997 that Kamco was restructured and mandated by the government to acquire non-performing loans from Korean financial institutions and dispose of them. Most banks preferred the second alternative, that is, sell the assets rather than reserve them. By the end of 1998, Kamco had bought NPLs worth some Won 44 trillion. In the process, banks had mostly been cleaned of their NPLs on their balance sheet. The average NPL to good loans ratio reported at end-1998 was only 7%. The process of sale continued in 1999.

What happened to the selling banks? The loans were bought with both a put option, as also at their fair market value, thus resulting in heavy losses for the selling banks. This could have forced many of the Korean banks into bankruptcy; as a matter of fact, many of them chose to merge into larger banks or merchant banks. This reduced the number of banks and merchant banks both. An April 1999 report [*Asia Bank Restructuring* by Fitch IBCA] reported that the number of commercial banks fell to 17 from 26, and merchant banks from 30 to 13. In addition, five were nationalized, five were recapitalized and banks were forced to cut costs by shedding some 30% of their staff.

Kamco's NPL sales and securitization

To fund the purchases of bad loans, Kamco has been both selling and securitizing its loans. There have been some 14 domestic bond issuances by Kamco by the end of 2001 [based on website at http://www.kamco.or.kr/eng/area/main1.htm]

In July-August 2000, Kamco came out with the first off-shore securitization of non-performing loans in Asia, minus Japan. The deal was ground-breaking and was later awarded several prizes as one of the best structured finance deals from Asia in 2000. See transaction in Figure 21.1.

The portfolio

Non-performing loans fall into three groups. They are either secured or unsecured loans in default for three months or longer, secured or unsecured loans that have received court approval for restructuring as part of corporate reorganization, or composition proceedings or workout company loans that have received creditors approval for debt restructuring.

The portfolio comprised 135 restructured corporate loans bought from Korean banks. Most of the loans were dollar denominated and were bought from six originating banks - Korea Development Bank (KDB), Korea Exchange Bank, Cho Hung Bank, Hanvit Bank, Shinhan Bank and Kookmin Bank — under various settlement and supplemental agreements.

The SPV structure

The deal included the establishment of two off-balance sheet SPVs, one layered on the other. The existence of two-tier SPV structure was explained by the requirement of the Korean law as also the need to issue securities to offshore investors. One was set up in Korea and the other in the Cayman Islands. Kamco sold the portfolio to the Korean SPC. The SPC then issued senior and subordinated notes that comprised the purchase price for the loans. The senior notes were credit-enhanced by the subordinated note and a credit facility provided by the KDB to the Korean SIC. The senior note was sold to the Cayman SPC.

The senior notes

The Cayman Islands' SPC in turn issued US$367 million in floating rate notes due 2009. The expected maturity of the notes is 4.7 years. These notes are listed on the Luxembourg Stock Exchange and were offered in the U.S. under Rule 144(a). The senior notes received rating BBB+ by Fitch IBCA, largely influenced by the large put option against KDC. KDC itself was rated BBB+.

To the author's knowledge, the notes were a sellout in the London market, reportedly oversubscribed by more than 2.5 times.

Credit enhancements

The most significant credit enhancement in the deal was put options provided by KDB as also by the respective originating banks. The put options were, in the first place, granted by the selling banks to Kamco when the loans were sold. Thereafter, they were assigned by Kamco to the Korean SPV. Under terms of the put option, the originating banks are obligated to repurchase the loans under certain circumstances. These include a payment default by the loan borrowers for a period of six months or longer or cancellation of the corporate reorganization or composition proceedings rendering payments of principal or interest, or both, impossible. The investors got a put option for nearly 60% of the notes against KDB.

This apart, there were other credit enhancements. There was a US$110-million credit facility granted by KDB, about 30% of the senior notes. In addition, the senior notes were also supported by junior notes at US$53 million, roughly 12% of the senior notes.

European NPL securitizations

There have been a range of NPL securitizations from Italy – of non-performing mortgage loans and leases. In addition, several NPL sell-downs have been done out of Germany as well, which might later find their way into the securitization market.

How does it actually happen?

The real miracle in securitization of non-performing loans is not to turning bad into good; it is not that the bad apple becomes a good apple when sliced, but rather that the good portion of the bad apple is sliced and given to outsiders, while the bad part is retained by the originator or other enhancers. Most non-performing loans securitizations have been supported by substantial over-collateralization or subordinated interests retained by the originating banks. Most of the Italian securitizations, for example, are credit-enhanced by a substantial extent of subordinated notes retained by the originator.

For the Korean non-performing loan securitizations, it is a put option with the Korea Development Bank that enhances the acceptability of the bonds.

That is as far as the creation of investor-acceptable securities is concerned. But on a macro basis, a more significant question is: The NPLs are merely being transferred from the originating banks into an SPV, and someone is still holding the baby, so is the exercise creating any value or merely giving an illusion of a value creation?

For several bank NPL securitizations, the value creation is the pooling of NPLs into an SPV that does not do banking but simply administers and resolves the bad loans. The reconstruction company works with a single and simple brief of resolving problem loans – not with the intent of recovering maximum value out of a defaulted loan but to recover the maximum that can be extracted with the shortest time span. The approach is more time value of money than absolute value as such. The existence of a specialized servicer duly equipped with appropriate legal powers results into better recoveries. Besides, as the funding of the NPL pool is done by the capital markets, the originating banks are completely freed of their problem loans, both in terms of administration and also funding.

Government receivables

Governments in various parts of the world have been users of securitization devices to raise funding from capital markets.

Why securitization of government assets?

The most common justification given for securitization of government revenues is socially beneficial investments by the governments. Governments of all nations have to invest in public goods such as healthcare and infrastructure. Some government spending is in sectors that do not have any identifiable revenues; there are some of these investments that have long-term revenues. The former should appropriately be funded by the general budgets of governments, but for the latter, if government finances are linked with capital markets, it enables a more efficient funding of social utilities, and reduces the burden on government finances.

Deficit financing and securitization

During 2004 and 2005, intensive debate erupted, particularly owing to rulings of Eurostat, as to whether securitization should be allowed to reduce government deficits. In view of the controversy, Greece dropped a proposal to securitize its taxes. We have included the Eurostat rules and decisions in this heading.

European government revenues securitizations

All over Europe, several instances of securitization of government revenues, government properties, or with explicit or implicit government support have recently taken place. Some notable transactions are: Sweden's Framtiden; Finland's Fennica; Italy's INPS; Portugal's Explorer; Belgium's EVE and Belsca.

Eurostat ruling

On July 3, 2002, Eurostat published the following rules on whether a securitization transaction can be allowed to reduce the fiscal deficit:

The decisions:

1. **Securitization of future flows not attached to a pre-existing asset is always to be treated as government borrowing**

When a government transfers to a SPV, or to another unit, specific future receipts that are not directly attached to an asset usually recorded in its balance sheet but resulting from activity undertaken by government, the securitization unit has no involvement in the activity at the origin of the flows specified in the contract and which are assumed to be used for repayment of its debt. This unit has no control on the generation of flows unlike the case where it has the full ownership of an asset. In national accounts, such arrangements are to be considered as government borrowing.

2. **The granting of guarantees by government to an SPV or to another entity implies an incomplete transfer of risk and is evidence that there was not an effective change in ownership of the assets. Therefore, in the case of a securitization operation undertaken with an SPV, it implies the reclassification of the SPV within the government sector, or the recording of an implicit loan from the SPV to the government.**

According to ESA95, the sale of an asset implies a complete transfer of "risks and rewards." It means that the seller no longer bears any risk on behalf of the purchaser or investors in the special vehicle created on purpose for securitization. Guarantees may be given by a government unit selling one asset, such that, finally, the latter would have to compensate any "failure" related to further asset "performance" (like insufficient repayments of loans and resale at a lower price than the purchase price). Such guarantees are evidence that no true sale has occurred and that the government unit has kept the ownership of the asset in the sense of national accounts. Therefore, the proceeds of a securitization transaction should be considered in this case as government borrowing, in most cases by reclassifying the SPV within the government sector.

3. **Whenever the securitization contract includes, in addition to the initial payment by the SPV to the general government unit, a clause on additional future payments from the SPV, specific provisions apply. In particular, whenever the difference between initial payment and the observed market price or market-based estimated price is higher than 15%, the transaction has to be treated as government borrowing.**

In cases where a securitization contract stipulates possible future payments to the general government unit, in addition to the initial payment, linked to future cash flows resulting from the management of the securitized assets, there is a need to assess whether a complete transfer of risk has occurred. In cases where the initial payment (sale price) is clearly lower than the observed market price or a market-based price estimated by independent experts, it is considered that the purchaser of the asset bears no real risk in this transaction and that the transaction is very close to a financial borrowing. With the support of a majority of CMFB experts, Eurostat has decided that such a "discount" should not exceed 15%. This upper limit corresponds to a reasonable effective transfer of risk from the respective general government unit to the SPV and can cover cases of sales of both financial and non-financial assets. Beyond this "acceptable margin", the whole transaction has to be treated as government borrowing, with an increase in government debt and no impact on deficit/surplus.

4. **The value of the initial transaction must be recorded as an amount of cash effectively paid by the SPV to the government. Possible additional payments might have an impact on net borrowing/net lending in the case of sales of non-financial assets only at the time they occur.**

ESA95 provides rules about the value of a financial transaction, and its counterpart, that are to be recorded in national accounts. It is defined as the amount of means of payment exchanged. This must be applied in the case of securitization arrangements. Therefore, where a sale price is lower than the "reference price" (but within a limit of 15% as specified above) only the sale price has to be considered. There may be an effect either on deficit/surplus and debt in the case of a sale of non-financial assets, or only on government debt in the case of a sale of financial assets. However, possible additional payments, of amounts that are uncertain at the inception of the securitization arrangement, could have a further impact according to the above-mentioned cases.

All securitization operations undertaken by the government in the current and in past years will have to be classified according to these decisions. Adjustments should normally appear in the Excessive Deficit Procedure (EDP) notification of August 2002.

Based on the above ruling, a £1.25 billion issue of bonds by London and Continental Railways (LCR) was taken as government borrowing. LCR is a public-private partnership project. The revenues securitized in the instant case were future flows from railway track rentals. There is a guarantee from the Department of Transport regarding payment of track access charges, which form the basic income stream of the transaction. In its ruling, the public accounting department of the U.K. government explained its decision: "The judgment required is whether the bondholders are at risk. If they aren't, because of a formal guarantee or an indirect equivalent, then the Government must be the risk holder. Although the debt raised by the securitization is not directly guaranteed, the details of the arrangements are such that government is judged to be holding the risk rather than the bondholders."[11]

By its ruling dated May 23, 2005, the Eurostat also included SCIP transaction as a part of the government's borrowing.

Italian securitizations

The Italian government has been an avid user of securitization. The government uses securitization under three broad captions:

- Securitization program for real estate assets (SCIP)
- Securitization of public sector receivables (SCIC)
- Securitization of social security contributions (SCCI)

The Italian government agency securitized delinquent social security contributions in a landmark transaction concluded in 1999. This was an issue of € 4.65 billion of floating rate notes (FRNs) by the Instituto Nazionale per la Previdenza Sociale (INPS), the Italian social security agency. A specific body Società di cartolarizzazione dei crediti INPS (SCCI) bought the receivables from INPS; in the first tranche, the total amount of receivables backing the funding was € 42.3 billion of receivables. The FRNs received a AAA rating.

Several series of the INPS transaction have been brought into the market. Some of the FRNs have already matured and been paid.

Under the transaction structure, INPS continues to be the collection agent, and INPS in turn does collection through several concessionaire who are paid a percentage of their collections.

In 2001, Italy raised € 3 billion by securitizing the net revenue from its state run lotteries for the next five years. Societa per la Cartolarizzazione dei Crediti e dei Proventi Pubblici a Responsabilita Limitata, an SPV owned by two Dutch foundations, bought the rights to the future net revenue until 2006 from the two main lottery games in Italy — the Lotto and Super Enalotto. The SPV financed the initial payment by issuing € 3 billion of floating rate notes (FRNs). The structure was cleverly designed so that the payment of the deferred purchase price by the SPV to the government could be interrupted under certain triggers to ensure timely repayment of the FRNs. This coupled with the other covenants as well as the significant over-collateralization and allowed the FRNs to see a AAA rating. Legally the structure was a sale of the lottery revenues and the government does not have to count the FRNs as part of its debt.

The Italian government also raised large amounts of money through securitization of real estate and other property under its SCIP program. The SCIP-1 program was fully repaid in December 2003. SCIP-2 issued notes in two tranches – in December 2002 and April 2005.

An S&P report[12] noted a total of 17 treasury-sponsored transactions rated by the rating agency. The initial outstanding amount on these transactions, to July 2005, totalled € 49.459 billion, and the outstanding amount at that time was € 29.7 billion.

The Italian model on delinquent social security contributions was followed by Portugal in € 1.66 billion transaction known as Explorer.

U.S. tobacco settlement receivables

Tobacco settlement revenue securitizations have been used by several U.S. municipalities to raise funds secured by their interest in the future rights to payments made under the tobacco master settlement agreement. The agreement refers to the November 1998 settlement with tobacco majors between the attorneys general of 46 states and the four largest U.S. cigarette manufacturers – Phillip Morris, RJ Reynolds, Brown & Williamson (a subsidiary of British American Tobacco PLC), and Lorillard Tobacco Co. (a subsidiary of Loews Corp.). Subsequently, more than 36 other manufacturers signed the settlement. The purpose of the master settlement was to resolve cigarette-smoking litigation between the governments and the tobacco companies and release the tobacco companies from past and present smoking-related claims, while providing continuing release of future state claims.

Most of the governments used securitization of the tobacco receivables to encash the settlement proceeds up front – basically to support their budgets.

However, under various suits, litigation against the tobacco companies continued. For example, in March 2003 there was an order against a tobacco company that the "light" cigarettes sold by them were fraudulent, and huge damages were awarded. Consequently, around August 2003 most of the tobacco bonds had been downgraded by the rating agencies.

Some of the lawsuits were subsequently resolved. In December 2005, the Supreme Court of Illinois cleared a lawsuit against Philip Morris. However, rating agencies maintained a negative outlook. In its report of December 15, 2005, S&P stated: "While Standard & Poor's considers the current corporate credit ratings on the Original Participating Manufacturers (OPMs), or those on their parent companies, to be an important part of its analysis when rating tobacco settlement-backed bonds, they are among many factors and risks considered. Even if the negative outlooks assigned to the ratings on the major tobacco manufacturers, or their parent companies, are revised to stable, it is likely that the negative outlook on the tobacco settlement-backed bonds would remain, reflecting numerous risks that are independent of the corporate OPM ratings . . . Lawsuits pending in various states, including Arkansas, California.

Kentucky, New York (Freedom Holdings versus Spitzer), Oklahoma, and Tennessee, challenge, on various grounds, the validity of one or both of the model statutes enacted by those states on the Master Settlement Agreement (MSA) itself. Although none of these pending lawsuits have invalidated the MSA or any model statutes, a temporary disruption of annual payments to the states and the tobacco settlement-backed trusts could occur if the plaintiffs ultimately succeed in these suits . . . The possibility also remains that the market share loss calculated by the independent auditor to the MSA for calendar year 2003 could ultimately result in a reduction of payments to the states (and trusts) vis-à-vis the nonparticipating manufacturer (NPM) adjustment."

Hong Kong toll revenues securitization

The Hong Kong government brought a much talked-about securitization of toll revenues in May 2004. Hong Kong Link 2004 Ltd., an SPV created for this purpose, sold bonds worth HK$6 billion on five government-owned tunnels and one bridge.

Financial future flows

This is yet another application of the securitization technology that has been in limelight over the last few years. Financial future flows refer to remittances coming into a bank, generally from hard currency countries. Banks from Turkey, and several Latin American countries have been engaged in this activity and the underlying ratings of these securities are driven by the ratings of the respective banks; most of these transactions draw upon a third-party enhancement and see insurance wraps or guarantees.

In a significant way, the securitization of financial future flows is unique; the inflow is not the asset or income of the recipient. For example, future flows by way of export revenues represent the income of the exporter, for which he has the right of disposal. However, for remittances a receiving bank is merely an agent for the purpose of remittance. Therefore, if it is securitizing the inflow, it is not securitizing an income. It is simply securitizing a cash flow.

The concept of securitization of remittances is to have a borrowing in foreign currency that is repaid out of the remittance flows. The corresponding liability to pay in domestic currency is discharged by the remittance bank out of its domestic resources. Therefore, remittance securitization is not a matching of incomes with debt service, but matching of the inflows with debt service.

One of the most common applications of remittance securitization is workers' overseas remittances. For instance, many Indians who work throughout the world send remittances of their earnings on a regular basis to Indian banks. The recipient bank receives foreign exchange, and pays in domestic currency to the recipient. If these receivables in foreign currency are used as the basis for servicing a foreign currency liability, the bank is able to borrow at efficient rates from international markets.

The securitization of remittances is not limited to workers' remittances; it commonly extends to "diversified payment rights," that is, payments in international currency for remittances happening as a counterparty bank.

Bank requirements for remittance securitization

The remittance securitization borrowing is based on the banks' continued ability to service its borrowings by a regular flow of the remittances. Hence, there is a great reliance on the continued presence of the bank in the remittance business. The remittance business itself is growing increasingly competitive, and new means of remittances are constantly being devised.

The bank must satisfy some basic requirements. For example, it must be financially strong and there should not be apprehension as to the closure of its business. It should be rated domestically investment grade and generally among the top 2–3 banks. The remittance business should be important to the bank.

Technological change and the remittance business

The stability of remittance flows also presupposes that the existing methods of remittance will remain operative. For instance, if globalization of banking reaches an extent that a recipient in India is directly allowed to access the account of the sender out of the country, the remittance mechanism may undergo a drastic change. With technological development and exchange control liberalization, there may be drastic changes in how people transfer their money from place to place. As email has brought about a complete change in the way people communicate – something difficult to imagine in the good old days of postal communication – there may be unimaginable changes in remittances as well.

Inventory securitization

In some European transactions, another interesting application of the concept of securitization has been securitization of physical inventories. A landmark deal has been the *Marne et Champagne* transaction originated from France. The Champagne deal faced financing problems at the originating company, leading to a downgrade of the securities from BBB to CCC with a negative watch. However, the transaction model was followed in several securitizations later.

These transactions are based on the sale of inventories, rather than the sale of financial assets as with traditional securitizations. This is another illustration of securitization used to replace traditional working capital funding from banks.

Case study: Rosy Blue diamond inventory securitization

Another case is the securitization of diamond inventories by a Belgian diamond trader called Rosy Blue. Here, Rosy Blue NV, on the starting day of the transaction, made sale of title, a stock of diamond inventories worth US$165 million. The buyer was an SPV, Rosy Blue Carat SA, which raised funding of US$100 million by issuing notes. The excess of the diamond stock remained with the SPV as an over-collateralization.

The stock sold, but was not physically put in the possession of the SPV. The SPV put the stock with the seller as a consignment, retaining legal ownership. Whenever any stocks are to be sold, the SPV made a sale, and therefore had the right to retain the sale proceeds, until the seller reinstates the stock of diamonds to the required over-collateralization levels. This is a revolving transaction, with the collateral being a physical asset, legally transferred to the SPV.

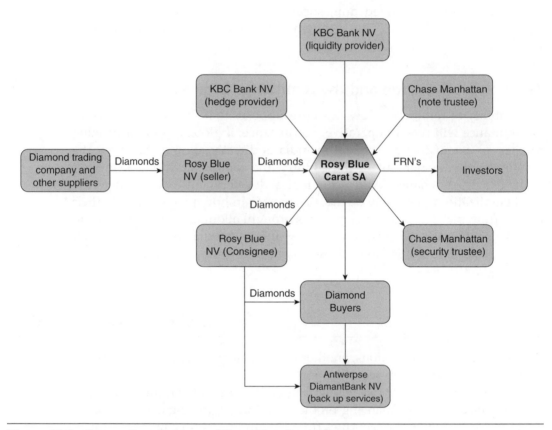

Figure 21.2   Transaction diagram of Rosy Blue Securitization

There is a notable difference between the whole business structure discussed above and the inventory securitization structure; in the present case, the structure is based on a true sale and not a secured loan.

The transaction in the present case was rated A, and there was only one class. Though there is a rating-dependence on the originator, the true-sale backed inventory securitization is similar in features to a revolving asset securitization. Like a revolving asset securitization, an inventory transaction has to depend on the originator for reinstatement, and not for performance as in the case of future flows or whole business transactions. Therefore, there is scope to apply asset-based rating principles in this case.

Potential products for inventory securitization

Sensing the potential for such transactions, rating agency Moody's issued a special report entitled "**Debut of Inventory Securitization in Europe: Moody's**

Rating Approach."[13] In the report, Moody's outlined features of a commodity that could be a candidate for inventory securitization:

- Regulated market with generally high barriers to entry.
- Organized open market and secondary market, such as Antwerp Diamond Index for Rosy Blue, champagne open market and inter-champagne market for Marne et Champagne.
- Liquidity and tradability of the inventory.
- "Durable" goods that do not deteriorate due to a longer-than-expected storage period.

Insurance securitization

In this section, we discuss an interesting development – securitization of the embedded value of insurance contracts. The risk transfer technology used for transferring risk of insurance contracts, such as catastrophe risk, is discussed in Chapter 22.

While risk securitization has been around for a while and securitization of future annuities or endowment contributions is also near routine, a new asset class of the securitization market has recently been introduced - securitization of value-of-in-force life insurance policies, or the embedded value of life insurance.

Unlike other alternative risk transfer devices, this securitization is not essentially a risk transfer device; it is predominantly a device to monetize the profits inherent in already-contracted life insurance policies. It is comparable to the securitization of the servicing fees of a servicer, the residual profits of a business, or the fees of asset managers.

In life insurance business, the key cash flows of the insurer consist of:

- Inflows:
  - Premiums
  - Annuities
  - Investment income and capital receipts
  - Fee income (for specific insurance contracts only)

- Outflows:
  - Policy benefits
  - Annuity payments
  - Investments
  - Surrenders
  - Expenses, both origination and continuing
  - Capital expenditure and investments
  - Taxes

The value of in-force life insurance policies tries to capitalize the net surplus out of these cash flows. Sometimes also known as "block of business securitization" (as the early usage of such funding was to refinance the initial expenses incurred in acquiring new blocks of policies), this funding method is based on structured finance principles whereby the residual income of the securitized block is monetized up front.

One of the early examples of this method is American Skandia Life Assurance Company (ASLAC). From 1996-2000, ASLAC issued thirteen securitization transactions designed to capitalize the embedded values in blocks of variable annuity contracts issued by ASLAC. The trusts issuing the notes are collateralized by a portion of future fees, expense charges, and contingent deferred sales charges (CDSC) expected to be realized on the annuity policies. In its 2000-2001 GAAP annual report, the company listed twelve outstanding issues from 1997 through 2000 with total initial issue value of $862,000.

Hanover Re has also used this device.

However, the most commonly cited example is that of National Provident Institutions (NPI), a U.K. based company that did a unique securitization in 1998, selling certain interests in an open pool of life insurance policies using the whole business securitization device used by several U.K. companies (discussed in Chapter 20). The transaction involved a huge amount of policies worth US$4.08 billion, with an embedded value of US$487 million.

In late 2004, Friends Provident Life and Pensions Limited raised core Tier 1 capital through an issue by Box Hill Life Finance of £380 million ($720.1 million) of floating rate notes, issued in two tranches.

Motivations for insurance securitization

One of the basic motivators for insurance securitization has been capital, as indicated by the declining *free asset ratio*. The free asset ratio measures the market value of the insurer's assets, minus its policy liabilities, essentially the economic capital or solvency of the insurer. The free asset ratio includes the implicit value of in-force policies (VIF). The implicit value is actuarially assessed net present value of future profits inherent in the current book of business. The *embedded value* of the insurer is said to be the total of the existing capital plus VIF.

The essential motive behind securitization of embedded value is to monetize the VIF. Under emerging insurance accounting rules, the VIF will not be considered as a part of the insurance capital in the future.[14]

On the other hand, the monetization of the surplus of in-force policies may be considered a part of capital if the repayment of the funding, raised by way of the transaction, is unambiguously linked to the surplus on the defined pool of policies. While the clean implicit item, unmonetized, requires regulatory clearance to be counted as capital, the funding way of the securitization of a surplus is a more definitive part of capital. Hence, the quality of regulatory capital improves as a result of the securitization.

Transaction structure

The crux of structuring the transaction is to look at residual profits from a pool of insurance policies; hence, the transaction is fairly similar to the whole business transactions discussed in Chapter 20. However, there is understandably no need to put the kind of financial covenants required in whole business transactions.

In addition, to have clean impact on regulatory capital, these transactions may use either a reinsurance vehicle or a contingent loan.

Case study: Box Hill Life Finance

In December 2004, Box Hill Life Finance transaction received preliminary ratings from S&P for issue of £380 million notes. The notes were guaranteed by Ambac and saw a rating of AAA, but the underlying rating was A-. The ultimate beneficiary holding the insurance policies was Friends Provident Life & Pensions (insurance originator). The transaction uses the reinsurance structure – the insurance originator sees reinsurance from a reinsurance SPV, which in turn has a contingent loan from the issuing SPV (the intermediary is involved in the process to give a group company loan, typical of U.K. transactions).

The policy book

The summary of the defined book is:

Table 21.3   Summary information of Life Insurance securitization case

	Contracts in force	In force premium (Mil. £)	Non-unit reserves (Mil. £)	Unit reserves (Mil. £)	Net present value (Mil. £)	Net present value (%)
Conventional non-profit life	233,436	27	113	N/A	93	11
Conventional non-profit pensions	138,157	7	2,492	N/A	252	31
Unit-linked life	294,253	107	2	1,680	83	10
Unit-linked pensions	505,330	116	26	2,732	139	17
Unitized with-profit life	370,965	145	N/A	2,835	164	20
Unitized with-profit pensions	413,814	79	N/A	2,702	94	11
Total	1,955,955	481	2.633	9,949	825	100

Note: Net present value assumed discount rate is 6%.
Net present value is the aggregate value of defined book surplus cash flows projected to arise in the future (under the base case assumptions) in respect of all policies in force as at May 31, 2004, discounted to December 15, 2004, assuming that cash flows are available on April 15 of each year following the calculation period.
N/A—Not applicable.

Transaction structure

The transaction is intended to provide regulatory capital support to the originator, so it is structured as a reinsurance contract with a reinsurance SPV. The reinsurance SPV receives from the originator a reinsurance premium, as also an annual accretion equal to "defined book surplus calculated in a given year less the annual premium." It is notable that this profit needs to be transferred to the reinsurance SPV, because the reinsurer needs to repay the loan it has from the lending intermediary.

The initial maximum liability of the reinsurer to the originator under the reinsurance agreement is £380 million, which increases each year by the benefit increase rate (the rate of residual surplus in the insurance contracts) and is reduced by the recapture amount (that is, the extent to which the incremental profits have been paid) and any claim in respect of that year. The aggregate maximum liability of the reinsurer is therefore the initial sum insured of £380 million, compounded for the term of the transaction (until April 15, 2019) at the benefit increase rate.

Several warranties have been laid down for continuation of the reinsurance contract, including:

- Origination procedures and servicing of the defined book in a manner expected of a diligent insurance company;
- Compliance with laws and regulations, including no mis-selling;
- Tax assumptions to remain unchanged;
- Investment of proceeds of the annuity book in accordance with the annuity-backed investment criteria and objectives;
- Responsibility for accuracy of all information;
- Requirement to act as a prudent insurer;
- Investment objectives and criteria for the reinsurer assets as per the reinsurer investment management agreement;
- Obligation to maintain an inflation hedge fully allocated to the defined book;
- The reinsurer regulatory surplus not being less than the defined book surplus (the conduit covenant); and

The reinsurer meeting regulatory capital requirements (the capital maintenance warranties).

Notes

1 John S Hillery: *Securitization of Intellectual Property, Recent Trends from the United States*, March 2004.
2 See http://www.pullmanco.com.
3 Manhattan Supreme Court Justice in July 2003 ruled that rather than possessing "a unique formula," Mr. Pullman merely used previously known techniques to analyze the numbers: *Pullman Group v. Prudential Insurance*, 600772/01.

4   So much so that one of the best selling fiction writers Linda Davies wrote a novel titled *Something Wild* that features the lives of music stars and also talks of Bowie Bonds. David Pullman was featured by Time as an innovator: http://www.time.com/time/innovators/business/profile_pullman.html, last visited December 26, 2005.

5   *Fortune,* April 28, 1997.

6   A brief description of several instances of music and other intellectual property securitization transactions may be found on http://www.ex.ac.U.K./~RDavies/arian/bowiebonds.html, last visited December 26, 2005.

7   See Chapter 23 on Legal Issues.

8   See Chapter 27 on Accounting Issues.

9   Press release on http://www.paulcap.com, last visited December 26, 2005.

10   Global Non-performing Loan Report 2004.

11   National Accounts Classifications, LCR Securitized Bonds August 2, 2005.

12   Report dated July 20, 2005: Performance Report on Italian Treasury Sponsored ABS transactions.

13   May 21, 2002.

14   For example, the Integrated Prudential Sourcebook of the FSA, U.K., Annex 2G.

Chapter 22

Synthetic Securitization and Other Risk Transfer Devices

A ll securitization is concerned with converting something into securities, hence the name "securitization." As asset securitization converts assets into securities, if the assets in question are synthetic rather than really transferred and securitized, this is a synthetic securitization. The synthetic technology comes from the world of derivatives, where a position of risk and return emulating an actual asset or exposure is created by a derivatives transaction. The basis of a synthetic securitization is a derivative or risk transfer transaction and the purpose is to synthetically replicate actual transfer of assets.

The fast growing world of synthetic securitization has spread very quickly to see immense structuring of CDOs, SME loan pools and certain forms of retail assets. The ease with which synthetic transactions can be constructed and executed allows for interesting combinations such as CDO squares, mixtures of credit and commodity and interest rate risks.

Cash vs. synthetic securitization

In a traditional securitization transaction, there is funding raised by the originator, as the originator transfers assets for cash. That is why generic securitization structures are known as cash structure securitization. Here, both the elements are important – transfer and cash.

In a synthetic securitization transaction, there is neither cash nor a transfer. First of all, the assets transferred are not transferred for real; they are merely transferred by way of a derivative contract. If the objective of the transaction is to transfer credit risk, then the derivative used is a credit derivative.

In a credit derivative, a credit asset is replicated by one party transferring credit risk to another. Let us think of a bank, say X entering into a credit derivative with another party, say bank Y, with reference to a counterparty, say M. The terms of the credit derivative are that A would keep paying a certain premium calculated on the value of this transaction. If during the term of the transaction M defaults on its obligations (not necessarily obligations to X) or goes bankrupt, Y makes certain protection payments to X. If there is no such default, the transaction closes on termination.[1]

This type of a credit derivative transaction is called a credit default swap – named in tune with interest rate swaps and seeking to transfer the risk of credit default of the counterparty M. The transaction puts Y, called the *protection seller*, in a position of risk that is symptomatic of an actual owner of the assets. To be rewarded for this protection provided, the protection seller earns from the *protection buyer* (X in our example above) a fee or premium, representative of the spreads that an asset owner would earn for owning a credit asset. One may notice that in the transaction above, the position of Y is the same as the owner of credit assets; Y has the exposure to M, just the same as Y would have had, if Y actually lent money to M.

In a typical credit default swap, the protection seller does not fund the asset for cash, and so does not get any compensation for funding; he bears the risk inherent in the asset, and so earns spreads representing the risk. Therefore, minus the funding, the protection seller has the same risk and reward as the asset owner. Thus, selling protection by way of a credit derivative is the equivalent of buying or creating a credit asset synthetically.

Understanding synthetic securitization is easy if the concept of synthetic credit assets is understood. In our example above, between X and Y, the credit asset has been synthetically transferred. It is not necessary for X to hold the credit asset in question; in fact, actual ownership of the credit asset is completely collateral to the transaction between X and Y. A synthetic securitization would arise when the assets acquired by the SPV are synthetic assets. In our example, if the transaction was an actual transfer of a credit asset, X with credit exposure in M would transfer the asset to Y. For a synthetic transaction, X, whether holding the credit asset in question or not, synthetically transfers the asset to Y, who creates the asset by selling protection.

A cash structure or generic securitization is aimed at two primary motives, leaving aside the consequential effects: Transfer of risk and rewards, as well as funding. When the portfolio of assets is transferred by the originating bank, presumably the risks and rewards are also transferred to the investors, who also fund the acquisition of the portfolio.

Often the bank's purpose is not funding but risk/reward transfer. Funding is either not an immediate concern, or if the risk is removed, can be taken care of by other traditional balance sheet means.[2] Therefore, if a bank aims to securitize to remove the risk/reward of a loan or bond portfolio, the bank can achieve the same by a synthetic transfer or a credit derivative, rather than an actual transfer for cash.

A synthetic securitization securitizes a debt portfolio synthetically, not actually. We emphasized earlier two features of a cash transaction – *cash* and *transfer* – with the originator raising cash and making a transfer. In a synthetic transaction, both are missing; the originator does not raise any cash, nor does he transfer any assets.

The modality of a synthetic transfer of assets usually involves a credit default swap. A credit default swap (CDS) is a credit derivative contract under which an asset up to a particular value (called notional value as such value needs to be the actual exposure of the protection buyer) will be bought by the protection seller if a certain *credit event*[3] takes place with reference to the asset, or the protection buyer will be compensated to the extent of the difference between the par value and fair value of the asset.

Synthetic securitizations resolve one of the most vexing problems of cash transactions – the transfer of assets.

Modus operandi

- The originator identifies the portfolio that he intends to synthetically transfer.
- The originator sets up an SPV.
- The SPV issues credit-linked notes (CLNs). A credit-linked note is a debt security, but with an underlying credit default swap. The face value of the notes is equal to the notional value of the credit default swap that each note holder implicitly writes. Each note holder becomes a protection seller and the note issuer becomes a protection buyer. Should the credit events take place, the principal, or interest, or both payable to the note holder would be offset by the amount of compensation payable under the swap.
- Thus, indirectly through the SPV, the originator buys protection equal to the sum total of CLNs issued by the SPV.
- The amount raised by CLNs is usually invested in a credit risk-free investment, such as government securities or like collateral. The idea is that there must be no counterparty risk as far the investors are concerned.
- The SPV in turn writes a credit default swap with the originator referenced to the reference portfolio.
- The protection buyer pays the agreed premium to the SPV. In addition, the SPV also earns coupon from the AAA investment made by it.
- If the credit risk event does not take place, the investors are paid the return on the collateral *plus* the risk premium paid. The risk premium acts as a premium paid to the investors to buy protection from the investors.
- Upon the occurrence of a credit risk event for which the originator has sought protection, the SPV will have to sell the collateral (unless the required payment can be met from undistributed interest income of the SPV) to the extent required to make payment to the protection buyer. Simultaneously, the holders of credit-linked notes will suffer a waiver/reduction of the interest and/or principal payable to them.
- The transaction is continued for its tenure, or until all obligors in the reference portfolio are satisfied/removed from the portfolio.

Structured credit risk transfer

The idea of structured credit risk transfer follows from the basic principles of structured finance. The essence of structured finance is to isolate a pool of assets from the generic entity risks of the originator and to fund these assets by creating a stacking order of liabilities that assume differentiated risks and returns on this pool. The economics of securitization essentially derive from this differentiation exercise.

If, for the pool of assets that we commonly have in a securitization transaction, we were to substitute a pool of synthetic assets, we may see the same principles of structuring that apply to any securitization will apply for synthetic securitization. The credit risks in the pool of synthetic assets may be sliced into several sequential slices, so that some provide protection to the other. The picture will be somewhat like that in Figure 22.1.

As is evident from the illustration of a simple credit derivative, the credit risk transfer in most synthetic securitizations is structured by classing or tranching. The protection buyer, the originator in the picture, is transferring a risk on a US$1 million portfolio to the SPV. The SPV is a special purpose vehicle, which does not have the credibility demanded of a swap counterparty; therefore, the SPV pledges collateral in favor of trustees who hold the same for the benefit of the originator and the investors, in that sequence.

The SPV, in turn, transfers the risk to the investors by issuing credit-linked notes; this is the money invested by the SPV to collateralize the protection that it sells to the originator. The credit-linked notes have an embedded derivative, in that the credit protection payments made to the originator on the reference portfolio will be netted off from the principal and/or interest on the CLNs. The CLNs are classified into four classes in this example; they can be put into more or less classes based on the same factors on which structuring are done for any securitization.

These classes are ramped up in a military-like structure of defense, as is the general case of subordinated securities. Class D is the first line of defense. Should the enemy in the form of credit losses attack, Class D must sacrifice its life before any damage is done to Class C. Class C must likewise say: "Only

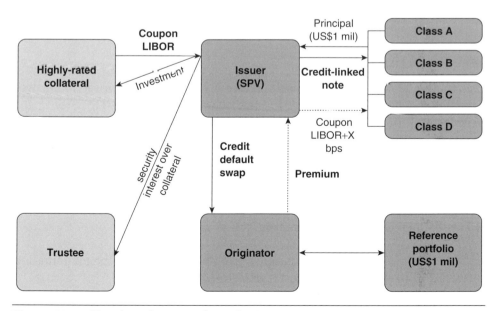

Figure 22.1   Simple unleveraged synthetic securisation

over my dead body will you touch class B!" Thus, Class B has the protection of both classes D and C, in that sequence. Class A has protection from all subordinate classes.

In a ratings parlance, we would say, Class A sees credit enhancement from B, C and D; B sees credit enhancement from C and D, and C is credit enhanced by D. The sizing of the subordinate classes is done with a particular rating target for the senior classes. For example, Class A will be typically rated AAA, and the rating agencies' requirement for a AAA rating for Class A in the given scenario is 15% credit enhancement, then classes B, C and D must add up to 15% of the total transaction size. The junior-most Class D is typically unrated.

Class D is the riskiest, as it bears the credit risk of the entire portfolio. If the value of Class D is 10% of the total size, Class D has 10 times as much risk as the portfolio risk. This is because Class D bears the risk of every obligor in the portfolio, and the portfolio size is 10 times the size of Class D. Obviously, Class D must obtain a sufficiently high coupon.[4]

The junior classes see a successively higher coupon – the weighted-average coupon (WAC) of the classes determines the required risk premium that the originator must pay to the SPV. It is evident from the picture above that the issuer (SPV) earns LIBOR from the investment collateral, but it pays a higher WAC to the investors. This spread (WAC – LIBOR) represents the price of the portfolio risk transferred, which the originator must pay as the premium to the SPV.

Thus, the pricing for the risk transfer in a capital market transaction is capital market-determined (based on the WAC, which itself is based on the coupon expected by different investors, in turn based on the ratings of the various classes). The more bottom-heavy is the structure, the better the rating of the senior classes, but the more the WAC and hence the higher risk premium. Thus, the sizing of the respective classes is a delicate balance between the rating target and the aggregate price for risk transfer.

Leveraged risk transfer

As a matter of fact, tranching itself creates leverage in the transaction; as we have noted, Class D is leveraged to the extent of (A+B+C+D)/D.

To (a) seek protection over a larger portfolio than the amount of funding involved and (b) provide higher coupon to the investors, most synthetic transactions use a leverage structure where the value of the reference portfolio is much higher than the value of the funding raised from investors. This is shown in Figure 22.2 (the sizing of the classes is only illustrative and may not be a good indicator.

The distinctive features of this transaction are:

- The value of the reference portfolio is US$1 billion, whereas the total funding raised from the capital market is only US$200 million.
- The balance is being covered by an unfunded *super-senior swap* for US$800 million.

- The super senior swap is also a CDS, similar to any ordinary CDS, with the only difference that the risk on this swap will be transferred to the counterparty only when all four classes A, B, C and D have been fully wiped out.
- The originator writes the super senior swap with the super senior swap counterparty. The originator writes the junior (junior to the super-senior) swap with the SPV. The swap with the SPV is fully funded by investor's money, which they put as subscription to the CLNs, which are pledged with the SPV. This is called a **funded swap**. The swap with the super senior swap provider is not normally funded or collateralized, hence it is called an **unfunded swap**.

Super-senior swap

We have noted in our example for leveraged risk transfer that the first-loss risk on the portfolio of US$1 billion will be first absorbed by the funded swap with the SPV (sequentially absorbed by the various classes bottom-up), while any remaining losses will be transferred to the super-senior swap counterparty.

Why is the super senior swap called "super senior?" This has to do with the risk/rating features of Class A. We have noted above that the one of the main purposes of having subordinate classes is to provide credit enhancement to the senior classes. Typically, in most real-life transactions, the sizing of the subordinate classes is worked out to ensure a AAA rating to the senior-most class (Class A in our example). In rating jargon, this means that Class A has the highest safety of principal and interest, while in plain English it means there is little perceptible risk at the time of the rating of any loss of interest or principal on this class. We also know that the super-senior swap is senior to

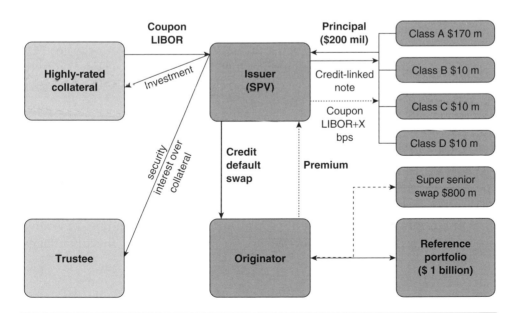

Figure 22.2 Leveraged synthetic securitization

Class A, which must be fully wiped off before any risk is transferred to the super-senior swap counterparty. This implies that the possibility of any risk transferred to the super-senior class is purely hypothetical. This swap is senior to the senior-most, which is why it is called super-senior swap.

Why is the super-senior swap required at all? If we understand that the risk being transferred to the super-senior swap is purely hypothetical, an originator should be indifferent between transferring this risk and retaining it. This risk is only catastrophic risk, which for a diversified portfolio is unlikely to lead to any losses except in extremely adverse situations. The super-senior swap protection is sought purely for regulatory reasons, for the catastrophic risk or the mark-to-market risk in case the portfolio suffers huge losses. Regulatory capital rules in some countries provide[5] that capital relief shall not be granted on an uncovered portfolio. If the portfolio is partly covered by a credit derivative, the capital relief shall be proportionately reduced.

As the risk transferred to the super-senior swap counterparty is from very small to purely negligible, the pricing of the super-senior swap is done taking care of the marginal risk of the losses eating into the subordination, as well as the fact that the swap eats up regulatory capital of the swap counterparty.[6] Therefore, in many cases the super-senior swap counterparty is effectively renting its surplus regulatory capital, and the swap premium represents rental for regulatory capital.

Impact of the super-senior swap on the cost of the transaction

The presence of a super senior swap in synthetic securitizations helps to reduce the weighted-average cost of the transaction. As is apparent, if the super senior unfunded swap was not there, the entire funding of the transaction would have to come from the funded Class A. For the sake of argument, even if Class A was broken into a super-senior Class A-1 and second Class A-2, the coupons payable on Class A-1 will include an element of spread the investors will expect. On the contrary, the super-senior swap, being unfunded, carries a lesser swap cost. Of course, the swap cost is market-determined and is affected by demand/supply forces, but as long as the cost is less than the credit spread on the funded AAA class, there is a cost-saving to achieve.

Advantages of synthetic securitization over cash transfers

Over time, synthetic securitization has become increasingly popular, particularly in Europe and Asia. Synthetic securitization resolves a number of vexing problems associated with cash transactions. The following are the advantages of synthetic securitization:

Minimizes funding and reinvestment problems

One of the most important advantages of a leveraged synthetic transaction is that the amount of funding raised from the investors is only a fraction of the total value of the portfolio on which risk is transferred. In practice, most synthetic securitizations use a partly funded, leveraged structure as shown before, and the actual leverage may only be more than what was used in our example. As in the example we took, the value of the reference portfolio was US$1 billion and the total funding raised from the market was US$200 million, thereby reducing the funding to 1/5th of the portfolio size. The balance portfolio is covered by a theoretical risk transfer to a super-senior swap counterparty or is not covered at all.

If the originator wants to achieve a similar objective in a cash structure, it would entail transfer of the entire portfolio of US$1 billion. Theoretically, the originator could still limit the capital market funding to US$200 million by buying back the super senior class of US$800 million, but there is still a transfer of the entire portfolio.

The inevitable result is that in cash securitizations, the funding exercise is far more elaborate. Synthetic transactions are much leaner and can be accomplished more easily than cash transactions.

The funding size leads to a major reinvestment problem for the originator. It is not easy to reinstate the portfolio that stands reduced by the transfer; reinvestment is both time-taking and leads to a negative carry problem. On the other hand, the originator completely avoids the reinvestment problem for synthetic securitizations as he does not have any cash to reinvest.

Splits the funding and the risk transfers

Synthetic securitization splits the funding and risk transfer aspects of securitization. The risk is transferred by way of credit derivatives. The funding can be taken care of by on-balance sheet sources, based on the capital relief obtained by the risk transfer. In fact, once the risks are removed by risk transfer, funding by regular balance sheet means should be only more convenient.

Alleviates transfer-related problems

Cash securitizations are built upon a "true sale" structure, implying that the originator must make a transfer of the portfolio to the SPV. The transfer must be legally perfected and done in a manner that will be respected in law and cannot be annulled by a bankruptcy court.

Transfer of a loan is by itself far more difficult than selling a car. A claim against a person is not the same as a claim on an asset[7] when it comes to transferring that asset. There are archaic requirements of law dating back centuries when it comes to selling a claim against a third person to a transferee.[8] These requirements vary by country, but these may include:

- In many countries, notification of the obligor is required for a transfer to be effective. In some countries, even consent of the obligor is required. This would imply the originator notifying each and every obligor that the obligation stands transferred to someone who is a rank stranger for the obligor. This is both logistically difficult as well as unfriendly to the obligor.

- In most systems, it is required that the whole of the obligation must be transferred and not a part. This would imply, for a portfolio of loans maturing at different points in time, the entire range of loans maturing at different times being transferred.
- In most systems, it is required that the transfer of the obligation is accompanied by a transfer of the securities or collateral that back up the loan. Once such securities are transferred, the originator obviously cannot give a further loan on the security of the same collateral, commonly done in lending practice.
- Only the receivables that exist can be transferred, not those that have not yet been created. This implies that any receivables to be created out of undrawn amounts or partly drawn amounts cannot be transferred.

Even after this, there is no certainty that the transfer will still be regarded as a valid sale in law. This is because of a recharacterization risk that looms large in such transactions where significant credit enhancements are provided by the originator. The legal rationale is that if the originator truly transfers his assets out, he must also cease to carry any risk on such assets. If he continues to support the assets with his own credit rather than the quality of the assets, the transfer may be treated as a funding taken by the originator rather than a true sale.

Even if a true sale, the sale can face a legal power of the court called consolidation, which means the originator and the SPV are treated as two outfits belonging to the same economic unit. In other words, the separate entities of the originator and the SPV are ignored and the two are treated as a unit – making the transfer redundant.

Thus, true sale issues have been a major worry for securitization transactions and often a great deal of legal costs, structuring complexity and a multiplicity of intermediate SPVs[9] are used to presumably reduce the legal uncertainty in securitizations.

True sale concerns become all the more acute when the assets are located in multiple jurisdictions, with each having a different set of requirements for transfer. As per essential legal principles, the receivables are located where the place of payment is.

Synthetic transactions steer absolutely clear of this by not relying on the transfer of obligations at all. It is not the obligations but merely the risk that is transferred in synthetic structures. The risk is transferred by a derivative structure, which is unconnected with what the originator does with the obligor.

Does not require artificial separation of origination and servicing functions

In cash structures, because of the true sale structure, there is an artificial separation of the ownership and servicing of the obligations. The house-owner becomes the housekeeper; that is, the originator who was the owner of the credit assets before assumes the role of a servicer of the obligations. In other words, as far as the obligors are concerned, all the servicing functions and all collection functions will still be discharged by the originator. In most cases, the obligors do not even come to know this role transition.[10] The originator's association with the obligor is so obtrusive that it almost puts a cloak on the transfer.

This artificial change of the originator role into a servicer role leads to an elaborate legal, logistical and systems exercise. The originator has to keep collecting the receivables but not co-mingle them with his own; he must maintain a segregation of what he collects on his own account and that he collects as an agent of the SPV, a tremendous burden on the systems for retail portfolios. He must transfer the agency collections immediately to the SPV or dispose as per the instructions of the SPV. He can and should charge a service fee for what he does, which is mostly nothing but his profits in disguise. He can be replaced in certain circumstances by a backup servicer, who must be identified up front, although that contingency is remote. The potential transfer of the servicing function to a backup servicer is again a greatly burdensome task; if the backup servicer has to be identified right away, there may be costs attached to this commitment as well.

The essence of all this is that the originator must, on the surface, keep on doing all that he was doing before the transfer, but agree behind the facade with the SPV that he is doing it as an agent.

The rigmarole of servicing/origination separation is completely ruled out in synthetic transactions. The originator's relation with the obligors is left untouched, both legally and on the surface.

Lower legal costs

Securitization requires massive legal documentation – for achieving the transfer of assets and the elaborate representations and warranties he gives, changing the role of the originator into a servicer and setting up the servicer responsibilities and transfer of collateral. All has to be done in a manner that will not lead a court to question the truth of the transaction. This requires hefty payments by way of legal fees for documentation, setting up the structure and vehicles, and opinions.

Besides, another important part of the legal costs is the duties and taxes payable on the transfer of receivables itself – stamp duties are payable in many countries on transfer of receivables. Some countries impose value-added tax on transfer of receivables as well.

Credit derivatives have a much simpler documentation. A few-page ISDA can do what cash structures take 200 pages to write on. There is no transfer of receivables – therefore, there are no stamp duties whatsoever.

No upfront taxation

Cash structure securitization mostly results in problems of upfront taxation of the originator's profits. The originator's profit equals the weighted average return of the portfolio less the weighted-average coupon payable to the investors. At the end of the day, the originator must capture that profit and extract it out from the SPV. Originators use various devices, often in combinations, to extract their profit – upfront gain on sale by way of difference between the transfer price and the carrying value, service fees, interest rate strip, clean up call option, interest rate swap,. While an upfront gain on sale is certainly taxable upfront, the other devices might defer the taxability of the profit. However, tax officials have an inherent right to question such deferment and accelerate the same to tax it immediately, particularly in cases where the gain on sale has been reported upfront in books of account.

For example, if an originator extracts his profit by way of an excess service fee, the tax officer might contend that this fee is nothing but a disguised deferred profit, which can be used to increase the fair value of the transfer and thus taxed immediately.

Any such contingency is ruled out for synthetic transactions where there is no transfer of the reference asset at all.

Avoids double taxation of residual profits

Another common problem with cash structures is the double taxation of the originator's residual income. Residual income refers to the income on the most subordinate piece in the liability structure of the SPV,[11] which is mostly held by the originator. The yield on this piece is mostly set such that the remaining profit in the SPV after servicing all external investors is swept by the originator.

For tax purposes, this may be treated as residual economic interest in the SPV, and therefore, equity of the SPV. Any payment to service equity is not allowable as a deduction for tax purposes, leading to a tax on such distribution as the income of the SPV. This very income, when received by the originator, will be treated as income again and is liable for tax. Thus, the originator's residual tax may come for tax twice unless the SPV is a tax-transparent or tax-free entity.

In contrast, the originator's profits on the portfolio in a synthetic transaction are not disturbed at all. He just pays the swap premium as the cost of buying protection and continues to pocket the entire credit spread on the pool. The credit default premium is paid to the SPV, which is an allowable expense, and the premium is an amount just enough to pay the WAC of the SPV, leaving no such residual profit to come for double taxation.

No accounting volatility

Cash structure securitizations are characterized by volatile accounting for income and assets by the originator. This is a result of the accounting standards on securitization accounting. The most important global accounting standards relating to securitization are the FAS 140 and the IAS 39.

The standards require off-balance sheet treatment for securitizations that qualify for such treatment. While the U.S. standard has been set up in a manner most prevalent in the market for an off-balance sheet treatment, the IAS 39 after its recent amendment seemingly makes it difficult for many securitizations to qualify for off-balance sheet treatment.[12]

When an asset has to go off the books, it must give rise to a gain or a loss on sale. Accounting standards require that in computing this gain or loss on sale, it is not merely the apparent gain on sale (that is, the difference between the transfer price and the carrying value of the portfolio) that should be considered, but also the retained elements of profit such as excess service fees, excess interest on a subordinated bond, excess discounting rate for a clean up call, interest rate strip and value of interest rate swap. That is, if the originator has set up the transaction as to create a source of profit in the future, this must also be brought up front and treated as a part of the consideration for computing the gain or loss on the sale. This source of future profit will also be simultaneously put up as an asset. That is, the accounting standards will lead to a gain on sale that is in excess of the apparent gain, leading to creation of ephemeral assets.

These sources of future profits are mostly subordinated and therefore uncertain. Over time, the originator is supposed to re-evaluate the assumptions made at the time of initial recognition of the gain on sale and the asset representing retained interests. The values of both will change based on the change in assumptions, leading to an extremely volatile accounting of income and assets by securitizers. A *Business Week* article some time back scoffed at such accounting practices: "Securitizations are all about guesswork. First, companies guess how much revenue they can expect at a particular time. Then they guess how much of that money they will need to back their bonds safely. Finally, they guess how much cash will be left over – and book that as profit... And guess what? Sometimes they guess wrong."[13]

Synthetic transactions remove the volatility in originator accounting as far as the gain on sale issue is concerned. As the assets are never sold in the first place, there is no question of any gain on their sale. The inherent gain on origination is captured over time as the assets pay off, and that is dealt with by normal revenue recognition principles. The only source of volatility on the originator's books is the value of the derivative, but if the derivative is a good hedge against the portfolio, the value of the derivative will only make good the losses on account of the impairment of the portfolio, thus removing or reducing volatility rather than creating or augmenting it.

As far as investor accounting is concerned, investment in synthetic securitizations may be as volatile as investing in subordinate tranches of cash securitizations.[14] That is the same as investing in any credit-sensitive asset. The volatility introduced by gain-on-sale accounting is alleviated completely in synthetic transactions.

Does not reduce book size

Quite often, banks and financial intermediaries see a source of pride in the growth of their balance sheet assets. Securitization results in assets going off the books, and therefore reduces the book size.

Credit derivatives, on the other hand, do not affect the asset-recognition on the books. The book size is not affected.

The best part is that while the financial books are not affected, the regulatory books are. For regulatory accounting purposes (RAP), credit derivatives mostly lead to a reduction in risk-weighted assets, and thus capital relief. With this relieved capital, a bank may create more leverage and therefore grow its book size.

Retains flexibility in customer service

Having flexible business relations with the obligors is most necessary with any financial intermediary. Most credit assets are the result of an on-going relation with the obligor. To retain this relationship, financial intermediaries serve the obligors, which often include prepayments, advance payments, waivers, rebates, rescheduling, further lending, change from one lending scheme to another and collateral waivers. In traditional securitization, as discussed, the house-owner changes into a house-keeper; for every little odd thing as white-washing the house or changing a dysfunctional fan, the originator will look to the trustees, now vested with security interests on the assets transferred to the SPV. This greatly reduces the business flexibility of the originator.[15]

On the other hand, credit derivatives do not, in any way, affect the business operations of the originator. If the portfolio is static and a particular obligor has to be prepaid, the only implication is that the notional value of the swap may have to be reduced. Most capital market transactions are done with dynamic portfolios with substitution rights reserved with the originator, so the originator may, subject to conditions, call back an obligor from the portfolio and reinstate another.

Bullet repaying notes

For synthetic transactions, the maturity profile of the notes is generally bullet repayment. For cash transaction, principal is usually paid down over time as the principal inherent in the assets in the pool is realized. For synthetic transactions, there is no principal repayment inherent in the assets (as the cash assets are actually the financial investments made by the SPV), and the swaps are normally for a fixed term. Fixed income investors prefer a bullet repaying investment than one that amortizes or pays an uncertain amount of principal over time.

Inefficiencies of a synthetic securitization

While discussing the factors that make a synthetic securitization preferable over a cash securitization, we must also note some inefficiencies and limitations of a synthetic transaction.

First, a synthetic transaction has an implicit funding inefficiency. The cash raised by issuing CLNs is typically invested externally in safe securities. The difference between the WAC of the transaction and the funding returns is paid by the originator as the swap premium to the SPV. If the originator was to use this funding himself, the implicit cost of the swap would only be the difference between the WAC of the transaction and the WAC (or marginal cost of funding) of the originator. This is simple to understand, because in that event the originator pays a coupon on the funding to the SPV, and in addition pays a swap premium. Assuming the originator will be prepared to pay a coupon equal to his WAC, the swap premium represents the difference between the coupons paid to the investors and the WAC of the originator. For obvious reasons, the WAC of the originator is higher than the returns on the external safe investment of funds by the SPV, so there is a funding inefficiency equal to the difference between such returns and the originator's WAC.

This funding inefficiency arises as the transaction aims to isolate the assets of the SPV from the originator. The assets in this case are the cash raised by issuing CLNs; if this was invested with the originator, the rating of the securities will face the risk of the originator's bankruptcy.

The second inefficiency is the super-senior swap; in a certain way, the super-senior swap is responsible for an extraneous cost on the entire transaction, as there is only a marginal risk transfer by way of the super-senior swap.

In addition, one must note a very significant limitation of synthetic transactions; they do not result in funding. If the idea of the originator in looking at a securitization transaction is funding, synthetic securitizations do not achieve that objective. That is why synthetic securitization is never used for funding-focused securitizations, such as future flows and whole business transactions.

Distinction between cash-funded and synthetic securitization

The table below sums up the differences between cash structure securitization and synthetic securitization:

Table 22.1 Differences between cash structure securitization and synthetic securitization

	Cash-funded securitization	Synthetic securitization
Purpose	To raise cash, raise liquidity, transfer portfolio of loans	To transfer risk on portfolios, manage regulatory and economic capital, reduce concentration.
Transfer of assets	Loans/credits are transferred from the balance sheet of the originator	There is no legal transfer of loans; only the risks are transferred using a credit derivative contract.
Off balance sheet treatment	Leads to loans going off the GAAP balance sheet	Does not lead to loans going off the balance sheet.
Impact on regulatory capital	To the extent of assets transferred, attains regulatory relief	To the extent of assets backed by cash or near cash collateral, attains regulatory relief; to the extent of assets covered by CDS from permitted/rated banks, reduces the risk weightage by replacement of the risk weights.
Accounting treatment	FAS 140/IAS 39 to be applied on the sale of the assets	FAS 133/IAS 39 to be applied by splitting the derivative and accounting for fair value changes in the derivative.
Regulatory compliances	Complicated and costly	As there is no true sale, very few legal and regulatory issues.
Risks of investors	Investors take risk in the collateral pool	Investors take the risk of the collateral, but the risks may include "credit events," which may be defined as to be more elaborate than a real loss.[16]

Balance sheet and arbitrage synthetic securitization

The idea of a synthetic credit asset pool can most effectively be used for arbitrage transactions – that is, when the purpose is not to transfer the risks of an asset pool held by an originator, but to accumulate a pool and then transfer the risk out to investors by issuing CLNs.

The methodology of an arbitrage synthetic securitization is explained at length below. Briefly, in a balance sheet transaction, there is an originator sitting with a pool of assets, the risks of which he transfers by buying a credit default swap from the SPV. The purpose of the originator is to manage regulatory and economic capital requirements on this pool.

In an arbitrage transaction, the sponsor (who takes over the role of the originator in a balance sheet transaction) constructs a portfolio with the objective of reaping arbitrage opportunities, either for himself or for the equity investors in the transaction. The credit assets are the reference entities on whom protection is sold by the SPV. The arbitrage is the difference between the premiums earned by selling protection on these entities and the coupons paid to the different classes of investors.

It would not be difficult to understand that in a cash synthetic transaction, the asset pool is the pool originated and held by the originator; therefore, the composition of the pool will reflect the actual names held by the originator. For arbitrage transactions, the portfolio is completely synthetic, and thus carefully constructed with the objective of maximizing the arbitrage revenues. Obviously, arbitrage revenues are maximized when the gap between premiums earned by selling protection and the weighted-average cost of the transaction implied by the coupons on the liabilities as well as the sizing of the liabilities are maximized.

Below, we take a closer view of balance sheet and arbitrage synthetic securitizations.

Elements of balance sheet synthetic securitization

Originator

The role of the originator in a synthetic securitization is that of a protection buyer under the credit derivative. However, unlike OTC derivatives where the reference asset is mostly a single name or a basket of rated or well-known obligors, the portfolio in a synthetic securitization is usually carved out of the portfolio held by the originator. The originator is the "originator" of the portfolio; he is the one who has created the portfolio.

This leads to two significant differences between a plain credit default swap transaction and one in a balance sheet synthetic securitization. One, the originator as the protection buyer is generally exposed to the assets for which he buys protection. Two, even while seeking protection under a credit derivative, the originator makes several representations and warranties regarding the portfolio originated by him, which are atypical of true sale type securitizations but very different from the implied warranties of the protection buyer in ISDA documentation.

The extent of these warranties depends on the nature of the assets; the more retail and dispersed is the portfolio, the more the need for such representations and warranties.

Obligor portfolio

The originator selects the obligor portfolio with respect to which the risk is to be transferred. The portfolio is obviously the one where the originator wants to reduce his balance sheet risk or concentration. While the balance sheet management motive of the originator is the basic consideration, there are numerous factors going into framing the balanced portfolio for risk transfer.

These factors include a weighted-average rating factor to be achieved that is based on the credit quality of the portfolio, individual obligor concentration, industry concentration, geographical concentration and diversity score.

Type of credit derivative

The credit derivative used in synthetic securitizations can be either a CDS or a TROR swap.[17] However, a CDS is more common, as it leads to payment of a certain premium to the SPV that will allow the SPV to pay the required coupon to the investors. The terms of a TROR swap, in which the originator pays a floating amount or variable total return and receives a fixed spread, will not easily fit into CLNs carrying a stipulated coupon.

The originator buys protection either by entering into a default swap with the SPV, or for non-SPV structures by issuing credit-linked notes himself. For SPV structures, the originator pays the premium that takes care of the negative carry involved in the financial assets and obligations of the SPV. For a direct issue of CLNs, the originator pays such a coupon on the CLNs, which inherently comprises a default swap premium.

Credit events and loss computation

The credit events for synthetic securitizations are not always the same as for OTC derivatives. The originator has greater control on the type of credit derivative he writes and the list of credit events he includes than in OTC transactions, although the risks transferred to the SPV ultimately impact the WAC demanded by the investors. However, a modification of the ISDA standard definitions is very often required by the exigencies of the case. For example, the portfolio might consist of corporate loans where failure to pay principal on a scheduled date may have a much larger notice or grace period under the obligor agreement itself, and so the typical OTC market grace period of two days is not appropriate for such a case.

Events like restructuring may not be suitable to be specified as events of default for SME loans where it is a common practice to agree to such requests.

If the reference portfolio is a portfolio of leases, the event of default may need to be defined in a specific manner.

The scope of the credit event definition is also modulated by the approach of the rating agencies accepting or not accepting certain events of default. For example, the following is a gist of the approach of Standard & Poor's in accepting/not accepting credit events:

- Obligation default is not accepted as a credit event as this may technically be construed to cover several technical defaults such as failure of interest cover.
- If assets are structured products, a rating downgrade to D level is acceptable as a credit event, because structured products do not default by way of "failure to pay" as in case of cash obligations.
- "Failure to pay" may be defined for structured products as failure to pay as per defined terms. Note that ISDA Subsequently came out with definitions in case of structured products.

The loss calculation methods also need to be spelt out in detail. If the portfolio is diversified and consists of a large number of small value loans each, the standard market practice of a dealer-poll valuation may not work. Methods of valuation need to be tailored to the requirements of the case.

Special purpose vehicle

A special purpose vehicle is brought in as an intermediary between the investors and the originator. Such an intermediary is required for cash structures so as to hold the assets as a repository for the investors. In synthetic structures, there is no transfer of assets at all, but an SPV is still commonly used for more reasons than one. These are:

- The funding put in by the investors is held and invested by the SPV. Had there been no SPV, the entire funding would be held by the originator, which will impose a counterparty risk on the originator, as the originator will be the obligor for such securities. One of the important objectives of rating the securities is that the rating is not dependant on that of the originator, but taking a counterparty risk on the originator will subject the rating of the transaction to the cap of the originator rating. Hence, the funding is housed into a specific vehicle distanced from the originator that cannot be treated as a part of the originator's bankruptcy estate, making the securities bankruptcy-remote as far the originator is concerned.
- Had the SPV not been there, the originator will be the issuer of the securities. For several cross-border issues, this will impose withholding tax requirements.

A typical SPV for a cross-border issuance is an offshore SPV usually located in a tax haven jurisdiction that will avoid withholding tax implications.

The SPV will be constituted in a manner conducive to the usual SPV treatment. Organizationally, an SPV can be either a company or, in several jurisdictions, a trust; the choice is essentially a balance of several factors including taxation and legal issues. These features include:

1. Independence of the SPV from the originator, so that the SPV cannot be treated as a subsidiary or subset of the originator and consolidated in the event of bankruptcy of the originator, or anyone else for that matter; this will require the SPV to be structured as an orphan with its equity holding widely dispersed or declared in trust for public charity.
2. Similarly, the SPV should be managerially independent and not be treated as an originator-controlled entity. Points 1 and 2 will ensure that the bankruptcy of the originator cannot impact the SPV in any manner.
3. The special purpose vehicle should be a "special purpose" entity with its business, purpose and functions limited by its constitutional documents. It should satisfy the conditions of bankruptcy remoteness discussed elsewhere in this Book.
4. The SPV should have no power to issue any further obligations.
5. The parties whose services the SPV uses on outsourcing basis or otherwise should undertake not to petition the SPV into bankruptcy.
6. The constitutional documents of the SPV should put restrictions on the power to amalgamate, merge or resolve to voluntarily wind up. Points 3–6 ensure that the SPV cannot go bankrupt or opt to wind itself up.

Assets of the SPV

Typically, the cash assets of the SPV, that is, the funding raised from investors is invested in risk-free securities. This increases the negative carry of the SPV – that is, the difference between the coupon payable to the investors and the coupon earned on the investments. To reduce the negative carry, a number of synthetic transactions allow the whole or a part of the funding to be transferred to the originator, as a prepayment against the swap and deposit. The funding, to the extent it is transferred to the originator, reduces the negative carry as the originator's cost of funding is expected to be higher than the return on risk-free investments. In such cases, however, the rating of the originator may serve as a cap on the rating of the securities unless other enhancements are introduced (see non-SPV structures below).

The SPV is primarily formed to acquire synthetic assets – by selling protection to a single originator or in arbitrage transactions to various protection buyers. The cash assets are only to support or collateralize the protection sold. Usually, in single-originator transactions, the SPV is cash-funded only to the extent required to achieve a AAA-rating for the highest of its liabilities; therefore, it is the size of the required credit enhancement for a AAA-rating that determines the size of the cash assets of the SPV. However, in arbitrage transactions, the SPV sells protection to various originators and cannot obviously be limited to the size of its cash funding, so a sizeable part of synthetic assets is not supported by cash assets but by stand-by facilities such as a liquidity facility.

Liabilities of the SPV

Liabilities of the SPV are the securities that it issues to the investors. These, like assets, can be either cash liabilities or synthetic liabilities. Cash liabilities are the funded securities, mostly in the form of CLNs. Synthetic or unfunded liabilities can be protection bought in form of credit default swaps. Here again, usually, based on the structure of the transaction single-originator transactions are motivated by capital relief and so the originator directly buys the unfunded credit default swap from high-rated institutions. However, for arbitrage transactions, the SPV is itself usually backed by default swaps.

The funded liabilities of the SPV are usually classed and structured, with the size of each junior class determined to provide a target rating to a senior class. Usually, the approach is top-down – the senior-most class is given a certain enhancement based on its target rating, and then that enhancement is successively split into several classes with each class credit-enhanced based on its target rating. The last of the classes is usually unrated and first-loss piece. (See below under Sizing of the Credit Enhancement.)

Non-SPV structures

Logistically, an SPV is required in cash structures for holding the assets to be isolated from the originator, to protect the assets from the bankruptcy risks of the originator. A ratings arbitrage – any of the securities of the SPV being rated above the originator – is theoretically not possible if any of the securities represent a claim against the originator. Synthetic transactions do not physically buy the assets of the originator – the assets are only synthetic. Therefore, there is no need to protect the "assets" (meaning, synthetic assets) of the investors. However, synthetic CDOs do have assets to the extent of the funding contributed by the investors. If this funding were to be pre-paid or invested in the originator, the claims of the investors are backed by a claim against the originator, and so are subject to the rating cap of the originator.

That is why, in synthetic structures as well, an SPV is typically introduced as an isolation device that holds the funding put in by the investors in its own assets, not being claims against the originator.

However, it is understandable that the cash assets of a synthetic transaction are only a fraction of the synthetic assets, and hence the need for originator-bankruptcy protection is significantly less prominent. Therefore, a number of synthetic securitizations have found it less necessary to involve a façade between the originator and the investors and have gone ahead with non-SPV structures. In a non-SPV structure, the securities offered to investors are issued by the originator himself, and therefore represent a claim against the originator.

The following circumstances justify a non-SPV structure:

- There are several jurisdictions where this risk of originator-bankruptcy could be addressed by the creation of a security interest that leads to "ring fencing" – a dedication of some specific assets of the originator which may be utilized by the security holder in the event of bankruptcy. If it is possible to dedicate assets of the originator to secure the investors their funding and insulate these assets from the generic bankruptcy risks of the originator, an SPV is an avoidable intermediary in a synthetic transaction. There have been some non-SPV synthetic securitizations particularly from countries where ring-fencing is a well-accepted legal principle.

- If the rating of a funded class is capped at the originator rating, with a higher rating assigned to the unfunded portion, an SPV becomes irrelevant. CIBC used a non-SPV structure in a transaction called Imperial II CDO where credit-linked notes are issued only against a mezzanine default swap. The senior swap is unfunded, and rated above the rating of the originator, but the senior-most of the credit-linked notes is rated at par with or lower than the rating of the originator. In this way, the investors' claim against the originator is noted rated above the rating of the originator, but the originator's claim against the senior default swap counterparty is rated above the rating of the originator.[18]

Sizing of the credit enhancement

As discussed, the principles inherent in sizing of the credit enhancement are the same as for any other securitization: The confidence level – (1-probability of losses) at any rating level – should be equivalent to the survival rate of like-rated corporate debt securities. The sequential process of this determination is:

- Probability of default for each of the credits in the pool is established; this may be based on the standard methods for assessing probabilities of default – structural models or hazard rate models, or the probabilities of defaults implied from market rates of credit spreads.
- The next issue is to establish correlation as between the different credits in the pool. There are several possible approaches; one is to take correlated obligors as forming one block and reduce them to a theoretical number to remove the intra-obligor correlation. Moody's had for some time used this method, and computed a **diversity score,** which indicated the theoretical number of uncorrelated obligors after eliminating the correlation in the pool. The other method is to put explicit inputs of correlations among the different obligors.
- A probability distribution of the different levels of portfolio losses is constructed based on observation, statistical methods such as binomial distribution, simulation approaches, or using one of the standard models such as Standard & Poor's CDO Evaluator or Moody's CDO-ROM. This probability distribution will provide us the different probabilities of defaults of a particular percent of the obligors in the pool. See, for instance, the accompanying Figure 22.3 generated by the S&P CDO Evaluator.
- For a target rating of a particular class, the probability of default of a like-rated corporate bond is taken. For example, if the default probability of a AAA-rated corporate bond is 0.02% over the last 10 years of rating migration history, we expect the credit enhancements at the level of the security

to absorb the default probabilities such that the right-hand extreme is left at or lesser than 0.02%. In other words, for a AAA-rated tranche, a loss probability of 0.02% or lesser is acceptable, so the cumulative probability of default from the right-extreme should not exceed 0.02% for a AAA-rating. Likewise, the historical default rate for an A-rated corporate bond is, say, 2%. So, we need to count the loss probability from the right-extreme such that it does not exceed 2%. At the 2% level, the portfolio loss could be 30% or higher. In other words, the probability of the portfolio loss being 30% or more is 2%, and that is comparable to the default probability of an A-rated bond.

- The required credit enhancement is based on the (1-recovery rate) multiplied by the above level of portfolio loss. If the recovery rate is estimated to be 40%, the required enhancement in the above case is 12%.
- Rating agencies also apply a certain adjustment factor to the default probability on account of a synthetic transaction not exactly mirroring the meaning of "default" in a cash transaction.
- The above will apply for a diversified portfolio. If the extent of correlation in the portfolio increases, the right-hand tail of the histogram (or the curve implied by it) will extend further, leading to a higher cumulative probability of the loss limited to a certain level.

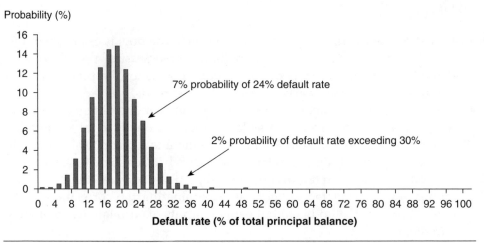

Figure 22.3   Probability Distribution of Portfolio Default Rates

Source: Standard & Poor's *CDO criteria* March 2002

Swap calculation agent

The swap calculation agent or the loss calculation agent is required in any credit derivative, and is present in a synthetic transaction as well. Mostly, the originator himself is named as the calculation agent, but in certain cases independent assessors or valuers may also be named.

Trustees

As for cash structure securitizations, the trustees are the ones who hold the security interest on the assets of the SPV. The SPV invests in the collateral and pledges the collateral in favor of the trustees. The trustees typically hold it as a trustee for:

- Originator;
- Class A investors;
- Class B investors;
- And so on

in that order of priority. In other words, the collateral will be first used to pay off the originator for the claims of the latter under the credit derivative. Thereafter, the collateral is held for the benefit of the senior class and subordinate classes in sequence.

Apart from being the mere holder of security interest, trustees in a synthetic securitization perform a significant role. The functions include:

- Ensuring compliance by all parties to the terms and conditions of the documents; in particular, ensuring that the reference obligations are selected in compliance with the stipulated conditions, and substitution of obligors is done in compliance.
- Ensuring the SPV uses the cash collected by it on the collateral and the CDS premium in the stated waterfall or allocation priority, typically meeting the expenses coupon to Class A, coupon to Class B and so on.
- Disposing the collateral to pay off the originator for any protection payments.

Super-senior swap provider

We have discussed the need and nature of a super-senior swap in leveraged portfolio risk transfers.

The super-senior swap counterparty is typically a highly-rated bank. The SPV is usually not a party to the super senior swap; it is mainly the originator who writes it directly with the counterparty.

Other swap counterparties

To remove various risks in the collateral, the SPV may enter into some other swaps. For example if the collateral returns a fixed coupon while one or more classes carry a floating coupon, the SPV may enter into an interest rate or basis swap to remove the interest rate risk. The prices of the collateral may fall due to a rise in interest rates; to remove this risk, the SPV might have to buy into a put option against a highly-rated entity to remove the price risk.

Arbitrage synthetic CDOs

We have briefly discussed the nature of arbitrage synthetic CDOs before. Here, the pool of assets of the CDO is a pool of corporate credits (or sovereigns and PSEs) with reference to which the CDO has sold protection. Thus, there is no particular originator aiming to reduce his balance sheet or regulatory capital. The transaction is usually set up by a sponsor, and the portfolio is selected and managed by a collateral manager, whose purpose is to earn management fees. The sponsor, who may also be the equity investor, is motivated by arbitrage considerations – earning a spread between the weighted-average return and the weighted-average coupon paid to the investors.

This arbitrage, like any arbitrage, is essentially a result of market inefficiency, but commonly arises because of diversity of the synthetic assets created by the CDO and the tranching of risks by multiple classes of liabilities issued by the CDO.

The distinctive features of synthetic arbitrage CDOs are:

- As against an originator in a balance sheet transaction, there is a collateral manager who puts together the whole show (see below on "collateral manager").
- The sponsor/arranger arranges one or more "equity investors" who take up the most subordinate tranche of the CDO. This tranche bears the leveraged risks and rewards of the entire portfolio. In a balance sheet transaction, this position is normally taken up by the originator himself.
- The size of the equity tranche determines the size of other classes, and therefore, the size of the CDO as a whole.
- With this funding, the synthetic CDO vehicle creates synthetic "assets" by selling protection in the market. The CDO vehicle becomes a protection seller as in the OTC market. The selection of the reference assets with reference to which and counterparties to whom the protection is sold is done as per the detailed provisions of the covenants. These selection criteria are similar to those applicable to balance sheet transactions and do not warrant any specific discussion.
- The funding raised from investors is typically invested in safe collateral. For certain hybrid structures (hybrid of cash and synthetic transactions) this funding may also be used to create cash assets.
- If the transaction is unleveraged, the total amount of protection sold will be equal to the funding raised from the investors. This will, however, not lead to any significant arbitrage.
- Therefore, more arbitrage synthetic CDOs sell significantly more protection than is the funding of the CDO, covering themselves with a super senior swap as in case of leveraged balance sheet transactions discussed before.
- The income of the CDO vehicle is the premium earned on protection sold to various protection buyers. Here, unlike balance sheet transactions, the pricing of the risk premium is market determined and goes in the same way as the OTC market.

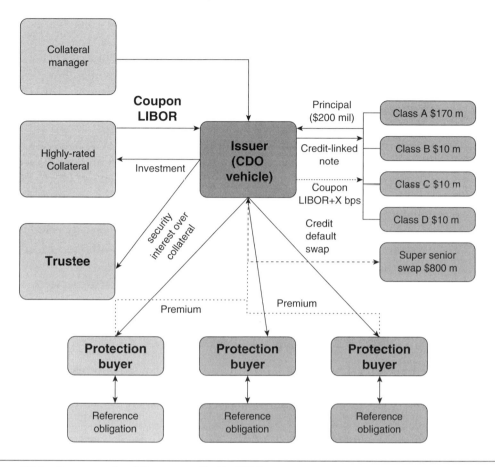

Figure 22.4   Leveraged arbitrage synthetic CDO

- The income so earned, plus the income earned from the collateral investments, is divided among the various "debt" (or rated) classes as per the coupon payable to them and the remaining income is distributed to the equity or unrated class. Thus the equity class takes the entire arbitrage income of the CDO.

Synthetic arbitrage vehicles have gained popularity of late. Dealers in credit derivatives have created arbitrage vehicles as an extension of their own trading desks.

Difference between arbitrage synthetic CDOs and balance sheet synthetic CDOs

- **Purpose**: As discussed above, the purpose of a balance sheet synthetic CDO is to manage the balance sheet of the originator either by transferring balance sheet risks or for regulatory relief. On the other hand, arbitrage CDOs are *created* players in the market; they operate just like any other derivatives dealer sourcing credit assets from various parties in the market. There is no capital relief objective, nor does the balance sheet treatment management of any particular originator play any role. Balance sheet synthetic CDOs have an identifiable originator who is its primary beneficiary; arbitrage vehicles are managed by a collateral manager but there is no primary beneficiary as such except, may be, a controlling holder of the equity class who gets a major share of the arbitrage profit. Typical CDO managers are asset managers having substantial asset management experience in the relevant asset class.

- **Composition of the pool**: The composition of the pool as between balance sheet and arbitrage transactions is substantially different. For balance sheet transactions, the pool is the pool synthetically transferred by the originator. For arbitrage transactions, it is constructed by selling protection, so the collateral manager has a lot of discretion in selecting names with the idea of making the pool as balanced, and yet, as remunerative as possible. The geographical, sectoral and industrial diversification attained in arbitrage transactions is substantially high.

  The other significant difference is that in arbitrage transactions usually the notional value per obligor is the same.

  Sometimes, arbitrage transactions might follow standard indices – such as the iTraxx index. In this case, the portfolio exactly matches the composition of the indices.

- **Debt/equity distinction**: The equity and debt distinction is more predominant for arbitrage vehicles. Though, technically, there is an equity class in every CDO (the most subordinated class being economically the equity), in most balance sheet CDOs this is picked by the originator himself. For an arbitrage vehicle, there are one or more equity investors motivated by the arbitrage opportunities, who are the residual risk/reward holders. The entire architecture of the transaction is built over equity size; the rest of the CDO is a cantilever structure built over the foundation of the equity.

- **Size**: Balance sheet CDOs are usually much larger in size to have any significant impact on the regulatory balance sheet of the originating bank. The usual size in the market is US$1 billion upwards. Arbitrage CDOs are comparatively smaller, as the size is predicated by the size of the equity.

- **Ramp up period**: Ramp period is the time taken by the CDO to create the assets. For balance sheet transactions, there is no need to allow any such time as the assets are to be transferred by an originator, and the assets are there already. For arbitrage transactions, the assets are to be acquired from the market, so there is some time allowed for the collateral manager to do so. This is called the ramp up period. The ramp period could typically be 3–6 months.

- **Nature of credit enhancements and warranties**: In a traditional asset-backed transaction, the assets are usually created by the originator as a part of the originator's business. Therefore, it is typical for the originator to give several representations and warranties regarding the assets; these act as inherent credit enhancements for the CDO. In arbitrage transactions, there are no more such representations than implied by standard ISDA documentation.

- **Typical terms of the credit default swaps**: For balance sheet transactions, the CDS of the CDO is with the originator, so the terms of the swap are essentially driven by the originator's hedging needs. For arbitrage transactions, the assets are created by writing CDS referenced to various standard counter-parties in the market; hence, the terms are mostly indicative of commonly prevailing terms in the credit derivatives market.

Collateral manager

As discussed before, the crucial agency in an arbitrage CDO is the CDO collateral manager who puts up the whole show together and over the life of the CDO runs the portfolio.

The CDO manager may or may not be the equity investor of the CDO. In case the CDO manager is also not the substantial equity holder, the motivation of the CDO manager is to expand the value of assets under his management and increase fee income. "An insurance company with a high-yield bond portfolio already has the expertise in place for the purchase and monitoring of those credits. To create the model portfolio for a potential CDO, the insurance company can simply increase the size of every position, which is virtually cost-free. In doing so, the company creates an annuity stream of asset management fees lasting the life of the transaction. Executing a CDO is simply a way for the investment advisor to leverage off a fixed cost base."[19] For synthetic transactions, managers having experience of managing synthetic investments are most likely to be the CDO manager.

Rating agency Moody's says: "Moody's looks for the collateral manager to possess the core competencies that will enable him/her to make sound investment decisions that are consistent with the spirit and letter of the governing documents. In turn, we then analyse the transaction assuming nothing more (or less) than such capable and effective management."[20]

OC and IC triggers for synthetic CDOs

The concept of structural protection in CDOs by putting leverage controls – over-collateralization test and interest coverage test – is discussed in the chapter on CDOs.

Application of OC and IC triggers to synthetic CDOs

OC and IC triggers essentially control the leverage of the transaction, with leverage indicated by the extent of junior liabilities to the total assets of the pool. The question of applying the OC/IC trigger will apply where the transaction has a reinstating feature; that is, the collateral manager has the right to reinstate an expired asset by a new asset. If the trigger is in place, instead of reinstating the collateral, the collateral manager reduces the size of the liabilities, typically by repaying the senior liabilities.

Synthetic balance sheet CDOs often have a reinstating feature. If the assets composed in the pool repay, prepay or amortize, the originator typically introduces further assets into the pool such that the total size of the pool remains constant. In such cases, triggers may be established. If the triggers are in place, then instead of new loans being introduced in the pool, the transaction size will be reduced, meaning the SPV will sell a part of the collateral to repay the liabilities.

In synthetic arbitrage transactions, triggers relating to mark-to-market value of the assets in the pool may be put.

Pay-down structure

While traditional cash securitizations, including cash CDOs, repay principal over the term of the transaction, synthetic CDOs normally have a bullet repaying structure (discussed earlier). Hence, there is usually no principal paydown over the term of the transaction and all classes of the notes may have a bullet maturity.

However, if the pool is static and the underlying assets have an amortizing nature, it may be necessary to reduce the total size of the pool along with the repayment of the assets in the pool. In such a case, the question of pay-down of the liabilities will arise. The basic principles of paying down the liabilities are the same as for any cash securitization – reiterated below for ease of reference.

Essentially, there are three kinds of pay-down structures:

Sequential paydown

A sequential paydown structure means notes are paid down sequentially, top down. It is sequential as amongst the various classes, and *pro-rata* within the class. The impact of a sequential pay-down is:

a. To reduce the leverage of the transaction;
b. To increase the percentage credit enhancement of the senior classes;
c. To increase the weighted average cost of the transaction; and
d. To reduce the return on equity class.

The above are mutually related and are not difficult to understand. A CDO is comparable to any highly-leveraged corporation – sequential pay-down means retirement of the highest-rated and therefore the cheapest debt class. Obviously, this increases the protection available to the senior class as the relative size of debt to equity comes down. Simultaneously, as the cheapest liability will be retired first, the weighted-average cost of the transaction goes up pushing down the returns of the equity class.

Hence, sequential paydown is an exceptional feature and should not be used indiscriminately. Sequential pay-down may increase the weighted-average cost of the CDO to an extent as to make it unviable and force the CDO to wind up early. On the other hand, if there is a serious breach of the OC/IC trigger, or it is intended to clean up the CDO, a sequential pay-down is a most workable device.

Pro-rata paydown

Pro-rata or proportional paydown means the cash available for repayment to investors is used to pay the various classes in proportion to their respective capital outstanding. A *pro-rata* repayment structure:

a. Maintains the leverage of the transaction;
b. Maintains the percentage credit enhancement available to the various classes;
c. Maintains the weighted-average cost of the transaction; and
d. Other things being equal, maintains the returns on the equity class.

In other words, a *pro-rata* repayment is no greater structural protection to the senior classes than to the junior classes. As it does not alter the extent of credit enhancement at any level, a pro-rated repayment cannot correct any breach of OC/IC triggers. Hence, a pro-rated structure is suitable where amortization of the notes happens otherwise than as a protective or corrective measure. For example, for a synthetic CDO referenced to a static pool, if the pool is amortizing over time, the CDO must also paydown the cash liabilities; this is not a paydown triggered by any breach or impending breach, so the best way is to paydown proportionally.

Fast-pay slow-pay structure

As a mid-way between sequential and proportional repayment, a fast-pay/slow-pay structure repays both the senior and junior classes, but pays more to the senior classes and less to the junior classes. Therefore, the senior class is the fast-pay class and the junior class is the slow-pay class. For example, if de-leveraging is taking place due to a breach of the OC test, instead of sequentially taking all the money to pay off the senior classes first, it may pay so much to the senior class as required to restore the OC test, and then pay off the two classes proportionally. The fast-pay/slow-pay device may be quite handy in cases where the OC/IC triggers are satisfied for the senior classes but not breached for the junior classes.

Evolution and growth of synthetic securitization

The device of synthetic securitization first developed in the CDO market, but later found extremely interesting applications in RMBS, CMBS and retail assets.

The first synthetic CDO emerged around 1997. This found a significant following in the European market as the European banks' assets are not suitable for a traditional CDO for several reasons already discussed, more specially the following – higher compliance costs for transfer of loans, lack of homogenous loan pools such as syndicated loans and better quality loans on the balance sheet with less motivation to put assets off-balance sheet.

There were two main early players who steered the synthetic CDO market and brought it to its present level of refinement – JP Morgan with its BISTRO structures and Citibank with C*Strategic, shortly known as C*Star.

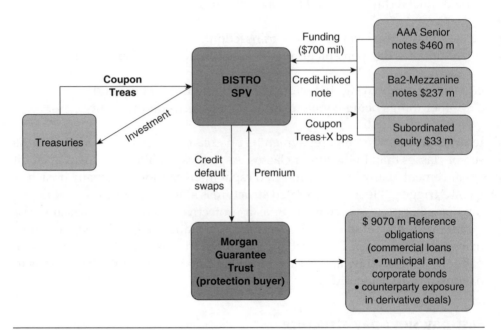

Figure 22.5   JPM's BISTRO structure December 1997

JP Morgan's first Broad Index Structured Trust Offering (BISTRO) was priced in December 1997. This CDO included exposure to over 300 investment-grade credits, adding up to US$9.7 billion. The exposure was acquired by JP Morgan from various other banks in the market, subject to a threshold level of risks that the originating banks retain. The funding raised from the market was just US$697 million in notes. This transaction was to mature on December 31, 2002. The money raised from investors was invested in U.S. Treasuries maturing also on the same date. The protection buyer was Morgan Guarantee Trust (MGT) under which MGT pays a semi-annual premium to the SPV equal to the difference between the Treasury yield and the coupon payable to investors.

The BISTRO structure has been refined and repeated over time.

Another repeat program for synthetic CDOs is the one run by Citibank. An early synthetic CDO for the European market was Citibank's C*Star (1999–1). The €4 billion, 10-year transaction was split into a senior tranche, made up of a €3.68 billion credit default swap, and a €280 million junior tranche available to institutional investors; it was thus issued in the funded form and was offered to investors. This was broken into three tranches – AAA, A and BB. Citibank kept the €40 million first-loss tranche. Thus, Citibank succeeded in transferring credit risk on a €4 billion portfolio by retaining risk only to the extent of €40 million. The underlying portfolio was 164 loans to 152 European corporations, half of which were not rated.

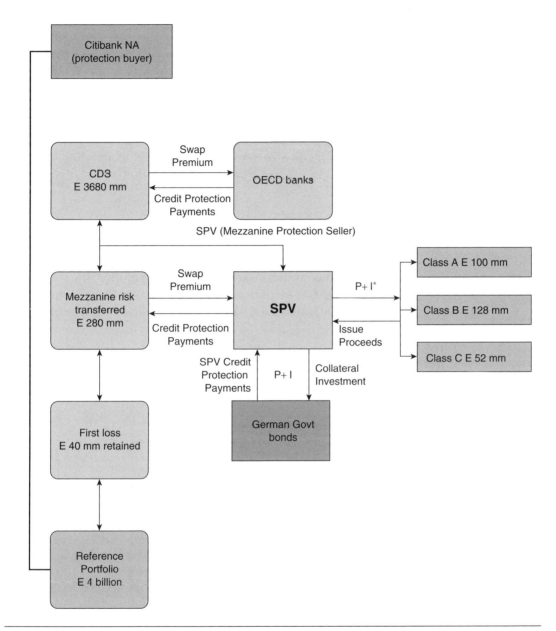

Figure 22.6 Citibank's C*Star 1999–1

Over time, synthetic CDOs have become extremely popular both in Europe and in the U.S. In Asian markets also, synthetic CDOs are drawing a lot of interest.

From purely balance sheet-based transactions, synthetic CDOs have grown far more into the arbitrage model. CDO squares, CDO cubes and interesting structures of leverage have been tried in the CDO market. For more discussion on synthetic CDOs, see Vinod Kothari's *Credit Derivatives and Synthetic Securitisation*.

Synthetic RMBS

The synthetic securitization technology, developed in the CDO market, is fast expanding into more traditional securitization classes and RMBS is an example.

Synthetic RMBS is seen having increased interest in the U.S. and European markets. There have been several examples of synthetic RMBS in Europe – for example, the transactions done under the Provide template of KfW, Germany. Below, we look at one of mega-size synthetic RMBS deal from ABN Amro:

Case study: ABN Amro's Shield 1 BV

In early December 2005, ABN Amro completed a mega synthetic RMBS transaction with several notable features; the funding size of the AAA-rated piece itself was substantial, which indicates a partial funding motive; the size of the portfolio backing up the transaction is itself gigantic – €22.81 billion, and it was reported that this transaction was the largest ever European RMBS transaction.[21]

In this deal, ABN Amro set up an SPV called Shield 1 BV. The SPV is a typical securitization vehicle. The SPV raised funds of €4.016 billion from the market by issuing six classes of securities. The particulars of the securities are:

Table 22.2 Securities in synthetic RMBS case

Class	Prelim. rating*	Prelim. amount (Mil. €)	Credit support at closing (%)	Interest	Legal final maturity
A	AAA	3000	4.62	Three-month EURIBOR plus a margin[22]	January 2014
B	AA	363	2.97	Three-month EURIBOR plus a margin	January 2014
C	A	284	1.68	Three-month EURIBOR plus a margin	January 2014
D	BBB+	150	1.00	Three-month EURIBOR plus a margin	January 2014
E	BB	159	0.27	Three-month EURIBOR plus a margin	January 2014
F	B	60	Note – except the cash reserve	Three-month EURIBOR plus a margin	January 2014

The ratings are Standard & Poor's as per its pre-sale rating report on November 29, 2005.

The following features may be noted as for the transaction structure:

- Usually, in synthetic transactions, the size of the AAA-rated tranche is small, as the idea of the transaction is not funding but to keep a larger part of the liabilities as unfunded super senior piece. In this case, the AAA piece itself is substantial, and in fact, the thickest of all classes. This indicates a partial funding motive – which is understandable as the cash collateral is kept with the originator.[23]

- The fact that the cash collateral is kept with the originator is also an important feature. Note that the rating of ABN Amro is AA on the date of the rating, and the short-term rating is A-1+. A bank deposit is a short-term deposit, possibly why the rating of the bank has not served as a cap on the rating of the notes, particularly as the trustees have the ability to remove the deposit from ABN Amro once the rating falls below A-1+. As the cash deposit is with the bank, the transaction does not lead to the funding inefficiency referred to earlier in this chapter.

- As may be noted, all the notes have a common legal final maturity, and in view of the replenishment rights (explained below), it is quite likely that the reference portfolio size will remain static throughout the term of the transaction; hence, it is most likely that the notes will be repaid by way of bullet repayment around six years maturity (the legal maturity is longer – about eight years, a common feature of the transactions). If this was a straight cash securitization, there would have been two significant differences – the term of the notes would have been much longer (the pool has a weighted remaining maturity of nearly 24 years), and there would be amortization of the notes over time. In addition, the notes will be subjected to prepayment risk. In the synthetic structure, the maturity of the notes does not match with the maturity of the underlying pool of mortgages. This allows for the bullet repaying structure of the notes.

- The protection buyer (ABN Amro) has the right of replenishment up to 20% of the initial pool size. Assuming that the amortization + prepayments in any year will not exceed 20%, and that the originator will have sufficient new originations to replenish the pool, it is most likely that the pool size will remain static over time. In other words, the pool size is static, but the pool is not.

- By way of credit enhancements, apart from the subordination structure, there is a trapping of excess spread, at the rate of 9 bps for the first two years, and 4 bps for the rest of the maturity of the transaction. Note that in typical cash securitizations, the excess spread provides the first level of credit enhancement in the transaction, unless the excess spread is partly stripped out by senior servicing fees or senior IO strip. However, in this case, the originator only pays as much as he wants. The accumulated excess spread will become a cash reserve. Once again it is notable that the cash reserve is built from the excess spread; in other words, if the excess spread in the pool dries down due to losses or prepayments, then the originator is not bound to introduce the excess spread in the cash reserve.

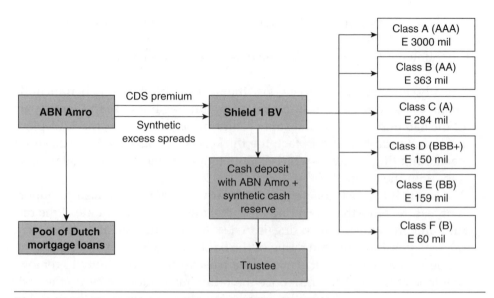

Figure 22.7   Transaction graphic of synthetic RMBS case

- The transaction does not require any interest rate swap, though the notes carry a floating rate. This is because the terms of the credit default swap require ABN Amro to pay the note interest and the senior expenses.

The pool at the transaction closing will consist of seasoned residential mortgage loans originated by the bank in The Netherlands. The weighted-average seasoning has been close to 60 months. The houses are owner-occupied, first houses. The mortgages are distributed across all regions of the country. The pool includes a number of different ABN AMRO products: interest-only mortgages (54.0% of the pool by value), annuity mortgages (3.6%), hybrid mortgages (22.5%), investment mortgages (1.6%), life mortgages (11.3%), linear mortgages (0.6%), and savings (6.4%). The loan-to-foreclosure value (LTFV) of the mortgages averaged at about 91%. However, the weighted average may be an illusion, as the highest LTFV goes to 130%.

The revolving nature of the transaction is subjected to usual restrictions – that the weighted-average LTFV of the revolving pool is not greater than the pool at closing, and that the product of weighted-average foreclosure frequency (WAFF) and weighted-average loss severity (WALS) on the replenishment date does not exceed the product at the inception by more than 0.25%.

The credit events and the loss computation procedure may be noted. Failure to pay an amount equal to four monthly installments leads to a "failure to pay" event. In addition, bankruptcy of the borrower is also defined as a credit event. Restructuring leading to a debit in the lender's profit and loss account is also a credit event.

The loss computation is based on actual foreclosure, supposed to happen within 11 months of the trigger event. However, if foreclosure is not completed within 11 months, the loss computation may be based on loss estimation, in which case the excess of actual realization later will be credited to the excess spread. The loss realization or estimation as above will first be set off against the cash reserve, and then will be allocated against the securities in reverse order of priorities.

Synthetic CMBS

In view of the ease with which synthetic transactions can be conducted, several European banks, particularly those in Germany, have taken CMBS transactions through the synthetic route.

Case study: Europa Three Synthetic CMBS

The Europa Three synthetic CMBS deal is the third one under the Europa template, which is one for synthetic CMBS assets originated by RHEINHYP AG, which later merged into EUROHYPO.

The Europa Three transaction transfers risk on a CMBS pool worth €1.44 billion, while the CLNs add to €322.15 million. The portfolio has 47 commercial mortgage loans in 10 jurisdictions.

The originator buys protection by way of a guarantee on the pool from an intermediary bank Bayerische Landesbank (BL). This is obviously required for Eurohypo to maximize the regulatory capital relief. BL, thereafter, slices the swap into three parts and buys protection against the junior swap from an undisclosed OECD bank, a mezzanine swap from Europa Three SPV, and the senior swap again from another undisclosed OECD bank.

Table 22.3 Securities in synthetic CMBS case

Class	Amount (€m)	Tranche CE %	Rating (Moody's/ S&P/Fitch)	WAL	Legal final	Type
Senior CDS	1,079.1	24.98%	[Aaa]/[AAA]/[AAA]	4.8 years	2051	CDS
A+	0.25	24.98%	[Aaa]/[AAA]/[AAA]	4.8 years	2051	CLN
A	93.0	18.51%	[Aa1]/[AAA]/[AAA]	6.2 years	2051	CLN
B	71.5	13.54%	[Aa2]/[AA]/[AA]	6.2 years	2051	CLN
C	69.0	8.74%	[A2]/[A]/[Λ]	6.2 years	2051	CLN
D	60.4	4.55%	[Baa2]/[BBB]/[BBB]	6.2 years	2051	CLN
E	28.0	2.60%	[Ba2]/[BB]/[BB]	6.2 years	2051	CLN
Junior CDS*	37.4	–	[PR]/[PR]	6.2 years	2051	CDS

The entire funding raised by the issue of CLNs is invested with Eurohypo, which the latter backs by *pfandbriefs* as far the funding of classes A+ to C is concerned, and MTNs as for classes D and E. As *pfandbriefs* have an automatic bankruptcy protection under German law, the collateral does not have to be concerned with the bankruptcy risk of the originator. As for the MTNs, the rating at that level is BBB or less, so bankruptcy dependence does not cause a rating drag.

A notable feature is that the transaction has static collateral, but with replenishment right based on prepayments expected at a 3% CPR. This is easy to understand for CMBS deals. This would mean, as the pool size is reduced, the originator will be motivated to reduce the total protection, and therefore, pay down the notes. However, the paydown structure has been as sequential, which would obviously increase the weighted-average cost of the transaction quickly and make it burdensome.

The credit events on the transaction are bankruptcy and failure to pay (50% of the amount due is not paid within 30 days), and the losses are realized principal losses and enforcement costs. Note that unpaid interest is not considered as a loss here. This goes in line with the nature of the first transaction between the originator and the intermediary bank as a guarantee. The credit default swaps on the capital market transaction also assume the nature of a counter guarantee, but possibly documented as default swaps.

Synthetic retail assets

It is interesting to see the increasing application of the synthetic technology to traditional ABS classes such as auto loans, retail leases and hire purchase contracts.

Case study: Lion Synthetic

In late 2003, HSBC brought to the market a transaction referenced to a pool of bus and taxi receivables in Hong Kong. Called Lion Synthetic, the total amount of notes issued under the deal amounted to HK$330 million.

The pool size was US$3 billion, consisting of 1,423 hire purchase contracts for buses, taxis and vehicles. As is notable from the table below, the subordinated class, Class D, has a credit enhancement of 2%, which means the terms of the credit default swap between HSBC and Lion Synthetic provide for a threshold risk of 2% retained with the originator. The transaction has a 5-year revolving period.

Table 22.4 Securities in synthetic retail auto loans case

Class	Rating	Initial Principal Balance	Scheduled Maturity Date	Legal Maturity Date	Credit Support
A	Aa2	HK$120 mil	11/18/2008	9/1/2009	9%
B	A2	HK$90 mil	11/18/2008	9/1/2009	6%
C	Baa2	HK$60 mil	11/18/2008	9/1/2009	4%
D	Private	HK$60 mil	11/18/2008	9/1/2009	2%

The cash collateral raised by issue of the notes is invested with HSBC as a deposit. Once again, the deposit is short term and the trustees have the right to remove the deposit and place it with another bank should the rating of HSBC fall.

Hybrid securitizations

Transactions, which are hybrids of cash and synthetic assets, are seen as growing in popularity. Hybrid transactions are basically arbitrage transactions. The meaning of hybrid securitization is one where the intention of the sponsor is to make arbitrage profits by investing in cash assets and exposing in synthetic assets.

Typical hybrid structures that have emerged in the market are securitizations that have a typical synthetic asset pool as for usual synthetic securitizations; in addition, the funding raised by issuing the CLNs is invested in cash ABS securities instead of investing the same in AAA-type collateral. The cash ABS usually have an average BBB rating. In other words, the transaction earns spreads from the synthetic assets, and cash returns from the cash assets. Where payments are to be made by the CDO on account of the synthetic asset losses, the cash collateral is not disposed off; on the contrary, amounts are drawn from the super senior unfunded swap. This amount is a sort of advance on the actual realization of cash from the cash ABS assets; first the amount drawn up from the super-senior swap is paid before the principal on the CLNs is paid down.

These structures essentially arise from the need to explore more and interesting arbitrage opportunities, and creating a mixture of uncorrelated cash and synthetic assets is another idea of increasing the arbitrage profits.

Investing in synthetic CDOs

Over the past few months, synthetic CDOs have become a fairly well-accepted product with investors. Synthetic CDOs allow investors to invest in fairly diversified portfolios. Synthetic arbitrage CDOs have also become very common and are believed to be more efficient than their cash counterparts due to, both, the higher spreads prevailing in the synthetic market and lower transaction costs.

Investing in CLNs and synthetic CDO tranches is essentially investing in a credit-sensitive product. Most synthetic CDOs are rated and rating agencies take into account various risks implicit in the CDO. However, investors in their own wisdom need to carefully consider the following factors:

- **Nature of the portfolio**: The most important source of strength/risk for any CDO, including synthetic CDOs, is the composition of the portfolio. Most synthetic CDOs aim at synthetically transferring diversified portfolio usually consisting of a large number of obligors, most of which are not rated. The obligation may or may not represent secured obligations. A careful understanding of the underwriting criteria and internal rating scores of the originator is important.

  One of the most important factors in analysis of the portfolio is the existence of correlation in the portfolio. There is no better way to assess the lack of correlation in the portfolio than by diversity standards – indicated by the concentration data in rating reports or Moody's diversity scores.

The extent of correlation directly affects the risks transferred to the senior classes. If the portfolio is concentric and correlated, losses may wipe off the first loss class and move up to the rated classes where investors are typically exposed.

There have been cases of synthetic CDOs consisting of exposure to a particular industry – aircraft loans[24] or shipping loans[25] and so on. However, investors in such industry-focused synthetic CDOs should clearly understand that investing in such CDOs is essentially taking an exposure, though diversified within the industry, in a particular industry.

Most CDO portfolios are dynamic, but the circumstances in which the originator can replace assets and the comprehensive replacement criteria become significant. If the originator has uncontrolled discretion as to replacement, there might be issues of moral hazard for the transaction.

For arbitrage transactions, the biggest risk, apart from the credit risk from the investors' point of view is the correlation risk. There are reasons to believe that the selection of assets by the sponsor is skewed so as to maximize the arbitrage profits of the transaction. For example, in a given rating band, the sponsor tries to pick up assets which have higher prevailing premiums than low premiums. But sector correlation can exacerbate the problem by having several defaults in the pool, in which case the credit support will be quickly depleted.

Granularity of the pool is another significant risk for arbitrage transactions. Most arbitrage deals will have around 100 credits in the pool. Obviously, these obligors do not default by percentage, they default by number. If the pool has fewer obligors, default of just a few may mean default of a sizeable percentage of the pool.

- **Motivations of the originator**: Investors should try to understand the originator's motivations – capital relief in most synthetic CDOs, but in some cases, the originator may also be trying to reduce excess industry concentration or economic capital.
- **Credit events**: The nature and width of the definition of credit events clearly relates to investors' risks. CDO transactions usually carve out variations of standard ISDA definitions as some standard ISDA terms may not be fit for reference obligations. Besides, the originator may aim at transferring certain risks not covered in standard ISDA terms – for example, some transactions even include a certain rating downgrade as a credit event. Obviously, comprehensive credit event definition increases the risk potential for investors. Investors may also note that certain credit events in ISDA documentation are liable to be interpreted as a credit event, although there is no default in commercial sense.[26]
- **Loss computation**: Another crucial issue in synthetic CDOs is the manner in which a loss will be computed on a credit event. Unlike OTC transactions where valuation is more transparent such as dealer polls, in synthetic CDOs, the reference obligations are not amenable to market valuation and the losses will be mostly assessed either based on actual recovery or estimated recovery rate. The computation is mostly done by the originator

himself as the calculation agent – of course, there are trustees to finally sanction the loss claim. There is, therefore, a trust reposed on the mechanism of loss computation and claim.

- **Retention of first loss by the originator**: Almost invariably, a first-loss piece is either retained by the originator, or the originator invests in the junior-most piece. The first loss piece absorbs first losses – and as losses on a portfolio take place over a time scale, the size of the first-loss piece comes down as the portfolio suffers losses. This reduces the credit enhancement for the rated classes and rating agencies often react with a downgrade action. However, there may still be no default for several years before the first-loss class is fully wiped out. Investors should carefully keep track of the movements in credit enhancement by subordinate classes as this is the surest indication of distance to default.

Insurance risk securitization and other methods of alternative risk transfer

The device of synthetic securitization is essentially a device of packaging a risk transfer in the form of issue of securities. The generic device of commoditization of risk, by transfer of risk to a special purpose entity and then embedding the same into marketable securities, has found several applications, and may find increasing number of applications in the future. Wherever a risk leads to a loss of money, the risk can be commoditized.

Some of the applications of risk transfer where the synthetic technology has been used include insurance risk, weather risk, risk of residual values of assets and risk of commodity prices going up or going down. Though *alternative risk transfer* is by itself a topic requiring elaborate treatment, in this section, we briefly discuss securitization of insurance risk and the activity going on in this market.

Alternative risk transfer

An insurance contract is essentially a device of risk transfer, from the insured to the insurer. Alternative risk transfer is the collective name given to devices of seeking risk protection using non-traditional routes, that is, other than through traditional insurance companies.

Apart from insurance risk securitization, the other usual methods are captive insurance companies and renting of insurance companies.

Insurance securitization

One of the most innovative applications of securitization technology is to securitize insurance risk. Here, the resulting product is not essentially a vehicle for raising finance but one for distributing insurance risk.

The essential idea is a combination of trading in insurance risk, a usual feature in insurance markets, and securitization technology. It is common for an insurance company to seek re-insurance cover from reinsurance companies. By adopting the risk securitization device, an insurance company seeks reinsurance cover not from a traditional reinsurance company, but from a re-insurance SPV, which in turn sells notes or securities to capital market investors. These investors will have to suffer either loss of principal, or loss of interest, or a substantial moratorium on repayment of principal, if a specific loss event against which the insurance has been given occurs.

Catastrophe bonds

Risk securitization technology was first employed to seek reinsurance cover against catastrophic risks – understandably so because the likely losses in catastrophes, though remote, were huge and could wipe off a reinsurance company's capital altogether. The resulting securitization product, which carried catastrophic risk, was called **catastrophe bonds** or **cat bonds**.

Non catastrophe risk securitization

The general use of the insurance risk securitization device has been for risks where the frequency is low and the loss severity is high. However, there have been some cases of non-catastrophe risk securitization as well.

Risk transfer by the insured

One of the interesting extensions of the cat bonds technology is a non-insurance company, a potential client of an insurance company, disinter-mediating the insurer and seeking insurance cover directly from capital markets by setting up an insurance SPV. This approach bypasses the traditional insurer, seeking risk cover by such methods is generically known as *alternative risk transfer*, indicating that this method is an alternative to the traditional insurance cover route.

The cat bonds market

Though the concept of cat bonds has existed since 1993, the market is a development of 1996 and 1997. Attempted cat issues in 1995 failed, but the market really caught on in 1996. Since then, there has been a spate of cat bonds issuance primarily in U.S. markets. The first issue of cat bonds by European issuer was in 1999 by a French reinsurer.

Most cat bonds have used the Cayman Islands as the jurisdiction for location of the reinsurance SPV, because of a permissive law there and promise of tax neutrality. This had led the National Association of Insurance Commissioners in the U.S. to draw up a cat bonds law, which when adopted would provide tax neutrality to cat bonds issued in the U.S. as well.

In 2002, several transactions of catastrophe risk securitization were noted:

Table 22.5 Some cat bonds transactions

Purpose	Sponsor	Risk amount ($million)	Peril	Risk Location
Redwood	Swiss Re	$194.0	Earthquake	California
Capital II	Swiss Re	6.0	Earthquake	California
St. Agatha Re	Lloyd's – Syndicate 33	33.0	Earthquake	California, New Madrid
K3	Hannover Re	230.0	Earthquake, hurricane, wind	U.S., Japan, Europe
Residential Re 2002	U.S.A	125.0	Hurricane	East/Gulf Coast, Hawaii
Fujiyama Ltd.	Dowa	68.0	Earthquake	Tokyo, Tokai (Japan)
		2.1	Earthquake	Tokyo, Tokai (Japan)
Pioneer 2002 Ltd.	Swiss Re	85.0	Hurricane	North Atlantic
		50.0	Windstorm	Europe
		30.0	Earthquake	California
		40.0	Earthquake	Central U.S.
		25.0	Earthquake	Japan
		25.0	All of the above	All of the above
Pioneer 2002 Ltd. (Sep. takedown)	Swiss Re	5.0	Windstorm	Europe
		20.5	Earthquake	California
		1.8	Earthquake	Central U.S.
Pioneer 2002 (Dec. takedown)	Swiss Re	8.5	Hurricane	North Atlantic
		21.0	Windstorm	Europe
		15.7	Earthquake	California
		25.5	Earthquake	U.S.
		30.6	Earthquake	Japan
		3.0	All of the above	All of the above
Studio Re Ltd.	Vivendi S.A. (through Swiss Re)	150.0	Earthquake	Southern California
		25.0	Earthquake	Southern California

Source: Guy Carpenter.

Over time, the price for catastrophe risk protection has come down, which has been explained by the increased supply of reinsurance protection. A report by Guy Carpenter explained the reasons for the reduction as under: "1. Abundant reinsurer capacity, the marketplace was highly competitive, leading to further softening in rates. 2. Part of the observed decline in rate on line is somewhat artificial. In a number of countries there has been a vertical upward movement in programs, which has the arithmetic effect of lowering rates, as rates on line decline as cover moves up. However, Guy Carpenter's analysis of layers with the same amount of risk still shows a marked decline in pricing."[27]

Despite the above, the market for catastrophe bonds has continued to grow steadily. "The catastrophe bond market continued its steady growth in 2004 and 2005. Outstanding risk capital totaled US$4.65 billion as of June 30, 2005, up from US$4.04 billion outstanding at year-end 2004 and US$3.45 billion at year-end 2003. Total issuance declined from the record high of US$1.73 billion in 2003 to US$1.14 billion in 2004, which was roughly on a par with 2002 levels. As of June 30, 2005, however, the market has already seen issuances totaling US$1.01 billion, approximately 88% of the 2004 total. Since 1997, 64 catastrophe bonds have been issued with total risk limits of US$9.68 billion."[28]

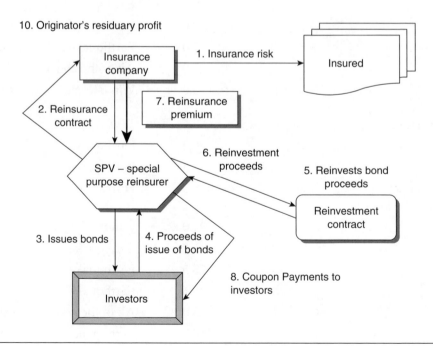

Figure 22.8 Basic process of insurance risk securitization: Before risk event takes place

Illustration of the cat bonds technology

In a typical cat bonds issuance, the insurance company would have written catastrophe risk insurance policies with the insured. In usual practice of insurance markets, the insurer will seek reinsurance for risk above a particular amount. In the securitization alternative, the insurance company sets up a special purpose reinsurance entity, to which it will transfer reinsurance for risk above the specific amount. The SPV will issue bonds in capital markets the proceeds of which will be reinvested in specific investments. The coupon to the investors will be paid from proceeds of these investments and the reinsurance premia paid by the insurance company. If no covered event takes place, investors earn the high returns based on returns from the reinvested funds and the insurance premia. If the insured event takes place, the risk above the amount absorbed by the insurance company is transferred to the investors through the SPV; the investors suffer either a loss of principal, or loss of interest, or both, or have to suffer a substantial moratorium on their investments. In other words, the reinsured risk is shared by the investors. See Figures 22.8 and 22.9.

Equity call option

There is yet another option in insurance securitization, called an equity swap, where the investors do not pay any amount up front, but agree to provide an equity contribution in the event of the insured event taking place. This is akin to calls on equity, where the issuer calls an uncalled equity (or exercises a put). The investors receive the coupon in the form of reinsurance premium, but the investors may putatively invest their funds in their own chosen investments.

Insurance securitization by non-insurance companies

The cat bonds technology has been used by potential customers to seek insurance cover from capital markets directly. Here, a potential insured sets up an insurance SPV that issues bonds in the market. The insurance premium is paid to the investors, along with coupon on the invested funds at LIBOR. In the event of the insured event taking place, investors have to take the risk based on the terms agreed.

The world's first case of non-insurance risk securitization was a Japanese amusement park called Tokyo Disneyland, which sought earthquake risk insurance through securitization. Since then, there have been some more instances. Though alternative risk transfer by non-insurance companies has received lot of attention, there has not been substantial activity because of stiff competition among insurance companies and prevailing cheaper costs of traditional insurance.

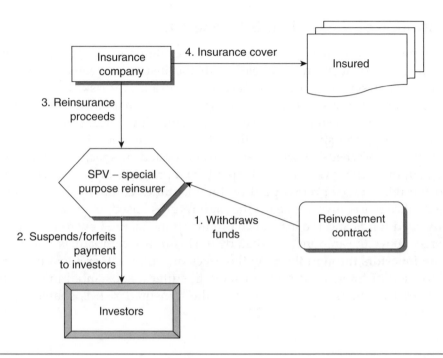

Figure 22.9   Basic process of Insurance risk securitization: After risk event takes place

Notes

1 For more on credit derivatives, see Vinod Kothari: *Credit Derivatives and Synthetic Securitization*

2 As a synthetic securitization reduces balance sheet risks, it creates fresh capacity for balance sheet funding. This is true both in regulatory sense and in economic sense. However, a synthetic securitization does not reduce the balance sheet size for financial reporting purposes.

3 There is an elaborate definition of credit events, but broadly standard documentation includes bankruptcy, failure to pay, acceleration, obligation default, moratorium and restructuring.

4 Theoretically, the structuring of the risk transfer is comparable to an inter-creditor arrangement where some investors agree to provide a first line of defense to others. It may be argued that the distribution of credit risk to the various classes is only a matter of allocation, and the weighted-average coupon of all the classes should be equal to the coupon for an unstructured risk transfer. However, this rule is seldom followed in practice; if this rule were applicable, the issuer will be indifferent as to the sizing of the individual classes.

5 The position may change under Basle II, which permits the risk-weighting of the uncovered senior position to be at par with that applicable to the senior-most of the rated securities. Regulatory aspects of credit derivatives are dealt with at length in Vinod Kothari's *Credit Derivatives and Synthetic Securitization*.

6 As a swap counterparty, the protection seller is required to keep regulatory capital for the risk, although theoretical, undertaken by providing the protection.

7   A claim against a person is referred to as an actionable claim or a chose in action; a claim over an asset in possession is called a chose in possession. See Chapter 23 on Legal Issues.

8   There is an attempt at harmonizing and modernizing the law relating to assignment or transfer of receivables; UNCITRAL has formulated a model law for assignment of receivables that will be circulated among member countries of the United Nations for adoption. See Chapter 23, also Appendix 2 to that chapter, on Legal Issues.

9   For example, the two tier SPV structure used in U.S. transactions.

10 Obligor notification is a requirement in many countries, but it is seldom ever done in practice. Such countries still recognize the transfer as an "equitable transfer."

11 This junior-most piece seldom takes the form of legal equity, but is nevertheless an economic equity of the SPV. The legal form can be preference shares with participation rights, subordinated loan and zero coupon bond.

12 See more in Chapter 27 on Accounting Issues

13 Business Week, October 26, 1998.

14 As a forceful example of volatility in investing in subordinate CDOs, cash or synthetic, American Express had to write off US$370 million in June 2001 on a $1.4 billion CDO portfolio.

15 In practice, the flexibility to an extent is retained by the originator retaining a call or substitution option for such assets needed back for obligor service. But the call back option is constrained by both legal and accounting restrictions, and is generally as complicated as the initial transfer itself.

16 As rating agency Fitch puts it: "Some of the considerations investors must grasp when analyzing synthetic deals include the potential linkage to the sponsoring entity (i.e. bank) via the credit derivative and the resultant structural risks; the composition of the reference obligations and the sponsor's credit culture, origination process and ability to substitute obligors; definitions of credit events and loss recognition for impaired assets; and, finally, appropriate policies for collateral investments." [Fitch Special Report on *Synthetic Securitization:Unique Structures, Analytical Challenges*, June 4, 2001]

17 A total rate return (TROR) swap is different from credit default swap. In this case, without having to depend on a default on a regular basis, the protection buyer will swap with the protection seller the total return, that is, all the coupon received plus appreciation minus depreciation, against a base rate + spread. Thus, the protection buyer replaces his actual return from a portfolio with an index-based return plus a spread.

18 Presumably, in such cases, the rating of the protection seller should act as a cap on the rating of the unfunded swap.

19 Banc of America Securities Asset-backed Research: *Collateralized Debt Obligations, An Introduction to Arbitrage CBOs and CLOs*, June 1999, p.9

20 Moody's: *Responses to Frequently Asked CDO Questions (Second of Series)* July 13, 2001

21 *Financial Times*, December 8, 2005.

22 *The Financial Times* report above states that the pricing ranged from 17 bps for the AAA class to 700 bps for the junior most class.

23 The news report in the Financial Times *ibid* also seemed to suggest that there was an apprehension in the market that the deal was also to part-finance an acquisition that the bank did in Italy.

24 IntesaBCI, an Italian Bank, launched its €1 billion synthetic securitization of aircraft loans vide Leonardo SPV in May 2001. After September 11, there have

been some downgrades on the junior classes, but many people have regarded this deal as a prototype for similar risk transfers to come. Journal **Asset Finance International** regarded this as the "bank finance deal of the year" – *Asset Finance International* April 2002.

25 As per Standard & Poor's Presale rating rationale, NIB Capital Bank NV's synthetic transaction called Latitude Synthetic is referenced to a portfolio of shipping loans.

26 See Chapter 2 of Vinod Kothari's *Credit Derivatives and Synthetic Securitization*

27 Guy Carpenter: 2005 The World Catastrophe Reinsurance Market. p. 2

28 Guy Carpenter: *Ibid* p. 5

Part IV: Technical and Operational Aspects

Chapter 23

Legal Issues in Securitization

The man who first discovered that a Debt is a Saleable Commodity ... made the discovery which has most deeply affected the fortunes of human race.

— Henry Dunning McLeod, *Principles of Economic Philosophy* (1872)

Legal issues relating to securitization tend to be quite complicated in most jurisdictions in the world, partly because many countries do not have well-defined laws relating to it and partly because most securitizations represent a delicate balance between pure financial transactions and real asset transfers. If this balance tilts a bit, an apparent securitization transaction might look no different from a loan with a senior ranking.

It is quite clear that one of the basic objectives of securitization is to allow the investors an undeterred claim on a section of assets of the corporation. If corporate laws were to respect such all-pervading inter-creditor arrangements in which some of the assets of a corporation – while still being the assets of the corporation – could be dedicated to a particular section of investors, possibly securitization could take place without a sale of assets and therefore, without an SPV.[1] Legally, the fulcrum of a securitization transaction is the sale of the assets by the originator, so most of the legal issues arise at that level. For the future, as some countries have already put in place corporate laws to allow a cellular company[2] – one with multiple cells of assets and obligations and each protected from other cells, securitization aims to fragment a corporation into several cells by putting up the assets into several SPVs and issuing securities from there.

The significance of legal issues in securitization

To say that legal issues are extremely significant in securitization is trite, as they are equally significant for any financial instrument. But to add some weight, let's say it is truer for securitization than other financial instruments.

Here is the reason; one of the distinctive features of securitization is that the repayment of securitized products is based on the assets transferred by the originator, and the structure does not primarily rely on a repayment obligation of the originator. In other words, securitization investors look at the assets transferred and isolated by the originator, and not at the originator himself. The rating agency rates the transaction free from the bankruptcy risk of the originator, as the isolation of the assets frees them from the same. This forms both the legal crux and the commercial substance of a securitization transaction.

This feature of securitization transactions gives them distinctive legal and commercial character, which is why they are preferred all over the world. An originator may run into financial problems, may close shop, or may go bankrupt, but securitization investors will not be affected as they are paid out of assets transferred by the originator. In the existence, prosperity or mortality of the originator, the investors look at the pool of assets. It is on this principle that securitized instruments are called asset-backed securities.

Such a pool of assets, however, is not good for the investors if the transfer is not a legally valid transfer or is liable to be revoked in extraordinary situations.

Therefore, one of the prime motives in designing the legal structure of the securitization transaction is to ensure that the transfer of assets by the originator is legally perfect, is irrevocable and irreversible, and such assets stay clear of any claims of the originator, his creditors, liquidator, or anyone else, serving the benefit of the investors. If the transfer of assets is challenged, the entire legal structure of the transaction collapses. Therefore, the legal sanctity of the transfer of assets is key to the safety, rating and marketability of the transaction.

Why are securitization legal issues complicated?

Securitization legal issues seem complicated to the extent of looking to be blown out of proportion, but the attention given to legal details is understandable in view of the need for bankruptcy remoteness and the originator-independent rating of transactions.

It is difficult to exactly point out why securitization legal issues tend to be complicated as well as uncertain, but a possible list could be:

- It is a new instrument; concerned parties (lawyers included) do not understand it too well, so they tend to protect against all sorts of imaginary risks, thus making the transaction complicated.

- In most countries, the legal structure for securitization has not been well defined. Most countries do not have sufficient laws, and even when they do, the laws are not clear enough. (You cannot blame the lawmakers for not being clear, as law always chases commerce, not the other way round.)
- Some complications are a result of the narrow requirements of bank regulatory bodies to achieve the benefit of capital relief.
- There is an apparent conflict in the securitization transaction itself; the originator apparently distances himself from the assets that he seeks to transfer, and at the same time he has to provide or organize sufficient credit enhancements to make the securities marketable, as also to reap the residual profits inherent in the assets.
- There are some judicial precedents (such as *Kingston Square)*, which we study in detail in this document, which have put to question more business-like structures; the result is structures that are contriving to be ironclad.

Securitization: The big picture

To understand the real nature of any transaction, it is necessary to look at the big picture because only looking at a part may result in a mistaken understanding. There is a famous tale from India on the problems of limited vision; the story of the elephant and five blind men, who had no idea what an elephant is like; they tried to comprehend an elephant by feeling it, but the animal was too big for any of them to touch it fully, so each took hold of a part of the animal's body – the trunk, teeth, legs, belly and tail. The one who felt the trunk said the elephant must be crooked like a jug handle. The one who held the teeth said it is smooth like a mirror. Likewise, the other three, respectively, thought the elephant must be like a thick wood log, a huge drum and a broom. None were incorrect, but only correct in part. They were each correct in isolation, but if any of them had been correct, the others must be incorrect. For instance, the elephant cannot be like a broom and a jug handle at the same time. No man looked at the big picture of a complete elephant and their comprehension suffered from the biggest problem – incompleteness or the bias of limited vision.

The transaction of securitization, like the elephant above, is composed of several sub-pieces. Looking at any of the pieces in isolation, one might have no idea of the big picture. First, there is a special purpose entity, which is like any other legal entity, except for the restrictions on its powers and very limited net worth. The originator does not own this entity, but nevertheless there is a residual beneficial interest in the entity that the originator directly or indirectly commands. Second, there is a transfer of legal interest in the assets of the originator, which in isolation looks like any other transfer of assets by a commercial entity to an independent, arms-length commercial entity. Third, there is a provision of some form as well as an extent of credit support to the transaction by the originator. This is almost universally the case, except for direct portfolio sales. While credit support can quite often be much higher, at least the residual interest of the originator – the excess spread – is almost always subordinated. The second and third parts are mutually inconsistent but look okay on a stand-alone basis. In a normal transaction of transfer, there is no credit support after the transfer. On the other hand, if it is a case of continuing credit support, it cannot be a transfer. Fourth, there is an issue of securities by the SPV, which are the SPV's securities and those of the originator. Once again, the reality is that those securities have the solitary backing of the assets originated or to be originated by the originator; thus, they have the explicit backing of the assets of the originator. Fifth, there is a recapturing of the excess spread by the originator, in some form or the other, as the investors in the securities have a limited interest in the assets of the SPV and the surplus flows back to the seller or the residual interest holder.

This big picture with all the pieces of the jigsaw puzzle put together looks very much like a limited recourse financing. In a straightforward secured-asset financing, the lender gives funding backed by the security of specific assets. The lender's interest is limited to repayment of his principal and return thereon. The residual value of the assets is the originator's profit from the assets. In the event of deficits or losses in the assets, the lender has the right to claim the money from the borrower, but in all limited liability corporates, the rights of the lender go no further than the equity of the corporation. The borrower, if he intends to keep the company going, may recapitalize the corporation, but there is no such obligation on the borrower, nor did the lender look at any such expressed or implied promise while giving the loan. The equity of the corporation serves the same purpose as the credit support in a securitization transaction.

Therefore, on a big picture basis, securitization does not look very different from collateralized lending; the difference is visual rather than real. It is important to understand that in financial structuring we are always concerned with visual differences.

The device of securitization reflects the intent of the parties to create a method of funding that is solely asset-backed. The investors have the backing of assets, and are not affected by post-origination risks of the originator's business, most significantly, bankruptcy risks. The transfer of assets to the SPV is not the heart of the transaction – bankruptcy and other risk-shielding devices are.

Current securitization practices have been unduly obsessed with the method rather than the result. The method commonly used is transfer, but what is more significant is the end-result – a bankruptcy-remote, asset-backed funding device.

Principal legal structures

Principally, securitization transactions from a legal viewpoint can take the following three structures:

- True sale structures – transactions where the issuer SPV acquires legal title over the collateral pool:

○ Existing assets versus future flows – from a legal standpoint, the distinction between existing assets and future flows may be important as future flows involve a transfer of an asset in the future, and that bankruptcy remoteness may be less an objective in future flows as the transaction has a substantial dependence on the originator's continued performance.

○ Single originator versus arbitrage transactions – the legal issues in arbitrage transactions are understandably different as the issuer acquires assets through marketplace transactions from various sellers. None of these sellers have a collusive relation with the issuer; hence the question of the issuer looking like a subset of the originator does not arise.

• Synthetic structures – where assets are not actually acquired by the issuer, but a stake in the assets is created by a synthetic transaction that replicates or emulates an actual transfer. Here, the legal issues are understandably very different as synthetic transactions do not involve any legal vesting of title in the assets in the issuer.

• Secured loan structures – the issuer does not acquire the assets as such but acquires legal security interest, which presumably will allow the issuer to realize the assets free from bankruptcy risk of the asset owner. This model, increasingly used in European transactions relies on specific laws (such as *pfandbrief* laws) or on security interest enforcement laws that respect the interest of a secured lender despite the borrower being bankrupt.

Generally speaking, unless the transaction has been designed as a synthetic transaction, the true sale structure is the most commonly used format of securitization. In the ensuing discussion, we are mostly dealing with true-sale type securitization structures.

What are the main legal issues?

The major legal issues in a typical true-sale type securitization of existing assets are:

• Is the transaction on the whole regarded as a valid transfer of receivables to the SPV or a mere financing arrangement?
• Are the assets being securitized good for transfer?
• What must be done to achieve a legally enforceable transfer of receivables to the SPV? What are the compliances required to do so?
• What must be done to protect the SPV from the bankruptcy of the originator?
• How should the SPV be organized?
• What needs to be done to protect against the bankruptcy of the SPV itself?
• What is the legal nature of the note/instrument issued by the SPV?
• Specific to the originator in question, are there any legal issues?

Securitization and loan obligations

The very basis of a true-sale securitization transaction is the transfer of receivables from the originator to the conduit, the SPV. Securitization differs from a usual monetary transaction in that the basis of the transfer of funds from the investors to the originator is not a loan obligation but a consideration for transfer of receivables. Many of the distinctive benefits of securitization flow from the fact that it is not treated as a borrowing transaction. The table below notes major differences between a monetary loan and a securitization transaction:

Table 23.1   Securitization and monetary loans: Major differences

	Securitization	*Loan*
Legal nature of the transaction	Transfer of pool of assets of the originator or of several originators	Normal monetary obligation of the borrower
Parties to the transaction	To allow the pool of receivables to be aggregated and kept intact, a collective investment medium, the SPV is formed; hence, there are three parties to the transaction – the originator, SPV (issuer) and the investors. In addition, depending on the structure of the transaction, there might be an indenture or security trustee to hold security interest over the assets for the benefit of investors	There are two parties to the transaction – the borrower and the lender; for participation of several persons in the loan, there might be an indenture trustee acting as a trustee for the investors
Relation with the debtors of the originator	Transfers claims against debtors/customers of the originator	No connection with the debtors of the originator
Nature of instrument acquired by investors	Either a fractional beneficial interest in the pool of receivables held by the SPV, or a debt obligation of the SPV	Debt obligation of the originator
Legal rights of the investors	Exercisable against the SPV, or through the SPV against the debtors of the originator	Exercisable against the originator
Treatment for regulatory purposes	Not treated as borrowing	Treated as borrowing
Effect on regulatory capital requirement	Normally frees up regulatory capital by reducing the size of risk-weighted assets	Does not free regulatory capital as has no direct relation with the size of the assets
Bankruptcy of the originator	Investors beneficially own the pool of assets transferred to the SPV	Investors have a claim against the originator; usual bankruptcy/distressed company protection available to the originator
Failure of the debtors of the originator	Depends upon recourse features; normally investors will suffer a loss	Investors will not be affected; they have a claim against the originator

The core difference between securitization and borrowing transactions is that while borrowing transactions are based on a promise of the borrower to pay, securitization transactions are, in a way, pre-paid at the very beginning as the originator transfers assets to the SPV up front. As an issuer of asset-backed securities, even the obligation of the SPV or the trustees is essentially obligation to distribute and not obligation to pay. If the assets transferred are a good value, securitization investors are better off than lenders. Against lenders, they have a prime, unfettered claim over the assets transferred into the SPV, unaffected by any distress or bankruptcy of the transferor. If the assets transferred are not a good value or are not adequately credit-enhanced, securitization investors may be worse than secured lenders; for a secured loan, to the extent of the residual unsatisfied part of the loan, the lender has a claim against the general assets of the borrower. Securitization investors have no claim on those assets of the originator that were not transferred to the SPV.

True sale or a mere tale

What happens if a securitization transaction is not treated for legal purposes as a true or valid securitization transaction? That is, a *recharacterization* of the transaction takes place in a judicial proceeding relating to the nature of the transaction. If there is still a monetary transaction between the investors and the originator, a court will most likely treat the transaction as a borrowing. However, as the intent of the parties at the inception was not a loan, they would not have created or perfected security interests in favor of the investors, relegating them to the position of unsecured creditors, if not worse. This means, while a true securitization makes investors better than secured lenders, a badly structured transaction may make them at best equal to, or even worse than, unsecured lenders.

Obviously, to create and maintain a distinctive superiority from usual monetary transactions, it is important that the securitization exercise is treated as a transfer of an asset by the originator and not as a loan-type commitment.

In other words, securitization must **look** different, and **be** different, from loans. The **form** and **substance** of securitization must be different from loans.

To ensure that the form and substance of securitization is different from loans, the following are the key elements:

> Box 23.1: The two faces of securitization: Or is it what it looks like?
>
> When or why do you need to ask: Is it what it looks like?
>
> Usually, everything and everyone is what it or one looks like.
>
> But there are exceptions – for example, your boss or your spouse (supposing they are not the same). Or securitization.
>
> The is-it-what-it-looks-like question arises when there are Inconsistencies between the outer face and inner face. Does this apply to securitization?

- The overall character of the transaction, taking all its parts together, must be one of transfer of assets and not a financial obligation of the originator.
- There must be a proper, legally recognized transfer of assets from the originator.

- The transfer must be substantive – that is, there must be a transfer of benefits and/or risks in the assets.

We take up each of these in the following sections.

The true sale question

True sale is a buzzword in the securitization industry. Before we get into the true sale question, let us understand its background.

Background of the true sale question

Why should we ask a true sale question?

When you sell your car, no one asks you whether you made a true sale or not. But imagine a case where you sell your car, but you still continue to possess it, may use it, and may also run the risks of repairs. Isn't it fair to ask what kind of a car sale was it, if everything stays as it was?

In a securitization transaction, the originator transfers certain receivables and assets, but apparently such receivables or assets are still within the originator's manifest control as he continues to collect and service the same. It is not the control that an owner has, but that the originator is not the owner is not openly manifest from the way the transaction is run. The originator may also retain some risks in the asset – for example, risk of default. And in a subtle way, the originator may also retain rewards in the asset. There is no outward manifestation of the sale, and there is a continued support given by the originator. No one comes to know about the sale except the seller and the buyer (we deal with the question of obligor notification later in this chapter).

The fact that apparently the originator continues to have a similar relation with the assets as before gives rise to an apparent question: Was the sale of the asset a true sale or a mere legal fiction?

Who can question the true sale?

If I say I have sold my car, and the buyer agrees he has bought the car, who can question it anyway?

What a document says is usually enforced as between the parties, but it does not necessarily bind the world at large. The job of a court, or bankruptcy court, or tax authority, or even an accountant is to give effect to the true nature – that is, the inner face of a document and not be guided simply by its language.

Also, the transaction of so-called securitization has significant impact on many interested parties – assuming the assets are sold, they are not available for the benefit of the rest of the creditors, claimants and shareholders of the corporate.

Therefore, a true sale question can be asked by a court, bankruptcy court, tax authority, accountant or any other external agency supposed to interpret and give effect to the transaction. However, the most likely situation in which the truth of sale is questioned is when the originator, after transferring assets, goes bankrupt, and the bankruptcy judge finds himself unable to use such assets to pay off the creditors and employees of the bankrupt company.

What if it is not a true sale?

If someone comes to a conclusion that what it looks like is not what it is, then he will also conclude what it really is. In other words, a court or other authority concluding that a purported securitization transaction is not a true securitization will also determine its true character. This is called **recharacterization** – that is, assigning to the transaction a character different from its apparent one.

Usually, when a securitization transaction is recharacterized, it will be characterized as a financial transaction – a loan. Quite obviously, if this happens at a time when the seller has gone into bankruptcy, the recovery value of the investments will come crumbling down. Ironically, true sale questions have been raised in several bankruptcies and sometimes successfully.

Notably, the question of bankruptcy remoteness, on which the structure of securitization is based, is rendered nugatory if the sale of the assets is put to question. If there is no sale in law, the SPV acquires no assets at all, and therefore, its bankruptcy remoteness has no meaning. Therefore, true sale is a far more significant issue in structuring securitizations than the bankruptcy remoteness of the transferee.

> **Box 23.2: Securitization: A question of substance**
>
> - The evident purpose of any securitization is to achieve legal superiority over traditional loans.
> - Towards this end, securitization is structured as a sale of assets, not funding on the security of assets.
> - The possibility exists, however, that a court would ignore the documentation and would treat the transaction as a substantive borrowing.
> - If so, a securitization investor would be worse than a secured lender, as he would not even hold a perfected security interest as required in most jurisdictions.
> - Moral: Calling it an apple is not enough: It must look and taste like one.

The question of substantive transfer or financing arrangement

One of the basic principles of law is that a court will try to give to an instrument such effect as the parties have intended. The intent of the parties is normally exhibited in their language, but at times there is a deviation between the language and the intent. That is usually when the parties entered into a particular mode of a transaction to achieve a desired tax or regulatory advantage, but the real intent of the transaction is different.

For securitizations as well, it is possible for a legal forum to come to a conclusion that the real intent of the transaction was not legal transfer of the receivables to the SPV but a financial transaction masquerading as a securitization. This approach is called the **substance over form** approach. The approach of a judicial forum in treating a securitization transaction as a financial transaction will lead to *recharacterization* as discussed before.

Substance over form is though a sacred principle in law, taxation and accounting standards; it is accounting standards that are the fastest to re-align accounting treatment to the substance ignoring the form. Taxation rules are next to catch up with the reality of the transaction – substance differing from form. And the courts are, by and large, the last and the most reluctant of the lot[3] to adopt the substance ignoring the form, as judicial machinery is accustomed to adopt and honor the language of any instrument and will generally refuse to go behind the language if its meaning is clear. This is based on the golden rule of interpretation that parties know what their intent is and they can write it efficiently; thus, what they wrote is their intent.

Therefore, the requirements for a "true securitization" from a legal point of view would be less stringent than those from a taxation viewpoint, and the latter would be less stringent than those from an accounting perspective.

The question of form versus substance is (a) subjective and therefore uncertain, and (b) limited by the extent to which one is prepared to probe into this question, as there is no such thing as "ultimate substance."

It is not difficult to see that once we agree that form and substance are not the same, the form is apparent, the substance elusive. The form is the same; the substance is how we see it. Thus, the form is objective, while the substance is subjective, so there is no safe harbor to probe into the substance of any transaction.

Questions of substance over form can be stretched only up to a limit. The form versus substance question needs to be reconciled to find a practical place somewhere between the extremes of form and substance. To say that every transaction is true to its form is extreme and absurd, because if the substance was always clearly revealed by the form, then there would be no scope for a dispute as to the intent of the transaction and no role for a lawyer or the court. "Ultimate substance" is another extreme, and is equally absurd because the ultimate substance of every financial instrument is the same – funding. The issue is not *what* the instrument tries to achieve, but *how*. A difference of method – structure used to achieve the ultimate end – has to be a difference of form, so we are back to relying on the form.

Therefore, a probe into the substance of a securitization transaction should be put under the limitation of being realistic. To expect that a securitization transaction should be like a commercial sale where the seller should have no retained risk and reward would make the model completely unrealistic, as no such securitization practically exists. To look at the eventual impact of the transaction on the originator is also not the right approach, as every securitization transaction results in funding, as every other financial instrument does. If there are differences in the effective method that the parties have employed in achieving the ultimate impact, a securitization transaction is different from a secured borrowing.

Case law on true sale

The potential for a judicial forum treating a documented transfer of receivables as a financing transaction depends upon the tendency of courts to go behind the apparent language of documents and look at the garbed intent. The golden rule of judicial interpretation is that courts go by the letters of a document and do not undertake an exploratory expedition into substance, which is anyway subjective.

Recharacterization, however, is an intellectual mind sport of world courts. The rationale is to an extent understandable – a bankruptcy court presides over a huge deficiency of funds and is trying to negotiate its way through unsettled claims of creditors, employees and the state; it finds Wall Street investors sitting pretty over assets that were "transferred" only ephemerally. A true sale in a securitization is a challenge to the bankruptcy court's own powers; to the extent the assets have been sold off, they are beyond the reach of the court, and what is beyond the reach is particularly tempting!

There have been cases where a securitization of receivables has been recharacterized by courts as a financial transaction. In addition, there are several cases in context of other financial instruments such as sale and leasebacks, factoring where courts have expounded principles for distinguishing between sale and financial transactions. Some of these cases are discussed below. For obvious reasons, we have mainly selected cases where either the true sale was rejected or the determination was inconclusive.

U.S. cases

Major's Furniture Mart

Major's Furniture Mart v. Castle Credit Corp. 602 F.2d 538 (3d Cir. 1979) is a prominent and oft-cited case on true sale. Major's Furniture Mart, a furniture vendor, used to sell furniture on credit to its customers. To finance itself, it entered into an agreement with Castle Credit whereby it sold the accounts receivables to Castle. The sale was with full recourse and Major's had to guarantee full performance of the account. Castle had the right to refuse the purchase of any particular account. The price paid by Castle for each account was "the unpaid face amount of the account exclusive of interest less a fifteen percent "discount" and less another ten percent of the unpaid face amount." Under this agreement, Major's sold a large chunk of receivables to Castle from 1973 to 1975. Major's sued Castle for returning the difference being the amount realized under the accounts and the amount actually funded by Castle.

To decide whether Major's had a claim to the differential money collected by Castle, the Court had to examine whether the agreement was in reality a sale of receivables or a mere financing agreement. If it was a sale, the seller conveyed full title and the buyer had full rights over the value. Major's claim was untenable if it was a sale. If it were a financing transaction, Castle had no control over the excess collected by it.

It is notable that financing transactions by way of transfer of account receivables (factoring transactions) are covered by Article 9 of the Uniform Commercial Code in the U.S. The Code provides that if the transaction is a financial transaction, the lender must return the surplus. U.C.C. § 9-502 (1990) provides:

(1) When so agreed and in any event on default the secured party is entitled to notify an account debtor or the obligor on an instrument to make payments to him whether or not the assignor was therefore making collections on the collateral, and also to take control of any proceeds to which he is entitled under Section 9-306.

(2) A secured party who by agreement is entitled to charge back uncollected collateral ... must proceed in a commercially reasonable manner and may deduct his reasonable expenses of realisation from the collections. If the security agreement secures indebtedness, the secured party must account to the debtor for any surplus, and unless otherwise agreed, the debtor is liable for any deficiency. But, if the underlying transaction was a sale of accounts or chattel paper, the debtor is entitled to any surplus or is liable for any deficiency only if the security agreement so provides.

The court applied the well-known reasoning that it is not bound to go by the label of a contract. Instead, the nature of the agreement is properly governed by the business activities of the parties. The court emphasized the fact that there was full recourse to the seller in the present case. Though it was not the court's contention that any recourse would recharacterize the sale of a receivable – there could be guarantees of quality of a receivable or its collectibility, but if all the risks were sought to be shifted to the seller, the case could well be taken as a financial exercise. The court noted the following elements of recourse provided by Major's:

(1) Major's retained all conceivable risks of uncollectibility of these accounts; (2) Major's warranted that the customers meet the criteria set forth by Castle; (3) Major's performed credit checks to make sure the criteria was met; (4) Major's guaranteed that the accounts were enforceable legally and fully collectible; (5) Major's was to indemnify Castle out of a reserve account for losses sustained due to customer default; and (6) Major's was to repurchase any account in default for more than 60 days.

The court put stress on the fact that by the sum of all covenants, all the risks of the underlying collateral were shifted to the originator:

"In the instant case the allocation of risks heavily favors Major's claim to be considered an assignor with an interest in the collectibility of its accounts. It appears that Castle required Major's to retain all conceivable risks of uncollectibility of these accounts. It required warranties that retail account debtors, e.g., Major's customers, meet the criteria set forth by Castle, that Major's performed the credit check to verify that these criteria was satisfied, and that Major's warrant that the accounts were fully enforceable legally and were "fully and timely collectible." It also imposed an obligation to indemnify Castle out of a reserve account for losses resulting from the customer's failure to pay, or for any breach of warranty and an obligation to repurchase any account after the customer was in default for more than 60 days. Castle only assumed the risk that the assignor itself would be unable to fulfil its obligations. *Guarantees of quality alone, or even guarantees of collectibility alone, might be consistent with a true sale, but Castle attempted to shift all risks to Major's and incur none of the risks or obligations of ownership. It strains credulity to believe that this is the type of situation ….in which there may be a "true sale of accounts … although recourse exists."* When we turn to the conduct of the parties to seek support for this contention, we find instead that Castle, in fact, treated these transactions as a transfer of a security interest."

The nature of recourse was a major factor in *Major's Furniture*. The court said: "The question … is whether the *nature* of the recourse … [is] such that the legal rights and economic consequences of the agreement bear a greater similarity to a financing transaction or to a sale."

At the end of the day, the court took the case as one of collateralized borrowing, and not a true sale.

Evergreen Valley Resort

Another notable case on recharacterization is *In re* **Evergreen Valley Resort**, 23 B.R. 659 (Bankr. D. Me. 1982). This case was based on the ruling in *Major's Furniture*. In this case too, the court regarded the purported sale of account receivables as a financing transaction and noted the following factors as indicative of a financing intent:

(1) Whether the creditor has a right of recourse to other assets of the debtor if the assigned assets fail to generate sufficient funds; (2) Whether the creditor's rights in the assigned property would be extinguished were the debt to be paid from some other source; (3) Whether the creditor must account to the debtor for any amount received from the assigned assets in excess of the debt; (4) Whether the assignment of assets acted to fully discharge the debt; and (5) Whether the agreement itself indicates an intent to create a security interest.

Endico Potatoes

In Endico Potatoes, Inc., and Others vs. CIT Group/Factoring, Inc., Second Circuit Nos. 1751, 1961 Decided: October 2, 1995, the court was examining a factoring transaction. Merberg was, prior to entering bankruptcy on May 10, 1991, a dealer in perishable agricultural commodities and other foodstuffs. CIT provided financing to Merberg and held security interests in all of Merberg's assets including its equipment, inventory, and most significantly, accounts receivable. CIT was making advances to Merberg on a revolving basis, against assignment of accounts receivables. The receivables were assigned by Merberg to CIT as a "contemporaneous transfer," that is, a transfer operating as and when the receivables were originated. CIT claimed that it had ownership interest in the accounts receivables, whereas, the contesting question was whether CIT's claim was no more than the claim of a secured lender.

The basic principles in this case were drawn from *Major's Furniture*.

"In determining the substance of the transaction, the Court may look to a number of factors, including the right of the creditor to recover from the debtor any deficiency if the assets assigned are not sufficient to satisfy the debt, the effect on the creditor's right to the assets assigned if the debtor were to pay the debt from independent funds, whether the debtor has a right to any funds recovered from the sale of assets above that necessary to satisfy the debt, and whether the assignment itself reduces the debt …. The root of all of these factors is the transfer of risk. Where the lender has purchased the accounts receivable, the borrower's debt is extinguished and the lender's risk with regard to the performance of the accounts is direct, that is, the lender and not the borrower bears the risk of non-performance by the account debtor. If the lender holds only a security interest, however, the lender's risk is derivative or secondary, that is, the borrower remains liable for the debt and bears the risk of non-payment by the account debtor, while the lender only bears the risk that the account debtor's non-payment will leave the borrower unable to satisfy the loan."

The court relied upon the following facts: (1) The recitals in the agreement made a reference to a loan given by CIT; (2) Merberg's outstanding debt was not reduced upon assignment; it was only reduced on actual realization of the receivables; (3) CIT could demand payment from Merberg at any time; (4) Merberg could discharge the debt at any time in which case CIT will not hold any interest in the receivables.[4]

The so-called assignment was recharacterized as a mere funding transaction.

Octagon Gas

There was another U.S. ruling where the court has treated a purported transfer of receivables as a financial transaction, but on a different ground altogether. In the case of **Octagon Gas Systems, Inc. v. Rimmer (In re Meridian Reserve, Inc** 995 F.2d 948 (10th Cir. 1993), the 10th Circuit court held that a transfer of an "account," that is, receivable for goods sold, can never be a true sale under the UCC and would always be treated as a security interest, based on the court's interpretation of article 9-102. This case was based mainly on the court's interpretation of the Code. The Permanent Editorial Board of the Uniform Commercial Code, however, has criticized this decision; later, a revision of Article 9 nullified the ruling by a specific provision in section 9-318(a) that states: "A debtor that has sold an account, chattel paper, payment intangible or promissory note does not retain a legal or equitable interest in the collateral sold." Therefore, this ruling is taken to be a precedent only for the limited purpose of understanding the nature of the challenge.

LTV Steel

In recent securitization history, there is no legal challenge as powerful as LTV Steel. LTV Steel, an integrated steel plant, had securitized receivables and current assets from 1994 to 1998 over several transactions. In December 2000, LTV filed for Chapter 11 bankruptcy. The debtors' counsel contended on the first days of the Chapter 11 hearings, that certain critical assets "sold" to non-debtor special purpose entities in connection with securitization arrangements still belonged to the company as the sale was not a true sale, but only artifice to disguise the true nature of the transactions, which were loans to LTV Steel secured by assets of LTV Steel. The bankruptcy court apparently accepted the argument and authorized their use of those assets on a post-petition basis.

The basis of the argument on behalf of the debtors was facts of the transaction, which were representative of almost the entire securitization industry. Therefore, if this transaction was not a true sale, most securitization transactions will not qualify as such. Among the factors cited by the debtors justifying a recharacterization were:

- Sweeping daily cash balance back to the parent (LTV);
- Settling inter-company transactions through book entry rather than by cash transfers;
- Sharing office space;
- Not providing separate employees;
- Not maintaining multiple accounts of each subsidiary;
- Parent's treasury officer managing treasury of subsidiaries;
- Different subsidiaries were merely subsets to hold different assets and different risks;
- Agreement requiring LTV to infuse fresh equity into steel SPV if the latter's equity deteriorates; and
- Residual interest retained by LTV

The interim order of the court held that even if the question of recharacterization was not settled, it could not be denied that LTV had some equitable interest in the assets it regularly transfers to the SPVs; all the court was doing at that stage was making orders for use of the cash collateral: "[T]here seems to be an element of sophistry to suggest that Debtor does not retain at least an equitable interest in the property that is subject to the interim order. Debtor's business requires it to purchase, melt, mould and cast various metal products. To suggest that Debtor lacks some ownership interest in products that it creates with its own labour, as well as the proceeds to be derived from that labour, is difficult to accept. Accordingly, the Court concludes that Debtor has at least some equitable interest in the inventory and receivables, and that this interest is property of the Debtor's estate. This equitable interest is sufficient to support the entry of the interim cash collateral order."

Obviously, the entire securitization industry was shaken by the case. A combined motion was filed on behalf of several large players and law firms. The matter was never finally decided by the court as the securitization funding in the case was replaced by DIP funding.[5]

As the decision in the case was never complete, it is feared by many that issues raised in this case have never been resolved. The significance of the LTV case cannot be over-emphasized, as rulings cited earlier related to factoring transactions. A present-day, representative securitization transaction was being tested for the first time. Some people hold that the LTV Steel ruling, or the absence of it, does not hold precedent value,[6] but others say the case may be a precursor to similar challenges in future.

Avianca future flow transaction

Another challenge to a future flow securitization transaction was made in Bankruptcy Court of the Southern District of New York in the case of *Avianca*. The Colombian airline had done future flows securitization in December 1997 of its ticket sales, in which receivables were transferred by way of a master trust agreement in New York. The challenge was to the transfer under the master trust agreement, as, in the view of the plaintiff, there was no true sale but a mere security agreement. Even if construed as a true sale, it was an executory contract, or unperformed obligations, which is avoidable under U.S. bankruptcy law.

U.K. cases

U.K. courts have a rich tradition on the question of form *versus* substance. Specific to an assignment of receivables, there are at least two significant rulings, discussed below.

George Inglefield

In *Re George Inglefield Limited* [1933] Ch. 1, a trader sold goods on hire-purchase basis to its customers. The hired goods along with the accounts receivables were bought by a finance company. The accounts receivables were bought by way of an absolute assignment, though the sale was not notified to customers. The buyer was a discounting house, which in English usage at that time was equivalent to today's receivables finance transaction. In this ruling, the transfer of receivables was regarded as a true sale. The court set three important conditions – if these conditions are satisfied, the transaction indicates intent of sale, rather than financing:

1. In a transaction of sale, the vendor is not entitled to get back the goods sold by returning to the purchaser the money that has passed between them. That is to say, in a usual sale of receivables, the transferor cannot re-acquire the receivables by returning the money he has received. If a right to repurchase exists, it might potentially disrupt the sale treatment.

2. In a transaction of sale, the purchaser is entitled to make a profit on the asset bought. If the transaction does not oblige the transferee to return the profit made on the receivables, it is most likely to be taken as a true sale than financing. In the case of *Major's furniture*, this was itself a question. In general, the buyer of receivables must be able to realize profit by selling them or realizing them, without being accountable to the seller to return the profit. On the other hand, if the buyer is only entitled to a fixed amount and has to return the surplus to the seller, the transaction is most likely to be regarded as a financing transaction.

3. The third condition is most critical; if the buyer of receivables does not realize the full price that he paid for the same, he cannot look to the seller for the balance. This is the famous recourse obligation of the seller. In *Major's Furniture*, recourse was a major factor; although it was also contended there that recourse by itself cannot be destructive of a true sale. However, if the recourse is general, and guarantees realization of full value to the purchaser irrespective of the payment on the underlying receivables, it is very likely that the transaction may be taken as a financing transaction.

The Court relied upon an old ruling in *Helby* v. *Matthews* [see later].

Other U.K. cases

In **Orion Finance v. Crown Financial Management** [1996] 2 BCLC 78, the court reviewed the above observations in *George Inglefield* and held that none of the three conditions mentioned could singly destroy the sale treatment. The court stated: "No single one of these features may be determinative. The absence of any right in the transferor to recover the property transferred is inconsistent with the transaction being by way of security; but its existence may be inferred, and its presence may not be conclusive. The transaction may take the form of a sale with an option to repurchase, and this is not to be equated with a right of redemption merely because the repurchase price is calculated with reference to the original sale price together with the interest since the date of the sale. On the other hand, the presence of a right of recourse by the transferee against the transferor to recover a shortfall may be inconsistent with a sale; but it is not necessarily so, and its absence is not conclusive. A security may be without recourse. Moreover the nature of the

> **Box 23.3: What could demolish a securitization transaction**
>
> As the recharacterization of an agreement is a matter of judicial discretion, none of the following is either conclusive or complete. They are, however, indicative:
>
> - Originator pays on fixed dates irrespective of collections from obligors.
> - Originator pays a fixed amount irrespective of collections.
> - Originator provides unlimited recourse on a general basis, not due to failure of warranties.
> - Transferee realizes a fixed amount and returns the difference to originator.
> - In actual operation, transferee did not look at the quality or nature of assets but merely looked at originator.
> - Amount advanced by transferee had nothing to do with the value of receivables.
> - Originator has a right to buy back assets at a price which indicates a fixed interest on amount advanced.

property may be such that it is impossible or at least very unlikely that it will be realized at either a profit or loss. Many financing arrangements possess this feature. The fact that the transferee may have to make adjustments and payments to the transferor after the debts have been got in from the debtors does not prevent the transaction from being by way of a sale."

The *Orion Finance* ruling is typical of the "neither this, nor that" approach in some recent rulings that hold in any such case of disputed character there is no clarity that preceding rulings can offer; thus, it is open for the court to decide the case one way or another. If this were to mean anything, it means that any such case will be taken to the House of Lords to decide. The *Orion Finance* ruling does not give any guidelines of its own, and at the same time undoes all the previous rulings on the matter, and so is a retrograde ruling. The only relief is that this was a case where the agreement expressly recorded that the transfer of receivables was for a matter of security and was construed as such.

In **Welsh Development Agency v. Export Finance Co. Ltd.** [1992] BCLC 148, a case apparently looking like a financing of stock but documented as a sale of goods by a presumptive borrower to the lender; was taken as a sale, not a financing transaction.

English tradition has been to distinguish transactions based on the intent of parties and the methods achieved by the parties to achieve that end. In **Lloyds & Scottish Finance Limited v. Cyril Lord Carpets Sales Limited & Ors.** [1992] BCLC 609, the House of Lords held that while "block discounting," a method of discounting bills of exchange, might achieve the purpose of funding, a discounting charge cannot be equated with interest. It held: "My Lords, the fact that the transaction consisted essentially in the provision of finance, and the similarity in result between a loan and a sale, to all of which I have drawn attention, gives to the appellants' arguments an undoubted force. It is only possible, in fact, to decide whether they are correct by paying close regard to what the precise contractual arrangements between them and the respondents were. Given that the trading agreement was a real contract, intended to govern the individual transactions which followed and (as is accepted) that it was not rescinded or varied, the ultimate question must be whether what was done can be fitted into the contractual framework which that agreement set up with such reasonable adaptations as should be needed in commercial practice and as should not transfigure the nature of the contract."

Canadian ruling in BC Tel's case

In *Metropolitan Toronto Police Widows and Orpahs Fund* vs. *Telus Communications* (BC Tel's case) [ruling dated January 21, 2003], the Canadian Supreme Court of Ontario virtually turned aside all arguments against a true sale and seemed to hold that if the parties had clearly written an intent of a true sale, the transaction would be treated as such:

"The wording of the Agreement throughout clearly indicates the intention of both parties that the transaction be a true sale. The Agreement is clearly crafted to use the language of a sale throughout. There are no references to a loan or to security or to payments of principal or interest on a loan. The true nature of the transaction can be determined not only by the wording of the Agreement but can also be gleaned from an examination of how the relationship in fact transpired and the conduct of the parties."

The court apparently relied heavily on Steven Schwarcz and others' article[7] distinguishing between credit recourse and economic recourse:

"The plaintiffs concede that recourse for collectibility is consistent with a true sale of accounts receivable but that an economic recourse which ensures a return unrelated to the collectibility of the accounts receivable is indicative of a secured loan transaction where the receivables serve simply as collateral."

The transaction in question was a full-recourse transaction. If the buyer did not have enough cash collected during a period, the seller at its option could either transfer an amount in cash or supplement the collections with substituted receivables. However, the court regarded this as a mere recourse of collectibility and not economic recourse: "The recourse available to RAC (buyer) under the Agreement is not in all events a full recourse with respect to collectibility and is not an economic recourse in the sense of a guarantee of repayment of the Outstanding Cash Payments and a calculated yield thereon." In the U.S. cases listed above, recourse has been a major factor in the determination of sale; therefore, this case has drawn a significant distinction.

Not only did the buyer have full recourse against the seller, the buyer was also obligated to return any excess collected over and above the scheduled investor payments. The buyer held such excess in trust for the seller. Logically, combining the credit recourse and the right of the seller to the entire excess should be nothing but the "economic recourse" referred to by the court, but the court was not inclined to be influenced by the presence of even this factor, held to be indicative of a financing intent in both *George Inglefield* [not singularly but in combination with other factors] as well as *Evergreen Valley*.

The court regarded the sale in this case as a true sale. As almost all the negative attributes in a true sale determination were present in *BC Tel*'s case, taking this case as a precedent would mean every securitization transaction that looks like and reads like a securitization transaction will indeed be regarded as one. The ruling has substantially reduced the scope for any recharacterization, but the court here has indeed taken a very optimistic view. The court has dismissed each negative attribute at a time, but not taken a holistic view as to what they all mean together. However, as a precedent value, the case will have a strong appeal as (a) this is a case that relates to present-day securitization transaction; and (b) it has discussed the case law on both sides of the Atlantic.

Safe harbor law

The risk of recharacterization is a risk of unsafe landing for a transaction. The issuer raises millions in funding a transaction professed to be a sale. Some legal counsel or the other would also give an opinion that the transaction is a true sale. And, when the question of "true sale" determination becomes most significant, that is, in bad time, a court may come to the conclusion that all read or believed so far was incorrect, and the transaction was not a true sale at all. This seems to suggest "What you wrote was not what you meant," and may be a substantial risk for capital market transactions where third-party investors are present.[8]

Also, there is great uncertainty as to what factors are relevant in such determination and what are not. The uncertainty in judicial treatment prompted a commentator to issue the following comment: a court could flip a coin, and find support for the characterization in case law.[9]

Therefore, an attempt was made in the U.S. to introduce a reform of bankruptcy laws whereby securitization transactions would be treated as such, at least in bankruptcy cases; that is, they were guaranteed a safe harbor.

In 2001, the Bankruptcy Reform Act sec. 912 sought to amend sec. 541 of Title 11, U.S. Code (Bankruptcy code) as follows:

> Any eligible asset (or proceeds thereof), to the extent that such eligible asset was transferred by the debtor, before the date of commencement of the case, to an eligible entity in connection with an asset-backed securitization, except to the extent such asset (or proceeds or value thereof) may be recovered by the trustee under section 550 by virtue of avoidance under section 548(a)

The above was provided as an exclusion from the bankruptcy estate – assets transferred in a securitization transaction would be out of the bankruptcy estate. Securitization transactions were defined as:

> The term "asset-backed securitization" means a transaction in which eligible assets transferred to an eligible entity are used as the source of payment on securities, including, without limitation, all securities issued by governmental units, at least one class or tranche of which was rated investment grade by one or more nationally recognized securities rating organizations.

An investment grade rating of at least a tranche was required. In addition, the transaction must be a securitization of "eligible assets."

> The term "eligible asset" means:
> (A) financial assets (including interests therein and proceeds thereof), either fixed or revolving, whether or not the same are in existence as of the date of the transfer, including residential and commercial mortgage

loans, consumer receivables, trade receivables, assets of governmental units, including payment obligations relating to taxes, receipts, fines, tickets, and other sources of revenue, and lease receivables, that, by their terms, convert into cash within a finite time period, plus any residual interest in property subject to receivables included in such financial assets plus any rights or other assets designed to assure the servicing or timely distribution of proceeds to security holders;

(B) cash; and

(C) securities, including without limitation, all securities issued by governmental units.

The above amendment sought to give a pre-determined meaning to "transfer." To scuttle a judicial probe into whether there has been a transfer or not, the amendment provided a written-in-granite certainty to transfer by defining it as:

(5) The term 'transferred' means the debtor, under a written agreement, represented and warranted that eligible assets were sold, contributed, or otherwise conveyed with the intention of removing them from the estate of the debtor pursuant to subsection (b)(8) (whether or not reference is made to this title or any section hereof), irrespective and without limitation of:

(A) whether the debtor directly or indirectly obtained or held an interest in the issuer or in any securities issued by the issuer;

(B) whether the debtor had an obligation to repurchase or to service or supervise the servicing of all or any portion of such eligible assets; or

(C) the characterization of such sale, contribution, or other conveyance for tax, accounting, regulatory reporting, or other purposes.

Quite obviously, this was an extremely aggressive legislative action, as it would eliminate any scope for judicial enquiry into whether an asset-backed securitization transaction was a true sale at all.

After the collapse of Enron, legal academia consisting of 35 law professors and deans wrote a letter of January 23, 2002, to a Senate group opposing the above proposed reform, which sought to give a safe harbor to securitization transactions. The industry, represented by the Bond Market Association, strongly supported the amendment, and opposed the views of the professors.

The amendment was finally dropped.

Safe harbor law in some states

While the Federal bankruptcy safe harbor provision could not be given effect to, safe harbors have been enacted by some states already.

Delaware

On January 17, 2002, the state of Delaware enacted the Asset-Backed Securities Facilitation Act, 6 *Del. C.* § 2703A (the "ABSFA"). The ABSFA effectively creates a safe harbor under Delaware state law for determining what constitutes a true sale in securitization transactions.

The ABSFA first provides that any "property, assets or rights purported to be transferred, in whole or in part, in the securitization transaction shall be deemed to no longer be the property, assets or rights of the transferor." Given the foregoing provision, to the extent Delaware law applies, the traditional legal criteria used in determining what constitutes a true sale in the context of a securitization is intended to be irrelevant.

The ABSFA further states that a "transferor in the securitization transaction … to the extent the issue is governed by Delaware law, shall have no rights, legal or equitable, whatsoever to reacquire, reclaim, recover, repudiate, disaffirm, redeem or recharacterize as property of the transferor any property, assets or rights purported to be transferred, in whole or in part, by the transferor." The ABSFA also provides that in "the event of a bankruptcy, receivership or other insolvency proceeding with respect to the transferor or the transferor's property, to the extent the issue is governed by Delaware law, such property, assets and rights shall not be deemed part of the transferor's property, assets, rights or estate."

Thus, effectively, the state law makes a securitization transaction completely free from risk of recharacterization.

International safe harbor law

Countries that have enacted specific laws on securitization have generally addressed the need for safe harbor by incorporating a specific provision. Here are some examples:

Italy

The Italian securitization law, called law no 130 of 1999, is an excellent model of a brief and crisp, yet all-comprehensive law.

Art. 3 of the law provides bankruptcy safe harbor. It says: "Receivables in respect of each transaction shall constitute property for all purposes separate from that of the company and that relating to other transactions. Legal actions may not be taken against each property by creditors other than the holders of the notes issued to finance the purchase of the relevant receivables." As the law applies "for all purposes," it provides a shelter in the event of bankruptcy as well.

The factors that make or mar a true sale

Looking at the above case law, it is difficult to draw to a reconciled, objective tally of the factors that matter and those that do not. There is no doubt that every transaction intended to look like a securitization transaction will read like one. In every such case, the seller would appear to "convey all the seller's right title and interest." But the question is whether the conduct of the parties is true to their language, a key task in a probe into the substance. In a substantive determination, a court could not be influenced by the nomenclature used by the parties, as a question of substance comes only when there is an allegation of a conflict between the word and the deed. A securitization transaction is a significant issue for the corporate corpus, as a chunk of assets moves away from the corporation and becomes unavailable for other creditors and shareholders. The question is whether the language of sale was merely used as a convenience by the parties or does the transaction exhibit the feature of a real sale, as in arms-length, commercial transactions.

English courts, as a matter of tradition rooted in common law, are more inclined to honor the expressed intent of parties than an implied intent. However, U.S. courts have an insatiable urge to question the substance of deals.

We draw below an inventory of the factors critical in determination. Two things must be noted: None of these factors are conclusive or exclusive, because each has been ruled out in some ruling, but what is required is a holistic view. And, one must construct the big picture of the elephant by looking at all its parts, and not just one document. Therefore, a combined reading of all the agreements relating to the transaction is important.

The role of language used by the parties

In several cases courts have made reference to the language used by the parties,[10] but the language cannot alone be determinative. It is true that unless the parties intend something illegal or wrong the purpose of law is to enforce the intent of the parties and not subvert it. Language is one of the most obvious indicators of intent, but it stops at the "obvious" stage. Justice V.R. Krishna Iyer, formerly of the Supreme Court of India, characteristically remarked: Language is a good guide to meaning, but a bad master to dictate.

Apparently, there must be no contradiction between what parties say and what they do. But it is trite to say that in life there are endless examples of conflicts between the word and the deed, the letter and the spirit. It is there that the intent as transpiring from the conduct of parties will take over the language. The conduct of parties must indicate intent of sale and purchase.

Recourse

There has been a substantial amount of sophistry about the role of recourse in transactions on sale of financial assets. Reference has been made to the article of Steven Schwarcz and others, entitled *Rethinking the Role of Recourse in the Sale of Financial Assets*.[11] The article drew a distinction between a mere recourse of collectibility (credit recourse) and economic recourse. Recharacterization must be done only where there is an economic recourse. "Recourse for collectibility merely improves the quality of the asset transferred. The purchaser with recourse cannot do better economically than the purchaser without recourse if the asset performs in accordance with its terms.

The economic terms of the transaction are defined by the cash flows of the asset itself and collectibility recourse is defined solely by the failure of the asset to perform. On the other hand, economic recourse in some fashion guarantees the return to the purchaser, without regard to the economic characteristics of the transferred asset."[12]

The authors of the article were trying to promote predictability – safe harbor. "Affording true sale treatment to a sale with recourse for collectibility also promotes predictability," which is valued by the bankruptcy laws. It has been reiterated in several rulings that recourse itself is not a decisive factor. Recourse is like a manufacturer's warranty of the quality of goods being sold. Endorsement of negotiable instruments with recourse is a common phenomenon since time immemorial. But recourse of collectibility, along with several other factors, may consummate an "economic recourse" that the authors suggest here. We cannot ignore the realities of a securitization transaction where the external investors have the right to only a certain rate of return, as the cash flow mechanics of the transaction divert the surplus cash to the residual interest holder, which in most circumstances is the seller himself. The risk of any downward variation is sheltered by the credit recourse, the chance of any profit is removed by the residual interest; the two together may seem to suggest guaranteeing a rate of return to investors.

If recourse is a negative attribute, what about other forms of enhancement? Invariably, in every securitization transaction the originator will use some forms of enhancement to absorb expected losses and to an extent even the unexpected losses. If recourse is a negative factor, so also must be subordination, or purchase of subordinated interest. The question of recharacterization is a question of substance, and if a court is influenced merely by the form of recourse, that would defeat the entire approach to substance. Invariably, the big picture of every securitization transaction involves profit-trapping devices, credit protection devices, and the rating given to a transaction is the manifestation of the predictability of the rate of return to the investors. If the rate of return to the investors were to be concomitant with the rate of return on the transferred portfolio, structured finance would lose its meaning.

For a transaction to be true sale there must be some difference between the so-called sale and mere money-lending. In a sale, the buyer must have some risk and reward that arise directly out of the performance of the portfolio of the asset and not out of the assurance of the seller. Any such risk and reward that matters to the transaction should be sufficient to hold out that difference. Additionally, it may be noted that risks and rewards are only two sides of the same coin; one generally indicates the other. For example, if a risk is transferred, the probability of not facing the risk is a reward. If a reward is transferred, the risk of not getting a reward is a risk.

Of all the forms of credit enhancement, full and generic recourse – an obligation to pay the scheduled amounts to the investors irrespective of the collections – is the most apparent negative attribute and should be avoided, as recourse is a loud promise to pay. It is not without reason, therefore, that bank regulators in most countries hate recourse.[13]

Residual interest

The seller's retention of residual interest may take various forms, such as retention of an interest strip above a certain percentage and residual interest by way of seller's share expressed as all that is left over after paying off the investors. Retention of an interest only strip at the time of transfer is only a partial assignment; the problems of partial assignment are different and are discussed later. It does not end the question over the whole intent of the transaction. Retention of seller's interest that would do damage to true sale is an understanding whereby the entire surplus left after paying off the investors belongs to the seller.

In isolation, this has been seen as innocuous in *George Inglefield,* but in that case the assignment was only required for paying the discounting company. However, in a true sale, the seller cannot have control on the profits of the buyer that arise after the sale. We have discussed above that recourse against a seller is like a warranty given by the seller on the quality of the goods, but in a commercial sale the seller cannot have a right to share the benefits if the asset performs better than expected.

Steven Schwarcz in his article *The Parts are Greater Than the Whole* says: "Several courts also have considered the existence of a transferor's right to any surplus collections, once the transferee has collected its investment plus an agreed yield as indicative of secured loan. The right of the transferee of the receivables to retain all collections of transferred receivables for its own account, even after the transferee has collected its investment plus yield, would therefore be a factor in favor of characterization of the receivables transactions as a true sale."[14]

Retention of residual profit is equivalent of the seller's call option, hated even for accounting purposes.[15] In terms of relative significance, retention of residual interest by the seller is louder as a factor against true sale than recourse, and the loud becomes ludicrous when the two get together.

Once again, a transaction might, and most likely would, subtly introduce retention of surplus by inserting an equity or economic equity in an SPV. For instance, the seller might have bought a zero-coupon bond of the SPV that has a redemption value high enough to sweep the surplus remaining after discharging all liabilities. The ultimate effect may be the same, but much difference is made by the fact that the surplus-trapping feature is embedded in a bond that is a marketable commodity.

Servicing by the seller

That the seller continues to service the transaction is only an outward manifestation of the transaction. The only problem it creates is that the seller does not *seem* to have sold the asset, as he still continues to do virtually everything he was doing before. But this is not a problem in a true sale characterization if certain conditions are met. As Steven Schwarcz puts it:

> In practice, the seller often is appointed as the collection agent
> initially. This is not necessarily inconsistent with sale characteriza-
> tion if (1) the seller as collection agent, will be acting as an agent for

the purchaser pursuant to established standards, much like any other agent, (2) the seller will receive a collection agent fee that represents an arm's length fee for these services, and (3) the purchaser has the right at any time to appoint itself or another person as collection agent in place of the seller.

Servicing consideration

A question closely related to the above is terms of the servicing arrangement. An originator agreeing to service a transaction at no or inadequate servicing fees, or on terms that are unrealistic, may lead to the conclusion that the servicing agreement is not independent and is a part of the package. For instance, if the servicing fee is completely subordinated, it appears as nothing but a way of sweeping the residual profit.

Uncertain sale consideration

Deferred sale consideration – the seller being entitled to a further price for sale of the asset depending on the residual left after paying all investors – is equivalent to the seller's interest referred to above. This leads to an indeterminable consideration that is not characteristic of a sale transaction. "Pricing mechanism may also be indicative of a secured loan to the extent the purchase price is retroactively adjusted to reflect actual rather than expected collections on payment streams" – Steven Schwarcz, *The Parts are Greater Than the Whole*, citing *Home Bond Co.* v. *McCheaney* 239 US 568 (1916) and *Dorothy* v. *Commonwealth Commercial Co.* 116 NE 143 (Ill. 1917).

Factors in determination of a sale

The discussion above focused on the features of a true sale. Before it can be a *true* sale, it must be a *sale*. In other words, the basic ingredients of a legal sale of receivables, as well as compliance with any procedure under law, are required before any sale can be considered a true sale. Therefore, adherence to these principles is a precursor to the determination of a true sale.

Requirements of valid transfer of receivables

Listed below are the general requirements for a legally acceptable securitization (the list is not complete). Also, there are local variations, but these principles are generally applicable to most jurisdictions:

Legal or legally enforceable transfer of receivables

The right to receive a sum from anyone is a property, as much as any other property, but the law does not treat receivables at par with other properties. The transfer of receivables is different from a transfer of any other asset.

Normally, the law provides for a specific legal procedure for transfer of receivables, as it is not just an agreement between the two parties present in the transaction, but it binds the debtors of the transferor who are not a party to the transaction.

The law provides for detailed procedure for transfer of receivables, legally referred to as *actionable claims*. At times it might be too cumbersome or practically difficult/undesirable to follow the legal procedure for transfer; in that case, the transferor may adopt an *equitable transfer* of the receivables, which does not create any legal rights in the transferee, but would vest in the transferee such rights that would effectively put the transferee in the position of a legal owner of the receivables.

Therefore, the securitization transaction must result in either a legal transfer or one that can be effectively treated as equivalent to a legal transfer. For detailed requirements of a legal or equitable transfer, see later in this chapter.

In common law, there are three types of transfer of receivables – assignment, novation and sub-participation. In securitization transactions, assignment is the most common form. The legal effect of the other modes of transfer will be covered later.

> **Box 23.4: Basic preconditions for legal transfer of receivables**
>
> - Receivables must exist at the time of assignment.
> - Receivables must be specific both by obligor and by obligation.
> - If the SPV is to have an independent right of action, the whole of the receivable must be transferred.
> - A receivable must be absolute and not dependent upon obligations of originator.
> - An underlying contract should not restrain transfer.

The receivables must exist at the time of the assignment

This principle is easily understandable: What does not exist, cannot be transferred. The underlying legal maxim is: *nemo dat quot non habet* – you cannot give what you do not have.

The law recognizes a debt-in-present and a debt-in-future at par. Thus, not only can a present obligation to pay is an asset transferable, but even a future obligation to pay is a transferable property. For example, if a loan, lease or mortgage transaction results in an obligation of the obligor to pay over a period of time, future obligations are also receivables and they are transferable at present.

However, many securitizations involve transfer of debt, which has not even been contracted. For example, take the case of securitization of a revolving asset or future sales – the debt obligation of the obligor will be created only in the future when the obligors, unidentifiable today, enter into a transaction with the originator.

Such securitization transactions represent an agreement on the part of the originator to transfer receivables in the future, as there cannot be any present transfer of such receivables. To this extent, the transaction contains a promise to transfer and does not result in any transfer at present. There is an implicit *future contract* in such transactions. In other words, an assignment of future revenues is only enforceable as an agreement to transfer receivables, and not as an agreement of transfer. See later for more discussion on legal issues in future flow securitization.

The receivables must be identifiable

The identifiability of the receivable is an obviously understandable condition. Identifiability refers to (a) the obligor whose debt is being transferred; and (b) if the obligor has several obligations to pay, which of these are being transferred. In absence of specifications as to the above, the securitization may only be creating a general interest limited to a monetary amount in the total assets owned by the obligor, which would defy the basic purpose of securitization. For example, a transfer of $1,000 worth of receivables out of a total pool of assets owned by the seller does not amount to a sale. The basic idea of a sale is that the rights of the seller must be vested in the buyer, and the rights of the seller are against the obligors. In the example above, the buyer cannot have any claim against any obligor; hence the sale merely creates a right against the seller or a right to participate, and not a right against any obligor.

Box 23.5: Common law rule against partial assignment

- Under common law, liabilities can be joint and several, but obligations can be either joint, or several, but where they are joint, they cannot be several.

- If the originator transfers only a fraction of his interest in receivables, he creates a joint right, which is not independently enforceable by either party.

- Both the joint-holders have necessarily to join in any action against the obligor.

- Hence, a fractional transfer can never give to SPV an independent legal right.

- However, equitable transfers can result in partial transfers.

A general assignment of book debt creates security interest and not absolute interest or the interest of the transferee. In a Canadian ruling, [*Canada Trustco v. Port O'Call Hotel Inc.* (1996) 27 D.L.R. (2nd) 147 (S.C.C.)], it was held:

"It would be absurd if a company were to fluctuate between having title to their book debts based on their ratio of debt to assets. Yet if a GABD (general assignment of book debt) is treated as an absolute assignment, this can be the only result, as the bank is limited to recovering the amount of the loan. Since the bank could not recover any book debts if the company has a surplus in their account, the book debts would belong to the company. When there was a deficit, some or all of the book debts would belong to the bank. Such a fluctuating state of affairs is inconsistent with the certainly required in commercial matters. I believe that the correct view is that a GABD represents a security interest with the legal title being with the lender and the equitable title remaining with the borrower."

The whole of a receivable should be assigned

This requirement is present in English common law, and is therefore applicable in all such countries where English common law is adopted. If there is an assignment of a receivable, then the whole of the receivable should be assigned, and not a part of it. If there is an agreement that gives rise to 60 payments over a period of 5 years, all of which are mutually unseverable, a transfer of the loan would amount to transfer of the whole of receivables; if an agreement seeks to transfer the first 30 and leave the rest with the seller, it amounts to a fractional transfer. Similarly, transfer of x% of the receivables creates a fractional transfer.

A fractional transfer is not bad in law – it only creates a joint interest of the transferor and transferee in the asset. None of the two can be said to have an independent interest in the asset. The basic contract law principle here is that an obligation can be a joint and several obligation, but a right can only be a joint right, or a several right, but not a joint and several right. This is a common position of English contract law, which provides that if there is a joint right, such joint right is exercisable only jointly – for example, sec. 45 of the Indian Contracts Act, mirroring the U.K. contracts law. This provision was inserted with a great insight; if joint rights were to be enforced independently or severally, the promisor or the obligor will be called upon to face multiple claims and litigation for the same right. Therefore, the law provides that "when a person has made promise to two or more persons jointly, then, unless a contrary intention appears from the contract, the right to claim performance rests, as between him and them, with them during their joint lives ..."

Based on this rule, in English law there has been a dispute of authority as to whether a part of an actionable claim could be assigned. The partial assignment rule is applicable in two cases – when the assignor himself holds a part of a receivable, or when the assignor holds the whole of a receivable but wants to transfer a part. In either case, the effect of the transfer will be to create a joint right in favor of the transferee on the receivable.

In English law, the authority on this issue has been divided; in *Skipper and Tucker* v. *Holloway and Howard* (1910) 2 KB 630, it was held that an ascertained part of a debt could be assigned. But around the same time in *Forster* v. *Baker* (1910) 2 KB 636, it was held that a part of a debt was not assignable. In an often-cited ruling in *Re Steel Wing Co. Ltd* (1921) 1 Ch 349, (1920) All ER Rep. 292, it was held that a part of a debt was not legally assignable but merely created an equitable interest against the debtor in favor of the transferee. This ruling was also accepted in *Walter & Sullivan* v. *J Murphy Ltd* (1955) 1 All ER 843.

In India also there have been divergent views in this regard. The English ruling in *Steel Wing* has been followed in *Rajamier* v. *Subramaniam* (1929) 52 Mad 465, and also *Ghisulal* v. *Gambhirmal* (1932) 62 Cal 510. The Patna High Court also reviewed English authorities in *Durga Singh* v. *KeshoLal* (1939) 18 Pat. 839 and held, in view of the meaning of "actionable claim," that even if a part of the debt was assigned, it could not be viewed as an actionable claim in law.

If a partial assignment is made, it results in creation of a joint right in the receivables in favor of the originator and the SPV. Neither the originator nor the SPV has a singular right or remedy. If there is any action to be brought against the obligors, the originator and the SPV must sue jointly. If any one of them has to sue, the suit will have to involve the other party as a respondent, for refusal to join in the suit.

Section 136 of the U.K. Law of Property Act 1925 clearly makes it a precondition for a legal transfer of receivables that the whole of the receivable should be assigned.

The assignor must not be the assignee

This is a simple rule of a transaction *inter vivos*, that is, between two or more parties. If the transferor transfers the asset to himself, the transaction has no significance. In some cases, there might be a *declaration of trust* by an originator – this is construed as transfer of beneficial interest to the beneficiaries of the trust, though there is no real legal transfer of the asset. Hence, the *inter vivos* rule is technically satisfied in this case.

It must be an assignment of rights, not obligations

Box 23.6: Assigned rights must be independent of obligations

- Rights are a property: They are transferable in accordance with legal procedure.

- However, obligations cannot be transferred except with the consent of the counterparty, that is, by novation.

- In many cases, the rights of the originator may be based on his obligations.

- Unless such rights are severable from the obligations, the rights cannot be assigned independent of the obligations.

- This may be an important limitation in many cases.

One of the very important principles of law is that assignment of rights is possible; assignment of obligations is possible only if the person to whom the obligation is owed gives his consent to the assignment. That would operate as a novation of the obligation, but as such, an assignment of an obligation is not permissible. This principle, originally enunciated in English law [*Tolhurst* v. *Associated Portland Cement Manufacturers* (1902) 2 KB 660] is now a part of U.S. law as well [*Corbin on Contracts*, (1951) Vol. 4, page 866]. The underlying rationale is easy; if an obligation were to be assignable, the creditor would face the unpalatable situation of having to enforce his right against a person with whom he never contracted.

In U.S. jurisdiction, there have been several rulings on assignment of contracts involving executory clauses – a contract requiring a performance of obligations by the transferor.

In India, the common law rule has been reiterated in several rulings. In *Jaffer Meher Ali* v. *Budge Budge Jute Mills Co* (1906) 33 Cal. 702, it was observed as follows: "The rule as regards the assignability of contracts in this country is that the benefit of a contract for the purchase of goods as distinguished from the liability there under may be assigned, understanding by the term *benefit* the beneficial right or interest of a party under the contract and the right to sue to recover the benefits created thereby. This rule is, however, subject to two qualifications: first, that the benefit sought to be assigned is not coupled with any liability or obligation that the assignor is bound to fulfill, and next that the contract is not one which has been induced by the personal qualifications or considerations as regards the parties to it."

In *Indu Kakkar* v. *Haryana State Industrial Development Corporation Ltd.* 1999 AIR 296 SC, the Supreme Court reiterated the rule as under:

"Assignment by an act of the parties may cause assignment of rights or of liabilities under a contract. As a rule, a party to a contract cannot transfer his liabilities under the contract without consent of the other party. This rule applies both at the common law and in equity (vide para 337 of Halsbury's Laws of England, Fourth Edition Vol. 9). Where a contract involves mutual rights and obligations, an assignee of a right cannot enforce that right without fulfilling the correlative obligations." The aforesaid principle has been recognized by a Constitution Bench of this Court in *Khardah Co. Ltd.* v. *Raymon and Co. (India) (P) Ltd.* (AIR 1962 SC 1810: (1963) 3 SCR 183) T. L. Venkataramiah, J. who spoke for the Bench observed thus:

"The law on the subject is well settled and might be stated in simple terms. An assignment of a contract might result by transfer either of the rights or of the obligations there under. But there is a well-recognised distinction between these two classes of assignments. As a rule obligations under a contract cannot be assigned except with the consent of the promisee, and when such consent is given, it is really a novation resulting in substitution of liabilities. On the other hand rights under a contract are assignable unless the contract is personal in its nature or the rights are incapable of assignment either under the law or under an agreement between the parties."

A receivable that involves a pending performance on the part of the transferor may be assigned, if the obligation could be severed from the rights. Usually, however, that will not be the case if rights are conditional upon the obligations.

Apparently this principle is not involved in securitizations; most securitization deals involve transfer of assets and not liabilities, so it is easy to fall into a trap on this principle. Many securitization transactions might contain an implicit, but not apparent, assignment of obligations; if there is a right with the originator that is based on an obligation of the originator, then an assignment of the right would amount to assignment of the obligation also. For example, take the case of a lease with a contract of service; say a lease of a photocopier where the lessor is also required to service the photocopier. The right to rental here is obviously conditional upon the servicing of the photocopier. Unless the agreement provides otherwise, the right is not severable from the obligation. Hence, the transfer of the right to receive the rental would also amount to transfer of the obligation to service.

If a right under a contract is based on an obligation, the right is not assigned unless the obligation has been satisfied. Assignment of such right stands on the same footing as the assignment of a future receivable. See later on assignability of future receivables.

There must not be contractual or other restrictions on transfer

Prima-facie, every right – nay, every property – is transferable. Therefore, rights under a contract or benefits of a contract are transferable by default. However, the underlying contract may contain restrictions on the right to transfer. It would be typical for contracts to specify that the rights under the contract are not transferable. If such restriction exists, it would attach immobility to the rights and they cannot be transferred except with the sanction of the counterparty.

The effect of anti-assignment clauses in the originating contract has been a subject matter of rulings in several countries. It is generally held that a contractual prohibition against transfer may operate against the obligor, but would not invalidate the contract between the assignor and assignee. Several law cases relating to efficacy of contractual restrictions have been reviewed in *Sydney Law Review*, Vol. 26, June 2004. In English law, the position is that if the parties have contractually prohibited or restricted assignment, full effect shall be given to it.[16]

The rights must not be personal rights

Certain rights are construed as rights of a specific person, and not rights that are in the nature of a property. Personal rights are not in the nature of property and are not assignable. For instance, the right of an employer to avail the services of an employee is a personal right. This principle does not have a frequent application to securitization transactions.

There must not be a right of set-off or claims against the originator

The law provides that in any securitization transaction, the transferee of the receivables acquires them with the equities and limitations that existed at the time of assignment. If the originator's right to receive was constrained by any set-off right with the debtor, the transferee cannot claim a stand-alone right to receive without being affected by a set-off. Set-off is the right of a debtor to adjust a claim against the originator from the debt payable to the originator. As a matter of general contract, when there is a right to receive from a person to whom a sum is also due, the right to set-off is available in absence of any contrary stipulation. Generally, loan, lease and mortgage documents specifically provide that the amount payable therein is not subject to any set-off, but wherever set-off is available or not specifically ruled out, the transfer of receivables will be subject to such set-off.

The obligor's right of set-off amounts to the originator's obligation, and transfer of any receivable subject to such right would amount to a transfer of obligations as well. If the transfer of the right can happen independent of the set-off right, it obviously causes a prejudice to the obligor, for which his express consent is required.

Methods of transferring receivables

In common law, three methods of transferring legal rights in receivables have been known: assignment, novation and participation.

Assignment

Assignment is a legal conveyance of rights in a receivable – similar to the transfer of any other property. Assignment in common law does not require the consent of the debtor, although notification may be required to prevent the debtor from claiming discharge on paying the transferor. Assignment is an assertion of the property rights of the transferor.

Novation

Novation is consensual, not unilateral. A novation happens when the obligor by express consent agrees to regard all benefits of contract as payable to the transferee. As noted, novation is the only effective means of transferring an obligation under a contract or a right based on an obligation. The usual method of a novation will be a tripartite agreement between the transferor, transferee and the debtor, where the debtor agrees to substitute the transferee for all the benefits under the contract accruing to the transferor. The obligations, if any, may be carried by the transferor, or may be assumed by the transferee.

Novation, though legally the most perfect way of transferring receivables, is logistically most cumbersome and seldom resorted to except for one-to-one transfers. In the normal course of securitization, not to speak of seeking the sanction of individual obligors, the originator may not even find it advisable to notify the obligors.

In civil law jurisdictions, novation is recognized. As a matter of fact, many civil law jurisdictions only regard a novation as a proper means of transferring receivables.

It is notable that the legal requirements for assignment discussed in this chapter, including registration and stamping of the assignment agreement, do not apply to novation. Novation is an agreement that effectively *creates* legal rights in favor of the transferee, but does not *transfer* them. Hence, a novation agreement will not be regarded as one transferring any receivables.

Sub-participation or participation

This is a bilateral agreement between the transferor and the transferee where the transferor agrees to allow the transferee to participate in the benefits of the contract with the obligor. There is no transfer of receivables; the transferor remains legally entitled as against the obligor. The obligor has no legal relation with the transferee. However, the transferee obtains a right against the transferor to benefits of the contract.

Participations are quite common in banking practice; banks reduce their concentration in particular transactions by inviting other banks to participate in the loan. From the viewpoint of bankruptcy, loan participation achieves the impact of a true sale as to the extent of a participation granted to the other bank, the loan is not taken as part of the bankruptcy estate of the originating bank. Case law on participations is reviewed in *Recharacterization Issues in Participating Loans* by John C. Murray.[17]

The U.S. Financial Accounting Standards Board has considered at length the nature of loan participations and has agreed, in an Exposure Draft, to apply the true-sale type treatment to loan participations, subject of course to several preconditions.[18]

Declaration of trust

Declaration of trust is the declaration by the transferor that he holds the asset for the benefit of the beneficiaries. Thus, there is no transfer of legal interest – the property continues to be held by the "transferor." There takes place a transfer of beneficial interest only. In many jurisdictions, transfer of beneficial interest is sufficient to lead to bankruptcy remoteness. Bankruptcy laws usually provide for exclusions from the bankruptcy estate the property held as a trustee. As the transferor post-declaration is merely a trustee, the property would be excluded from his bankruptcy estate. Declaration of trust is commonly used as a device to avoid problems relating to transfer.

Legal systems and assignment of receivables

English common law

Securitization involves transfer of debts payable by third parties. There are two basic reasons for which there are specific legal procedures on transfer of receivables in most jurisdictions, particularly under those following the Anglo-Saxon or English common law pattern:

If transfers of receivables were not recorded, there would be confusion as to title. For movable properties, the prima-facie indication of title is possession. Movable properties are acquired by acquiring possession thereof, and transferred by parting with it. Hence, delivery becomes the common mode of transfer of movables, which is acceptable under common law. For immovables, the question of acquiring and effecting delivery does not arise. Hence, the law requires dealings in immovables to be the subject matter of registration. All dealings in immovables under the Anglo-Saxon law require registration, and registration acts as a prima-facie, though not exclusive or conclusive, evidence of such dealings. For intangibles, such as receivables, the delivery of the property is not possible, as the asset does not satisfy physical attributes. Hence, to make clear and beyond doubt the record of dealings in intangible properties, legal systems generally require all dealings in intangible properties such as actionable claims to be recorded in writing whether registered or not. The second reason, particularly applicable for receivables, is that unless there was a written record and a notice of any dealings to the debtor, the debtor would face serious difficulty in facing legal claims from totally unrelated parties. The debtor would be forced to recognize and honor claims from parties that he never knew of. With these two objectives in view, the Anglo-Saxon legal system requires written records of dealings in receivables. This means Anglo-Saxon law treats receivables at par with immovable properties. As immovable properties require conveyance, transfer of actionable claims would also require a conveyance.

> **Box 23.7: Assignment of receivables and legal systems**
>
> - Transfer or assignment of receivables is governed by prevailing legal system.
> - Common law regards a receivable as any other property – transferable without sanction of the debtor.
> - Debtor notification may or may not be required.
> - Civil law systems regard rights against parties as personal rights, not properties; generally require debtor sanction.

In addition, as a common law principle, obligor notification, that is, a notice to the debtor that the receivable has been transferred, is also required (see later for the intent of this requirement and the implication if it is not fulfilled).

This requisite is not to put any fetters on the right of parties to deal in their properties. The intention of these legal requirements is not to make receivables or intangibles any less freely transferable property than other property. The requisites of written record are only an instrument of such dealings to establish title clearly. If these requisites can be otherwise satisfied, the law should not prima-facie have any objection to dealings in receivables. Transferability of loans and other claims against third parties is key to securitization markets the world over. "The ability to trade a receivable without permission of the obligor began the foundation for U.S. securitization markets."[19]

Roman-Dutch law or civil law

Under Roman-Dutch law (followed in parts of Europe, large parts of Africa, Latin America, Sri Lanka and Indonesia), properties were classified as those which required *mancipation* and those that did not. Mancipation referred to a legal recording of the transfer of properties. Mancipation was required for *land, animals, and slaves* – these three were the tools or inputs required for agriculture.

There is no requirement that receivables should be transferred subject to a conveyance. However, most civil law jurisdictions do not treat a right to receive as a property. Therefore, rights against persons are assignable only subject to the consent of the debtor or based on notification of the debtor in a particular way.

Transfer of receivables in civil law countries is, therefore, conditional upon a sanction of the debtor. Some present day agreements put in a clause whereby the debtor gives sanction at the origination stage itself – a clause in the underlying agreement to the assignment. However, it is not certain whether such a sanction would be recognized as consent to assignment, giving the assignee legal rights to the receivable.

Procedure for assignment of actionable claims

We have based this discussion partly on the provisions of English property law and on the Indian Transfer of Property law. The Transfer of Property Act in India is modeled on the Law of Property Act, U.K. Most of the principles relating to transfer of receivables in Indian law are the same as they apply to common law countries. Therefore, this discussion is of generic significance.

The essential legal requirements for assignment are contained in sec. 136 of the U.K. Law of Properties Act, to which section 130 of the Indian Transfer of Property Act corresponds. Section 136 of the Law of Properties Act provides:

> 136(1) Any absolute assignment by writing under the hand of the assignor (not purporting to be by way of charge only) of any debt or other legal thing in action, of which express notice in writing has been given to the debtor, trustee or other person from whom the assignor would have been entitled to claim such debt or thing in action, is effectual in law (subject to equities having priority over the right of the assignee) to pass and transfer from the date of such notice –
> (a) the legal right to such debt or thing in action;
> (b) all legal and other remedies for the same; and
> (c) the power to give a good discharge for the same without the concurrence of the assignor."

The key provisions of Indian law and laws of some other countries are in Appendix 3 of this chapter.

Briefly stated, the requirements of English/Indian law relating to assignment of receivables are as follows:

1. Receivables are taken as actionable claims.
2. Transfer of actionable claims possible "only by execution of an instrument in writing," as per sec. 130 of the Indian Transfer of Property Act/sec. 136 (1) of the British Law of Property Act.
3. Such written instrument shall be regarded as a conveyance; as such an instrument seeks to transfer property. It is notable that instruments *by which* a property is transferred are regarded as conveyance, while instruments that *merely record* a transfer are not treated as such. As the assignment

agreement is a legal necessity, it is an agreement by which the receivables are transferred; hence, it is to be treated as a conveyance.

4. Unless the receivable is taken to be an interest in immovable property, the receivable will be treated as a movable property.
5. English law requires obligor notification as a condition precedent, as it provides for "of which express notice in writing has been given." The requirements of obligor notification and its impact are discussed later below.

Let us have a detailed review of these provisions.

Meaning of debt or actionable claims

A debt and actionable claim can be used interchangeably, except to the extent of specific differences enacted by law. In Indian law, "actionable claim" means a claim to any debt, other than a debt secured by mortgage of immovable property or by hypothecation or pledge of movable property or to any beneficial interest in movable property not in the possession, whether such debt or beneficial interest be existent, accruing, conditional or contingent. [Sec 3 of Indian Transfer of Property Act]

It may be noted that the above definition **excludes**:

*   Transfer of a loan secured by immovable property
*   Transfer of a loan secured by hypothecation or pledge of movable property
*   Transfer of "securities" – instruments treated as marketable securities such as shares and debentures
*   Transfer of negotiable instruments.

Thus, claims to lease rentals, hire-purchase receivables, credit card receivables, or other receivables will be treated as actionable claims. Regarding receivables under loan secured by mortgage of immovable properties, the view is that such a receivable would itself be regarded as an immovable property – see **Mulla** on *The Transfer of Property Act*, 1995, pages 1010–11. Another relevant provision here is sec 8 of the Indian Transfer of Property Act (noted below). According to this section, when the loan secured by the mortgage is transferred, there will be a transfer of the mortgage also, which again may amount to a transfer of an interest in immovable property. In several cases such as *Perumal* v. *Perumal* (1921) AIR 196 (Mad.), *Bank of Upper India* v. *Fanny Skinner* (1929) AIR 51 (All), *Villa* V. *Petley* (1934) 148 IC 721, it has been held that a mortgage is an immovable property and cannot be transferred otherwise than by a registered instrument.

In sum:

*   If there is an assignment of any debt other than the debt under a loan secured on movable properties, the provisions of sec. 130 of the Indian Transfer of Property Act are applicable.
*   If there is an assignment of mortgage debt secured by immovable property, the provisions relating to transfer of immovable properties will be applicable.

- If there is a transfer of a debt secured by hypothecation or pledge of movable property, it is assignable without compliance with sec. 130.

Instrument in writing

Under the English/Indian law provisions cited, there are two essential requirements for an assignment of actionable claims, instrument in writing, and obligor notification.

Sections 130–137 of the Indian Transfer of Property Act contain provisions relating to assignment of actionable claims. In view of their importance in regulating assignments, these are in Appendix **3** to this chapter.

Another significant provision is sec. 8 of the Indian Transfer of Property Act, which provides that where a debt is transferred, then, unless a different intention is expressed, all securities for such debt will also stand transferred. However, arrears of interest for the time up to the transfer will not be transferred.

Sec. 130 of the Indian Transfer of Property Act requires that transfer on an actionable claim shall be effected only by the execution of an instrument in writing, signed by the transferor, and such transfer shall be complete and effectual upon the execution of such instrument, whether a notice to the debtor is given or not. The transferee of the actionable claim gets, on the strength of such instrument, lawful rights to recover the claim from the debtor in his own name, without any reference to the transferor.

> **Box 23.8:** Assignment of actionable claims under common law
>
> - Receivables are mostly treated as actionable claims. Exceptions may be receivables secured on immovable property and movable property.
>
> - Assignment of actionable claims can be done by a written instrument.
>
> - Such instrument, as it transfers receivables, is regarded as conveyance.
>
> - Conveyance may/may not require public registration.
>
> - Most conveyances are stamped.
>
> - This will not apply for novation.

Obligor notification

The provision of sec. 136 of the Law of Property Act clearly requires a written notice to the obligor. Thus, an expressly written notice of the assignment is necessary to complete the assignment against the obligor. This is also true for most other common law countries.

In England and common law countries, an assignment of actionable claims where notice of assignment has not been given to the obligor is treated as an **equitable assignment** (see later in this chapter for details). In *Performing Right Society* v. *London Theatre of Varieties* (1924) AC 1, it was held that although the assignor could not transfer his legal title to the assignee, equity would recognize the assignment of his equitable interest, provided that the assignor was joined as party to the action, either as plaintiff if he consented to the action or as defendant if he did not. Thus, the impact of an equitable assignment is that the assignee will obtain a good discharge if he pays the assignor (*Brandt* v *Dunlop Rubber Co.* (1905) AC 454). Notice to the debtor is also essential if the assignee is to have priority over subsequent assignees: *Dearle* v. *Hall* (1828) 3 Russ. 1.

In other words, the absence of obligor notification creates a problem of priorities; in absence of such notification, subsequent transferees that are notified will have a priority. Obligor notification is comparable to, or rather the basis of, the present-day system of registration or perfection of security interests.[20] The instrument of transfer *creates* the interest of the transferee, and the notification *perfects* it. Present-day legal systems have, in many countries, replaced the system of obligor notification with that of public registry, which serves as a notification to the world at large.

In India in 1900, the requirement of notice to obligors was removed and the transfer was made effective upon execution of the instrument. However, a proviso to sec. 130 enables the transferor of an actionable claim to deal with it, and such dealing shall be valid against such transfer unless the debtor has express knowledge of such transfer. This rule seems to be similar to English law on equitable assignment; hence, there is no basic difference between English law and Indian law except that what is recognized by English law as equitable assignment is a legal assignment in India, although ineffective as against the obligor without express notice – Indian courts do not recognize equitable rights as distinct from legal rights.

Under the Transfer of Property Act [sec. 131], a notice of assignment can be given by the transferor, or in case the transferor refuses to give the notice it can be given by the transferee. This is a significant safeguard as it is the transferee whose interest is adversely affected in the absence of a notice of assignment. Commenting on the pre-1900 text of the corresponding sec. 132, which did not allow for the transferee to give notice, it was held in *Ragho v. Narayan* (1897) 21 Bom. 60 that not allowing the transferee to give notice of assignment was a slip, as the notice was required for perfection of interest of the transferee.

In practice of securitization, obligor notification is merely reserved as a power with the transferee, as it is logistically difficult and originator-unfriendly to do so, and more so, unnecessary where servicing is retained with the transferor. The power is exercised only in those remote situations where servicing is transferred.

Cases where conveyance or obligor notification is not required

In Indian law, the requirement of conveyancing or notification does not apply in the following cases:

> 1. Claims secured by mortgage of immovables or by pledge or hypothecation of movables, as excluded from the definition of actionable claims. 2. Stocks, shares, debentures, or other instruments that are for the time being by law or custom, negotiable, or any mercantile document of title to goods. – Section 137.

An understanding of the exemption under sec. 137 is crucial to explain the intent and operation of sec. 130 of the Act. The exemptions given in the section are two. One is for instruments that were, at the time of enacting the law, known as marketable instruments – shares, stocks and debentures, and mercantile documents of title to goods, such as railway receipts and bill of lading. The other exception is for instruments that might later, by law or custom, emerge as marketable instruments. The list of such instruments is open-ended. Sec. 137 affords dynamism to the law contained in the Transfer of Properties. Obviously, the lawmaker enacting the law way back in time was futuristic. Apart from exempting what was known and dealt in as marketable securities then, the lawmaker visualized that more such instruments might emerge in future. This goes on to reflect the basic intention of sec. 137. The section obviously does not put fetter on the transferability of such claims, which are known to be transferable. The debtor, at the time of originating a debt comprised in a marketable instrument, possibly should be aware of the possibility of any dealings in the claim, and so cannot take grudge against such transfers. Further, the exemption is only for negotiable instruments. The law pertaining to negotiable instrument generally provides for negotiation by endorsement and delivery, unless the instrument is a bearer instrument. The fact of endorsement serves the basic purpose of the section – a written record of the dealings in the claim by way of a written instrument.

Mode of transfer of actionable claims

Whereas the essential scheme of the section is to prescribe the mode of transfer of actionable claims, courts have over the years taken a very liberal stand on the mode of transfer. The full Bench of Karnataka High Court held in the case of *Simon Thomas* v. *State Bank of Tranvancore* (1976) KLT 554 (FB) that no particular words or any particular form needs to be adopted for transfer of actionable claims. The purpose of the section is served if there is an intention to transfer the claim and such intention is recorded in writing. Notably, though, sec. 130 requires the transfer to be effected by written instrument, but the provisions of the Registration Act do not require compulsory registration of such an instrument. The Bombay High Court in *Jivraj* v. *Lalchand and Co.* (1932) 34 Bom. LR 837 held that even in oral transfer of actionable claims, subsequently recorded, would serve the purpose of the section. In a recent case, the Calcutta High Court did not enforce compliance with the requirements of sec. 130 at all for assignment of a fixed deposit in a bank. This is reflective of the liberal attitude taken by courts in strict compliance with sec. 130, provided the intention of the transferor to transfer his claim in the debt is transparent and evident on record.

Equitable assignment

What is equitable assignment?

English law has for a long time had a practice of equitable transfers. Equitable transfer means a transfer where the substantive commercial intent of the parties is clear, but which is made without complying with some or the other legal procedure laid down in law. That is to say, it is an assignment that is complete as between the assignor and the assignee, but not complete in the eyes of law. For example, for immovable properties, a registered conveyance is a legal necessity, but even if this procedure is not followed, the transfer of property is valid as an equitable transfer. Similarly, under U.K. law, even if obligor notification is not given, but the receivables have been transferred it is paid for by the transferee.

The underlying premise in an equitable transfer is that if the transferor and transferee have evidently agreed to transfer the former's rights to the latter, for which the latter has paid the former and the transfer is not legally perfect owing to technical formalities not being complied with, the transfer must still operate as valid as between the transferor and the transferee. An equitable transfer cannot give any rights to the transferee as against the obligors; it merely binds the transferor to honor what he has undertaken. Therefore, in English common law, it is a trite position that the assignee does not have a right of action against the obligor in his own independent capacity; if he intends to sue the obligor, he must be joined by the assignor either as a plaintiff or as a defendant. [*Performing Right Society* v. *London Theatre of Varieties* (1924) AC 1; *Three Rivers District Council* v. *Governor and Company of the Bank of England* (1995) 4 All ER 212]

Equitable transfers are well understood in several countries such as England, Hong Kong, Australia, Malaysia, and Singapore.

Indian courts do not have a general tradition of recognizing equitable transfers of property. [To wit, "the law of India, speaking broadly, knows nothing of that distinction between legal and equitable property in the sense in which it was understood when equity was administered by the Court of Chancery in England." *Tagore* v. *Tagore* (1872) 9 Beng. L R 37]. However, reinforcing the liberal view of sec. 130, courts have consistently paid scanty attention to compliance of the provisions of this section where parties' intents were clear. The Indian Supreme Court clearly laid down this principle, in the case of *Bharat Nidhi Ltd.* v. *Takhatmal* (1969) AIR (SC) 595. In this case, the court gave virtual *carte blanche* to parties willing to transfer actionable claims by holding that there can exist an equitable transfer of actionable claims, even outside sec. 130. Based on the Supreme Court's ruling, there would be deemed to be an equitable transfer of actionable claims if the intention is available as a matter of written record. Even a subsequent document witnessing that receivables have been assigned would serve the purpose of sec. 130. The above ruling was recently reviewed and approved of in a case pertaining to the granting of power of attorney in *Canara Bank* v. *Tecon Engineers* 80 Comp. Cas. 325 (Ker.). The court relied upon *Palmer* v. *Carey* in deciding what would constitute equitable assignment. A reference to a specific fund out of which payments to the assignee would be made would constitute such equitable assignment.

Why equitable assignment?

Why do entities resort to equitable assignments? Essentially, to avoid the difficulties involved in a full-scale legal transfer. These difficulties may either include having to notify the debtors (as under U.K. or Hong Kong law) or the stamp duties associated with a conveyance that transfers the receivables (as in the U.K. and India). Some preconditions for affecting an equitable transfer are:

- There must be an express intention on the part of the transferor to assign receivables.
- The receivables must be identified.
- The buyer must have paid the consideration.
- Though the obligor is not notified, the transaction must be carried between the transferor and transferee as if a full scale transfer has taken place. Therefore, the seller must not be paying from his general funds, but out of either a specific fund or collections from the receivables.
- To allow the transferee to proceed against the obligors if the need arises, the transferor should be given a power of attorney authorizing the transferee to collect payments from the obligors.
- To support and strengthen the power of attorney specified above, a mandate should also be given requiring the obligors to pay the transferee.

Problems with equitable assignment

Box 23.9: Equitable assignments

- Legal provisions for assignments may be difficult to comply with due to:
  - Conveyance and stamping problems
  - Debtor notification
  - Partial transfer
- Hence, parties may resort to equitable assignment, that is, without complying with required legal formalities.
- It is a contract enforceable in equity against the transferor, but does not create any right against the debtor.

If the equitable assignment route outlined above was without any problems, there was no reason for people to opt for a legal assignment of receivables. However, the equitable assignment route has several inefficiencies, and so as far as possible securitization transactions must adopt legal assignments:

- **Wrong dealing by the originator may expose the transferee to problems:** If the transferor, having done an equitable assignment, re-transfers the asset and the second transferee serves notice on the obligors, the second transferee will have priority, though this is an arguable question.
- **Tax laws may not recognize equitable transfers:** Tax laws may not recognize incomplete, legally inefficient transfers of receivables; this may involve problems of the originator having to treat the securitization transaction as a mere borrowing in every sense.
- **Court rulings about the validity of equitable assignments have been fact-based:** In rulings like the Indian case of *Bharat Nidhi Ltd.*, the courts were concerned with the typical modality of the transaction – the power of attorney and payment out of a specific fund. Also, this was a case where the assignment was for the purpose of security, not transfer of a legal interest. The general applicability of the securitization concept is limited by these restraints. Also, the absence of a few factual features may tilt the judicial opinion, which is a big legal risk.

- **Not independent of the originator:** Legal suits will be filed in the name of the originator, which creates dependence on the originator. All action for enforcement such as repossession will have to depend on the originator.

Stamp duty on securitization: General

Stamp duty is a tax payable on the document effecting a transaction. Usually stamp duties are payable on conveyances. As noted before, it is a requirement of law that an assignment of actionable claims is done on the strength of a written instrument; therefore, a conveyance is required for transfer of receivables and a conveyance attracts stamp duty.

Various countries have stamp duties applicable on securitization. These include the U.K., Australia and Malaysia (exempted in certain cases, see later). In India, a transfer of receivables by a written instrument will also be subject to stamping at the rates applicable to conveyances. These rates are fixed by the state governments but could be anywhere between 3 and 16% (with the exception of states that have specifically provided for lower duties; see later).

Stamp duty is an antiquated tax; it belongs to an age when commercial transactions were put on documents that were authenticated by the seal or stamp of the state, and thus was called stamp duty.[21] In the present age of technology increasingly heading towards paperless contracting, it is appropriate that stamp law should be replaced by a tax on the transaction rather than documents.

FAQs on stamp duty on securitization

The quick questions and answers may need to be read in context of local law – stamp duty is basically a local law, and there are no generally acceptable principles of stamp law applicable across the world.

Why applicable to securitization transaction?

As discussed above, stamp duty arises as securitization involves a document by which transfer of receivables (actionable claims or choses in action, as they are called in law) are transferred.

What attracts the duty – the transaction or the instrument?

Stamp duty is a tax on the instrument, not the transaction.

What is the chargeable amount for duty purposes?

It depends on the law that levies the duty. Normally, the duty is paid on (a) the nominal value of assets transferred by the instrument or (b) on the consideration paid for the transfer. It is most likely that the consideration shall be treated as the present fair value of the asset, and so duty shall be applicable to the consideration. For example, if receivables worth $100 are transferred by an instrument for which the purchaser pays $80, the duty is payable on $80.

What are the common ways to avoid the duty?

The following are commonly used devices to avoid stamp duty:

- Equitable assignment – the assignment is not perfected but is kept as an equitable assignment creating a trust between the assignor and assignee.
- Oral assignment – the duty being a duty on the instrument and not the transaction, so an oral agreement to assign would likely not be liable to the duty (see more below).
- Shifted jurisdiction – as stamp duty is applicable on the instrument, jurisdiction depends on the place where the instrument is executed. If the instrument is executed at a place where the duty is affordable or not applicable, the instrument will escape duty. For transactions taking place in the U.K., it is a common practice for documents to be signed in Ireland. One must, however, note the *differential duty provisions*, discussed below. These provisions, applicable in most cases, require payment of differential duty when the instrument executed outside the jurisdiction physically comes into the jurisdiction.
- Incompleted offer – another device commonly used when the assignor makes an offer to transfer, not completed by the assignee by acceptance, as legally, an acceptance is required for an agreement to be completed.
- Exempted transfers – in U.K. stamp law, for example, transfers to certain group entities and mortgages are exempt. There are exemptions in several other countries (see later). If the SPV can qualify as a group entity, the originator's document transferring the receivables may not come for duty. Amendments made in 2000 provide that intra-group relief will not be available if the seller can exercise voting control over the SPV. This condition directly clashes with accounting and regulatory requirements of independent SPVs; hence, it is unlikely that this exemption will be of any use in securitization transactions.

Can the duty be avoided by oral agreements?

Oral agreements can obviously not be stamped, as there is no instrument that can be stamped. To avoid stamp duty, however, one cannot envisage keeping the transaction completely undocumented as that would be chaotic. The solution is to have a post-facto document, in the nature of a record of a transaction that has taken place, evidencing whatever was agreed between the parties. The legal view is that such a recording document is not a document *by* which the transaction was effected, and so would not require stamping.

However, stamp laws of many jurisdictions define an "instrument" for stamping purposes as including an instrument that records or manifests a transaction. So, one must be careful using this defense.

Can the duty be applicable to agreements electronically signed and stored?

As discussed earlier, stamp law is antiquated law; it does not keep pace with present-day technological developments. If an agreement is electronically signed and stored, there is no application of stamp law, as stamps cannot be affixed on something that is intangible. Certain countries such as the U.K. have updated their stamp laws to provide for payment of stamp duty on electronic documents as well.

What is the duty applicable to revolving asset securilization?

A revolving asset securitization involves one document entered at present, under which there will be a regular substitution of assets over a period of time. Each time the existing assets becomes exhausted, new assets are transferred into the pool. A question arises as to whether such future transfer of receivables is also to be stamped. Going by the view that the duty is on the document, the duty is limited to the value of the assets transferred *by* the instrument, irrespective of transfers taking place in the future. Moody's in a special report entitled *An Overview of U.K. Stamp Duty and its Impact on U.K. Securitization Transactions* also concurred with this view, citing *Cory (Wm) & Son Ltd* v. *IRC* (1965) AC 1088.

What is the duty applicable to future receivables securitization?

Going by the view above, the duty is applicable only to the present transfer of receivables by the document, not future transfers.

Is the duty applicable to transfer of pass-through securities?

A pass-through certificate is pro-rated interest in receivables held by the SPV in trust. Hence, transfer of a pass-through certificate is only a transfer of beneficial interest or a re-alignment of the proportions in which beneficial interest is recorded by the SPV. There is no transfer of assets as the SPV continues to hold the receivables. Thus, there is no stamp duty applicable on transfer of pass-through certificates.

Moody's in the above document have opined that the grant of trust interest by the trustees by issue of notes is NOT a stampable transfer, as the trustees do not transfer any asset, but merely indicate beneficial interest. By the same ground, transfer of such notes is only a re-adjustment of beneficial interests, and will not, therefore, be liable to duty.

Is there any duty on issue of pass-through certificates?

Duty may be applicable on issuance of a bond or note, but no duty by way of a conveyance arises on issue of pass-through notes, for the reason mentioned above. The Moody's report cited above also agrees with this view.

Avoiding stamp duty by shifting jurisdiction

Stamp duty in most jurisdictions has a territorial basis; it is applicable at the place of execution of the instrument. For example, if duties are applicable in the U.K., they can be avoided by executing the agreement outside the U.K., say in Ireland or the Netherlands. In India, as stamp duty is a provincial issue and some states have reduced stamp duty on securitization, a securitization normally documented in a particular state would be shifted to a low-duty jurisdiction, say Maharashtra.

While the temptation to execute agreements in no-duty or low-duty jurisdictions is understandable, one has to appreciate the **differential duty provisions**.

Differential duty provisions are found in stamping laws of almost all jurisdictions. The differential duty provisions provide that where an instrument pertains to a property situated in the state or a matter or thing done or to be done in the state (here referred to as "the situs state"), and the agreement relating thereto is executed outside the state (referred to as "the agreement state"), then the agreement will be stampable in the situs state to differential duty, that is, the difference between the duty payable in the situs state over the duty paid in the agreement state, if the agreement physically comes to the situs state.

For example, if an agreement is executed in the Netherlands where it relates to a matter or things in the U.K., and after execution the agreement comes to the U.K., it will be charged to differential duty in the U.K.

In India, for instance, the reduction in stamp duty has been effected in Maharashtra, followed by some other states; for stamping cost reasons as well as logistical convenience, most securitizations are still entered in Maharashtra. If the assignment agreement is entered in the State of Maharashtra to avail the lower duty, does it take care of the problem to be faced in the situs state if the agreement enters that state? Note that the agreement may have to enter the situs state for several purposes, including the purpose of enforcement. The differential duty issue poses several questions:

- What is the situation of the "receivable," as the "situs state" for an assignment will be the state where the receivables are situated?
- What would be differential duty liability if the receivables are located in many states?

Situation of "receivables"

The agreement of assignment is evidently an agreement relating to a property and not an agreement for a matter or thing to be done. Therefore, the situation of the property will decide the right of the situs state to differential duty. It should be clear that what is being transferred by way of assignment is not an interest in the property of the originator or the securities held by him but an interest in the receivables. Therefore, what is not material is the location of physical assets; what is material is the location of the receivables. A debt arising out of a contract is deemed to be situated at a place where it is properly recoverable by action – generally at the place where the debtor resides. [Halsbury's Laws of England, Vol. 8, page 434]. Location of the residence of the debtor is obviously relevant only when the parties have not mutually agreed upon a place of payment. Where such a place has been agreed upon, that decides the location of the receivable. Hence, the place where the receivables are to be paid under the underlying agreements will be the place of location of the receivables.

Position for multi-state properties

The differential duty provisions of states contain no mechanism for applying the differential duty for multi-state location of properties. Assume that an assignment agreement relates to receivables in State X and in State Y, and is executed in Y to take benefit of lower duty. Now, if the agreement enters State X after execution, will it be liable to differential duty? If so, on how much, as the agreement relates to a composite property that has a multi-state location? As no machinery provision exists for applying differential duty in such cases, one is inclined to think that the provision will not be applicable. It is no premise in taxing statutes for the interpreter to supply provisions that do not exist, and so there is no rationale in thinking of any proportions in which the assets will be split. In fact, the intent of the differential duty provisions was basically anti-avoidance, and no avoidance intent exists in the present case as the agreement was executed in the state where the property existed, although in part.

Stamp duties on transfer of securities of the SPV

If the securities of the SPV are issued as certificates of beneficial interest, can such beneficial interest also be regarded as property, giving rise to a stamp duty on each transfer of the property?

Beneficial interest versus equitable interest

In legal parlance, the true nature of the interest of investors in the assets held by the SPV is not a beneficial interest but an equitable interest. This is true in case of securities of the SPV being beneficial interest certificates. There is often a wrong interchange of the terms "beneficial interest" and "equitable interest" and in common parlance, we tend to equate the two. Beneficial interest arises when one person holds a property *on behalf of* another. For example, A holds a property on behalf of B; B is the beneficial owner of the property and A is the legal or nominee owner. A's interest in the property is merely that of a nominee; A does not have any rights of his own but merely proxies for B. Equitable interest arises when A holds a property not on behalf of B, but *for the benefit of B*. That is, A is not a nominee for B; he holds the property in his own rights, but he does not have a right to derive a personal benefit out of the property

Box 23.10: Transfer
of investors' interest:
Stamping implications

- Nature of investors' interest in SPV assets is equitable interest, not beneficial interest.

- Equitable interest means ability to force the SPV to use assets for the benefit of investors.

- Equitable interest, strictly speaking, is not a property.

- Hence, transfer of interest by investors inter se should not require any stamping, as no property is transferred.

- This will not apply to debt securities issued by SPV, or in systems that regard equitable interest as property.

as he holds it for the benefit of B. In the first case A is the agent or nominee for B. In the second case, A is a trustee for B. In the first case B has beneficial interest in the property; B is the shadow owner and can compel A's discretion on the property. In the second case B is merely a *cestui que trust* and can only compel A to ensure that A does not derive any personal benefit from the property, but the beneficiary of an equitable estate cannot control the discretion of the trustee.

In eyes of law, a beneficial interest in property is a property in itself. But an equitable interest in a property is not a property in strict sense as there are no property rights that the beneficiary can exercise against the trustee except for proper execution of a trust. English law may have a different rule here; under English law, equitable rights are legally enforceable in courts of equity.

Legal nature of investors' right for securitizations

The SPV in securitization transactions holds receivables in its own right, and only declares a trust in favor of the investors. Therefore, it cannot be said that the SPV holds the receivables on behalf of the investors, but merely for the benefit of the investors. As such, any transfer of interest in an SPV by the investors would be a transfer of equitable interest and not beneficial interest.

Equitable interest in trust property is transferable; trust laws provide for such transfers. For example, sec. 58 of the Indian Trusts Act empowers a beneficiary of a trust to transfer his equitable interest.

Hence, in common law jurisdictions, transfer of investor's interest in securitization pools will not be regarded as transfer of property and should not require any stamping.

There are two notable exceptions to what is stated above:

- In many jurisdictions, the concept of a trust simply does not exist. Hence, there will be no distinction between a beneficial interest and equitable interest.

- In several securitization structures, the SPV issues debt securities, not beneficial interest certificates. These securities may be treated at par with other debt securities.

Stamp duty on securitization transactions: Indian case

This section is not only of direct relevance to the Indian market, but is of general interest as we review the Indian experience and draw lessons out of it that are applicable to any country that faces a similar problem.

Stamp duty on securitizations is a common feature of common law countries and the generic reasons and remedies have been discussed above. India is a common law country and requires stamping on conveyances. An agreement by which receivables are transferred is a legal requisite, so it will be treated as a conveyance and stamped.

Stamp duty in India is a provincial subject: each state imposes its own duties. All states without exception impose stamp duties on conveyance, the rate of duty varies from state to state. However, as an important source of revenue for state governments, the duty ranges from 5 to 16%.

Evidently, no securitization transaction can bear the brunt for this kind of duty; therefore, reduction of stamp duties on securitization is a regulatory aim.

Reduction of stamp duty by Maharashtra

The lead was taken by Maharashtra, a western Indian state that is economically one of the most advanced in the country, with its capital Mumbai being the country's financial capital.

Maharashtra took an inordinately welcome step and drastically cut down the rates of stamp duty on securitized instruments with effect from April 1994. The step was based on the realization that there was never intent to stamp such instruments to duty when the duty was originally thought of, and in any case, the basic documents creating the receivables have already been duly stamped. The state government accordingly brought down the rate of duty on securitization of receivables to 0.1% of the value securitized, from the ad valorem rate of 3% contained in the Act. The Notification to this effect, no. STP 1094/CR – 369/ (B) – M-1 dated May 11, 1994 reads:

"In exercise of the powers conferred by clause (a) of section 9 of the Bombay Stamp Act, 1958 (Bom. LX. of 1958), the Government of Maharashtra hereby reduced with effect from the 1st April, 1994 the duty with which an instrument of securitization of loans or of assignment of debt with underlying securities is chargeable under (a) of Article 25 of Schedule I to the said Act, to fifty paise for every Rs. 500 or part thereof of the loan securitized or debt assigned with underlying securities and in case of an instrument of assignment of receivables in respect of use of credit cards to two rupees and fifty paise for every rupees 500 or part thereof."

Other states follow

The example set by Maharashtra has been followed by a number of states; for example, Gujarat, Tamil Nadu, Karnataka and West Bengal have notified differential rates of stamp duty on securitization instruments.

Lessons from India

The Indian example of the taxmen in some states taking action in making securitizations possible has led to several lessons that may be of value, both to Indian legislators and those from other countries facing similar problems:

- Given the stamp duty incidence originally goes back to an era when securitization or factoring was non-existent, it simply fails to realize huge transactions in receivables as a common feature of the present-day financial world, and so if the government does not address the problem of stamp duty on transactions in receivables, securitization will simply not take place. Securitizations in India did not take place before 1994 or adopt a circuitous equitable assignment route.

- If the government has the power to waive or reduce duties by a basic legislative instrument, it should do so by using its legislative powers rather than administrative powers. For example, India is a typical case where stamp duty is a provincial revenue and is imposed by state governments. However, there is a federal control on the duty power – on certain instruments listed in the Constitution, the duties are not within the control of the states, although they are charged by the states. If the states merely exercise their provincial powers, it leads to a lopsided situation where some states would relax the duty and some would not, or some would not do so for some transactions.

  If India's central government saw a rationale to amend the Constitution to put securitization stamp duty outside the legislative powers of the state governments (as for negotiable instruments, shares and receipts), the present inter-state differences could have been avoided. Also, it would not have been necessary to get relaxation notifications from so many states, a major task. Right now some states have a reduced duty, which results in confusion.

  o The drafting of the notifications leaves a lot of scope for confusion. The Tamil Nadu notification takes a narrow scope, but the obvious intent of the Maharashtra and other state notifications was to grant a generic exemption to securitization transactions. However, there are at least some areas for confusion:

    - The Maharashtra notification refers to Article 25 (a) of the stamp schedule. This article relates to agreement for transfer of a movable property. As noted before, if a receivable secured by an immovable property is transferred, such an agreement is treated as transfer of an immovable property that may be covered by a different article. As the reference in the notification is to a particular article, it is doubtful whether it would even cover cases where transfer of mortgage loans is involved.

    - The notification refers to transfer of receivables with the underlying security. We have noted before that sec. 8 of the Transfer of Property Act provides that a transfer of a receivable will be accompanied by transfer of the underlying security. However, if the originator deliberately wants to transfer the receivable without transferring the security, the question is whether the relaxed duty under the notification will still be applicable. Except if one were to go by a very technical literal interpretation, the answer will be in the affirmative. The intent of the government could only have been to *allow* a transfer of receivables with the security, and not to *restrict* the same. The wording in the notification could only have been to make it clear that it covers transfer of securities as well. There is obviously no reason why the government should insist necessarily on a transfer of receivables with the security.

Stamp duty relaxations in other countries

Realizing that the imposition of a stamp tax on securitization transactions is not conducive for the transactions to take place, several countries have either exempted or substantially relaxed stamp duty requirements on securitization transactions.

Malaysia

Malaysia has exempted stamp duty on transactions of securitization where the transaction has been approved by the Securities Commission. The text of the exempting STAMP DUTY (EXEMPTION) (NO.6) ORDER 2000 is as under:

Citation and commencement
1. (1) this order may be cited as the Stamp Duty (exemption) (no. 6) order 2000
(2) This order shall be deemed to have come into operation on 30 October 1999.

Interpretation
2. For purposes of this order -
"Assets" means claims or securities or properties;
"Credit" enhancement in relation to an asset includes -
(a) The process of insuring risk associated with purchasing or funding of assets by means of securitization;
(b) Any other similar process related to purchasing or funding of assets by means of securitization;
"Securitization" means any arrangement approved by the Securities Commission for the funding or proposed funding of assets that have been or are to be provided by the holder or holders of those assets, by issuing bonds to investors and by which payments to investors in respect of the instruments or entitlements relating to such issuing of bonds are principally derived, directly or indirectly, from such assets;
"Special" purpose vehicle means any company incorporated in Malaysia that has been approved by the Securities Commission for the purpose of Securitization

Exemption
3. The instruments specified in the schedule executed on or after 30 October 1999, but not later than 31 December 2000 for the purpose of Securitization are exempted from stamp duty

SCHEDULE
(1) Any instrument that operates to transfer, convey, assign, vest, effect or complete a disposition of any legal or equitable right or interest in or title to, assets or charges or mortgages or other documents in relation thereto (referred in this schedule as "those rights"), to or in favor of a special purpose vehicle

(2) Any instrument that operates to effect charges, assignments trust deeds or any letters of guarantee or any other documents for the credit enhancement of the assets

(3) Any instrument that operates to transfer, convey, assign, effect or complete disposition of any of those rights in connection with the repurchase of those rights from the special purpose vehicle to or in favor of the person or persons from whose those rights were acquired for the purpose of securitization

Made 26 January 2000
on behalf and in the name of the Minister of Finance

Australia

Australia is another jurisdiction where transfer of actionable claims in many provinces is liable for steep duty. Relaxations have been given, as in New South Wales, where duty is not chargeable on MBS transactions. Section 282(3) of the Duties Act provides for exemption for:

(a) *the issue or making of a mortgage-backed security, or*
(b) *the transfer or assignment, of or other dealing with a mortgage backed security, or*
(c) *the discharge, cancellation or termination of a mortgage backed security.*

A mortgage-backed security has been defined as:

a) an interest in a trust that entitles the holder of or beneficial owner under the interest:

(i)   to the whole or any part of the rights or entitlements of a mortgagee and any other rights or entitlements in respect of a mortgage or any money payable by the mortgagor under the mortgage (whether the money is payable to the holder of or beneficial owner under the interest on the same terms and conditions as under the mortgage or not), or

(ii) to the whole or any part of the rights or entitlements of a mortgagee and any other rights or entitlements in respect of a pool of mortgages or any money payable by mortgagors under those mortgages (whether the money is payable to the holder of or beneficial owner under the interest on the same terms and conditions as under the mortgages or not), or

(iii) to payments that are derived substantially or, if the regulations prescribe the extent, to the prescribed extent, from the income or receipts of a pool of mortgages, and that may, in addition, entitle the holder or beneficial owner to a transfer or assignment of the mortgage or mortgages, or

b) a debt security (whether or not in writing) the payments under which by the person who issues or makes the debt security are derived substantially or, if the regulations prescribe the extent, to the prescribed extent, from the income or receipts of a pool of mortgages, or

c)   any of the following:

   (i)   an interest in a trust creating, conferring or comprising a right or interest (whether described as a unit, bond or otherwise) of or on a beneficiary in a scheme under which any profit or income in which the beneficiaries participate arises from the acquisition, holding, management or disposal of prescribed property, or any instrument that evidences such a right or interest;

   (ii)   a security (whether or not in writing) the payments under which by the person who issues or makes the security are derived substantially from the income or receipts of prescribed property;

   (iii) an interest in a trust, a debt security (whether or not in writing), an instrument or property that creates an interest in or charge over an interest in a trust, a debt security (whether or not in writing) or other instrument or property, to which paragraph (a) or (b) or subparagraph (i) or (ii) of this paragraph applies, but does not include an instrument or property comprising; or

d)   a mortgage; or
e)   the transfer of a mortgage; or
f)   a declaration of trust; or
g)   an instrument of a class or description of instruments, or property of a class or description of property, prescribed not to be a mortgage-backed security for the purposes of this definition.

Other countries

Ireland

Certain designated mortgages and assignment of interest in such mortgages is exempt from duty under sec. 15 of the Securitization (Proceeds of Certain Mortgages) Act, 1995. In addition, there is no stamp duty on issue or transfer of notes by SPVs.

Singapore

By way of notification dated June 28, 2005, the Monetary Authority of Singapore granted several exemptions to securitization SPVs. Included therein was the exemption from stamp duty on transfer of assets to "authorized" SPVs under section 74 of the Stamp Duties Act.

Secured loan structures

As mentioned, securitization structures have in some jurisdictions taken secured loan structures as well. In such cases, the SPV as the issuer of securities does not buy the assets – it simply gives a loan to the originator. The loan is backed by a security interest on the receivables as also the relevant properties that give rise to the receivables. In other words, all that would, in normal true sale cases, have been assigned by way of a sale to the SPV is here assigned by way of a mortgage or other admissible form of security interest.

As true sales generally appear to be difficult in continental European countries, and costly and cumbersome in the U.K., secured loan structures have increasingly been used in Europe.[22]

As for choosing between the secured loan structure and the true sale structure, the following factors are relevant:

- From the viewpoint of giving a predominant right over the assets, a true sale is a stronger method of conveyance. A true sale conveys absolute property in the asset, whereas a secured loan conveys only security interest. Creation of security interest, in countries that have efficient security interest laws, should allow the secured lender to have the right of sale of the secured property to recover the loan amount. The residual generally belongs to the borrower.[23] In fact, that is precisely what is required in securitization transactions, as investors are neither interested nor generally allowed to participate in the residual value of the assets.
- Secured loan structures are advisable only in countries that have firm security interest laws. A robust security interest should allow the secured lender the right, without judicial intervention, to assert a claim on the asset in the event of failure of the debtor to pay. Ideal security interest laws are automatically bankruptcy-remote, as the secured lender is allowed to enforce security interests outside of bankruptcy proceedings, or take foreclosure action before commencement of bankruptcy proceedings.
- Many countries allow, for secured loans, an enforcement or foreclosure only subject to judicial intervention. This might slow down the recovery of the asset, and in the event of the judicial authorities taking a view that is investor-adverse, the transaction might suffer.
- However, if the secured lender takes foreclosure action after the commencement of bankruptcy proceedings, there might be common provisions in bankruptcy laws that allow either parallel claims or prior claims over those of a secured lender, such as the interest of workmen, and agriculturists.
- The advantage in true sale structures is that a true sale, unless successfully challenged, vests the transferee with a predominant, clear right on the asset that is not subjected to any judicial intervention or bankruptcy interference. On the other hand, as the quintessence of a securitization transaction is funding, a secured loan transaction is less cumbersome and truer to its purpose. It does not lead to transformation of the role of the originator into a servicer, and therefore, retains the originator's transaction with the customers. In addition, a secured loan avoids all the typical problems associated with an absolute transfer such as stamp duties, fractional transfers and residual interests.

The U.K. is one of the countries where secured loan structures have worked well.[24] The method of securing the loan, with fixed and floating charges, was discussed in Chapter 14 on whole business securitization. There is no *true sale*, but there should be *true control* of the lender over the assets of interest. A true control would imply the ability of the lender to take preventive action – step in before the commencement of bankruptcy, or after commencement to be able to enforce the security interest outside of the bankruptcy. Notably, if true control is established, the rating of the transaction is not controlled by the rating of the transferor, although a loan is an obligation of the borrower. Sufficiently *asset-backed*, the securities will get an asset-backed rating.

In view of the increasing use of secured loan structures in Europe, rating agencies have issued specific legal criteria documents for the European market. For example, see *Standard & Poor's European Securitization Legal Criteria*, dated March 23, 2005.

Standard & Poor's expects that security interest creation in the secured loan structure will provide a functional equivalent of a true sale; in other words, the probability of the secured assets not being available for realization and repayment to investors is the same as is the permissible tolerance at the particular rating level. The rating agency investigates four issues to admit security interest as a functional equivalent – analysis of assets, enforceability of the security interest, true control and liquidity.

The asset analysis is the same as for true sale transactions.

The second issue is the enforceability of the security interest. Here, the efficiency of the security interest enforcement laws becomes critical. U.K. insolvency law, for example, allows a secured lender to enforce security interest even after the borrower has gone into insolvency. "Creditors who are fully secured are largely unaffected by the liquidation process. They can remove their security from the pool and realize it to satisfy what is due to them, accounting to the liquidator for any surplus."[25] However, there might be challenges to the security interest itself, a concern that needs to be evaluated based on the jurisdiction concerned. For example, in Germany secured loan transactions can be complicated by the legal rule that allows a liquidator to petition the court for return of "excess security." In other words, if a creditor or insolvency officer of the transferor can convince a court that the value of property provided as security for the loan was substantially in excess of the amount due, the excess can be released from the security package.

The third issue is one of true control. Control here means the priority of the SPV's interest over the secured asset over other claimants, and the ability to control its own conduct in such enforcement.

For priority, one needs to evaluate several possible circumstances due to which the SPV's interest over the secured assets may be questioned. There might be issues of conflicting, competing or overriding claims. For example, if the debtor has ceded pari passu or prior security interest over the asset, the security interest of the SPV may be subordinate or proportional. Possessory claims generally override non-possessory security interest; for example, for goods kept in a warehouse, the warehouse owner has a lien over the goods to the extent of his unpaid warehouse rentals.

Bankruptcy laws of many countries provide for preferential claims of certain classes of creditors, notably, wages of workers, pensions, tax claims and crown debts. In many cases, these claims may also arise due to several other laws; for example, tax statutes often entitle the authorities to attach the assets of the borrower to realize delinquent tax dues. This is where security interests and true sales differ; as the assets continue to be those of the corporate, there are possible conflicting or overriding claims that may arise by myriad statutes.

Distressed companies' protection legislation may also come in the way of enforcement of security interests. Many countries have laws to provide protection to entities to allow them to restructure or reorganize their businesses.

The institutional framework for enforcement of security interests may also be an issue. In many countries, self-help repossession may be possible, but some countries may provide for a certain agency to cause such enforcement. The costs of such an agency are deductible from the proceeds of the asset.

Will the secured lender have control over the timing and conduct of the enforcement of security interest? The insolvency laws of many countries require seeking the leave of the insolvency court before the secured lender does a self-help repossession. While seeking the leave may be a mere formality, it may cause delays and fetters.

The fourth issue is liquidity. While insolvency causes legal or practical delays in collection of the assets, the noteholders still need to be paid and so the transaction has to build sufficient liquidity (either a cash reserve or a liquidity facility) to use during such period.

Fixed and floating charges

U.K. corporate laws have a concept of fixed and floating charges; fixed charges mean a security interest over an ascertainable asset, while floating charges mean a security interest over a generic asset, generally working capital and the residual assets of an enterprise. Whether a charge is a fixed or floating charge depends not merely on the language of the security document but on whether the security interest holder had effective control over the asset in question.[26] Fixed charges have a priority over floating charges, but as floating charges can be enterprise-wide, the floating chargeholder has a special right to appoint "administrative receivers" under U.K. insolvency laws. The right as to appointment of administrative receivers was significantly curtailed by the Enterprise Act, but then capital market transactions have been excluded.

- The issuer should hold a first-priority, fixed charge over the assets of the transferor. Standard & Poor's will focus on whether the security package defeats the claims of existing or potential creditors of the transferor, including any preferential creditors. Considerable emphasis will be placed on first-priority, fixed security interests (which as a matter of English law rank ahead of all other creditors, including preferential creditors and holders of floating security). First-priority, fixed security interests should secure in full the principal and interest on the asset-backed securities.
- There are appropriate assets and adequate realization (cash flow security, not market value security). The assets over which the first-priority, fixed

security is granted by the transferor will be highly relevant and security over them, when realized, must be adequate to repay investors. A transaction that relies on the cash flow generated by the assets could default if forced to rely on the market value realized through the sale of assets. Where assets are receivables representing a known and certain income stream (including receivables expected to generate repayments for the secured loan), security over them should be realized through the transfer of the originator's rights in those assets to the issuer (and not a sale on the open market). True control is achievable under such a cash flow security as there should be little risk to full and timely payment. Where the security is over the transferor's real property assets, the administrative receiver may have to sell those assets to realize the security. A forced sale may mean that the security over the real assets, once realized, is insufficient to provide full payment to the investors. Under such a market value security, there is clearly a threat to true control. Standard & Poor's will focus on the security package in favor of the issuer to determine whether, and to what extent, it meets full payment concerns.

- There is a first-priority, floating charge over all the transferor's present and future assets not caught by the fixed charge (floating charge). The combination of floating charge and fixed charge (or the floating charge alone, if it is over substantially the whole of the originator's assets) is needed to block administration and appoint an administrative receiver. Under English law, secured creditors with lower priority than the issuer may appoint an administrative receiver in relation to the transferor. Theoretically, the issuer loses control (but not priority) over the enforcement of its security if another general charge is first to appoint an administrative receiver. From a rating perspective, if the secured loan transaction is properly structured, this risk may not necessarily lead to the conclusion that there is no control. For example, the fixed charge and floating charge mean that the issuer has priority over other existing secured creditors. Where there is no prospect of the issuer subordinating its security to existing or subsequent secured creditors, the issuer will usually be able to overreach the appointment of another administrative receiver by appointing its own. By doing so, this issuer also takes control of the transferor's charged assets. In so far as this involves additional cost to the issuer, Standard & Poor's will generally look for appropriate support in the structure.
- The balance between a fixed and floating security should be such that the floating charge is not primarily relied on to generate funds to repay investors. Floating charge holders do not have priority over preferential creditors (including employees and tax authorities). Further, a secured creditor's realization is always subject to equities, so that where, for example, valid general law set-off rights are exercised by a borrower against the transferor, the resulting reduction in the value of the security will be borne by the issuer. It is possible to cut short the build up of set-off rights in relation to assets secured by a fixed charge by giving notice of the charge to borrowers (in true sale structures the set-off risk may be similarly contained). Notice of floating charges does not cut short the build up of set-off risk, a risk that continues until the floating charge crystallizes.

- There is an agreement by the transferor not to create any further fixed or floating security over its assets that secure the secured loan structure or not to do so until any new secured creditor is party to an inter-creditor agreement giving priority to rated debt.

Secured loan structures vs. true sale structures

As the above analysis reveals, security interests have been used over centuries in both direct lending transactions and capital market transactions. Inefficiencies of the secured lending mechanism are evident over this long history – competing, conflicting or overriding claims. Sometimes, a statute may empower a claimant, typically a government authority, to freeze all assets of the corporate, putting the securitization transaction to a deadlock.

The essence of a securitization transaction is the rating arbitrage, which is justified by moving away a section of the assets of the corporate and protecting the same from all competing or conflicting claims. If a secured borrowing achieves such proofing, securitization is not required. At the same time, if a mere transfer of assets to a mythical entity called the SPV could immunize assets from all claims, then corporates would be free to move all except junk away from their generic balance sheets.

Therefore, one must understand the limitations of both the secured loan structure and the true sale structure. Ideally, laws should provide for on-balance sheet isolation; the assets staying with the corporate, but in a separate cell that is protected against all claims other than those of specific investors. True sales try to achieve that result, albeit by artificial separation into an artificial body called the SPV. The off-balance sheet treatment given to such transactions may not be desirable, but legal isolation is the spirit. However, given the fact that such legal isolation requires hiving off of assets to an entity that is admittedly a made-for-this-purpose parking place, such transactions must look like a sale to an arms-length independent buyer; this leads to all the rigmarole associated with true sales such as separation of the servicing function, establishment of a fair sale consideration and recapturing of the excess spread.

Secured loan structures, on the other hand, are much older, much simpler and much more easily understood by everyone concerned. Given the relative merits and demerits of the two methods, secured loan structures may be used where true sales are inconvenient, cumbersome or very costly. Also, there might be intermediate alternatives, such as creation of participation rights and declaration of trust, discussed earlier in this chapter.

Quite significantly, it may be noted that international accounting standard IAS 39 permits off-balance sheet treatment even in case of secured loan structures, subject to certain conditions. See the chapter on accounting issues later.

Legal issues in synthetic structures

Synthetic structures are discussed at length in another chapter on synthetic securitization. In synthetic structures, there is no sale of the asset in law, so there are no issues relating to true sale. The sale is only virtual, by way of a credit default swap transaction between the transferor and the transferee. Therefore, the only legal issues relate to the validity of a credit default swap. These issues are discussed at length in Vinod Kothari's *Credit Derivatives and Synthetic Securitization.*[27]

The legal structure of a synthetic transaction is as follows:

- The originator identifies the pool to be securitized.
- The SPV is set up/identified.
- The originator writes a credit default swap or a guarantee with the SPV whereby the SPV commits to make certain protection payments to compensate the originator for losses in the pool. The default swap might be triggered in relation to losses above a particular value; that is, there might be threshold risk that is absorbed by the originator himself.
- Detailed terms of the credit default swap should provide, among other things, (a) what will constitute a "credit event" for the purpose of making of claims by the originator; (b) how will the losses be computed for a credit event. In normal credit default swap transactions, the terms of the swap provide for physical settlement – the protection buyer transferring the defaulted asset to the protection seller and claiming the full par value of the asset from the protection seller. However, for SPV as a protection seller, it will be futile to provide for a physical settlement. Hence, the swap may provide for a cash settlement based on a certain valuation of the defaulted asset.
- The SPV, in turn, issues credit-linked notes (CLNs) to investors. The terms of the credit-linked notes provide that if there are losses in the asset pool above a threshold level requiring the SPV to make protection payments to the originator, the SPV will be entitled to write off the principal and/or interest accrued and payable to the investors.
- The SPV invests the collateral raised by the issue of the CLNs in specified investments.
- These investments, such as the cash assets of the SPV, are collateralized in favor of the trustees. The trustees hold the collateral for the benefit of (a) first, the originator, to the extent of the protection payments due to the originator; (b) then, the various classes of notes, in order of priority.

As there is no sale of assets for synthetic transactions, legal issues typical of true sales do not arise in synthetic securitizations. The originator enters into a credit default swap and buys protection. Briefly, the legal issues are:

- **Legality of a derivative:** In the jurisdiction concerned, is a derivative transaction legal? Derivatives are a big global business and their legality is generally not questionable, but there may be restrictions on the types of derivatives, or derivatives players, in different countries.
- **Credit default swap or a guarantee:** Is it proper for the originator to buy a hedge in the form of a credit default swap or a straight guarantee? A guarantee is a more traditional form of buying a hedge, but once again as guarantees have a long history, they have several preconditions and restrictions

inherent, most significantly that the claims of the protection buyer cannot exceed the actual losses suffered by him. Credit default swaps, on the other hand, are completely independent of the actual losses of the protection buyer. Once again, the legal principle will be substance over form; no matter what an instrument is called, its substance will define its legal character. If a transaction is documented as a credit default swap, but in fact merely seeks to compensate the protection buyer for actual losses suffered by him, then it is to be treated as a guarantee and will be subjected to all restrictions/preconditions applicable for a guarantee.

- **Definition of credit event and determination:** The most critical issue in a credit default swap is whether the credit event has been triggered. Generally, the parties will sign an ISDA-type credit default swap confirmation, but as credit events for balance sheet transactions may have to be tailored to suit requirements,[28] they may be defined uniquely. If the credit event has occurred, how is its determination done? For ISDA transactions, there might be reliance on "publicly available" sources of information, which, obviously, is unsuitable for balance sheet synthetic transactions. A typical method may be the originator serves notice of a credit event upon the trustees.

- **Valuation of defaulted assets:** As mentioned earlier, the usual method of protection payments for balance sheet transactions will be cash settlements, where the valuation of the assets may be required. The detailed method of who will do the valuation and on what basis will have to be laid down. Balance sheet synthetic transactions may also opt for "fixed recovery swaps" or "binary swaps" instead of the defaulted assets being valued, where the protection seller pays a pre-fixed amount to the protection buyer.

- **Structuring of the SPV:** The structuring of the SPV and the criteria to be satisfied by the SPV are the same as for any other securitization transaction (see below).

Bankruptcy-remote securitization

One of the basic aims in securitization is to ensure that the assets transferred to the SPV are not affected by any claims of or against the originator. In other words, the assets transferred to the SPV are the paramount property of the SPV with no claims of any other creditors. At the same time, the SPV should be a bankruptcy-remote entity. Therefore, the transaction is not affected by an entity risk other than the asset risk; that is, the obligors.

From this viewpoint, there are four basic steps to be taken:

- Perfection of legal interest in the SPV
- No prior claims of any person
- No consolidation of the SPV with the originator
- No clawback

Perfection of legal interest

Perfection of legal interest implies the creation of legal rights in the receivables in favor of the SPV. The legal procedures regarding assignment of receivables have been discussed earlier. Due care must be taken to ensure a transfer of legal interest to the SPV. If the local law imposes any requirement for perfection or filing, the same must be complied with.

If the securitization transaction has passed on legal interest in the receivables to the SPV, the liquidator of the originator in bankruptcy does not have any right against the receivables. This would be true even if the originator is assigned the role of collection. As collection or servicing agent, the originator has no better rights than those of a postman. Hence, the liquidator's rights will be limited to only such rights as the originator himself had.

Priority of claims

Priority means the supreme legal rights of the SPV on the assigned receivables. There are two inherent thoughts: (a) There should not be any existing claims against the assigned receivables, either of the obligor himself (such as a claim for set-off, waiver or cross-default) or on any other party (such as rights created in favor of other creditors already); and (b) there should not be any subsequent claims of any third party such as claims of workers of the originator and preferred creditors.

As far as pre-existing prior claims are concerned, the law provides that the transferor of any receivables transfers them with the same equities and disabilities existing at the time of transfer (this issue was discussed earlier). Any prior claims, set-off or other rights existing at the time of assignment would constrain the rights of the SPV.

If any prior rights existed at the time of assignment, those would also affect the predominant rights of the SPV. For example, if any tax claim, claim of a creditor or a security interest in a specific receivable exists at the time of assignment, the SPV would acquire the same subject to such a pre-existing right.

A usual situation finds the originator with outstanding loans where the lenders have security interest in *all present and future assets* of the originator. In law, a general security interest such as a charge over all present and future assets is a floating charge, and a **floating charge** is vacated when the asset is sold. However, if the lender's interest was a **fixed charge,** the SPV would be affected by such a charge.

> **Box 23.11: Four potential threats to rights of SPV/investors**
>
> - Transfer of interest by originator was not legally perfect, or was not a "true sale."
>
> - Transfer of interest was a true sale, but is subject to overriding, prior claims that are transmitted to the SPV.
>
> - Transfer of interest was a true sale, but the SPV holding such interest is treated as substantively a subset of the originator, clubbing the assets and obligations of the two.
>
> - The transfer was a transfer in anticipation of originator bankruptcy, and so is voided by court.

Next is the question of subsequent prior claims on the assets of the originator. There are the usual statutory preferential claims in winding up, which are either dues to the state or dues of workers that are treated as preferred claims; they take priority over claims of all secured creditors. For example, refer to sec. 529, 529A and 530 of the Indian Companies Act. However, none of these rights to preferential payments shall affect the SPV holding legal rights in receivables, as the receivables already stand transferred to the SPV and have since become the property of the SPV.

Protecting against consolidation

Consolidation, lifting or piercing the corporate veil refer to the right of judicial or other authorities to disregard the veil of separate legal entities that dissociates the originator from the SPV, treating the two as one. In other words, it means the aggregation of the assets of the SPV with those of the originator. This is possible if the judicial authority comes to a reckoning that the creation of a separate legal entity in the form of the SPV was merely an arrangement or colorable device, that the SPV is only an alter ego for the originator, and that the whole scheme is not to be given any legal effect.

See a later heading for more about consolidation.

Protecting against clawback

Clawback refers to legal provisions that entitle an authority, normally in cases dealing with bankruptcy, to treat any transfer of assets, even those legally made, as void and so can claw back or reclaim the assets already transferred. Such claw-back provisions are normally applicable to a company in bankruptcy.

This bankruptcy rule is called a **rule to avoid transfers in contemplation of bankruptcy**. The underlying rationale is that certain transfers if made immediately before bankruptcy of an entity will be regarded as transfers made in contemplation of bankruptcy, a fraudulent preference, and will be avoided or held illegal.

Take, for instance, sec. 53/54 of the Indian Provincial Insolvency Act, 1920 and sec. 55/56 of the Presidential Towns Insolvency Act, 1909. Similar clawback provisions exist in insolvency laws of most countries, for example, sec. 588FG of the Australian Corporations Act.

Section 53 of the Provincial Insolvency Act provides that any transfer of property made may be annulled by the court if the transferor is adjudged insolvent within two years after the date of such transfer. An exception is made for "transfers in good faith and for valuable consideration." The power is a discretion vested with the court.

The effect of the above provision is not to make mandatory the voiding of transfers made two years prior to bankruptcy, so transfers made in "good faith" are protected and securitization deals would not be killed by sec. 53, even if the originator files for bankruptcy soon after the assignment. But good faith, like beauty, lies in the eyes of the beholder, and so one must be particularly careful for securitizations made by distressed or potentially distressed companies.

Structuring the SPV

Securitization structures mostly employ a special purpose vehicle for the purpose of holding title to the receivables, receiving and passing through incomes. It may be noted that SPVs are normally not needed for factoring, which largely use the same methodology.

The concept of SPVs is not limited to securitization transactions. These vehicles are used for several other purposes too, such as project finance and synthetic leases. Special purpose entities came under sharp focus after the bankruptcy of Enron, which had overused the SPV device for several motives that were understandably ulterior.[29] In the realm of securitization, SPVs are used not merely for issuing securities, but also for creating a loan, holding a credit derivative, intermediary SPVs and holding real estate. In conduit transactions, there are SPVs at each level where a pool is acquired and transferred to the pool.

Why an SPV?

It is easy to appreciate that in securitization transactions a transfer of receivables is one of the basic objectives; if the originator were to create the securities himself, the basic purpose of bankruptcy remoteness will be lost.

The SPV is brought in as an intermediary to hold the receivables that the originator transfers.

The role of the SPV is essentially to serve as a conduit between the multifarious investors and the single/multiple originators. If there was one originator and a single purchaser of the receivables, the SPV was not required; this emphasizes the point that the essential role of the SPV is to legally facilitate the transaction by enabling various investors to participate in a pool of receivables without legally breaking up the pool into many holdings of each investor. In other words, the SPV is like a body corporate (not necessarily incorporated); the investors hold an undivided interest in the SPV and the SPV in turn holds interest in the pool of receivables. No investor is a direct legal owner of the pool; the investors are, however, beneficial owners of the undivided pool and collectively become the beneficial owner of the whole of the receivables.

Legal considerations

The structuring and constitutional documents for the SPV are largely a legal issue. The issue is important from the viewpoint of defining:

- the mode and ease of formation of the SPV;
- ensuring its existence only for a specific purpose and limiting the scope of its activities;
- limiting the existence of the SPV only until the satisfaction of the securitization transaction;
- ensuring that fiduciary responsibilities will be applicable to those in charge of the SPV;

- ensuring that the SPV can hold properties in its own name/in the name of an agent, and can without much difficulty file legal suits and protect its property rights;
- ensuring the tax transparency of the SPV – the tax applicable on the SPV does not lead to any duplication of taxes with that applicable to investors;
- ensuring that the SPV holds the receivables in its own right, and thus would not be affected by the obligations of the originator;
- ensuring that the SPV is not treated as a subset of the originator so that the assets/liabilities of the originator are merged with those of the SPV.

The organizational form of the SPV, therefore, depends on the local jurisdiction as to which form effectively serves all the above objectives.

Organizational forms of SPVs

The organizational forms of SPVs differ from country to country and the choice may be influenced by purely local factors. There is no clear reason to favor one form over another across countries.

Essentially, the following organizational forms of SPVs are prevalent:

1. A single purpose company
2. Trust
3. Limited partnership
4. LLCs
5. Special forms

Corporations

Corporations are the most commonly used form of a legal vehicle in present times. Most countries have a fairly easily understandable system of incorporation, recognition and administration of corporations or companies. Therefore, this type of legal vehicle may be quite easy to use. However, in many countries, the choice of the corporate form would be limited by the difficulties in forming a company, required minimum capital and costs in forming, and more importantly, the ease in winding up the company after formation.

Trusts

A trust is a great gift of English jurisprudence and trusts as an organizational concept is much older than companies. Before incorporation of companies began, the concept of an unregistered company was formed on a deed of settlement, wherein the directors of the company were trustees, and the company was a trust. Foundations of modern corporate law are embedded in the trust principles. The concept of trusts exists in most jurisdictions, while it is not necessary to have a specific law on formation of trusts, as trusts are more a concept than an organizational form.

What is a trust?

A common misnomer is to look at a trust as an entity. A trust is not a legal entity. There is no such body or entity named a trust; a trust is simply the confidence reposed in the trustees to hold a property. A trust comes into existence when a property is transferred to someone (trustee) to hold for the benefit of someone else (beneficiary). The obligation to hold the trust property for the benefit of the beneficiary is the trust. A property being transferred to the trustee is essential for a trust to come into existence.

A trust is not a separate entity; the trustee is the entity that runs a trust. All property belonging to the trust is held in the name of the trustees.

While a trust is not a *separate legal entity*, it is nevertheless a *separate legal property* as legal provisions provide a safeguard against the property held by the trustee being commingled with that of either the trustee or someone else.

Trusts and securitization

Barring specific local issues, trusts are a very convenient mode of organizational entity for securitization transactions. Trusts are very easy to form; they are formed by mere transfer of property to be held in trust or by mere declaration that the property will be held in trust. They are very easily demolished; a trust is extinguished when the purpose of the trust is satisfied. A trust is not a creation of law, so it does not require any elaborate formalities for its formation or extinction.

In addition, unless the SPV issues a debt instrument, the real relationship between the SPV and investors is that of a trust. The SPV is the fiduciary and the investors are the beneficial owners of the property. So, even if the SPV is permanently organized as a company, it acts as a trustee in relation to the investors.

Analogous to provisions against winding up of companies (see the section on constitutional documents of SPVs), in case of trusts, the trust must be irrevocable.

LLCs

The concept of a limited liability company requires specific legislation; for example, each of the states in the U.S. has enacted LLC legislation. It is the intermediary between a company and a partnership. The advantage of LLCs is that under tax laws, they enjoy the tax transparency (or freedom from double taxation) as applicable to partnerships, while they can still enjoy limited liability. LLCs are therefore, essentially, limited liability partnerships. LLCs are very commonly used in securitization transactions.

Special forms

Certain countries have introduced specific forms of organization for securitization transactions. For example, the French law has a concept of *Fondos* that runs securitization transactions. Protected cell company legislation has been enacted by some countries that make it possible to have one entity with several cells, each cell containing protected assets and liabilities.

Bankruptcy remoteness of SPVs

What makes the SPV bankruptcy-remote? In law, there can be no guarantee that an entity will not become bankrupt. There is no guarantee of immortality as well. It is the structure and the scope of operations of the SPV that reduces the chances of bankruptcy or premature mortality of the SPV to remoteness; therefore, it is called a bankruptcy-remote entity. It is not a *bankruptcy-proof* body.

One who rides a horse might fall, one who crawls cannot. A king may become a pauper, a pauper cannot become bankrupt. An SPV is an entity without substance, without profits, losses, liabilities or net worth. It does not have net worth beyond the bare minimum required to come into existence as a vehicle; it does not need any such net worth as by its schematics it is prohibited from taking any risks or losses. It does not have any creditors other than the investors who bought its securities; those investors will not have any temptation to file for bankruptcy or winding up the SPV as it has nothing more than the assets that it holds beneficially or in trust for those very investors. As it is a body without wealth, it is without worries. It is, so to say, *pre-pauperized*, and so bankruptcy-remote.

Another precondition of bankruptcy remoteness is that the chances of consolidation of the SPV with the originator or any other substantial interest holder must be ruled out. This is ensured by structuring the SPV as an independent.

Conditions for bankruptcy remoteness

Rating agencies have over time developed criteria for bankruptcy remoteness. The essential basis in rating an asset-backed security on the strength of the assets and not the issuer is the fact that the issuer is a non-issue, or a non-substantive entity and no more than a stand-alone, ever-staying bundle of assets. This is the concept of bankruptcy remoteness of SPVs; as the special purpose vehicle is unlikely to go into bankruptcy, the rating need not be concerned with the credit of the issuer. The conditions of bankruptcy remoteness are discussed below:[30]

Restriction on objects and powers

The fundamental SPE characteristic is that the entity's objects and powers be restricted as closely as possible to the bare activities necessary to effect the transaction. The purpose of this restriction is to reduce the SPE's risk of insolvency due to claims created by activities unrelated to securitized assets and the issuance of the rated securities.

Rating agencies require that the organic documents of the entity constrain the SPE to those activities needed to ensure sufficiency of cash flow to pay the rated securities. The organic documents are the preferred locus for this constraint for two reasons: These documents are publicly available and provide some measure of public notice of the restriction, rather than merely notice to the parties to a particular transaction; an organic restriction is less likely to become lost in the organizational files and more likely to remind the management of the SPE to act in accordance with its charter. Where possible, this limited objects clause, as well as other SPE criteria, should also be in covenants with the appropriate transaction documents (deed of trust).

In brief, the SPE should not engage in unrelated business activities.

Debt limitations

An SPE should be restricted from incurring additional indebtedness except in cases where such indebtedness would not affect the rating on its *existing* indebtedness. An existing rating could be affected if holders of the additional indebtedness have an incentive to file the SPE to gain access to the SPE's cash flow and assets. Therefore, additional indebtedness either expressly subordinated to, or rated the same as, existing indebtedness should not in principle affect the rating of existing indebtedness. Additional indebtedness includes any monetary obligation or other obligation that may involve the payment of money, such as covenants by the SPE to remove liens and indemnify.

Non-petition agreement

Rating agencies generally require a non-petition language in any agreement between the SPE and its business creditors whereby the creditors agree not to file the SPE into bankruptcy and not to join in any bankruptcy filing. These creditors include those who render services to the SPE as auditors and trustees.

The independent director

An SPE acts through its board of directors, general partner, management committee or managing member. For a corporation, business is conducted under the direction supervision of the board, although day-to-day management of the corporation is generally delegated by the board to the corporate officers. The directors are elected by the shareholders, the corporation's owners. Major decisions possibly taken by the board include filing the corporation into bankruptcy, and so it is this concern that is behind the request for an "independent director" in respect of corporate SPEs or the equivalent for other forms of SPEs.

In many structured transactions, the SPE is sought to be established by a non-SPE operating entity parent. This parent may, at times, be unrated or have an issuer credit rating below the issue credit rating of its subsidiary debt. Moreover, the directors of the parent may well serve as the directors for the subsidiary. Interlocking directorates present a potential conflict of interest. If the parent becomes insolvent, although the subsidiary is meeting its debt and is otherwise in a satisfactory financial state, there may be an incentive for the parent to cause the subsidiary to "voluntarily" file for bankruptcy, thus paving the way for a consolidation of its assets with the parent. However, if the subsidiary has at least one director independent from the parent and this director's vote is required in any board action seeking bankruptcy protection for the subsidiary or the amendment of its organic documents, the subsidiary may be less likely to voluntarily file an insolvency petition.

Accordingly, rating agencies require organic documents of an entity seeking to be considered an SPE to recite that in voting on bankruptcy matters an independent director would take into account the interests of the holders of the rated securities.

No merger or reorganization

This requirement attempts to ensure that while the rated securities are outstanding the bankruptcy-remote status of the SPE will not be undermined by any merger or consolidation with a non-SPE or any reorganization, dissolution, liquidation or asset sale. Rating agencies generally also require that the SPE not amend its organizational documents without prior written notice to the agency. Should the issuer credit rating of the merged or consolidated entity be lower than the rated obligations, the rating on the SPE's obligations may be adversely affected.

Separateness covenants

Separateness covenants are designed to ensure that the SPE holds itself out to the world as an independent entity; this follows the theory that if the entity does not act as if it has independent existence, a court may use principles of piercing the corporate veil, alter ego, or substantive consolidation to bring the SPE and its assets into the parent's bankruptcy proceeding. The involvement of an overreaching parent is a threat to the independent existence of the SPE. "Piercing the corporate veil" is the remedy exercised by a court when a controlling entity, such as the parent of an SPE, so disregards the separate identity of the SPE that their enterprises are seen as effectively commingled. The remedy can be sought, by creditors with claims against an insolvent parent who believe funds can be properly traced to the subsidiary. The "alter ego" theory is used when the subsidiary is a mere shell and all its activities are in fact conducted by the parent.

Substantive consolidation is discussed later in this chapter.

An important element of rating agencies' bankruptcy-remote analysis is the existence of legal comfort that the SPE would not be substantively consolidated with its parent. In this regard, the entity should observe certain separateness covenants. These covenants, as listed by Standard & Poor's[31] are:

- To maintain books and records separate from any other person or entity;
- To maintain its accounts separate from those of any other person or entity;

- Not to commingle assets with those of any other entity;
- To conduct its own business in its own name;
- To maintain separate financial statements;
- To pay its own liabilities out of its own funds;
- To observe all corporate, partnership or LLC formalities and other formalities required by the organic documents;
- To maintain an arm's-length relationship with its affiliates;
- To pay the salaries of its own employees and maintain a sufficient number of employees in light of its contemplated business operations;
- Not to guarantee or become obligated for the debts of any other entity or hold out its credit as being available to satisfy the obligations of others;
- Not to acquire obligations or securities of its partners, members or shareholders;
- To allocate fairly and reasonably any overhead for shared office space;
- To use separate stationery, invoices and checks;
- Not to pledge its assets for the benefit of any other entity or make any loans or advances to any entity;
- To hold itself out as a separate entity;
- To correct any known misunderstanding regarding its separate identity; and
- To maintain adequate capital in light of its contemplated business operations.

No free-floating assets, no net worth

A requirement of bankruptcy remoteness is that the SPE either beneficially conveys all assets to the investor (as for pass-through certificates) or grants a security interest over all its assets for the benefit of the noteholders. The purpose of this general security interest is primarily to diminish the incentives for any potential third-party creditor to seek to initiate insolvency proceedings against the SPE. To the extent that there are no free-floating and available assets for such a creditor to seize or share in, the likelihood of such an action is reduced.

Generally speaking, SPVs should be restricted to only financial assets and not real assets. In other words, the SPV should not own or lease real estate. In certain CMBS transactions, the SPV is made to own properties. If the SPV owns properties, clearly it has a net wealth because the property generally has value exceeding the outstanding amount of notes. This is usually taken care of by a seller's interest, such that the excess of the property value over outstanding amount of notes belongs to the seller.

Limitations in constitutional documents

The organic documents of the SPV, whether corporation (memorandum and articles of association) or trust (trust deed), must limit its objects and powers. This and other restrictions required for bankruptcy-remote SPVs (see later in this chapter) should be found in the constitutional documents.

The following limitations should be imposed in the constitutional documents to make the SPV bankruptcy remote:

- The company's purpose should be limited. The purpose will depend on the function of the SPV. Issuer SPVs will have the purpose of acquiring the assets of the originator, issuing securities and all ancillary functions.
- The company's ability to incur indebtedness should be limited. The nature of the limitation will depend on the limited liability company's role in the transaction.
- The company should be prohibited from engaging in any dissolution, liquidation, consolidation, merger or asset sale and amendment of its articles of organization as long as the rated obligations are outstanding.
- The company must have an independent director. Preferably, the majority of the Board must be independent.
- The unanimous consent of the independent directors and members should be required to (i) file, or consent to the filing of, a bankruptcy or insolvency petition or otherwise institute insolvency proceedings; (ii) dissolve, liquidate, consolidate, merge or sell all or substantially all of the assets of the corporation; (iii) engage in any other business activity; and (iv) amend the company's organizational documents.
- The company should agree to observe the "Separateness Covenants" (see above).

Ownership structure of the SPV

The ownership structure of the SPV is important from the viewpoint of the originator's control over winding up of the SPV, consolidation risk and a number of regulatory purposes. Hence, it has become a significant issue in present-day securitizations.

Typically, the ownership capital of SPVs is a nominal amount. This amount is declared by the holder to be held for public charitable purposes. As the beneficial interest is the holding, once diffused there is no clear beneficial owner of the SPV, which becomes an *orphan company*.

Even where there are identifiable owners of the SPV, it must be ensured that the SPV does not become the subsidiary or affiliate of any person, leading to questions on its independence.

Multi-use SPVs

As the SPV is a *special purpose* entity, does the purpose – to be special purpose – have to be limited to a single securitization transaction? In other words, can there be one SPV, the holder of assets of various transactions, with various sets of investors?

The easiest answer to this question is based on whether the assets belonging to different series of investors may be kept mutually segregated. In general, all assets of a company belong to all investors and all creditors and there are no "pools" or subsets within a company. However, an SPV may hold out to be a trustee for various series of investors, in which case each such pool of assets will be distinguished by different trust formations.

The other way to ensure a multi-use SPV is to build terms in the issuance of the securities of each scheme that each scheme is non-recourse as far as the general assets of the SPV are concerned, as well as the assets of various other schemes.

Consolidation of the SPV

One of the perceived threats to securitization structure is the possibility that a court, tax authority or other agency would treat the SPV and the originator as one. The very essence of securitization, it may be noted, is to decompose the company, break and take away its assets into a separate entity that has legal rights of its own over the properties transferred to it. If consolidation of the assets of the SPV is done with those of the originator, it would amount to a nullification of the process of securitization. The true sale will lose its meaning if a consolidation takes place, as one cannot be making a true sale to oneself.

Meaning of equitable consolidation

The action of a judicial or other authority in treating the SPV and the originator as the same is called **lifting or piercing the veil of legal entity**; this concept allows an authority to lift the veil of separate legal entity that separates the SPV from the originator, treating the two as one. This doctrine is also called **the doctrine of substantive consolidation**.

In most countries, courts have a power to consolidate two entities and treat them as one. The U.S. Bankruptcy Code [sec.105] provides for such inherent power. Consolidation is essentially a matter of judicial discretion, so circumstances that may increase the likelihood of the substantive consolidation of separate entities include the following: (1) creditors having dealt with the separate entities as a single economic unit in extending credit, (2) fraudulent transfers of assets among the separate entities, (3) extreme entanglement of the affairs of the separate entities, and (4) disregard of the distinct legal identities of the separate entities. See generally *Collier on Bankruptcy* ¶100.06; *In re Augie/Restivo Baking Co.*, 860 F.2d 515 (2d Cir. 1988); *Fish* v. *East*, 114 F.2d 177 (10th Cir. 1940); *In re Vecco Construction Industries*, 4 B.R. 407 (Bankr. E.D.Va. 1980).

General principles of consolidation

Consolidation or lifting the corporate veil is the determination by the court that entities separated by the mere cloak of incorporation should be treated as one. This implies the court regards the separateness of the entity as a myth. Some general tests were developed to use such an approach in the U.S. case of *Fish* v. *East*:

- The parent owns all or a majority of the capital stock of the subsidiary;
- There are common directors and officers;
- The parent corporation finances the subsidiary;
- The parent corporation is responsible for incorporation of the subsidiary;
- The subsidiary has grossly inadequate capital;
- The parent company pays the salaries or expenses or losses of the subsidiary;
- The subsidiary has no independent business from the parent;
- The subsidiary is commonly referred to as a subsidiary or as a department or a division of the parent;
- Directors and executive officers of the subsidiary do not act independently but take direction from the parent; and
- The formal legal requirements of the subsidiary as a separate and independent corporation are not observed.

Buckhead America ruling

On first viewing, it seems unlikely that a proper case of securitization would be reversed by substantive consolidation. But the short history of securitization has already seen one case where a securitization SPV has been consolidated with the originator: *In re Buckhead America Corporation* 161 B.R. 11 (Bankr. D. Del. 1993).

In this case, Days Inn of America, a motel franchiser, transferred its franchise fee receivables along with its trademark and related goodwill to an SPV called Days Inn Receivables Funding Corp. The SPV issued US$155 million in notes secured by franchise fee receivables. Soon after this transaction, rated by S&P as BB+, the originator filed for bankruptcy. The originator's administrator received a comprehensive offer for its total business; to reacquire its franchise rights that stood transferred to the SPV, the originator took the SPV also to bankruptcy. This was done despite the usual protection against SPV bankruptcy, such as the existence of an independent director and a clause in the constitutional documents requiring consent of all directors for bankruptcy application.

The bankruptcy court ordered the consolidation of the originator with the SPV.

It appears that in this case, the investors in the SPV were themselves inclined to have the SPV consolidated, and this was one of the reasons cited in the ruling for consolidation. However, the ruling set up a precedent that pushed the U.S. securitization industry into building additional walls of protection against SPV consolidation.

Kingston Square

There was another case where the originator himself, along with the investors and professionals, orchestrated involuntary winding up proceedings against the SPVs and finally succeeded in doing so: *In re Kingston Square Associates*, 1997 WL 594707; 214 B.R. 713 (Bankr. S.D.N.Y. 1997). The facts of this are peculiar to the case and had a lot to do with the role of the independent director, who the Court held was not "independent."

LTV Steel

The LTV Steel case, noted earlier, was also essentially a case for consolidation, pleading that the SPV and the originator were in fact the same commercial entity.

Legal rights of the investor: Legal nature of the investor's right

One of the important legal issues in securitization, from the viewpoint of the investor, is the nature and scope of the rights of the investors. This can have several sub-questions:

- What are the rights the investor can have against the originator?
- What are the rights of the investor against the SPV?
- What are the rights of the investor against the obligor?
- What are the rights of the investor as holder of "security"?

Investor's rights against the originator

In securitization transactions, the originator transfers assets to the SPV, which in turn issues securities to the investors or issues beneficial interest certificates to the investors. The originator has only such obligations to the SPV as are expressly contained in the documentation between them. Normally, there are warranties relating to the assets being transferred, but these warranties relate to any deficiencies in the assets as existing at the time of the transfer. Subsequent thereto, the originator may be liable for recourse expressly under-taken by him.

Legal relation between the originator and the investors is shielded by SPV. The SPV could be a trust or a company. If it is a trust, the investor is merely a participant or beneficiary in the trust, and so does not have any legal rights against the originator. If it is a corporation, the investor merely holds the securities of the corporation – in either case, having no direct rights against the originator.

Therefore, even if the SPV has any rights against the originator, such rights are exercisable by or in the name of the SPV, not by the investor directly. It may also be noted that the investor holding fractional interest in the assets held by the SPV cannot take any action against the originator in his own name.

Investor's rights against the SPV

The SPV stands in a fiduciary capacity as against the investors. It is holding the assets transferred to it in trust for, and for the benefit of, the investors.

Though it holds the receivables in its own name, it holds the same for benefit of the investors.

The legal rights of the investor against the SPV depend on the structure of the SPV as a trust or corporation.

If the SPV is organized as a trust, the investor is a beneficiary of the trust. The legal rights are those arising out of the Trusts law and the rich tradition of law of trusts. If the SPV is a corporate, normally the securities will be issued as bonds: therefore, the rights will be the same as those of a bond-holder under corporate laws and further as contained in the terms of issue of the bonds.

If one were to take the Indian Trusts law as a common law model of trust statutes, in case the SPV is a trust, the beneficiary has the following rights:

- Right to the rents and profits, that is, right to receive a share of income from the trust – sec 55.
- Right to specific execution – that is, right to force the trustee to carry out the provisions of the trust deed – sec 56.
- Right to inspect and take copies of the trust deed, accounts and vouchers of the trust – this is a very significant right. Note that in case of companies, even shareholders do not have the right to inspect the books of account of the company. – Sec. 57.
- Right to transfer beneficial interest. This section clearly provides for trans-fer of beneficial interest. This provides for an unlimited right to transfer the beneficial interest in the SPV – sec. 58
- Right to sue for the execution of the trust – sec. 59
- Right to proper trustees. The beneficiary has right to ensure that proper trustees are appointed to manage the trust. Certain persons are disquali-fied from being appointed as trustee, such as a person domiciled abroad, an alien enemy, a person having an interest inconsistent with that of the beneficiary, a person in insolvent circumstances, and, unless the personal law of the beneficiary allows otherwise, a married woman and a minor. Besides, there is a very important provision in the section which provides that if the trust relates to management of money, there will be at least two trustees. Needless to elaborate, the management of the SPV does relate to money: therefore, it is necessary for the SPV to have at least two trustees. – Sec. 60
- Right to compel the trustee to do his duty – sec. 61.

Most significantly, as the trust deed will invariably provide that the SPV will take appropriate action against the obligor/originator for delinquencies, the beneficiary can force, through court action, the SPV to take steps to recover delinquent sums.

The SPV owes fiduciary duty to the beneficiary. The SPV may be controlled by the originators; in such cases, the trustees looking after the SPV have an onerous duty of unrivaled loyalty towards the beneficiaries. For breach of faith or dereliction of duty, the trustees may be liable personally.

Investor's rights against the obligors

Here again, the legal relation between the obligors and the beneficiaries is that of the latter beneficial owner of the trust interest. Any action against the obligors can be taken only by the SPV and not by the beneficiaries. Of course, the beneficiaries may force the SPV to take steps against the obligors.

Investor's rights as holders of "security"

Can the investors claim any rights or relief as investors in a "security"? The answer to this question depends on the definition of "security" under the relevant law.

This has obviously to depend on the meaning of the term "security" under the relevant securities legislation. If the SPV issues bonds or notes, they surely are securities. If the SPV issues pass-through certificates indicating beneficial interest in the assets of the SPV, the issue whether such paper is a security or not has to depend on the local law.

If the SPV is a trust and the note issued by the SPV is a beneficial interest in the SPV's property, it is hard to treat such investment as a security as it is akin to an interest in a commonly owned estate. The following ruling from a U.S. circuit court is relevant in this context:

In particular circumstances, it may be held that mere creation of beneficial interest by the SPV does not amount to issue of securities. In *Steinhardt Group Inc.* v. *Citicorp* 96-7757 (U.S. Ct. App. 3rd Cir.) September 12, 1997, a bank created a securitization transaction to remove non-performing assets from its books. The bank created a limited partnership ("Bristol") to issue debt and equity securities to investors. Another limited partnership ("Steinhardt") was to hold over 98% of the interest of Bristol. Specifically, the transaction involved the securitization of a pool of delinquent residential mortgage loans and real estate owned as a result of foreclosed loans. After obtaining title, Bristol was to obtain bridge financing from the bank to underwrite a public offering. Steinhardt agreed to an equity contribution in Bristol, but later sued the bank alleging that the bank knew that several assumptions underlying its pricing model were false, and that it concealed information from Steinhardt, causing the assets to be overvalued. The District Court granted the bank's motion to dismiss, holding that Steinhardt's investment in Bristol did not constitute an "investment contract" under federal securities law because a common enterprise was not established. Steinhardt appealed, claiming that the securitization transaction was an "investment contract" within the meaning of the Securities Act of 1933.

To receive protection as an investor under the Securities Act, it must first be demonstrated that the instrument used was a "security," as defined. The Act specifically enumerates certain security instruments and also contains a catchall category of "investment contracts." The U.S. Supreme Court has interpreted an "investment contract" to require: (1) an investment of money, (2) in a common enterprise, (3) with profits to come solely from the efforts of others. *SEC* v. *W. J. Howey*, 328 U.S. 293 (1946). The Third Circuit Court found the first test was met by Steinhardt. The Court then moved to the third prong, which requires that the investment be made for a profit and that the investor not had more than minimal control over the performance of the investment. The court found that Steinhardt had veto power over any material action taken by Bristol, could remove general partners without notice, and had other significant rights and powers. Such substantial control meant that the instrument underlying the transaction was not a security and therefore, the transaction received no protection under the Act. The Third Circuit concluded that where a limited partner retains such pervasive control over its investment in a limited partnership, that it cannot be deemed a passive investor, the transaction does not constitute an investment contract and so a security. Accordingly, dismissal of Steinhardt's claim was appropriate.

Issuance of asset-backed securities is clearly covered by the SEC's regulatory regime, and recently the U.S. SEC has come out with regulations on registration and disclosures for the issuance of asset-backed securities.

Legal nature of a future flow securitization

The meaning and structure of a future flow securitization has been discussed earlier.

Future flow securitization is one of the most exciting applications of securitization, particularly for emerging markets, and it is very likely that there will be increased use of this device in the future. Many future flow transactions have strong potential to run into defaults, when the legal nature of the transaction will be called in question.[32]

It is, therefore, important to understand the enforceability of a future flow securitization. As discussed earlier, in law, what does not exist cannot be transferred, but there may be an agreement to transfer it. There are several possible situations as follows:

Table 23.2   Possible situations on transferability of receivables

There is a debt that is payable immediately	Transferable
There is a debt contracted today, but payable in future	Transferable
There is an identifiable debt, not existing today, but ascertainable	Transferable in future, but there can be binding promise to transfer it
There are debts to arise from an existing, identifiable asset that exists today	Income from an identifiable source is transferable
Debts to arise from an unidentifiable asset, or unidentifiable debt	Not transferable
Expectancy as to income	Not transferable

Assignability of future flows

General rule

The general rule about future flows is that the transfer will be consummated in the future, when the transferee will automatically acquire the right to the receivable. As a matter of fact, talking about a right of the transferee, even before the receivable has come into being, is of no avail as no such right exists and can be exercised. So, the real issue for future flows is whether future receivables can be assigned now, such that the assignment is a binding promise and becomes a transfer contemporaneously as the receivables arise.

Common law

Under common law principles, the position on transferability of future debt can be very complicated. On one hand, we have a simple and logical maxim of law: How can you transfer what you do not have (*nemo dat quod non habet*)? You can transfer it when you have it, but you cannot transfer now what you do not have as of now. On the other hand, there are rulings that seemingly suggest that future debt can also be transferred now. One such leading case cited world-over is *Tailby* v. *Official Receiver* (1883) 13 AC 523.

Tailby v. *Official Receiver* involved the equitable assignment by way of mortgage of all of the book debts – those already existing and those yet to come into existence – of a company. When the assignor company went into bankruptcy, the official liquidator questioned the validity of an assignment of future debt and claimed rights over the amount received from debts created after the date of assignment. The House of Lords rejected this argument. The court recognized that an assignment may be vague in the sense of "indefinite and uncertain" in which case it will be ineffective. However, an assignment of all of the future book debts of a company was, agreeably, upon their coming into existence, to be identified with certainty. This, in the opinion of the House of Lords, was the standard to be met: "When there is no uncertainty as to identification, the beneficial interest will immediately vest in the assignee." Therefore, the issue in question as far as assignment is concerned is not whether the debts exist or not, but whether the assignment is of identifiable and ascertainable debt.

There is no real conflict between the common law rule of *nemo dat quod non habet* and the ruling in *Tailby*. Tailby merely recognizes a future flow transfer in the future, as automatically operative as and when the debt is created. Therefore, there is an agreement *to* transfer today, which matures into an agreement *of* transfer as and when the debt is created.

The *Tailby* ruling has been followed by several cases, notably in India in *Bharat Nidhi Ltd* v. *Takhatmal* (1969) AIR SC 313.

Other countries

It has always been believed that agreement to assign future flows will be taken to be a promise under New York law.[33] In the recent *Avianca* case (see under True Sale case law), transfer of the future flows has been challenged.[34]

In a recent French ruling as well, the transfer of future flows has been challenged. The ruling is the decision of the commercial section (*Chambre commerciale*) of the French *Cour de cassation* dated April 26, 2000, which held that the transferee of assigned receivables under the Dailly law was unable to recover the sums due by the transferor's debtor resulting from an ongoing contract (*contrat à execution successive*) after the opening judgment of bankruptcy proceedings against the transferor. This decision is deemed applicable to the transfer of future receivables to French securitization vehicles.

What if future flows are explicitly transferable?

Some legislations, like the UNCITRAL model law (see later in this chapter and Appendix 1) seek to provide that future flows are transferable. In fact, the position of law does not change much even if future flows are explicitly made transferable. The main issue in enforceability of a transfer is who has the asset – the seller or buyer. If the transfer is a sale immediately, the buyer receives the property immediately. If the transfer is a sale in future, the buyer gets the property only in the future. For a future receivable, what is transferred does not exist. For what does not exist, it is not a question as to who owns it. The ownership issue will arise only when the receivable comes into being. This is when the buyer seeks to own the asset. Common law rules that provide that the sale of a future flow is valid today but effective in the future provide for exactly this result; the asset automatically becomes the property of the buyer in future when it comes into existence, without any consent or concurrence of the buyer.

However, in the event of a bankruptcy of the originator in the meantime, will the liquidator of the seller be able to avoid the promise for transfer of receivables, taking it as an onerous promise or executory contract? It remains to be seen if the UNCITRAL-type model permitting transfers of future receivables is adopted, whether bankruptcy law provisions empowering the liquidator/ trustee to avoid onerous contracts cease to apply.

Structuring future flows

Thus, it should be clear that a future debt can be transferred only when it actually arises, although an agreement can effectively be entered into now for transfer in the future. While all assignments of future flows are promises to transfer, the key question is one of enforceability of the promise against the subject matter – the receivables. The answer is given by the above ruling; the question primarily hinges on the identifiability of the receivables. For example, a promise to assign all the ticket sales of a particular aircraft, all the ticket sales from a particular territory, all receivables from particular customers or receivables paid by use of particular credit cards are examples of a binding promise as the subject matter is easily identifiable. But revenues from aircraft that are yet to be acquired are unbinding promises, as they are based on a pure conjecture.

In a typical future flow transaction, the receivables come into existence over a period of time and they are automatically transferred as and when they arise. However, what happens if the receivables do not arise at all? For example, if US$1,000 was advanced for purchase of air ticket receivables over a period of time, and US$20 worth of ticket receivables have already been transferred. Now, the aircraft stops flying altogether. It would not require a great elaboration to understand that the US$980, as still an amount advanced against a promise to sell air ticket receivables in future, is an unsecured advance. If at this point, the airline was to go in bankruptcy, the investor who advanced the money would be no better than an unsecured creditor of the airline. Thus, there are two possible ways to give to the investor an elevated status:

Provide the investor with a security interest on the aircraft. That is, the investor has a right to the ticket receivables as and when they are created, and a security interest on the aircraft. This will keep the investor at par with secured creditors.

Provide that the investor has a right to ticket receivables, irrespective of who flies the aircraft. This may be an important right. As discussed earlier, if a source of income exists, income from the source can be sold, and such an agreement to sell income would be construed as a usufructuary mortgage, which will operate even against the buyer of the property. That is, if the aircraft in question is operated by someone who buys it from the subject company, the ticket receivables still belong to the investors.

Future flow securitization documents have to be very skillfully drawn to protect investors from having to queue up in bankruptcy courts. Future flows are substantively close to collateralized lending, but it must be ensured that the true sale either becomes questionable or insignificant, and investors are relegated to a position worse than secured lending.

Legal issues in arbitrage transactions

Arbitrage transactions are where the SPV is a conduit that buys receivables of several originators. This is commonly the case with ABCP conduits, CDOs and several CMBS transactions.

There are several legal issues that would never arise in arbitrage transactions. For instance, true sale questions will become much less challenging. As the SPV buys receivables from various sellers in the market, the transactions are bound to be arms-length transactions at fair value. There is little apprehension about collusive relations between any such originator and the SPV. Likewise, a question of consolidation of the SPV with any of the originators does not arise.

However, conduits engage in on-going activities of acquisition of assets and issuance of liabilities. They cannot have debt limitations and asset limitations of the sort that SPVs typically have. Their net worth cannot be unsubstantial, as the residual interest in the conduit does have residual profits.

The other significant issue in conduits is that they seem to be actively engaged in business, and issues might arise whether they need license based on the line of activity they are engaged in. For example, can the conduit be regarded as an investment company or a finance company?

Ideal legal framework for securitization

Having noted the numerous difficulties posed by the nouveau concept that is securitization, it is important to dwell upon what should be the contents of an ideal legislative framework for securitizations. Several countries have incorporated specific legal rules for securitization transaction. Italy was one of the latest countries; South Korea has a separate set of laws as does Japan.

In the next section, we will deal with the efforts of UNCITRAL to harmonize laws regarding transfer of receivables.

Specifically on the issue of securitization, the following from the **European Securitization Forum** may be noteworthy:[35]

Insofar as possible, standardization/homogeneity of the structure and terms of the underlying receivables/credit obligations that are securitized.

Legal, regulatory and tax provisions/mechanisms that enable asset originators to sell or otherwise convey a broad range of assets to securitization issuing vehicles. Examples of such provisions and mechanisms would include a basic legal framework governing the creation, transfer and perfection of ownership and security interests in collateral; the absence of material restrictions on the types or terms of financial assets that may be securitized; the absence of significantly burdensome borrower consent or notifications requirements in the event of transfer; and the absence of onerous gain recognition or taxation requirements upon the transfer of assets into a securitization vehicle.

A bankruptcy and insolvency regime that provides certainty and predictability in the method of isolating transferred assets from the bankruptcy or insolvency estate of the seller and its creditors.

A legal framework that permits the creation and recognizes the status of special purpose securitization vehicles.

Access to adequate and accurate current and historical data concerning the composition, characteristics and performance of an originator's receivables.

Timely and widespread access to sufficiently detailed information concerning the performance of outstanding securitization transactions, including both security level and collateral level performance data.

Competitive rating agency involvement in the local securitization market, free of substantive ratings regulatory requirements or other governmental and regulatory constraints.

UNCITRAL initiative for uniform law on assignment of receivables

Legal difficulties with 19th Century laws on assignment of receivables have already been noted.

The United Nations Commission on International Trade Law (UNCITRAL), an international body for harmonization of trade-related law, has discussed the issue of a harmonized legal framework for assignment of receivables. UNCITRAL has taken over the assignment of framing and recommending such model law by different countries. This initiative has been going for some years, and several sittings of the committee formed for this purpose have already taken place.

A draft of the convention was adopted in July 2001. So far, as per the latest information on the UNCITRAL website,[36] only one country has accepted the convention, which is Luxembourg on June 12, 2002. At least five such countries are required to adopt before the convention may be in force.

By its very nature, UNCITRAL models are applicable to cross-border assignments or to assignment of cross-border receivables. However, it would be advisable for countries to adopt the basic framework of UNCITRAL law for local assignments as well.

UNCITRAL drafts some basic changes in the approach on transfer of receivables; it seeks to recognize as enforceable transfer of receivables, either present or future, and whether in full or a fractional transfer.

In view of the significance of this law in the context of securitizations, some significant extracts from the convention are extracted as Appendix 1 to this chapter.

Appendix 1

Extracts from UNCITRAL Convention

**UNITED NATIONS CONVENTION ON THE ASSIGNMENT
OF RECEIVABLES IN INTERNATIONAL
TRADE PREAMBLE**

The Contracting States,

Reaffirming their conviction that international trade on the basis of equality and mutual benefit is an important element in the promotion of friendly relations among States,

Considering that problems created by uncertainties as to the content and the choice of legal regime applicable to the assignment of receivables constitute an obstacle to international trade,

Desiring to establish principles and to adopt rules relating to the assignment of receivables that would create certainty and transparency and promote the modernization of the law relating to assignments of receivables, while protecting existing assignment practices and facilitating the development of new practices,

Desiring also to ensure adequate protection of the interests of debtors in assignments of receivables,

Being of the opinion that the adoption of uniform rules governing the assignment of receivables would promote the availability of capital and credit at more affordable rates and thus facilitate the development of international trade,

Have agreed as follows:

CHAPTER I
SCOPE OF APPLICATION

Article 1
Scope of application

1. This Convention applies to:

(a) Assignments of international receivables and to international assignments of receivables as defined in this chapter, if, at the time of conclusion of the contract of assignment, the assignor is located in a Contracting State; and

(b) Subsequent assignments, provided that any prior assignment is governed by this Convention.

2. This Convention applies to subsequent assignments that satisfy the criteria set forth in paragraph 1 (a) of this article, even if it did not apply to any prior assignment of the same receivable.

3. This Convention does not affect the rights and obligations of the debtor unless, at the time of conclusion of the original contract, the debtor is located in a Contracting State or the law governing the original contract is the law of a Contracting State.

4. The provisions of Chapter V apply to assignments of international receivables and to international assignments of receivables as defined in this chapter independently of paragraphs 1 to 3 of this article. However, those provisions do not apply if a State makes a declaration under article 39.

5. The provisions of the annex to this Convention apply as provided in article 42.

Article 2
Assignment of receivables

For the purposes of this Convention:

(a) "Assignment" means the transfer by agreement from one person ("assignor") to another person ("assignee") of all or part of or an undivided interest in the assignor's contractual right to payment of a monetary sum ("receivable") from a third person ("the debtor"). The creation of rights in receivables as security for indebtedness or other obligation is deemed to be a transfer;

(b) In the case of an assignment by the initial or any other assignee ("subsequent assignment"), the person who makes that assignment is the assignor and the person to whom that assignment is made is the assignee.

Article 3
Internationality

A receivable is international if, at the time of conclusion of the original contract, the assignor and the debtor are located in different States. An assignment is international if, at the time of conclusion of the contract of assignment, the assignor and the assignee are located in different States.

Article 4
Exclusions and other limitations

1. This Convention does not apply to assignments made:

(a) To an individual for his or her personal, family or household purposes;

(b) As part of the sale or change in the ownership or legal status of the business out of which the assigned receivables arose.

2. This Convention does not apply to assignments of receivables arising under or from:

(a) Transactions on a regulated exchange;
(b) Financial contracts governed by netting agreements, except a receivable owed on the termination of all outstanding transactions;
(c) Foreign exchange transactions;
(d) Inter-bank payment systems, inter-bank payment agreements or clearance and settlement systems relating to securities or other financial assets or instruments;
(e) The transfer of security rights in, sale, loan or holding of or agreement to repurchase securities or other financial assets or instruments held with an intermediary;
(f) Bank deposits;
(g) A letter of credit or independent guarantee.

3. Nothing in this Convention affects the rights and obligations of any person under the law governing negotiable instruments.
4. Nothing in this Convention affects the rights and obligations of the assignor and the debtor under special laws governing the protection of parties to transactions made for personal, family or household purposes.
5. Nothing in this Convention:

(a) Affects the application of the law of a State in which real property is situated to either:

(i) An interest in that real property to the extent that under that law the assignment of a receivable confers such an interest; or
(ii) The priority of a right in a receivable to the extent that under that law an interest in the real property confers such a right; or

(b) Makes lawful the acquisition of an interest in real property not permitted under the law of the State in which the real property is situated.

CHAPTER II
GENERAL PROVISIONS

Article 5
Definitions and rules of interpretation

For the purposes of this Convention:

(a) "Original contract" means the contract between the assignor and the debtor from which the assigned receivable arises;
(b) "Existing receivable" means a receivable that arises upon or before conclusion of the contract of assignment and "future receivable" means a receivable that arises after conclusion of the contract of assignment;

(c) "Writing" means any form of information that is accessible so as to be usable for subsequent reference. Where this Convention requires a writing to be signed, that requirement is met if, by generally accepted means or a procedure agreed to by the person whose signature is required, the writing identifies that person and indicates that person's approval of the information contained in the writing;

(d) "Notification of the assignment" means a communication in writing that reasonably identifies the assigned receivables and the assignee;

(e) "Insolvency administrator" means a person or body, including one appointed on an interim basis, authorized in an insolvency proceeding to administer the reorganization or liquidation of the assignor's assets or affairs;

(f) "Insolvency proceeding" means a collective judicial or administrative proceeding, including an interim proceeding, in which the assets and affairs of the assignor are subject to control or supervision by a court or other competent authority for the purpose of reorganization or liquidation;

(g) "Priority" means the right of a person in preference to the right of another person and, to the extent relevant for such purpose, includes the determination whether the right is a personal or a property right, whether or not it is a security right for indebtedness or other obligation and whether any requirements necessary to render the right effective against a competing claimant have been satisfied;

(h) A person is located in the State in which it has its place of business. If the assignor or the assignee has a place of business in more than one State, the place of business is that place where the central administration of the assignor or the assignee is exercised. If the debtor has a place of business in more than one State, the place of business is that which has the closest relationship to the original contract. If a person does not have a place of business, reference is to be made to the habitual residence of that person;

(i) "Law" means the law in force in a State other than its rules of private international law;

(j) "Proceeds" means whatever is received in respect of an assigned receivable, whether in total or partial payment or other satisfaction of the receivable. The term includes whatever is received in respect of proceeds. The term does not include returned goods;

(k) "Financial contract" means any spot, forward, future, option or swap transaction involving interest rates, commodities, currencies, equities, bonds, indices or any other financial instrument, any repurchase or securities lending transaction, and any other transaction similar to any transaction referred to above entered into in financial markets and any combination of the transactions mentioned above;

(l) "Netting agreement" means an agreement between two or more parties that provides for one or more of the following:

    (i) The net settlement of payments due in the same currency on the same date whether by novation or otherwise;

(ii) Upon the insolvency or other default by a party, the termination of all outstanding transactions at their replacement or fair market values, conversion of such sums into a single currency and netting into a single payment by one party to the other; or

(iii) The set-off of amounts calculated as set forth in subparagraph (l) (ii) of this article under two or more netting agreements;

(m) "Competing claimant" means:

(i) Another assignee of the same receivable from the same assignor, including a person who, by operation of law, claims a right in the assigned receivable as a result of its right in other property of the assignor, even if that receivable is not an international receivable and the assignment to that assignee is not an international assignment;

(ii) A creditor of the assignor; or

(iii) The insolvency administrator.

Article 6
Party autonomy

Subject to article 19, the assignor, the assignee and the debtor may derogate from or vary by agreement provisions of this Convention relating to their respective rights and obligations. Such an agreement does not affect the rights of any person who is not a party to the agreement.

Article 7
Principles of interpretation

1. In the interpretation of this Convention, regard is to be had to its object and purpose as set forth in the preamble, to its international character and to the need to promote uniformity in its application and the observance of good faith in international trade.

2. Questions concerning matters governed by this Convention that are not expressly settled in it are to be settled in conformity with the general principles on which it is based or, in the absence of such principles, in conformity with the law applicable by virtue of the rules of private international law.

CHAPTER III
EFFECTS OF ASSIGNMENT

Article 8
Effectiveness of assignments

1. An assignment is not ineffective as between the assignor and the assignee or as against the debtor or as against a competing claimant, and the right of an assignee may not be denied priority, on the ground that it is an assignment of more than one receivable, future receivables or parts of or undivided interests in receivables, provided that the receivables are described:

(a) Individually as receivables to which the assignment relates; or

(b) In any other manner, provided that they can, at the time of the assignment or, in the case of future receivables, at the time of conclusion of the original contract, be identified as receivables to which the assignment relates.

2. Unless otherwise agreed, an assignment of one or more future receivables is effective without a new act of transfer being required to assign each receivable.

3. Except as provided in paragraph 1 of this article, article 9 and article 10, paragraphs 2 and 3, this Convention does not affect any limitations on assignments arising from law.

Article 9
Contractual limitations on assignments

1. An assignment of a receivable is effective notwithstanding any agreement between the initial or any subsequent assignor and the debtor or any subsequent assignee limiting in any way the assignor's right to assign its receivables.

2. Nothing in this article affects any obligation or liability of the assignor for breach of such an agreement, but the other party to such agreement may not avoid the original contract or the assignment contract on the sole ground of that breach. A person who is not party to such an agreement is not liable on the sole ground that it had knowledge of the agreement.

3. This article applies only to assignments of receivables:

(a) Arising from an original contract that is a contract for the supply or lease of goods or services other than financial services, a construction contract or a contract for the sale or lease of real property;

(b) Arising from an original contract for the sale, lease or license of industrial or other intellectual property or of proprietary information;

(c) Representing the payment obligation for a credit card transaction; or

(d) Owed to the assignor upon net settlement of payments due pursuant to a netting agreement involving more than two parties.

Article 10
Transfer of security rights

1. A personal or property right securing payment of the assigned receivable is transferred to the assignee without a new act of transfer. If such a right, under the law governing it, is transferable only with a new act of transfer, the assignor is obliged to transfer such right and any proceeds to the assignee.

2. A right securing payment of the assigned receivable is transferred under paragraph 1 of this article notwithstanding any agreement between the assignor and the debtor or other person granting that right, limiting in any way the assignor's right to assign the receivable or the right securing payment of the assigned receivable.

3. Nothing in this article affects any obligation or liability of the assignor for breach of any agreement under paragraph 2 of this article, but the other party to that agreement may not avoid the original contract or the assignment contract on the sole ground of that breach. A person who is not a party to such an agreement is not liable on the sole ground that it had knowledge of the agreement.

4. Paragraphs 2 and 3 of this article apply only to assignments of receivables:

    (a) Arising from an original contract that is a contract for the supply or lease of goods or services other than financial services, a construction contract or a contract for the sale or lease of real property;

    (b) Arising from an original contract for the sale, lease or license of industrial or other intellectual property or of proprietary information;

    (c) Representing the payment obligation for a credit card transaction; or

    (d) Owed to the assignor upon net settlement of payments due pursuant to a netting agreement involving more than two parties.

5. The transfer of a possessory property right under paragraph 1 of this article does not affect any obligations of the assignor to the debtor or the person granting the property right with respect to the property transferred existing under the law governing that property right.

6. Paragraph 1 of this article does not affect any requirement under rules of law other than this Convention relating to the form or registration of the transfer of any rights securing payment of the assigned receivable.

CHAPTER IV
RIGHTS, OBLIGATIONS AND DEFENCES

SECTION I
ASSIGNOR AND ASSIGNEE

Article 11
Rights and obligations of the assignor and the assignee

1. The mutual rights and obligations of the assignor and the assignee arising from their agreement are determined by the terms and conditions set forth in that agreement, including any rules or general conditions referred to therein.

2. The assignor and the assignee are bound by any usage to which they have agreed and, unless otherwise agreed, by any practices they have established between themselves.

3. In an international assignment, the assignor and the assignee are considered, unless otherwise agreed, implicitly to have made applicable to the assignment a usage that in international trade is widely known to, and regularly observed by, parties to the particular type of assignment or to the assignment of the particular category of receivables.

Article 12
Representations of the assignor

1. Unless otherwise agreed between the assignor and the assignee, the assignor represents at the time of conclusion of the contract of assignment that:

   (a) The assignor has the right to assign the receivable;
   (b) The assignor has not previously assigned the receivable to another assignee; and
   (c) The debtor does not and will not have any defenses or rights of set-off.

2. Unless otherwise agreed between the assignor and the assignee, the assignor does not represent that the debtor has, or will have, the ability to pay.

Article 13
Right to notify the debtor

1. Unless otherwise agreed between the assignor and the assignee, the assignor or the assignee or both may send the debtor notification of the assignment and a payment instruction, but after notification has been sent only the assignee may send such an instruction.

2. Notification of the assignment or a payment instruction sent in breach of any agreement referred to in paragraph 1 of this article is not ineffective for the purposes of article 17 by reason of such breach. However, nothing in this article affects any obligation or liability of the party in breach of such an agreement for any damages arising as a result of the breach.

Article 14
Right to payment

1. As between the assignor and the assignee, unless otherwise agreed and whether or not notification of the assignment has been sent:

   (a) If payment in respect of the assigned receivable is made to the assignee, the assignee is entitled to retain the proceeds and goods returned in respect of the assigned receivable;
   (b) If payment in respect of the assigned receivable is made to the assignor, the assignee is entitled to payment of the proceeds and also to goods returned to the assignor in respect of the assigned receivable; and
   (c) If payment in respect of the assigned receivable is made to another person over whom the assignee has priority, the assignee is entitled to payment of the proceeds and also to goods returned to such person in respect of the assigned receivable.

2. The assignee may not retain more than the value of its right in the receivable.

SECTION II
DEBTOR

Article 15
Principle of debtor protection

1. Except as otherwise provided in this Convention, an assignment does not, without the consent of the debtor, affect the rights and obligations of the debtor, including the payment terms contained in the original contract.
2. A payment instruction may change the person, address or account to which the debtor is required to make payment, but may not change:

    (a) The currency of payment specified in the original contract; or
    (b) The State specified in the original contract in which payment is to be made to a State other than that in which the debtor is located.

Article 16
Notification of the debtor

1. Notification of the assignment or a payment instruction is effective when received by the debtor if it is in a language that is reasonably expected to inform the debtor about its contents. It is sufficient if notification of the assignment or a payment instruction is in the language of the original contract.
2. Notification of the assignment or a payment instruction may relate to receivables arising after notification.
3. Notification of a subsequent assignment constitutes notification of all prior assignments.

Article 17
Debtor's discharge by payment

1. Until the debtor receives notification of the assignment, the debtor is entitled to be discharged by paying in accordance with the original contract.
2. After the debtor receives notification of the assignment, subject to paragraphs 3 to 8 of this article, the debtor is discharged only by paying the assignee or, if otherwise instructed in the notification of the assignment or subsequently by the assignee in a writing received by the debtor, in accordance with such payment instruction.
3. If the debtor receives more than one payment instruction relating to a single assignment of the same receivable by the same assignor, the debtor is discharged by paying in accordance with the last payment instruction received from the assignee before payment.
4. If the debtor receives notification of more than one assignment of the same receivable made by the same assignor, the debtor is discharged by paying in accordance with the first notification received.
5. If the debtor receives notification of one or more subsequent assignments, the debtor is discharged by paying in accordance with the notification of the last of such subsequent assignments.

6. If the debtor receives notification of the assignment of a part of or an undivided interest in one or more receivables, the debtor is discharged by paying in accordance with the notification or in accordance with this article as if the debtor had not received the notification. If the debtor pays in accordance with the notification, the debtor is discharged only to the extent of the part or undivided interest paid.

7. If the debtor receives notification of the assignment from the assignee, the debtor is entitled to request the assignee to provide within a reasonable period of time adequate proof that the assignment from the initial assignor to the initial assignee and any intermediate assignment have been made and, unless the assignee does so, the debtor is discharged by paying in accordance with this article as if the notification from the assignee had not been received. Adequate proof of an assignment includes but is not limited to any writing emanating from the assignor and indicating that the assignment has taken place.

8. This article does not affect any other ground on which payment by the debtor to the person entitled to payment, to a competent judicial or other authority, or to a public deposit fund discharges the debtor.

Article 18
Defenses and rights of set-off of the debtor

1. In a claim by the assignee against the debtor for payment of the assigned receivable, the debtor may raise against the assignee all defenses and rights of set-off arising from the original contract, or any other contract that was part of the same transaction, of which the debtor could avail itself as if the assignment had not been made and such claim were made by the assignor.

2. The debtor may raise against the assignee any other right of set-off, provided that it was available to the debtor at the time notification of the assignment was received by the debtor.

3. Notwithstanding paragraphs 1 and 2 of this article, defenses and rights of set-off that the debtor may raise pursuant to article 9 or 10 against the assignor for breach of an agreement limiting in any way the assignor's right to make the assignment are not available to the debtor against the assignee.

Article 19
Agreement not to raise defenses or rights of set-off

1. The debtor may agree with the assignor in a writing signed by the debtor not to raise against the assignee the defenses and rights of set-off that it could raise pursuant to article 18. Such an agreement precludes the debtor from raising against the assignee those defenses and rights of set-off.

2. The debtor may not waive defenses:

    (a) Arising from fraudulent acts on the part of the assignee; or
    (b) Based on the debtor's incapacity.

3. Such an agreement may be modified only by an agreement in a writing signed by the debtor. The effect of such a modification as against the assignee is determined by article 20, paragraph 2.

Article 20
Modification of the original contract

1. An agreement concluded before notification of the assignment between the assignor and the debtor that affects the assignee's rights is effective as against the assignee, and the assignee acquires corresponding rights.
2. An agreement concluded after notification of the assignment between the assignor and the debtor that affects the assignee's rights is ineffective as against the assignee unless:

   (a) The assignee consents to it; or
   (b) The receivable is not fully earned by performance and either the modification is provided for in the original contract or, in the context of the original contract, a reasonable assignee would consent to the modification.

3. Paragraphs 1 and 2 of this article do not affect any right of the assignor or the assignee arising from breach of an agreement between them.

Article 21
Recovery of payments

Failure of the assignor to perform the original contract does not entitle the debtor to recover from the assignee a sum paid by the debtor to the assignor or the assignee.

Appendix 2

Model Legal Opinion
for a Securitization Transaction

[Letterhead of Law Firm]

[Date]

[Name and address of Principal trustee of the SPV/Merchant banker]
Re: Securitization of [mortgage loans]

Dear Sirs:

We have acted as counsel to [originator], a company under the Companies Act, *** ("**Originator**"), in connection with the securitization of receivables arising out of the several mortgages [as listed in the Schedule annexed hereto] by assigning the same to the [Special purpose vehicle] formed for this purpose.

We have examined

(a) the constitutional documents of the originator;
(b) models of the agreements, guarantees and other documents with reference to which the mortgage loans have been given by the originator from time to time (herein collectively referred to as "the loan documents");
(c) the drafts of the deed of assignment, constitutional documents of the special purpose vehicle, power of attorney and other documents in connection with the assignment of the aforesaid receivables (herein collectively referred to "the assignment documents").

We have not examined:

(a) each and every mortgage loan document individually;
(b) any legal cases or other disputes pending with the mortgagors in connection with any of the mortgages abovementioned;
(c) compliance or otherwise with any of the internal procedures of the originator with respect to such loans;
(d) verification of either the existence of the borrowers or the mortgaged properties;

(e) physical possession of the security documents in relation to the mortgages;

(f) [more].

Based on the foregoing, and upon such investigation as we have deemed necessary, and subject to the qualifications and exceptions herein contained, we are of the opinion that:

1. Originator is duly incorporated under the laws of the land, and as on the date of expression of this opinion, is not an insolvent company with the meaning of the [** Insolvency Act].

2. Originator has the power under its Organisational Documents [Memorandum of Association/charter] and applicable law to:

    (a) carry on the business of giving loans in respect of the mortgages referred to above;

    (b) be engaged in the business of giving such loans with reference to the [relevant Act/Rules/Directions], **** etc;

    (c) [in case of private money lenders] be engaged in the business of money-lending under the provisions of the [relevant Act] ***/applicable State law.

We are not aware of any legal provision/restraint that should generally vitiate the business of the originator or materially adversely affect the rights of the originator with respect to business transacted/to be transacted.

3. All borrowers are citizens of [country]. The internal procedures of the Borrower provide for conducting routine checks to ensure that the Borrowers are legally empowered to take loans from the Originator.

4. Based on a general examination of relevant documents, we note that the Borrower has taken all action necessary under its Organizational Documents and applicable law to authorize the execution and delivery of the Loan Documents and the performance of its obligations there under and has duly executed and delivered the Loan Documents.

5. The Loan Documents, if properly executed, would create

    (a) in favor of the originator a valid and enforceable right over the properties mortgaged/charged in favor of the originator and would empower the originator to evoke the guarantees under the agreements of guarantee;

    (b) against the borrowers a valid and binding unconditional obligation to pay the instalments or other sums referred to in the loan documents, and in default thereof, to hand over to the originator vacant possession of the property/asset mortgaged/charged in favor of the Originator except as may be limited by insolvency or other similar laws affecting the rights and remedies of creditors generally and general principles of equity;

(c) as against the guarantors a valid and binding unconditional, independent, coextensive and mutually unexclusive obligation to pay the sums guaranteed under the loan documents.

6. Based on such test scrutiny of the loan documents as was considered appropriate by us, we report that:

(a) the loan documents have properly been filled up and executed;

(b) the loan documents are properly stamped and registered (where required);

(c) original documents in respect of the mortgages have been obtained by the originator and have been kept in the safe custody of the originator;

(d) we are not aware of any legal lapses, non-compliances or other failures that should have a general and substantial impact on the rights of the originator under the loan documents.

7. There are no such covenants/conditions [or, the following are the covenants/conditions] to be complied with by the Originator under the loan documents which might have a direct bearing on the right of the Originator to enforce all/any claims of the originator under the loan documents.

8. The form and structure of the assignment agreement is such as would:

(a) not violate any of the terms of conditions of the loan documents/any applicable law of the land/common law principles;

(b) convey to the assignee a legally enforceable right in the debts assigned therein;

(c) not require notice of such assignment to the debtors/borrowers/guarantors;

(d) allow the assignee to make claim against the debtor/borrower for all or any sum due under the loan agreements without the originator having to join as a party/front for the assignee;

(e) vest in the assignee all the rights and claims of the originator in respected of the property/assets mortgaged/charged in favor of the originator under the loan agreements.

9. The assignment agreement is/is proposed to be duly stamped under the laws of the [applicable jurisdiction], and that the assignment agreement would not be liable to differential duty if taken out to [jurisdiction] to be enforced there.

10. The special purpose vehicle is duly constituted as a trust/company under the applicable laws.

11. The powers of the special purpose vehicle are duly defined in the constitutional documents and such powers put the following limitations on the special purpose vehicle:

(a) the SPV will not employ any employee or other agent and would not incur any liability for expenses in relation to any employee of any other person.

      (b) the SPV shall not be entitled to borrow in any form from any person.

      (c) the SPV shall not be engaged in any other business or activity except in relation to the present transaction.

12. The issuance of the securities by the SPV does not amount to a "public offer" under any of the rules/guidelines of the [securities regulator] and is otherwise in compliance with such rules and guidelines.

Yours truly,

Appendix 3

Provisions of the Indian Transfer of Property Act

TRANSFERS OF ACTIONABLE CLAIM

130. (1) The transfer of actionable claim whether with or without consideration shall be effected only by the execution of an instrument in writing signed by the transferor or his duly authorised agent, shall be complete and effectual upon the execution of such instrument, and thereupon all the rights and remedies of the transferor, whether by way of damages or otherwise, shall vest in the transferee, whether such notice of the transfer as is hereinafter provided be given or not:

Provided that every dealing with the debt or other actionable claim by the debtor or other person from or against whom the transferor would, but for such instrument of transfer as aforesaid, have been entitled to recover or enforce such debt or other actionable claim, shall (save were the debtor or other person is a party to the transfer or has received express notice thereof as hereinafter provided) be valid as against such transfer.

(2) The transferee of an actionable claim may, upon the execution of such instrument of transfer as aforesaid, sue or institute proceedings for the same in his own name without obtaining the transferor's consent to such suit or proceedings, and without making him a party thereto.

Exception.- Nothing in this section applies to the transfer of a marine or fire policy of insurance or affects the provisions of section 38 of the Insurance Act, 1938 (IV of 1938).

Illustrations

(i) *A* owes money to *B*, who transfers the debt to *C*. *B* then demands the debt from *A*, who, not having received notice of the transfer, as prescribed in section 131, pays *B*. The payment is valid, and *C* cannot sue *A* for debt.

(ii) *A* affects a policy on his own life with an Insurance Company and assigns it to a Bank for securing the payment of an existing or future debt. If *A* dies, the Bank is entitled to receive the amount of the policy and sue on it without the concurrence of *A*'s executor, subject to the proviso in sub-section (1) of section 130 and to the provisions of section 132.

NOTICE TO BE IN WRITING SIGNED

131. Every notice of transfer of an actionable claim shall be in writing, signed by the transferor or his agent duly authorized in this behalf, or, in case the transferor refuses to sign, by the transferee or his agent, and shall state the name and address of the transferee.

LIABILITY OF TRANSFEREE

132. The transferee of an actionable claim shall take it subject to all the liabilities and equities to which the transferor was subject in respect thereof at the date of the transfer.

Illustrations

(i) *A* transfers to *C* a debt due to him by *B*, *A* being then indebted to *B*. *C* sues *B* for the debt due by *B* to *A*. In such suit *B* is entitled to set off the debt due by *A* to him; although *C* was unaware of the date of such transfer.

(ii) *A* executed a bond in favor of *B* under circumstances entitling the former to have it delivered up and cancelled. *B* assigns the bond to *C* for value and without notice of such circumstances. *C* cannot enforce the bond against *A*.

WARRANTY OF SOLVENCY OF DEBTOR

133. Where the transferor of a debt warrants the solvency of the debtor, the warranty, in the absence of a contract to the contrary, applies only to his solvency at the time of the transfer, and is limited, where the transfer is made for consideration, to the amount of value of such consideration.

MORTGAGED DEBT

134. Where a debt is transferred for the purpose of securing an existing or future debt, the debt so transferred, if received by the transferor or recovered by the transferee, is applicable, first, in payment of the costs of such recovery: secondly, in or towards satisfaction of the amount for the time being secured by the transfer; and the residue, if any, belongs to the transferor or other person entitled to receive the same.

ASSIGNMENT OF RIGHTS UNDER POLICY OF INSURANCE AGAINST FIRE

135. Every assignee, by endorsement or other writing, of a policy of insurance against fire, in whom the property in the subject insured shall be absolutely vested at the date of the assignment, shall have transferred and vested in him all rights of suit as if the contract contained in the policy had been made with himself.

INCAPACITY OF OFFICERS CONNECTED WITH COURTS OF JUSTICE

136. No Judge, legal practitioner or officer connected with any Court of Justice shall buy or traffic in, or stipulate for, or agree to receive any share of, or interest in, any actionable claim, and no Court of Justice shall enforce, at his instance, or at the instance of any person claiming by or through him, any actionable claim, so dealt with by him as aforesaid.

SAVING OF NEGOTIABLE INSTRUMENTS

137. Nothing in the foregoing sections of this Chapter applies to stocks, shares or debentures, or to instruments which are for the time being by law or custom, negotiable, or to any mercantile document of title to goods.

    Explanation.- The expression, "mercantile document of title to goods," includes a bill of lading, dock-warrant, warehousekeeper's certificate, railway-receipt, warrant or order for the delivery of goods, and any other document used in the ordinary course of business as proof of the possession or control of goods, or authorizing or purporting to authorize, either by endorsement or by delivery, the possessor of the document to transfer or receive goods thereby represented.

Provisions of the laws of Australian States on assignment of debts

The Conveyancing Act 1919 of the New South Wales provides as under:

12 Assignments of debts and choses in action

Any absolute assignment by writing under the hand of the assignor (not purporting to be by way of charge only) of any debt or other legal chose in action, of which express notice in writing has been given to the debtor, trustee, or other person from whom the assignor would have been entitled to receive or claim such debt or chose in action, shall be, and be deemed to have been effectual in law (subject to all equities which would have been entitled to priority over the right of the assignee if this Act had not passed) to pass and transfer the legal right to such debt or chose in action from the date of such notice, and all legal and other remedies for the same, and the power to give a good discharge for the same without the concurrence of the assignor: Provided always that if the debtor, trustee, or other person liable in respect of such debt or chose in action has had notice that such assignment is disputed by the assignor or anyone claiming under the assignor, or of any other opposing or conflicting claims to such debt or chose in action, the debtor, trustee or other person liable shall be entitled, if he or she thinks fit, to call upon the several persons making claim thereto to interplead concerning the same, or he or she may, if he or she thinks fit, pay the same into court under and in conformity with the provisions of the Acts for the relief of trustees.

Notes

1   This view has gathered more force with the submissions of the American Securitization Forum to the FASB, of an alternative method of accounting where the assets of the SPV will appear as a segment on the balance sheet of the originator. See details on Vinod Kothari's editorial website http://vinodkothari.com/secedit.htm, simultaneously published in Asset Securitization Report, August 1, 2003.

2   Also called a protected cell company.

3   The inclination of a court to go into the substance question is essentially the tradition of judicial approach. Some countries are known as "form countries" while some others get a reputation of being "substance countries."

4   English common law has for ages treated such a sale as a conditional sale, treated as a variant of a mortgage. If a transfer of property is made with the understanding that upon discharge of the debt, the property will be re-conveyed to the original owner, it is a mortgage by way of conditional sale.

5   Debtor-in-possession (DIP) funding is a special funding organized during a bankruptcy resolution with the sanction of the court.

6   "The LTV Steel ABS Opinion is predicated on unusual circumstances and, therefore, it is not likely to open the floodgates for ABS challenges in bankruptcy" Robert Stark: "Viewing the LTV steel ABS opinion in its proper context", *Journal of*

Corporation Law, Winter 2002. Some have even held that the Court was influenced by psychic factors such as the location of the Court near to LTV's headquarters, and the presence of several Congressmen in the hearings. – Kenneth N. Klee and Brendt C. Butler: "Asset-backed securitization, special purpose vehicles and other securitization issues" *Uniform Commercial Code Law Journal*, Vol. 35, No. 2.

7 "Rethinking the role of recourse in the sale of financial assets," *The Business Lawyer*, November 1996.

8 The presence of third-party investors was considered to be a crucial factor in *Frank Lyon and Company*, a tax case dealing with sale and leaseback transactions.

9 Robert D. Aicher and William J. Fellerhoff: *Characterisation of a Transfer of Receivables as a Sale or a Secured Loan Upon Bankruptcy of the Transferor* 65 AM. BANKR. L.J. 181 (1991).

10 For example, *In re Golden Plan of California, Inc.*, 829 F.2d 705 (9th Cir. 1986).

11 *The Business Lawyer*, November 1996. In fact, this is a report, citing opinions of nine legal experts.

12 p. 171

13 See Chapter 29 on Regulatory Issues.

14 *Colombia Business Law Review*, 1993, No. 2, p. 147.

15 See the chapter on Accounting for Securitization.

16 *Linden Gardens Trust Ltd* v. *Lenesta Sludge Disposals Ltd*, [1994] 1 AC 85.

17 Available on the web at: http://www.firstam.com/faf/html/cust/jm-summaries. html, last visited December 13, 2005.

18 Exposure Draft dated August 11, 2005; see more in the chapter on Accounting Issues.

19 Frederick Feldkamp in "Asset securitization: The alchemist's dream," *International Financial Law Review*, London, 2000.

20 For more, see Vinod Kothari: *Securitization, Asset Reconstruction and Enforcement of Security Interests*. For details and latest edition information, see http://vinodkothari.com/arcbook.htm.

21 The early stamp laws referred to stamping "every skin or piece of vellum or parchment, or sheet or piece of paper, on which shall be engrossed, written or printed."

22 See Standard & Poor's report "Securitization without true sales: They do things differently in Europe" (published on October 6, 2003).

23 Except in English mortgage and mortgage by way of conditional sale, where a decree of foreclosure vests the lender with a proprietary interest in the property. For details, see Vinod Kothari's *Securitization, Asset Reconstruction and Enforcement of Security Interests*. For latest edition information, see http://vinodkothari.com/arcbook.htm.

24 Legal provisions about fixed and floating charges and recognition of the floating chargeholder holding a generic security interest on the assets of the borrower exist in all those countries that have structured corporate laws based on the U.K. pattern. Obviously, floating charges have no meaning for non-corporate borrowers.

25 Goode, RM: *Principles of Corporate Insolvency Law*, 1997, p. 167.

26 Significant recent judicial pronouncements have been made on the concept from House of Lords, recently in the case of *National Westminster Bank plc* v. *Spectrum Plus Limited & others* [2005] U.K.HL 41, and before that, in *Cosslett* and *Brumark* case. For details, see Vinod Kothari: *Securitization, Asset Reconstruction and Enforcement of Security Interests*.

27 For details and latest edition information, check at http://vinodkothari.com/crebook.htm

28 See, for example, the case studies of RMBS and CMBS transactions in the chapter on Synthetic Securitization.

29 See, for details, the Powers Committee report, February 1, 2002.

30 Based on S&P's SPV criteria.

31 Legal Criteria for Structured Finance Transactions, April 2002.

32 For instance, for the *Avianca* – see *ante* in this chapter.

33 Mark Raines and Gabrielle Wong: "Aspects of Assignment of Future Cash Flows under English and New York Law" *Duke Journal of Comparative & International Law*, Spring 2002.

34 See earlier in this chapter.

35 Subsequently, the ESF has come out with a detailed exposure draft of the Securitization Framework. See the full text at http://www.europeansecuritisation.com.

36 http://www.uncitral.org/en-index.htm, last visited on August 31, 2003.

Chapter 24

Legal Documentation for Securitization

Needless to say, documentation is the very heart of a securitization transaction. Like the constitution of a nation, the very source of legal powers, obligations, covenants and compliances by the parties in a transaction is contained in the transaction documents.

Securitization documents must have the standard features required for any other contractual documents – brevity, simplicity, objectivity and readability. As the transactional documents will govern the transaction for years to come, the meaning must be objectively understandable, irrespective of the availability of the author of the document to interpret it.

Unfortunately, while the International Swaps and Derivatives Association (ISDA) has done a commendable job in the standardization of derivatives documentation, a similar standardization and "incorporation by reference" of securitization documents is unheard of. The result is every securitization document repeats pages after pages of standard definitions, warranties and conventions, whereby crucial operative clauses are submerged under a heap of words.

Basic structure of documentation

Barring differences in transaction structure, a securitization transaction would involve the following steps:

1. A special purpose entity is brought into existence. If the SPE is to be a company, the company is incorporated. If it is to be a trust, depending on the law or practice in the country concerned, the trust is brought into existence by way of an independent settlement or by declaration of trust by the trustee.
2. The seller agrees to transfer the receivables to the SPV.
3. The SPV appoints the seller as a collection and servicing agent.

4. The SPV issues either pass-through certificates or debt securities. For debt-type certificates, there will be a creation of security interest on the assets of the SPV in favor of the trustee for the investors.
5. Offer documents: Whether a prospectus or an information memorandum will depend on the nature of the offering and the securities regulations of the country concerned.

The basic documentation to achieve the above will be:

- The pooling and servicing agreement: The document by which receivables are transferred that includes detailed representations and warranties of the seller, undertaking of the servicer, the servicing fees and the excess service fees.
- The trust deed: The document by which the SPV is formed or the trustee agrees to hold the property in trust for the investors, issues pass-through certificates, describes the waterfall and the rights of various classes of the pass-through certificates.
- Offer documents.

The pooling and servicing agreement

The pooling and servicing agreement derives its name from the fact that the transferor agrees to "pool" the receivables – constitute the pool by identifying the receivables to be transferred, transfer them, and agree to collect and service the transaction. If identifiable assets are being transferred with no obligation on the part of the transferor to "pool" them over time, the jargon "pooling" may be inappropriate and a simple assignment or transfer agreement may be used.

The main clauses of the PSA agreement are discussed below. Notably, we will not go into details that are required specifically for a transaction.

Identification of asset to be assigned

One of the most critical clauses in the receivables transfer agreement or the pooling and servicing agreement is to identify what is to be transferred. The receivables arise under the origination agreement (for example, the loan agreement) with the obligor and there are various elements of receivables there under, apart from interest and principal. In addition, receivables may arise from various collateral sources, such as insurance companies, any guarantees or derivatives and any other collateral. Receivables may also arise by sale of collateral on foreclosure of any security interest. In short, it is necessary to identify the ambit of what is being transferred to the SPV.

The receivables may be present or future receivables. The identification for future receivables is even trickier, as the origination agreement also does not exist at the time of the agreement. Usually, for future flows, a variable interest in a larger mass of receivables is transferred; the variable interest itself depends on the schedule of payments due to the investors. The excess of the actual mass of receivables over the variable interest remains untransferred or the seller's own interest in the receivables.

For both present and future receivables, the "cut-off" date from which the transfer of the asset will be operative is important. For future flows, it is also important to define the terminal date until when the transfer will continue.

Identification of receivables must also deal with any deduction or set off that the obligor makes. Normally, a transaction would be much cleaner if the receivables are free from set off or deduction, but sometimes a deduction may even be a supervening obligation, such as a withholding tax. In such cases, is the transferor bound to make good the deduction or is the benefit of the deduction to be transferred to the transferee?

How to identify receivables

The identification of receivables is usually done either through the definitions clause or through the conveyance clause (see below).

Samples

1. **Sale of lease receivables:**

"**Lease Receivable**" means, with respect to any Lease at any time, all Scheduled Payments then or thereafter payable by the Obligor under such a Lease, together with all supplemental or additional Payments required by the terms of such a Lease with respect to insurance and other specific charges, *excluding* any such payments or charges that constitute charges for excessive wear and tear of the Equipment or any reimbursements for any sums paid or payable by the Seller, or any sales-tax, or other taxes.

"**Scheduled Payments**" mean, with respect to a Lease Receivable, the remaining rent installments (exclusive of any amounts in respect of insurance or taxes) payable by the Obligor under the related Lease.

Notes:

1. Note the exclusion here. There is no question of assignment of reimbursements for actual expenses, such as sales-tax and inspection costs. This is excluded by defining Scheduled Payments to mean only the rent installments.
2. Similarly, reimbursements for depletion in the residual value of the asset are also not assigned. This would be necessary to protect the tax-acceptable nature of the lease. Besides, if the residual value of the asset is not transferred, a payment made towards depletion in the value of the asset (say on account of capital repairs) is essentially towards depletion in residual value, and therefore, ought not to be transferred.

2. **Sale of residential mortgage receivables:**

Seller does hereby convey: "All the right, title and interest of the Seller in and to the Mortgage Loans. Such conveyance includes, without limitation, the right to all distributions of principal and interest due with respect to the Mortgage Loans after the Cut-off Date, together with all of the Seller's rights under any Insurance Proceeds related to the Mortgage Loans, and the Seller's security interest in any collateral pledged to secure the Mortgage Loans, including the Mortgaged Properties."

Notes:

1. This one is an all-pervasive clause and there are no exclusions made; the entire right, title and interest of the mortgage lender in the mortgage loan, as well as the security interest in the mortgage property, is being conveyed to the transferee. This kind of all-pervasive transfer is recommended only on a careful construction of the mortgage origination document, as there might be receivables in the nature of reimbursements or indemnities that may logically still be the interest of the mortgage lender.

3. Auto loans/hire purchase agreements:

Seller does hereby convey all right, title and interest of the Seller in, to and under:

(a) The Receivables sold on each such date, as listed in Schedule A to the relevant Receivables Sale Agreement, and all moneys received thereon after the Cut-off Date;

(b) All security interests in the Vehicles granted by Obligors pursuant to the Receivables sold and any other interest of the Seller in such Vehicles;

(c) All proceeds and all rights to receive proceeds with respect to the Receivables sold from claims on any physical damage, credit life or disability insurance policies covering Vehicles or Obligors and any proceeds from the liquidation of such Receivables;

(d) All rights of the Seller against Dealers pursuant to the agreement of the Seller with the Dealers and the assignment by the Dealers of the origination agreements;

(e) All rights under any Service Contracts on the related Vehicles; and

(f) All proceeds of any and all of the foregoing.

Notes:

1. For hire purchase agreements, the word "security interest" may be defined to include the retention of title to the vehicles.
2. Notably, there is an assignment of any payments on account of dealers' warranties as well.
3. Note that the reference to Dealer, in (d), relates to origination of the loans/leases by a network of dealers, who subsequently assign the loan to the finance company/bank.

4. Future flows:

Seller does hereby convey all right, title and interest in the variable amount of Receivables set forth below (such amount, herein referred to as "Purchased

Receivables"). The Purchased Receivables will be nebulous and limited to the following variable amounts:

(a) During each Collection Period that does not occur during an Early Amortization Period and until an Acceleration, an amount equal to the sum of (i) 100% of the amount required during any such Collection Period for servicing of investors, (ii) any additional amounts payable during such Collection Period with respect to any outstanding Series of Certificates and (iii) any amounts necessary to be deposited to the Reserve Accounts, if any, of each outstanding Series such that the funds in each such Reserve Account are equal to the Required Reserve Amount for each such Series; or

(b) During any Collection Period during an Early Amortization Period, an amount equal to the sum of … (set out here the amount required for early amortization trigger) or

(c) During any Collection Period following an Acceleration, an amount equal to all collections on Receivables deposited into the Bank Account during such a Collection Period.

"Receivables" shall mean the following property, wherever located and whether now or hereafter existing, created or acquired: (a) all existing and future contingent payment rights and other indebtedness that (i) arise from the sale of (specify the source of receivables, such as the sale of tickets or any goods) by the Seller to Customers (these are either designated customers, or all customers paying by way of a designated mode of payment), and (ii) are generated by the Seller and evidence rights to payments from time to time owing (after giving effect to any adjustment, discount or other price reduction from time to time) by such Customers, together with (b) all interest, dividends and returns on, and other investments and proceeds of, such property (including without limitation cash, general intangibles, deposit accounts, securities, certificates and instruments).

Notes:

1. The specification of a variable amount of receivables is a very important feature of this document. Essentially, the definition of "receivables" is very wide and covers not only all receivables from particular customers but also all proceeds from reinvestment of such property. However, out of this mass, what is actually conveyed is only the portion equal to the amount required for investor service.

2. In common law, this is a case of a fractional transfer, as the transferee does not have any definite claim against any particular obligor. The transferee's claim against any or all customers ranks parallel (in terms of joint ownership) to that of the transferor.

Conveyance clause

This is the clause that brings about the conveyance – the transfer. Usually, in terms of sequence, this is the first clause after the definitions. A typical conveyance clause says: "In consideration hereof, the Seller does hereby transfer, assign, make over, and otherwise convey, without recourse, to the Purchaser ..."

The meaning of "does hereby... convey" is that execution of the agreement amounts to conveyance. If the parties need to make a distinction between an agreement to convey and the actual conveyance,[1] then the conveyance clause may be an executory clause; that is, the seller irrevocably agrees to convey.

Registration, stamping, etc.

In many cases, conveyance is also accompanied by delivery of the loan documents, particularly for mortgages. If that is the practice, the physical handing over of the documents may also be recorded here. In many jurisdictions, the transfer of receivables may require registration or filing; the agreement may provide for such filing by either the transferor or transferee. In many countries, the transaction of conveyance is subject to registration fees, stamp duties and documentary tax. The agreement needs to make clear provisions as to who will bear these costs.

Restrictions on re-transfer, etc.

The conveyance clause vests absolute property in the asset to the transferee: therefore, by default, the transferee gets all such rights over the asset as the transferor had. This will include the right to sell, pledge, transfer, encumber or otherwise deal with the asset. Should it be desired (as is common for sale to SPVs) that the transferee does not re-transfer the asset, the limitation may be specified here. It is preferable that the restriction be spelt out clearly.

Transfer of rights, not obligations

Another important point to make in the conveyance clause is the exclusion of any of the obligations of the transferor to the obligors. A clause to the following effect may be inserted here:

> "Nothing herein shall constitute, and nothing herein is intended to result in an assumption by the Purchaser, or any Beneficiary, of any obligation of the Seller, the Servicer, the Transferor or any other Person in connection with the Receivables or under the Origination Agreement or under any agreement or instrument relating thereto, including, without limitation, any obligation to any Obligor.

Any continuing or future transfers

A number of transactions may require a transfer of assets over time; it would be important for the agreement to provide what are the rights or obligations of the transferor to transfer such assets, whether the transferee has an option to decline such transfers, what will be the criteria for selection of such assets, what will be the maximum amount up to which the transferee will accept further transfers, the manner of making such transfers and the settlement of consideration.

Contingency of the transfer not being regarded as true sale

The intention of the parties, obviously, is to have the transaction treated as a true sale. However, there is an inevitable risk of recharacterization. This is more so for future flows. Hence, it might be sensible to (a) express the intent of the parties – for the transfer to operate as a sale of legal and beneficial interest in the asset to the transferee; (b) provide a standby clause to protect investor interest, so that if the transfer is not regarded as a sale, it will be regarded as a secured borrowing. This will ensure investors have the rights over the collateral.

Sample:

> It is the intention of the Parties that the sale and assignment contemplated by this Agreement shall constitute an absolute sale of the Receivables from the Seller to the Purchaser, and vest all legal and beneficial interest therein to the Purchaser. Without prejudice to the above, if the sale and assignment contemplated hereby is held not to be a sale by any authority or for any statutory purposes, then, this agreement shall be deemed to be an agreement of mortgage by the Seller, and the Seller hereby grants to the Purchaser interest in all of the Receivables, by way of mortgage, to secure payment of all such sums as the Seller, as a Servicer under this agreement is obligated to make. In such contingency, the Seller shall agree to enter into such documentation, and/or do such filing or registration as may be required to give effect to the above.

Consideration for the transfer

The consequence of the conveyance is consideration for the transfer. The manner in which the consideration is paid to the seller could differ from case to case. A common way is for the transferee to pay the consideration in a determinable amount of cash at the time of the conveyance; in such cases, the amount may be specified. In several pooling agreements, the transfer of assets will take place over time, and therefore, the documentation will have to mention the manner of computing the consideration, such as discounting future receivables at a particular discount rate.

Yet another common way of settling the consideration up front is the issuance of certificates or securities by the SPV; the SPV simply buys receivables and transforms the same into securities which is "paid" as consideration to the seller, for the seller to offload to investors. This method goes well with the nature of the purchaser as a special purpose entity. In other words, the initial transaction between the seller and the purchaser is merely an exchange.

A part of the consideration may also be reserved as *deferred sale consideration* – basically a profit-trapping device for the seller to sweep any remaining profits in the SPV. The deferred sale consideration may be an amount or a formula, such as the excess of the trust property remaining after discharging all beneficiary payments and meeting all trust expenses.

Conditions precedent

Conditions precedent refers to those events without which the transaction contemplated by the parties will not go ahead, and therefore, the agreement will be rendered ineffective *ab initio*. For example, it may be a condition precedent for the seller that the SPV has been successful in raising funding to the extent contemplated; the transfer of receivables does not make sense if investors have not been lined up. Concurrence of parties may also be a condition precedent.

If the transaction contemplates regular sales of receivables, the conditions precedent to any such sale may also be mentioned.

Representations and warranties of the Seller

This is by far the most "spacious" part of securitization documentation, filling in a lot of pages. Representation and warranties are a significant part of the documentation, as the seller makes certain affirmative or negative statements about himself as well as the quality of the receivables sold. Breach of the representations and warranties allows the purchaser to require the seller to repurchase the receivables or to demand compensation.

The purpose of making the representations and warranties is to provide the basic assurance required as to merchantability of what is being sold – the receivables. The representations and warranties should not be extended to provide ongoing credit support: that would be taken as a credit enhancement. There are regulatory implications of giving representations and warranties that are in the nature of credit enhancement.[2]

Broadly, the seller's representations are (a) representations about himself; and (b) representations about the receivables. The former are largely standard representations applicable for most business transactions. The latter are partly standard representations, and partly make assertions about the quality, age and collateral backing of the receivables.

As stated, an attempt may be made to remove the standard representations from individual documents and incorporate them by reference to some central industry document, as in the case of ISDA. In any case, most are implicit warranties; their absence from a documentation is unlikely to do any damage to the counterparty.

Standard representations about the Seller

We put in below standard representations, translating them into a standard language applicable in most cases:

(i) **Status.** The Seller is duly organized and validly existing under the laws of the jurisdiction of its organization or incorporation and, if relevant under such laws, in good standing;

(ii) **Powers.** The Seller has the power to execute this Agreement and any other documentation relating to this Agreement to which it is a party, to deliver this Agreement and any other documentation relating to this Agreement that it is required by this Agreement to deliver and to perform its obligations under this Agreement and any obligations it has under this agreement or any similar agreement to which it is a party and has taken all necessary action to authorize such execution, delivery and performance;

(iii) **No Violation or Conflict.** Such execution, delivery and performance do not violate or conflict with any law applicable to it, any provision of its constitutional documents any order or judgment of any court or other agency of government applicable to it or any of its assets or any contractual restriction binding on or affecting it or any of its assets;

(iv) **Consents.** All governmental and other consents that are required to have been obtained by it with respect to this Agreement or any other agreement for the purpose of this transaction to which it is a party have been obtained and are in full force and effect and all conditions of any such consents have been complied with; and

(v) **Obligations Binding.** Its obligations under this Agreement and any other document relating to the transaction to which this agreement pertains, constitute its legal, valid and binding obligations, enforceable in accordance with their respective terms (subject to applicable bankruptcy, reorganization, insolvency, moratorium or similar laws affecting creditors' rights generally and subject, as to enforceability, to equitable principles of general application) regardless of whether enforcement is sought in a proceeding in equity or at law.

(vi) **Ordinary business activity**: The execution of this Agreement by Seller as also the consummation of the transaction contemplated by this agreement, are in the ordinary course of business of the Seller, and will not result into any breach of any corporate law or procedure, contractual restriction under any other business transaction or borrowing or financial arrangement, will not result into any default or acceleration of any other material agreement.

(vii) **Absence of Litigation.** There is not pending or, to its knowledge, threatened against it or any of its holding company or affiliates, any action, suit or proceeding at law or in any equity or before any court, tribunal, governmental body, agency or official or any arbitrator that is likely to affect the continued business powers of the Seller, or legality, validity or enforceability against it of this Agreement or the transaction contemplated by this Agreement, or its ability to perform its obligations under this Agreement.

(viii) **Accuracy of Information**. No written information, financial statement, document, book, record or report furnished or to be furnished by the Seller to the Purchaser, Underwriter, Rating agency, due diligence auditor or otherwise in relation to the transaction contemplated by this Agreement is or shall be inaccurate in any material respect as of the date it is or shall be dated or furnished, or contains or shall contain any material misstatement of fact or omits or shall omit to state a material fact or any fact necessary to make the statements contained therein not materially misleading.

Standard representations about the Receivables

Each Receivable (or where the language so warrants, with respect to each Receivable):

(i) **Compliance with the law** Complies at the time it was originated or made, and at the date such Receivable is sold by the Seller to the Purchaser, complies, in all material respects, with all requirements of Applicable Law (the word "applicable law" may be defined to include all laws applicable to the jurisdictions, rules, regulations, statutory guidelines or interpretations, code of practice).

(ii) **Enforceability of the Receivables** Was originated under an origination agreement that was not a fraud or misrepresentation, or based on fraud or misrepresentation by any party concerned, and represents the genuine, legal, valid and binding payment obligation in writing of the Obligor, enforceable by the holder thereof in accordance with its terms and all parties to each Receivable had full legal capacity to execute and deliver such Receivable and all other documents related thereto and to grant the security interest purported to be granted thereby.

(iii) **Conveyance of good legal title**: Immediately prior to the sale of Receivable, the Seller has, and by these presents, would convey to the Purchaser, good and marketable title to each Receivable free and clear of all liens, encumbrances, security interests and rights of others.

(iv) **Jurisdiction:** Has been originated by way of an origination agreement in the Acceptable Jurisdiction (either name the country or the province or define the term) either by the Seller or a person lawfully acting on behalf of the Seller in the ordinary course of the Seller's business, with full authority to originate the Receivable;

(v) **Security interest:** Creates or shall create a valid, subsisting and enforceable right to receive money as specified in the origination agreement along with (as applicable) (a) ownership interest over a physical asset; (b) first priority perfected security interest over a physical asset; (c) other rights as may be specified in the origination agreement, in favor of the Seller;

(vi) **Sufficiency of the rights:** Originated by an origination agreement that contains customary and enforceable provisions such that the rights and remedies of the holder thereof shall be adequate for realization of the Receivable and against the collateral of the benefits of the ownership or security interest;

(vii) **No variation**: (Except as has been expressly made known to the Seller) the origination agreement in respect of the Receivable has not been amended, or rewritten or collections with respect thereto deferred or waived, and no Receivable has been satisfied, subordinated or rescinded, or the relevant security interest released in whole or in part;

(viii) **Unconditional obligation of the Obligor**: Represents an unconditional obligation of the Obligor to make payment under the origination agreement, and there is no performance, obligation, service or any other condition to be performed by the Seller, Servicer or any other person;

(ix) **No obligor right to set off**: Except as specified herein, the Obligor has no right of set off, deduction, counterclaim or any other right whereby any Receivable as provided for in the origination agreement may be wholly or partly reduced, satisfied, adjusted or otherwise adversely affected in any manner;

(x) **Predominance of Seller interest**: To the best knowledge of the Seller, the Seller has sole interest in the Receivables and in the ownership or security interest related thereto, and except for the security interests in favor of the Seller, the Receivables are free and clear of all security interests, liens, charges, and encumbrances and to the best knowledge of the Seller no right of rescission, set-off, counterclaim or defence has been asserted or threatened with respect to any Receivable;

(xi) **No prior sale or agreement to sell**: The Seller has not done or agreed to do any sale, encumbrance, pledge, assignment, or any other dealing in the whole or any part of the Receivable, nor created any legal or equitable interest including interest of participation therein;

(xii) **Correctness of information**: The information set forth in the Schedule of Receivables or otherwise provided to the Purchaser is true and correct, or is based on the records of the Seller, which the Seller attests as true and correct in all material respects on the Cut-off Date;

(xiii) **Update of records to mark sale**: Immediately upon sale of Receivable, the Seller would have appropriately marked or made appropriate records in all books, accounts, database or other record of the Seller to enter therein the fact that the Receivable stands sold to the Purchaser;

(xiv) **Fairness in lending practices**: The lending practices used by the Seller in origination of the transaction were legal, ethical and as per standard industry practices of conscionable conduct;

(xv) **Compliance with underwriting standards**: The origination agreement was originated generally in accordance with the underwriting standards in effect at the time origination, and was diligently underwritten following standard procedures of the Seller's business (if appropriate, make a schedule of important underwriting criteria – this provides an important protection to the investors against accounts that go delinquent due to original defect); and

(xvi) **General prudence**: Generally, the Seller is not aware, and after exercising due diligence, could not have been aware, as of the Cut-off Date, of any facts or circumstances that render the transaction contemplated by this agreement as an unacceptable investment, or would cause the Receivable to become delinquent, or otherwise would impair the value of the Receivable.

Specific representations about the Receivables

As may be understandable, these specific representations are specific to the asset in question and generalization is not possible. We give below samples of some representations and warranties for some types of collateral:

Residential mortgage
Each Receivable (or where the language so warrants, with respect to each Receivable):

(i)   **Original and remaining maturity:** Has a remaining maturity, as of the Cut-off Date, of not more than * months; and has an original maturity of not more than ** months;

(ii)   **Remaining principal balance:** Has a remaining Principal Balance as of the Cut-off Date of not more than $***;

(iii) **Past due:** Is no more than 30 days past due as of the Cut-off Date (also, the following condition may be put: was not more than 90 days past due at any time from the date of its origination up to the Cut-off Date), and no funds have been advanced by the Seller, or Seller's affiliate, or anyone acting on behalf of any of them to the Obligor to pay any of the Obligor's dues under the origination agreement to the Seller;

(iv)   **No default:** No default, breach, violation or event permitting acceleration under the terms of any Receivable has occurred, and the Seller has not waived any of the foregoing.

(v)   **No statutory obligations on mortgage property:** There are no delinquent taxes, ground rents, water charges, sewer rents, assessments, insurance premiums, leasehold payments, including assessments payable in future installments or other outstanding charges affecting the related mortgaged property.

(vi)   **Insurance of mortgage property:** All buildings on the mortgage property are insured by insurance with an approved insurer, against loss by fire, hazards of extended coverage and such other hazards as are customary for the type of the mortgage property or the area where the mortgaged property is located. All such insurance policies name the Seller as the mortgagee and loss payee, and all premiums due thereon have been paid. The terms of the origination agreement or the mortgage obligate the Obligor/mortgagor to keep effective all such insurance at mortgagor's cost and expense, and on the Mortgagor's failure to do so, authorizes the holder of the mortgage to maintain such insurance at mortgagor's cost and expense;

(vii) **Title insurance policy:** (Make similar provisions as above, if the mortgages are supposed to have been covered against the mortgagor's title);

(viii) **Pool insurance/primary mortgage insurance:** (Make similar provisions as above, if the mortgages are supposed to have been covered against the mortgage pool insurance).

(ix)   **Enforceability of the mortgage:** All requirements of law as to stamping, registration, filing, or enforceability of the mortgage have been duly complied with and the mortgage is a first, subsisting valid legal lien of the mortgagee;

   (x) **Completion of disbursement/no holdbacks:** The mortgage loan has been fully disbursed and the Seller is not obligated to make any further or future advances there under. All costs, fees and expenses incurred in making or closing the origination transaction have been paid, and the Seller is not entitled to any refund of any amounts paid or due in respect of the origination agreement;

  (xi) **Loan to value ratio/debt to income ratio:** The mortgage in the origination agreement does not have, at the time of origination, a loan-to-value ratio of more than **%; debt-to-income ratio of more than **%;

 (xii) **Consolidation of Seller advances**: All advances made by the Seller in relation to the mortgage have been consolidated with the outstanding principal balance in respect of the origination agreement, and the Seller will not have any claim on the Receivables or the mortgage property subsequent to consummation of this agreement.

Commercial mortgage receivables

The representations and warranties in commercial mortgage transactions are substantially similar to those above. Rating agency Duff and Phelps published a special report titled **DCR Examines Latest Legal Issues Regarding Mortgage Loans,**[3] wherein a standard set of representations and warranties for CMBS transactions was listed. Most are the same as above; we mention only the additional and partly additional clauses (elaborated, simplified and standardized by the author):

   (i) **Condition of Mortgaged Property.** Each Mortgaged Property is in good repair and condition, free of any material damage.

  (ii) **Local law compliance.** Each Mortgaged Property including any extension or improvement thereof is in full compliance with all applicable local laws (this word might either be defined or elaborated in relation to the local laws relating to construction, zoning, town planning, easements, use and operation of the property, safety standards); all inspections, licenses and certificates required have been obtained and are in full force and effect. There are no encroachments, improvements on adjoining properties that materially encroach upon such Mortgaged Property so as to materially and adversely affect the value or marketability of such Mortgaged Property.

 (iii) **Environmental Compliance.** The Mortgaged Property fully complies with environmental laws, guidelines of any international body or norms which are applicable to the Mortgaged Property.

  (iv) **Insurance.** Each Mortgaged Property and all improvements thereon are covered by insurance policies providing coverage against loss or damage sustained by

   a. fire and extended perils included within the classification "All Risk of Physical Loss" in an amount not less than the principal balance of the Mortgage Note and sufficient to prevent the Mortgagor from being deemed a co-insurer; such policies provide coverage on a full replacement cost basis and contain no deduction for depreciation;

b. business interruption or rental loss insurance in an amount at least equal to 12 months (or 18 months for specialty properties) of operations of the Mortgaged Property;

c. flood insurance (or other natural hazards depending on the area where the property is located);

d. acts of terrorism, vandalism, riots, outbreaks, or other similar risks

e. comprehensive general liability insurance in amounts as are generally required by contemporary prudent commercial mortgage lenders for similar properties; and

f. workers' compensation insurance; [other insurance as applicable to specific circumstances and criteria].

The insurer with respect to each policy is qualified to write insurance in the relevant jurisdiction and has a claims paying ability rating from the Rating Agency of not less than "A".

The insurance policies contain a standard mortgage clause naming the mortgagee, its successors and assigns as additional insured's, and provide that they are not terminable and may not be reduced without thirty (30) days prior written notice to the mortgagee; all premiums due and payable through the Closing Date have been made; no notice of termination or cancelation with respect to any such policies has been received by Seller. Each Mortgage requires that the Mortgagor maintain insurance as described above or permits the mortgagee to require insurance as described above. The Mortgage for each Mortgage Loan provides that proceeds paid under any such casualty insurance policy will (or, at the mortgagee's option, will) be applied either to the repair or restoration of the related Mortgaged Property or to the payment of amounts due under such Mortgage Loan.

(v)   The Seller has inspected or caused to be inspected each related Mortgaged Property within the last 12 months.

(vi) Each Mortgaged Property consists of an estate in fee simple in real property[4] and improvements owned by the Mortgagor. The buildings and improvements on the Mortgaged Property are owned by the Mortgagor and are used and occupied for commercial purposes in accordance with applicable law. [If there are any leasehold mortgages, see representation below against **ground leases**]

(vii) **Transfers and Subordinate Debt.** The Mortgage contains a "due on sale" clause, which provides for the acceleration of the payment of the unpaid principal balance of the Mortgage Loan if, without the prior written consent of the holder of the Mortgage, the property subject to the Mortgage, or any interest therein, is directly or indirectly transferred or sold. The Mortgage prohibits any further pledge, encumbrance or lien on the Mortgaged Property, whether equal or subordinate to the lien of the Mortgage, without the prior written consent of the holder of the Mortgage.

(viii) **Ground Leases.** With respect to any Mortgage Loan that is secured by an unencumbered interest of the Mortgagor as lessee under a ground lease ("Ground Lease") of the related Mortgaged Property, the Seller hereby represents and warrants to the Purchaser that:

  (i) such Ground Lease or a memorandum thereof has been duly recorded; such Ground Lease permits the interest of the lessee there under to be encumbered by the related Mortgage and does not restrict the use of the related Mortgaged Property by such lessee, its successors or assigns in a manner that would materially adversely affect the security provided by the related Mortgage; and there has been no material change in the terms of such Ground Lease as its recordation, except by written instruments all of which are expressly declared to the Purchaser;

  (ii) the lessor under such Ground Lease has agreed in such Ground Lease (or in another writing included in the related Mortgage File) that such Ground Lease may not be amended, modified, canceled or terminated without the prior written consent of the Mortgagee and that any such action without such consent is not binding on the mortgagee, its successors or assigns;

  (iii) such Ground Lease has an original term (or an original term plus one or more optional renewal terms that under all circumstances may be exercised, and will be enforceable, by the mortgagee) that extends not less than ten years beyond the stated maturity of the related Mortgage Loan;

  (iv) such Ground Lease is not subject to any liens or encumbrances superior to, or of equal priority with, the Mortgage other than any encumbrances specifically permitted herein; and such Ground Lease is, and provides that it shall remain, prior to any mortgage or other lien upon the related Fee Interest;

  (v) such Ground Lease does not permit any increase in the amount of rent payable by the lessee there under during the term of the Mortgage Loan;

  (vi) such Ground Lease is assignable to the Purchaser and its assigns without the consent of the lessor there under;

  (vii) as of the date of execution and delivery hereof, such Ground Lease is in full force and effect and no default has occurred under such Ground Lease nor is there any existing condition which, but for the passage of time or the giving of notice, would result in a default under the terms of such Ground Lease;

  (viii) such Ground Lease (or other written agreement signed by lessor) requires the lessor to give notice of any default by the lessee to the Mortgagee; and such Ground Lease (or other written agreement) further provides that no notice given there under is effective against the Mortgagee unless a copy has been given to the Mortgagee;

(ix) a mortgagee is permitted a reasonable opportunity (including, where necessary, sufficient time to gain possession of the interest of the lessee under such Ground Lease through legal proceedings or to take other action so long as the Mortgagee is proceeding diligently) to cure any default under such Ground Lease that is curable after the receipt of notice of any such default before the lessor there under may terminate such Ground Lease; and all rights of the Mortgagee under such Ground Lease and the related Mortgage (insofar as it relates to the Ground Lease) may be exercised by or on behalf of the Mortgagee;

(x) such Ground Lease does not impose any restrictions on subletting which would be viewed as commercially unreasonable by an institutional investor; and the lessor there under is not permitted to disturb the possession, interest or quiet enjoyment of any subtenant of the lessee in the relevant portion of the Mortgaged Property subject to such Ground Lease for any reason, or in any manner, which would materially adversely affect the security provided by the related Mortgage;

(xi) under the terms of such Ground Lease and the related Mortgage, taken together, any related insurance proceeds (other than in respect of a total or substantially total loss or taking) will be applied either (A) to the repair or restoration of all or part of the related Mortgaged Property, with the mortgagee or a trustee appointed by it having the right to hold and disburse such proceeds as repair or restoration progresses, or (B) to the payment of the outstanding principal balance of the Mortgage Loan, together with any accrued interest thereon; and

(xii) under the terms of such Ground Lease and the related Mortgage, taken together, any related insurance proceeds or condemnation award in respect of a total or substantially total loss or taking of the related Mortgaged Property will be applied first to the payment of the outstanding principal balance of the Mortgage Loan, together with any accrued interest thereon (except in cases where a different allocation would not be viewed as commercially unreasonable by a prudent commercial mortgage lender, taking into account the relative duration of such Ground Lease and the related Mortgage and the ratio of the market value of the related Mortgaged Property to the outstanding principal balance of such Mortgage Loan); and until such principal balance and accrued interest rate are paid in full, neither the lessee nor the lessor under such Ground Lease will have the option to terminate or modify such Ground Lease without the prior written consent of the mortgagee as a result of any casualty or partial condemnation, except to provide for an abatement of the rent.

(ix) **Defeasance.** Each Mortgage Loan containing provisions for defeasance of mortgage collateral either (i) requires the prior written consent of, and compliance with the conditions set by, the holder of the Mortgage Loan, or (ii) requires that (A) defeasance may not occur prior to the time permitted by applicable rules (e.g., REMIC rules), (B) the replacement collateral consist of government securities in an amount sufficient to make all scheduled payments under the Mortgage Note when due, (C) independent certified public accountants certify that the collateral is sufficient to make such payments, (D) the loan be assumed by a Single-Purpose Entity designated by the holder of the Mortgage Loan, and (E) counsel provide an opinion that the trustee has a perfected security interest in such collateral prior to any other claim or interest.

Equipment lease receivables

Once again most of the standard clauses above are applicable. Below, we focus only on the clauses that have a distinctive applicability to equipment lease contracts:

(i) The Receivable arises from a bona fide lease of the Equipment described in the related Lease, and such Equipment is in all respects in accordance with the requirements of such Lease, has been delivered to and unqualifiedly accepted by the lessee there under, is in possession of the Obligor/lessee thereof, is not being subleased by such Obligor/lessee to any other Person (or, in case any sublease is permitted by the lease agreement, specify the conditions to which the sublease may be subjected, and also provide that where Obligor has subleased the Equipment to sublessee, the Obligor remains liable under the original lease or sale of such Equipment);

(ii) Receivable, together with the related Lease and Equipment, comply with all applicable laws and regulations;

(iii) Receivable arises under a Lease that is a non-cancelable, unconditional, hell or high water agreement;[5]

(iv) Receivable, together with the Equipment and all proceeds thereof, are not subject to any Adverse Claim of the lessee, or any other Person;

(v) In respect of any Receivable arising under a Lease of Equipment, such Lease requires the Obligor to maintain the Equipment in good and workable order and provides that, in the event of any loss, damage or destruction of the Equipment covered by or the subject of such Lease, the Obligor will replace such Equipment with same-or-better model Equipment in same-or-better configuration or the Purchaser will receive from an insurer or from the Obligor as self-insurer, an amount not less than the Repurchase Price of the Lease Receivable (specify the method of computing the repurchase price);

(vi) In respect of Receivable as also the Equipment, all taxes, assessments, fines, fees and other liabilities have been paid when due;

(vii) The Seller (i) is the owner of, or has a first priority perfected security interest in, each item of Equipment subject to the related Lease, free and clear of any Adverse Claim and (ii) has granted a first priority perfected security interest in such Equipment to the Purchaser;

(viii) If a purchase option or early termination option exists with respect to the related Lease, the payment required in connection with the exercise of such purchase option or early termination option is in an amount sufficient to recover the Repurchase Price;

Future flows

For future flows, the sale of the receivables will legally take place when the receivables are originated in future. The conditions subject to which the purchaser buys the receivables are, therefore, more in the nature of covenants of the seller to be complied with at the time of sale. These are, in addition to the representations listed above (to the extent applicable), similar to loan-type restrictions on the borrower's business. These are discussed under the heading Covenants below.

Consequences of breach of representations

Breach of representation is a breach of promise on the part of the seller, and the transaction documentation would usually provide for three alternative remedies:

- If the breach is corrigible, the seller will be given a time within which he must correct the breach.
- If not, the seller would be required to substitute the receivable failing the representation by a like receivable, which complies with the same.
- As the second option may be difficult in many cases, the seller would mostly be required to repurchase the receivable that fails the representation.

In the last case, it is important to specify the method of repurchase and the computation of the repurchase price. Usually, it is not a particular receivable that will fail to comply with the representation; a particular origination agreement will be disqualified, leading to a repurchase of all the receivables under the agreement. Therefore, computation of the repurchase price needs to be done by applying a discounting rate, which quite likely is the initial discounting rate minus a penalty.

Sample:

Upon the discovery by any Party (a defined term, including the servicer, trustee or beneficiary) of a breach or breaches of any of the representations and warranties of the Seller, the party discovering such breach shall give prompt written notice to the other parties. The Purchaser shall promptly notify the Seller of such breach and (i) where, in the opinion of the Purchase, the breach is curable, request that the Seller cure such breach within ** days; (ii) where either the Seller fails to cure the breach within ** days of the notice referred to in (i) above, or, in the opinion of the Purchaser, the breach is not curable, the Seller shall either (a) substitute a origination agreement in respect of which the breach has been notified, by an acceptable replacement origination agreement (as specified below) or (b) repurchase such origination agreement from the Purchaser and forthwith pay the Purchase Price.

A replacement origination agreement shall be acceptable to the Purchaser, and shall further satisfy the following criteria:

(i) have an outstanding Scheduled Principal Balance, not greater than nor materially less than the Scheduled Principal Balance of the substituted origination agreement (the amount of any shortage shall be paid for in cash by the Purchaser, which shall be treated as a prepayment under this transaction);

(ii) at the time of substitution have an internal rate of return equal to or exceeding that of the substituted origination agreement;

(iii) have a Loan-to-Value Ratio no higher than the Loan-to-Value Ratio of the substituted origination agreement;

(iv) have a remaining term to maturity no greater than (and not more than one year less than) the substituted origination agreement;

(v) be of the same or better credit quality classification as that of the substituted origination agreement;

(vi) comply with each representation and warranty relating to the Receivables set forth herein; and

(vii) at the time of substitution have not been delinquent for a period of more than ** days or more than once in the ** months immediately preceding such date of substitution (notably, this criteria may be more stringent than that in the representations and warranties in the original clause).

No Receivable or origination agreement may be substituted more than once.

No substitution shall be made after the expiry of ** months from the cut-off date.

Upon acceptance of substitution by the Purchaser, the substituted origination agreement shall be deemed to have been subject to this agreement and shall be added to the Schedule of origination agreements forming part of this agreement, and shall, from the date of such substitution, be subject to all the terms and conditions herein.

For repurchase laid down herein, the repurchase price shall be computed as follows:

There are several alternatives available – the repurchase may be treated as a case of prepayment – which is what it is from investor viewpoint – and the method of computing the prepayment consideration as applicable to the obligor may be applied to the seller's repurchase. In cases where the payments under the origination agreements may be distinguished as between principal and interest, the required payment might be outstanding principal balance, any interest overdue, interest unto the next monthly payment date at the implicit rate of return, and a prepayment penalty. In case where the concept of principal and interest is not applicable (e.g., lease payments, future flows), the receivables may be present-valued.

Immediately after substitution or repurchase, the Purchaser shall cause the substituted or purchased origination agreement to be released, and shall execute such document (e.g., conveyance), at the cost of the Seller, as may be required to give effect to the same.

Continuing covenants of the seller

While conditions precedent are the preconditions to the operation of the transfer, the conditions subsequent or continuing covenants of the seller are the conditions that the seller agrees to satisfy over the period of the transaction.

The extent to which the seller's continuing covenants are important to a transaction depends on its nature; standard securitizations of existing receivables do not have much dependence on continuing obligations of the seller except in a servicing role. Reinstating transactions have a continued relation with the seller. On the other extreme, future flows are transactions that are highly dependent on continuing conditions of the seller. Obviously therefore, the scope of continuing covenants is the maximum for future flows.

For future flow-type securitizations, the continuing covenants are of two types – *positive covenants* and *negative covenants*. Positive covenants require compliance by the seller, while negative covenants are restrictions placed on the seller.

We give below sample covenants for a future flows deal. It may be noted that in most future flows, the seller is also the servicer; thus, there is an element of servicers' obligations (see below) inherent in these covenants:

Affirmative covenants

Until the termination date (a defined term) the Seller shall:

(i) **Compliance with Laws:** Comply in all material respects with all applicable laws, rules, regulations and orders with respect to it and which may affect its business and properties. (The Standard Representations and Warranties relating to the Seller's business call for a continued compliance for future flows. They might either be inserted here, or incorporated by reference).

(ii) **Payment of Taxes:** Pay and discharge, before the same shall become delinquent, all taxes and other statutory obligations imposed upon it or upon its property, unless such taxes or other obligations are genuinely contested; and generally ensure that any tax or statutory obligation does not result into any preferential claim of the government, or any statutory lien on property of the Seller;

(iii) **Compliance with law relating to transfer:** Comply in all material respects with all applicable local laws (define the term) relating to the origination, purchase, sale of Receivables and the transactions contemplated by the origination agreements, and maintain all authorizations, approvals, licenses, consents or registrations required to enable the Seller to perform its obligations;

(iv) **Maintenance of Records:** Keep and maintain accurate and complete books and records and other information reasonably necessary and sufficient to permit verification of the accuracy of the reports to be furnished by the Seller;

(v) **Maintenance of Assets:** Maintain and preserve all of its assets and properties which are necessary for the conduct of its business in good working order;

(vi) **Employment of Personnel:** Employ, or contract the services of, appropriately trained personnel necessary to the performance of its obligations here undertaken;

(vii) **Maintenance of Insurance:** Maintain or cause to maintain property and casualty insurance with responsible and reputable insurance companies in accordance with applicable law and, in any event, in amounts no less than, and covering its properties and business no less comprehensive than such is in place on the Closing Date, unless such insurance is not available on commercially reasonable terms;

(viii) **Origination volumes:** Ensure that for any ** consecutive months, the average revenues of the Seller on account of the sale/supply/rendering of the subject transaction (for example, exports, ticket sales, royalty) does not fall below the average over the last ** years, or an amount of $****, whichever is higher. (Similar operational triggers may be put here as covenants);

(ix) **Performance of Obligations with respect to Customers:** Perform from time to time, to the extent commercially desirable by the nature of its dealings, comply with its obligations to Customers and with respect to such other action related thereto as is necessary to satisfy all conditions to the payment obligations of Customers on the Receivables;

(x) **Provision of information:** Provide to the Purchaser on a continuing basis as also as and when demanded the following information (a) quarterly financial statements; (b) break up of turnover in respect of the asset/goods/services to which the transaction relates; (c) break up of Customers, including customers not covered by this agreement; (d) such other information (either identify, or empower the Purchaser to instruct);

(xi) **Accuracy of Reports:** Each report, schedule, financial statement, book or record to be furnished at any time to the Trustee, the Holders of Certificates, any Collateral Agent or any Rating Agency in connection with any of the Transaction Documents will be accurate in all material respects as of its date or (except as otherwise expressly disclosed at the time) as of the date so furnished and will be in the English language or accompanied by a true and correct English translation thereof, and no such document will contain any untrue statement of a material fact or will omit to state a material fact necessary in order to make the statements contained therein, in the light of the circumstances under which they are or will be made, not misleading.

Negative Covenants of the Seller

(xii) **Dissolution or Winding-up, change in business:** The Seller shall not wind up, dissolve, merge or sell substantially all of its assets, nor permit any material change in its business, corporate character, nor merge or demerge or cause any other early amortization or acceleration event (both these are to be defined);

(xiii) **Rights of Certificate holders and Trustee:** The Seller shall not do anything or refrain from doing anything that would impair in any material respect the rights and interests of the Purchaser of the Beneficiaries, including, without limitation, sale, disposal, encumbrance or any other dealing in the Receivables, or any other asset that gives right to the Receivables, granting, or consenting to the exercise by any person of, any right of withdrawal, deduction or set-off in respect of or against Receivables;

(xiv) **Termination of Transaction Documents:** The Seller shall not contest, cancel or terminate, or purport to contest, cancel or terminate, any of the Transaction Documents or amend, modify, supplement or change in any manner any term or condition of any of them or any of the origination agreements, or underwriting policy with respect to the origination agreements;

(xv) **Instructions to Customers:** The Seller shall not give Customers any instructions contrary to or inconsistent with the provisions hereof;

(xvi) **Limitations on charges or security interests:** Until the terminal date (or until any amount remains outstanding to a Beneficiary), the Seller will not assume or incur or suffer to be created, assumed or incurred or to exist any charges or lien on any of its properties or assets (including, without limitation, Receivables), except for the following exclusions:

    a.   Liens existing or created on the date of this Agreement;

    b.   Liens in favor of any Governmental Authority to secure progress, advance or other payments pursuant to any contract or provision of any statute;

    c.   Liens (including, without limitation, the interest of the lessor under any capital lease) on property or assets existing at the time of the acquisition thereof or to secure the payment of all or any part of the purchase price or construction cost thereof or to secure any indebtedness incurred prior to, at the time of, or within six months after, the acquisition or completion of such property or assets for the purpose of financing all or any part of the purchase price or construction cost thereof;

    d.   Any extension, renewal or replacement, wholly or in part, of any Lien referred to in the foregoing;

    e.   Liens for taxes or statutory outgoings not yet due which are being contested in good faith;

    f.   Liens under law or liens for claims of any unpaid seller, banker, transporter, workman or mechanic, where any direct or indirect sanction of the Seller is not required;

g. Any attachment or judgment Lien, unless the judgment it secures shall not, within 30 days after the entry thereof, have been discharged or execution thereof stayed pending appeal, or shall not have been discharged within 30 days after the expiration of any such stay;

h. Deposits to secure the performance of bids, trade contracts (other than for borrowed money), leases, statutory obligations, surety and appeal bonds, performance bonds and other obligations of a like nature incurred in the ordinary course of business; and

i. Other Liens incidental to the conduct of the Seller's business or the ownership of its property and assets that are incurred in connection with the borrowing of money or the obtaining of advances or credit or capital leases; *provided, however*, that the indebtedness secured thereby does not exceed in the aggregate for the Seller an amount equal to *****.

Clean-up call

The entire transaction, including the duties of the seller, servicer and trustees will be terminated on the option to terminate – the clean-up call exercised by the seller. Clean-up call is an option, and is typically exercised only when the outstanding principal balance falls below a certain amount, say 10%. Here again, provisions need to be made for the repurchase price. The clean-up call option may also inherit a method of recapturing seller's profits as the purchase price may be set close to the amount outstanding on account of the investors.

Servicing covenants

The servicing agreement may also be a part of the transfer agreement or a stand alone agreement. The advantage of having a stand alone agreement is that servicing obligations are transferable. The advantage of a common pooling and servicing agreement is brevity.

The servicer clauses contain extremely important provisions relating to the administration of the receivables. Most of these relate to routines that the transferor follows for his own receivables; for receivables not transferred, the originator does it nevertheless and when the receivables have been transferred, the transferor has to do these tasks. The draftsman must understand that the transferee is a special purpose entity with no body or soul, and so all functions with respect to the receivables will have to be carried out by the servicer.

As the essence of securitization transactions lies in the independent portability of servicing arrangements, the servicing clauses should be as objective as possible, so that the same provisions with minimal alterations may be applied to a successor servicer as well.

Below we discuss the significant servicing clauses:

Appointment, termination

The appointment of the transferor (or that of an independent) as a servicer is an important condition precedent for most securitization transactions. Servicing is not only the very function that converts the receivables into value, but is also from the transferor's viewpoint a significant source of extracting profits from the transaction.

The appointment clause simply appoints the servicer as such, to service the Receivables for and on behalf of the Purchaser and the Beneficiaries.

The termination clauses relate to events of default by the servicer, his termination and the appointment of a backup servicer. These are discussed separately below.

Servicing standard and basic servicing functions

The servicing standard clause provides for a general guidance on the standard of servicing that the servicer is expected to follow. Most often, this clause also gives a listing of the important servicing functions of the servicer. Securitization agencies such as Fannie Mae have come out with detailed pronouncements on servicing standards.[6]

Sample

> **Servicing standard:**
>
> The Servicer agrees that its servicing of the Receivables shall be carried out in accordance with (either specify the guidelines, for example, Fannie Mae guidelines, or annex the important procedures) customary and usual procedures of institutions that are primarily engaged in the business of servicing the type of Receivables to be serviced hereunder; Provided, that in any event the Servicer shall exercise at least the degree of skill and attention that the Servicer exercises with respect to similar receivables that it services for itself or others (the foregoing standard of care being referred to as the "Servicing Standard").
>
> **Basic servicer duties:**
>
> The Servicer's duties shall include all those functions of collection, administration and customer service that the Servicer does in respect of receivables serviced for itself, and without affecting the generality of the above:
>
> 1. collection and posting of all payments; monitoring the same on regular basis, investigating delinquencies; issuing payment receipts if required;
> 2. responding to inquiries of Obligors on the Receivables; providing outstanding payment schedules or any information required for tax or other purposes by Obligors;

3. monitoring the security interest created by Obligors;
4. accounting for collections and furnishing monthly and annual statements to the Purchaser (add other parties, if important);
5. monitoring the status of all insurance policies (list all policies relevant here – in respect of the security interest, physical asset);
6. enforcing all the rights of the Seller as originator under the origination agreements at the cost and expense of the Servicer; and
7. performing all other functions specified in the agreement.

Power and authority of the Servicer:
To the extent consistent with the servicing standards, the Servicer shall follow customary standards, policies, and procedures and shall have full power and authority, acting alone, to do any and all things in connection with such managing, servicing, administration and collection that it may deem necessary or desirable. Without limiting the generality of the foregoing, the Servicer is hereby authorized and empowered by the Purchaser to do the following on behalf of, and under the authority of the Purchaser:

1. to execute and deliver, to the extent customary, any and all instruments of satisfaction or cancelation, or of partial or full release or discharge, and all other comparable instruments, with respect to the Receivables and with respect to the security interest; provided, that the Servicer shall not, except pursuant to an order from a court of competent jurisdiction, release an Obligor from payment of any unpaid amount or waive the right to collect the unpaid balance of any Receivable; (one may make provision for notification of any such release or satisfaction to be given promptly or on regular intervals to the Purchaser);
2. to take any action in law or as permitted by the security agreement an action to enforce security interest, including appointment of the Servicer himself, or an officer or agent of the Servicer, or any other person, as a receiver;
3. to commence, in its own name or in the name of the Purchaser, a legal proceeding to enforce a Receivable or to commence or participate in any other legal proceeding (including, without limitation, a bankruptcy proceeding) relating to or involving a Receivable, an Obligor or security interest provided in respect of the Receivables. If the Servicer commences or participates in such a legal proceeding in its own name, the Purchaser shall thereupon be deemed to have automatically assigned such Receivable to the Servicer solely for purposes of commencing or participating in any such proceeding as a party or claimant, and the Servicer is authorized and empowered by the Purchaser to execute and deliver in the Servicer's name any notices, demands, claims, complaints, responses, affidavits or other documents or instruments in connection with any such proceeding. The Purchaser shall furnish the Servicer with any powers of attorney and other documents as may be reasonably required and take any other steps which the Servicer may deem necessary or appropriate for this purpose. (Important provision needs to be made for legal costs: generally the cost

of legal enforcement is to be borne by the Servicer himself; provision is made for reimbursement of legal expenses provided the recovery from an enforcement action exceeds the amount of Receivables due, or where an amount is recovered specifically pertaining to such expenses – say, costs awarded by a Court);

4. to collect and enforce any proceeds under Insurance policies or to agree to the application of any insurance proceeds to restoration/repair of the insured property;
5. to agree to any subordinated financing on the security interest or the creation of a subordinated security interest on such asset; provided that in no circumstances the Servicer shall consent to the creation of a senior or parallel security interest;
6. to waive any late charges or penalties payable by the Obligors; and
7. to waive any prepayment penalties.

Limitations on powers of the Servicer
The Servicer shall not, except with the specific approval of the Purchaser:

1. Make or permit any modification to the origination agreement or otherwise give any waiver or reduction that would reduce the amount of any Receivable or reduce the internal rate of return inherent in the Receivables;
2. Agree to any subordination, release or impairment of the security interest;
3. Do any other act or thing or refrain from doing the same that is likely to have an adverse impact on the Receivables or the interest of the Purchaser therein.

Consideration for servicing: Servicing fee

This is another very important provision of the overall structure of the transaction. As stated, the servicing fee is not merely a compensation for the costs and efforts of the servicer, but quite likely also a way of capturing the excess profits of the transferor.

If there is an element of profit capture involved in the service fee, the structure would usually provide for a distinction between the service fees and the excess service fees (which may be alternatively named, for example, as base service fee and the supplemental servicing fee). The service fee is usually expressed as a rate to be applied to the scheduled principal balance of each origination transaction (e.g., the scheduled principal of each loan). The excess service fee may also, likewise, be defined either as a rate, or in some cases, as the excess of the cash flows of the purchaser over the amount required for investor service. Both these are extremely important provisions for modeling the transaction and should be very clearly spelt out.

The break up of the service fees into normal and excess service fees is not a formality; it has important repercussions particularly in extreme events such as the bankruptcy of the servicer.[7]

Apart from servicing fees, the servicer is quite often also entitled to reimbursement of certain specific expenses; these must be clearly spelt out in the documentation.

Mode of collections and servicer advances

These clauses provide for the detailed logistics of the transaction – the manner of collection of the receivables and the cash flow, routing ultimately to the Purchaser or the beneficiaries, any servicer advances and the recovery thereof.

In most securitization transactions, collections are first pooled in a separate bank account from which they are used to pay off investors. The mechanics of the actual flow of cash into the bank accounts is a matter of logistics of the transaction.

Periodic (monthly, if payments made to the investors are monthly) servicer advances is a common feature of most securitization transactions. The servicer typically makes an advance payment equal to the scheduled collections for the month and reimburses himself of such advances from collections made during the month. Any unreimbursed amount is to be recovered from the next months' collections. If any receivable is declared delinquent, the transaction will have to distribute the loss on account of delinquency to the investors (in order of priority in losses), which means the servicer will be reimbursed to the extent of delinquent payments from out of the payments due to investors.

Typically, the normal as well as the excess service fees are deducted from the payments made to the purchaser's account. In addition, as the servicer makes servicer advances, the late fees are also generally retained by the servicer.

Provisions also need to be made for reinvestment of the balances into the special account into which the collections are being pooled; the period for which the cash may be reinvested, where might it be reinvested, and the treatment of the gains/losses on reinvestments.

Samples

The Servicer shall deposit into the Special Account within two Business Days of receipt by the Servicer, the following payments and collections received or made by it subsequent to the Cut-off Date:

(i) All payments on account of principal, including Principal Prepayments, on the origination agreements;

(ii) All payments on account of interest on the origination agreements, including prepayment charges, less the Servicing Fee and the Excess Servicing Fee;

(iii) All insurance proceeds, other than proceeds to be applied to the restoration or repair of the security interest or released to the Obligor in accordance with the Servicer's normal servicing procedures, net of expenses directly in connection therewith, unpaid servicing fees and unreimbursed Servicer Advances;

(iv)   All proceeds of any repurchase by the Seller of any origination agreements;

(v)   Any amount received on account of enforcement of any security interest, including foreclosure; and

(vi)   Any other amounts required to be deposited hereunder.

In the event that the Servicer shall remit or deposit any amount not required to be remitted or deposited herein, the Service may at any time withdraw such amount from the Special Account.

All funds deposited in the Special Account shall be held by the Servicer in trust for the Beneficiaries until disbursed in accordance herewith.

Any investments of amounts on deposit in the Special Account shall be made by the Servicer in Eligible Investments, which shall mature not later than the second Business Day preceding the next distribution date. All such Eligible Investments shall be made in the name of the Purchaser for the benefit of the Beneficiaries. All income and gain net of any losses realized from any such investment shall be for the benefit of the Servicer[8] and shall be subject to withdrawal at its direction from time to time.

Monthly advances

The flow of funds usually is from the collection account into which the monthly collections are pooled; payments are made to an account for payment to the investors. In this account, the servicer is required to make monthly advances.

Sample:

The Servicer shall, on each advance date, make an advance amount, equal to the aggregate of scheduled monthly payments (net of prepayments already made), less the servicing fee and excess servicing fee. The Servicer shall be obligated to make any such advance payment only to the extent that the corresponding monthly payment, in the good faith judgment of the Servicer, has not become non-recoverable (for which, see clause below). Such advances shall be deposited in the Investor Account.

The Servicer shall be entitled to be reimbursed from the Special Account for all advances made by the Servicer.

If the Servicer has made a determination that any monthly payment from an Obligor has become non-recoverable, the Servicer shall evidence such determination by a certificate of a responsible officer, setting the reasons for such determination.

Cash reserves

Maintenance of a certain cash reserve is a very common feature of most securitization transactions. Usually, the excess service fee is a subordinated item in the waterfall; therefore, the reserves are built out of the excess profits collected over time. Alternatively, the transferor might be required to transfer cash immediately towards the reserve account.

The clause dealing with the reserve account needs to specify the amounts to be transferred to the reserve account, utilization of the reserve account, and restoration of its balance.

Reporting requirements

The servicer is required to furnish periodic reports to the purchaser, as also to the trustee and rating agencies. The reporting clause sets out the frequency of the servicing report (normally monthly) and its contents. Some of the common reports are:

- Monthly Report of deposits into and withdrawal from the special account, broken into categories
- Monthly reports (usually in electronic format and so commonly referred to as the monthly tape) to the trustee to enable the trustee to prepare distribution schedule to the investors
- Annual report giving a full review of the servicer's activities and whether the servicer has duly complied with such obligations

Termination of servicer

The servicing function is performed by the servicer as the agent of the purchaser. Termination of servicing function and its migration to a backup servicer is an exceptional event in securitization transaction for several reasons. First, the servicer retains customer relations in normal course and there is least outward manifestation of the sale of the receivables as far as the customers are concerned. Termination of servicing would mean loss of customer relations, loss of business reputation, and a straight erosion of confidentiality. Two, migration of servicing is not easy at all; this has been experienced in several instances in the past. Three, servicing is an important source of profit for the transferor and migration of servicing may mean loss of servicing profits, unless the excess service fees continue to remain payable to the original servicer even after the termination of servicing.

The circumstances in which termination will take place are partly standard, such as breach of servicing contract, co-mingling of cash flow and lack of servicing standard. Partly, however, these might be specific to the case, such as any continued deterioration in the business of the servicer or any credit default by the servicer.

Sample

Servicer termination event shall mean any of the following:

(a) Any failure by the Servicer to deposit into the Special Account any proceeds or payment required to be so deposited under the terms of this Agreement that continues unremedied for a period of two Business Days after written notice is received by the Servicer (this may or may not include the failure to make servicer advances);

(b)   Failure on the part of the Servicer to duly observe or perform any other covenants or agreements of the Servicer set forth in this Agreement, which failure continues unremedied for a period of 30 days after knowledge thereof by the Servicer or after the date on which written notice of such failure shall have been given to the Servicer;

(c)   Any representation, warranty or statement of the Servicer or in statement in any certificate, report or other writing delivered pursuant hereto or thereto shall prove to be incorrect in any material respect as of the time when the same shall have been made, and, within 30 days after knowledge thereof by the Servicer or after written notice thereof, such breach remains unremedied;

(d)   The occurrence of any Bankruptcy event[9] with respect to the Servicer, or any winding up petition;

(e)   Any rating agency shall lower or withdraw the outstanding rating of the Beneficiary instruments because the existing or prospective financial condition or servicing capability of the Servicer is insufficient to maintain such outstanding rating.

Consequence of Servicer Termination event

(a)   If a Servicer Termination Event shall occur and be continuing, the Purchaser may, by notice given in writing to the Servicer, terminate all of the rights and obligations of the Servicer under this Agreement. On or after the receipt by the Servicer of such written notice, all authority, power, obligations and responsibilities of the Servicer under this Agreement automatically shall pass to, be vested in and become obligations and responsibilities of the Successor Servicer; Provided, that the Successor Servicer shall have no liability with respect to any obligation which was required to be performed by the terminated Servicer prior to the date that the successor Servicer becomes the Servicer or any claim of a third party based on any alleged action or inaction of the terminated Servicer.

(b)   The terminated Servicer agrees to cooperate with the successor Servicer in effecting the termination of the responsibilities and rights of the terminated Servicer under this Agreement, including, without limitation, the transfer to the successor Servicer for administration by it of all cash amounts that shall at the time be held by the terminated Servicer for deposit, or have been deposited by the terminated Servicer, in the Special Account or thereafter received with respect to the Receivables and the delivery to the successor Servicer of all relevant records and electronic databases to enable the successor Servicer to service the Receivable. The Purchaser and Servicer agree to take all consequential and ancillary steps required to migrate the servicing to the successor Servicer.

(c)   Upon any termination of, or appointment of a successor to, the Servicer, the Purchaser shall give prompt written notice thereof to each Obligor.

The Trust Deed

There is no diametric distinction between the purpose of the PSA and that of the trust deed, except that they deal with two different aspects of the same transaction. The PSA deals with the transaction between the seller and the purchaser; the trust deed deals with the relations between the beneficiaries and the trustee. Therefore, it is advisable, although not necessary, to keep the trust deed and the PSA distinct. One of the advantages of a distinct documentation is that beneficiaries do not have access to the terms of the transfer between the transferor and the purchaser; as the trust law in most countries compels a copy of the trust deed to be delivered to the beneficiaries.

The main clauses in the trust deed relate to the holding of the trust property by the trustee in trust for the beneficiaries, the rights of the beneficiaries to the trust property and their mutual priority, the issuance of certificates/notes or bonds, payment waterfall, recording of any transfers of in beneficial interests, revocation and satisfaction of the trust.

We discuss the main clauses of the trust deed below:

Acceptance of trust

This is a standard clause that brings the trust into existence. Unlike a corporation, a trust is not an entity; it is simply the trust reposed in respect of the property held by the trustee. The transferor transfers property to the trust, and the trust agrees to hold in trust for the beneficiaries: this brings the trust into existence. Thus, trust is an obligation attached to a property – an obligation to hold the property for the benefit of the beneficiaries and not the trustee himself.

In accepting the trust, the trustee declares the obligation to hold the property in trust.

Definition of trust property

As in the case of "receivables" for the PSA a very careful definition is required for the trust property. The trust property is the subject matter of the trust. Essentially, the trust property will consist of the receivables transferred by way of sale under the PSA, the benefits arising out of any of the collateral agreements, any credit enhancements, any reinvestment of the cash flows arising and any accretion arising out of the same. In addition, any physical property acquired by way of foreclosure of any of the security agreements will also form part of the trust property.

Samples

The trust property shall include:

a.   the initial corpus of the trust;[10]
b.   any amount paid by the Beneficiaries for acquisition of beneficial interest in the trust, to the extent the same has not been invested in acquiring the Receivables;

c. the Receivables listed in the schedule to the Pooling and Servicing agreement, including all interest and principal received or receivable by the Seller on or with respect to the origination agreements after the Cut-off Date, but not including payments of principal and interest due and payable on the origination agreements on or before the Cut-off Date;

d. any physical asset or interest therein, or any other asset acquired as a result of enforcement of any security interest created in respect of the Receivables;

e. any amount lying in or deposited in any of the accounts in which payments to the Trust are to be made, or from which the payments to the Beneficiaries are to be made;

f. any insurance policies with respect to the origination agreements; and

g. all proceeds of the conversion, voluntary or involuntary, of any of the foregoing into cash or other liquid property.

Issuance of certificates

Here, the trustee obliges himself to issue certificates evidencing the beneficial interests of the investors. Most likely, there will be various classes of certificates each having well-defined rights. The rights of the various classes to trust property and to payments by the trust may be set out in clauses dealing with the rights of the certificate holders. This clause will provide that the issue by the trustee of certificates under its hands shall be deemed to be an evidence of beneficial interest of the holder thereof, in accordance with the rights of the certificate holders detailed in the agreement.

The provisions relating to any depository for certificates (for issuance in dematerialized format), transfer of certificates, maintenance of register of certificate holders, issue of duplicate certificates and transmission of certificates will also need to be provided for here. These are standard provisions in the case of any marketable instruments.

Distribution of cash flow

The waterfall clause, or the manner of appropriation of cash flows, is an extremely important part of a securitization structure. The essential edifice of the transaction rests on this clause. This is the clause that makes the senior investors and external agencies safe.

The distribution of cash flows is made in a particular order of priorities. A similar clause, in reverse order of priorities, needs to be made for distribution of realized losses: that is, as the origination agreements are determined to be delinquent, the losses are distributed to the various classes. The loss distribution reduces the principal balance outstanding of the various classes, bottom up. The manner of determination of the losses may be prescribed in detail.

Sample distribution clause

On each distribution date, not later than XX:00 a.m. the Trustee shall cause to be made the following transfers and distributions from the

Investor Account in accordance with the following priorities (such transfers and distributions to be based solely on the information contained in the Servicer's Certificate delivered on the related Determination Date:

1. to the Servicer, to repay any outstanding Servicer Advances;
2. on an *inter-se pari passu* basis, to each of the collection banks, the bank of the Collection account, and accountants, its respective accrued and unpaid fees and expenses;
3. to the Servicer or backup servicer, the Servicing Fee;
4. to the Trustee, the trustee's fees;
5. transfer of money into Reserve Account until the Reserve Account is equal to the greater of X% of the outstanding principal balance of all origination agreements or $XXXX, whichever is more;
6. to the Senior Certificates, *pro rata*, any accrued interest for the distribution period for such Class, plus any unpaid accrued interest remaining unpaid;
7. to the Mezzanine Certificates, *pro rata*, any accrued interest for the distribution period for such Class, plus any unpaid accrued interest remaining unpaid;
8. to the Junior Certificates,[11] *pro rata* any accrued interest for the distribution period for such Class, plus any unpaid accrued interest remaining unpaid;
9. to the Servicer, for payment of excess service fees;
10. to the holders of the Senior Certificates, the scheduled principal distribution amount, towards reduction of the current outstanding principal thereof, until the principal balance is reduced to zero;[12]
11. to the holders of the Mezzanine Certificates, the scheduled principal distribution amount, towards reduction of the current outstanding principal thereof, until the principal balance is reduced to zero; and
12. to the holders of the Junior Certificates.

Reporting by the Trustee

The investors receive periodic reports about the pool performance and investor servicing from the trustee. As there is no formal investor reporting requirement by law,[13] the transaction documents lay down the contents of the trustee's report.

Duties of the Trustee

This clause sets out the duties, defences and indemnities of the trustees. Normally, securitization transactions are serviced by independent trustees, who are paid a trusteeship fee for acting as such. The trustees do not assume any liability for the payments due to the investors, except on account of gross negligence.

Trust law under the Anglo-Saxon jurisdictions has existed for a long time now and is much older than the concept of corporations. Trustee duties are elaborately set out in the trust law; most of these hold for securitization trustees as well. Therefore, if the country has a trust law, it might be useful to make a reference to the trustee duties under such law. However, some exclusions as set out below are important to make.

Sample:

[Standard provisions about appointment, qualifications, disqualifications, powers and duties of trustees, which are common for most business trusts, are not being mentioned here]

The Trustee shall, as long as the trust is not extinguished hold the trust property in trust for the beneficiaries and perform such duties and only such duties as are specifically set forth in this Agreement.

The Trustee, upon receipt of all certificates, statements, reports, documents or data furnished to the Trustee that are specifically required to be furnished hereunder shall examine them to determine whether they conform to the requirements of this Agreement. The Trustee shall have no duty to recompute, recalculate or verify the accuracy of any certificate, so furnished to the Trustee.

No provision of this Agreement shall be construed to relieve the Trustee from liability for its own negligent action or negligent failure, willful misfeasance or bad faith.

The Trustee shall not be personally liable except for the performance of such duties and obligations as are specifically set forth in this Agreement, no implied covenants or obligations shall be read into this Agreement against the Trustee and the Trustee may conclusively rely, as to the truth of the statements and the correctness of the opinions expressed therein, upon any certificates or opinions furnished to the Trustee and conforming to the requirements of this Agreement which it reasonably believed in good faith to be genuine and to have been duly executed by the proper authorities respecting any matters arising hereunder.

The Trustee shall not be personally liable with respect to any action taken, suffered or omitted to be taken by it in good faith in accordance with the direction of Beneficiaries evidencing not less than 25% of the Voting Interests allocated to any class of Certificates (or, provide for senior certificates).

No provision of this Agreement shall require the Trustee to expend or risk its own funds or otherwise incur any financial liability in the performance of any of its duties hereunder or in the exercise of any of its rights or powers if it shall have reasonable grounds for believing that repayment of such funds or adequate indemnity against such risk or liability is not reasonably assured to it.

The Trustee shall not be deemed to have knowledge of any event of default or potential event of default, unless an appropriate officer of the Trustee shall have received written notice thereof from the Servicer, the Seller or a Beneficiary, or an appropriate officer of the Trustee has actual notice thereof, and in the absence of such notice no provision hereof requiring the taking of any action or the assumption of any duties or responsibility by the Trustee following the occurrence of any event of default or potential event of default shall be effective as against the Trustee.

Draft of the Investor Certificate

The text and tone of the certificate to be offered to the investors depend on the nature of the instrument – certificate, note, bond or debenture. In addition, the required details and the references to local securities legislation also are, understandably, bound to differ. Stressing the general terms of the certificate, we give below a draft of the broad form of the certificate:

Certificate No.

Class _____

Date of Pooling and Servicing Agreement and Cut-off Date:

First Distribution Date:

Servicer:

Assumed Final Distribution Date

Pass-through Rate

Percentage Interest: _____%

Aggregate Initial Current Principal Amount of this Certificate as of the Cut-off Date: $_____

Initial Current Principal Amount of this Certificate as of the Cut-off Date: $_____

Securities Regulation numbers (if any)

MORTGAGE PASS-THROUGH
CERTIFICATE SERIES ***

Evidencing a percentage interest in the distributions allocable to the Class * Certificates with respect to a Trust Fund consisting primarily of a pool of mortgage loans sold by ****** (Seller)

This Certificate is payable solely from the assets of the Trust Fund, and does not represent an obligation of or interest in Seller, the Servicer or the Trustee referred to below or any of their affiliates or any other person (collectively referred to as "the Parties"). Neither this Certificate nor the underlying Mortgage Loans are guaranteed or insured by any governmental entity or by the Parties. None of the Parties will have any obligation with respect to any certificate or other obligation secured by or payable from payments on the Certificates.

This certifies that _____ (name of the holder) is the registered owner of the proportionate interest evidenced by this Certificate (obtained by dividing the Initial Current Principal Amount of this Certificate by the aggregate Initial Current Principal Amount of all Class * Certificates, both as specified above) in the beneficial ownership interest of Certificates of the same Class as this Certificate in a trust (the "Trust Fund") generally consisting of mortgages loans secured by residences, (collectively, the "Mortgage Loans") sold by the Seller. *** will act as master servicer of the Mortgage Loans (in such capacity, the "Servicer," which term includes any successors thereto under the Agreement referred to below). The Trust Fund was created pursuant to the

Pooling and Servicing Agreement dated as of the Cut-off Date specified above (the "Agreement"), between the Seller, the Servicer and the Trustee. A summary of certain of the pertinent provisions of which is set forth hereafter. Full copy of the Trust Deed was offered to be examined by the Holder which was declined. To the extent not defined herein, capitalized terms used herein shall have the meaning ascribed to them in the Agreement. This Certificate is issued under and is subject to the terms, provisions and conditions of the Agreement, to which Agreement the Holder of this Certificate by virtue of its acceptance hereof assents and by which such Holder is bound.

*** Set here the interest distribution terms.

This Certificate is one of a duly authorized issue of Certificates designated as set forth on the face hereof (the "Certificates"), issued in ** Classes. The Certificates, in the aggregate, evidence the entire beneficial ownership interest in the Trust Fund formed pursuant to the Agreement.

The Certificate holder, by its acceptance of this Certificate, agrees that it will look solely to the Trust Fund for payment hereunder and that the Trustee is not liable to the Certificate holders for any amount payable under this Certificate or the Agreement or, except as expressly provided in the Agreement, subject to any liability under the Agreement.

This Certificate does not purport to summarize the Agreement and reference is made to the Agreement for the interests, rights and limitations of rights, benefits, obligations and duties evidenced hereby, and the rights, duties and immunities of the Trustee.

The Agreement permits, with certain exceptions therein provided, the amendment thereof and the modification of the rights and obligations of the Seller, Servicer and the rights of the Certificate holders under the Agreement from time to time by the Parties with the consent of the Holders of Certificates evidencing Voting Interests aggregating not less than **%. Any such consent by the Holder of this Certificate shall be conclusive and binding on such Holder and upon all future Holders of this Certificate and of any Certificate issued upon the transfer hereof or in lieu hereof whether or not notation of such consent is made upon this Certificate. The Agreement also permits the amendment thereof, in certain limited circumstances, without the consent of the Holders of any of the Certificates.

As provided in the Agreement and subject to certain limitations therein set forth, the transfer of this Certificate is registerable with the Trustee upon surrender of this Certificate for registration of transfer at the offices or agencies maintained by the Trustee for such purposes, duly endorsed by, or accompanied by a written instrument of transfer in form satisfactory to the Trustee duly executed by the Holder hereof or such Holder's attorney duly authorized in writing, and thereupon one or more new Certificates in authorized denominations representing a like aggregate Percentage Interest will be issued to the designated transferee.

No service charge will be made to the Certificate holders for any such registration of transfer, but the Trustee may require, if applicable, reimbursement of statutory expenses relating to such transfer.

Notes

1 Sometimes, difficulties of stamp duty may suggest that the actual instrument of transfer be kept different from the assignment agreement embodying the commercial and other detailed terms. This may also be desirable if the conveyance requires registration.

2 See Chapter 29 on regulatory issues.

3 October 1998. Duff and Phelps was later taken over by Fitch.

4 Also referred to as freehold property.

5 This is applicable for financial leases. For operating leases, suitable modification has to be made. For detailed exposition of financial and operating leases, see Vinod Kothari's *Lease financing and hire purchase*. For the latest edition, see http://india-financing.com

6 Fannie Mae's servicing standards may be viewed online at http://www.allregs.com/efnma/[last visited August 24, 2003]. Servicing requirements are now also required to be disclosed at length in offer documents as per SEC's Regulation AB. See chapter dedicated to the said regulation.

7 For example, in Conseco Finance's case. See also Chapter 25.

8 For bond-type transactions, where reinvestments are made for the longer term, the benefits from reinvestments obviously accrue to the bondholders.

9 This may be defined with reference to ISDA's standard documentation – see definition in ISDA Master agreement. Under ISDA documentation, an entity suffers a bankruptcy event, (1) if it is dissolved (other than pursuant to a consolidation, amalgamation or merger); (2) becomes insolvent or is unable to pay its debts or fails or admits in writing its inability generally to pay its debts as they become due; (3) makes a general assignment, arrangement or composition with or for the benefit of its creditors; (4) institutes or has instituted against it a proceeding seeking a judgment of insolvency or bankruptcy or any other relief under any bankruptcy or insolvency law or other similar law affecting creditor's rights, or a petition is presented for its winding-up or liquidation, and, in the case of any such proceeding or petition instituted or presented against it, such proceedings or petition (A) result in a judgment of insolvency or bankruptcy or the entry of an order for relief or the making of an order for its winding-up or liquidation or (B) is not dismissed, discharged, stayed or restrained in each case within 30 days of the institution or presentation thereof; (5) has a resolution passed for its winding-up official management or liquidation (other than pursuant to a consolidation, amalgamation or merger); (6) seeks or becomes subject to the appointment of an administrator, provisional liquidator, conservator, receiver, trustee, custodian or other similar official for it or for all or substantially all its assets; (7) has a secured party take possession of all substantially all its asset or has distress, execution, attachment, sequestration or other legal process levied, enforced or sued on or against all or substantially all its assets and such secured party maintains possession, or any such process is not dismissed, discharged, stayed or restrained, in each case within 30 days thereafter; (8) causes or is subject to any event with respect to it which, under the applicable laws of any jurisdiction, has an analogous effect to any of the event specified in clauses (1) to (7) (inclusive); (9) takes any action in furtherance of, or indicating its consent to approval of, or acquiescence in, any of the foregoing acts.

10 In many cases, the trust is brought into existence by settlement of a nominal amount, and thereafter, the trust acquires further property with the money provided by the beneficiaries.

11   If the junior certificates are of the nature of residual interest certificates, as in the case of REMICs, they will be entitled to all the interest remaining after discharging other classes.

12   This is a sequential paydown structure. For paydown structures and their significance, see Paydown Structures in this book.

13   Various industry bodies have come out with investor reporting standards. For example, the European Securitisation Forum, has framed investor reporting requirements: http://www.europeansecuritisation.com/pubs/esfguidelines.pdf. Additionally, also see Commercial Mortgage Securities Association, U.S.: http://www.cmbs.org/standards/IRP.html; Australian Securitisation Forum, http://www.securitisation.com.au/Newsletters/July2000.pdf

Chapter 25

Operational Issues in Securitization

T he true worth of a house is not its beauty but how functionally convenient it is; thus, the true worth of a securitization transaction lies in its ability to collect and relegate the cash flows and retire investors' actual claims. Hence, operations hold the key to the efficiency of the transaction, and in the absence of operational strength, the legal health of the transaction has no meaning.

Significance of operational risks

Operational risk in securitization transactions has been the highlight of attention in recent years, and clearly operational risks are more significant than the risks of legal structure.

A survey by Standard & Poor's[1] confirms that the structured finance market regards operational risks as a major area of concern. More than 2/3rds of participants identified operational risk as a major area of concern, and 78% regarded servicer quality as a major area of focus.

The main area of operations in securitization is handled by servicers, and some administrative functions are handled by the trustees. Below, we focus on the role of servicers and trustees and the risks inherent therein.

Types of servicers

As the origination, servicing and resolution of assets become increasingly fragmented, the usual hold-all function approach to retail assets is giving way to specialized services. Broadly speaking, for residential and commercial mortgages, three types of servicing functions have emerged:

- Primary servicer: The one who originated the loan and maintains the franchise with the obligors. Usually, it is the originator who has regular dealings with the borrower.
- Master servicer: At the transaction pool-level, the master servicer is responsible for ensuring the smooth functioning of the entire transaction, including adherence by each servicer of the servicing functions.
- Specialized servicer: Normally brought in when an asset becomes non-performing. Essentially, this is the servicer having expertise in resolution of such problem loans. The loan might end up in foreclosure, may be restructured or may otherwise be corrected.
- Backup servicer: Generally a stand-by servicer who would step in if there are any events of default with the primary or master servicer. We take up backup servicers later in this chapter.

For CMBS transactions, there might be more than one master servicer, particularly in conduit or fusion conduit deals.

The servicing models that have emerged show the following pattern:

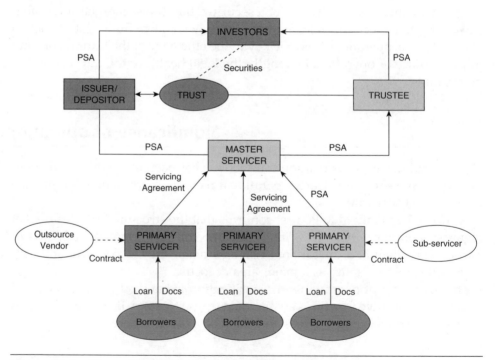

Figure 25.1   Normal RMBS servicing model

The allocation of functions between the primary and the sub-servicers may not be very clear. For CMBS transactions, the Commercial Mortgage Securities Association has developed a recommended splitting of functions between the primary servicer, sub-servicers and special servicer. This is available at: http://www.cmbs.org/standards/CMBSFunction%20Guide%20w_white%20paper.pdf, last visited December 27, 2005.

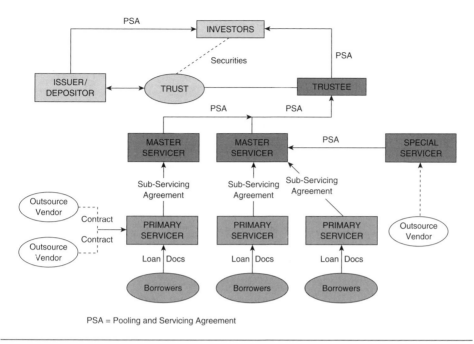

Figure 25.2   Normal CMBS servicing model

Servicer strengths

Servicing is essentially a process-oriented job and requires organizational strengths to accomplish the processing within defined time and up to standards expected in the market.

Staff strengths

Servicing demands both knowledge and experience – knowledge of the business processes inherent for the asset type involved and experience in handling the same. Experience in the relevant industry for a fair length of time shows the ability of the servicer to provide value addition.

Organizational structure

The servicing entity should be organizationally designed to support servicing requirements. At the same time, the organizational structure should keep space for growth and continual updates of the required functionalities. The organizational structure should provide for systems of supervision and review to monitor performance and compliances at various levels.

What type of organizational structures is best suited for efficient servicing organizations? While the question certainly cannot have absolute answers, rating agency S&P feels centralized platforms usually represent a potential for greater economies of scale. Depending on the servicing activity, a combination of transactional and functional departments – e.g., payment processing versus asset/portfolio analysis – usually results in lower per-loan servicing costs. The rating agency feels outsourcing and/or off-shoring transactional-based activities (such as bank lockbox and tax/insurance third-party service providers) and certain functional-based activities (such as call centers, customer service, property inspections and financial statement analysis) also may result in lower costs, and may provide a level of experience not available within the organization.

Training

As organizations continuously need to hone skills, prepare for succession management and have resource development, they need to spend on training. Training has become an essential part of every learning organization, but it is considered very significant in the servicing industry. Training is also seen as a motivator as the employees feel motivated by the fact that their employer is spending on their personal development. Depending on the job being performed by the employee concerned, training is required for both soft skills as well as the technical skills required for the job.

Staff turnover

The servicer's organization should be stable and resilient to periodical jerks. Employee turnover is an indicative measure of the stability and general management of a company. High turnover is detrimental to efficiency and profitability. Rating agency S&P says that it observes a higher turnover rate in residential mortgage and other consumer product servicing industry, of close to 15% to 20%, while for commercial products, it is low at about 5% to 10%.

Systems

Servicing being process-oriented, investment in systems and technology is a significant strength in servicing business. A proper servicing system should exist, and wherever possible, the servicer should make use of external technology support such as for automated dialing and/or document imaging systems. A review of how effectively and efficiently the various systems are integrated to avoid manual re-handling of data is addressed, along with system controls and administration of security functions within each system.

Business continuity planning and disaster recovery can be critical issues. Most servicing organizations maintain data back-up, protection against fire, piracy and breakdown. As continuity in servicing is significant, most servicing organizations also maintain alternate sites to shift the servicing location, should it be required. Ideally, the alternative system hot site and the business recovery site should be at least 25 miles from a company's main servicing location to ensure adequate power and minimize inaccessibility or transportation disruptions. Both the system recovery and business continuity plans must be tested at least annually to ensure workability. The servicer should target ability to recover functionality within 48 hours of the disaster event.

Internal controls

Existence of robust internal controls is key to any process-oriented business. Critical in ensuring adequate internal controls are: (a) Procedure Manuals; (b) Internal audit.

Procedure manuals are important for standardization of responses as also for continuity of operations. Adherence to systems and procedures is the key focus of internal audits.

Loan/asset administration

As the servicer's main function is to process the assets and payments, the servicer must demonstrate functional proficiency in processing the asset. The various components of asset administration include:

- Establishing new loan records, including testing the correctness of data, intimation to the borrower and apprising the borrower of his responsibilities.
- Document tracking: This will be relative to the nature of the transaction, and may include, ensuring the physical documents, for example mortgages, and also relevant filings such as security interest perfection.
- Payment processing: The duties for payment processing should be well laid, and there must be reporting and reconciliation systems to eliminate errors. Where appropriate, lock box services should be used.
- Insurance: Once again, this would be relative to the type of asset, but in most cases there would be some insurance taken to insure against the risks relating to the asset.
- Taxes and other compliances: Monitoring necessary tax and other compliances is important.
- Investor reporting: Appropriate investor reporting formats and well-differentiated allocation of duties on investor reporting are critical to servicing function.
- Obligor service: Servicers are responsible not only for interface with the investors but also with the obligors. One of the most common obligor service jobs is to intimate the obligor on his outstanding amount and answer queries about any charges in the invoices.
- Servicer advances: Servicers are commonly required to support the transaction with advances for any delinquent interest and principal, and sometimes for tax and insurance payments. Such advances and reconciliation of the amounts advanced and netted off on regular basis are necessary.
- Asset aging analysis: One of the critical servicing jobs is to be able to manage the collections effectively, for which aging analysis of the receivables is most important.

- Delinquency minimization: Servicers are supposed to have well-established systems for handling delinquencies. The follow up sequence – automated dialers, letters – are well laid down. If there is a manual follow up, the response should be documented at all times.

Servicer qualities

S&P has listed[2] expected qualities for servicers for asset classes. Being significant, we deal with these briefly below.

Consumer finance

This includes credit card and other forms of consumer credits. Here, the servicer should demonstrate the following abilities:

- Effective credit card utilization monitoring and portfolio retention initiatives.
- Demonstrate effective fraud detection procedures.
- Customer service environment that provides satisfactory degree of customer care, including an automated call distribution system, voice response unit, and Internet site for customer inquiries, transactions and overall productivity management.
- Management of delinquent portfolios including monitoring roll rate migration, FICO scoring and behavior modeling, loss mitigation counseling, and effective skip tracing.
- Demonstrate sound collection procedures with appropriate staff allocations and product-specific experience levels.
- Collection staff training including extensive FDCPA requirements and testing, soft skills instruction and negotiation techniques.
- Satisfactory oversight of collection staff, including continuous call monitoring, scoring and feedback as well as periodic refresher training and certification courses.
- Effective procedures for payment plans, and matrix of approval levels for staff, middle and senior management. Satisfactory history of cure rates, promise-to-pay success rates versus recidivism rates.
- Demonstrate procedures for timely charge-off of delinquent accounts between 120 and 180 days and review by senior management.
- Maintain effective procedures for recovery of post-charge off assets including internal and external initiatives.

If the servicer is a special servicer, that is, for delinquent consumer finance transactions, the servicer should demonstrate the following:

- Demonstrate effective portfolio due diligence of acquired portfolios to ascertain effectiveness of prior collection effort and likelihood of recovery based on primary, secondary or tertiary nature of portfolio.

- Post-purchased review of pricing model and technology to determine efficacy of purchasing decisions.
- Demonstrate development and implementation of recovery models. Review recovery assumptions and case histories of purchased portfolios.
- New loan set up should be executed from electronic file downloads due to the higher volumes.
- Extensive data scrubbing of all new portfolios, including effective identification of skip tracing needs.
- Procedures for borrower contact, repayment and/or restructuring plans, settlement authorizations, including automated promise-to-pay monitoring, and required daily monitoring of collections.
- Extensive FDCPA training and compliance monitoring.
- Daily portfolio-specific recovery modeling and goal planning for each collector and team.
- Technology and degree of system interface between call center(s), servicing systems, and alternative payment vehicles (speed pay, quick collect, Western Union).
- Accepting additional collateral, short payoffs or liquidations, and appropriate analysis templates for decision-making.
- Rigorous monitoring of restructured assets.

Commercial finance servicers

This will include equipment leases, commercial loans and SME loans. Here, the critical abilities include:

- Demonstrate controls for tracking sales tax, personal property tax and UCC filings. Maintain sufficient staff, systems and expertise to proactively monitor lessee compliance and credit positions, administer lease modifications, perform lease-end re-marketing and dispositions of used equipment, and engage in reasonable inventory valuation practices.
- Demonstrate sound collection procedures with experienced staff allocated to higher delinquency levels.
- Demonstrate an adequate recovery performance history through channels such as equipment resales, deficiency collections and lease modifications. Realized residual values should be tracked and reasonable.
- Maintain an appropriate charge-off policy, typically between 120 and 180 days, and monitoring of charge-off recoveries, which should have a neutral effect on earnings and reserves.
- Demonstrate sufficient procedures and documentation controls regarding resolution approvals.

Franchise loan servicers

As franchise lenders' security interests extend over a variety of business assets, it is necessary for the franchise loan servicer to be able to monitor a variegated set of security interests. The demonstrable abilities include:

- To the extent applicable, based on the loan's collateral, monitor the status of real estate taxes and other levies against the loan collateral/borrower that could negatively affect lien position, and take appropriate measures.
- Maintain sound procedures to track the status of all applicable security interest filings and take appropriate action to ensure that security interest filing renewals are completed before their expiration dates.
- Collect and analyze franchisee's operating statements at least semi-annually (preferably quarterly) and identify negative trends. The financial review process should include a fixed charge coverage ratio analysis calculated at the unit and corporate borrower level.
- Maintain watchlist functions so that loans experiencing negative trends or potential default issues are monitored more intensively.
- Follow proactive collection procedures for borrowers with past due payments.
- Monitor borrowers' loan covenant compliance and take prudent action regarding any such non-monetary defaults.
- Perform collateral site inspections no later than after a loan enters the watchlist stage.
- Possess acceptable credit analysis skills among staff for identifying and evaluating key elements of franchise concept, unit and borrower performance.
- Proactively identify and implement the optimal strategy and tactics for recovering troubled franchise assets.
- Have sufficient staffing levels and asset manager industry experience for executing franchise loan workout plans.
- Management staff experience demonstrates success in resolving troubled franchise credits, including credits in bankruptcy.
- Acceptably track all key activities covering the special servicing process.
- Demonstrate expertise in evaluating the correct course of action relating to each asset, and with adequate documentation substantiate asset recovery recommendations and decisions.
- Asset business plans are prepared within the first 90 days or less of delinquency.
- Show acceptable controls regarding decision-making and approval processes.
- Control third-party vendor engagements through standardized agreements, competitive bidding, management approvals and centralized tracking.

Commercial mortgage-backed finance servicers

Primary servicers

- As applicable, perform all duties according to Commercial Mortgage Securities Association industry standards, and regulatory requirements (i.e. REMIC rules) for CMBS portfolios.
- Maintain adequate procedures for monitoring and disbursing real estate taxes. Penalties for late payments should be tracked separately on a dollar per loan count basis.

- Have acceptable procedures for tracking security interest filing expirations and obtaining continuations with adequate lead-time, usually six months.
- Have sound procedures for obtaining, spreading, normalizing and analyzing property financial data. Including NOI adjustments and debt service coverage ratio (DSCR) calculations.
- Maintain sound procedures for obtaining periodic inspection reports and monitoring related follow up actions.
- Maintain tracking of borrower requests, and act promptly and expeditiously in responding to those requests.
- Have formalized loan watchlist procedures.
- Have adequate early delinquency/default collection efforts. This includes sufficiently proactive time lines for telephone and written borrower contact.

Master servicers

- Properly track individual PSA requirements on specific deals and closely track sub-servicer compliance.
- Have procedures for wire remittance from sub-servicers, and their reconciliation, including procedures for tracking and balancing reports received from sub-servicers having more than one securitization issue.
- Have good procedures in place for tracking and monitoring P&I advances.
- Monitor special servicer performance in handling its assets, updating valuations/appraisal reductions, and recoverability testing of advances.
- Monitor material fluctuations in collateral value, taking such fluctuations into account as part of the decision-making process regarding advances and determination of non-recoverability.
- Demonstrate understanding of the impact of non-recoverability determination, and take reasonable steps to prevent cash flow interruptions to investment-grade certificate-holders.
- Monitor late reporting/remitting and tax disbursement penalties incurred by sub-servicers.
- Routinely monitor sub-servicer tracking and disbursement reports relating to taxes, insurance, reserves and UCC refilings to identify exceptions.
- Routinely monitor and require sub-servicers have adequate D&O, E&O, and force-placed insurance coverage in place on all loans as a matter of policy.
- Maintain sound procedures for tracking insurance loss drafts and claims disbursements.
- Track sub-servicer delinquency reporting and collection activity.
- Have adequate procedures for overseeing sub-servicer handling of borrower/property financial statements and property inspections.
- Maintain an integrated watchlist for all master serviced loans (i.e. primary plus sub-serviced loans).
- Have adequate procedures for authorizing advances and tracking reimbursements.

- Maintain appropriate staffing and procedures for approving borrower requests such as modifications and assumptions.
- Have an adequate sub-servicer on-site audit program conducted with a frequency commensurate with each sub-servicer's volume.
- Routinely ensure that all compliance certificates, financial statements and reports required by PSAs are forwarded and reviewed on a timely basis.

Special servicers

- The company should have a demonstrated track record of resolving problem assets. If the company's track record is of short duration, the achievements may be based on the prior experience of key managers for overseeing and disposing of troubled loans/REO.
- Possess expertise in handling a variety of assets types, although company may have a concentration of experience with one particular property type.
- Demonstrate an ability to evaluate the correct course of action relating to each asset. Policies are in place to maximize the recovery proceeds of each asset, taking into account the interests of all certificate-holders and out-lined within the framework of the resolution business (loan or REO) plans.
- Exercise judicious management of all trust assets and expenses during the workout process.
- Require the creation of individual asset (loan) business plans within 90 days of transfer to the special servicer (usually a 150-day delinquency benchmark). Plans are approved through proper delegations of authority.
- Properly document all specific asset management recommendations, including foreclosures, restructures, note sales and borrower settlements, with proper delegation of authority for approvals.
- Have procedures in place for transferring assets from loan to REO status with timely notifications to all internal and external parties.
- Have procedures in place for REO management. REO business plans and budgets should be prepared within 60 to 90 days of acquisition of title.
- Maintain procedures for selecting, engaging and overseeing third-party property managers.
- Require formalized procedures for property management company financial reporting.
- Review monthly property manager financial reporting, which is done by in-house staff having accounting and audit backgrounds.
- Maintain procedures for monitoring property manager reporting compliance and bank account activity and reconciliations.
- Follow formalized and sound procedures for REO dispositions.
- Follow recovery actions that are consistent with REMIC rules and time constraints.
- Select, engage, and monitor brokers with adequate controls. Listing agreements should not be longer than six months, and can be canceled by notice from the property owner. Sales offers are substantiated and approved by senior management.

- Control third-party vendor engagements through standardized agreements, competitive bidding, management approvals, approved vendor lists, and system tracking.
- Maintain an acceptable process for review of appraisal and environmental reports. No foreclosure actions are completed without an environmental review from a qualified expert.
- Manage the legal function through an approved counsel list. Billings are closely monitored.

Residential mortgage servicers

Primary servicers

- As applicable, perform all loan servicing-related duties in accordance with investor guidelines and prudent industry practice.
- Demonstrate acceptable and efficient loan boarding procedures that maximize automation and ensure acceptable data integrity controls.
- Demonstrate satisfactory controls in payment processing environment with proper handling of live checks and research items as well as solid oversight of vendor relationships.
- Maintain an investor accounting, reporting and remitting structure that is functionally driven providing for the requisite segregation of duties among reporting, remitting and reconciling functions.
- Maintain satisfactory investor accounting and default management ratings from the respective GSEs.
- Maintain satisfactory USAP[3] rating and compliance.
- Perform rate adjustments on ARM loans in accordance with investor and regulatory guidelines.
- Maintain satisfactory compliance with RESPA[4] guidelines in all escrow administration functions.
- Demonstrate solid oversight of vendor relationships for escrow administration functions (i.e., hazard and flood insurance, real estate tax bill procurement).
- Maintain provisions for force placed hazard and flood insurance coverage via an insurance carrier with an acceptable claims paying ability rating.
- Demonstrate satisfactory compliance with lien release statutes in all 50 states.
- Maintain effective customer service, and depending on volumes, provide an automated call distribution system, voice response unit and Internet site for customer inquiries, transactions and overall productivity management.
- Demonstrate sound collection procedures and timelines in accordance with minimum standards specified by investors and agencies.
- Have satisfactory training in FDCPA[5] and other applicable regulations.
- Maintain acceptable collection technology including an autodialer or power-dialer for calling campaigns and call center productivity management.

- Maintain additional technology as needed, including credit scoring and behavior modeling, workflow automation, advanced telephony, and call scripting.
- Perform periodic property inspections on delinquent loans to ensure that all collateral is sufficiently monitored and protected against loss.
- Have appropriately aggressive and proactive focus on loss mitigation via mailing and calling campaigns.
- Maintain demonstrated ability to perform net present value analysis to determine best exit strategy.
- Demonstrate acceptable foreclosure and bankruptcy timeline management pursuant to investor guidelines.
- Maintain proactive case management and attorney oversight.
- Maintain effective REO property management marketing and disposition procedures including asset management guidelines, marketing plan, vendor organization and oversight, eviction and marketing timeline management, and sale results.

Sub-prime servicers

- Develop and implement aggressive collection timelines that address the credit profile of various nonconforming borrowers.
- Hire and retain experienced nonconforming collectors.
- Implement and encourage employee career-pathing to retain experienced collectors and minimize turnover.
- Provide in-depth collection training, including extensive FDCPA instruction, soft skills training and negotiation techniques, as well as role-playing in a simulated call center environment.
- Nonconforming servicers should perform welcome calls within five to ten days of a new loan closing to reinforce terms of the repayment obligation and to encourage positive pay habits.
- The nonconforming servicer should track the contact rate on welcome calls.
- Bilingual collectors should be on staff in accordance with specific portfolio demographics.
- Expanded collection calling hours, including evenings and weekends, should be in place to optimize contact with recalcitrant borrowers.
- Credit scoring and behavior modeling technology should be in place to strategically align calling campaigns with the latest borrower profiles.
- Advanced telephony should be utilized for optimum contact opportunities including inbound call volume.
- Consistent and frequent call monitoring to ensure that collectors remain effective and are following regulatory guidelines.
- Monthly property inspections to ensure that collateral is not compromised.
- Demonstrate advanced analytical environment capable of measuring and tracking roll rate migrations; promise-to-pay.
- Success rates, short-term repayment plan, cure rates, prime time calling percentage, best time to call criteria.

- Effective skip tracing environment, including skip tracing locate rate percentage.
- Demonstrate early loss mitigation initiative in advance of foreclosure referral. Advanced-loss mitigation analytics should include fully automated net present value analysis, including updated borrower financial statement and property valuation, resulting in best exit strategy workout plan.
- Full and complete file review prior to foreclosure to ensure that the collection effort has been exhaustive and that all regulatory guidelines have been met.
- Automated (electronic) file referral to approved counsel.
- Maintain corporate-approved list of external counsel for representation in foreclosure and bankruptcy cases.
- Maintain dual track of loss mitigation and foreclosure to ensure that foreclosure sale is the last resort.
- Closely manage foreclosure and bankruptcy timelines with external counsel. Issue monthly report cards on attorney performance.

Special servicers

- Highly experienced default management team to perform due diligence on distressed asset portfolios.
- Demonstrate proficiency at portfolio triage, including rapid assessment of incoming distressed portfolios, identification of assets requiring immediate attention, development of action plans and assignment of resources for new assets.
- Effectively manage flow of new assets into servicing stream.
- Identify reasons for default and make loan cash positive if possible.
- Demonstrated advanced portfolio analytics and attorney oversight methodologies.
- Demonstrated skip tracing abilities, including advanced technology tools, skip tracing locate rate.
- Highly experienced collection staff averaging more than five years industry experience.
- Implementation of early and proactive loss mitigation approach.
- Fully automated net present value analysis based on current borrower financial statement and property valuation, best exit strategy developed.
- Highly experienced foreclosure and bankruptcy team that can track problem assets, court delays, chronic filers and maximize timeline compliance. Expeditiously move for lift of stay in all cases.
- Aggressive dual path strategy combining loss mitigation efforts with proactive foreclosure timeline management.
- Provide adequate documentation to substantiate asset recovery strategies and decisions.
- Exhibit acceptable controls over decision-making and approval processes.
- Demonstrate strong vendor management methodologies including standardized agreements, competitive bidding process, management approval matrix, independent monitoring and tracking.

- Exhibit formalized and prudent procedures for REO management and disposition.
- Asset managers should have extensive REO management experience.
- Utilize cash for keys to expedite property vacancy where cost-effective.
- Select, engage and monitor brokers with adequate controls. Sales offers are substantiated and approved by senior management.

Master servicers

- Demonstrated ability to track individual pooling and servicing agreements (PSA) on specific deals and closely monitor sub-servicer compliance.
- Master servicing guide published on the Intranet.
- Exhibit adequate procedures for establishing wire remittance arrangements with new sub-servicers as well as reconciling incoming wires from sub-servicers.
- Exhibit satisfactory segregation of duties among the investor accounting and reporting functions.
- Satisfactory procedures and system security for reconciling unpaid principal balances to scheduled balances.
- Sound procedures for tracking and balancing reports received from sub-servicers administering multiple issues.
- Sound procedures for tracking and monitoring principal and interest advances.
- Monitor late reporting and remitting penalties incurred by sub-servicers.
- No unreconciled items aged more than 90 days.
- Routinely monitor sub-servicer tracking and disbursement reports for escrow items.
- Master servicers routinely monitor requirements that sub-servicers have adequate insurance coverage in force on all loans.
- Maintain sound procedures for tracking insurance loss drafts and claims disbursements.
- Routinely review sub-servicer delinquency reporting and collection activity.
- Exhibit sound procedures for authorizing advances and tracking reimbursements.
- Ensure adequate staffing, expertise and procedures for administering special requests such as modifications and assumptions.
- Adequate sub-servicer review program mandating periodic on-site audits based on loan volume and criteria watchlist as well as routine desk reviews.
- Annual compliance process for all sub-servicers pursuant to master servicing participation program. Ensure that all compliance certificates, financial statements, and required reports are received on a timely basis.
- Maintain exception-based tracking system for trailing documents.
- Maintain website for investor downloads and access to pool-level transaction data.

Servicing transition

Securitization transactions are presumably independent of the originator due to the legal isolation the transaction achieves due to "true sale." However, the truth of the sale might turn out to be a glib illusion if the servicing platform is so intimately originator-dependent that it is difficult to perceive its transfer. Transferability of servicing has been a key issue in several securitization transactions, either because the servicing fees were impractically fixed or because the servicing was intrinsically dependent on the originator's organization.

Conseco Finance's securitization transactions showed that impractical fixation of servicing fees can disrupt the performance of a transaction. As one would presumably do when the originator is the servicer, the servicing fees were subordinated, and were meager. When Conseco filed for bankruptcy, the servicing had to be transferred. The servicing fee was 50 bps and it was subordinated, which means the servicer would get nothing unless there was an excess spread. This is a kind of "onerous asset" that can be avoided in bankruptcy proceedings, which is what the company pleaded before the court. The court increased the servicing fee to 125 bps and made it senior to the noteholders, thereby reducing the excess spread of the transaction.

There have been some cases where successful transfer of servicing function has been possible, such as when Guardian Savings and Loan failed, wherein Financial Security Assurance as the guarantor was able to have the servicing transferred.

In the case of Spiegel and NextCard as well, the servicing fee was too low to attract a back up servicer.

The portability of the servicing function is quite dependent on the nature of the collateral. Rating agency S&P shows[6] the following graphic where the left side shows increasing degree of servicer dependence, with the serving platform being difficult to transfer:

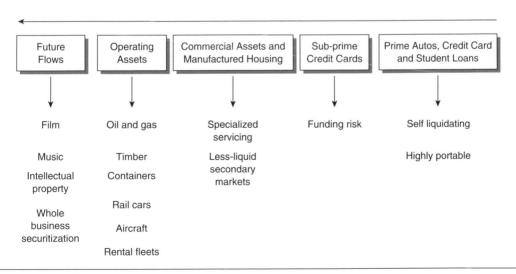

Figure 25.3   Operating risk spectrum

Backup servicer

As is evident from difficulties faced in several transactions, the portability of the servicing is itself a problem, and more significantly, the willingness of the backup servicer to pick up servicing as per terms assumed in the transaction cannot be assumed. Adequate backup servicing arrangements are key to the transaction.

Backup servicers may be classified into *hot, warm* and *cold*. The jargon comes from IT business where these terms are used for backup servers. A hot backup servicer is a sort of an alternate that keeps itself in absolute readiness to take over the servicing anytime. Generally, a hot backup will upload collateral data from the primary servicer more frequently, often weekly, and in many cases will shadow service the assets in question to assure the most seamless transfer possible should the need for the same arise. Obviously, hot backup servicers are quite expensive to retain.

Warm backup servicers update data from the primary servicer less frequently, usually monthly, and therefore are less expensive to keep on standby.

Cold backups perform the least frequent monitoring of the primary servicing data, providing updates possibly quarterly or even semi-annually.

As every backup arrangement implies a cost, one must take a practical view to organize the backup arrangement. However, a mere right to appoint a backup servicer, or a commitment on the part of a backup servicer to take over servicing, is meaningless unless accompanied by the readiness to do so.

Reporting by the servicer

Pursuant to Regulation AB, the role of the servicer and the reporting by servicer has been a topic for intensive discussion in the industry. Among other things, Regulation AB requires a certification along with a 10-K report to be filed by each servicer servicing 10% or more of the pool. For details, refer to Chapter 28.

Apart from regulatory intervention on servicer reporting, industry bodies have over time tried to evolve minimum servicer reporting standards. The Commercial Mortgage Securities Association (CMSA), for example, has investor reporting package in operation for several years. The Australian Securitization Forum and the European Securitization Forum have all come out with investor reporting standards.

Regulation or industry standards apart, the servicer reporting requirements are laid down in the pooling and servicing agreement. See Chapter 24 for some model clauses.

Role of trustees in operation of the transaction

The role of trustees in securitization transactions is far from standardized. The institution of trustees comes up for purely logistical reasons or to comply with legal requirements, but investors seem to place increasing reliance on the trustees.

The legal role of trustees is to act as a single window conduit for the investors. Trustees hold the legal title over the assets or the securities in trust for the investors. They enforce all covenants on the part of the contracting parties, and ensure that the servicer is performing his duties as per contract. The trustees would seek a noteholders' vote in exceptional circumstances.

In addition, the traditional role of the trustees includes acting as authenticating agent, registrar, transfer agent, asset and account custodian and analytics provider, in addition to holding legal or security interest on the assets. These responsibilities can be expanded or reduced by a trust deed. Sometimes, trustees may get involved in actual operations and provide services as backup servicers. But trustees taking over the role of servicers may raise issues of conflict of interest.

Like most other spheres of activity, technology is fast entering to make trustees' discharge of duties more efficient. An article by Patrick Tadie of the Bank of New York mentions[7] how technology is assisting trustees in better discharge of trustee functions:

- **Covenant maintenance.** An automated electronic ticker system enables periodic reviews of an ABS covenant to be conducted on an ongoing basis for the life of a transaction.
- **Funds collection and investment.** Electronic collection and tracking technologies facilitate the flow of incoming cash from servicers and its eventual investment according to the bondholder's wishes.
- **Bond analytics.** Proprietary programs calculate cash flow waterfalls and allocate bond payments for multi-class structures; historical data-capture systems help generate customized reports for issuers, projecting valuations for residuals under varying economic assumptions.
- **Investor communications.** The Internet, proprietary electronic bulletin boards and automated voice response systems enable communication with investors through multiple channels, in addition to telephone and face-to-face interactions with relationship managers.

As for servicers, there have been attempts to standardize trustees' reports too. For instance, the Bond Market Association has finalized a format of trustee report for CDOs.[8]

Fraud risk

Among the operational risks in an asset-backed transaction, the risk of fraud cannot be under-rated. Fraud risk remains present in every sphere of activity, but there is reliance on several independent agencies each handling a fragment of the transaction in securitizations. This is the perfect setting for a fraudster, who takes advantage of the fact that there is no one with "overall" responsibility for the transaction; each party has a split-segment of responsibility. The servicer is concerned only with what he paid for, the originator is presumably hands-off, and the trustees are legal watchdogs who step into action only when they are made to smell something wrong.

While instances of systematic ponzi-type devices exist in the past, such as Towers Healthcare, one of the recent instances of fraud in asset-backed securities was National Century. National Century Financial Enterprises (NCFE) filed for bankruptcy in November 2002 and brought to the fore some unique risks of mishandling securitization funds. NCFE specialized in healthcare funding and used to buy healthcare receivables from several healthcare centers in the U.S. These receivables were securitized.

Shortly before the bankruptcy filing, it was revealed that the company was misusing the funds collected on behalf of its securitization clients. Investigations revealed frauds by the company's top bosses, resulting into filing of the bankruptcy petition. Approximately US$3.5 billion worth of asset-backed securities defaulted. The sad part is that some of the classes were rated AAA by more than one rating agency.

Investors have sued the trustees as well as the placement agencies.[9] The SEC has sued the former principal executives of the company.[10]

Notes

1 Structured finance market opinion survey confirms operational risk remains a serious concern for securitization professionals, report dated February 24, 2005.

2 Servicer Evaluation Ranking Criteria, September 21, 2004.

3 Uniform Single Attestation Program – a Mortgage Bankers Association standard

4 Real Estate Settlement Procedures Act.

5 Fair Debt Collection Practices Act.

6 Backup servicer plays vital role in non-commodified securitizations, June 20, 2005.

7 Article at http://www.iflr.com/?Page=17&ISS=17633&SID=524704 last visited December 27, 2005.

8 See http://www.bondmarkets.com/market/CDO_Trustee_Template.pdf, last visited December 27, 2005.

9 City of Chandler, et al., v. Bank One, N.A., et al. (D. Az.); Metropolitan Life Ins. Co. v. Bank One, N.A. (D.N.J.); Bank One, N.A. v. Poulsen, et al. (S.D. Ohio), State of Arizona et al. v. Credit Suisse First Boston Corporation et al., in Superior Court of Arizona.

10 CNN news on December 21, 2005. Full text of the SEC complaint is at: http://www.sec.gov/litigation/complaints/comp19509.pdf, last visited December 28, 2005.

Chapter 26

Tax Issues in Securitization

No business is a good business if the tax officer understands it.

— *Vinod Kothari*[1]

Lack of clear provisions on the taxation of securitization transactions can have very negative implications. Therefore, many countries that consciously tried to promote the concept of securitization have provided a clear taxation framework for such transactions. In the absence of specifically enacted principles, the general body of tax law may not be enough or efficient to treat securitization transactions with the neutrality they deserve.

Securitization is not a business, but a transformation of assets into securities. SPVs that are introduced as vehicles of transformation are not substantive entities; they cannot accumulate income or make profits. Therefore, prima facie, a fiscal system should keep a basic securitization transaction free from additional tax. The best way of ensuring this is to ignore the existence of an SPV that is not an entity with substance to demand the attention of the taxman. However, in several present-day transactions, SPVs are far from being mere conduits or transformation devices. They redistribute incomes, paying a certain section of investors in priority over others. They might accumulate and reinvest income the same way as any other corporation. These are cases when taxation laws would not find much difference between a special purpose entity and a substantive business entity. That is, if an SPV plays any redistributive role and creates mismatch between the accrual of income (a) had the SPV not been in picture; and (b) if such income is redistributed by the SPV, there is a justifiable claim to treat the SPV as a regular taxable entity.

In fact, if the law provides tax immunity to SPVs, there is potential for misuse. An entity might transfer its own income to an SPV, park it there and defer its receipt, while accumulating the income with the SPV. Therefore, an ideal tax regime may treat an SPV as a conduit to the extent it distributes its income, and levy tax to the extent it retains income. While this may be a sweeping generalization, the real world taxation of SPVs must take into account several aspects.

An appropriate tax regime for securitization transactions must be concerned not merely with the taxation of SPVs, but also the taxation of the originator at the time of transfer of the pool, taxation of the residual excess profit, taxation of the SPV, and taxation of investors.

In essence, the significant questions from taxation viewpoint are:

1. Will the transaction be treated for tax purposes as sale or financing?
2. What will be the tax treatment of securitized receivables at the time of their sale in the originators' hands?
3. What will be the tax treatment on receipt of the underlying income and its pass-through/pay through to the investors?
4. What will be the tax treatment of the special purpose vehicle?
5. What will be the tax treatment of the outlay and receipts in the investors' hands?
6. What is the applicability of withholding taxes on each of the underlying payments?

In the opinion of the author, tax issues relating to securitization, in most countries other than those with framed specific tax rules, have not been taken seriously enough. The world's most developed securitization market, the U.S., has specific provisions relating to pass-throughs, REMICS and FASITs,[2] and therefore, the tax treatment is well defined. In some growing markets like Italy, tax rules have been laid down. In many other markets, the SPVs are, for various reasons, domiciled in tax havens. For the remaining limited number of domestic transactions, the number of transactions that have accumulated so far is probably not enough for tax laws to give concerted attention to securitization as a mode of financing. It is quite likely that many of the present-day SPVs would lose their tax neutrality if properly exposed to basic tax rules.

Concept of tax neutrality or tax transparency

As James M. Peaslee & David Z. Nirenberg say: "Tax planning in the securitization area is generally defensive rather than offensive. Transactions are undertaken for non-tax reasons and the role of tax planning is to avoid unnecessary incremental taxes that would make transactions uneconomic. Offensive tax planning involves generating net tax benefits or possibly also relying on very technical readings of the tax law to achieve unanticipated results."[3]

It is difficult to envisage securitization being used for tax benefits, although the ingenuity of tax planners might run farther than the analytical wisdom of either this author or any taxman. Hence, the important concern in taxation of securitization is to ensure that it is tax neutral; that is, it does not result in unwarranted incremental tax impact.

The basic objective of an ideal tax regime for securitizations should be based on the nature of the securitization vehicle. If the vehicle is merely a passive conduit between the investors and the originator, the conduit should be tax neutral or tax transparent. If the conduit amounts to an active framework for re-configuration of the cash flows transferred by the originator, such that the conduit amounts to a virtual satellite company, the conduit should be taxed on entity taxation principles.

Tax transparency means the securitization conduit or SPV should be seen as a mere conduit or collective name for the investors. It should not be seen as a taxable entity by itself. The tax applicable on the entire collection of income by the SPV and its distribution to the holders of the notes/certificates should be the same as for individual recipients. This is based on the principle that the SPV is not, unlike regular business entities, engaged in business activities. It is merely a conduit, a facade for investors. It is formed for a special purpose and it does not have or retain any income of its own.

On the other hand, if the tax laws were to tax the income in the hands of the special purpose vehicle, there would be double taxation of income to the extent of equity or residuary interest of the originator. If the SPV issues its own securities as debt securities, then the income earned by it from the receivables will be offset against income distributed on the debt securities, so there is normally an element of residuary interest of the SPV, distributed as equity dividend or residuary profits.

If a securitization transaction is not tax neutral, it would introduce an element of double taxation, which adds to the cost of securitization. The weighted-average cost of the transaction goes up, and in many cases, the transaction would become unviable.

When is securitization tax neutral?

A securitization will be tax neutral if it does not impose any significant tax burden on the transaction as a whole. That is to say, there is no significant difference between the taxability of all the parties concerned comparing a securitization and a plain financial transaction.

In a plain financial transaction, the originator creates and holds assets, and finances them. The creation of assets leads to a return, and the financing has a funding cost. The originator is taxed on his spread, that is, the difference between the rate of return and the funding cost. This spread is taxed over a period of time. The lenders are taxed on the interest they earn; as a whole, the originator and the lenders pay tax on the total returns from the transaction.

If we transform the above scenario into a securitization transaction, the originator becomes the originator and seller of the assets, and lenders become investors in the securities of the SPV. When the originator sells assets, logically, he must accelerate and make his profit upfront. If he does so, the timing of taxes change, as the taxes are preponed.

The other threat to tax neutrality is, at the SPV level, if any of the distribution made by the SPV is treated as a distribution and not as cost. The basic tax principle is that an expense is allowable to offset income, but a distribution or application of the income, such as a dividend, is not a deductible expense. Therefore, to the extent the distribution made by the SPV will be treated as distribution, the SPV will have an income (as to that extent, it would not have admissible expenses), and so the SPV will be taxed on the income. The recipients of the income will obviously also be taxed on the income received by them.

Threats to tax neutrality

Thus, the threats to tax neutrality are:

1. There is an acceleration of income at the time of the sale of assets by the originator; to this extent, there is a timing difference between a financial transaction and a securitization transaction.
2. The SPV's existence as an intermediary between the seller and the investors is not ignored for tax purposes, that is, the SPV is not treated as a *pass-through* or *see-through* entity; and the SPV is not able to offset entirely its income against expenses, that is, external expenses and the distribution made to investors, due to any of the following:

   (a) The whole or any part of the funding raised by the SPV is treated as substantive equity; therefore, the servicing thereof is treated as dividend, and so is not allowed for tax purposes;
   (b) The SPV is left with a residual profit after all distribution to investors; this may be the originator's residual interest, but because it is in the nature of a distribution, it will be taken as income of the SPV;
   (c) The timing of the income of the SPV is taken as per the income/ principal composition of the underlying receivables, whereas the timing of the interest expenses of the SPV is based on a bond coupon, leaving a timing difference between the two.

Substance of the transaction: Sale or financing

The first significant tax issue is whether, based on the entirety of the transaction, the transaction should be treated as a sale of assets by the originator or a financial arrangement.

A tax authority must treat a securitization transaction as a sale, as that is what it is made out to be. However, a tax officer may look at the big picture, connecting all the bits and pieces of the transaction together, and come to a conclusion that the transaction does not satisfy the attributes of a sale; instead, it must be treated as a financing transaction, as if the originator had borrowed money on the security of the collateral apparently sold to the SPV.

Giving a securitization transaction a sale treatment amounts to ignoring its legal form and looking at its substance. Such substance-based taxation is perfectly understandable, and either explicit or implied powers exist with tax authorities all over the world.

Whether a securitization transaction is treated as an on-balance sheet or off-balance sheet transaction from accounting standpoint is not by itself decisive of whether it will be treated as a sale or financing from a tax viewpoint. There are several instances when a transaction, treated as financing from an accounting viewpoint, is treated as a real transaction from a tax viewpoint, such as treatment of financial leases in many countries.

We note below the differences between sale treatment and financing treatment:

Sale treatment/financing treatment

If the receivables are accorded a sale treatment, the originator is deemed to have sold an income-producing asset, and so will cease to earn an income from the asset in future to the extent such asset is sold. The asset in question becomes the asset of the buyer (the SPV, or in a see-through approach, the investors) and the income that the seller would have made now becomes income of the buyer.

At the time of sale of the asset, the seller may also have made a profit (loss); that is, the excess (deficit) of the sale proceeds of the asset over the tax-admitted carrying value (in most cases, the cost or written-down value) of the asset. This profit (loss) will also be brought to tax.

For example, if an auto finance transaction was to give an income of $10 on a $1,000 funding over a period of 5 years, and is now sold for a price of $1,030, the tax treatment will be as follows: the entire income of $10 per year, otherwise taxable over 5 years, would now cease to be the income of the seller. On the other hand, the gain on sale, that is $1,030–1,000 = $30 will be taken as business profit in the year of sale.

Table 26.1 Tax treatment of securitization transactions

Sale treatment	Financing treatment
The entire income from the transaction over its period is accelerated	The income from the underlying transaction is taxed over time as before
The difference between the nominal value of receivables and the amount raised by securitization is allowed as "discount"	The "discount" is spread over the term of the securitization instrument
In result, the gain/loss on securitization is taxed immediately	In result, the gain/loss on securitization is taxed over the term of the transaction
The income that the originator were to make becomes the income of the SPV	As there is no sale but a mere financing, the income of the SPV is only the amortized amount of discounting charges earned by it, that is, similar to interest income

On the other hand, if a financial treatment is given, the fact of there having been a sale of receivables will be ignored. The discount charges on the receivables will be allowable to the SPV as a loan-type expense and the income from the receivables will continue to be taxed over time. The difference in treatment is essentially the same as for accounting purposes; for an illustration of the financing treatment, see the chapter on **Accounting for Securitization**.

Situations in which financing treatment is applicable

Needless to say, an originator would prefer to have the financing treatment from a tax viewpoint, as that avoids having to pay immediate tax on the accelerated income from the transaction. We have earlier elaborated on the concept of tax neutrality; tax neutrality is automatically attained if a financing treatment is given, as the entire taxation on the transaction will be as if it is a financing transaction.

The following situations are essentially where the financing treatment would be applicable:

- There is no sale of the asset in law;
- There is sale in law, but for tax purposes, the tax law specifically provides for financing treatment;
- There is a sale in law, but the tax law ignores the legal form and captures the economic substance, treating the transaction as in-substance financing; and
- If the law treats the transaction as a "transfer of income" and not a transfer of an "income-producing asset."

No sale in law

Where receivables in question have not been legally sold, the transaction has not achieved the legal effect of sale, and therefore, there is no question of the tax treatment of a sale being accorded. In other words, a legal or beneficial transfer of the asset is required for tax purposes before there can be any question of sale treatment. As to what qualifies for a sale treatment in law is discussed in the chapter on **Legal Issues**. Barring local differences, a sale of future flows will not be treated as a sale at least at the time when the sale agreement is signed. A future sale of reinstating assets in a credit card transaction cannot come for sale treatment, although there may be recognized income based on future transfers.

There is no question of sale of the asset in synthetic transactions; merely the risks and rewards are transferred.[4] There is also no question of a sale in a case where the transaction is based on a secured loan.

This is not to suggest that a legal true sale controls a "sale" from tax viewpoint. The concept of "sale" in tax laws is closer to economic ownership than legal ownership (see below).

No sale of economic ownership

There may be sale in law, but not an economic sale; there might be an economic sale, but not a sale in law. Tax laws are concerned, in most countries, with an economic sale. An economic or substantive sale occurs when the risks and rewards relating to ownership of an asset are transferred. New risks and rewards may be created, but those must be, on a holistic basis, different from the risks and rewards that prevailed before the transaction took place. In other words, if the risks and rewards of the asset owner remain unaffected by the transaction, the fact of a sale occurring is economically insignificant.

The leading case law on transfer of economic ownership is the U.S. Supreme Court ruling in *Frank Lyon Co.* v. *United States*, 435 U.S. 561 (1978). In this case, the Court cited a series of cases on the meaning of transfer of title for tax purposes:

> This Court, almost 50 years ago, observed that "taxation is not so much concerned with the refinements of title as it is with actual command over the property taxed – the actual benefit for which the tax is paid." *Corliss* v. *Bowers*, 281 U.S. 376, 378 (1930). In a number of cases, the Court has refused to permit the transfer of formal legal title to shift the incidence of taxation attributable to ownership of property where the transferor continues to retain significant control over the property transferred, e.g., *Commissioner* v. *Sunnen*, 333 U.S. 591 (1948); *Helvering* v. *Clifford*, 309 U.S. 331 (1940). In applying this doctrine of substance over form, the Court has looked to the objective economic realities of a transaction rather than to the particular form the parties employed. The Court has never regarded "the simple expedient of drawing up papers," *Commissioner* v. *Tower*, 327 U.S. 280, 291 (1946), as controlling for tax purposes when the objective economic realities are to the contrary. "In the field of taxation, administrators of the laws, and the courts, are concerned with substance and realities, and formal written documents are not rigidly binding," *Helvering* v. *Lazarus & Co.*, 308 U.S., at 255. See also *Commissioner* v. *P. G. Lake, Inc.*, 356 U.S. 260, 266–267 (1958); *Commissioner* v. *Court Holding Co.*, 324 U.S. 331, 334 (1945). Nor is the parties' desire to achieve a particular tax result necessarily relevant, *Commissioner* v. *Duberstein*, 363 U.S. 278, 286 (1960).

In this case, dealing with a sale and leaseback transaction, the Court ultimately held the sale of the asset to be an economic transfer:

> "… we hold that where, as here, there is a genuine multiple-party transaction with economic substance which is compelled or encouraged by business or regulatory realities, is imbued with tax-independent considerations, and is not shaped solely by tax-avoidance features that have meaningless labels attached, the Government should honor the allocation of rights and duties effectuated by the parties."

In the *Frank Lyon* case, the court was impressed with the fact that there were independent third-party investors who had invested in the transaction based on its legal character as a sale; this argument is applicable to most securitization transactions as well. However, the mere fact that external investors are present is not enough; tax officers would be well within rights to hold the sale to be a contrivance if one or more of the following situations exist:

- The sale is a mere contrivance aimed at some benefit by an artificial sale-type treatment; for example, the ability to write losses on sale of the asset;
- The risks and rewards apparently transferred have been re-acquired by a series of transactions;
- The transferor has guaranteed payments to the so-called buyers of receivables; and
- Circumstances where a true sale in law can be challenged exist.

Specific tax provisions for financing treatment

Specific provisions in law may exist that may provide for financing treatment to the transaction. This is not a very common situation unless tax laws have been specifically aimed at simplifying the taxation by having the transaction treated as financing.

Substantive financing treatment

This possibility relates to the applicability of tax principles on the substance of the transaction. This is also, as in legal issues, a situation of *recharacterization;* that is, despite the transaction being a legal sale, it is treated as a financing transaction for tax purposes.

What justifies such recharacterization for tax purposes, even though the legal fabric of the transaction has been accepted? The question of substance of securitization transactions has been dealt with from a legal standpoint in the chapter on **Legal Issues** and from an accounting standpoint in the chapter on **Accounting Issues**. It has also been discussed in the chapter on Legal Issues that the severity of concerns in the substance approach is not the same for legal, tax and accounting purposes. Legal interpretation is more a matter of legal rights of parties, as shown by their intention and the court should generally try to give effect to the parties' intent unless there is an ambiguity. Accounting issues are concerned with substance as the basic approach, although for securitizations there is a departure from substance and a leaning towards the financial components.

From a tax viewpoint, the substance approach is a general power of tax authorities to replace form with substance, if there are glaring inconsistencies in the form of the transaction. Usually a tax officer is not supposed to ignore the façade of the transaction to look into substance, unless the form is a mere contrivance or a device to garb the substance. But the tax officer has before him the different bits and pieces of the transaction, including any recourse, swap, put options or call options the seller may have written or acquired.

Specific to securitization transactions, the possibility of a financial-substance-treatment from originator viewpoint is practically limited. As would be noted from the table above, if a securitization transaction is treated as a sale of receivables, the underlying income is accelerated, as well as the expenses on the transfer of receivables. Normally, the income would exceed the expenses, as the rate of return on the underlying assets would be more than the total costs, including funding and up-front expenses. Therefore, a sale-treatment results in a net taxable income up front. However, if the transaction were to be treated as a financial transaction, the same income would be taxed over a period of time by way of allocated income and financial expense.

If a sale treatment results in more up-front income recognition, a tax officer would normally not have the temptation to question the sale treatment and opt for financing treatment. The taxpayer would not have any such choice, as in most systems, having described and documented a transaction as a sale, a taxpayer would not be allowed the liberty of assailing his own assertion to treat the transaction as financing.

However, where the originator transfers low-yielding or non-performing assets, such as bank securitizations, there may arise an up-front loss on securitization. That would be the case when the rate of return on underlying assets is lower than the overall cost of securitization.

From a taxation viewpoint, the following points of significant difference from a legal and accounting approach should be noted:

> **Box 26.1: Tax treatment of securitization as finance transaction**
>
> - Sale treatment of securitization would result in up-front recognition of gain, that is, difference between the inherent rate of return of the portfolio over the cost of securitization.
> - Therefore, sale treatment leads to acceleration of tax liability.
> - Therefore, where securitization is documented as a sale, there is little chance of it being taken as financing by the tax officer.
> - However, if it results in up-front loss recognition, such an approach is not ruled out.
> - Basically, a tax officer can ignore legal form only if it is a nominality.

- Parties should be taxed as in a traditional financial transaction, if they understand clearly at all times that the transaction is a financial transaction, but the sale treatment is given merely to garb the intent of the parties.
- The apparent character of the transaction should be disregarded only when it is a nominality or mere nomenclature. Usually, there is a motive in choosing the nomenclature; it is not necessarily a mutual fraud against the revenue; it might even be convenience, or some regulatory advantages. If the parties have adopted a certain nomenclature only to serve a particular purpose, while their true intent is different and they understand their true intent as such, the tax officer should relegate the transaction back to its intended character and not the subterfuge adopted by parties.
- The end result or the ultimate effect of a transaction is not relevant in determining substance: if the substantive features of the subject transaction differ from a financial transaction, the apparent nature of the transaction should be regarded.

- Accounting treatment cannot govern the tax treatment. As noted in the chapter on **Accounting Issues**, the approach of accounting standards on securitization hinges on its legal features, and almost every transaction that amounts to a legal true sale will be given a sale treatment in books. However, the legal or accounting treatment cannot control the tax treatment.

Substantive sale by the SPV: Precondition for a see-through approach

The sale versus financing question may be an overall question – for the transaction as a whole – or may be looked at from the originator's or SPV's view. If the transaction as a whole is regarded as financing, there is no sale from the seller to the SPV, and hence, no question of onward sale by the SPV to the investors. However, if the originator makes a tax acceptable to the SPV, the next question is whether the SPV has transferred beneficial interest in the receivables to the investors, and thus made a "sale" for tax purposes. If the answer is in the affirmative, the SPV does not own the asset, and so will not have an income; the transaction will attain a see-through treatment. However, if the issuance of certificates or securities by the SPV is regarded as financing, the SPV is taken to be the owner of the asset, and so shall have to report income for tax purposes.

The principles for sale *versus* financing treatment for the SPV are the same as for those of the originator. There must be a transfer of economic ownership by the SPV. With this theme, some U.S. IRS rulings over time have given rise to the following list of situations that in combination may justify a financing treatment for the SPV:

- Revolving period for principal reinvestment;
- Payment mismatch (e.g., monthly pay collateral vs. quarterly pay debt);
- Use of excess spread to pay principal on debt so that the debt can be retired before the collateral is repaid;
- Existence and the size of the present value of the equity in the issuing entity;
- Nomenclature used in the transaction (i.e., labeling the securities as bonds or notes);
- Interest rate cap (i.e., a debt-like cap at an objective rate or an equity-like cap at the weighted-average rate of the loans);
- Right of the Issuer to call the debt at a point significantly earlier than a typical clean-up call (This may also be treated as financing for GAAP); and
- Use of a floating rate index for interest on the debt different than the index on the underlying loans.

Transfer of income, no transfer of asset

The next situation where, for tax purposes, a transaction is treated as financing and not a sale refers to a common rule in taxes, called **transfer of income without transferring the asset.** This means, if there has been a splitting of income from ownership of an asset – if someone continues to own an asset but diverts the income out of it, the income will continue to be taxed in the hands of the transferor.

Applicability of this principle would depend on the nature of the receivable. Essentially, a securitized receivable can be either an income from an asset, or an asset in itself. For example, the lease rentals emanating out of an asset are for tax purposes not an asset in itself, but income from an asset. On the contrary, the asset is deemed to have been beneficially sold as if a mortgage loan or an auto finance deal, and the installment is regarded as asset. Loan receivables are an asset as are credit card receivables. For commercial real estate, securitization of rental income is a case of transfer of income, not backed by a transfer of assets. The distinction between assets and income out of an asset may be quite thin, and often confusing. For example, if a lease, one argument can be that the right to receive the rental income is itself an asset, but for tax purposes, it would be crucial to examine whether the originator, in this case the lessor, continues to own an underlying asset from which such an income emanates.

Tax treatment in the originators' hands

One of the fundamental questions concerning securitization, both in terms of accounting rules and tax purposes, is whether there is a sale of the receivable. We have discussed above the principles for distinguishing between sale and financing treatment.

The basic tax issues for the originator are:

- If the transaction results in a sale of assets, will he be charged tax on the gain/loss on the sale up front?
- How would his servicing fees be taxed?
- How would any residual income from the transaction be taxed?
- What will be the taxation of retained interests?

Each of the above questions is related to a fundamental larger question – taxability of the originator's profit on the asset. The profit, as we have mentioned before, represents the weighted-average return inherent in the portfolio over the weighted-average cost of the transaction; this profit must enter the tax stream at some time. There are several ways of capturing this profit in a transaction:

- Up-front encashment by transferring receivables at higher than their carrying value or at a lower discounting rate than the weighted-average IRR
- Servicing fees
- Residual interest security – an investment in the SPV by way of a loan, zero-coupon bond, or residual income bond that allows the originator to sweep the remaining profit in the SPV
- A clean-up call, whereby all remaining receivables may be swept at a lower price
- Retention of an interest rate strip

- Interest rate swap
- Deferred sale consideration – the amount that remains with the SPV after repaying all investors is added to the consideration for sale of the asset as deferred sale consideration.

The taxability of the originator's profits would depend on the method of profit extraction used; usually a combination of methods is used. The essence of these profit extraction methods is the timing of the extraction or encashment of the profit – up front, over the period of the transaction or at the end of the transaction. Quite obviously, with an up-front extraction method in which the sale proceeds exceed the tax carrying value of the asset, there will arise a taxable gain on sale.

However, with servicing fees and other over-term or end-of-term extraction methods, the taxability may be deferred.[5] This is in spite of the fact that the servicing charges or residual interests may result in an accounting gain on sale. That is to say, based on well-accepted principles, tax accounting and GAAP accounting need not coincide, and the gain for tax purposes may be lower than for accounting purposes.

The other possible contention is that if the originator has residual interest in the assets he has transferred, such residual interest is also a form of consideration for the transfer; the value of such consideration is nothing but income. The counterargument to this can be that taxation cannot be based on uncertain or contingent income that is contractual but not certain. One needs to be concerned with local tax laws in answering the basic question as to taxability of the gain on sale for the originator.

Originator taxation where tax laws are not clear

Tax laws of most countries would not have clear provisions relating to securitization. In the face of provisions that are not designed to clearly cover securitization, how does one navigate and find tax answers? Let's take the case of Indian tax laws. The principles relating to diversion of income without transferring the asset exist in tax laws of most countries in some form or the other. Therefore, the following discussion may be of relevance to most countries.

Sec. 60 of the Indian Income-tax Act provides the following on diversion of income:

> *All income arising to any person by virtue of a transfer whether revocable or not and whether effected before or after the commencement of this Act shall, where there is no transfer of the assets from which the income arises, be chargeable to income tax as income of the transferor and shall be included in his total income.*

The above provision makes it clear that whoever might receive an income, whether with or without the right to receive it, the onus of paying tax will vest in the person who owns the asset from which the income arises. Transfer of income without transferring an asset is a form of application of income. The tax rule is that application of income is different from accrual of income. Income continues to accrue in the hands of the one who owns the asset.

One classic example of a sale of income without sale of underlying asset is *Provat Kumar Mitter* v. *CIT* 37 ITR 91 (Cal.) affirmed by the Supreme Court in 41 ITR 624, where the assessee transferred dividends out of shares without transferring the shares. The dividend income was held to be taxable in the hands of the assessee only. For the transfer of lease receivables, it is apparent that the asset from which the income arises – the physical asset – continues to be owned by the lessor. The lessor continues to own residuary interest in it, over and above the right to benefit from such part of the lease consideration as may not have transferred to the investors. Hence, lease rentals will continue to be taxed in the hands of the lessor. However, for securitization of hire-purchase receivables or loan receivables, the only asset claimed by the originator is the right to receive the installments. When such an asset is transferred, the income therein is also transferred to the transferee of the receivable. The discount suffered by the originator on transfer of the asset would be allowable as an expense – see the Supreme Court ruling in *Madras Industrial Investment Corporation* 225 ITR 802 (SC). The discount on issue of an instrument (called original issue discount – *OID*) is an important tax issue and generally most tax statutes would provide for specific tax treatment of *OID*. Hence, in cases such as securitization of lease receivables, house rent receivables and hotel rent receivables, transfer of receivables is not accompanied by transfer of the asset, which is distinct from the right to receivables. In such cases, the income from the asset will continue to be taxed in the hands of the originator. The position would be different if the receivable were the only "benefit" arising out of the physical asset, because such a transfer of a benefit amounts to a transfer of the asset itself in substance. At the same time, the originator will also continue to be eligible for capital allowances based on ownership of the asset. This is despite the fact that the originator has transferred all rewards and risks in as much as he has transferred the right to receive the income. But then, apart from the right to receive income, the lease originator also has the right to enjoy the residual value of the asset. It is for this reversionary interest that he has not transferred (and for which he still stands to the position of risk and reward), on which he would remain eligible to claim capital allowances. If the receivable itself is the only asset, then transferring the receivables should be taken to be a transfer of the asset, because an asset without the right to benefit out of it is no asset. In such a case, the entire amount of receivables upon transfer should be deemed to have been accelerated, and the discounting charges paid thereon should be deductible as the cost of such acceleration. The following explains this situation:

Case 1: Where receivables and not the asset transferred

This rule is applicable when there is a substantive asset over and above the right to receivables, such as lease rentals securitization, housing rent or hotel receipts securitization. The asset owner will continue accruing the income. In compensation, the asset owner will continue claiming capital allowances on the asset.

Case 2: When the asset itself is transferred

This rule is applicable when the receivable is the only substantive asset of the originator. On transfer, the income ingrained in the receivable will be deemed to have been transferred to the transferee. The resulting gain – the excess of the sum realized over the cost at which the asset is outstanding – will be considered to be the business profit of the originator.

Tax treatment of the special purpose vehicle (SPV)

Taxation of the SPV is one of the most crucial tax issues in a securitization transaction. The ultimate cost of a securitization transaction would be increased if SPV taxation leads to a double taxation of originator income. In some cases, the very economics of the transaction may be frustrated, leaving investors at a loss if the burden of taxes on the SPV undermines the assets available to the investors.

Three alternative ways of taxing the SPV

There are three possible approaches to SPV taxation:

- The SPV is treated as tax-transparent or a tax-spared entity.
- The SPV is charged to tax in a representative capacity.
- The SPV is charged to tax as a taxable entity in its own right.

Box 26.2: Three approaches to SPV taxation

- Pass-through or tax-spared entity: The SPV is not treated as taxable entity; investors are taxed in individual capacity on their share of income.
- Representative taxation: The SPV is taxed as representing investors. The SPV pays tax usually at a maximum marginal rate; investors do not pay tax on their share in the income.
- Entity level tax: The SPV pays tax on its income net of investor servicing. Investors pay tax on income received by them. Originator's share is taxed twice.

See-through tax treatment or SPV as tax-transparent entity

The legal framework of a securitization transaction is that the originator transfers financial assets to the SPV, and the SPV legally holds such assets but only as a fiduciary for the investors. The income emanating from such assets becomes the income of the SPV, and the SPV distributes such income among the investors in accordance with the terms of the scheme.

The SPV does not have an ownership interest in the asset; the legal interest it acquires is merely a logistic convenience to the investors. The income the SPV receives only mirrors the income of the investors. The whole existence of the SPV is not economically substantive. Therefore, the SPV may be regarded as having sold the asset beneficially to the investors, and so its existence with reference to the assets may be ignored. This is called the *conduit principle*, or *pass-through taxation* or *see-through taxation*.

If conduit tax principles are applied on the SPV, the SPV is viewed as nothing but a collective device or a compendious name for the investors. In other words, the investors are viewed as receiving what is legally received by the SPV. The SPV is transparent; in other words, the tax law can see the investors receiving the income received by the legal fiction that is the SPV. In this case, no tax is imposed on the SPV as it is not deemed to be receiving any income. The tax is imposed on the investors, relative to their share of income.

Conduit treatment would normally be applicable only when the SPV is a passive entity, as in simple pass-through transactions. It does not actually receive or reinvest any income. It merely distributes incomes to investors and is virtually only a collective conduit for the body of investors who actually receive the income. The SPV is a legal way of relating the investors to the originator, and does not have any further role. In such cases, the existence of the SPV is ignored for tax purposes.

It is difficult to generalize this law across countries, but some elementary principles that should be internationally important are:

- The SPV may have any organizational form to qualify for tax-transparent treatment. If it is a company, it is still holding the assets in a fiduciary capacity; thus, there is a trust relation between the investor and the SPV.
- The trustee must have no discretion as to application of income.
- Generally speaking, the share of income received by the investors must exactly mirror a rateable portion of the income received by the SPV.
- It is important to understand that see-through taxation means the income of the beneficiaries therein must be the income received by the SPV, and not the income that remains after paying all interest costs. In other words, the see-through principle applies to the gross income of the SPV and not its residual income.
- Tranching of income amounts to reallocation. If an SPV reallocates incomes, there is a basic difference between an SPV and a normal tax paying entity. In such a case, it is difficult to envisage the SPV as a tax-transparent entity.
- There must not be an equity class eligible for unspecified, residual portion of the income from the transaction.

Representative taxation of SPV income

Representative tax means the SPV is charged tax on the income, but the tax is deemed to be a tax on behalf of the investors. In other words, if the SPV pays tax on the collective income, there is no tax payable by the investors. This is generally the case with regular business associations, called associations of persons, or firms or other unincorporated bodies.

There is no double taxation of income in representative tax, as with conduit tax principles. However, the essential difference between conduit tax and representative tax treatment is one of tax rates. In conduit taxation, investors pay tax in their personal capacity, based on the rates of tax applicable to each. In representative tax, the SPV becomes a representative entity and pays tax at the rates applicable to such a body. Once the income has been taxed in representative capacity, there is no further tax on the share of income in the investors' hands.

Representative tax is certainly not very conducive to securitization transactions. Representative taxation leads to a problem of marginal rates of taxation; usually tax laws would provide for a representative taxpayer paying tax at the maximum marginal rate. Thus, investors pay more tax than in an individual capacity.

Entity-level taxation

Entity-level taxation means the SPV is treated as an independent taxable entity in its right, not in a representative capacity. Any income received or deemed to be received by the SPV is deemed to be its income, and any income distributed by the SPV is deemed to be the expense of the SPV and the income of the investors.

> **Box 26.3: Entity-level taxation of SPV**
>
> - If the SPV issues debt securities payable on fixed dates and carrying fixed coupon, it is going to be taxed as a taxable entity.
> - The entire income transferred by the originator will be taken as income of the SPV.
> - Against this, the coupon paid to investors is an expense, and so a set-off.
> - The structure should aim at matching the income and expense.
> - The residuary income of the originator will be servicing the equity and will be taxed in the hands of SPV.

Entity-level taxation results in double taxation as strictly both the SPV and the investors are charged to tax. However, as the income of the investors is a set-off for the SPV, double taxation arises only to the extent that the income distributed by SPV does not qualify for a tax deduction in the hands of the SPV.

Basically, a distribution by the SPV will be treated as an expense, if it is a payment towards **debt** or **charge against income**. If the payment by the SPV is a payment towards **equity** or **a distribution** or **application of income**, such payment will not be deductible for tax in the hands of the SPV and is still chargeable to tax in the hands of the recipient.

Normally, a payment is treated as payment towards equity if it is based on the profits of the enterprise. In securitization transactions, the residuary interest of the originator is in the nature of equity interest; therefore, the residuary profits of the originator will not qualify for tax benefit in the hands of the SPV but will be taxed as profit in the hands of the originator.

Securitization transactions where the SPV uses a bond structure, such as CMO, CLO or CBO structures would clearly fall under entity-level taxation principles. Here, what is done to avoid double taxation is the back-to-back matching of the incomes and expenses of the SPV. In other words, the income of the SPV by of interest is matched with the expenses on investor coupon, leaving the originator surplus which is subject to double taxation.

Whether the SPV is organized as a trust or a corporation, if it issues debt securities carrying fixed coupon and fixed repayment dates, collateralized by the cash flows from the originator, the SPV cannot avoid being treated as a taxable entity.

Distinction between debt and equity: The crux of entity-level taxation

The conditions of pass-through taxation are stiff, and they may not be complied with in many cases. In addition, there may not be any clear rules relating to pass-through transactions in many countries. Therefore, SPVs may have to reconcile with the entity-level taxation approach.

Under the entity-level approach, the key to tax neutrality is the ability to match the income of the SPV with its expenses so as to neutralize the effect of taxability. The income of the SPV is what it is entitled to on the assets transferred to it. The expenses are what the SPV, primarily, pays to the investors. On first impression, what the SPV earns is what it distributes among investors, so the income of the SPV must by definition be zero.

However, there is a very significant question here. If the SPV pays money to investors that may be regarded as a distribution or dividends, and the same is not treated as an expense of the SPV, this will lead to double taxation. For tax purposes, the servicing of a class will be treated as a distribution if the class can be treated as an equity class and not a debt class.

Debt or equity distinction

The debt versus equity distinction is a fundamental income tax principle, not limited to securitization transactions. There are rulings on this all over the world. It would be beyond the scope of this book to offer details of this issue, but basic principles are derived that would be crucial to decide whether the debt of the SPV may be wholly or partly characterized as equity for tax purposes.

In a U.S. ruling, there were 13 non-exclusive characteristics, called Mixon factors (after the name of the case) that were held to be useful in distinguishing between debt and equity:

1. The name given to the certificate evidencing the indebtedness;
2. The presence or absence of a fixed maturity date;
3. The source of payments, i.e., whether the recipient of the funds can repay the advance with reasonably anticipated cash flow or liquid assets;
4. Whether the provider of the funds has the right to enforce payment;
5. Whether the provider of the advance gains an increased right to participate in management;
6. The status of the contribution in relation to regular creditors;
7. The intent of the parties;
8. Whether the recipient of the advance is adequately capitalized;
9. Whether there is an identity of interest between the creditor and the shareholder;
10. Source of interest payments, i.e., whether the recipient of the funds pays interest from earnings;
11. The ability of the corporation to obtain loans from outside lending institutions;

12. The extent to which the recipient used the advance to buy capital assets; and

13. Whether the recipient repaid the funds on the due date (Mixon factors). [*Estate of Mixon v. United States*, 464 F.2d 394, 402 (5th Cir. 1972).]

Avoiding double taxation

As double taxation of originator income is a significant drag on the transaction and undermines the originator's profits, it is necessary in securitization transactions to avoid double taxation. There are two common ways of avoiding taxation of the SPV – **a tax haven domicile of the SPV** and **availing tax neutrality under a specific law**.

Tax haven incorporation of the SPV is a very common device. If the SPV is incorporated in a tax haven jurisdiction, the key issues are: (a) whether there is a double tax avoidance treaty with the host country; and (b) whether the scope of activities of the SPV in the host country is such that the SPV can be deemed to have a "permanent establishment" in the host country and liable to tax in the host country. Typically, a permanent establishment in the host country can be avoided if there are no employees and no office in the host country.

The other mechanism would be to structure the SPV in a way that it qualifies for tax exemption under a specific law, say the REMIC law in the U.S., or Italian rule on tax-neutral SPVs.

Tax haven incorporation of the SPV

To avoid double taxation of the SPV's residuary income, it is common to place SPVs in popular tax haven jurisdictions such as the Cayman Islands, Isle of Man and Gibraltar.

If the SPV is based on a foreign jurisdiction, the payments that the originator passes on to the SPV are payments made to a foreign entity, in which case, withholding tax implications may arise. These are reviewed in a later section.

The other significant issue is that although the SPV is legally domiciled in a foreign country, it may still be subject to tax as a resident in the country of the originator. This is based on a tax principle by which an entity is regarded as a resident in a jurisdiction if it has a **permanent establishment** in the jurisdiction.

The general tax rule is that a permanent establishment will arise in a jurisdiction if the entity is managerially controlled from that jurisdiction, no matter where it is incorporated. [Permanent establishment includes a place of management, branch, office or factory or the presence of dependent agents with authority, habitually exercised, to conclude contracts in name of offshore enterprise; limited use of facilities, e.g., display, storage, maintenance of merchandise or for purchases of merchandise or collecting information, do not constitute a permanent establishment.] "Control" is itself an abstraction. In the context of securitizations, a relevant issue is who controls the affairs of the SPV. As noted in the chapter on Legal Issues, SPVs are normally shell entities and their actual ministerial work is handled by an administrator, normally the originator himself. The Board of Directors of the SPV may also be controlled by the originator. Therefore, a question arises as to whether the SPV can be deemed to be controlled from the jurisdiction of the originator, thus bringing it back to tax in the origination country.

A "permanent establishment" cannot be deemed to exist in the originator country merely because the administrative or ministerial tasks relating to collection and servicing are carried out in the originator country. Therefore, to avoid being domiciled in the originator country, the board of directors of the SPV is comprised of independent directors, so the SPV does not have any office or address in the originator country.

U.S. taxation rules for securitization

Under the U.S. tax laws, the following situations may find taxation of SPVs:

* Grantor trust
* Owner trust
* REMIC
* FASIT (since deleted)
* Other entities

Grantor trusts

There are special tax rules for non-discretionary trusts that beneficially hold assets for the grantor, that is, the author of the trust. Here, the trustees hold the assets solely as per the direction of the grantor.

Sections 671 to 679 of the IRC contain provisions on grantor trusts. A grantor trust is charged to tax on so much of the interest as it does not convey to the beneficiaries. Sec. 671 provides that when the grantor or another person is deemed the "owner" of any portion of a trust, such an owner is then required to include in computing his or her taxable income those items of income, deductions and credits against tax of the trust that are attributable to that portion of the trust. Remaining items of income, deductions and credits against tax are taxed to the trust or beneficiary as applicable, in determining taxable income. The grantor is not treated as "owner" in respect of such a share of its income as it may have been already beneficially apportioned to the beneficiaries.

There are several restrictions on grantor trusts, such as restrictions on reversionary interests.

In pass-through securitization transactions, the holders of the pass-through certificates will be deemed to be the substantive owners of the trust, and so the income will be taxed in the hands of the investors rather than the trust itself. This is a completely see-through treatment; even the expenses of the trust are treated as expenses rateably apportioned among the investors. The pass-through certificates of Ginnie Mae, Fannie Mae and Freddie Mac qualify for grantor trust treatment, as per several rulings of the IRS.

There were several rulings of the revenue on whether senior/subordinate structures would qualify as pass-through certificates. One of these is Sears Regulations[6] in 1984. These regulations provided: "an 'investment' trust will not be classified as a trust if there is a power under the trust agreement to vary the investment of the certificate holders. *See Commissioner* v. *North American Bond trust*, 122 F 2d 545 [4]-2 USTC 9644] (2d Cir. 1941) *cert. Denied*, 314 U.S. 701 (1942). An investment trust with a single class of ownership interest, representing undivided beneficial interest in the assets of the trust, will be classified as a trust if there is no power under the trust agreement to vary the investment of the certificate holders. An investment trust with multiple classes of ownership interests ordinarily will be classified as a business entity under 301.7701-2; however, an investment trust with multiple classes of ownership interests, in which there is no power under the trust agreement to vary the investment of the certificate holders, will be classified as a trust if the trust is formed to facilitate direct investment in the assets of the rust and the existence of multiple classes of ownership interests is incidental to that purpose."

By way of an example, it said where there are two classes A and B paying sequentially, then the trust will not be regarded as a trust but as a business entity:

> A corporation purchases a portfolio of residential mortgages and transfers the mortgages to a bank under a trust agreement. At the same time, the bank as trustee delivers to the corporation certificates evidencing rights to payments from the polled mortgages; the corporation sells the certificate to the public. The trustee holds legal title to the mortgages in the pool for the benefit of the certificate-holders but has no power to reinvest proceeds attributable to the mortgages in the pool or to vary investments in the pool in any other manner. There are two classes of certificates. Holders of Class A certificates are entitled to all payment of mortgage principal, both scheduled and pre-paid, until their certificates are retired; holders of Class B certificates receive payments of principal only after all Class A certificates have been retired. The different rights of the Class A and Class B certificates serve to shift to the Holders of the Class A certificates, in addition to the earlier scheduled payments of principal, the risk that mortgages in the pool will be pre-paid so that the holders of the Class B certificates will have "call protection" (freedom from premature termination of their interests on account of prepayments). The trust thus serves to create investment interests with respect to the mortgages held by the trust that differ significantly from direct investment in the mortgages. As a consequence, the existence of multiple classes of trust ownership is not incidental to any purpose of the trust to facilitate direct investment and, accordingly, the trust is classified as a business entity under 301.7701-2.

Notably, when a trust is taxed as a business entity, it is taxable in its own right, and not as a representative taxpayer.

Owner trusts

A pass-through certificate is a certificate of ownership interest. As the trust distributes all ownership of its assets by way of pass-through certificates, it is left with no ownership.

However, subsequent transactions such as CMOs see the trust issuing debt-type instruments. As the trust will raise funds by issuing debt, the trust will be treated as the owner of the property – thus, the concept of owner trust. An owner trust is taxed on the same basis as a partnership entity. That is, the tax it pays is on behalf of the partners.

REMIC rules

To encourage CMO structures, REMIC rules were specifically inserted. We have noted before[7] the historical setting under which the REMIC law was passed. The basic purpose of the REMIC law is to shift the burden of taxation of the whole transaction on residual income class, discussed below. However, as the residual income class need not have any substantial amount or percentage of investment in the whole structure, most REMICs have a nominal (say, US$100) worth of residual class, and the rest of the classes are treated as substantive debt of the REMIC.

What is a REMIC?

- Real estate mortgage investment conduits (REMICs) are securitization entities that come for special treatment under Federal tax laws. The REMIC rules are contained in sections 860A to 860O of IRS regulations and contain a way out for the pass-through rules under which securities with multiple payback periods could not have been issued and the certificates had to mirror the pay-in period of the collateral pool. Most U.S. RMBS transactions adopt either the pass-through or the REMIC status. CMOs are generally structured for tax purposes as REMICs.
- A REMIC must buy only qualifying mortgages. Qualifying mortgages include obligations principally secured by an interest in real property, and includes pass-through certificates and interest in other REMICs. Amendments made in 2004, effective January 1, 2005, allowed REMICs to buy interests in reverse mortgages as well.
- A REMIC does not have to be a separate legal entity. It can simply be a section of the mortgage pool. So, under one legal entity, for example, under one trust, there can be more than one REMIC.
- The REMIC itself is a tax-transparent entity. There is no entity-level tax on the REMIC. Tax is imposed on the holders of interests in the REMIC.

REMIC interests

- Every REMIC must designate two classes of interests – regular and residual interests.
- Regular interests can be of more than one class, but residual interests can only have one class.

- Regular interest is comparable to a conventional bond with a fixed principal and interest on a fixed or floating rate. A residual interest can have any characteristic.
- As residual interest in a REMIC can be of only one class, where the structurer desires to have various interests which cannot be characterized as regular interests, the REMIC is broken into several REMICs, one investing into the other. For instance, if the originator intends to strip interest above 8% in a mortgage pool, and also intends to sell an IO strip of 8%, the first REMIC will acquire the entire pool and sell uncertified interest of 8% in the mortgage pool, retaining the balance. The second REMIC will buy the 8% interest and sell the PO portion and the IO portion separately.

Taxation of REMIC interest holders

- The broad principles of taxation of REMICs are as follows; the REMIC itself is not taxed, but the interest holders are.
- The entire income of the REMIC is taken as the income of the residual interest holders, and the interest paid on the regular interests is taken as if it were a deductible expense. In other words, the (total income of the REMIC – interest on regular interests) is allocated to the residual class holders as their income. As mentioned above, in view of any minimum amount of residual interest, this has the effect of treating almost the entire regular interest in the REMIC as a debt and achieving tax neutrality.

FASIT rules

The FASIT rules were inserted in 1996 to create tax-efficient securitization vehicles for non-MBS asset classes. These rules are contained in section 860H to 860L of the IRC. Regulations have also been framed, albeit after a gap of four years since the enactment of the law.

Repeal of FASIT rules

"(F)rom beginning to end, almost nothing relating to FASITs has been done right," comment leading tax authors James M. Peaslee & David Z. Nirenberg.[8] Enron had reportedly misused the FASIT tax exemption for several high coupon transactions. The Joint Committee on Taxation's Enron report recommended repeal of FASIT exemption, and it was repealed effective January 1, 2005. Existing FASITs were grandfathered.

The discussion below applies only to the grandfathered vehicles.

Principles of FASIT taxation

The basic principles of FASIT taxation are:

- As in the case of a REMIC, a FASIT will not come for an entity-level tax, nor will it be taxed as a trust or partnership.

- FASIT has a single class of ownership interest and one or more classes of regular interests. The tax burden of the entire transaction is shouldered by the ownership class. The regular interests are treated as the debt of the FASIT and therefore the residual income taxable to the ownership interest is only the income that remains after paying all regular interests.
- FASITs are permitted to invest in fixed-rate debt instruments, specified floating-rate debt instruments, inflation-indexed debt instruments and credit card receivables. Additionally, FASITs may hold beneficial interests in, or coupon and principal strips created from, these types of instruments.
- As a structural difference between REMICs and FASITs, FASITs are consolidated, for tax purposes with the holder of the ownership interest. Therefore, there are conditions laid down as to who can be an eligible holder of ownership interest.
- The holder of ownership interest may be a single domestic taxable corporation.
- Gain on sale rules have been incorporated into FASIT regulations. Transfer of assets to a FASIT triggers recognition of gain on sale to the holder of ownership interests.

Other entities

As noted before, if an SPV is treated as a business entity, it will be taxed on income less expenses. The key consideration of distinction between debt and equity has already been noted before.

Thin capitalization rules and SPV taxation

Tax laws of many countries provide for thin capitalization rules. The intent of these provisions is that, generally speaking, expenses on servicing of debt are allowable as an expense. Serving of equity is taken as a distribution and not as an expense. Every business requires a certain degree of equity or risk capital. However, with increasing sophistication of financial instruments, it is possible to structure an instrument that looks like debt but has the economic impact of equity, such as a subordinated debt. This would have the effect of exhibiting a servicing, which is really a servicing of equity as that of debt, and so would make an unjustifiable claim for tax expenditure.

To counter the tendency, tax laws of many countries put in a thin capitalization rule providing that if the entity is thinly capitalized (indicated mostly by the debt-to-equity ratio), then the servicing of debt, or a certain part of the debt, will not be allowed as an expenditure. For instance, see Division 820 of the Income Tax Assessment Act 1997 of Australia.

This existence of thin capitalization and loan relationships also suggests related party transactions, because a lender lending to a thinly capitalized entity under circumstances that are not commercially sustainable indicates an affiliation.

How does this rule affect SPVs? SPVs are, by their very constitutional feature, nominally capitalized. If thin capitalization rules are applied to SPVs, several transactions with the SPVs will be subject to transfer pricing rules or will lead to disqualification of expenses. The only way out of this seems to be specific exemption from thin capitalization rules. For instance, sec. 820.39 of the Income Tax Assessment Act 1997 of Australia provides an exemption from the thin capitalization rules to an SPV on satisfaction of certain conditions (primarily bankruptcy remoteness as per criteria of an international rating agency).

Taxation of SPVs where no specific provisions exist: India

In most countries, specific provisions on taxation of securitization transactions would not be in place. As a case to illustrate how SPVs would be taxed when tax laws are silent, we take up the case of India.

In India, an SPV may:

- Either be exempt from tax altogether;
- Or be taxed in a representative capacity;
- Or be taxed in an independent capacity.

The form of organization of the SPV does not matter; if the SPV is organized as a company, it might still be regarded as a trustee for investors. If it is organized as a trust, it may still be taxed as an entity and not as a representative of the investors.

The broad principles for the three alternative taxing schemes are the same as discussed earlier. Specific reference to the rules is made below:

Non-discretionary trust treatment

Tax laws make a distinction between discretionary trusts and non-discretionary trusts. Non-discretionary trusts are similar to the U.S. concept of grantor trusts, where the trustees are simply fiduciaries and work under a pre-fixed formula. In non-discretionary trusts where the share of the beneficiaries to the income of the trust is well defined, the income of the beneficiaries is determinate and ascertainable. In such cases, though the tax officer has a right to tax the trust in a representative capacity, such tax cannot be any different from the taxability of the beneficiaries. Therefore, there is no motivation on the part of the tax officer to tax the trust.

The rules about discretionary trust taxation were laid down by the Supreme Court in its landmark ruling in *CWT* v. *Trustees of H. E. H. Nizam's Family (Remainder Wealth) Trust* (1977) 108 ITR 555 (SC), holding that the principles of representative taxation apply only where the shares of beneficiaries are not determinate. In other words, a trust is by itself not a taxable entity in India; a trust merely comes for vicarious tax if the shares of the beneficiaries are not determinate. The rule of discretionary trusts was once again *Commissioner Of Income-tax* v. *Kamalini Khatau* 209 ITR 101 (SC):

"A discretionary trust is a trust whose income is not specifically receivable on behalf or for the behalf of any one person or wherein the individual shares of the beneficiaries are indeterminate or unknown. The rate of tax payable by trustees upon the income of a discretionary trust is that which would be paid upon such income by an association of persons. Where, however, such income or a part thereof is actually received by a beneficiary, tax shall be charged thereon at the rate applicable to the total income of the beneficiary if this benefits the Revenue."

Representative capacity

Representative taxation arises only when one person receives income on behalf of others; if a person receives income on his own behalf, he cannot be charged to tax on a representative basis. Thus, if the SPV issues debt securities that constitute obligations, the income it receives will be an income on its own behalf and not for investors, thus resulting in entity-level tax and not representative tax.

The following are the essential principles of representative tax:

1. All representative assessees shall be liable to the same duties, responsibilities and liabilities and the tax incidence upon him shall be as if the income were received by the beneficiary. [Sec. 161 (1A)]. Under this provision, the SPV can be taxed for the income deemed to be received by the SPV on behalf of the several investors, but such tax will be revenue-neutral, since this amount of tax cannot exceed the tax individually payable by the beneficiaries on such income. Obviously therefore, the revenue will not resort to representative tax in such a case.
2. Exceptions to this rule are made in sec. 161 (1A), 164 (1), 164 A and 167B. When the trust falls under any of these exceptions, its income shall be charged to tax at the maximum marginal rate, that is, at the maximum slab applicable to individuals.

One would think even if the trust were to fall under any of the exceptions mentioned above, yet the trust would anyway have nil income, as what the trust is deemed to receive is to be netted off by what the trust pays to the beneficiaries, and the net result is invariably zero. In this proposition, difficulties in actual administration might arise because the trust becomes a separate assessable entity and also that a revenue-minded tax officer may regard the income of the trust as income and the expense as the appropriation of such income and not an expense, and hence tax the whole of the receipt. To avoid tax at a maximum marginal rate, the trust must ensure it does not fall under the provisions of sec. 161 (1A), 164, 164 A and 167B.Sec. 161 (1A) applies if any part of the income deemed to be received by the trust comprises business income. If the trust is not actually engaged in business activity, but is merely holding property and issuing beneficial interest certificates, the trust is deemed to receive income only on behalf of the beneficiaries, who may be treating the acquisition of receivables or income as business income. If any one of the participants in the scheme receives the income as business income, the revenue will thereby get the right to tax the trust to representative tax and at the maximum marginal rate. As this strange provision, inserted with anti-avoidance intent, is applicable, the trust must ensure that none of the participants hold the investment in securitized receivables as a business investment. Sec. 164 (1) applies where the shares of the beneficiaries in the income of the trust are not known. That is not the case here, as the shares of the investors are known by the amount of investment made by them. Proviso to sec. 164 (1) and sec. 167 B apply to associations of persons (AOPs). These provisions apply to AOPs whose members – any of them – have income above the maximum that is exempt from tax. The trust in the instant case cannot afford to omit from the investor base all persons having taxable incomes. Hence, it would be ridiculous to get caught in these provisions. There are two escapes to provisions of tax applicable as AOP: First, claim that the trust in the instant case is merely a grantor trust that does not have any common objective except that property is held on behalf of a group of persons for the sake of convenience. An association of persons has a community of objective, formed for carrying out such objective; there is no such common objective served by the trust, except of name lending to the group of participants. The second, care to be observed for escaping sec. 167B is to avoid the definition of "body of individuals." If not an AOP, the trust could be regarded as a body of individuals. For this, the escape is simple: As a participant in the scheme, include a person who is not an individual (such as a company).

Admittedly, the set of provisions dealing with trusts and AOPs is quite complicated, and obviously not designed to deal with the kind of trusts the securitization exercise is going to create. However, in respect of several venture capital funds, there have been rulings of the Authority for Advance Rulings holding the see-through of pass-through nature of the trust in situations where the trust is non-discretionary.

Entity-level tax

Adequate attention has not been given to circumstances in which some of the "beneficial interest certificates" of the trust may be treated as debt for tax purposes, leaving the entire burden of tax on the residual certificates. While it is true that the income of the trust will be taxed in the hands of the beneficiaries where their shares are determinate, if the trust issues various classes and some classes have limited interest to claim payment, they may be regarded as debt. The distinction between debt and equity, discussed at length earlier, will apply here; a beneficial interest is merely an interest to claim distribution, while a debt is a right to claim money. Beneficial interest is not an actionable claim but a mere equitable right. If the certificates issued by the trust create a right to claim money, it would be proper to construe them as debt rather than as beneficial certificates.

Deductibility of expenses by the SPV

If the securitization deals are carried through SPVs, questions may arise from a tax viewpoint as to what is the nature of the SPV – a business entity, a limited purpose entity or a non-entity.

Questions as to the deductibility of expenses incurred by the SPV on raising capital, rating and administration of the trusts have been raised for an Australian securitization vehicle called First Australian National Mortgage Acceptance Corporation (FANMAC). The business of the company was to administer securitization trusts where each trust would represent the money raised from investors and utilized in buying mortgages.

Question arose as to the deductibility of expenses incurred by the company on rating and sourcing. It was argued on behalf of the revenue that either the company was not engaged in any business as it was not formed for the purpose of earning any profit, or that the expenses could be said to be revenue expenses as they related to the formation of the trusts or sourcing of the resources.

The Federal Court of Australia held as follows, in *Fanmac Limited* v. *Commissioner of Taxation* 91 ATC 4703 22 ATR 413:

> The taxpayer argues that its business consists of the establishment of trusts through which the process of **securitization** takes place and that this is an operational function whereby the mortgages acquired are pooled for sale to investors as medium to long term securities; and that the pooling process is a normal operational feature of the taxpayer's business. Viewed in this way, the taxpayer says, the cost of establishing such trusts is a normal operating expense. The expenditure, which did not obtain for the taxpayer any tangible asset or advantage of an enduring kind, was analogous to the cost of marketing or "packaging" a product and the following description of Dixon C.J., in *Vacuum Oil Co. Pty. Ltd*. v. *Federal Commissioner of Taxation* (1964) 110 CLR419 at 434 is applicable here:
>
> > "... there is no sufficient reason for treating the expenditure as made on capital account. It appears to me clearly expenditure incurred in the process of marketing the commodity and to be expenditure which is not made once for all but is likely to be repeated, and not to be sufficiently identified as outside the ordinary conduct of business."
>
> Alternatively, the taxpayer says, it is accurate to characterize the establishment of the Trust as forming part of the business activities of the taxpayer, rather than something done to enlarge the framework within which the taxpayer carried on its business; it was not the first trust established by the taxpayer nor the last. In the present case, if the only relevant activity of the taxpayer were the instant trust, there would be much to be said for the view that this item of expenditure was an affair of

capital. But in my view, this would be to take too narrow a view of what the taxpayer was doing. It is appropriate to describe the relevant activities of the taxpayer as the carrying on of the business of establishing, marketing, managing and administering trusts that issue fixed-rate securities. The item of expenditure took place within that framework and as part of that process. Similar items of expenditure were incurred by the taxpayer from time to time. These considerations suggest that the items took their character from the processes of the operations of the business rather than constituted a part of the structure of the business. In this sense, this item should in my view be characterized as something incurred on revenue account.

Tax treatment in the hands of the investors

In securitization transactions, the taxation of investors is a derivative of the taxation of the SPV. Investors are essentially participants in the pool of interests – the SPV. Hence, here again, there are three possible choices:

- Investors are charged to tax ignoring the SPV as an entity at all.
- Investors are not charged to tax as the tax paid by the SPV is treated as tax paid on behalf of the investors.
- Investors are treated as holding securities issued by the SPV: They are taxed on what they earn by holding or transferring such securities.

> **Box 26.4: Three approaches to investor taxation in securitization**
>
> - Investors pay tax on what the SPV receives and redistributes, applicable in clear pass-throughs. Investor income is his proportion in income transferred periodically by originator.
> - SPV pays tax in representative capacity: Investors are not taxed.
> - Investors are taxed as if they hold a debt security typically the case if a bond structure has been used.

First possibility: Pass-through investors

If the investors are deemed to be receiving income divided by the SPV, and the existence of the SPV is ignored for tax purposes, investors receive what the obligors pay. The SPV plays no role in the transaction except distributing incomes to a plural investor base.

In this case, each investor pays proportional tax on what is earned by the investor. As the investor has acquired a proportion of the flows redirected by the originator, the investor's income is the proportion of income that the originator redirects.

Take the following example to understand proportional redirection. Let us suppose the originator transfers the following cash flow, where the originator was to receive equated repayments inclusive of an imputed interest and repayment of principle, computed as:

Table 26.2 Imputed interest working in mortage installments

Year	Installment	Outstanding principal	Interest paid	Principal repaid
1	100,000	£411,140.73	£49,336.89	£50,663.11
2	100,000	£360,477.62	£43,257.31	£56,742.69
3	100,000	£303,734.93	£36,448.19	£63,551.81
4	100,000	£240,183.13	£28,821.98	£71,178.02
5	100,000	£169,005.10	£20,280.61	£79,719.39
6	100,000	£89,285.71	£10,714.29	£89,285.71

Let us suppose the cash flows have been apportioned among 1,000 pass-through certificates; each investor holding one pass-through certificate will be deemed to be receiving income which is $1/1000^{th}$ of the income mentioned in Column 4 above. In actual administration, the originator will provide a certificate as to the income comprised in the repayments made, based on which the investors pay tax on their income.

Second possibility: SPV taxed in representative capacity

If the SPV has been charged to tax in a representative capacity or as an association of persons, the tax paid by the SPV is deemed to be a tax paid on behalf of the investors. Therefore, in such a case, the investors are not required to pay any tax on the distributed income.

In the above example, the entire income mentioned in column 4 of the above table will be taxed in the hands of the SPV. Let us suppose the SPV pays tax at a 30% rate. The remaining cash flows, after tax, are distributed to investors, who do not pay any tax on their income.

Third possibility: SPV issues debt securities

If the SPV issues debt securities, investors pay tax on the coupon rate specified on the security. For example, if the portfolio in the example above were to be funded by issuing debt of $400,000 carrying an 11% coupon, investors will pay tax on the outstanding nominal value at the coupon rate.

Withholding taxes

Depending on the tax regime concerned, domestic transactions and/or cross-border transactions are subject to withholding taxes. The concept of withholding tax or tax deduction at source is that a certain assumed rate of tax should be applied on a payment at the time of making it, retained by the source, and remitted to the government as advance against tax payment. While domestic withholding tax may or may not exist in the country, withholding tax on interest payments in international transactions is a global feature.

The question of withholding tax arises when there is a payment or a credit. In securitization transactions, payments arise at the following stages:

- When the SPV pays for the assets bought from the originator.
- When the SPV collects payments from debtors.
- When the SPV passes on payment to the investors.

Usually, the question of any withholding tax at the time of payment by the SPV to the originator will not arise, as the SPV pays to the originator for the purchase of the receivables. Even if the transaction of securitization is so structured as to amount to a pay-through structure, there is no payment of interest as such at zero time, as it is the SPV that is paying the discounted value of receivables to the originator.

For collections that the SPV makes from the debtors, withholding tax will be applicable based on the nature of the transaction; the securitization deal does not disturb the original transaction between the originator and the debtor. Therefore, any withholding tax, if applicable, will continue to be applicable. From the viewpoint of logistical convenience in operating the scheme, it would be far better to select assets where there are no pre-paid taxes.

Essentially, the question is whether the payments made by the SPV to the investors will be deemed to be carrying interest. Here one possible view could be that the SPV is merely a conduit and is rechanneling the income from the debtors to the investors. It is only a payment device or a conduit; it is not collecting income in its own right and paying it on account of its own liabilities. This would be particularly a strong view to take with pass-through structures.

However, in pay-through and bond structures, payments made by the SPV are not merely a redistribution but a payment of interest, and so would normally suffer withholding tax.

An Indian ruling on the matter

In India, the only decided case on securitization has dealt with this issue. The Madras Appellate Tribunal ruling relates to facts that may be said to be relevant for a "pay-through structure", that is, one where there is no total transfer of beneficial interest in the underlying receivables. The assessee company was Vishwapriya Financial Services and Securities Ltd. [*Vishwapriya Financial Services & Securities Ltd.* v. *ITO* {1997} 60 ITD 401 (Mad.)] Vishwapriya was one of the earliest entrants to securitization in India.

The company was pooling investors' money and investing in various fixed income investments. Direct matching of receipts and payout was obviously not there, generally considered a prerequisite for pass-through securitization. The company had also guaranteed a fixed rate of return, again a feature destructive of the pass-through securitization structure, as the originator should sack off all his risk in the receivables. However, the company contended that it was only an agent for the investors; it was only investing money as an agent for the investors and there was no debtor-creditor relationship between it and the investors. Therefore, when the company made payments to the investors, no case of deduction of tax at source arose.

The Tribunal analyzed the meaning of "interest" for the purposes of application of withholding tax. It held that sec 2 (28A) of the Income tax did not necessarily require a debtor-creditor relation for applicability of the provisions. It is enough if there was an "obligation" to pay money. Looking at the features of the scheme, there was a guaranteed return and pooling of funds whereby the investors had no idea of what were the investments from their funds, the money the company was paying to investors was a kind of obligation. Therefore, withholding tax was applicable.

The case went a long way in affecting the Indian market for securitizations; pass-throughs are distinguishable on facts, and the feeling of this commentator is that the case for tax exemption on pass-throughs becomes stronger with this ruling. But unfortunately, none of the Indian securitizations at present are pass-throughs; not only is there a recourse to the originator (meaning the payments are guaranteed), there are even usual clauses that require the originator to pay the receivable over to the investors even when the originator has not collected the same from the debtors. This may well be taken as covered by the Vishwapriya ruling, and accordingly the payment made over by the originator may be regarded as payment for a debt, and the withholding tax at the applicable rates may be slapped.

The present case was not on taxability of the SPV, as there was no SPV employed by the company in the case. The company itself was collecting and paying over the receivables deemed to belong to the investors. A trustee was appointed to oversee this function. One is not sure from the case whether the tax officer made a claim that the income deemed to belong to the investors was taxable as the income of the company, and the amount paid by the company is only a claimable expense. If this was claimed, the company may face a further problem, as the payments it makes may be distinguished between repayment of debt and return on debt, with only the latter being deductible as an expense.

Exemption from withholding tax

Clearly, the economics of securitization transactions may be distorted if withholding taxes are imposed. Several countries have tried to override this by providing specific exemptions from withholding taxes.

For example, in Italy, the decree 35 of March 14, 2005, amending law 130 provides for withholding tax exemption on the notes of issuers issued to noteholders resident in jurisdictions outside Italy that are (1) not resident for tax purposes in a tax haven country (as defined by the Italian ministry of finance) and (2) resident for tax purposes in a country that allows for an adequate exchange of information if the notes have been deposited in accordance with the provisions of Italian tax laws and all the relevant requirements have been fulfilled. Special exemptions have been provided for institutional investors.

In Spain too exemption has been given. The Law 23/2005 was published on November 19, 2005, in Spain's Official Journal. The 2nd Final Provision of this

Law exempts securitization bonds issued by Spanish asset-backed and mortgage-backed Fondos from a withholding tax for non-resident bondholders provided that these bondholders are not tax haven residents.

In Ireland as well, Section 110 of the Taxes Consolidation Act grants a specific exemption from withholding tax on interest payable by the SPV where the recipient is resident in a country with which Ireland has a tax treaty. Alternatively, if the notes issued are in the form of quoted Eurobonds and a non-Irish paying agent is used, interest may be paid free of withholding tax irrespective of the residence of the noteholder.

Notes

1 In a public meeting with the Central Board of Direct Taxes.
2 FASITs were subsequently repealed effective January 1, 2005.
3 Supplement V to their book: Federal Taxation of Securitization, p. 1.
4 Situation may be arguable if a total rate of return swap where the entire risk and rewards are exchanged by a completely new set of risks and returns. The point is so far not settled in tax laws. See, for further details, Vinod Kothari: *Credit Derivatives and Synthetic Securitization.*
5 This applies except when there are specific rules to include the value of retained interests while computing gains on sale.
6 So called, these were issued in pursuance of an offer by Sears Mortgage Securities Corp of fast pay and slow pay certificates.
7 Chapter on RMBS markets.
8 Supplement V to their book, *Ibid*, p. 123.

Chapter 27

Accounting for Securitization

Acounting rules have been a significant concern for all entities opting to securitize their receivables, and for good reason, as one of the prime motives in the exercise was to put off the asset, and in some cases the liability, off the balance sheet. Off-balance sheet funding reached a new level of controversy with the bankruptcy of Enron and the disclosure that it hid a substantial amount of its assets off-balance sheet by forming special purpose entities. The controversy was, properly speaking, one relating to hiving off substance in shell entities – called special purpose vehicles, but the people, unable to realize that special purpose entities were not limited to securitization, identified off-balance sheet accounting in general with securitization.[1]

Most of the key benefits of securitization over traditional funding are an off-shoot of the accounting treatment; hence, the accounting treatment is simply one of the very crucial issues in securitization. Off-balance sheet financing has been quite popular for diverse reasons, elegantly explained as "putting capital to more efficient use" and "keeping the parent balance sheet lean." However, the central desire that works here is the common urge in our stressful lives: *Ars longa vita brevis* – small capital and endless ambitions, short life and a lot to do, a small piece of land and a mighty mansion to build, small means and boundless desires. Off-balance sheet funding is essentially meant to extend leverage.

Securitization is not the only means to achieve off-balance sheet funding. The history of accounting standards globally has been to nab off-balance sheet devices even as innovators keep devising new methods of taking things off the books. This chase can be seen for leasing transactions, guarantees, derivatives, and so on. For securitization, present-day accounting rules generally permit assets to go off the books, and the rules about SPVs generally permit those assets to stay off the books. However, if the evolutionary process of accounting standards is an indication, the rules that qualify assets to go and stay off the books will become stricter over time.

Securitization accounting in flux

Securitization accounting has been in a state of disequilibrium for quite some time, and the fact that this should be so for an instrument that is new and fast growing is unfortunate.

At the end of 2003, the International Accounting Standards Board issued several amendments to the accounting standard on financial instruments, which included provisions on de-recognition (and securitization should mostly be concerned with de-recognition) of financial assets. It was generally felt that these amendments had substantially changed the approach of international accounting standards and brought the same closer to the substance-over-form accounting and farther from the U.S. approach.

The U.S. FASB also seemed to be in a great state of confusion. While securitization accounting standards have never really settled down, with the replacement of FAS 125 by FAS 140, there was some spark of brilliant rethinking coming from the FASB all the time. Responding to some of the proposed changes to FAS 140, the American Securitization Forum stated: "We are concerned that the Board has taken too casual an attitude towards the direct and indirect costs to reporting entities in responding to the series of changes in GAAP affecting securitizations over the past six years."[2]

What initially started as an Emerging Issues Task Force matter on servicing rights and certain issues relating to QSPEs, in the course of discussions developed into a major debate that seemed to touch the very fabric of the securitization industry. The U.S. FASB suggested new conditions for qualifying SPEs, which, in the opinion of the industry, would make it difficult for any SPE to achieve the QSPE status. As an alternative, the securitization industry suggested a new form of accounting treatment where the SPE will not be off-balance sheet but a segment on the balance sheet of the originator.[3]

This would have broadly been in line with the U.K. accounting treatment under FRS 5.

In the course of developments, in mid-2005 the split saw amendments to FAS 140 into three distinct areas – Transfers of Financial Assets (essentially relating to QSPEs), Servicing of Financial Assets and Hybrid Financial Instruments. On each of these, exposure drafts were issued.

In December 2005, it was reported that the Board would issue final statements on the Servicing Rights and Hybrid Instruments in the first quarter of 2006 and on Transfers/QSPEs in the second quarter. Details of the exposure drafts, progress and conclusions until the end of 2005 are discussed later in this chapter.

The Basic Accounting rule: Substance over form

With accounting rules, the basic issue is: Whether the securitized asset will be put off-balance sheet? The answer is obvious: It should be off-balance sheet if the asset has been sold or transferred. If the asset has been sold, the funding raised thereby should also be off-balance sheet as it represents the consideration for sale of receivables. If the asset has not been sold, it would stay on the balance sheet, and the amount raised in the process would be accounted for as if it were a loan on the collateral of the asset. Thus, the key issue for consideration is whether securitization of receivables represents a sale of the asset and the resulting funding the sale proceeds thereof, or does it represent collateral for a loan and loan liability, respectively.

Most securitization transactions are made to look like a sale of the receivable by the originator. Hence, the legal form is almost invariably one of transfer of receivables. The legal document would mostly look like a transfer of receivables from the originator to the SPV. Apparently, there is a good temptation to regard every securitization as a case of the sale of receivables, and consequently achieve an off-balance sheet effect.

However, accounting rules put stress on the substance of a deal over its legal form. Hence, one has to see whether the securitization deal in substance amounts to a sale of receivables. Talking of substance as a concept is different from form; one looks at the inner content and effect of a deal rather than the form in which such effect has been given. Usually, substance and form go hand in hand, but when the two are different, marginally or drastically, the accountant would look at the substance in precedence over the form. This means, it is possible:

- To securitize receivables in a way in which the form and substance of the deal is the sale of receivables; this would be accorded a sale treatment.
- To securitize receivables in a way in which the form is not one of sale, but the substance is one of sale; this is apparently a rare situation and it would be difficult for accounting standards to digest this situation. However, there is a possibility under the new IAS 39 where there is no sale in law and yet the asset is given a sale treatment due to a pass-through arrangement – see later in this chapter.
- To securitize receivables in a way in which the form is one of sale, but the substance is not one of sale; this would not be accorded a sale agreement.

It should be evident from the above discussion that the accounting treatment for a so-called securitization transaction may not exactly match with (a) its legal treatment; (b) its tax treatment; (c) its regulatory treatment for regulations relating to financial intermediaries. The essential form-*versus*-substance principle should guide the accountant in formulating the right accounting treatment; the accountant should not be controlled by the legal treatment of the transaction, although in a very significant way, global accounting standards for securitization do look at legal considerations, because one of the factors to examine is whether the assets securitized would continue to be available to the creditors and liquidator of the originator. At the same time, it would be pertinent to note that the legal treatment of a transaction should not be affected by its accounting treatment.

Accounting for sale, or accounting for securitization?

The sale of the asset and its securitization are two distinct and mutually independent steps. Securitization implies merely conversion of an asset or interest in a security. There are transactions of securitization that are not based on a sale at all – for example, secured loan structures and synthetic structures. On the other hand, there might be a sale of an asset by the enterprise, and there may be no securitization at all; for example, A sells the asset to B, and B simply retains the asset without converting the same into any securities.

Accounting standards relating to securitization are essentially aimed at accounting by the originator; hence, they are more concerned about the sale than the securitization. As such, in general these accounting standards are intended to be applied even when there is no securitization at all – for instance, bilateral loan sales or portfolio sales.

One may note that the material part of IAS 39 relates to "de-recognition" and the U.S. standard FAS 140 is concerned with accounting for "transfers." Both de-recognition and transfer relate to the first leg of a securitization transaction – transfer of the asset from the originator.

The issuance of securities or beneficial interests by the SPV might also be treated as a "sale," that is a transfer of beneficial interest. But in any event, "securitization" – the issuance of securities – is not at the heart of the accounting standards on securitization.

Sale of financial assets versus sale of non-financial assets

Another important feature of accounting standards for securitization is that these standards are related to transfers of financial assets and do not relate to transfers of non-financial assets.

For instance, a transfer of a physical asset is not covered by accounting standards on securitization. Securitization by transfers of physical assets is not completely unseen, but such transfers will be dealt with by usual standards relating to transfer of physical assets.

Similarly, certain rights or interests transferred for the purpose of securitization are not financial assets, such as future flows. A future flow is not an existing claim to a financial asset, and so is not a financial asset until it ripens into a receivable. The accounting standards relating to securitization would apply to a future flow only where it becomes an existing receivable.

On the other hand, transfer of assets such as bonds or fixed income securities will be covered by the standard, as these assets are "financial assets."

Development of accounting principles on securitization

One of the earliest statements on accounting principles for securitization is the U.S. Financial Accounting Standards Board's (FASB) Statement No. 13 on Accounting for Leases (FASB 13).

FASB 13 distinguishes between receivables assigned with recourse and without recourse. The basic accounting treatment is contained in Para 116 and 117 of the Statement no. 13 on Accounting for Leases. Para 116 of the Statement provides that in a financial lease, subsequent sale of the receivables or the lease property will not negate the treatment given to the lease initially. Instead, profit or loss on the sale will be accounted for at the time of sale. This is applicable for sales without recourse.

However, as securitization, particularly of mortgage receivables, became a common happening, the FASB was forced to issue a specific accounting standard dealing with securitizations. It was commonly understood that if receivables have been sold without recourse, it is obviously a "sale" of receivables. However, it was an open question as to whether even "with recourse" transfers could be treated as "sales."

Until 1983, it was generally felt that only the sale of receivables without recourse could qualify as sales. By this time, however, mortgage receivables securitization had become a common practice[4] and most of the sales of receivables to the agencies were sales with recourse. To deal with assignment of receivables with recourse, the Financial Accounting Standards Board issued in November 1983 Statement No. 77 on Accounting for Receivables Sold with Recourse. This Statement was based on a "predominant characteristic approach." Under SFAS No. 77, if a transaction "purports" to be a bona fide sale, the transferor's obligation under the recourse provisions can be reasonably estimated, and if certain other qualifying criteria are met (i.e., no calls or puts on transferred assets, control of assets has been relinquished), the transaction is treated as a sale. Besides, piecemeal guidance on securitization was also contained in SFAS No. 76, Extinguishment of Debt; SFAS 122, Accounting for Mortgage Service Rights; and FASB Technical Bulletins No. 84-4, Technical Bulletin no 85-2 relating to CMOs.

Effective 1997, FSAB 77 was replaced by a more detailed accounting standard called The Financial Accounting Standards Board's Statement No. 125, Accounting for Transfers and Servicing of Financial Assets and Extinguishments of Liabilities (FAS 125). FAS 125 was issued in June 1996 as part of a larger exercise relating to off-balance sheet financing that was going on since 1986.

FAS 125 was until then the most comprehensive accounting standard on securitization. The fact that such an elaborate accounting standard was to remain in effect for merely four years is an indication of the fast growing world of structured finance transactions. FAS 125 was later replaced by the even more detailed FAS 140.

While development of FAS 125 was going on, the International Accounting Standards Committee (IASC) also seized on the issue of reporting on financial instruments. The IASC had first issued an Exposure Draft on accounting for Financial Instruments in 1991 (E 40), which was expounded and issued as

Exposure Draft (E48) in early 1994. This became a Standard (Accounting for Financial Instruments, IAS 32). IAS 32 is mainly concerned with presentation – classification of financial instruments and disclosures.

However, with the explosive development of off-balance sheet derivatives, the IASC had still to make further refinement in its accounting standard dealing with financial instruments, and finally came out with IAS 39. This statement includes provisions on de-recognition, which directly relate to securitization transactions.

The Accounting Standards Board of the United Kingdom issued in 1994 FRS 5, related to reporting the substance of transactions, which includes detailed provisions about accounting for securitizations.

Most other countries have adopted their own versions of IAS 39, either with degrees of localization, or as is. Australia has adopted an accounting standard similar to IAS 32/ IAS 39. South Africa has replicated IAS 39 into its own list of standards. Canada usually falls in line with U.S. accounting standards and has adopted a standard similar to FAS 140. International Accounting Standards are effective for implementation in several countries. Other countries have either adopted IAS 39 or moderated/modified the same to suit their own local requirements.

Thus, the major guides to accounting principles for securitization presently are the following:

- FASB 140
- IAS 39
- FRS 5

IAS 39, like most statements from the IASB, is more a statement of principles than a detailed exposition of rules; on the contrary, the FASB has an almost insatiable urge to pen down the minutest details and so prefers to go into rules. With the amended version of IAS 39, some significant differences have come about between IAS 39 and FAS 140 in so far as it relates to securitization transactions. FRS 5, on the other hand, has adopted a completely different approach.

The accounting standards on securitization transactions are still evolving; FAS 140 is almost sure to undergo major changes, while IAS 39 has been recently revised and most countries are in the process of implementation of a revised IAS 39.

Sale treatment vs. loan treatment

Broadly speaking, the two key issues concerning accounting for a securitization transaction are:

- Is there a sale of an asset(s)?
- Is there a gain/loss on such a sale?

As is evident, the second question is only consequential; there is no question of a gain or loss on sale if the answer to the first question is negative. Therefore, the most crucial question is whether the transaction results in a sale of the asset of the transferor, and more specifically in the context of securitization, a sale of financial assets of the transferor?

Legally, a securitization transaction would generally lead to assignment of receivables from the originator to the SPV; therefore, there will be a legal sale of such receivables to the SPV. However, based on accounting principles, the transaction may either be treated as a sale or a mere financial transaction by transferring the receivables as a matter of security.

Generally speaking, any originator would prefer to achieve "sale treatment" of securitization transactions for books of account and "loan treatment" for taxation purposes. Discussed below are the requirements of various accounting standards as to when to treat securitization as a "sale." Giving a sale-type treatment means it is recognized that the originator has sold certain assets (receivables) and has raised an amount by selling such assets. On the other hand, giving a "loan" treatment would put the substance of the transaction before its legal form, and treat the transfer of receivables as a mere matter of security, keeping the assets as well as the receivables on the balance sheet of the originator.

Importantly, the sale-type or loan-type treatment will not have any impact as to the manner of accounting by the investor in such receivables. In either case, the investor recognizes his investment as an investment (see investor accounting later in this chapter).

Impact of sale vs. loan treatment

A sale treatment for accounting purposes is preferred because it entitles the originator to put the assets off the balance sheet. At the same time, a "financial" or "loan treatment" for tax purposes is preferable because the gain made on assignment of receivables will not be immediately taxable.

The following is a comparative picture of the effect of the two treatments on the originator's books:

Table 27.1 Comparing sale treatment and loan treatment

	Sale treatment	Loan treatment
Asset	Put off books	Keeps on books
Liability	Stays off books	Keeps on books
Income	Accelerates	Continues as usual
Discounting charges	Netted off from revenue	Amortized over the term of the receivables

Sale treatment leads to off-balance sheet accounting, which is responsible for several of the advantages of securitization. One of the immediate objectives of the originator may be to capture the excess spread inherent in the assets and put it as a profit up front. The advantage of increased leverage and the resulting lower weighted-average cost of funding may also be frustrated if the liability is reflected as on-balance sheet liability. It is likely that if the assets are not put off the books, even capital relief may not be available and the assets may be treated as on-balance sheet for regulatory capital purposes. Hence, on-balance sheet accounting may simply spoil the party.

Therefore, the key question is: **Under what conditions may assignment of receivables be treated as a sale of such receivables?**

The basic philosophy: From retention of risk to a predominant characteristic

It is important to understand the basic philosophy behind the stipulations of securitization accounting standards.

One of the simplest approaches in deciding the proper manner of securitization accounting would have been whether there is any impact on the risks and rewards of the originator, on the receivables transferred, as a result of securitization. Take a case where the originator transfers certain receivables but undertakes full obligation on account of recourse. There is no material change in the risk carried by the originator on the transferred assets as a result of securitization. When the receivables were on his books, he was liable to pay for the liabilities contracted against such receivables. Now when he has legally assigned the receivables, he still has the same liability as he has an obligation of 100% recourse. It is unlikely that the transferor would retain all the risks and bargain away all the rewards; therefore, one must assume that if the risks are retained, the residual rewards would also have been retained. As there is no transfer of risks and rewards, the transaction should not be recorded as a securitization but as a mere financing transaction.

100% recourse is not a very common feature of securitizations; in most cases, the originator retains a limited risk by way of limited recourse, either in the form of over-collateralization or a cash reserve. Let us say the originator retains a 10% risk on account of recourse; the risk in the portfolio, as measured historically, is a default rate of 4%. The recourse risk undertaken by the originator is significantly higher than the apprehended risk. If the receivables were on the originator's books as before, the risk would possibly have been 4% delinquency. Now that the originator has assigned the portfolio, the risk would, in all probability, still be the same as the originator has recourse obligation up to 10%.

If retention of risk was the only consideration, even this transaction would have been disregarded as a proper sale of receivables and would have been accounted for as a financial transaction. This is what

> **Box 27.1: Accounting substance of securitization**
>
> - While accounting for most financial instruments is based on risks and rewards, accounting for securitization has been influenced more by market practices.
>
> - In securitization accounting, an originator could retain definite risk and reward in the portfolio, and still treat the transaction off the books.
>
> - Securitization accounting follows a components approach: Specific components of risk retained are kept on books and the balance put off.

was implied by the traditional approach on assignment of receivables years ago in FAS 13 and the like. However, while writing FAS 77, the standard setters in the U.S. jettisoned the risk-reward approach and adopted the "predominant characteristic approach." The so-called dominant character was largely based on the legal nature of the transaction being a sale in law. There were critics of this approach at that time;[5] however, it seems market exigencies prevailed and the FASB permitted assets to be put off the books even for retention of substantial risks by the transferor.

The justification given for this approach was as follows: Imagine a case where the company in question bought a 10% risk, say as a limited guarantor or recourse provider, in a portfolio owned by someone else. If the apprehended risk is less than 10%, the company in question is assuming virtually the entire risk in the portfolio. That does not mean the whole portfolio comes on the books of the company, as what comes on the books is only the extent of obligation assumed – 10%. Another ground favoring the predominant characteristic approach was that in most market transactions the transferor lost economic benefits of the portfolio, while there was risk-retention to some extent as credit enhancer. If the risk-retention criteria were followed, this portfolio would stay on the books of the transferor despite the loss of economic benefits of ownership.

Thus, under FAS 77, assets would be put off the books if the dominant characteristic of the transaction was a sale.

Unspinning the yarn: The components approach

FAS 77 was still an "all or none approach," that is, the transaction had the predominant features of a sale and would result in the whole of the asset going off the books. On the contrary, if it was predominantly a collateralized borrowing, the whole of the asset would stay on the books. With increasing sophistication in financial markets, there were numerous transactions where financial assets were unraveled into various threads, with some of these being retained and some transferred. Under this approach, the predominant feature of the transaction was not relevant; the components transferred, whether predominant or not, would go off the books and those retained would stay on the books.

According to this approach, in every securitization transaction there are components of risk or rewards that are retained by the originator and there are components that are transferred. The purpose of fair accounting would be served if the components retained by the originator are kept on his books. Thus, under FASB 125, almost every securitization, complying with basic conditions, would be given a sale treatment to the extent of components of risk transferred to the SPV. The detailed reasoning as to how the FASB considered the alternative approaches of FRS 5, IAS 32 and finally decided upon the components approach are given in Paras 99 to 106 in Appendix B to FASB 125.[6]

Among alternative approaches, the linked presentation approach in the U.K. FRS 5 was also discussed. Para 103 does not give a reason for not adopting the linked presentation approach, except this vague statement: "That approach (linked presentation) had some appeal to the Board because it would have highlighted significant information about transactions that many believe have chrematistics of both sales and secured borrowings. The Board observed, however, that the linked presentation would not have dealt with many of the problems created by the risks-and-rewards approach." [Para 103]

The FAS 125 ushered in the components approach to recognition/de-recognition of financial assets. FAS 140 continue with the same approach and it seems to an extent to show market practices have also been shaped by the accounting standard and vice versa. Practices of exploding assets into components and trading in some components and retaining the others have grown over time.

IAS 39, pre-amendment in 2003, adopted the components approach, although the exposure drafts had initially recommended the risk-rewards approach – see Exposure draft E48. Even the lone dissenting voice of the U.K. standard setters is slated to merge into a so-called convergence exercise. The U.K. ASB issued FRED 30, expected to fall in line with IAS 32/39. However, the revised version of IAS 39 is curious and a bit complicated mix of risk-rewards approach and the "partial de-recognition" approach.

In retrospect, it is difficult to say whether the components approach has contributed greatly to better reporting in financial statements. Most people see this as an improvement over the FAS 77 approach,[7] but there are many who feel that the linked presentation approach should better serve the purpose.[8] It is, of course, common logic that if greater caution is exercised at the time of letting assets go off the books, many worries about bringing back such books by way of consolidation would be reduced.

Continuing involvement approach: The JWG version

The Financial Instruments Joint Working Group of standard setters (JWG) partly redefined or rechristened the components approach in what they preferred to call a "continuing involvement" approach. Under the JWG discussion paper on financial instruments, a transfer has substance if the transferee is either a substantive business entity (meaning, not an SPV), or the transferred components have been put beyond the reach of the transferor or transferor's creditors (meaning a true sale). Para 51 provides that the transferor should de-recognize the financial asset if the transferor has no continuing involvement in the asset.

Para 52 goes on to define the meaning of continuing involvement. "A transferor will have no continuing involvement in a financial asset if it neither retains any of the contractual rights that resulted in that asset nor obtains any new contractual rights or contractual obligations relating to the asset, i.e., if it has no interest in the future performance of that asset and no responsibility to make payments in the future in respect of the asset under any circumstance." At the same time, Para 50 clarifies that retention of a servicing right and a clean up call would not amount to continuing involvement. Para 52, quoted above very succinctly and forcefully, brings about the condition for de-recognition, but this is the strict version of the risk-rewards

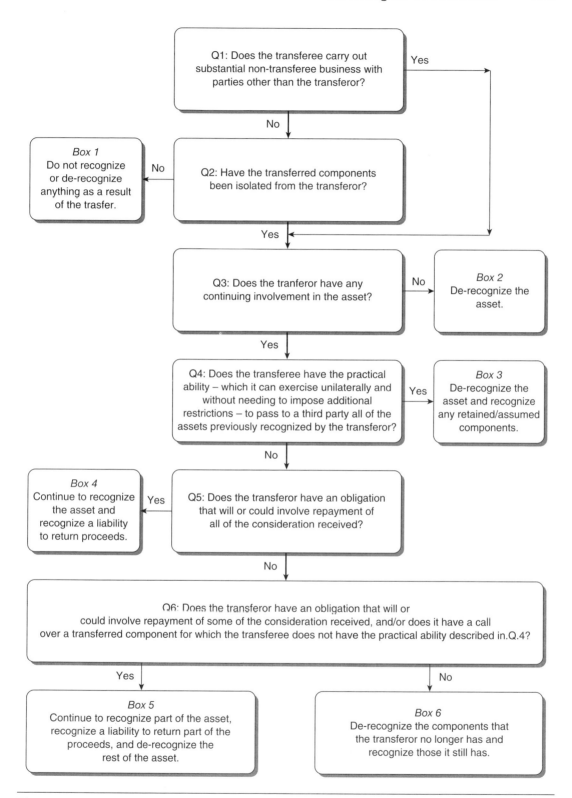

Figure 27.1   Continuing involvement approach

approach. Para 53 further elaborates that recourse provisions and other guarantees against the unfavorable performance of the asset, agreements to re-acquire the asset, and options written or held relating to the asset will be seen as vitiating the condition of "no continuing involvement."

In the application guide to the paper, a graphic under Para 234 clarifies any doubts as to the "continuing involvement" condition. It is clear that even where there has been an isolation of assets or their components, if there is a continuing involvement, a de-recognition shall not be affected.

Subsequent to the JWG's discussion paper, the International Accounting Standards Board adopted the "continuing involvement approach" in the revised IAS 39. However, both the definition of "continuing involvement" and the implications thereof were substantially altered.

We discuss IAS 39 more elaborately later in this chapter.

Preconditions for sale treatment: A wrap-up of various accounting standards

There would be no difficulty in treating a non-recourse assignment as a "sale," as the originator does not assume any recourse and the assignment is treated as off-balance sheet. Some other basic conditions, for example, that the originator should not have a right of buy-back should be satisfied.

The basic issue is, therefore, cases where the originator retains a degree of risk by retention or by his continuing involvement with the transaction as a servicer. It is difficult to expect real life transactions to be completely without retention of risks and rewards. Hence, the crux of accounting standards on securitization is to deal with cases where there is a degree of retention of risks and rewards by the seller.

According to FASB 77, a transfer of receivables with recourse was to be accorded a sale treatment if the following conditions were satisfied:

1. The transferor surrenders control of the future economic benefits embodied in the receivables. Control has not been surrendered if the transferor has an option to repurchase the receivables at a later date.
2. The transferor's obligation under the recourse provisions can be reasonably estimated. Lack of experience with receivables with characteristics similar to those transferred or other factors that affect a determination at the transfer date of the collectability of receivables may impair the ability to make a reasonable estimate of the probable bad debt losses and related costs of collections and repossessions. A transfer of receivables shall not be recognized as a sale if collectability of the receivables and related costs of collection and repossession are not subject to reasonable estimation.
3. The transferee cannot require the transferor to repurchase the receivables except pursuant to recourse provisions.

Thus, the test to treat an assignment as a sale, even though with recourse, was the possibility of reasonably measuring the risk of such recourse, and the fact that such risk was not material.

Under FASB 77, a securitization was either treated as a sale or not treated as a sale. In other words, based on the overall character of the transaction, the accountant took a view to treat the transaction either as a true sale or as a financing transaction. However, FASB 125 triggered a new approach, as discussed earlier – the components approach. To wit: "The board decided to adopt as the basis for this Statement a *financial components approach* that focuses on control and recognizes that financial assets and liabilities can be divided into a variety of components."

The key conditions for treating a securitization as a sale of financial assets are set out in Para 9, in which there can be a transfer of financial assets or a portion of a financial asset; it will be accounted for as a sale if (a) there is a legal transfer of the asset so as to put the asset beyond the reach of the transferor or the transferor's claimants; (b) the transferor surrenders control over such assets. There are two points to be noted – the standard talks about transfer of either a financial asset or a portion of an asset; that is, there may be a qualifying transfer of even a portion of a financial asset that may be recorded in the books. And, a transfer is recognized as a sale to the extent of consideration received for it; if the consideration is merely a beneficial interest in the assets transferred, then the transfer is ignored.

The key considerations in recording a transfer as a sale are legal transfer and surrender of control. Whether the transfer is a legal transfer is a matter of governing law. It is not very common for accounting standards to use the law as the basis for determining the accounting treatment, as the basic accounting rule is: Legal form gives way to commercial substance. However, the FASB has clearly recorded the fact that in giving overriding significance to legal treatment, the FASB was driven by practices in securitization transactions where rating agencies and investors were concerned about "true sale" considerations from a legal viewpoint. [Para 118 of FASB 125] Thus, the FASB states: "Because legal isolation of transferred assets has substance, the Board decided that it could and should serve as an important part of the basis for determining whether a sale should be recognized." [Para 119]

The other basic element is surrender of control. According to Para 9, control is taken to have been surrendered if all the following conditions are satisfied:

- The transferred assets have been isolated from the transferor; this is essentially a legal feature, implying that there must have been a legal transfer of the assets from the transferor in a manner to isolate the assets from the transferor, the transferor's creditors or a liquidator.
- The transferee is entitled to sell or pledge the transferred assets without any constraints or the transfer is made to a qualifying SPV whose holders are entitled to sell or pledge the securities of the SPV free of any constraints.
- The transferor does not maintain effective control over the transferred assets through a buy-back right.

As the basic approach in FAS 125 has been followed in FAS 140, we discuss the basic requirements for de-recognition as per FAS 140 below.

As far as international accounting standards are concerned, the essential principle originally enshrined in Exposure Draft 48 (later IAS 32) of the

International Accounting Standards Committee was based on retention of risks. Para 30–31 of the Exposure Draft allowed a sale treatment if the risk retained by the seller of the receivables by keeping a liability of recourse could be measured, and if such risk was not substantial, the transfer of receivables could be treated as a sale thereof. However, in IASC's Exposure Draft 62 (IAS 39), the approach was quite similar to the FASB 77 – retention of control. Accordingly, a financial asset is to be removed from the balance sheet as per the following principles:

> An enterprise should de-recognise a financial asset or a portion of a financial asset when, and only when, the enterprise realizes the rights to benefits specified in the contract, the rights expire, or the enterprise surrenders or otherwise loses control of the contractual rights that comprise the financial asset (or a portion of the financial asset).

Further:

> A transferor has not surrendered or otherwise lost control of a transferred financial asset if:
>
> (a) it has the right to rescind the original transfer without fully compensating the transferee; or
> (b) it is both entitled and obligated to repurchase or redeem the transferred asset on terms that effectively provide the transferee with a lender's return on the cash or other assets received in exchange for the transferred asset.
>
> A lender's return is one that is not materially different from that which could be obtained on a loan to the transferor that is fully secured by the transferred asset.

Further:

> A transferor has not surrendered control of a transferred financial asset unless one or more transferees has the ability to obtain the benefits of the transferred asset. That ability is demonstrated:
>
> (a) if the transferee is free to either sell or to pledge approximately the full fair value of the transferred asset; or
> (b) even if the transferee is a special-purpose entity whose permissible activities are limited, but either the special-purpose entity itself or the holders of beneficial interests in that entity have the ability to obtain substantially all of the benefits of the transferred asset.
>
> The ability of the transferee to obtain the benefits of a transferred asset also may be demonstrated in other ways.

FRS 5 adopted a different approach; it classified the accounting treatment for securitizations (and for that matter, for most other financial instruments) into three possibilities – removal of securitized assets; non-removal but linked presentation of the asset and the corresponding liability; and separate presentation of the asset and the liability. According to FRS 5, the same three approaches would apply to the originator as to the issuer – the SPV.

The first approach – according the sale treatment to the transfer of the asset – would be determined on the basis of the following two questions:

(a) Whether the originator has access to the benefits of the securitized assets and exposure to the risks inherent in those benefits (referred to below as benefits and risks); and

(b) Whether the originator has a liability to repay the proceeds of the note issue (that is, the notes issued by the SPV).

A linked presentation would be appropriate where the originator has retained risks and rewards on the securitized assets, but it is absolutely certain that the downside exposure of the originator is limited to a fixed monetary amount.

The complexity inherent in the mosaic of approaches adopted by these three standard-setting bodies is very likely to leave accountants in other countries in a fix. If one is from a country other than the U.S. or U.K., or a country not expressly following IAS 39, the predicament is how exactly to account for securitizations.

Below, we take up a consolidated view of the requirements of different accounting standards and recommend a synthetic approach to securitization accounting.

The legal vs. substantive transfer: Applicability in "form" countries

It is clear from the development of accounting standards on securitization that the U.S. standards have influenced those in the rest of the world. U.S. standards, in turn, are influenced by the legal nature of the transaction.

One of the primary requirements under the U.S. accounting standards is legal transfer, which has the effect of deprivation of the equity owners or creditors of the entity from laying hands on the transferred assets. Therefore, the assets of the entity cease to be available to owners and creditors, hence justifying off-balance sheet treatment. Therefore, the condition that there must be a legal transfer of the asset is understandable. Another feature of the U.S. accounting standards is that a legal transfer of the asset, having the effect of legal divestment, is sufficient to at least partly put the asset off the balance sheet. In other words, even if substantive risks and rewards have been retained, a legal transfer of the components of the asset would put such components off the balance sheet.

However, while applying the U.S. standards to the rest of the world, one should not ignore differences in judicial approaches in different countries. The U.S. is well known as a substance country; U.S. courts are inclined to question the legal form of a transaction and be guided by substance. There have been numerous cases in the U.S. when transactions of securitization have been recharacterized as financings. Needless to emphasize, there have been many more such rulings in relation to a number of other financial instruments. However, the judiciary in many countries is inclined to go by the golden rule that the language adopted by the parties best describes their intention, and therefore, the legal form of the transaction must generally prevail. It is not the courts cannot question the legal form, but they generally do not. These countries are, to use a common expression, called "form countries."

The clash between form and substance is difficult to imagine in a U.S. jurisdiction. If a transaction has the substance of financing but a form of securitization, the transaction should be treated as financing in law, and therefore, also in accounting. But in a form country, it is quite likely that a court, and therefore a legal counsel, goes by the legal character of the transaction alone and treats it as a securitization transaction even if its underlying character may be financing. In such cases, it would clearly not be appropriate to treat the legal nature as the guide for the accounting treatment.

Therefore, it is necessary that accounting standard setters and accountants in form countries carefully apply the "legal transfer criteria" and back it up with economic substance.

Preconditions for sale accounting:
A synthetic approach

The following discussion is based on a consolidated study of different accounting standards and differences in approach, wherever applicable:

Legal/legally enforceable transfer of identifiable receivables

Generally speaking, accounting standards insist that the transfer of the asset must be such that under local law it would be recognized as a sale.

We have earlier noted why securitization accounting standards have used the legal character of the transaction as the basis for determining the accounting treatment.[9] The transfer, for this purpose, must be such as would deprive the equity owners or creditors of the entity from laying hands on the transferred assets, so that such assets are no more the assets available to the owners and the creditors, hence justifying off-balance sheet treatment. Any method of legal transfer that has the effect of depriving owners and creditors of the entity of the asset should be treated as a transfer for this purpose. The methods of transfer are unimportant; the effect should be that a court would recognize the transferee having been vested with the asset and the transferor divested of the asset.[10]

Thus, it is important to note that a transfer of receivables cannot be recognized as a sale for accounting purposes unless it is a true sale for legal purposes.[11] There might be cases, particularly in "form" countries, where a transfer would be a true sale in law but is not regarded as a sale for accounting purposes, but the opposite is not true. This principle signifies that for a transfer to be recorded as sale on the books, the requirements of the local law as to a perfected legal sale must be satisfied.

As it is necessary that the transfer must be a legal transfer, all requirements of governing law relating to a transfer of receivables automatically fasten to a sale treatment. Identifiability of receivables is an understandable legal requirement. Both in law and for accounting purposes, unless the receivables are identifiable so as to be able to distinguish between those that stand transferred and those that remain with the originator, the assignment will not be recognized as a sale. The identification problem may be quite prominent in small ticket transactions or revolving assets (such as credit cards) where the originator transfers a huge number of small ticket assets.

Partial transfers

Accounting standards consistently talk of a partial de-recognition, but a pertinent question is can a transfer of a part or a fraction of an asset be treated as a transfer in law at all? And, if the legal nature is a precondition, can such transfer lead to an off-balance sheet treatment? It is notable that in most countries, legal requirements do not completely rule out a partial transfer but rather result in creation of a joint interest between the transferor and the transferee. The issues relating to partial transfers have been discussed at length in the chapter on **Legal Issues**, but please note that partial or fractional transfers are not illegal; they merely create joint rights. For accounting purposes, the issue for the transferor is not whether the transferee has an independent legal right to sue the obligor, but whether the transferee has acquired legal interest to the extent the transferor has transferred it. The answer to this question, for partial transfers, is in the affirmative. Therefore, there should be no hesitation in giving off-balance sheet treatment to partial assignments.

Transfer of existing receivables

One of the easily understandable conditions for sale treatment of securitization is that it should be a transfer of assets existing on the balance sheet. If the asset in question does not exist, the transfer cannot be regarded as a "sale." In other words, any securitization of future flows will not qualify for off-balance sheet treatment. Legally speaking, the nature of a future flow securitization is an advance agreement for a transfer of an asset as and when that asset comes into existence.

Transfer, but transfer for what purpose?

Accounting standards have insisted on a transfer of the asset, so an important question is the purpose of the transfer of the asset. There might be differing approaches to recognizing a transfer for the purpose of bankruptcy or creditor rights, for the purpose of taxes on transfers or transactions or for the purpose of general property law. Which of these considerations are relevant here?

As the accounting standards emphasize, the relevant consideration is whether the assets have been put beyond the claim of the creditors and the liquidator of the transferor. Obviously, claims of the creditors/liquidator on the assets of the transferor arise on receivership, administration, bankruptcy or similar proceedings. Financial statements in usual circumstances are prepared on a "going concern" basis in which the bankruptcy value of assets is not a factor. It might be queer, but securitization accounting is to an extent based on a bankruptcy presumption, as the key question posed is if the entity goes into liquidation, would the liquidator be able to lay hands on these assets?

Cases of no transfers at all

In cases where there is no transfer of assets, the question of de-recognition would mostly not arise. These include:

- Synthetic transactions; and
- Secured loan structures.

Legal transfer vs. revocable transfers or asset lending transactions

The transfer, for the purpose of recording a sale, must be absolute and irrevocable. There are several instances of inchoate transfers or transfers with retained options that are not treated as transfers for accounting purposes.

In practice, a revocable transfer and a transfer with a call option held by the transferor have the same implications. A revocable transfer is one where the transferor may revoke the transfer and recall the asset. A callable transfer is one where the transfer can exercise a call option and force the transferee to resell the asset.

A transfer with a repurchase agreement, typically referred to as a ready forward agreement, has the same effect as a revocable transfer, with the only difference that the repurchase is not at the option of the transferor but is pre-contracted.

Under FAS 140.9.c, a repurchase agreement entered concurrent with transfer is treated as secured borrowing. There is also a contention that a repurchase agreement gives to the transfer the legal character of an asset loan, as if the asset had been lent and not sold.

Surrender of control

The second key condition for de-recognition of assets is surrender of control. The first condition was that the transferor must sell the asset and the second is that he must, after such a sale, not continue to control the asset to his advantage. In other words, post-transfer the asset must be the asset of the transferee, free from the clutches of the transferor. The transferor has not relinquished the assets if he continues to control the asset. An old word of law can easily explain the concept of surrender of control: Usufructs. The transfer must be such that the usufructs are also transferred to the transferee. What will be the usufruct, or fruits of the asset, depends on the nature of the asset, but in context of financial assets, a generic way to describe usufructs would be the benefit of appreciation or any accretion to the value of the asset. If the transferor controls the profits of the transferee in any manner, the condition of surrender of control would be defeated.

The principal condition for surrender of control is that the transferee of the receivables must have unconstrained ability to trade in the receivables without any significant restrictions put in by the originator. In case of transfer to the SPV, the investor should have unconstrained ability to trade in the securities of the SPV; trading in the securities of the SPV apparently achieves the effect of trading in the assets held by the SPV.

FASB conditions for surrender of control

While the condition of surrender of control in a broad sense should mean anything by which the transferor controls the profits of the transferee, the FASB has reduced it to a set of three rules, contained in Para 9:[12]

a.   The transferred assets have been isolated from the transferor – put presumptively beyond the reach of the transferor and its creditors, even in bankruptcy or other receivership.
b.   Each transferee (or, if the transferee is a qualifying SPE, each holder of its beneficial interests) has the right to pledge or exchange the assets (or beneficial interests) it received, and no condition both constrains the transferee (or holder) from taking advantage of its right to pledge or exchange and provides more than a trivial benefit to the transferor.
c.   The transferor does not maintain effective control over the transferred assets through either (1) an agreement that both entitles and obligates the transferor to repurchase or redeem them before their maturity or (2) the ability to unilaterally cause the holder to return specific assets, other than through a clean-up call.

First condition legal transfer: The first condition in Para 9 simply means the transfer must be a legal transfer. We have discussed the meaning of legal transfer in this context and its relevance to off-balance sheet treatment.

Second condition – transferee's right to sell or pledge: The transfer must mimic a transfer as in a commercial arms-length transaction. The buyer of an asset in a commercial transaction has the right to use, consume, abuse, sell, pledge or otherwise deal with the asset. The right to sell is inherent in every commercial purchase of an asset. On the contrary, if the seller has simply allowed the buyer to retain the asset but not re-transfer it, he controls the buyer's rights, and therefore, the surrender of control becomes questionable. On the other hand, if the seller has not controlled the ability of the buyer to sell or pledge the asset, the seller has surrendered the control. Therefore, in case the seller transfers the asset to a substantive business entity, he must not restrict the buyer's right of transfer or pledge. For transfers to special-purpose entities, the transferee entity continues to hold the asset and is generally prohibited from selling or pledging the asset, but investors can reap the same effect as selling or pledging the asset by selling or pledging the securities of the SPV.

The FASB further requires the transferee to be a qualifying SPE. The concept of qualifying SPE was originally meant to define what exactly is an SPE, where the free transferability of the assets could be curtailed. But in the way the conditions of QSPEs have been laid down, the concept of QSPEs has become in itself a serious and historically controversial issue. We shall take up the concept of QSPEs later.

Third condition – no call option and redemption obligation: The transferor might also effectively control the transferred assets through a call option. A call option is effectively a tool for controlling the profits of the buyer, as the seller will exercise the option when it is profitable for him to do so. With the call option with the seller, the buyer can make no more than a certain yield based on the "strike price" of the call option, and therefore, the seller cannot be said to have really sold the asset. Even if the transferor has an agreement that is a futures contract, either to repurchase (or to redeem – essentially the same thing) the transferor cannot be said to have surrendered his control over the asset.

Call options that do not vitiate surrender of control: There are several call options that do not destroy the condition of surrender of control. These are as follows:

1. **Clean-up call option:** A clean-up call option is an industry practice that allows the transferor to buy back the assets or buy out the outstanding securities of the SPV after the outstanding asset values have been reduced substantially; therefore, the transaction has become uneconomic to be serviced. In typical industry practice, clean-up call options are exercised when the outstanding values fall below a specified percentage; the practice varies from 1% to 10%. Accounting standards put a limit of 10%; that is, a right to call the asset where the outstanding asset balance is more than 10% is not treated as a clean-up call option and would vitiate off-balance sheet treatment.
2. **Embedded callability in the transferred assets:** Sometimes the assets transferred might themselves have an embedded callability. For example, a prepayment option in a mortgage loan or a call option in a bond. Transfer of such assets inherently containing a callability feature does not vitiate the surrender condition, as it is not the transferor trying to retain economic benefits by such a call option.
3. **Call option must be at a fixed price:** A call option, at fair value of the transferred asset, is really no different from a restriction on transfer or the right of first refusal. A transferor holding an option to buy the assets at their market values is effectively not controlling the benefits of the buyer. Such an option is economically worthless as the value of any option is the

difference between the market price and the strike price. Therefore, such an option does not vitiate the surrender condition.[13] The FAS 140 only adds that in such a case, the transferor must also not be holding the residual value of the asset, such that coupled with the right to buy-back at what is apparently a fair value, and the residual value, he is able to resurrect the asset with all its value. [Para 53]

4. **ROAPs for random assets:** A removal of accounts provision (ROAP) is a provision in securitization documents that either entitles or requires the transferor to remove, or remove and substitute, certain transferred accounts or assets in certain circumstances. One example may be a ROAP for defaulted assets or assets that breach representations and warranties. By way of an option, the transferor might also have a ROAP for excess assets – that is, if the amount of assets actually held by the SPV exceed those required in terms of the transfer documents (for example, return of over-collateral). In such cases, an option to remove some assets would not defeat the surrender condition, provided it relates to randomly selected assets. [Para 54 with Para 87 (a)]

5. **Obligation to buy back:** What defeats the surrender of control condition is an option to buy back and not an obligation. A transferor might be obliged to buy back assets, for example, on the failure of representations and warranties or for a retained recourse. In such cases, there is no retention of a benefit by the transferor, and hence, no impact on the condition of surrender of control.

Options that do vitiate surrender of control condition:

1. **Call options on the securities of the SPV:** The idea of a transferor retaining a call option on the assets is essentially the transferor retaining his control over the economic benefits of the asset. The same purpose may be fulfilled by the transferor retaining a call option on the securities of the SPV. Therefore, a call option on the securities of the SPV also vitiates the surrender condition. [Para 52, FAS 140]. Obviously, such an option would defeat a sale accounting only if it is entered into with all, or substantially all, the holders of the securities of the SPV. Entering into derivatives with a section of investors cannot be said to cast an impact on the sale accounting on the entire transfer of assets to the SPV.

2. **Futures on the securities of the SPV:** Though not explicit by FASB's pronouncements, any futures on all or substantially all the securities of the SPV should also have the same impact as a futures on the assets transferred to the SPV.

IAS conditions on surrender of control

The IAS 39 has been revised and the standard has shifted emphasis from surrender of control to transfer of risks and rewards, as well as continuing involvement. These are taken up below under an independent discussion on the de-recognition conditions under IAS 39.

FRS 5 approach – transfer of risks and rewards

In accounting parlance, risks and rewards are generally considered to be crucial; for example, accounting for leases is based on whether risks and rewards on the leased assets have been transferred.

FRS 5 is, however, essentially based on the transfer of risks and rewards. The risk in the receivable is the risk of having to pay the notes issued by the SPV, without being able to collect the receivables. The benefit or reward is the ability to transfer the receivables at their fair market value.

FRS 5 enumerates the following risks and rewards relating to loan receivables (applicable to all transactions carrying an apparent or implied interest):

The main benefits and risks relating to loans are as follows:

Benefits:

The future cash flows from payments of principal and interest.

Risks:

(i)   Credit risk (the risk of bad debts);

(ii)   Slow payment risk;

(iii)   Interest rate risk (the risk of a change in the interest rate paid by the borrower. Included in this risk is a form of basis risk, i.e., the risk of a change in the interest rate paid by the borrower not being matched by a change in the interest rate paid to the transferee);

(iv)   Reinvestment/early redemption risk (the risk that, where payments from the loans are reinvested by the lender before being paid to the transferee, the rate of interest obtained on the reinvested amounts is above or below that payable to the transferee); and

(v)   Moral risk (the risk that the lender will feel obliged, because of its continued association with the loans, to fund any losses arising on them).

Most securitization agreements do provide for normal warranties of the originator; these pertain to the enforceability, legal validity, credit worthiness of the receivables at the inception of the agreement, etc. Such a covenant would not disqualify the securitization from sale treatment. However, if the originator assumes any liability for any subsequent deterioration in the quality of the receivables, a de-recognition or sale treatment would not be appropriate.

Most securitizations would carry some or the other credit enhancement from the originator and may be in the form of over-collateralization, retained cash or retained fees. Therefore, the originator retains risk of default to the extent of the credit enhancement provided. Not every such limited recourse would disqualify the transaction from de-recognition; one has to evaluate whether the recourse amounts to a significant retention of risk. For example, if in a securitization of receivables worth $100, and the expected loss on account of delinquencies/delays is $0.5 while the originator has assumed recourse up to $5 – up to 10 times the expected loss value, the originator has assumed significant risk of default, in which case a de-recognition would not be appropriate. In the same case, if the expected loss value was $10, and the recourse was limited to $5, a de-recognition was possible, with separate disclosure for the guarantee/security undertaken by the originator.

FRS 5 recommends linked presentation in cases where the originator has a limited risk on the receivables. The ultimate impact of this may be the same as under FASB 125, but the difference in approach is certainly important.

Arms length transaction at fair values

As a normal requirement, the sale of the receivables should be on "parties at arms length basis," that is, the terms should be concluded to indicate that the transfer of receivables is at a fair price.

Qualifying SPV[14]

For a transfer of financial assets to go off the books, transfer to an SPV is not required. The buyer may be a substantive operating entity – engaged in any business. But in that case, there must be no restriction on the resale, transfer or pledge of the assets by the buyer.

The concept of qualifying an SPE (QSPE) is linked with the condition that the transferee must be free to resell the assets. This condition is normally not required to be complied with when the transferee is QSPE. In that case, the condition is modified to apply to the securities of the SPE, as these securities become the asset-based replicas of the assets held by the SPE. Therefore, to achieve a securitization transaction – result in creation of asset-backed securities that trade as beneficial interests in the assets transferred by the transferor, the SPE must meet certain qualifying tests that lead to the concept of a qualifying SPE or QSPE. To reiterate, if the SPE is not a qualifying SPE, the securities of the SPE will not be viewed as a proxy for the assets of the transferor, in which case the assets themselves must be transferable without restriction and not merely the securities of the SPE.

There are, of course, other consequences of the SPE as a QSPE, such as it does not require consolidation and is not treated as a variable interest entity under FIN 46R.[15]

The essential idea of the QSPE, therefore, was simply as an entity that does not have substantive businesses or business interests, so as to be regarded as more than the assets of the transferor. However, while enacting rules as to what a QSPE is, the standard-setters have defined what a QSPE can do, leading to a complicated definition of QSPEs. Notably, there are no such detailed conditions in IAS 39, not even in the revision of IAS 39.

The QSPE conditions were laid down in Para 26 of FASB 125 as the following:

a.   It is a trust, corporation or other legal vehicle whose activities are permanently limited to:

1)   Holding title to the transferred assets.
2)   Issuing beneficial interests in the form of debt or equity securities. These include the rights to receive all or portions of specified cash inflows, including senior and subordinated rights to interest or principal inflows

to be "passed through" (e.g., multi-class participation certificates) or "paid through" (e.g., notes or bonds) and residual interests.

3) Collecting cash proceeds from assets held, reinvesting in eligible investments pending distribution and perhaps servicing the assets held.

4) Distributing proceeds to the holders of its beneficial interests.

b. It has a standing at law distinct from the transferor. If the transferor holds all of the beneficial interests, the trust has no standing at law, is not distinct, and thus is not a qualifying SPV; the transaction is neither a sale nor a financing. The true test here is whether the transferor gives up the ability to unilaterally dissolve the trust and reclaim the individual assets. Special-purpose entities that issue debt or equity interests to parties unaffiliated with the transferor usually meet the condition of having standing at law distinct from the transferor because the transferor may not dissolve the entity without any involvement by the third-party holders of the beneficial interests.

Para 35 of FAS 140 made these conditions substantially more elaborate, more verbose, and as a rule-maker always does, more complicated.[16] Elaborate discussion has gone into what are the assets that the QSPE may hold, and in what circumstances it may sell assets. The conditions of Para 35 are discussed below.

Demonstrably distinct legal entity

The QSPE must be a distinct legal entity and must be demonstrably distinct from the transferor. As per Para 36, the QSPE is demonstrably distinct if it cannot unilaterally be dissolved by the transferor. The transferor will have such ability if the transferor holds all the equity capital, or all the beneficial interest, or all the voting rights in the SPE. In light of this, it should be apparent that the ability to dissolve the SPE is the antithesis of the transfer itself. If the originator has the right to dissolve the SPE, it is equivalent to a call option, which denies off-balance sheet treatment in the first place.

Limits on permitted activities

Para 35.b states that the activities of the SPE (1) are significantly limited, (2) are entirely specified in the legal documents that established the SPE or created the beneficial interests in the transferred assets that it holds, and (3) may be significantly changed only with the approval of the holders of at least a majority of the beneficial interests held by entities other than any transferor, its affiliates, and its agents. The meaning of this condition is that the entity must satisfy its "special purpose" test. It must not be a substantive business entity and such restriction should be constitutional.

What assets may be held by the SPE

Para 35.c contains a long list of what all assets may be held by the SPE. Again, the rule-maker's flair for detailing is visible.

Passive financial assets of the transferor

Essentially, SPEs are formed for acquiring the assets of the transferor. However, a QSPE must hold only passive assets. The idea of a QSPE is of an inanimate bunch of assets and not a business enterprise. Decision-making is the crux of an operating business, and therefore, the QSPE must be brain dead; it must not need to decide, as it is constitutionally unable to decide, thus it must not buy any asset that requires decision-making; that is conveyed by the term "passive assets." An asset is passive if it does not entail decision-making by the holder, except decisions on servicing. For example, holding an equity share is holding an ownership in an operative business and is therefore not a passive investment. Holding any other instrument that either singularly or in combination allows the exercise of control over the investee is also not passive. Derivatives entailing call options or other similar rights of the holder are also not passive and cannot be held by a QSPE. However, swaps such as interest rate swaps, or protection bought by way of a credit default swap or a total rate of return swap do not require any managerial decision-making.

QSPEs should not hold substantial equity stakes, as equities may involve voting and the QSPE should not have the ability to vote or exercise a significant influence over any enterprise.

What is passive? The intent of the SPE making investments is not trading or actively managing a portfolio, but investing so as not to keep money idle. The SPE cannot be intending to maximize the returns or value out of investment by actively dealing with the investments. For example, "an SPE has cash balances that will not be distributed to beneficial interest holders for 200 days. The documents that establish the SPE give it the discretion, in these circumstances, to choose between investing in commercial paper obligations that mature in either 90 or 180 days. This discretion does not preclude the SPE from being qualifying. If, in these circumstances, the SPE also has the discretion to invest in 270-day commercial paper with the intent to sell it in 200 days, the SPE is not qualifying."[17]

Passive derivatives[18]

Para 35.c.2, read with Para 40, provide huge details on what derivatives an SPE can hold, with what notional values and with whom. This clause allows a QSPE to hold passive derivative financial instruments that pertain to beneficial interests (other than another derivative financial instrument) issued or sold to parties other than the transferor, its affiliates or its agents. The essential idea of this clause is two-fold – that the derivative must be passive, and must seek to mitigate the risk only of the beneficial interests (the securities of the SPE) held by independent outsiders and not the originator himself. The idea that went behind limiting the risk-mitigation to only the securities offered to outsiders was essentially to curb a possible exploitation of the SPE route by transferors who could transfer their risk-prone assets to SPEs, hold beneficial interests themselves, and buy protection from SPEs for such beneficial interests, thereby apparently removing the risk. Alternatively, it has also been argued that transferors may not try to park their derivatives in QSPEs and thereby avoid the provisions of derivatives accounting in FAS 133.[19] The way the requirement has been put is quite aggressive; it says the notional value of the derivatives does not exceed the outstanding value of securities issued to outsiders, nor is it expected to exceed. "Expected to exceed" may be quite a difficult scenario as the size of the asset pool and consequently the size of the securities are affected by prepayment risk. Therefore, QSPEs have to enter into callable swaps or into swaptions to ensure that the notional value of derivatives does not exceed the outstanding value of securities.

Guarantees or collateral

A QSPE may hold financial assets (for example, guarantees or rights to collateral) that would reimburse it if others were to fail to adequately service financial assets transferred to it or to pay obligations in a timely manner due to it and that it entered into when established, when assets were transferred to it, or when beneficial interests (other than derivative financial instruments) were issued by the SPE. The key point in this condition is that any risk-mitigant relating to assets that the SPE holds must have been bought when the asset was transferred to it and not subsequently. The purpose of this restriction is to possibly relate the guarantee to the very act of acquisition of assets and not as a discretion exercised subsequently.

Servicing rights

A QSPE may, of course, hold servicing rights on the assets it holds. It cannot be a servicer for others' assets.

Temporary non-financial assets

SPEs under this accounting standard are meant for transfer of financial assets and must be limited to such assets. In general, QSPEs cannot hold non-financial assets, except those temporarily acquired in enforcement of the financial assets held by it. For instance, if an auto loan is foreclosed and the physical asset is repossessed, the SPE can temporarily hold it. The same would be true on foreclosure of a mortgage. For financial lease transactions, the QSPE's interest in the residual value of assets will be permitted only if the same is guaranteed by the lessor or someone else. It should be important to note that the lease receivables for operating leases are not financial assets.

Temporary cash surpluses

Pending distribution, the QSPE may hold cash and investments purchased with that cash. The investments should be appropriate for the purpose of meeting the mismatch (that is, money-market or other relatively risk-free instruments without options and with maturities no later than the expected distribution date). The essential idea is that the QSPE must not make itself into an investment company. The investment activity is incidental and is merely a stop-gap operation.

When can QSPEs sell assets?

Equally verbose is Para 35.d that defines the circumstances when QSPEs may be permitted to sell assets. Generally speaking, SPEs are incorporated asset pools; they are expected to hold assets and realize them and not trade in them. Therefore, the restriction on the sale is understandable. The essential idea conveyed by this Para is that QSPEs must not be allowed to sell assets with a view to make profit.

As for what it does or buys, a QSPE must not use discretion in when or what it sells. Therefore, the sale must be triggered as an automated response to the following:

Adversities relating to its assets

If a trigger is listed in the legal documents of the SPE relating to a defined adverse change in the value of assets of the SPE, the SPE may be automatically required or permitted to sell its assets. Para 42 gives several examples of powers that might result into a sale, without breaching the QSPE condition. These are illustrations only, and once again the basic idea is non-discretionary, preprogrammed sale:

a) A failure to properly service transferred assets that could result in the loss of a substantial third-party credit guarantee;
b) A default by the obligor;
c) A downgrade by a major rating agency of the transferred assets or of the underlying obligor to a rating below a specified minimum rating;
d) The involuntary insolvency of the transferor; and
e) A decline in the fair value of the transferred assets to a specified value less than their fair value at the time they were transferred to the SPE.

On the contrary, Para 43 gives examples of sales that are not pre-programmed but require decision-making, and so are destructive of the QSPE condition:

a. A power that allows an SPE to choose to either dispose of transferred assets or hold them in response to a default, a downgrade, a decline in fair value, or a servicing failure;
b. A requirement to dispose of marketable equity securities upon a specified decline from their "highest fair value" if that power could result in disposing of the asset in exchange for an amount that is more than the fair value of those assets at the time they were transferred to the SPE; and
c. A requirement to dispose of transferred assets in response to the violation of a non-substantive contractual provision (that is, a provision for which there is not a sufficiently large disincentive to ensure performance).

It is on this ground that many of the CDOs and other conduit programs that buy and sell assets on an ongoing basis are often not treated as QSPEs.

The rights for CMBS transactions, where the servicing of delinquent loans is handed over to specialized servicers that need a lot of discretion to deal with the defaulted loans, were considered by FASB staff and several case specific solutions, such as the ability to hold a foreclosed property temporarily for sale, have been found.

Exercise of option by the investors

The SPV might be compelled to sell the whole or a part of its assets upon exercise of a right vested in the beneficial interest holders or investors in securities of the SPE. Examples of this include a put option, exercise of a discretion to cause an in-kind distribution, or partial dissolution of the SPE.

Exercise of permitted ROAPs

We have discussed earlier that the transferor, by way of a common practice, in certain circumstances has a power to remove some of the transferred accounts that may include a right to replace them. Unless the exercise of such ROAP may be regarded as a call option denying de-recognition (as discussed earlier), the SPE may have to sell its assets back to the transferor in such cases.

Terminal sale by the SPE

On a fixed or determinable date, the QSPE may have to sell its assets. Here, Para 45 provides that the QSPE has the power to transfer its assets to parties other than the transferor.

What if the SPE is not a QSPE?

If the SPE is not a QSPE, sale treatment is not denied; the transferee SPE would then be viewed as any other buyer. It must buy the asset as in an arm's-length commercial transaction. There must be no restrictions on the right of the buyer to resell or pledge the asset.

In addition, the beneficial interests in the SPE held by the originator will not be treated as consideration for the sale. That is, to the extent the transferor holds the beneficial interest in a non-qualifying SPE, there is no sale of the asset. [Opening line of Para 9]

For the purposes of consolidation, an SPE that is not a QSPE does not avail of the general immunity from consolidation granted by Para 46. An SPE may also be a variable interest entity and be liable to consolidation based on variable interests as per FIN 46.[20]

More restrictions on QSPEs

The exposure draft of proposed changes to QSPE conditions, issued on June 10, 2003, and later revised on August 11, 2005, proposed further restrictions on QSPEs. Briefly speaking, the proposed statement would prohibit an entity from being a qualifying SPE if any of the beneficial interest holders have more than one type of "involvement" and derive a non-trivial benefit.

While the language of the exposure draft may be convoluted, it puts several restrictions on SPEs to have liquidity or credit support, other than liquidity support from servicers.

Para 45A proposed to be inserted by the August 11 Exposure Draft states:

If its governing documents permit rollovers of beneficial interests, no party (including its consolidated affiliates or agents) has the opportunity to obtain a more-than-trivial incremental benefit by virtue of having more than one type of involvement with the entity. *Opportunity to obtain a more-than-trivia incremental benefit* refers to a party's opportunity, as a result of holding a combination of rights or obligations, to enhance its rights or to minimize its obligations related to the qualifying SPE in comparison to the opportunities associated with the same rights or obligations if each right and each obligation were held by separate, unrelated parties. *Involvement with the entity* refers to conditional or unconditional rights to receive assets from the entity or obligations to deliver assets to the entity as well as decision-making authority or obligations to provide services to the entity. The types of involvements include:

a. An obligation to provide liquidity to support the issuance by a qualifying SPE of beneficial interests that will be rolled over, regardless of the form of the obligation. Some examples include a line of credit, letter of credit, and an obligation to purchase assets or beneficial interests. Obligations of servicers of financial assets are not subject to these requirements if the servicing contract includes only the terms and conditions customarily included in arm's-length contracts to service the same types of assets.

b. Enhancement of the credit quality of the beneficial interests issued by a qualifying SPE regardless of the form in which that enhancement is provided. Some examples include a subordinated right to cash flows from the assets of a qualifying SPE, a guarantee of either the collectability of the qualifying SPE's assets or payment of its liabilities, and options to put impaired assets.

c. A right or obligation to specify the terms and conditions of the beneficial interests that the qualifying SPE issues, to decide which investors to sell them to, to decide when to issue beneficial interests, or any combination thereof (to direct the financing activities of the SPE). Those rights and obligations are constrained by paragraph 35(b), which states that the qualifying SPE's permitted activities must be entirely specified in the legal documents that established the qualifying SPE or created the beneficial interests in the transferred financial assets it holds and must be significantly limited.

Whether that party has an opportunity to obtain a more-than-trivial incremental benefit from combinations of involvements requires consideration of the specific facts and circumstances. Beneficial interests issued by a revolving-period master trust are not considered rollovers if the proceeds are applied to reduce the transferor's interest.

For latest developments on the exposure draft, see Vinod Kothari's website at http://vinodkothari.com/accouningissues.htm.

Sale-treatment: Balance sheet and revenue impact

If the transaction is to be given a sale treatment, the originator must recognize up-front gain or loss on the sale. The sale and the gain (loss) on sale treatment have a cause-consequence relationship. If there is a sale, it must lead to one of three consequences: The asset is sold exactly at its carrying value, and hence, there is no gain or loss on sale, or there is a gain or loss based on whether sale proceeds exceed or fall short of the carrying value. That is why sale treatment accounting is also called gain-on-sale accounting. While this principle sounds simple enough, it may be easily understood that computing gain/loss on sale in securitization is not as easy as when we sell our car, because under the components approach, we need to view each retained thread of the original asset as a component and ascribe a value to it.

Gain-on-sale accounting is not optional; if the conditions for sale treatment are satisfied, the originator has to recognize gains or losses up front and remove the asset to the extent of interest transferred.

Para 11 of FASB 140 requires that where the transaction amounts to a sale and conditions for off-balance sheet accounting are satisfied, the assets sold will be de-recognized and all assets or liabilities incurred in the process and the retained interest, if any, will be accounted for. The assets and liabilities acquired in the process of securitization were not on the balance sheet already, so these will be brought on the books. The retained interests indicate a proportion of interest in the transferred receivables, so the value of retained interest is carved out of the sale proceeds of the receivables.

Briefly, the consequences of transfer of assets are:

- If the transfer is not a sale at all, there is no impact on the asset accounting.
- If the transfer is a sale, the carrying value of the asset is split between components retained and components transferred [Para 10]. From this, we find the carrying value of the sold components. Notably, the unsold components stay on the balance sheet at the carrying value.

  - Now there are two situations. If the conditions of Para 9 are not satisfied, there is still a sale of the sold components, but this sale is not to be recorded as sale. In this case, the cash or other considerations received are treated as a collateralized borrowing.
  - In case the conditions of Para 9 are satisfied, go to the next.

- If the conditions of Para 9 are satisfied, the sold elements go off the books, and the assets/liabilities created as a result of the sale are brought on the books. The cash or other considerations received from the transfer, plus the value of any asset created minus the value of any liability created due to transfer, is the total consideration received by sale of the sold components.
- The excess (deficit) of the total consideration as above, over the carrying value of the sold components, is the gain (loss) on sale.

Dissecting the asset into components

The components approach is the key principle behind FAS 140, and to the extent IAS 39 permits partial de-recognition, the approach is inherent in IAS 39 as well. The philosophy that financial assets are a string of many threads is carried down to valuation. Thus, in all cases even if the sale does not qualify for off-balance sheet treatment, a splitting of the carrying value of the asset into its components is done.

There are two points to be noted here. First, the very idea behind splitting the asset value into component values is applicable where some components are retained and some are transferred. If the sale results in transfer of the entire asset with no retention at all, there is no question of split accounting. Two, the rationale of split accounting, even in cases where off-balance sheet treatment is not accorded, is that in such cases there is still a collateralization of the asset of the transferor (or de facto borrower), and such collateralization is to the extent of the components transferred.

So, Para 10, applicable even in cases where conditions of Para 9 are not satisfied, mandates splitting the carrying value of the asset into (a) servicing asset, (b) beneficial interest in the transferred asset (applicable only where the transferee is a QSPE – see rationale before),[21] (c) retained undivided interests and (d) the transferred components – components other than those that are retained. The meaning of each of these retained elements is discussed below.

In the normal course of business when an asset is originated and held, the profits that the originator earns from the asset do not have to be dissected. However, the profits relate to various functions or utilities – origination profits, funding profits, profits for servicing the asset, profits for absorbing one or more risks relating to the asset. Once the asset is securitized, it becomes important to segregate these profits as the originator may transfer some while retaining others.[22]

Split accounting is done on the premise that the carrying value of the whole asset pre-transfer was attributable to these various threads. The splitting is done in proportion to the fair values of each of the retained components and the fair value of the transferred components. We discuss below the computation of fair values of each of these components.

Funding component

In most securitization transactions, the funding component – the amount invested in originating the financial asset – is transferred. In most cases, it would be easier to identify the retained components, so that all that is not retained is transferred.

Servicing asset

Servicing includes all functions, other than funding, that a financial asset would require before it is converted into cash.[23] Servicing is, therefore, a function or series of functions. The accounting concept that treats this function as an asset or liability is essentially the consideration involved – the servicing fees. Where financial assets are transferred, a servicing function is typically not, and so there arises the need to consider a servicing asset or liability. If the servicer is paid for the servicing function, the excess of the fees over the costs is an asset, and vice versa is a liability. If the servicer is not paid for the servicing function, the servicing costs to be incurred represent a liability. As it would be unlikely that the servicing costs would exactly be offset by the servicing revenues, in all cases of retained servicing there would arise a servicing asset or servicing liability.

Sometimes in securitization practice, a distinction is made between normal servicing fee and excess servicing fee. The latter is essentially the originator's profit, but documented as a servicing fee. For accounting purposes, no distinction is made between the two.

It is notable that servicing revenues in accounting jargon include all that the servicer gets by way of the servicing contract, as defined in the servicing agreement. This would typically include the normal and excess service fees, late charges and float.

Beneficial interests in securitized assets

The transferor may also retain beneficial interest in the assets by acquiring, for example, a seller's share in the transferred assets or a deferred sale consideration. These are considered as retained assets only if the SPE is a QSPE. If the SPE is not a QSPE, the asset is not deemed to be transferred to the extent of such beneficial interests.

Undivided interests

The transferor might also make a fractional transfer and retain an undivided interest in the asset. For instance, x% of the asset may be retained, or all the interest or x% of the interest, or interest above a certain rate.

Valuing the components

Valuing the retained components

Valuation of components is all the art and is the reason for all the confusion there is in gain-on-sale accounting. The reason is not difficult to understand; there is no reliable or uniform basis for valuing some components that are not like segments of an orange, but as unmarketable as its seeds, pulp or peel. The FASB sits on a high altar and frames a biblical rule: "Quoted market prices in active markets are the best evidence of fair value and shall be used as the basis for the measurement, if available." [Para 68] "If quoted market prices are not available, the estimate of fair value shall be based on the best information available in the circumstances. The estimate of fair value shall consider prices for similar assets and liabilities and the results of valuation techniques to the extent available in the circumstances. Examples of valuation techniques include the present value of estimated future cash flows,[24] option-pricing models, matrix pricing, option-adjusted spread models, and fundamental analysis."

Most of the retained components are usually retained, so obviously there is no marketplace for them. As such, there are no market values. Use of valuation techniques listed by FASB is prone to several subjectivities, such as cash flows are not easily predictable and for present valuation purposes, the discounting rates are highly variable.

Computation of fair values of several assets, for which ready markets do not exist, has become the way of life in financial accounting, as increasingly accounting standards require such fair valuation.

All valuations relate to projected cash flow

We are concerned here with the valuation of the retained components, which represent a share, at a particular level of priority in the cash flow waterfall, in the cash flow of the transaction. The cash flow is projected, and therefore, key to making all accounting estimates of the fair values of retained interest is the cash flow model of the transaction.

The cash flow model is not merely a set of hypothetical numbers, but based on all assumptions relevant to the transaction – contractual cash flows, prepayment rate, delinquency rate, default rate, structural protections and features of the transaction. Not only should these assumptions be based on realism, they should also be back tested on an ongoing basis.

Please refer to the chapter on cash flow modeling for securitization.

Valuation devices

Present valuation techniques provide a useful device for valuation of a stream of cash flows. However, unlike a certain stream of cash flows such as for bonds or fixed income securities, retained interests have unique features.

There might be various reasons for volatility in residual cash flows. In fact, many of these factors might result into volatility for senior cash flows as well:

- Subordination of the cash flows and inherent leverage that magnifies the impact of uncertainty on the subordinated cash flows;
- Prepayment or partial payments;
- Delayed payments;
- Defaults; and
- Structural protection triggers that might, under certain circumstances, trap the residual cash flows and redirect them into a cash reserve.

In short, the retained interests might reflect a high degree of uncertainty. It is notable that not all residual cash flows may have same or similar uncertainty. For example, quite often servicing fees may be payable on senior basis before the noteholders' coupon. If so, the risk inherent on the servicing fee cash flow is not credit risk, but merely the risk of the pool size changing because of prepayment.

There are two possible approaches in valuing such uncertain cash flows: Use a suitably risk-adjusted rate (a higher discounting rate) to value such cash flows, or assess various probable outcomes with their respective probabilities to find expected values, and then use a risk-free discounting rate to present-value. The first approach, in FASB parlance,[25] is traditional discounting approach and the second approach is the expected cash flow approach.

In either case, the components for present valuation are:[26]

a. An estimate of the future cash flow, or in more complex cases, series of future cash flow at different times;
b. Expectations about possible variations in the amount or timing of that cash flow;
c. The time value of money represented by the risk-free rate of interest;
d. The price for bearing the uncertainty inherent in the asset or liability; and
e. Other, sometimes unidentifiable factors including illiquidity and market imperfections.

It is also notable that the FASB "found the expected cash flow approach to be a more effective measurement tool than the traditional approach in many situations." [Para 45 of FASB Statement of Concepts no. 7: Using Cash flow Information and Present Value in Accounting Measurements]

Traditional discounting approach

Under the traditional discounting approach, a single set of cash flows is predicted, although subject to the uncertainties inherent therein. For instance, if the computation involves estimating the present value of a servicing fee that is subordinated, we will take the cash flows on accounting of servicing based on a single set of assumptions. As this cash flow is subject to uncertainty, we will use a discounting rate that best suits the uncertain nature of the cash flows. The choice of discounting rate is the trickiest part of the traditional approach. The following factors may be noted:

- The discounting rate for a residual cash flow cannot be the same as the weighted-average rate of return of the pool. The weighted-average rate represents a certain degree of risk; that risk, when taken to the level of residual cash flow, has been accentuated because fixed claims have first been taken against that risk.
- The originator's weighted-average cost of capital is also not an appropriate measure of the risk of the residual cash flows. While the originator holds the residual cash flow on his balance sheet and thus it is a balance sheet asset, it would be wrong to assume that this asset is funded from the overall balance sheet of the originator. In fact, a residual cash flow is appropriately funded entirely from the equity of the originator.
- Even from a regulatory capital viewpoint, the residual cash flow representing retained interest is a deduction from the regulatory capital.

- If the returns from the pool are comparable to the return on assets (ROA) in corporate finance, the residual cash flow is comparable to return on equity (ROE).

Hence, if the cash flows are residual, an appropriate discounting rate may be the seller's return on equity, on returns on risk-adjusted capital (RAROC – risk-adjusted return on capital). However, there is no consistency on this and a survey of published accounts of several major securitization entities reflects wide variation in the use of the discounting rate. In fact, discount rates used have been widely different over the years.[27]

Expected cash flow approach

Under the expected cash flow approach, we can visualize various outcomes relating to cash flows, and their probabilities. For instance, if the retained interest relates to a cash inflow that is dependent on the rate of prepayment, we might take various possible prepayment rate scenarios, compute the cash flow under each, and then present-value them using a risk-free rate of interest.[28] The next thing is to assign probabilities (based on experience, based on expectations) and then compute the probability-weighted present values. That is the fair value of the cash inflow.

The expected cash flow approach sounds quite logical, but requires technological support for efficient computation of retained interest in different scenarios. There are several factors that affect residual cash flows, which, in turn, might be affected by several other factors, some common and some different. For example, the prepayment rate and default rate are two significant factors. If one visualizes at a very basic level ten different prepayment scenarios and ten different default scenarios, we have 100 combinations of probable scenarios. This computation may be as aggressive as the computation of an option-adjusted spread.[29]

Example of component valuation

The essential idea in component valuation is the value recorded for the retained component should, as much as practicable, be the same as would be realized over a period of time. The accountant must take good care in this sensitive area of measuring a future inflow (outflow) and putting it on books as an asset (liability). The idea should be to be conservative in measuring future inflows and outflows.

Example 1: A simple example

Assume we have a mortgage portfolio for a weighted-average remaining tenure of 15 years, carrying a weighted-average annualized percentage rate (APR) of 12%. We would transfer the portfolio at its carrying value, that is, $1,000 and allow the SPV to pay a servicing fee of 5% (ignore the actual service expenses for the purpose of this example). The service fee is subordinated to the coupon and other expenses of the SPV, which may be taken at 7%. As the servicing fee is subordinated and equal to (weighted return of the pool – coupon rate), it essentially means the servicing fee will capture all residual cash flows after payment of the investors' principal and coupon. At the time of inception, the prepayment rate is taken at 100 PSA and the charge-off rate is assumed to be 1%.

We first compute the servicing fee cash flow on the above assumptions (taking mortgage payments to be annualized, for the sake of simplicity). We might only add that the workings below ignore the actual service expenses; if we took the same into account, the service fees as computed below should be reduced by the amount of the servicing expenses. All workings here have been oversimplified; they are taken on an annual basis to reduce the number work. The results are shown in Table 1 (See CD Excel Worksheet Example 1).

Using the discounting model

Under the discounting model, the fair value of the service fees is computed by present-valuing the projected cash flow at an appropriate discounting rate. Using a discounting rate of 15% (this rate is higher than the APR of the mortgage portfolio), we find fair value of the service fee is $153.75.

This fair value has captured (a) the impact of prepayments; (b) the impact of the charge-offs; and (c) the impact of the higher discounting rate of 15% instead of the coupon rate of 7%. If the annual mortgage payment on the initial outstanding balance – $146.82424 – was simply sold at a discount rate of 7%, the transferor would have encashed a profit of $337.26. This is the same as the fair value of the service fees, if we were to eliminate prepayment, eliminate charge-offs and use a discounting rate of 7% for present-valuing the service fee cash flow in our example.

Using the expected value model

Under the expected value model, one is supposed to predict different scenarios, assign probability of occurrence to each, and then compute expected value by multiplying the probabilities to the present value under each scenario. Let us estimate three scenarios: Charge-off rate of 1% and prepayment rate of 100 PSA (probability 60%); charge-off rate of 1.5% and prepayment rate of 150 PSA (probability 20%); and a charge-off rate of 0.8% and prepayment rate of 80 PSA (probability 20%).[30]

We compute the present values using a 5% discounting rate (assuming that is a good representation of a risk-free rate). The present values and probabilities are shown below:

The last column computes the probability-weighted present values in each scenario, and the sum is the expected value, the fair valuation as per this method. The substantial difference between the two fair valuations is explained by the huge difference in the discounting rates used in the two calculations.

Valuing the transferred components

Valuing the transferred components is quite easy, as the consideration paid for the transfer is the fair value of the transferred components.

Allocation of the carrying value to components

One of the key features of the components approach is that it views a financial asset as composed of several components. One can envision a financial asset as made of several parts, such as a computer or machine. If there are retained components in the process of securitization, it implies some components are being transferred while some are not. The task is to allocate the carrying value of the composite asset that existed before securitization to the components that are split in the process. This is required, because (a) there is no question of computing any gain/loss on the components that are not transferred; (b) as the retained components will stay on the balance sheet at their proportionate carrying value, the carrying value of the composite asset must be split into components retained and components transferred.

The allocation of the carrying value of the composite asset is done in the proportion of the fair values of transferred components and retained components. This is the most reasonable basis for allocation, as the carrying values of the components would presumably bear the same proportion as the fair values.

Example 2

Let us work out the allocation of values as obtained in Example 1. Say we use the discounted value approach, where fair value of the servicing interest was found to be $153.75. Thus, we see the following numbers:

Carrying value of the composite asset	1,000
Fair value of the transferred component	1,000
Fair value of the retained interest	153.75

To split the carrying value of the composite asset, we use the ratio of 1000:153.75. Thus, the carrying value of the components would be:

Carrying value of the transferred component	1000* 1000/1153.75
	= 866.74
Carrying value of the retained interest	1000*153.75/1153.75
	= 133.36

Table 27.2   Workings for example 2

Year 1	Actual annual payment 2	Actual interest 3	Actual principal recovered 4	Actual outstanding principal begin 5	Charge-off 6	Pre-paid 7	Net outstanding principal of mortgages 8	Net outstanding principal of notes 9	Principal repaid on notes 10	Coupon payable on notes 11	Service fees 12
1	146.82424	120	26.82424	1000	10	24	939.17576	1000	60.82424	70	40
2	141.69462	112.70109	28.993526	939.17576	9.3917576	45.080436	855.71004	939.17576	83.46572	65.742303	37.56703
3	133.21454	102.6852	30.529334	855.71004	8.5571004	51.342602	765.281	855.71004	90.429037	59.899703	34.228402
4	123.54452	91.83372	31.710802	765.281	7.65281	45.91686	680.00053	765.281	85.280472	53.56967	30.61124
5	114.52256	81.600064	32.922501	680.00053	6.8000053	40.800032	599.47799	680.00053	80.522538	47.600037	27.200021
6	106.09811	71.937359	34.160752	599.47799	5.9947799	35.96868	523.35378	599.47799	76.124212	41.96346	23.97912
7	98.222456	62.802454	35.420002	523.35378	5.2335378	31.401227	451.29901	523.35378	72.054767	36.634765	20.934151
8	90.847774	54.155882	36.691892	451.29901	4.5129901	27.077941	383.01619	451.29901	68.282823	31.590931	18.051961
9	83.925641	45.961943	37.963698	383.01619	3.8301619	22.980971	318.24136	383.01619	64.774831	26.811133	15.320648
10	77.404483	38.188963	39.21552	318.24136	3.1824136	19.094482	256.74894	318.24136	61.492415	22.276895	12.729654
11	71.224656	30.809873	40.414783	256.74894	2.5674894	15.404937	198.36174	256.74894	58.387209	17.972426	10.269958
12	65.307514	23.803408	41.504106	198.36174	1.9836174	11.901704	142.97231	198.36174	55.389428	13.885322	7.9344694
13	59.526375	17.156677	42.369698	142.97231	1.4297231	8.5783385	90.594549	142.97231	52.377759	10.008062	5.7188923
14	53.604624	10.871346	42.733278	90.594549	0.9059455	5.4356729	41.519653	90.594549	49.074896	6.3416184	3.623782
15	46.502011	4.9823583	41.519653	41.519653	0	0	3.553E-14	41.519653	41.519653	2.9063757	2.0759826
TOTAL									1000		153.75

PV OF SERVICING FEE AT DISCOUNTING RATE OF 15%

Notes

1. The actual mortgage payment in Col. 2 has been computed by amortizing [Excel: net outstanding balance/(pv(APR%, balance no of years, 1)] the net outstanding balance of the mortgages, as in Col. 8 (net of charge-off and prepayment). The interest in Col. 3 is obtained by applying the APR on the outstanding mortgage balance. Principal in Col. 4 is the difference between the mortgage payment and the interest.

2. Prepayment rate for year 1 has been taken as 2.4%, year 2 as 4.8% and year 3 as 6%. This is admittedly an oversimplification of PSA speed that rises by a step function of 0.2% every month.

3. The principal repaid on the notes in Col. 10 is the sum of actual principal recovered, prepayment and charge-off. The charge-off affects the service fees as the latter are subordinated. The net outstanding balance of the notes in Col. 9 is obtained after deducting successively the principal repayments in Col. 10. The coupon rate of the notes is applied on the principal balance of the notes.

4. The service fees in Col. 12 are the residual cash flow. That is to say, the actual mortgage payment, plus prepayment, minus principal repaid on the notes, minus coupon on the notes.

Valuing the assets/liabilities created in securitization

There is a difference between retained interests, and assets and liabilities arising by way of securitization referred to in Para 11.b. The retained interests are what have not been transferred, while the assets/liabilities here are those arising as a result of the transfer. For instance, the simplest and the most common asset received in the exchange is cash. In addition, the transferor might receive a financial asset such as securities of the SPE, a derivative asset. These form the consideration for the transfer, and therefore, are a part of the sale proceeds. The consideration for transfer might also be negative, in the form of liabilities, say a recourse liability. An obligation to service the portfolio (unless covered by servicing fees) is also a liability and should be treated as a negative consideration.

It is notable that the retained interests under Para 10 include only interests – assets. The consideration for the transfer under Para 11.b includes both assets and liabilities. Thus, if a liability arises as a result of the transaction, it cannot be treated as a retained interest but will be reduced from the consideration.

While the retained assets are still continued at carrying value (as we split carrying value of the asset into components), the assets/liabilities received/ incurred as a result of securitization are put in books at fair value. For example, if any subordinated securities are received, the same shall be measured at fair value and added to the cash consideration received. Similarly, if any recourse liability is undertaken by the transferor, the same shall be fair-valued and deducted from the sale consideration for computing the aggregate consideration for the transfer.

It is important to understand that the fair valuation here as well, as for retained interests, requires estimation of cash flows. For instance, the fair value of a liability on account of recourse is not the amount of recourse liability undertaken by the transferor as a credit enhancer, but the potential liability the transferor might have to suffer based on estimated delinquencies in the receivables.

Example 3

Let us say that in the facts stated in Example 1, the transferor undertakes a recourse liability for all assets that go bad within 3 months of the transfer. The fair value of this liability (expected value approach will be handy here) is computed to be $50. As the cash consideration received is $1,000, the net value of the consideration will be taken to be $950.

What if fair values cannot be computed practicably?

Para 71 of FAS 140 provides that where fair values cannot be determined practicably, then:

(a) If it is an asset, the value of the asset should be taken as nil; and
(b) If it is a liability, there will be no gain on sale recorded and the liability will be taken as equal to the gain on sale or value of contingencies as per FAS 5, read with FIN 14.

Computation of gain or loss

We have gone through the steps needed to compute the gain or loss on sale. To summarize, the steps involved are:

a.   Take the carrying value of the asset before transfer;
b.   Take the cash consideration received as a result of the transfer;
c.   Compute the fair value of assets and liabilities received/incurred as a result of the securitization;
d.   Add the value of assets in c. to b. and deduct the value of liabilities in c. from the consideration in b. The result is the fair value of the transferred component;
e.   Compute the fair value of the retained components;
f.   Apportion the carrying value of the asset in a. in the ratio of (i) the fair value in d. and (ii) the fair values in e. This will give (iii) the carrying value of the transferred component and (iv) the carrying value of the retained component; and
g.   Deduct from the fair value in d. the carrying value in f. (iii) the difference is the gain/loss on sale.

Example 4

Let us take the assumptions in Example 1, and the further information in Example 3 – the fair value of the recourse obligation – as $50. The computation of the gain on sale is:

	$
Carrying value of the asset as per books	1,000
Cash consideration for transfer	1,000
Value of the recourse obligation	–50
Fair value of the transferred component receivables	950
Fair value of the service fee (first computation in Example 1)	153.75
Splitting the carrying value in the ratio of 950: 153.75	
Carrying value of the transferred component	860.70
Carrying value of the servicing fee	139.30
Gain on sale	89.30

The resulting accounting entries will be as under:

		$
Cash	Debit	1,000
Recourse obligation	Credit	50
Receivables (asset)	Credit	950

(To record the assets and liabilities created in the transaction, and take the net impact as consideration for transfer of receivables)

		$
Servicing asset	Debit	139.30
Receivables	Credit	139.30

(To carve out the servicing fee asset from the carrying value of the asset)

		$
Receivables	Debit	89.30
Gain on transfer	Credit	89.30

(To recognize the gain on transfer and square off the receivables account)

The recourse obligation and the servicing asset are balance sheet items. The gain on sale is a revenue item. The asset account is completely squared off.

Example 5

Let us take another example to illustrate the computation of the gain on sale. Say the originator has assets with a carrying value of $1,000, transferred for a cash consideration of $1,050. The transaction gives rise to an interest rate swap whereby the transferor would swap the fixed rate of interest in the asset port-folio for a floating rate, valued at $70. The transferor also has a clean-up call option, valued at $40. The servicing asset carries a fair value of $100, and the recourse obligation has a value of $60.

First, we need to compute the fair value of the transferred component below:

	$
Consideration for transfer	1,050
Value of interest rate swap	70
Value of call option	40
Value of the recourse obligation	−60
Hence, fair value of the transferred component	1,100

There is a retained interest, so the carrying value of the asset will be split as between the transferred interest and the retained interest in proportion to their respective fair values. Note the apportionment below:

		Proportion	Apportioned carrying value ($)
Fair value of transferred interest	1,100	.91667	916.67
Fair value of retained interest	100	.08333	83.33
Total	1,200	1.00	1,000

The computation of the gain on sale and the accounting treatment are now explained as:

	$
Consideration for transfer	1,050
Value of interest rate swap	70
Value of call option	40
Value of the recourse obligation	−60
Fair value of receivables	1,100
Carrying value of receivables	1,000
Apportioned carrying value as per tabulation above	916.67
Gain on sale	183.33

The resulting accounting entries will be:

Cash	Debit	1,050
Interest rate swap	Debit	70
Call option	Debit	40
Recourse obligation	Credit	60
Receivables	Credit	1,100

(To record the assets and liabilities created in the transaction, take the net impact as consideration for transfer of receivables)

Retained servicing asset	Debit	83.33
Receivables	Credit	83.33

(To record retained interest by apportioning the carrying value)

Receivables	Debit	183.33
Gain on transfer	Credit	183.33

(To recognize the gain on transfer and square off the receivables account)

What happens to the servicing asset?

FAS 140.13 provides that a servicing asset or liability shall be amortized in proportion to and over the period of the set servicing fee. In addition, over the period of the servicing, any impairment in the value of the service fee will also have to be accounted for.

Leaving aside the issue of impairment, let us consider the amortization of the servicing asset. The servicing asset in our computation (a) is a discounted value of the servicing fees over time, (b) has been further reduced to its proportionate carrying value, and is not being carried at the discounted value itself. Therefore, amortization of the servicing fee over time would include taking to revenue (a) a financial component based on the discounting rate and (b) a component proportionate to the gain on sale that is inherent. Thus, amortization of the service fees would take to revenue every year an element equal to the discounting component as well as the gain component. Table 27.2 demonstrates this:

Example 6

Let us amortize the service fees in Example 1 for the carrying value apportioned therein, that is $133.36, assuming over time, the service fees remain what they were estimated to be.

Table 27.3 *IRR for amortization 19.46%*

Year	Service fees received	Amount taken to revenue	Amount taken against asset val.	Balance sheet val. of asset
Initial value of servicing fee $133.36				
1	40	25.95773	14.04227	119.3177
2	37.56703	23.22449	14.34254	104.9752
3	34.228402	20.4328	13.7956	91.17959
4	30.61124	17.74757	12.86367	78.31592
5	27.200021	15.24373	11.95629	66.35963
6	23.97912	12.91651	11.06261	55.29702
7	20.934151	10.76324	10.17091	45.12611
8	18.051961	8.783529	9.268431	35.85767
9	15.320648	6.979484	8.341164	27.51651
10	12.729654	5.355926	7.373729	20.14278
11	10.269958	3.920673	6.349285	13.7935
12	7.9344694	2.684822	5.249647	8.54385
13	5.7188923	1.66301	4.055883	4.487967
14	3.623782	0.873556	2.750226	1.737742
15	2.0759826	0.338241	1.737742	−5.8E-10

Notably, the amortization rate here is 19.46%, while the discounting rate used for discounting the service fee was 15%, due to the gain on the unsold component involved.

There is yet another approach to amortization of the servicing fees over time – valuation of the servicing fee at the end of each reporting period by computing the fair value of the remaining expected servicing flows. The approach has the advantage of (a) taking into account the pool values that actually remain at the end of such period, and therefore, being historically correct; (b) being able to review the assumptions on prepayments and defaults based on actual experience, and therefore, be more realistic. We will take up this approach in our next work example.

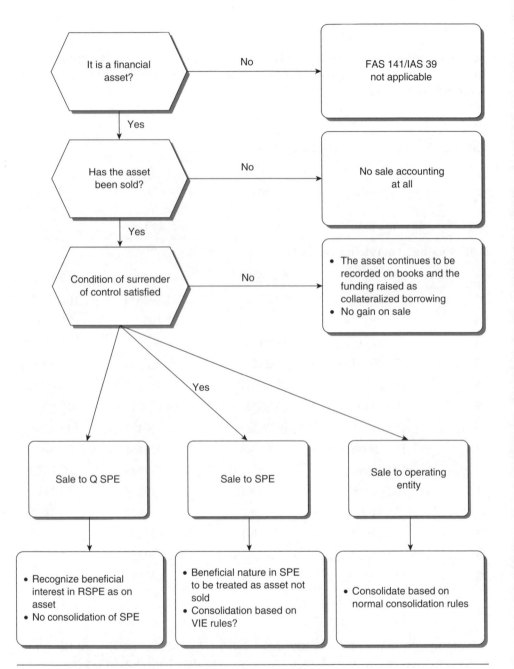

Figure 27.2   Securitization accounting: An overview

What happens to the recourse liability?

As with servicing assets/liabilities, all other assets and liabilities, either representing a retained interest or one created as a result of the securitization transaction, need to be revalued each reporting period. Thus, any actual losses on account of recourse will first dip into the recourse liability account before affecting the current revenue; the current revenue will only be affected to the extent of the increase in the value of the recourse liability remaining after such a set-off.

Retained interest valuation in a real life case

In Chapter 8, we took an example of a real life securitization transaction for the purpose of cash flow modeling. As projected cash flow is so significant for the purpose of retained interest valuation, we use the same example of retained interest working. It may be recalled that this is a pool of auto loan receivables with a carrying value (outstanding principal) of $1 billion. The pool has a weighted average APR of 5.855% and a remaining maturity of 53 months. Five different securities have been issued, for a total value of $1 billion to refinance this pool – Class A-1, A-2, A-3, A-4 and Class B. The particulars of the securities are (numbers in 000s):

Table 27.4   Securities and coupons in real life example

Securities	Nominal	Coupon
Class A-1	220,000	3.50%
class A-2	215,000	4.25%
Class A-3	350,000	4.50%
Class A-4	192,500	5%
Class B	22,500	6%
	1,000,000	

The originator has two residual interests – a 50 bps servicing fee, and all residual cash flows after the coupons on the securities have been paid and the required cash reserve has been created.

The cash flows were projected in Chapter 8's Example 12 worksheet. We have used the same worksheet, with the relevant workings for this chapter, as with Chapter 27's Worksheet 2 Retained Interest valuation in the Capital One case.

Value of the servicing fee

We make a simplified assumption that (a) the servicing is done by the originator or affiliate entity; and (b) that half of the servicing fee is the servicing expense.

The servicing fee is a senior item in the waterfall, senior to all external investors. This makes the servicing fee even senior to Class A, which has an AAA rating. In this sense, the servicing fee is super-senior, and hence, almost risk-free. For valuation, a risk-free discounting rate may be used. In Chapter 27's Worksheet 2, for retained interest valuation, we have used a 3% discounting rate to compute the value of the servicing fee.

Valuation of residual interest

For valuing the residual cash flows, two approaches may be used – an expected value approach and a risk-adjusted discounting rate approach. Consistent with industry practice (see the example below from a leading company's published accounts), we have used a risk-adjusted discounting rate of 12% for these cash flows. Essentially, the appropriate discounting rate for valuing the originator's residual interest should be the return on economic equity in the type of collateral.[31] The results are in (Worksheet 2).

Computation of gain on sale

Having found the values of the servicing asset and the residual interest, the computation of a gain on sale has been done in (Worksheet 2). The brief results are:

Table 27.5   Computation of gain on sale in example

	Fair value	Carrying value	Gain on sale
Servicing asset	5,350.92631	5,267.82	
Residual interest	10,425.35	10,263.43	
Transferred assets	1,000,000	984,468.7	15531.2528
Total	1,015,776.28	1,000,000	

Gain on sale accounting: Guesswork?

Securitization accounting by the originator is based on an estimate of residual profits left over in the transaction, and so is highly judgment-oriented. While subjectivity in valuation of residual interests just cannot be avoided, it is interesting to note the assumptions that go behind such valuations and the impact of changes in the assumptions on the values. The following are extracts from an Annual Report of GE:[32]

Key assumptions used in measuring the fair value of retained interests in securitizations and the sensitivity of the current fair value of residual cash flows to changes in those assumptions are noted in the following table. These assumptions may differ from those in the previous table as these related to all outstanding retained interests as of December 31, 2004.

Table 27.6   Illustrative disclosure of impact of assumptions in retained interest valuation

(Dollars in millions)	Equipment		Commercial real estate		Other assets		Credit card receivables	
DISCOUNT RATE(a)	7.3	%	8.6	%	6.7	%	11.3	%
Effect of:								
10% Adverse change	$	(10)	$	(13)	$	(19)	$	(9)
20% Adverse change	(20)	(26)	(37)	(17)				

PREPAYMENT RATE(a)	9.4	%	3.2	%	1.1	%	12.2	%
Effect of:								
10% Adverse change	$	(6)	$	(4)	$	(9)	$	(35)
20% Adverse change	(12)	(9)	(19)	(65)				
ESTIMATE OF CREDIT LOSSES(a)	1.8	%	0.4	%	0.5	%	8.0	%
Effect of:								
10% Adverse	$	(11)	$	(8)	$	—	$	(34)
20% Adverse change	(23)	(17)	(2)	(67)				
Remaining weighted average lives (in months)	35	101	62	8				
Net credit losses	$	54	$	7	$	25	$	465
Delinquencies	78	38	10	256				

IAS 39 revised and securitization

The revised IAS 39 was made effective for accounting periods beginning on or after January 1, 2005. While the standard made several changes in the accounting for derivatives, one of the significant areas that the standard made amendments on was de-recognition. As securitization amounts to de-recognition of an asset accounted for as such on the balance sheet, securitization transactions are clearly affected by amendments. The focus of the discussion below is on amendments effected by IAS 39 (Revised), while the generic principles discussed above still hold.

As for FAS 140, the accounting standard is applicable only in matters of de-recognition of a previously recognized "financial asset." The asset in question must be a financial asset, for example, loans, receivables, bonds, securities, and the asset being securitized must be already recognized as such on the balance sheet. Hence, IAS 39 will have no application to securitization of future flows that sell assets not currently on the balance sheet (it may apply in the future, though, when the relevant receivables are recognized by the seller). It also does not apply to the sale of physical assets such as commercial real estate, inventory, and intangible assets such as intellectual property.

The key distinctive features of IAS 39 are:

1. De-recognition of fractional assets only under specific conditions

The principles of de-recognition apply to a composite financial asset – the asset recognized by the originator. These principles cannot be viewed with reference to a part of an asset, except on satisfaction of specific conditions. For instance, if I have a loan book worth $1,000, I cannot contend that the book consists of a senior interest worth $800 and a junior interest worth $200, and that I have transferred the whole of the senior interest. Application of de-recognition principles to the part of an asset will apply only in three situations listed in Para 16 (b):

(a) Specifically identifiable cash flows from an asset

If specifically identifiable cash flows from an asset are transferred, such a part may be de-recognized subject to satisfaction of conditions specified by the standard, as discussed below. For example, in a pool of loans, principle and interest are specifically identifiable cash flows. If the principal is retained and interest is transferred, de-recognition to the extent of interest is permitted.[33] The reverse also holds true. What is the meaning of "specifically identifiable cash flows," and in particular, specifically identified by what or whom? It sounds reasonable to presume that specific identification may be in the originating document or in books of account. For example, in a pool of loans, servicing fees cannot be said to be a "specifically identifiable cash flow," as no borrower pays servicing fees separately from the overall consideration for the loan.

(b) Fully proportionate share of cash flows from an asset

This clause permits the application of fractional de-recognition to *pro rata* share of cash flow from a financial asset. For example, if x% of receivables from a loan is transferred, and (1–x%) is retained, it is possible to apply the de-recognition principles to x% transferred. It is important to note the precondition that the part retained and the part transferred must be fully proportionate in all respects. If the part retained is subordinated to the part transferred, it cannot be viewed as a transfer of a fraction of an asset. It is not clear, however, whether the fraction must be a constant or may vary over time. An instance may be the seller's interest in a credit card transaction. The investors' interest is generally a specific amount, and the excess of the value of the asset over the investors' interest is the seller's interest. The seller's interest is proportionate, but the proportion itself will vary over time. Going by the purpose of this condition, there should not be an objection to treating this case as a transfer of a fractional interest. Notably, the term "fully proportionate" should refer to a fraction that distributes the significant risks affecting an asset proportionately.

(c) Fully proportionate share of specifically identifiable cash flows from an asset

This clause is a combination of the two situations discussed above. For example, transfer of all interest but with retention of an IO strip, which is a fully proportionate share in a separately identifiable cash flow – interest – should qualify for fractional de-recognition. Once again, it is important to note that the fraction retained should neither be senior nor subordinated to the fraction transferred. That is to say, credit enhancing IO strips are not sought to be covered by this clause.

Implications of fractional de-recognition principle

The provisions of the Standard on fractional de-recognition are quite significant. With the stress on the components approach underlying the U.S. standard, it is possible for originators to contend that they have transferred components of a composite asset. The de-recognition approach will be applicable to the entire asset and not components, unless one of the situations above is applicable.

However, the following points should be noted:

- It is not that partial de-recognition is ruled out. In fact, in the continuing involvement approach, the most likely scenario under the Standard, the most likely result will be partial de-recognition. The implication of the above conditions is that we cannot apply the conditions of de-recognition as per this standard only with reference to a fraction.
- The rule does not apply if the original asset itself was a fraction. For example, if someone acquires the servicing rights over an asset, and such rights are transferred, what is transferred might have originally been a fraction of an asset, but as for the seller under reference, it is transfer of the composite asset.
- The rule is applicable to de-recognition, not to recognition. Even if the fractional approach is not permitted for the seller, for the buyer whatever fraction the buyer buys is recognized as an asset in the books of the buyer.

2. True sale is not a precondition

One of the most significant changes, almost silently brought about by the Standard, is that true sale is not a precondition under IAS 39 for de-recognizing an asset. There may be a de-recognition without a true sale, and there may not be a de-recognition even while there is a true sale. This principle reinforces the essential accounting rule that the treatment for transactions is not driven by the legal form, but by the commercial substance. Notably, this feature of the IAS 39 is significantly different from the conditions of FAS 140 where legal sale and the resulting bankruptcy remoteness are essential for off-balance sheet treatment.

That true sale is not a precondition for de-recognition comes from a combined reading of Para 18 and Para 19. Para 18 provides:

> 18. An entity transfers a financial asset if, and only if, it either:
> (a) transfers the contractual rights to receive the cash flows of the financial asset; or
> (b) retains the contractual rights to receive the cash flows of the financial asset, but assumes a contractual obligation to pay the cash flows to one or more recipients in an arrangement that meets the conditions in Paragraph 19.

That is to say, transfer of the contractual right to receive the cash flows (which obviously means legal title to the cash flows) is not necessary if the "transfer" meets the conditions listed in Para 19. The conditions listed in Para 19 were referred to in the exposure draft as a pass-through arrangement. We use the same term and discuss the conditions below.

Conditions of pass-through arrangement

If the contractual right to the cash flows is not transferred, but the holder creates for himself a back-to-back, pass-through obligation putting himself in the position of a mere collecting and distributing conduit; the transaction, not being a sale, may still result in off-balance sheet treatment. Para 19 states:

> 19. When an entity retains the contractual rights to receive the cash flows of a financial asset (the 'original asset'), but assumes a contractual obligation to pay those cash flows to one or more entities (the 'eventual recipients'), the entity treats the transaction as a transfer of a financial asset if, and only if, all of the following three conditions are met.
>
> (a) The entity has no obligation to pay amounts to the eventual recipients unless it collects equivalent amounts from the original asset. Short-term advances by the entity with the right of full recovery of the amount lent plus accrued interest at market rates do not violate this condition.
>
> (b) The entity is prohibited by the terms of the transfer contract from selling or pledging the original asset other than as security to the eventual recipients for the obligation to pay them cash flows.
>
> (c) The entity has an obligation to remit any cash flows it collects on behalf of the eventual recipients without material delay. In addition, the entity is not entitled to reinvest such cash flows, except for investments in cash or cash equivalents (as defined in IAS 7 Cash Flow Statements) during the short settlement period from the collection date to the date of required remittance to the eventual recipients, and interest earned on such investments is passed to the eventual recipients.

The conditions above are not difficult to understand. The underlying spirit is that the holder of legal title should be left with no economic interest in the asset other than holding the legal title and should have created no obligation to pay anything to the "transferees" other than from the cash flows of the assets. The first condition specifies that the holder of the asset is not obliged to pay except from the cash flows of the "transferred" asset. Advances, such as servicer advances or payments by way of a liquidity facility, would not militate against this condition unless they provide support for losses. The second condition indicates the creation of a lien of the "transferees" over the asset. Once again, the legal form of the lien is not important, as long as it curbs the liberty of the holder. Notably, it is also not important that such "lien" should be bankruptcy-remote. The third condition requires that the holder of the asset cannot receive and not remit the cash flows. Devices whereby reinvestments are permitted to bridge the practical gap between collection and repatriation do not violate this condition; however, the interest on such reinvestment should be used for the benefit of the ultimate beneficiaries.

The essence of the pass-through arrangement is that if the holder of the asset holds on to the chaff of legal title, but transfers all pith and substance of the cash flows, continuing his interface in the transaction as a collecting and paying device, the transaction should lead to off-balance sheet treatment.

Condition 1 and 3 also imply that physical separation of cash flows of the "transferred" asset is done. Commingling might imply that the holder of the asset is paying the obligation, not merely repatriating the cash flows.

Illustrative situations where a pass-through rule should apply

This author believes that as the undertone of the pass-through rule is to make a legal form of transfer unimportant, bankruptcy-remoteness[34] from a legal viewpoint is not a precondition for off-balance sheet treatment. Hence, full effect should be given to the pass-through rule without being prejudiced by legal forms of the "transfer." Illustratively, we note some situations where the pass-through rule may/may not apply:

- Secured loan form of sale, but pass-through obligation: The secured loan method is extensively used in several countries. If the arrangement satisfies condition 1 and 3 (condition 2 is obviously satisfied under terms of the security arrangement), off-balance sheet treatment may be applied subject to satisfaction of other conditions of the Standard.
- Sub-participation: Quite often, sub-participation form of transfer is used, whereby the "transferee" is allowed to participate in cash flows to a certain extent. Most of these arrangements comply with the conditions of fractional de-recognition discussed earlier, as also the conditions of pass-through arrangement.
- Issue of obligations by the SPV: De-recognition of the asset acquired by the SPV may also be possible under the pass-through rule. We will revert to this issue later in context of accounting for SPVs.
- Synthetic transactions: Can a synthetic transaction lead to off-balance sheet treatment? In a synthetic transaction, there is neither a true sale nor a transfer of cash flows. Hence, there is no question of an off-balance sheet treatment in case of synthetic transactions.

3. Risk and rewards given a new thrust

Under FAS 140, the legal sale of the asset takes priority over transfer of risks and returns. The undertone of IAS 39 is to rely on transfer of risks and rewards. This seems to be like revival of an age-old accounting rule, lost in the past due to inclination of the Standard on financial instruments towards the U.S. standards.

While transfer of substantially all risks and returns relevant to the asset is not a precondition for de-recognition, the Standard puts a negative condition; where substantially all risks and returns are retained, the asset will not be de-recognized. Para 20 (a) and (b) provide as follows:

> *(a) if the entity transfers substantially all the risks and rewards of owner-ship of the financial asset, the entity shall derecognize the financial asset and recognize separately as assets or liabilities any rights and obligations created or retained in the transfer.*
>
> *(b) if the entity retains substantially all the risks and rewards of owner-ship of the financial asset, the entity shall continue to recognize the finan-cial asset.*

The phrase "substantially all the risks and rewards" should not be limited to credit risks. For example, if the transferor provides significant recourse for credit losses, it cannot be concluded that there is retention of substantially all the risks and returns. There are various risks concerning an asset, which would differ based on the nature of the asset. For example, for several assets, prepayment may be a significant risk. While the originator does retain the risk for credit losses, he transfers the risk of prepayments, as pre-paid cash flows are passed over to the investors. Similarly, there might be interest rate and other risks relating to the asset.

Risks and rewards are mutually supportive; if there is retention of substan-tially all risks, it should normally follow that there is retention of substantially all rewards too, because rewards are essentially for shouldering risks. The returns to the transferee are, then, in the nature of a lender's rate of return. On the con-trary, if there is a transfer of risks, say, prepayment risk, then it should follow that there is transfer of rewards too – for example, the cost of the prepayment option. If there is a risk, the possibility of not suffering the risk is itself a reward. If there is a reward, the possibility of not receiving the reward itself is a risk.

The other significant point is that as the risk/reward question is essentially one of substance over form, technicalities should not come in the way of real-ization of substance. Notably, if the transaction has been split in various pieces, all the pieces of the jigsaw puzzle should be put together to look at the complete picture. For instance, if the risks are transferred by one document, and are re-acquired by another (say, a put option given to the buyer), the big picture is still one of no transfer of risks.

The situation of retention of substantially all risks/returns will normally arise only where the transaction virtually puts the transferee in the position of a lender, paying fixed cash flows on fixed dates, irrespective of actual collec-tions or losses. It is difficult to envisage such a transfer to satisfy the test of a "true sale" as well.

4. Hierarchy of conditions for de-recognition

Para 20 (c) envisages the situation that will be applicable in most securitiza-tion transactions. As we have noted above, Para 20 (a) envisions a case where substantially all risks/rewards are transferred, and Para 20 (b) a case where substantially all risks/rewards are retained. Both of these are unlikely in most securitization transactions. Hence, Para 20 (c), which envisages situations in which risks/rewards are neither completely transferred nor completely retained, is the most likely scenario.

In this case, there are two alternatives – the seller surrenders control over the asset [Para 20 (c) (i)] or the seller does not surrender control [Para 20 (c) (ii)]. Surrender of control is elaborated by Para 23, which provides: "If the transferee has the practical ability to sell the asset in its entirety to an unrelated third party and is able to exercise that ability unilaterally and without needing to impose additional restrictions on the transfer, the entity has not retained control. In all other cases, the entity has retained control." The transferee for securitization is the SPV, and generally, it is appropriate to expect that the SPV will not have the legal or practical ability to sell the assets, either in entirety or otherwise. In fact, one of the defining parameters of SPVs is that it does not have the discretion to sell down the asset. Hence, Para 20 (c) (i) is designed for asset sales and not typical securitization transactions.

Para 20 (c) (ii) is applicable in case control has not been surrendered. In this case, the continuing involvement approach is used, explained below.

Briefly, the hierarchy of conditions governing de-recognition is shown in Figure 27.3.

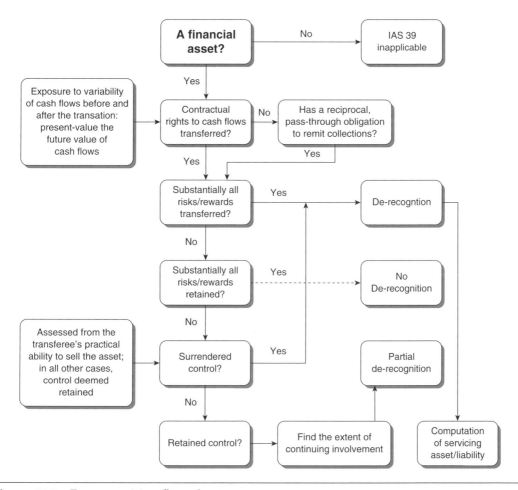

Figure 27.3 De-recognition flow chart

5. The continuing involvement approach

As noted above, the continuing involvement approach is the most likely case applicable to securitization. Paras 30–35 deal with the continuing involvement approach. A continuing involvement is a case of partial de-recognition. While the continuing involvement approach may, in principle, be different from the components approach of the U.S. FAS 140, in practice, the application of the continuing involvement approach may give rise to similar results.

Meaning of continuing involvement

All cases where some, but not all, risks/returns in the asset are retained by the seller will come under continuing involvement, unless it is a case of surrender of control. As continuing involvement means retention of risks/returns, the seller is obviously exposed to changes in the value of the transferred asset. Thus, Para 30 provides that "The extent of the entity's continuing involvement in the transferred asset is the extent to which it is exposed to changes in the value of the transferred asset."

Continuing involvement does not mean mere retention of control. For instance, retention of servicing by itself does not amount to continuing involvement.

Where there is a continuing involvement, measurement of the extent to which there is a continuing involvement may sound a challenge. While the U.S. standard requires fair valuation of the retained components, IAS 39 provides guidance on the measurement of continuing involvement in certain specific cases, discussed below.

Continuing involvement for guarantees, etc.

Where the continuing involvement is in the form a guarantee, the transferor's continuing involvement is to the extent of the guaranteed amount [Para 30 (a)], that is, the maximum amount of consideration that the seller may be required to return on account of guarantee. While the Para speaks of guarantees, it would obviously apply to a case of over-collateralization, as over-collateralization is also a guarantee to pay from specific assets, recourse and substitution obligations.

To be meaningful, Para 30 (a) should be read with Para 31, which provides that where an entity continues to recognize an asset due to continuing involvement, it will also recognize the relevant liability. It also provides that the value of the liability should be such that the net of the retained asset and the associated liability reflects the value of the retained interest. For unfunded guarantees,[35] the seller does not have any right to cash flow; hence, there is no asset to retain on the books of the seller. There is a liability – the liability to absorb losses to the extent of guaranteed amount. Hence, on the face of it, Para 30 (a), which requires retention of an asset to the extent of the liability on account of returnable consideration, is confusing. For example, if a seller were to transfer an asset worth $1,000, retain a subordinated investment worth $100 and have an obligation to suffer losses due to recourse, say $50, the value of the retained asset will be $100 and the value of resultant liability will be $150. But if the liability is unfunded, there is no question of booking an asset; it is just the value of the liability of $50 that will come on the books.

The above treatment also applies for written or purchased options with reference to the asset. A common example of a purchased option may be a clean-up call option.

Continuing involvement for residual interests

Para 34 provides for splitting the value of the asset between transferred portions and retained portions. This approach is similar to the components approach of the U.S. standard.

6. Dealing with the servicing asset

The Standard explicitly provides for recognition of the servicing asset or liability in each case where a full de-recognition is applicable. Para 24 provides: "If an entity transfers a financial asset in a transfer that qualifies for de-recognition in its entirety and retains the right to service the financial asset for a fee, it shall recognise either a servicing asset or a servicing liability for that servicing contract. If the fee to be received is not expected to compensate the entity adequately for performing the servicing, a servicing liability for the servicing obligation shall be recognised at its fair value. If the fee to be received is expected to be more than adequate compensation for the servicing, a servicing asset shall be recognised for the servicing right at an amount determined on the basis of an allocation of the carrying amount of the larger financial asset in accordance with Paragraph 27."

A significant difference between the U.S. standard and the IAS 39 is notable; the U.S. standard looks at the servicing asset itself as a component, while the recognition of the servicing asset or liability is permitted/required only in cases where a financial asset qualifies for de-recognition in its entirety. As we have noted, most cases of securitization will, in greater likelihood, not qualify for full recognition, and the servicing asset is permitted to be brought in books only in very limited cases.

7. Booking of gain on sale under continuing involvement approach

Para 34 clearly permits recognition of gain or loss in cases where the continued involvement relates to a part of the financial asset. The allocation of the carrying value of the asset between the part retained and the part transferred is done on the basis of fair values, largely on the same basis as already discussed above.

8. Examples of the continuing involvement approach

The Application Guidance provides several illustrative situations in relation to de-recognition. The points relevant to securitization are:

Assume an entity has a portfolio of prepayable loans whose coupon and effective interest rate is 10% and whose principal amount and amortized cost is $10,000. It enters into a transaction in which, in return for a payment of $9,115, the transferee obtains the right to $9,000 of any collections of principal plus interest thereon at 9.5%. The entity retains rights to $1,000 of any collections of principal plus interest thereon at 10%, plus the excess spread of 0.5% on the remaining $9,000 of principal. Collections from prepayments are allocated between the entity and the transferee proportionately in the ratio of 1:9, but any defaults are deducted from the entity's interest of $1,000 until that interest is exhausted. The fair value of the loans at the date of the transaction is $10,100 and the estimated fair value of the excess spread of 0.5% is $40.

The entity determines that it has transferred some significant risks and rewards of ownership (for example, significant prepayment risk) but has also retained some significant risks and rewards of ownership (because of its subordinated retained interest) and has retained control. It, therefore, applies the continuing involvement approach.

To apply this Standard, the entity analyzes the transaction as (a) a retention of a fully proportionate retained interest of $1,000, plus (b) the subordination of that retained interest to provide credit enhancement to the transferee for credit losses.

The entity calculates that $9,090 (90% $10,100) of the consideration received of $9,115 represents the consideration for a fully proportionate 90% share. The remainder of the consideration received ($25) represents consideration received for subordinating its retained interest to provide credit enhancement to the transferee for credit losses. In addition, the excess spread of 0.5% represents consideration received for the credit enhancement. Accordingly, the total consideration received for the credit enhancement is $65 ($25 + $40).

The entity calculates the gain or loss on the sale of the 90% share of cash flows. Assuming that separate fair values of the 10% part transferred and the 90% part retained are not available at the date of the transfer, the entity allocates the carrying amount of the asset in accordance with Paragraph 28 as follows:

	Estimated fair value	Percentage	Allocated carrying amount
Portion transferred	9,090	90%	9,000
Portion retained	1,010	10%	1,000
Total	10,100		10,000

The entity computes its gain or loss on the sale of the 90% share of the cash flows by deducting the allocated carrying amount of the portion transferred from the consideration received, i.e. $90 ($9,090 − $9,000). The carrying amount of the portion retained by the entity is $1,000.

In addition, the entity recognizes the continuing involvement that results from the subordination of its retained interest for credit losses. Accordingly, it recognizes an asset of CU1 000 (the maximum amount of the cash flows it would not receive under the subordination), and an associated liability of CU1 065 (which is the maximum amount of the cash flows it would not receive under the subordination, i.e. CU1 000 plus the fair value of the subordination of CU65).

The entity uses all of the above information to account for the transaction as follows:

	Debit	Credit ($)
Original asset	—	9,000
Asset recognized for subordination or the residual interest	1,000	—
Asset for the consideration received in the form of excess spread	40	—
Profit or loss (gain on transfer)	—	90
Liability	—	1,065
Cash received	9,115	—
Total	10,155	10,155

Immediately following the transaction, the carrying amount of the asset is CU2 040 comprising CU1 000, representing the allocated cost of the portion retained, and CU1 040, representing the entity's additional continuing involvement from the subordination of its retained interest for credit losses (which includes the excess spread of CU40).

In subsequent periods, the entity recognizes the consideration received for the credit enhancement (CU65) on a time proportion basis, accrues interest on the recognized asset using the effective interest method and recognizes any credit impairment on the recognized assets. As an example of the latter, assume that in the following year there is a credit impairment loss on the underlying loans of CU300. The entity reduces its recognized asset by CU600 (CU300 relating to its retained interest and CU300 relating to the additional continuing involvement that arises from the subordination of its retained interest for credit losses), and reduces its recognized liability by CU300. The net result is a charge to profit or loss for credit impairment of CU300.

Financing treatment and linked treatment

Where the securitization transaction does not qualify for a sale or de-recognition treatment, it is given a financing treatment. In other words, notwithstanding the legal acceptability of the assignment of receivables, the receivables continue on the balance sheet of the originator and the amount raised by the assignment of receivables is accounted for as a liability.

The financing treatment is premised on the presumption that the form of the transaction may be a legal transfer of the receivables, but its substance is mere financing.

If the transaction is given a financing treatment, the receivables will remain on the balance sheet and would be removed as and when they are collected. On the other hand, the "liability" on account of the amount to be paid to investors will be recognized at its present value and would be removed based on the amortization of the liability over a period of time.

It may be noted that under the financial components approach, almost every securitization transaction would qualify for an off-balance sheet treatment to the extent of the components transferred. The financing treatment is essentially a concept under the U.K. accounting standards. Para 21 of FRS 5 requires a financial treatment when there is no significant change in the entity's risks and rewards on the transferred assets. Para 22 suggests a sale treatment only when all significant risks and rewards are transferred by the originator. However, most securitization transactions would not qualify for either extreme. There, Para 26 of FRS 5 for linked presentation would apply.

FRS 5 recommends a linked presentation when there is retention of risks and rewards by the originator, but the financing is ring-fenced. Ring fencing arises when the payments would be made out of a dedicated asset or fund, and there is no possibility of a claim against the originator other than the claim against the specific funds dedicated. For example, a recourse obligation to the extent of an over-collateralized receivable would be a case of ring-fencing, but if there is a general recourse undertaken by the originator against his own assets, the case would not qualify for linked presentation.

If a linked presentation approach is adopted, the value raised by assigning the receivables is netted off from the value of the receivables on the balance sheet, that is, the liability is netted off from the asset.

In all other cases, FRS recommends a separate presentation, that is, the asset and the liability will both be recognized as their full values. Text of relevant extracts from FRS 5 is appended to this chapter. FRS 5 incited global attention recently as it was suggested to the FASB[36] that the FASB adopt an approach similar to the linked presentation suggested under FRS 5.

Comparative view of sale and financing treatment

If the transaction of securitization is given a sale treatment for accounting purposes, the revenue statement of the originator will recognize, on the date of making the assignment, a profit or loss as the difference between the carrying value of the assigned receivables and the amount raised by assigning the receivables.

This illustration is a simplified case where there is no retained interest, nor any asset/liability arising as a result of the transaction.

For example, if receivables of $25 per month, for next 60 months (total nominal value Rs. 1500) were carried at a carrying value of $980 (based on the outstanding principal value), and are transferred for a price of $1,030, there is an immediate gain of $50 ($1,030 – 980). If the said receivables are transferred for a price of $950, there is an immediate loss of $30.

For the sale treatment, the gain or loss is treated as the gain or loss of the accounting period when the securitization takes place and taken to revenue straightaway.

For a "loan type treatment," the receivables will be carried on the books, as if the securitization had not been effected and the income from which will be accounted for every period as per the accounting policy of the originator. The "discount" on the issue of the securitized note – the difference between the nominal value of the assigned receivables and the price at which they are sold – will be spread over the tenure of the note so as to represent a fixed charge on the outstanding principal value of the note.

The application of this accounting policy will be illustrated in the following illustration.

Assume the following are the amounts receivable under a transaction for the next five years: Year 1: $320; Year 2: $320; Year 3: $320; Year 4: $320; and Year 5: $320. As per generally acceptable accounting principles, these receivables should be recognized at their present value computed at the implicit rate of return in the original transaction. If assuming the transaction was based on an outflow of $1,000, the accounting treatment is reflected in the computations below:

Table 27.7   Example of financing treatment

Basic assumptions: The transaction	
Outflow	−1,000
Year 1	320
Year 2	320
Year 3	320
Year 4	320
Year 5	320
IRR	18.03%
Discounted value after 1 year @ 16%	895.42

Chart showing carrying value/ financing income of original transaction

	Ostndg. investment	Installment	Financing income	Capital recovery	Carrying value as at year end
Year 1	1000.00	320.00	180.31	139.69	860.31
Year 2	860.31	320.00	155.12	164.88	695.43
Year 3	695.43	320.00	125.39	194.61	500.82
Year 4	500.82	320.00	90.30	229.70	271.12
Year 5	271.12	320.00	48.88	271.12	0.00

(Continued)

Let us say the transaction is securitized at the beginning of year 2
SALE TREATMENT

Carrying value as per books	860.31
Amount received by assignment	895.42
Gain on assignment	35.11

Revenue account:

	Expenditure		Income	
Year 1	Normal financing cost	Year 1	Financing charges	180.31
Year 2		Year 2	**Gain on securitization**	35.11

Loan treatment
Amortization of the securitization instrument

	Amount raised	Installment	Apprtned discount	Amortization	Balance
Year 2	895.42	320.00	143.27	176.73	718.68
Year 3	718.68	320.00	114.99	205.01	513.67
Year 4	513.67	320.00	82.19	237.81	275.86
Year 5	275.86	320.00	44.14	275.86	0.00

Revenue account:

	Expenditure			Income	
Year 1	Normal financing cost		Year 1	Financing charges	180.31
Year 2	Apprned discount	143.27	Year 2	Financing charges	155.12
Year 3	Apprned discount	114.99	Year 3	Financing charges	125.39
Year 4	Apprned discount	82.19	Year 4	Financing charges	90.30
Year 5	Apprned discount	44.14	Year 5	Financing charges	48.88

Disclosures by the originator

FASB 140.17 imposes disclosure requirements mainly dealing with the nature of restrictions on assets transferred and the controls retained on such assets, servicing assets retained, any other asset or obligation acquired and policy for amortization thereof.

A. For all servicing assets and servicing liabilities:

   (1) The amounts of servicing assets or liabilities recognized and amortized during the period;

   (2) The fair value of recognized servicing assets and liabilities for which it is practicable to estimate that value and the method and significant assumptions used to estimate the fair value;

   (3) The risk characteristics of the underlying financial assets used to stratify recognized servicing assets for purposes of measuring impairment in accordance with FAS 140.63; and

   (4) The activity in any valuation allowance for impairment of recognized servicing assets – including beginning and ending balances, aggregate additions charged and reductions credited to operations, and aggregate direct write-downs charged against the allowances – for each period for which results of operations are presented.

B. If the entity has securitized financial assets during any period presented and accounts for that transfer as a sale, for each major asset type (for example, mortgage loans, credit card receivables and automobile loans):

   (1) Its accounting policies for initially measuring the retained interests, if any, including the methodology (whether quoted market price, prices based on sales of similar assets and liabilities, or prices based on valuation techniques) used in determining their fair value;

   (2) The characteristics of securitizations (a description of the transferor's continuing involvement with the transferred assets, including, but not limited to, servicing, recourse and restrictions on retained interests) and the gain or loss from sale of financial assets in securitizations;

   (3) The key assumptions used in measuring the fair value of retained interests at the time of securitization (including, at a minimum, quantitative information about discount rates, expected prepayments including the expected weighted-average life of prepayable financial assets and anticipated credit losses, if applicable); and

   (4) Cash flows between the securitization SPE and the transferor, unless reported separately elsewhere in the financial statements or notes (including proceeds from new securitizations, proceeds from collections reinvested in revolving-period securitizations, purchases of delinquent or foreclosed loans, servicing fees and cash flows received on interests retained).

C. If the entity has retained interests in securitized financial assets at the date of the latest statement of financial position presented, for each major asset type (for example, mortgage loans, credit card receivables and automobile loans):

   (1) Its accounting policies for subsequently measuring those retained interests, including the methodology (whether quoted market price, prices based on sales of similar assets and liabilities, or prices based on valuation techniques) used in determining their fair value;

(2) The key assumptions used in subsequently measuring the fair value of those interests (including, at a minimum, quantitative information about discount rates, expected prepayments including the expected weighted-average life of prepayable financial assets, and anticipated credit losses, including expected static pool losses, if applicable);

(3) A sensitivity analysis or stress test showing the hypothetical effect on the fair value of those interests of two or more unfavorable variations from the expected levels for each key assumption that is reported under (2) above independently from any change in another key assumption, and a description of the objectives, methodology and limitations of the sensitivity analysis or stress test. [See earlier – extracts from annual report of GE showing the above disclosures];

(4) For the securitized assets and any other financial assets that it manages together with them:

   (a) The total principal amount outstanding, the portion that has been de-recognized, and the portion that continues to be recognized in each category reported in the statement of financial position, at the end of the period;

   (b) Delinquencies at the end of the period; and

   (c) Credit losses, net of recoveries, during the period.

   Disclosure of average balances during the period is encouraged, but not required.

Accounting for the SPV

The SPV, whether organized as a company or a trust, would need to prepare its own accounts.

The SPV's basic assets are the initial equity or corpus normally contributed by the originator, and the assets transferred by the originator. The assets transferred by the originator to the SPV would include the receivables, an over-collateralization receivables or cash retention (if transferred by way of a true sale, as opposed to transferred by way of a collateral) and any third party guarantees. On the other hand, the SPV passes on to the investors in form of equity, debt, certificates of beneficial interest, or commercial paper interest in the pool of receivables transferred to it.

While there might be circumstances where the originator may retain the receivables on its balance sheet, it would not be proper for the SPV to de-recognize the receivables from its own balance sheet. For example, even where the originator has retained significant risks and rewards in the receivables, it cannot be said that the SPV would not account for the asset or corresponding liability on its balance sheet.

However, for pass-through securitizations, where the SPV is acting as a mere conduit, such that the amounts raised by issuance of the notes is no more or no less than the beneficial interest in the assets acquired, then the SPV does not have to record the assets acquired by it in a fiduciary capacity. Such assets are not the beneficial assets of the SPV; therefore, the SPV does not record either the assets acquired as a fiduciary or the securities issued indicating beneficial interest. In a typical pass-through securitization, the SPV will have no residual interest, no leftover or no asset that is not passed through to investors. In such a case, the SPV may elect not to recognize the asset on its balance sheet. Hence, grantor trusts for pass-through transactions do not usually prepare any books of account for the assets transferred by the originator.

On the other hand, if the securities of the SPV are construed as debt-type securities, the SPV will record the assets acquired by it as its assets, and the corresponding certificates/securities issued to investors as liabilities.

Consolidation of SPV accounts with the originator

The issue of consolidation of SPV accounts with the originator is in itself a very sensitive issue. It would be easy to appreciate that the very purpose of off-balance sheet treatment of securitization would be frustrated if the SPV's accounts are consolidated. What goes off-balance sheet as a result of securitization comes back on-balance sheet of the originator by way of consolidation.

Where the SPV is the subsidiary of the originator, consolidation would be required in all such countries for which group accounts are required. [Group accounts are currently not required in India.] Even where the SPV is not a direct subsidiary, there might be situations when it might be treated as a quasi-subsidiary. FRS 5 [Para D18] gives the following guide to treatment of quasi-subsidiary: If the originator has residuary interest in the SPV – if the net assets of the SPV belong to the originator or if the originator has risks in the net assets of the SPV – the SPV will be treated as the quasi-subsidiary of the originator. FRS Para D19 says: "In general, where an issuer's activities comprise holding securitized assets and the benefits of its net assets accrue to the originator, the issuer will be a quasi-subsidiary of the originator. The issuer will not be a quasi-subsidiary of the originator where the owner of the issuer is an independent third party that has made a substantial capital investment in the issuer, and has benefits and risks of its net assets."

SIC 12 on consolidation

The International Accounting Standards Board has also issued an interpretation called SIC 12 where a similar view was taken. SIC 12, issued in respect of IAS 27, provides as follows:

8. An SPE should be consolidated when the substance of the relationship between an enterprise and the SPE indicates that the SPE is controlled by that enterprise.
9. In the context of an SPE, control may arise through the predetermination of the activities of the SPE (operating on "autopilot") or otherwise. IAS 27.13 indicates several circumstances which result in control even in cases where an entity owns one half or less of the voting power of

another entity. Similarly, control may exist even in cases where an entity owns little or none of the SPE's equity. The application of the control concept requires, in each case, judgement in the context of all relevant factors.

10. In addition to the situations described in IAS 27.13, the following circumstances, for example, may indicate a relationship in which an entity controls an SPE and consequently should consolidate the SPE (additional guidance is provided in the Appendix to this Interpretation):

(a) In substance, the activities of the SPE are being conducted on behalf of the entity according to its specific business needs so that the entity obtains benefits from the SPE's operation;

(b) In substance, the entity has the decision-making powers to obtain the majority of the benefits of the activities of the SPE or, by setting up an "autopilot" mechanism, the entity has delegated these decision-making powers;

(c) In substance, the entity has rights to obtain the majority of the benefits of the SPE and therefore may be exposed to risks incident to the activities of the SPE; or

(c) In substance, the entity retains the majority of the residual or ownership risks related to the SPE or its assets in order to obtain benefits from its activities.

While it seems that in most cases, an SPV will require consolidation due to the above treatment of quasi-subsidiaries, a new gateway of escape is the pass-through rule under the revised IAS 39. We have referred to Para 19 of the IAS 39 earlier. While the SPV acquires contractual rights to the cash flows and does not transfer the same to the investors, it assumes pass-through obligations. Importantly, it is not obliged to pay anything unless it actually receives the cash flow on the asset. It has no right to retain the cash flows after it actually collects the same. The reinvestments done by the SPV are typically only to bridge the maturity mismatch. The SPV also is contractually debarred from transferring the asset or pledging the same. Unless the SPV is a reinvestment-type vehicle, as for CDOs or ABCP conduits, the SPV may easily qualify as a pass-through vehicle, and therefore, the assets may be removed from the books of the SPV. Therefore, though the consolidation under SIC 12 may apply, it may still keep the assets off the balance sheet.

Consolidation of variable interest entities under U.S. gaps

Post-Enron, there was a substantial controversy about special purpose vehicles and their possible misuse. Special purpose vehicles were publicly seen as a device to dodge tax and accounting scrutiny. A special purpose vehicle is like a secret bank locker – its owner or beneficiary cannot be established on a primary appearance and it is still safe as it is a hived-off bundle of assets with only specific assets or activities. As the voting capital in special purpose entities is abysmally low (and would typically be declared for public charity or otherwise widely dispersed), such entities could not come for consolidation based on their voting capital.

Therefore, U.S. standard setters set on a "whodunit" kind of mission to spot the real beneficiary of special purpose entities. The result was an interpretation called FIN 46 that deals with consolidation of certain entities on a basis other than voting control. Thus, FIN 46 is an exception to the usual consolidation rules in Accounting Research Bulletin (ARB) 51.

FIN 46 was, soon after its introduction, replaced by FIN 46 (Revised) in December 2003. The references to FIN 46 below are to the revised interpretation.

FIN 46 is, therefore, an exception to the normal accounting rule requiring consolidation based on voting control. A new term was coined for this purpose – variable interest entities – to which the new consolidation rule would be applicable. A variable interest entity (VIE) is essentially nothing but an accounting jargon for the commercial world phrase "special purpose entity." What the FASB is trying to do here, as is quite common with lots of FASB definitions, is to identify a special purpose entity by its features.

What is a variable interest entity?

The Interpretation identifies two key features of an SPE – inadequacy of at-risk capital and exercise of absentee control by the *de facto* owner of the entity and not the front-running equity holders who are mere nominalities. There is no substantive definition of a variable interest entity such as the fact that a special purpose entity is not allowed to enter substantive business operations or the fact that it is structurally bankruptcy-remote and is nothing but an incorporated shell. On the other hand, the FASB thought it appropriate to focus on two features – inadequacy of capital and lack of control by the apparent voting shareholders. Possibly, that best suits the purpose of the Interpretation as an exception to the general rule where equity holders are regarded as the owners of the entity.

Para 5 provides that an entity will be subject to consolidation as per this interpretation if *any* of the following features are satisfied:

- The total equity investment at risk is not sufficient to permit the entity to finance its activities without additional subordinated financial support provided by any parties;
- As a group the holders of the equity investment at risk lack any one of the specified characteristics of a controlling financial interest; and
- The voting rights of some investors are not proportional to their obligations to absorb the expected losses of the entity, their rights to receive the expected residual returns of the entity, or both and substantially all of the entity's activities either involve or are conducted on behalf of an investor that has disproportionately few voting rights.

The underlying spirit of the interpretation lies in the way SPVs are constituted. The distinction between variable interest entities and other business enterprises is based on the nature and amount of the equity investment and the rights and obligations of the equity investors. If the total equity investment at risk is not sufficient to permit the entity to finance its activities, the parties providing the necessary additional subordinated financial support will not permit an equity investor to make decisions that may be counter to their interests. That means that the usual condition for establishing a controlling financial interest – a majority voting interest – does not apply to variable interest entities. Consequently, a standard for consolidation that requires ownership of voting stock or some other form of decision-making ability is not appropriate for such entities.

We discuss below the features of variable interest entities.

Inadequacy of at-risk capital

The first significant feature is the inadequacy of at-risk capital. As a common feature of SPEs, entities are thinly capitalized; the support for losses of the entity comes not from the legal capital of the entity but in some other form of first-loss support. The capital, being insignificant, should not be the basis of consolidation.

Para 5 also provides anti-avoidance safeguards that define what will or will not be counted as equity for the purposes of determining sufficiency. For instance, such investment includes, if reported as equity in the reported statements, the residual beneficiary capital, even if not entitled to voting rights. But it does not include amounts provided, directly or indirectly, to equity owners by others, such as by way of fees or contributions, or amounts financed by loans or guarantees on loans by others.

As for any entity, the insufficiency of capital is to be judged in relation to the expected losses of the entity. The expected losses of a VIE are defined in Para 8 as the expected negative variability in the fair value of its net assets. As the adequacy of the at-risk investment is to be tested relative to expected losses, the term "expected losses" itself becomes significant. A complete Annexure (Annexure A) is devoted to illustrating what are expected losses. Briefly, expected losses are not losses in an accounting sense, but expected losses in a statistical or financial sense – variability of the residual income of the enterprise. Statistically, the "expected loss" is the probability-weighted fair value of the deviations of various expected outcomes from their mean or expected value.

By Para 9, there is a presumption that if the equity investment is not at least 10% the total assets of the enterprise, it is inadequate unless there are definite escape routes available; for instance, the expected losses can be shown to be lower than 10% based on quantitative analysis or qualitative evidence.

Absentee ownership

The second feature of a VIE is that equity owners are not those who really run the show; they are there just as a legal facade. This is obvious because if the equity is insignificant and substantive risk absorption is taking place by those who would have a subordinated investment at stake, the latter would not let the equity owners run the business. Therefore, if the equity holders lack any of the following features of financial control, the entity is a VIE:

(a)   The entity has no voting capital or the voting capital does not have the discretion relating to the entity's activities. Usually, SPEs are either pre-programmed, so as to rule out discretion, or the decision-making is done by some named director who is otherwise not a majority on the Board.
(b)   The equity owners are not exposed to expected losses, because of an absorption by other subordinated investors, or due to guarantees from others.
(c)   The equity owners do not have the right to enjoy the residual returns of the enterprise, for instance, by capping the same.

Disproportionate voting rights

The irrelevance of equity as an indication of control can be also be established if some class of investors has voting rights that are disproportionate to their obligation to absorb the expected losses or their right to enjoy the expected residual returns of the enterprise.

What is a variable interest?

Once we establish an entity as a VIE, we need to establish who the variable interest holder is. In practice, it would be more difficult to answer this question than to simply identify a variable interest entity. By definition: "The investments or other interests that will absorb portions of a variable interest entity's expected losses if they occur or receive portions of the entity's expected residual returns if they occur are called variable interests." [Para 6] That is to say, he who bears those expected losses or enjoys expected residual returns that are sealed off for the equity owners are the variable interest holders. While equity is an investment, a variable interest does not have to be an investment, indicated by the use of the words "investment or other interest." For instance, the ability to earn variable fees is a variable interest.

Para 12 lays down that if the variable interest is only in specific assets of the entity, it may still be regarded as the variable interest for the purpose of the interpretation as the interest is in majority of the assets of the entity by fair value.

Consolidation based on variable interests

For VIEs, consolidation will not be based on equity, but on variable interests. That is, the one who has a majority of the variable interests will consolidate the VIE. Such a majority holder is called the primary beneficiary. The words "primary beneficiary" are a euphemism; as in cases where the variable interests are asymmetrically divided, one entity absorbs the expected losses and another enjoys the residual rewards, so consolidation is based on losses. The position of primary beneficial interest is to be established after taking into account the interests held by all "related parties," the latter term meaning the same as under FAS 57. In addition, the holdings of *de facto* agents of the beneficiary shall also be included. The *de facto* agents, under Para 16, include the following:

a. Other VIEs of which the beneficiary is the primary beneficiary.
b. A party whose contribution was funded by the beneficiary.
c. An officer, agent or governing board member of the beneficiary.
d. A party that has an agreement that it cannot sell, transfer or encumber its interest without the consent of the beneficiary, or one that is connected with the beneficiary due to a close business relationship such as between a service provider (say a law firm) and a client.

Exception for QSPEs

The Interpretation is not applicable to QSPEs covered by Para 35 of FAS 140, or grandfathered SPEs under the previous accounting standard FAS 125. While this exception is a major relief for a larger part of the securitization industry, the problem of consolidation is focused in cases where the SPE does not qualify under FAS 140 (see the earlier pages on QSPEs). Also note that on April 30, 2003, the FASB decided to amend the conditions for QSPEs to make these conditions more elaborate.

Impact of FIN 46 on structured finance

Rating agency Standard & Poor's in early April narrated the results of a survey of the opinions of the structured finance industry, nearly two months after the effective date for implementation of FIN 46. It reported that "the majority of securitization professionals worldwide report that they are overwhelmingly frustrated, skeptical and confused by the new set of rules for off-balance-sheet financing, characterizing it as an unnecessary and costly burden on an otherwise healthy market. Moreover, the regulation fails to adequately tackle the problem of corporate malfeasance that it was originally designed to address, market participants said."[37] "Respondents were consistently incisive, reproachful and vehement in their criticism of FASB's year-long process of developing and vetting FIN 46, conveying in strong, pointed language their dissatisfaction with FASB's responsiveness to the securitization market and their disappointment with the final Interpretation, which many construe as an overly broad, "over-reaching" measure which is treating a very specific abuse (inadequate and misrepresentative corporate disclosure)."

A total of 470 participants from the U.S. and Europe participated in the survey. Most also felt that the market would adapt itself with new structures that simply cosmetically re-engineer SPEs to fall out of the definitions of the Interpretation.

Attaining sale treatment for accounts and loan treatment for taxes

One of the important objectives of any securitization structure is to see the best of both worlds – off-balance sheet treatment for books and loan treatment for taxation.

Off-balance sheet book treatment confers several advantages to the originator:

- The originator recognizes an immediate gain on sale thus boosting his reported profit.
- The originator de-recognizes the asset and the liability, thus reducing balance sheet size.
- As the assets are off the balance sheet, and the spread on securitization is booked as a fee income, the Return on Assets (RoA) increases.
- As the liability is off-the-balance-sheet, the D/E ratio is not affected/comes down.
- The regulatory capital requirements (a percentage of risk-weighted assets) are reduced as the assets are put off the balance sheet.

At the same time, an originator would prefer that the securitization transaction should be treated as a debt for tax purposes, as:

- Tax on income, that is, the gain made on securitization, will not be applicable immediately but will be apportioned over the period of time; and
- Withholding tax will be applicable, at the rate applicable to normal debt transactions.

Given the fact that the tax principles and accounting principles are not harmonious, it is possible to achieve both the above objectives. The structure required for tax purposes to qualify as a debt would depend on the provisions of the relevant law. Or, there might be a specific tax provision dealing with securitizations as already incorporated in several countries.

Accounting for revolving asset securitizations

A revolving asset securitization involves a current transfer of assets and a forward agreement to replace amortizing assets with new assets. For example, for credit card receivables, a set of existing obligations is transferred currently, and when they are paid off, the amount received is released to the originator to buy fresh receivables.

The special features of rollover securitization from an accounting viewpoint will be first that the gain to be recognized as a sale will be limited to the pool of receivables transferred at the present time. The gain on transfers to be made over time will be recognized as, and when, the transfers are made. [FAS 140.78]

Two, to the extent there is a promise to transfer receivables generated over time, there is a forward contract by the originator. The forward should be accounted for as per the usual accounting policy relating to forwards [FAS 133/IAS 39]. The essential principle of accounting for forwards is that the value of the forward, at zero time, is zero, but over time, as the receivables will be contracted at the rates prevailing over time, there is a gain or loss depending upon whether the rates have moved up or down. The common practice is to compute the fair value of the IO strip as the difference between the portfolio yield and the base rate of the transaction. See more in Chapter 8 on Credit Card Receivables.

FAS 140.79 makes clarifying provisions about transfer of assets to master trusts. A master trust is essentially a pot that holds assets for the seller, until such time and to the extent the assets are transferred to the issuer vehicle. Therefore, mere transfer of assets to a master trust is not a sale to give rise to any sale accounting.

Accounting for future flow securitization

Future flow securitization represents transfer of assets that do not exist, such as the sale of ticket receivables by an airline or rentals by a property company.

Here again, there is no current transfer of assets; legally, a future flow securitization is an agreement to transfer receivables as and when the receivables are brought into existence. As securitization accounting standards are concerned with securitization of financial assets, future flow securitizations are not covered by securitization standards until the assets in question come into existence.

There is no question of any sale treatment to future flow securitization; as the assets transferred do not exist on the books, there is nothing that can be taken off the books. All future flow securitizations will, therefore, be given a loan-type treatment to begin with, and the amount raised will be taken as sale proceeds for assets only when the relevant assets are created. For practical purposes, accounting for securitized future flows is, therefore, no different from accounting for an income that has not been transferred.

Receivables under financial leases and hire-purchase contracts are pre-committed assets of the originator and are usually on the balance sheet. Receivables under operating leases are usually accounted for by the originator as income as and when received. Therefore, securitization of financial leases will qualify for an off-balance sheet treatment based on the other conditions discussed earlier. However, securitization of operating leases will be given a financial treatment.

Investor accounting

An investor holds a securitization investment as a regular investment. Investments are financial assets, and their accounting is governed by accounting standards prevalent on accounting for financial instruments. For jurisdictions following international accounting standards, the relevant standard is IAS 39, and the relevant U.S. accounting standards are FAS 115 and FAS 133, the latter relating to derivatives and embedded derivatives.

Broadly, investors may recognize financial assets held by them in four categories – originated loans, hold-to-maturity (HTM) investments, available-for-sale (AFS) assets, and trading assets and trading liabilities. Originated loans are loans originated by the enterprise, not the case with securitization investments even if they are pass-throughs. HTM investments are those intended to be held to the maturity of the instrument. AFS assets are those not necessarily intended to be held to maturity – that is, at an opportune time, they may be sold. Trading assets are assets held with short-term trading intent.

The income-recognition rules are different for each of these classes. Briefly, HTM investments are carried at amortized value; amortization may be done at a consistent rate, usually the IRR of the asset. AFS assets are required to be fair-valued at each reporting date, but the gain or loss on fair valuation may be taken to shareholders' equity. Trading assets are to be marked to market, that is, fair-valued at all times.

HTM characterization of assets has certain problems of rigidity, and therefore, accountants would categorize securitization investments, based on intent, as either AFS or trading assets. In either case, the mark-to-market valuation will be required.

How do investors mark a securitization investment to market? If trading quotations are available, that is the best, most reliable method. If not, fair valuation has to be done by applying one of the several valuation models. DCF models are normally used, applying a discounting rate appropriate to the rating of the investment, after projecting cash flows based on the portfolio performance as reflected by regular servicing information.

EITF 99-20

This interpretation was issued by the FASB for specific credit and prepayment sensitive investments in securitization transactions. EITF 99-20 remained one of the most controversial issues in accounting for securitization transactions in 2001 and was responsible for massive write downs by a number of securitizers, particularly in the CDO segment.

EITF 99-20 was effective in the first quarter of 2001.

EITF 99-20 was essentially meant as guidance to Para 14 of FAS 125. Para 14 of the FAS 125 related to investor accounting for retained interests in securitizations that are credit or prepayment-sensitive. It said: "Interest-only strips, loans, other receivables, or retained interests in securitizations that can contractually be pre-paid or otherwise settled in such a way that the holder would not recover substantially all of its recorded investment shall be subsequently measured like investments in debt securities classified as available-for-sale or trading under Statement 115, as amended by this Statement."

Para 14 of SFAS 140 also provided: "Interest-only strips, retained interests in securitizations, loans, other receivables, or other financial assets that can contractually be pre-paid or otherwise settled in such a way that the holder would not recover substantially all of its recorded investment, except for instruments that are within the scope of Statement 133, shall be subsequently measured like investments in debt securities classified as available-for-sale or trading under Statement 115, as amended (paragraph 362)."

It was apparent that this portion of the statement applied only:

- To retained interests in securitizations, and not if someone other than the securitizer makes investment in such piece. For example, the accounting for the originator retaining a B piece in a securitization was covered by this Para, but accounting by an external investor buying such piece was not covered by this Para, but rather covered by SFAS 115.
- This Para applied only where the retained interest could be contractually pre-paid or could be settled without the originator recovering the whole of his recorded investment.

However, EITF 99-20 did not merely amplify the requirements of the Standard, but carried it further when it provided that the requirements of EITF 99-20 would be applicable to both investors and originators.

Scope of EITF 99-20

EITF 99-20 covers all securitization tranches [ABS, MBS, CDO that are accounted for under FAS 140] other than the following:

- As for the credit-sensitive test, those either guaranteed by the government or GSEs or entities with similar credit quality, or those adequately covered by subordinations to ensure that the possibility of credit loss is remote; and
- As for the prepayment sensitive test, agency POs are not covered; IOs or other instruments with prepayment risk are covered.

Entities that are covered include investors as well as originators.

Under FAS 115, the investor could hold an investment either as an HTM or AFS. For HTM, amortized cost treatment is permitted under the accounting standards. However, EITF 99-20 applies even in cases when the investment is HTM.

Periodic income accounting under EITF 99-20

Periodic income of yield to be recognized on a retained component is the IRR of the investment. The IRR at inception is determined by equating the initial apportioned carrying amount (for the originator) or the actual cost (for a purchaser) with the expected cash flows from the retained component. At the inception of the deal, this IRR would supposedly equal the rate at which the fair value of the retained piece was computed.

At any balance sheet date, the amortized cost is:

Initial investment (as above)
Add: accreted yield as per IRR calculated above
Less: actual amount received, whether interest or principal
Less: any impairment discussed later.

The IRR will be periodically and prospectively recomputed based on the amortized cost and the revised estimates of future cash flows.

When is impairment required?

Impairment is required where the estimate of future cash flows is revised – either with reference to time or with reference to the amount being received. This will require a recomputation of fair values that will result in an impairment.

Other securitization accounting standards

The Institute of Chartered Accountants of India issued a Guidance Note on Accounting for Securitization, which essentially adopts the IAS 39 approach. The accounting standard is applicable only for securitization transactions, and not for a bilateral sale of financial assets.

The Guidance Note provides for de-recognition as well as computation of gain on sale in certain conditions. The conditions for gain on sale are as under:

- Surrender of control by the originator
- Acquisition of control by the SPE
- De-recognition not allowed where:
  - Creditors of the originator can attach the transferred assets
  - SPE does not have the right to deal with the transferred assets
  - Originator has a call option and obligation

Illustration of the computation of gain on sale is given, modeled on FASB 140 illustrations.

The guidance note also provides for accounting by SPVs and requires assets and liabilities to be recorded by the SPV. Notably, the accounting standard is silent on pass-through transactions. However, as a matter of basic accounting principle, if a transaction amounts to a pass-through, the SPV conveys beneficial interest to the investors and has, therefore, no assets left to record on its balance sheet. More importantly, the beneficial interest certificates are not certificates of liability, but merely an indication of beneficial interest.

The accounting standard clarifies that for future flow transactions, the financing will be recorded as a liability on the balance sheet.

Securitization accounting standards have been adopted in several other countries – Canada, Japan and Malaysia. Most of these have adopted either the FAS 140 approach or the IAS 39 approach, with modifications to suit local requirements. In Chapter 3 on review of different markets, we have also included, wherever available, information on accounting standards.

Servicing rights and QSPE amendments

As noted before, securitization accounting standards, particularly the U.S. standards, have constantly been in a flux. There are at least two areas identified by standard-setters, in which comprehensive amendments are expected. At the time of this writing, a new standard FAS 156 had been issued to make amendments to FAS 140 relating to servicing assets/liabilities, and amendments are also expected as regards qualifying SPEs.

FAS 156 on servicing assets/liabilities

In March 2006, the FASB issued FAS 156, a new standard that makes amendments to FAS 140 relating to servicing assets and liabilities (references below to "servicing assets" also include references to "servicing liabilities"). The major thrust of the amendments is to require initial valuation of servicing assets/liabilities and fair values, and to permit, but not insist upon fair valuation of servicing assets and liabilities on an ongoing basis. In addition, comprehensive disclosure requirements regarding servicing assets (liabilities) have also been imposed. The amendments are effective for financial years beginning on or after September 15, 2006.

One of the amendments is to introduce a definition of "undivided interests" defined as "Partial legal or beneficial ownership of an asset as a tenant in common with others. The proportion owned may be pro rata, for example, the right to receive 50 percent of all cash flows from a security, or non–pro rata, for example, the right to receive the interest from a security while another has the right to the principal." The definition seems similar to the concept of fractions of financial assets in IAS 39. The concept of undivided interests replaces the existing concept of "retained interests."

While fair valuation of servicing assets is required at inception, the subsequent valuation may be done based on either amortization method, or fair valuation method. The amortization is to be done based on fair value of the servicing assets. In case of the fair valuation option, changes in fair value are to be taken to current earnings. The election is to be done based on each "class" of securitized assets, and applied consistently over such class. "Classes" are identified based on either market information required for fair valuation, or entity's own risk management methods, or both.

The comprehensive disclosure requirements are as under:

For all servicing assets

(1) Management's basis for determining its classes of servicing assets
(2) A description of the risks inherent in servicing assets and, if applicable, the instruments used to mitigate the income statement effect of changes in fair value of the servicing assets. (Disclosure of quantitative information about the instruments used to manage the risks inherent in servicing assets, including the fair value of those instruments at the beginning and end of the period, is encouraged but not required.)

(3) The amount of contractually specified servicing fees (as defined in the glossary), late fees, and ancillary fees earned for each period for which results of operations are presented, including a description of where each amount is reported in the statement of income.

For servicing assets subsequently measured at fair value:

(1) For each class of servicing assets, the activity in the balance of servicing assets (including a description of where changes in fair value are reported in the statement of income for each period for which results of operations are presented), including, but not limited to, the following:

   (a) The beginning and ending balances
   (b) Additions (through purchases of servicing assets, assumptions of servicing obligations, and servicing obligations that result from transfers of financial assets)
   (c) Disposals
   (d) Changes in fair value during the period resulting from:
       (i) Changes in valuation inputs or assumptions used in the valuation model
       (ii) Other changes in fair value and a description of those changes
   (e) Other changes that affect the balance and a description of those changes

(2) A description of the valuation techniques or other methods used to estimate the fair value of servicing assets. If a valuation model is used, the description shall include the methodology and model validation procedures, as well as quantitative and qualitative information about the assumptions used in the valuation model (for example, discount rates and prepayment speeds). (An entity that provides quantitative information about the instruments used to manage the risks inherent in the servicing assets, is also encouraged, but not required, to disclose a description of the valuation techniques, as well as quantitative and qualitative information about the assumptions used to estimate the fair value of those instruments.)

For servicing assets subsequently amortized in proportion to and over the period of estimated net servicing income or loss and assessed for impairment or increased obligation:

(1) For each class of servicing assets and servicing liabilities, the activity in the balance of servicing assets (including a description of where changes in the carrying amount are reported in the statement of income for each period for which results of operations are presented), including, but not limited to, the following:

   (a) The beginning and ending balances
   (b) Additions (through purchases of servicing assets, assumption of servicing obligations, and servicing obligations that result from transfers of financial assets)

(c) Disposals

(d) Amortization

(e) Application of valuation allowance to adjust carrying value of servicing assets

(f) Other-than-temporary impairments

(g) Other changes that affect the balance and a description of those changes

(2) For each class of servicing assets, the fair value of recognized servicing assets at the beginning and end of the period if it is practicable to estimate the value

(3) A description of the valuation techniques or other methods used to estimate fair value of the servicing assets. If a valuation model is used, the description shall include the methodology and model validation procedures, as well as quantitative and qualitative information about the assumptions used in the valuation model (for example, discount rates and prepayment speeds). (An entity that provides quantitative information about the instruments used to manage the risks inherent in the servicing assets, is also encouraged, but not required, to disclose a description of the valuation techniques as well as quantitative and qualitative information about the assumptions used to estimate the fair value of those instruments.)

(4) The risk characteristics of the underlying financial assets used to stratify recognized servicing assets for purposes of measuring impairment in accordance with Paragraph 63

(5) The activity by class in any valuation allowance for impairment of recognized servicing assets – including beginning and ending balances, aggregate additions charged and recoveries credited to operations, and aggregate write-downs charged against the allowance – for each period for which results of operations are presented.

If the entity has securitized financial assets during any period presented and accounts for that transfer as a sale, for each major asset type (for example, mortgage loans, credit card receivables and automobile loans):

(1) Its accounting policies for initially measuring the retained interests that continue to be held by the transferor, if any, and servicing assets, if any, including the methodology (whether quoted market price, prices based on sales of similar assets or prices based on valuation techniques) used in determining their fair value

(2) The characteristics of securitizations (a description of the transferor's continuing involvement with the transferred assets, including, but not limited to, servicing, recourse, and restrictions on retained interests that continue to be held by the transferor) and the gain or loss from sale of financial assets in securitizations

(3) The key assumptions used in measuring the fair value of retained interests that continue to be held by the transferor and servicing assets, if any, at the time of securitization (including, at a minimum, quantitative

information about discount rates, expected prepayments including the expected weighted-average life of prepayable financial assets, and anticipated credit losses, if applicable)

(4) Cash flows between the securitization SPE and the transferor, unless reported separately elsewhere in the financial statements or notes (including proceeds from new securitizations, proceeds from collections reinvested in revolving-period securitizations, purchases of delinquent or foreclosed loans, servicing fees and cash flows received on interests that continue to be held by the transferor).

If the entity has retained interests that continue to be held by the transferor in securitized financial assets that it has securitized or servicing assets or servicing liabilities relating to assets that it has securitized, at the date of the latest statement of financial position presented, for each major asset type (for example, mortgage loans, credit card receivables and automobile loans):

(1) Its accounting policies for subsequently measuring those retained interests, including the methodology (whether quoted market price, prices based on sales of similar assets and liabilities or prices based on valuation techniques) used in determining their fair value

(2) The key assumptions used in subsequently measuring the fair value of those interests (including, at a minimum, quantitative information about discount rates, expected prepayments including the expected weighted-average life of prepayable financial assets, and anticipated credit losses, including expected static pool losses, if applicable)

(3) A sensitivity analysis or stress test showing the hypothetical effect on the fair value of those interests (including any servicing assets) of two or more unfavorable variations from the expected levels for each key assumption that is reported under (2) above independently from any change in another key assumption, and a description of the objectives, methodology and limitations of the sensitivity analysis or stress test

(4) For the securitized assets and any other financial assets that it manages together with them:
   (a) The total principal amount outstanding, the portion that has been de-recognized, and the portion that continues to be recognized in each category reported in the statement of financial position, at the end of the period
   (b) Delinquencies at the end of the period
   (c) Credit losses, net of recoveries, during the period (Disclosure of average balances during the period is encouraged, but not required.)

Amendments regarding QSPEs

The issues expected to be taken by these amendments are:

1. Reconsideration of the concept of requiring that an entire financial asset first be transferred to a qualifying SPE (or other entity that is not consolidated with the transferor) to meet the requirements for sale accounting for

transactions that involve transfers of portions of financial assets unless the resulting portions meet the definition of a participating interest; it appears this issue is the same as the fractional approach rule of the IAS 39.

2. Consideration of issues related to definition of a participating interest, including:
   a. Definition of recourse;
   b. Whether to permit a transferor to allocate third-party guarantees, such as government guarantees, unequally among participating interest holders;
   c. Whether to permit any other exceptions to the allocation of cash flows with unequal priority, recourse, or subordination; and
   d. How to define an individual financial asset for purposes of applying the requirements of Paragraph 8A.

3. Consideration of issues related to isolation, including:
   a. Whether to require that a hypothetical legal analysis be performed that considers the impact of direct and indirect support arrangements by an affiliate of the transferor, including entities included in the consolidated group of the parent entity of the transferor, as if the support were provided by the transferor in evaluating whether transferred assets are isolated;
   b. Whether isolation for transactions involving a qualifying SPE requires a hypothetical true sale analysis of arrangements between a beneficial interest holder and the transferor, its consolidated affiliates, or its parent, as if those arrangements were made by the transferor directly [Paragraph 9(e)];
   c. Whether to clarify what is meant by "any arrangement or agreement made in connection with a transfer;"
   d. Whether implementation guidance provided by Paragraphs 27A and 27B should be expanded to include jurisdictions that do not require a "true sale" of financial assets to place transferred financial assets beyond the reach of a transferor, its affiliates and agents, including in bankruptcy or receivership;
   e. Whether the specific implementation guidance provided for jurisdictions under U.S. bankruptcy law should be included in the implementation guidance provided in Paragraphs 27A and 27B; and
   f. Whether Board members would object to Paragraphs 9(d) and 9(e) being merged under Paragraph 9(a).

4. Consideration of issues related to the application of Paragraph 9(b), including:
   a. The application of Paragraph 9(b) to transferors' beneficial interests;
   b. The application of Paragraph 9(b) to multi-step transfers, including those involving bankruptcy-remote entities;
   c. The application of Paragraph 9(b) to transfers from one qualifying SPE to another qualifying SPE.

5. Consideration of whether a qualifying SPE must issue more than 10% of the fair value of its beneficial interests to outside parties to meet the requirements of a qualifying SPE.

6. Reconsideration of provisions for initial measurement of a transferor's beneficial interest.

7. Consideration of whether to provide additional measurement guidance on the subsequent measurement of a transferor's beneficial interest.

8. Consideration of the removal of Paragraph 40 in its entirety and the modification of Paragraph 35(c) 2 of Statement 140 to remove the restriction on a qualifying SPE from holding derivative financial instruments that do not pertain to the beneficial interests of the qualifying SPE.

9. Reconsideration of the restrictions on rollovers of beneficial interests.

10. Consideration of whether to provide additional guidance on the permitted activities of a qualifying SPE.

11. Consideration of permitting a qualifying SPE to hold certain equity instruments such as titling trust certificates and money-market investments.

12. Reconsideration of the effective date and transition provisions.

Appendix 1

Extracts from FRS 5: UK Accounting Standards Board

Application note on securitization:

Application Note D – Securitized assets

Features

D1 Securitization is a means by which providers of finance fund a specific block of assets rather than the general business of a company. The assets that have been most commonly securitized in the UK are household mortgages. Other receivables such as credit card balances, hire purchase loans and trade debts are sometimes securitized, as are non-monetary assets such as property and stocks. This Application Note applies to all kinds of assets.

D2 The main features are generally as follows:

(a)   The assets to be securitized are transferred by a company (the 'originator') to a special purpose vehicle (the 'issuer') in return for an immediate cash payment. Additional deferred consideration may also be payable.

(b)   The issuer finances the transfer by the issue of debt, usually tradeable loan notes or commercial paper (referred to below as 'loan notes'). The issuer is usually thinly capitalized and its shares placed with a party other than the originator – charitable trusts have often been used for this purpose – with the result that the issuer is not classified as a subsidiary of the originator under company legislation. In addition, the major financial and operating policies of the issuer are usually predetermined by the agreements that constitute the securitization, such that neither the owner of its share capital nor the originator has any significant continuing discretion over how it is run.

(c)   Arrangements are made to protect the loan noteholders from losses occurring on the assets by a process termed 'credit enhancement'. This may take the form of third party insurance, a third party guarantee of the issuer's obligations or an issue of subordinated debt (perhaps to the originator); all provide a cushion against losses up to a fixed amount.

(d)   The originator is granted rights to surplus income (and, where relevant, capital profits) from the assets – i.e. to cash remaining after payments of amounts due on the loan notes and other expenses of the issuer. The mechanisms used to achieve this include: servicing or other fees; deferred sale consideration; 'super interest' on amounts owed to the originator (e.g. subordinated debt); dividend payments; and swap payments.

(e)   In the case of securitized debts, the originator may continue to service the debts (i.e. to collect amounts due from borrowers, set interest rates, etc.). In this capacity, it is referred to as the 'servicer' and receives a servicing fee.

(f)   Cash accumulations from the assets (e.g. from mortgage redemptions) are reinvested by the issuer until loan notes are repaid. Any difference between the interest rate obtained on reinvestments and that payable on the loan notes will normally affect the originator's surplus under (d) above. The terms of the loan notes may provide for them to be redeemed as assets are realized, thus minimizing this reinvestment period. Alternatively, cash accumulations may be invested in a 'guaranteed investment contract' that pays a guaranteed rate of interest (which may be determined by reference to a variable benchmark rate such as LIBOR) sufficient to meet interest payments on the loan notes. Another alternative, used particularly for short-term debts arising under a facility (e.g. credit card balances), is a provision for cash receipts (here from card repayments) to be reinvested in similar assets (e.g. new balances on the same credit card accounts). This reinvestment in similar assets will occur for a specified period only, after which time cash accumulations will either be used to redeem loan notes or be reinvested in other more liquid assets until loan notes are repaid.

(g)   In certain circumstances, for example if tax changes affect the payment of interest to the noteholders or if the principal amount of loan notes outstanding declines to a specified level, the issuer may have an option to buy back the notes. Such repurchase may be funded by the originator, in which case the originator will re-acquire the securitized assets.

D3 From the originator's standpoint, the effect of the arrangement is usually that it continues to obtain the benefit of surplus income (and, where relevant, capital profits) from the securitized assets and bears losses up to a set amount. Usually, however, the originator is protected from losses beyond a limited amount and has transferred catastrophe risk to the issuer.

Analysis

D4 The purpose of the analysis is to determine the following:

(a)   the appropriate accounting treatment in the originator's individual company financial statements. There are three possible treatments:

  (i)   to remove the securitized assets from the balance sheet and show no liability in respect of the note issue, merely retaining the net amount (if any) of the securitized assets less the loan notes as a single item ('de-recognition');

  (ii)   to show the proceeds of the note issue deducted from the securitized assets on the face of the balance sheet within a single asset caption (a 'linked presentation'); or

> (iii) to show an asset equivalent in amount to the gross securitized assets within assets, and a corresponding liability in respect of the proceeds of the note issue within creditors (a 'separate presentation');

(b) The appropriate accounting treatment in the issuer's financial statements. Again there are three possible treatments: de-recognition, a linked presentation or a separate presentation; and

(c) The appropriate accounting treatment in the originator's groups accounts. This involves issues of:

> (i) whether the issuer is a subsidiary or (more usually) a quasi-subsidiary of the originator such that it should be included in the originator's group accounts; and
>
> (ii) where the issuer is a quasi-subsidiary, whether a linked presentation should be adopted in the originator's consolidated accounts.

Each of these is considered in more detail below.

(a) Originator's individual accounts

Overview of basic principles

D5 The principles for determining the appropriate accounting treatment in the originator's individual company financial statements are similar to those applied in both Application Note C – 'Factoring of debts', and in Application Note E – 'Loan transfers'. It is necessary to establish what asset and liability (if any) the originator now has, by answering two questions:

(a) whether the originator has access to the benefits of the securitized assets and exposure to the risks inherent in those benefits (referred to below as 'benefits and risks'); and

(b) whether the originator has a liability to repay the proceeds of the note issue.

Where the originator has transferred all significant benefits and risks relating to the securitized assets and has no obligation to repay the proceeds of the note issue, de-recognition is appropriate; where the originator has retained significant benefits and risks relating to the securitized assets, but there is absolutely no doubt that its downside exposure to loss is limited, a linked presentation should be used; and in all other cases a separate presentation should be adopted.

D6 The benefits and risks relating to securitized assets will depend on the nature of the particular assets involved. In the case of interest-bearing loans, the benefits and risks are described in paragraph E6 of Application Note E – 'Loan transfers'.

De-recognition

D7 De-recognition (i.e. ceasing to recognize the securitized assets in their entirety) is appropriate only where the originator retains no significant benefits and no significant risks relating to the securitized assets.

D8 While the commercial effect of any particular transaction should be assessed taking into account all its aspects and implications, the presence of all of the following indicates that the originator has not retained significant benefits and risks, and de-recognition is appropriate:

(a)   the transaction takes place at an arm's length price for an outright sale;
(b)   the transaction is for a fixed amount of consideration and there is no recourse whatsoever, either implicit or explicit, to the originator for losses from whatever cause. Normal warranties given in respect of the condition of the assets at the time of the transfer (e.g. in a mortgage securitization, a warranty that no mortgages are in arrears at the time of transfer, or that the income of the borrower at the time of granting the mortgage was above a specified amount) would not breach this condition. However, warranties relating to the condition of the assets in the future or to their future performance (e.g. that mortgages will not move into arrears in the future) would breach the condition. Other possible forms of recourse are set out in paragraph 83; and
(c)   the originator will not benefit or suffer if the securitized assets perform better or worse than expected. This will not be the case where the originator has a right to further sums from the vehicle that vary according to the eventual value realized for the securitized assets. Such sums could take a number of forms, for instance deferred consideration, a performance-related servicing fee, payments under a swap, dividends from the vehicle, or payments from a reserve fund.

Where any of these three features is not present, this indicates that the originator has retained benefits and risks relating to the securitized assets and, unless these are insignificant, either a separate presentation or a linked presentation should be adopted.

D9 Whether any benefit and risk retained are 'significant', should be judged in relation to those benefits and risks that are likely to occur in practice, and not in relation to the total possible benefits and risks. Where the profits or losses accruing to the originator are material in relation to those likely to occur in practice, significant benefit and risk will be retained. For example, if for a portfolio of securitized assets of 100, expected losses are 0.5 and there is recourse to the originator for losses of up to 5, the originator will have retained all but an insignificant part of the downside risk relating to the assets (as the originator bears losses of up to ten times those expected to occur). Accordingly, in this example, de-recognition will not be appropriate and either a linked presentation or a separate presentation should be used.

Linked Presentation

D10 A linked presentation will be appropriate where, although the originator has retained significant benefits and risks relating to the securitized assets, there is absolutely no doubt that its downside exposure to loss is limited to a fixed monetary amount. A linked presentation should be used only to the extent that there is both absolutely no doubt that the noteholders' claim extends solely to the proceeds generated by the securitized assets, and there is no provision for the originator to re-acquire the securitized assets in the future. The conditions that need to be met in order for this to be the case are set out in Paragraph 27 and explained in Paragraphs 81–86. When interpreting these conditions in the context of a securitization the following points apply:

condition (a) (specified assets) – a linked presentation should not be used where the assets that have been securitized cannot be separately identified. Nor should a linked presentation be used for assets that generate the funds required to repay the finance only by being used in conjunction with other assets of the originator;

condition (d) (agreement in writing that there is no recourse; such agreement noted in the financial statements) – where the noteholders have subscribed to a prospectus or offering circular that clearly states that the originator will not support any losses of either the issuer or the noteholders, the first part of this condition will be met. Provisions that give the noteholders recourse to funds generated by both the securitized assets themselves and third party credit enhancement of those assets would also not breach this condition;

condition (f) (no provision for the originator to repurchase assets) – where there is provision for the originator to repurchase only part of the securitized assets (or otherwise to fund the redemption of loan notes by the issuer), the maximum payment that could result should be excluded from the amount deducted on the face of the balance sheet. Where there is provision for the issuer (but not the originator) to redeem loan notes before an equivalent amount has been realized in cash from the securitized assets, a linked presentation may still be appropriate provided there is no obligation (legal, commercial or other) for the originator to fund the redemption (e.g. by repurchasing the securitized assets).

D11 These conditions should be regarded as met notwithstanding the existence of an interest rate swap agreement between the originator and the issuer, provided all the following conditions are met:

(a)   the swap is on arm's length, market-related terms and the obligations of the issuer under the swap are not subordinated to any of its obligations under the loan notes;

(b)   the variable interest rate(s) that are swapped are determined by reference to publicly quoted rates that are not under the control of the originator;

(c)   at the time of transfer of the assets to the issuer, the originator had hedged exposures relating to these assets (either individually or as part of a larger portfolio) and entering into the swap effectively restores the hedge position left open by their transfer. Thereafter, where the hedging of the originator's exposure under the swap requires continuing management, any necessary adjustments to the hedging position are made on an ongoing basis. This latter requirement will be particularly relevant where any prepayment risk involved cannot be hedged exactly.

The conditions for a linked presentation should also be regarded as met, notwithstanding the existence of an interest rate cap agreement between the originator and the issuer, provided that, in addition to all the above conditions being met, the securitization was entered into before September 22, 1994.

D12 In the case of securitizations of revolving assets that arise under a facility (e.g. credit card balances), a careful analysis of the mechanism for repaying the loan notes is required in order to establish whether or not conditions (b) and (f) in Paragraph 27 are met. For such assets, the loan notes are usually repaid from proceeds received during a period of time (referred to as the 'repayment period'). The proceeds received in the repayment period will typically comprise both repayments of securitized balances existing at the start of the repayment period and repayments of balances arising subsequently (for example arising from new borrowings in the repayment period on the credit card accounts securitized). In order that the conditions for a linked presentation are met, it is necessary that loan notes are repaid only to the extent that there have been, in total, cash collections from securitized balances existing at the start of the repayment period equal to the amount repaid on the loan notes. This is necessary in order to ensure that the issuer is allocated its proper share of any losses.

D13 It will also be necessary to analyze carefully any provisions that enable the originator to transfer additional assets to the issuer in order to establish whether or not conditions (b) and (f) in Paragraph 27 are met. To the extent that the originator is obliged to replace poorly performing assets with good ones, there is recourse to the originator and a linked presentation should not be used. However, where there is merely provision for the originator to add new assets to replace those that have been repaid earlier than expected (and thus to 'top up' the pool in order to extend the life of the securitization), the conditions for a linked presentation may still be met. For a linked presentation to be used, it is necessary that the addition of new assets does not result in either the originator being exposed to losses on the new or the old assets, or in the originator re-acquiring assets. Provided these features are present, the effect is the same as if the noteholders were repaid in cash and they immediately reinvested that cash in new assets, and a linked presentation may be appropriate.

Separate Presentation

D14 Where the originator has retained significant benefits and risks relating to the securitized assets and the conditions for a linked presentation are not met, the originator should adopt a separate presentation.

Multi-originator programs

D15 There are some arrangements where one issuer serves several originators. The arrangement may be structured such that each originator receives future benefits based on the performance of a defined portfolio of assets (typically those it has transferred to the issuer and continues to service or use). For instance, in a mortgage securitization, the benefits accruing to any particular originator may be calculated as the interest payments received from a defined portfolio of mortgages, less costs specific to that portfolio (e.g. insurance premiums, payments for credit facilities), less an appropriate share of the funding costs of the issuer. The effect is that each originator bears significant benefits and risks of a defined pool of mortgages, whilst being insulated from the benefits and risks of other mortgages held by the issuer. Thus each originator should show that pool of mortgages for which it has significant benefits and risks on the face of its balance sheet, using either a linked presentation (if the conditions for its use are met), or a separate presentation.

(a) Issuer's accounts

D16 The principles set out in paragraphs D5 to D15 for the originator's individual financial statements also apply to the issuer's financial statements. In a securitization, the issuer usually has access to all future benefits from the securitized assets (in the case of mortgages, to all cash collected from mortgagors) and is exposed to all their inherent risks. Hence, de-recognition will not be appropriate. In addition, the noteholders usually have recourse to all the assets of the issuer (these may include the securitized assets themselves, the benefit of any related insurance policies or credit enhancement, and a small amount of cash). In this situation, the issuer's exposure to loss is not limited, and use of a linked presentation will not be appropriate. Thus, the issuer should usually adopt a separate presentation.

(b) Originator's group financial statements

D17 Assuming a separate presentation is used in the issuer's financial statements but not in those of the originator, the question arises whether the relationship between the issuer and the originator is such that the issuer should be included in the originator's group financial statements. The following considerations are relevant:

(a) Where the issuer meets the definition of a subsidiary, it should be consolidated in the normal way by applying the relevant provisions of company legislation and FRS 2. Where the issuer is not a subsidiary, the provisions of this FRS regarding quasi-subsidiaries are relevant.

(b) In order to meet the definition of a quasi-subsidiary, the issuer must give rise to benefits for the originator that are in substance no different from those that would arise were the entity a subsidiary. This will be the case where the originator receives the future benefits arising from the net assets of the issuer (principally the securitized assets less the loan notes). It is not necessary that the originator could face a possible benefit outflow equal in amount to the issuer's gross liabilities. Strong evidence of whether this part of the definition is met is whether the originator stands to suffer or gain from the financial performance of the issuer.

(c) The definition of a quasi-subsidiary also requires that the issuer is directly or indirectly controlled by the originator. Usually securitizations exemplify the situation described in Paragraphs 34 and 98, in that the issuer's financial and operating policies are in substance predetermined (in this case under the various agreements that constitute the securitization). Where this is so, the party possessing control will be the one that has the future benefits arising from the issuer's net assets.

D18 It follows that it should be presumed that the issuer is a quasi-subsidiary where either of the following is present:

(a)   the originator has rights to the benefits arising from the issuer's net assets; i.e. to those benefits generated by the securitized assets that remain after meeting the claims of noteholders and other expenses of the issuer. These benefits may be transferred to the originator in a number of forms, as described in Paragraph D2 (d); or

(b)   the originator has the risks inherent in these benefits. This will be the case where, if the benefits are greater or less than expected (e.g. because of the securitized assets realizing more or less than expected), the originator gains or suffers.

D19 In general, where an issuer's activities comprise holding securitized assets and the benefits of its net assets accrue to the originator, the issuer will be a quasi-subsidiary of the originator. Conversely, the issuer will not be a quasi-subsidiary of the originator where the owner of the issuer is an independent third party that has made a substantial capital investment in the issuer, has control of the issuer, and has the benefits and risks of its net assets.

D20 Where the issuer is a quasi-subsidiary of the originator, the question arises whether a linked presentation should be adopted in the originator's group financial statements. It follows from paragraph 37 that where the issuer holds a single portfolio of similar assets, and the effect of the arrangement is to ring-fence the assets and their related finances in such a way that the provisions of Paragraphs 26 and 27 are met from the point of view of the group, a linked presentation should be used.

Required Accounting

Originator's individual financial statements

De-recognition

D21 Where the originator has retained no significant benefits and risks relating to the securitized assets and has no obligation to repay the proceeds of the note issue, the assets should be removed from its balance sheet, and no liability shown in respect of the proceeds of the note issue. A profit or loss should be recognized, calculated as the difference between the carrying amount of the assets and the proceeds received.

Linked presentation

D22 Where the conditions for a linked presentation are met, the proceeds of the note issue (to the extent they are non-returnable) should be shown deducted from the securitized assets on the face of the balance sheet within a single asset caption. Profit should be recognized and presented in the manner set out in Paragraphs 28 and 87–88.

The following disclosures should be given:

(a) a description of the assets securitized;
(b) the amount of any income or expense recognized in the period, analyzed as appropriate;
(c) the terms of any options for the originator to repurchase assets or to transfer additional assets to the issuer;
(d) the terms of any interest rate swap or interest rate cap agreements between the issuer and the originator that meet the conditions set out in Paragraph D11;
(e) a description of the priority and amount of claims on the proceeds generated by the assets, including any rights of the originator to proceeds from the assets in addition to the non-recourse amounts already received;
(f) the ownership of the issuer; and
(g) the disclosures required by conditions (c) and (d) in Paragraph 27.

D23 Where an originator uses a linked presentation for several different securitizations that all relate to a single type of asset (i.e. all the assets, if not securitized, would be shown within the same balance sheet caption), these may be aggregated on the face of the balance sheet. However, securitizations of different types of asset should be shown separately. In addition, details of each material arrangement should be provided in the notes to the financial statements, unless they are on similar terms and relate to a single type of asset, in which case they may be disclosed in aggregate.

Separate presentation

D24 Where neither de-recognition nor a linked presentation is appropriate, a separate presentation should be adopted, i.e. a gross asset (equal in amount to the gross amount of the securitized assets) should be shown on the balance sheet of the originator within assets, and a corresponding liability in respect of the proceeds of the note issue shown within liabilities. No gain or loss should be recognized at the time the securitization is entered into (unless adjustment to the carrying value of the assets independent of the securitization is required). Disclosure should be given in the notes to the financial statements of the gross amount of assets securitized at the balance sheet date.

Issuer's financial statements

D25 The requirements set out in Paragraphs D21–D24 for the originator's individual financial statements also apply to the issuer's financial statements. For the reasons set out in Paragraph D16, in most cases the issuer will be required to adopt a separate presentation, in which case the provisions of Paragraph D24 will apply.

Originator's consolidated financial statements

D26 Where the issuer is a quasi-subsidiary of the originator, its assets, liabilities, profits, losses and cash flows should be included in the originating group's consolidated financial statements. Where the provisions of Paragraph

D20 are met, a linked presentation should be applied in the consolidated financial statements and the disclosures required by Paragraphs D22 and D23 should be given; in all other cases a separate presentation should be used and the disclosure required by Paragraph D24 should be given.

Indications that de-recognition is appropriate (securitized assets are not assets of the originator)	Indications that a linked presentation is appropriate	Indications that separate presentation is appropriate (securitized assets are assets of the originator)
Originator's individual accounts		
Transaction price is arm's length price for an outright sale	Transaction price is not arm's length price for an outright sale	Transaction price is not arm's length price for an outright sale
Transfer is for a single, non-returnable fixed sum.	Some non-returnable proceeds received, but originator has rights to further sums from the issuer, the amount of which depends on the performance of the securitized assets.	Proceeds received are returnable, or there is a provision whereby the originator may keep the securitized assets on repayment of the loan notes or re-acquire them.
There is no recourse to the originator for losses.	There is either no recourse for losses, or such recourse has a fixed monetary ceiling.	There is or may be full recourse to the originator for losses, e.g.: the originator's directors are unable or unwilling to state that it is not obliged to fund any losses; noteholders have not agreed in writing that they will seek repayment only from funds generated by the securitized assets.
Originator's consolidated financial statements		
Issuer is owned by an independent third party that has made a substantial capital investment, has control of the user, and has benefits and risks of its net assets.	Issuer is a quasi-subsidiary of the originator, but the conditions for a linked presentation are met from the point of view of the group.	Issuer is a subsidiary of the originator.

Notes

1 A U.S. Senate Subcommittee that investigated some structured finance transactions of Enron [U.S. Senate Permanent Subcommittee On Investigations Report On Fishtail, Bacchus, Sundance, And Slapshot: Four Enron Transactions Funded And Facilitated By U.S. Financial Institutions January 2, 2003] had the following to say: "The cumulative evidence from the three Subcommittee hearings demonstrates that some U.S. financial institutions have been designing, participating in, and profiting from complex financial transactions explicitly intended to help U.S. public companies engage in deceptive accounting or tax strategies. This evidence also shows that some U.S. financial institutions and public companies have been misusing structured finance vehicles, originally designed to lower financing costs and spread investment risk, to carry out sham transactions that have no legitimate business purpose and mislead investors, analysts, and regulators about companies' activities, tax obligations, and true financial condition."

2 Letter dated July 28, 2003.

3 See letter dated July 28, 2003: "If FASB does not accept our key suggestions (or make other appropriate changes), the resulting guidance will not be operational, and we urge FASB to consider a new start. In Part VI of this letter we discuss the matched presentation, which we view as an attractive alternative in those circumstances."

4 See chapter on RMBS.

5 "Current literature (referring to FAS 77) uses legal form as the principal discriminating criterion as to whether a transaction should be treated as a sale or collateralized loan. Many have suggested that economic substance should be used to make this distinction. A transaction could be classified as a sale when most of the economic benefits and rights, as defined by prescribed rules, have been relinquished. This approach has been used in other areas, such as lease accounting via SFAS No. 13. Such an approach is objective, thus promoting comparability. The attest function is also well structured under this approach. An auditor has only to determine if 1) the triggering prescribed conditions exist and 2) if the applied accounting treatment is dictated by the prescription." Kane, Gregory D: "Accounting for securitized assets," *CPA Journal*, July 1995.

6 As regards the risk-rewards approach, the FASB apprehended difficulties in implementation. "The number of different risks and rewards would vary depending on the definitions used. Questions would arise about whether each identified risk and reward should be substantially surrendered to allow de-recognition, whether all risks should be aggregated separately from all rewards, and whether risks and rewards should somehow be offset and then combined for evaluation ... Moreover, viewing each financial asset as an indivisible unit is contrary to the growing practice in financial markets of disaggregating individual financial assets or pools of financial assets into components." [Para 101].

7 For example, Kravitt, Jason: in *Introduction to Securitization* at http://www.securitization.net/knowledge/transactions/introduction.asp: "The new financial components approach is an attempt to break out of these conceptual traps as all securitizations will divide risks and rewards among both the transferor and transferee leaving such transactions difficult to characterize with certainty by those who believe that risks or rewards should be the determinative factors. The idea behind the financial components approach is that a pool of assets and their attendant liabilities can be divided into an unending succession of conceptual risks and benefits. Rather than agonizing over how much of each must be transferred and

to whom, find a sale (or a financing) of all of the assets and liabilities at issue, why not recognize that the transferor and transferee may each record on their own balance sheets those aspects of the assets that they control, and those liabilities for which they are liable. This will create balance sheets that are less misleading than balance sheets constructed on the basis of an all-or-nothing formulation that by definition must be at least partially misleading."

8   See, for instance, a comment letter by Deloitte Touche to FASB dated September 24, 1999: "We believe that the linked approach is a simpler alternative to the current accounting model, given its complexities. The linked approach permits proceeds that qualify for the linked presentation to be netted against the portion of the financial assets sold. This approach results in the de-recognition of the financial assets in the balance sheet to the extent of proceeds and it avoids considerable difficulties. We believe a linked presentation is conceptually consistent with a definition of control that focuses on control over benefits. In many instances, particularly when the transferor has provided some form of credit enhancement, the transferee acquires an interest in the cash flows of an asset and the transferor transfers its rights to those cash flows. However, the asset itself generally cannot be physically separated into the portion sold and the portion retained to enable each party to control its portion of the underlying asset. As a result, control over the underlying asset is shared and relegated to provisions in trust documents or other agreements that are acceptable to both the transferor and transferee. In instances in which control is specified by these agreements, it is particularly difficult to assess it without focusing on the control over benefits. The linked presentation recognizes the transfer of the rights to cash flows of the underlying asset, but the retention of benefits."

9   We have also noted why, in form countries, an approach solely based on a legal nature may lead to very unhappy results.

10 Thus, various methods such as equitable transfers, participations and declaration of trusts may lead to off-balance sheet treatment.

11 There is an exception under IAS 39 – see later.

12 Text of FAS 140 has been revised by FAS 156, in March 2006. See later in this chapter.

13 This could also be understood in option pricing language. The value of any option is the difference between its market price and strike value. If the strike price is the same as the market value, the option always has a zero value and should, therefore, be disregarded.

14 An Exposure Draft has already been issued to revise the prevailing QSPE conditions and amendments to the standard may be expected in 2006. See later for discussion of the Exposure Draft.

15 See later in this chapter.

16 That is not the end. The FASB has already decided to bring another amendment to FAS 140 to further amplify these conditions. At the time of writing this [December 2005], the FASB had come out with a revised exposure draft on which the comment process had ended and a new standard is expected in 2006. For latest developments, see Vinod Kothari's website at http://vinodkotharicom/accountingissues.htm.

17 Rosenblatt, Johnson and Mountain: *Securitization Accounting*, 7th edition, p. 11.

18 For discussion on an Exposure Draft on Hybrid Financial Assets that deals with the derivatives held by a QSPE, see later in this chapter.

19 Rosenblatt, Johnson and Mountain: *Securitization Accounting*, 7th edition, p. 12.

20 See later in this chapter.

21 Refer to the heading What if an SPE is not a QSPE?

22 Splitting a single asset into components and looking at whether some of them have been transferred might sound internally fallacious. For example, if one has an asset with r% return, which is funded with a non-recourse loan with $(r - x)$% cost, should the funding profit to the extent of x% be brought on books? Why should the components approach be applicable only where the asset has been transferred, if each component can be looked as an asset? Note that IAS 39 lays down that the whole of a financial asset, and not a part of it, may be treated as a financial asset, except if certain conditions are satisfied.

23 Para 61 puts it thus: "Servicing of mortgage loans, credit card receivables, or other financial assets commonly includes, but is not limited to, collecting principal, interest, and escrow payments from borrowers; paying taxes and insurance from escrowed funds; monitoring delinquencies; executing foreclosure if necessary; temporarily investing funds pending distribution; remitting fees to guarantors, trustees, and others providing services; and accounting for and remitting principal and interest payments to the holders of beneficial interests in the financial assets. Servicing is inherent in all financial assets; it becomes a distinct asset or liability only when contractually separated from the underlying assets by sale or securitization of the assets with servicing retained or separate purchase or assumption of the servicing."

24 FASB Concepts Statement No. 7, *Using Cash Flow Information and Present Value in Accounting Measurements*, discusses the use of present value techniques in measuring the fair value of an asset (or liability) in paragraphs 42–54 and 75–88. The Board believes that an expected present value technique is superior to traditional "best estimate" techniques, especially in situations in which the timing or amount of estimated cash flows is uncertain, as is often the case for retained interests in transferred financial assets. Concepts Statement 7 also discusses in Paragraph 44 the steps needed to complete a proper search for the "rate commensurate with the risk" in applying the traditional technique.

25 FASB Statement of Concepts no. 7: Using Cash flow Information and Present Value in Accounting Measurements.

26 Para 23 of FASB Statement of Concepts no. 7: Using Cash flow Information and Present Value in Accounting Measurements.

27 As disclosure standards require disclosure of assumptions used in valuing retained interest, including discounting rate, one can see the disclosures in published accounts of several major securitization entities. Some examples are shown later in this chapter.

28 The risk-free rate of discounting is used because the risk of variations has been factored in the probabilities. However, another possible argument is in the expected valuation approach, the risk of the prepayment rates/default rates being higher or lower than those used in the base case assumption has been discounted. The risk inherent in the asset class itself has not been factored. Therefore, the appropriate discounting rate in the expected valuation is not the risk-free discounting rate, but the APR of the pool.

29 For more on computation of option-adjusted spread, see the relevant chapter.

30 The spread of the probabilities is just based on conjecture, but there is a method that goes behind it. By a normal distribution rule, probabilities concentrate around the most likely scenario, obviously the base assumption. The dispersion there will have probabilities reducing based on how far the dispersion is from the average.

31 For further discussion on this, refer to Chapter 9.
32 Public domain document at http://www.ge.com/ar2004/note_29.jsp, last visited December 18, 2005.
33 While future interest itself is not a recognized asset yet, the value of the composite asset may be split between value of principal and value of interest.
34 Bankruptcy remoteness is an issue only in the event of bankruptcy, while accounts are prepared under the going-concern presumption.
35 A subordinated investment or over-collateralization may be viewed as funded guarantees – guarantees along with investment of cash or collateral by the seller.
36 See Vinod Kothari's website at http://vinodkothari.com/secedit.htm.
37 S&P: *Is FIN 46 the Wrong Solution to the Right Problem? Securitization Professionals Share Their Views in Standard & Poor's SF Market Opinion Survey*, April 11, 2003.

Chapter 28

Regulation AB: Securities Regulation on Asset-backed Securities

I n April 2004, the SEC came out with proposal for a new set of regulations for public offers of asset-backed securities. Effective March 8, 2005, the U.S. Securities Exchange Commission has promulgated regulations applicable to issue of mortgage and asset-backed securities, called Regulation AB (17 CFR 229). The rules impose registration, disclosure and regular reporting requirements for asset-backed securities. The rules are applicable for any initial offer made after December 31, 2005.

To understand the scope and implications of Regulation AB, it might be helpful to understand the broad regime for issue of securities under the SEC regulations.

Overview of SEC regulatory regime

The genesis of the regulation is sec. 5 of the Securities Exchange Act, which provides that unless a registration statement is in effect as to a security, it shall be unlawful for any person, directly or indirectly, to sell such security through the use or medium of any prospectus or otherwise; or to carry or cause to be carried any such security for the purpose of sale or for delivery after sale.

Section 4 provides exceptions to the generic prohibition. Sec 4 (2) provides that private placements do not have to comply with Sec. 5. Regulation D provides general conditions for issue and sale of securities for which a registration statement has not been filed under sec. 5. Securities issued by way of a private placement are regarded as "restricted securities;" their resale is not permitted except under a registration statement or in accordance with exemptions under rule 144 or rule 144A. Rule 144 essentially imposes a one-year holding period unless the securities are resold by way of another private placement and continue to be restricted in the hands of the buyer. Thus, private placements under sec. 4 (2) and regulation D do not result in creation of a public market in securities, and hence do not concern the SEC's explicit scope of operation.

Rule 144A provides another exemption – for resale of securities to qualified institutional buyers (QIBs). QIBs include insurance companies, investment companies, small business investment companies, employee benefit plans, employee benefit trusts, business development companies, savings and loans associations, foreign equivalents and investment advisers.

Another offering or sale not requiring registration with the SEC is Regulation S, which relates to offers outside the U.S.

Scope of Regulation AB

As Regulation AB does not affect exempted transactions, offers seeking exemption under rule 144A or Regulation S will not be concerned with Regulation AB.

Prior to the issue of Regulation AB, issue of asset-backed securities was covered by filings under Form S-3[1] (applicable only for issuers satisfying certain conditions). Form S-3 was amended in 1992 to include investment grade ABS, but the definition of "asset-backed securities" under the rule was still restrictive.

Broadened definition of "asset-backed securities"

Among other things, Regulation AB adopts a modernized definition of asset-backed securities that seeks to cover most of the prevalent collateral classes. The revised definition is:

> Asset-backed security means a security that is primarily serviced by the cash flows of a discrete pool of receivables or other financial assets, either fixed or revolving, that by their terms convert into cash within a finite time period, plus any rights or other assets designed to assure the servicing or timely distributions of proceeds to the security holders; provided that in the case of financial assets that are leases, those assets may convert to cash partially by the cash proceeds from the disposition of the physical property underlying such leases.

The details backing up the definition are provided in the rules. The following are significant points:

- The issuer of the securities must not be an investment company and must be a special purpose entity "limited to passively owning or holding the pool of assets, issuing the asset-backed securities supported or serviced by those assets, and other activities reasonably incidental thereto."
- The pool does not consist of NPAs; delinquent receivables are permitted to the extent of no more than 50% by dollar volume.
- As the definition above suggests, in case of lease transactions, apart from the identifiable receivables, the securities may also be paid from out of residual value. However, the residual dependence should not exceed 65% in value of the pool in case of motor vehicles, and 50% in other cases.

- The "discrete pool" requirement of the definition will not be taken as having been breached in the following cases:

  o Master trusts
  o Prefunding period
  o Revolving period of up to 3 years.

What is not covered in "ABS"

- As is quite obvious from the definition above, synthetic transactions are not covered as they are not backed by a pool of receivables or other financial assets.[2]
- On the face of it, future flows-based transactions and intellectual property receivables transactions will also not fall under the definition as they cannot be said to be backed by "discrete pools."
- Based on the requirement that the issuer of securities should be a passive entity owning the assets, neither an investment company nor someone who actively manages the assets, it may be said that managed CDOs will also not fall under the rule.
- As discussed above, private placements to QIBs that claim exemption under rule 144A are not covered by Regulation AB.

What if it is not covered by Regulation AB?

It seems that if the asset-backed securities are not covered by the definition in Regulation AB, they will have to take the rule 144A route.

In the past, rule 144A issues have been numerous by number, but small in percentage. Data for the first 9 months of 2005 reveal that the percentage share of rule 144A offerings is quite small:

Table 28.1   Worldwide Securitization Volume   −09/30/2005

	9M-05 issuance ($Mil.)	No. of deals	Market share (%)	9M-04 issuance ($Mil.)	No. of deals	Market share (%)	'05-'04 change (%)
U.S. Public ABS	$569,848.9	580	40.0	$471,029.2	576	43.1	21.0
U.S. Rule 144A ABS	46,009.8	251	3.2	50,378.5	270	4.6	-8.7
U.S. Public MBS	362,506.2	493	25.4	231,622.9	422	21.2	56.5
U.S. Private ABS	3,300.0	2	0.2	1,035.7	2	0.1	218.6
Non-U.S. ABS and MBS	145,838.1	176	10.2	157,407.1	247	14.4	-7.3
U.S. Commercial MBS	113,800.1	80	8.0	70,379.8	77	6.4	61.7
Non-U.S. Commercial MBS	49,519.1	69	3.5	23,530.9	61	2.2	110.4
Worldwide CDOs	134,770.8	324	9.5	88,242.1	289	8.1	52.7
Worldwide Total	**1,425,593.1**	**1,975**	**100.0**	**1,093,626.1**	**1,944**	**100.0**	**30.4**

Source: Asset Backed Alert

Contents of the Prospectus

Regulation AB is mostly all about disclosures in the offer documents for asset-backed securities.

Cover page contents

These contents are essentially very close to what is commonly disclosed in offer documents. These include the sponsor/depositor,[3] and the issuing entity; the title of the securities with series number, if any; classes of securities; asset type being securitized; a statement that the securities are the obligations of the issuing entity and those of the sponsor, depositor or affiliates; aggregate principal amount of each class and the total aggregate principal, and in case the class carries no principal, a statement to that effect; interest rates applicable, and for floating rates, the reference rate and the spread; the distribution frequency; credit enhancement for each class and identify the enhancement provider.

Transaction summary and risk factors

Once again, the information required here is a systematic, structured set of what is most commonly found in most of the offer documents. The summary page will contain the following:

- Transaction participants, including the sponsor, depositor, issuer, trustee and servicers and their respective roles, any originator, and any significant obligor. "Significant obligor" means a debtor, property or lease implying a credit risk of 10% or more of the pool size.
- The pool assets, including material characteristics of the asset pool and cut-off date for establishing the composition of the asset pool.
- Basic terms of each class of securities offered. In particular:
  - Classes offered by the prospectus and any classes issued in the same transaction or residual or equity interests but not offered in the prospectus;
  - Interest rate or rate of return on each class offered;
  - Expected final and final scheduled maturity or principal distribution dates, if applicable, of each class of securities offered;
  - The denominations in which the securities may be issued;
  - Distribution frequency;
  - Summarize the flow of funds, that is, waterfall among the classes offered, classes not offered, and other fees and expenses to the extent necessary to understand the payment characteristics of the offered classes. This is essentially the cash flow waterfall;
  - Early amortization, liquidation, or other triggers that might alter the waterfall structure;
  - Any optional or mandatory redemption or termination features;
  - Credit enhancements and loss distribution, including any enhancement provider, and how losses not absorbed by the enhancement will be allocated to the securities;

- Any outstanding series or classes of securities backed by the same asset pool or otherwise have claims on the pool assets. Also, whether any additional series or classes of securities may be issued backed by the same asset pool, and circumstances under which those additional securities may be issued. Whether security holders' approval will be taken for such issuances and whether security holders will receive notice of such issuances;
- If the transaction will include prefunding or revolving periods, indicate:

    - The term or duration of the prefunding or revolving period;
    - For prefunding periods, the amount of proceeds deposited in the prefunding account;
    - For revolving periods, the maximum amount of additional assets that may be acquired during the revolving period, if applicable;
    - The percentage of the asset pool and any class or series of the asset-backed securities represented by the prefunding account or the revolving period, if applicable;
    - Any limitation on the ability to add pool assets;
    - The requirements for assets that may be added to the pool;
    - If pool assets can otherwise be added, removed or substituted (for example, in the event of a breach in representations or warranties regarding pool assets), summarize briefly the circumstances under which such actions can occur;

- Servicing fees: The amount or formula for calculating the fee, source thereof, and the priority in the waterfall.
- Federal income tax issues material to investors of each class of securities offered.
- Ratings and whether the issue or sale of any class is conditioned on the assignment of a rating by one or more rating agencies. If so, identify each rating agency and the minimum rating that must be assigned.

Sponsor/originator information

This section includes partly the most general and obvious inputs on the name of the sponsor and character of his organization. More specifically, the document should disclose how long the sponsor has been in securitization business, particularly for the assets in case. The document should disclose his experience in origination, acquiring and securitizing such assets, and information about his own assets of the type being securitized that may be material for understanding the performance of the pool. Also, it should disclose whether any prior securitizations organized by the sponsor have defaulted or experienced an early amortization triggering event.

The prospectus describes the sponsor's material roles and responsibilities in its securitization program, including whether the sponsor or an affiliate is responsible for originating, acquiring, pooling or servicing the pool assets, and the sponsor's participation in structuring the transaction.

A separate section requires similar details about the originator as well.

Static Pool Information[4]

One of the most significant parts of the disclosures is about the pool. While the caption used for this section is "static" pool information, the disclosures provide for both static and revolving pools. The requirement for the prior securitized pools, or for limited experience with prior securitizations, of originations by vintage years, requires fairly copious data.[5] The information requirements are as under:

- For amortizing, that is, static pools, the following:
  - Information regarding delinquencies, cumulative losses and prepayments for prior securitized pools of the sponsor for that asset type in case.
  - If the sponsor has less than three years of experience securitizing assets of the relevant type, then information as to delinquencies, cumulative losses and prepayments by vintage origination years regarding originations or purchases by the sponsor.
  - The information about prior securitized pools or vintage origination years should cover a time frame of 5 years or so long as the sponsor has been in relevant business, whichever is less. The prior securitized pool/vintage origination year information will present the following:
    - Delinquency, cumulative loss and prepayment data, by way of a time series, in periodic increments such as monthly or quarterly, over the life of the prior securitized pool or vintage origination year, with the most recent period being no later than 135 days of the date of first use of the prospectus.
    - Summary information for the original characteristics of the prior securitized pools or vintage origination years. This should include, with appropriate modifications for the nature of the collateral:
    - Number of pool assets; original pool balance; weighted-average initial pool balance; weighted-average interest or note rate; weighted-average original term; weighted-average remaining term; weighted-average and minimum and maximum standardized credit score or other applicable measure of obligor credit quality; product type; loan purpose; loan-to-value information; distribution of assets by loan or note rate; and geographic distribution information.

- For revolving asset master trusts, the document should provide data regarding delinquencies, cumulative losses, prepayments, payment rate, yield and standardized credit scores or other applicable measure of obligor credit quality in separate increments based on the date of origination of the pool assets. Subject to case-specific variations, the document should provide such data at a minimum in 12-month increments through the first five years of the account's life (e.g., 0–12 months, 13–24 months, 25–36 months, 37–48 months, 49–60 months and 61 months or more).

To prevent securities litigation based on the disclosures as above, the rules provide that information about previous securitized pools, securitized any time before January 1, 2006 (effective date of the Regulation), will not be deemed to be a part of the Prospectus.

Depositor

If the depositor is an entity different from the sponsor, information about the deposit, broadly on the lines of that for the sponsor, needs to be provided.

Issuing entity

Information about the issuer – the SPE – needs to be provided. SPEs have so far been the Da Vinci's Code of Wall Street law firms. However, rules require SPE information that is far more copious than currently being disclosed:

- Issuer's name and form of organization, including the state or other jurisdiction of organization of the SPV, with the governing documents filed as an exhibit.
- Permissible activities and restrictions on the activities of the issuing entity under its governing documents, including any restrictions on the ability to issue or invest in additional securities, to borrow money or to make loans to other persons. Provisions, if any, in the governing documents that might allow modification of the issuing entity's governing documents, including its permissible activities.
- Scope of the issuer's discretion as to administration of the asset pool or the asset-backed securities, and the person or persons authorized to exercise such discretion.
- Issuer's assets, apart from the pool assets; and liabilities, apart from the asset-backed securities. The fiscal year end of the issuer.
- If the issuing entity has executive officers, a board of directors or similar, information required by Items 401, 402, 403 and 404 of Regulation S-K. Item 401 requires detailed information about directors and executive officers, item 402 requires details of executive compensation, item 403 requires details of shareholding or beneficial interests held by such directors or executives, and item 404 requires details of related party transactions.
- Terms of any management or administration agreement regarding the issuing entity, with the copy filed as an exhibit.
- Capitalization of the issuing entity and the amount or nature of any equity contribution to the issuing entity by the sponsor, depositor or other party.
- Description of the sale or transfer of the pool assets to the SPE and creation (and perfection and priority status) of any security interest in favor of the SPE, the trustee, the asset-backed security holders or others, material terms of such agreements, with the copies of the agreements filed as an exhibit.
- If the pool assets are securities, the market price of the securities and the basis on which the market price was determined.

- If expenses incurred in connection with the selection and acquisition of the pool assets are to be payable from offering proceeds, the amount of such expenses. If such expenses are to be paid to the sponsor, servicer, depositor, issuing entity, originator, underwriter, or any affiliate of the foregoing, the type and amount of expenses paid to each such party.
- Bankruptcy remoteness: Any provisions or arrangements included to address the following issues:

  - Whether any security interests granted in connection with the transaction are perfected, maintained and enforced.
  - Whether declaration of bankruptcy, receivership or similar proceeding with respect to the issuing entity can occur.
  - Whether in the event of a bankruptcy, receivership or similar proceeding with respect to the sponsor, originator, depositor or other seller of the pool assets, the issuing entity's assets will become part of the bankruptcy estate or subject to the bankruptcy control of a third party.
  - Whether in the event of a bankruptcy, receivership or similar proceeding with respect to the issuing entity, the issuing entity's assets will become subject to the bankruptcy control of a third party.

- If any of the assets of the issuer are held by someone else on its behalf, the arrangements instituted to hold such pool assets on behalf of the issuing entity.

Servicer information

The Regulation provides for chunks of details about servicers. In fact, the need for servicing details may bring about significant structural changes in servicing practices. The information requirements are as under:

- Multiple Servicers: Where servicing is done by multiple servicers, (e.g., master servicers, primary servicers and special servicers)

  - Clear introductory description of the roles, responsibilities and oversight requirements of the entire servicing structure and the parties involved.
  - Identification of:
    - Each master servicer;
    - Each affiliated servicer;
    - Each unaffiliated servicer that services 10% or more of the pool assets;
    - Any other material servicer responsible for calculating or making distributions to holders of the asset-backed securities, performing workouts or foreclosures, or other aspect of the servicing upon which the performance of the pool assets or the asset-backed securities is materially dependent.
  - The information about servicers below will be provided for each servicer identified above who services 20% or more of the pool assets.

- Servicers information (as noted above, this is to be given for each of the servicers identified above, servicing 20% or more of the pool of assets):

- The servicer's name and organizational form.
- How long the servicer has been servicing assets, with general discussion of servicing of any type of assets, but details of experience in performing the tasks assigned in the transaction in case. Material information as to the size, composition and growth of the servicer's portfolio of serviced assets of the type in case should be provided.
- Any material changes to the servicer's policies or procedures in the servicing function during the past three years.
- Information regarding the servicer's financial condition.

- Servicing Agreements and Servicing Practices.

  - Material terms of the servicing agreement and the servicer's duties, with the servicing agreement filed as an exhibit.
  - The manner in which collections on the assets will be maintained, such as through a segregated collection account, and the extent of commingling of funds that occurs or may occur from the assets with other funds.
  - Any special or unique factors involved in servicing the specific type of assets, such as sub-prime assets, and the servicer's processes and procedures designed to address such factors.
  - Servicer advances – the extent to which the servicer is required or permitted to provide advances of funds, including interest or other fees charged for such advances and terms of recovery by the servicer of such advances. Statistical information on servicer advances on the pool assets and the servicer's overall servicing portfolio for the past three years.
  - The servicer's process for handling delinquencies, losses, bankruptcies and recoveries, such as through liquidation of the underlying collateral, note sale by a special servicer or borrower negotiation or workouts.
  - Any ability of the servicer to waive or modify any terms, fees, penalties or payments on the assets and the effect thereof on the potential cash flows from the assets.
  - If the servicer has custodial responsibility for the assets, the arrangements regarding the safekeeping and preservation of the assets, such as the physical promissory notes, and procedures for segregation thereof from other serviced assets. If no servicer has custodial responsibility for the assets, disclosure of the fact, and particulars of the custodian.
  - Any limitations on the servicer's liability under the transaction agreements.

- Back-up Servicing. The material terms regarding the servicer's removal, replacement, resignation or transfer, including:

  - Provisions for selection of a successor servicer and financial or other requirements that must be met by a successor servicer.
  - The process for transferring servicing to a successor servicer.
  - Provisions for payment of expenses associated with a servicing transfer and any additional fees charged by a successor servicer.
  - Arrangements, if any, already made regarding a back-up servicer, and identity thereof.

Trustees

Apart from general information about the trustee's name, organizational form and prior experience, the information required here will include the trustee's duties and responsibilities, both under the transaction documents as also under applicable law. In addition, the Prospectus shall disclose any actions required by the trustee, including whether notices are required to investors, rating agencies or other third parties, upon an event of default, potential event of default (and how defined) or other breach of a transaction covenant and any required percentage of a class or classes of asset-backed securities that is needed to require the trustee to take action.

Other details include limitations on the trustee's liability, trustee's indemnity and the priority of any such claims in the waterfall, any contractual provisions or understandings regarding the trustee's removal, replacement or resignation, as well as how the expenses associated and the expenses relating to such replacement.

Pool assets

Arguably the most copious item requiring information under the Regulation is the data and details about the pool assets. It is not that such information is currently missing, but the fact that there is a standardized inventory of information required would possibly make offer documents more complete as well as bulky.

By way of a general comment, the regulation provides that if the pool information would lead to better understanding when broken into distribution sub-groups, then such information broken into sub-groups should be provided. Wherever any averages or weighted averages are disclosed, the maximum and minimum should also be disclosed. The required information is:

- General Information regarding Pool Asset type and Selection Criteria:
  - A brief description of the type or types of pool assets to be securitized.
  - A general description of the material terms of the pool assets.
  - Underwriting criteria used to originate or purchase the pool assets, including any changes therein and exceptions.
  - The method and criteria by which the pool assets were selected for the transaction.
  - The cut-off date for pool composition.
  - If legal or regulatory provisions (such as bankruptcy, consumer protection, predatory lending, privacy, property rights or foreclosure laws or regulations) may materially affect pool asset performance or payments or expected payments on the asset-backed securities, identification thereof and their effects.
- Pool characteristics: Material characteristics of the asset pool, which, subject to case-specific variations, should include:
  - Number of each type of pool assets.

- Asset size, such as original balance and outstanding balance as of a designated cut-off date.
- Interest rate or rate of return, including types such as fixed and floating rates.
- Any capitalized or uncapitalized accrued interest.
- Age, maturity, remaining term, average life (based on different prepayment assumptions), current payment/prepayment speeds and pool factors, as applicable.
- Servicer distribution, if different servicers service different pool assets.
- If the pool is made of loans or similar receivables:
  - Amortization period.
  - Loan purpose (e.g., whether a purchase or refinance) and status (e.g., repayment or deferment).
  - Loan-to-value (LTV) ratios and debt service coverage ratios (DSCR), as applicable.
  - Type and/or use of underlying property, product or collateral (e.g., occupancy type for residential mortgages or industry sector for commercial mortgages).
- If receivables arise under a revolving account, such as credit cards:
  - Monthly payment rate.
  - Maximum credit lines.
  - Average account balance.
  - Yield percentages.
  - Type of asset.
  - Finance charges, fees and other income earned.
  - Balance reductions granted for refunds, returns, fraudulent charges or other reasons.
- Percentage of full-balance and minimum payments made.
- If the pool is made of commercial mortgage receivables, then:
  - For each mortgaged property:
    - The location and present use.
    - Net operating income and net cash flow information, and components thereof.
    - Current occupancy rates.
    - The identity, square feet occupied by and lease expiration dates for the three largest tenants.
    - The nature and amount of all other material mortgages, liens or encumbrances against such properties and their priority.
  - For each commercial mortgage, by dollar value, 10% or more of the asset pool, as measured as of the cut-off date:
    - Any proposed program for the renovation, improvement or development, estimated cost thereof and financing method.
    - The general competitive conditions to which such properties are or may be subject.

- Management of such properties.
- Occupancy rate expressed as a percentage for each of the last five years.
- Principal business, occupations and professions carried on in, or from the properties.
- Number of tenants occupying 10% or more of the total rentable square footage of such properties, principal nature of business of such tenant, principal provisions of the leases – rental per annum, expiration date and renewal options.
- The average effective annual rental per square foot or unit for each of the last three years.
- Prospective Schedule of the lease expirations for next 10 years stating the number of tenants, area in square feet, annual rentals represented by them and percentage of gross annual rentals.

- Whether the pool assets are secured or unsecured, and the nature of collateral.
- Standardized credit scores of obligors (such as FICO scores) and other information regarding obligor credit quality.
- Billing and payment procedures, including frequency of payment, payment options, fees, charges and origination or payment incentives.
- Information about the origination channel and origination process for the pool assets, such as originator information (and how acquired) and the level of origination documentation required.
- Geographic distribution, such as by state or other material geographic region. If 10% or more of the pool assets are or will be located in any one state or other geographic region, then any economic factors specific to the region that may have bearing on the pool cash flows.
- Other concentrations material to the asset type (e.g., school type for student loans).

- Delinquency and Loss Information for the pool including statistical information.
- Sources of Pool Cash flow: If the cash flow is to support the securities come from different sources (such as rentals and residual values for leases), provide the following information:

  - Disclose the specific sources of funds with percentage of each, with description of any assumptions, data, models and methodology used to derive such amounts.
  - Residual Value Information: If the pool has leases or other assets with a residual dependence, the following needs to be disclosed:

    - Estimation of residual value, including an explanation of any material discount rates, models or assumptions used, and who selected such rates, models or assumptions.
    - Any procedures or requirements incorporated to preserve residual values during the term of the lease, such as lessee responsibilities, prohibitions on subletting, indemnification or required insurance or guarantees.

- The procedures for realization of the residual values, and who would do so, including experience of the entity concerned.
- Whether the residual values are lessee-guaranteed and the percentage of such leases.
- Any lessor obligations under the leases, and potential effect on securities from failure by the lessor to perform its obligations.
- Statistical information regarding estimated residual values for the pool assets.
- Summary historical statistics on turn-in rates, if applicable, and residual value realization rates over the past three years, or such longer period as is material to an evaluation of the pool assets.
- The effect on security holders if not enough cash flow is received from the realization of the residual values; whether there are any provisions to address this contingency, and how any surplus cash flow will be allocated.

- Representations Warranties and Repurchase Obligations: Summary of any representations and warranties made concerning the pool assets by the sponsor, transferor, originator or other party to the transaction and the remedies available for a breach, such as repurchase obligations.
- Claims on Pool Assets: Description of any material direct or contingent claim of parties other than the holders of the asset-backed securities have on any pool assets. Also, any material cross-collateralization or cross-default provisions on the pool assets.
- Revolving Periods, Prefunding Accounts and Other Changes to the Asset Pool: If the transaction contemplates a prefunding or revolving period, the following information as to addition, removal and substitution of the assets needs to be provided, including situations where any additional securities (as for master trusts) may be issued:

- The term or duration of any prefunding or revolving period.
- For prefunding periods, the amount of proceeds to be deposited in the prefunding account.
- For revolving periods, the maximum amount of additional assets that may be acquired during the revolving period, if applicable.
- The percentage of the asset pool represented by the prefunding account or the revolving account.
- Triggers or events that would trigger limits on or terminate the prefunding or revolving period and the effects of such triggers.
- When and how new pool assets may be acquired during the prefunding or revolving period, and if, when and how pool assets can be removed or substituted.
- Any limits on the amount, type or speed with which pool assets may be acquired, substituted or removed.
- The acquisition or underwriting criteria for additional pool assets to be acquired during the prefunding or revolving period, including a description of any differences from the criteria used to select the current asset pool.

- Who has the authority to add, remove or substitute assets from the asset pool or to determine if such pool assets meet the acquisition or underwriting criteria. Also, disclosure of whether or not there will be any independent verification of such person's exercise of authority or determinations.
- Any requirements to add or remove minimum amounts of pool assets and any effects of not meeting those requirements.
- If applicable, the procedures and standards for the temporary investment of funds in a prefunding or revolving account pending use (including the disposition of gains and losses on pending funds) and a description of the financial products or instruments eligible for such accounts.
- The circumstances under which funds in a prefunding or revolving account will be returned to investors or otherwise disposed of.
- Whether, and if so, how, investors will be notified of changes to the asset pool.

Significant obligors

The meaning of "significant obligor" has already been noted above. Briefly, it means an obligor with a 10% or more credit exposure or property constituting 10% or more of the security in value of the pool.

The generic information requirement for significant obligors includes names, organizational form, and the nature of concentration and material terms of the agreements with the obligors.

A specific requirement is provision of selected financial information for all significant obligors (for properties, only the net operating income from the property is required). The selected financial information is the same as that required under Item 301 of Regulation S-K. Item 301 of Regulation S-K requires disclosures of last 5 years' data as to:

> net sales or operating revenues; income (loss) from continuing operations; income (loss) from continuing operations per common share; total assets; long-term obligations and redeemable preferred stock (including long-term debt, capital leases, and redeemable preferred stock; and cash dividends declared per common share.

For significant borrowers involving 20% or more concentration, financial statements of the obligor need to be provided.

The obligor data as above need not be provided if the obligor in question is a sovereign.

If the obligor happens to be the issuer of an asset-backed security, then, in lieu of the financial data provided above, the information required under Regulation AB for such issuer may be filed. Likewise, for foreign obligors, the information provided by financial statements of the obligor may be reconciled to U.S. generally accepted accounting standards.

Transaction structure

This is yet another caption where detailed disclosures are required. The itemized list of required details is:

- Description of the Securities and Transaction Structure:
  - The types or categories of securities that may be offered, such as interest-weighted or principal-weighted classes (including IO (interest only) or PO (principal only) securities), planned amortization or companion classes or residual or subordinated interests.
  - The flow of funds for the transaction, including the payment allocations, rights and distribution priorities among all classes of securities, and within each class, with respect to cash flows, credit enhancement or other support features, any features that adjust the rate of return on the asset-backed securities, or preserve monies that will or might be distributed to security holders. In the flow of funds discussion, information as to the trapping of any cash (such as in reserve accounts, cash collateral accounts or expenses) and the purpose and operation of such requirements should be given.
  - The interest rate or rate of return on the securities and how such amounts are payable. Determination of the rate frequency of such determination. Clear information about any reference rate or rates should be given.
  - How principal, if any, will be paid on the asset-backed securities, including maturity dates, amortization or principal distribution schedules, principal distribution dates, formulas for calculating principal distributions from the cash flows and other factors that will affect the timing or amount of principal payments for each class of securities.
  - The denominations in which the securities may be issued.
  - Any changes to the transaction structure that would be triggered upon a default or event of default (such as a change in distribution priority among classes).
  - Any liquidation, amortization, performance or similar triggers or events, and the rights of investors or changes to the transaction structure thereupon.
  - Whether the servicer or other party is required to provide periodic evidence of the absence of a default or of compliance with the terms of the transaction agreements.
  - Overcollateralization or undercollateralization, if any.
  - Any provisions contained in other securities that could result in a cross-default or cross-collateralization.
  - Any minimum standards, restrictions or suitability requirements regarding potential investors in purchasing the securities or any restrictions on ownership or transfer of the securities.
  - Security holder vote required to amend the transaction documents and allocation of voting rights among security holders.

- Distribution Frequency and Cash Maintenance: Frequency of distribution dates for the asset-backed securities and the collection periods for the pool assets. Description of how cash held pending distribution or other uses is held and invested, and the length of time. Identification of the party or parties with access to cash balances and the authority to invest cash balances. Authority to make any decisions regarding the deposit, transfer or disbursement of pool asset cash flows and whether there will be any independent verification of the transaction accounts or account activity.
- Fees and Expenses: This requires a tabulation of an itemized list of all fees and expenses on the transaction. The list should indicate the purpose, the recipient, the source of funds for such fees or expenses, and the distribution priority. If not a fixed amount, the formula used to determine such fees or expenses should be disclosed. The information should also include circumstances in which such fees and expenses could be changed, and in particular, whether they can be changed without notice to security holders, for example, for a change in transaction party.[6]
- Treatment of Excess Cash flow: The information about disposal of residual cash flow also used to be garbed in uncertain language in the offer documents. The Regulation requires details as to disposition of residual or excess cash flow, also the identity of the person who owns any residual or retained interests to the cash flows if such person is affiliated with the sponsor, depositor, issuing entity or any interested party. Any requirements to maintain a minimum amount of excess cash flow or spread from, or retained interest in, the transaction should be disclosed, together with any actions that would be required or changes to the transaction structure that would occur if such requirements were not met. Any features or arrangements to facilitate a securitization of the excess cash flow or retained interest from the transaction should also be disclosed.
- Master Trusts: If the transaction is a part of a master trust structure, information regarding the additional securities that have been or may be issued needs to be given to understand their effect on the securities being offered, including the following:

  - Relative priority of such additional securities to the securities being offered and rights to the underlying pool assets and their cash flows.
  - Allocation of the cash flow from the asset pool and any expenses or losses among the various series or classes.
  - Terms under which such additional series or classes may be issued and pool assets increased or changed.
  - The terms of any security holder approval or notification of such additional securities.
  - Who has the authority to determine whether such additional securities may be issued, and conditions to such additional issuance, if any, and whether or not there will be an independent verification of such person's exercise of authority or determinations.

- Optional or Mandatory Redemption or Termination: If any class of the securities have an optional or mandatory redemption or termination feature, the following needs to be disclosed:
  - Terms for triggering the redemption or termination.
  - The identity of the party that holds the redemption or termination option or obligation, and if such party is an "affiliate" of the transaction players.
  - Redemption or repurchase price or formula for the same.
  - The procedures for redemption or termination, including any notices to security holders.
  - If the amount allocated to security holders is reduced by losses, the policy regarding any amounts recovered after redemption or termination.
  - Note that the rules provide that the title of any class of securities with an optional redemption or termination feature that may be exercised when 25% or more of the original principal balance of the pool assets still outstanding must include the word "callable," – this requirement for a master trust will be applicable with reference to 25% or more of the original principal balance of the particular series.
- Prepayment, Maturity and Yield Considerations: The document will describe models, including the related material assumptions and limitations, used for projecting cash flow patterns on the pool assets. To understand the impact of prepayment or payment rate:
  - The document will explain the degree to which each class of securities is sensitive to changes in the rate of payment on the pool assets (e.g., repayment or interest rate sensitivity), and the consequences of such change. The document will provide statistical information of such effects, such as the effect of prepayments on yield and weighted average life.
  - Special allocations of prepayment risks among the classes of securities, and whether any class protects other classes from the effects of the uncertain timing of cash flow.

Credit enhancements and enhancers

- Mechanisms of credit enhancement:
  - Any external credit enhancement, such as bond insurance, letters of credit or guarantees.
  - Any mechanisms to ensure that timely payments, such as liquidity facilities, lending facilities, guaranteed investment contracts, and minimum principal payment agreements.
  - Any credit-enhancing derivatives.
  - Any internal credit enhancement, such as subordination provisions, over-collateralization, reserve accounts, cash collateral accounts or spread accounts.
- Credit enhancers: If any entity or group of affiliated entities is liable or contingently liable for payments representing 10% or more of the cash flow supporting any offered class of asset-backed securities, the document will

provide information about such enhancers, including name, organizational form and character of the enhancer. If the enhancer provides up to 20% support to any offered class, financial data about such enhancer (with details similar as for "significant obligors") need to be provided. If any enhancer provides more than 20% support to any class of offered securities, the financial statements of the enhancer need to be appended.

Derivatives

If the transaction is backed by any derivatives, such as interest rate swaps or currency swaps, the details about such derivatives and derivatives counterparties need to be given. These details are substantively similar to those for credit enhancers above.

Tax Matters

The Prospectus should provide a clear and understandable summary of the tax treatment of the transaction as also of the securities – owning, purchasing and selling the same. If the tax consequences for different classes may be different, the same should be disclosed.

The substance of counsel's tax opinion, including identification of the material consequences upon which counsel has not been asked, or is unable, to opine should also be disclosed.

Legal proceedings

This caption requires disclosures as to legal proceedings which are fairly common.

Reports and accessing of SEC reports

This caption requires disclosure of regular investor reports, if any. In addition, the prospectus will disclose whatever reports will be filed with the SEC, and that the public may access and read the reports, as also the websites where reports filed with the SEC may be retrieved.

Affiliations and relationships

This item requires disclosure of any affiliations between any of these parties: Servicer; Trustee; Originator; Significant obligor; Enhancement or support provider; any other material parties related to the transaction. The last caption may include derivatives counterparties, not explicitly listed.

Rating information

Here, information as to ratings, rating agencies, and minimum ratings are to be given. Arrangements as to regular monitoring of the ratings are also to be disclosed.

Servicers' reports

By Sec. 240.13a-18 of the Regulation, the annual report on Form 10-K for any class of asset-backed securities must include a servicer's report regarding its assessment of compliance with the servicing criteria. The servicing criteria have been listed in item 1122 of Regulation AB. The servicer will make a statement of the service's responsibility for assessing compliance with the servicing criteria applicable to it; a statement that the servicer used the criteria listed below to assess the compliance; an assessment of the compliance and any material instance of non-compliance; and a statement that a public accounting firm has issued an attestation report on the party's assessment of compliance with the applicable servicing criteria as of and for the period ending the end of the fiscal year covered by the Form 10-K report.

By laying down the elaborate servicing criteria and enforcing their compliance, the regulators have, in fact, created tight control on the servicing function. The servicing function is evidently a very significant function for any asset-backed transaction, but servicing is not unique to securitization; servicing is inherent in every balance sheet transaction as well. In addition, it seems the SEC's servicing considerations have been concerned not only with the interest of the investors, but also with obligors' interest – for example, returning of money held in trust for the obligors, or not charging a late fee to an obligor unless there was a default on the part of the obligor. There are no corresponding controls or reporting requirements of how any originator deals with his own obligors in case the pools are not securitized.

The servicing criteria are as under:

Servicing criteria

- General Servicing Considerations:
  - Policies and procedures are instituted to monitor any performance or other triggers and events of default in accordance with the transaction agreements.
  - If any material servicing activities are outsourced to third parties, policies and procedures are instituted to monitor the third party's performance and compliance with such servicing activities.
  - Any requirements in the transaction agreements to maintain a back-up servicer for the pool assets are maintained.
  - A fidelity bond and errors and omissions policy is in effect on the party participating in the servicing function throughout the reporting period in the amount of coverage required by and otherwise in accordance with the terms of the transaction agreements.
- Cash Collection and Administration:
  - Payments on pool assets are deposited into the appropriate custodial bank accounts and related bank clearing accounts within two business days of receipt, (or such number of days specified in the transaction agreements).

- Disbursements made via wire transfer on behalf of an obligor or to an investor are made only by authorized personnel.
- Advances of funds or guarantees regarding collections, cash flows or distributions, and any interest or other fees charged for such advances, are made, reviewed and approved as specified in the transaction agreements.
- The related accounts for the transaction, such as cash reserve accounts or accounts established as a form of over-collateralization, are separately maintained (e.g., with respect to commingling of cash) as set forth in the transaction agreements.
- Each custodial account is maintained at a federally insured depository institution as set forth in the transaction agreements.
- Unissued checks are safeguarded so as to prevent unauthorized access.
- Reconciliations are prepared on a monthly basis for all asset-backed securities related bank accounts, including custodial accounts and related bank clearing accounts. These reconciliations:
  - Are mathematically accurate;
  - Are prepared within 30 calendar days after the bank statement cut-off date, or such other number of days specified in the transaction agreements;
  - Are reviewed and approved by someone other than the person who prepared the reconciliation; and
  - Contain explanations for reconciling items that are resolved in 90 calendar days of identification (or such other number of days specified in the transaction agreements).
- Investor Remittances and Reporting:
  - Reports to investors, including those to be filed with the Commission, are maintained in accordance with the transaction agreements and applicable Commission requirements. Specifically, such reports:
    - Are prepared in accordance with timeframes and other terms set forth in the transaction agreements;
    - Provide information calculated in accordance with the terms specified in the transaction agreements;
    - Are filed with the Commission as required by its rules and regulations; and
    - Agree with investors' or the trustee's records as to the total unpaid principal balance and number of pool assets serviced by the servicer.
  - Amounts due to investors are allocated and remitted in accordance with timeframes, distribution priority and other terms set forth in the transaction agreements.
  - Disbursements made to an investor are posted within two business days to the servicer's investor records, or such other number of days specified in the transaction agreements.
  - Amounts remitted to investors per the investor reports agree with canceled checks, or other form of payment, or custodial bank statements.

- Pool Asset Administration.

  - Collateral or security on pool assets is maintained as required by the transaction agreements or related pool asset documents.

  - Pool assets and related documents are safeguarded as required by the transaction agreements.

  - Any additions, removals or substitutions to the asset pool are made, reviewed and approved in accordance with any conditions or requirements in the transaction agreements.

  - Payments on pool assets, including any payoffs, made in accordance with the related pool asset documents are posted to the applicable servicer's obligor records maintained within two business days after receipt, (or such other number of days specified in the transaction agreements), and allocated to principal, interest or other items (e.g., escrow) in accordance with the related pool asset documents.

  - The servicer's records regarding the pool assets agree with the servicer's records with respect to an obligor's unpaid principal balance.

  - Changes with respect to the terms or status of an obligor's pool asset (e.g., loan modifications or re-agings) are made, reviewed and approved by authorized personnel in accordance with the transaction agreements and related pool asset documents.

  - Loss mitigation or recovery actions (e.g., forbearance plans, modifications and deeds in lieu of foreclosure, foreclosures and repossessions, as applicable) are initiated, conducted and concluded in accordance with the timeframes or other requirements established by the transaction agreements.

  - Records documenting collection efforts are maintained for delinquent assets in accordance with the transaction agreements, at least a monthly basis, or such other period specified in the transaction agreements, and log the entity's activities in monitoring delinquencies, including, for example, phone calls, letters and payment rescheduling plans in cases where delinquency is deemed temporary (e.g., illness or unemployment).

  - Adjustments to interest rates or rates of return for pool assets with variable rates are computed based on the related pool asset documents.

  - Regarding any funds held in trust for an obligor (such as escrow accounts):

    - Such funds are analyzed, in accordance with the obligor's pool asset documents, on at least an annual basis, or such other period specified in the transaction agreements;

    - Interest on such funds is paid, or credited, to obligors in accordance with applicable pool asset documents and state laws; and

    - Such funds are returned to the obligor within 30 calendar days of full repayment of the related pool asset, or such other number of days specified in the transaction agreements.

  - Payments made on behalf of an obligor (such as tax or insurance payments) are made on or before the related penalty or expiration dates, as indicated on the appropriate bills or notices for such payments, provided that such support has been received by the servicer at least 30 calendar days prior to these dates, or such other number of days specified in the transaction agreements.

- Any late payment penalties in connection with any payment to be made on behalf of an obligor are paid from the servicer's funds and not charged to the obligor, unless the late payment was due to the obligor's error or omission.
- Disbursements made on behalf of an obligor are posted within two business days to the obligor's records maintained by the servicer, or such other number of days specified in the transaction agreements.
- Delinquencies, charge-offs and uncollectible accounts are recognized and recorded in accordance with the transaction agreements.
- Any external enhancement or other support is maintained as set forth in the transaction agreements.

Servicing criteria under Regulation AB and those in the servicing agreement

The servicer's responsibilities as to servicing the pool are defined by the servicing agreement. The servicing criteria listed in the Regulation do not become the law of servicing – they are not intended to be, as the SEC's scope of operation is not to lay down laws as to how parties should conduct their business of dealing with their obligors. If one or more of the servicing functions, inherent in the servicing functions above, has not been assumed by the servicer in a particular transaction or is not relevant to the nature of the collateral, the servicer may make a disclosure as to the inapplicability of the particular point.

What if a servicing function has not been complied with by the servicer? Non-compliance is not a breach of SEC regulations; non-disclosure is. As far as the non-compliance is concerned, the consequences will be as per the servicing agreement between the parties.

Certifications and Sarbanes Oxley implications

The servicer makes a compliance statement. The statement is very strongly worded. It says: "The servicer has fulfilled all of its obligations under the agreement in all material respects throughout the reporting period," and if there has been a failure to fulfill any such obligation in any material respect, the servicer specifies each such failure known to such officer and the nature and status thereof.

Since these statements became a part of the 10-K reports, they have the same legal significance and sanctity, including the consequences of misstatement, as any other 10-K report. In addition, the person responsible for signing the Sarbanes-Oxley Section 302 Certification must certify that all of the reports on assessment of compliance with servicing criteria and their related attestation reports required to be included in the 10-K have been included as an exhibit to the 10-K, except as otherwise disclosed. Further, any material instances of non-compliance described in such reports must be disclosed in the 10-K.

Notes

1 Form S-3 is one of the several forms used for SEC registration statements relating to issue of securities. Form S-1 is the basic form applicable where no other form applies. S-3 is a brief form for shelf registration. For foreign issues, the forms are labeled as F-1, F-3, etc.

2 Synthetic transactions were excluded despite ISDA's representation – see ISDA representation dated March 8, 2005.

3 The term depositor in U.S. parlance typically means the entity that acquires receivables and transfers them to the issuer.

4 Static pool information of several leading securitization originators is available on their respective websites. Some illustrative website addresses are:
www.bearstearns.com/transactions/bsabs_i/2006-he1/
http://www.capitalone.com/staticpool
http://www.citimortgagembs.com
http://www.countrywidedealsdata.com?CWDD=01200601
http://www.gmacrfcstaticpool.com
http://www.gs.com/staticpoolinfo/
http://www.morganstanley.com/institutional/abs_spi
http://www.regab.c-bass.com
http://www.securitieslink.com/staticpools {wells fargo}
http://www.triadfinancial.com/absdata
http://www2.salliemae.com/SEC_investors/pdf/regab_noncons20060111.pdf

5 Also see SEC's guidance on Regulation AB, on SEC website at: www.sec.gov/interps/telephone/cftelinterps_regab.pdf, last visited April 11, 2006.

6 Reference seems to be the change of servicer.

Chapter 29

Regulatory and Economic Capital in Securitization

This chapter examines the regulatory capital issues in securitization. Other regulations, such as the Regulation AB imposed by U.S. securities regulators, have been discussed in Chapter 28. Regulatory issues primarily concern the treatment for securitization for the purpose of regulatory capital. **Regulatory capital** refers to the capital required by banking and financial supervisors as the minimum capital for financial intermediaries. We also examine the impact of securitization for the purpose of economic capital, that is, the minimum capital required for survival of a firm in a situation of uncertainty.

Regulatory capital issues are very important, understandably because one of the prime considerations, particularly for a bank, is the possible capital relief the bank receives. Capital relief has been a significant motivator for most international banks, as relieved capital allows banks to create more banking assets with a given amount of regulatory capital, and so, to put regulatory capital to more efficient use. Regulatory conditions determine whether, and to what extent, a bank's regulatory capital will be relieved due to securitization.

The regulator's concerns

Bank regulators internationally have fixed minimum capital requirements for banks. The issue of capital adequacy is considered directly relevant to the soundness and health of the banks, and consequently, the financial system. Therefore, it is one of the essential functions of bank regulators to ensure that banks have adequate capital.

Capital adequacy requirements are defined on a national or zonal level by bank regulators. Similar requirements are mostly applicable to non-banking financial intermediaries such as term lending institutions, finance companies and specialized financing bodies. The broad pattern of such regulations is set up as per an international convention under the aegis of the Bank for International Settlements (BIS).

The framework for bank capital adequacy that has existed for years was framed in accordance with a BIS concordat of 1988. However, from mid-1999 the BIS has been discussing a replacement of the 1988 regulations with a new standard, commonly referred to as BIS-II or Basle-II. If this is Basle II, the existing standard may be referred to as Basle I.

Both under Basle I and Basle II, the main concern of the regulators is adequacy of capital in the banking system. The need for minimum capital puts a limit on the extent to which banks can grow relative to their capital size. In other words, the power of banks to leverage their capital and raise borrowed money gets controlled. Capital is, after all, required for meeting risks, and one of the primary risks that banks undertake is credit risk, as the assets of banks are basically credit assets. Therefore, both Basle I and Basle II are concerned with laying down capital requirements for banks based on their risk-weighted assets.

Securitization reduces the capital requirement by removing the assets from the balance sheet of the bank; the consequence of sourcing of funds is not reflected as a liability. Thus, if a bank securitizes its assets, and the value of the assets consequently comes down, the bank's existing capital is relieved as there is a reduction in required capital, and so the bank is said to receive a **capital relief.**

The regulator's concern here is simple; securitization does not completely eliminate the risks a bank carries in its loan portfolio. On the other hand, it merely limits the risk to a defined amount, represented by the extent of recourse or collateral provided by the bank. Sometimes, even after securitization, the bank might maintain such obtrusive relation with the issuing vehicle that the legal transfer of the assets might seem illusory. Therefore, the primary concerns of bank regulators to securitization are:

- Is the legal transfer of assets accompanied by real transfer of risks and returns or has it made no difference to the substantive beneficial position of the bank?
- What is the extent of risk retained by the bank, and if so, what is the extent of risk capital required by the bank?
- Does the securitization transaction pose any unique liquidity risks, for example, due to the inherent early amortization triggers?
- How are the risks inherent in the asset to be allocated to different classes of structured securities?

Background of regulatory concerns

With increasing bank activities in securitization, bank regulators in all significant countries have issued guidelines for a regulatory approach to securitization. These have evolved over time and with the issuance of Basle II, which has an extensive section dealing with securitization, the regulatory capital treatment that was different seems to be converging.

The key to the regulators' concerns is the extent of risk that a securitization transaction either occasions or leaves unremoved. Capital is a cushion against risks; therefore, a regulator must first identify risks, and then provide for capital requirements to meet such risks.

The early regulatory guidelines specifically aimed at securitization have been primarily concerned with simple securitization structures. However, more recent guidelines have been concerned with several complex structures where risks are stripped, repackaged and transferred.

GAAP accounting and RAP accounting

It is notable that there are significant differences between the impact of securitization for normal bookkeeping purposes and regulatory purposes. In securitization parlance, these two treatments are referred to as **GAAP accounting** and **RAP** accounting. RAP does not refer to any separate set of books that banks have to maintain, but to the periodic reports that banks have to send on their income and financial condition.[1]

The formal concept of RAP accounting for banks in the U.S. for securitization transactions was removed effective January 1997, when FAS 125 became effective. However, as differences between capital relief standards and off-balance sheet standards persist, the word RAP accounting survives.

For GAAP purposes, a securitization may qualify for an off-balance sheet purpose and only the retained interests or acquired assets may be put on the balance sheet; however, for regulatory purposes, a bank may be required to have more, or less, capital than before based on the extent of risk retained. Thus, the fact that an exposure has been put off the balance sheet for reporting purposes is not enough for regulatory purposes.

Generally speaking, the requirements for capital relief are stricter than those for off-balance sheet reporting. Banking capital requirements are overwhelmingly based on risks and rewards, and formally, there is no "financial components" approach adopted for regulatory purposes.

Legal transfer and regulatory issues

Banking regulators are not greatly concerned with accounting treatment, but they are certainly clear that for an asset to be removed from the regulators' books there must be a legal transfer of the asset. A formal legal transfer is a pre-requisite for regulatory capital relief in most countries.

Risks and responsibilities in securitization

The following are the common risks and responsibilities highlighted in regulatory statements of most countries:

Basic minimum requirements

All regulatory statements highlight that the transaction in question must comply with basic meaning requirements. For instance, there must be a true sale; in addition, there must be transfer of risks and rewards.

Servicing responsibilities

Securitization shifts the role of the transferring bank from owner of assets to a servicer. The servicing role throws a burden on the resource and technology commitments of the bank to ensure efficient, error-free execution of servicing obligations. A bank that owns assets does servicing as well, but the moment the servicing role is split, it is like servicing the assets of others.

Information systems

Securitization throws incremental responsibilities on the servicing bank's information systems. There are regular reporting requirements as to investors, trustees and rating agencies. The ability to process to supply accurate information on the performance of underlying assets, in a timely manner, to investors, rating agencies and investment bankers is critical to a smooth securitization presence.

Risks inherent in securitization activities

Reputation risk   Reputation risk is significant to a bank as a successful presence in the banking business requires a bank not only to be sound but to be perceived as sound. Reputation is a key capital of banks on which they source their funding, both from capital markets and retail depositors. Although securitization often allows issuers to transfer loss exposure and remove assets from the balance sheet, transferring banks typically do not detach themselves completely from the transferred assets. In market perception, it is not the issuing special purpose entity that is taken to be the issuer; it is the bank. The assets, after all, have been originated by the bank and a bunch of poorly performing assets reflects on the underwriting standards of the bank.

This risk is obviously more pronounced for those issuers who intend to maintain a continuing presence in the securitization markets.

Strategic risk   Strategic risk is the risk arising from adverse business decisions or improper implementation of those decisions. One crucial strategic decision is whether securitization itself adds value to the bank. There are other related issues as to what assets to securitize, frequency and volumes. Before initiating a securitization transaction, management should perform a risk assessment that compares the strategic and financial objectives of securitization activities to the various risk exposures and resource requirements. In the present context, a bank management may also consider whether securitization of assets for cash is preferable or the synthetic securitization route is better. These decisions should be reviewed periodically.

Credit risk   It is important to understand how securitization will affect the credit risk inherent in a bank's credit assets. Securitization transfers or at least limits the credit risks of the transferring bank to the extent of the first loss retained by the bank. Thus, unexpected losses are transferred to the investors.

However, a bank must understand that securitization exposes the collection efficiency of the bank to public knowledge. Once the assets are securitized, regular servicing reports will go out to investors that will give, among other things, details of delinquent collections. Thus, the credit management of the bank will become obvious to the market at large.

To avoid this, banks quite often engage in some form of "cherry-picking" – selection of assets designed to ensure that delinquencies are minimized. This, however, has the effect of leaving a weaker bank at the end of the day. Regulatory norms in most countries require that assets must be randomly selected.

It is also important that the bank checks with reasonable frequency (a) the compliance with the agreed underwriting standards; and (b) the validity of the models based on which the default and repayment behavior of the collateral was projected.

Transaction risk   Transaction risk in the context of securitization is the inability of the parties to understand the needs of the transaction and therefore leave gaps in servicing or performance as per agreed terms or expected standards. Important servicing responsibilities are assumed by the transferring bank – transaction processing, collection and controls and investor reporting. Many of these reports require assimilation of data from several places. The existence of technology and the ability to understand the needs of the servicing obligation, process data are key components of the servicing transaction. Lapse in this performance may expose the bank to not only reputational risk but even legal liabilities.

Liquidity risk   Liquidity risk is the paucity of cash to meet liabilities that require timely payments. In a plain securitization transaction, the transferor's liquidity requirements are limited to meeting recourse or warranties, if any. However, liquidity risk also encompasses how a securitization plan fits into the overall liquidity management of the bank. If securitization is a one-time effort to raise funding, it leads to creation of a huge liquidity immediately as assets are transferred, but this also implies elimination of a regular source of inflow on which the bank had been dependent. This is just another side of a securitization transaction, as the transaction replaces future cash flows by cash flows today.

Another serious issue in liquidity risk is the inherent premature termination triggers. This is particularly true for revolving transactions. The bank builds a continued reliance on securitization as a source of rotating funding. Premature termination triggers are often hit when the bank passes through some tough time – e.g., when origination volumes fall. If rotating funding is withdrawn at this stage by an acceleration clause, the going gets tougher for the bank. Like the old adage about banking: Lend an umbrella when the sun shines, and ask for it back as it starts raining; securitization funding complies more strictly with this rule than most other modes of funding.

As early amortization triggers spell a strong reason for liquidity risk, bank management may create a suitable system for timely warning. For example, if origination volumes falling over three successive months hit the trigger, the bank may create a system that sounds an alarm one month ahead.

OCC, U.S. has listed several factors to consider in liquidity management:

- Number of transactions or volume of securities scheduled to amortize in any particular time period;
- Management's plans and timing for meeting future funding requirements,
- Existence of early amortization triggers;
- Analysis of viable alternatives if substantial amounts of liquidity are needed quickly; and
- Operational concerns associated with re-issuing securities.

Compliance risk   Compliance risk refers to risks of non-compliance with laws, regulations or other mandatory instruments, for example, guidelines of the financial regulator. Securitization transactions are becoming increasingly complicated, and there is a diverse array of statutory instruments affecting them. In many countries, securitization transactions attract stamp duties and value added taxes. It is important to seek proper legal counsel to ensure proper compliance.

Overview of Basle-II norms

The Bank for International Settlements is the international body which, among other things, frames international guidelines on the supervision of banks and financial institutions in the world. The extant risk-based capital standards are based on the 1988 concordat that has been implemented in most countries.

The process of revising and replacing the 1988 standards for BIS II (Basle II or Basle II) started in mid-1999, and, after a series of drafts and consultations, the final version of Basle II was issued in June 2004.[2] A revised version, incorporating certain amendments to the market risk or trading book treatment, was released on November 15, 2005.[3] The framework should be available for implementation by the end of 2006, and for more advanced approaches, from end-2007. National regulators are expected to set their own timeframe for implementation.

The implementation of Basle II seemed mired in doubts with the apprehensions of the U.S. regulators, after the results of Quantitative Impact Study (QIS 4) were released. U.S. regulators were concerned that if Basle II is implemented for U.S. banks, the existing capital requirements will be greatly depleted, which is not a result that they would like to see. Therefore, U.S. agencies have come up with a revised proposal, popularly known as Basle IA.[4] This is discussed later in this chapter. In Europe, however, the European Parliament passed the Capital Requirements Directive on September 28, 2005, thus paving the way for its adoption by the 25 European Union member countries as per the schedule recommended by the BIS. The U.S. agencies subsequently issued a notice of proposed rule-making on March 30, 2006 for a four-quarter parallel run starting January 2008 and to implement Basle II, hopefully, in 2009.

The major changes brought about by Basle II are:

- While the existing capital standard was almost entirely dedicated to capital requirements, the Basle II proposes, what is called three pillars of bank supervision: Minimum capital requirements (Pillar 1); Supervisory review of capital adequacy (Pillar 2); and Public disclosure requirements (Pillar 3). (In this chapter, our focus, understandably, is only on Pillar 1).
- As for Pillar 1, the earlier capital ratio of 8% of risk-weighted assets remains unchanged. Changes are in the risk weightings. The 1988 requirements are based on straight-jacket risk weight of 0%, 20%, 50% and 100%, assigned to various assets irrespective of the risk assessment of the respective assets. Under the Basle II norms, risk weightings are purported to be more closely aligned to an underlying risk of the asset or the portfolio.
- A categorical change of approach is to place greater reliance on the internal risk assessments by banks; therefore, there is a new approach of risk-weighting where the risk weights are based on internal ratings assigned by the banks. This approach is called the IRB approach and may be regarded as a very significant feature of the new standard.

It is also important to understand what is common between Basle I and Basle II. First, the 8% capital rule is still the same. The distinction between Tier 1 and Tier 2 also continues, and the limit for Tier 2, included in the minimum 8% capital, still continues to be 100%. In other words, out of the minimum 8% capital, there must be no more than 4% of risk-weighted assets out of Tier 2 capital, but it is perfectly okay if Tier 1 is 5% and Tier 2 is 3%. The Tier 3, meant for market risk, also remains unchanged.

The meaning of Tier 1 and Tier 2 also, barring minor modifications, remains the same as under the 1988 standard, that is to say:

Tier 1 (a) Paid-up share capital/common stock
          (b) Disclosed reserves
Tier 2 (a) Undisclosed reserves
          (b) Asset revaluation reserves
          (c) General provisions/general loan-loss reserves
          (d) Hybrid (debt/equity) capital instruments
          (e) Subordinated debt

Credit risk, market risk and operational risk

Another distinguishing feature of Basle II is that it stipulates capital requirements for market risk, that is, non-idiosyncratic risk of changes in market factors such as prices of securities and operational risk. As for securitization transactions, there is no specific treatment on account of market risk or operational risk. Therefore, much of the discussion below focuses on the credit risk capital requirements.

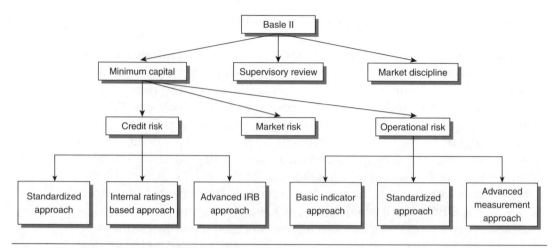

Figure 29.1   Basle II – Viewed from a distance

Three approaches to risk assessment

The three approaches below relate to credit risk capital.

One of the fundamental features of the new rules is that it tries to align the risk weighting to the economic risk of the asset or the portfolio. For measurement of the economic risk, there are three possible approaches:

- Standardized approach
- Foundation internal ratings-based (IRB) approach
- Advanced IRB approach

Under all three approaches, capital is a function of (1) probability of default (PD) (2) Loss given default, that is loss severity (LGD), and (3) exposure at default, that is, the actual amount outstanding at the time of default (EAD). However, the difference in the three approaches is how the above measures are computed.

The standardized approach is substantially similar to the current standard, except for the fact that the risk weights for different categories of assets have been substantially changed. The risk weights are laid down by the supervisory guidelines, as per recommendations contained in Basle II. Unlike the existing guidelines, the risk weights are not the same across all assets of a particular class. For example, all sovereign claims are not 0% risk-weighted; the risk weighting is based on external credit assessment. The same is true for business exposures. Certain retail exposures such as residential mortgage loans are being given lower risk weight.

The IRB approaches, either basic or advanced, are the most innovative aspects of the Basle II norms, and allow banks to use their internal economic capital models for assessment of required capital. Thus, the objective is to narrow down, to the extent of eliminating, the gap between economic capital and regulatory capital. The regulators simply supply the formulae, and the banks are supposed to provide inputs relating to the attributes of the portfolio.

The inputs are: (1) Probability of default (PD), over a given time horizon; (2) Loss given default (LGD), that is, the percentage loss (reciprocal of recovery percentage), in case a default occurs; (3) Exposure at default (EAD), that is, the amount of the exposure likely at the time when the default occurs, and (4) Maturity (M), that is, the remaining maturity of exposure. Under the IRB approach, while (1) above is assessed based on an internal rating assigned by the bank, (2), (3) and (4) are based on supervisory formulae, that is, these are laid out in the rules.

   The difference between the foundation IRB approach and the advanced IRB approach is that in the latter case, the values of (2), (3) and (4) above are computed by the bank based on its own assessment, while for the former approach, these are fixed by the supervisory guidelines. As far as the probability of default is concerned, the banks must compute it themselves in either case, as that is the very hallmark of the IRB approaches.

Table 29.1   Three approaches to credit risk

	Standardized approach	*Internal ratings-based approach*	*Advanced internal ratings-based approach*
Probability of default	Not relevant, as risk weights are laid down by rules	Computed, based on internal ratings of the bank	Computed, based on internal ratings of the bank
Loss given default	Not relevant, as risk weights are laid down by rules	Standard LGD laid down by rules	To be computed by the bank
Exposure at the time of default (EAD)	Not relevant, as risk weights are laid down by rules	Based on conversion factors laid down by rules	To be computed by the bank

Basic approach to securitization

The approach of the Basle II norms for securitization is the elimination of capital arbitrage. Under the 1988 norms, capital arbitrage was one of the prime movers responsible for securitization transactions, as banks were able to relieve capital by retaining a much smaller first-loss piece than 8%, the capital required under the 1988 norms. "The Committee believes that it is essential for the New Accord to include a robust treatment of securitisation. Otherwise the new framework would remain vulnerable to capital arbitrage, as some securitisations have enabled banks under the current Accord to avoid maintaining capital commensurate with the risks to which they are exposed. To address this concern, Basel II requires banks to look to the economic substance of a securitisation transaction when determining the appropriate capital requirement in both the standardized and IRB treatments."

Among the significant features of the Basle II approach to securitization, the highly subordinated or the first-loss piece in a securitization transaction calls for deduction from capital. This is so under both the standardized and the IRB approaches, and this is true for both the originating bank as well as the investing banks, leaving aside finer differences in either case.

The capital treatment is applicable to both cash securitizations and synthetic securitizations. We deal with the capital requirements for synthetic transactions later in this chapter. The discussion below applies only to cash transactions.

Substance over form

The Basle II norms, as most regulatory statements, prefer to look at a securitization transaction based on its economic substance rather than legal form. "Since securitisations may be structured in many different ways, the capital treatment of a securitisation exposure must be determined on the basis of its economic substance rather than its legal form. Similarly, supervisors will look to the economic substance of a transaction to determine whether it should be subject to the securitisation framework for purposes of determining regulatory capital." Despite this general remark, it is difficult to envisage regulators discarding the accounting treatment of a transaction for financial reporting purposes, although it is clear that accounting standards could not care less for the economic substance of securitization transactions.

Prerequisites for regulatory relief

The norms set certain prerequisites for regulatory off-balance sheet treatment that are common for both the standardized as well as the IRB approach. These are:

Significance of risk transfer

Significant credit risk associated with securitized exposures must have been transferred to third parties. Apparently, the norms do not bar the transferor's retention of risks; it provides, positively, that there must be a transfer of significant risks. The language of this rule might give an impression that in cases where the originator's risks are capped, this condition should be taken to be satisfied. However, in Pillar 2 norms,[5] the BIS have extended the risk-transfer concept in a new supervisory dimension. Para 786 provides: "If the risk transfer is considered to be insufficient or non existent, the supervisor can require the application of a higher capital requirement than prescribed under Pillar 1 or, alternatively, may deny a bank from obtaining any capital relief from the securitisations." Accordingly, the supervisory expectation is that, to achieve some capital relief, an originator is expected to have transferred some risk to third parties. Therefore, the capital relief that can be achieved will correspond to the amount of credit risk that is effectively transferred.

The Second Pillar guidelines provide several illustrative situations where the risk transfer is insignificant:

- Cherry-picking of assets, such that the assets transferred are distinctively different from the assets retained.
- Retention or repurchase of significant amounts of risk. "Retaining or repurchasing significant securitisation exposures, depending on the proportion of risk held by the originator, might undermine the intent of a securitisation to transfer credit risk. Specifically, supervisory authorities might expect that a significant portion of the credit risk and of the nominal value of the pool be transferred to at least one independent third party at inception and on an ongoing basis." [Para 787]

Isolation and surrender of control

This condition is similar to that under the accounting standards. The transferor should not maintain effective or indirect control over the transferred exposures. The assets are legally isolated from the transferor in such a way (e.g., through the sale of assets or through sub-participation) that the exposures are put beyond the reach of the transferor and its creditors, even in bankruptcy or receivership. These conditions must be supported by an opinion provided by a qualified legal counsel. As this requirement is substantially similarly worded as under FAS 140/IAS 39, the conditions relating to surrender of control as under the accounting standards should be deemed applicable here as well. Further, the norms provide that the transferor will be deemed to have retained control if the transferor: (i) is able to repurchase from the transferee the previously transferred exposures to realize their benefits; or (ii) is obligated to retain the risk of the transferred exposures – [Para 554 (b)].

Retention of a call option, as provided for above, indicates retention of control over the asset by the bank. Generally speaking, clean-up calls are permitted and are economically insignificant [Para 797]. However, if the call option is related to a date, and not the pool value falling below a certain percentage, the date should not be sooner than the duration – the weighted-average maturity of the asset.

No economic recourse

The norms stipulate that the securities issued are not obligations of the transferor. Thus, investors by purchasing the securities only have claim to the underlying pool of exposures. Does that rule out recourse? Experts have made distinction between credit recourse and economic recourse; economic recourse being the situation where the transferor assumes, putatively, obligation to discharge the securities. Credit recourse implies the right of the transferee to fall back upon the transferor if some of the assets do not pay. Thus, right of the transferee to seek recourse for delinquent assets may not be the equivalent of creating an obligation on the part of the transferor to pay the securities. But a generic recourse, coupled with other circumstances such as sweeping back of profits of the transferee, may imply an economic recourse.

In addition, in the guidance on Pillar 2, there are several paragraphs on provision of explicit or implicit credit support to the transaction. Implicit support might arise due to repurchase of delinquent assets. The regulators seem to be in favor of *clean break criteria*, that is, complete isolation of the assets. "The provision of implicit (or non-contractual) support, as opposed to contractual credit support (i.e., credit enhancements), raises significant supervisory concerns. For traditional securitisation structures the provision of implicit support undermines the clean break criteria, which when satisfied would allow banks to exclude the securitized assets from regulatory capital calculation". [Para 791] When a bank has been found to provide implicit support to a securitization, it will be required to hold capital against all of the underlying exposures associated with the structure as if they had not been securitized. It will also be required to disclose publicly that it was found to have provided non-contractual support, as well as the resulting increase in the capital charge (as noted above). The aim is to require banks to hold capital against exposures for which they assume the credit risk, and to discourage them from providing non-contractual support [Para 792]. In other words, it is clear that the regulators would frown upon provision of implicit support not provided for in the contractual documents. So much is the regulatory disapproval of implicit support that the BIS even suggests punitive action. Para 793 provides: If a bank is found to have provided implicit support on more than one occasion, the bank is required to disclose its transgression publicly and national supervisors will take appropriate action that may include, but is not limited to, one or more of the following:

- The bank may be prevented from gaining favorable capital treatment on securitized assets for a period of time to be determined by the national supervisor;
- The bank may be required to hold capital against all securitized assets as though the bank had created a commitment to them, by applying a conversion factor to the risk weight of the underlying assets;
- For purposes of capital calculations, the bank may be required to treat all securitized assets as if they remained on the balance sheet;
- The bank may be required by its national supervisory authority to hold regulatory capital in excess of the minimum risk-based capital ratios.

Transferee to be SPE

The norms require that the transferee is an SPE and the beneficial interests in the SPE are transferable and pledgeable without restriction. Though this condition is worded similar to the qualifying SPE (QSPE) condition in FAS 140 and ostensibly, the intent is similar too, the elaborate restrictions on what an SPE may or may not be able to do are not found here. The norms do contain[6] a definition of SPE as under: "An SPE is a corporation, trust, or other entity organized for a specific purpose, the activities of which are limited to those appropriate to accomplish the purpose of the SPE, and the structure of which is intended to isolate the SPE from the credit risk of an originator or seller of exposures. SPEs are commonly used as financing vehicles in which exposures are sold to a trust or similar entity in exchange for cash or other assets funded by debt issued by the trust." The definition does not confine the decision-making or discretionary powers of the SPE.

Clean-up calls

Clean-up calls must satisfy the following conditions: (1) it must be exercisable at the discretion of the transferor; (2) it must not be structured to avoid allocating losses to be absorbed by credit enhancements or positions held by investors or otherwise structured to provide credit enhancement; and (3) it must only be exercisable when 10% or less of the original underlying portfolio or reference portfolio value remains. See also the heading Isolation and Surrender of Control above.

Hands-off approach

The securitization does not contain clauses that (i) require the originating bank to alter systematically the underlying exposures such that the pool's weighted-average credit quality is improved unless this is achieved by selling assets to independent and unaffiliated third parties at market prices; (ii) allow for increases in a retained first-loss position or credit enhancement provided by the originating bank after the transaction's inception; or (iii) increase the yield payable to parties other than the originating bank, such as investors and third-party providers of credit enhancements in response to a deterioration in the credit quality of the underlying pool.

Generic principles for securitization

While the three different approaches to computing capital – standardized approach, IRB approach and advanced approach – are discussed below, here we mention some general rules applicable to each type of securitization:

- The basic approach is that to the extent the assets in a securitization have been replaced by securities and retained interests, the bank will be required to provide capital only for the retained interest. This is, of course, subject to the qualifying conditions discussed above.
- Credit support provided by the bank by any means, say, over-collateralization, would be considered as a retained interest.
- In certain circumstances, the rules require deduction for a particular security or interest. Where the rules require deduction, the deduction will be 50% from Tier 1 and 50% from Tier 2.

- However, to the extent of any increase in equity resulting out of securitization, the deduction should be only from Tier 1 [Para 562]. The requirements of this paragraph are likely to confuse, and there are two possible opinions:

  - *First opinion:* The increase in equity as a result of securitization is the "gain-on-sale," that is, the profit booked by virtue of the transaction. The standard is not an accounting standard, so it is not against booking of profit, the domain of accounting standard-setters. It is also illogical for the standard to provide for rejection of gain on sale in all circumstances. Para 562 is placed immediately after Para 561, which requires splitting of deduction between Tier 1 and Tier 2. Therefore, Para 562 modifies the requirement of Para 561 to provide that the deduction, required under Para 561, should be entirely out of Tier 1 to the extent of the gain-on-sale recognized, and the balance should be split 50:50 between Tier 1 and Tier 2. This view is logical because the deductions required for securitization are only to the extent of retained interest. In fact, if all gains-on-sale were to be reversed (second view below), then the provision in Para 564, that gain on sale will not be recognized in case the bank provides implicit support, would become meaningless. This author is in favor of the first view.
  - *Second opinion:* The gain-on-sale will not be part of the regulatory capital in either case. In other words, the gain-on-sale should always be disregarded as a part of regulatory capital. The underlying rationale is that the value of the gain-on-sale, unless it is a realized profit, is always subordinated, and so is a part of the first-loss support. The Quantitative Impact Study 5 worksheet issued by the BIS seems to take the second view and include the entire gain-on-sale as deductible from Tier 1.

- To resolve this, distinction must be made between credit-enhancing, gain-on-sale and non-credit enhancing profit. Usually, a residual interest is a subordinated position, but that is not always so. For example, in several cases, the residual interest may actually be senior – say, service fees. Or, the gain-on-sale may represent a cash profit, if the pool is sold at a premium. The question of reversing any such gain-on-sale does not arise.[7]

- If the gain-on-sale is reversed, then the next issue is – when does one include it as a part of the equity? After all, when the residual income captured in the gain-on-sale is realized, it needs to be included, if it was not included at inception. This would mean a complete departure from accounting rules, because in GAAP accounts, the residual income would have largely been captured up front and the subsequent receipt would mainly lead to amortization.

- A similar rule in the Capital Requirements Directive of the European Union, Art. 57 says: "In the case of a credit institution which is the originator of a securitization, net gains arising from the capitalization of future income from the securitized assets and providing credit enhancement to positions in the securitization shall be excluded from the item specified in point (b)." That is to say, capitalized profits are to be excluded only to the extent they provide credit enhancement.

- To the extent the profit is encashed, it is no more future margin income, and hence the question of applying the above rule does not apply. To the extent it is not credit enhancing or subordinated, but merely deferred in time, based on the discussion above, it is not appropriate to exclude such gains from the computation of Tier 1 capital.

Capital rules under standardized approach

If the underlying assets being securitized were risk-weighted under the standardized approach, the securitization exposure must also be treated under the standardized approach. There is a similar requirement for IRB approach (see later).

Under the standardized approach, the risk-weights to the retained/acquired exposure are based on the rating of the component. The rules relating to ratings – external credit assessment institutions – are the same as those for other exposures, with one exception; private ratings do not qualify for securitization transactions. In addition, the rating agency must have securitization experience. The following table illustrates the ratings-based, risk-weights:

	Originator	*Investor*
Unrated most senior position	"Look-through approach," i.e., average risk-weights applicable to the obligor pool	"Look-through approach," i.e., average risk-weights applicable to the obligor pool
Second-loss or better, unrated position in ABCP programs	Subject to certain conditions, 100% or highest risk-weights of the obligors, whichever is higher	Subject to certain conditions, 100% or highest risk-weights of the obligors, whichever is higher

Long-term ratings		
AAA to AA–	20%	20%
A+ to A–	50%	50%
BBB+ to BBB–	100%	100%
BB+ to BB–	Deduction from capital	350%
B+ or below or unrated	Deduction from capital	Deduction from capital

Short-term ratings		
A-1/ P-1	20%	20%
A-2/ P-2	50%	50%
A-3/ P-3	100%	100%
Any other rating, or unrated	Deduction from capital	Deduction from capital

As is evident, the rules require deduction from capital for all below-investment grade tranches for the originator and all B+ or lower-rated tranches for the investing bank. The norms provide that deduction of capital will be split 50:50 against Tier 1 and Tier 2 capital. However, to the extent any future marginal income has been accounted for in books, there will be a deduction from capital (see the author's view earlier).

Capital rule for liquidity facilities

Eligible liquidity facilities

For eligible liquidity facilities (discussed below), risk weight applicable to the highest risk-weighted exposure covered by the facility should be applied to convert the facility into its credit-equivalent amount. The credit conversion factors (CCF) for eligible liquidity facilities are 20% for facilities with original maturity of 1 year or less, and 50% for original maturities exceeding 1 year.

To be an eligible liquidity facility, the following rules must be complied with:

1. A liquidity facility must not be a credit enhancer: in circumstances such that a draw-down is certain or otherwise.
2. The facility must be subject to an asset quality test or similar safeguard whereby it cannot be drawn if the assets have already been in default.[8]
3. The liquidity facility should not be drawn down after other available credit enhancers, from which the liquidity facility could benefit, have been used. In other words, the liquidity enhancer should still have the benefit of credit enhancements.
4. Drawn liquidity facility must not be subordinated.
5. There must be provision for the termination of the facility if the asset class becomes substandard.

Essentially, the idea of the above preconditions is that the liquidity support must not be tantamount to credit support for the transaction. The liquidity facilitator must take all precautions that a third-party support provider normally takes.

If not eligible

If the liquidity facility is not eligible as per the above list, then the risk weight is the highest risk weight applicable to the exposure covered by the facility and the CCF is 100%.

Market disruption liquidity facilities

If the liquidity facility is available only for a general market disruption, it can go with a 0% CCF, or in other words, not require any capital as long as it is not drawn up. Program-wide liquidity facilities may qualify as a general market disruption, defined as a situation where several SPVs are not able to roll over their paper because of a widely prevailing liquidity crisis in the market.

Overlapping exposures

If a liquidity facility also amounts to, for example, a credit enhancement, it is a case of overlapping exposures. In such cases, the overlapping amount is to be included only once, and with higher risk weight.

Capital rule for servicer advances

A servicer is entitled to give servicing advances, provided they are senior to other claims as regards reimbursement. The norms provide that as per national discretion, servicing advances may be given a 0% CCF; this implies that the unutilized amount of servicer advances will not be risk-weighted; whatever has already been used by the transferee becomes an on-balance sheet exposure and should be 100% risk-weighted.

Capital rule for revolving securitizations

The speciality of revolving asset securitizations, from the viewpoint of capital requirements, is the risk of early amortization. As a general principle, the norms require the originating bank to hold capital against assets that are subject to an early amortization provision, that is, the assets may revolve back with the bank. However, this is not applicable for replenishing structures, where an early amortization trigger will only put a curb on the power of the bank to add more assets into the structure, and the assets do not revert to the bank.

Overview of the capital rules for early amortization

The following is the hierarchy of different situations under the early amortization rule:

- Replenishing and revolving structure: For replenishing structures, that is, those where early amortization merely curbs the ability of the bank to add more assets into the pool but the assets do not come back to the bank, there is no need to provide capital for the early amortization risk. For revolving structures, the early amortization risk needs to be provided for.
- The early amortization risk is provided for against the investors' share, that is, the share of assets that has been put off the balance sheet. As for the seller's share, it is anyway on the balance sheet and is risk-weighted as a retained interest.
- For off-balance sheets subject to early amortization, we will apply risk weight to the CCF, calculated as per the rules below.
- To apply the CCF, we distinguish between controlled and uncontrolled early amortization.
  - o In brief, a controlled amortization is where the bank has the required liquidity backup, and the amortization speed does not exceed certain limits.

- For both controlled and uncontrolled amortization, we distinguish between uncommitted and committed credit lines.
- In both committed and uncommitted lines, we distinguish between retail and non-retail credit lines.

  ○ For uncommitted retail credit lines, the required CCF is based on the ratio of (a) the prevalent 3-month average excess spread to (b) the excess spread prevalent at the "trapping point," that is, the point where the transaction requires the excess spread to be retained in the SPV.

- Having thus converted the investors' interest at the appropriate CCF, and applied risk weight thereon, we compute capital for the revolving transaction.
- But there is a cap here – the total capital cannot exceed the capital that would have been required if the asset had not been securitized, or the risk-weighted capital on the retained exposure, whichever is higher.

Revolving and reinstating securitizations

To understand the complex matrix applicable to early amortization, we first need to understand distinction between revolving structure and reinstating structure. A credit card securitization is an example of a revolving transaction; once the early amortization triggers (EATs) are in place, the draw-downs by the cardholders will start coming on to the books of the bank. A CLO with a revolving period is an example of reinstating transaction – during the so-called revolving period; the bank had the ability to add further assets. If the OC/IC triggers fail, the bank will not be able to add further assets to the pool, but the assets do not start reverting to the bank. So, while revolving transactions entail liquidity risk, reinstating transactions do not. The probability of the asset reverting to the bank on EATs applied for a revolving transaction is similar to an off-balance sheet exposure, and should, therefore, be converted at a CCF.

To qualify for a reinstating transaction, the transaction may fall under the following situations (they appear to be non-cumulative):

- Replenishment structures where the underlying exposures do not revolve and the early amortization ends the ability of the bank to add new exposures;
- Transactions of revolving assets containing early amortization features that mimic term structures (i.e., where the risk on the underlying facilities does not return to the originating bank);
- Structures where a bank securitizes one or more credit line(s) and where investors remain fully exposed to future draws by borrowers even after an early amortization event has occurred;
- The early amortization clause is solely triggered by events not related to the performance of the securitized assets or the selling bank, such as material changes in tax laws or regulations.

In most cases of early amortization, the last condition above will not be satisfied, as the triggers will mostly relate to the performance of the assets.

However, the first condition will exclude transactions like CLOs or revolving synthetic CDOs.

Controlled and uncontrolled early amortization

The CCFs are different for controlled and uncontrolled amortization – lower for controlled amortization, and higher for uncontrolled amortization. An amortization is controlled if it satisfies the following cumulative conditions:

(a) The bank must have an appropriate capital/liquidity plan in place to ensure that it has sufficient capital and liquidity available in the event of an early amortization. This is a qualitative condition and can only be checked by the supervisors.
(b) Throughout the duration of the transaction, including the amortization period, there is the same *pro rata* sharing of interest, principal, expenses, losses and recoveries based on the bank's and investors' relative shares of the receivables outstanding at the beginning of each month. In other words, during the early amortization period, the seller's share should not become subordinated.
(c) The transaction must set a period for amortization that would be sufficient for at least 90% of the total debt outstanding at the beginning of the early amortization period to have been repaid or recognized as in default; and
(d) The pace of repayment should not be any more rapid than would be allowed by straight-line amortization over the period set out in criterion (c).

For transactions adopting a pass-through type amortization, relegating all principal collections to repayment of the notes, it seems condition (c) and (d) above will be satisfied. However, if there is a stated repayment date for the notes or for master trusts where the amortization speed is fast so as to reduce the seller's share on a more than proportionate basis, the transaction might be treated as uncontrolled amortization.

Committed and non-committed exposures

The distinction here is based on whether the bank has committed a particular amount of lending, or the facility is uncommitted. Credit card debt is an example of uncommitted facility, as the bank does not agree to provide credit up to any particular limit. Defined lines of credit, for example, home equity, may be committed lines of credit.

Retail and non-retail exposures

The meaning of retail exposures is as generally defined in the document (see Para 70 for definition of retail exposures). One of the principal requirements is granularity; that exposure on one counterparty does not exceed 0.2% of the total portfolio.

Comparison of the prevailing excess
spread with that at the trapping point

The CCFs for uncommitted retail lines are based on the size of the prevailing excess spread, relating to the excess spread at the point when it would be trapped within the structure. A trapping point refers to the point where, as per the credit enhancement structure of the transaction, the excess spread will be trapped and will not be allowed to be released to the seller to retain more credit support in the transaction. Generally speaking, transactions provide for trapping of excess spread if the level of excess spread falls below a particular percent. We are supposed to compare the existing 3-month average excess spread with the excess spread when the trapping will be applicable. If there is no trapping point laid down in the transaction, it is deemed to be 4.5%.

Controlled amortization:			3-month average excess spread/excess spread at trapping point	CCF for investors' share
	Uncommitted credit			
		Retail	1.33 or more	0%
			1.33–1	1%
			1–.75	2%
			.75–.50	10%
			.50–.25	20%
			Less than .25	40%
		Non-retail		90%
	Committed			90%
Uncontrolled	Uncommitted credit	Retail	1.33 or more	0%
			1.33–1	5%
			1–.75	15%
			.75–.50	50%
			Less than .50	100%
		Non-retail		100%
	Committed			100%

Figure 29.2   Excess spread trapping point and CCF

Internal ratings-based approach

As for the standardized approach, the IRB approach should be applied for securitization transactions, if the underlying assets being securitized were treated for capital purposes under the IRB approach. For the investing bank, the approach may be used if the bank is permitted by the supervisor to use IRB approach. Under the IRB approach, the capital rules for the transferring bank and the investing bank are substantially the same. Notably, the IRB

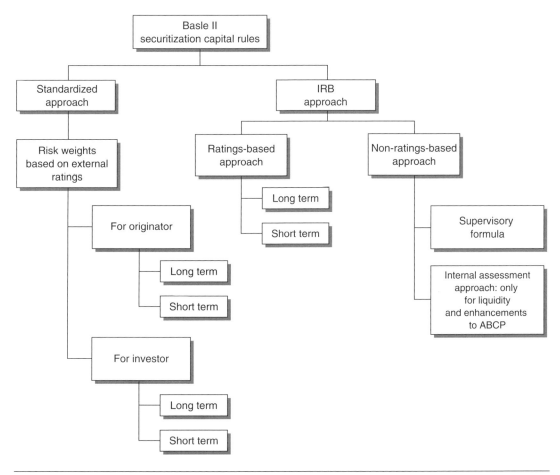

Figure 29.3 Basle II approach to securitization capital computation

approach for securitization transactions is different from the IRB approach for loan exposures; the latter is based on banks' estimates of probability of default, while for securitizations, as the risk is based on pools of assets and the risk is tranched, the risk estimates are either based on the rating agencies' ratings, or are based on the IRB capital required for the pool pre-securitization.

Understanding the inputs: K_{IRB}, L and T computation

Under the IRB approach, the impact of a securitization transaction on the capital requirement is related to K_{IRB}. Therefore, it is imperative that the concept of K_{IRB} is well understood. K_{IRB} is the capital (expressed as a fraction) required under the IRB approach for the pool of assets securitized, pre-securitization. The K_{IRB} is based on probability of default, loss given default, exposure at the time of default, and the maturity of the exposure. The BIS norms have explained the computation of capital under the IRB approach extensively; this, not being within the scope of this book, is not being discussed here.

There are two other essential inputs: the extent of credit enhancement available to a tranche (L), and the thickness of the tranche (T).

L is the ratio of (a) the notional amount of all securitization exposures subordinate to the tranche in question to (b) the notional amount of exposures in the pool. This is the simple concept of credit enhancement available to a tranche.

T is defined as ratio of (a) the nominal size of the tranche of interest to (b) the notional amount of exposures in the pool. This is the size of the tranche expressed as a fraction.

Example 1

Let us say, for example, the total size of a transaction is 100, shared by five classes as under:

Classes	Ratings	Relative size	L	T
A	AAA	82	0.18	0.82
B	AA	6	0.12	0.06
C	BBB	4	0.08	0.04
D	BB	5	0.03	0.05
E	unrated	3	0	0.03
Total		100		

The L for Class D is the support provided by Class E, in fraction, which is 0.03 or 3%. The thickness of Class D is 0.05 or 5%. Likewise, the L and T of the respective classes are computed above.

Three situations under the IRB approach

There are three alternative, non-optional situations under the IRB approach:

- The ratings-based, or RBA approach, is to be applied where the securitization exposure has either actual or inferred ratings.
- The supervisory formula, or SF approach, is applicable where there are no actual or inferred ratings.
- The internal assessment approach, or IAA, is applicable for liquidity and credit enhancements to ABCP programs.

RBA approach

The RBA is applicable where the tranche is either rated or a rating may be inferred.[9] Under the RBA approach, the risk weights are to be based on a table – one each for a short-term rating and a long-term rating. This is the case under the standardized approach as well.

Under both long-term and short-term ratings, the risk-weighting depends on three factors: (a) the rating assigned or inferred; (b) the granularity of the pool; and (c) the seniority of the tranche in question.

As for seniority of the tranche, a tranche is regarded as senior if it is entitled to first claim on all the assets of the transaction. This would mean, generally speaking, first claim in the waterfall, but obviously after ignoring external costs such as expenses and swap payments. The document gives several examples of positions that may be regarded as senior:

- In a typical synthetic securitization, the "super-senior" tranche would be treated as a senior tranche.
- In a traditional securitization where all tranches above the first-loss piece are rated, the most highly rated position would be treated as a senior tranche.
- Usually a liquidity facility supporting an ABCP program would not be the most senior position within the program; the commercial paper, which benefits from the liquidity support, typically would be the most senior position.

The granularity of the pool is based on whether the effective number of obligors in the pool (**N**) is 6 or more. The effective number of obligors in the pool is not just the number of obligors in a pool, but is computed by a measure of diversity as under:

$$N = \sum_i (EAD)^2 \ divided\_by \ \sum_i (EAD^2)$$

That is to say, the squares of the sum of all the exposures in the pool are divided by the sum of the squares of all exposures in the pool. This would tend to reflect the concentricity in the pool. By way of a simple illustration, if there are 5 exposures in a pool, each of $100, N comes exactly to 5 [500^2/ (100^2)*5]. However, as we increase the size of any one constituent, say, the first one is taken to be $1,000 instead of $100, N drops down to 1.8846.

The working of N is based on *Herfindahl Index of Concentration*. According to this index, the effective number of equally weighted components of a portfolio is the reciprocal of (sum of squares of weights of each item in the portfolio). The Herfindahl Index is the sum of squares of the weights, that is, percentage share, of each component, and the reciprocal of the Index is the effective number. This is based on a simple logic that if the relative weight of an item in the portfolio goes up (portfolio is concentric), the Index goes up, and therefore, the effective number comes down.

Under long-term ratings, the risk weights are given in the three columns below. Col. 1 is for a highly granular pool, and a highly senior tranche. If N > 500 and the position is senior, then Col. 1 is applicable. Here the risk-weights, particularly for senior tranches, are quite low. If N < 6, that is, the portfolio is highly concentric, the risk weights in the third column below will be applicable. In all other cases, the risk weights in the second column will be applied. The idea is simple – the second column is the base case, applicable in general.

The first column is one of reduced weights to account for the senior position. The third column is one of higher weights to take into account the concentric risks in the pool.

Table 29.2   Of long-term ratings-based risk weights

	1	2	3
AAA	7%	12%	20%
AA	8%	15%	25%
A+	10%	18%	35%
A	12%	20%	35%
A–	20%	35%	35%
BBB+	35%	50%	50%
BBB	60%	75%	75%
BBB–	100%	100%	100%
BB+	250%	250%	250%
BB	425%	425%	425%
BB–	650%	650%	650%
Below BB– and unrated	Deduction	Deduction	Deduction

The following table gives the risk weights for short-term assigned or inferred ratings. The columns, 1, 2 and 3 are the same as in the table above.

Table 29.3   Of short-term ratings-based risk weights

	1	2	3
A-1/P-1	7%	12%	20%
A-2/P-2	12%	20%	35%
A-3/P-3	60%	75%	75%
All other ratings/unrated	Deduction	Deduction	Deduction

Example 2: RBA computation

Let us take the numbers in Example 1 above. In addition, let us assume the K_{IRB} for the pool is 0.05, or 5%. Let us also assume the N for the portfolio is more than 6. If the originating bank picks up class E, since L+T < K_{IRB} the entire tranche retained will call for reduction from capital.

If the bank invests in class D, the portion up to K_{IRB} (that is, 2%) will call for deduction, while the balance 3% will be treated as per Col. 2 above, viz., 425% risk-weight.

The SF approach[10]

As discussed above, the SF approach is applicable where ratings or inferred ratings are not available for a tranche. Here, the risk weights are based on four essential inputs: K_{IRB}, L, T, N and LGD. The LGD factor is the weighted-average loss given default, that is, (1 − Recovery rate in the event of default).

In case the L + T are less than or equal to K_{IRB}, the entire tranche will be a deduction from capital.

In other cases, the capital requirement is given by the greater of (i) .0056*T; (ii) the capital charge S (L + T) − S (L) as per the supervisory formula given below. The intent of (i) is to fix a supervisory floor of 56 basis points capital requirements in all cases. The intent of (ii) is to compute the capital for the tranche of interest which basically takes risk at level (L + T) − (L). The supervisory formula for S (L) is as under:

$$S\,(L) = K\,(L) + K_{IRB} - K\,(K_{IRB}) + (d.\ K_{IRB}/\omega)\,(1 - e^{\omega(K_{IRB}{}^{-L})/K_{IRB}})$$

Note that ω has been given a supervisory value of 20. Therefore, $1/\omega$ equals 0.05, and so on.

The calculation of d above is based on a series of recursive parameters, as per the following formulae:

$$h = (1 - K_{IRB}/LGD)^N$$
$$c = K_{IRB}/(1 - h)$$
$$V = \frac{(LGD - K_{IRB})K_{IRB} + 0.25(1 - LGD)K_{IRB}}{N}$$
$$f = \left(\frac{V + K_{IRB}^2}{1 - h} - c^2\right) + \frac{(1 - K_{IRB})K_{IRB} - V}{(1 - h)\tau}$$
$$g = \frac{(1 - c)c}{f} - 1$$
$$a = g \cdot c$$
$$b = g \cdot (1 - c)$$
$$d = 1 - (1 - h) \cdot (1 - Beta[K_{IRB}; a, b])$$
$$K[L] = (1 - h) \cdot ((1 - Beta[L; a, b])L + Beta[L; a + 1, b]c).$$

The formula is based on results of credit risk measurement models in tranching of risks. This formula is recursive; it takes results of a lot of other variables. To understand these, we apply the numbers taken in Example 1.

Example 3: Computation under the SF approach

We take the numbers from example 1, with the assumption that the ratings are not available. Let us say, a bank acquires Class C. The K_{IRB} of the transaction is 0.05 (as already assumed before). The L and T here are 0.08 and 0.04 respectively. We take LGD as 0.45, or 45%. Let us say, N = 10.

$$h = (1 - K_{IRB}/LGD)^N$$

Hence,
h = (1 − 0.05/.45)^10 = 0.307946148

Next,
$c = K_{IRB}/(1-h)$

Hence,
$c = 0.05/(1-0.307946148) = 0.072249$

Next,
$v = ((LGD - K_{IRB}) K_{IRB} + .25 (1 - LGD) K_{IRB})/N$

Hence,
$v = ((.45 - .05).05 + .25(1 - .45).05)/10 = 0.0026875$

Next,
$f = [\{(v + K_{IRB}^2)/(1-h)\} - c^{2]} + \{(1 - K_{IRB}) K_{IRB} - v\}/(1-h)\tau$
where $t = 1000$

Hence,
$f = [\{(0.0026875 + .05^2)/(1-0.307946148)\} - 0.072249^2] + \{(1-0.05).05 - 0.0026875\}/(1-0.307946148).1000 = 0.0023407$

Next,
$g = [\{(1-c) c\}/f] - 1$

Hence,
$g = [\{(1-0.072249). 0.072249\}/0.0023407] - 1 = 27.636476$

Next,
$a = g.c$

Hence,
$a = 27.636476. 0.072249 = 1.99669979$

Next,
$b = g. (1-c)$

Hence,
$b = 0.799148. (1 - 0.0023407) = 25.639776$

Next,
$d = 1 - (1-h). \{1 - BETA (KIRB; a, b)\}$ where BETA refers to cumulative beta distribution.

Hence,
$d = 1 - (1-0.307946148). (1 - BETADIST (0.05, 1.99669979, 25.639776) = 0.5767596$

Next,

K (l) = (1 – h). {(1 – BETA(l; a, b).l) +BETA (l; a + 1, b).c}

Hence,

K(l) = (1 – 0.307946148).((1 – BETADIST(0.08, 1.99669979, 25.639776).0.08) + BETADIST(0.08, 2.99669979, 25.639776). 0.0023407) = 0.6757231

Similarly, the value of K (K_{IRB}) will be computed, by working out the Beta's at 0.05 instead of 0.08. We get the value of:

K (K_{IRB}) = 0.686551823

Putting these values in the formula for S (L), we get the value:

= 0.05 + 0.6757231 – 0.686551823+ 0.5767596*(0.05/20)*(1 – EXP (20*(0.05 – 0.08)/0.05)) = 0.040613136

Internal assessment approach

The internal assessment approach (IAA) is applicable to liquidity and credit enhancements provided by the bank to ABCP transactions, whether sponsored by the bank or by others. Here, the basic theme is on the exposure of the bank under such programs, the bank will be allowed to (a) give an internal rating based on its own assessment of the risk inherent in such exposure; and (b) based on such rating, to compute the capital as per the RBA risk weights.

There are several conditions that the bank must satisfy before it qualifies to use the internal ratings. These are:

- For the unrated exposure to qualify for the IAA, the ABCP itself must be externally rated and subject to the RBA. This obviously means the transaction should not have been risk-weighted under the standardized approach.
- The internal assessment of the credit quality should be akin to one used by rating agencies, and must at least be equivalent of investment grade rating when initially assigned. The internal assessment must be used in the bank's internal risk management processes, including management information and economic capital systems, and generally must meet all the relevant requirements of the IRB framework.
- For banks to use the IAA, the local supervisors must be satisfied with the rating methodologies used in the process. Banks are required to demonstrate to the supervisors how these internal assessments correspond with the relevant ECAI's standards.
- The bank's internal assessment process must identify gradations of risk. Internal assessments must be mapped with external ratings to allow the supervisors to do one-to-one correspondence of internal assessments with external ratings.

- The stress factors used in determining credit enhancement requirements must be at least as conservative as the publicly available rating criteria of the rating agencies.

  o In case the ABCP program has ratings by two rating agencies, or the rating methodologies of two rating agencies are different, the bank uses the one that is more conservative.
  o When selecting rating agencies to externally rate an ABCP, a bank must not go for "rating shopping" to find the agency with less restrictive rating methodologies.
  o Generally speaking, if the rating methodologies for an asset or exposure are not publicly available, then the IAA may not be used. However, in certain instances, for example, for new or uniquely structured transactions, not currently addressed by the rating criteria, a bank may discuss the specific transaction with its supervisor to determine whether the IAA may be applied to the related exposures.

- Internal or external auditors, a rating agency, or the bank's internal credit review or risk management function must perform regular reviews of the internal assessment process and assess the validity of those internal assessments. If the bank's internal audit, credit review, or risk management functions perform the reviews of the internal assessment process, then these functions must be independent of the ABCP program business line, as well as the underlying customer relationships.

- The bank must track the performance of its internal assessments over time to evaluate the performance and refine it as necessary.

- The ABCP program must issue guidelines on what kind of assets it buys and should lay down parameters, such as type of asset being purchased; type and monetary value of the exposures arising from the provision of liquidity facilities and credit enhancements; loss waterfall; and legal and economic isolation of the transferred assets from the entity selling the assets. The program should:

  a. exclude the purchase of assets that are significantly past due or defaulted;
  b. limit excess concentration to individual obligor or geographic area; and
  c. limit the tenor of the assets to be purchased.

- A credit analysis of the asset seller's risk profile must be performed and should consider, for example, past and expected future financial performance; current market position; expected future competitiveness; leverage, cash flow and interest coverage; and debt rating. In addition, a review of the seller's underwriting standards, servicing capabilities and collection processes should be performed.

- The ABCP program should have collection processes established that consider the operational capability and credit quality of the servicer. The program should mitigate to the extent possible seller/servicer risk through various methods, such as triggers based on current credit quality that would preclude co-mingling of funds and impose lockbox arrangements that would help ensure the continuity of payments to the ABCP program.

- The loss estimates of assets must consider all sources of potential risk, such as credit and dilution risk.[11] If the seller-provided credit enhancement is sized based on only credit-related losses, then a separate reserve should be established for dilution risk, if material for the particular exposure pool. In addition, in sizing the required enhancement level, the bank should review several years of historical information, including losses, delinquencies, dilutions and the turnover rate of the receivables. Furthermore, the bank should evaluate the characteristics of the underlying asset pool, e.g., weighted-average credit score, identify any concentrations to an individual obligor or geographic region, and the granularity of the asset pool.
- The program must incorporate structural triggers such as wind down triggers specific to a pool of exposures.

U.S. regulatory requirements: Historical

As securitization volumes have been significant, U.S. regulators have had regulatory statements on securitization for quite some time.

Regulators talk risk

Regulators have been commenting on the risks inherent in securitization transactions in several of their communiqués.

OCC September 1996 guidelines

One of the early regulatory statements in the U.S. was the September 1996 guidelines of the Office of Controller of Currency.[12] The overall tone of these guidelines is to protect investors against irregularities of a growing market: "Securitized receivables remain susceptible to the same economic influences that have troubled consumer and business borrowers in the past." Thus, though the OCC intends to encourage banks to securitize, it wants to warn bank managements of the inherent risks: "The OCC recognizes securitization as a progressive and effective financial intermediation and risk management tool. A bank should make the strategic decision to participate in securitization activities in the context of its overall growth, profitability objectives, funding alternatives, and operational capacities. Management should have a clear understanding of which risks are transferred to the investors or credit enhancers and which remain with the bank even after the assets have been sold." In addition, the OCC wants to caution banks against being enticed into a business they do not understand well: "The availability of funding through securitization should not entice issuers to enter a business line in which they have only limited expertise or experience. For example, banks that were successful at underwriting or servicing high quality paper may not be as successful with lesser quality, sub-prime paper, given the different skills needed for servicing higher risk loans."

The OCC guidelines provided an inventory of the risks perceived in securitization activities of banks: Reputation, Strategic, Credit, Transaction, Liquidity and Compliance. Besides, as for capital requirements, the guidelines provided that if the seller retained significant recourse, the seller will be required to hold full capital against transferred assets. "In asset sales where the seller provides recourse to the buyer, the selling institution generally must hold capital for the full outstanding amount of assets transferred. There are exceptions for low-level recourse, specific small business obligations, and certain mortgage-related transactions. Low-level recourse limits the risk-based capital charge to the lower of the bank's maximum contractual exposure under the recourse obligation or the amount of capital that would have been required had the assets not been transferred."

The guidelines also talked of implicit recourse, that implied by the action of the bank in substituting performing assets for those that turn non-performing.

FRS guidelines of July 11, 1997

The Division of Banking Supervision and Regulation of the Federal Reserve System issued a letter addressed to Federal Reserve Banks, number **SR 97-21 (SUP)** dated **July 11, 1997.** By this time, obviously, securitization activity among U.S. banks has become very widespread. This regulatory statement was directed at making Federal bank regulators aware of the risks posed by securitization transactions that "while not new to banking, may be less obvious and more complex than the risks of traditional lending activities." By this time, complaints that securitization was encouraging sub-prime lending had also been abuzz: "The heightened need for management attention to these risks is underscored by reports from examiners, senior lending officer surveys, and discussions with trade and advisory groups that have indicated that competitive conditions over the past few years have encouraged an easing of credit terms and conditions in both commercial and consumer lending."

As this was a letter to the bank regulators, it stressed the need for inspectors to evaluate the risk management systems in banks that were active in securitization and secondary trading in credits, in cash form or synthetic form.

Highlighting the fact that in many cases, removal of assets from the books may not be commensurate with removal of credit risks, the regulators treated assumption of first-loss position on portfolios as "direct credit substitutes." The concept of direct credit substitute goes as follows: If a bank while transferring its own portfolio retains a first-loss position to the extent of credit risk inherent in the portfolio, the bank continues to have the same risk as it had before transferring the asset. On the other hand, if a bank takes a first-loss position or subordinate investment in a portfolio securitized by someone else, say a conduit, the position is the same as for risks in an originated portfolio. It may be noted that this was the time when asset-backed commercial paper conduits had already become commonplace in U.S. banking. Hence, the regulator commented: "Banking organizations that sponsor certain asset-backed commercial paper programs, or so-called "remote origination" conduits, can be exposed to high degrees of credit risk even though it may seem that their notional exposure is minimal. Such a remote origination conduit lends directly to corporate customers referred to it by the sponsoring banking organization that used to lend directly to these same borrowers. The conduit funds this lending activity by issuing commercial paper that, in turn, is guaranteed by the sponsoring banking organization. The net result is that the sponsoring institution has much the same credit risk exposure through this guarantee as if it had made the loans directly and held them on its books. However, such credit extension is an off-balance sheet transaction and the associated risks may not be fully reflected in the institution's risk management system."

As far as regulatory capital is concerned, the regulators did emphasize that the nature of risks retained in many securitization transactions may not be apparent and therefore, the minimum capital requirements may be suitably altered according to situations: "When evaluating capital adequacy, supervisors should ensure that banking organizations that sell assets with recourse, assume or mitigate credit risk through the use of credit derivatives, and provide direct credit substitutes and liquidity facilities to securitization programs, are accurately identifying and measuring these exposures and maintaining capital at aggregate levels sufficient to support the associated credit, market, liquidity, reputational, operational, and legal risks."

Risk-based capital rules

As early as on June 29, 1990, the Federal Financial Institutions Examination Council (FFIEC) published a request for comment on recourse arrangements. The publication announced the agencies' intent to review the regulatory capital, reporting, and lending limit treatment of assets transferred with recourse and similar transactions. The FFIEC decided to review the reporting and capital treatment of recourse arrangements and direct credit substitutes that expose banking organizations to credit-related risks. In the meantime, the OTS (responsible for supervision of Thrifts) implemented some of the FFIEC's proposals (including the definition of recourse) on July 29, 1992.

On May 25, 1994, the agencies published a notice containing a proposal to reduce the capital requirement for banks for low-level recourse transactions (transactions in which the capital requirement would otherwise exceed an institution's maximum contractual exposure); to treat first-loss (but not second-loss) direct credit substitutes like recourse; and to implement definitions of "recourse," "direct credit substitute," and related terms. The 1994 Notice was implemented by the different agencies (OCC, Board and the FDIC) on different dates around first half of 1995.

Low-level recourse rules

The 1995 rules established what was known as the "low-level recourse" rule. Assets which were accounted for as sales under GAAPs could qualify for this rule. Under this rule, if there was a recourse liability retained by the transferring bank (which includes over-collateralization or other forms of credit enhancement), the risk-based capital required by the bank would be equal to the contractual liability for recourse. Under the low-level recourse principle, the institution holds capital on approximately a dollar-for-dollar basis up to the amount of the aggregate credit enhancements. However, if an institution does not contractually limit the maximum amount of its recourse obligation or if the amount of credit enhancement is greater than the risk-based capital requirement that would exist if the assets were not sold, the low-level recourse treatment does not apply. Instead, the institution must hold risk-based capital against the securitized assets as if those assets had not been sold.

The essence of this rule is that the capital requirement would be the lower of the risk-based capital required pre-securitization or the extent of credit enhancement provided by the transferor. The low-level recourse is typically reported by the "direct reduction method" (meaning, the capital is reduced to the extent of the credit enhancement) or the "gross-up method" (meaning, the risk-weight is 1250% (at 8% capital requirement).

Concerns on retained risks

The regulators began expressing concerns on retained risks in securitization transactions when sub-prime assets were rampantly being securitized. On December 13, 1999, Inter-agency Guidance cautioned against gain-on-sale accounting coupled with substantial retained risks: "The creation of a retained interest (the debit) typically also results in an offsetting 'gain-on-sale' (the credit) and thus generation of an asset. Institutions that securitize high yielding assets with long durations may create a retained interest asset value that exceeds the risk-based capital charge that would be in place if the institution had not sold the assets (under the existing risk-based capital guidelines, capital is not required for the amount over 8% of the securitized assets). Serious problems can arise for institutions that distribute contrived earnings only later to be faced with a downward valuation and charge-off of part or all of the retained interests."

Thereafter, proposed rules were issued in March 2000 to elaborately deal with retained risks and residual interests in securitization transactions. This finally culminated in new capital rules of November 29, 2001.

November 2001 rules

The November 2001 rules were framed under the backdrop of the prevailing practice among banks of booking gains on sale on high-risk assets and still being required to keep only 8% capital. The rules made specific provisions about recourse, residual interests and direct credit substitutes. Each of these concepts was elaborately defined. Detailed discussion of each of these concepts follows:

Meaning of recourse

Recourse is defined for regulatory capital purposes as: "Any arrangement in which an institution retains risk of credit loss in connection with an asset transfer, if the risk of credit loss exceeds a *pro rata* share of the institution's claim on the assets."

There are two significant features of this definition; that recourse implies retention of *more than proportionate risk* and that recourse arises only when risk is *retained*, not acquired. Retention of proportionate risk is merely retention of a proportion of the asset, and the regulatory rules on recourse will not apply in such case. By the second feature, if risk is acquired on an asset originated by someone else, it is not a case of recourse but a direct credit substitute as discussed below.

More than proportionate risk can be retained in several ways, such as legal recourse, substitution and subordinate participation. Each of these falls under the broad caption of recourse.

An agreement to provide liquidity is not recourse, but if such liquidity facilities are subordinated to external liabilities, it is tantamount to recourse. Servicing obligations is also not recourse, but for the servicer responsible for credit losses, such obligation serves as a credit enhancement and would, therefore, be taken as recourse.

Credit risk, and not other risks

Another significant issue is that assumption or retention of risks other than credit risk is not covered by capital adequacy rules. For example, if the originator retains interest rate risk, it is not a case of retention of risks or recourse for the purpose of the capital adequacy guidelines.

Implied recourse also covered

Another issue which regulators have clarified is that "recourse" for the purpose of capital rules includes any recourse in form or substance, even if the recourse is not contractual but is implicit. Such implicit recourse may be implied by the conduct of the bank.

Breach of representation or warranty

Repurchase or recourse on account of a breach of representation or warranty is not taken as recourse. However, any representations or warranties that create exposure to default risk or any other form of open-ended, credit-related risk from the assets that is not controllable by the seller or servicer is treated as recourse.

The regulatory practice is to treat "standard representations and warranties" as not amounting to recourse. The standard warranties are those that refer to an existing state of facts that the seller or servicer can either control or verify with reasonable due diligence at the time the assets are sold or the servicing rights are transferred. These representations and warranties will not be considered recourse or direct credit substitutes, provided the seller or servicer performs due diligence prior to the transfer of the assets or servicing rights to ensure that it has a reasonable basis for making the representation or warranty. The term "standard representations and warranties" also covers contractual provisions that permit the return of transferred assets in the event of fraud or documentation deficiencies, (i.e., if the assets are not what the seller represented them to be).

Examples of "standard representations and warranties" include:

- seller representations that the transferred assets are current (i.e., not past due) at the time of sale;
- that the assets meet specific, agreed-upon credit standards at the time of sale;
- or that the assets are free and clear of any liens (provided that the seller has exercised due diligence to verify these facts).

Examples of a non-standard representation and warranty are:

- an agreement by the seller to buy back any assets that become more than 30 days past due or default within a designated time period after the sale.
- that all properties underlying a pool of transferred mortgages are free of environmental hazards. This representation is not verifiable by the seller or servicer with reasonable due diligence because it is not possible to absolutely verify that a property is, in fact, free of all environmental hazards. Such an open-ended guarantee against the risk that is unknown but currently existing and may be discovered in the future would be considered recourse or a direct credit substitute. However, a seller's representation that all properties underlying a pool of transferred mortgages have undergone environmental studies and that the studies revealed no known environmental hazards would be a "standard representation and warranty" (assuming that the seller performed the requisite due diligence). This is a verifiable statement of facts that would not be considered recourse or a direct credit substitute.

Meaning of direct credit substitute

The meaning of direct credit substitute is closely related to that of recourse, and in fact, complements the latter. "The term 'direct credit substitute' refers to an arrangement in which a banking organization assumes, in form or in substance, credit risk associated with an on- or off-balance sheet asset or exposure that was not previously owned by the banking organization (third-party asset) and the risk assumed by the banking organization exceeds the *pro rata* share of the banking organization's interest in the third-party asset." Thus, while recourse implies a more-than-proportionate risk in the bank's transferred assets, a direct credit substitute is a similar position on assets of a third party. A subordinated interest, letter of credit or, in certain circumstances, even a credit derivative could be treated as a direct credit substitute.

Meaning of residual interests

Compared to recourse and direct credit substitutes, residual interests are balance sheet assets. In GAAP parlance, a residual interest is a retained interest. The regulatory statement defines residual interest as "any on-balance sheet asset that represents an interest (including a beneficial interest) created by a transfer that qualifies as a sale (in accordance with generally accepted accounting principles) of financial assets, whether through a securitization or otherwise, and that exposes a banking organization to any credit risk directly or indirectly associated with the transferred asset that exceeds a *pro rata* share of that banking organization's claim on the asset, whether through subordination provisions or other credit enhancement techniques." Examples of residual interests are credit-enhancing interest only strips (usually the residual interest after paying the investors' interest and other expenses on the trust), spread accounts, cash collaterals, retained subordinated interests, accrued but uncollected interest of a credit enhancing capacity, and similar on-balance sheet assets that function as a credit enhancement. Over-collateralization is also a residual interest.

For residual interests that do not qualify for ratings-based capital treatment as per the table below, the bank needs to hold dollar-for-dollar capital: "A bank must maintain risk-based capital equal to the remaining amount of the residual interest that is retained on the balance sheet (net of any existing associated deferred tax liability), even if the amount of risk-based capital required to be maintained exceeds the full risk-based capital requirement for the assets transferred."

Ratings-based risk weights

In line with the Basle proposals, U.S. regulators had adopted a ratings-based capital rule. The regulations are contained in 12 CFR part 3, appendix A (OCC); 12 CFR parts 208 and 225, appendix A (Board); 12 CFR part 325, appendix A (FDIC); and 12 CFR part 567 (OTS). The risk weights are different, as in the case of Basle, for long-term and short-term ratings.[13] These are as in the tables below:

Table 29.4   Long-term ratings-based risk weights under U.S. regulations

Long-term rating category	Examples	Risk weight
Highest or second highest investment grade	AAA or AA	20%
Third highest investment grade	A	50%
Lowest investment grade	BBB	100%
One category below investment grade	BB	200%
More than one category below investment grade, or unrated	B or unrated	Not eligible for ratings-based approach

Short-term ratings-based risk weights under U.S. regulations

Short-term rating category	Examples	Risk weight
Highest investment grade	A-1, P-1	20%
Second highest investment grade	A-2, P-2	50%
Lowest investment grade	A-3, P-3	100%
Below investment grade	Not Prime	Not eligible for ratings-based treatment

Notably, the ratings-based approach is applicable to all asset-backed securities, whether retained or acquired, including residual interests, recourse obligations, except credit-enhancing IO strips.

The regulations make a distinction between "traded" and untraded positions; a traded position is a marketable security, that is, at the relevant time there is a reasonable expectation that an unaffiliated investor may buy that position relying on the rating. For a traded position, the rules require rating by only a rating agency. For an untraded position, the rating must be assigned by more than one rating agency and in case of any difference, the lower rating will be given regard.

For residual interests that do not qualify for ratings-based treatment (they are unrated or B or below rated) will call for dollar-for-dollar capital, as against the low-level recourse rule earlier. Notably, this is not the case for off-balance sheet recourse and direct credit substitutes, for which the low-level recourse rule continues to apply.

U.S. regulators apply an inferred rating to a super-senior position, that is, an unrated position senior in all respects to a rated position. In this case, the risk-weights for the unrated senior position will be based on that for the rated position immediately below it.

Internal ratings-based approach

The regulators have also permitted internal ratings-based approach for direct credit substitutes for ABCP programs. Unlike the Basle proposals, detailed formulae for working out capital under the IRB approach have not been laid down by the regulators, but reference has been made to software that would map internal ratings to those of the rating agencies.

The conditions to be satisfied to adopt the IRB approach are:

1. The internal credit risk system is an integral part of the bank's risk management system, which explicitly incorporates the full range of risks arising from a bank's participation in securitization activities;
2. Internal credit ratings are linked to measurable outcomes, such as the probability that the position will experience any loss, the position's expected loss given default, and the degree of variance in losses given default on that position;
3. The bank's internal credit risk system must separately consider the risk associated with underlying loans or borrowers, and the risk associated with the structure of a particular securitization transaction;
4. The bank's internal credit risk system must identify gradations of risk among "pass" assets and other risk positions;
5. The bank must have clear, explicit criteria that are used to classify assets into each internal risk grade, including subjective factors;
6. The bank must have independent credit risk management or a loan review personnel assigning or reviewing the credit risk ratings;
7. The bank must have an internal audit procedure that periodically verifies that the internal credit risk ratings are assigned in accordance with the established criteria;

8. The bank must monitor the performance of the internal credit risk ratings assigned to non-rated, non-traded direct credit substitutes over time to determine the appropriateness of the initial credit risk rating assignment and adjust individual credit risk ratings, or the overall internal credit risk ratings system, as needed; and

9. The internal credit risk system must make credit risk rating assumptions that are consistent with, or more conservative than, the credit risk rating assumptions and methodologies of the rating agencies.

If the conditions above have been satisfied, the direct credit substitute exposure will be risk-weighted as per the table above.

Basle IA

On October 20, 2005, federal regulators initiated dialogue process for a proposal to amend the existing risk-based capital rules. It appears that the implementation of Basle II will be delayed for several reasons. One, "the complexity and cost associated with implementing the Basel II framework effectively limit its application to those banking organizations that are able to take advantage of the economies of scale necessary to absorb these expenses. The implementation of Basel II would create a bifurcated regulatory capital framework in the United States, which may result in regulatory capital charges that differ for similar products offered by both large and small banking organizations." Two, as the preliminary results of QIS 4, which were released earlier in 2005, prompted concerns with respect to the (1) reduced levels of regulatory capital that would be required at individual banking organizations operating under the Basel II-based rules, and (2) dispersion of results among organizations and portfolio types. Because of these concerns, the issuance of a Basel II notice of proposed rule was postponed while the Agencies undertook additional analytical work. The notice was issued on March 30, 2006.

In the meantime, U.S. federal regulators have proposed amendments to the existing risk-based capital rules. Highlights of the proposed changes seek to increase the number of risk-weight categories, use LTV ratios in relation to risk weights for residential mortgage exposures, higher risk weights to 90-days' past due receivables, more risk-sensitive capital weights for retail, small business and commercial exposures, and require a risk-based capital charge for early amortization features in revolving asset securitizations. Some of these proposed changes are in line with Basle II; therefore, Basle IA seems to be a half-way house to Basle II.

We take up below the proposals relevant for securitization transactions:

Ratings-based risk weights

The proposal seeks to adopt ratings-based risk weights for most exposures, as against the exiting rule that applies to certain exposures only. In addition, the number of risk-weight slabs is proposed to be increased. Unlike Basle II, there is no distinction between risk weights applicable to the originator and the investor in securitization transactions, but the existing proposal in the Recourse Final Rule about sub-investment grade and unrated exposures is to be retained. The proposed risk weights are as follows:

Table 29.5 Illustrative risk weights based on external ratings

Long-term rating category	Examples	Risk weights
Highest two investments grade ratings	AAA/AA	20%
Third-highest investment grade rating	A	35%
Third-lowest investment grade rating	BBB+	50%
Second-lowest investment grade rating	BBB	75%
Lowest investment grade rating	BBB–	100%
One category below investment grade	BB+, BB, BB–	200%
Two or more categories below investment grade	B and lower	350%

Table 29.6 Illustrative risk weights based on short-term external ratings

Short-term rating category	Examples	Risk weights
Highest investments grade ratings	A-1	20%
Second-highest investment grade rating	A-2	35%
Lowest investment grade rating	A-3	75%

Capital requirements for early amortization

In line with Basle II, the proposed rule lays down capital requirements for the early amortization risk inherent in revolving securitizations. The proposals relate the capital charge to position of the 3-month average excess spread with the excess spread at the trapping point; however, distinction between controlled and uncontrolled early amortizations found in Basle II is missing here. The proposed capital requirements are:

Table 29.7 Example of credit conversion factor assignment by segment

3-month average excess spread	Credit conversion factor (CCF)
133.33% of trapping point or more	0%
less than 133.33% to 100% of trapping point	5%
less than 100% to 75% of trapping point	15%
less than 75% to 50% of trapping point	50%
less than 50% of trapping point	100%

FSA U.K.'s guidelines for capital relief

The Financial Services Authority, U.K. (FSA) had issued detailed guidelines [FSA Guidelines on Securitization and Loan Transfers dated June 29, 1998] for regulatory treatment of securitization. These have been improvised over time. The FSA has published interim prudential rulebooks for banks, building societies and other intermediaries regulated by the FSA. The rules applicable to banks are contained in SE section of the Interim Prudential Rulebook of the FSA.[14] From December 31, 2004, the FSA has begun the process of integration of the sectoral rulebooks for different financial intermediaries into a consolidated set.

General

The FSA's rules are applicable to both securitization and asset transfers and these rules are available on the SE section of the prudential rulebook. The rules applicable to securitization are substantively the same applicable to bilateral asset transfers, with some additional stipulations for securitization.

FSA defines securitization as "a process by which assets are sold to a *bankruptcy remote special purpose vehicle* (SPV) in return for an immediate cash payment. The cash payment is raised by the SPV issuing debt securities, usually in the form of tradable notes or commercial paper."

The "clean break" policy

Like all other regulators, the FSA is concerned about the possible repercussions of securitization on a bank. Of these, the most obvious is retained risk. The FSA cautions that even if a bank achieves a legal transfer of assets and therefore caps its risks, there might be a reputational risk that might linger on. This would be particularly so in cases where the transferring bank retains a continued involvement with the assets. As a solution, the FSA recommends a "clean break" policy: "The solution for the FSA has been to implement the policy of "clean break." A bank, once it has securitized assets, should not have any further involvement with those assets except in accordance with the policy in this chapter. This should be the case both explicitly and implicitly, i.e. any reputational linkage between the assets of the originator/sponsor should be broken so far as is possible."

According to the FSA, this can be achieved by:

(a) The immediate legal separation of the seller from the assets and their new owner;
(b) As far as possible, the complete economic separation of the seller from the assets and their new owner;
(c) Presentational or "moral" separation of the seller from the assets and their new owner; and
(d) The identification of the retained risks for capital or other coverage purposes.

Role of banks in securitization

Banks may play *primary* and *secondary* roles in securitization; a primary role implies the bank being a party to the transaction of securitization, whereas a secondary role is that of a facilitator or service provider. In primary role, banks may be originators, or a sponsor or repackager (implying repackaging in arbitrage transactions, sponsors of CDOs or ABCP conduits). In a secondary role, banks may be servicers, liquidity providers, credit enhancers and underwriters.

The prudential and capital relief guidelines are different for originators and repackagers; therefore, it is essential to distinguish between the two. The FSA rules also provide that for repackaging, the assets repackaged must be investment-grade, third-party assets; in case they are below investment-grade, the repackager will be treated as originator. In the repackaging role, up to 10% of originated assets, and likewise up to 10% of below-investment-grade assets are allowed.

For each of these roles, the regulators describe the potential risks to which the bank may be exposed. Barring fine details, these risks are broadly the same as those discussed in context of the U.S. regulations.

Methods of transfer

The FSA would recognize various legal methods of transfer, provided they satisfy the precondition of giving to the bank a "clean break." Four methods of asset transfer have specifically been approved in the rules; other methods, particularly in other jurisdictions, may be permitted based on legal opinion and prior FSA approval. The four methods approved are – assignment, novation, sub-participation and declaration of trust.[15] Other methods of transfer are permitted, provided they are backed by legal opinion and prior approval of the FSA.

Assignment is the legal transfer of the rights (and not the obligations) arising out of a contract. Assignments may be legal or equitable. The FSA would recognize *silent assignments*, that is, where obligor notification is not given,[16] as a valid clean break device, provided:

(a)   the volume of assets to individual borrowers sold on a silent assignment basis should be subject to appropriate internal controls;

(b)   the seller should keep under careful review the risks that follow on from this position as it remains the lender of record and therefore will be the focal point for pressure from the borrower.

Novation is a transfer of the rights of the lender achieved by amending the originating agreement with the borrower; therefore, the borrower's express consent is a must. In the FSA's view, a novation is the cleanest method of risk transfer.

Declaration of trust implies that the transferor continues to hold assets but declares that he holds them in trust for the intended transferee (the SPV). Hence, there is a transfer of beneficial interest, without there being a legal transfer. The FSA accepts declaration of trust subject to the preconditions as for silent transfers.

Sub-participation is not a transfer of the asset in legal sense, but creation of an obligation on the part of the "transferor" to allow the "transferee" to participate in the receivables from the asset, either wholly or in part. Therefore, this is a non-recourse funding on back-to-back basis. As there is no unconditional obligation on the part of the "transferor" to pay to the participant, it is not treated as an obligation of the "transferor" but a transfer of the asset. For the participant, it is treated as an exposure on the underlying borrower (and not against the "transferor").

Conditions for primary role

The following are general conditions applicable:

For both single loans and loan packages

(a) The transfer does not contravene the terms and conditions of the underlying loan agreement and all the necessary consents have been obtained;

(b) The seller has no residual beneficial interest in the principal amount of the loan (or that part which has been transferred) and the buyer has no formal recourse to the seller for losses;

(c) The seller has no obligation to repurchase the loan (or fund the repayment of a sub-participation), or any part of it, at any time;

The seller may, however, retain an option to repurchase performing assets provided the balance outstanding has fallen below 10% of the original outstanding (that is, a clean-up call option). Any other call option is also prohibited.

An exception to this restriction on repurchase obligation is where the obligation arises from warranties given in respect of the loan at the time of its transfer, provided that these are not in respect of the future credit-worthiness of the borrower. The warranties must relate to matters not outside the control of the transferor. Environmental warranties may be given, but these should restrict liability to legislation in force at the time of sale, not at any time in the future otherwise they may be regarded as constituting a warranty on matters outside the originator's control.

Notably, under the FSA norms, there is an exception for a conduit sponsor or re-packager; a sponsor or re-packager may have a repurchase agreement with the SPV. The important limitation here is that the repurchase must be for investment grade assets and at market prices. For defaulted assets, the repurchase may be at nominal values. As the repurchase has to be at market value, the value of the put or call option, by definition, is zero, and therefore, the option loses its meaning.

(d) The seller can demonstrate that it has given notice to the buyer that it is under no obligation to repurchase the loan (or fund the repayment of a sub-participation), nor support any losses suffered by the buyer, and that the buyer has acknowledged the absence of obligation; if the seller is a subsidiary of a bank, the parent bank may provide a guarantee in respect of the seller's obligation to the SPV as to the seller passing on payments it receives in respect of the securitized assets. However, the guarantee can go no further than the obligations of the seller itself.

(e) The documented terms of the transfer are such that, if the loan is rescheduled or renegotiated, the buyer and not the seller would be subject to the rescheduled or renegotiated terms; and

(f) Where payments are routed through it, the seller is under no obligation to remit funds to the buyer unless and until they are received from the borrower.

Payments voluntarily made by the seller to the buyer in anticipation of payments from the borrower must be made on terms under which they can be recovered from the buyer if the borrower fails to perform.

Additional requirements for loan packages

For transfer of loan pools or portfolios, the seller has additional responsibility of pooling. The process of packaging loans together and selling them as a block or pool can compound risks. The commercial reputation of the originator is committed because of its close association with the scheme; such a commitment may jeopardize the existence of a clean break and there may be pressure to support any losses of investors. Therefore, there are additional conditions laid down for pooling obligations:

(a) The FSA expects the servicing agent and originator to have evidence available in their records that their auditors and legal advisers are satisfied (i) that the terms of the scheme protect them from any liability to investors in the scheme, other than liability for breach of express contractual performance obligations as servicing agent or originator or for breach of warranty made with respect to the assets in conformity with the other requirements of these rules, or liability for any other matter wholly within the control of the originator; (ii) that the terms of the scheme comply with U.K. accounting standard FRS5;[17] and (iii) that the terms of the Scheme comply with FSA's policy. This should be confirmed in writing to the FSA.

(b) The servicing agent and originator must be able to demonstrate that they have taken all reasonable precautions to ensure that they are not obliged, nor will feel impelled, to support any losses suffered by the scheme or investors in it. This requirement may be met by any offering circular (or other analogous documentation) containing a highly visible, unequivocal statement that neither the servicing agent nor the originator stand behind the issue or the vehicle and will not make good any losses in the portfolio.

(c) The seller must not hold any share capital or any other form of proprietary interest in the SPV. In addition, the SPV should be an independent, in terms of control as well as composition of the Board of Directors.

(d) The provision of insurance cover by a subsidiary of the bank against loss, e.g., mortgage indemnity insurance, may be viewed as unacceptable support, despite this being an arms-length transaction.

(e) The name of a company used as vehicle for a scheme must not include the name of the servicing agent or the originator nor imply any connection with either.

(f) The servicing agent or originator must not bear any of the recurring expenses of the scheme. Credit enhancements may be offered based on conditions discussed separately below.

(g) A servicing agent or originator may not fund a vehicle or scheme and in particular may not provide temporary finance to a scheme to cover cash shortfalls arising from delayed payments or non-performance of loans which it administers. Liquidity facilities are discussed separately below.

(h) The seller or primary party should not enter into any swap arrangement with the SPV whereby the former bears the losses of the latter. The rules clarify that this does not apply to interest rate swaps and exchange rate swaps; therefore, the obvious reference is to total rate of return swaps or credit default swaps.[18]

Conditions for replenishing assets and revolving credits

Like most other regulatory statements, the FSA puts certain additional conditions for replenishing asset transfers, such as for credit cards, where the transferor continues to transfer assets on a continuing basis. The conditions here are similar to those under the Basle or U.S. norms. These are:

(a) The asset quality of the pool is not materially altered by the addition;

(b) Any change to the quality of the assets remaining with the originating bank is either not material or is acceptable to the regulators.

(c) (for revolving credit securitization only) There is no change in the liquidity implications of the securitization resulting from the addition; and

(d) There are no unacceptable changes to the "moral" risks to the originator signaled by the addition.

For revolving credits, that is, those assets where the borrowers enjoy a revolving credit facility where the drawn amount at any time is uncertain, there are additional risks perceived by the regulators. It is common to securitize such credits using a master trust or similar structure where the transferee issues a seller interest and investor interest, the seller interest representing the excess of the actual receivables at any time over the investor interest.

The FSA's fundamental policy with regard to revolving credits is "that the arrangements for the securitization should ensure the full sharing of interest, principal, expenses, losses and recoveries on a clear and consistent basis. This principle implies, among other things, the need for full loss-sharing on the stock of receivables in the pool throughout the revolving period of the securitization, since the investors' share of the receivables is removed in full from the originating bank's balance sheet for the whole of that period."

The FSA makes distinction between the *aggregated structure* and the *disaggregated structure* – the former implying a case where the entire receivables pool held by the master trust is regarded as a homogenous pool from which distributions are made to the seller and investors based on the respective shares held by each. For disaggregated structures, the respective assets are appropriated against originator interest and investor interest separately. For aggregated structures, the concern of the regulators is that the seller might face liquidity risk when the scheduled amortization period commences; usually, the scheme provisions require a repayment of investor principal out of aggregated collections, which includes even repayment of the principal on financings done after the commencement of the amortization period. Thus, the originator may be actually paying for investor interest out of its own liquidity rather than that generated from the assets. To allay this fear, the FSA requires the seller to demonstrate that the repayments made by the borrowers during the amortization period will be sufficient to pay 90% of the principal repayments to investors.

Most revolving and reinstating transactions carry early amortization features. Early amortization triggers are *economic triggers* and *non-economic triggers*. The former includes various indicators of a deterioration of the quality of the pool. The latter includes exogenous events like tax factors and insolvency of the originator. Economic triggers are a sort of credit support; the FSA accepts these triggers provided it is satisfied that when hit, the bank may be able to reduce its own origination volumes broadly in line with the early amortization.

Capital treatment

Subject to compliance with the conditions above, a bank transferring assets is able to remove the assets from its supervisory balance sheet, and hence attain capital relief. There are provisions for credit enhancements, discussed below.

Capital treatment for credit enhancements

Any arrangement that, in form and substance, covers the losses and risks on the pool of the assets is a credit enhancement. Purchase of investment-grade securities of the SPV is not treated as a credit enhancement if the same are protected by sufficient enhancement themselves.

The FSA has put several conditions to be satisfied by the credit enhancer bank itself:

(a) The credit-enhancement facility is limited in amount and duration and there should be no recourse to the enhancing bank beyond the contractual limits;

(b) The SPV and/or investors in a bond issue have the clear right to select an alternative party to provide the facility; in other words, the enhancement should be structured as a support to an independent party;

(c) The facility is documented separately from any other facility provided by the bank;

(d) The transaction should be undertaken at the initiation of the scheme;
(e) The details of the facility should be disclosed in any offering circular or other appropriate documentation; and
(f) Payment of any fee or other income for the facility is not further subordinated, or subject to deferral or waiver, beyond what is already explicitly provided for in the applicable order of priority and other payment entitlement provisions.

For capital treatment, the regulators make a distinction between *first-loss* and the *second- or subsequent-loss* credit enhancement. First-loss is defined as the support that bears the brunt of the credit risk on the assets held by the SPV, as required for bringing the SPV's securities to investment grade. Subsequent tiers of protection are treated as second-loss facility. From the language, it is clear that if there are several sequential classes of securities below investment grade, they should all be treated as first-loss classes.

The capital treatment for an originator for credit enhancements is as under:

- For a first-loss facility, the originator may either deduct the facility from capital or may provide for capital as if the assets had never been transferred. Effectively, therefore, the capital requirement is the lower of the first-loss portion, or the capital required for on-balance sheet assets.
- For a second-loss facility, the originator should deduct the amount of the facility from the capital. As noted earlier, investment in investment grade securities is not treated as a credit enhancement under FSA norms; therefore, this should not be applied to purchase of investment grade paper.

The capital treatment for a sponsor or repackager is:

- For a first-loss facility, the sponsor/repackager must deduct the amount of the facility from capital fully. Therefore, here is a provision for dollar-for-dollar capital.
- For a second-loss facility, the sponsor/repackager might only provide risk-weighted capital.

Conditions for liquidity facility

The primary regulatory concern for liquidity facilities is the same as by other regulators – that the facility may not be a credit enhancement in disguise. Therefore, the FSA provides for a set of conditions to be satisfied:

(a) The facility is provided on an arm's length basis and is subject to the bank's normal credit review and approval processes;
(b) The facility may be reduced or terminated should a specified event relating to a deterioration in asset quality occur;
(c) The facility should be conducted on market terms and conditions;
(d) The facility is limited in amount and duration; there is no recourse to the bank beyond the fixed contractual obligations provided for in the facility;

(e) The SPV and/or the note trustee representing the investors have the clear right to select an alternative facilitator;

(f) The facility is documented separately;

(g) Payment of any fee or other income for the facility is not further subordinated, or subject to deferral or waiver, beyond what is already explicitly provided for in the waterfall;

(h) The facility may not be drawn for the purposes of credit support;

(i) The facility documentation clearly defines the circumstances under which the facility may be drawn and prohibits drawing in any other circumstances;

(j) The facility will provide for repayment of advances within a reasonable time period;

(k) The funding is provided to (or via) the SPV and not directly to investors;

(l) Proceeds of drawings under the facility cannot be used to provide permanent revolving funding, or be for the express purpose of purchasing underlying assets held by an SPV;

(m) The funding cannot be used to cover losses recorded by the SPV; and

(n) Drawings under the facility are not subordinated to the interests of investors, except that drawings may be subordinated to other liquidity facilities if tiered liquidity facilities are used in a scheme. Such subordination should be clearly set out in the offering circular or other appropriate documentation.

Consultation paper on revised capital rules

In line with the CRD of the European Union (see below), the FSA U.K. released in January 2005 a Consultation Paper, entitled Strengthening Capital Standards. Broadly, the proposals will institute Basle II type capital requirements, generally as per CRD (see discussion below on the CRD).

EU capital directive

The EU has circulated the Capital Requirements Directive (CRD). The circulation of the CRD has been approved by the Economic and Finance Ministers to the European Parliament's legislative resolution. The CRD reflects the Basel II rules on capital measurement and capital standards agreed at the G-10 level. The Commission proposed the Directive on July 14, 2004 and it was approved by the European Parliament on September 28, 2005.

The CRD defines securitization as:

"a transaction or scheme, whereby the credit risk associated with an exposure or pool of exposures is tranched, having the following characteristics:

(a) payments in the transaction or scheme are dependent upon the performance of the exposure or pool of exposures; and

(b) the subordination of tranches determines the distribution of losses during the ongoing life of the transaction or scheme."

Sub-section (4) of section 2 deals with securitization. The requirements broadly reflect the recommendations in Basle II.

Regulatory requirements in other countries

The German financial supervisory body has issued guidelines on securitization that draw from international experience. A brief description of these guidelines has been given under the country profile of Germany – see Chapter 3 entitled **The World of Securitization**.

The Hong Kong Monetary Authority (HKMA) has also issued guidelines that are broadly in line with those of Bank of England. The important requirements are:

- The offering documentation must clearly state that the originating bank is not liable for any losses of the SPV and does not stand behind the SPV. This is to ensure that the sponsoring bank does not have any moral risk on the securitization transaction.
- Any losses must be borne by the SPV and subsequently by the investors. No credit support should be provided by the originating bank. If any support is provided by way of subordinated loans to the SPV, the amount of such loans should be deducted from the capital of the bank.
- There must be no obligation upon the originator to buy back any loans, including delinquent loans. An option with the originator to buy back loans, however, does not militate against this requirement.
- To prevent against investors viewing the SPV as a subset or alter ego of the originator, it is required that the SPV must not borrow the name of the originator. The originator may appoint only one director on the board of the SPV and must not bear the expenses on the SPV.
- Transfer of loans by the originator must not violate any of the conditions of the underlying loan agreements.

Securitization and economic capital

Meaning of economic capital

Capital is a cushion against bankruptcy. Capital is required to protect against losses arising from contingencies. A contingent loss is a risk, and there are various sources of risk to a bank or financial intermediary. The primary sources of risk to a bank are credit risk, market risk and operational risk. The capital standards discussed above impose requirement of capital primarily to protect against credit risks.

While the risk-based capital standards discussed above, in their pre-Basle II form, apply the same risk weightage to all corporate exposures, irrespective of the quality of the asset or the portfolio, economic capital is the measure of real economic risk inherent in banking assets. Most banks have of late put in place economic capital models as regulatory capital standards, which have been found to be of little use in assisting banks to compute the capital required for what is the most basic use of capital – bankruptcy risk protection.[19]

Economic capital models have only one element of consistency – their purpose. But each bank may have its own approach to economic capital and therefore there is no industry standard as far as measurement of economic capital goes.

Expected and unexpected losses

Credit risk can expose the bank to two types of losses – *expected losses* and *unexpected losses*. The expected loss is the weighted-average loss – weighted based on the probabilities of different loss levels. Mathematically, the expected loss is the expected value of different probabilities of losses. Unexpected losses measure the diversion from the average; the fact that at a certain level of probability, the actual loss may be more or less than the average. We are not concerned with the actual loss being less than the expected value, as that is no risk at all. But if there is a certain level of probability that the actual loss might exceed the expected loss, there must be capital to meet the same. Mathematically, the unexpected loss is the deviation of the loss from the mean value.

As the unexpected loss may be high with a low chance (for instance, there is a 0.01% chance that the loss might go up x amount), economic capital is the capital needed to save the bank from bankruptcy, that is, to meet losses up to a confidence level. If we have provided for economic capital at 0.01% chance of a higher loss, we have covered the bank with 99.99% *confidence level*. The confidence level is the extent of probabilities up to which the economic capital would meet the loss.

Notably, economic capital is not needed for expected losses, as the loss is anyway expected and must have been priced out in pricing the credit. In other words, that loss would be covered by the spreads or profits of the bank.

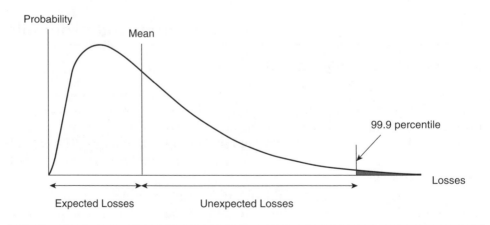

Figure 29.4 Illustrating economic capital

The curve above shows various levels of losses and their respective probabilities; there are losses going up, although with increasingly less chance to the right hand side. If capital is provided equal to the mean and the 99.9% (cumulative probabilities up to this point), there is only a 0.01% chance that the loss will exceed the capital.

> A trite analogy is the story of a man who measured the average depth of a river he was to cross and compared it with his own height to see if he could wade through it. The result is an easy guess. As one may realize, the man considered the average depth of the river but did not consider the deviation from the average depth that was important to save him from sinking.

Economic capital is needed to save the bank from sinking – bankruptcy – in those cases where the portfolio risk deviates from the mean or expected losses. If deviations are measured in terms of standard deviations, one can compute the required economic capital as the number of standard deviations for a given level of confidence, or in other words, to reduce the chances of bankruptcy to a given extent.

The confidence level itself is set with a target rating in mind. For example, some banks target reducing the risk of bankruptcy to 0.03%, considered to be the historical default rate on AA-rated corporate bonds, as this level of economic capital would make the bank a primary candidate for an equivalent rating.

How is economic capital computed?

Economic capital models may broadly be classified into *default paradigm* models and *mark-to-market models*. Default paradigm models try to assess the unexpected losses on account of default. A mark-to-market paradigm recognizes losses due to decline in market value of an asset that has not actually defaulted.

As is evident from the graphic above, there are two key inputs for a default-based economic capital model – the probabilities of default (PD) and the loss given default (LGD). In case the loan is an amortizing loan, another element is the exposure at the time of default (EAD). The probabilities of default at different levels are referred to as *probability density function*. Evidently, the most critical task in economic capital computation is inputting the PDs.

Arguably, the internal credit rating of the customer is critical in estimating the PDs. These, in turn, could be based on internal scoring models or could draw upon external information, including analysis of financial data. Banks might try to map their internal ratings with those by the rating agencies to be able to use the default matrices of rating agencies. The default matrices of rating agencies rely on the rating transition matrices, the probabilities of an entity with a certain rating going into default.

The approach where unexpected losses of each asset in a portfolio is computed, and thereafter aggregated to compute the capital required for a portfolio, is called the *bottom up* approach. On the other hand, if losses are assessed based on an aggregate portfolio, the approach is called *top down* approach.

For mark-to-market model, capital is required not merely based on default, but to cover against losses on impairment of the value of credit assets. That is to say, capital is needed not merely to provide for a technically defaulted asset but is required much ahead of default to meet losses in valuation of the credit asset. Losses in valuation arise when the fair value of credit asset declines. Hence, under this method, capital is required based on decline in fair values.

The fair value, in turn, may be computed based on a discounted cash flow (DCF) basis or based on risk-neutral valuation (RNV). The DCF approach computes the present value of future contractual cash flow at discounting rates reset to reflect the credit spreads applied by the market (based on yield curves) on similarly rated credits. Thus, as the credit quality of an asset deteriorates, the credit spread goes up, and hence the fair value of the asset comes down.

The RNV approaches bases itself on Robert Merton's analysis of a loan being an option written in favor of the equity holders to declare bankruptcy and transfer the assets of the firm to the lenders. Under this approach, instead of taking into account the contractual cash flows of the borrower, the contingent cash flows are taken into account. The contingent cash flow is the par value if the borrower does not default and the recovery rate in case the borrower defaults. Obviously, there is a linkage between the default paradigm model discussed above and the RNV model. The only difference is that under the RNV model, instead of computing merely the losses at the time of default, the valuation of the loan is done by applying risk-neutral discounting rates over the contingent cash flows.

Regulatory arbitrage

As existing regulatory norms require banks to hold capital based on a certain risk weight irrespective of the risk of the asset, securitization helps banks to obtain a regulatory capital relief by reducing the capital from the regulatory haircut to the economic capital. Assuming a bank provides sufficient credit enhancement to cover unexpected losses up to an investment grade rating, the bank will need to provide first-loss cover at a confidence level sufficient to get a BBB rating. If this first-loss retention is a deduction from capital, the bank exposes its capital only equal to economic capital, and thus, receives capital relief to the extent of the excess of regulatory capital over economic capital.

This is known as regulatory capital arbitrage.

Basle II norms try to bridge the gap between regulatory capital and economic capital. To the extent this is effective, regulatory capital arbitrage as a motive for securitizations will become redundant.

Notes

1 These reports may have different market names: for example, call reports (Consolidated Report on Condition and Income), as they are referred to in the U.S.

2 International Convergence of Capital Measurement and Capital Standards: A Revised Framework

3 The reference to paragraph numbers in this chapter is to the revised version of November 2005.

4 The Advance Notice of Proposed Rule was published on October 20, 2005, and is available at http://www.fdic.gov/regulations/laws/federal/2005/05basel1020. html, last visited December 27, 2005.

5 Notably, Pillar 2 is a supervisory discretion.

6 Para 552.

7 The issue seems to have evoked similar response from the industry. For example, in his testimony, June 22, 2004, before House Financial Services Committee on New Basel Accord Private Sector Perspectives, Adam Gilbert of JP Morgan stated as follows: "We acknowledge that when FMI and reserve accounts are available to absorb losses they are still at risk and therefore should be deducted. However, this treatment should be limited to gains that remain at risk. Banks should not be required to deduct crystallized gains. For example, mortgage-backed securitizations sell their future margin income strips and lock in the profit upon securitization. More generally, banks should not be required to deduct gains when the securitization *locks in* an arbitrage, i.e. banks can buy assets in one format (single-name credit exposures) and repackage the risk for sale in another format (portfolio-tranched credit exposures). The bank's gains should only be deducted when they pertain to amounts which remain at risk due to the future performance of the exposure pool." [at http://financialservices.house.gov/media/pdf/062204ag.pdf, last visited December 27, 2005]

8 Requirements of Para 452 to 459 define when an asset is in default.

9 Ratings may be inferred only for unrated senior positions; where there are rated positions subordinated to the unrated position and certain other operational conditions, listed in Para 617, are satisfied. In practice, this would mostly apply for super-senior tranches, where an inferred rating is equal to the senior-most rating to rated tranches.

10 For the theoretical foundations of the model, see *Model Foundations for the Supervisory Formula Approach*, by Michael B. Gordy, July 2004.

11 When the amount of a receivable suffers a reduction on account of set-offs or deductions, such as netting off of mutual claims, the amount of receivables are diluted, other than on account of default. This is dilution risk.

12 OCC 96-52 *Securitization – Guidelines for National Banks* September 25, 1996.

13 The risk weights are different from those under BIS Consultative Paper 3, but it may be noted that at the time when U.S. regulators framed these proposals, consultative paper 1 was only available.

14 June 2001 version, amended from time to time. The version used here is latest version is available on FSA site at http://fsahandbook.info/FSA/html/handbook, last visited December 28, 2005.

15 These methods of asset transfer have been discussed in the chapter on Legal Issues.

16 By definition, a silent assignment would be treated as an equitable assignment in law.

17 See for details, the chapter on Accounting for Securitization

18 These are credit derivative contracts. For more details, see Vinod Kothari's *Credit Derivatives and Synthetic Securitization*. For latest information, see http://vinod-kothari.com/crebook.htm

19 Apart from the fact that regulatory risk standards are unrelated to the real risk, the relevance of regulatory standards to capital needs has also been greatly reduced by regulatory arbitrage devices, particularly asset securitization by leading banks. "Spurred by opportunities for regulatory capital arbitrage created by the above anomalies, securitization and other financial innovations are rendering the formal RBC ratios increasingly less meaningful, at least for the largest, most sophisticated banks. Through securitization, in particular, large banks have lowered their RBC requirements substantially without reducing materially their overall credit risk exposures." David Jones and John Mingo, Board of Governors of the Federal Reserve System: *Industry Practices in Credit Risk Modeling and Internal Capital Allocations: Implications for a Models-based Regulatory Capital Standard*, January 29, 1998.

Part V: Investing in Asset-backed Securities

Chapter 30

Investing in Securitization Instruments

I n this chapter, we discuss the experience of investors in investing in securitization transactions. In addition, we specifically examine the aspects in securitization transactions that investors will need to analyze. Some general investor concerns, as the benefits of securitization to investors, the legal issues from investors' viewpoint, taxation issues and accounting issues have been noted earlier under relevant chapters. We have also taken up investors' financial analysis of securitization transactions in an earlier chapter.

As noted before, securitization transactions have mostly drawn institutional investors. The demand for securitized products has been quite strong, and over the years, securitized products have been bought and have been traded at very fine spreads to comparable high grade investments such as U.S. Treasuries or LIBOR.

However, the securitization market is still comparatively a new market. Most countries are only beginning to enter into securitization transactions. Legal systems in most countries are still not mature enough. The lawyers and courts have yet to understand the nuances of securitization. Therefore, the level of interest evinced today may well prove to be an overdrive, if investor prudence precedes the novelty of the instrument and the associated zeal.

Distinguishing between securitization instruments and other fixed income investments

While asset-backed securities[1] look like other fixed income securities, there are certain features that are significantly different.

Irregular cash flows

Most asset-backed securities will have irregular cash flows, as they pass on prepayments to investors. A straight corporate security is a claim on the borrower, which the borrower pays on stated intervals. There might be a callability option on corporate bonds as well, but for asset-backed securities, the prepayment arises due to prepayments, foreclosures and repayments on the collateral pool. Normally, in pass-through as well as in bond-type structures, prepayments of principal will be passed on to investors by retiring the principal. This may not be true for reinstating type transactions, but there too, acceleration triggers pose a prepayment risk.

Thus, the timing as well as the speed of asset-backed investments might be irregular.

Derived cash flows

By definition, asset-backed investments are investments in the underlying collateral pool. From the viewpoint of risk as well as returns, investors need to be concerned about the pool characteristics.

Average maturity as a mark of duration

Asset-backed investments are similar to an amortizing loan: periodic distributions by the SPV will include both interest and principal. Besides, principal payment may be liable to acceleration due to prepayment speed or other factors. Hence, the duration relevant for asset-backed securities is the weighted-average maturity of the pool.

Callability and extension risk

All mortgage-backed and asset-backed investments have a callability and extension risk. Callability implies the risk of principal is paid faster than the schedule. Extension risk is the opposite of callability; it implies the tenure of the security extended due to lower prepayment levels. The risk of callability is essentially a reinvestment risk, as investors may be forced to reinvest the returning cash flows at the current, and possibly, reduced rates. Extension risk, on the other hand, affects investors in a period of increasing interest rates.

Both prepayment risk and extension risk are two sides of the same coin. Both imply a repricing risk passed on to the investor. For numericals on the measurement of callability risk, see Chapter 10.

Investors' concerns in securitization investments

This section focuses on investors' concerns and risks inherent in securitization investments.

Price discovery

In view of the unique features of asset-backed securities, investors' major concern is price discovery. That this is a major area of concern from investors' viewpoint was confirmed by an investors' survey conducted by Greenwich Associates, on behalf of the American Securitization Forum.

Credit risk

The most significant risk that is bound to concern investors is the credit risk of the underlying asset pool. The level of this risk is a function of the quality of the portfolio and the credit enhancements. However, a hard look at the credit quality is one of the most important things for an investor, because the investor has put in his money on the strength of the assets and not the quality of the originator.

A study of the credit risk is a primary responsibility of the rating agency assigning rating to the transaction, but key investors do their own analysis based on the data contained in offer documents.

The credit risk of the portfolio is itself a complex matrix built around several variables. Some of these are discussed below:

Diversification

Diversification is one of the most important sources of comfort to the investors. Diversification minimizes the correlation that might exist in the performance of individual obligors during certain economic events. For example, the CMBS market is representative of a less diversified pool, with the value of each individual mortgage high enough. There have been a number of cases where several mortgage obligors have defaulted at the same time. In other words, there is a high degree of correlation present. However, when the obligor population comes from different walks of life, possibly deriving their own income from different economic sectors, the chances of certain economic events affecting a large section of the obligors are minimized. There have been cases of an overall crisis, such as the Thai currency crisis, but even in such eventualities, the Thai cars securitization transaction did not default.

In the parlance of BIS new capital regime norms, this is referred to as *granularity* of the portfolio.[2]

Loan-to-value ratio

Default is also a function of the obligor's propensity to pay. Economic events may affect the obligors' ability to pay, but the willingness of the obligors to pay is driven by several factors, of which, in an asset-backed financing market, the loan-to-value (LTV) ratio is certainly one of the most important factors.

In financial economics, a loan is a contingent claim on the assets of the obligor; if the assets of the obligor fall below the liabilities, an obligor declares bankruptcy. In asset-based funding language, this translates into the following; if the value of the asset falls below the outstanding amount of the funding facility, the borrower has an incentive to declare a default, irrespective of his residual assets. The loan-to-value ratio determines the amount of the loan to the value of the asset, and the movement of the two over time. Thus, a low

LTV ratio ensures a borrower's positive equity at all times, and thus is a great protection against default.

There are several international studies mapping the behavior of defaults with the LTV ratio. For example, the following tables show the impact of LTV on the default probability, loss severity and expected losses in various countries:[3]

Table 30.1   Rating agency default probability assumptions by LTV by country for BBB rating

Default Probabilities

LTV ranges	Australia	Germany	Holland	Spain	U.K.	U.S.	Six country averages relative to 75.01–80%
<= 40	2.00%	2.00%	3.00%	3.00%	2.00%	1.20%	0.39
40.01–50	3.00%	3.00%	3.00%	3.00%	3.00%	1.80%	0.49
50.01–60	3.00%	3.00%	3.00%	4.00%	4.00%	2.50%	0.56
60.01–65	4.00%	3.00%	3.00%	4.00%	5.00%	3.00%	0.62
65.01–70	4.00%	4.00%	4.00%	4.00%	6.00%	3.70%	0.73
70.01–75	6.00%	4.00%	4.00%	5.00%	6.00%	4.60%	0.84
75.01–80	6.00%	5.00%	5.00%	6.00%	7.00%	6.00%	1
80.01–85	7.00%	6.00%	6.00%	7.00%	8.00%	8.10%	1.2
85.01–90	9.00%	7.00%	7.00%	8.00%	10.00%	11.00%	1.48
90.01–95	11.00%	9.00%	8.00%	10.00%	13.00%	15.10%	1.88
95.01–98	14.00%	10.00%	9.00%	12.00%	16.00%	20.60%	2.31
98.01–100	16.00%	12.00%	10.00%	16.00%	18.00%	23.20%	2.69

Table 30.2   Rating agency loss severity assumptions by LTV by country for BBB rating

Loss Severity

LTV ranges	Australia	Germany	Holland	Spain	U.K.	U.S.	Six country averages relative to 75.01–80%
<= 40	0.00%	0.00%	0.00%	0.00%	0.00%	0.00%	0
40.01–50	0.00%	0.00%	0.00%	0.00%	0.00%	0.00%	0
50.01–60	7.50%	3.90%	10.10%	12.70%	0.00%	0.00%	0.15
60.01–65	16.50%	12.70%	18.00%	22.30%	8.54%	6.54%	0.4
65.01–70	24.30%	20.20%	24.80%	30.60%	16.29%	14.29%	0.63
70.01–75	31.00%	26.80%	30.60%	37.70%	23.00%	21.00%	0.83
75.01–80	36.90%	32.50%	35.80%	44.00%	28.88%	26.88%	1
80.01–85	42.10%	37.50%	40.30%	49.50%	34.06%	32.06%	1.15
85.01–90	46.70%	42.00%	44.40%	54.40%	38.67%	36.67%	**1.29**
90.01–95	50.80%	46.00%	48.00%	58.80%	42.79%	40.79%	**1.41**
95.01–98	52.30%	47.50%	49.30%	60.50%	44.32%	42.32%	1.46
98.01–100	54.50%	49.60%	51.20%	62.80%	46.50%	44.50%	**1.52**

Collateral quality

The obligor's propensity to pay is also directly affected by the quality of the collateral. The higher the quality of the collateral, the more is the propensity to pay. Mathematically, the lower the loan-to-value ratio at a given time, the more is the propensity to pay. Quality of the collateral may be purely an academic value, if the SPV cannot lay hands on the collateral and convert it to value. This will be determined by foreclosure procedures for confiscating the collateral, physical and logistical ease in doing so and the ability to dispose of it.

In some cases, obligations are completely unsecured, such as credit card receivables. Here, obviously, the investor relies upon the very high extent of diversification.

Servicer quality

Also very important is the ability of the servicer in terms of systems and administrative ability to efficiently manage the receivables. Efficient administration of receivables with proper collection and follow up machinery itself reduces the chances of default. Coupled with this, the servicer must also be capable of tracking the collateral and if required, repossessing it. Where the value of the collateral is important, the servicer must also have regular inspection and valuation systems in place. The servicing risk, a significant part of the operational risk in a securitization transaction, has been discussed at length in Chapter 25.

Counterparty risk

This relates to the risk of the credit enhancers. The credit enhancers might include the originator himself. It will also include all parties who have provided credit enhancement for the transaction. Investors are likely to rely on the ratings of the enhancement providers.

There may be a number of ancillary facilities such as swaps in a securitization transaction. Exchange rate swaps are most common in international sourcing. Interest rate swaps are also quite common. The quality of the swap counterparties is also critical for the investors.

Transaction legal risk

This represents the possibility that some of the fundamental legal assumptions in the transaction are proven invalid. For example, a court may disregard the SPV's title over the receivables recharacterizing the whole transaction as a financial transaction. Or, the SPV may be consolidated with the originator, and so on. Even if the SPV's rights over the receivables are honored, the actual safety of the collateral could still be open to question due to minor technical issues.

Tax risk

Tax uncertainties may sometimes affect the investors. If the SPV is liable to entity-level taxes and the payments to investors are treated as payment to equity holders, the entire cash flows in the transaction may be subjected to unprecedented taxes. Sometimes, the underlying cash flows may be subjected to a withholding tax requirement. These are risks that concern investors and they need to study these risks carefully.

Cash flow risk

Cash flow risk is certainly one of the most important risks in the transaction. The risk may encompass:

- Risk of delayed payments
- Risk of prepayments

Risk of delayed payment may be covered by the credit enhancements, particularly the cash collateral and the over-collateralization provided by the originator. Therefore, normal expected levels of delinquencies will be well covered.

However, what is not covered is the risk of prepayment. The prepayment risk as it affects investors has already been discussed before. We have also discussed prepayment risk in asset-backed securities at length (see Chapter 6).

Another risk relevant for the investors is the risk of cash flow commingling; that the collections on account of securitized receivables will be commingled with those of the originator. This is essentially answered by a proper transaction structure and payment tracking mechanism.

Reinvestment risk/basis risk

There are two ways movements in interest rates may affect investors. If the underlying cash flows are variable in response to interest rate movements, the investors will be directly affected by such movements.

In reconfigured cash flows, the SPV may have cash available between two scheduled payment dates to investors. This has to be reinvested, and the reinvestment rates will vary based on interest rates prevailing. Though it is common for securitization transactions to have guaranteed investment contracts, the guaranteed rate is mostly not a nominal rate but a spread above a prevailing basis rate. Thus, changes in basis rate will affect the investors.

Flow of information

Investors have also voiced concerns about the flow of information on securitization investments. For corporate finance securities, the information requirements are laid down by corporate laws, which over the years have tried to introduce standardization in reporting, data transparency and audits. For asset-backed securities, most of the corporate reporting requirements are inapplicable. Hence, investors have complained that the data are inadequate, late, not standardized and unavailable at a centralized location.

Fraud

Among the operational risks of asset-backed securities, fraud by the parties – obligors, originator or servicer – remains a risk that has not substantially surfaced still, but the case of National Century healthcare receivables was an adequate pointer to the possibility. In Chapter 25, we have discussed fraud risk.

Performance of securitization investments

The history of securitization transactions so far has been very happy; there have been cases of default and there have also been cases of fraud, but the general experience has been quite good.

Several factors have been responsible for the almost clean record of securitization transactions. One, the rating agencies have played a major role in proper evaluation of underlying risk. Rating agencies have viewed securitization default as a direct determinant of their reputation. Thus, in some cases, they have even used moral pressures upon parties concerned to ensure payments to investors. Similar is the role played by investment bankers. In one case of unrated securitization, a Mexican company called Ahmsa failed on its future flows securitization; the investment banker owned moral responsibility and made a 25% payment to investors.

The spreads on securitization transactions have varied, both regionally and over periods. However, in general securitization investments have proved worthy of what was expected out of them – a tool for risk diversification and sound, professionally rated investment.

As far as the historical performance of securitization transactions is concerned, the performance has varied by asset class and by region. Certain asset classes, such as prime residential mortgages, have proven to be the safest. Classes like home equity loans, or in the U.S. context, manufactured housing loans, were known to be risky, and therefore, registered more defaults and downgrades. The same is true in the CDO market; the performance of arbitrage and speculative grade CDOs has been very volatile.

We take a quick look at some performance parameters:

Performance of RMBS transactions

Moody's published a paper titled "Performance of U.K. residential mortgages 1985–2000." In this report, Moody's estimated that the projected lifetime loss (cumulative loss) in a pool of U.K. residential mortgages with an average life of 8 years has a mean of 1.14%, with a standard deviation of 1.24% (the worst performing origination year was in 1989 with a lifetime loss of 4.5%). The average loss severity rate was estimated to be 24%.

In the RMBS segment, the agency pass-throughs and CMOs form a distinctive class by themselves. Here, the issue is not the risk of rating downgrade or default, but more about spread compression, valuation due to interest rate changes and negative convexity. As MBS investments have a negative convexity, they have a compensating higher nominal rate. They perform well in periods of low interest rate volatility. Apart from interest rate volatility, a connected issue is the extent of refinancing activity. If refinancing activity is less, the prepayment speeds in MBS come down, which has a positive value for MBS investors as they reap a higher coupon but do not face the adverse consequence of negative convexity.

As regards private-label securities, in terms of rating stability, RMBS has historically been one of the safest of structured finance classes. Upgrades in RMBS have consistently been several times of the downgrades; the reasons for upgrades could be amortization of the securities, or sequential repayment. The table below from S&P[4] shows the upgrades and downgrades on RMBS over several years:

Table 30.3   Standard & Poor's RMBS rating upgrades and downgrades, 1980–2004

	Upgrade	Downgrade	Upgrade-Downgrade Ratio
1980	1		N/A
1981			N/A
1982		3	N/A
1983		4	N/A
1984			N/A
1985		7	N/A
1986		6	N/A
1987		7	N/A
1988		25	N/A
1989	50	6	0.33
1990	7	292	0.02
1991	2	101	0.02
1992	13	34	0.35
1993	27	31	0.57
1994	132	62	2.13
1995	74	55	1.35
1996	43	30	1.10
1997	96	56	1.71
1998	55	67	1.31
1999	132	29	4.55
2000	552	164	3.37
2001	551	64	0.61
2002	634	106	5.95
2003	1,192	96	12.42
2004	1,427	69	20.65

N/A=Not applicable.

The private label MBS market in the U.S. over the last few years has been characterized by intensive competition resulting in features such as negative amortization and interest-only mortgages. These have been a matter of concern for everyone, including Federal banking regulators.[5] Therefore, there have been concerns about the quality of private label RMBS products going forward. A research report from Nomura Securities said: "We recommend that investors use caution when going down in credit for several reasons. First, there has been a large increase in the number of IO loans and negatively amortizing option-ARMs in Prime and Alt-A deals. For instance, 35% of loans in Alt-A deals in 2005 had negatively amortizing features and 31% of loans had IO features according to LoanPerformance data. This compares unfavorably with pools from three years ago, when the negatively amortizing percentage was 1% and IOs were only 9%."[6]

Historically, there have been instances of defaults in RMBS. There were, for example, 22 defaults in 2001. The number of defaults rose to 50 in 2003, but a larger number of these were due to the default of a guarantor. In 2004, there were 34 defaults, mostly due to performance of the collateral. Despite defaults, the loss severity has been low. The loss severity in the U.S. RMBS market has been reported by Standard & Poor's (S&P). S&P's analysis below relates to the period July 2001 to June 2002:

Table 30.4 Recoveries of default RMBS credit classes by initial credit rating and collateral, July 1, 2001, to June 30, 2002.

Original rating	Prime		Sub-prime		Grand Total	
	Count	Recovery rate (%)	Count	Recovery rate (%)	Count	Recovery rate (%)
AA	3	91			3	91
A	1	99	1	87	2	93
BBB	1	99	3	78	4	83
BB	1	100	3	93	4	94
B	4	94		0	5	75
CCC	1	100	1		1	100
Total/average	11	95	8	75	19	87

Source : Standard and Poor's.

Performance of CMBS transactions

The S&P study cited above also gave recovery rates in respect of CMBS classes. Not surprisingly, the recovery rates have been quite high in CMBS default. Tables 30.6 and 30.7 reflect this:

Table 30.5 Recoveries of defaulted RMBS classes by underlying collateral and original credit rating, as of June 30, 2002*

Original rating	Prime		Sub-prime		Title I§		High LTV loans¶		Defaults with recoveries		Total defaults
	Count	Recovery rate (%)	Count	Recovery rate (%)	Count	Recovery rate (%)	Count	Recovery rate (%)	Count	Recovery rate (%)	Count
AAA	3	96							3	96	3
AA	19	75			1	73			20	75	26
A	2	55	1	87					3	66	9
BBB	9	66	6	61	1	98	1	77	17	67	18
BB	8	61	6	74			1	76	15	67	15
B	22	47	8	7					30	36	30
CCC	1	100							1	100	1
Total/ Average	64	63	21	45	2	85	2	77	89	60	102

*Of the total 102 defaults, 89 have information available for the recovery computation. § Title I RMBS are backed by FHA-insured home improvement loans. ¶ High LTV loans are those with loan-to-value ratios exceeding 100%.

Table 30.6 Summary count of defaults of structured finance securities by asset type, inception to June 30, 2002

Periods*	ABS	CMBS	RMBS	TOTAL
First period: Inception to June 30, 2001	17	14	83	114
Second period: July 1, 2001, to June 30, 2002	27	18	19	64
Total: Inception to June 30, 2002	44	32	102	178

* The inception dates are 1985 for ABS, 1985 for CMBS, and 1978 for RMBS.

Table 30.7 Recovery of defaults CMBS credit classes by initial credit rating, July 1, 2001, to June 30, 2002

	Defaults with recovery	
Original rating	Count	Recovery rate (%)
BB	8	97
B	10	98
Total/Average	18	98

The table below includes recovery rates on CMBS classes that had defaulted before the period covered by the survey, and the recoveries were going on during the period; it states recoveries up to June 30, 2002:

Table 30.8 Recoveries of defaulted CMBS classes by original credit rating, as of June 30, 2002

	Defaults with recovery		Total defaults
Original rating	Count	Recovery rate (%)	Count
AA	1	89	3
A	1	0	3
BB	9	97	10
B	16	79	16
Total/Average	27	83	32

Thus, quite clearly, CMBS has proved itself to be a high-recovery class.

In view of the performance of CMBS, investors' liking for CMBS has consistently increased over time. A Nomura Securities report[7] made an analysis of the collateral performance, spreads and the AAA credit support for several classes of asset-backed securities. For CMBS, the spreads are calculated based on 10-year AAA spreads over swap rates for the like period. The collateral performance is based on 60-day and 90-day delinquency, foreclosure and REO data for commercial mortgages. The credit support data is the weighted-average of credit enhancement at AAA level for CMBS deals issued during the relevant time.

Logically, if the collateral performance is worsening, the credit enhancement levels should go up and the spreads should widen. On the contrary, the market has exhibited declining levels of AAA credit enhancements in the face of worsening credit quality. The following graphic[8] shows this:

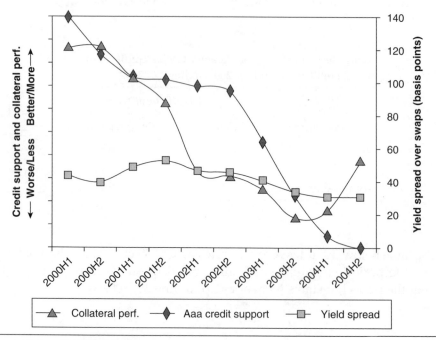

Figure 30.1   CMBS Trends

Performance of credit card ABS

The Nomura paper referred to above does a comparative study of the performance of credit card ABS as well. The three comparative measures are collateral performance, spreads and AAA credit support. In this case, the collateral performance is based on monthly charge-offs in bank credit cards. The spreads are based on 5-year AAA spreads to swaps. The credit support level is based on a weighted-average of AAA credit enhancements for the issuances during the periods. The results, shown in the graphic below, show a high degree of stability:

Performance of other ABS classes

Nomura Research tracked[9] the defaults on asset-backed classes in the U.S. issued from 1990 to mid-2001. This excluded the RMBS and CMBS classes, as well as CDOs. This study tracked the defaults of classes that were investment grade at the time of issue, and subsequently, either actually defaulted, or were downgraded to default status. Nomura classified "defaults" into four classes:

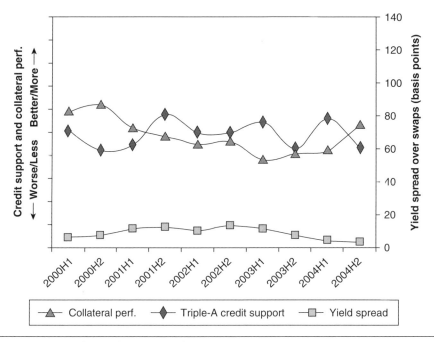

Figure 30.2   Credit card ABS trends

defaults, near-defaults, major downgrades and minor downgrades. Near-default means the downgrade was to CCC or worse, just before default. Major default is defined as a downgrade from AAA, or a downgrade from investment grade to below-investment grade. Minor defaults include all other downgrades.

The rating migrations are given in the table below:

Table 30.9   Cumulative event frequencies by asset class (by no. of deals; including all deals)

Type	Defaults	Near defaults (and worse)	Major downgrades (and worse)	Minor downgrades (and worse)	Number of deals
Utility receivables	0	0	0	0	30
Student loans	0	0	0	1	244
Cards – Bank	4	4	17	21	909
Sub-prime autos	9	10	10	13	437
Cards – Retail	2	2	5	5	140
Autos prime	1	2	20	30	801
Home equity	62	74	124	139	2300
Equipment	15	18	20	27	346
Other	61	78	104	117	936
Aircraft receivables	7	18	32	32	107
Manufactured Housing	107	119	146	155	249
Total	268	325	478	540	6499

Note: Each column includes the values in all the other columns to its left.

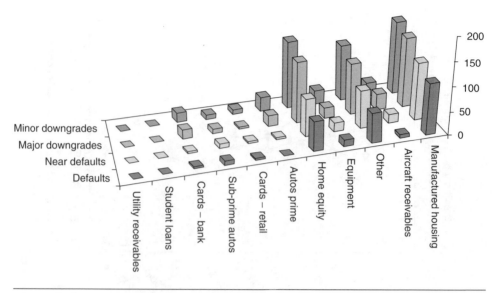

Figure 30.3   Comparative view of ABS defaults

The following generalizations have been made based on this study:

- Some asset classes showed notably low frequencies of adverse credit events: (1) bank credit cards, (2) prime auto loans, (3) student loans, (4) utility receivables. As for aircraft receivables, post-2002 study, there have been several adversities in the aviation segment, as several airline companies have gone into bankruptcy. Therefore, there has been a general worsening noted in the aircraft receivables segment.
- The equipment leasing sector historically showed strong performance. But over the 2003 and 2004 periods, there has been a general weakening of this segment as well.
- For the home equity segment, there were a substantial number of defaults, near-defaults, and downgrades, but it also represents the largest sub-population among the asset classes, with 2,300 deals. If one were to calculate the default frequencies against the sub-population deals that did not carry bond insurance, the results would worsen for all the home equity frequencies.
- The manufactured housing segment registered a number of downgrades, and a high frequency of defaults. The shame of the ABS market lies in this segment, but this was known to be a sub-prime quality collateral.

Rating agency S&P in the study cited above gave recovery rates in several classes of asset-backed securities. As may be noted, and understandably so, the recovery rates in asset-backed securities differ by collateral – the lowest being in the case of synthetic securities, which are clearly meant to transfer risk of bankruptcy of an obligor to the investors.[10]

Table 30.10 Recoveries of defaulted ABS credit classes by initial credit rating and collateral, July 1, 2001, to June 30, 2002

Original rating	Credit cards		Franchise loans		Manufactured housing loans		Synthetic securities		Defaults with recovery	
	Count	Recovery rate (%)	Count	Recovery rate (%)	Count	Recovery rate (%)	Count	Recovery rate (%)	Count	Recovery rate (%)
AAA	2	93							2	93
A	2	0	5	100					7	71
BBB			4	78			6	10	10	37
BB			4	75	1	24			5	65
B			3	100					3	100
Total/Average	4	47	16	88	1	24	6	10	27	62

Default experience in structured finance instruments: What rating transitions do not reveal

The default experience and recovery rate in structure finance instruments have been quite very satisfying so far, but there is something in the statistics published by the rating agencies that does not reveal the full picture.

Rating agency Moody's candidly puts it:

"There are several reasons for the confusion related to the low default frequency of ABS/MBS securities – key among them is the room, in structured transactions, for severe, prolonged credit deterioration that falls short of a legal default.

A default in a structured finance security could lag a severe and permanent credit impairment for a prolonged time period. Unlike corporate debt, structured finance instruments commonly write down the rated notes. While this write-down is a clear signal of credit impairment, it is not generally a "default" under the terms of the binding documents of the structured finance security.

In addition, CDO indentures typically do not treat the PIKing [paying in kind] of CDO notes as "defaults" even though it is clear that the investors of many PIKing tranches may not recoup their full investment. There are several deals in the market where there have been material and permanent impairment to the asset pools collateralizing the notes, although the legal default may not occur until the stated maturity of the notes – up to 30 years in some cases.

Thus, even though structured finance securities have endured few defaults to date, the default rates are skewed by the unique terms of these deals. With time, increased default rates in this asset class should begin to materialize.

Adding further confusion, the structured finance market, especially for lower-rated securities, is rather young. Because the market lacks the benefit of the abundant data that surrounds the corporate debt market, it is currently difficult to compare default and loss rates between these two asset classes accurately.[11]

Evaluation of an ABS Investment

Societe Generale ABS Research have put together a very readable piece entitled **Asset backed Securities Practical Guide for Investors**. In this document, they talk about five stages or aspects in evaluation of an asset-backed investment. These are:

Collateral evaluation

Needless to say, collateral is the most crucial aspect of analysis of an ABS investment, as this is the cash cow of the transaction. This is the material that the investment would be made of.

Collateral evaluation examines the credit of the collateral portfolio. Significant aspects to examine here are:

Quality of the obligors

One must carefully distinguish between the retail and wholesale portfolios. A retail portfolio is highly granular and is appraised based on statistical features of the portfolio. Wholesale portfolios, on the other hand, are analyzed based on due diligence of the transactions.

Data about the collateral performance are generally set out in detail in the rating rationale.

Maturity profile of the obligors and reinstating features

A static portfolio may be analyzed based on its past performance, but in many cases, the portfolio is either dynamic, or is a portfolio of reinstating assets, which will constantly evolve over time. In such a case, a very careful analysis of the safeguards required to maintain the quality of the portfolio is required.

Underwriting quality

The quality of the asset is itself a function of the underwriting standards. The credit policy subject to which the origination was done needs to be carefully appraised. In addition, the selection of the receivables, their composition, and how the relative industry concentration compares with that of the rest of the originator's portfolio should be studied to ensure that the originator is not trying to sack off excess concentration in some industry into the SPV. The underwriting quality becomes extremely significant for receivables to be created over time – such as reinstating assets and future flows.

Credit enhancement

Credit enhancement for the first losses usually comes from the originator himself – irrespective of the form of enhancement, it essentially means the originator's equity in the transaction. Some forms of credit enhancement also serve as liquidity enhancement – for example, cash deposit.

The extent of required enhancement would have been worked out by the rating agencies based on the mean expected losses and standard deviations. Apart from the extent of the credit enhancement, the source of the enhancement is itself very important. For instance, if the first loss enhancement were to come from the obligor himself, the very meaning of credit enhancement is lost, as the obligor is the party responsible for the loss itself.

The concept of credit enhancement is closely related to the degree of correlation in the portfolio. As the correlation increases (or, the number of obligors in the portfolio reduces), credit enhancement as a certain percentage of the pool loses meaning. To take an extreme example, if it was a fully correlated portfolio, which is the same as a single obligor portfolio, any obligor default would mean the entire exposure at default, less the recovery rate, is lost. Thus, the probability of losses reaching to the senior classes varies inversely with the correlation in the pool.

Cash flow mechanics

Investors need to carefully understand the cash flow mechanics of the transaction and the protection, or the lack of it, inherent therein. There are at least two important points to be studied carefully – the reinvestment powers of the SPV and any sequential pay-down triggers. Reinvestment might significantly alter the quality of the collateral and expose the investors to a risk of mandatory reinvestment, although the collateral quality is deteriorating. Sequential payment triggers are required to protect the senior investors from adversities. Sequential payment increases the weighted-average cost of the transaction substantially, and therefore, should be resorted to only in emergencies.

Legal structure

As for any commercial transaction, the legal structure of the transaction is an important issue for investors. As an asset-backed investment, investors draw their security from the asset collateral. The collateral must, therefore, be free from risk during the pendency of the transaction and also during extreme events such as bankruptcy. Bankruptcy should not be brushed aside as a remote contingency, as many securitization transactions have passed through originator bankruptcies. The legal strength of the transaction lies in whether the transaction would withstand the test of the originator's bankruptcy and whether the SPV would be able to sustain the collections even when a very important party to the transaction is removed and replaced.

Links with the seller

Though most securitization transaction is dependent on the seller for credit enhancement and servicing, the higher the extent of seller domination, the higher is the vulnerability of the transaction due to seller's entity risk. For example, a transaction relying on a total rate of return swap[12] written by the seller or an interest rate swap with the seller take a counterparty risk on the seller.

Notes

1 Unless specified or implied by context, in this chapter, we use the words "asset-backed securities" as including mortgage-backed securities.
2 For more on computation of N, the number of effective obligors in a pool, see our chapter on Regulatory Issues.
3 Tables based on Fitch data: source.
4 RMBS Rating Transitions 2004, January 21, 2005.
5 On December 20, 2005, financial regulators issued guidance on nontraditional mortgage products. The Joint Release said: "These nontraditional mortgage products include 'interest-only' mortgage loans where a borrower pays no principal for the first few years of the loan and 'payment option' adjustable-rate mortgages where a borrower has flexible payment options, including the

potential for negative amortization. Institutions are also increasingly combining these mortgages with other practices, such as making simultaneous second-lien mortgages and allowing reduced documentation in evaluating the applicant's creditworthiness. ... While innovations in mortgage lending can benefit some consumers, the agencies are concerned that these practices can present unique risks that institutions must appropriately manage. They are also concerned that these products and practices are being offered to a wider spectrum of borrowers, including subprime borrowers and others who may not otherwise qualify for more traditional mortgage loans or who may not fully understand the associated risks of nontraditional mortgages." [at http://www.fdic.gov/news/news/press/2005/pr12805.html, last visited December 28, 2005].

6 US Fixed Income 2006 Outlook/2005 Review, December 15, 2005.

7 "Structured finance trends – Yield spreads, credit support, and collateral performance – The Big Picture," June 27, 2005.

8 Nomura Securities: *Ibid.*

9 Or, rather, tracks, as this is presumably an ongoing research. See Nomura Fixed Income Research: *ABS Credit Migrations* updated March 5, 2002. The later data cited here are from *ABS Credit Migrations* dated December 7, 2004.

10 In the instant case, the obligor in question was Enron, where recovery rates were assumed to be 10%.

11 *Responses to Frequently Asked CDO Questions (Second of Series)* July 13, 2001.

12 This is a form of a credit derivative. For details, see Vinod Kothari's *Credit Derivatives and Synthetic Securitization*. For latest edition information, see http://vinodkothari.com/crebook.htm.

Index

Title of Cases